Verbal Aspect in the Greek of the New Testament, with Reference to Tense and Mood

Studies in Biblical Greek

D.A. Carson
General Editor

Vol. 1

PETER LANG
New York • San Francisco • Bern • Baltimore
Frankfurt am Main • Berlin • Wien • Paris

Stanley E. Porter

Verbal Aspect in the Greek of the New Testament, with Reference to Tense and Mood

PETER LANG
New York • San Francisco • Bern • Baltimore
Frankfurt am Main • Berlin • Wien • Paris

Library of Congress Cataloging-in-Publication Data

Porter, Stanley E.
    Verbal aspect in the Greek of the New Testament, with Reference to
    Tense and Mood.
    (Studies in Biblical Greek; vol. 1)
    Revision of the author's thesis.
    Bibliography: p.
    Includes index.
    1. Greek language, Biblical—Aspect. 2. Greek language, Biblical—
Tense. 3. Greek language, Biblical—Mood. 4.Greek language, Biblical—
Verb. 5. Bible. N.T.—Language, style. I. Title. II. Series.
PA847.P67   1989, 1993   487′.4   88-32803
ISBN 0-8204-0847-6   CIP
ISBN 0-8204-2423-4 (PBK)
ISSN 0897-7828

CIP-Titelaufnahme der Deutsche Bibliothek

Porter, Stanley E.:
Verbal aspect in the Greek of the New Testament, with reference to tense and
mood / Stanley E. Porter. - New York; Berlin; Bern; Frankfurt/M.; Paris;
Wien: Lang, 1989, 1993
    (Studies in Biblical Greek; Vol. 1)
    ISBN 0-8204-0847-6
    ISBN 0-8204-2423-4 (PBK)
NE: GT

The paper in this book meets the guidelines for permanence and durability of
the Committee on Production Guidelines for Book Longevity of the
Council on Library Resources.

© Peter Lang Publishing, Inc., New York 1989, 1993, 2003

Printed in the United States of America.

TABLE OF CONTENTS

EDITOR'S PREFACE

Studies in Biblical Greek is an occasional series of monographs designed to promote and publish the latest research into the Greek of both Testaments. The Series does not assume that biblical Greek is a distinct dialect within the larger world of koine: on the contrary, the assumption is that biblical Greek is part and parcel of the hellenistic Greek that dominated the Mediterranean world from about 300 B.C. to A.D. 300. If the Series focuses on the corpora of the Old and New Testaments, it is because these writings generate major interest around the world, not only for religious but also for historical and academic reasons.

Research into the broader evidence of the period, including epigraphical and inscriptional materials as well as literary works, is welcome in the Series, provided the results are cast in terms of their bearing on biblical Greek. In the same way, the Series is devoted to fresh philological, syntactical and linguistic study of the Greek of the biblical books, with the subsidiary aim of displaying the contribution of such study to accurate exegesis.

It is particularly gratifying to salute Dr. Stanley E. Porter's revision of his doctoral dissertation as the inaugural volume of the Series. Of few dissertations can it rightly be said that the work is both meticulously researched and frankly ground-breaking. This is one of the exceptions. I particularly welcome this study because of its explanatory power. In the dominant Greek grammars of our day, students are taught such labels as "historic present" and "gnomic aorist," but even where they are accurate descriptions of particular pragmatic uses it is not clear why an "historic present" might be called up to displace an aorist, why a "gnomic aorist" should be found where some might have expected a present. Dr. Porter's work is the first attempt to present a fully rigorous analysis of Greek verbal aspect, applying the categories of systemic linguistics to New Testament Greek with a competence and a comprehensiveness that spans two major fields of learning. The result is a theory that provides more than labels: it explains.

D.A. Carson
Trinity Evangelical Divinity School

AUTHOR'S PREFACE

The major assertion of this work in biblical Greek linguistics is that the category of synthetic verbal aspect--a morphologically-based semantic category which grammaticalizes the author/speaker's reasoned subjective choice of conception of a process--provides a suggestive and workable linguistic model for explaining the range of uses of the tense forms in Greek. An introduction places this work within the fields of linguistics and hermeneutics. Chapter 1 traces the history of Greek grammatical discussion from the ancients to the moderns, showing that tense-forms have traditionally been explained in terms of temporal categories, but that in some recent research the importance of verbal aspect has been recognized. Chapter 2 sets out a model of the three major aspectual categories using systemic linguistics, in which a verbal network consisting of distinct, formally-based verbal systems in opposition is posited as providing a stringent non time-based model for understanding Greek verbal usage. Chapter 3 responds to a possible objection that tense usage in the NT is not typical on the basis of Semitic influence by showing that in no cases of verbal aspectual usage is there evidence of interference from Semitic languages. Questions regarding multilingualism and the nature of NT Greek are discussed. Chapter 4 treats the major aspectual opposition in Greek: perfective (Aorist) and imperfective (Present/Imperfect) in the assertive attitude (Indicative), explaining the range of pragmatic uses--historic Present, gnomic tenses, etc.--as manifestations of essential semantic aspectual categories. Chapter 5 applies the same procedure to the stative (Perfect) aspect. Chapter 6 analyses conditional sentences, a major discourse mode in Greek, using non time-based aspectual categories and attitude of the protasis for classification. Chapter 7 discusses the Aorist, Present and Perfect tenses in the non-assertive attitude, including Subjunctive, Optative, and Imperative. Chapter 8 applies aspect and syntax to discussion of several problematic areas regarding the Participle and Infinitive. Chapter 9 shows that the Future form is not fully aspectual or attitudinal, but that it grammaticalizes expectation. And chapt. 10 accounts for the few exceptions to the rule that verbs occur in aspectual opposition by showing that such verbs-- e.g. φημί, εἰμί--play a special role in the verbal structure, especially the latter, which forms a vital component of periphrastics. Catenative constructions are treated in an appendix.

This work has benefited from the help and suggestions of many friends and colleagues: Mr. N.J.C. Gotteri (Sheffield), Rev. Prof. J.W. Rogerson (Sheffield), Rev. Dr. A.C. Thiselton (St. John's College, Durham), Dr. G.C. Horrocks (Cambridge), Mr. P.E. Satterthwaite (Cambridge and Manchester), Dr. J. Shanor (Irvine, California), and Rev. Prof. D.A. Carson (Cambridge and Chicago), who made the resources of GRAMCORD available, as well as invited this volume to inaugurate the series, Studies in Biblical Greek, from Peter Lang. Special thanks also go to Michael Thompson for advice on computer preparation of this manuscript, and especially to my parents. This work was substantially complete in July 1987, although I have tried to include later material which has come to my attention.

Presentation format conforms to MLA standards, with a few noteworthy exceptions: biblical abbreviations follow those in *JBL*; extra-biblical abbreviations are by author abbreviations found in Liddell/Scott, with abbreviated English titles of works (editions are standard; departures from them are noted); and references to secondary sources within the body of the work are by author and (usually) the first noun of the title, except for grammars, where the author's name alone is used.

INTRODUCTION:
GREEK GRAMMAR AS
HERMENEUTICS,
WITH AN INTRODUCTION TO
SYSTEMIC LINGUISTICS

0. INTRODUCTION. This work, integrating both linguistic theory and analysis of numerous examples from a sample language,[1] applies a version of systemic linguistics to discussion of the semantic category of verbal aspect in the Greek of the NT. The major assertion is that the category of synthetic verbal aspect--a morphologically-based semantic category which grammaticalizes the author/speaker's reasoned subjective choice of conception of a process--provides a suggestive, workable and powerful linguistic model for explaining the range of uses of the tense-forms in Greek. To my knowledge this is the first rigorous and thorough application of systemic linguistics to the verbal network of ancient Greek.

---

[1]Although a range of ancient Greek writings is drawn upon, the major focus is the Greek of the NT analysed in terms of a single linguistic model. This comprises a profitable corpus for the following reasons: (1) One cohesive document includes a variety of texts (e.g. narrative, non-narrative, etc.) by at least eight authors. (2) The corpus compares favourably in size to other major collections analysed by scholars. For example, Mandilaras (59), in his treatment of verbal aspect in the papyri, bases his findings upon papyri with 3,525 individual verb forms, compared to the 28,000 contained in the NT. The text of the NT, by comparison, is approximately as large as if not larger than the corpus of Homer's Iliad, of Homer's Odyssey, of Sophocles, of Aeschylus, of Thucydides, of Xenophon's Hellenica and Anabasis combined, and almost as large as that of Herodotus, to name only a few well-known extra-biblical authors. Individual biblical books are comparable in size to other well-known classical texts: e.g. Plato's Apology approximates the size of Paul's Romans or 1 Corinthians. All of these have served as primary texts for scholarly analysis (e.g. Chantraine [2 vols.]; Moorhouse). (3) The Greek of the NT comprises a reasonable representation of the common language variety of the hellenistic world (see chapt. 3). (4) Karleen (*Syntax*, 3) states, "little modern syntactic work has been done on [the NT]."

1. RECENT DISCUSSION OF LINGUISTICS IN BIBLICAL
STUDIES. Since Barr published his *Semantics* (1961), biblical scholars have been forced to reckon with the role modern linguistics plays in interpretation of the sacred texts of Christianity (other scholars argued similarly before Barr [e.g. Birkeland, "Reflexions"] but he did so with persuasive force; see Tångberg, "Linguistics"; Erickson, *Barr*, who summarizes Barr's work up to 1974). Not all scholars welcomed Barr's penetrating comments about various abuses of modern structural linguistics (e.g. Friedrich, "Semasiologie"; Hill, *Words*, esp. 1-9; Boman, Review; Barr responded to critics in "Sense"),[2] like contrasting Hebrew and Greek thought patterns on the basis of perceived linguistic differences, using questionable etymologies to establish lexical data, and confusing word and concept, to name a few (see also Barr, "Hypostatization"; *Words, passim*, etc. [see bibliography]). Insights from structural linguistics were first appropriated in the study of lexis (e.g. Sawyer, *Semantics*; Burres, *Semantics*; Silva, *Change*), but of late an ever-growing number of scholars have shown sensitivity to the importance of various forms of structural linguistics in understanding grammar as well, resulting in monograph-length studies devoted to biblical syntax and semantics (e.g. Kieffer, *Essais*; Louw, *Semantics*; Silva, *Words*; Schmidt, *Grammar*; Wonneberger, *Syntax*; Nida et al., *Style*; Levinsohn, *Connections*).[3]

Biblical Greek scholars cannot be blamed for being overly cautious in adopting structural linguistics, especially in semantics,[4] since the field itself is one of ever-increasing diversity and specialization in method and approach. Most linguists agree that semantics is concerned with meaning in language, although its relation to such areas as phonology, morphology, and syntax is a matter of wide disagreement. In one sense, semantics must always have been at the heart of analysis of language, since to recognize a sound or written unit as significant is to attribute some 'meaning' to it. In another sense, however, the

---

[2]Much has been written on this issue. To the complaint often voiced that Barr was destructive rather than constructive cf. Max Black, *Models*, 242: "There will always be competent technicians, who, in Lewin's words, can be trusted to build the highways 'over which the streamlined vehicles of a highly mechanized logic, fast and efficient, can reach every important point on fixed tracks.' But clearing intellectual jungles is also a respectable occupation. Perhaps every science must start with metaphor and end with algebra; and perhaps without the metaphor there would never have been any algebra."

[3]Not all these studies are beyond criticism: see Ronca, Review; Collinge, Review of Wonneberger; Hewitt, Review. The best survey of semantics from a biblical scholar's perspective is Thiselton, "Semantics of NT Interpretation"; cf. Nida, "Implications"; Poythress, "Analyzing."

[4]Gibson (*Logic*) is quick to point out the shortcomings of various post-Barr biblical scholars, but his criticism in many instances seems overly harsh: e.g. he castigates Moule for entitling his book *Idiom Book*, when it treats the wider concerns of grammar and not specifically what is called idiom in linguistics (118-22). Cf. Thiselton, Review.

study of semantics as a discipline is only about a century old, and much more recent as an accepted discipline for the linguist. Though Bréal first coined the term semantics in his *Essai* (1897), semantics was long out of fashion primarily because of the influence of Bloomfield (1933), who argued against mentalistic theories of meaning and strove for a 'scientific' estimation of language (*Language*, esp. 139-57).[5] The last thirty years, however, have seen a significant increase in concern for semantics as part of the science of linguistics, in Britain beginning especially with the work of Firth (esp. *Papers*; *Selected Papers*) and Ullmann (esp. *Semantics*; *Principles*) and culminating to date in Lyons's two volumes, *Semantics* (see also *Structural Semantics*, esp. 1-90; *Introduction*, 400-81; *Language, Meaning* ; and *Language and Linguistics* , 136-75; cf. Leech, *Semantics*; Palmer, *Semantics*). The discussion of semantics has emphasized the fact that questions of meaning in language cannot be avoided, but that more precise, objective, and principled means must be formulated by which meaning may be discussed. (Robins [*History*, 198-240] traces the history of 20th-cent. linguistics, which is more complex than my short paragraph can convey.)

Kempson, for example, has recognized that linguistic theory is part of the general approach of the sciences, i.e. it is concerned with "construction of a system of abstract concepts which will account most adequately for the particular properties which languages display" (*Theory*, 1). From the standpoint of biblical studies this is very much akin to Thiselton's assertion that the semantics of biblical language is an aspect of hermeneutics ("Semantics of Biblical Language"). Many biblical scholars have come to realize that their analyses of biblical texts do not occur apart from an interpretative model, i.e. presuppositionless exegesis does not occur, but all interpretation occurs within an interpretative context (the classic essay is by Bultmann, "Exegesis"; cf. Stanton, "Presuppositions"; G. Turner, "Pre-Understanding"). It has long been a commonplace for discussion in the humanities (and is now increasingly being accepted in the hard sciences) that the paradigms or models of interpretation in a given discipline change or shift, perhaps not with regularity but on a regular basis, as subsequent generations reassess and expand a given body of data (Kuhn, *Structure*; cf. MacIntyre, "Crises"; Strug, "Paradigm").[6] Such is the case with hermeneutical models used for interpretation of written texts, and, as importantly, such is the case with grammars of any language,

---

[5]A mentalistic theory is contained in Ogden/Richards, *Meaning*, though the book never uses the term "semantics" except in the appendix by Malinowski on primitive languages (298).

[6]For a critique see Suppe, *Structure*, esp. 1-232, 617-730. Also noteworthy is Popper, *Conjectures*, esp. 3-30. Application and assessment for theology are found in McFague, *Theology*, 67-144; Ratsch, *Philosophy*, esp. 13-105.

including (perhaps especially) an ancient language. As Hainsworth asserts, "Language, as described in grammars, is a convenient fiction" ("Greek," 856; Lyons [*Language and Linguistics*, 43] calls a language system a "theoretical construct"). This assertion implicitly contains an important distinction between the use of a language by a native speaker, and the grammarian's assessment of what transpires when a particular language is used (see Lyons, *Semantics*, 25-31; cf. *Language and Linguistics*, 38: "practical familiarity with language tends to stand in the way of its objective examination").

When the grammarian constructs his grammar of a language, using a particular linguistic model, what standards can be established for verification and falsification? The task for a "purely epigraphic language" (the terminology is from Collinge, "Reflexions," 79, cf. 79-82) such as ancient Greek is made more difficult because there are no native speakers to give opinions on the use of their language, the corpus of available material is limited, a skewing of registers (the oral level is completely missing) results, and the social context is difficult to recover. These factors, however, rather than causing despair should make more pressing the need to reevaluate constantly the interpretative models employed and to rely more heavily upon formal linguistic features of the extant corpus. Kempson notes that

> the development of linguistic theory has generally followed a particular pattern: (i) constructing an abstract system (a theory) to account for a certain part of language structure, (ii) investigating the consequences of setting up such a system, and (iii) rejecting the system if it predicts certain facts which do not in fact obtain, and (iv) substituting an alternative system which is compatible with the facts. (*Theory*, 1)

Kempson realizes that the creation and alternation of theories is not quite so simple, though her abstraction of the process is essentially, though idealistically, correct. Several additional factors must also be taken into account. (1) Certain theories have a higher emotional appeal attached to them. This occurs for any number of reasons, but may include such factors as the personality of the originator of the theory or of its greatest proponents (Robins, *History*, 5), vested interests in the theory (like printing new textbooks), sheer length of time that a theory has been held, and supposed myths about its origin. In studying Greek grammar appeal is often made to the hellenistic grammarians and the comparative philologists of the 19th cent. as providing a definitive model (Gleason ["Contributions," 48] says, "Biblical scholars should deal just as critically with their tools as with their subject matter; by and large they have not done so with their linguistic tools"). (2) Competing theories may be current at the same time, especially in humanities subjects where the data are inherently ambiguous. In linguistics itself,

Chomskian and other forms of transformational-generative grammar, Pike's tagmemics, Hudson's word grammar, and systemic linguistics, to name only a few of the more prominent, are currently viable linguistic models within Britain. Though there is some question within the hard sciences about the co-existence of competing models (e.g. wave and particle theories of electromagnetic radiation), it is reasonable to believe that in the humanities, although certain models may appear better suited to particular purposes than others, models can co-exist (e.g. Wonneberger [*Syntax*] uses an early form of Chomskian grammar to create 37 rules for the syntax of NT Greek, but he does not discuss verbal aspect or *Aktionsart*). (3) The data for observation, especially in the humanities, are not objectively distanced from the observer, but are intimately part of the interpretative process, i.e. there are no uninterpreted facts (see Lyons, *Language and Linguistics*, 40-46). Instead, certain facts are agreed upon as constituting the essential data that must be explained (Kempson, *Theory*, 2; see Thiselton, *Two Horizons* , esp. 293ff., for similar findings in recent hermeneutical theory). In discussing Greek verbal structure, for example, an adequate explanation of the 'gnomic' uses of the tenses must constitute one portion of the data treated. As Gleason says, "the appraisal of a linguistic work can only be done within the framework of some general understanding of language, that is, a theory of linguistics" ("Contributions," 50).

In such a relativistic context, it may appear difficult to decide upon criteria for evaluation of a suitable linguistic model. Three criteria, however, demand satisfaction for any grammatical model to be considered adequate (P. Armstrong, "Conflict," 346-48):[7] (i) in treating the data a model must be inclusive, i.e. it must incorporate within its explanatory model the largest number of pertinent pieces of data with the fewest items excluded;[8] (ii) it must result in rational discourse, i.e. the results must be open for discussion and analysis by others, not merely grasped by the original investigator; and (iii) it must provide creative and provocative conclusions that offer potential for further analysis (Fawcett [*Linguistics*, 10] argues for the model that works). The construction of a grammar of a language, therefore, is a process of

---

[7]Lyons, *Structural Semantics*, 1-5; Robins, *History*, 5, cf. 3; Wonneberger, *Syntax*, 57-66; Moravcsik, "Introduction," 16-18, propose criteria of adequacy. See Butler, *Linguistics*, 227-30.

[8]This is reminiscent of the converse of Sapir's dictum that "all grammars leak." The ideal is to create a grammar that leaks less than competing models, always striving to incorporate greater numbers of pertinent facts. Collinge ("Reflexions," 83), however, provides a welcome reminder: "If an economic description of the *valor* of a structure, or a systemic term found in it, leaks some few apparently intractable examples, it is immaterial whether these are resolved by the admission that the analyst cannot know the full context or by his allowing for a feature of *parole* (provided one or other admission is credible)." Cf. similarly Berry, "Teacher," 53-61; McKay, 214.

constantly reassessing the data and making adjustments in the interpretative grammatical framework to arrive at a more convincing and powerful explanation. At times, when the previous model seems no longer satisfactory, the use of a new model becomes incumbent upon the linguist. Such a major shift in linguistics was seen as a result of the work of de Saussure, and such has occurred in the history of Greek grammar as well. (See chapt. 1 for historical survey and analysis.) Although the Stoic grammarians included analysis of kind of action, most of the hellenistic grammarians, while recognizing the importance of morphologically-based verbal categories, emphasized a primarily time-based framework (see Robins, *History*, 29; Lyons, *Introduction*, 313; idem, *Semantics*, 704), which failed significantly in its treatment of the Aorist, Present and Future tenses. This model provided the basis for virtually every subsequent treatment until the work of Curtius in the mid-19th cent., although some continue to utilize this framework. Curtius recognized that Greek verbs, although organized into categories according to morphology, were concerned primarily with describing 'kind of time' (*Zeitart*). This model was accepted readily by the comparative philologists of the 19th cent., like Delbrück and Brugmann, who utilized this understanding of Greek verbs to make detailed comparison of Greek with other languages. Despite its obvious limitations in attempting to arrive at objective descriptions of the various kinds of actions described, this model became the standard model for many classical Greek grammars and virtually every NT Greek grammar. In the 20th cent., after the advent of structural linguistics, several grammarians have attempted various approaches to the Greek verb on the basis of verbal aspect (to be defined below), having in common a structuralist view of the Greek language, i.e. the Greek language treated on its own terms comprises a self-referring language system. Only a few grammarians have proceeded very far in terms of a whole grammar of Greek, though serious efforts in the area are to be noted and welcomed (cf. Robertson, 32: "It is not possible then to write the final grammar of Greek either ancient or modern"; Cadbury, "Vocabulary," 153: "Although the language of the Greek NT has been studied as long and as intensively as that of any body of writings, the resulting knowledge in any generation cannot be regarded as final"). The theoretical models applied to analysis of the Greek language have traditionally been very few in number, and the previous attempts to describe Greek verbal usage have major, serious flaws that leave large portions of the language inadequately explained. In hopes that a new perspective might help to clarify several problematic areas, a previously relatively unused linguistic model, systemic linguistics, is drawn upon. (Butler [*Linguistics*, 40-57] treats systems as the 'deep structure' of systemic linguistics; cf. Hudson, "Grammar," 804-05; Fawcett, *Linguistics*, 4-18, 69ff.)

2. SYSTEMIC LINGUISTICS: AN OVERVIEW. This analysis of Greek verbal structure exploits a functional linguistic model of fairly recent provenance, systemic linguistics (its chronological development is traced in Butler, *Linguistics*; see also Morley, *Introduction*; Hudson, "Grammar"; and the essays in Halliday/Martin, *Readings*; Halliday/Fawcett, *Developments*). It is a functional paradigm, thus it defines language in terms of its use as an instrument or tool for communication and social interaction. The study of any language, according to this model, occurs within a framework of actual language usage and provides a reciprocal relationship with its setting or context (see Dik, *Functional*, 4-5, who compares functional and what he calls formal [or transformational] paradigms; cf. Halliday, "Form," in Halliday, *Halliday*. I use "formal" as synonymous with morphologically-based features). In other words, the language must be studied in its "context of situation" (Firth, *Papers*, 144, 181, cf. 226).[9] It is prima facie much more reasonable and potentially promising to approach a 'dead' language from a functional paradigm, in which instances of real language are cited, than from a 'formal' (psychological) model which must test user competence against an already finite set of sentences, with no possible recourse to native speakers for verification (see Lyons, *Structural Semantics*, 19. As Kempson [*Theory*, 7] says, "A collection of recorded speech events can therefore never record more than a subset of the required set of sentences"). The text of the NT constitutes a suitable corpus of material.

Systemic linguistics has generated a recent, significant increase in writing (see Butler, *Linguistics*, 231-44; add Halliday/Fawcett, *Developments*). Rather than summarize the entire theory, much of which addresses problems beyond the modest scope of this work, I assume basic principles found in major work by Fawcett, Berry, Butler, Gotteri, and Halliday, and select for special attention items most important for a discussion of verbal aspect in light of a systemic linguistic model. Gotteri makes a helpful start when he defines systemic linguistics as follows:

> The term "systemic linguistics" can be used of any variant of system-structure theory in which language is interpreted as essentially a vast network of interrelated sets of options. The structure of a language (wordings or other syntagmatic realisations) is regarded as

---

[9]Systemic linguistics is the child of Firthian linguistics: see Firth, *Selected Papers*, esp. 1-11. For a critical assessment see Lyons, "Theory"; Butler, *Linguistics*, 4-13; Kress, *Halliday*, x-xv. It is possible to appreciate the work of Firth while recognizing the limitations of his programmatic, provocative and undeveloped statements.

8

manifesting choices made from interdependent paradigmatic options, which between them constitute the language's potential for conveying meaning. ("Comparison," 31)[10]

This definition contains several ideas that require comment.

    a. Although from its inception systemic linguistics has shunned several of the principles of structuralist linguistics as defined by de Saussure (*Course*, esp. 65ff.; see Culler, *Saussure, passim*; cf. Fawcett, "Semantics," 132), several fundamental principles held in common are worth defining briefly (others that are assumed include the priority of synchronic over diachronic analysis and linguistics as a descriptive science). The first is the concept of system, although systemic linguistics has adapted this terminology. Within a given language, any meaningful component is part of a system of similar available choices, and these systems of choices are arranged into a network. As Halliday ("Sketch," 3, in Halliday, *Halliday*) says, "The system network is the grammar."[11] This work treats the verbal aspectual system as one of two major systems (the other being finiteness) of the Greek verbal network. Thus the verbal network in Greek, though it may have developed in any number of ways, developed within it an aspectual system with three individual aspect systems--perfective (»»Aorist); imperfective (»»Present/Imperfect); stative (»»Perfect/Pluperfect)--which must be considered in relation to each other, not independently and certainly not primarily in relation to Sanskrit or Latin, both languages often alluded to in discussion of ancient Greek (see e.g. Holt, *Etudes*, 5; Robertson, 46-48; McKay, "Syntax," 44-45, who recognize this problem). Although with an epigraphic language the corpus is limited, and analysis must be done from the interpreter's standpoint, the use of the concepts of system and network bind evaluation to actual instances in opposition to other possible selections within the language, primarily in terms of the language itself before formulation of translational equivalents.

    b. Systemic linguistics sees language as a network which specifies the choices available in a given system and displays them graphically. Fawcett calls this "the expression of knowledge as procedures," in which "the availability of such a choice is always dependent on the selection of a logically prior feature" (*Linguistics*, 19; cf. Halliday, "Chain," 84-87; "Sketch," 3-6, in

---

[10]Morley, *Introduction*, v-vi: systemic linguistics accounts "for the nature of the linguistic system available to the native speaker of a language and for the selection of options which a person makes when using the language. . . . The meaning options are then realised as component elements of the language structure. . . ." Cf. Berry, *Introduction*, 1.21-32.

[11]See Halliday, "Categories," 67-70; "Features," 58-73; "Structure," 122-31, all in Halliday, *Halliday*; Berry, *Introduction*, 1.141-76; Fawcett, *Linguistics*, 19-25 ("System networks are not merely a notation: they are a conceptual model" [20]); Butler, *Linguistics*, 40-45; J. Martin, "Meaning," 17; Hasan, "Dream," 185.

Halliday, *Halliday*). (1) To display a network is not to say that a speaker or writer actually makes a conscious choice at every juncture, since use of language by a native speaker lies beyond the scope of what this model strives to delineate. For example, it is implausible that a Greek speaker consciously determined--if he were to use an Imperative--that he would select the features [+aspectual / +finite: -assertion: +direction] to arrive at the realization »»Imperative, yet this is the set of semantic choices that he seems to make in Greek, nonetheless. (2) Movement through a network system does not imply temporal progression, but it does display a set of selected semantic features. Despite various conceivable ways of drawing the same network, each network ideally is elegant, i.e. it captures the generalizations of the language and breaks them down into their constituents in the most economical and symmetrical fashion (cf. Fawcett, "What," 8). To use a given language a speaker or writer makes certain increasingly specific semantic choices, i.e. the progression is from broader to more delicate, and these constitute the necessary conditions for subsequent choices, until a specific realization is arrived at. A realization statement for the verbal network consists of a selection expression of semantic features and a specific verb form, and the convention in this thesis for labelling this is »», e.g. »»Imperative (see below. Hierarchy is very important in systemic linguistics [Gotteri, "Comparison," 34]; see Berry, *Introduction*, 1.104-40; Martin, "Meaning," 16-26). For example, the entry condition for making a verbal statement as opposed to a verbless statement must be satisfied before selecting the semantic features of the verbal component itself, such as aspect and attitude. (3) In any given system not all choices are always available. Certain choices either are not possible or have never been felt necessary by the speakers of a given language (cf. Fawcett, *Linguistics*, 65-66, on "facilitation," in which certain combinations of choices are repeatedly made). Displaying the choices in a network graphically allows the implications to be grasped more firmly. For example, in classical Greek speakers grammaticalize three numerical designations for the verb: singular, dual, and plural. These might be arranged in a network display in two ways, since networks/systems may be drawn in various ways, according to their purposes. The one on the left makes no further distinction in delicacy but displays all three formal choices at the same level of specification. The one on the right sees an opposition between singular/non-singular, and treats the latter at a further level of delicacy as a second of two choices (see Fawcett, "What," 10-14). Capital letters are used for system names, and small letters for the terms within a system:

This system differs from the one in hellenistic Greek where it is no longer utilized by speakers (a number of earlier authors do not use it as well):

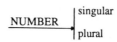

A speaker of classical Greek has three choices (or two sets of choices) available, whereas the speaker of hellenistic Greek has two choices, as the network display makes clear.

    c. In systemic linguistics, there are two types of networks: non-semantic and semantic taxonomies (Gotteri ["When"] refers to "bogus networks" for non-semantic taxonomies; cf. Fawcett, "What"; Halliday, "Structure"; Martin, "Meaning," 30-37). Semantic taxonomies or networks have been treated above when speaking of choice within the verbal aspectual system. Non-semantic taxonomies are employed for displaying networks of formal choices. Their uses are four: "explaining the use of various forms," "checking the consistency of your terminology," checking "the completeness of your coverage," and determining "the applicability of your generalisations. . ." (Gotteri, "When," 7). The convention adopted here (suggested by Fawcett) is to utilize slanted-line diagrams in non-semantic taxonomies. For example, the formal choice of VOICE in Greek might be displayed thus:

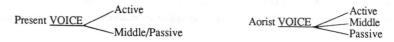

The networks for semantic choices, i.e. semantic choices realized by formal means, use straight-line diagrams. Thus the diagram for VOICE might be as follows:

---

[12]So Zwicky, "Markedness," 133; cf. Fawcett, *Linguistics*, 19. Or should this be displayed as follows?

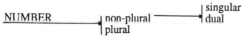

VOICE
- -restrictive (»»Active)
- +restrictive
  - +benefit (»»Present M/P, Aorist Middle)[13]
  - -benefit (»»Present M/P, Aorist Passive)[14]

Semantic networks are at the heart of this thesis (Fawcett ["What," 6] gives the following criteria for a semantic network to be considered usable: realization rules, holistic, and generative/analytic).

Several other conventions for diagramming should be noted.

a — b / c   if a, then b or c

a — b \ c   if a, then b and c

a \ b / — c / d   if a and b, then c or d

a \ b / — c   if a and b, then c

d. Whereas there is a dispute among systemic linguists whether formal categories convey meaning (Huddleston, "Features"; Fawcett, *Linguistics*, 5-6, 39-45; cf. idem, "What," 1-4), previous work in analysing verbal networks has shown that systemic linguistics benefits greatly when it makes an overt and conscious distinction between the form and function of a given linguistic item, especially with reference to verbal choices (see esp. Gotteri, "When," in response to idem, "Note"; Fawcett, *Linguistics*, 43; idem, "Generating," 157. Bolinger [*Meaning*, 1-21] cites Firthian linguistics as carrying discussion forward in this area; cf. Dahl, *Tense*, 21). For Greek this may not seem an important point to make, since it has long been recognized that Greek is a language with a relatively stable morphological basis, especially in the verb. In fact, it is all the more important to stress the relationship between the two.[15] For example, Participle is a form, and in Greek it may be an element of the subject, predicate, adjunct (e.g. temporal or causal Participle), or complement

[13]Joseph, "Greek," 338.

[14]See Barber, "Voice," 16-24; cf. Rijksbaron, 126ff. Barber argues convincingly that the Middle and Passive should be linked, rather than the Active and Middle, which might be posited if the history of the language were being considered. The identical formal realization for Middle and Passive in the Present prompts thought that lack of formal differentiation may result in vagueness rather than ambiguity in VOICE, although the Middle itself seems vague (see Carson, *Fallacies*, 77-79). See my chapt. 10 on ambiguity and vagueness.

[15]See Panhuis, "Endings," 106-07, 110-11, who notes the form/functional relation of Person in Greek. Functionally 1st and 2d Person are shifters, and 3d Person is a non-shifter. These two are also related to the speaker, person spoken to, and something outside of these two (Jesperson, *Philosophy*, 54). These correspond to the sound symbolism of the endings: μ, σ, τ, moving from the least obstruent (μ) to a fricative (σ) to a complete stop (τ). Thus the "cline of person" is "underscored by a phonological hierarchy . . ." (110).

(object of a verb) in clause structure. To identify the form is not to delimit its function. For tense names, as will be seen below, it is especially crucial that formal and functional categories be distinguished, since the names Aorist, Present, Imperfect, Perfect, Pluperfect, Future, are all formal titles, formulated around at least three concepts: time, kind of action, and lack of specification (Lyons [*Semantics*, 704] relabels the tenses: Present imperfect [»»Present]; present Perfect [»»Perfect]; past Imperfect [»»Imperfect]; past Perfect [»»Pluperfect], calling the Pluperfect "misleading"). But these do not describe the use or function of any of these forms, e.g. the Present used in past-time contexts ('historic' Present). There is in grammar no necessary correlation between a formal name and the function(s) of the form(s), although a strong case can be made for this correlation clearly existing in Greek (see chapt. 2).[16] I follow the convention of capitalizing all formal terms--Subjunctive, Participle, Aorist Indicative--and retaining lower case spelling for functional categories--e.g. perfective, attitude, stative, etc. Quotations retain their original spellings. There is a temptation to alter quotations, but since many fall victim to vagueness in their tense terminology, a vagueness which has repercussions for their tense analyses, it is better to be faithful to the original (for further discussion of why capitalization is adopted to separate formal and functional titles see Porter, "Terminology").

   e. *"Meaning* implies *choice"* (Bazell, *Form*, 51; see also Lyons, *Structural Semantics*, 25-30; idem, *Introduction*, 413-14, 415-19; Dahl, *Tense*, 12; cf. Collinge, "Reflexions," 88, esp. 99-100; Jakobson, "Struktur"). Since systemic linguistics deals with language as it is actually evidenced in usage, systemic linguistics takes seriously the dictum of structural semantics that an element is only meaningful if it is defined wholly in terms of other elements. A given linguistic phenomenon that is wholly predetermined, i.e. there is no choice between this and some other grammatical unit, offers little for a discussion of meaning. For example, certain verbs in Greek offer no formal choice of tense systems, like εἰμί. Thus it is meaningless to classify the forms εἰμί, etc., ἤμην, etc., as part of the Present/Imperfect conjugation, since there is no Aorist conjugation, etc. (see chapt. 10). Systemic linguistics--with its use of systems in networks that are constructed around choice--is well suited to exploit this concept by displaying all possible and conceivable oppositions within a given network. For example, at the level of the semantic category

---

[16]As Gildersleeve ("Evolution," 206) says: "Where form survives anywhere, function survives everywhere." Cf. Gotteri, "Speaker's Right," 77, who notes that "the alternative to delimiting one's data in this way seems to be to embark on a global and frankly unmanageable investigation of how Polish [or Greek] talks about processes, situations, the world, the universe and everything."

realized by the word (and any structure of which it is an element) it is impossible to find principled grounds for distinguishing among ingressive, constative, and effective Aorists. The verb form is, simply, the Aorist. And there is no further choice that makes discussion of such concepts as ingressive, constative, and effective meaningful. The meaningful choice of the Aorist occurs in relation to the Present/Imperfect and Perfect/Pluperfect tenses. Thus semantic choices may be defined in terms of what is not chosen, in contrast with the items that are chosen, emphasizing that a distinction is made, rather than striving to find an appropriate metalanguage to define every semantic category fully. The concept of meaning as choice also serves to bridge the gap between form and function, since it must be admitted that to differentiate semantic categories without formal realizations undermines not only the principle of form/functional relation but principled means for differentiation (Halliday ["Grammar," 88-98, in Halliday, *Halliday*] showed early that form and function are integral in semantic analysis; Zwicky ["Markedness," 137] uses the term "iconicity").

    f. All networks must contain a series of realization statements that show how selection of particular features (selection expressions) are translated into the data of the language itself (realization) (Fawcett, *Linguistics*, 50-53, 115-24; cf. Fawcett, "What," 4-6 [he calls them "realization rules"]; Butler, *Linguistics*, 59-62; Berry, *Introduction*, 2.18-50; Huddleston, "Features," esp. 67, 69; Halliday/Martin, "Notational Conventions," 10-12, in Halliday/Martin, *Readings*. There is some discussion about whether selection expressions may result in semantic or formal realizations). In this work componential analysis is often utilized to make realization statements more precise (a major treatment of this approach is Nida, *Analysis*). There has been much justified criticism of componential analysis of late (e.g. Kempson, *Theory*, 86-102), especially when it is utilized in defence of making specific ontological statements about the qualities of certain linguistic items (this occurs mostly in lexical studies). In a systemic semantic network componential analysis need not assert anything about ontological qualities, but may convey as a "simple calculus" (Kay/Samuels, "Analysis," 49) the semantic component of a given choice within a system and provide a more complete translation into the metalanguage of the particular qualities realized by a given form (cf. Lyons, *Structural Semantics*, 80: "'Componential analysis' is as valid as the relations upon which it is based and which it may conveniently summarize"). A formal taxonomy might have the following realization statement:

<u>Realization statement</u>
Selection expression
a:b
a:c
a:d:e
a:d:f

Realization
=
=
=
=

The semantic network of VOICE (see above) might appear as follows:

<u>Realization statement</u>
Selection expression
-restrictive
+restrictive: +benefit
+restrictive: -benefit

Realization
=   »»Active
=   »»Middle
=   »»Passive

Often reference will only be made to the most delicate semantic choice in a system, but selection of, for example, [+benefit] implies inheritance of the bundle or accumulation of all previous semantic choices (Hasan ["Dream," 187] calls this "systematic path inheritance").

g. Systemic linguistics distinguishes between (syntagmatic) chain and (paradigmatic) choice. Paradigmatic choice--the choice of a single linguistic item as distinct from other linguistic items of the same class that might fulfil the same function--is fundamental to systemic linguistics, since the choices that are made in any network are at any given point selections along the paradigmatic axis (Gotteri, "Comparison," 32; cf. Berry, *Introduction*, 1.52-56; Lyons, *Structural Semantics* , 59: "I consider that the theory of meaning will be more solidly based if the meaning of a given linguistic unit is defined to be the set of [paradigmatic] relations that the unit in question contracts with other units of the language [in the context or contexts in which it occurs]"; idem, *Introduction*, 70-81). Syntagmatic choice emphasizes the linear relation of given linguistic items (structure) (see e.g. Halliday, "Structure"). While many systemic linguists are concerned with syntagmatic choice, especially at the larger ranks, this work places its emphasis on paradigmatic choice as crucial for syntagmatic meaning. The semantic choice of verbal aspect, realized in a particular verbal form and placed in the predicate slot (see Berry, *Introduction*, esp. 1.63-65) at the rank of clause, determines the verbal aspect for the entire clause in which the particular verbal item occurs. The individual item with its semantic meaning as a verbal category is influential upon the entire semantics of the greater context of situation.

h. Although many systemic linguists do not make this distinction, and it is a point of contention among a number of linguists outside this model (e.g. Lyons, *Semantics*), it is useful to distinguish semantics from pragmatics, or "what the forms mean" (semantics) from "what speakers mean when they use the forms" (pragmatics) (Gotteri, "Note," 49; cf. "When," 13).[17] In the case of Greek verbal structure, semantics can be defined as analysis of the essential meanings of the individual verbal aspects which allows their usage in a variety of contexts. These contexts may differ, for example, in relation to temporal reference. (Grammarians have various ways of defining this difference: e.g. Dahl, *Tense*, 3-19; Bache, *Aspect*, 54-60; Comrie, *Aspect*, 41-51.)[18] Another useful way of making this distinction is in terms of code and text (see Gregory/Carroll, *Language*, 75-98). Code refers to the shared meaning-system encoded in grammatical, syntactical and lexical items, such that the utterances speakers produce, despite individual variations, are "describable in terms of a particular system of [linguistic] rules and relations" (Lyons, *Introduction*, 52, cf. 140-41, on idealization of linguistic data at this level; Butler, *Linguistics*, 40-57). Grammar determines the verbal range of an individual, i.e. the "range of meanings which that person can express," and the ways in which these meanings are realized in the specific formal features of the language. Texts then exist as the "operational instances" of language as code (Gregory/Carroll, 75, 84). The code is the network of verbal choice that speakers draw upon when creating their individual instances of text (Fawcett insists upon the close connection between semantics and formal realization in generating text). A valuable point of connection between the two is the concept of implicature. Comrie recognizes that there is a profitable "distinction between the meaning of a linguistic item, in terms of its conventionalised semantic representation, and the implicatures that can be drawn from the use of a linguistic item in a particular context" (Comrie, *Tense*, 23; cf. Lyons, *Semantics*, 592-96). Thus implicature applies to what is implied by the use of the particular verbal aspect within a given set context.

> The separation of meaning from implicature thus enables us first to give a more accurate characterisation of the meaning of a linguistic form, and secondly, given a theory of implicatures, to account for the implicatures that are assigned to linguistic forms in the absence of any cancellation of those implicatures. (Comrie, *Tense*, 25)

---

[17]Within systemic linguistics, the semantics/pragmatics distinction is often not made, though Gotteri ("When," 9) finds it a "useful fiction." Levinson (*Pragmatics*, 5-47) attempts to define pragmatics.

[18]At this point discussion could turn to discourse analysis. While this work concentrates upon semantics, it recognizes the importance of the issue of text analysis, without being able to discuss it in detail. For a useful treatment see Brown/Yule, *Analysis*, esp. 27-67, 190-222.

For example, the essential semantic feature of the Future is [+expectation]. One of the common implicatures of such semantic meaning (though not the only one) is future reference (see chapt. 9).

i. Producing translations is not to be seen as the sole purpose of studying a language. Exploiting the translational value of ancient texts has long been an item of high priority for scholars. In systemic linguistics, with its emphasis upon meaning as choice within a given system network, the ability or lack of ability to translate a given linguistic item into another language, or even into a concise description in a metalanguage, must be viewed with appropriate scepticism. For example, in translating Hebrew tenses, since the Imperfect and Perfect often occur in identical temporal contexts (e.g. Psalm 23, where the Imperfect verbs in vv 1b-3 are often rendered identically with the Perfect verbs in vv 4ff.), many scholars neglect the formal difference in arriving at identical translational equivalents, thus neglecting the important distinction in verbal aspect. Most examples within this work are translated, but the purposes of the translations vary from being literalistic renderings to interpretative glosses, depending upon the particular point being made, and they are not to be used to evaluate the particular concept being discussed. As Gleason says, "Translation is a very inadequate means of expressing meanings and must always be used with great caution" (*Introduction*, 77; "Linguistics," 15-16; "Contribution," 54-55; cf. Robertson, *Minister*, 90-91; Lyons, *Structural Semantics*, 97-99: translations [of terms for skills, etc.] "cannot claim to be adequate statements of meaning in any scientific sense" [98]).

CHAPTER 1:
RESEARCH INTO TENSE,
AKTIONSART AND ASPECT

0. INTRODUCTION. As late as 1974, Rydbeck, commenting on the state of research into NT grammar, said, "today research into post-classical Greek in general and NT Greek in particular has come almost to a standstill." One of the reasons he gives for this is that "there is a prevalent but false assumption that everything in NT Greek scholarship has been done already" ("What Happened," 427; announced earlier by Moule, *Language*, 1ff.). This assumption is rightly open to question. The state of discussion of aspect[1] in NT Greek--in its terminology, assumptions, and conceptual framework--is still only the tentative result of a history of previous debate. Though this debate began with the Greeks themselves, from a linguistics standpoint it is relatively recent. This chapter summarizes the major work that has treated the question[2] offering a critique along primarily two lines: difficulties evidenced (i) within individual treatments and (ii) in opposition to systemic linguistics as a theoretical model. The discussion divides into six sections: hellenistic Greek grammars, 19th-cent. and traditional grammars, comparative philology and *Aktionsart*, transitional approaches, structural linguistics and aspect, and

---

[1] "Aspect" is apparently a translation by Ch. Ph. Reiff in 1828-29 of the Russian word *vid*, a loantranslation from Greek, εἶδος (see Pollak, *Studien*, 32; Bache, *Aspect*, 5), whose history has little if any bearing on its semantic definition and current linguistic use.

[2] For histories of discussion see Herbig, "Aktionsart," 171-86 (the first to apply *Aktionsart* to modern European languages); Wackernagel, *Vorlesungen*, 13-39, 149-57; Holt, *Etudes*, 1-13; Schwyzer, 2.248-56; Schlachter, "Verbalaspekt," 22-34; Pollak, *Studien*, 30-47; Wilkinson, *"Aspect,"* 22-30. For a summary of major 19th-cent. disputants see Meltzer, "Lehre." Gonda (*Rgvedic*, 18) says: "what . . . will strike the reader of the books and articles devoted to this chapter of Greek syntax considered as a whole is their almost chaotic character"; Verkuyl, *Nature*, 6, 7.

grammars of hellenistic Greek from Winer to the present, with appendixes on 'perfectivizing' prefixes (1A) and dissenting theories (1B).

It would be wise, however, to express a caveat regarding tense terminology. In major linguistics books a common complaint is voiced about categories used to describe verbal action (e.g. Lyons, *Introduction*, 304ff.). *Inter alia* the problems include the desire to relate all verbal action to past, present, and future time; the tendency to believe that temporal reference is "necessarily an inflexional category of the verb"; and the neglect of other categorial uses of tense forms, such as aspect, deixis and various temporal and modal functions (Lyons, *Semantics*, 677ff. [quotation 678]).

Grammarians have traditionally been concerned with the range of linguistic entities in one language (and often many more languages), and they feel obliged to say something meaningful about tense, without taking sufficient time to consider fully such a problematic area. Thus they often speak along traditional lines and further obscure an issue of central importance (see the large number of attempts at grammars of English and Slavonic languages, besides general linguistics books). Some of the difficulty is caused by the abstruse nature of the categories of tense and aspect themselves, since they are related to each other and to other verbal categories, such as Mood. One of the most basic facts about the names for tense categories is that they are based on typical functions, but this is potentially very misleading. In English, it is commonly said that there are two forms of the Present tense: the simple Present and the progressive Present, so called because they are often used with present meaning. But it is significant how few times English speakers actually use the simple Present. The progressive Present seems much more common not only in present but also future contexts. The progressive Present seems to have a range of legitimate temporal functional uses, unified around an aspectual quality, the progressive kind of action. This illustrates the crucial problem of maintaining the difference between a tense category's formal name and its functional uses, in which a formal name is often mistakenly understood to represent the range of functional uses available (Lyons, *Semantics*, 683: "Indeed, it is no exaggeration to say that there is probably no tense, mood or aspect in any language whose sole semantic function is the one that is implied by the name that is conventionally given to it in grammars of the language. Furthermore, it is undoubtedly the case that the terms conventionally used to describe the functions of the tenses, moods and aspects in certain languages are very misleading. This point must be borne constantly in mind"). In the following discussion, therefore, these general problems in tense terminology must be remembered. Whereas they do not excuse errors or minimize the necessity of formulating clearer and more accurate definitions, they do allow a certain generosity and the acknowledgment that to venture an opinion on tense terminology is to invite almost certain criticism.

1. HELLENISTIC GREEK GRAMMARS. Whereas the earliest Greek writers had a fundamental understanding of time, they took much longer to formulate a theory of temporality.[3] They were slower yet in their formulations of grammatical theory.[4]

a. Dionysius Thrax. The first (extant) Greek grammar is attributed to the Alexandrian scholar Dionysius Thrax (c. 120 B.C.) (the Greek text is in

---

[3]See Hom. Il. 1.70, speaking of Calchas the diviner, ὃς ᾔδη τὰ τ᾽ ἐόντα τὰ τ᾽ ἐσσόμενα πρό τ᾽ ἐόντα (who [knew] already all things that are and that are expected and the things previous); Pl. Rep. 392D; E. Daught. Troy 468; Rev 1:8; see my chapt. 2. Plato and Aristotle are usually credited with making the distinction between a verb and a noun, with Aristotle stating that the verb (ῥῆμα) is "the thing that indicates time" (τὸ προσσημαῖνον χρόνον; Int. 16B6; cf. 16B6-25).

[4]For details of the history of linguistic discovery in the ancient world see esp. Robins, *History*, 9-44; *Theory*, 1-47. Treatments of ancient Greek grammatical scholarship can be found in Steinthal, *Geschichte*, esp. 1.307-17; Sandys, *History*, esp. 103-64; Pfeiffer, *History*, esp. 234ff.; Pinborg, "Antiquity"; Hoffmann, "Paratasis," 1-8; Hovdhaugen, *Foundations*, chapt. 3.

Bekker, *Anecdota Graeca*, 2.638; scholastic scholia on various points in Dionysius's treatment of the verb can be found on 2.887-91).[5] His short, structured γραμματική devotes sect. 15 to the verb (ῥῆμα), which he divides into eight categories. Concerning the tenses or times (χρόνοι), he says there are three: ἐνεστώς, παρεληλυθώς, μέλλων (present, past and future [it is noteworthy that this definition uses two Perfect Participles and a Present Participle]), and four different kinds of past tense: παρατατικόν, παρακείμενον, ὑπερσυντέλικον, ἀόριστον[6] (the Imperfect, Perfect, Pluperfect, and Aorist), with three relationships among the tenses: ἐνεστῶτος πρὸς παρατατικόν, παρακειμένου πρὸς ὑπερσυντέλικον, ἀορίστου πρὸς μέλλοντα (Present to Imperfect, Perfect to Pluperfect, Aorist to Future) (note ambiguity whether formal or functional categories are being specified for the Present and Future). This can be represented diagramatically:

Past	Present	Future
παρεληλυθώς	ἐνεστώς	μέλλων

παρατατικός
παρακείμενος
ὑπερσυντέλικος
ἀόριστος

And the oppositions thus:

ἐνεστώς	-	παρατατικός
παρακείμενος	-	ὑπερσυντέλικος
ἀόριστος	-	μέλλων

This brief description illustrates several points.

(1) Dionysius does not make clear whether his temporal categories correspond to particular verbal forms, though the forms he selects as labels seem to argue against this (Pulgram, "Functions," 251-52). Since he differentiates four past forms, the temporal terms appear to be a mixed grouping--present or future may correspond exactly to a single verb form (though Dionysius does not state this) but past is a type with four sub-types. Dionysius does not clarify how the four past forms are related, since his work does not contain a syntax of the verb (Dinneen ["Linguistics," 62] notes that Dionysius never got beyond individual words in his analysis).

(2) Dionysius recognizes that binary relationships exist between the tense names, though his reasoning is unclear. The relation of Present to Imperfect in Dionysius seems to be that of temporality, but this cannot be the basis for Perfect to Pluperfect, since they are both listed as past forms (the categorization of the Perfect as a past tense is surprising, and open to serious question even as a general pattern of usage). And the relation of Aorist to Future is obscure. Robins notes that the proportions may have been constructed on morphological grounds (the word and paradigm method) with the Imperfect built upon the Present stem, the Pluperfect built upon the Perfect stem, and the Aorist and Future evidencing the sigmatic stem though not being etymologically related (Robins, *History*, 36. The presence of the sigma in the Aorist and Future may have 'fooled' the ancient Greeks, as it has many modern scholars). This may be correct, since one of the scholia

---

[5] Some doubts have been cast on the authenticity of Dionysius's authorship: Pfeiffer (*History*, 271-72) endorses the traditional view of authorship while questioning arrangement of the manuscript as original; against Pinborg ("Antiquity," 103-06), who, referring to the work of di Benedetto, argues for a 3d cent. A.D. composition. For a summary and critical discussion of the entire treatise see Robins, "Dionysius Thrax."

[6] Herbig ("Aktionsart," 175) claims that in Dionysius the term "aorist" is found for the first time. For elucidation of these terms see the scholia in Bekker, *Anecdota Graeca*, 2.889-90.

makes such a correlation in expanding upon Dionysius's theory (Bekker, *Anecdota Graeca*, 2.890-91.), unless Dionysius had a scheme similar to that of the Stoics' in mind (see below).

(3) Dionysius's scheme is clearly temporally oriented. On the basis of his recognition of three temporal categories he attempts to subsume all other verbal uses, creating very forced results, including failure to treat verb forms that may be non-past referring, but especially regarding what he calls past tenses. Perhaps this is why Dionysius's outline does little more than provide a list of categories. As Robins says, Dionysius's "failure to give proper recognition to the aspectual dimension in the semantic structure of the Greek tenses must be considered a definite loss of insight" (*History*, 36; Gonda, *Rgvedic*, 17. Schwyzer [2.249] disagrees, claiming that though both Dionysius and the Stoics made time "den Oberbegriff . . ., so erscheinen doch als Unterbegriffe die Begriffe des *Verlaufes* oder der 'Erstreckung' . . . oder der *Nicht-Vollendung*, der *Vollendung* und der zeitlichen *Unbestimmtheit*. . . ." But nowhere does Dionysius state this).

b. Stoic grammars. By comparison the Stoic grammarians present a much more sophisticated picture of the Greek verb, found primarily in a scholia by Stephanos on Dionysius's grammar (selections are from Bekker, *Anecdota Graeca* , 2.891-92; see Haberland, "Note," 173-76, who notes the difficulties in interpreting the Stoic comments; and Collinge, "Greek," 17-19, who doubts their existence). Working with essentially the same terminology as the Alexandrians, the Stoics do not set out a purely temporal paradigm but work from tense-form oppositions,[7] defining tenses according to both temporal distinctions and kind of action. Thus the Stoics define the Present as the present incomplete (ἐνεστὼς παρατατικός), ὅτι παρατείνεται καὶ εἰς μέλλοντα (because it stretches even into the future). In other words, ὁ . . . λέγων ποιῶ καὶ ὅτι ἐποίησέ τι ἐμφαίνει καὶ ὅτι ποιήσει (the one who says "I am doing" shows both that he did/does something and that he will do something). By analogy the Imperfect is the past incomplete (παρῳχημένος παρατατικός), which means that ὁ . . . λέγων ἐποίουν, ὅτι τὸ πλέον ἐποίησεν, ἐμφαίνει, οὔπω δὲ πεπλήρωκεν, ἀλλὰ ποιήσει μέν, ἐν ὀλίγῳ δὲ χρόνῳ (the one who says "I was doing" shows that he did/does more, and he is not yet finished, but that he will do more, but in a little while[8]). "Therefore the Present and the Imperfect are related because both are without completion and they possess the same sounds," e.g. τύπτω and ἔτυπτον (an earlier scholia on Dionysius remarks that the Present-Imperfect, the Perfect-Pluperfect and even the Aorist-Future oppositions are joined according to sound [κατὰ τὴν φωνήν] and what they signify [κατὰ τὸ σημαινόμενον] [Bekker, 2.890-91]).

If the event is complete, however, the verb used is the ἐνεστὼς συντελικός because it represents τὴν συντέλειαν τῆς ἐνεργείας (the accomplishment of the action), and is divided into the Perfect (παρακείμενος) and the Pluperfect (ὑπερσυντέλικος). Since they both represent past accomplishment (τελείως παρῴχηται) and possess the same representative elements (χαρακτηριστικὰ στοιχεία), the Stoics elucidated a strange relationship between the Perfect and Pluperfect on the basis of the Aorist (ἀόριστος . . . ἐκλήθη πρὸς ἀντιδιαστολὴν τοῦ παρακειμένου καὶ ὑπερσυντελίκου [the Aorist is chosen to distinguish between the Perfect and the Pluperfect]. The Attic Future, so called by the Stoics, is also listed as a future manifestation of

---

[7]On the Stoic view of time see e.g. D L. 7.141, who, believing time is ἀσώματον (incorporeal), says τὸν μὲν παρῳχηκότα καὶ τὸν μέλλοντα ἀπείρους, τὸν δ᾽ ἐνεστῶτα πεπερασμένον (that which is past and that which is future are infinite, but that which is present is finite). Cf. scholia on present time as the meeting point of past and future (Bekker, *Anecdota Graeca*, 2.889-90); Arist. Int. 5A7-8. Steinthal (*Geschichte*, 1.300-08) thinks philosophical interests govern the Stoics' grammatical analysis; cf. Frede, "Principles," esp. 32-35.

[8]ἐν ὀλίγῳ . . . χρόνῳ may be rendered "in short, briefly," possibly referring to the explanation itself, but this is discounted by the μέν . . . δέ construction and its placement.

the Perfect form, though recognized as rare). Having determined that the Aorist is used for the past, τοῦ ἄρτι τοίνυν τῷ ἀορίστῳ διδομένου γίνεται παρακείμενος, οἷον ἐποίησα ἄρτι-- πεποίηκα, τοῦ δὲ πάλαι προσνεμομένου ὁ ὑπερσυντέλικος γίνεται, οἷον ἐποίησα πάλαι-- ἐπεποιήκειν (therefore the act being represented by the Aorist as just occurring becomes the Perfect, as in "I just did"--"I have done." And the act assigned to the distant past becomes the Pluperfect, as in "I did formerly"--"I had done"). Regarding the nature of the Aorist itself, the Stoics only say, ὁ . . . ἀόριστος κατὰ τὴν ἀοριστίαν τῷ μέλλοντι συγγενής (the Aorist according to its indefiniteness is related to the Future). (The Stoics debate why the Future is not called the Aorist Future, but conclude that the Aorist is named according to its boundaries, while the Future is not [is this a recognition of the problem of tense terminology?].)

The Stoic scheme, therefore, is as follows:[9]

	Time	Past (παρῳχειμένος)	Present (ἐνεστώς)	Future (μέλλων)
Action				
Incomplete (παρατατικός)		παρατατικός	ἐνεστώς	
Complete (συντελικός)		ὑπερσυντέλικος	παρακείμενος	
Undefined (ἀόριστος)		ἀόριστος		μέλλων

This scheme is presented less systematically by Apollonius Dyscolus (A.D. 2d cent.).[10]

Though the Stoics are to be commended for their attention to both temporal content and kind of action conveyed by verbs, and for their attempt to elucidate tense categories through apparent formal oppositions (they cite several examples of the appropriate form with each definition), the exact nature of the system has apparently eluded them.[11]

(1) Most obviously, the Stoics have failed to develop a complete system that elucidates all the verbal forms and functions (especially such an important form as the Aorist, where it is defined in terms of ἄρτι and πάλαι [see Pinborg, "Antiquity," 92; Haberland, "Note," 175-76]), since they are bound within a temporal framework similar to Dionysius's. For example, the Aorist like the Future is left undefined, and it is not compared to the Present and Imperfect, but only the Perfect and Pluperfect. And their categories make no reference to past-referring Presents or Perfects, present-referring Imperfects and Pluperfects, as well as non-Indicative usage.

(2) The Stoics have failed to define terms clearly. Besides failing either to define or to make explicit the relation between the Aorist and Future (apart from seeing their non-participation in the incomplete/complete opposition), the Stoics evidence terminological difficulty in defining the other tense forms, as seen in the repetition of terms within their conceptual framework, sometimes according to temporal reference, sometimes according to kind of action.

(3) Although reference to "incompleteness" is made, the definitions of the Present and Imperfect, through use of the concept of futurity to define incompleteness, are temporally bound

---

[9]See Robins, *History*, 29; cf. Steinthal, *Geschichte*, 1.309. Pinborg ("Antiquity," 93-94) presents and criticizes schemes by other scholars; Hiersche ("'Aspect'") disputes an aspectual analysis (he uses the categories of *Aktionsart*). Their common features preclude analysis individually, although several are noticeably more complex than the evidence warrants.

[10]Bekker, *Anecdota Graeca*, vol. 2, trans. in Householder, *Syntax*. Holt (*Etudes*, 3; followed by Wilkinson, *"Aspect,"* 22ff.) attributes the Stoic position directly to Apollonius Dyscolus, while Steinthal (*Geschichte*, 1.310-ll) differentiates Apollonius from the Stoics proper, though recognizing their common terminology.

[11]Holt (*Etudes*, 3) calls their theory "ingénieuse." Steinthal (*Geschichte*, 1.315) is more to the point: "So blieb die Theorie der Temporal in der Stoa durchaus inconsequent, teils weil man theoretisch alle Bestimmtheit der Zeit von dem Verhältnisse zur Gegenwart abhängig machte, teils weil man sich durch die tatsächlich vorliegenden Formen irre führen liess."

(many modern grammarians fall victim to this same fault), as are the definitions of the Perfect forms (see Hiersche, "'Aspect,'" esp. 280-281, 283). The distinction between Perfect and Imperfect is also muddled, since the Perfect is called ἐνεστὼς συντελικός but is said to represent past accomplishment and is defined in terms of ἐποίησα ἄρτι. The statement that the ὑπερσυντέλικος is best represented by ἐποίησα πάλαι is not much clearer. But it is these definitions that have been adopted by many modern grammarians. To use ἀόριστος at all can only confuse the matter, however, since the term is left undefined. The problem appears to stem from the Stoics' over-dependence upon temporally-based definitional categories even for kind of action, so that since they could not conceive of the Future or Aorist in terms of specific 'aspectual' relations they were compelled to leave them outside the system proper (see Arist. Nic. Eth. 1173A34-B4; Pl. Thaeat. 155B-C [see chapt. 2]). As Pollak says, their system was based "allerdings also Attribute des χρόνος, der den Überbegriff bildet" (*Studien*, 31; Robins [*Theory*, 35-36] suggests the Stoics' problem stemmed from dependence upon meaning rather than form. This is only part of the problem). The Greeks cannot be faulted only for an insufficient metalanguage; the definitions and understandings themselves are not comprehensive or fully satisfactory.

As Robins rightly says, whereas "an author's work is important as part of the intellectual and literary life of the times and civilization in which he lived and wrote," more importantly it "represents a stage in the history and development of the subject he is concerned with" ("Dionysius Thrax," 68). Dionysius Thrax and the Stoics performed groundbreaking work in Greek grammar, and the former especially has had a formative influence on subsequent work (Robins, 67-68; cf. Robertson, 824, who laments Dionysius's influence even into the 20th cent.). As Friedrich says, "The traditional theories of Dionysius Thrax and the Stoics partly recognized the aspectual character of Ancient Greek, but erred seriously by overemphasizing tense, by defining aspect in terms of completion, and by inadequately characterizing the relation between the aorist and the future" ("Theory," S9). This should not discourage later grammarians, however, from striving for a better understanding of the subject, believing that the Greeks spoke the final word on Greek grammar. Certainly their abilities to use the language far exceeded those of modern scholars, yet their efforts at describing their own language were, unfortunately, rudimentary and even in places misleading.

2. 19TH-CENTURY AND TRADITIONAL GRAMMARS. Between the hellenistic age and the 19th cent., many significant scholars made important contributions to discussion of verbal usage, such as the Latin grammarians, J. C. Scalinger, Samuel Clarke and Jacob Harris (see e.g. Herbig, "Aktionsart," 180-83; Holt, *Etudes*, 5-6; Wilkinson, *"Aspect,"* 23ff. For an overview see Robins, *History*, 45-163.). A thorough discussion cannot be attempted here. The thread of the history resumes with the 19th cent., when there was a significant increase in work not only in Greek grammar but in linguistic study in general (Jankowsky, *Neogrammarians*, 12, 39; cf. Fries, *Linguistics*, 37ff.; Danker, *Century*, 57ff.). Even as recently as the 19th cent., the grammarians comprise roughly two groups: those resembling a. Dionysius Thrax and b. the Stoics.

   a. Of those resembling Dionysius, Madvig (87-97) and Krüger (162-75) both treat tense forms as absolutely temporally based, and apparently formulate their descriptions on the basis of representative pragmatic usage. Consequently many ambiguities and peculiarities in verbal usage do not find ready explanation. For example, Madvig claims there is little difference between the Aorist and Imperfect (Th. 2.6.1), labels present-referring and customary usage of the Aorist as peculiar (Isoc. 1.1; Pl. Rep. 566), and claims that the historic Present is used for lively connected narrative (X. Anab. 1.1.3). Krüger posits a completely synonymous use of the tenses in contexts where, for example, the Aorist and Imperfect are mixed, since he invokes no other semantic feature than temporality.

   Jelf's standard English classical Greek grammar (2.51-73) also establishes temporal relations as the primary criterion for the predicate. He divides the three temporal categories into absolute and relative tenses, the former expressing action "without reference to any other action" and the latter having "reference to some other action expressed by some other predicate" (51). Arguing logically, Jelf claims there are three absolute and nine relative tenses, including periphrastics. This elegant--though formally repetitious--scheme attempts to understand verbal action in the relative tenses on the basis of their relations, but since the entire scheme is formulated around temporal criteria (e.g. coincidence, antecedence, consequence), the plan is unhelpful. (In treating pragmatic usage he speaks in terms of incomplete, complete, and momentary action, but this is clearly secondary to his major formulation and often related to lexical conception of an event; see below on *Aktionsart*.) And Jelf's failure to define functional categories adequately (he explains the names of the tenses with English examples [54]) leads to confusion, as illustrated in his detailed discussion, where, though he admits to kinds of action, he treats such instances as the Present used for the Future, the Imperfect for the Present, and the Aorist instead of the Present, Imperfect, Perfect, and Pluperfect. In many places Jelf's pragmatic descriptions are correct, but in others he has obvious difficulties. Regarding the historic Present Jelf takes refuge in its use as an absolute tense to bring an event "more vividly before the mind" (55), although use in relative clauses would seem to argue against this (Hdt. 5.91; cf. X. Anab. 1.7.16); concerning Present verbs with Perfect meaning he dismisses this as arising from the "sense of the verb" rather than the "force of the tense" (56; X. Cyr. 6.1.45 with οἴχεται; Hom. Od. 15.403 with ἀκούεις); to the Aorist in non-momentary or non-past contexts (Hom. Il. 13.300; S. Ant. 303) he devotes a section on "peculiar usages" (63-66); and with reference to the Moods he notes that they are not strictly temporal, although if this is true, his scheme has little basis for describing how the Moods function. (His treatment does actually define the non-Indicative Moods in terms of temporal pragmatic usage [74ff.].)

   As late as 1924 Meillet and Vendryes (*Traité*, 294-97) continue in this mould, mentioning only the temporal function of the primary (present) and secondary (past) endings.

   b. The Stoic-influenced grammarians are more plentiful. P. Buttmann, at the turn of the 19th cent. ([1st ed. c. 1800] 125-26, on verb forms [he treats three temporal divisions and a manifold number of past tenses], and 407-15, on verbal functions), recognized that "die Bedeutungen können gründlich erst in der Syntax entwickelt werden" (125). Consequently, he defined tense usage relationally: the Aorist is a narrative tense and the Perfect is not; the Perfect represents "vollendete und abgeschlossene" action while the Present "unvollendete und geschehende" (407); the Aorist is momentary past while the Imperfect is durative past (408). Despite his temporal dependence for the Indicative, Buttmann identifies incomplete, momentary and resultive characters of the Present, Aorist and Perfect. A recognizable difficulty, however, is when Buttmann notes that, though incomplete and momentary events are expressed in present and future times through single forms, the non-Indicative Moods have double forms throughout (409). Like the Stoics, however, Buttmann apparently misconstrues the nature of the kind of action by defining the tenses in temporal terms (complete, incomplete and momentary) and by apparently trying to use them as objective descriptions of the action itself. As a result Buttmann, for example, describes the empiric Aorist as "einen besondern Gräcismus häufig der Aorist" (411); recognizes the unmarked nature of the Aorist, though he says it can replace the Imperfect or Pluperfect if temporal indicators are sufficient (408; X. Mem. 1.6.14); claims the Present and Future are durative and momentary, although there are no double forms in the Indicative; recognizes present value of the Aorist in τί οὐ questions; and defends the historic Present (X. Anab. 1.7.16) as possible because of great freedom in choice of tense forms in Greek (412).

As late as 1897, Jannaris continues virtually the same Stoic scheme (esp. 433-45; see also Sandford, 167-68, 172-73; F. Thompson, esp. 138-41). After distinguishing nine categories (three temporal categories by three kinds of action) he includes a note that the effective and durative Presents (e.g. ποιῶ, "I do" and "am doing") have no separate single form (180, cf. 433, 435). This initially follows from a temporal view of verbal action. He applies this model to all the non-Indicative Moods as well (433). In his treatment of individual tenses, Jannaris states that, for example, the historic Present represents the past transferred to the present (Th. 1.91), in animated speech the Present is used for future reference (although both of the classical examples he cites--Th. 6.91; D. 19.32--are conditional statements), the Present stands for the Perfect, the gnomic Aorist transfers general truths to the past (again his only classical example--D. 2.9--is a conditional statement), the Perfect stands for the Aorist, and the Future is the present transferred to the future.

A similar system is promoted by Goodwin in his grammar and special treatment of the verb (*Grammar*, 268ff.; *Syntax*). In his *Syntax*, Goodwin formally distinguishes seven tense forms, gives temporally-dependent estimations of kind of action (going on, finished, or simply taking place), and then relates them to absolute (Indicative) or relative time (normally non-Indicative Moods). Since the Present "represents an action as *going on* at the time of speaking or writing" (8), and "as the limits of such an action on either side of the present moment are not defined, the present may express a customary or repeated action [Pl. Phaed. 58A] or a general truth [A. Ag. 857]" (9). This definition presents further problems for the historic Present (X. Anab. 1.1.1; Hdt. 1.63), use of the Present with πάλαι (Pl. Gorg. 489C), Presents with so-called perfect sense (Hom. Il. 15.223), and Presents of complete action (Th. 6.20). His definition of the Perfect as an action already finished at present time, besides being temporally oriented, must admit exceptions, as Goodwin himself recognizes (Pl. Theaet. 114B; Men. Fr. 598 where no continuance of result is seen; Isoc. 1.2 with no past action). His definition of the Aorist as a "simple *occurrence* in past time" (16) is controverted by: examples speaking of a state or condition (D. 30.33), though he admits that the difference between the Aorist and Imperfect is related to the perspective of the speaker (16-17); verbs of speaking where he sees no semantic difference between Aorist and Imperfect forms (Th. 1.72, 79), and Aorists used of present (S. Aj. 536; Ar. Knights 696) or future (E. Alc. 386) reference. His inclusion of a special discussion of gnomic and iterative tenses (53-56) shows that his temporally-based system finds it difficult to treat these uses except as something noteworthy.

In his *Grammar*, Goodwin proposes again an essentially temporally-based system, but with a concretizing of the categories regarding kind of action. A difficulty in formal and functional terminology is evidenced when he asserts that the gnomic Aorist is a primary tense, since it refers to present time and the historic Present is a secondary tense, since it refers to past time (271), forgetting that primary and secondary tenses are determined on formal criteria.

Kühner, in the German original from which Jelf is a translated adaptation (Kühner/Gerth, 1.129-200 [1955 reprint of the 3d ed., 1897]; see Lejnicks, *Morphosyntax*, 45-58, who follows Kühner/Gerth), adheres to the same 19th-cent. neo-Stoic scheme. Thus, though he includes a knowledgeable discussion of kind of action (he uses the term *Aktionsart*--see below), his model of the Indicative is based upon absolute temporal categories (131). He defines the Aorist as referring both to a simple fact (*Faktum schlechthin*), thus as an event complete in itself; and to a fully represented event, thus momentary (cf. his chart that includes no present-referring momentary form [131]). His definition of the Present as delineating an event in its development or movement, thus without limitation and hence durative, is temporally bound, as is his definition of the Perfect as a state resulting from a completed event (130). Kühner makes disclaimers regarding the terminology of *Aktionsart* (e.g. momentary does not mean occurring in a moment), but these reveal an attempt to unite what might be called subjective and objective views of the action (131). Several further difficulties emerge. Kühner defines the historic Present in terms of the speaker transferring himself to the time of the event to maintain his definition of absolute present reference, though it is questionable whether this definition handles instances where Aorist and Imperfect verbs also occur (Hdt. 3.129ff.); admits that the Present is often used where the event belongs to the past but is in present view by the speaker, though several examples are troublesome (X. Mem. 3.5.26; Anab. 4.6.17; Pl. Gorg. 503C; Kühner admits that several are used like the Imperfect); and recognizes the future-referring Present as one of the original uses of the tense, though this also occurs with verbs of going. Though Kühner defines the Imperfect as the Present in the past, this presents difficulties in examples that do not show development (Th. 4.28; he maintains that the Aorist and Imperfect are not mixed though he is at pains to explain why [143-44, cf. 154, 157]). And he recognizes the difficulty of Perfects without reference to a past event (Th. 1.144.1) and instances where an event not yet begun is treated as completed (X. Cyr. 4.2.26). Kühner claims that Aorist verbs from durative roots are inceptive (Hdt. 2.137; this example is debatable), but Hdt. 1.16.1 calls this formulation--lacking formal criteria--into question (Ἄρδυος δὲ βασιλεύσαντος ἑνὸς δέοντα πεντήκοντα ἔτεα ἐξεδέξατο Σαδυάττης ὁ Ἄρδυος, καὶ ἐβασίλευσε ἔτεα δυώδεκα [and after A. reigned for forty nine years, S., the son of A., succeeded him, and he reigned twelve years]). His treatment of the gnomic Aorist as a single concrete case is unsatisfying (Isoc. 1.6), as is his treatment of present and future-referring usage (D. 23.206) and questions with τί οὐ (X. Cyr. 2.1.4).

In as recent a grammar (revised) as Smyth's (esp. 412-76; see also Bizos, 118-26), still widely used, this system continues. Though he recognizes that the tenses represent the "time of an action" and the "stage of an action" (412), he lists time of action first, describes its relative and absolute uses (when he notes that the actual time may be different from that denoted by the tense, he seems to have confused tense terminology regarding name and function), and constructs a diagram in which he lists only the seven tense forms. Regarding kind of action, he creates a tense-system listing continued, completed, and simple attainment (in which he, like the Greeks, places the Aorist and Future), though he notes that the Present stem may denote aoristic action and the Future continued or aoristic action. Smyth reveals further confusion over formal and functional criteria when he lists the gnomic Aorist, perfect Aorist and present Imperfect as primary tenses, and makes the apparently contradictory remarks that "the tenses of the moods except the indicative do not express time in independent sentences" (415) and that the Subjunctive, Optative and Imperative always refer to future time. He explains the use of the tenses in temporal terms alone, causing difficulties. After defining the Present as representing a present state or action, Smyth lists the Present of customary action (D. 19.46); the Present of general truth (Men. Sent. 11); and Present for the future (Pl. Gorg. 505C), though he qualifies it as referring to "what is immediate, likely, certain, or threatening" (421); historic and annalistic Presents (X. Cyr. 2.1.19; Anab. 1.1.1); and Present for the Perfect (X. Anab. 1.4.8). He recognizes the Imperfect appearing in contexts where present reference would be expected (X. Anab. 4.8.1). Although Smyth says the Future denotes future action, he also notes gnomic (Pl. Rep. 603E) and jussive (D. 24.39) uses. His definition of the Aorist as expressing "the mere occurrence of an action in the past" (429) is apparently incompatible with the gnomic Aorist (Hes. Works 218), even though he invokes reference to a typical case; present or dramatic Aorist (S. El. 668); and future Aorist (E. Alc. 386 [in the apodosis of a conditional statement]). He admits as well that ingressive Aorist verbs need not be ingressive (430).

3. COMPARATIVE PHILOLOGY AND *AKTIONSART*. During the 19th cent., a few grammarians grew uncomfortable with traditional tense definitions. As early as 1836, Rost, though ascribing temporal categories to the verb, realized, "um die eigenthümliche Bedeutung eines jeden Tempus genau zu bestimmen und sicher aufzufassen, ist nothwendig, dass man ausser dem Begriffe der Zeit auch den Stand der Handlung welche in dem Verbum ausgedrückt ist, berücksichtige. . ." (559; 559-72 on the tenses in general). Though he reconciles the two systems--action and time--by the same scheme as proposed by many mentioned above, Rost is able to move further in his understanding by paying particular attention to the verbal action of the individual tenses. (He also opposes the Aorist to the Imperfect rather than the Future.)

a. Most credit for making grammarians aware of the issue of verbal kind of action goes to Curtius, who was the first to attempt a reconciliation of comparative linguistics and Greek philology (see Pedersen, *Discovery*, 89, cf. 89-90; Jankowsky, *Neogrammarians*, 200-12). He recognized the need for "considerable revision" of the "doctrine of the use of the tenses." (His works include *Die Bildung der Tempora und Modi im Griechischen und Lateinischen sprachvergleichend dargestellt* [1846; Eng. trans. *Verbs*], *Griechische Schulgrammatik* [1852] and *Erläuterungen zu meiner griechischen*

Schulgrammatik [1863]. I cite the authorized translation of the last, *Elucidations*, 207-18, on the verb, a theory first presented in *Verbs*, 2ff.) Curtius asserted that ἐγένετο, ἐγίγνετο and ἐγεγόνει (become) are distinguished from each other along quite different lines than distinguish ἐγίγνετο and γίγνομαι, or ἐγεγόνει and γέγονα. This difference requires a new term--*Zeitart* or "kind of time." Whereas *Zeitstufe* (lit. time-step, left untranslated by Curtius's translator) refers to external time or the relation of "the action to the speaker" (208), *Zeitart* refers to internal distinctions: continuous (Present stem), completed (Perfect stem) and *eintretende* (Aorist stem).[12] Discussing the Aorist, Curtius discounts use of the term "momentary" (though later grammarians reinstated it) since it creates the temptation to measure the difference in lapse of time, e.g. νικᾶν and νικῆσαι (conquer), ἔβαλλε and ἔβαλε (throw), whereas when an artist affixed ΕΠΟΙΗΣΕ or ΕΠΟΙΕΙ (make) to his work his choice did not depend on the actual length of time in creating the work but "on his intention to lay stress either on the simple fact that he was the artist, or on the labour spent upon it" (209). He also distinguishes the Aorist's *Zeitart* from a beginning or impending act, from a continuing act, and from an incomplete act (while recognizing the term's ambiguity). In describing *Zeitarten*, Curtius compares the Aorist to a point, which has no size, as the Aorist does not take "extension in time" (212) into account. But then Curtius expands his definition by noting that since an aoristic action is opposed to a continuing one, it may be ingressive--e.g. ἐρασθῆναι (to fall in love), the "starting-point of a line"; or effective--e.g. ἀγαγεῖν (to carry away), "the culmination of an act" (213). The Present by contrast is equated with a line, having indefinite extension, and the Perfect with "a surface bounded by lines, since it is completely limited in every direction" (213).

    b. The importance of Curtius's groundbreaking work cannot be overestimated; however, only one major grammarian adopted his terminology: Stahl (74-87, on theory of tense; 87-220, on tense usage; he rejects the term *Aktionsart*, since, he argues, not every verb refers to an action or event [74]):

> Das Tempus bezeichnet einen zeitlichen Bereich des Verbalbegriffs. Der Bereich einer Erscheinung wird ebenso nach der Zeit bemessen wie der Bereich einer Substanz nach ihren räumlichen oder begrifflichen Umfange. Wir unterscheiden nun den Bereich einer Erscheinung an sich und den Bereich einer Erscheinung im Verhältnisse zur Zeit der Aussage, und nennen jenen Zeitart, diesen Zeitstufe. (74)

Stahl differentiates an action as "durative" (*dauernde*), "complete" (*vollendete*) and "in and for itself" (*an und für sich*), corresponding to the Present, Perfect and Aorist stems as the three *Zeitarten* in Greek (74). (Note that he departs from Curtius in his definition of the Aorist.) Stahl rigorously follows this regime, finding that a *Zeitart* corresponds to its verbal stem, with choice of

---

[12]Curtius (*Elucidations*, 209) acknowledges adopting this term from Rost and Krüger; see the note, 210-12, where he discusses the French grammarian Thurnot's objections to his new terminology, since Thurnot posits only simultaneous, anterior and posterior action as expressed by the verb.

tense dependent on the individual author's conception of the action and temporal reference secondary. Stahl's helpful theory adumbrates the later work of Jacobsohn, Hermann, and McKay (see below), though Stahl also creates unnecessary difficulties. For example, although Stahl reasonably entertains general, past, present, and future uses of the Present, he poses the difficulty of the Perfect Present (X. Anab. 2.1.4; 5.7.29; Pl. Euth. 3E; he finds the same problem with the Imperfect: Hom. Il. 1.188; D. 20.48). Regarding the Perfect, Stahl depends upon a temporal definition which posits a past event, though this causes difficulties with the intensive Perfect (Hes. Works 207; Hom. Od. 5.400) and the extensive Perfect (Hom. Od. 8.134). Although Stahl reasonably argues that the Imperfect and Aorist differ not in temporal reference but in *Zeitart*, and since he argues that the augment bestows past reference, he must explain the empiric Aorist (Pi. Ol. 12.10), as well as the Perfect Aorist (S. Trach. 500).

Problems of a more general nature are also present. (1) The term *Zeitart* itself is questioned, since it does not appear to some to describe the nature of the concept being defined. Terms like *duration, momentary, punctual* are seen not as descriptions of kinds of time but as kinds of action. As Herbig ("Aktionsart," 185-86) says, "Zeit in den Zusammenhangen Zeitart und Zeitstufe etwas Verschiedenes bedeutet." (2) Criticism is found with Stahl's almost iron-clad (Gildersleeve would say overly-repetitious) description of verbal usage according to tense form (Gildersleeve, "I.--Stahl's Syntax . . . Tenses," 389-409). For example, Gildersleeve questions: whether the Future ought not be considered a Mood only (391); the conception of the Present as purely durative (here Gildersleeve follows most 19th-cent. grammars) (392); Stahl's formulation of the Imperfect as interrupted and uninterrupted (393), since duration is subjective; his multiplication of categories (394); and what Gildersleeve calls Stahl's "tiresome defense" of the right of the author to choose the verbal *Zeitart* he wishes (394). He concludes by declaring that little of Stahl's work is new and acceptable (409). Gildersleeve's reaction is surprising, since in many respects Stahl went beyond Curtius or his contemporaries.

An interesting contrast can be made to Gildersleeve's own grammar (esp. 79-122; see "Problems," 241-60, where he endorses a morphologically-based aspectual system along the lines of Curtius, disputing the terminology of the comparative philologists, e.g. regarding punctual or momentary Aorists; cf. "Brief Mention," 23 [1902] 106). Gildersleeve displays (80) a chart of verbal usage which apparently confuses form and function, in particular regarding the Present (cf. 82-83), and treats the "stage of action" (continuance, completion, attainment) with the "period of the action" (79). Thus he links temporal and kind-of-action meanings to tense stems, with his individual expositions of tenses temporally based. His terminology is tempered compared to many grammars (e.g. he refers to the "Present anticipating the Future" [83]), though he does not explain tenses using "kind of action" (cf. "Present for Perfect" [87]). Consequently, several apparent difficulties may be mentioned. Gildersleeve justifies the specific and universal presents as what occurs in English (81), though this fails to account for the historic Present (Pl. Phaed. 84D [cf. his 86 on annalistic Present]), which he must call "especially strange" (85); and the Present for the Perfect (X. Anab. 2.1.4), whose particularity may be increased by the problem of English translation. Since he emphasizes the Perfect of maintenance of result, Gildersleeve treats the intensive Perfect as an old form (Ar. Birds 944) and the emotional Perfect (S. Aj. 139) as unusual. He also distinguishes the ingressive Aorist as an item particularly favourable to the 1 Aorist, though he admits 2 Aorist uses as well (X. Cyr. 1.5.2; this distinction cannot be maintained on any principled linguistic grounds); and argues for the Aorist for the Perfect (Isoc. 5.19-21) on the basis of the Aorist being next of kin for verbs that form no Perfect (but cf. D. 9.26).

Since Curtius, major thought about Greek verbal usage has concentrated upon reassessing the importance of the kind of action represented by the verb. But this does not mean that all were in agreement, only that the struggle for definition had begun in earnest.

c. Delbrück shows in his Greek syntax (*Grundlagen*, 80-114, on the tenses) the transition to the purely comparative philology which dominated classical linguistics well into the 20th cent. Giving credit to Curtius, he realizes that the stems of the Present, Aorist and Perfect show different *Aktionen* (duration, event, complete event), in all Moods, with time only indicated by the augment (80). He then posits, however, that individual lexical items offer choices for stem meanings, which should form the basis of a grammar of the Greek tenses, rather than working from the tenses to the individual verbs (81-91). Delbrück's dependence on Indo-European (IE) languages is also evident. He argues for example: the Perfect stem is the oldest of IE verbs; the Future is not necessarily punctual since it probably did not originate from the Aorist Subjunctive; the Aorist as in Vedic originally had two senses based on the sigmatic and non-sigmatic forms; and the many Present stems reflect the IE verb's ability to build many verbs out of a common root (94, 97, 100, 111-12). But he readily acknowledges that his conclusions were only tentative and that much research was needed in the area of Greek tenses.

d. Perhaps the most important name in late 19th-cent. discussion of the Greek verb was Brugmann. In 1885 in his Greek grammar, he coined the term *Aktionsart* to describe the kind of action indicated objectively by a verb (538-41, on *Zeitstufe* and *Aktionsart* in general; 541-70, on tense usage). He begins his section on tenses boldly:

> Das System der sog. Tempora des idg. Verbums diente von Haus aus nicht dazu, die subjectiven, ausserhalb der Verhandlung selbst liegenden Zeitstufen der Gegenwart, Vergangenheit und Zukunft auszudrücken. Vielmehr dienten sie zur Charakterisierung der Aktionsart, d.h. der Art und Weise, wie die Handlung vor sich geht. (538)

Claiming to find this concept in Apollonius Dyscolus he says further that all forms of the IE verb were originally timeless, and in Greek all non-Indicative tense forms remain timeless, "aber keine ohne Aktionsart" (538).

For Brugmann, *Aktionsart* is determined by verbal stem (root plus affix) so that a different stem offers a different conception of the action. He offers the following scheme:

1. Punctual *Aktionsart*--an event is complete, gathered up in a moment. One can speak of momentary, perfective and aoristic action, shown mainly through the Aorist: e.g. βα (go).[13]

---

[13]The origin of this terminology actually lies with Mutzbauer, *Grundlagen*, 1.11: "Die Bedeutungen des Praesens- und Aoriststammes scheiden sich scharf nach dem Prinzip der Anschaulichkeit. Und zwar lässt sich die Bedeutung des Praesensstammes einer Linie, die des Aoriststammes einem Punkte vergleichen." He then divides the point action into momentary (*Moment*), inceptive (*Anfangspunkt*) and terminative (*Schlusspunkt*).

2. Cursive *Aktionsart*--an event develops without limits as a single act inside itself, so that beginning and ending are not in view. The Present stem usually has this meaning, which can be referred to as linear (he only gives German examples).

3. Terminative *Aktionsart*--exit or endpoint is displayed, regardless of whether the action in itself is cursive or punctual, e.g. ἀγνύναι (smash).

4. Iterative *Aktionsart*--repeated action is represented, e.g. ⁻σκον suffix.

5. Perfective *Aktionsart*--action of the Perfect stem, in which a state of the subject results from a previous event, e.g. βέβηκα, "I have come and now am here."

6. A prefix can perfectivize a verb.

Brugmann then characterizes the various stems according to their *Aktionsarten*, asserting with Delbrück that to understand the contrast of the tense stems one must not proceed from a general concept but from each single verb (cf. Brugmann, *Kurze . . . Grammatik*, 2.493-94, for an outline of the same scheme of *Aktionsart* for all IE languages; 494-551, for discussion of the verbal stems; see also Delbrück, *Syntax*, 2.13ff.). Under the Present stem he lists ἵστημι (stand) and γίγνομαι (become) as iterative; δάμνημι (subdue), δάκνω (bite), ὄρνυμι (rouse) and τίνω (pay) as linear-terminative; ⁻σκω verbs such as φάσκω (say) as terminative; ιο suffixed verbs and κλαίω (weep) as cursive. Originally these verbs supposedly had no Aorist form because of the nature of the action, though later sigmatic Aorist forms developed by analogy. Other forms had both Present and Aorist roots to start, others just Aorist. According to Brugmann, the original classes of verbs were then assigned tense classifications on the basis of their *Aktionsart*, the punctual being claimed as Aorists, the non-punctual as Presents. This led to organizing different roots opposite each other even though the forms did not correspond (i.e. suppletive verbs), like λέγω/εἶπον.

In his exposition of the various tense forms, Brugmann shows how *Aktionsart* is exemplified. For example, the Aorist can represent ingressive (ἐδάκρυσα--I began to cry), effective (ἔπεσον--I fell down; ἤγαγον--I led), or constative (ἐποίησα--I did) action, depending not on the Aorist but on the perspective of its particular verbal root. Therefore, durative roots that later formed Aorists are described as complexive (Hdt. 2.133; Th. 5.5). Likewise the difference between an intensive (τέθηλε--I am blooming) and accomplished (μέμνημαι--I have remembered; cf. Pl. Crito 46A) Perfect is the meaning of the root. He also notes an intensive use (Ar. Peace 335), though he dismisses it as a late phase; and a transitive use in which an Aorist or Imperfect could be used (Hom. Il. 5.66). The Future, being a mixed tense from the IE Future and the sigmatic Subjunctive Aorist, may be punctual (βήσομαι--I will come), non-punctual (ἔσομαι--I will be) or both (ὄψομαι--I will see/observe) depending on the root. Also the Present may be punctiliar (e.g. εἶμι--I come, νέομαι--I come) as well as durative.

e. The number of works fostered by this method is large. One obvious descendant of the comparative school of thought is the comparative grammar. For example, Wright finds five essential *Aktionsarten* --momentary, cursive, perfect, iterative and terminative (252-55), while Buck traces Greek back to its parent language with three essential "aspects" (*Grammar*, 238-40, who recognizes the terminology of "aspect" as having a broader sense than in Slavonic to cover disparate, non-technical distinctions that differ from language to language [240]).

The most significant work, however, is by Wackernagel (*Vorlesungen*, 149-86; see also Romano, "Significato," who applies his findings to Xenophon). On the basis of Slavonic, he claims that the differentiation of *Aktionsarten* (153) reflects the conception of the action by the speaker not the factual state of the event. When applied to Greek, however, Wackernagel accepts uncritically (154-56) the kinds of action (*Aktionsarten*) posited by the other comparative philologists: punctual, terminative, cursive, and the role of perfectivizing prefixes, as objective descriptions of action. In applying these categories to Greek tenses, Wackernagel argues for both a characterization of each tense and distinctions based upon the roots of individual words. For the Present tense, he states that since a form like φημί only shows a root (φη) and an ending (μι) and no augment for past tense or sigma for futurity, it must only be used for present reference, though there is no present element per se (157-58), and it does not exclude uses like the gnomic. He depends upon the IE Present to explain that certain verbs (εἶμι, ἔρχομαι [come]) have future meaning (Hom. Il. 1.169; John 14:3) since they are punctual Presents, as in Slavonic usage; and that the historic Present is based upon an original timeless use of the Present (157-66). In comparison of the Imperfect and Aorist, he differentiates the meanings of the 1 (sigmatic) and 2 Aorists, claiming that the 2 Aorists were closer in meaning to the Imperfect, since the Aorist forms probably were not synonymous originally, though now no difference can be detected (171). He also cites examples where the Aorist is near to the Present (ἔκλαυσα [break]; ἐδάκρυσα [cry]; S. Aj. 270 [175-76]), and after prolonged discussion sees the gnomic Aorist as reflecting the original timelessness of the Aorist, as in Slavonic (Hes. Works 218; Jas 1:24 [178-81]). The Future divides its *Aktionsart* between punctual and non-punctual roots on the basis of point of view (197), though some scholars cite different forms, e.g. ἔξω/σχήσω (203). The above discussion samples some of Wackernagel's disparate statements regarding Greek, intermixed with discussions of other languages. Though he recognizes *Aktionsarten* as subjective he constructs a model along the lines of the comparative philologists. Though his practice of interpretation, especially in the non-Indicative Moods, is often morphologically determined, it is virtually always violable on the basis of diachronic study or apparent, translational meaning.

The second type of work fostered by this approach is the historical Greek grammar, especially by Kieckers (13-29). His first distinction is between time and kind of action, noting that time only applies to the Indicative. After briefly defining the four most important *Aktionsarten* or *Aspekts* (imperfective, perfective, perfectual, iterative) and perfectivizing prepositions, and claiming a correlation between tense stem and *Aktionsart*, such that the Present is imperfective and the Aorist perfective (this explains the difference between χαρίζασθαι and χαρίσασθαι [show kindness]), and the Perfect perfectual, all with a mixture of examples from Greek and other languages (13-15), Kieckers extends his categories. He claims there are also perfective Present verbs, thus explaining the future-referring Present (εἶμι [I go]); and perfective *Aktionsart* with punctual and terminative meaning (15-16). When he discusses usage of the forms, Kieckers almost completely disregards his previous discussion, listing a number of uses of each verb. Present: general or timeless, actual, timeless with πάρος (earlier) or πάλαι (for a long time), historic Present, resultive, conative, future, and prophetic; Imperfect; historic Aorist, in which "Die dauer des Vorgangs spielt dabei keine Rolle" (23); the ingressive Aorist; gnomic Aorist, in which "der Aorist is . . . zeitlos gebraucht" (25); Perfect, intensive and iterative; Pluperfect; Future, in which one form can be imperfective or perfective, as well as modal (volitive); and the Future Perfect. Kieckers's treatment is included more for its exemplary value than its explanatory powers, illustrating the persistence of this model. Its limitations are noteworthy. (1) The categories of *Aktionsart* are derivative. While Kieckers recognizes a correlation with stem forms, he lacks a theoretical basis for clarifying the relationship. (2) The treatment of *Aktionsart* has little influence on formulation of categories of usage, which are uncoordinated. He does not clarify how he arrives at the sub-categories of Present usage or why they are sub-categories. Treatment of the Aorist lists several major categories, also uncoordinated. (3) The Greek examples given are generally few and often made up, and they are often overshadowed by examples from German and Slavonic languages. Overall the treatment is disappointingly uninformative, not only because it does not advance treatment of Greek itself but because it leaves fundamental assumptions unexamined.

f. A survey of a number of important publications in response to Brugmann *et al.* is worth making. The amount of material is overwhelming, since it includes articles in comparative philology, Slavonic and other IE languages, as well as purely theoretical discussions (see Schwyzer, 2.246-48, for bibliography; for a summary of the comparative philological approach represented by Brugmann and Delbrück [known as the Neogrammarians] see Jankowsky, *Neogrammarians*, 124-43; Ivic, *Trends*, 58-64; cf. also Robins, *History*, 164-97).

(1) There is a noteworthy range of disagreement regarding the internal structure of the Greek verbal edifice. For example, Brugmann lists 32 different stem classes arranged under twelve headings in IE (*Flexionslehre*, 86-390, with some duplication) and 16 of these (not counting sub-classifications) are applied to Greek (*Grammatik*, 312-62). Brugmann does not believe that each class represents a particular function, since he conveniently divides them into various *Aktionsarten* (see above). But even these categories are questionable. For example, δάμνημι (bring under the yoke) and ὄρνυμι (rouse), both characterized as linear-terminative, seem to be terminative in opposite ways. And how linear-terminative differs from strict terminative, e.g. εὑρίσκω (find), or even iterative, e.g. γίγνομαι (become), is unclear. Brugmann himself notes that terminative can be used with a cursive or punctiliar root. The categories of *Aktionsart*, therefore, are more than root-based categories alone.

(2) An even more fundamental difficulty is to arrive at proper categories of *Aktionsart* (see e.g. Streitberg, "Benennung," 72-74, who is acutely aware of the terminological difficulties, though he endorses the terms imperfective/perfective, since the grammarian can give his particular meaning to them, he contends; cf. Review, 57-67. For very thorough listings of the secondary literature regarding verbal categories see footnotes to Brugmann, 538-70; Schwyzer, 1.247-301; see also Brunel, "L'aspect.")

Sarauw ("Syntaktisches," 145-49) argues against the terms punctual and punctual-perfective, noting that every action lasts some moment in time, so the beginning and ending cannot be linked directly, as the punctual event must be if characterized as a mathematical 'point.' He likens the point instead to one on a piece of paper with a certain extension. Therefore every verb represents a certain duration, and there is no such category as the punctual verb as an objective description of an event (cf. Brugmann's [540 n. 2, 541 n. 1] response to such criticism, and my chapt. 2).

Streitberg ("Perfektiv," 311-13) objects to any conception of a perfective verb other than one of completion. Since every verb of whichever *Aktionsart* expresses an event that has duration, he claims, when this common element is removed all that is left for a perfective verb is the moment of completion (he objects to Delbrück's use of the term "punctual" [313-14]). Streitberg also criticizes the use of *punctual* and *terminative* as conceptions of the same verbal root (Aorist in Greek, though he refers to the Slavonic Perfect), since the two are contradictory notions, referring to unlimited and limited action (313-14; Herbig ["Aktionsart," 209] finds a "durative-perfective Aktionsart" of the Aorist in ἐβασίλευσε τριάκοντα ἔτη [he reigned thirty years]).

Pedersen ("Vorschlag," 152-53; cf. "Lehre," 220-24) throws the debate into further terminological confusion when he argues on the basis of Slavonic and Gothic that the category of terminative verbs is misleading, since examples in fact can be punctual, iterative, and even durative. Instead, since every verb called punctual has a fixed termination it is better to refer to single-time and iterative-terminative, and possibly durative-terminative action. Regarding the category of iterative verbs, however, Herbig believes such a category is only psychological and not morphological, and dependent on adverbial modifiers ("Aktionsart," 214-16; he believes the Ionic σκον-suffix is already devoid of iterative significance).

This brief treatment is not designed to discredit the quest for verbal *Aktionsart* in itself, but to illustrate that these categories are neither strictly morphologically based, in the sense that a morphological pattern automatically conveys a particular *Aktionsart*, nor descriptively objective. They are convenient logical constructs grounded not in description of usage in an individual language but in argument from logical conceptions (see Streitberg, "Perfektiv," 313, who recognizes this) and the interpretative framework of comparative philology, thus providing a convenient and perhaps useful fiction in the guise of linguistic objectivity.

This method is potentially misleading when trying to gain insight into the nature of a particular language, especially one as morphologically based as Greek. For example, Brugmann in disputing Stahl's view that the Aorist is used to represent the event in and of itself states, "Aber ebensogut kann das Präsens in diesem Sinn gebraucht werden in Fällen wie *der Vogel fliegt*" (541; cf. Kieckers, 14). This German example says nothing about Greek usage. Hartmann's monumental study of the difference between the Aorist and the Imperfect falls victim to the same criticism. On the basis of a hypothesis about the original similarity in form between the two verbal categories and comparisons with various other languages, he concludes that certain categories of Aorists are not differentiated functionally from Imperfects ("Aorist und Imperfektum," 48 [1919]; 49 [1920]). On the basis of these previous studies, Hartmann can find no semantic differentiation between use of the Aorist and Imperfect in, for example, Luke 1-4 ("Aorist und Imperfektum im Griechischen," 327), only stylistic differences (contra Sarauw, "Syntaktisches," 151, who cites Hdt. 2.175.3, noting that ἐκόμισεν is not punctual but "concentrated," since it refers to the three year period during which the monolithic shrine was brought [ἐκόμιζον] from Elephantine). Also troublesome is Herbig ("Aktionsart"), whose argument constantly alternates between the theoretical and linguistically eclectic.

(3) Stahl (75) argues that, rather than suffixes of the Present stem containing meanings found in IE, (a) a special *Aktionsart* has not been indicated for every suffix, (b) with each single suffix the assumed sense is not employed with all constructed verbs, and (c) it must remain doubtful if the assured sense does not lie already in the tense itself. Taking -σκω as an example, Stahl argues it does not have a single fundamental meaning since it may be construed as inchoative with γηράσκω (I grow old), γιγνώσκω (I know) or μεθύσκω (I get drunk), iterative in Imperfect forms, e.g., ἐμέθυσκον (I was getting drunk), and neither in πάσχω (I suffer), εὑρίσκω (I find), βόσκω (I nourish), or θνήσκω (I die). For the NT, as Moulton, a follower of the comparative-philological school, notes, "In prehistoric Indo-Germanic these stems may have carried some functional distinctions, but it is difficult to prove these distinctions in all cases, and most of them were obsolete before Hellenistic Greek arose, even if they could be claimed for earlier periods" (Moulton/Howard, 183).

g. Regarding *Aktionsart* several points may be clarified.

1. Determining *Aktionsart* is an attempt to define *objectively* the kind of action conveyed by a verb. Therefore such terms as punctual, iterative, terminative, cursive, perfective, linear are used.

2. Such conceptions are *not* based strictly upon morphological criteria since similar forms are often subordinated beneath varying descriptive categories. As Schlachter says, in the quest for *Aktionsart* the morphological point of view has been "nahezu vergessen," with the only formal element of large interest being the prefix ("Verbalaspekt," 24).

3. The categories themselves are subjective constructs of highly questionable pertinence. As Klein states, "grundsätzlich könnte man von der Annahme ausgehen, dass es so viele Aktionsarten gibt, wie es denkbare Beschreibungskategorien eines verbalen Vorgangs gibt" (*Tempus*, 104. He continues: "Als relevant dürfen jedoch nur solche aktionsartlichen Kategorien gelten, die Auswirkungen auf eine mögliche Selektionsbeschränkung der Aspektsetzung oder auf weitere Syntaktische Kompatibilitäten besitzen"; see also Bache, *Aspect*, 10). Perhaps this is the most important point to make regarding *Aktionsarten*.

4. Whereas verbal roots may have conveyed *Aktionsart* at an earlier stage (e.g. in proto IE) these categories are not applicable to Greek from at least Homer onwards.[14] Resorting to terms such as "ingressive," "effective," "constative" Aorist is an appeal to non-formally based grammatical categories, lacking any objective grammatical standard for deciding their character. As Klein once more states, "die besondere Schwierigkeit aktionsartlicher Untersuchungen besteht darin, dass die Aktionsarten 'nicht zur Ausbildung fester grammatikalischen Kategorien gelangt' sind" (*Tempus*, 104, quoting W. Hanckel, *Die Aktionsarten im Französischen* [Diss., Berlin, 1930] 7).

5. Attempts to equate *Aktionsart* with tense categories have no basis of support in discussion of *Aktionsart*, since tenses are treated as merely convenient ways to describe general tendencies. Appeal is made to the verbal root (see above), lexis or time. An appeal to lexis is seen when it is argued that a certain verb is perfective (e.g. ἀκούω) since in one's lexical understanding one hears a noise and its importance remains. An appeal to temporal distinctions is seen in such headings as "Present used for/as a Future" (this terminology also neglects formal/functional differences) or when an Imperfect is treated as an Aorist since both refer to an event in past time and are found in parallel constructions (a classic example using translational value of individual lexical items is Riemann, "La question," 585-99).

6. These criticisms can be summarized in this way (see Schlachter, "Verbalaspekt," 25). (a) Proponents of *Aktionsart* claim it to be an objective method of characterizing action when in fact it is arbitrary and subjective, since the hearer must construe the meaning apart from any principled grammatical means of determination, such as morphology (Schlachter, 36. That determining *Aktionsart* is subjective, in that it attempts to summarize or characterize an event as punctual, etc., was recognized by B. Faddegon in *Donum natalicium Schrijnen* [1929] ll9ff., 127, as stated by Debrunner, Review of Koschmieder, 89 n. 1). (b) Without formal (morphological) criteria, comparative philologists lack an objective basis upon which to treat systematically all the variables present in Greek (kind of action, temporal distinction), without creating strained categories. (c) The terminology is temporally based; and the *Aktionsarten* are contradictory, mutually exclusive and (ironically) highly subjective appraisals of verbal action. (d) The problem can be laid at the feet of several causes, one being the comparative-diachronic method, since comparative philologists lack sensitivity to any one language as object of analysis. Since they function under the dictum that "what is not historical in linguistics is not scientific" (Ivic, *Trends*, 61), they tend to lose sight of the conception of any one language as a whole and to focus instead upon particular features found in many languages as evidence of the original IE. Also to blame are the failure to conceive of each language as a system in its own right, overreliance on temporal distinctions to establish suitable parallel contexts as well as to formulate tense labels, and failure to distinguish the value of tense categories. (e) One of the enduring features of the work of comparative philology, however, is to re-establish (from the hellenistic grammarians) that formal verbal tense categories, such as Aorist, Present, Perfect, as well as the forms of the various Moods, have a history that predates the hellenistic grammarians and even Homer, reaching back to the formative stages of Greek. And although the comparative philologists went far beyond the tense categories in formulating conceptions of Greek verbal usage, their recognition of and dependence upon these categories as comprising the starting point of any discussion of tenses are notable. These tense categories, at the heart of the Greek language, are to be treated as linguistic constructs (i.e. various forms are recognized as belonging to the same tense category), which are susceptible to principled

---

[14]Crisafulli (*Aspect*, esp. 1-33) attempts to demonstrate that lexical meaning is determinative for what he calls "aspect" (durative and punctiliar; actually this is a theory of *Aktionsart*), but he is forced to examine only primary verbs (i.e. those that have been in the language from earliest times) and exclude secondary verbs (i.e. those formed later from non-verbal stems or other verbal stems). Besides the evident problems of determining root meaning (translational values are crucial for him), the circularity of his logic is evident. It comes as no surprise that what he determines are durative roots appear most frequently in Present/Imperfect forms, and punctiliar roots in Aorist forms, though even here such a rule is far from absolute.

evaluation, unlike *Aktionsart*. Therefore, though Greek may appear to have many *Aktionsarten*, these are better viewed as contextual abstractions on the basis of lexis (i.e. attempts to describe each action objectively) and their verbal use must be subsumed under tense forms though *not* temporal categories.[15] Subsequent evaluation of Greek grammatical discussion endorses the results presented above.

4. TRANSITIONAL APPROACHES. a. As early as 1919 Harrison (*Aspects*), in a romanticized treatment of Russian and Greek, posited a direct correlation between Russian aspects and Greek tense forms.[16] The next significant development in study of aspect and *Aktionsart* was an incisive review by Jacobsohn of Wackernagel's *Vorlesungen* (369-95, esp. 378-86). After noting several difficulties Wackernagel and his school have in using IE to define *Aktionsarten*, and utilizing Semitic languages as a starting point, Jacobsohn concludes that there are two ways of conceiving of action: subjective aspect, "wie der Sprecher Verlauf der Handlung ansieht" (379; Jacobsohn is much more inclusive in his definition of aspect, listing such items as Moods as well as tenses [379, 381]), and objective *Aktionsart*, "als Beziechnungen eines besonderen, ausserhalb des Subjekts gegebenen objektiven Tatbestandes" (381),[17] though he affirms that the border between the two is flexible (386). Jacobsohn also argues that the verbal prefix is used in Greek to transform a durative tense into perfective action, treating this at the level of *Aktionsart*, though he says that this construction is to be considered at the level of grammar and not lexis (381-82). (Porzig ["Aktionsart," 152-53] takes up Jacobsohn's terminology, attempting to show that aspect is strongly morphologically based; contra Schlachter ["Verbalaspekt," 27-28], who criticizes Jacobsohn's definitions of the aspects, notes the lack of boundaries for what constitutes an *Aktionsart*, and points out Jacobsohn's failure in practice to fulfil his morphological differentiation.)

Soon after Jacobsohn, Hermann published an article which posits a solution for understanding the Greek Aorist ("Aktionsart," 207-28, similar to

---

[15]See Miller, *Tense*, 203-04. I follow his definition of lexis as a feature that is best handled by an "appropriate entry in a dictionary" of Greek, since the feature is "peculiar to one verb or to a group of verbs rather than being a general characteristic of the verb system" (204). See Pollak, *Studien*, 35-39, for others who argue for this position regarding Greek, including Leroy, "L'aspect"; Kravar, "Approche," 963, besides Jacobsohn and Hermann (see next section); cf. Klein, *Tempus*, who contrasts the morphological/grammatical concept of aspect with the lexical/semantic category of *Aktionsart* (77). The latter depends upon a single verb's meaning and the influences of context (103).

[16]Comparative philologists would have little to do with Harrison's explanation of the origin of aspect: "Some rather profound spiritual need must surely have prompted this distinction of aspect which is at once the dominant characteristic and the crowning glory of the Russian language" (*Aspects*, 11).

[17]The first to differentiate aspect and *Aktionsart* is reputed to be S. Agrell, who applied them to Slavonic languages in his *Aspektänderung und Aktionsartbildung beim polnischen Zeitworte: ein Beitrag zum Studium der indogermanischen Präverbia und ihrer Bedeutungsfunktionen*, Lunds Universitets Arsskrift NS 1, IV.2 (Lund, 1908). He distinguished aspect as the main category of Slavonic tenses (imperfective and perfective) and *Aktionsart* as functions of verbal composites which mark the kind or way the event is completed (see Pollak, *Studien*, 34, for summary).

K.W.L. Heyse in 1856 when he differentiated subjective and objective time; see Herbig, "Aktionsart," 185). He claims, "man hat bisher nur übersehen, dass zweierlei durcheinandergeworfen wird, was scharf zu trennen ist, weil es auf zwei verschiedenen Ebenen liegt" (207). The difference between ἐβασίλευον and ἐβασίλευσα "liegt lediglich in der Auffassung des Sprechenden" (207-08). Hermann devises a scheme of subjective *Aktionsart* (Hdt. 1.16.1)--complexive and cursive--and objective *Aktionsart*--durative and non-durative, with ἐβασίλευον/ἐβασίλευσα as complexive and durative, and ἐβασίλευσα as cursive and non-durative. All "Geschehene usw. dauern oder nichtdauern und alle Prädikate entweder durativ oder nichtdurativ sind" (211).[18] Despite the fact that Hermann has defined two subjective systems, has not sufficiently differentiated their relationship, confuses form and function in defining their uses (since he treats them on the same level), and maintains the same reductionistic terminology for *Aktionsarten* (e.g. ingressive, effective, and momentary non-durative *Aktionsarten* [213, 224-25]), he distinguishes the major issues involved. (Schlachter ["Verbalaspekt," 29-30] criticizes Hermann for blurring his subjective and objective categories, failing to maintain morphological distinctions, and psychologizing when differentiating categories.) It is unfortunate that his so-called structural analysis of the Greek language falls far short of the expectations he created.[19]

Jacobsohn, in clarifying his position ("Aspektfragen," 293-318, esp. 305-18), disputed Hermann's limitation of *Aktionsart* to durative and non-durative, rightly recognizing that action "objectively" speaking is manifest, but that a speaker may view an event in different ways, *Aspekte*, which he characterizes as forming the pair durative/perfective (Hom. Il. 16.175 vs. 180; cf. Od. 16.118-19). Although the definition of terms may differ from language to language, he claims they are best expressed around formal verbal oppositions. This distinction between lexis as *Aktionsart* and subjective perspective as aspect is significant, but Jacobsohn is hesitant to exploit its implications, arguing that *Aktionsart* is "stärker empfunden als beim Aspekt" (316), on the basis of his reconstructed history of the Greek language (308-10). If he had examined modern Greek, however, he would have seen that aspect has grown in

---

[18]Hermann traces a somewhat different history of IE verb development than does Jacobsohn, equating different *Aktionsarten* with different stems, which may not have been associated phonetically (ὁράω and εἶδον) or which developed different forms from the same stem (ἔχω and ἔσχον) (222). Hermann implies that aspectual categories were already present when *Aktionsarten* began to develop, whereas Jacobsohn claims aspect developed slightly later.

[19]Cf. Hermann, "Altgriechischen Tempora," 583-649, where he defines conceptually the major categories of *Zeitdauerarten* (durative, terminative, circuitous, punctual, momentary and coincidental [591-95]) solely on the basis of his conception of how events should occur. His application to Greek (611-19, cf. 607-10) is an imposition of these categories, not a structural analysis of the language itself. Rather than utilizing the insights of structural linguistics (whose accomplishments he realizes [esp. 585ff.]), his treatment lacks formal criteria for evaluation, conflates categories such as the Imperfect and Aorist, disregards contextual factors, and is much more like Brugmann's treatment than any other.

importance (especially in its equation with morphological categories),[20] while *Aktionsart* is still a matter of lexis. In any case, on the basis of the work of Jacobsohn and Hermann the major categories were distinguished upon which subsequent structural linguists might draw in their formulations of aspect in Greek verbal systems. (Svensson [*Gebrauch*, 1-9] recognizes the difference between aspect as a subjective category [perfective/imperfective] and *Aktionsart* as an objective category [iterative, intensive, inchoative, etc.] but chooses to treat verbs of saying from the standpoint of *Aktionsart* [10ff.].)

b. The major grammatical work to display sensitivity to this approach was written as late as 1950: Schwyzer's Greek grammar, begun as a revision of Brugmann's grammar and completed (vol. 2) by Debrunner (2.248-301, on tense and aspect; Lohmann [Review, 353] labels Schwyzer's grammar "als eines der grossen, repräsentativen Werke am Abschluss einer Epoche der europäischen Sprachwissenschaft," apparently referring to comparative philology; cf. 357-59 on aspect). Schwyzer distinguishes aspect and *Aktionsart* at the outset, using Hermann's work as a basis. He defines *Aktionsart* as pertaining to the difference between complete and incomplete action, and formulates two "Hauptaspekte"--the confective which "sieht einen Vorgang oder eine Handlung als Ereignis, als schlechthin geschehen, vollendet," and the infective which "betrachtet den Verbalinhalt ohne das Moment der Vollendung, einen Zustand als lediglich zuständlich, einen Vorgang oder eine Handlung als noch unabgeschlossen, noch geschehend, verlaufend" (252). Schwyzer (252-53) also rejects the terms *perfective* and *imperfective* because he believes they are too similar to traditional tense designations; he rejects visual depictions (linear, punctual, etc.) as well. He claims that all three tense categories in Greek are essentially aspectual (254, 257). Despite his formulation of an aspectual system, and although his discussion of pragmatic usage of individual tenses is in many ways exemplary since he primarily categorizes according to temporal reference, Schwyzer adopts a specific application quite similar to that of earlier comparative philologists. (1) Since he posits only two major aspects, he must place the Perfect in one of the categories--the infective (τέθνηκε, βέβηκε), though he also introduces the term "stative" (252, 257, 263, where he reserves it for the intransitive active Perfect), and suggests the two aspects are combinable in confective-infective and vice versa Presents (e.g. πείθω, Ar. Wasps 784; D. 24.6). (The Future is modal [265].) Aspect, therefore, is based upon morphological and not morphological or synthetic criteria, with apparently no principled means for distinguishing them. (2) He asserts that the Indicative has absolute temporal meaning (254, 256, 269), an assertion which causes unnecessary problems, since he acknowledges that the non-Indicative Moods are solely aspectual (304).

Thus though the Present stem, which he posits as an abstracted category (256 n. 2), is usually aspectually infective, Schwyzer finds confective Presents in verbs of future meaning (εἶμι, νέομαι) and the historic Present (X. Anab. 1.8.26) (his distinction between the expressive and inexpressive historic Present is grammatically unfounded [271-73]). And he includes Presents with the temporal scheme of a past event with present status (D. 20.141). As he says, "die häufige Beschränkung eines Verbs auf das Präsenssystem verbürgt keinen bestimmten Aspekt" (259). His

---

[20]Thumb (*Handbook*, 151-78) shows the same facts from a comparative philologist's standpoint.

temporal rigidity for the Indicative fails to explain the future Present and the timeless Present (S. Phil. 121), which he attributes to an early timeless Present (Schwyzer believes the aspects preceded time-based tenses [253]). His claim that the augment is a past-time indicator presents problems with the non-past Imperfect (X. Hell. 2.1.21; Pl. Phaedr. 230A), as well as the completed Imperfect in contradistinction to its aspect (Hom. Il. 7.471ff.). Regarding the Aorist and Imperfect, though he acknowledges most Aorists are built on confective roots (contra ἐφόρησε, among several other infective Aorists [257]) and Imperfects on infective, Schwyzer recognizes a weakening of the confective sense to one of factiveness or non-infectiveness (e.g. Anacr. 8D: ἔτεα πεντήκοντά τε κἀκατὸν Ταρτησσοῦ βασιλεῦσαι [to rule as king of T. 150 years; 261]), although he argues that "das Gefühl für die Verschiedenheit der beiden Systeme vom Altertum bis zum heutigen Tag lebendig geblieben ist" (262). While claiming that the Aorist Indicative is past-referring (he says this use is "geläufigen"), he distinguishes a category for "immediate" (*unmittelbare*) past, though a distinction from present-referring is not convincing in several examples (S. Phil. 1314: ἥσθην πατέρα τὸν ἀμὸν εὐλογοῦντά σε [I enjoy your praising my father]; cf. also E. Supp. 1161; S. El. 668; Aj. 536); and tries to avoid the implications of a future-referring Aorist Indicative (Th. 6.80.2). Four categories of usage for typical situations or events, including the gnomic Aorist (Isoc. 1.6), are recognized as well. Since he posits a present use of the Perfect, Schwyzer encounters the same problems as in discussion of the Present, in which past (X. Hell. 7.1.41), future (X. Anab. 1.8.12) and even nontemporal (Hdt. 7.130.1) uses do not seem to conform to rigid absolute temporal conceptions. A further problem is Schwyzer's major emphasis on the difference between the intensive and resultative Perfect, for which the Aorist is "gleichwertig" (287; Rev 5:7), though no criteria are given upon which to make such a determination.

    c. A recent syntax of the verb by Rijksbaron, written in light of linguistic theory (esp. 126ff. on Voice), has made use of Schwyzer's terminology. Much of his treatment is sensitive to issues of Greek language, particularly his distinction of lexical from grammatical meaning (3-4), and dismissal of the resultative Perfect (36). Surely because of the constraints of space, much of his theoretical discussion remains perplexing. Rather than seven, Rijksbaron distinguishes five tense stems (Present, Aorist, Perfect, Future, Future Perfect), each of which has a semantic value: not-completed (imperfective), completed (confective), stative (stative-confective), future, future state (1-2), although not only is it questionable whether all tense stems should be treated on the same plane but the criteria for determining each semantic feature are mixed. This is reflected in a chart (6), similar to those of earlier grammarians. Though he includes "verbal action" as one axis of his grid, he categorically rejects as "untenable" the view that the tense forms are "aspect stems" (he entertains *Aktionsart* [4]), claiming that the difference, for example, between the Aorist and the Imperfect is "point of orientation" or order of events, although he freely admits that "substitution of one form for another usually changes the information and thus influences the way in which a speaker may proceed with, for instance, a narrative" (3, cf. 12-15). Rijksbaron wishes to invoke relative temporal reference for the tenses on the basis of simultaneity, anteriority and posteriority, except in the Indicative where absolute tense is present, i.e. with relation to the moment of utterance, distinguishing the tenses according to primary and secondary endings. He says there is no primary Aorist Indicative since the Aorist stem is complete. Although he claims not to countenance "aspect," Rijksbaron's formulation of tense as synthetically based is closer to the traditional formulation of aspect than *Aktionsart*. This is further seen in his treatment of tense usage in non-Indicative Moods, where temporal distinctions do not obtain, except possibly in the Imperative (5), although he reintroduces temporal differences with the Infinitive and Participle. In discussion of individual tense usage, though Rijksbaron is obviously sensitive to issues of absolute and relative tense, he gives no justification of, for example, generic (either habitual or universal/timeless--are these the same?) use of the Present (Pl. Lach. 179B; Hdt. 2.68.1), completed use of the Imperfect (Hdt. 5.24.1; Lys. 12.6-7), or historic Present. Rijksbaron admits that "Strictly speaking this historic use conflicts with the fundamental value(s) of the primary present indicative" (22), claiming instead that this gives it a special status for highlighting decisive actions (E. Med. 1156-69) or making enumerations (X. Anab. 1.1.10). Justifying the first usage, Rijksbaron makes the possibly contradictory remarks that the historic Present creates an "eyewitness-effect" (24), while it also highlights significant moments in a person's life. Rijksbaron also notes use of the Aorist Indicative (1st Person) of verbs of emotion, arguing that "the speaker had begun to feel the emotion concerned before his interlocutor finished speaking" (28-29), though Ar. Wasps 983 appears to contradict this, as does the gnomic Aorist, where Rijksbaron states it does not have past value (Hdt. 1.194.4).

There is much to be learned from these grammars, but their dependence upon older, well-criticized schools of thought leaves them lacking in theory and explanatory power.

5. STRUCTURAL LINGUISTICS AND ASPECT. a. The first structural linguistic approach to aspect[21] was published in 1943 by Holt (*Etudes*, 14-47, on ancient Greek). After an historical survey (2-12), Holt makes the important observation that previous attempts to adjudge aspectual values of the Greek verb suffered from lack of a systematic structural approach, i.e. failing to note that iterative/non-iterative is a different kind of opposition than Imperfect/Aorist (13; cf. 14-15, where he claims failure to formulate an appropriate metalanguage for the Aorist/Imperfect opposition has hindered study). He instead argues for a differentiation between a language's expression (form) and content (function). After noting that on the basis of the distribution of verbal forms alone (he charts the seven forms [16]) the Greek tenses cannot be temporally based, he explores the verbal stems, believing rightly, "dans la langue il ne peut pas exister plus d'unités dans le plan du contenu qu'il ne ce trouve d'unités dans le plan de l'expression," e.g. ποιῶ/ποιήσω (17, cf. 1, 15).

Using Hjelmslev's view of language-structure with aspect as morphematic,[22] Holt argues for a system of inflectional aspectual oppositions which includes the Perfect as positive (devolutive), the Present as its negative (evolutive), as in οὐδὲ βουλεύεσθαι ἔτι ὥρα ἀλλὰ βεβουλεῦσθαι ("ce n'est plus le moment de délibérer mais d'avoir délibéré," Pl. Crito 46A [28]), and the Aorist as neutral (zero) (Holt draws here on Brøndal ["Structure"], who provides a complex and purely theoretical scheme of oppositions), with the Future non-aspectual. Citing X. Anab. 2.3.22, 23 (ἐπεὶ μέντοι ἤδη αὐτὸν ἑωρῶμεν ἐν δεινῷ ὄντα, ἠσχύνθημεν . . . προδοῦναι αὐτόν . . . . ἐπεὶ δὲ Κῦρος τέθνηκεν, οὔτε βασιλεῖ ἀντιποιούμεθα τῆς ἀρχῆς

---

[21]There have been many structural approaches to aspect in languages other than Greek. See bibliography, esp. in Comrie, *Aspect*. Many of these treatments do not clearly distinguish aspect, *Aktionsart*, and lexis (as treated here). This section does not treat approaches to or those based upon modern Greek, e.g. Seiler, *L'aspect* (cf. idem, "Problematik"); Bakker, *Imperative* (see my chapt. 7), and Paraskevas-Shepard, "Choosing." See Wilkinson, *"Aspect,"* 16-17, 206-17, who shows how Russian aspectual categories are not informative for study of ancient Greek, as does Maclennan, *Problema*, 33-54, who in analysing Holt and Ruipérez shows the difficulties of formulating a convincing aspectual theory of Greek in light of dependence upon Slavonic studies.
[22]See Hjelmslev, "La structure," 122-47; "Essai d'une theorie," 160-73, in *Essais* (1971), whose method is ruggedly structuralist, formulating a language-system wholly apart from categories of meaning. Cf. "Analysis," 27-35, in *Essais* (1959).

["mais quand nous avions compris qu'il était en danger, nous avons eu honte de le trahir . . . . mais après la mort de Kyros, nous ne disputons pas au roi la possession de son trône"] 21), he determines that aspectual selection is homonexual (internal), whereas temporal determination is heteronexual (external).[23] The positive term is the most delimited since it represents "l'état obtenu par un procès antérieur" (28), whereas the negative term is the process without its termination. The Aorist is allowed to remain undefined, as in the Greek writers, adopting Meillet's definition that the Aorist represents "the process pure and simple without consideration of duration" (32). This explains, Holt claims, terminative, ingressive and complexive action (Th. 1.1). (Holt also distinguishes a group of derivative aspects, equivalent to Hermann's objective *Aktionsarten*, consisting of σκ endings and reduplicated Presents, though he claims most of the distinctions have disappeared in classical Greek [34-39].)

Holt correlates the flexional forms with tense forms, positing the future as positive, the present as negative, and the past as neutral. Since he recognizes that the tense labels represent frequent uses (40), he explains the use of past and present tenses for future time on the basis of their negative or neutral characters. His conception of time as a realization of prospective, improspective and neutrospective categories (43), as differentiated from logical categories (e.g. the present as a point where past and future meet) allows him flexibility. When reconciling tense to aspect, however, he posits that, "c'est le morphème de temps qui détermine le morphème d'aspect," as illustrated by the following chart (44):

	+	0	-
+	Perfect Future		Future
0	Perfect	Aorist	Present
-	Pluperfect		Imperfect

He then explains such uses of the Aorist as gnomic (or present) (44) by the fact that the Aorist is temporally and aspectually neutral.

Holt is to be commended for composing the first structural analysis of aspect, especially in realizing the importance of inflexional aspect (35; cf. 45-46, where he makes inflexional aspect subordinate to derivative aspect, i.e. aspect subordinate to *Aktionsart*), and in attempting to relate time to aspect (esp. 39ff.). Though he set the tone for subsequent discussion among structural linguists, there appear to be several shortcomings to his method.

(1) Despite his protestations he does not depart significantly from a strictly logical analysis (23, 26ff.). His constructs are not apparently based upon an investigation of the Greek language so much as the Hjelmslevian model imposed on Greek. And if it is posited that the tenses function to convey meaning (as seems true from analysis of the language and so most grammarians and linguists), then Holt has dissociated his theory from this factor (even Schlachter, though he states that "im Altgriechischen bilden die Aspekte eben kein 'System'" ["Verbalaspekt," 67], believes that differences of aspect are realized by temporal morphemes [68]). For example, Holt recognizes that the Aorist is basically a past tense according to usage but claims this is of no importance since the form is really non-temporal and non-aspectual in his system, though he also says it is solely aspectual (44). And though vague temporal reference of the Present allows for past reference (42), he also claims that the historic Present is independent of the value of its temporal direction (21 n. 1) and has the same sense as the Aorist aspect (?) (33).

(2) His desire to put all choices on the same level (aspectual as well as temporal) fails to differentiate terms clearly. For example, he claims that the tense forms in Greek are both temporal and aspectual morphemes, but never says what it means that the Perfect and Present are 0 temporally, and how this relates to the Pluperfect and Imperfect being -. His description of the Aorist as neutral in both spheres does not fit his treatment of the Aorist as a past tense and as

---

[23]This distinction between internal and external time is taken up by later linguists such as Lyons and Comrie (see below), by which two different aspects may enter into the same function simultaneously, but whereby two tenses may not do so.

parallel with the Present in various contexts, such as the gnomic. And despite his rejection of binary choices (24-25), the supposition of a 0 term apart from the meaningful opposition of + and - appears to be the same. It is questionable whether his formulation is helpful: on the one hand he argues that the temporal morpheme is predominant yet he also argues for a wide range of temporal usage especially for the Aorist and Present.

(3) Despite his recognition that it is impossible to define a term solely by its diverse uses (23), Holt's definition of the individual aspects is apparently confused. The semantic feature that differentiates Perfect (συντελικός) from Present (ἀτέλη) does not appear to be termination, as if the Present had no quality of itself (would it not be 0 then?). It does not follow that the Perfect must indicate the state attained by an anterior process (τέθνηκε, λέλογχα, λέλοιπα [28]), simply because it occupies a unique "zone" and is the least frequent and thus most specific, unless Holt is following the ancient Greek grammarians, a dubious aid to his scheme. He dismisses intensive Perfects (βέβρυκε, κέκραγε, etc.) as simply lexis and translation (29), though he includes perfective Presents (ἀκούω). He never specifies what it means for the Future to be an aspect. And it is not clear why the Aorist as the unmarked term would entail ingressive, etc., action or have the sense of the Perfect (33).

(4) Holt says time is predominant in determining aspect (44), showing a theory of aspect which is undermined by such things as the past-referring Aorist and the present-referring Present, since these are predominant uses that a theory must explain. The Future as delimited appears to be a logical rather than Greek-specific formulation. And his theory provides little help for understanding use of non-Indicative tense forms, where aspect alone is in effect, since the Aorist and Present are the predominant opposition. (Holt treats none of the non-Indicative uses of the Greek verb, though he acknowledges their relative temporal reference [40].)

(5) Holt must rely upon meaning, though he attempts to develop a system with reference only to structure. His movement between the two (form and function) is unclear. (Lyons [*Structural Semantics*, 111-17] essentially adopts Holt's system, followed by Erickson ["OIDA," from *Semantics*, esp. 297-303], whose construction of models based upon English lexical meaning and whose illogical shifting of formal/functional categories show up the weaknesses of Holt's analysis. See my chapt. 5.)

b. Ruipérez has eliminated many of the problems of Holt's work in perhaps the most thorough structural analysis of the Greek verb (*Estructura*, 1-44, for theoretical formulation; see also "Neutralization"; "Quelques vues"; he is followed by Louw, "Aspect"). Ruipérez bases his analysis on a Jakobsonian/Prague model from phonetics, though he departs slightly by positing that the unmarked member of an opposition may either be neutral or form a privative opposition (negative) (17-19). Not equipollent, the marked member always has an unmistakable value. The basic structure of the Greek verbal system, according to Ruipérez, is built upon two sets of oppositions, one for aspect the other for temporal reference.

The basic opposition is between the Perfect (expressing the state resulting from an action, τέθνηκε, ἕστηκα, πεποίηκα, κέκτημαι) and the Present/Aorist, in which the Perfect is marked for its termination, not cessation or duration (45-65). Thus Present (Hom. Il. 5.472) or Aorist (Th. 5.5.1) verbs can be used where it is fitting to find a Perfect. In the Perfect, verbs with transformational semantemes (verbs illustrating a modification of the subject) emphasize the subsequent state (θνήσκειν [die], χαίρειν [be happy]), while verbs with non-transformational semantemes (excluding any modification) are known as intensive Perfects (εἶναι [to be], κεῖσθαι

[lay]).[24] The same verb, e.g. βέβηκα (go), may fit both categories of semanteme, since the category is based upon meaning, not phonetic form. Through this division, Ruipérez claims to be able to eliminate the exceptions pointed out by previous scholars (e.g. δέδορκα, γέγηθα).

The secondary opposition is between the Present and Aorist, with the Present marked for durativity and the Aorist unmarked for aspectual value (67-89), i.e. not emphasizing termination, punctuality, etc. After criticizing various theories designed to differentiate the Present and Aorist, Ruipérez claims that the Present/Aorist opposition is neutralized in the Indicative since there is no Aorist Indicative with present value (see 72), and attempts to find aspectual ideas in present time are the result of explorations of *parole*. Partial neutralization occurs also in the Aorist Subjunctive and Optative Moods (Ruipérez claims they are predominant over the Present), where the Aorist is unmarked and the Present marked. Regarding traditionally applied verbal concepts of ingressive, perfective, etc., Ruipérez sees arbitrariness in trying to judge externally objective fact through subjective use of verbs (e.g. θανεῖν may not be ingressive but perfective in relation to νοσεῖν [to be ill]), but instead he divides along the lines of transformational and non-transformational semantemes: the former is either momentary (ἀστράψαι [flash lightning]) or durative (νοσεῖν [be ill]), while the latter is either momentary (βῆναι [take a step]) or indifferent. He attributes certain other of these conceptions of action, such as iterative and inchoative, to realizations of *parole*. The only values the Aorist actually has are punctuality (Hdt. 1.1 [negative value]), and indifference to any aspectual distinction (Hdt. 5.28.1). In the Present tense only the opposition μίμνω/μένω (remain) maintains an aspectual distinction of its own (cf. 119-24). The Aorist is the unmarked member because it both expresses action without aspectual qualifications and displays complex values (e.g. ingressive, complexive, iterative, factive, inchoative, etc.). The Present on the other hand has a clear, unified durative value (but not necessarily lasting a long time [Hom. Il. 2.785]), and its possibility of selection for purely subjective reasons in place of the Aorist when the writer wants to contemplate the development of an action (not necessarily temporal duration) are known (Lys. 12.4: οὑμὸς πατὴρ Κέφαλος . . . ἔτη δὲ τριάκοντα ᾤκησε [neutral Aorist], καὶ οὐδενὶ πώποτε οὔτε ἡμεῖς οὔτε ἐκεῖνος δίκην οὔτε ἐδικασάμεθα οὔτε ἐφύγομεν [neutral Aorist], ἀλλ᾽ οὕτως ᾠκοῦμεν [descriptive Imperfect] δημοκρατούμενοι ὥστε μήτε εἰς τοὺς ἄλλους ἐξαμαρτάνειν μήτε ὑπὸ τῶν ἄλλων ἀδικεῖσθαι [descriptive Present] [my father C. lived for thirty years and for no one ever did we nor he ever prosecute nor defend, but thus we were living in a democracy in order neither to offend others nor to be treated unjustly by others] [85]).

In temporal relations, Ruipérez opposes future with present/past, the basic notion being futurity. Ruipérez notes that futurity is different from present and past. In the future the verbal content has not been verified but comes from an act of the will. Thus the Future, without being exactly the same as the Subjunctive and Optative, has a certain modal character, including desiderative (E. And. 1076), imperatival (Pl. Prot. 338A), prospective (Hom. Od. 14.512), purely temporal (Lys. 24.6), but also past (Ael. Nat. Anim. 16.11), present (Hdt. 1.173), and gnomic (Arist. Nic. Eth. 1123A27) uses, the last three manifestations of *parole*, as are Present with future reference (Th. 6.91.3) and Aorist with future reference (Hdt. 8.102.2) (91-94). In the opposition of present/past, the determination is complicated by *parole* in which the forms can be used for various temporal references (habitual Present, Simon. 7.65), but the fundamental idea seems to be present-ness (Theoc. 1.135; Th. 1.144.1), considered from a psychological standpoint as the natural position of the speaker facing events without taking into account his situation in the line of time (96). This psychological factor allows for the general Present (Hom. Il. 16.384), rhetorical Present (Th. 6.91.3), or historic Present (see 147-57). The past is the unmarked member and thus able to express past time (negation of the present) or be indifferent (neutral), in such cases as the

---

[24]The terms *transformational* and *non-transformational* semantemes are difficult not only to translate but to grasp conceptually, since the terminology is reminiscent of transformational grammar. In some ways the terms harken back to the division between stative and dynamic verbs, but I have decided to stay with Ruipérez's terminology rather than increase the risk of misconstruing him. See criticism five below.

general Aorist (Hes. Works 240), or Aorist in similes or maxims (Hdt. 2.47.1) (91-100). Thus the psychological system of the Present and the indifference of the preterite work together.

Ruipérez has devised an appealing scheme depicting the relationships among the aspects. In particular the differentiation of the Perfect from the Aorist/Present is convincing. But his scheme presents problems at several points as well.

(1) He does not devise a model which shows a relationship between aspect and tense, leaving each system to function independently. Thus how to determine the pertinent neutralizations is not explained. Neither does he explain why the Present works according to psychological principles, especially with reference to tense, while the Aorist subsumes categories of usage according to *langue* and *parole*.

(2) Ruipérez fails to define the nature of the aspects in the most widely used Mood, the Indicative. To say that the opposition of Present and Aorist is neutralized in the Indicative (72) not only leaves too much outside the system but neglects much evidence that the Present Indicative has aspectual meaning (cf. Jones, Review, 127). Ruipérez's analysis begins by positing no meaningful opposition between the Present and Aorist Indicatives, but this reflects a formulation of aspect along time-based categories and apparently makes the temporal axis predominant. When Ruipérez extends this model to posit neutralization in the Subjunctive and Optative Moods as well, his theory seems to have failed to account for a fundamental opposition throughout the Greek verbal edifice.

(3) More specifically, his definition of the Perfect contradicts the evidence he cites. He claims the Perfect represents verbal action after its termination yet includes examples of what he labels intensive Perfects emphasizing initial action (πέφευγα [flee]). His appeal to transformational and non-transformational semantemes does not solve this. (Adrados ["El metodo," 26] argues that Ruipérez's concept is actually more unified than even he posits.)

(4) The distinction between *langue* and *parole* is important, but Ruipérez treats *parole* as if it were synonymous with 'aberrations.' He must show how the aberrations are connected and not really aberrant at all. For many of them he intimates that a misconstruction of lexical choice is at the heart but he must show more convincingly that the gap between *langue* and *parole* is bridgeable. When analysing any language--especially an ancient one--the outwardly evidenced phenomena must be adequately explained. To posit that much falls outside the norm and thus cannot be accounted for creates an unverifiable system.

(5) Perhaps most seriously, Ruipérez's differentiation between transformational and non-transformational verbs is problematic. It is difficult to see why φεύγειν (flee) is transformational and τρέχειν (run) or πέτεσθαι (fly) is non-transformational, or χαίρειν (be happy) and νόσειν (be ill). Rather it seems that Ruipérez's aspectual categories contain not only what has been termed aspect as a morphological category, but lexical choice, which compels him to formulate distinctions of *Aktionsarten*, e.g. ἀστράψαι (flash lightning) or βῆναι (take a step) as momentary. He provides only a rough model for differentiating these.

(6) Kahane (Review, 326) points out Ruipérez's difficulty regarding differentiation of the unmarked term in the opposition Present and Aorist in the non-Indicative Moods on the basis of duration. What if the basic notion is punctuality? Then the marked term is the Aorist and the unmarked is the Present. Besides Ruipérez's use of *Aktionsart*, this suggests the necessity of firmer criteria for determining the marked and unmarked terms (Collinge [Review of Ruipérez, 61] argues rightly that a phonetically-based opposition cannot be applied directly to syntax. This is a shortcoming in Ruipérez's formulation).

c. Friedrich likewise improves on his predecessors ("Theory"). After defining aspect (following Roman Jakobson) as a category dealing with temporal values inherent in a verbal process without view to the participants and the language event, he differentiates three devices for coding aspect: the inherent radical, the derivational-thematic, and adverbial-compositional (S5), choosing to concentrate on the derivational-thematic. In Homeric Greek, Friedrich contends, aspect "involves several subcategories related to one another through a hierarchy of markedness and differential latency" (S9), with the primary opposition being durativity. Thus he first discusses the durative tenses (Present and Imperfect) versus the Aorist, neither of which is inherently marked for time. Under the Present, Friedrich easily subsumes such uses as iterative (ἵημι [speak]), future, past (Hom. Il. 18.386), etc., on the basis of the primary durative aspect. He does similarly with the Aorist, subsuming traditional grammatical notions such as momentary (ingressive, resultative) and limited. Comparison of forms as well as "semosyntactic criteria" (S13) leads him to conclude that the Aorist is the unmarked member in the equipollent opposition.

Under verbal themes not marked for duration, Friedrich groups the categories of realized/nonrealized, defining the Perfect (or consequent) as the marked category. This not only includes an inherent temporal element derived from the concept of past completion and general condition, it also intersects with the category of intransitivity, which points to self-realization. Most Perfects are intransitive, Friedrich asserts, though the transitive tends to past meaning [and is hence more often found in aoristic contexts?]. Friedrich supports these verbal categories not only with reference to recent literature in linguistics but also with extended treatment of a select set of examples, concluding that the thematic categories are evidenced textually. He also provides a "categorial cube" (S25) to illustrate the relation of tense and aspect to mood.[25]

Friedrich's scheme is tidy, well-exemplified, succinct in explanation, but problematic as an overall framework. (1) He gives the following diagram of the Greek verbal edifice:

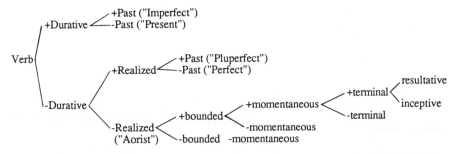

This system is formulated upon the standard of durativity. But according to Friedrich's definition of the Perfect as combining various aspectual and temporal criteria, and being the most clearly marked tense form, as well as his specific address of the issue of Aorist versus Imperfect (and by implication the Present), his fundamental opposition should be Aorist:Present, and the Perfect differentiated separately (as per Ruipérez). Friedrich's distinctive feature notation (which he uses well to illustrate his theoretical conceptions) displays this:

---

[25]Less to the point is Friedrich's comparison of Greek aspect with aspect in other languages (S28-S34) and an attempt at an axiomatic theory of aspect (S34-S37). This appears to be the correct procedure for establishing linguistic universals and departs fundamentally from the technique employed by many traditional approaches. Rather than imposing models of related languages upon Greek to flatten out its linguistic contours, Friedrich explores aspect among various languages and uses the findings to make generalizations and comparisons.

Present-Imperfect	[+Duration	]
Aorist	[-Duration	]
	[>Past	]
Perfect	[-Duration	]
	[+Real	]
	[+State	]
	[>Intransitive	]

The Perfect is the tense form with the most features (the most marked) and, therefore, should not be linked directly with the Aorist in opposition to [+Duration] (cf. Dahl, *Tense*, 72-73).

(2) Friedrich's [>Past] feature under Aorist does not apply to the non-Indicative Moods and is only a tendency in the Indicative, as he himself notes: "The aorist also lacks obligatory past reference in the oblique moods and certain other, less important cases. The aorist participle, although it usually refers to an antecedent act, is obligatorily marked only for aspect. . . . In other words, past tense is an implication of the aorist forms [he attributes this to the augment and the endings, an assertion questioned in chapts. 2 and 4], but it ranges from a limited probability to a weak connotation to zero. The one exception is the fact that the aorist necessarily refers to the past in contrary-to-fact constructions" (S11). He does not pursue suggestive comments about the difference between semantics and pragmatics.

(3) While Friedrich is too temporally oriented in his argument for the Present and certainly for the Perfect (Friedrich is clearly dependent upon Chantraine regarding the Perfect; see my chapt. 5), his definition of the Aorist fails on other grounds. His definition is not equipollent as he claims but is rather a privative opposition which neutralizes a too-temporally based feature, i.e. duration. His definition cannot account for such well-noted uses as τριάκοντα ἔτη ἐβασίλευσε (he ruled for thirty years), thus indicating that durativity is probably not the essential semantic feature. And his criteria for determining markedness, especially including analysis and comparison of pragmatic usage, do not clarify the use of the tense forms.

(4) Friedrich is right in differentiating the three means for encoding aspect, but his terms are misleading. His "inherent-radical" is tantamount to *Aktionsart*, and "adverbial-compositional" (see below) is solely dependent upon context. Greek aspect, it is argued below (and Friedrich shares this in emphasizing derivational-thematic aspect), is fundamentally morphologically determined. The other "influences" (not to be called aspects) must be posited in terms of pragmatic interpretation of morphologically-based aspect. Thus Friedrich's diagram nowhere shows where he passes from aspect proper to *Aktionsart*. If he wishes to include *Aktionsart* he has only gone partway, neglecting categories for the Perfect and Present, for which instead he substitutes temporal categories. The result is a potentially useful scheme misled by its desire to be too inclusive.

d. Comrie, in the first full-length English treatment of aspect (*Aspect*), goes far to correct Friedrich in his evaluation of Greek aspect?[26] Comrie's text focuses primarily on the Slavonic languages but he includes able discussions of other languages, including ancient and modern Greek. Comrie differentiates aspect from tense as a way "of viewing the internal temporal constituency of a situation" (3), although he considers both to be time categories, with aspect concerned with "situation-internal time" and tense with "situation-external time" (5). He devotes an entire chapter to the important distinction between aspect and tense, including a further differentiation between aspect and voice (66-86). Comrie as well differentiates aspect as a grammatical category from

---

[26]Unfortunately, Dahl (*Tense*), who follows Comrie (see e.g. 24), delivers much less than he promises, and is not systematically reviewed here.

Aktionsart as a lexical or lexical/derivational category (see 6 n. 4; cf. 41-51 where he treats *Aktionsarten* as inherent meanings in various lexical items). In defining the exact nature of the major aspectual categories--perfective, imperfective (16-40), and Perfect (52-65)--Comrie draws upon a variety of languages, attempting to devise particular definitions for each language, although he uses terms prominent in Slavonic study. He supplements his references to aspect as a grammatical category with discussion of other formal and syntactical 'aspectual' oppositions (though not all are relevant to Greek). In a worthwhile chapter on markedness Comrie distinguishes the kinds and degrees of markedness available not only among languages but within languages themselves (111-22). Regarding ancient Greek in particular (see his language guide [127]), Comrie posits two oppositions--between the Perfect and non-Perfect forms and between the Aorist and non-Aorist, contending that the Future is an aspectless temporal form (see his helpful section on the benefits of feature analysis to display sets of oppositions [130-32]). Although Comrie has single diagrams of the tense forms of ancient and modern Greek (96), he does not construct any further diagrams to illustrate the relations of temporal and aspectual reference.

Comrie would no doubt expect to be criticized in general for the lack of space devoted to each language and the fact that his knowledge of Greek appears limited. Bache has offered a damaging critique of the fundamental structure of Comrie's theory (*Aspect*, 6ff., esp. 18-20; "Aspect," 58ff. His criticism extends to Lyons, *Semantics*, 714ff.; and Mussies, *Morphology*, 265ff., as well). (1) "If the definition of aspect as a matter of 'viewing' situations is correct [as Bache and Comrie argue] then aspect has little to do with 'event-time' as such" (Bache, *Aspect*, 18). Not only is it misleading, but it is probably wrong to call both aspect and tense time categories. (2) Comrie's definition of aspect as a view of internal temporal constituency appears to be an attempt to define the objective nature of an event, and thus is a theory of *Aktionsart*. This is seen as well in the particular universal "aspectual" categories he defines, which focus upon the nature of the action itself and "are not grammaticalized in a specific language" (Bache, "Aspect," 62). (Comrie lists typical aspectual oppositions as Perfective/Imperfective, and under Imperfective, Habitual/Continuous, and under Continuous, Nonprogressive/Progressive [25]. He clearly has crossed from aspect to *Aktionsart*. As Vet [Review, 383] points out, lexis is the cause of such notions, rather than sentential semantics.) (3) When Comrie establishes his aspectual hierarchy (see [2] on their dependence upon *Aktionsart*), "it appears that there are no uniform criteria for the subdivisions of 'imperfectivity' to justify the setting up of six related aspects . . ." (Bache, "Aspect," 60). Many of these categories appear to be "inherent meanings rather than members of generic aspectual oppositions" (62).

Further criticism of Comrie may be made. (1) He retains the terms Perfect and perfective (though he differentiates the two by capitalization) as functional terms but he needs to be more precise to avoid confusion. The mixing of formal and functional definitions is troublesome in formulating proper tense terminology for Greek. Even more troublesome is Comrie's definition of the Perfect as indicating the "continuing present relevance of a past situation" (*Aspect*, 52). As Bache points out, the specific temporal reference of this definition to past and present times renders this a definition according to *Aktionsart*, not aspect (*Aspect*, 20). (2) Comrie's examples are not numerous enough to provide a clear illustration of the point he is making. He thus selects the well-known ἐβασίλευσε to support ingressive meaning of the Aorist. Besides the fact that this formulation contradicts his definition of perfective aspect as a view from outside the action (Vet, Review, 383), an exploration of further examples would have shown the lack of regularity in such formulations, since the non-morphological categories in Greek are matters of lexis and not aspect. (Perhaps the problem stems from over-reliance on Goodwin's grammar [19].) (3) Comrie claims that the Aorist Indicative is primarily (12 n. 1) or essentially (127) a past tense. This ambiguous formulation conveys two different ideas. The first formulation is of a statistical probability (the Aorist Indicative is often used with reference to past time), and the second is a semantic one. But neither one is adequate to account for non-past uses of the Aorist Indicative (e.g. gnomic, timeless) and hence to arrive at a formally-based analysis of the semantics of the Aorist in the Indicative and non-Indicative Moods.

As an introduction to aspect as a semantic term, especially with reference to other semantic categories like temporal recognition, however, Comrie's book has performed a most commendable and long-awaited service and is not likely to be quickly bettered.

e. Whereas the above are the best-known theoretical discussions of Greek verbal aspect, and each makes a significant contribution to the present study, there are also several Greek grammars which use aspect as the fundamental tense-form category.

(1) The French grammarians Chantraine (2.183-204, on tenses; cf. "Questiones"; "Remarques") and Humbert (133-54 [the 3d ed. is virtually unchanged from the 1st ed.]; "Aspect"; followed by Druet, "L'aspect," 97-101) recognize the importance of aspect (cf. Meillet/Vendryes, Traité, esp. 267-93; Carrière, Stylistique, 58ff. A recent summary of the "French" school is in Loriaux, "Notes," esp. 50 [1982] 49-53). Whereas Chantraine puts undue emphasis upon temporal uses of the tense forms (183), asserting that past reference is indicated by the augment, he does note in "exceptional" cases that aspect is predominant (e.g. present sense of the Aorist: Hom. Il. 2.114 [184]). In non-Indicative Moods he recognizes that the tense form indicates the verbal process only, without temporal significance, although he does note that the anterior use of the Aorist Participle is typical (187-88). In his "Remarques," he emphasizes the use of aspectual forms as reflecting the subjective value of aspectual choice, and demonstrates these clearly in the Subjunctive and Optative Moods; in "Questiones," he applies this to the Imperative.

Although Chantraine's aspectual system is not clearly defined in his grammar (he defines the Aorist as punctual [189] and as "l'action pure et simple" [187]), Humbert begins with the assertion that it is difficult to render the Greek tenses since the Greeks had a different psychological view than does modern man (Humbert's affinities with Guillaume are noted, see appendix 1B). After debunking the traditional view of tenses formulated on temporal conceptions (133-34), he asserts, "la notion d'aspect est fondamentale en grec" (the ambiguity of his stance is noteworthy, however, since he continues: "ce mot, traduit du sl. vid [all. Aktionsart ou Aspekt], exprime différentes perspectives. . . ." [but see above]). And "c'est l'aspect qu'expriment les thèmes dits temporels" (134). He juxtaposes the durative (Present) and punctual (Aorist) as well as determined and indetermined uses (see appendix 1A on Brunel for the source and meaning of these terms). Humbert then shows that, for example, the Aorist and Imperfect are always distinguished, being selected according to the subjective view of an action by the author, though a concrete value is thus attached to each tense/aspect for the interpreter. Humbert is careful to define the Aorist as "not the present" as opposed to its having a specific quality, thus supposedly warranting its characterization as punctual, although he notes that punctuality or duration is strictly in the speaker's perception (Lys. 12.4). The Perfect stands isolated from this first and primary opposition. Relying upon Chantraine, Humbert does not show how the Perfect is related in the system of choice to the other tense forms, though he defines its function and compares various uses, with the stative Perfect temporally closer to the Present (Hom. Il. 22.52) and the resultative closer to the Aorist (S. Trach. 486).

In his application, Humbert tries to maintain aspectual predominance, readily sacrificing temporal reference in such cases as the atemporal (S. Aj. 536) and gnomic (Hom. Il. 9.320) uses of the Aorist, though he does differentiate such categories as constative, inchoative (Th. 6.55) and terminative (A. Prom. 204-08). These are not morphologically determined, nor are the examples he cites clearly provable on lexical grounds. For example, in A. Prom. 204-08 (οἱ δὲ τοὔμπαλιν / σπεύδοντες, ὡς Ζεὺς μήποτ᾽ ἄρξειεν θεῶν, / ἐνταῦθ᾽ ἐγὼ τὰ λῷστα βουλεύων πιθεῖν / Τιτᾶνας, . . . / οὐκ ἠδυνήθην [and some who were desiring the opposite, that Z. never would rule the gods--I then advising the best things was not able to persuade the T.s]), line 206, οὐκ ἠδυνήθην, need not be rendered "I was in the end incapable of persuading," but simply "I was not able [through the course of argument] to persuade." Humbert's categories are limited to subjective contextual and lexical interpretations by the reader rather than the author. This confusion is seen further in Humbert's definition of the Present as an elastic tense which in its spatial representation of duration falsifies reality (137), as in the historic Present (E. El. 9-11). This contradicts his theoretical formulation of aspect and misses the point of the subjective choice of aspectual interpretation by the author by limiting the concept of duration to a temporal (extending over time) rather than aspectual/conceptual category. He makes a similar temporal comparison in his definition of the uses of the Perfect, as noted above.

Far less successful is Ruijgh (*Autour*, 229-36), who does not advance discussion in his outline of the tenses or in his definition of their semantic values. On the basis of psychological opposition he defines future, stative-resultive, durative and confective action, in relation to an absolute temporal scheme. His distinctive contribution is that "l'aspect est lui aussi une catégorie d'ordre temporel" (231). (Ruijgh uses few examples from real Greek.) Thus ἀνέῳξα τὴν θύραν ὅτε ἔγραφεν / ἔγραψεν ἐπιστόλην contrasts a concurrent subordinate event with an antecedent one (I opened the door when he was writing / had written the letter); and βούλομαι γράφειν / γράψαι ἐπιστόλην contrasts a continuing writing with an accomplished act (I have in mind a certain time of writing / having accomplished the writing of a letter). (Cf. Ruijgh, Review of Hettrich; "L'emploi.") That his is not a definition of aspect is seen in chapt. 2, as is the unhelpful dependence upon a strictly time-based view of Greek tenses. The principle of ordering is examined more carefully in my chapts. 4 and 8.

(2) McKay (esp. 136-41, 214-24, on aspect, clearly differentiated from discussion of tense, 141-48; cf. also his many articles; he is followed by

Wilkinson, *"Aspect,"* esp. chapt. 1, on Homeric Greek) recognizes from the outset the difference between *Aktionsart* as a lexical distinction and aspect as a category "by which the author (or speaker) shows how he views each event or activity in relation to its context" (136). McKay defines four aspects: the imperfective for an activity in process, the aorist which expresses a "whole action or simple event," the perfect for "the state consequent upon an action," and the future "expressing intention" (136). These correspond directly to the Present, Aorist, Perfect and Future tenses (McKay uses aspect as the classificatory term and tense for its divisions). McKay stresses the importance of the "subjective attitude of the speaker or writer" (137) in selection of aspect in Greek, and his renaming of the Present as "imperfective" helps him to untangle confusing Greek tense terminology, though he retains the term "future" despite his argument for it as an aspectual category (Pl. Apol. 37B). His tacit equation of standard tense forms with aspectual categories is not argued explicitly. In an appendix (214-24), McKay utilizes his insights into aspect to solve several supposed conundrums in Greek. For example, he maintains clear distinction between the Aorist and the Imperfect (X. Anab. 3.3.5) even with initial verbs of saying (Hdt. 7.63), though interpretative significance may not be the same; the lack of temporal significance in the Aorist Participle (Hdt. 1.111-12); the aspectual integrity of the historic Present (cf. "Remarks"); and the gnomic and present uses of the Aorist as aspectually determined (X. Cyr. 1.2.2). McKay's application of aspect terminology in discussion of tense is less certain, especially since here he appears to stress typical uses (e.g. "The *present tense* is mostly used to describe a process taking place either in present time or without specific reference to time. . . " [141]) at the expense of his theoretical formulation. His lexical distinction of action and stative verbs is clearly an English formulation that is akin to *Aktionsart*. McKay conflates *Aktionsart* and aspect when he notes that though the Aorist expresses an action simply as an event, pure and undefined, the action itself may be momentary, prolonged, etc., simply because it is the residual aspect (138-39). This misses the point of his own argument for defining the Aorist as a specific aspect, as opposed to calling it unmarked (137). This oversight is carried forward when he differentiates the Aorist Indicative as referring to "a complete action or mere occurrence in the past" (144) and then lists ingressive, constative and effective uses (he does not actually label this last use, though he distinguishes it as a category). He does, however, note timeless (D. 20.15), dramatic (Ar. Knights 696), and iterative (X. Cyr. 7.1.10-11) uses. His definition of the Future is equally problematic since he notes that it refers to "statements of intention" as well as futurity (147), thus casting doubt upon it as an aspectual category, as well as Mood. His definitions of the historic Present as "a means of enlivening a narrative" (142) and of future reference of the Present (Th. 6.91.3) lack a legitimate explanation according to aspect.

(3) A comparison might be made with Moorhouse's *Syntax* of Sophocles (esp. 181-213, on tense; cf. Palmer, "Language," 146-49), which shows familiarity with recent linguistic discussion. Moorhouse invokes the two schemes of verbal reference (time and aspect), claiming that "when the tenses are used in the indicative, these two functions are expressed simultaneously" (181). After defining aspect as representing the "manner in which the action

etc. is envisaged as occurring by the speaker" (181), Moorhouse says this is "basically temporal, showing not *when*, but *how* the action occurs in relation to time" (181). This subtle distinction seems to reveal a hesitancy to release traditional conceptions of the tenses. Moorhouse defines three aspects: perfective (state resulting from a preceding action); durative (imperfective, linear); and aoristic (confective, punctual) (the Future is "indifferent" regarding aspect). He defines the aoristic negatively "as not showing the special features of the other two aspects" (181). But when he says that thus "It may show the negative of duration in a punctual sense, either inceptive . . . or terminative" (181) it seems that traditional language is once more being invoked at the expense of clarity. Moorhouse's application to Sophoclean usage is similar to Ruipérez's discussion, claiming the durative aspect of the Present may be neutralized so that it can take aoristic aspect. This is not Ruipérez's argument actually, but rather is designed to handle examples of non-durative verbs (Ant. 443: καὶ φημὶ δρᾶσαι κοὐκ ἀπαρνοῦμαι τὸ μή [and I say I did it and I do not deny it]), which appears to be a formulation according to *Aktionsart*. Similar difficulties are found in the Present for the Perfect (Trach. 347) and historic Present, where Moorhouse decides on the basis of lexis whether a particular usage is durative or punctiliar (184-87), and treatment of the Imperfect recognizes the correlation between pragmatic categories and aspect (188-93). Although the Aorist is laden with traditional categories of inceptive, terminative and perfective use, Moorhouse recognizes that the contemporary Aorist arises from its aspect, since substitution with a present would be "inappropriate aspectually" (195). And his temporal definition of the Perfect runs afoul of intensive use (El. 283: κλαίω, τέτηκα, κἀπικωκύω ["I weep, pine, and lament"]). The modal uses of the Future are noted as well, as are aspectual distinctions of the non-Indicative Moods, where Moorhouse stresses relative time (208), noting that placement of the Participle is important (Aj. 237ff. [212-13]).

Despite difficulties, McKay's, and to a lesser degree Humbert's and Moorhouse's, grammar provides a firm basis for future study of Greek grammar. The necessary task seems not so much a recognition of the importance of aspect (though as appendix 1B shows, not all are convinced), but a concise definition and legitimate application of semantic categories to actual usage, in particular with reference to temporal and aspectual distinctions.

6. GRAMMARS OF HELLENISTIC GREEK FROM WINER TO THE PRESENT. The student of the Greek NT fortunately has been endowed with many grammars. The underlying tense-models that form the basis of the major grammars' discussions of verbal usage are presented here. The survey is divided into three major chronological sections: a. early 19th-cent. rationalistic grammars, b. comparative-historical grammars, and c. new alternatives (cf. Schmidt, *Grammar*, 3-13; "Study," 27ff.; see also Milligan, "Grammar"; Metzger, "Grammars"; Danker, *Century*, 76ff.).

a. **Early 19th-century rationalistic grammars.** 1. The first NT grammar of major significance was written by Winer (1822).[27] Winer remarks that NT grammarians have been "chargeable with the grossest mistakes in regard to the tenses" (330). By this he means,

> the aorist refers to the past simply (the simple occurrence of an event at some past time, considered as a momentary act) . . . the imperfect and the pluperfect always have reference to subordinate events which stood related, in respect of time, with the principal event (as relative tenses); and lastly, the perfect brings the past into connexion with the present time, and represents an action as a completed one, in relation to the present time. (330-31)

The Present hence "expresses present time in all its relations" (331). This brief description clearly sees the tenses as time based, overlooking any systematic relation or clear definition of the kind of action (except for the troublesome Perfect, and note the definition of the Aorist as momentary). (Winer also asserts, "Strictly and properly speaking, no one of these tenses can ever stand for another. . ." (331), but for him this has nothing to do with kind of action.)

The problems become evident in Winer's explication of individual tenses. The Present, he says, is "used for the future in appearance only" (Matt 26:2 [331]). This confuses form and function, since he seems to say that the Present form *only appears* to function futuristically, but he does not say how that would differ from actually functioning futuristically. His description of the Present as "used for the aorist" (John 1:29 [333]) is focused on temporal reference ("when the narrator wishes to bring a past event vividly before us") and neglects kind of action, though his treatment of Present for preterite "indicates a state which commenced at an earlier period but still continues" (John 15:27 [334]). He recognizes a durative sense of the Imperfect, though his statement that it can take the place of the Aorist is again temporally based (Luke 10:18). The Aorist is interpreted in terms of its translation as a Pluperfect (Acts 5:24), or as a Future but again "only in appearance" (John 15:6 [345]). He defines the Perfect in terms of something past set in relation to the present (Luke 13:2), which he draws out in contexts where the Perfect and Aorist occur together (Luke 4:18), though he has difficulty explaining strictly present uses of the Perfect (John 20:29). And although he claims that the Future "does not always indicate pure actual futurity" (Luke 22:49 [348]), in discussing examples he often argues for a temporal conception (Matt 7:24). Regarding the non-Indicative Moods Winer has a reasonable conception of their relation to reality (351), but his bold comment about the temporal value of the tenses is not followed up with an application to them. Though amply supplied with pertinent examples, Winer's grammar is of dubious value as a grammatical model, since he does not account for alternation in tense forms with similar temporal reference, i.e. he does not recognize a category concerned with kind of action; restricts the tenses temporally; and imposes a logical grid which results in confused terminology, in which some verb forms "appear" (but only appear) to function as other forms.

2. Winer's perspective is found in several other grammars as well. A. Buttmann gives no fully systematic exposition of the tenses but it is clear that his 'system' is temporally based (194-206). Problems of sparseness and organization may be due to the fact that Buttmann's grammar of the NT was

---

[27]For a survey of grammars known to him see Winer, 1-11. I follow the 1882 Eng. trans., esp. 330-51, on the tenses. Winer's grammar provides a fascinating publishing history. See Schmidt, *Grammar*, 71-72, 98 (line 6 should read 1855).

designed as a commentary upon or supplement to his father's (P. Buttmann) classical Greek grammar (treated above). He is concerned essentially with whether one tense can be substituted for another, for example Aorist for Perfect or Pluperfect, Present for Future, with only sporadic reference to the kinds of action referred to by the tenses. He notes only in passing that the Aorist "expresses something momentary" and the Imperfect/Present "continuous" (200), with the Present Participle adding the idea of incompleteness or contemporaneousness and the Aorist Participle that of completed past (201). Viteau (esp. 2-3) as well does not refer to kind of action, establishing the tense system as strictly temporal. And Abbott fails to describe tense systematically regarding either kind of action or time of action, an unfortunate lacking in his compendious work.

3. Green (8-30) follows in the tradition of many Greek grammarians in giving prominence to temporal distinctions, though without neglecting to make some observations regarding kind of action. He describes the Present/ Imperfect as "continued or habitually repeated action" (10); the Aorist as excluding duration, with the action "presented as occupying, as it were [?], a point of time" (12); and the Perfect/Pluperfect as expressing the "lasting, unvarying effect of some terminated action" (17). (The Future is called prospective [26].) These descriptions, not systematically formulated, are suggestive but Green's treatment is still time-based. Consequently, Green refers to "special cases" of the Present with general truths (Jas 1:15), since he must see the time as extending in either direction; the future-referring Present for events "viewed as certainly fated" (John 21:23 [11]); and the Present with reference to past time treated under the Aorist (Mark 2:4). Examples of non-momentary action in the Aorist must be viewed in their completion, though he also cites Aorists used when a specific time of duration is expressed (John 2:20; Heb 11:23 [15]). The "peculiar" gnomic Aorist (1 Pet 3:6) and the present Aorist (Phlm 19, which most grammarians would call an epistolary Aorist) are admitted as well. And he gives no formal guidelines for distinguishing permanent Perfects (Mark 11:2) and terminated-action Perfects (Heb 11:17). (See also P. Thompson, *Tenses*, 17ff.)

4. Burton, much like the Stoics, discusses the tenses under two functions: the progress of the action (the chief function) and the time of the action.[28] He claims that "in general" the Present/Imperfect denote action in progress; the Perfect, Pluperfect and Future Perfect represent completed action; the Aorist "represents the action indefinitely as an event or single fact" (6); and the Future denotes either progressive or indefinite action. Burton presents a

---

[28]Burton is to be commended for his introduction, in which he distinguishes between form and function, claiming he deals with "the various functions of the various verb-forms of the Greek of the New Testament" (1). He notes that tense terms, while once intended to designate function, are now used conventionally (2). Burton also differentiates synchronic and diachronic study of languages: "Our interpretation of the phenomena of language in its later periods can hardly fail to be affected by a knowledge of the earlier history. Strictly speaking, however, it is with the results only of the processes of historical grammar that the interpreter is concerned" (3, cf. 4).

relatively advanced theoretical view of kind of action. He does not however indicate whether dividing the tense forms according to the progress of the action is morphologically determined (aspect) or lexically dictated (*Aktionsart*). Neither does he justify his terminology, for example the apparent contradiction of saying the Aorist describes a single fact and is "indefinite" as well (Phil 4:ll; 1 Pet 1:24; Acts 28:30).

Burton's application is also problematic. For example, though he recognizes that the Present tense originally probably had no time reference he is overly restrictive of its present function in NT Greek (7-8), forcing such uses as gnomic Present (2 Cor 9:7), aoristic Present (Acts 16:18), historic Present (Mark 11:27), and Present for the Future (Mark 9:31) to appear as aberrations. In none of these just-mentioned categories does he elucidate progressive action. In fact, he claims the opposite, arguing that the aoristic Present is used of an action "conceived of as a simple event," which "is a distinct departure from the prevailing use of the Present tense to denote action in progress" (9). Burton apparently overemphasizes pragmatic conceptions and this results in overly optimistic attempts to give English equivalents for Greek functions.

Regarding the Aorist Burton is more specific in linking his (contradictory?) view of the action to all uses of the tense. He distinguishes "as respects the point of view from which the action is looked at . . . three functions of the tense common to all its moods" (17): indefinite or historical Aorist for describing an event in its entirety (John 1:11), inceptive (2 Cor 8:9) and resultative (Acts 27:43). These views apparently contradict his definition of the tense as denoting action indefinitely or as a single fact, unless the definition is based on objective action and the three subcategories solely on a subjective viewpoint (note that his definition on 7 is used for the historical Aorist on 19). But later he argues, "the distinction between momentary, comprehensive, and collective is in respect to the Future tense, as in respect to the Aorist, a distinction which primarily has reference to the facts referred to and only secondarily to the writer's conception of the facts" (33-34). Problems of *Aktionsart* need not be repeated here.

Burton takes his approach further with the Future, noting that, whereas it may be either progressive or aoristic, neither category can be "justified from the point of view of pure grammar" even though they are "real distinctions" (32). Burton's failure to formulate his initial theory regarding the basis of verbal kinds of action seems to undermine his discussion here, which seems dependent upon *Aktionsart* when he argues that context and lexis must be determinative (33), although he recognizes that future reference is only one of several uses, including imperative (Jas 2:8), gnomic (Rom 5:7), and deliberative (Luke 22:49). In his section on the Perfect and Pluperfect no set of criteria is given for distinguishing various functional categories, but he generally follows a temporal conception in which use of the tense "implies a past action and affirms an existing result" (Acts 5:28). This causes problems especially for the Perfect of existing state (Matt 27:43), intensive Perfect (John 6:69), and aoristic Perfect (2 Cor 2:13).

Though inconsistent between theory and practice, and bound to the older grammatical categories, Burton actually advanced study of NT Greek considerably, especially the non-Indicative Moods (see my chapt. 7), utilizing for the most part Greek of the NT alone. It is a shame that more of his theoretical understanding was not clearly defined and adopted by subsequent scholars (see also Nunn, 10-11, 65-80).

b. Comparative-historical grammars. The next major group of NT grammars to be considered are all based upon or utilize the models of comparative philology. For the most part, this is the point at which NT grammar remains for the time being.

1. In 1896, Blass, the classicist, published his *Grammatik des neutestamentlichen Griechisch* (esp. 187-202, a translation of Blass's 1st ed. [1896] with appended notes incorporating his 2d ed. [1902]), designed as a special investigation of hellenistic Greek presupposing knowledge of the classical language (see Schmidt, *Grammar*, 6-7, 72-73). Blass's model resembles Burton's in many ways, dividing tense usage into two functions: expressing an action and an absolute time-relation, except for the Future. He recognizes that the non-Indicative Moods only denote the former. The Present/Imperfect denotes an action viewed in its duration or progress, including actions which have not reached completion. The Imperfect shows its greatest distinction, according to Blass, in comparison with the Aorist (completion), though he singles out certain Aorists which lexically "prefer the form of incompleted action" (191): κελεύω, προστάσσω, παραγγέλλω (order). And the Perfect is perceived as resembling a unity of the Present and Aorist (Acts 5:28), usually emphasizing present meaning, with replacement of the Aorist not uncommon, especially in Revelation (e.g. 5:7). The Future only expresses future time. The non-Indicative Moods differentiate action and not time reference, for example, the Present Imperative is used for general precepts and the Aorist for individual cases. Whereas Blass's terminology for kind of action is promising, his equation of Present form with present time causes several difficulties. He claims that in some cases the Present "may be regarded as a point of time" (187), evidenced in the aoristic Present (Acts 9:34; 16:18) and the historic Present (John 1:29), which he argues is used for "lively, realistic narrative" (188). He also treats the Present with future-reference (John 14:3), although he does not say how this is related to kind of action, only to present time in cases of verbs of movement (John 3:8). Blass makes instructive comments on the difference between the Imperfect and Aorist in kind of action, e.g. Blass's rule for use of ἔλεγεν and εἶπεν, in which individual utterances of an individual person are said to be denoted by the Aorist, whereas utterances of an indefinite number of persons are denoted by the Imperfect, although he notes several major exceptions with longer speeches (Luke 6:20) and additional remarks (Mark 4) (192). His terminology for the Aorist is inaccurate, however, since there are many events which do not refer to completion (see above), for example, inchoative Aorists (Acts 15:12) and gnomic statements (John 15:6). Blass's conception of the Perfect is too temporally oriented, necessitating a series of exceptions such as in John 1:15 (κέκραγεν [shout]) with present meaning and 2 Tim 4:7 (τετέλεκα [complete]) with aoristic meaning, although Blass insists that these do not affect "the correctness of the employment of this tense" (199). Whereas Blass is probably correct that the Future does not express kind of action, he must also qualify his assertion that it is simply a time-based tense when he notes modal functions (imperative [Matt 5:43] and supposition in conditional statements [Matt 26:33]) and gnomic uses (Rom 5:7). These problems seem to stem from a failure (a) to justify the connection betwen tense and kind of action, (b) to differentiate aspect from *Aktionsart*, (c) to reassess the temporal basis of grammatical categories, and (d) to conceive of verbal usage as systematically structured throughout.

Blass's grammar went through three editions before his death and was taken through the 10th ed. by the comparative philologist Debrunner. The 10th ed. with supplementary notes by Debrunner was translated into English by Funk (Blass/Debrunner, esp. 166-81, on tense). Since then it has gone through another five editions, though surprisingly much of it is identical with or even briefer than (though with some new examples) the English edition (Blass/Debrunner/Rehkopf, 263-88, on tense). Because of completeness I refer primarily to the English ed., making reference to the latest German edition where it provides helpful elucidation. Blass/Debrunner begin with a clear exposition of their approach to tense: "the original function of the so-called tense stems of the verb in Indo-European languages was not that of levels of time (present, past, future) but that of *Aktionsarten* (kinds of action) or aspects (points of view)" (¶ 318). They differentiate five important *Aktionsarten* in NT Greek: (1) punctiliar (momentary) in the Aorist stem, including ingressive (ἐβασίλευσεν [became king]), effective (ἔβαλεν [hit]), and constative (ἐποίησεν [he made]) action; (2) durative (linear or progressive) in the Present stem (γράφω [I am writing (now)]); (3) iterative in the Present stem (ἔβαλλεν [threw repeatedly (or each time)]); (4) perfective in the Perfect stem, where a past action results in a condition or state (ἕστηκεν [he placed himself there and stands there now]); and (5) perfectivizing by addition of a prefix (Blass/Debrunner/Rehkopf [¶ 318 n. 5] subordinate [5] to a footnote).

As seen above in sect. 3, this model is problematic. (a) The failure to recognize a difference between *Aktionsart* and aspect, after the recent work in linguistics, is very surprising. (b) The *Aktionsarten*--that is what the labels are--are morphologically linked to their respective stems. (c) The conception of the Aorist action as punctiliar or momentary is problematic in any scheme, especially that of *Aktionsart*. (d) There is an apparent mixing of categories by including (5), in which a verb would change *Aktionsart* (but not morphological stem) on the basis of the prefix (see appendix 1A). (e) Blass/Debrunner seem bound by their temporal definition of tense forms, as their definition of Moods shows and and their application of tense usage exemplifies. For example, the aoristic Present is posited "where a punctiliar act taking place at the moment of speaking is to be denoted. . . . since the punctiliar aorist stems form no present" (Acts 9:34; ¶ 320). This formulation according to *Aktionsart*, in which ἰᾶταί σε Ἰησοῦς Χριστός (is this a Present?) is translated "he heals you in this moment in which I proclaim it to you," violates the morphological system above, neglects the subjective nature of aspect, and misconstrues the Aorist. Similar criticism can be made of the historic Present (John 1:29ff.; ¶ 321), perfective Present, especially with ἀκούω (Luke 9:9; ¶ 322), and futuristic Present, which discussion disregards aspect or *Aktionsart* (Matt 11:3; ¶ 323). Whereas the contrast of linear and punctiliar action is useful in drawing contrasts between the Imperfect and Aorist, this scheme fails to be convincing in particular instances but leads to some distinctions closer to a theory of aspect, when Blass/Debrunner say that the Imperfect is used to represent a past action as being in progress (Acts 5:26; ¶ 327). But the ingressive (Acts 15:12) and complex Aorist clearly cannot be seen as punctiliar or momentary, as in Acts 28:30, where the author says Paul remained (ἐνέμεινεν) in his own room for two years (¶¶ 331, 332). And Blass/Debrunner define the gnomic Aorist (Jas 1:24) as standing for a non-existent perfective Present (?) or referring to a specific case (¶ 333), apparently because they are reliant on traditional temporal categories. (These same categories are maintained for the non-Indicative Moods [¶¶ 335ff.].) When discussing the Perfect, Blass/Debrunner are overly reliant upon temporal reference to explain use of present (¶ 341) and aoristic (¶ 343) Perfects (see on Blass above). Despite contradicting their assertion that the Future "is the only tense which expresses only a level of time and not an Aktionsart" (¶ 348), Blass/Debrunner recognize gnomic (Rom 5:7) and relative (Matt 20:10) uses.

Failure to define terms clearly, as well as a surprising neglect of criticism of the last thirty years, has rendered a major work unfortunately less than optimally useful.

2. Moulton stands as perhaps the finest comparative philologist of Britain's NT Greek grammarians. In his *Prolegomena* to *A Grammar of the Greek NT* (esp. 108-51; cf. "Characteristics," 10 [1904] 353-64, 440-50; see Barrett, "Classics," for recent review and appreciation of Moulton), he makes full use of the latest German criticism, implying that he is introducing *Aktionsart* into English grammatical parlance, though he is not afraid to assert his own findings. He posits that the many different Greek stem classes once had *Aktionsarten*, although his language is ambiguous: he could be referring to the conjugations or the tenses themselves. He contends that stems were later blurred until three remain: the Aorist is punctiliar, regarding action as a point and thus in its entrance (ingressive), completion (effective), or as a whole (constative--"a line reduced to a point by perspective"); the Present is durative or linear; and the Perfect denotes "what began in the past and still continues" (109). On the basis of formal criteria he also designates iterative verbs (reduplication with ι) and verbs of ambiguous formal history, e.g. ἔφην (say), or which may have only one or both of the above *Aktionsarten*, e.g. ἐνεγκεῖν (bear). He also notes the perfectivizing force of prefixed verbs. Criticisms of Blass/Debrunner above seem to apply equally well here, with the added stricture that Moulton fails to appreciate that tense categories are not strictly root based, which would solve such problems as defective and ambiguous verbs (see my chapt. 10). Moulton bases his argument on prehistoric use to show that certain Presents are not linear, but punctiliar, such as aoristic Presents (Acts 16:18). He claims this accounts for the future reference of some Presents, such as ἀποθνήσκομεν (1 Cor 15:32 [120], but in Matt 26:18 ποιῶ is not "punctiliar"). Claiming that the only difference between Present and Future here is the note of assurance, he seems to have overlooked kind of action, though his recognition that past temporal usage also comports well with the Present form (historic Present; P.Par. 51 [2d cent. B.C.]) allows him to admit that "the Present is not primarily a tense, in the usual acceptation of the term" (120). Concerning the Aorist, Moulton has a somewhat imprecise conception of ingressive usage, etc. For example, he recognizes that "two or even three" of the kinds of Aorist action "may be combined in one verb" (130): e.g. ingressive βασιλεύσας ἀναπαήσεται ("having *come to his throne* he shall rest" [Agraphon, P.Oxy. 654.8-9, Clement of Alexandria] and constative ἐβασίλευσαν μετὰ τοῦ Χριστοῦ χίλια ἔτη ("they *reigned* a thousand years"; Rev 20:4). He also recognizes the place of the timeless Aorist (Luke 10:18), although this is made unnecessarily complex because, after he has made much of the augment as a past time indicator (129), he must posit an "original" usage from Sanskrit (134-35). And while his treatment of the difference between Present and Aorist prohibitions shows the value of distinguishing kind of action (122-26), his definition of the Aorist Participle as punctiliar requires him to see it as past referring (126-27) except in particular idiomatic uses (Matt 22:1; Acts 10:33 [131]; he sees no evidence for subsequent reference of the Aorist Participle as in Acts 25:13 [132]). Moulton's discussion of the Perfect (see these views discussed in my chapt. 5) seems too concerned with its temporal distinctions from the Aorist, and for the Future he opts for punctiliar usage in many cases on the basis of its similarity in form to the Aorist Subjunctive, although he notes a mixed usage

(e.g. in Mark 14:28 προάξω [go before you] is progressive and in 1 Thess 4:14 ἄξει [will bring] is punctiliar).

3. In the United States, this line of thought was perpetuated by Robertson's massive grammar (esp. 821-910, on tense, who is followed uncritically by Carpenter, *Aktionsart*; and Trotter, *Use*, both his Ph.D. students). Robertson, in tracing the history of Greek verb stems, recognizes the influence of both the individual words and the tense constructs, concluding that there exist three essential kinds of action: the momentary or punctiliar, the linear or durative, and the perfected or completed, as well as perfectivizing prefixes (823, 826-28; sufficient comment on this terminology has already been made). Robertson equates each category with a particular tense, but this is hardly legitimate according to *Aktionsart*, since Robertson's three kinds of action are too restrictive, not taking into account categories such as terminative, iterative, causal, etc. He then invokes the influence of individual verb roots for such categories. For example, in John 1:14 he sees "constative" (ἐσκήνωσεν [lived]), "ingressive" (ἐγένετο [became]), and "effective" (ἐθεασάμεθα [saw]) Aorists (829). Robertson thus argues both for the mixing of the Aorist and Imperfect on the basis of root (*Aktionsart*) and distinction on the basis of tense (882). He says the Aorist "tells the simple story," while the Imperfect "draws the picture" (883), just the opposite of Weinrich's conception (see appendix 1B). The basis for his distinctions appears to be translation alone. Though he perceptively notes the faulty nature of tense terminology, in which some refer to kind of action (Aorist, Perfect, Imperfect) and some to time (Present, Future) (825-26), this scheme does not promise its resolution.

Starting from the premise that each tense is distinct (830), Robertson debates all of the suggested possible categories, focusing upon pragmatic usage. For example, he argues that constative, ingressive, and effective Aorists are all *Aktionsarten* under the *Aktionsart* "punctiliar" (?) (830-31). He admits that these logical categories are not "a tense-notion at all," since "at bottom only one kind of aorist (punctiliar in fact or statement)" exists (834). "Sometimes it will not be clear from the context what the *Aktionsart* is" (835). This helps to explain the gnomic use (John 15:6), but since he has posited that the augment is a past-time indicator (825), he must invoke the "original timelessness of the aorist indicative" (836). And he claims that there is no instance in the NT of a present-referring Aorist, only instances referring to an event that has just happened (Matt 9:18 [842]), which seems to be an unnecessarily time-bound definition. Discussing the specific (= punctiliar) Present, Robertson mixes categories when he lists the historic Present apparently on the basis of temporal reference not kind of action. On the other hand he also lists the futuristic Present since it is "generally punctiliar or aoristic" (869). For the Future, of which he notes modal uses (872ff.), Robertson argues that punctiliar and durative *Aktionsarten* are maintained, sometimes in the same form (πείσομεν [persuade] in Matt 28:14 and 1 John 3:19), although he gives no criteria for determination, and asserts that the form's origin is in punctiliar Presents or Aorist Subjunctives, hence most Futures are punctiliar (870-72). Robertson's description of durative *Aktionsart* contains many of the same categories as under the punctiliar heading, showing inadvertently that morphology or tense form itself cannot explain the different functions in his "system." Robertson's category of "Presents as Perfects" (John 11:28) shows the problem best: "Here the form is that of the present, but the root has the sense of completion" (881), although the same may be said of progressive, iterative, and inchoative Presents. Robertson gives priority to the root (lexical) meaning, but retains (temporal) tense categories when convenient (Robertson has essentially no system beyond his basic three *Aktionsarten*). Regarding the perfected state, he mixes such categories as present Perfect, intensive Perfect and extensive Perfect (he later subordinates the last two under the first), arguing that "the past perfect and future perfect are both built upon the present perfect stem" (892). He seems to imply there are several Perfect forms but they all look the same, and in fact asserts that "No single graph for the perfect can therefore be made" (893). And none of his suggestions covers his "'Aoristic' Present Perfect" (898-902).

Robertson, though occasionally arriving at perceptive formulations, appears in many ways to be the least systematic thinker of the major NT Greek grammarians (cf. Dana/Mantey, 176-208, who follow Robertson very closely).

Chamberlain (67-80), following Robertson, attempts a resolution of certain problems in tense definition when he recognizes that the kind of action fundamental to a tense is different from *Aktionsart*, though it may be related. He defines the linear or durative action as action in progress; the punctiliar as simple, undefined (aoristic) action; and the perfect as completed action, recognizing from the outset that the same action may be observed from any one of these viewpoints (67). Unfortunately, it appears contradictory to say that aoristic action is undefined, simple, and punctiliar. And Chamberlain's relation of this scheme to tense, which he sees as secondary, is highly reminiscent of 19th-cent. models equating a form to each tense category. When he defines *Aktionsart* later (69) he seems to meld kind of action with *Aktionsart*. Nevertheless, his incipient formulation of an aspectual system is to be noted.

4. Radermacher follows in a similar vein (2d ed., 148-56). In a preliminary bibliography acknowledging familiarity with Hartmann's discussion of the Aorist and Imperfect, he adopts a distinction between description (*Aktionsart*?) and the describer (aspect?). In reference to description one can choose to focus upon the entrance, duration or conclusion, and in reference to the describer one can choose to view the action in its duration, repetition, or factuality. Unfortunately Radermacher does not develop this rough outline of an aspectual/*Aktionsart* system or show the precise relation between the categories. As seen already, however, attempts to limit "objective" description are problematic. When Radermacher elucidates his verbal model, however, he posits a traditional temporal construct of past, present and future time, fitting into his three kinds of action. Thus he posits two Future forms (Future Perfect and Future), a Present form that can have several *Aktionsarten* (factive, event, duration) and past and future temporal references, and four past forms (Pluperfect, Perfect, Imperfect, Aorist) (reminiscent of Dionysius Thrax?). With this scheme it is unclear why he singles out the historic Present (Mark 1:40) for special notice (155-56). In the Indicative, he argues that the Perfect has lost its distinctive meaning to the Aorist, though in the non-Indicative Moods he claims the durative or iterative use of the Present and the momentary use of the Aorist are maintained. This model--clearly dependent upon its predecessors--appears unclear in its treatment of form and function, and the temporal references of the tense forms.

5. Abel (249-68) takes a step backward in his insistence that the temporal axis is predominant over kind of action, which is temporally-based as well. He defines the three kinds of action as "l'idée verbale pure et simple ou

l'idée de la mise en acte," "le fait en train de se réaliser," and "l'état résultant de l'action accomplie" (250), correlating with the Aorist, Present and Perfect tenses, although in his chart (249) Abel lists two kinds of action for the Aorist, the first above and "Le fait d'entrer dans tel ou tel état." Abel has done much work in compiling lists of examples of pragmatic usage from classical, NT and papyric Greek, and sufficient criticism of many of these categories has been levelled above. Throughout his grammar Abel, however, rarely discusses usage in terms of kind of action. Hence a noticeable lack is his discussion of the Present expressing a simple act (John 10:32 [252]) and the Perfect (257-58). Of the Future (259), he claims that its indifference to kind of action allows it to be durative, instantaneous, inchoative, effective, conative, etc. (Matt 24:5-15), although he gives no criteria apart from the Future's origin in the Aorist (he does recognize modal usage [258]). In many cases, however, Abel seems to assume that on the basis of kind of action a range of pragmatic uses is available. Therefore, he says that "Pour donner plus de vie au récit d'un événement passé, on emploie le présent (historique), qui se trouve mêlé à des temps passés" (Matt 3:13 [250]), as well as recognizing other past-referring (Luke 9:9) and future uses (Mark 9:31) (254), and several uses of the Imperfect (conative [Acts 7:26] and volitive [Acts 16:22]). Abel's discussion of the Aorist, while recognizing the appropriateness of the tense as "le temps historique par excellence" (255), treats the gnomic use as a natural expression of its kind of action (Luke 4:24 [256]). Abel's discussion of the non-Indicative Moods wisely stresses kind of action as well, although his characterizations are open to question. For example, his description of the Present Imperative referring to general rules and the Aorist Imperative to particular cases runs afoul of Luke 11:3 (cf. Matt 6:11) and Matt 5:4 (cf. Luke 6:30) (261-62). Perhaps it is in what Abel does not express overtly that his book proves most helpful.

6. In his *Idiom Book* (5-19; cf. *Language*, esp. 22-23) Moule defines "kind of action" as a morphologically-based category which captures the writer's conception of the action, and places the time of action in a subordinate position. Unfortunately, he labels this *Aktionsart* (not aspect) and lists three *Aktionsarten*: linear, punctiliar, and perfect. To move to an analysis of the verb roots themselves is thus natural. For example, Moule recognizes that the Present is normally linear, but continues that there "are some English simple Presents ('punctiliar') which correspond to Greek Presents" (7). But it is questionable that John 4:19; Acts 17:22; 2 Cor 7:8; Mark 10:35 have any compelling reason in Greek (much less English) to be aspectually punctiliar. His discussion of the Imperfect wisely notes that the elementary use (linear) has many interesting nuances, such as inceptive (Mark 1:21), conative (Mark 9:38), iterative (Luke 21:37), and desiderative (Acts 25:22). With reference to the Aorist he sees it as past in the Indicative due to the augment, though this certainly fails to explain the gnomic (1 Pet 1:24; Jas 1:11), which he consequently questions (12-13). And his adoption of the ingressive category (1 Cor 4:8) fits poorly with a punctiliar conception, as do the Aorists he labels as linear (Acts 28:30; Eph 2:4). In discussing the Perfect Moule falls back upon a temporal conception, although he recognizes exceptions "which cannot be explained away" (14): 2 Cor 2:13; 7:5; 11:25; 1 John 4:14; Matt 13:46; 25:6 and possibly 5:10. Unfortunately, rather than critically examining his *Aktionsart* definition of the Perfect, he allows the exceptions to stand. After a promising beginning, Moule seems unable to evaluate the fundamentals of tense definition, fails to conceive of the Greek verbal network as an interconnected system, and thus treats each tense in isolation (and often according to English translation).

7. N. Turner, in the *Syntax* to *A Grammar of NT Greek* (esp. 59-89; followed closely by France, "Exegesis"), specifically addresses the issue of

"aspect and tense." Recognizing that temporal indicators arose late in IE, he states: "essentially the tense in Greek expresses the kind of *action*, not time, which the speaker has in view and the *state* of the subject, or, as the Germans say, the *Aspekt*" (59). But like Moule he continues by saying that the tense-systems indicate this point of view and *Aktionsart* is the term used by grammarians (!). There are two: continuous or linear, and instantaneous or punctiliar (Turner's definitions appear to be temporally based). Usually these are to be equated with the Present and Aorist stems; however, sometimes the Aorist is noncommittal regarding duration, seeing the action as a whole. The augment indicates past time, so that forms without it are contemporary or not concerned with time at all. (The Future is a temporal tense and "considerations of *Aktionsart* do not often [?] intrude" [60], though he later claims it is "usually punctiliar" [86].) Turner begins well when he says that "tense-stems indicate the point of view from which the action or state is regarded" (59), understanding aspect as the *morphologically* (tense form) based system of recent semantic investigation. But he undermines this by adopting the term *Aktionsart*, which is not a synonym (he makes little reference to bibliography on this issue), and redefines tense-stem to mean root lexical meaning.

Turner's exposition of usage is disappointing, possibly because he relies on *Aktionsart* (see Horsley, *Context*, 49-69, for a thorough critique of Turner's approach, revealing that Turner is heavily dependent upon Mayser [see below] for his categories). For example, on the basis of his assertion that "Greek has no present stem with a punctiliar root" (60) and the supposed ambiguity of translation of the Present by the English punctiliar present and progressive (he creates a false dilemma using English grammar), he claims Greek is ambiguous since it uses the linear Present stem in the Indicative. He neglects possible Aorist usage, which he discounts because of the augment (cf. his discussion of gnomic [Luke 7:35] and proleptic [John 15:6] Aorists, where he unsuccessfully tries to reconcile the presence of the augment with punctiliar kind of action and non-past reference [73-74]). He then says that the historic Present "is an instance where *Aktionsart* and tense-forms do not coincide" with the Present having "punctiliar action" (60), never stating why this cannot be linear past action, as in the Imperfect. Recognition of punctiliar Presents (see examples from Moule above) further undermines his point (64). The term "Perfective Present" (62) seems misleading, since it confuses lexis, aspect and formal/functional distinctions; and his adoption of Moulton's definition of the futuristic Present (see above) also reveals his time-based definition of tense forms.

Turner recognizes the classical distinction between the Imperfect and Aorist (apart from ἔλεγεν and εἶπεν), although he claims choice is dictated by habit. Regarding the Aorist, Turner claims that *Aktionsart* must be viewed with caution, since the categories collapse with linear Aorists (Acts 1:21). This apparently results from his "punctiliar and momentary meaning" (71), in which few (no?) verbs fit comfortably. Though trying to maintain the punctiliar view, while admitting lexis is important, Turner overtheologizes his renderings of the ingressive Aorist: e.g. Luke 19:41, "he burst into tears" (ἔκλαυσεν [71-72]), when "he cried over it [the city]" would suffice. He maintains the importance of the specific instance in the gnomic Aorist, though he assumes a timeless Aorist exists. For the Perfect, Turner describes the *Aktionsart* as combining the Aorist and Present with an interval after the past event or on the fulfilment of the process (τέθνηκα? [die]) (81-82), a rather too loose and temporally-bound definition which allows confusion with the Aorist and Present (e.g. perfective Aorist [Matt 27:20]), as well as revealing that all his tense-forms are defined temporally. Turner adopts Chantraine's view of the history of the Perfect (see my chapt. 5), using it to explain present Perfects (82) and resultative Perfects (83).

Turner applies his definitions to the non-Indicative Moods, though his definitions leave him to conclude that the "problem of *Aktionsarten* of the tenses is by no means solved as yet for the NT" (75). (Cf. Goetschius, whose book--though for beginners--makes a rudimentary attempt at the problems of linguistics and in particular aspect, in sects. 88, 95, 227, 246, 257, 332(2); contrast Funk, 216-19, who perpetuates the comparative philological approach.)

8. Mateos is careful to distinguish his terms more precisely (*Aspecto*, esp. 19-39), though he does not consider secondary literature outside the NT grammars. He first distinguishes grammatical aspect (he lists a conglomeration of terms like durative, punctual, etc.) from semantic aspect, which distinguishes words with stative and dynamic meaning (19-20). This latter opposition, he believes, forms the heart of the former, and the two together are the constituent elements of the three forms of verbal aspect: lexematic, morphematic, and syntagmatic. (The term "aspect" is much broader than used elsewhere in this work, except for Friedrich.)

Lexematic aspect primarily distinguishes stative and dynamic lexemes, for example, action verbs are continuous, instantaneous, or resultative (21, 22-23, 29-30). Morphological aspect refers to morphemes as particular verbal realizations used to carry the lexemes (21, 30-32), though Mateos sees the lexeme as the governing factor. Syntagmatic aspect concerns the other factors in a sentence, like auxiliaries, subjects and complements--whether they are singular, plural, determined, indetermined--temporal reference, and adverbs (21-22, 32-39).

Though Mateos wisely shows that there are many categories to consider in discussing aspect, he has not progressed significantly beyond the 19th-cent. discussion. It appears otherwise at first reading, since he uses the term "aspect," consciously rejecting *Aktionsart* (20), though his broad definition of aspect overlooks many other important distinctions mentioned above. His model is essentially a version of *Aktionsart*, in which morphological aspect (note that the word takes on a different sense) is governed by external factors, like syntax and lexis. His basing of the model on lexis (the rest of the book contains a discussion of the lexis of Greek verbs) seems dictated by Spanish. Mateos discusses the nature of Spanish verbs first and then applies these results to Greek. His discussion of Greek morphological aspect, more a treatment of the tenses per se, does recognize an essential nature for each tense form (Present is punctiliar or durative [?]; Aorist is punctiliar; Perfect is resultive; Future is future [?]), which nature is maintained in the non-Indicative Moods, though lexis--always prominent--exerts a controlling influence on the tense form selected. Overall, Mateos lacks a clear systematic treatment of the arrangement of these constituent elements.

c.   New alternatives. 1.   Before more recent works are treated, several works on the papyri may be noted. a. The first is by Mayser (2, 1.130-223). Though his is a comprehensive listing of the available material, when discussing the verb Mayser lacks systematic treatment, instead presenting categories organized in the Indicative according to temporal distinctions. In his only brief exposition of *Aktionsart*, in the Aorist Mayser posits a punctual-momentary fundamental meaning with manifestations as ingressive (PSI 333.1 [256 B.C.] ἡμῖν συνέβη ἀγωνιᾶσαι [it happened that we became angry]), effective (P.Magd. 42.7 προσαπήγαγέν με εἰς τὴν φυλακήν . . . [he took me away to the prison) or constative (P.Magd. 42.7 [221 B.C.] . . . καὶ συνέσχεν ἐφ᾽ ἡμέρας δ [and locked me up for four days]) (141-43). In contrast to the Present, Mayser claims that the Perfect penetrates more and more into the Aorist and becomes a narrative tense, so that a promiscuous use of both tenses results (P.Magd. 12.8 [218 B.C.] οὐδένα λόγον ἐποιήσαντο, ἀλλὰ ἐγβεβλήκασί με ἐκ τῶν κλήρων [they took no account, but cast me out by casting lots][29] [139ff.]). On the basis of a tacit understanding of *Aktionsart*, Mayser is careful to assert a distinction between the Aorist and Present (punctiliar and durative) in the non-Indicative Moods, though his practice reverts to temporal distinctions. For example, regarding the Aorist and Present Participles, Mayser asserts they are timeless, only differentiating *Aktionsart*, but that therefore the Present is usually contemporaneous and the Aorist antecedent (168, 172). This *non sequitur* is not confirmed by Mayser's own examples, which include at least simultaneous and antecedent use of both.

b. Mayser's approach is in striking contrast to that of Mandilaras (esp. 54-56, 57-60; cf. *Studies*, 9-50), who acknowledges the problems of aspect and *Aktionsart*. He states that though the papyri preserve all the tense forms of classical Greek, "their use is considerably limited owing to the encroachment of the synthetic verbal forms, i.e. the infinitive and participle, upon the territory of the finite verb system" (54). Apart from the opposite probably being the case (see Blass/Debrunner, ¶¶ 388ff.; Turner, *Syntax*, 134ff.), this forebodes a misunderstanding of the relation of aspect to tense, apparently confirmed when he states,

> Aspect depends not only on the use of the particular tense, but also on the meaning of the particular verb involved. Sometimes too, adverbial expressions in the sentence point to a differentiation of aspect, which the tense alone could not determine definitely. Other factors which can create a special situation in which "aspect" is differentiated are (a) the use of compound verbs, (b) the personal style of the writer, and (c) the kind of document. (54)

Though he never states how these factors fit together, Mandilaras seems to have given an expanded definition of *Aktionsart*, not aspect.

Mandilaras then shows both how one tense form may have various temporal uses (ἔγραψα [I write/wrote] P.Gen. 52[v].3-5 [4th cent. A.D.] and P.Lond. 237.3 [c. A.D. 346]) and how different tense forms may have the same temporal reference but should not be equated, for example, Perfect, Aorist and Imperfect (verbs of saying in P.Lond. 404.8 [c. A.D. 346], P.Oxy. 1668.9-11 [3d cent. A.D.], and P.Oxy. 1683.20-21 [4th cent. A.D.]). He then reasonably concludes, "in the tense-usage of these [papyri] writers, aspect was their primary consideration, to which precise indication of time was frequently subordinated" (56). This discussion is closer to a morphological/aspectual treatment of verbal usage (cf. the next paragraph where he reiterates the perfectivizing influence of prefixes and the effect of adverbs). Mandilaras concludes by citing the standard classical and hellenistic grammars to show that since each cites a different number of uses of the Aorist, verbal aspect has evolved: "In examining the uses of the aorist in Classical and Hellenistic Greek we see that the latter (more than Classical Greek) enhances aspect at the expense of time. This is due to the development of the aorist towards an aspectual tense" (56). It is difficult to see how the number of categories cited in a grammar can be equated with development of verbal aspect. These seem to be purely arbitrary categories used to explicate pragmatic usage.

---

[29]This example is susceptible to other analyses, but is listed here as one of Mayser's. Perhaps a better reading is to see the Aorist as simply stating a simple fact, and the Perfect, reinforced by the strong adversative, stressing the state the speaker found himself in, i.e. thrown out by an arbitrary method. This would better explain the use of the tense forms, each of which had both Aorist and Perfect forms available.

To conclude that the Aorist is developing into an aspectual tense (?) seems rather nonsensical. In his subsequent discussion of the confusion of tenses (57-60) Mandilaras, though still mixing aspectual and temporal categories, recognizes that though temporal reference may be the same with different verb forms, they are not necessarily synonymous: the tenses were used quite self-consciously and with recognized functions.

In discussion of tense usage, Mandilaras assumes an aspectual perspective, noting and usually endorsing the linear perspective of the Present/Imperfect (here he is able to differentiate aspect from *Aktionsart* [94]), and the punctiliar nature of the Aorist (156), though it is not clear how the punctiliar idea applies to such sub-categories as the constative (he introduces a logical adjustment; BGU 423.16 [2d cent. A.D.] ὅτι με ἐπαίδευσας καλῶς ["because you educated me well"; 160]), ingressive (BGU 113.8-10 [14 B.C.]), perfective, or continual (P.Rein. 19.11-12 [108 B.C.]) Aorist. Mandilaras argues clearly for aspectual predominance in the Perfect and shows clear evidence of its continued, distinctive use into 1st cent. A.D., though his dependence on traditional categories is troublesome. For example, he claims that the Perfect in general is the tense of emphasis (221) but yet he calls the resultative Perfect emphatic (224), and the intensive Perfect (P.Petrie ii 11 [1].4-5 [3d cent. B.C.] ἐὰν γὰρ σὺ παραγένηι, πέπεισμαι ῥαιδίως με τῶι βασιλεῖ / συσταθήσεσθαι [for if you give support, I am convinced that I will easily engage the king in battle]) complies with his definition only because he attributes to it the "original use of the tense" (222). It is not altogether clear what Mandilaras means when he speaks of the Future, arguing that it "displays no real variation of aspect" morphologically but then claiming it is "punctiliar" since it presents the Aorist in its simplest form (181).

2. Though there is great awareness of the issues regarding aspect, much work remains to be done, in particular in definition of terms, differentiation of aspect and *Aktionsart*, realization of formal and functional differences, and creation of workable systematic linguistic structures. It is only within the last few years that workable solutions have been made. To conclude this section three grammatical works may be noted.

a. First is the work of McKay. His Greek grammar is discussed above, but the position he outlines there is used in several significant articles which treat the NT (see esp. "Syntax"; "On the Perfect . . . NT Greek"; "Aspect"). Voelz ("Language") is dependent upon McKay's scheme in an appendix where he treats *Aktionsart* (he is unwilling to abandon this terminology). Claiming that in hellenistic times a change in tense meanings occurred (here he differs from McKay), particularly regarding the Present, he categorizes its meaning as "essentially connective: a speaker or writer using it connects the verbal action to the person doing the acting; the aorist [is] non-connective or neutral: its occurrence concentrates attention upon the act itself, not upon the relationship which may exist between it and an actor" (967). Admitting that this system is "very subjective and subtle" (969), he uses this in support of his claim that increased use of the Aorist in hellenistic Greek was the result of foreign users unacquainted with the language's subtleties. The criticisms directed at McKay regarding his scheme may be noted, since Voelz essentially repeats it (969 n. 484). His argument for "connectedness" of the Present is likewise not convincing. There is no substantial reason why the Present shows connectedness between the event and speaker in a way that the Aorist or another tense does not (especially the Perfect?), unless this is simply rejuvenation of a traditional *Aktionsart* theory, in which the durative Present is construed as more connected because it elapses over time, whereas the Aorist is punctiliar and hence distant and past (see 968 n. 484 for implications to this effect). And when Voelz treats usage, he does not utilize his scheme. He argues that the historic Present (Mark 5:35-42) is "the equivalent of the aorist (or imperfect [?]), i.e., as a 'zero tense' taking its meaning from its context" (947) (see my chapt. 4).

b. In 1963, Zerwick (esp. 77-99) published in English his Greek grammar, noting that his translator J.P. Smith had contributed "certain additions, notably in the chapters on the 'tenses' and the 'moods'" (v). In discussing tenses, Zerwick mentions the problem of traditional tense labels, realizing that they point to much more than temporal distinctions, although his formulation is not as precise as one might hope: "'aspect' is an essential element of the Greek 'tenses' (leaving out of account the future) and hence is always distinguished by the form, whereas the time of the action is expressed in the indicative only, and in the other moods is either lacking or secondary" (77; he also provides an insightful analysis of the difference between absolute and relative time). The aspects are three: a "simple realization . . . without reference to continuation or repetition but simply 'globally,'" i.e. the Aorist; an "activity in progress or habitual (repeated) or simply as this *kind* of activity or activity tending to a given end," i.e. the Present or Imperfect; and a "completed act resulting in a 'state of affairs' which is predicated by the verb as holding for the present time," i.e. the Perfect (77). These apply in all the Moods, he claims. Whereas his formulations of the Present and the Perfect are too temporally oriented, the validity of his model must be recognized, in which choices are made according to subjective authorial need (78). Whereas most scholars explain Aorist usage in terms of punctuality, Zerwick does not assume this burden in his definition, yet in his practical application he imposes it. For example, he claims δός (give) in Matt 6:11 refers to a "definite petition" and in Luke 9:23 the verbs assume the "once for all" nature of the cross (78). If anything he seems to overinterpret the Aorist (1 John 2:1; cf. 3:9 [82]). He also posits inceptive (John 20:31) and effective (Acts 28:14) categories, though he does not treat them as necessary interpretations. Regarding the other tenses, he maintains aspectual distinctions between the Imperfect and Aorist (Mark 6:41), even in verbs of speaking, and Perfect and Aorist (cf. John 9:29 and Matt 5:21ff.). And his insights into the aspectual nature of Participle usage (see 85ff.) are helpful. The only difficult category is where he speaks of the Present standing for the Future (93-94), in which he argues for Aramaic influence. Overall, however, Zerwick's grammar is a long awaited effort in the study of aspect and the NT Greek verb.

c. Last, attention is drawn to a small and rather rudimentary grammar by Durie (288-95). Like Zerwick, he takes an aspectual approach to the verb, defining aspect as "how the author looks at the event in relation to other events" (288). Durie believes there are four aspects: durative, future, aorist and perfect. Despite the terminological problem, as noted repeatedly above, Durie makes an effort to distinguish aspect from English equivalents (289-91). Claiming there are really only two temporal conditions in Greek, present and past (his calling them tenses might be confusing), Durie defines the Future as an aspect, since it refers to imaginary events and describes intention or expectation (Mark 8:35 [292]). Like Ruipérez, Durie finds duration as the essential verbal feature in Greek and constructs a model accordingly (294):

Participation of the Subject
   in the event
Realized State of the Subject in
   consequence of an event
Expectation of the Subject
   concerning the event
Minimal Subject Affectedness

Durie is to be commended for adopting a morphologically-based aspectual system, though presumably for reasons of space and the nature of the grammar he does not clearly justify these categories. And his attempt at a system using dichotomies showing markedness is helpful. Durie's scheme, however, is open to criticism. (a) He does not show clearly how his definition of aspect correlates with his diagram. The diagram makes no mention of "other events." (b) He fails to show that duration is the essential quality distinguishing marked from unmarked forms. If the future is an aspect (see chapt. 9), it surely is the most marked and should be distinguished first, then the perfect. The emphasis on duration tends toward a distinction upon temporal grounds (*Aktionsart*). (c) Durie's labels appear to be askew. For example, duration implies nothing about participation in the event that the aorist aspect does not. Also, Durie seems to be trying both to define the aspects and to classify them; the results are mixed. In fact, he has four different kinds of labels--the durative relational, the perfect functional, the future attitudinal, and the aorist essentially unclarified.

    7. **CONCLUSION.** This survey, brief in its individual treatments but long in its accumulated data, shows the history of research into the nature of Greek verbal usage, the methodologies employed, the unsatisfactory nature of most treatments, and the tremendous potential for future work. Thus Rydbeck's statement that "there is a prevalent but false assumption that everything in NT Greek scholarship has been done already" ("What Happened," 427) is rightly vindicated. Certainly progress has been made, but virtually all of the major NT grammars adhere firmly to the comparative-philological approach, a method out of touch with current linguistic thought but, more than that, apparently with the Greek language itself. Only a very few more recent works show signs of incorporating recent semantic research into their discussions of verbal usage. Subsequent chapters define a consistent methodology for discussing Greek verbal usage and then apply these findings to a range of examples.

APPENDIX 1A:
PERFECTIVIZING PREFIXES

0. INTRODUCTION.[1] Many scholars, like Brugmann (548-50) and Delbrück (*Syntax*, 2.146-70), followed by NT grammarians like Blass/Debrunner (¶ 318) and Moulton (111-15), have argued that the prefix has a perfectivizing force on the simplex verb. Purdie ("'Aktionsart'"; using Herbig, "Aktionsart," as her foil), supported by Thumb ("Aktionsart"), gives a lengthy rationale for such an argument, positing that the Aorist simplex in Homer conveys a "perfect" significance in an overwhelming number of cases. As Greek verbs evolved, she believes, the Aorist became a constative tense, eventually losing its original perfective force and compelling use of verbs with prefixes (σύν, κατά, διά esp.) to give a force like that of the original Aorist. Since her discussion is virtually solely in terms of characterizing the objective nature of the process (*Aktionsart*), as well as a fundamental misconstrual of categories, it can be passed over.

Meltzer ("Perfektivierung"), however, in an article finding its terminology in Curtius and foreshadowing Stahl and his successors, begins by redefining tense along the lines of *Zeitart*, rejecting much of Delbrück's terminology. Instead of dividing use of the Aorist into perfective and constative, therefore, he opts for an overriding perfective sense in contrast to the imperfective (Imperfect), thus reinforcing the formal and functional bonds between *Zeitart* and tense. He describes the role of the prefix as that of "perfektivierend" (320) to distinguish it from the idea that affixing of the prefix seems to "change" the verb into another formal category. The uses of the tenses are consistent, therefore, with the prefix serving in context to give shadings to the meanings of the tense categories.

1. BRUNEL. The most far-reaching work in scope and influence, however, has been Brunel's treatment of "preverbs" (*L'aspect*). He posits two levels of aspect or better *Aktionsart*: the momentary/progressive/perfective and the determined/undetermined. Finding the second opposition in Slavonic verbal usage he asserts that each Greek verb has the same aspectual distinctions, evidence of which is displayed in verbs with variant forms (e.g. ἀνύω/ἀνύτω [accomplish]; μένω/μίμνω [remain]; ἔχω/ἴσχω [have]; -άνω ending) and those with forms that are confused in Aorist and Imperfect meanings (e.g. ἔφην). The number of verbs in these categories, however, is not large, thus the opposition must be established primarily through prefixes. The prefix has several roles: to maintain its individual (local) semantic value, to form a new lexical unit with the simplex verb, or to change an undetermined verb into a determined one.

Most of Brunel's book is given over to citing numerous examples that show various effects of prefixes. (I have examined usage in the NT of the verbs Brunel cites, with the NT containing approximately one-fourth of the approximately three hundred verbs he treats. The results here are a distillation.) In discussing prefixes that show permanence he cites ἐμμένω (continue), but Th.

---

[1]It is often argued that prefixes began as prepositions, which began as locative adverbs: so Kühner/Gerth, 1.448-53, 526-54; Wackernagel, *Vorlesungen*, 165-67; Schwyzer, 1.417-27. Origin in the adverb has been argued against by Hessinger ("Status").

2.2.1; 2.23.3; 8.31.4 differ from Th. 1.5.3, the first three giving a limited period of time (all Aorists) (as in Acts 28:30 [Imperfect]; cf. John 7:9 with μένω) and the last a custom (Perfect). (This is close to Acts 14:22; Gal 3:10 [with κατάραν (curse) followed by ἐπικατάρατος used apparently synonymously]; Heb 8:9 with ἐμμένω speaking of a permanent spiritual condition, but cf. verses with μένω: e.g. John 3:36; 12:34, 46; 6:56; 2 Cor 3:11; 9:9; Heb 7:24.) ἐπιμένω (abide) is cited in Ar. Clouds 196 (Aorist) with a limited temporal reference, as in Acts 10:48 (Aorist), but cf. Rom 6:1; Phil 1:24 (both Presents), etc., where no definite period is stated, usage Brunel recognizes in comparable passages from classical literature (S. Trach. 1176; E. Supp. 624 [cf. E. Phoen. Maid. 223]). κατέχω (retain; Pl. Apol. 39C-D) seems to be emphatic (though "retenir" [24] is not much different from use of ἔχω in Mark 3:22) but the sense is not always the same in the NT (cf. Acts 27:40; 1 Cor 7:30; 11:2; Luke 4:42; 8:15); likewise Acts 19:22 with ἐπέσχεν (Aorist) does not have Brunel's limited sense and contrasts with Luke 14:7; Phil 2:16 (both Presents). While Luke 22:28; Gal 2:5 may conform to Brunel's conception of διαμένω (remain; Pl. Prot. 344B-C) as presenting "la durée de la situation comme un résultat" (31), 2 Pet 3:4; Luke 1:22 are dissimilar (cf. 1 Thess 1:10 with ἀναμένω with X. Anab. 5.1.5). And ἀναλογίζομαι (think) refers to reflection in Heb 12:3 (Aorist), like X. Hell. 2.4.23 (Imperfect), but so do 1 Cor 13:5; 2 Cor 10:11 (both Presents) with λογίζομαι, as in X. Hell. 2.4.28 (Aorist), as Brunel admits.

Verbs of result with a prefix marking direction display a clearly local use in many cases.[2] Though δείκνυμι (show) is formally determined on account of the suffix νυ, Brunel believes it functions otherwise, though NT examples with ἐπιδείκνυμι seem similar (Matt 16:1; 22:19; 24:1; Luke 17:14; Heb 6:17), and Brunel's distinction that ἀναγκάζω (compel; Pl. Prot. 345E, 346B) is used for general obligations is not upheld in the NT (Mark 6:45 par. Matt 14:22; Acts 26:11; 28:19; Gal 2:3; 6:12; ἐπαναγκάζω does not appear in the NT apparently because its function is handled sufficiently by the simplex form). ἀκούω already has a determined meaning, Brunel states, and the distinction that εἰσακούω expresses "la réalité de l'audition" (68) is untenable, when John 4:42 (Perfect) accomplishes the same with the simplex, as is a differentiation of σκοπέω (watch for) and ἐπισκοπέω (Rom 16:17; Heb 12:15) (Brunel invokes difference in voice to account for the prefixed form). Brunel admits that εἰσακούω has other senses as well: e.g. E. El. 416, where the hearing is new, yet carries the strength of certainty. ἐπακούω (listen to) only occurs in 2 Cor 6:2 in a quotation of Isa 49:8 (LXX). λανθάνω (escape) though formally determined is used undeterminedly, according to Brunel, since the Present simplex λήθω is rare. Though λήθω does not appear in the NT, λανθάνω still seems to be "determined" in some instances, e.g. 2 Pet 3:5. ἐπαισχύνομαι (be ashamed) referring to specific situations rather than sentiments alone (Pl. Soph. 247B-C) seems contradicted by 2 Tim 1:12. And 2 Tim 3:8 (Perfect) with καταφθείρω (destroy) contradicts Brunel's description of the word emphasizing termination rather than continuation (S. Oed. King 331, cf. 272). Certainly Luke 2:16; Acts 21:4 with ἀνευρίσκω (find) show an effective discovery, but so does εὑρίσκω (Matt 7:8; Luke 15:9; John 1:45; Acts 8:40) (Brunel's distinction between X. Anab. 7.4.14 and 19 on the basis of the prefixed form is unclear). ἀναπείθω (persuade) is used in Acts 18:13 (Present) of persuading to a position contrary to standards, but so is the simplex in Acts 26:28; Rom 2:8 (both Present). συναρπάζω (seize) as Brunel says conveys a sense of grasping strongly (S. Aj. 16; Present) but so does Acts 8:39 (Aorist) with the simplex. And Acts 12:12; 14:6 conform to Brunel's dictum that συνοράω (συνεῖδον) (see) dignifies "voir en anême temps, à la fois" (109), but so does John 1:48 with the simplex.

---

[2] ἐπιμέλομαι (look after), καθέζομαι (sit down), καθίζω (sit down), καθίστημι (put in charge/set down), ἀνοίγω (open up), συλλαμβάνω (seize; except Luke 1:24?); ἐπέρχομαι (come upon), προσέρχομαι (come to), εἰσέρχομαι (enter), ἐπιβαίνω (get upon), συμπίπτω (fall), ἐπιστρέφω (turn toward), ἐπεγείρω (stir up).

68

Of prefixes that distinguish elongation, again many retain their local meanings.[3] ἀποτίνω (pay back) as Brunel says signifies "l'abandon de ce qu'on donne en payment" (121), but so does 2 Thess 1:9 with the simplex (cf. Pl. Phaed. 81D with a similar phrase). λύω (loose) in the NT may also mean "delivrer" (121), as does ἀπολύω (Acts 13:3; 16:35). (Brunel's distinction of Pl. Phaed. 62B; 83A; 84A from 64E; 67A; 81D; 113D, reasoning that "cette seconde notion ["delivrer"] peut être exprimée par le simple lui-même, mais avec valeur indéterminée," is not convincing.) Of ἀποπνίγω (choke) Brunel says it is the normal term for "faire mourir étouffé" (130) and it is used this way in the NT (Luke 8:7, 33), though the simplex is used in Matt 13:7; Mark 5:13. διασώζω (save) is used in the NT in several different senses--of healing from illness (Matt 14:36; Luke 7:3) and of physical safety (Acts 23:24; 27:43; 28:1, 4; 1 Pet 3:20), both duplicated by the simplex with an apparently equally effective result (Matt 9:21; Acts 27:20, 31). While most uses of διατάσσω (command) conform to Brunel's dictum of being addressed to distinct persons or situations (cf. 1 Cor 7:17), the simplex is used similarly (Acts 15:2; Matt 28:16).

In the section on departure and fulfilment, several verbs show local use of the prefix.[4] ἀφικνέομαι in Rom 16:19 means, as Brunel states, "I arrive," but so does the simplex in classical Greek (see Liddell/Scott, *Lexicon*, s.v. ἱκνέομαι. It does not appear in the NT), as does ἀπαντάω (meet) (Mark 14:13; Luke 17:12) (Brunel recognizes that the prefixed form replaces the simplex in these cases). Brunel contrasts δέχομαι as material acceptance with ἀποδέχομαι as intellectual acceptance (Acts 2:41), but this does not hold in the NT, where ἀποδέχομαι may refer to receiving people (Luke 8:40). Brunel's distinction of τελέω (finish) from ἐκτελέω as "le simple exprimait un procès indefini, le composé note un dénouement précis" (A. Pers. 228 [203]) does not explain simplex use (Matt 13:53; 26:1; 17:24; Luke 18:31; 22:37).

In the section on achievement,[5] contrary to Brunel, ἐκτρέφω (feed) in Eph 5:29 (Present) does not mean the action pursued up to the moment when the child becomes an adult. And it is difficult to estimate the intensive value of ἐκπληρόω (fulfil) in Acts 13:33 (Perfect) (cf. Matt 1:22 with simplex, similar to X. Cyr. 5.3.24 [both Aorists]). διαφθείρω has two distinct senses in the NT, the one meaning "corruption" following classical usage (2 Cor 4:16; 1 Tim 6:5; Pl. Apol. 24C; X. Mem. 1.1.1), and the other meaning "destruction" similar in meaning to the simplex (Luke 12:33; Rev 8:9). Brunel argues that μανθάνω (learn) however is already perfective (θ and ανω), though the prefixed form makes certain the determined aspect (Matt 6:28). Whereas most NT uses of κατανοέω (think) conform to classical usage as "comprendre, saisir par la pensée" (236), Acts 27:39 says the boatmen did not recognize the island as Miletus until landing (Acts 28:1), and Jas 1:23, 24 say one looking at himself in the mirror immediately forgets his appearance when he turns away. Brunel's distinction of ἐργάζομαι (perform) from κατεργάζομαι on the basis of the former describing the instinct and the latter the author of an action (relation to determined/undetermined is unclear) does not hold in the NT (John 5:17; 6:28; 1 Cor 4:12; Gal 6:10).

2. NT GRAMMARS. Brunel's book, not readily available though referred to in Blass/Debrunner and Turner without specific citations, shows the wide variance in definitions and methods employed in asserting that a compound is "determined." Of the NT grammars that refer to perfectivizing prefixes, a similar treatment as above could be made, but analysis of three words often cited is sufficient: ἀπόλλυμι, συναρπάζω, and ἀποθνήσκω (ἀποκτείνω). Moulton argues regarding ἀπόλλυμι (destroy) that the recurrent phrase οἱ ἀπολλύμενοι "the perishing" implies "the completion of the process of destruction" or "the sense of an inevitable doom" (114). Moulton may be correct that virtually every NT example has the sense of complete destruction, but

---

[3]ἀποστρέφω (turn away), ἀπονίπτω (wash), ἀπολούω (wash), ἀποφεύγω (flee), ἐκφεύγω (flee), ἐκκαθαίρω (clean out), ἐκλείπω (leave), ἐκφύω (put out), διαφεύγω (escape), ἀποκρύπτω (hide), ἐξεγείρω (raise up).

[4]ἀποστέλλω (send out), ἐκφέρω (carry away), ἐκβαίνω (go out).

[5]ἐξαπατάω (deceive) is local.

the range of this lexical item must be considered. (a) It is not possible to temper the concept of destruction very much. (b) The sense of certainty he gives the term is unjustified, since escape is provided in several instances (Matt 8:25; Luke 15:17). (c) The simplex does not occur in the NT (it is obsolete in hellenistic Greek by Moulton's admission), thus leaving the writer no choice of lexical item. (d) The previous points are further proof that the prefix is not inherently perfective, since Brunel asserts that ὄλλυμι is itself determined. The duplicate function with the compound perhaps explains the simplex's passing out of use. (Brunel [132] attributes the determined sense to the nasal suffix.)

Moulton also makes much of the use of συναρπάζω in Luke 8:29, claiming that it "denotes not the temporary paroxysm, but the establishment of a permanent hold." The interpretation of συν here depends upon the fact that its normal adverbial force is "no longer at work" (113). συναρπάζω is also found in Acts 6:12; 19:29 when Paul or his companions are arrested and dragged before authorities, and Acts 27:15 when Paul's ship is seized by a fierce wind off Causa, all with the Aorist. One would expect the prefix to make Luke 8:29 approximate the Aorists but the senses are different, with only Acts 27:15 similar. Instead the sense Moulton gives to συναρπάζω is attributable to the use of the Pluperfect rather than the prefix, since Acts 6:12; 19:29 do not emphasize a state like the demoniac experienced.

Concerning ἀποθνήσκω (and ἀποκτείνω) Moulton begins by trying to explain the use of the Present-stem prefixed form. He asserts that θνήσκω is "to be dying" and ἀπέθανον "to die," so he queries how ἀποθνήσκω functions. He discovers: iterative (1 Cor 15:31) and frequentative (Heb 7:8; 10:28; 1 Cor 15:22; Rev 14:13) uses (Moulton distinguishes the iterative as repeated action by the same agent and frequentative as recurring to different individuals, obviously a lexical and not a grammatical distinction); future use (John 21:23; 1 Cor 15:32); and durative use (Luke 8:42; 2 Cor 6:9; Heb 11:21). He claims the last use replaced the simplex since the linear-perfective expressed the simplex's meaning sufficiently, denoting the whole process leading up to "an attained goal" (114). Actually this does little to reinforce Moulton's position. (a) He notes strictly durative uses of the compound (the other uses he mentions can be subsumed under the imperfective grammatical aspect as well), though Rom 6:9 and 1 Cor 15:31 may be included also. Thus the prefix is not strictly perfectivizing. (b) He admits the simplex is obsolete (114 n. 4; the Perfect of the simplex occurs in the NT). Therefore one must ask what choice the author had to convey the durative meaning and it is ἀποθνήσκω, as Moulton admits. (3) Moulton cannot argue that the linear-perfective is sufficient to fulfil the simplex's function, since he himself notes that the concept of death implies having "the goal in sight" (114; Brunel [90] recognizes the relation between θνήσκω and its composite forms is "plus abstraite"). Therefore any of the verbal forms, on the basis of lexical meaning, is inherently perfective. The same reasoning applies to ἀποκτείνω, since κτείνω does not occur in the NT. (Brunel claims the simplex represents "une action qui se poursuit sans cesse" [127] and the composite "la réalisation effectives dáctes particuliers" [128].)

3. CONCLUSIONS. The findings of this investigation may be summarized briefly.

a. Brunel mixes two categories he calls aspect--morphological/grammatical and lexical. The second of his oppositions (determined/undetermined) is not based on any grammatical rules but upon the meaning of individual lexical items. The presence of the prefix, however, does not guarantee any particular function. Instead, the concepts of determined/undetermined are loose categories to describe a variety of interpretations. For example, he utilizes transitivity and voice in support of his argument for determinedness (see Debrunner, Review of Brunel, 286, who not only cites Brunel's mixed bag of features for determining perfectivization, but questions his interpretation of classical examples).

b. Robertson (562-63) is correct when he describes four broad categories of the effect of the prefix (Brunel recognizes these as well): no effect at all; local; intensive (κατεσθίω--eat up) or perfective; and altered meaning of the simplex verb. As Moulton admits, "the actual majority of examples preserve the original meaning" (114; see also Debrunner, Review of Brunel, 287; and Herbig, "Aktionsart," 222ff., who argued in 1896 that the prefix never lost its original meaning completely and thus only occasionally displayed "perfectivizing" force). And it can be noted from the many examples Robertson cites as "perfective" that many are no more than local: ἐκφεύγω (escape) Heb 2:3; διατηρέω (keep continually) Luke 2:51; συντηρέω (keep together [safely]) Mark 6:20; διασπάω (draw in two) Mark 5:4; κατακαίω (burn up) Acts 19:19; συνέχω (hold together) Luke 8:45. It cannot be denied that the prefix may add a different meaning to the simplex, in fact one often pointing to completion, termination or intensification, but that this is a matter of lexical not aspectual alteration.

c. The major criticism of Brunel's proposal is the same one levelled against *Aktionsart:* grammatical aspect is being confused with lexical *Aktionsart.* In understanding prefixed verbs it must be realized that each has a lexical meaning that interplays with a particular context (lexical meaning is an extrapolation from an accumulation of contexts), which context is verbally determined by aspect. Therefore, verbal aspect as properly understood is not altered by prefixes. As Debrunner says, "Wenn es überhaupt eine Aktionsartenbedeutung der Präverbia gegeben hat, so hat sie auf keinen Fall die des Aorists beseitigt; denn der Gegensatz Präsensstamm-Aoriststamm ist noch im heutigen Griechisch so sicher und scharf wie im Altgriechischen und wohl in der idg. Urzeit!" (Review of Brunel, 285).

d. In an article published in 1946, seven years after his book, Brunel ("L'aspect") argues for essentially the same distinctions that are concluded above, but with some significant modifications: whereas the prefix may function in a number of ways, each use must be determined in relation to use of the simplex verb; and whereas this may be realized in an aspectual opposition, it is essentially a lexical phenomenon bearing on *Aktionsart* (or what he calls "l'ordre de procès"). This significant shift in his position has not been noted for the most part by scholars following Brunel's earlier work.

APPENDIX 1B:
DISSENTING THEORIES

0. INTRODUCTION. Although a growing number of linguists and grammarians over the last forty years have recognized the importance of aspect in Greek verbal usage, several notable scholars have expressed displeasure with such a scheme. Two such approaches are singled out: the 1. "temporal priority" and 2. "morphological disbelief" approaches.

1. TEMPORAL PRIORITY. In the secondary literature, two temporal priority approaches to "aspect" are found. **a.** Koschmieder's scheme (*Zeitbezug*, esp. 47-51, 72-78) is formulated around two opposite temporal movements, that of time itself from future to past (*Zeitbezug*) and that of the "I" from past to future (*Zeitrichtung*). The intersection of the temporal line and the "I" as a pointer on the line (before is future, behind is past, immediate is present) determines what Koschmieder would call "aspects." Drawing upon Polish and Russian, Koschmieder posits that Greek is a language with established grammatical categories for treating temporal movement (48). The Present indicates movement of past to future (*geschehend*), the Aorist of future to past (*geschehen*) and the Perfect a combination of the two. Using the comparison of stretching a rubber band until it breaks, he claims to show that the present is merely a point joining the past and future, and can only be spoken of using the Present tense. Thus the answer to the question "Was machst du da?" cannot take the "Aorist." The Greek Participle shows the contrast more clearly: the Present Participle represents "occurring" action and the Aorist the event that has "occurred" (48-49).

Koschmieder has rightly been attacked from all sides, although only a few of the criticisms, particularly those referring to Greek, are discussed. (a) Debrunner has argued that other languages, such as Hebrew, in fact clearly have tense forms that are purely aspectual (Review of Koschmieder; cf. Schlachter, "Verbalaspekt," 35ff., for summary and critique), and that Greek is best seen as one of these languages (if not the Slavonic languages as well). Koschmieder ("Grundfragen") replies that the Aorist is a past tense form, but that coincidentally it may be best translated with present reference, especially with verbs of speaking. Koschmieder has undermined his argument, since his temporal categories are apparently merely formal categories; when applied to usage they lose their significance. (b) Hermann ("Aspekt und Aktionsart") has attacked the logical contrast that Koschmieder imposes, arguing that aspect has nothing to do with temporal movement (472) and that the scheme cannot treat adequately such phenomena as punctual Presents and historic Presents. Though Koschmieder makes it clear that time itself as interpreted through language is a construct (though to argue with Koschmieder that the present is only a psychological construct could, as Hermann says [475-76], be construed to mean the past and future are artificial as well), his insistence upon primarily temporal categories is untenable in Greek. (Hermann ["Aspekt und Zeitrichtung"] reiterates his feeling that Koschmieder's scheme has nothing to do with the fundamental aspectual oppositions in Greek; cf. also Gonda, *Rgvedic*, 19 n. 66.) In fact, Koschmieder admits he overstated his case ("Grundfragen," 300).

b. Guillaume (*Temps et verbe*), using the French language, creates a model which includes temporal, aspectual, and modal relations. Guillaume shows how important is sound methodology in conjunction with actual observation of language. (His psychological hypothesis makes virtually no reference to Greek usage.) He establishes two temporal lines--Imperfect, Present, Future, and Pluperfect, Perfect, (Future Perfect). These two lines are connected by the Aorist, standing at the point of present reference, which is nothing more than the point where past and future intersect. Guillaume lays modal usage over this initial structure to create a comprehensive picture of Greek verbal use.

Whereas Guillaume's depiction of the Indicative may have some basis in fact temporally, and his attempt at integrating discussion of modality, a feature neglected by many other grammarians, is to be commended, (1) he neglects much more by not establishing why the two temporal lines should be differentiated in the first place (other than for formal difference). Guillaume seems to make some unfounded assumptions regarding the nature of time itself. (2) The two lines are not actually parallel, since the Pluperfect in relation to the Perfect is not the same as the Imperfect to the Present. This scheme appears arbitrary. (3) The Aorist displays a variety of uses that gives it flexible temporal reference. Therefore, it is difficult to believe with Guillaume that the Aorist is nothing more than a cipher or a connecting point, without any character of its own, and that the only distinguishing characteristic is a flexible temporal reference. And Guillaume has essentially eliminated any "aberrant" uses of other tenses. (4) Most damagingly, the overlay of the Moods imposes temporal restrictions on verbal functions that are best considered to be non-temporal in Greek (see Holt, *Etudes*, 10-12, for summary and critique of Guillaume; cf. Schogt, "'Temps,'" for a critical estimation). Consequently, British and American linguists have ignored Guillaume's *a prioristic* psychologization regarding tense (so Contreres, Review. But see Hirtle, *Aspect*, who uses Guillaume. It has been suggested to me that Guillaume's writing in French may be the primary cause of his neglect among English-speaking linguists).

2. MORPHOLOGICAL DISBELIEF. The many attempts to discredit morphologically-based aspectual distinctions can be traced back to 19th-cent. and to earlier 20th-cent. grammars. Several scholars have recently addressed the issue. **a.** Szemerényi has been the most outspoken critic of morphologically-based aspect in Greek. He argues that, since the 17th cent., when Slavonic aspectual opposition was first discussed, there has been an increasing tendency to find aspect in all IE languages. But Szemerényi argues there is nothing in Greek (or any other IE language) that can represent the thorough-going dualism of Slavonic verbs (he does not address the issue of modern Greek!). If it is accepted that the Slavonic system was not inherited, another explanation must be found for the origin of the verb systems, which Szemerényi sees in tense and mode. This he claims agrees with the formal evidence, in which present and past tenses were first opposed and later the future and perfect grew up, whereas the differentiation of the Present and Aorist systems was secondarily established (*Einführung*, 286-88, 310; "Origin").

In an earlier article, Szemerényi cites several other scholars in support of his position ("Views"). He uses Galton's work on Slavonic aspect, supplemented by work by Machek, to show that aspect was not inherited from IE but was a later development. Szemerényi makes several apparent mistakes, however. (1) Even if IE did not have an aspectual system as later found in Slavonic languages (here speculation confronts speculation), this does not preclude that the tendency was present from the start but required time for development. (2) To reason that since Greek did not inherit the Slavonic system it could not have developed its own system (as Slavonic did according to Szemerényi) is a *non sequitur* (see Friedrich, "Theory," S29). It seems logically, formally and textually certain that Greek developed aspectual categories in its tenses by the time of Homer at the very latest and that these continued to develop, up to modern Greek. (3) Szemerényi does not interpret Galton correctly. In his section on Greek verbs, Galton argues that Slavonic did develop later forms on its own, but that Greek too developed aspectual oppositions, already noted to various degrees by the hellenistic Greek grammarians themselves (Szemerényi ["Origin," 1 n. 1] finds it convenient to cite recent research by Hiersche disputing "aspectual" oppositions in the hellenistic grammarians). In fact, Galton distinguishes aspect and *Aktionsart*, claiming that verbal roots (reflecting aspect) were later suffixed to differentiate *Aktionsarten* (Galton, *Aorist*, 128-33; reiterated in "Verbalaspekt"; cf. *Functions*, and "Theory").

b. Szemerényi turns also to Weinrich ("Tense"), who posits that aspectual theories, though dating back to the Stoics, are incredibly complex but grammar is in reality "fundamentally a simple system" (32). Instead he posits a system of tense (though not time) alone. (1) Weinrich divides tense forms according to their speech attitude. The narrative tense group includes the preterite, pluperfect, etc., and the discursive tense group the present, perfect and future. In each category there is a zero tense (the first listed respectively). (2) Weinrich notes that the tenses (excluding the zero tense) give different perspectives, the perfect and the pluperfect being retrospective and the future and conditional being prospective. He believes that such concepts as present and past time, since they are not linguistic categories, are better treated this way. (3) Weinrich notes the dimension of *relievo*, in which some tenses give background narration and others foreground narration.

Applying his findings to Greek, Weinrich (*Tempus*, esp. 288-93) labels verbs with primary endings as discursive and those with secondary endings as descriptive or narrative tenses. The major difference between the Imperfect and Aorist is one of *relievo*, the former giving background and the latter foreground. For example ἐβασίλευε means "he ruled as king," as background to the description, while ἐβασίλευσε means "he ruled as king," as the principal subject, since it is new and upsetting. The gnomic Aorist thus describes its parabolic content factually or descriptively, gathering up the high points.

A response to Weinrich should be evident. (1) There is serious question whether he has in fact devised a clearer system. Although Weinrich ("Tense," 41) calls his theory "unassailable," Bache (*Aspect*, 22) notes that this makes the theory itself "rather suspicious," as does his overly simple characterization of his opponents' theories of time and tense. His scheme of verbal usage is complex and uncoordinated, and his further exposition of the Moods, in which the levels are not adumbrated, makes for confusion. Just because a system is complex, however, it need not be wrong, though it must be stated that Weinrich has not proved that aspect systems are in fact overly complex. (2) Weinrich's system is inconsistent in its division between the uses of the Indicative and other Moods. For example, it is not clear why the Present and Aorist Infinitives should have both discursive and narrative capacities, and maintain their background and foreground capabilities. As Bache (*Aspect*, 23-24; cf. Pollak, "Aspekt," 158) points out, Weinrich's system itself is time-bound in its treatment of examples, and the theory of aspect that he disputes is actually a theory of *Aktionsart*, since he refers to characterizations of the action itself (cf. Weinrich, *Tempus*, 155). (3) What Weinrich (290-91) says about the contrast between Aorist and Imperfect is undermined by the description he quotes from Wackernagel that the Aorist is used for a series of events and the Imperfect for the single description. The NT confirms this general pattern, with the Aorist appearing much more as the "background" narrative tense. Fajen ("Tempus," 38-41) shows, using the section that Weinrich cites in X. Anab. 1.1-3 and ff., that in fact Weinrich's theory is unable to account for much verbal usage, including not only the Aorist/Imperfect but the function of the Present and Perfect tenses. (4) In final assessment, there is nothing inherently contradictory about Weinrich's scheme and a theory of aspect (Fajen [41] argues that "das griechische System, unbeeinflusst vom lateinischen, ist beträchtlich verschieden von dem der modernen westeuropäischen Sprachen"; cf. Louw, "Aspek," 16). Aspect is a semantic category, while his scheme addresses pragmatic usage. As Bache (*Aspect*, 24) says, "the problem with Weinreich's [sic] theory of tense is that it confuses grammatical meaning with literary function. An analysis of the stylistics of certain linguistic items cannot and should not replace an analysis of grammatical meaning." In fact, Weinrich's differentiations are probably governed by aspectual factors he fails to recognize.

3. CONCLUSION. Whereas several dissenting theories discount the importance of verbal aspect in Greek, none of them provides a more promising alternative, although several include insights that might enhance discussion.

CHAPTER 2:
A SYSTEMIC ANALYSIS OF
GREEK VERBAL ASPECT

0. INTRODUCTION. A competent semantic description of tense usage in Greek must account for and explain at least the following sets of instances according to a unified semantic theory. The most persuasive explanation will delimit a defined number of specific, shared semantic features which describe the largest number of kinds of examples, i.e. an adequate explanation must account for the tokens of its type (Lyons, *Semantics*, esp. 28-29). As McKay (214) says, "The test of any hypothesis therefore is not that it resolves all doubts but that it offers the most consistent explanation, leaving few anomalies" (cf. Collinge, "Reflexions," 83; Berry, "Teacher," 53-61).

1. Present Indicative[1]

Matt 8:25: κύριε . . . ἀπολλύμεθα (lord . . . we are perishing)
Mark 11:27: καὶ ἔρχονται πάλιν εἰς Ἱεροσόλυμα (and they were coming again into J.)
Matt 26:18: πρὸς σὲ ποιῶ τὸ πάσχα μετὰ τῶν μαθητῶν μου (with you I am going to make the passover with my disciples)
Matt 7:19: πᾶν δένδρον μὴ ποιοῦν καρπὸν καλὸν ἐκκόπτεται καὶ εἰς πῦρ βάλλεται (every tree not making good fruit is cut off and thrown into the fire)
2 Cor 9:7: ἱλαρὸν γὰρ δότην ἀγαπᾷ ὁ θεός (for God loves a joyful giver)

2. Aorist Indicative

2 Cor 11:25: τρὶς ἐραβδίσθην, ἅπαξ ἐλιθάσθην, τρὶς ἐναυάγησα (three times I was beaten, once I was stoned, three times I was shipwrecked)
Luke 16:4: ἔγνων τί ποιήσω (I know what I intend to do)
John 17:14, 18: ὁ κόσμος ἐμίσησεν αὐτούς. . . . κἀγὼ ἀπέστειλα αὐτοὺς εἰς τὸν κόσμον (the world is going to hate them. . . . I am going to send them into the world)
Eph 5:29: οὐδεὶς γάρ ποτε τὴν ἑαυτοῦ σάρκα ἐμίσησεν (for no one ever hates his own body)

---

[1]Unlike many grammars, even those which recognize the non-temporal nature of non-Indicative forms (see chaps. 4 and 7), this discussion begins with the Indicative.

Luke 7:35: καὶ ἐδικαιώθη ἡ σοφία ἀπὸ πάντων τῶν τέκνων αὐτῆς (wisdom is justified by all her children)

3. Perfect Indicative

Matt 21:27: καὶ ἀποκριθέντες τῷ Ἰησοῦ εἶπαν, οὐκ οἴδαμεν (answering, they said to Jesus, "we don't know")
Acts 10:45: ὅτι καὶ ἐπὶ τὰ ἔθνη ἡ δωρεὰ τοῦ ἁγίου πνεύματος ἐκκέχυται (because the gift of the holy spirit had been poured out upon the Gentiles)
Jas 5:2-3: ὁ πλοῦτος ὑμῶν σέσηπεν καὶ τὰ ἱμάτια ὑμῶν σητόβρωτα γέγονεν (your riches are going to rot and your garments are going to become moth-eaten)
2 Pet 2:19: ᾧ γάρ τις ἥττηται, τούτῳ δεδούλωται (for by what someone is overcome, by this he is enslaved)
1 John 3:14: μεταβεβήκαμεν ἐκ τοῦ θανάτου εἰς τὴν ζωήν (we are transformed from death into life)

1. GRAMMATICALIZATION OF TENSE. The discussion of possible solutions to understanding tense usage in Greek must proceed from fundamental terminology. In his recent, thorough treatment of tense, Comrie notes, "the establishment of the correct meaning of a grammatical category like tense is by no means straightforward, so that even for a language as thoroughly studied as English there remains controversy concerning the definition of the various tenses" (*Tense*, ix; cf. Dahl, *Tense*, esp. 103-28; Bache, *Aspect*, 15-25; Lyons, *Semantics*, 677-90). As noted in chapt. 1, temporal reference of tense forms comprises one of the major components, if not the major component, of many descriptions of the use of the Greek tenses.

Comrie defines "tense" as "the grammaticalisation of location in time," i.e. that a particular location in time is established by use of a grammatical category like tense (*Tense*, viii, cf. 1; Dahl, *Tense*, 23; Lyons, *Semantics*, 678: "Tense, in those languages which have tense, is part of the deictic frame of temporal reference: it grammaticalizes the relationship which holds between the time of the situation that is being described and the temporal zero-point of the deictic context"; idem, *Introduction*, 304-06). Though the distinction between grammaticalization and lexicalization is often an item of debate, especially in matters of translation (see Lyons, *Semantics*, 234-37; Collinge, "Reflexions," 84; Dahl, "Review," 490), it is less of a problem within a language like Greek, where grammaticalization of tense is both fully obligatory (i.e. a tense form must be selected when using a verb) and morphologically bound (i.e. the change of tense forms requires a change in the morphology of the verb). Periphrastics appear to be an exception to this rule. This is more apparent than real, since virtually all major tense categories in Greek are able to be constructed apart from periphrastic formations, with periphrasis involving the word complex (see my chapt. 10 for discussion)? Traditionally, time is depicted for discussion as a line.

before	contemporaneous	after

zero time

chart 1[3]

In terms of absolute tense, in which the point of reference or zero time is the present/contemporary moment (Comrie, *Tense*, 6, 36; cf. idem, *Aspect*, 2; Dahl, *Tense*, 24), the present tense must include the present moment, though many grammarians have noted the difficulty of this conception. "It is relatively rare for a situation to coincide exactly with the present moment," Comrie continues (37, cf. 38), thus "a more characteristic use of the present tense is in referring to situations which occupy a much larger period of time than the present moment, but which nonetheless include the present moment with them" (see also Lyons, *Structural Semantics*, 111-17).

Applying this to the Greek examples above, it becomes clear according to a principle of contrastive substitution (see Curtius, *Elucidations*, 209; Bache, *Aspect*, 1; cf. Collinge, "Reflexions," 89 n. 1, as well as several grammarians analysed in chapt. 1)--by which the identical form is used in different temporal contexts--that Greek does not grammaticalize absolute tense with the Present, since only Matt 8:25 clearly makes reference to present time as defined above. It might be argued that Matt 7:19--what is best called an omnitemporal use (see below and chapt. 4)--includes present reference as one of its points of reference, since it describes an event that happens with regularity, i.e. it has happened in the past, is the kind of thing that happens now, and seems likely to occur in the future, but this is not its most obvious or indeed best explanation (cf. chapt. 4, where scholars discussing the gnomic Aorist [omnitemporal] often use the event's occurrence in the past as justification for an explanation of the tense form along temporal lines).[4] This explanation is inadequate for 2 Cor 9:7, where a theological statement--characteristic of timeless usage (see chapt. 4)--is made, and Matt 26:18 can only by a stretch of the imagination be made to

---

[2]See Comrie, *Tense*, 10-12, 8-9. He distinguishes the "sum total of expressions for locating in time" as: lexically composite expressions (e.g. μετὰ τούτου [after this], ἐν τούτῳ [while, when], etc.), lexical items (e.g. νῦν [now], ἄρα, τότε [then], ἄχρι, ἕως, μέχρι [while], ὅταν [when/whenever], ἐπάν [after], ἡνίκα [when/whenever], ὅτε, ἐπείδη, ὁπότε [when], ὡς [when, since], πρίν [before], etc.), and grammatical categories, like tense forms.

[3]Lyons, *Introduction*, 305; contra Comrie, *Tense*, 2: is his chart in error?

[4]Comrie (*Tense*, 39-41) claims there are not habitual or gnomic tenses in English, since the features of repetition or universality are events that do overlap with the present or use time adverbials. I conflate both into the category of omnitemporal.

include a specific present moment, since the passover is future to the dialogue. The most convincing example is Mark 11:27, what is traditionally recognized as the historic Present (see chaps. 3 and 4 for discussion). Explanations of the historic Present along traditional lines often involve transference of either the speaker into the past or the past event into the present (see e.g. Delbrück, *Grundlagen*, 80ff.; Brugmann, 555-56; Eriksson, *Präsens*, esp. 8-24). The sheer inventiveness of the theories, by which in a single stretch of text (e.g. John 1:35-42; cf. X. Anab. 1.1.10) one would be required to move constantly from past to present, illustrates that present reference is not to be inferred from pragmatic use of the tense form. Thus it may be concluded that Greek does not grammaticalize present reference in the Present tense form, since the same form may be used with a variety of temporal and non-temporal references. As Robertson (881-82) says, "Since the pres. ind. occurs for past, present and future time it is clear that 'time' is secondary even in the ind." He articulates what most grammarians recognize in their categorizations of usage of the Present (cf. Moulton, 120).

It is possible, though highly unlikely, that Greek would fail to grammaticalize tense in only one tense category. In fact it appears that Greek does not grammaticalize tense in any of the three major tense categories. (The Future calls for separate discussion; see my chapt. 9; Comrie, *Tense*, 43-48; Dahl, *Tense*, 103-12.) Comrie defines the past tense as locating "the situation in the past, without saying anything about whether that situation continues to the present or into the future, although there is often a conversational implicature that it does not continue to or beyond the present" (*Tense*, 41). Even if the event may continue into or beyond the present this proves unsatisfactory for the Greek Aorist tense usage cited above, apart from 2 Cor 11:25 and possibly Eph 5:29. Eph 5:29 may have in mind a past event of a man hating his own body, though the importance of the usage, especially in a context concerned with the relations of men and women, is that this kind of event has significance for the past, present and future (omnitemporal). Luke 16:4 has no indication that a past event is in mind since the unjust steward has just wondered out loud what he might do when the master kicks him out and he must fend for himself. He then exclaims "I know!" Attempts to explain this as a consistent use of the past-referring Aorist (see e.g. Rijksbaron, 28-29, who also cites Ar. Peace 1066; Birds 983; E. And. 918-19; cf. Moorhouse, 195-96) must redefine what is meant by present time to a point in time that cannot be captured in any use of language, since it is past long before it can be referred to. John 17:14, 18 have future reference, as seen from the temporal progression conveyed in the prayer of Jesus, who is recorded saying that the world is going to hate his followers (v 14; cf. 15:18, where the Present is used of the world hating the disciples, but it is in the protasis of a conditional statement), and just as he was sent into the world, he is going to send his disciples (v 18). There is no antecedent reference to either in the Gospel to this point (contra Winer, 346, who equates their sending with their calling). Luke 7:35 contains an enigmatic statement of Jesus with no apparent temporal reference (timeless) (see Péristérakis, *Essai*, for treatment of non-past referring Aorist). There is no indication of past reference, and it may in fact be construed as future-referring, positing a time when wisdom will have its day of justification, though the timeless use seems more appropriate. Thus the range of usage of the Aorist form indicates convincingly that Greek does not grammaticalize temporal reference in the Aorist, even in the Indicative (see my chapt. 4).

The Perfect reveals the same situation. The standard definition of the Perfect tense (see below and chapt. 5) already tacitly recognizes that the Perfect may refer to several temporal points (the grammars note this; see chapt. 5), with the consequence that it does not grammaticalize absolute temporal reference (e.g. Winer, 341-43; Robertson, 892ff.; Burton, 37ff.; cf. Mandilaras, 222-28; Goodwin, *Syntax*, 13-16; Humbert, 146-49). Several examples make this point clear. Matt 21:27 refers to a present event, when the Jewish authorities are asked directly if John the Baptist was from heaven or from men. They answer that they do not know. By contrast, Acts 10:45 is set in a past context when the author narrates the amazement of those of the circumcision at the coming of the holy spirit upon the Gentiles. Jas 5:2-3 logically suggests a future use of the Perfect, because of reference by the author to the future destiny (ταῖς ἐπερχομέναις [v 1]) of the material possessions of the rich. 2 Pet 2:19 describes an omnitemporal state of affairs in which the author says that the thing by which one is overcome, by this one stands enslaved. And 1 John 3:14 refers to being transferred by God from death to life, as a result of loving the brothers. Thus the Perfect, along with the other two Indicative verb tenses in Greek, does not grammaticalize absolute temporal reference. (Bache [*Aspect*, 15] says, "tense [in the traditional sense] is not a universal category since not all languages known today possess verb forms expressing time distinctions. Time may of course be a universal category, but if it is, it is not obvious that it is a purely linguistic one.")

One of the problems with investigating tense distinctions in languages is that the names for tense categories are often based only on typical functions of the tense forms concerned, and do not capture the full range of functions that a given category may express (see Porter, "Terminology"). This is potentially very misleading, because it is tempting to see the typical function that motivates the form name as *the* function, i.e. to treat a short label as far more informative and exhaustive than it really is. (Dahl [*Tense*, 3-10] distinguishes prototypical from focused and extensional from intensional meanings of tense/aspect categories. My chapt. 1 shows that most grammars of Greek have taken a prototypical view, although some are extensional ["we divide the extension of a term into different regions, one of which we--for whatever reason--look upon as 'basic' or 'primary' with regard to the others" (9)] and others intensional ["the 'meaning' or 'sense' of the word consists of several components . . ., one or more of which are then said to be primary or basic with regard to the others" (90)].) As Lyons says,

> Indeed, it is no exaggeration to say that there is probably no tense, mood or aspect in any language whose sole semantic function is the one that is implied by the name that is conventionally given to it in grammars of the language. Furthermore, it is undoubtedly the case that the terms conventionally used to describe the functions of the tense, moods and aspects in certain languages are very misleading. This point must be borne constantly in mind. (*Semantics*, 682)

In the Greek examples above, for example, the Present is used in contexts referring to present time, future time and past time, besides omnitemporal and timeless contexts. The verb tense form is exactly the same in all cases. This can be analysed in several ways. Some might say there is something unusual about a Present that allows it to refer to the future (it is the Present of assured result, or some such thing) or the past (as if the past event were occurring in the present), etc. Better still, perhaps, this form has a variety of temporal uses, the present being one and the future and past being others equally legitimate. While tense names in a language are based on some typical function, this function is usually not the only function of the form concerned, and a speaker risks causing considerable confusion if he fails to make clear that the name often only reflects one of several functions.

Regarding NT Greek, Robertson (825 [1st ed. 1915]) and Nunn (66 [1st ed. 1912]) in the early 1900s recognized the problem of Greek tense terminology (more recently see Carson, *Fallacies*, 69). Regarding classical Greek, Bolling ("Teaching") recognized in 1917 that the tenses in Greek are indifferent to time (see more recently Masterman, "Terminology"; McKay, 128ff.; idem, "Syntax," 44ff., among his several articles). But the problem persists. The "Present" and "Future" are temporal categories while "Imperfect" and "Perfect" are named according to the kind of action or the way the action is described. And the "Pluperfect" seems to combine both (Lyons [*Semantics*, 704] calls the term "misleading"). It cannot be suspected from this that, for example, the Imperfect is related morphologically to the Present. And there is the "Aorist." Many grammarians say that this rubric comes from the Greek ἀ-όριστος, "without boundary" or "undefined" (see chapt. 1 for examples throughout the history of discussion of Greek grammar). The term was first devised by the hellenistic Greek grammarians themselves, as seen above in chapt. 1, with Dionysius Thrax linking the Aorist and Future together, calling them both undefined. Grammarians since have been fooled on more than one occasion into thinking then that the tense function itself is unspecified, but perhaps the Greeks themselves were fooled (if indeed they thought this).

A simple solution to this problem of Greek tense terminology would seem to be to standardize the terms on the basis of temporal reference, but this will not work for several reasons, not least of which is that time is (as many grammarians recognize) of no direct consequence in the non-Indicative Moods (see chapts. 4 and 7 for discussion), besides the major problem of tense substitution noted above. A second solution would be to realize that the Greek tenses are not based essentially upon a temporal understanding of verbal action and to reformulate the names accordingly. But tense labels are rather seductive. Robertson remarks regretfully: "the names cannot now be changed, though very unsatisfactory" (826; cf. Carson, *Fallacies*, 69).

Three tentative ways of alleviating the difficulty of tense terminology suggest themselves. The first is to recognize the difference between verbal form and function. When Greek grammars speak of punctiliar Presents, future Presents, inceptive Aorists, they are speaking of two different things. They are speaking of a verbal form--Present, Aorist, Perfect--used in a certain function--it refers to present time, future time, etc. (Bache [*Aspect*, 15] notes: "The traditional distinction between 'time' and 'tense,' . . . was a formal one: 'tense' was used to refer to *language-specific* forms conveying certain [supposedly] *universal* 'time' qualities; that is, tense was a formal category whereas time was a notional category.") Using traditional tense terminology, there seem to be two ways to avoid confusion. One would be to capitalize all form names and use small initial letters for functions. So the term "past Present" is a Present form used of past time. This provides a neat shorthand to keep the two categories separate, but it is just a shorthand and does not address the problem, that tense is not grammaticalized in Greek verb forms. The second suggestion is that perhaps the shorthand ought to be clarified. For example, "the Aorist form used of present time" and "the Perfect form used of past time" may take longer, but they are certainly clearer. This once more shows up the difficulty of tense terminology in Greek, however. The phrase "Present used of past time" (or "with past time reference") still says nothing about the basis of the Greek tense system, which cannot be formulated along absolute temporal lines. Therefore tense categories must include some component to reflect their essential semantic (non-temporal) component. McKay has done this partly when he labels the Present form the "imperfective." But he does not need to keep the term Aorist either, since it is treated by grammarians as anything but undefined. (McKay should, it seems, eliminate the term Future as well, since he believes it constitutes an aspectual and not solely a temporal category [136-37]; "Syntax," 44ff., and his other articles; see my chapt. 9.) The difficulties with this scheme, however, are self-evident. First, it eliminates the boundary between form and function so that the metalanguage is ambiguous on whether formal or functional criteria are being invoked, and, second, it makes a too facile equation of form with function (though this equation seems warranted in Greek verbal usage).

To state that Greek does not grammaticalize temporal reference, however, says nothing about its ability to refer to time (it is a common misunderstanding that the two are necessarily linked; see Comrie, *Tense*, 3-5). Many instances can be cited in Greek literature where authors seem specifically to distinguish temporal moments,[5] and no one would deny that within the literature itself there is narrative (past context), description ('present' context), etc. One syntactical example might be indirect discourse in hellenistic Greek. Following a primary or secondary tense form the same tense form is maintained (except in a few examples where the Optative is used [e.g. Imperfect and Pluperfect]).[6] Thus in Gal 2:14 (εἶδον ὅτι οὐκ ὀρθοποδοῦσιν [I saw that they were not walking uprightly]) the author shifts the point of temporal reference, but uses a Present form for reporting a past event. In other words, the alternatives to not grammaticalizing tense are not simply that a language has no concept of time (see Comrie, *Tense*, 3, 7-8) but that the language uses other means, such as deictic indicators (see below; Comrie, *Tense*, 13-18). Another way of formulating this is to say that in Greek the sentence is tenseless, while the proposition is tensed, i.e. the sentence does not grammaticalize temporal reference, while propositions do on the basis of deixis (see Lyons, *Semantics*, 679). When deixis is defined more specifically below it is noted that certain tenses tend to be used in certain kinds of contexts (e.g. Aorist in narrative, Present in description). Two factors must be distinguished here. The first is a unifying semantic category (or essential or basic/typological meaning at the level of code) of tense usage and the second is a pragmatic category (or secondary meaning at the level of text) (Dahl, *Tense*, 9-11). I am primarily concerned with defining the essential semantic component(s) of tense usage in Greek, i.e. use of the tense forms at the level of code or network which allows various pragmatic manifestations at the level of text. I share Comrie's belief that "in the characterisation of the meanings of tense . . ., the more flexible approach provides a more accurate characterisation of the linguistic system." There is a "distinction between a context-dependent meaning and interpretation fostered by specific contexts" (Comrie, *Tense*, 19). A helpful category here is implicature, by which is

---

[5]Hom. Il. 1.70: ὃς ᾔδη τά τ᾽ ἐόντα τά τ᾽ ἐσσόμενα πρό τ᾽ ἐόντα (who [knew] already the things that are and the things that are expected and the things previous) (cf. E. El. Fr. 3.15); Pl. Rep. 392D: διήγησις οὖσα τυγχάνει ἢ γεγονότων ἢ ὄντων ἢ μελλόντων (it is a narration of the things that have come about, that are and that are intended); cf. Pol. 301E-302B; Phil. 39C; Parm. 141D-E; E. Daught. Troy 468: πάσχω τε καὶ πέπονθα κἄτι πείσομαι (I am suffering and I have suffered and I intend to suffer); Rev 1:8: ὁ ὢν καὶ ὁ ἦν καὶ ὁ ἐρχόμενος (the one who is and who was and who is coming); cf. D L. 7.141. It is noteworthy that in none of these examples are the Aorist, Present and Future tenses used of past, present, and future time as some would expect. Instead, the Perfect and Present are each used for past reference, and the Present is used for future reference. In no instance here is the Aorist Participle used.

[6]This is very similar to use of indirect discourse in classical Greek, except for decreased use of the Optative following secondary tense forms in hellenistic Greek. Greek follows a sequence of tense rule in indirect discourse (see Comrie, *Tense*, 104ff.) with the less heavily marked attitudes serving as default forms.

meant "the distinction between the meaning of a linguistic item, in terms of its conventionalised semantic representation, and the implicatures that can be drawn from the use of a linguistic item in a particular context" (Comrie, *Tense*, 23, cf. 18-26; Lyons, *Semantics*, 592-96. I use the term as it has been applied to the area of tense usage and not solely as it was first used by Grice ["Logic"]).

2. INTRODUCTION TO VERBAL ASPECT. What might be the unifying semantic category of Greek tense usage? To answer that question a second set of examples must be explained (this is suggested by Curtius, *Elucidations*, 209; Bache, *Aspect*, 1ff.; Collinge, "Reflexions," 89 n. 1; and several grammarians [see chapt. 1]).

Luke 21:10: τότε ἔλεγεν αὐτοῖς (then he was saying to them)
Luke 20:41: εἶπεν . . . πρὸς αὐτούς (he said . . . to them)
Acts 20:38: τῷ λόγῳ ᾧ εἰρήκει (the word which he spoke)

Luke 24:18: οὐκ ἔγνως τὰ γενόμενα ἐν αὐτῇ ἐν ταῖς ἡμέραις ταύταις; (you don't know the state of things in [Jerusalem] in these days?)
John 5:42: ἔγνωκα ὑμᾶς (I know you)
John 21:17: σὺ γινώσκεις ὅτι . . . (you know that . . .)

These select sets of examples are especially useful for this discussion. A comparison of the examples cited at the outset of the chapter arranged according to their temporal categories--present, past, future, omnitemporal, timeless--would provide a similar set for examination. The set directly above, however, uses words for saying in three different tense forms--Imperfect, Aorist, Pluperfect (historic Present and past-referring Perfect could be included as well), and words for knowing in three different tense forms-- Aorist, Perfect, and Present. An explanation of the tense forms must not only be able to account satisfactorily for the varied temporal usage of the same tense form (as above) but it must be able to explain several factors about use of these tense forms: why these two sets of three current Greek tense forms with similar temporal reference are semantically distinct. (This is asserted not only on the basis of their co-existence in the same code but on the basis of the tendency in Greek not to waste multiple forms on the same function [see Rose, *Tenses*, esp. 43; Adrados, "Observaciones," 12; cf. Bolinger,*Form*, 1-20].)

In chapt. 1 it is seen that several scholars from Brugmann to the present have proposed a category called *Aktionsart* (kind of action). But *Aktionsart* fails to explain the above set for two major reasons (see Bache, "Aspect"; *Aspect*, 9ff. Forsyth [*Grammar*, 17-31] defines *Aktionsarten* as "*procedural* forms and nuances" [19]).

(i) On the basis of similar lexical content, a theory of *Aktionsart* would be compelled to argue that all three examples depict the event of speaking in the same way. From the standpoint of objective description of the event this may well be true. This not only fails to satisfy an innate sense that each of the three conceives of the event differently (so too most grammars), even if the difference is slight or even unexpressible in German or English translation, but it fails to explain why the Greek language maintained triplicate (if not quintuple!) forms with identical conception of the action, as well as similar temporal reference.

(ii) *Aktionsart* attempts to characterize the objective kind of action of an event by use of a lexical item (see my chapt. 1; cf. Louw, "Aspek," 24). Therefore, there is no reason to limit the number of tenses, but they could conceivably multiply to reflect the numerous (or even infinite) ways an event may be conceived (e.g. Roussel [*L'aspect*, 8-31] posits 25 major aspectual categories and under them 123 subcategories). Not only did this never happen in Greek--its tense system remained stable for over 1000 years (McKay, 214)[7]--but this analysis provides no principled means for discriminating the various tense uses on the basis of formal criteria (see Bache, "Aspect," 60-67; *Aspect*, 9-14).

A second explanation has been discussed more widely in recent linguistic literature and has been tentatively explored by several grammarians of Greek. The category is that of verbal aspect.[8] This work, in arguing for application of the linguistic semantic category of verbal aspect, asserts that, rather than on the basis of temporal reference, Greek verbal usage must be stringently reformulated on the basis of systemic application of the grammatical category of synthetic or formally-based verbal aspect (Comrie,*Aspect*, 87-88). Several linguistics books give general definitions of aspect without being particularly helpful in the definition of Greek verbal aspect. For example, Hockett says that aspect does not deal with location of an event in time but with "temporal distribution or contour" (*Course*, 237). Several distinctions help to make my formulation more precise.

1. Tense categories in Greek have been a recognized component of the language since earliest attempts to make descriptive categories. Plato distinguished between the nominal (ὄνομα) and verbal (ῥῆμα) components of sentences, as did Aristotle (who added a third category),[9] though it was Aristotle who apparently posited that verbs signal temporal reference (ῥῆμα δέ ἐστι τὸ προσσημαῖνον χρόνον, to use the language of Int. 16B6). Both Plato and Aristotle wrote provocative statements that many linguists note as an early recognition of "aspectual" categories. Thus Collinge ("Reflexions," 80) concludes, "Nobody would now deny some sort of 'aspect' distinction, answering to the formal ablaut difference, in the Greek present and aorist verb stems" (cf. Armstrong, "Aorist," 11; Kravar, "Approche," 961).

[7]Humbert ("Aspect," 22) traces the evolution of the subjectivity of aspect from classical Greek up to the highly objective, bifurcated structure in modern Greek, with the major shift from ancient to modern Greek occurring in the 6-7th cents. Paraskevas-Shepard ("Choosing") argues that modern Greek continues to be aspectually based, although P. Hoffmann ("Paratasis," 8-26) argues that a transformation from aspectual to temporal reference occurred in neoplatonic writing of certain Stoic writers (esp. Simplicius and Damascius) to characterize "being" according to extension in time.

[8]The semantic category of verbal aspect was foreshadowed by Curtius, *Elucidations*; Jacobsohn, Review, esp. 378-86; idem, "Aspektfragen," 305-18; Rose, *Tenses*, esp. 5-7. The major treatments of verbal aspect with reference to Greek are Holt, *Etudes*, 14-47; Ruipérez, *Estructura*; Friedrich, "Theory"; Comrie, *Aspect*. Several of the recent grammars that make use of this category are Humbert, 133ff.; McKay, 136-41, 214-24 (see his articles); Moorhouse, 18; Mandilaras, 54ff.

[9]E.g. Pl. Soph. 262A-263D; Crat. 399A-C, 424E-425A; Parm. 151E-152A; Arist. Poet. 1457A10 30; Int. 16A13ff.; 19B5-14; Rhet. 1404Bff. (cf. 1413B-1414A); see Dinneen, "Linguistics."

For example, Pl. Thaeat. 155B-C: ὕστερον ἀλλὰ τοῦτο εἶναι ἄνευ τοῦ γενέσθαι καὶ γίγνεσθαι ἀδύνατον; . . . εἰμὶ γὰρ δὴ ὕστερον ὃ πρότερον οὐκ ἦ, οὐ γενόμενος· ἄνευ γὰρ τοῦ γίγνεσθαι γένεσθαι ἀδύνατον (later, however, this is the case: apart from 'to come about' indeed it is impossible 'to be coming about' . . . for later I am indeed what I was not previously, not 'coming about'; for apart from 'coming about' it is impossible 'to come about') appears to posit a fundamental aspectual opposition, in which one cannot exist without the other; and Arist. Nic. Eth. 1173A34-B4: ἡσθῆναι μὲν γὰρ ἔστι ταχέως ὥσπερ ὀργισθῆναι, ἥδεσθαι δ᾽ οὔ, οὐδὲ πρὸς ἕτερον, βαδίζειν δὲ καὶ αὔξεσθαι καὶ πάντα τὰ τοιαῦτα. μεταβάλλειν μὲν οὖν εἰς τὴν ἡδονὴν ταχέως καὶ βραδέως ἔστιν, ἐνεργεῖν δὲ κατ᾽ αὐτὴν οὐκ ἔστι ταχέως, λέγω δ᾽ ἥδεσθαι (for it is possible to enjoy pleasure quickly as it is to be angry, but not to be enjoying oneself, and not more quickly than another, as it is to walk or grow and such things. On the one hand, it is possible therefore to transform into a pleasurable condition quickly or slowly, but not to operate in relation to it quickly, so I speak of enjoying oneself) posits meaningful oppositions, apparently contrasting a condition with an event seen in progress.[10] The Stoics, some of the earliest grammarians, maintained a distinction between τὸ σημαῖνον and τὸ σημαινόμενον (e.g. D L. 7.62), very similar to the later fundamental distinction in structural linguistics (the distinction between *signifier* and *signified*; see de Saussure, *Course*, 65ff.). As noted in chapt. 1, the Stoics attempted a description of the Greek verb edifice. Though it can be argued that their use of a temporal category--though widely followed--is inadequate, their use of a primitive form of aspect is commendable. The most significant feature is their semantic categorization according to formal criteria, i.e. they distinguished clearly among the various tense forms, and then they attempted on the basis of their semantic grid to describe the essential feature of each. In short, they utilized their distinction between form and function but also showed how the two converge on individual verb tense forms.[11]

The Stoic method of categorizing tenses formally was not only adopted by other hellenistic grammarians (see chapt. 1), but by virtually all grammarians of Greek through to the present, although the same semantic grid was not employed. In this sense, discussion of tenses in Greek, along the very similar lines of the theory of systemic linguistics utilized here, has: recognized the difference between formal and functional categories; acknowledged a close relationship in Greek between formal classes and their unified functional semantic features; and attempted to interpret their relationship within a number of grids, often formulated around conceptions of time and kind of action. The tacit recognition by the earliest grammarians of Greek, the Greeks themselves, through to present day expositors, that within an individual tense category the morphology may be variable (there is virtually never explicit address of this in treatment of tense categories [see Humbert, *Histoire*, 24], though in the discussion verbs of varied morphology are used) points to early

---

[10]Bakker (*Imperative*, 28-29) refutes Ruipérez (*Estructura*, 85), who argues for an ingressive meaning for the Aorist. Even if Ruipérez is correct here (there is evidence within Aristotle's selection that the philosopher was concerned to make a point in relation to one particular lexical item for his philosophical purposes), it does not necessarily follow for all Aorist verbs.

[11]The Stoics attempted similarly principled classifications for Aristotle's σύνδεσμος, ὄνομα and a new category μεσότης (adverbs). It is noteworthy that their attempt to distinguish proper nouns (ὄνομα) and common nouns (προσηγορία), not morphologically distinguishable categories, did not endure in later writers. See D L. 7.57-58; Bekker, *Anecdota Graeca*, 2.842; Robins, *History*, 28; Diver, "System," esp. 45-49.

recognition of verbal tense categories as dynamic constructs, i.e. the tense label for the verbal unit is used to delimit a class of varied morphologically-based items.

2. It has already been argued that the verb tense categories are incapable of referring objectively to varied kinds of action (*Aktionsarten*). Lexical items are better suited to this purpose, though here too it must be seen that selection of an individual item, within the confines of obligatoriness in a language, is a reasoned and not arbitrary subjective decision, as Lazzeroni rightly recognizes ("L'aspetto," 89, treating adverbs of rapidity with Present verbs as one factor influencing reasoned choice. Others are suggested below--e.g. deictic indicators, syntax, etc.). In reference to the second set of examples above (each employing lexical items from the same paradigm), it is noteworthy that in the first group each sentence has past temporal reference and in the second group each has present temporal reference. Rather than reflecting a temporal distinction or a differing objective characterization of the kind of action, each choice of verb tense reflects an attempt by the speaker to grammaticalize his conception of the process. Since tense is fully obligatory in Greek, the speaker is called upon to use one verb tense form as opposed to some other verb tense form in virtually every verbal situation. As Dahl (*Tense*, 12) says, "in choosing a certain form you voluntarily or involuntarily convey a piece of information, viz. the information that the conditions for the appropriate use of that form are fulfilled. . ." (Dahl goes on to say that one makes a commitment to the truth of that information. This does not follow.) This choice of tense form is best treated as the grammatical realization of a fully exclusive semantic choice of verbal aspect, one of a succession of choices described more fully below (cf. Collinge, "Reflexions," 99, on the terminology of choice; Forsyth [*Grammar*, 35] says, "if the narration of a series of events in the perfective past tense can be 'translated' directly into the [imperfective] present historic mode of narration without the addition of new lexical items, this indicates that the verbs concerned constitute valid aspectual pairs"). Indirect discourse in Greek provides clear evidence of the aspectual nature of Greek tense forms. Despite the shifting temporal sphere of reference the verbal aspect of the original statement is maintained. This applies whether the Indicative, Subjunctive, Optative, Infinitive or Participle is used. (The fact that either the original tense form or the Optative after a secondary tense form could be selected in classical Greek points both away from the Optative as necessarily past-referring [see Hulton, "Optative," 140-41] and toward a tense-sequence rule. It also directs renewed attention to appreciating the semantic qualities of the Moods, since choice is available; see Palmer, *Mood*, 163-67.)

These verbal constructs appear as part of a verbal system. For example, in Arist. Poet. 1457A16ff. Aristotle refers to the Present (βαδίζει), Perfect (βεβάδικε) and Aorist (ἐβάδισε) of the verb βαδίζω: τὸ δὲ βαδίζει ἢ βεβάδικεν προσσημαίνει τὸ μὲν τὸν παρόντα χρόνον τὸ δὲ τὸν παρεληλυθότα . . . τὸ γὰρ ἐβάδισεν; ἢ βάδιζε πτῶσις ῥήματος κατὰ ταῦτα τὰ εἴδη ἐστίν (βαδίζει or βεβάδικεν signifies on the one hand the present time and the other the past [?] . . . and ἐβάδισεν? βάδιζε is a category of word according to these forms [i.e. questioning or commanding]) (1457A17-18, 22-23). Virtually every Greek verb, with the noteworthy exception of a few aspectually vague verbs (see chapt. 10), appears in opposition to at least another verb in its paradigm. This is not to say that every verb maintains every possible verb form, since in fact many do not (or at least the extant evidence is lacking), but that virtually every verb maintains at least one meaningful opposition, often the Present/Aorist (see Moulton/Howard, 225-66, for examples in the NT, apart from those that are completely regular), though a small number have only Present/Perfect,[12] and a few only Aorist/Perfect.[13] A number of verbs with incomplete paradigms (often called defective verbs) combine roots to form a complete paradigm (suppletive forms).[14] And as ancient Greek continued to add vocabulary throughout its linguistic evolution, new verbs continued to be formed also (see Moulton/Howard, 225ff.; Palmer, *Grammar*, 122ff.). Besides further illustrating that tense categories in Greek are dynamic constructs, this process illustrates the apparent lack by language-users of confusion among tense forms in Greek. Confusion of individual lexical items in certain forms is not common, but confusion of broad tense categories on a large scale is unusual if not unknown. For example, ἔβην could have served as the Imperfect of βα, but ἐβαίνον was considered the Imperfect, thus distinguishing the two (see Schwyzer, 1.673, 640).

3. Tense usage is not dependent upon lexis, otherwise there is no accounting for the number of different tense forms in Greek that may be used with the same lexical item within the same temporal contexts. The question of lexis within systemic linguistics and then within the Greek language is one that should receive greater attention in future research. The tension in the discussion is between recognizing the complexity and importance of the lexicon and a compulsion to include it within any language model (Fawcett, *Linguistics*, 57, 59), and the treatment of grammar as a level of abstraction removed from individual items. Although Halliday attempted a complete separation of the two at the outset (Halliday, "Categories," 69, in Halliday, *Halliday*; cf. "Lexis"), later work has come to recognize the place of the lexicon as the greatest level of delicacy in the grammar (Hasan, "Dream"). In other words, each individual lexical item may be seen as forming a class of which it is the only member (see esp. Berry, *Introduction*, 2.51-76; Butler, *Linguistics*, 128-35). This model, therefore, recognizes that there are instances in which the lexicon must be considered at the level of grammatical discussion, but without it becoming an overriding focal point that detracts from analysis of other systems and the relationships among them. Lexis as the most delicate grammar may provide a point at which *Aktionsart* can be joined with a theory of verbal aspect (cf. Miller, *Tense*, 203-04; Klein, *Tempus*, 77, 103; Leroy, "L'évolution"; idem, "L'aspect"; Kravar, "Approche"; Wilmet, "Aspect grammatical"; see Pollak, *Studien*, 35-39).

4. When interpreting an author's subjective selection of a particular verb tense, interpretation is objective in the sense that the form the author

---

[12]σήπω/σέσηπα (rot); σκύλλω/ἔσκυλμαι (distress); ῥώννυμι/ἔρρωμαι (strengthen); περιρραίνω/περιρέραμμαι (sprinkle); πιέζω/πεπίεσμαι (press); -οἴχομαι/ᾤχημαι (go); τραύω/τέθραυσμαι (bruise); βδελύσσομαι/ἐβδέλκυγμαι (loathe); βιβρώσκω/βέβρωκα (eat); ἀμφιέννυμι- ιάζω/ἠμφίεσμαι (clothe), etc.

[13]ἐρρέθην/εἴρηκα (say); ἧξα/ἥκω (come). The smaller number is perhaps explained by the Aorist being less heavily marked; thus its lack of status in the system made rarely used forms easily expendable (or possibly never necessary to create).

[14]E.g. ἔρχομαι/ἦλθον; ἐσθίω/ἔφαγον; λέγω/εἶπεν (ἔλεξα)/εἴρηκα; φέρω/ἤνεγκα; ὁράω/εἶδον/οἶδα; see Strunk, "Überlegungen," 16-19; Stork, *Usage*, 402-03; Schwyzer, 2.257-58.

utilizes is the grammatical realization of a specific set of semantic features selected from the possible meaning choices in the system network (cf. realization statement). Each of the three tense forms in Greek (see chapt. 9 on the Future) may be used in a variety of contexts, often distinguished according to temporal reference; conversely, the three may appear together in similar contexts. The essential semantics of a given form are distinct, despite the contextual variables. The two sets of examples treated above illustrate that this criterion is satisfied.

In the previous sections (1-4), a description of Greek tense usage has been given that has focused upon correlating a formal category (verb tense forms) with a semantic category, verbal aspect. As Comrie notes, "the term 'aspect' tends to be less familiar to students of linguistics than are terms for the other verbal categories such as tense or mood . . ." (*Aspect*, 1). The existent metalanguage connected with aspect is introduced to avoid the circle of which Bache speaks:

> the very existence in the Slavonic languages of the category of aspect makes it imperative to provide for aspect in our metalanguage whether or not this categorial potential is realized in e.g. the Germanic languages. The setting up of the metalinguistic category of aspect is clearly justified even if we do not aim at cross-linguistic applications and comparisons. Conversely, however, we cannot legitimately discuss the particular problem of aspect as a productive category in modern non-slavonic languages without having first established aspect as a metalinguistic category. (*Aspect*, 27)

It is surprising how many grammars of Greek introduce the category of aspect without a sufficient definition or any definition at all (e.g. Rijksbaron, 1ff., who claims to analyse the verb according to modern linguistic principles) and how many linguistics books use the term as if its definition were almost self-explanatory (e.g. Lyons, *Introduction*, 313ff.; Robins, *Linguistics*, 208).

The following is a concise definition of verbal aspect used in this work: Greek verbal aspect is a synthetic semantic category (realized in the forms of verbs) used of meaningful oppositions in a network of tense systems to grammaticalize the author's reasoned subjective choice of conception of a process. Similar though not identical definitions may be found in several recent works: Humbert, *Histoire*, 18-19; idem, "Aspect," 22; Comrie, *Aspect*, 1-6, esp. 4; McKay, 136 (followed in his other works); Wilkinson, *"Aspect,"* 2; Louw, "Aspek," 24; Loriaux, "Notes," 50 (1982) 49; Forsyth, *Grammar*, 1-2; cf. Rose, *Tenses*, 6-78. (Many unfortunately give the impression that the subjective choice is wholly arbitrary [against this see Lazzeroni, "L'aspetto," 89; Forsyth, *Grammar*, 2]. I attempt to show otherwise.)

To avoid the tense terminological difficulties mentioned above the traditional tense-form names are retained to represent the formal paradigms as abstracted constructs that developed early in Greek usage and are now hallowed by tradition. But consistent functional names for the representative verbal conceptions of action must be devised as well. The following have been selected: perfective (»»Aorist), imperfective (»»Present/Imperfect), stative (»»Perfect/Pluperfect). These terms are recognizably taken from Slavonic linguistics, and not only provide possibilities for dialogue in general linguistic theory (e.g. typology), but they seem to provide descriptive labels which encapsulate the essential semantics of each aspectual category. In a recent, provocative essay on verbal aspect, Louw voices strong discontent with traditional conceptions of verbal aspect ("Aspek"; see also Gonda, *Rgvedic*, chapt. 1), rightly criticizing several scholars for defining aspect merely in terms of finding, for example, a durative feature in the Present.[15] To some extent he sets up a straw man, but admittedly many previous attempts have been deficient. After summarizing a number of previous treatments of tense usage, he argues that an acceptable model must get away from imposing from without a set of translational values but must work from the essential features of each verb form used in relation to one another (21, 24-25).

There are several different ways to arrive at a formulation of the semantic qualities of each verbal aspect. I present four as helpful perspectives on the same fundamental network. (Dahl [*Tense*, 1] recognizes the elusiveness of defining the semantic qualities of aspect; cf. Jakobson, "Implications," 271-72, who is optimistic that the search for invariants such as aspect is attainable.)

    a. Verbal opposition. Verbal oppositions, without indicating more specifically in the metalanguage what their semantic features entail, can be established in terms of marked pairs. (The best exposition of markedness is Zwicky, "Markedness"; see also Comrie, *Aspect*, 111-22; Greenberg, *Universals*, chapts. 3 and 4; Lyons, *Semantics*, 305-11; Bache, *Aspect*, 60-73; contra McKay, 137; Wilkinson, *"Aspect,"* 12-15, who dispute the ability to establish verbal opposition.) Binary oppositions are often spoken of in terms of privative oppositions, in which case one aspect might be considered [+imperfective], while the other in its binary pair might thus be [-imperfective].[16] But this is not a convincing explanation for several reasons. (1) In Greek none of the tense forms is formally unmarked, i.e. each form has distinguishing formal features (see Zwicky, "Markedness," 137-39, on "iconicity"): e.g. the Perfect has reduplication or augment and non-thematic endings; the Pluperfect also has lengthened connecting vowels, besides reduplication; the Present often has a lengthened stem and/or suffixal endings; the Imperfect has an augment besides the Present stem; and the Aorist has the augment (Indicative only) and often the sigmatic connecting consonant (the Aorist is the least heavily marked). (2) In the Present and Aorist opposition distributional marking is not highly significant,

---

[15]Louw seems to begin by implicitly characterizing aspect as *Aktionsart*, although he later distinguishes the two (23-24). He also suffers from the major fault of insisting that absolute tense is one of the major categories of temporal reference (25-26).

[16]Appeal to instances of usage to dispute marked and unmarked pairs is problematic, since whenever an example is cited, one can easily cite an opposing case. Hence appeal is made here to other criteria in the first instance.

although the Present/Imperfect tends to be used slightly more in the Greek of the NT. (3) Implicational markedness with regard to tense-category irregularities and syncretism of the Present Middle/Passive points to the Present/Imperfect as the marked tense. (4) Semantic marking is the most difficult to evaluate, especially when attempting to define verbal aspect. There is no apparent evidence that in Greek any of the verbal aspects is semantically unmarked (contra Haberland, "Note," 182). In fact, this work argues that even within the binary oppositions all members contribute semantic weight to the verbal component of the clause. Greek verbal aspect, therefore, appears to function on the basis of equipollent binary oppositions, in which while each aspect is not identically weighted, at the least each contributes semantically in an identifiable way (see Friedrich, "Theory," S14).

On the basis of the concept of markedness in Greek verbal aspect (see chapts. 4 and 5 for treatment of the specific aspects involved), the binary pairs can be arranged in two oppositions. The Perfect tense (stative aspect) is the most heavily marked formally, distributionally and semantically, and forms an opposition with the Present/Aorist (imperfective/perfective) opposition (see Ruipérez, *Estructura*, 45ff.). Within the Present/Aorist, the imperfective aspect on the basis of formal markedness, a slight distributional advantage, and semantic markedness is the more clearly marked member of the equipollent opposition with the perfective aspect (see e.g. McKay, 138; idem, "Syntax," 46ff.; Lyons, *Introduction*, 314-15; cf. Comrie, *Aspect*, 127; contra e.g. Ruipérez, *Estructura*, 67-89; "Neutralization"). The perfective aspect as the least heavily marked may be called the "default" aspect, however, since it "is felt to be in Greek more usual, more normal, less specific. . ." (Comrie, *Aspect*, 111; see Dahl, *Tense*, 19, on the distinction between markedness as a formal classification and default as a semantic or functional category). Because of formal similarities of the Present and Perfect, and unique formal features of the Aorist, all of which reinforce the above analysis, the oppositions may be represented in the following way.

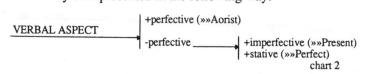

VERBAL ASPECT

+perfective (»»Aorist)

-perfective _____ +imperfective (»»Present)
+stative (»»Perfect)

chart 2

Rom 6:7-11 illustrates this semantic opposition cogently. Paul says that the one who is dead (ὁ . . . ἀποθανών [Aorist Participle]) is justified (δεδικαίωται [Perfect Indicative]) from sin. The marked stative aspect seems to form a summary term for the following interplay of imperfective and perfective aspects. In all the instances the perfective aspect constitutes the underlying assumption for the comparatively marked new information provided by the imperfective aspect. If we are dead (ἀπεθάνομεν) with Christ, then we are believing (πιστεύομεν) that we will live with him, knowing (εἰδότες) that (if) Christ is raised (ἐγερθείς) from the dead, then he no longer dies (ἀποθνῄσκει) and . . . death no longer dominates (κυριεύει). What he died (ἀπέθανεν), he died (ἀπέθανεν) to sin once for all. But what he lived (ζῇ [Present with past reference]), he lived (ζῇ) to God. Thus you yourselves count (λογίζεσθε) yourselves dead to sin but alive (ζῶντας) to God in Christ Jesus. (Cf. Epict. 1.1.32: ἀποθανεῖν με δεῖ. εἰ ἤδη, ἀποθνῄσκω . . . [it is necessary for me to die. If already I am dying].)

b.   Visualization.   If each aspect represents the author's grammaticalized "conception" of a process, it is logical to ask what that picture might be. In **a.** above it was noted that the stative was the most heavily marked aspectual category, and that the imperfective and perfective were in some ways on an equal level, although the imperfective seemed slightly more heavily marked. Thus the descending order of complexity should correspond to the conception of the process by the speaker. Traditionally, as noted in chapt. 1, the tenses have been characterized as follows: Perfect conveys past or antecedent action with present or current consequences; Present conveys durative or iterative action; and Aorist conveys punctiliar action. These are crude and, as will be shown in more detailed individual treatments of the aspects (chapts. 4 and 5), grossly misleading, since they place the perspective in terms of the event itself and since they are formulations according to differing criteria.   Instead, a suggestive correlation has been made by the Russian scholar Isachenko, which is adopted here.[17]   Let me draw the picture of a parade. If I am a television correspondent in the BBC helicopter flying over the parade, I view the parade or process in its immediacy from a vantage outside the action as "perfective," i.e. in its entirety as a single and complete whole. If I am a spectator sitting in the grandstand watching the parade pass by in front of me, I view the process immersed within it as "imperfective," i.e. as an event in progress. And if I am the parade manager considering all of the conditions in existence at this parade, including not only all the arrangements that are coming to fruition but all of the accompanying events that allow the parade to operate, I view the process not in its particulars or its immediacy but as "stative," i.e. as a condition or state of affairs in existence. There are three important points to this analogy (besides the obvious fact that all analogies are only meant to be helpful and not definitive comparisons). (1) External temporal reference is not a factor here, i.e. there is not necessarily anything inherently past, for example, about the perfective aspect. Consequently the term "complete" is used of the perfective aspect rather than "completed," which implies past temporal reference (Comrie, *Aspect*, 18). (2) Although each aspect is describing the same set of circumstances, each contributes a unique perspective on the process. (3) None is an objective description of the process, but each represents the speaker's subjective conception.   Thus "progress" rather than "durative," and "complete" rather than "punctiliar" are used to shift the emphasis to the perspective of the observer and away from any characterization of the process itself.

---

[17]See Murphy, *Usage*, 21, quoting A.V. Isachenko, *Grammaticheskij stroj russkogo jazyka v sopostavlenii s slovackim*, Morfologija II (Bratislava, 1960), followed by Miller, *Tense*, 45.

In Rom 8:11, when Paul says ὁ ἐγείρας Χριστὸν ἐκ νεκρῶν (the one who raised Christ from the dead), he views the resurrection of Christ as a complete event. When Paul uses the Imperfect in 2 Cor 1:9 (τῷ θεῷ τῷ ἐγείροντι τοὺς νεκρούς [the God who is in progress raising the dead]), he views the process as one that is in progress. And in 2 Tim 2:8 (Ἰησοῦν Χριστὸν ἐγηγερμένον ἐκ νεκρῶν [Jesus Christ raised from the dead]), the author emphasizes the state of Christ's risenness (cf. Metzger, "Grammars," 481).

    c. Planes of discourse. Drawing upon the insights of "perceptual psychology," Wallace ("Figure" [quotation 201], cf. 213, where he notes the connection with Gestalt psychology) and Hopper ("Aspect," esp. 213-16) attempt to reconstruct traditional understanding of aspect (Wallace also treats Mood and tense)[18] utilizing studies of discourse analysis that divide the planes of discourse into two: "foreground and background." As Hopper says: "It is evidently a universal of narrative discourse that in any extended text an overt distinction is made between the language of the actual story line and the language of supportive material which does not itself narrate the main events" ("Aspect," 213; whereas Hopper focuses upon narrative, Wallace applies this model to non-narrative discourse as well). Thus in Greek the Aorist is the background tense which carries the discourse and the Present/Imperfect is the figure or foreground tense (see e.g. Kühner/Gerth, 1.157; Gildersleeve, 91; Schwyzer, 2.275; contra Wallace and Hopper). It is noteworthy that in Greek often the basic narrative is laid down by the 3d Person Aorist, a common trait of the background tense, while the Imperfect/Present introduces significant characters or makes appropriate climactic references to concrete situations, typical of the foreground tense. Also, when an extended noteworthy description is given, the foreground tense is used. (See Wallace, "Figure," 212, cf. 214; and Hopper, "Aspect," 216, for categorization of linguistic features. Rijksbaron [12-13] and Weinrich [*Tempus*, 288-93; "Tense"] follow Wallace and Hopper.) Wallace only indirectly refers to other possible tense categories (209, 210; on 216, he notes the problem of tense in his system), but it is possible to posit a third plane of exposition, called here frontground. Rather than seeing the Perfect as giving further background information, it seems to provide a narrower range of the characteristic features (214) of the figure tense: it is discrete, well-defined and contoured, apparently much more so than the Present/Imperfect and certainly the Aorist tenses. Wallace's hypothesis, which seems helpful for discussion of Greek tenses, is "that linguistic categories . . . function to differentiate linguistic figure from linguistic ground: the speaker uses such categories to structure an utterance . .

---

[18]It is not necessary to make a thorough critique of Wallace to appreciate his contribution. He finds himself caught in a dilemma between seeing the tenses as confused on temporal reference and not wanting to deny that "time is an important semantic property of the categories of tense" (203). Also, his attempt at a universal grammar leads him to make mistakes in his treatment of and application to individual languages (e.g. 204, 208, 215)

. into more or less salient portions, and the listener uses such categories as clues to interpreting the speaker's verbal picture" (214). The relation of the tenses may be represented as follows:

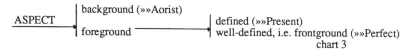

chart 3

In Acts 16:1-5, the author uses the Aorist to establish the basic framework of events: he (Paul) arrived (κατήντησεν) in Derbe and Lystra, where there was a disciple named Timothy. The (defined) foreground aspect (Imperfect) is then used to highlight a significant feature about this new character, Timothy: he was commended (ἐμαρτυρεῖτο) by the brethren. The background line then continues with the Aorist (ἠθέλησεν [want]; ἐξελθεῖν [go away]; λαβών [take]; περιέτεμεν [circumcise]). The reason for his circumcision is then given with the frontground aspect, reinforced by the (defined) foreground aspect: for all knew (ἤδεισαν [stative]) that his father was (ὑπῆρχεν [imperfective]) Greek. Doctrine is obviously important in this passage, thus when the narrative continues, since the mission of Paul and his companions is related to teaching and building up churches, the (defined) foreground aspect is used (διεπορεύοντο [pass through]; παρεδίδοσαν [entrust]; φυλάσσειν [guard]), with the frontground aspect again employed to describe the dogma being guarded: the one determined (τὰ κεκριμένα) by the apostles and elders in Jerusalem. The successful result, again in the (defined) foreground aspect, is church growth (ἐστερεοῦντο [grow]; ἐπερίσσευον [grow rich]). The next narrative incident (16:6) continues with the background aspect (διῆλθον [pass through]).

d. Systemic display. A systemic display of the Greek verbal network, using componential notation, provides a graphic representation of the Greek verbal network (see chart 4) (cf. Collinge, "Reflexions," 99-100, who provides his own system for the Greek verb [100 n. 1]). As noted in the introduction, this work attempts an explanatory model of verbal aspect for Greek, as part of a larger network of the entire language (still to be written). It is not possible to argue exhaustively here for every distinction (explanation of most categories, and all those concerned with verbal aspect, are to be found within their respective chapters), but significant comment is made to enable consideration of the model proposed (traditional grammarians should recognize many of the distinctions made here but placed within a conceptual grammatical whole). Componential analysis provides a succinct and useful means of noting the semantic features accumulated in a trip through the systems within the network from broader to more delicate distinctions.[19] To avoid the major difficulties over mentalism and hypotheses about where meaning resides (universalism), no claim is made for the components apart from their use as relational terms within a given network to summarize

---

[19]Componential analysis has been both widely endorsed and stringently criticized. The chief proponent is Nida, *Analysis*, see also Goodenough, "Analysis." Criticism is found in Kempson, *Theory*, 86-102. For summary see Lyons, *Introduction*, 474-81; *Semantics*, 317-35, with bibliography.

conveniently in notational form the relations among members (see Lyons, *Structural Semantics*, 80).

At the rank of clause, once a choice to communicate a particular process has been made (this is similar to Fawcett [*Linguistics*, 72-74] on the primary choice of whether to communicate), the speaker must choose to grammaticalize the structure of the predicate by means of a verbal group which consists of a verb form (periphrastics are complex words consisting of a vague auxiliary verb and a Participle, the Participle requiring its own trip through the network; see chapt. 10). This analysis of structure is further suggestive of the form-functional correlation in Greek. Elegance requires that each selection expression results in onely one formal realization. Thus each formal element has a unique set of semantic features (helpful here are Gotteri, "Note"; "Speaker's Right"). This model for paradigmatic selection of the verb excludes consideration of two kinds of clause: verbless clauses, and clauses that have predicates realized by aspectually vague verbs. In verbless clauses, there is no verbal aspect, since there is no verbal expression, and attempts to read in unexpressed verbal components are unwarranted except in those places where secondary ellipsis has occurred (see chapt. 10). There are also in Greek a very few verbs which do not offer paradigmatic formal choice, and are thus aspectually vague. These verbs are not numerous, though they warrant special analysis (εἰμί [I am]; -εῖμι [I go]; κεῖμαι [I lie]; φημί [I say]; see chapt. 10).

Within the network of Greek verbal usage two simultaneous systems present the broadest choice: ASPECTUALITY and FINITENESS. The FINITENESS system distinguishes the semantic distinction between limitation on the verbal expression through Person [+finite] and lack of limitation [-finite]. Greek has a plethora of personal forms [+finite] resulting in realization of finite verb forms. Greek also has two types of [-finite] items, which may function as elements in the structure of the predicate, although their lack of limitation makes them more compatible with functioning as elements in subjects, complements and adjuncts. They have very similar syntactical distribution, and selection between them requires choice between two further semantic features, [+factive presupposition] and [-factive presupposition]. These are realized respectively by the »»Participle and the »»Infinitive (see chapt. 8). It becomes clear from discussion below that the ASPECTUALITY system must also be chosen when the feature [±factive presupposition] is selected (ATTITUDE is blocked, because its dual entry condition is not met).

As established above, the essential semantic feature of Greek verbal usage is verbal aspect. The ASPECTUALITY system requires choice of [+expectation] or [+aspectual]. It is at this point that the peculiarities of the Future form are confronted (see chapt. 9). In any explanation, the Future stands out because of its odd formal paradigm and limited distribution. In hellenistic Greek several of the more difficult forms were already eliminated, such as the »»Future Perfect or the »»Future Optative. (These forms are realized within this network utilizing asterisks; this device--which blocks all other features--is unwieldy, but used to provide a more complete network. Surely the difficulty in establishing these verbal relations within the network reflects their instability and, consequently, the reasons for their demise.) It appears that many of the little-used forms were created by analogy to fill the Future paradigm in line with other verbal forms (see chapt. 9). Perhaps its late development in Greek verbal structure is then reflected in the virtual independence of the form in relation to the rest of the network. Its place in the ASPECTUALITY system reflects that the Future is related to a way of viewing the action, although it is not best seen as fully aspectual, since formal paradigmatic choice is not offered. [+expectation] offers a simultaneous choice of [+finite] realized by »»Future Indicative or [-finite] realized by »»Future Participle or Infinitive.

Semantic choices which are fully aspectual distinguish two subsystems, ASPECT 1 and ASPECT 2. The [+perfective] aspect is the least semantically marked (see above and chapt. 4), in equipollent opposition to the [-perfective] aspects. This is the broadest aspectual opposition in Greek. The [+perfective] aspect is realized by a single simple form, »»Aorist, while the [-perfective] aspects offer a subsequent more delicate choice (ASPECT 2) between [+imperfective] and [+stative] aspect. There are both formal (e.g. Voice, primary endings, etc.) and semantic (e.g. foregrounding) reasons for positing this aspect as more delicate, the most important being the realization of [±remoteness] in the [+assertive] attitude. The distinction of [+remoteness] and [-remoteness] is the closest that Greek verb forms approach to tense forms as realizations of temporal semantic features (see Lyons, *Semantics*, 819; cf. Comrie, *Tense*, 83-101). This is on the basis of their use within a limited number and kind of contexts, such as narrative and I.b. conditionals (see chapts. 4 and 6), in which the speaker stands distanced from the process he describes. Selection of [+imperfective: +remoteness] is realized by the »»Imperfect Indicative, and [+imperfective: -remoteness] by »»Present Indicative, and selection of [+stative: +remoteness] is realized by the »»Pluperfect Indicative, and [+stative: -remoteness] by the »»Perfect Indicative.

A more delicate system than ASPECTUALITY, but simultaneous with ASPECT 1 is ATTITUDE,[20] entered when [+aspectual / +finite] are selected. This semantic feature grammaticalizes the speaker's view of the process in relation to his conception of reality. Hence he makes a choice between [+assertion] and [-assertion]. This is the distinction (to use more traditional terminology) between epistemic and deontic modality, the former expressing a commitment to the process and the latter expressing a volitional orientation, both revolving around the kind of commitment the speaker makes to the statement. [+assertion] is realized by »»Indicative, while [-assertion] is realized by the non-Indicative Moods. The semantic overlap between the use of »»Subjunctive, »»Optative and »»Imperative in Greek has long been noticed and debated. All seem to focus upon the volitional element (although this term is not used here because of the confusion surrounding it in the secondary literature; see Palmer, *Mood*, 96-97). The volitional element alone, semantically labelled here [+direction], is realized by »»Imperative (see Lyons, *Semantics*, 823ff.). The volitional element with a visualization of it, labelled here [+projection], requires the more delicate simultaneous choice [±contingency]. [+projection: +contingency] is realized by »»Optative, while [+projection: -contingency] is realized by »»Subjunctive. When [+assertion] is selected, a simultaneous choice in the ASPECT 1 or 2 and possibly REMOTENESS systems is required, but if [-assertion] is selected only a choice of ASPECT 1 or 2 is simultaneously required, since REMOTENESS is blocked. This network of verbal systems accounts for all formal choices of individual verb forms found in hellenistic Greek. If the co-selection feature of [+expectation] with [+contingency] or [+stative] is included, the network should be complete for classical Greek as well.

This semantic network highlights several features of the Greek verbal network (see appropriate chapters for extended discussion).

(1) [+perfective] offers no choice in the REMOTENESS system, unlike the [+imperfective] and [+stative], which realize a choice between [±remoteness]. Thus descriptions of so-called ingressive, effective, constative, etc. Aorists, while they may be pragmatic categories worth considering (among many other pragmatic analyses), confuse form and function, as well as semantics and pragmatics, and cannot be justified on principled systemic grounds (it has also been shown that such categories are self-contradictory within their sphere of usage, *Aktionsart* [see chapt. 1]). Such categories are better seen as lexical and contextual interpretations of a particular

---

[20]Many grammarians use the terms "mode/modality" for the semantic feature realized by the Mood in Greek. "Attitude" is selected to avoid confusion with modality as a technical term in systemic linguistics for the means of conveyance within registers (see Fawcett, *Linguistics*, 85), and because it seems to reflect in the metalanguage what is conveyed by the feature, i.e. the speaker's attitude toward or view of the process in relation to reality. On the issue of attitude (although he adopts traditional terminology) see Palmer, *Mood*, esp. 4-5; cf. *Modality*, 4-5, 7. The distinctions made here follow recent work performed by a number of grammarians, esp. Gonda, *Character*. See also Lyons, *Semantics*, 452, 736.

semantic category, always realized formally by the Aorist. Thus the ingressive ἐβασίλευσε (he began to rule [Rom 5:17]) is different in meaning from ἐκάθισαν (they began to sit [Matt 23:2]) on the basis of lexis, not grammar. Many examples may be labelled constative or even effective just as well. For example ἐβασίλευσε in Rom 5:14 surely cannot be confined to an ingressive meaning (Rom 5:17 is questionable as well, since this is a pragmatic interpretation).

(2) The Future is semantically peculiar within the Greek verbal network. The difficulty highlights its late development in distinction both to aspect proper and to attitude, but it also makes noteworthy that [+expectation] is a significant semantic feature in any realization statement.

(3) Aspectually vague verbs (virtually by definition) have a slightly different network, which excludes aspectual differentiation. Whereas the concept of aspectually vague verbs has been recently introduced (see Porter/Gotteri, "Ambiguity"), it certainly seems helpful, especially in understanding periphrasis, which can be explained therefore with the same network. The aspectually vague verb serves as the auxiliary while the systems for [+aspectual] and [+factual presupposition] establish the aspect of the word-complex (see chapt. 8).

(4) It is a noteworthy feature of Greek that the negated Aorist Imperative is very rare (see Chantraine, 2.230; Moorhouse, 221; Louw, "Prohibitions," 43; Stephens, "Origins": e.g. Hom. Il. 4.410; 18.134; Od. 24.248; S. Fr. 493; Ar. Thes. 870; see chapt. 7), and that the negated Aorist Subjunctive serves as the Aorist prohibition, as most grammarians recognize (see chapt. 7). But the network calls for further examination at this point, since [+direction] »»Imperative negated, according to this network, is not semantically equivalent to [+projection: -contingency] »»Subjunctive with negation (often posited as equal to the negated Aorist Imperative). A case can be made that the network has correctly captured a significant though subtle semantic difference, since the Aorist is incompatible with both the [+direction] semantic feature and negation (a marked feature). Instead a negated perfective command uses »»Subjunctive, which on the basis of its unmarked semantic features appears compatible with negation. But perhaps a more plausible explanation revolves around the volitional nature of [-assertion], in which negation of the less heavily marked perfective direction was felt too semantically vacant, so that the negated perfective projection was substituted. The similarity of the semantic selection expressions of the two forms, while not perhaps explaining fully the use of the negated Aorist Subjunctive as a command, does at least illustrate that this is semantically an understandable usage.

Analysis of the Greek verbal network shows that each semantic selection must be considered in relation to opposition and choice. The Greek language is not to be considered a series of discrete, disjoint forms but is to be viewed as a coordinated network of verbal semantic choices arranged in coherent systems. As Lyons says, "Few parts of a language-system illustrate better than its aspect-system does the validity of the structuralist slogan: *Tout se tient* ('Everything hangs together')" (*Semantics*, 714; quotation from Meillet). Perhaps this network renders several of the complexities of Greek verbal usage less daunting, both for scholars and those contemplating teaching others about it. The scheme also clears away several confusing factors often introduced in descriptions of the Greek language (e.g. how disparate temporal functions can be implicated from the same form), by labelling clearly the exact semantic relationships among the features, and hence the semantic features of the formal realizations. The distinction between semantics and pragmatics is thus vindicated, since the Greek code, or what the individual forms mean, stands behind the range of applications to which a form may be put by the individual speaker, including various temporal references.

3. DEICTIC INDICATORS AND TEMPORAL REFERENCE.

It has now been established that the tense categories in Greek are not time based, but aspectually based. Thus when a speaker refers to an event he grammaticalizes an aspectual choice, and the three synthetic aspects-- perfective, imperfective, stative--have been defined. Two other topics have been addressed less directly--attitude and time. The question which must now be answered is this: if the tenses in Greek are primarily aspectually based and thus do not refer to any specific absolute time, how is it possible to speak of different times of processes in Greek? This section treats two topics: the relations of aspect, tense and attitude; and the role of deixis.

Aspect is not properly speaking a temporal category, but it is related to tense (and attitude) in the sense that all three of these categories are concerned with processes which occur in time and the realm of time is their semantic domain (cf. Comrie, *Aspect*, 5; Bache, *Aspect*, 18-20; Lyons [*Semantics*, 687] notes that what is often called "tense" refers actually to "aspect" in many grammars). This domain includes three possible temporal points: the time of speaking or writing (S), the time at which a specific process occurs (P), and the time of all processes a writer or speaker may refer to at a given moment (R). Tense seems to be a matter of the relationship between reference time (R) and process time (P), i.e. the reference time is the point of view from which the situation at process time is considered. Greek does not grammaticalize absolute tense, where the speech time is equated with the present; rather, Greek maintains relative tense in all tenses and Moods, i.e. where the time of a situation is relative to a time not necessarily the point of speaking (Comrie, *Tense*, 36-82), and where any tense category may be used in any of the temporal contexts (see above). Aspect grammaticalizes how a specific process (P) is viewed from the perspective of the speaker (S), i.e. it is viewed with regard to its constituency as opposed to external time. And attitude grammaticalizes the relationship between the speaker (S) and reference time (R), i.e. the quality of statement about the event. This can be summarized in graphic format (Comrie, *Aspect*, 3; Johnson, "Theory," 148-49 [for chart, modified here. He follows Reichenbach][21]). Dahl (*Tense*, 29-31) suggests a fourth point of reference, temporal frame. This must be taken into account (as I believe it can be by the temporal categories listed above; see chapt. 4) but seems better handled in terms of discourse analysis rather than grammaticalization (see also Lyons, *Semantics*, 809-20; "Deixis," 112-15):

---

[21]Johnson's view does not "contrast" ("Theory," 148) with Comrie's nearly so much as he thinks (see Comrie, *Tense*, 118-30), since Comrie implies the three pivots which Johnson makes explicit: "Verb aspect involves reference to one of the temporally distinct phases in the evolution from event through time" (152).

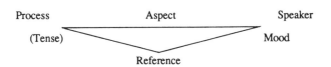

Process   Aspect   Speaker

(Tense)   Mood

Reference

Aspect, therefore, grammaticalizes how a specific process (P) is viewed by the speaker. Attitude grammaticalizes the speaker's perspective (S) on the point of reference (R). And time is a non-grammaticalized category of temporal reference established on the basis of deixis. It is both imaginatively and logically possible to conceive of any given number of temporal categories, and the simple fact that various languages have differing numbers attests to this. In light of the traditional historical discussion, dating back to the Greeks, three temporal categories of past, present and future may be retained. The non-temporal basis of Greek verbal aspect suggests introduction into the metalanguage of two additional categories: omnitemporal and timeless reference. "A timeless proposition is one for which the question of time-reference . . . simply does not arise. . . . An omnitemporal proposition. . . is one that says that something has been, is and always will be so" (Lyons, *Semantics*, 680). From what has been said above it is clear that verbal aspect is essentially non-temporal, but that pragmatic usage may implicate its allied manifestation, timeless usage. Its converse--omnitemporal reference--is thereby suggested as well. In this sense *aspect* is non-deictic, whereas temporal reference is deictic (Lyons, *Introduction*, 315, 306; Comrie, *Aspect*, 2, 3; idem, *Tense*, 14; Dahl, *Tense*, 25; Bache, *Aspect*, 3-4, cf. 105-09 for a similar scheme using deixis), since verbal aspect may and essentially does function apart from temporal specification. All temporal reference in Greek, therefore, is not absolute but relative time, "where the reference point for location of a situation is some point in time given by the context, not necessarily the present moment" (Comrie, *Tense*, 56; cf. *Aspect*, 1-6).

Deixis is defined by Lyons as "the location and identification of persons, objects, events, processes, and activities being talked about, or referred to, in relation to the spatiotemporal context created and sustained by the act of utterance and the participation in it, typically, of a single speaker and at least one addressee" (*Semantics*, 637; cf. *Introduction*, 275-80, 304-17; "Deixis"). In Greek four deictic categories can be profitably distinguished: person, time, discourse, and social deixis. (See Levinson, *Pragmatics*, 54-96; cf. Lyons, *Semantics*, 637-90; Comrie, *Tense*, 13-18.) This discussion sets aside the theoretical issues of a theory of discourse, as well as questions more pertinent to general linguistics, while formulating a workable model for Greek, although many of the issues overlap (see Brown/Yule, *Analysis*; Halliday/Hasan, "Text"; Comrie, *Tense*, 26-35, for integrative approaches).

a. Person deixis. As Levinson states, "as speakers switch, so the deictic centre on which the rest of the deictic system hangs, is itself abruptly moved from participant to participant" (*Pragmatics*, 68). Hence in hellenistic Greek the basic grammatical distinctions are 1st, 2d and 3d Person, Singular and Plural (the Dual is not of concern). Person deixis is essential to the language, since it establishes the parameters and relations of the participants. Two points may be made. (1) 1st and 2d Person are distinctly different from 3d Person. With 1st Person the speaker is included [+speaker] and 2d Person the addressee is included [+addressee], while 3d Person does not necessitate addressee or speaker inclusion [-speaker, -addressee], though it may (Mark 14:51?). Thus no role is set for the participants. In Greek 3d Person is the unmarked Person (see Greenberg, *Universals*, 44-46). This analysis is helpful in that if the reader is aware of the context of discourse and its participants, use of 1st or 2d Person enables more exact deictic placement. With the 3d Person, however, while the speaker and addressee may be included, this is not required. For example, in the Sermon on the Mount, Jesus begins the beatitudes in 3d Person (Matt 5:3-10), but then switches to 2d Person (Matt 5:11ff.), perhaps having included his audience in the 3d Person portion. The use of 3d Person in narrative is thus instructive (see Dahl, *Tense*, 112-20). Not only does it point to narrative as the unmarked discourse type (as opposed to descriptive or admonitory discourse, for example), but it is the least precise in establishing direct temporal reference, since another participant beyond the speaker and addressee may be introduced whose relation to the events of the discourse is unknown. (2) Person deixis is vital to the language, since it places an event in relation to set persons. 1st Person Singular attributes a speech-act to oneself (2 Cor 10:1), which is different from attributing an event or speech-act to the addressee in 2d Person (2 Cor 10:7; cf. Rom 7:7), and very different from mere reportage. Thus an authority and credibility structure on the basis of proximity to the speaker attaches especially to 1st and also to 2d Persons that is lacking in 3d Person, thereby reinforcing its status as the unmarked Person.

Three special uses of person deixis warrant mention. (a) The first occurs where the person or thing that comprises the Person is explicit. For example, in Matthew, note how many pericopes from 2:1ff. have Jesus as subject of the opening sentence (3:13; 4:1; 8:14, 18; 9:9, 35; 10:5; 11:25; 12:1, 15; 13:1, 53; 14:13; 15:21, 29, 32; 16:13, 21; 17:1; 19:1; 20:17; 21:12; 22:1; 23:1; 24:1; 26:1, 26, 31, 36; 27:11). Knowledge of the time of the person's life enables temporal distinctions to be made. Not all examples are easy to determine, for example, the use of Christ. In Col 1:27 it seems he is now present, but Eph 5:29 (ὁ Χριστὸς τὴν ἐκκλησίαν, with ἐκτρέφει [feed] and θάλπει [take care of] understood) is not clear temporally.

(b) The second is 1st Person Plural where the author appears to exclude himself as an individual in an attempt to include himself and all others sharing a common belief as a whole. (Greek does not grammaticalize an inclusive and exclusive 1st Person Plural pronoun, as do some languages; see Levinson, *Pragmatics*, 69; Rogers, "'We,'" 139-40.) In many places in the epistles traditionally ascribed to him, Paul speaks in terms of general Christian experience (although this is not his only use of the 1st Person Plural). For example, in Titus 3:3-6, he says we (ἡμεῖς) were previously (ποτε) ignorant, etc., but when the kindness and philanthropy of τοῦ σωτῆρος ἡμῶν θεοῦ (our saviour God) appeared, he saved us (ἡμᾶς; cf. Rom 15:4) not by works which we (ἡμεῖς) performed but according to his mercy through the holy spirit, which he poured out upon us (ἡμᾶς) richly through Jesus Christ our (ἡμῶν) saviour. The introductory sections to Pauline epistles often contain noteworthy 1st Person Plural usage: e.g. Rom 1:5 (cf. v 6 with ὑμεῖς); 2 Cor 1:4ff., where Paul speaks of the one who comforts us (ἡμᾶς) in order that we may be able (δύνασθαι ἡμᾶς) to comfort, followed by several 1st Person Plural verbs in the protases of conditional statements; Eph 1:3ff. Cf. 1 Thess 3:1, 2, 6 (Moulton ["Notes," 7 (1903) 107] cites parallel instances in the papyri: P.Teb. 55 [2d cent. B.C.], 58 [111 B.C.]; P.Amh. 37 [2d cent. B.C.], 144 [5th cent. A.D.], P.Fay. 117 [A.D. 108]).

(c) Pronouns used in 3d Person are important. For example, in Rom 3:23; 5:12 Paul's use of πάντες (all) gives the proposition an omnitemporal sense, while ὅσοι in Rom 2:12 renders the proposition timeless, since a law of nature is not established but a hypothetical and non-deictically bound instance is cited. It is noteworthy that not only does person deixis not clarify the temporal reference but theological constructs cannot be established simply on the basis of verb tenses.

b. Time deixis. It is unnecessary here to develop various theories of the organization of space and time, but whereas it is important to "distinguish the moment of utterance (or inscription) or *coding time* (or CT) from the moment of reception or *receiving time* (or RT)" (Levinson, *Pragmatics*, 73) in some languages, such does not apply to Greek. Temporal deixis is best seen as referring to the participant at CT, and it is always the case that RT is treated as identical to CT, whether it be narrative, description, present-reference, or even epistolary writing, unless other indicators are introduced (e.g. John 20:30-31, with shift to 2d Person). (Levinson [73-74] suggests that epistolary tenses can be explained on the basis that the CT and RT are not identical in these contexts. This seems to apply only to languages that grammaticalize temporal reference in tense forms, although it may also call this analysis into question for certain languages. See my chapt. 4.)

There are three classes of time deictic indicators. (1) Lexical items, such as mentioned above. For example, a present temporal indicator includes the present (this is to be seen as a space of time and not a point). νῦν is a good example in John 8:52, though it may also serve as a logical indicator in John 8:40. Other words that may be used as indicators are ἄρτι, ἤδη, πάλιν, ὡς, τότε, πάντως, ἕως, μέχρι, ὅταν, πρίν, etc. (2) Anaphoric words, especially near and remote demonstratives, the article, and pronouns. Though some grammarians would not want to classify these words as anaphoric, in Greek this seems the most concise means of classification. Use of the article in Greek is not an easy issue to resolve, especially in relation to anaphora, but the best concise description seems to be Carson's (*Fallacies*, 83, cf. 82-84; cf. Karleen, *Syntax*, 46-55):

Articular	=	definite	generic
Anarthrous	=	indefinite, i.e. qualitative	non-generic (individual)

The articular is the marked form in Greek on the basis of its additional morphological element and its anaphoric use in definite statements (Acts 10:4), as well as generic statements (Luke 10:7), where reference appears to be made to a known state of affairs. (It has long been recognized that the article is related to the demonstrative morphologically; see Robertson, 755; cf. Lyons, *Semantics*, 652-54.) Demonstratives, though primarily denoting proximity to the speaker (see Lyons, *Semantics*, 646-53), help to establish temporal reference in the surrounding world. For example, Matt 3:1 uses ἐκείναις (those just referred to) to establish which ἡμέραις (days) are specified. Pronouns serve as substitutes for nouns, noun-substitutes, and nominal substitutes (relative pronouns function similarly to the second use below). In some cases they merely make more explicit (or emphatic) the grammaticalized subject of a given verb (Matt 10:16), though a more important function is to refer specifically to some antecedent (Acts 10:2), and hence to what the antecedent refers (see Lyons, *Semantics*, 660). The first is less help in establishing temporal reference, while the latter is susceptible to the problem of cataphoric reference as well (John 1:19), in which the pronoun precedes the item to which it refers. (3) References to places. For example, in 1 Cor 15:32, Paul refers to fighting wild beasts in Ephesus. Whether these beasts are to be taken literally or figuratively, in either case the article arguably gives past temporal reference to the protasis of this conditional, referring to a previous period in Paul's ministry.

c. Discourse deixis (text deixis). "Discourse, or text, deixis concerns the use of expressions with some utterance to refer to some portion of the discourse that contains that utterance (including the utterance itself)" (Levinson, *Pragmatics*, 85). This category is potentially the most important and most helpful in discussing temporal reference in Greek, since it focuses on larger units, but it is also bound by serious limitations, since it is dependent upon all of the other deictic categories to a large degree, i.e. all the other categories are found within discourse, including person, time, and place deixis.

Establishment of discourse deixis may require several sets of features besides those already discussed. They include: (1) connectives, e.g. γάρ, οὖν, ἄρα, καί, δέ, μέν . . . δέ, μέντοι, τὸ λοιπόν, ἐν τούτῳ, ἄχρι, μέχρι, ὅταν, ὅτε, etc. These words, often occurring near the beginning of an utterance, establish connections and relationships with the preceding discourse unit, whether it be conclusion, continuation, contrast, etc. (2) Main story indicators. This is closely related to topic/discourse, theme/rheme concepts (Berry, *Introduction*, 1.77-82; cf. Lyons, *Introduction*, 334-37), in which a story line maintains its flow by adding to what has already been given. In Greek this movement may be indicated not only by connectives, but by alteration in word order. (Levinson [*Pragmatics*, 88-89] seems to argue that this applies only to "relationship fixed word-order languages" [88]. While it may be more difficult in non-fixed word-order languages like Greek, since distinct word-order patterns have been observed, the concept can be entertained. Perhaps deixis has played a larger part in Greek word-order than previously realized. See Levinsohn, *Connections*; Dover, *Order*; Denniston, *Style*, 41-98.) For example, John 1:1ff. is well crafted. After the introductory ἐν ἀρχῇ (in the beginning) the sentences tend to alternate predicate-subject, subject-predicate, with each subject or predicate maintaining continuity while the second element introduces something new. Thus v 5 is past-referring, since it maintains the alternation of subject-predicate-complement (v 4) with subject(=complement)-predicate, and ἐν τῇ σκοτίᾳ forms the topic for v 5b: καὶ ἡ σκοτία αὐτὸ οὐ κατέλαβεν (and the darkness did not overcome it). (3) Entire discourse units. This is very close to what might be called literary forms or types (the terminology is particularly difficult in this area, but the concepts seem helpful at this point if they are used apart from entertaining larger ontological questions). For example, an epistle creates different expectations than does an historical narrative, and knowing the literary form and purpose help to establish the unit's temporal reference.

 d. Social deixis. This category is perhaps the most difficult to apply in Greek and of the least value for temporal deictic indication. It concerns those language structures that "encode the social identities of participants (properly, incumbents of participant roles), or the social relationship between them, or between one of them and persons and entities referred to" (Levinson, *Pragmatics*, 89). The Vocative qualifies for mention here, since it singles out a single person or group of persons for address, and is a grammatically unattached element "invariably marked for speaker-referent relationships: there is no such thing, it seems, as a socially neutral summons or address" (92). See e.g. Matt 15:28 with an individual; and Luke 24:25 with a group. Lesser addressees may also be mentioned, for example in the introductions of Paul's epistles.

 4. STANDARD PATTERNS OF VERBAL USAGE. The final major concern of this chapter is to answer a particular question: if tense forms are non-temporal in reference why does the Aorist refer to the past in the great majority of uses, and the Present to the present? An appropriate response must distinguish several points.

 Most explanations of Greek tenses appeal to temporal reference in virtually all instances. Since it can now be recognized that the tense forms are not primarily temporal but essentially aspectual the need for imposing temporal categories at the semantic level is eliminated, i.e. analysis of a given utterance can begin from the non-temporal reference of the verb.

 While it may be true that (according to traditional analysis) the Aorist most often is used in past-referring contexts and the Present in present-referring contexts (this widely held assumption [see chapt. 1] often goes unstated even in otherwise helpful grammatical works on Greek), and while the sentences in which they occur may continue to do so even under another analysis, the argument marshalled here is strictly a statistical and terminological one, claiming that the best understanding or approximation of the semantic range of a grammatical category is its majority usage (extensional meaning; Dahl, *Tense*, 9; cf. Bache, *Aspect*, 54-60). This argument is flawed for several reasons. (1) Because it artificially limits its explanatory power, this explanation is incapable of adequately describing any grammatical category fully and thus fails to account for actual counter-examples, especially those that do not fall within the statistical probability (see Louw, "Waarde," 25). (2) It gives undue weight to that which occurs often instead of that which can and does occur, even if in small numbers. (3) It fails to recognize that there is no necessary correlation between a grammatical category's semantics and the number of times it is used. If an adequate semantic category is to be defined, sufficient attention must be paid to all potential uses, including those which are infrequent; to characterize them as odd or deviant is to place greater stress on primary usage than is warranted. The most convincing and adequate grammatical explanation must encompass the widest range of uses under a single explanatory head (intensional meaning), relegating the fewest number to the category of those beyond comprehension. (4) This approach has been seduced by tense terminology. As mentioned above, it is often tempting to see the typical function that motivates the form name as *the* function, i.e. to treat a short label as far more informative and exhaustive than it really is.

A more adequate explanation recognizes at least a functional difference between semantics at the level of code and pragmatics at the level of text (Gregory/Carroll, *Language*, 75-85; see my chapt. 3). This work attempts to explain the Greek verbal network at the level of code (the speakers' shared meaning-system encoded in grammatical, syntactical and lexical items), though it must be remembered that instances of language are always instances of pragmatic usage. The connection between these two is made through the concept of verbal implicature, defined as "something that can be inferred from the use of a certain linguistic category or type of expression, although it cannot be regarded as belonging to its proper meaning" (Dahl, *Tense*, 11). (The term implicature suggests a range of issues in linguistics, not all drawn upon here; see Levinson, *Pragmatics*, 97-166; cf. Fawcett, *Linguistics*, esp. 245ff.) To discuss the essential semantic features of a verb tense as distinct from its usage in a specific instance is to make "the distinction between the meaning of a linguistic item, in terms of its conventionalised semantic representation, and the implicatures that can be drawn from the use of a linguistic item in a particular context" (Comrie, *Tense*, 23, cf. 23-26, 26-35, on integrating grammatical and discourse considerations; *Aspect*, 41-51). As Comrie continues,

the separation of meaning from implicature thus enables us first to give a more accurate characterisation of the meaning of a linguistic form, and secondly, given a theory of implicatures, to account for the implicatures that are assigned to linguistic forms in the absence of any cancellation of those implicatures. (*Tense*, 25)

Implicatures can be cancelled, whereas the essential meaning cannot. This represents a significant shift from the traditional explanation of why, for example, the Aorist tends to be past-referring and the Present to be present-referring. The traditional explanation views the primary usage at the pragmatic level as the controlling feature for defining the semantics of the form, and this estimation is often absolute-tense based, while the explanation offered here looks to the essential semantic features as governing the range of pragmatic usage. From a theoretical standpoint alone, the latter is more satisfying, since it not only abides by a meaningful hierarchy, but it has greater explanatory power in its treatment of actual usage, with the fewest number of exceptional instances (the network above tries to spell out some of the implications of this). But the traditional understanding of tenses has persistent force, being advocated even by McKay, who says that "an action described as present in time must almost inevitably be regarded as a process and so require the present tense of the imperfective verb" (145), and Dahl, who says that "single, completed events [perfective aspect] will in the 'typical cases' be located in the past" (*Tense*, 79, cf. 81-84; cf. Rijksbaron, 2; Comrie, *Aspect*, 41-42; Bache, "Aspect," 67-68). Not only does this formulation seem to be derived from a theory of *Aktionsart* in trying to describe the objective status of the process itself, something McKay is sensitive to and elsewhere rejects (137 n. 1), but it seems to be formulated around a mentalist view, i.e. trying to reconstruct the psychological conception of time within speakers' minds.

Although implicature does not dictate tense usage, but to the contrary tense usage governs implicature, nevertheless, a much-evidenced correlation can be seen between temporal reference, speaker's conception, and tense usage, related to what Dahl calls "conventionalization" (*Tense*, 11). Patterns of textual usage readily illustrate that certain textual conditions become associated with particular tense forms (e.g. Aorist in narrative contexts; Present in descriptions), such that use of the tense form in the textual environment readily implicates the conventionalized meaning. To determine why the Aorist is used in a large number of past-time contexts and the Present in a large number of present-time contexts, traditional grammars of Greek begin with consideration of the various pragmatic uses at the level of text, listing a number of categories of usage and (sometimes) attempting to find a unifying thread that holds these together. This leads many grammars to incorporate the bipartite scheme of time and kind of action to explain the range of usage, arguing sometimes that one and sometimes the other is predominant. As seen in chapt. 1, these attempts are often unsatisfactory, with potentially confusing and contradictory criteria often forcing the evidence.

Since it has been established on the principle of substitution that the tense forms in Greek are aspectually and not temporally based, verbal aspectual semantics apart from temporal considerations constitutes the logical starting point for an explanation of the wide range of pragmatic usage often discussed by grammarians. Perfective verbal aspect has least concern from a speaker's standpoint for the movement, development, progress of a process. Thus Comrie says that "the perfective looks at the situation from outside, without necessarily distinguishing any of the internal structure of the situation" (*Aspect*, 4; his attempt to correlate aspect with "situation-internal time" and tense with "situation-external time" [5; repeated in *Tense*, 6] runs contrary to his view of aspect as non-deictic and shifts to a view of aspect as *Aktionsart*; see Bache, *Aspect*, 18, for criticism). The imperfective verbal aspect, on the other hand, is concerned from a speaker's standpoint with the movement, development or progress of a process. Thus Comrie says that "the imperfective looks at the situation from the inside, and as such is crucially concerned with the internal structure of the situation" (*Aspect*, 4). The stative verbal aspect is the most complex of the verbal aspects, since it is not concerned with the process itself, as are the perfective and imperfective, but with a point of observation removed from it, with the speaker grammaticalizing reference to a condition or state that depends upon the process. This characterization is not designed to introduce a temporal progression between past event and present result, but explains why the stative aspect may be found in both present and past contexts with surprising regularity (Louw, "Aspek," 25, 26; "Waarde," 25; contra Comrie, *Aspect*, 52-53, and most Greek grammarians; see my chapt. 5]), as well as in future, omnitemporal and timeless contexts. In this way, temporal implicature is perhaps less relevant for the stative than the other two aspects at the level of pragmatics, and the mixture of usage of the Perfect form within predominantly Aorist or Present/Imperfect contexts illustrates this. For example, in 1 John 1:1-4, Perfect verbs parallel with Aorist and Present verbs have caused controversy, almost certainly because of a temporal conception of the tense forms rather than because of aspectual pragmatic difficulties.

The range of usage of the imperfective and perfective aspects is more difficult to explain, although an adequate model which avoids strict mentalism can be constructed. The analysis seems to entail two major assumptions: a temporal conception, in which the past is seen as in some way secure, established, and distant, while the present is seen as in flux, evolving, and at hand (see Entwistle, *Aspects*, 184; cf. Jespersen, *Philosophy*, 257; Lyons,

Semantics, 677); and a literary conception, in which the default tense is considered most compatible with the unmarked literary category. This distinction of literary categories has been variously characterized as that between narrative and description (Louw, "Waarde," 25), narration and commentary (Weinrich, *Tempus*, 288-93; "Tense"), historic and experiential modes (Lyons, *Semantics*, 688; cf. "Deixis," 117), or temporal sequence such as narrative or series of instructions versus exposition, description or argumentation (Nida *et al.*, *Style*, 110) (cf. Demetr. 19: τρία δὲ γένη περιόδων ἐστίν, ἱστορική, διαλογική, ῥητορική [the kinds of periods are three: narrative, dialogue, exposition]). Although the categories cannot be sharply bifurcated, since narrative contains description, and vice versa, these two coordinates are complementary. The past is the realm in which security is believed to lie, and hence is considered more "objective." Though the processes require interpretation and even rearrangement, they are not thought to change. When the chronological thread or background events of an account are selected for simple narration, the Greek speaker readily uses the aspect most compatible with this conception: perfective. The perfective aspect is used to characterize the process in its entirety and as a whole, with no specific reference to its internal consistency and with no regard for its internal movement. As McKay says, the perfective is "used when the speaker or writer had no special reason to use any other" ("Syntax," 46). Thus in sections of the Gospels, and other Greek narrative literature, the basis of the narrative is carried by a string of Aorist verbs. This does not deny that other aspects are used in like contexts, but on the basis of their increased semantic weight their use automatically selects and marks reference to the process (thus in one context an author may choose to mark the process and in another he may choose not to). This explanation is recognizably circular in that it is asserted that the default tense form, the Aorist, is used in unmarked contexts, narrative, while the unmarked context or literary convention governs use of the perfective aspect. But this is not a vicious circle, since the default quality of the Aorist can be explained on other lines as well (see above); rather, it helps explain a major pattern of Greek usage (on the Imperfect and Aorist see chapt. 4). (Dahl [*Tense*, 79, 113] claims this pattern holds for a number of languages as well.)

On the other hand, the present is thought to be still evolving, in progress, and at hand, thus the imperfective aspect is suited for use by a speaker to express the more subjective nature of this foreground process. The perfective aspect could be used but this would not conceive of it as in progress but in its wholeness and completeness. The present, by its nature still not established, both relies upon the contexts of past events (thus reinforcing narrative of past events as the unmarked context) to ground its sequence of events, but it to a large extent holds establishment in abeyance, since the process of which it is a part (see above for definition of present as not punctiliar but a space on either side of "now") must still be seen through to completion (see Louw, "Aspek," 22, who speaks of the "tension" that the Present creates in such literary types as memorabilia, commentary and philosophical discussion; cf. van Gronigen, "Considérations," 56). Again, the perfective aspect may be used in such non-past contexts, and such use is not unnatural Greek, although it is not the primary usage of the tense form or the tense form most frequently found in such contexts.

An important correlation between verbal aspect and context is seen. The distinction between narrative and non-narrative, not designed as a rigorous discussion of genre, seems almost self-evident in Greek writing, and one which cuts across boundaries such as poetry, epic, history, etc. For example, within a dialogue of Plato one might reasonably find narrative as well as much non-narrative material. The most heavily marked aspect [+stative] is used freely in various temporal contexts, within both marked and unmarked discourse; the [+imperfective] also functions within the two major temporal spheres, including the unmarked discourse, narrative; and the least heavily marked [+perfective] aspect is less readily used in marked contexts. (The future was apparently not of the same standing in speakers' minds as were the past and present, and thus [+assertive] attitude tends to avoid such temporal implicatures; see chaps. 4 and esp. 9. Lyons [*Introduction*, 314-15] entertains the notion of bi-temporal languages.) This formulation--maintaining the priority of Greek verbal semantics at the level of code but recognizing the primary pragmatic usages of the forms--goes a long way toward a fuller understanding of the nature of Greek verbal usage.

5. CONCLUSION. On the basis of contrastive verbal substitution, it is clearly shown that tense forms in Greek are not primarily time based (i.e. tense is not grammaticalized in Greek) but that they are aspectually based. Greek verbal aspect is defined as a synthetic semantic category (realized in the forms of verbs) used of meaningful oppositions in a network of tense systems to grammaticalize the author's reasoned subjective choice of conception of a process. The Greek verbal aspects are three: perfective, imperfective, and stative. In light of traditional grammatical analysis, recent work with grammatical models, and development of system networks in systemic linguistics, these aspectual categories may be helpfully defined through various means of vizualization, including display in a semantic verbal network with formal realizations. These models are helpful since translation is not a reliable guide to formulation of meaningful tense distinctions, especially in the area of

verbal aspect, where by definition speakers may choose to conceive of a process in various ways. Because temporal reference is relative and not absolute in Greek, deictic indicators play an important part as the grammatical means by which temporal distinctions are made. And the relation of semantics to pragmatics, or the code shared by Greek users and their resultant texts, is best formulated in terms of implicature, which accounts for patterns of tense-form usage.

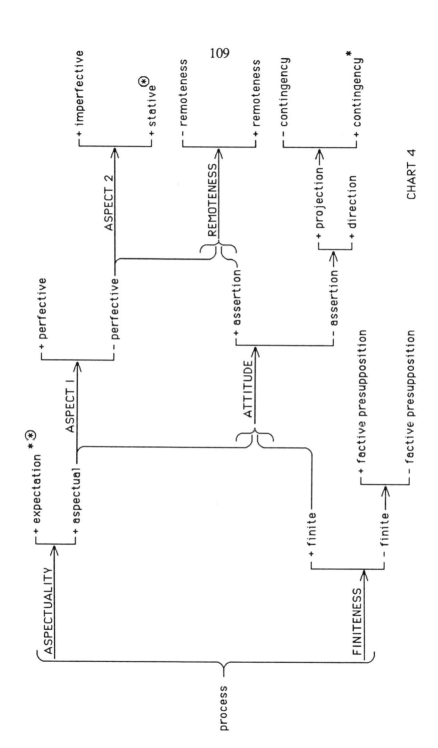

CHART 4

CHAPTER 3:
THE INFLUENCE OF
SEMITIC LANGUAGES
ON VERBAL ASPECT
IN THE NEW TESTAMENT

0. INTRODUCTION. An objection that might be raised to the major assertion of this work--that verbal aspect provides a controlling model for discussion of use of the tense-forms in the Greek of the NT--is that verbal usage in the NT is not representative of Greek verbal usage in general because of Semitic-language influence. If it can be proved that Semitic influence has altered verbal usage to any significant degree, then this analysis must be altered before it can be applied to the NT (though the NT can still be investigated as a corpus). If it can be shown that no usage in the NT cannot reasonably be explained along the lines of secular Greek usage or its natural development, then the investigation can proceed unhindered. In this chapter, therefore, general views regarding the language of the NT are summarized to demonstrate the current diversity of opinion, supposed instances of Semitic influence on the verbal structure of the NT are considered, and some conclusions are drawn about the Greek of the NT, in light of linguistic analysis of the 1st cent. hellenistic language milieu.

1. THE LANGUAGES OF PALESTINE AND THE NATURE OF NT GREEK. Since the first significant studies of Semitic influence on the NT published by Wyss, Pasor and Trom in the mid 17th cent., there has not been a lack of interest in this topic (see Vergote, "Grec," cols. 1321-44 [he is clearly biased against the Deissmann school, cols. 1361-67]; Maloney, *Interference*, 7-34; Irmscher, "Streit"), though the issues involved are diverse and not easily defined (Silva, "Bilingualism," 199). Treatments of Semitic influence on the Greek of the NT usually concentrate on two issues: a. the current languages of 1st-cent. Palestine, and b. various theories regarding the nature of the Greek of the NT.

    a. The question of the languages used in Palestine during the 1st cent. overlaps with the question of what language Jesus spoke. Answers to these questions have been offered since Erasmus and the Renaissance, and, as Silva notes, comprise a "complex, and at times amusing, history of research" (*Change*, 3). (Meyers/Strange [*Archaeology*, 62-91]; Schürer [*History*, 20ff.]; Leclercq ["Note"]; Fitzmyer ["Languages"] summarize the physical and linguistic evidence for Hebrew, Aramaic, Greek and Latin.)

    1. It has long been agreed by scholars that Aramaic was the predominant language of Palestinian Judaism (Büchsel, "Sprache," 133-42) and almost certainly one of the languages, if not the primary language, of Jesus; Dalman's conclusion--that though Jesus might have known Hebrew, and probably spoke Greek, he certainly taught in Aramaic (*Jesus*, 1-37; Lapide ["Insights," 483-86] summarizes the major proponents of the Hebrew versus Aramaic debate)--has held sway with a majority of scholars (see Black, *Approach*, 16 n. 1, cf. 47-49). The Aramaic hypothesis rests securely upon the fact that, though Greek was the language of the Greek and Roman Empires, it never fully replaced Aramaic (an important Semitic language brought back to Palestine after the exile) in Palestine, as evidenced by not only the biblical writings of Daniel and Ezra, but a large amount of inscriptional, ossuary, epistolary (Bar Kokhba), papyric, and literary evidence, especially from Qumran. It was once thought that Aramaic had entered a period of decline in the two cents. on either side of Christ's birth, but in the last 50 years many important discoveries have been made (see esp. Fitzmyer/Harrington, *Manual* [esp. xi]; Beyer, *Texte*). While it is likely that Jesus' primary language was Aramaic (Black, 15; cf. Brown, "From Burney"; Haenchen, *John 1*, 52-66 [bibliography 52-55]; Rajak, *Josephus*, esp. 230-32, cf. 46-64, 174-84), this position is argued primarily by logical and historical inference, since Jesus is not recorded as using Aramaic apart from odd quotations (e.g. Mark 15:34). Also, the majority of texts is of literary quality, some quite late, while the inscriptional evidence (much of which could be Hebrew) is limited mostly to proper names (Fitzmyer, "Languages," 520). Nevertheless, this theory has many important supporters, such as Wellhausen, Dalman, Joüon, Bardy, Matthew Black, Wilcox, Fitzmyer, Feldman, and, most notoriously perhaps, Torrey (see bibliography).[1]

    2. Others have maintained, however, that some form of Hebrew, whether Biblical or Mishnaic, had a far greater importance in 1st-cent. Palestine than is often suspected. In a lengthy article in the *Jewish Quarterly Review* (1908) and later in his *Grammar* (1927), Segal ("Hebrew," esp. 670-700, 734-37; *Grammar*, 5-19), followed in his major formulations especially by Birkeland (*Language*, 1-40; see also Chomsky, "What"; Kutscher, "Mishnaic," cols. 1592-93; idem, *History*, 115-20), proposed that Mishnaic Hebrew, rightly considered the linguistic evolutionary offspring of Biblical Hebrew, much evidenced in the Rabbinic writings and independent of Aramaic (which Birkeland contends was reserved for the upper classes), was a prominent Jewish vernacular at all social levels from approximately 400 B.C. to A.D. 150. The Judean Desert documents, including those from Qumran (which outnumber those in Aramaic) but especially the Hebrew Bar Kokhba letters, have given further credence to the theory of vernacular Hebrew (Barr, "Language," 20; cf. Gundry, "Milieu," 405-07), though ossuary, numismatic, and literary (Ben Sira, Mishnah) evidence can also be found. Several scholars disagree with Segal over the exact nature of this Hebrew and its extent of use: Birkeland contends it is a dialect of

---

[1]The debate over which dialect of Aramaic was spoken--that based on the Targums of Onkelos (Kutscher *et al.*) or the Palestinian Targums (Kahle *et al.*)--is still unsettled: Kutscher, "Language," esp. 9, 12-16; Kahle, "Pentateuchtargum" (also *Geniza*, esp. 191-208). Cf. Jeremias, "Vorgeschichte"; Ott, "Muttersprache"; Rüger, "Problem"; Black, *Approach*, 15-49; Wilcox, "Semitisms," 986-92. See Kaufman, "Methodology," for insightful analysis.

Mishnaic Hebrew overwhelmingly predominant at the lower social levels, and Lapide ("Insights," 486-500), following Ferguson ("Diglossia"), proposes that Mishnaic Hebrew was the bridge language between Hebrew (high language) and Aramaic (low language) in the Palestinian diglossic milieu, but they have been followed to the extent that (Mishnaic) Hebrew is thought to have been a probable language of the 1st cent., and a possible if not probable language of Jesus, by Manson, Emerton, Barr, Grintz, and Rabin, among others (see bibliography). It must be noted, however, that though Jesus may have known sufficient Hebrew to read in Luke 4:16-30 (cf. Acts 26:14), and Hebrew was certainly in use in Palestine, at least by the Jewish leaders, "evidence for colloquial Hebrew is not abundant," with an almost complete lack of Hebrew inscriptions in Palestine (Fitzmyer, "Languages," 529).

    3. Other scholars have argued strongly for the predominant role of Greek in 1st-cent. Palestine and, hence, in the ministry of Jesus. Their arguments rest firmly on, among other facts, the role of Greek as the *lingua franca* of the Roman Empire, the trilingual nature of the Judean Desert material, including Greek Bar Kokhba letters (see Lifshitz, "Papyrus," for the texts; Howard/Shelton ["Letters"] propose a reconstruction which suggests that Hebrew writing by this group was limited to a very few), inscriptional, ostraca, and ossuary evidence (Goodenough, *Symbols*, 121-50), literary evidence (e.g. Josephus's writings), and most importantly the linguistic fact that the NT has been transmitted in Greek from its earliest documents (Sevenster [*Know Greek*] discusses the evidence). Abbott, Argyle, Smith, Sevenster, N. Turner, Lieberman, Mussies, Treu and Hengel, among others (see bibliography), have argued in various ways that Greek was in widespread use in the multilingual society of 1st-cent. Palestine. There seems to be nothing to have prevented any Palestinian resident from learning Greek, certainly as a second and often as a first language, though the ability of the average resident is still an unquantifiable factor. (The degree of Greek penetration of rural Palestine is discussed in Jones, *City*, 289-95; Rajak, *Josephus*, 46-64; Hengel, *Judaism*, 58ff.; Feldman, "How Much"; cf. Kraabel, "Synagogue." A distinction must be made between Greek language and Greek culture.)

    It is not possible here to settle the various issues regarding the linguistic milieu of 1st-cent. Palestine, except to say that the archeological, linguistic and sociological evidence seems to indicate that the region was multilingual, including at least Aramaic and Greek in widespread and frequent use, and Hebrew as a possible vernacular but certainly a written language, with Latin a fourth language used primarily by the Romans in political and administrative matters. Therefore, the likelihood that Jesus, along with most Gentiles and Jews, was multilingual himself is secure. (See Fitzmyer, "Languages," 531: "the most commonly used language of Palestine in the first century A.D. was Aramaic, but . . . many Palestinian Jews, not only those in hellenistic towns, but farmers and craftsmen of less obviously Hellenized areas used Greek, at least as a second language. The data collected from Greek inscriptions and literary sources indicate that Greek was avidly used. In fact there is some indication . . . that some Palestinians spoke only Greek. . . . But pockets of Palestinian Jews also used Hebrew, even though its use was not widespread"; Schürer [*History*, esp. 20-28, 74-80] is less optimistic. Dalman, Black, Rabin, Gundry, Barr, Fitzmyer, Bardy, Sevenster, Birkeland, Emerton, Turner, Lapide, Sparks, Leclercq, de Waard, Olmstead, Rajak, and Meyers/Strange, among others, mention the possibility of at least a trilingual community.)

    b. A more important debate for this work centres upon the nature of the Greek of the NT. The proposals have ranged from positing a pure koine derived directly from Attic Greek to a heavily Semitized translation Greek, and all points in between. Though the history of this debate is well known (see esp. Voelz, "Language," 894-930; as well as Vergote, "Grec," cols. 1321-24; Maloney, *Interference*, 7-34; cf. N. Turner, "Thoughts"; McKnight, "'Holy Ghost'"), a recounting of the major positions of the last one hundred years shows that consensus is still lacking.

 1. Deissmann, first in his *Bible Studies* (1895 *Bibelstudien*, 1897 *Neue Bibelstudien*; Eng. trans. 1901) and later in *Light from the Ancient Near East* (1908), was the first to make widely known the importance of the then recently-discovered Egyptian papyri and hellenistic inscriptions (on these events see C.E. Turner, *Papyri*, 17-41; Barclay, "NT," 54ff.), although the papyrologists were anticipated by almost 50 years by E. Masson in the preface to his translation of Winer (Harris, "Greek," 54-55) and J.B. Lightfoot in lectures delivered in 1863 (Moulton, 242). Arguing against the views that NT Greek fulfilled classical standards or that it was part of a "Biblical" Greek (including the LXX) inspired by the Holy Spirit, Deissmann maintained that the Greek of the NT was part of the body of Egyptian or popular Greek of the hellenistic age. Recognizing the role of the LXX as a translated document, he thereby discounted any "written Semitic-Greek" as ever being a spoken or literary language. He recognized that certain portions of the Gospel material were translations of Aramaic into Greek, though he questioned the ability to reconstruct a *Vorlage* (unlike the case of the LXX). Most hellenistic Jews, Deissmann maintained, knew Greek as a first language, so that investigation of the NT documents must proceed from their examination as philological artifacts, not of the literary language of the time but of the vast body of hellenistic Greek, before application of secondary tests as to their Semitic "feel." Though he limited himself almost exclusively to investigation of lexicographical items, he maintained (almost inevitably for Deissmann) that a lexical item of the NT could be paralleled in hellenistic Greek: e.g. γραμματεύς (scribe), ἱλαστήριος (propitiation), λειτουργέω (serve), νόμος (law), ἀγάπη (love), καθαρίζω (cleanse). Deissmann was advanced in his consideration of the problems of multilingualism and linguistic development (*Studies*, 63-85; *Light*, 1-145; *Philology*, 39-65; "Griechisch"; see Silva, "Bilingualism"; Horsley, "Views," 393-98, for recent, generally positive evaluations).

 Deissmann's theories were soon applied to grammar, as well as lexis, by Moulton in a series of articles in the *Classical Review* (1901) and *Expositor* (1904), and his *Prolegomena* to *A Grammar of NT Greek* (1906). After examining volumes of papyri, Moulton found numerous parallels to many NT grammatical constructions, some previously thought to be foreign to Greek: e.g. instrumental ἐν (1 Cor 4:21), found abundantly at Tebtunis; restrictions of the Dative Case; encroachment of the Accusative, among many others. Recognizing the revolutionary character of Deissmann's discoveries and Thumb's similar philological findings, he concluded that biblical Greek, "except where it is translation Greek, was simply the vernacular of daily life," without "serious" dialectical differences and very much a predominant language in the bilingual environment of Palestine (Moulton, 4, 5 [quoted]; "Notes"; "Characteristics"; "NT Greek"; and *Science*; see also Thumb, *Sprache*, esp. 102-201; "Greek").

 Moulton was later followed by many others, including Thackeray, Radermacher, Robertson, Milligan, Meecham, Goodspeed, Trom, Colwell, Costas, and most recently Rydbeck, Koester and Browning, besides Silva and Horsley (see bibliography), though often with suggestive modifications. For example, Cadbury (e.g. "Luke," followed by others, has noted the possibility of Luke following the model of the LXX. Rydbeck (*Fachprosa*, 186-96), while affirming that the Greek of the NT shares a common grammatical base with all other *Fachprosa* (popular literature, papyri, etc.), denies that through these documents one can know the *Vulgärsprache* spoken during the hellenistic period (cf. Kurzová, "Griechische," 218-24, who disputes Rydbeck at this point; and Pax, "Probleme," 560-62, who questions his concept of *Fachprosa*). W. Howard, who completed vol. 2 of Moulton's *Grammar*, included an appendix on Semitisms (411-85 [cf. Howard, "Language"; Moule, 171-91]). And Malherbe (*Aspects*, 31-59) rightly emphasizes the range of literary accomplishment of the NT documents.

This position, therefore, holds that: (a) hellenistic Greek was the natural product of linguistic development; (b) hellenistic Greek was essentially a single variety of language; (c) the Greek of the NT, while influenced by Semitic contact (especially LXX), remained recognizably Greek; and (d) this can be demonstrated through comparison of significant examples, whereby supposed instances of Semitic influence can for the most part be paralleled by examples from extra-biblical Greek.

Others have found greater fault, however, with the Deissmann-Moulton hypothesis. For example, some have questioned the purity of Alexandrian or Egyptian Greek, hence its validity as a standard for establishing the nature of hellenistic Greek. One group has maintained that Alexandrian Greek came under Semitic (primarily Hebrew) influence because of the large Jewish population in the region. The papyri then already had a Semitic cast, hence their closeness to NT Greek. (See Ottley, *Handbook*, 165; Dalman, *Words*, 17; Courtenay James, *Language*, 57-75; more recently Turner, *Insights*, 184, citing Burney, *Origin*; cf. Turner, "Thoughts," 47. de Waard ["Σημιτισμοί"] argues this for Palestinian Greek, without adopting the Gehman/Turner hypothesis [see below].) Another group, following L.-T. Lefort (1928), has argued that the Alexandrian Greek of the papyri was influenced by Egyptian Coptic, which is, according to this view, similar syntactically to the Semitic languages. (See Vergote, "Grec," cols. 1353-60; Gignac, esp. 1.46-48; idem, "Language"; idem, "Papyri," 157-58.) This would result in apparent linguistic similarities between NT Greek, influenced by Aramaisms, and the papyri, influenced by Coptic (McKnight, "'Holy Ghost,'" 90; cf. Richards, "Grammar," 289-90; Thumb, *Sprache*, 170-74; and Moulton, 38-40, 242, who already rejected this possibility). As Teodorsson has indicated (*Phonology*, esp. 25-35), however, these arguments, though plausible, suffer from the fundamental problem that no other kind of Greek has ever been found in Egypt (Mandilaras [50] notes that since Vergote's examples of Coptic date from the 3d cent. A.D. they may evidence Greek influence). Thus there is no evidence of a previous 'pure' Greek, no evidence of the creolization process, and no evidence of this Greek being considered to depart from the acceptable norms of hellenistic Greek.

2. A theory with more support over the years, or at least more argumentative force, has maintained that the Gospels and at least the first part of Acts, and possibly Revelation, are translations directly out of Aramaic. A serious weakness of early attempts by, for example, A. Meyer, Wellhausen,[2] E. Nestle, and Dalman (see Black, *Approach*, 1-14; Wilcox, *Semitisms*, 1-12; idem, "Semitisms," 979-86), was a failure thoroughly to support Aramaic reconstructions of the supposed original text, as Dalman himself admits (*Words*, 43 71). Black claims (2), however, that a few of Wellhausen's results have endured, for example, explaining Matt 23:26 (καθάρισον [cleanse]) and Luke 11:41 (δότε ἐλεημοσύνην [give alms]) on the basis of confusing the two Aramaic words *dakkau* (purify) and *zakkau* (give alms) (Wellhausen, *Einleitung* [2d ed.], 27). Later, armed with a wealth of supposed evidence, on the basis of such criteria as apparent mistranslations, ambiguity in the Aramaic text, and parallels with the LXX, Torrey (*Translated Gospels* [quoted below]; *Composition*; "Fact"; "Origin"; "Aramaic"; *Apocalypse*, esp. 13-48), followed in many respects by Burney, Montgomery, Burrows, and de Zwaan, argued vociferously that the Gospels, Acts 1-15, and Revelation were early translations from Aramaic originals. Rather than depicting the translators as bunglers, however, he depicted, for example, the Gospel "writers" as pious men who did an admirable job of translation in an attempt to preserve "the wording of the original text" (lviii), enabling reconstruction of the underlying original, though the final Greek may be, in Torrey's own words, "inexcusable" (liv) as idiomatic Greek. Though much of his writing is devoted to positing plausible reconstructions (he translated all four Gospels), the lack of an Aramaic *Vorlage* with which to compare his results renders his conclusions necessarily circular. Also, as Black points out, *most* of his examples of mistranslations, like Burney's, are "open to grave objection." For example, of Torrey's claim that the translator of Mark 7:3 misread Aramaic

---

[2]Cf. editions of Wellhausen's *Einleitung*. In ed. 1 (7-43) he emphasizes the Semitic (Aramaic) element standing behind the Gospels, while in ed. 2 (7-32) he places slightly more stress on the Gospels as part of the koine. Torrey ("Julius Wellhausen") criticizes Wellhausen's failure to take the next (for Torrey) logical step in ed. 1 to argue for translation.

ligmar as Hebrew *ligmodh,* Black says (1) the Hebrew could only be printed *l*gomedh*, (2) the Aramaic word does not appear in the lexica, and (3) the Hebrew word never means "fist" (5, cf. 7-14, where he examines the criterion of mistranslation and questions its value as scientific proof). Beyer (*Syntax,* 11) concludes, "Die meisten Vorschläge angeblicher Semitismen (besonders von Torrey und Burney) sind auch gar klein Widerlegung wert" (see Marcus, "Notes," for a scathing review of Torrey, although Payne ["Semitisms"], realizing Torrey is virtually overthrown [135], recognizes the impressiveness of evidence on the basis of mistranslation [139]).

More recently Black, Wilcox, and Fitzmyer have attempted a similar quest, though they have generally been much more circumspect (noteworthy exceptions are Zimmermann, *Origin,* esp. 3-23; Lachs, "Elements"; G. Lee, "Translation"; Schwarz, *"Und"*), appreciating the varied Aramaic textual tradition, the tension between translation Greek and original Greek within the same texts, and the varied textual traditions of the NT. And their conclusions are stated cautiously, not polemically. (See Black, *Approach,* 15-49, 271-80; Wilcox, *Semitisms,* 17-19, 180-85; idem, "Semitisms," 993-1021; Fitzmyer, "Study"; although Reiser [*Syntax,* 6-7] questions several of Black's major proposals.)

They have not convinced all Semitists, however. Beyer (*Syntax,* 17-18) has argued as recently as 1968 that the Johannine writings have a Hebrew and not an Aramaic *Vorlage;* Carmignac ("Studies") has posited a Hebrew original for the Synoptics; Thompson (*Apocalypse,* esp. 2-6), following in a long tradition which includes Charles, posits a Hebrew source for Revelation; and G. Howard (*Gospel;* cf. "Was") claims to have discovered an early, independent version of Matthew in Hebrew.[3]

All of these variations on the Semitic theme believe that: (a) the Greek NT arose from a heavily Semitic environment; (b) portions of the Greek of the NT are not explainable in terms of the Greek language itself, i.e. internally many passages cannot be understood readily as Greek and externally no suitable parallels can be mustered; (c) linguistic crossover can be substantiated at significant junctures (even though proponents must rely on a very small corpus of Semitic documents, often much later than the NT); and (d) a meaningful distinction between Aramaic and Hebrew sources can be made and sustained throughout an entire document or set of documents.

3. A theory which has aroused more controversy than any other of late is that of Gehman on the LXX ("Character"; "Hebraisms"; "Ἅγιος") and N. Turner on the NT ("Unique Character"; *Syntax,* 1-9; *Style,* 1-10; *Insights,* 174-88; "Language"; "Quality"; "Thoughts"; "Biblical Greek"; cf. "Gospels," where his ideas are forming; "Literary Character," where he notes the literary Greek qualities of several NT writers). The theory harkens back to the late 19th cent., when some (represented by Rothe and Cremer) believed that the NT was written in a unique Holy Ghost Greek (see Vergote, "Grec," cols. 1326-27; cf. Turner, *Syntax,* 9; "Biblical Greek," regarding the question of a "Holy Ghost language"). Gehman and Turner have modified the position to argue for a Jewish-Greek dialect in use in Palestine in the 1st cent. Recognizing the Semitic element in the Gospels and other NT books, Turner claims that Semitic influence alone inadequately explains all the linguistic phenomena, especially since, for example, use of ἐκεῖνος, position of ἕνεκα, and constructions with πᾶς in the NT and the LXX indicate a "family resemblance" (*Syntax,* 5, citing studies in "Unique Character"). Turner also asserts that the NT displays an "almost complete lack of classical standards in every author" (*Syntax,* 2 [listed on 2-3]; cf. "Literary Character"). He therefore concludes that Jesus, as well as his disciples, the NT writers and possibly many others, used in regular conversation a Greek influenced by the Semitic languages spoken in Galilee at that time. In kind very similar to LXX Greek, Turner maintains, this Greek was very different from the Greek of the papyri; it "was a distinguishable dialect of spoken and written Jewish Greek" (*Insights,* 183). Though Gehman suggests this may have been a temporary linguistic condition

---

[3]Howard believes that a Hebrew text found in a 14th cent. Hebrew treatise by rabbi Shem-Tob ben-Isaac ben Shaprut is possibly the document referred to by Papias (Eus. Hist. 3.39.16). He relies on linguistic characteristics; supposed puns, word-connections, and alliterations; and theological issues (e.g. the divine name, Jesus and the law). Many of his criteria cut two ways. Howard admits that it is unclear whether the Hebrew or Greek version came first.

brought about by Jews passing from Semitic to Greek language,[4] Turner believes that the period was not transitional nor the language artificial. As he states, "Biblical Greek is so powerful and fluent, it is difficult to believe that those who used it did not have at hand a language all ready for use" (*Insights*, 183, basing his conclusion at least in part on his "'Testament.'" Dating, style and recensions of this document are all problematic). In apparent common reaction with Turner to Deissmann, Black goes so far as to call biblical Greek "a peculiar language, the language of a peculiar people" ("Languages," 11; see also Charles, *Revelation*, cxliii; Grant, "Hebrew," 122; Thompson, *Apocalypse*, 108; Horton, "Reflections").

Turner, Gehman and their followers seem to posit that: (1) a blending of Greek and Semitic languages is a linguistically acceptable category for discussion; (2) such a blend in fact occurred in heavily Semitic Palestine and Alexandria; and (3) clear instances of such a combination can be detected in the documents available and can only be adequately explained by such a theory.

The three major positions represent three very different views of the language of the Greek NT.[5] Several significant examples often posited as illustrating the influence of Semitic languages on verbal aspect of the Greek of the NT are now discussed in order to evaluate critically the views just presented.

2. POSSIBLE INSTANCES OF SEMITIC INFLUENCE UPON NT GREEK. a. Introduction.

In this section those instances the major grammars and reference books cite as illustrating Semitic influence on the verbal systems of the NT are explored. Several points guide discussion. (See appendix 3A for outlines of Semitic verbal edifices.)

1. This treatment focuses upon use of grammatical categories, in particular verbal aspect, and not translation (or mistranslation) of individual lexical items, though this has been the preoccupation of many studies of Semitic and LXX influence on the NT (e.g. Kennedy, *Sources*; Hatch, *Essays*, 3-35; Abbott, *Essays*, 65-109; Dodd, *Bible*, pt. 1; Hill, *Words*; Silva, *Change*; Hemer, "Reflections"; cf. Sanders, *Tendencies*, 190-209, who distinguishes linguistic from cultural Semitisms, claiming the former are analysable while the latter are too abstruse).

2. The concern is not with individual instances but with the cumulative evidence of several examples of the same phenomenon (Payne ["Semitisms," 136] and Turner [*Insights*, 175] note that this is the only one of Torrey's criteria valid for determining translation). In this way it is possible to formulate rules for entire books and possibly the entire NT, rather than speculating about the significance of only a single item.

3. The Hebrew OT is treated synchronically, without regard for the diachronic development of its language, since the LXX translators and other 1st-cent. readers would have regarded it in this light.

4. Two general approaches to determining Semitisms in the NT have been proposed: (a) assume priority of the Semitic source and put the burden of proof upon the NT to justify a particular construction (Ottley, *Handbook*, 163-65; so most scholars, including Black and Wilcox, and recently Thompson, *Apocalypse*); or (b) put the burden of proof upon those arguing for a Semitic source to prove that a particular construction is impossible in the NT or highly unlikely to occur as often as it does (Munck, "Deux notes," 127ff.). The second is preferable, since the NT

---

[4]The concept of interlanguage is irrelevant here, since it refers to "the language of a learner who is in the process of acquiring a given foreign language . . ." and not a language community. For discussion see Arabski, *Errors*, 9ff.

[5]Contra Voelz, "Language," 925, who argues "there is no longer any serious division in the scholarly world concerning the general nature of NT Greek." He claims the Semitic view, with support from Turner, is preeminent. It is also the position he endorses (925-30).

documents are extant Greek documents in a Greek linguistic milieu, with the possibility of "good Greek" being used by those whose mother tongue is Semitic (Munck, 149). Since Semitic influence on Greek is not merely a matter of circumstances but of measurable alteration, the burden of proof must lie with those who argue for Semitic influence. As Payne ("Semitisms," 136) says, "It requires a reasonable quantity of Semitisms before deciding that a particular passage was clearly influenced by a Semitic language." Reiser (*Syntax*, 13) is even more explicit: "Eine sprachliche Erscheinung im Neuen Testament, sei sie lexikalischer, phraseologischer, syntaktischer oder stilistischer Natur, sollte mit Hilfe des Semitischen erst dann erklärt werden, wenn sie aus dem Griechischen nicht hinreichend erklärbar ist" (cf. Thackeray, 29-30). This differs for treatment of the LXX, since the LXX is a translated document, and discussion of Semitic influence may begin from this assumption and means of comparison.

    5. There are three levels of Semitic influence: (a) direct translation (e.g. Mark 15:34 = Matt 27:46, whether Aramaic or Hebrew); (b) intervention, when a form that cannot reasonably be formed or paralleled in Greek must be attributed to the influence of a Semitic construction (e.g. temporal ἰδού for either Aramaic אֲרֵי or Hebrew וְהִנֵּה, Luke 13:16: ἔδησεν ὁ σατᾶν ἰδοὺ δέκα καὶ ὀκτὼ ἔτη [Satan bound (her) for 18 years]; Moulton/Howard, 447); (c) enhancement, when a rare construction that can be paralleled in Greek has its frequency of occurrence greatly increased due to associations with Semitic literature (e.g. adjectival attributive Genitive, Rom 8:21: τὴν ἐλευθερίαν τῆς δόξης [the glorious freedom]; cf. Hdt. 4.136.3: αἱ . . . ἡμέραι ὑμῖν τοῦ ἀριθμοῦ [your numbered days]; see Moulton/Howard, 440; Porter, "Genitive"). Whereas (c) plays a significant role in tracing diachronic change in a language, only (b) constitutes what can legitimately be called a Semitism, since it represents an incursion by Semitic language and not a linguistic change that can be accounted for within the parameters of Greek linguistic development. This is similar to Moulton's distinction of primary (b) and secondary (c) Semitisms (Moulton/Howard, 16; cf. de Zwaan, "Use," 54).

    6. A Hebraism is defined as a Semitism that can be fairly confidently attributed to Biblical or Mishnaic Hebrew and an Aramaism as a Semitism that can be attributed to Aramaic. This distinction, not always essential, is fairly standard at least since Dalman (*Words*, esp. 36-42; see e.g. Payne, "Semitisms," 135-36; Sanders, *Tendencies*, 190-209). And a Septuagintalism is a construction in the LXX of prominence disproportionate to other hellenistic Greek usage (and perhaps passed on to the NT), though it does not necessarily follow that it constitutes a Semitism, e.g. οὐ μή (see J. Lee, "Features," 18-23, who notes that though οὐ μή is frequent in the LXX there is no Semitic equivalent).[6] On the basis of the place of the LXX in 1st-cent. Judaism and Christianity, its relation to the Hebrew OT, and its being a translated document, the distinct possibility exists that the LXX could have exercised independent influence upon the language of the NT.

    7. A diachronic use of a range of Greek literature is justified in finding parallels to supposed Semitisms. Every language has a history, i.e. every synchronic system is the product of diachronic development (though not always logical and direct); therefore, citation of a hellenistic Greek construction occurring in earlier Greek helps to determine its use in relation to Semitic languages. Continuity in Greek verbal aspect from the classical through to the hellenistic periods (see chapt. 2) obviates the need to distinguish register (literary, non-literary, etc.) at this level of analysis, since verbal aspect is a semantic category (not a pragmatic one) functioning at the level of code, not text (see below) (see Reiser, *Syntax*, 32-35, who makes helpful distinctions for analysis of style).

    8. A preliminary, random study of the translation of verbal forms in the LXX from the Hebrew OT reveals the following:

---

[6]I depart from the standard definition of a Septuagintalism as a Semitism that has had a formative influence upon the language of the LXX: e.g. Dalman, *Words*, 41; Sanders, *Tendencies*, 199. Beyer (*Syntax*, 11) curiously defines a Septuagintalism as a construction rendered incorrectly from Hebrew into Greek.

ORIGINAL	TRANSLATION INTO GREEK
Hebrew Perfect/converted Imperfect	=Aorist in 80-90%/cases
Hebrew Imperfect/(converted Perfect)	=Future in 65%/cases and Present Indicative occasionally
Hebrew Participle	=Present Participle and Present Indicative in most cases, though Aorist Participle and Indicative occur
Hebrew Infinitive	=Aorist Infinitive and Indicative, and Present Indicative and Future all occur

Ottley's results, on the basis of essentially the same conception of the Hebrew tenses, are virtually identical, though he notes that the Present Participle is used more often than the Aorist Participle in the LXX, perhaps reflecting influence of Mishnaic Hebrew on the translators of the LXX (see appendix 3A). Several distinguishing features of this representation are: a surprisingly large number of Optatives and a large number of Futures used for the Hebrew Imperfect, which makes the LXX read unnaturally in many places (see Conybeare/Stock, ¶¶ 74, 75; Ottley, *Handbook*, 120-22), again suggesting possible influence of Mishnaic Hebrew (Blau, "Hebräisch," 97); infrequent occurrence of the Imperfect, usually translating the Perfect/converted Imperfect (e.g. Gen 7:18, 19); and a relatively small number of Perfects and Pluperfects, which often translate a Hebrew Perfect. Thompson (*Apocalypse*, 42-43) argues that the Greek Perfect is often used to render a non qal (oblique) Hebrew stem. Though this is true in several instances (e.g. Gen 9:2, 3; see Thompson for others), enough examples of the qal rendered by the Greek Perfect render this statement of minimal value (e.g. Gen 8:8, 11).

9. This study essentially clarifies and responds to the major arguments made by proponents of Semitic influence. Statistics on the NT rely heavily on Moulton/Howard's appendix on Semitisms. I have found their statistics accurate, though I have compared them with those who see a fairly heavy Semitic influence on the NT. If an error is made, probably the numbers will err toward seeing a stronger Semitic influence. The large number of instances referred to in any given construction (see 2 above) makes a slight numerical error relatively insignificant, however.

Examples of Supposed Semitic Influence upon the Greek of the NT

1. προστιθέναι used adverbially to render יסף (to add, increase = πάλιν, again)

While this idiom has been cited repeatedly as the sole Hebraism in Josephus (W. Schmidt, *De Flavii Iosephi elocutione observationes criticae* [1894], 514-17, cited in Deissmann, *Studies*, 67 n. 1; Thumb, *Sprache*, 125; Moulton, 233; Thackeray, 53, etc.), its presence in Josephus, who has a literary, tending toward an Atticistic style, makes one hesitant to view it as a clear Semitism. (Deissmann [*Studies*, 67 n. 1] calls it a lexical item, while Johnson ["Septuagint," 336] claims it is found in the papyri, though he cites no examples.) Thackeray has argued in fact that Josephus's usage in e.g. Ant. 6.287; 4.21; 14.157, 352 does not have the pleonastic sense of "again" but contributes semantically, while other instances (Ant. 19.19, 48) betray the hand of a Greek assistant who modelled his writing on Thucydides ("'Aramaism,'" 361-64).

In the NT, προστιθέναι is used only eighteen times (sixteen in the Gospels and Acts), with only five instances, all in Luke-Acts, following the patterns found in the LXX, where the sense of "again" is quite pronounced: (a) προσέθετο (προσέθηκεν) λαβεῖν (τοῦ λαβεῖν), is predominant in the LXX with 109 instances (e.g. Gen 4:2; 8:12), (b) προσέθετο (προσέθηκεν) καὶ ἔλαβεν is only found nine times (Thackeray, 52-53), and (c) προσθεὶς (προσθέμενος) ἔλαβεν (e.g. Job 27:1; Esth 8:3; Gen 25:1; 38:5), according to Thackeray, has approximate classical parallels (Thackeray [52-53], though he gives no examples, must be referring to the adjunctive Aorist Participle preceding the finite Aorist verb, a configuration that needs no illustration).

Pattern (a): Luke 20:11, 12: καὶ προσέθετο ἕτερον πέμψαι δοῦλον . . . καὶ προσέθετο τρίτον πέμψαι. Does this mean that "the farmer again sent another servant" (Marshall [Luke, 729] argues that προστίθημι means "to do another act of the same kind") or does it have the Greek meaning that the "farmer brought himself to send another servant" (Thackeray, "'Aramaism,'" 364)? The former interpretation approximates examples in the LXX, and is paralleled by Matt 21:36 and Mark 12:4 (πάλιν ἀπέστειλεν), though the sentence is acceptable Greek. This construction seems to reflect use of the lexical item, προστιθέναι, since the Aorist in narration is not of itself noteworthy. Acts 12:3: προσέθετο συλλαβεῖν καὶ Πέτρον. It is unlikely that Herod "again arrested Peter," since this is the first instance of Herod arresting Peter recorded in Acts. More likely the meaning is either an extension of the classical meaning, he "agreed to arrest Peter" after seeing the success with the Jews of his killing of James, or he "proceeded to arrest Peter." In either case the Semitic meaning is not appropriate. (Bruce [Acts, 243] calls it a Semitic construction, though his translation is compatible with a Greek understanding. Mandilaras ["NT," 24] cites an example of [a] in P.Oxy. 2182.14 [A.D. 166]: προσθέντος πεμφθῆναι ἐπ' αὐτόν.)

Pattern (b): Luke 3:20: προσέθηκεν καὶ τοῦτο ἐπὶ πᾶσιν [καὶ][7] κατέκλεισεν τὸν Ἰωάννην ἐν φυλακῇ. Here προσέθηκεν is necessarily independent as a predicate: "he added even this to all the things [and] locked up John in prison." The Semitic meaning of "again" or "repeat" is misleading. Plummer (Luke, 97) dismisses this pattern as not being Semitic.

Pattern (c): Luke 19:11: προσθεὶς εἶπεν παραβολήν. Whereas the Semitic meaning is appropriate--"He again spoke a parable" (Plummer, Luke, 438-39)--the syntax is not unnatural Greek, again indicating use of the lexical item.

The small number of examples, the appropriateness of the Semitic understanding in an even smaller number, and the parallels in Josephus discount Semitic intervention in Greek verbal aspect, though in an insignificant number of instances LXX enhancement may be entertained. This construction is better seen as use of a particular lexical item.

2. Constructions with ἐγένετο

This construction is one of the most widely discussed supposed Semitisms. (Major treatments include Johannessohn, "Biblische καὶ ἐγένετο"; Beyer, Syntax, 29-62; Delebecque, "Vivante formule," 123-65; Thackeray, 50-52; Fitzmyer, Luke, 1.118-19. Cf. Reiling, "Use.")

In the Hebrew OT, as Driver states, the writers often used וַיְהִי in narrative to prepare the reader for description of the action, i.e. as a historical narrative tense (Treatise, 89. Beyer [Syntax, 29-30] romanticizes this construction by claiming that ἐγένετο and its following verb are linked in an especially strong bond that gives the construction "Spannung und Eleganz." He concludes with

---

[7]The better evidence excludes καὶ (א* B D J), though it is included in א2 A C L W Y C f1, 13 Maj.

a *non sequitur*: "So verwundert es nicht, dass diese Konstruktion in anderen semitischen Sprachen nicht vorhanden ist." This construction cannot be Mishnaic Hebrew or Aramaic, since neither has consecutive tenses [Dalman, *Words*, 32; Segal, *Grammar*, 73]). Often in the LXX (around 400 out of approximately 745 instances of ויהי in the OT) the verb forms part of a larger construction translated with ἐγένετο (or another form of γίνομαι), an intervening temporal phrase and a resumption of the sentence. The intervening temporal phrase in Hebrew may consist of a preposition (often ב) and substantive (e.g. 1 Kgs 11:29), or occasionally simply a substantive (e.g. 2 Kgs 4:8, 11); a preposition and Infinitive (e.g. Gen 4:8); a conjunction (usually כאשר) and finite verb (e.g. Gen 29:10); and a few times a nominal sentence (e.g. 1 Kgs 20:39). Also, two or more temporal phrases may be used. The sentence may resume with any of a number of constructions. The most common (around 75%) is ו and an imperfective verb (e.g. Gen 4:8). Almost all of the rest continue with והנה (and behold) and: a substantive and Participle (e.g. Gen 24:15); a substantive and prepositional expression (e.g. 1 Kgs 18:7 without ἐγένετο in LXX); a linked nominal sentence (e.g. Gen 42:35); a substantive (e.g. 2 Kgs 2:11); a Participle and nominative sentence (e.g. 1 Sam 30:3); or Gen 29:25 (והנה-הוא לאה) [and behold it was Leah]).

The following translational patterns are found in the LXX. (a) ἐγένετο . . . ἦλθε. (b) ἐγένετο . . . καὶ ἦλθε. (c) ἐγένετο . . . ἐλθεῖν. Pattern (a) appears 145 times, (b) 269 times, and (c) only once: 3 Kgdms 11:43: καὶ ἐγενήθη ὡς ἤκουσεν Ἰεροβοὰμ . . . κατευθύνει (and it happened as J. heard . . . he came straight off). These approximately 400 instances are very close to the original number of examples in the Hebrew OT. In all but about 50 cases the initial ו is translated with καί, the others using δέ, especially in Genesis and Exodus (Beyer, *Syntax*, 31).

In the NT, ἐγένετο constructions with intervening temporal clauses are found predominantly in the Gospels and Acts, and then mostly in Luke.[8] Pattern (a) usually occurs with καί (Matt--5; Mark--2; Luke--14) otherwise δέ; (b) usually occurs with καί (Matt--1; Luke--8) otherwise δέ; and (c) occurs only twice with καί (Mark--1; Acts--1) otherwise with δέ. The statistical distribution is as follows (see Moulton/Howard, 426-27, for detailed chart; Beyer [*Syntax*, 31] includes Mark 2:15, the D readings in Acts, and Acts 10:25).

---

[8]ἐγένετο occurs in these books and the NT elsewhere, but not with the sense of "it came to pass" and not in one of the three patterns discussed. ἐγένετο is found approximately 13 times total in Matthew, 18 in Mark, 71 in Luke, 54 in Acts, 17 in John, 7 in Paul, and 23 in the remaining books.

(a) ἐγένετο . . . ἦλθε.		(b) ἐγένετο . . . καὶ ἦλθε.		(c) ἐγένετο . . . ἐλθεῖν.	
Matthew	5	Matthew	1	Matthew	0
Mark	2	Mark	0	Mark	1[9]
Luke	22	Luke	11	Luke	5[10]
Acts	0[11]	Acts	0[12]	Acts	16[13]
				(7 in Acts 1-15)	

Several important observations may be made. The first set of comments is concerned with the entire grammatical construction.

Direct dependence upon the Hebrew by the LXX is considered an unavoidable conclusion by most scholars, since pattern (b), the predominant pattern in the Hebrew OT, is also the predominant pattern in the LXX. And the non-translated books shun the pattern, using instead συνέβη and the Infinitive (cf. also Gen 41:13; 42:38). The evidence is strong, but not unequivocal, because of uneven distribution in the LXX. The preponderance of pattern (b) is on account of the later historical books (in Judges through to 4 Kingdoms pattern [b] occurs 164 times to 26 of pattern [a]), which, known for their stilted Greek, follow (b) rather slavishly, while the Pentateuch, especially Genesis and Exodus, and the prophets prefer pattern (a). In the Pentateuch and the prophets pattern (a) occurs 78 times (Genesis 34, Exodus 12, prophets 28) while (b) occurs 51 times (Genesis 25, Exodus 12, prophets 12). (Thackeray notes, for example, that in Genesis the Hebrew text has a second ו in 30 of 34 cases where pattern [a] without either καί or δέ appears, whereas 4 Kingdoms only omits καί twice [5:7; 6:30] when it appears in the original.)

This level of dependence does not hold for the NT, however, especially in verbal usage. (1) The most slavishly literal pattern, (b), is actually the most sparsely used, occurring in Matthew and Mark only at Matt 9:10: καὶ ἐγένετο αὐτοῦ ἀνακειμένου ἐν τῇ οἰκίᾳ, καὶ ἰδοὺ πολλοὶ τελῶναι καὶ ἁμαρτωλοὶ ἐλθόντες συνανέκειντο τῷ Ἰησοῦ καὶ τοῖς μαθηταῖς αὐτοῦ (and it happened as he was staying in the house, and behold many tax collectors and sinners came and sat down to eat with Jesus and his disciples). Even this example adapts the Semitic pattern, since the intervening Present Genitive absolute has no exact correspondence in Hebrew (Beyer, *Syntax*, 45), although it is used in the LXX (Exod 34:29; 1 Kgdms 30:1; 2 Kgdms 6:16; 13:30; 3 Kgdms 3:20; 13:20; 4 Kgdms 2:11; 8:5, 21; 13:21; 19:37). The Genitive absolute also occurs in pattern (a) Luke 9:37 (Aorist); 11:14 (Aorist); 20:1 (Present); and pattern (c) Luke 3:21 (Aorist and Present); Acts 16:16 (Present); 22:17 (Present). The subject-predicate order (instead of predicate-subject) of the second clause, with the adjunctive Participle preceding the verb, is more idiomatic Greek than the usual pattern of the Hebrew or LXX, although the LXX uses this pattern in a few places as well (Gen 26:32; 29:10, 23; Exod 2:11; Num 22:41; Josh 5:13; 1 Kgdms 24:17). And the use of καὶ ἰδού warrants further consideration (see below).

(2) Delebecque argues that all of the examples of pattern (b) in Luke (and by implication Matt 9:10) should be classified as examples of (a), except for Luke 19:15, since they contain either καὶ αὐτός or καὶ ἰδού before the second verb ("Vivante formule," 133-53). In pattern (a) the asyndetic second verb juxtaposes the first, he claims, whereas in pattern (b) connective καί coordinates a second verbal concept. It appears to Delebecque, however, that in Luke 19:15 (καὶ ἐγένετο ἐν τῷ ἐπανελθεῖν αὐτὸν λαβόντα τὴν βασιλείαν καὶ εἶπεν φωνηθῆναι αὐτῷ τοὺς

---

[9]See also Mark 2:15, which has γίνεται and no temporal clause.

[10]Luke 16:22 does not have a temporal clause.

[11]There is a textual variant at Acts 4:5 in D, which would give one instance in Acts. This would not alter the overall statistical significance greatly.

[12]There is one textual variant in D at Acts 2:1 and a questionable construction at 5:7. These would not alter the significance greatly.

[13]Moulton/Howard (427) do not include Acts 10:25, but do include 27:4. Acts 28:8 does not include temporal clauses.

δούλους τούτους [and it happened that when he came back, having received the kingdom, that he said for his servants to be called to him]) the connective καί is used after the fashion of the LXX translation with καί of the Hebrew *waw* in the apodosis after a temporal or conditional subordinate clause (cf. Luke 2:21, 27-28; 7:12; Acts 1:10). This is facilitated, Delebecque claims, by Greek usage, where καί follows a temporal clause: e.g. Hom Il. 1.493-95: ἀλλ᾽ ὅτε δή ῥ᾽ ἐκ τοῖο δυωδεκάτη γένετ᾽ ἠώς, / καὶ τότε δὴ πρὸς Ὄλυμπον ἴσαν θεοὶ αἰὲν ἐόντες / πάντες ἅμα (but when indeed the twelfth morning after that one came, then the gods who are all eternal came to O.); cf. Od. 2.107-08; Th. 8.27.5: ὡς δὲ ἔπεισε, καὶ ἔδρασε ταῦτα (as he advised, thus he did these things); cf. Hdt. 1.79.2 (Delebecque [130-31; 131 n. 14] lists further examples; cf. Most, "Did Luke"). Delebecque argues further that in Luke 5:12; 24:4 with καὶ ἰδού, and 5:1, 17; 8:1, 22; 9:51; 14:1; 17:11; 24:15 with καὶ αὐτός, the καί functions not as a connective between the verbs but as part of a formulaic syntactical unit (recognizably Greek although perhaps enhanced by הֵנִּה).

καὶ ἰδού announces the idea or person Luke wishes to emphasize: e.g. Luke 5:12: καὶ ἐγένετο ἐν τῷ εἶναι αὐτὸν ἐν μιᾷ τῶν πόλεων καὶ ἰδοὺ ἀνὴρ πλήρης λέπρας (then it happened, when he was in one of the cities, [that] there was a man covered with leprosy). This unique sentence lacks a verb in the second major clause, though this does not alter Delebecque's interpretation. Luke 24:4: καὶ ἐγένετο ἐν τῷ ἀπορεῖσθαι αὐτὰς περὶ τούτου καὶ ἰδοὺ ἄνδρες δύο ἐπέστησαν (then it happened, while they were perplexed about this, [that] two men stood by them).

καὶ αὐτός may either express an accompanying idea: e.g. Luke 5:1-2: ἐγένετο δὲ ἐν τῷ τὸν ὄχλον ἐπικεῖσθαι . . . καὶ αὐτὸς ἦν ἑστὼς παρὰ τὴν λίμνην . . ., καὶ εἶδεν (then it happened, while the crowd was gathering around, [that] he was standing beside the lake . . . and saw . . .) (see also 5:17; 14:1; 17:11-12). Though this theoretically could be an example of pattern (c), Delebecque argues for treating it as pattern (a) on the basis of parallels with καὶ ἰδού (Luke 5:17), and emphasis in Luke on Jesus' teaching, in which stress on "seeing" (the first use of εἶδεν in Luke) would shift the emphasis.

Or καὶ αὐτός may add a specific detail: e.g. Luke 24:15: καὶ ἐγένετο ἐν τῷ ὁμιλεῖν αὐτοὺς καὶ συζητεῖν καὶ αὐτὸς Ἰησοῦς ἐγγίσας συνεπορεύετο αὐτοῖς (and it happened, while they were conversing and discussing, [that] Jesus approached and travelled with them) (see also 8:1; 22; 9:51). (Fitzmyer does not make this twofold distinction, labelling all uses except Luke 24:15 as unstressed καὶ αὐτός.)

The result is that only a single example remains in the slavishly Hebrew category, the rest now being classified as pattern (a) influenced by the LXX. Fitzmyer (*Luke*, 1.121) recognizes the force of the argument regarding καὶ αὐτός, though he is more sceptical about καὶ ἰδού. (Johannessohn ["Biblische καὶ ἐγένετο," 204] cites only three examples of the καὶ αὐτός-like construction in the LXX: 3 Kgdms 22:32; 1 Kgdms 14:15; and 18:19, with αὐτή. He argues [203] that only Luke 19:15 and 5:1 constitute pure Hebrew renditions.)

(3) Pattern (a) represents a more idiomatic rendition of the pattern.[14] Though it seems dependent upon the LXX, it reverses the tendency to use pattern (b) by not placing a resumptive καί or δέ before the second verb, and is similar to the freer rendition of the Pentateuch.[15] Two

---

[14]Pattern (a) is now found occasionally in modern Greek, according to R. McKinley (cited in Moulton/Howard, 428), though it is not used to translate any of the same passages in the modern Greek NT. See ΤΑ ΙΕΡΑ ΓΡΑΜΜΑΤΑ. Moulton (17 n. 1) cites Thumb (*Sprache*, 123): "What appears a Hebraism or Aramaism in the Bible must count as Greek if it shows itself as a natural development in the MGr vernacular." While Pernot ("Greek," 105) calls the Gospels the first examples of modern Greek writing, this principle needs to be used very carefully.

[15]Maloney (*Interference*, 85) cites a single reconstructed (using the Greek version) example in Aramaic (4QEn^b 1.i.2), though it is too much to argue for this as a pattern in Aramaic. This pattern does not seem to appear in Mishnaic Hebrew either, which lost consecutive tenses (see Segal, *Grammar*, 73).

further observations may be made. (i) All examples of pattern (a) in Matthew use a ὅτε temporal clause: Matt 7:28; 11:1; 13:53; 19:1; 26:1, which has no exact equivalent in Hebrew and is fairly rare in the LXX, though it is idiomatic Greek (Gen 34:25; Judg 14:11 B; Esth 2:8 [LXX]. See Beyer, *Syntax*, 42, on Hebrew originals).

(ii) Luke uses the ἐν τῷ + Present Infinitive temporal construction in most cases of pattern (b) (though in 5:17; 8:1, 22, he uses ἐν + substantive). In pattern (a) Luke uses ἐν τῷ + Present Infinitive in 1:8; 9:33; 11:27; 17:14; 18:35; 24:51 and the Aorist Infinitive in 24:30 (εἶναι in 2:6; 9:18; 11:1), but he also uses ὡς + Aorist Indicative in 1:23, 41; 2:15; 19:29; the Genitive absolute (see above); ἐν + substantive in 1:59; 2:1; 7:11; and μετά + substantive in 2:46; 9:28. (Mark 4:4 uses ἐν τῷ + Present Infinitive while 1:9 has ἐν + substantive.) It is often argued that ב + Infinitive translated by ἐν τῷ + Infinitive is distinctly Hebraic (see Beyer, *Syntax*, 32-52, on temporal phrases).[16]

Though the construction is a natural translation of ב + Infinitive construct, several factors militate against Semitic interference in Greek verbal aspect. (1) Both Present and Aorist Infinitives appear in Greek, revealing aspectual choice not present in Semitic use of the Infinitive. (2) ἐν τῷ + Infinitive with a temporal meaning appears occasionally in older Greek, and seems to have increased in frequency during the hellenistic period (see Moulton, 215, cf. 249): e.g. Pl. Theaet. 167E: ἐν δὲ τῷ διαλέγεσθαι σπουδάζῃ τε καὶ ἐπανόρθοι τὸν προσδιαλεγόμενον (while discussing he might desire and improve that discussed previously) (cf. S. Aj. 554: ἐν τῷ φρονεῖν γὰρ μηδὲν ἥδιστος βίος [for while knowing nothing of life's pleasure . . .], a disputed example). P.Oxy. 743.35-37 (2 B.C.): ἐν τῷ δέ / με περισπᾶσθαι οὐκ ἠδυνάσθην / συντυχεῖν Ἀπολλω(νίῳ) τῷ Λιβικῷ (while [trans. "on account of" in edition] I was distracted I was unable to meet A. L.). Mandilaras (344) considers the use temporal, a use he finds in hellenistic Greek, though Mayser (2, 1.328-29) only finds two examples. Plu. Marc. Cato 9.4: στρατιώτου δὲ μὴ δεῖσθαι τὰς μὲν χεῖρας ἐν τῷ βαδίζειν, τοὺς δὲ πόδας ἐν τῷ μαχέσθαι κινοῦντος (he did not need a soldier moving his hands while marching and his feet while fighting). The NT and other Greek literature display a temporal meaning alongside others, whereas Hebrew ב + Infinitive is only seldom not temporal. Thus even the apparently stereotyped and LXX-dependent ἐν τῷ + Infinitive is better seen as an instance of Semitic enhancement, not interference (Soisalon-Soininen [*Infinitive*, 81-82] concurs).

(4) It is commonly agreed that Luke is capable of writing some of the most polished Greek of the NT (e.g. Norden, *Kunstprosa*, 2.483; and, more recently, Fitzmyer, *Luke*, 1.109), so it would be surprising to find him slavishly imitating Semitic style without some definite purpose. The examples bear this out. In Acts, he uses pattern (c) (all with δέ) virtually exclusively, a pattern

---

[16]An argument against Aramaic background for the Gospels might be found in use of ἐν τῷ + Infinitive, since spoken Aramaic does not have an equivalent (Dalman, *Words*, 32).

with other Greek parallels,[17] and he alters the pattern away from the Hebraic model fairly significantly in several instances: e.g. Acts 9:3: ἐν δὲ τῷ πορεύεσθαι ἐγένετο αὐτὸν ἐγγίζειν τῇ Δαμασκῷ (while he was going it happened that he came near to Damascus), where he places the temporal phrase first, separating δέ from ἐγένετο and the beginning of the sentence. Acts 10:25; 21:1: ὡς precedes ἐγένετο. Acts 21:5: ὅτε precedes ἐγένετο. This mitigates possible Semitic intervention, which the nine examples in Acts 16ff. (16:16; 19:1; 21:1, 5; 22:6, 17; 27:44; 28:8, 17) confirm. In the Gospel Luke uses pattern (c) six times: 3:21 (with ἐν τῷ + Aorist Infinitive and Aorist and Present Genitive absolutes); 6:1, 12 (with ἐν + substantive); and 16:22 (without a temporal clause). In the Lukan infancy narratives (a) occurs twice (1:8; 2:6) and (c) once (3:21); pattern (b) does not occur. Even Maloney (*Interference*, 85-86) must admit that pattern (a) cannot be a literal translation of Hebrew and, though maintaining (c) is non-Greek, that it too is not Hebrew or Aramaic. The resumptive Infinitive in this construction is usually an Aorist, though this too varies, with Luke 6:1; Acts 9:3; 28:8 (as well as Mark 2:23) using the Present Infinitive. The fact that ἐγένετο constructions appear almost exclusively in Luke, besides arguing against Aramaic originals for the Gospels, seems to argue that Luke captures the flavour of the LXX (enhancement) by using these constructions stylistically (Beyer, *Syntax*, 30 [but cf. 60]; Johannessohn, "Biblische καὶ ἐγένετο," 207, 210-11; Delebecque, "Vivante formule," 164-65); to argue Semitic or Hebrew intervention is not possible (contra Beyer, 60), since Luke also shows himself capable of varying his usage, rendering the phrase in accord with both the respected LXX pattern (a) of the Pentateuch, and the more hellenistic pattern (c). Whether in Luke any lines of movement can be detected among the three patterns is pure speculation, since Mark gives no appreciable help. A plausible scenario could see Luke altering pattern (b) to the freer (a) in the Gospel, though this does not seem to account fully for the absence of pattern (b) in Luke 1-2. Another scenario could see Luke emphasizing pattern (c) with suitable lexical and syntactic changes to give a sense of the LXX.

---

[17]These parallels relate mostly to impersonal verbs, the most important of which is συμβαίνω, found in Acts 21:35: συνέβη βαστάζεσθαι αὐτὸν ὑπὸ τῶν στρατιωτῶν διὰ τὴν βίαν τοῦ ὄχλου (it happened that he was carried by the soldiers because of the violence of the crowd); cf. Tob 3:7 AB. This occurs in the Greek books of the LXX, esp. 2 and 3 Maccabees: 2 Macc 3:2; 4:30; 5:2, 18; 9:7; 10:5; 12:34; 13:7; 3 Macc 1:3, 5, 8; 4:19. See also Th. 2.61.2; Plb. 3.11.3; 31.26.8; PSI 333.1 (256 B.C.); P.Lille ii 13.2 (3d cent. B.C.); P.Magd. 11.2 (A.D. 222); 12.4 (A.D. 218); P.Par. 6.17 (A.D. 126) (see Jelf, 2.335-36; Mayser, 2, 1.307-08; Winer, 407). Moulton (17), who sees modern Greek parallels, Moulton/Howard (427-28), and Fitzmyer (*Luke*, 1.118) argue that pattern (c) is a natural extension of common Greek usage. Use of γίνομαι (imperfective) is known in hellenistic writings: e.g. Mark 2:15 (καὶ γίνεται κατακεῖσθαι αὐτὸν ἐν τῇ οἰκίᾳ αὐτοῦ [and it happened that he reclined in his house]); P.Par. 49.29 (c. 160 B.C.); P.Lond. i 41.8 (A.D. 161), as Beyer (*Syntax*, 31 n. 4) recognizes, but Maloney (*Interference*, 207-08 nn. 130, 131) argues against this, since Mark's is an historic Present. 1 Kgdms 14:1 (καὶ γίνεται ἡμέρα καὶ . . . [and a day came in . . .]) is not truly parallel. Other tenses are also used with both συμβαίνω and γίνομαι; see Mayser, 2, 1.307.

Even if the case here presented is not entirely convincing that verbal usage of ἐγένετο constructions in the NT shows more enhancement by the LXX than direct Semitic interference, the case remains unmade that the use of ἐγένετο in narrative is anything other than normal Greek aspectual usage. (1) In most instances in the Gospels (unlike much of the rest of the NT), the ἐγένετο construction is used in the initial position of a sentence when resuming a narrative, and even to begin an entire section, which pattern, while apparently Semitic, also conforms to classical rhetorical word order and use of ἐγένετο.[18] (2) This pattern provides very little information regarding verbal aspect, and more regarding lexical choice. Luke and the other Gospel writers use the Aorist of γίνομαι in most cases, in keeping with statistical probabilities (and parallel with the classical use of συμβαίνω). In describing the progression of a narrative in Greek, as most grammarians agree this construction does (e.g. Moulton, 16; Winer, 760), what other tense form would be more natural? Or better, is this not a likely choice with γίνομαι?

3. Aorist for the Semitic Perfect

Several authors note passages in the NT which use the Aorist Indicative when arguably a present event is being described, suggesting influence of a Semitic Perfect (e.g. Moulton/Howard, 458-59; Black, *Approach*, 128-30; Turner, *Syntax*, 72; idem, *Style*, 16, 33; Thompson, *Apocalypse*, 37-42). A culling of the more prominent examples reveals the following as useful for exploration:

Matt 3:17; 6:12; 12:18; 13:24 = 18:23 = 22:2; 17:5; 23:2
Mark 1:11
Luke 1:47ff. (*Magnificat*); 1:68ff. (*Benedictus*); 3:22
2 Pet 1:17

a. Matt 3:17 = Mark 1:11 = Luke 3:22; Matt 17:5 (cf. Matt 12:18): ἐν ᾧ/σοὶ εὐδόκησα; 2 Pet 1:17: εἰς ὃν ἐγὼ εὐδόκησα

The use of the Aorist to capture God's judgment of Jesus given at the time of his baptism (or transfiguration) has sparked many and varied interpretations: e.g. inceptive Aorist, in which God became pleased with Jesus at some earlier time (Burton, 29; Lane, *Mark*, 58; cf. Winer, 347, who says Matt 3:17 is explained "very simply" this way); summary or constative Aorist referring to the thirty previous blameless years of Jesus' life or his preincarnate existence (G.G. Findlay, cited by Moulton/Howard, 458; Burton, 29; Gundry, *Use*, 32 [with bibliography]; Zerwick, 83: global Aorist); constative Aorist referring to the specific act of baptism (Burton, 29; Gundry, *Matthew*,

---

[18]See esp. Th. 5.45.4: καὶ ἐγένετο οὕτως (and thus it came about). Cf. Th. 1.100.1; 2.97.1; X. Hell. 4.5.11 (cf. 3.2.2, with ὡς δὲ ταῦτα ἐγένετο [and as these things took place]); Philostr. Life Apoll. 1.4; P.Wisc. II 48.3 (2d cent. A.D.): . . . οὐδὲν ἐγένετο; Sallust. 4: ταῦτα δὲ ἐγένετο (these things came about). The LXX shows similar usage in 4 Kgdms 4:8, 11 (καὶ ἐγένετο ἡμέρα καί [and day came and]). Blass/Debrunner, ¶ 472(3).

53); resultative Aorist, viewing the baptism or transfiguration as the crowning event to date (Turner [*Syntax*, 72] would probably describe the verb in this way); Aorist of proximate past, reflecting an ancient use of the Aorist allegedly on the basis of Sanskrit (Moulton, 135; Robertson, 842); perfect Aorist, i.e. the Aorist has taken on the meaning reserved for the Perfect tense (Fitzmyer, *Luke*, 1.479); gnomic Aorist (Robertson [837] questions this interpretation, while admitting the timeless Aorist as perfectly legitimate Greek); Aorist translating a Hebrew stative Perfect (Allen, *Matthew*, 29; tentatively Taylor, *Mark*, 162; Black, *Approach*, 128[19]); or timeless descriptive Aorist (Plummer, *Luke*, 100; Cranfield, *Mark*, 56; Robertson, 837).

Most of these proposals are easily questioned. Since there is no clear evidence of confusion of the tenses in hellenistic Greek, especially of the Aorist used for the Perfect, the theory of the perfect Aorist remains a problem of English translation ("am pleased"). Proposals of inceptive, constative, or resultative Aorists are dismissed on three grounds. (1) Their past temporal orientation demands a previous event. An historic Aorist is not to be dismissed categorically, but a consensus on the referential act has not been forthcoming. (2) Greek makes no formal distinction of these categories, thus each remains an Aorist describing a complete and here unspecified act. (3) Theological tendencies seem to have influenced selection of a particular exemplary act, none of which seems relevant to the particular Gospel at the point narrated. The Sanskrit Aorist must be dismissed not only because Greek does not grammaticalize remote and proximate past but because the proposal relies upon an untenable historical-comparative philology requiring a writer *and* reader to have known Sanskrit to communicate intelligibly. The gnomic or omnitemporal Aorist is used to specify regularly occurring (often natural) events, which are not being described here.

Whereas a past-referring Aorist may still be a possibility, two theories worth considering in more detail are the Semitic Perfect and the timeless descriptive Aorist. The argument for the Semitic Perfect must establish a probable line of connection between the Greek text and a Semitic source. It is not enough to posit that the language of Jesus and 1st-cent. Palestine was Aramaic.[20] εὐδόκησεν ἡ ψυχή μου (*Approach*, 128; see also Grant, "Hebrew," 119 on Mark 1:11). This is misleading, however, since the text is absent from Isa 42:1, which reads Ιακωβ ὁ παῖς μου, ἀντιλήμψομαι αὐτοῦ· Ισραηλ ὁ ἐκλεκτός μου, προσεδέξατο αὐτὸν ἡ ψυχή μου (Jacob my child, I will receive him. Israel my elect my soul receives him). The text Black cites, found most closely approximated in Matt 12:18, is in Theodotion and Symmachus, followed by Codex Marchalianus (Q). The possibility exists that a second Greek tradition was in use in the 1st cent., although no clear record of it exists for this verse apart from Matt 12:18 (Dodd, "NT," 107; contra Gundry, *Use*, 111-13; Stendahl, *School*, 10). The second possibility is direct mediation of the

---

[19]Black does not present any systematic discussion of his conception of the Hebrew or Greek tenses. It is worth noting, however, that his definition of the Semitic Perfect coincides well with the standard description of the range of uses of the Greek Aorist: the Perfect "corresponds, not only to the aorist, but to the perfect and present tenses in the latter use of present states or general truths" (*Approach*, 128). This makes it very surprising to see his justification of exploring the Aorist as Semitic on the grounds that "the [Aorist] tense defies analysis on Greek lines" (128).

[20]Dalman (*Words*, 280) argues that "there is no occasion for inquiry as to the Aramaic original," since a re-translation into Aramaic is quite different from any Semitic text.

Hebrew text itself. Though most scholars agree Isa 42:1 is the source of at least the verb εὐδόκησα, they have also examined Ps 2:7; Exod 4:22-23; and Gen 22:2, 12, 16.[21]

Whereas theological contacts between the OT and NT texts may be evident here, the verbal correlations are more difficult. And Bauckham (*Jude*, 205-10) discusses the strong possibility that 2 Pet 1:17 may be independent of the Gospel versions (cf. Bretscher, "Exod 4:22-23," 30, who notes that it follows Exod 4:22 "almost exactly"). The forms of the 'quotation' in the NT differ: Matt 3:17; 17:5 have 3d Person οὗτός ἐστιν and Mark 1:11; Luke 3:22; 2 Pet 1:17, 2d Person σὺ εἶ. Apart from the apparent difference in audience perception required by these constructions, and the difficulty in determining which is earlier,[22] even the 2d Person construction does not correspond exactly to Ps 2:7 (LXX) υἱός μου εἶ σύ or (MT) בני־אתה (lit. my son [are] you)[23] in anything other than the words υἱός μου and possibly σὺ εἶ (in Mark 1:11; Luke 3:22). Also the LXX is anarthrous unlike the NT, which has articular ὁ υἱός. Elsewhere in the NT when Ps 2:7 is quoted its word order is reproduced (cf. Acts 13:33; Heb 1:5; 5:5). Though it must be granted that the NT writer could have altered the word order, the evidence of linguistic dependence is lacking. If the author used the OT passage he seems to have been free to alter it to acceptable Greek phrasing in order to expand the complement to ὁ υἱός μου ὁ ἀγαπητός.

Regarding use of εὐδόκησα, Isa 42:1 MT reads בחירי רצתה נפשׁי (my chosen my soul delights in [Perfect]).[24] Two major differences in the Greek text are apparent. First is the syntax, in which the defective Hebrew version (Hooker, *Jesus*, 71-72) is rewritten in idiomatic Greek. The second is the change from the Hebrew circumlocution with נפשׁ to 1st Person in Greek. Though it is not difficult to conceive of the reasons for this latter change, according to Marshall, only once is such a change made in the LXX (Job 30:25) ("Son," 335 and n. 2, though he claims that the 1st Person construction can be a "legitimate, free translation").

The major difficulty seems to be the desire to translate εὐδόκησα with an English Present tense (e.g. Torrey, *Four Gospels, loc. cit.*), though it is not entirely obvious that such a reading is the best translation of Isa 42:1 MT. For example, Marshall indicates that Isa 42:1 MT records a past event (*Luke*, 156; he leaves the specific referent ambiguous), in which case a major argument for a Semitic Perfect in the baptism and transfiguration passages is eliminated. Apart from a past-referring Aorist, which seems unacceptable to most scholars, if a non-past referring Aorist is still argued for, no objection to this construction as natural Greek need be posited, since Matt 3:17; Mark 1:11; Luke 3:22; Matt 17:5; 2 Pet 1:17 are acceptable Greek syntax. The focus upon finding a specific temporal reference in the realm of past, present or future often encumbers discussion of Greek tense-forms. As several commentators and grammarians have argued, the statement "this is/you are my beloved son, in whom/you I am pleased" appears to be timeless, i.e. no deictic indicator in the context establishes a referential temporal sphere. This fits the context, whether the

---

[21]Isa 42:1: e.g. Carson, "Matthew," 109; Taylor, *Mark*, 162 (he suggests several other allusions); Schürmann, *Lukasevangelium*, 1.192-93; cf. Dodd, "NT," 106-09; Ps 2:7: e.g. Dalman, *Words*, 276-80; Moo, *OT*, 112-22; Marshall, "Son," 326-36 (who also entertains Gen 22:2; cf. *Luke*, 154-57); Gundry, *Use*, 29-32 (cf. *Matthew*, 53); Stendahl, *School*, 144 (though he says it "is not a quotation in the true sense"); Exod 4:22-23: Bretscher, "Exod 4:22-23," though he realizes this does not apply to the εὐδόκησα clause (310-11); Gen 22:2, 12, 16: Best, *Temptation*, 169-73, though his primary concern is ἀγαπητός.

[22]Gundry (*Matthew*, 52-53) argues that the 2d Person is original and that the 3d Person reflects Matthew's diction (cf. Luz, *Matthäus*, 1.156, who uses the change in Person to argue that the voice from heaven is merely a quotation of Isa 42:1), while Bretscher ("Exod 4:22-23," 302) claims that the Matthean version is correct since John 1:34 seems to allude to it.

[23]This difficulty is reflected in the alternative reading in Luke 3:22 D, which follows Ps 2:7: υἱός μου εἶ σύ, ἐγὼ σήμερον γεγέννηκά σε.

[24]εὐδοκέω renders other words besides רצה in e.g. 2 Kgs 22:20; Mal 2:17; 1 Chr 29:23; Jer 2:37. See Lentzen-Deis, *Taufe Jesu*, 191-92.

event is the baptism or the transfiguration. In the midst of the narrative a voice speaks from heaven, pointing out a specific individual, Jesus, as the beloved son, and one in whom the father takes pleasure.

A possible parallel is Arr. 1.1.1-2, where the historian comments upon the trustworthiness of his sources: Πτολεμαῖος . . . καὶ Ἀριστόβουλος . . . ὅσα μὲν ταὐτὰ ἄμφω περὶ Ἀλεξάνδρου τοῦ Φιλίππου ξυνέγραψαν, ταῦτα ἐγὼ ὡς πάντη ἀληθῆ ἀναγράφω. . . . ἀλλ' ἐμοὶ Πτολεμαῖός τε καὶ Ἀριστόβουλος πιστότεροι ἔδοξαν ἐς τὴν ἀφήγησιν (whatever things both P. and A. write concerning A. son of P., I write as entirely true . . . . but P. and A. seem to me more faithful in the narration). Like the NT examples cited, these Aorists may be referring to past inscripturation and assessment, although the discourse does not make this explicit or necessary. The relation of the sources to the final historical document seems to reinforce a timeless use. Therefore, even if the NT and OT passages treated above show close theological and even grammatical similarity, nothing in the verbal usage points to non-Greek use of the tenses. (Gundry [*Matthew*, 53] argues that the NT turns a timeless use of the Hebrew stative Perfect in Isa 42:1 into a historical Aorist, showing that even with an OT background, the use of a tense in Greek must be judged independently.)

b. Matt 6:12

In the midst of the Aorist Imperatives of the Lord's Prayer is found ἀφήκαμεν in v 12 (Luke 11:4 has ἀφίομεν, which, along with ἀφίεμεν, is a variant reading in Matt 6:12; see Metzger, *Commentary*, 16). Several interpretations have been proposed: e.g. Aorist of proximate past (Moulton, 140; Robertson, 842); substitute for a Semitic Perfect "which is not actually a past tense," the instance reflecting Jesus' original language (Turner [*Style*, 33] argues against Aramaic as the original language; Black [*Approach*, 129] cites Joüon, *L'Evangile de Notre-Seigneur Jesus Christ* [1930], attributing it to an Aramaic Perfect; and others, including McNeile, *Matthew*, 81; Lohmeyer, *Lord's Prayer*, 181; Jeremias, *Prayer*, 92, 102-04; Beare, *Matthew*, 178; Hill, *Matthew*, 138; cf. Grelot, "L'arrière-plan," 548, who recognizes the difficulty in deciding upon the exact Semitic verbal form); or the timeless perfective Aorist.

With so much written on the Lord's Prayer, it is difficult to summarize the many issues (see Lohmeyer, *Lord's Prayer*, 160ff.; Jeremias, *Prayers*, 82-107). Although the probabilities are high that Jesus delivered the Lord's Prayer in Aramaic (Burney, *Poetry*, 112-13; Lohmeyer, 27-29; Jeremias, 85-94 [cf. idem, *Theology*, 193-203]; Grelot, "L'arrière-plan," 541) or possibly in Hebrew (Carmignac, *Notre Pere*, 29-52, cf. 230-35), the question remains whether use of the Aorist ἀφήκαμεν[25] is ungrammatical and, therefore, whether Semitic verbal usage has significantly influenced Greek verbal usage in this instance. The past-referring Aorist seems inappropriate on account of the lack of deictic indicators and the difficulty in positing a past event during the instruction of a prayer that includes exemplary teaching on behaviour (cf. Torrey, *Four Gospels*, loc. cit., who translates: "as we forgive"). Several scholars have noted, however, that the fifth petition in Matthew constitutes a conditional-like statement (Abrahams, *Studies*, 95-100; Moule, "'. . . As we forgive . . .'," 69ff.; Lohmeyer, 168-84). Though it is debated whether Judaism contained a conditional concept of repentance in its liturgy (the evidence seems to point away from it[26]), a conditional-like view can be found in Matthew. The prayer seems to be saying that if/as/when we forgive others, then God forgives us (see Bonnard, *L'Evangile*, 86-87, on the sense of ὡς here: "as," without chronological value, making the one dependent upon the other but expressing simultaneity eschatologically). This need not imply a temporal or simplistic causal

---

[25]ἀφήκαμεν is an Aorist, not a Perfect. See Moulton/Howard, 241; contra Moule, "'. . . As we forgive . . .'," 68ff.; Manson, "Lord's Prayer," 109; Guelich, *Sermon*, 294 (who claims it refers to a "past, completed action"); Beare, *Matthew*, 178.

[26]See Abrahams, *Studies*, 95-100, who cites Sir 28:3 and *m. Yoma* (end) as examples outside liturgical use. Moule ("'. . . As we forgive . . .'," 69ff.) adds others, including (70 n. 4) one citation of a conditional statement from the Afternoon Service for Sabbath, *Abot* 4.13, though the example is not clear.

formulation of forgiveness, since the conditional statement merely posits the condition and its result. The construction is rewritten in the prayer to conform to the command-like structure, thus placing the protasis after the apodosis. This interpretation is supported by Matt 6:14-15, where Jesus is recorded as giving true conditional statements on forgiveness. Whereas the Semitic verb may be behind this entire formulation of the Lord's Prayer,[27] the conditional-like statement presents no problem as acceptable Greek. Cf. similar constructions in the NT: Matt 10:25; John 3:12; 10:35, 36; 15:20; 18:23; Acts 11:17; 23:9; Rom 3:3; 6:8; esp. 11:17-18; 15:27; 1 Cor 4:7; 9:11; 2 Cor 3:7-8; 7:8; Gal 2:17; esp. Col 3:1; 1 John 4:11, with Aorist verbs in the apodoses of conditionals (see Péristérakis, *Essai*, 12-27, for classical examples).

c. Matt 13:24; 18:23; 22:2

Black (*Approach*, 129) and Turner (*Style*, 33) contend that all three uses of ὡμοιώθη in Jesus' teaching reflect Semitic Perfects of general truth, as do many commentators, such as Hill, *Matthew, loc. cit.*; Zerwick (84) entertains the gnomic Aorist; Moulton (140) suggests the timeless Aorist; Robertson (835) posits the effective Aorist; and Carson argues for a past-referring Aorist ("ΟΜΟΙΟΣ," 277; cf. Gundry, *Matthew, loc. cit.*; Bonnard, *L'Evangile*, 199).

Carson has made a strong case for taking the Aorist ὡμοιώθη as past-referring in Matt 13:24; 18:23; 22:2 (he argues also for ὁμοιωθήσεται as future-referring) on the basis of the three parables referring to what the kingdom of God "has become like." If Carson's contextual reading is correct, then the argument for Semitic influence is negated, since he can explain the verbal usage on the basis of the Greek language itself. Several other factors, however, must be considered. Carson appears to be correct to distinguish stages in the coming of the kingdom as depicted in the Gospels, but he tries to prove this on the grounds that the Aorist is past-referring (and the Future is future-referring), when clear temporal deictic indicators are lacking. Apart from a theological pre-understanding of kingdom, the context seems to demand a timeless descriptive use of the Aorist, similar to that found in Pl. Rep. 510A. Socrates and Glaucon are speaking, and Socrates compares the relation between reality and truth in a proportion: ὡς τὸ δοξαστὸν πρὸς τὸ γνωστόν, οὕτω τὸ ὁμοιωθὲν πρὸς τὸ ᾧ ὡμοιώθη (as the opinion is to the knowable, so is the likeness to the thing of which it is a likeness). The context makes clear that a past reference of ὡμοιώθη not only is unnecessary but seems to ruin the parallelism of the proportion. Instead, Carson's point can be made on the basis of attitude, contrasting that which is asserted as being in existence (Indicative) with that which is expected (Future).

d. Matt 23:2

Jesus reportedly says that "upon the seat of Moses ἐκάθισεν the scribes and the Pharisees." Again there are several proposals put forward: e.g. ingressive or inceptive Aorist, where the scribes and Pharisees "came to sit," emphasizing the existing result on the basis of the affirmation of the previous fact (Burton, 29-30; cf. Moulton, *Einleitung*, 220 note [cited in Moulton/Howard, 458]); effective Aorist, meaning "they seated themselves"; constative Aorist, meaning "they sat" (Richards, "Grammar," 284, who concludes that Matt 23:2 may represent a number of examples that "defy analysis on Greek lines"); gnomic Aorist (Zerwick, 84); perfect Aorist, meaning "they took their seat and still sit" (Turner, *Syntax*, 72); or Semitic Aorist reflecting a Hebrew Perfect and reminiscent of Ps 1:1 with its three Perfects rendered by three Aorists (ἐπορεύθη, ἔστη, ἐκάθισεν) (Moulton/Howard, 458; cf. also Turner, *Syntax*, 2; idem, *Style*, 3; Wellhausen, *Einleitung* [1st ed.], 25; Black, *Approach*, 28; Grant, "Hebrew," 119).

A refutation of most of these proposals can be found under a. above. In this instance the Semitic Perfect would be plausible, except that a Greek idiom has been overlooked, in which καθίζω (+ ἐπί) means "to sit on X's seat" or "to succeed X." Carson ("Matthew," 472), who notes this usage, cites Exod 11:5; 12:29; 3 Kgdms 1:35, 46; 2:12; 16:11; 4 Kgdms 15:12; Ps 131:12; J. Ant. 7.353. See also Ar. Clouds 254; Th. 1.126.10. Thus Matthew says that the

---

[27]Gundry (*Matthew*, 108) argues that "Matthew has simply assimilated the verb [ἀφήκαμεν] to its aorist tense in the first clause. At most, the Aramaic perfectum praesens is a happy coincidence"; cf. Grelot, "L'arrière-plan," 548.

scribes and the Pharisees succeeded Moses, with the past-referring use of the Aorist making good sense of the passage.

e. Luke 1:47-55 (*Magnificat*) and 1:68-79 (*Benedictus*)

Of all the passages in the NT, probably the Lukan hymns are cited as, if not translated directly from Hebrew (Torrey, *Translated Gospels*, 28), the most heavily Semitic through influence of the LXX (Farris [*Hymns*, 31-66] surveys the major issues, deciding they came from Hebrew sources [62]). As Blass/Debrunner (¶ 4[2]) say, "the language of the LXX appeared to be very appropriate to a solemn and dignified style; the two hymns in Luke 1:46-55 and 68-79, both couched entirely in the style of the OT, afford the best examples of this. . . ." Whereas there is an abundance of material in the scholarly literature on parallelism, vocabulary, and syntax of the hymns, little is written in explanation of the Aorist verb forms. This includes the major grammars and Black, who devotes several pages to parallelism (*Approach*, 151-56) but only mentions the verbs briefly.[28] The verbs which seem to give the most difficulty are 1:47, 51-53, 68b, 70. (Farris treats the noticeable shift to the Future in 1:48b [119] and 76 [138-39]. While no one seems to mention these as Semitisms, could they be an imitation by Luke of the LXX, with a Future juxtaposed to an Aorist ?)

1:47b: ἠγαλλίασεν appears to be used in parallel with the Present verb in v 47a. It has been interpreted as: e.g. ingressive Aorist (Brown, *Birth*, 336); Hebrew consecutive Imperfect which, though normally referring to the past, can take present value (Marshall, *Luke*, 82; cf. Zerwick, 85, citing Joüon; Farris, 117-18, who says the verb functions "in precisely the same way as the present of v 46b," but translates it "has rejoiced"); Hebrew stative Perfect (Black, *Approach*, 151; Winter, "Magnificat," 343, who contends that the hymn [vv 46b-55] is a Maccabean Psalm of Thanksgiving sung after a victorious battle and placed here by Luke); or unmarked timeless Aorist (Fitzmyer, *Luke*, 1.366) in opposition to the marked Present. Buth has argued a variation of the last proposal in support of direct translation from Hebrew. Positing that Hebrew evidences alteration of tense forms as "rhetorical, non-semantic, structural" devices ("Tenses," 67), and citing supposed examples in the Psalms and QL, Buth reconstructs the Hebrew original and argues that Luke 1:47 is a faithful rendition.[29]

It has long been known that tense alternation is not only a phenomenon of Hebrew poetry but Greek as well (e.g. E. Med. 272, 707, 791), including

---

[28]Farris (*Hymns, passim*) has a good survey, as does Segert, "Structures"; on tense alternation in Hebrew poetry see Berlin, *Dynamics*, 35-36; Kugel, *Idea*, 18-19; and for examples Dahood, *Psalms*, 3.420-24.

[29]Buth's theory is not convincing. (1) He misunderstands the nature of verbal aspect and its relation to tense and the referential world; (2) he confuses his terminology, referring to the Hebrew tense forms by formal characteristics, temporal reference and kind of action depicted; (3) his examples, supported by comparison with the LXX, Peshitta and Targums, are not convincing (see de Vries, "Syntax"); (4) he does not consider the full range of possible solutions, e.g. privative opposition in Hebrew; and (5) his solution does not work for vv 51-53 (see below).

hellenistic poetry. In the Greek Anthology, in 5.212,[30] the speaker euphorically states that the sound of love is always (αἰεί) springing about (δινεῖ, Present) in his ears, and his eyes present (φέρει, Present) tears as an offering (lines 1-2). He continues that neither the night nor daylight sleep (οὐδ᾽ ἡ νύξ οὐ φέγγος ἐκοίμισεν, Aorist), but already (ἤδη) he lies under its charm (Present verb) (lines 3-4). The Aorist is used here with a present, timeless, or omnitemporal sense (anything apparently but past), in parallel with Present forms. A contrasting formal pattern is found in 5.3, where the poet says that dawn has come (ἔβη, Aorist)[31] and the rooster, heralding (κηρύσσων, Present Participle) it, has been crowing for a long time (πάλαι . . . ἄγει, Present). These examples argue against necessarily finding Semitic intervention in the poetry of the Lukan hymns, although Semitic enhancement on the basis of a Semitic source may remain a possibility. As Segert ("Structures," 1441) says, "Even though Greek is a language of different linguistic family [from Semitic languages], its inflectional character and its syntactic flexibility allowed a quite faithful rendering of those poetic structures and devices of Hebrew and Aramaic poetry which were not strictly bound to their phonological features."

> 1:51-53: The six Aorists may be interpreted as: e.g. gnomic Aorists (Zerwick, 84; Brown, Birth, 363, who asks why, if the verbs summarize God's normal way of acting, the Present was not used); prophetic Aorists based presumably on the Hebrew prophetic Perfect (Brown, 363); other acceptable translations of Hebrew Perfects (Ellis, Luke, 32-33; Zerwick, 85); or past-referring Aorists.

Farris argues (Hymns, 114-16) that the hymn's eschatological tension demands more than simple reference to a past event (constative Aorist) or to God's certain fulfilment in the future (prophetic Perfect). After rejecting the argument for a gnomic Aorist on the basis of the supposed fact that there are "few examples of the gnomic aorist in NT Greek" (114) (see chapt. 4), and rejecting an argument for translation of the Hebrew Perfect since this would isolate vv 51-53 from the rest of the passage and ruin the relation to both v 49 and vv 54-55, Farris argues for a solution that he claims does justice to the hymn's complexity, i.e. he tries to combine all the solutions. He believes the verb refers to (1) the great thing God has done, i.e. the coming of Christ; (2) the characteristic nature of God's act; and (3) the consequences of the action which reach into the coming age. "In fact," he says, "so decisive is the event that one can speak as if the age to come had already arrived, in the aorist [?]" (115-16). Farris concludes, "The Magnificat speaks of a past event with future, indeed eternal, consequences. This eschatological tension between the fulfilled and the not yet to be fulfilled is not entirely uncharacteristic of the New Testament" (116). Perhaps theologically this is not uncharacteristic of the NT, but it surely is uncharacteristic of the Aorist. Farris unloads his theology of the hymns on the six Aorists in vv 51-53, combining them in a way which does little to clarify use of the Aorist itself. While the Aorist has the semantic capability of referring to a past event, an event with future consequences, a present reality, and God's characteristic way of acting, it is highly unlikely pragmatically that a writer would use a single Aorist with all of these implicatures. Farris rather attempts to use the Aorist to bolster his theological conceptions. His final appeal to authority--claiming that several notable scholars have interpreted the Aorist this way--is an unfortunate weakness in his argument. Rather, Farris has shown that, though the theology of the passage may be complex, the deictic indicators establish the past-referring Aorist as a perfectly acceptable interpretation of these Aorists. The general reference to God's past mercy in v 50 provides an immediate context for reference to his behaviour in the past, vv 51-53, confirmed by his reference to OT Israel in v 54. Brown (Birth, 363), however,

---

[30]This poem is attributed to Meleager. Though born in Gadara in Syria (140 B.C.) and educated in Tyre, he became "a master of Hellenistic love poetry" and died in Greece, probably never returning home (Hengel, Judaism, 83-85, quotation 84).

[31]Gow/Page render ὄρθρος ἔβη as "the dawn-twilight has passed" (1ine 17), retaining the past sense of the Aorist, although they admit in their notes: "ἔβη: has passed, though we know no close parallel for this aor. See however Gildersleeve Gk Synt. ¶ 249" (Anthology, 2.26), where he refers to "When the perfect is used as a present, the aorist may take a perfect translation" (108).

overstresses the necessity for the Aorist to refer to a specific past event. He believes he has circumvented the difficulty by claiming that, though the "definite action in the past" referred to is the death and resurrection of Jesus, the author places the words on Mary's lips after that event (cf. D. Brown, "Aorist," 77). The theological constructs (Farris is right in seeing the eschatological thrust) are provided not by the Aorists themselves but by the entire argument of the hymn (cf. Tannehill, "Magnificat," 274 n. 26, who notes the "remarkable use of the aorist tenses" in vv 51-54).

1:68b, 70: The Aorists may refer to God's past actions in Israel's redemption (Farris, *Hymns*, 135), though Marshall wisely notes, "the question of the timelessness of the verb arises" (*Luke*, 90; see my chapt. 4).

This brief summary allows several closing observations.

(1) For virtually every example, some scholars posit that the Aorist can be explained along Greek lines, whereas others contend that an appeal to Semitic background or influence must be made. In the particularly difficult cases cited the explanations by the standard grammars (besides often being contradictory) often fail to satisfy, usually because there is an overdependence upon interpreting the Greek Aorist in the Indicative, as essentially temporal rather than aspectual.

(2) As observed in chapt. 2 (cf. chapt. 4), the Aorist in Greek first and foremost indicates perfective aspect but may, though does not necessarily, implicate relative temporal reference by means of various deictic indicators. In those cases where deixis is not limited, the Aorist can be used omnitemporally (gnomic Aorist seems to fall into this category), timelessly (without reference to a specific time), as well as present and future-referring, leaving perfective aspect as the essential semantic component.

(3) The Biblical Hebrew Perfect is aspectual (see appendix 3A), and as Black and others have stated, may be used for past, present or future temporal reference. An interesting correlation is seen. In the examples cited it is possible to posit Semitic enhancement of the perfective Aorist by the Semitic Perfect. This is entirely in keeping with the pattern observed in the LXX as well. But in this, the author does not necessarily depart from acceptable use of the Greek verb.

(4) The question is one of where to place the emphasis. The most likely place to find Semitic influence on verbal aspect is in Luke 1-2 (the hymns), and there is no doubt that these hymns reflect Semitic poetic style in their structure and language (they probably echo the Psalms via the LXX), but even here the verbal pattern is consistent and wholly within the scope of Greek usage. In a writer such as Luke this argues for conscious, stylistic imitation of the LXX to enhance his final product.

4. Historic Present and Imperfect for Aramaic Participle
a. Historic Present

Since Allen on Mark and Burney on John to the present, scholars have argued that the proportionately high frequency of this usage argues for an Aramaic *Vorlage*. (For figures see Moulton/Howard, 456; Hawkins, *Horae Synopticae*, 144-49; Kilpatrick, "Present" [who discusses the numbers on the basis of textual variants]; Osburn, "Present" [disputing Kilpatrick]; Burney, *Origins*, 87-90 [contra Colwell, *Greek*, 64-67]; O'Rourke, "Present," 585-90; Mussies, *Morphology*, 333. Page ratios are my own, rough figures.)

Mark 151 instances (72 speaking)	2.55/page	(Nestle/Aland)
Matthew 93 instances (68 speaking)	1.08/page	(Nestle/Aland)
Luke 11 instances (8 speaking)	.11/page	(Nestle/Aland)
John 164 instances (121 speaking)	2.27/page	(Nestle/Aland)
Acts 13 instances (11 speaking)	.15/page	(Nestle/Aland)
Revelation 153 instances (111 speaking)	3.18/page	(Nestle/Aland)

From analysis of the Aramaic verbal systems (see appendix 3A), just such a transference could be expected, but Aramaic scholars today do not seem to consider this pattern distinctly Aramaic (Sanders, *Tendencies*, 253). And this is rightly so, as the historic Present is universally attested in Greek literature as a marked use of the imperfective aspect in narration. (See Eriksson, *Präsens*, esp. 8-24 [see grammars also, e.g. Stahl, 90-92], though he defines the historic Present as a stylistic use of the Present to introduce a point thought by the author to be important in the description of a series of events. I instead emphasize the role of verbal aspect in tense usage [see chapt. 4].)

Though Homer is said not to use the historic Present but confine himself to the Imperfect (this judgment can be questioned; see Lilja, *Style*, 101-03), it is found in a variety of ancient Greek writings, from the earliest historians (Lilja, 104ff.), to the tragedians (e.g. A. Pers. 191-207; the prologues of Euripides [except Medea] and the dialogues of Sophocles), to the major historians (e.g. Hdt. 9.64.2 [cf. 9.63.2]; Th. 4.117.3 [cf. 4.117.1]; X. Anab. 1.1.1; 1.2.5ff.),[32] and even to Plato very occasionally (e.g. Crito 43B; Lach. 184D). Eriksson concludes that the historic Present in hellenistic writing died and was never fully revived in historical narrative prose, but remained in the *Volkssprache* and was employed in classicistic historical writing (*Präsens*, 112). Thus the *Volkssprache* and the classicistic and artistic language at this point stand roughly in opposition to the literary prose (113), perhaps accounting for Polybius's relatively low frequency of usage (e.g. 1.9.3; 2.25.2;[33] Colwell [*Greek*, 65] blames Epictetus's lack of narrative). LXX

---

[32]Thackeray (*Septuagint*, 21 n. 1) provides the following statistics for the first three books of the major historians: Herodotus 206 historic Presents (.52/page), Thucydides 218 (.73/page), and Xenophon 61 (.52/page). (Page ratios are correlated with Nestle/Aland text.)

[33]Thackeray (*Septuagint*, 21 n. 1) counts 40 in the first three books (.11/page, the same approximate rate as in Luke), while Eriksson (*Präsens*, 30) counts 20 in Book 1, 5 in Book 2, 9 in Book 3, 10 in Book 4, and 9 in Book 5. Cf. de Foucault, *Recherches*, 127-28.

usage in the historical books is relatively frequent, though not excessive (337 occurrences),[34] while the papyri display a full range of uses spanning the 2d cent. B.C. to the 4th cent. A.D. (e.g. BGU 291.8-13 [c. A.D. 170]; see Mayser, 2, 1.131-32; Mandilaras, 109). Several postclassical Greek historians evidence the use of the historic Present as well, including Dionysius of Halicarnassus, Nicolaus of Damascus, Arrian, and Herodian,[35] with Josephus using the historic Present more than almost any other historical writer.[36] Noteworthy is Apollodorus, who in one section (3.11.1-15.4) of about 20 pages uses approximately 110 historic Presents (5.5/page; the figures for Apollodorus are my own).

It seems, (1) the use of the historic Present is a thoroughly Greek phenomenon. The only possible Semitic influence could be enhancement by the LXX in Mark, John or Revelation, but this seems unlikely, since frequency of usage is highly variable among the non-biblical Greek writers. The Synoptics display a wide range of frequency themselves, Luke having the lowest frequency, with a clear majority of instances occurring with verbs of saying, which Eriksson cites as one of the most frequent uses in Greek literature (*Präsens*, 15-17; Kilpatrick ["Present," 261] notes frequency of φημί in Acts as an Atticism), though it is not the only one. As Black (*Approach*, 130) claims, "There is nothing specially Semitic about the tense" (contra Turner, *Style*, 20).

(2) Though grammarians generally agree that the historic Present may be used dramatically to create a more vivid narrative than the Aorist or Imperfect can (Brugmann, 555, *et al.*), the essential question is whether the Present assumes perfective aspect (perhaps as punctiliar [Turner, *Syntax*, 61; Blass/Debrunner, ¶ 321]) or whether imperfective aspect is maintained (Mandilaras, 108; Moulton, 120), or possibly both (Robertson, 867). Debates about whether the narrator depicts himself as present at the time of the event or whether the narrator projects himself back into the event or brings the event forward to the present, seem to miss the importance of verbal aspect (see my chapt. 4).

(3) On the basis of the contrasting frequency in Mark and the Johannine writings,[37] it appears that Luke regarded the historic Present as inappropriate, perhaps (though not necessarily)

---

[34]232 in the four books of Reigns (.68/page) including 151 in 1 Kingdoms (1.72/page), 25 in Job (.24/page), and 24 in the historical sections of Exodus. This argues against Aramaic influence, since these books derive from Hebrew. See Hawkins, *Horae Synopticae*, 213.

[35]See Eriksson, *Präsens*, 39-69, on Dionysius who roughly averages 1/page in his Archaeology; 70-75 on Nicolaus; 83-101 on Arrian who averages 1.62/page; 102-07 on Appian who averages .2/page; and 108-11 on Herodian who averages 1/page.

[36]Josephus averages 1.88/page in Antiquities and 1.75/page in Jewish War. Ericksson notes that the ratios range from .73/page to almost 4/page in various books. Though Eriksson recognizes places where Josephus's use of the historic Present seems foreign, he contends that Josephus is typical of postclassical writers in conforming to classical norms acquired through imitation of classical writers and in his general tendency to form certain typological uses (*Präsens*, 76).

[37]Thompson (*Apocalypse*, 35-37) argues that, since the historic Present was "never used on a large scale" (36-37) in hellenistic Greek and usually then only with verbs of saying, "*present verbs with past sense*" represent the Hebrew Participle. But cf. Apollod. 3.11.1-15.4 with ἐπιτρέπω (permit), πίπτω (fall), ἀνάγω (go up), μίγνυμι (mingle), γαμέω (marry), ἐλαύνω (drive), κρύπτω (hide), παραγίνομαι (be present), καθαίρω (cleanse), λαμβάνω (receive), γίνομαι (become), τυγχάνω (obtain), κτείνω (kill), ἀφικνέομαι (arrive), ἀγωνίζομαι (compete), ἀνάπτω (fasten), δίδωμι (give), among others, none verbs of saying. Mussies (*Morphology*, 333-36) argues along temporal lines against the historic Present reflecting Semitic influence in Revelation, since the shift in tenses (often Past-Present-Future) reflects an author who was competent in the Greek tenses: why would he use all three if he could use just the Present to represent the Hebrew Participle? Charles (*Revelation*, 1.cxxiii) essentially concurs that John's use of the Present and Future tenses is not arbitrary, though there may be cases where a Present instead of a Future or past tense shows Hebraic influence (Rev 9:8f., 17-20; 13:11f.).

because he regarded it as a vulgarism or because he was influenced by hellenistic literary prose, while the other Gospel writers tended toward the *Volkssprache* (see Moulton/Howard, 456; Eriksson, *Präsens*, 26 n. 2). Of his eleven instances, five are found in Parables (Luke 13:8; 16:7, 23, 29; 19:22) and might be better considered timeless usage (see chapt. 4). The six other instances are 7:40; 8:49; 11:37, 45; 24:12, 36. Moulton/Howard (456) are wrong to posit that, like Luke, Matthew removes the historic Present when possible, since of Matthew's 93 examples only 21 are to be found in Mark; 72 are his own. Thus this construction cannot be used to prove the priority of Mark: what if Matthew or Luke were prior? In that case they did not change Mark but the reverse occurred (Sanders, *Tendencies*, 253).

b. Imperfect

The same basic arguments as in **a.** above are often made for the supposed proportionately high frequency of the Greek Imperfect in the NT, citing the following statistics (Moulton/Howard, 457; cf. Hawkins, *Horae Synopticae* , 51, who includes ἔφη [Mathew 15, Mark 6, Luke 7, Acts 15, John 12]; see my chapt. 10):

Matthew	79	=	1.16/page
Mark	222	=	5.4/page
Luke	252	=	3.5/page
Acts	314	=	4.5/page
John	165	=	3.1/page

Some think that, since in Aramaic the Participle is often used in place of a Perfect in narrative (Stevenson, *Grammar*, 56-57), the Greek Imperfect in the NT occurs as a translation. W. Allen finds support in Theodotion's version of Daniel, where of 64 Imperfects used to translate the Aramaic, four correspond to a Perfect, twelve to an Imperfect, 27 to a Participle, and 21 to a periphrastic Participle with הוה ("Aramaic," 329).

It is clear, however, (1) to argue for translation of the Participle by the Imperfect is simply to argue for a consistent rendering of the aspect of the Aramaic Participle, since the Aramaic Participle even with הוה is still imperfective (Margolis, *Manual*, 81; cf. Joüon, "Aramaïsmes," 215-17). This would be significant only if the frequency were such to draw attention to the number of Imperfects. (2) The flexible temporal usage of the Aramaic Participle (see appendix 3A) makes the lines of influence tenuous. To claim that the Imperfect of the NT is influenced by Semitic languages would require an exceptional number of Imperfects similar to the noteworthy use in Theodotion. (3) In selected passages used for comparison, Appian and Polybius use the Imperfect in relation to the Aorist 7 times and 1.5 times as frequently as Mark does, making it implausible that Mark's usage is dictated by Semitic intervention or enhancement (Moulton, cited in Moulton/Howard, 457); Josephus uses the Imperfect in relation to the Aorist with about the same frequency as Mark and far exceeding Matthew and Revelation (Robertson, 839, citing Gildersleeve and Schlachter); and John uses the Imperfect almost as frequently as Epictetus, and in relation to the Aorist less frequently than Herodotus, Thucydides, Xenophon, Appian, and Polybius (so Colwell, *Greek*, 68-71). Black (*Approach*, 130) admits there is nothing specially Semitic about the Imperfect. (Turner [*Syntax*, 64] and Radermacher [150] see the Imperfect retreating before the Aorist in hellenistic Greek.)

5. Present Participle in Periphrastic Tenses with εἰμί

Parallels in Greek from Homer on can be found (Kühner/Gerth, 1.38-39; Mayser, 2, 1.223-24), although Blass/Debrunner (¶ 353) discount this evidence, which Robertson (376) calls "abundant" (see my chapt. 10). Proponents of Semitic influence argue that periphrastics occur proportionately more frequently in the NT than in extra-biblical Greek, particularly with regard to the so-called periphrastic Imperfect, although the periphrastic Future (eight instances) and periphrastic Present occur fairly rarely (Moulton-Howard, 451).[38] Hence Blass (203) argues that one cannot fail to notice "the influence of Aramaic." The statistics for periphrastic Imperfects are as follows (based upon my chapt. 10; Turner [*Syntax*, 88] and Moulton/Howard [452] provide different lists):

Matthew	=	7		John	=	1
Mark	=	12		Paul	=	6
Luke	=	26			(incl. Pastorals)	
Acts	=	28		Others =		1

(1) Most proposed examples in John are fairly easily discounted on formal (see chapt. 10) as well as functional grounds, since "ἦν exhibits a certain independence in all references. . ." (Blass/Debrunner, ¶ 353[1]). Perhaps this accounts for Burney's failing to cite this construction as evidence of an Aramaic *Vorlage* for John, even though he notes the construction in the LXX and Theodotion (Moulton/Howard [452] note this; see Burney, *Origins*, 52-53).

(2) The examples reveal some interesting facts: Matthew tends to avoid this construction, but agrees with Mark in two instances (Matt 7:29 = Mark 1:22; Matt 19:22 = Mark 10:22) out of four parallels. And Luke reproduces Mark only once (Luke 4:31 = Mark 1:22) in four parallels, though they agree elsewhere (Aland synopsis does not recognize the Lukan parallel). This kind of finding prompts Howard to observe, "It is so often introduced by Luke when absent from the Marcan source that one hesitates to suggest its frequency in cc. 1, 2 in 'Proto-Luke,' and in Acts 1-12 as evidence of fidelity to Aramaic originals" (Moulton/Howard, 452; cf. Hartman, *Constructions*, 23-27, who posits several explanations). Though Moulton (226) admits "the imperfect is the only tense in which correspondence is close enough to justify much of a case for dependence," Wilcox on Acts (*Semitisms*, 123; cf. "Semitisms," 1017, where he sees a stronger Semitic influence, followed by Black for the Gospels (*Approach*, 130), is "rather inclined to doubt the value of the construction in Acts as a 'Semitism,' and in particular as an Aramaism."

(3) Several scholars have argued that the periphrastic Imperfect originates with the LXX, since the Semitic languages cannot account for the form and since Luke, known to be LXX-oriented, introduces many of the instances in the NT, possibly for stylistic reasons (Tabachovitz, *Septuaginta*, 41-47; Aerts, *Periphrastica*, esp. 52-75; Hartman, *Constructions*, 12-13, 23-27; following Björck, *HN ΔIΔAΣKΩN*, 41-73 [who attributes this to NT innovation]). If this is true (it is doubtful; see chapt. 10), the most that can be argued for this construction is LXX enhancement.

(4) This construction, like most other periphrastic constructions, can be paralleled in other hellenistic Greek, where periphrastics seem to be increasing in frequency (see chapt. 10 for examples).

6. Constructions with ἀποκριθεὶς εἶπεν

This construction is supposedly based upon the LXX rendering of וַיַּעַן וַיֹּאמֶר. It appears frequently in the Gospels and Acts, except John:

---

[38]Conybeare/Stock (¶ 72), noting classical Greek evidence, conclude that enhancement is all that can be claimed for periphrastic constructions in the LXX.

Matthew	=	45	John	=	0
Mark	=	15	Acts	=	5[39]
Luke	=	39			

In the Synoptics and Acts ἀποκριθείς could be considered strictly redundant in approximately ten cases (see chapt. 8): Matt 11:25; 22:1; 28:5 (possibly 17:4; 24:2); Mark 10:51; 11:14; 12:35; 14:48 (possibly 9:5; 10:24); Luke 13:14; 14:3; 22:51 (cf. Moulton/Howard, 453. Note that ἀποκρίνομαι is used outside of this pattern in the Synoptics and Acts).

(1) The LXX and NT are at the least idiomatically Greek, even if translating the Hebrew converted Perfect as an Aorist Participle or as an Aorist Indicative, with Presents and Imperfects used as well, thus pointing to use of lexical items and not to influence upon verbal aspect (Turner, *Syntax*, 155 n. 2; Doudna, *Greek*, 126; Carter, untitled, 249; Blass/Debrunner, ¶ 420[1]). Cf. approximate parallels: Hom. Od. 4.203: τὸν δ᾽ ἀπαμειβόμενος προσέφη ξανθὸς Μενέλαος (answering him, golden-haired M. said); Pl. Prot. 314D: ἀποκρινόμενος εἶπεν; P.Par. 35.30 (163 B.C.): ἀπεκρίθησαν ἡμῖν φήσαντες; cf. PSI 340.5-8 (257 B.C.) (Mandilaras, "NT," 26).

(2) The low number of cases of a redundant Participle points away from the phrase as direct imitation and toward at most enhancement by the LXX (and its varied idiomatic renderings) of NT Greek, using components that approximate Semitic/LXX constructions. Doudna (*Greek*, 125) goes further and says that appearance of the phrase in 2 Macc 7:8 indicates "the locution was present in the koine" (contra Turner, *Style*, 51). (Dalman [*Words*, 25] acknowledges that the idiom "was unknown in genuine Aramaic.")

Burney contends that, instead of the Participle, John uses a finite verb, ἀπεκρίθη (-θησαν), fashioned after an Aramaic finite verb. Of the 78 total instances in John, eleven occur with a connective particle opening a sentence, but in 46 instances ἀπεκρίθη is not followed by a companion verb of speaking (both perfective and imperfective forms are used) characteristic of OT usage. (Burney [*Origin*, 52-54] claims there are only two cases of unconnected verbs in the Aramaic chapters of the OT [Dan 5:17; 6:14] and two in the whole Hebrew OT [Cant 2:10; Ps 118:5].) It appears (1) the 46 instances (59%) without a companion verb follow accepted Greek usage of tense forms and display no Semitic influence. (2) Of the remaining 32 instances, the eleven with a connective particle reveal at best an augmented rendering of the asyndetic Aramaic, and thus at most enhancement. (3) Since the remaining 21 instances show the same verbal patterns as other idiomatic Greek examples it is difficult to posit Aramaic interference into or enhancement of verbal aspect, especially in light of Dalman's opinion. In John's case, as Colwell posits (*Greek*, 14), the line of influence may lead from John back to the Synoptics.

7. Pleonastic λέγων for לאמר

The Hebrew Infinitive construct לאמר, found approximatey 870 times in the OT, is rendered in the LXX by a form of the Present Participle of λέγω approximately 770 times (90%) and another form of the Present 20 times (2%), with about 80 appearances going untranslated. Even though λέγω is used elsewhere in the LXX, this constitutes the vast majority of instances.

Usage in the LXX has led several scholars to argue for Semitic influence on the widespread use of λέγων in the NT (Thompson, *Apocalypse*, 69-70 [who mislabels this the infinitive absolute]; Moulton/Howard, 454). Claiming "there is limited evidence for similar use of λέγων in classical Greek" (70), Thompson differentiates two distinct meanings of λέγων rendering לאמר: (1) the simple meaning "to say" (e.g. 2 Kgdms 2:22; Isa 49:9; Zech 7:3), and (2) as an introductory formula equivalent to "thus" with another verb of speaking (e.g. Gen 1:28; 8:15; Exod 7:1), which Thompson claims is the predominant group. This differentiation--if such a distinction is necessary--finds parallels in all periods of Greek.

---

[39]There is a textual variant at Acts 8:37.

(1) Th. 2.65.1: τοιαῦτα ὁ Περικλῆς λέγων ἐπειρᾶτο (saying such things, P. attempted); Pl. Apol. 29C: ὃς ἔφη . . . λέγων πρὸς ὑμάς (who said . . . saying to us); cf. Gorg. 512C1; J. Jew. War 1.515: πάντα λέγων τε . . . γίνεται (saying all things . . . he became); P.Fay. 123.15-16 (A.D. 100): ἐλήλυθεν . . . Τεύφι/λος Ἰουδαῖος λέγων ὅτι (T. the Jew came saying); Rev 5:11-12: καὶ ἤκουσα φωνὴν . . . λέγοντες φωνῇ μεγάλη (and I heard a voice . . . saying in a great voice [hanging Nominative]).

(2) Hdt. 1.88.2: ὁ δὲ αὐτὸν εἰρώτα λέγων (he asked him thus); cf. 1.118.1: ἔφη λέγων (he said thus); 1.125; Epict. 4.8.26: καταγγέλλων καὶ λέγων (announcing thus); BGU 624.15 (A.D. 284-305): πόλλα . . . με ἠρώτησε λέγων (he answered me many things thus); Matt 3:1-2: Ἰωάννης ὁ βαπτιστὴς κηρύσσων . . . λέγων (John the Baptist preaching . . . thus).

This example is very important, (1) especially in probing the theory of LXX translation. Apparently on the basis of secular Greek precedent the translators of the LXX utilized a Greek construction that shows a distinct aspectual preference (imperfective) when rendering a verbal form without aspectual designation in Hebrew. This may confirm that the LXX translators had begun to formulate some concept about the Hebrew Infinitive, i.e. placing upon it an aspectual designation similar to that in Mishnaic Hebrew (see appendix 3A). This may also evidence a widespread consideration in Greek of the act of speaking as "imperfective," although instead of pointing to Semitic influence on Greek this would point to the possibility of a Greek tendency influencing the translators of the LXX. (2) On the basis of secular Greek parallels, heavy usage of λέγων in the NT is at most a well-accepted Greek idiom enhanced by the LXX, especially since it appears in the "characteristically Greek material" of Luke-Acts (Turner,*Style*, 52, though he also claims the form is "on its way out" [150]; cf. Cadbury,*Style*, 170). Turner sees the solecism of the undeclined Participle, especially in Revelation, as foreshadowing later Greek development, until in modern Greek the Participle has but one indeclinable form (*Syntax*, 315), while Conybeare/Stock (¶ 79) attribute the disappearance of the Participle to the influence of biblical Greek (this is highly questionable).

Several other patterns suggested as evidencing Semitic influence may be dismissed.

1. The Infinitive absolute is only rendered literally once in the LXX, Josh 17:13: ἐξολεθρεῦσαι δὲ αὐτοὺς οὐκ ἐξωλέθρευσαν = הוֹרֵישׁ‎ לֹא‎ הוֹרִישׁ‎ (they did not destroy them completely) (see Thackeray, 47-50; "Renderings," 597-601), although Symmachus* reads ἴστε γινώσκοντες at Jer 49:22; cf. 1 Kgdms 20:3: εἶπεν γινώσκων οἶδεν ὁ πατήρ σου ὅτι ([David] said, "Your father knows indeed that"). The Infinitive absolute with a verbal adjunct only appears once in the NT, using the Participle: Eph 5:5: τοῦτο . . . ἴστε γινώσκοντες ([you] know this completely).[40] This is apart from direct quotations of the OT (Matt 13:14; Acts 7:34; Heb 6:14) (Blass/Debrunner, ¶ 422). This construction is found in other Greek: e.g. A. Prom. 447-48; E. Bacc. 1050; X. Cyr. 8.4.9; P.Teb. 421.12-13 (3d cent. A.D.) (see Jelf, 2.371; Kühner/Gerth,

---

[40]On whether ἴστε is an Indicative or Imperative see Barth, *Ephesians*, 2.563; and whether the verbs are even to be linked, Moulton, 245.

2.99-100; cf. Blass/Debrunner, ¶ 422. The Participial construction does not seem to appear in the untranslated books of the LXX [Thackeray, 49]).

2. The use of the Infinitive, whether articular, following a preposition, or serving as a complement (see Moulton/Howard, 448-51), does not relate directly to the issue of verbal aspect because of flexibility in rendering the Semitic Infinitive with verbs of various aspects and nonverbal phrases; it does not present enough examples of any single form to formulate generalities (one exception might be ἐν τῷ + Infinitive in Luke-Acts, already discussed); and it has parallel forms and uses in ancient Greek. Thumb ("Value," 201) asserts that hellenistic Greek reflects Ionic Greek, primarily in the retention of the Infinitive over a ἵνα clause. Might it be that Luke, rather than reflecting Semitic influence, is reflecting literary Ionic? (See Turner, *Syntax*, 140-46; Blass/Debrunner, ¶¶ 398-404, for references and bibliography.)

3. Resolution of the Participle (or very rarely the Infinitive) into a finite verb (see Moulton/Howard, 428-30) does not relate directly to the issue of aspect but to Mood and syntax, and certainly does not present enough examples for a generalization except perhaps in Revelation. Charles (*Revelation*, 1.cxliv-vi; *Lectures*, 30-36) argues that a finite verb is used in 1:5-6, 18; 2:20, 23; 14:2, 3; 20:4 instead of a Participle, and 13:15 instead of an Infinitive. Burney ("Construction," 371-76) suggests Rev 1:5; 2:2, 9, 20, 23; 3:9; 7:14; 13:11; 14:2, 3; 15:2, 3; and John 1:32; 5:44, as well. Note that in Charles's own reconstructions he posits an Infinitive or Participle of the same aspect as the finite verb, thus discounting Semitic influence on verbal aspect (cf. *Studies*, 89). Mussies (*Morphology*, 326-28), discussing the examples proposed by Charles, discounts all but one (an OT quotation). Resolution of the Participle into a finite verb can be paralleled in Greek from Homer through to the papyri: e.g. Th. 1.57.4; 1.58.2; Epict. 1.27.1; BGU 846 (2d cent. A.D.) (see Kühner/Gerth, 2.100; Jannaris, 505-06; Mandilaras, 366; Moulton/Howard, 428-29; Colwell, *Greek*, 27-28).

4. The Participle substituting for a finite form (see chapt. 8), often an Imperative or finite verb, is often discussed (see Blass/Debrunner, ¶ 468; Black, *Approach*, 130-31; Wilcox, *Semitisms*, 121-23; Moule, 179; Mussies, *Morphology*, 324-26; Charles, *Studies*, 86-87; Thompson, *Apocalypse*, 67-69; on Participles with "imperatival" force see esp. Daube, "Participle," 467ff.; Davies, *Paul*, 130-36, 329; Kanjuparambil, "Participle"; Moulton, 223-35; Turner, *Insights*, 165-68; Frisk, "Participium," 431-32; Salom, "Use"). This is primarily a question of Mood and not aspect; is limited in occurrence in the NT (e.g. Rom 12:9ff.), being virtually absent from the Gospels apart from Codex Bezae (D) (see Black, *Approach*, 130-31; Moulton, 224-25); and can be shown to be legitimate hellenistic Greek (see Moulton, 223; Mandilaras, 372; Salom, "Use"; cf. Mayser, 2, 1.340-46, who attempts to explain examples as anacoluthon or mere slips. In that case the Greek is sloppy, but not necessarily Semitic).

5. Other pleonastic auxiliaries (Moulton/Howard, 452-56) relate more to matters of lexis or represent syntactical patterns; have little bearing on the question of influence on Greek verbal aspect; conform where definable to the standard patterns of verbal usage; and are difficult to determine, since the question of redundancy is very subjective. Hunkin ("'Pleonastic'") provides a convincing argument against seeing ἄρχομαι as redundant in the NT writings, citing classical examples (X. Cyr. 1.1.5; Anab. 3.1.26, 34, etc.). (Cf. Thackeray, who, finding a number of examples of ἄρχομαι + Infinitive in Josephus Antiquities, makes a problematic distinction between classical and non-classical use, concluding that this, the only Semitism in Josephus [!], results from the "over-working of a form of expression, correct but unusual in good Greek, because it happened to correspond to a phrase that was frequent in the Semitic language" ["'Aramaism,'" 370]. He is followed by Doudna, *Greek*, 111-17; cf. C. Turner, "Usage," 28 [1927] 352-54, on Mark.)

6. Any pattern of asyndeton or use of καί (parataxis) is clearly a matter of syntax and not aspect, and on the basis of the distinction between Greek periodic and linked styles (Arist. Rhet. 1409A-B; [Longin.] Sublime 21; Thumb [*Sprache*, 129] finds this feature in Aristotle himself) is not unique to Semitic idiom. On parataxis in pre-hellenistic Greek see Tate, *Progress*, 1-4 (e.g. Hom II, 1.259; Od. 16.448; Hdt. 3.53 [cf. Hom. Il. 1.500-02]); and on hellenistic Greek see Reiser, *Syntax*, esp. 99-137. Brock (Review, 27) cites P.Oxy. 2435, contemporary with the Gospels (mid 1st cent.), in which Germanicus Caesar's visit to Alexandria Egypt in A.D. 18 is

recorded (cf. Radermacher, 218). The narrative portions use καί much as do the Gospels, he notes. On asyndeton in classical writers see Denniston, *Style*, 99-123; and in Epictetus see Colwell, *Greek*, 10-13, who finds striking parallels with the Gospel writers.

I have not discussed all the possible Semitic influences on the NT, a task that has been attempted with various degrees of thoroughness and success by others. And I have not discussed possible examples of Semitisms in the LXX which the NT clearly lacks, such as the overuse of the Future and the Optative. But I have discussed those examples which would seem to indicate the greatest potential influence on Greek verbal aspect, distinguishing between direct translation, intervention, and enhancement. Broadly speaking, after analysis of the impact of Semitic verbal structure on the verbal structure of the Greek NT, there is no reason to believe in sizable or influential portions of direct translation, no clear instances of Semitic intervention, and only several cases of enhancement, and these limited primarily to Luke, known for his conscious imitation of the LXX (recognized by virtually all scholars from before Moulton [13-19] to Dalman [*Words*, 37-41] to Sparks ["Semitisms . . . Gospel"; "Semitisms . . . Acts"] to Turner [*Style*, 45-63]).

3. GREEK OF THE NT AS HELLENISTIC GREEK. **a. Introduction.** The significance and importance of hellenistic Greek as the *lingua franca* of the Greco-Roman world is only now being appreciated. This section evaluates from a linguistic perspective the major findings, incorporating previous discussion in this chapter. This section is not designed to evaluate all the various data available but to synthesize and assess according to sound linguistic principles. Frösén (*Prolegomena*) discusses in detail the secondary literature. His reconstruction, though suffering some terminological difficulties, essentially follows my history of the language (see Mussies, Review, 89-94, for summary). (Helpful on this issue are Hudson, *Sociolinguistics*, esp. 1-72, 191ff.; Pride/Homes, *Sociolinguistics*; Gregory/Carroll, *Language*.)

b. It is well beyond dispute that there are few if any sections in the NT that are still held to be literal translations from Semitic sources, apart from OT quotations (including those taken from the LXX) and arguably Luke 1-2 (Riddle ["Logic"] calls the theory of translation into serious question; see appendix 3B on Martin's statistical efforts to determine Semitic sources). In a recent reassessment of attempts to find the underlying Aramaic structure in Jesus' words, Hurst ("Role") makes several trenchant criticisms.

(1) Scholars who make such attempts fail as linguists to appreciate the problems of polysemy in vocabulary: "One of the underlying assumptions of biblical study this century has been the idea that words have only one basic meaning which is more or less immutable and can be directly and painlessly discerned in whatever context they appear" (64). Barr among others has shown the lack of consideration of this factor among biblical scholars.

(2) Many biblical scholars have a naive view of translation theory, failing to realize that "Since words are polysemic, the word which [a translator] chooses will represent *only one*

meaning of the original word by only one of its own meanings " (64). Use of δόξα is instructive. A semantic shift of *kabod* from "worth, dignity" to "radiance" (Ezek 1:4ff.) was so powerful that it caused a shift in δόξα from "opinion" to "divine splendour." If the correlation of the two were not known, a retranslation of Ezek 1:28 (LXX) according to the standards of most Gospel retranslation would probably not use *kabod* (67-68). Traditional attempts to recreate the Aramaic of Jesus' time have assumed that each word has a principal meaning and that there is only one, or possibly two, Aramaic words underlying the Greek (67-69), neglecting the element of choice within each language's system of signs (63-66).

(3) These same scholars have a naive view of language, until very recently misconstruing Aramaic as essentially static over four or five centuries (68-69). Much of this difficulty is caused by the lack of contemporary evidence for 1st cent. Aramaic that Jesus could have spoken, 'requiring' use of non-contemporary material (71-72). Another difficulty is failure to appreciate various linguistic levels or styles (71). Hurst (73-74) points to semantic field theory within the context of recognition of semantic tolerance as the way forward in this discussion, although he concludes that "If there is evidence of targumic or dynamic equivalence techniques in the gospels, it would be worse than useless to attempt a reconstruction of one Aramaic term out of a given Greek term" (75).

Even Black, an advocate of the Aramaic source hypothesis, admits that only in the words of Jesus can translation from Aramaic be considered and that in the majority of cases the "'translation' is not literal but literary; in other words, it is doubtful if it can be justly described as translation at all in some cases. . . . The Evangelists, that is to say, are for the most part writing Greek Gospels, even where they are dependent upon sources" (*Approach*, 274), with two exceptions: parable of the sower (Mark 4:2-9) and parable of the well-behaved guest (Matt 20:28) (but here he depends on D).

c. The major works on the relationship between Semitic languages and NT Greek have concentrated upon the lexicon. It is admitted that some of the technical and theological vocabulary of the NT has been secured through Hebrew influence, either directly or via the LXX (see Silva, *Change*, 60-95, for a list; cf. Simpson, *Words*; and Hemer, "Reflections," who look to extra-biblical Greek usage). Unfortunately, much of this research is theologically motivated and not sound lexicography, as Barr (*Semantics*) was the first to point out in a strong way (see also Louw, "Wordbook"; Poythress, "Analyzing"; Gibson, *Logic*; Louw, *Semantics*; Hurst, "Role"). Concerning the rest of the vocabulary, however, the issue is far from settled. Many, like Hatch, have argued vociferously that much of the NT vocabulary is wholly unique to the NT and LXX, while few since Kennedy have set such a study in its overall relation to the whole biblical vocabulary. Only very recently, however, have the results of structural linguistics been applied to NT vocabulary (e.g. Burres, *Semantics*; Silva, *Words*; idem, "Style"; Erickson, *Semantics*; cf. Thiselton, "Semantics of NT Interpretation").

Silva's study (*Change*, 60-95, for treatment of individual words, and 97-139, for analysis; cf. "Borrowing"; "Semitisms") of semantic loan words, i.e. those words used in the Semitic bilingual environment of the NT that evidence changes in meaning (as opposed to words attributable to theological lexicon, literary creativity or pure accident), concludes that Aramaic influence is almost negligible (.5 of 1% of NT vocabulary has been influenced by Aramaic) and LXX/Hebrew influence is also extremely small (about 1.5% of NT vocabulary is Hebraically motivated). By comparison, in Turner's latest article on NT vocabulary ("Jewish"), he treats many of the same words as does Silva but leaves the impression that NT vocabulary is heavily influenced by the LXX and Hebrew sources: "both new words and meanings have come upon the scene through religious influence, revolutionizing the language if not altogether creating a new dialect (as becomes ever more credible when the semasiological changes are considered alongside syntactical evidence)." He continues, "Incidentally, we hope that a survey of these words will indicate the uniqueness of the Biblical Greek vocabulary and will caution the NT exegete against neglecting the new meanings and against relying over much on secular parallels" (169).

Why these two different views? (1) Both Silva and Turner are in surprising agreement about significant words that evidence some semantic shift, though Silva's treatment is more systematic, thorough and conservative in its estimations. For example, Silva describes use of ἀγάπη/ἀγαπάω in terms of a shift in hellenistic Greek due to the semantic shift of κυνέω (kiss to impregnate) and φιλέω (love to kiss), rather than reliance upon rather doubtful LXX usage (2 Kgdms 13:15), meaning "lust" (*Words*, 96, using Joly, *Vocabulaire*, 33; Barr, "Words"; cf. Turner, "Jewish," 149, who merely says, "Most important of all, ἀγάπη finds no clear instance in secular Greek of pre-Christian date"). (2) Silva has analysed the words in relation to the greater number of words that are supposed to be Semitically coloured and these in light of the entire NT vocabulary, whereas Turner lets the few speak for the whole, setting no larger context. As J. Lee emphasizes, even though several religious or ethical terms in the NT may depend on Semitic influence, for linguistic purposes the entire vocabulary must be considered, with no lexical item inherently more important than another (*Study*, 22-23). (3) Silva defines his terms much more precisely, using the categories of Ullmannian linguistics (e.g. *Semantics*; *Principles*, are both widely quoted by Silva), to establish classifiable results, whereas Turner utilizes essentially the same method that has been employed in biblical lexicography for years (this is not to imply that those who see significant change are either unscientific or must posit Semitic influence: e.g. Gingrich, "Greek NT"). For example, Silva (*Words*, 79) plots the development in meaning of ἐκκλησία from "assembly" to "church" and of ἀλήθεια from "truth" to "Christianity" as instances of semantic conservatism, while Turner ("Jewish," 152, who lists ἀλήθεια, ἐκκλησία, νόμος and παραβολή) says that "light from the papyri on such old words . . . is trivial and unhelpful for the NT, nor can such words be semantically assessed except in the richness of their Christian contexts." This is not to say that biblical scholarship can only formulate worthwhile results when it utilizes the techniques of modern linguistics, however. Abbott, in his critical review of NT vocabulary designed in part to illustrate the shortcomings of Hatch's methods and results (similar to Turner's), concluded that the NT vocabulary outside technical terms is basically untouched by Hebraic (LXX) influence. And Abbott wrote 85 years ago (*Essays*, 69; cf. Kennedy, *Sources*, as well).

d. If the Greek of the NT is not so heavily Semitized in lexicon or grammar as once supposed, what then is its nature? Often it is said that the Greek of the NT is "bad" or "sloppy."[41] But bad or sloppy compared to what? Usually the answer is in comparison to a select number of written texts of classical Greek. First, though the problems of investigation are manifold, since there are no native speakers, recent investigations of spoken Attic indicate that even texts such as Aristophanes's plays are for the most part "literary portrayals" of speech (Dover, "Colloquial," 16). After an examination of what sources there are, Dover intimates there may have been a sizable gap between spoken and written classical Greek, with spoken Greek evidencing parataxis, short sentences, and a slang vocabulary, all possible linguistic correlations with the papyri. Teodorsson ("Variation," esp. 68-71)

---

[41]Discussion of NT Greek is often conducted in the same terms as discussion of some modern languages. As Milroy ("Equality," 66) says: "It is usual for linguistic scholars to adhere to some variant of the doctrine of linguistic equality, i.e. to claim that different languages, or different dialects of a language, cannot be shown to be 'better' or 'worse' than (or 'superior' or 'inferior' to) one another. . . . Despite this, non-linguists have always believed that some languages, or dialects, are 'superior' to others, and they have often been prepared to express their views very strongly indeed. Commonly, minor deviations from Standard English (for example) are branded as 'barbarisms,' 'illiteracies,' etc., and it is clear that most people regard some regional varieties of a language as inferior to the 'standard'; views are also expressed on the superiority of one *language* to another, and these go back some centuries. . . ." Cf. Milroy/Milroy, *Authority*, 3ff.

even argues on the basis of iotacism (see Pl. Crat. 418B-D) that modern Greek pronunciation had already developed an "innovative subdialect" (68) in classical Attic, and was "probably used in everyday speech by the majority of the population" (71). (On the non-Attic features of Attic Greek see Schwyzer, 1.127-28; Costas, *Outline*, 46 nn. 2, 3, 5, 6; see below on style [register], where a similar continuum probably held for classical Greek.) Second, as Thumb says, "There are philologists who are accustomed to characterize all modifications of classical Greek as due to the decline or deteriorating of the language" ("Value," 182; cf. *Sprache*, 181. Moulton [*Science*, 8] characterizes the language of the NT as "the great literature which many classical scholars have despised because in the interval of four centuries the Greek language dared to grow"). The failure to understand the natural process of linguistic development remains the primary stumbling block to understanding hellenistic Greek. Greek has one of the longest known histories of any language variety, perhaps only comparable to Indian and Chinese (Thumb, "Value," 181-82). Hellenistic Greek must be acknowledged as a fact of linguistic history, having many common features with Greek of other periods, yet with its own unique characteristics--both progressive and retrogressive--developed historically. To claim that it is inferior Greek is akin to making the absurd claim that 19th or 20th-cent. English is inferior to Chaucerian English because it lost its distinctive syntax or Renaissance English because it lost its expressive Shakespearean phrasing. As Deissmann says of the Greek of the NT, it "is neither good nor bad" (*Philology*, 61). Those who make such distinctions Moulton calls "pedants of classical learning" (*Introduction*, 9). No one language-period can be held up as the standard language of a culture for all time. As Blass (3) says, "the Hellenistic language as a whole is in its own way not less subject to rules nor less systematic than Attic." Writers like Dionysius of Halicarnassus or Plutarch who were part of the Attic revival in hellenistic Greek, like Edmund Spenser and John Skelton in their day, were reactionaries, who, idealizing a past era, attempted to retard the natural progress and development of language. Thackeray's findings comport well with modern sociolinguistic discussion of language (see esp. Hudson, *Sociolinguistics*, 30ff.), when he (21) says, "the κοινή is not estimated at its true worth when regarded merely as a debased and decadent Greek. Though it abandoned many of the niceties of the older language, it has some new laws of its own. It does not represent the last stages of the language, but a starting-point for fresh development."

Before discussing more specifically the nature of the Greek of the NT, two important issues must be distinguished. (1) The first is the relationship between Greek and Hebrew verbal aspect. Each language variety maintains its own verbal systems which function autonomously, i.e. every variety has a network of verbal systems which language-users have developed to handle linguistic situations demanding use of a verbal component. Recognition of this prompted Deissmann (*Studies*, 69) and grammarians like Robertson (45) to argue that there is no correlation between the tenses of Greek and Hebrew. (McFall [*Enigma*, 184-85] hints at this throughout his work. Is this a residual strain of the Sapir-Whorf hypothesis, touted by Boman in his radical differentiation between the Greek and Hebrew minds? See Barr, *Semantics*, 21-45, 295; Lyons, *Language and Context*, 303-12.) They are correct at the level just discussed above--no language variety needs another variety to create its verbal patterns, hence each is independent.

Yet on another level, if there is to be communication between differing language groups, there must be some basis for intertranslation. In Greek, aspect is best defined morphologically but these broad morphological categories encompass specific contextual pragmatic uses, e.g. an Aorist (perfective aspect) can be used gnomically, narratively, etc. But when linguists use such terms as "perfective," "imperfective" and "stative" they mean that there seems to be something typological about this semantic category and quite probably other languages (Wallace, "Figure," 201; cf. Greenberg, *Universals*, 25-30). No language is wholly autonomous. (The fact that translation can occur is proof of this.) And it is probably possible to map the ranges of meaning among aspectual systems of various language varieties (Anderson, "'Perfect,'" 227). When these correlations are realized it is possible to speak of relationships among verbal systems, and it is upon this principle that the preceding investigation has been conducted.

Aspect appears to be the broadest choice in both the Greek and Semitic verbal networks (with the exception of Mishnaic Hebrew). The findings of this chapter reveal as well that the verbal network is unaffected in its structure by Semitic influence. Thackeray (27) states this conclusion more strongly: "The influence of Semitism on the syntax of the Jewish section of the Greek-speaking world was probably almost as inappreciable as its syntactical influence on the κοινή as a whole, an influence which may be rated at zero" (cf. Helbing, *Grammatik*, I-XII). This is further confirmed by the consistency of the networks of Greek verbal aspect from classical through to hellenistic times (McKay, 214; Humbert, "Aspect").

(2) The second issue is the nature of the language of the LXX (still useful is Swete, *Introduction*, 289-314). Gehman, using a simple argument, reasoned that the LXX reflected the common speech of Alexandrian Egypt: "The object of a translator obviously is to render a document clearly into the vernacular." On the basis of apparent difficulties in the text of the LXX when compared to the MT and since "it is well-known that the Greek of the LXX is the koine" (though there are differences), Gehman claims, "we can hardly avoid speaking of a Jewish Greek, which was used in the Synagogues and in religious circles" ("Character," 81, cf. 90). Swete (299), admitting the limitations of the translation ("the manner of the LXX. is not Greek, and does not even aim at being so"), contends the Alexandrian Jews wrote as they spoke Greek. (Rydbeck [*Fachprosa*, 186-99] finds the question as to the nature of the common spoken language absurd. He overstates his case. While exact details of pronunciation are not known, it is within reason to believe that the spoken variety was grammatically very similar to the written if account is taken of differences of register. By Rydbeck's reasoning, i.e. since no samples of spoken language exist no informal calculation can be made, nothing could be known about any language of the pre-recording device era.)

Gehman's argument provides necessary points for observations about the LXX. (a) It is not necessarily true that the object of a translator is to render a document into the vernacular. It is not even clear that the translators themselves always understood the original text (Barr, *Typology*, 15); in fact, the opposite often seems to be the case (Lee, *Study*, 18), since their work contains a variety of oddities, including neologisms, transliterations, and odd syntax.[42] Brock describes quite clearly how difficult a task translation of the LXX was: "the Greek translation of the Pentateuch was an undertaking totally without precedent in the Hellenistic world," since there was no tradition of Greek translation of oriental religious documents. The LXX still stands as the only long oriental religious text to have been translated into Greek ("Phenomenon," 12, 14; see Rabin, "Process," for a modern linguistic perspective on translation in the ancient world; Bickerman, "Septuagint," 175-99, for application to the LXX; Nida, *Science*, 11-29, for a history of translation).

This novelty is reflected in the overall translation itself, although Barr ("Sense," 381) disputes the difficulty of it (cf. *Words*, 188-94). It contains a mixture of literal and free translation within certain sections (for example the Pentateuch with its legal and literary sections), and the translation itself essentially developed chronologically from freer to more literal on the basis of a growing rigidness in the conception of inspiration (cf. the Pentateuch with the historical books with Judges B). The result is often a compromise, which is not consistently literal or free (Brock, "Phenomenon," 16, 18, 20-21; cf. "Aspects," 69-79). Thus Barr (*Typology*, 5ff., cf. 283; in contention with Thackeray, 13) gives six standards for trying to judge the various ways a translation may be literal and free, at the same time. As a result many passages just do not read well, as even Gehman admits ("Character," 81; 90): "The language of the LXX certainly would have caused trouble to a Greek who was not acquainted with the psychology of the Hebrew language [sic], its idioms, and its constructions." As Rabin notes, however, translations of religious texts especially display a great amount of "semantic tolerance" for deviations from close verbal correspondence between the texts ("Process," 9-10; while Büchsel ["Sprache," 142] calls the LXX an interlinear version and in this sense a Jewish Greek language).

(b) Gehman, by maintaining that the LXX is part of hellenistic Greek, while acknowledging that there are peculiarities in the language, tacitly acknowledges the difference between the idealized language and functional variation, especially as found in translated documents (Rabin, "Process," 13). Gehman's failure to distinguish along these lines, however, leads him to an unwarranted conclusion. The fact that the LXX utilizes Greek with a distinctly Hebrew cast in certain places, which no one would deny, even Deissmann or Moulton, does not mean that there was any Jewish Greek language in existence (Rabin, "Process," 25; Brock, "Phenomenon," 32). Of course, it does not say there was not, except for the basic difficulty of comprehension; thus Olley (*"Righteousness,"* 11) rightly calls Gehman's formulation a *non sequitur*. Comparison between Jewish writings originally in Greek and those translated shows a marked contrast, according to Lee (*Study*, 14-15), with the latter heavily Semitized. This argument was already stated by Deissmann (*Studies*, 69 n. 1) and Thackeray (27-28), and, Lee contends, never refuted.

(c) The fact that the Semitisms in the LXX are not consistent and the translators vary in their use of expressions can often be attributed not to a Jewish Greek language but to hesitance in deciding among a literal translation, a paraphrase (Brock, "Aspects," 74-79; Barr, *Typology*, 5-10), or even an apparent departure from the Hebrew text. For example, the Hebrew idiom for "to ask someone about peace, i.e. to greet" (שאל ל שלום) is rendered literally in Judg 18:15 B (ἠρώτησαν αὐτὸν εἰς εἰρήνην; this is often the case in the later historical books), while Gen 43:27 has ἠρώτησεν . . . αὐτοὺς πῶς ἔχετε (he asked them, "How are you?") (see Thackeray,

---

[42]For example, neologisms include ἀκροβυστία (uncircumcised); ἀναθεματίζω (curse); ὁλοκαύτωμα (burnt offering); σκανδαλίζω (cause to sin); σπλαγχνίζω (have compassion) (see Swete, *Introduction*, 307, cf. 315-30; Thackeray, 39). Transliterations include Judg 5:7 A (φραζων; פרזון); Judg 8:7 and 16 (הברקנים is rendered βαρκοννιμ and βαρακηνιμ respectively) (Tov, "Translators," 55). Perhaps the oddest syntactical example is ἐγώ εἰμι with a finite verb, e.g. Judg 5:3 B: ἐγώ εἰμι ᾄσομαι [τῷ κυρίῳ] (I am/will sing [to the Lord]) (Thackeray, 55). Thackeray ("Translators," 272-73) gives the explanation that the 1st Person Hebrew pronoun was translated ἐγώ εἰμι in certain literalistic contexts, thus leading to use of two finite verbs in the translation, e.g. Judg 5:3. See Tov, "Translators," for other examples.

40-41; Lee, *Study*, 24-30, and appendix I, 150-51; cf. Barr, *Typology*, 46). This kind of "inconsistency itself argues against the existence of a Jewish Greek" (Brock, "Phenomenon," 32; cf. Psalm 18 [LXX 17] with 2 Samuel 22; 2 Kgs 18:13-20:19 with Isa 36:1-39:8; and Mic 4:1-5 with Isa 2:2-4, where in each pair the Hebrew text is essentially identical but the Greek significantly different [cited in Caird, *Language*, 123 n. 1]). Lee (15) argues in fact that the "kind of Greek found . . . in the Pentateuch is confined to books that are known to be translations, or are generally thought to be translations. Jewish works composed originally in Greek show nothing like the same degree of Semitic influence. Clearly this leads to the conclusion that the supposed 'Jewish-Greek' is a result of translation, and did not exist as a spoken language." Instead it illustrates the tension between men who knew Greek trying to render a sacred Hebrew text into their vernacular and yet maintain the sacred quality. (Kennedy [*Sources*, 21-45], followed by Thackeray [28-31], realized that Greek was probably the native language of the translators, while noting the vulgar elements caused by translation; contra Walters, *Text*, 169-70.) The LXX, therefore, is hellenistic Greek at the grammatical level, but still translation Greek, as Deissmann and Moulton asserted. Both factors must be considered (Psichari ["Essai," esp. 173ff.] appreciates them).

Why then is there so much unresolved controversy over the nature of the Greek of the NT? Much of the difficulty stems from stereotypes of the Deissmann-Moulton position. Calling his own position polemical, Deissmann (*Studies*, 175; cf. *Philology*, 51) admitted that he overstated his case when he underestimated the non-Greek character of the translated books of the LXX. As Silva states, however,

> The views of Adolf Deissmann and others have received less than fair press. . . . For example, the standard (and almost wearisome) characterization nowadays is that Deissmann made a major contribution to the field but that he took his views to an extreme and so they need considerable modification; yet when concrete instances of modifications are given, they often turn out to be items that had been readily admitted by Deissmann himself. ("Bilingualism," 199. Barclay ["NT"] provides an example of the characterization Silva mentions)

Deissmann's assertion that the LXX is written in "Semitic-Greek" and that the "Hebraisms" (his term) possibly influenced the language of early Christianity, though they did not affect the syntactic structure, is often overlooked (*Studies*, 67, 69-70: "no one ever spoke, far less used for literary purposes," the language of the LXX). He even later expanded his position to include "the sayings of Jesus" as "examples of translators' Greek" (*Philology*, 49).

Moulton also is often criticized for failing to account fully for Semitic influence.[43] Moulton, however, constantly revised his stance on certain issues of Semitic influence, as the appended notes to his *Prolegomena* attest (e.g. ἐν τῷ + Infinitive [215, 249]), but these reassessments are of degree not kind, as is evident from appended notes to reinforce his original position or to add more evidence (e.g. periphrastic Imperfect [215, 249]; πᾶς with negative =

---

[43]Reiser (*Syntax*, 2) notes that after Moulton's, Deissmann's and Thumb's deaths, the field was left open to those positing the Aramaic hypothesis.

οὐδείς [80, 245-46]). In his final writings on the subject in vol. 2, though he admits that "some applications of the principle" were "too rigorous" (14) and that "*overuse* of a rare locution" (15) may be called a Semitism (e.g. use of ἐνώπιον and ἰδού in James) here he makes his important distinction between primary and secondary Semitisms. Moulton himself actually moved from a position of seeing the Greek of the NT as "Hebraic Greek" to simply "common Greek" on the basis of his extensive study of the papyri.[44]

Scholars also have failed to define clearly what a "dialect" or "language" is, especially a Jewish Greek dialect (scholars in linguistics seem to have the same trouble).[45] As observed earlier, Turner contends that he has "tried to expose consistently the almost complete absence of classical standards" in NT Greek. This could be a convincing argument only if one were synchronically comparing NT Greek with classical Greek (if not an impossible surely an unwarranted task). Does not Turner overstate his case, however, referring to a "complete absence" of rules? He states further, "It is not that Biblical Greek has no standards at all, but pains must be taken to discover them outside the sphere of classical Greek, even outside secular Greek altogether." If Greek does not provide the standards for Greek, would the result not be something categorically different? As Turner indeed says, "Biblical Greek is a unique language with a unity and character of its own" (*Syntax*, 2, 3, 4, respectively). As McKnight understates, "It seems fair to say that Dr. Turner sees Biblical Greek as a unique language comparatively unrelated to the previous development of Greek and possibly influencing its later development" ("'Holy Ghost,'" 91; cf. "'Biblical Greek'"). In fact, Turner does argue that Jewish Greek continued to be used, witness the 3d cent. A.D. "Testament of Abraham" ("'Testament'"), though he claims here that "in numerous cases an Hebraic idiom has popularized and extended one which was already fairly familiar in Greek" (223). Examples of enhancement do not justify calling the Greek "unique." Moulton and Deissmann argued similarly.

What does Turner mean by "unique"? He cannot mean that the NT is unique because it does not reflect the Attic, hellenistic or papyri documents at

---

[44]Moulton ("Characteristics," 9 [1904] 67) notes that his beginner's Greek grammar, published in 1895, included a definition of hellenistic Greek as "*Hebraic* Greek, colloquial Greek, and late Greek," changed to "Common Greek . . ." in subsequent editions. Moulton himself proposed the appendix on Semitisms for vol. 2 of his grammar.

[45]E.g. a recent linguistics textbook remarks, "Linguistically, the world is a true mosaic. . . . and any attempt to draw boundaries beyond the individual forces ultimately arbitrary decisions. . . . It is difficult to specify criteria for distinguishing between a dialect and a language. Probably the two most commonly cited (though misguided) criteria are mutual intelligibility and possession of literature. . ." (Atkinson/Kilby/Roca, *Foundations*, 346-48). Cf. Haugen, "Norm," 98-99, who traces the problematic nature of the distinction between language and dialect back to the Greeks.

every point, since no one argues that. If he means that the hellenistic Greek of the NT at points differs morphologically or syntactically from Attic, that is admitted as well (pronunciation probably varied according to region; though difficult to determine, this alone cannot be what Turner means). He must mean that NT Greek differs from all other examples of hellenistic Greek (except the LXX).[46]

The question of language/dialect becomes crucial here (see esp. Hudson, *Sociolinguistics*, 21-72, esp. 37, though he claims no firm distinction between language and dialect can be drawn). Turner, Gehman, and their followers seem to be confused about the terms "dialect" and "language," as have been traditional grammarians, so that for them if there are irregularities between the NT and papyri the result must be a new "language." By this definition there would certainly be many "languages" or varieties in the NT alone, just as there would be in England and in the United States today, although this runs contrary to most grammarians' sense that many dialects make up a language, and not vice versa (Haugen ["Dialects," 99] states that "'language' [is] always the superordinate and 'dialect' the subordinate term"). But this is far different from the point Turner *et al* . seem to be making, in which they refer to broad varieties. In this instance it is better to define dialect and language as do modern classical philologists (Lyons, *Introduction*, 33-36; cf. Thumb, *Sprache*, 162-63). When they refer to dialects they refer to the kind of broad phonological, morphological, and lexical differences that distinguish Attic from Doric from Ionic, etc. as independent IE regional languages or dialects[47] On the basis of this definition, most Greek philologists see Greek passing from the age of "dialects," with no single prestige language, to the ascendance of a single dialect, Attic Greek, which formed the basis (along with the

---

[46]This can only be a difference of degree and not of kind, since Turner cites hellenistic and earlier Greek parallels (though differing ratios of usage) in his largest grammatical study, containing treatments of ἐκεῖνος, ἕνεκα and πᾶς ("Unique Character," 208-13; *Syntax*). But in a test of repetition of prepositions he shows that the NT books have approximately the same ratio as Thucydides 1, contra LXX Ezekiel (B text) (*Syntax*, 275). What does this mean?

[47]See Buck, *Dialects*, 141-72; Costas, *Outline*, 32-40, on their changing fortunes. Buck (136) states: "syntactical differences between the dialects are much less striking than those of phonology and inflection. To a considerable extent they consist merely in the conservation in some dialects of early forms of expression which have become rare or obsolete in literary Greek, and in a less strict formalization of usage"; and Hainsworth ("Greek," 86) says: "The idea of dialectal difference could not have failed to be universally familiar. . . . At the deeper level of syntax, and even in lexicon, the Greek dialects remained very similar. There is almost no evidence that local dialect ever formed a barrier to communication." As Herodotus says (8.144.2): τὸ Ἑλληνικὸν ἐὸν ὅμαιμόν τε καὶ ὁμόγλωσσον (the Greeks being of one blood and of one tongue); cf. Th. 3.94.

regularizing influence of literary or official Ionic) of hellenistic Greek.[48] During the Imperial period of Alexander (educated by the Athenian Aristotle, who used a pre-hellenistic Greek himself; c. 332 B.C.), the already ascendant regional variety, Attic, due especially to its cultural and economic superiority initiated under Philip II of Macedon, began a process of simplification and systematization (Meillet, *Histoire*, 241-44, 247-51; Radermacher [1st ed.], 4-6; Thomson, *Language*, 35; Costas, *Outline*, 58) on the basis of the interplay of linguistic innovation and tradition.[49] As the various propogators (soldiers, merchants, etc.) of Greek moved further from their language bases and mingled with those still using other regional dialects, the result was a standard variety or "common dialect."[50] As this language spread, Palmer notes, startling consequences of foreigners speaking Greek could have been expected, but these are "reasonably slight," essentially confined to enrichment of the lexicon (*Language*, 175; cf. Costas, *Outline*, 43, 49-50) and local variances in pronunciation.[51] Virtually every scholar of hellenistic Greek recognizes the presence of Semitisms, but they are seen as not affecting the essential grammatical structure or code of the language (e.g. Semenov, *Language*, 80-

---

[48]On the history of hellenistic Greek see esp. Schwyzer, 1.116-31; Meillet, *Histoire*, 245-54; Costas, *Outline*, 27-71, esp. 41ff.; Browning, *Greek*, 19ff.; Humbert, *Histoire*, 115-26; Moulton, "Characteristics," 9 (1904) 217-25, 310-20; and López Eire, "Atico," 377-92, who emphasizes the sociological dimension, esp. Attic treaties, which brought Ionic into influence; cf. Mickey, "Consciousness," 35-36; Teodorsson, "Variation," 72-74. Palmer (*Language*, 189-90; cf. Teodorsson, 72-74) claims the influence of the other dialects was negligible in comparison (he is refuting the theory of Kretschmer [*Einleitung*, 410-17], endorsed by Schwyzer [1.120-21], that hellenistic Greek was a mosaic of the ancient Greek dialects; see Vergote, "Grec," col. 1362) and only confined to isolated points, except in Crete and Rhodes where Doric gave the most resistance (see Hemer, "Reflections," 68 n. 8).

[49]E.g. stress over pitch was emphasized, further pronunciation changes occurred, vowels were reduced, the personal endings of verbs and nouns were simplified, the final ν was used more frequently though often assimilated, prepositions that did not go out of use were used increasingly with the Accusative, particles disappeared, μι verbs were replaced by ω forms, sigmatic Aorists (1) tended to replace non-sigmatic (2) Aorists, the Optative virtually disappeared, the Dual was completely eliminated, the Middle Voice was reduced in importance, the Subjunctive with ἵνα began finally to replace the Infinitive, the Dative Case eventually disappeared as the Accusative increased, use of ἄν expanded, and periphrasis increased in frequency. See Browning, *Greek*, 30-36; Semenov, *Language*, 93; Costas, *Outline*, 58-70.

[50]Moulton (*Introduction*, 1) idealizes the language as "a medium of expressing thought adapted uniquely to the requirements of writers who were to proclaim to the world a universal religion," and (10) "literary Attic could never have served, as did its despised successor, to make a world-speech ready at the provided time."

[51]Browning (*Greek*, 23) cites Strabo (8.1.2) on the loss of distinct varieties in Italy. Thumb, though defining five different pronunciation-areas (*Sprache*, 167-69), also notes the inflexibility of hellenistic Greek in relation to other languages (152); Radermacher ([1st ed.] 8), however, asserts that whereas the period before the decline of Rome was conservative, the later period of hellenistic Greek was more radical and open to outside influence.

97).[52] Hellenistic Greek then held sway as a single essentially sub-dialectless variety until the Byzantine and modern periods, when modern Greek again developed dialectical distinctives.[53]

If NT Greek is clearly a sub-variety of hellenistic Greek, however, why then the "resistant strangeness" (Palmer, *Language*, 194)? This may be explained in terms of the distinction between code and text, or grammar and style (Gregory/Carroll, *Language*, 75-85; Fawcett, *Linguistics*, esp. 245; Halliday, "Register variation," 60-75, in Halliday/Hasan, "Text"; Milroy, "Equality," esp. 66, 69-70, who makes a useful distinction between the *speaker* and the *linguistic system* to which he has access).[54] When Deissmann contends that the LXX and the Greek of the NT are examples of profane or vulgar Greek, he seems to be speaking at the level of code, referring to the speakers' shared meaning-system encoded in grammatical, syntactical and lexical items, such that the utterances speakers produce, despite individual variations, are "describable in terms of a particular system of [linguistic] rules and relations" (Lyons, *Introduction*, 52). Texts then exist as the "operational instances" of language (Gregory/Carroll, *Language*, 75). The difference between code and text is realized in the difference between grammar and style. Grammar determines the verbal range of an individual, i.e. the "range of meanings which that person can express," and the ways that these meanings are realized in the specific formal features of the language, while style describes the range of possible manifestations of code, i.e. registers (Gregory/Carroll, *Language*, 84;

---

[52]The spread of Greek to Palestine, in which another language was indigenous, mirrors a previous period when prehistoric Greek extended throughout Greece to peoples whose native tongues were not Greek, according to the traditional theory of Greek origins (e.g. Costas, *Outline*, 27-29). More recent analysis sees Greek developing internally: Chadwick, "Prehistory," 812-19.

[53]There are various theories on the origin of modern Greek. Kretschmer (*Einleitung*, 410-17) and Costas (*Outline*, 73-74) attribute modern dialects to the gap between spoken koine and the literary koine encouraged by the Atticists; Semenov (*Language*, 80-97) argues that koine died out and modern Greek evolved from vulgar Greek (he seems to draw too firm a distinction between the two); and Frösén (*Prolegomena*, 59ff.) raises the question of diglossia and creolization. Teodorsson (*Phonology*, 25-35) disputes Frösén's assertion on the basis that there is no evidence of a creole language, but only of koine Greek; and creoles are a transitional mix of two different languages (i.e. broad varieties), which Attic and hellenistic Greek were not, especially if spoken Attic resembled papyric language (see above). Thumb (*Sprache*, 170-75) already recognized this.

[54]Silva ("Bilingualism," 216-18) makes a distinction between *langue* and *parole* (see de Saussure, *Course*, 7-17). This distinction has been widely criticized not only because of de Saussure's fragmented presentation in the *Course* (the concepts seem to appear late in his writings compared to other foundational concepts, so Engler, "European Structuralism," 864), but because of similarity to Chomsky's psychologized distinction between competence and performance (Lyons, *Semantics*, 29; Palmer, *Semantics* [1st ed.], 7), and difficulties in defining the relation between the two concepts, of finding where *langue* is located and what it consists of, and of determining how syntax fits the schema (Godel, "Saussure's Theory," 488-92; Culler, *Saussure*, 29-34). See Spence, "Hardy Perenniel."

64-74 on register; cf. Hudson, *Sociolinguistics*, 48-53, who distinguishes register from dialect, though skeptical about the status of both; Halliday, "Register variation," 66-67, 74, in Halliday/Hasan, "Text," who sees register focusing on semantics, and dialect upon phonology, vocabulary, grammar, etc.). As Dover states,

> if one were asked to give an account of the author's "language"--that is to say, the author's language as opposed to the common factors of the language of the nation to which he belongs--the result might not differ in kind from what is presented as an account of his "style".... Style is an epiphenomenon of language, a grasp of aspects of language.
>
> (*Order*, 66)

Many biblical scholars have tacitly recognized this distinction (e.g. Deissmann, Robertson, Moulton, Thumb, Torrey, Radermacher, Turner, Rydbeck, Rabin, J.A.F. Sawyer, among others; cf. Nida *et al.*, *Style*, 51-53), though their seeming failure to articulate it is to a large extent responsible for the impasse in discussing the nature of the Greek of the NT.

The difficulty, however, is caused by several factors. One is the abundance of material available for comparison. As Thomson says, scholars possess a "fuller knowledge of Hellenistic Greek, spoken and written, than of any other ancient language" (*Language*, 36; cf. Kennedy, "Source Criticism," 127). A second is the lack of contextual indicators. As Collinge says, "it is still too rarely seen that in the interpretative process of relating text to context it is usually hard, and often impossible, to know the situation in which the text was uttered" ("Reflexions," 82; Halliday, "Register variation," 62-63, in Halliday/Hasan, "Text"). A third is that definition of register requires a "multi-dimensional analysis" (Hudson, *Sociolinguistics*, 51; cf. Milroy/Milroy, *Authority*, 118-25, on communicative competence), including societal status, field, tenor, and mode, such that discrete categories are highly problematic. A good example is "romances" of the 1st-2d cents., where, depending upon the features selected, Achilles Tatius, Philostratus's Life of Apollonius or Longinus's Daphnis and Chloe could be classified as non-literary or literary (see Perry, *Romances*, 3-43, esp. 33, where he calls the romance of "humble and demotic character"). Written hellenistic Greek, therefore, can be divided into various stylistic groupings along a broad continuum (in this sense registers existed in written hellenistic Greek). This scheme is not meant to be definitive, merely suggestive (Reiser, *Syntax*, 31-35; cf. Frösén, *Prolegomena*, 185, for spoken Greek; Hudson, *Sociolinguistics*, 43-44, on accent and dialect).

vulgar:	papyri concerned with personal matters, monetary accounts, letters, etc.
non-literary:	official and business papyri, inscriptions, scientific texts, and longer texts, e.g. Epictetus, Apollodorus, Pausanias[55]
literary:	Philo, Josephus, Polybius, Strabo, Arrian, Appian[56]
Atticistic:	Dionysius of Halicarnassus, Plutarch, Lucian[57]

Where would the NT writers fit in this scheme? Wifstrand ("Problems") divides the corpus into five basic categories: Paul; John; the Synoptic Gospels and Acts; Revelation; and the Catholic Epistles. He would claim that many of the authors write what might be called non-literary hellenistic Greek, though Revelation might be considered vulgar in places and certainly Paul, Luke (the author of Luke-Acts), and the authors of the Catholic Epistles (particularly Hebrews, James and 1 Peter) often attain to a literary quality. (Deissmann undervalued the literary qualities of the NT writers; see Costas, *Outline*, 55; Malherbe, *Aspects*, 31-45; Turner, "Literary Character," esp. 112-14; Rudberg, "Partizipien"; Howell, "St. Paul"; Köster, "Did Paul.") For example, Luke in comparison with the other Synoptics often chooses the (from a purist's point of view) better Attic word or expression,[58] and narratives like the prodigal son (Luke 15:11-32) are of recognizably artistic standard

---

[55]Mandilaras (45-46; "Confusion," 9-12) recognizes such a division. This level encompasses Rydbeck's *Sprachliche Zwischenschicht* , though he discounts the importance of the "vulgar" and conflates the literary and Atticistic (*Fachprosa*, 177, 179); cf L. Alexander, "Preface"; *Luke-Acts*, 18ff. The equation of the NT with *Fachprosa* has been justly criticized by Pax ("Probleme," 560-62; cf. Kurzová, "Griechische," 220ff.) for failing to consider other than syntactic factors, such as art, style and situation, and, I might add, subject matter. López Eire ("Atico," 379, 387f.) looks to Thucydides as the major figure behind the *Volkssprache*.

[56]This distinction encompasses the theory of Meillet and Mayser that hellenistic Greek evolved from the written and cultured Attic Greek. See Meillet, *Histoire*, 249-54; Mayser, 1.3-4. Rademacher (*Koine*, 33-34) contends that the rhetorical schools in their zeal for hellenistic culture were the primary force in killing any remnant of local languages.

[57]See Costas, *Outline*, 72-74; Rademacher, *Koine*, 51-52. Costas disputes Rydbeck's (*Fachprosa*, 191) claim that the Atticists did not arise formally until the 2d cent. A.D.; cf. Frösén, *Prolegomena*, 88. Colwell ("Language," 480-82) divides koine into literary and non-literary, calling the literary artificial due to its Attic imitations, and the non-literary "beyond description except in paradox" since there is no standard. This is problematic. On the part played by Atticistic tendencies in NT textual transmission see e.g. Kilpatrick, "Atticism"; cf. Michaelis, "Attizismus."

[58]E.g. νομικός (lawyer) instead of γραμματεύς (scribe); and medical terminology: ῥῖψαν (Luke 4:35) for σπαράξαν (Mark 1:26) (throw down/convulse); παραλελυμένος (Luke 5:18) for παραλυτικός (Mark 2:3) (paralytic); γενόμενος ἐν ἀγωνίᾳ (Luke 22:44) for ἤρξατο ἐκθαμβεῖσθαι (Mark 14:33) (become distressed); κλινίδιον (Luke 5:19, 24) for κράββατος (Mark 2:4, 11) (bed); ἰκμάς (Luke 8:6) for ῥίζαν (Mark 4:6) (root); βελόνη (Luke 18:25) for ῥαφίς (Mark 10:25; Matt 19:24) (needle); κακῶς ἔχειν (Luke 7:2) for βασανιζόμενος (Matt 8:6) (be sick); πλήμμυρα (Luke 6:48) for βροχή (Matt 7:25) (flood). See Cadbury, *Style*, 46.

(Robertson, 84-85).[59] Paul at times waxes lyrical (1 Corinthians 13). And 1 Peter and James are marked by figurative language (e.g. sincere milk of the word [1 Pet 2:2]; crown of life [Jas 1:12]), intense and intimate tone (note use of commands), and use of abstract substantives,[60] stylistic features that some Apostolic Fathers adopted, though they do not exhibit the Semitic elements which were particularly suited for the subject matter of James and 1 Peter. Wifstrand asserts that the language of James and 1 Peter, since it was the language of "common ground" and the language of the Greek synagogue and not a special dialect, was in phonology, accidence, syntax, word formation and vocabulary-ordering hellenistic Greek (even though they display Semitic elements) and ideally suited for later use by the Church Fathers. (Cf. Turner, "Language," 659, who recognizes division along Wifstrand's lines; and Moulton, *Science*, 20-21; and Lee, "Speech," 9-10, who make similar analyses; Radermacher [*Koine*, 65-66] believes education [cf. 51] made the Church Fathers better writers than the NT authors.)

How do these results comport with the multilingualism of the 1st cent.? (See Silva, "Bilingualism," 206-10; Moulton, 6-8; Vergote, "Grec," cols. 1360-67, esp. cols. 1366-67, who recognize this issue as important.) Much material has been written on multilingualism of late, and there are many variables which cannot be addressed directly (e.g. degree of language contact, development of linguistic sense, age of language acquisition), but although little specifically addresses the issues in this study, several observations from a linguistic standpoint may elucidate what has already been discussed in this chapter (see Oksaar, "Bilingualism," esp. bibliography; Baetens Beardsmore, *Bilingualism*, 152-78, bibliography; cf. Mohrmann, "General Trends").

(1) Regarding the linguistic environment of the LXX, i.e. Alexandrian multilingualism, the prestige language of that community was hellenistic Greek (see Haugen, "Problems," 278, on prestige language; Teodorsson, *Phonology*, esp. 13-35; Kapsomenos, "Griechische," 220ff., on Greek in Egypt), since it was the *lingua franca* of the dominant political, educational, and economic powers, Greece and Rome. On the basis of Greek being the native tongue of the translators and the prestige of their language,[61] linguistic interference--or "those features which distinguish the

---

[59]He cites J.C. Robertson in the *Classical Weekly* (March 9, 1912) 139: "In literary excellence this piece of narrative is unsurpassed. Nothing more simple, more direct, more forceful can be adduced from among the famous passages of classical Greek literature. . . . Yet its literary excellence is not accidental. The elements of that excellence can be analyzed."

[60]E.g. ἐγκράτεια (self-control); ἀνομία (lawlessness); πλάνη (error); παράβασις (transgression); ματαιότης (folly); ἐπιείκεια (equity); μακροθυμία (patience); πραΰτης (gentleness); ὑπομονή (endurance). Note how many of these words are Pauline as well.

[61]Brock ("Phenomenon," 34) does not give full credit to the likelihood of the native language of the translators being Greek (see above). The fact that a translation into Greek was necessary at all increases the likelihood immeasurably. Horsley ("Views," 400 n. 8) claims that the alternative to the translators of the LXX being a well-educated elite who knew koine Greek well is that they spoke a Semitized Greek indicative of a "ghetto mentality," whose existence is highly unlikely.

155

speech [or language] of a bilingual from that of a monoglot" (Baetens Beardsmore, *Bilingualism*, 43)--should be most prevalent in the influence of Greek, the donor language, on the Semitic or recipient languages. Rabin maintains that such was the case regarding verb tenses ("Hebrew and Aramaic," 1024). It is granted that lexical transfer occurred from the secondary to the primary language, in apparent contradiction to the general tendency (Baetens Beardsmore, 59), but this is understandable in light of the necessity of acquiring religious terminology (a positive transfer [Baetens Beardsmore, 60] or "need-filling motive" [Brennan, *Structure*, 16]), along with the fact that the "vocabulary of a language, considerably more loosely structured than its phonemics [sound system] and its grammar, is beyond question the domain of borrowing *par excellence* " (Weinreich, *Languages*, 56; cf. Hudson, *Sociolinguistics*, 46-47).

(2) The multilingual environment was slightly different in Palestine. Though the prestige language was still Greek, it was probably a second language for several NT writers, the first being Aramaic, though for Luke, the author of Hebrews, and probably Paul, this was almost assuredly not so (Dalman [*Words*, 41] admits this regarding Luke). The permeability of Greek to Semitic vocabulary is understandable, since the primary language is transferring to the secondary, although it is unwise to overstate the extent of this transfer (several studies have noted the Greek elements in rabbinic writings: e.g. Lieberman, *Greek*; Rosén, "KOINE").

Would not grammatical items transfer as well? Several factors militate against this. (a) Greek was able to maintain a "communicative norm" (Haugen, "Norm," 93), meaning that those using the language were not isolated from other speakers and thus vulnerable to forgetting Greek language patterns, since the needed reinforcement was provided by the constant use of Greek in social, economic, educational and even religious circles.

(b) Linguists question whether grammatical categories can be transferred by speakers, and whether, if a transfer should occur, there can be any lasting structural effect on the recipient language (see Weinreich, *Languages*, 29). If such a transfer is possible (and it seems rare), it would only occur if an elementary correspondence between the sending and receiving languages is present. Whereas Gehman argues that "in the transition period a generation has a smattering of the tongue of the forefathers without having become thoroughly immersed in the new vernacular" ("Character," 90), i.e. there is a compromise language between Greek and Hebrew, linguists are in virtually unanimous agreement that there is no such language as Gehman describes, in which basic grammatical categories are mixed (Haugen, "Problems," 287-88). The above treatment of verbal aspect confirms this for the Greek of the NT.

(c) Whereas a particular speaker's language may be affected by an acquired language, these accidents rarely have any lasting influence on his native tongue itself or the acquired tongue (Haugen, "Problems," 280; Deissmann [*Studies*, 175] recognized this principle of multilingualism). Even if it could be proved therefore that a biblical writer came under the influence of a particular Semitic grammatical construction, it is highly unlikely such an influence would be reflected in the written language in any lasting way (Munck, "Deux notes," 139), and it almost certainly would have no bearing on the structure of Greek itself. And even then, a multilingual can return to "correct" usage (Oksaar, "Bilingualism," 499).

(d) In a given language variety some semantic distinctions are harder to avoid expressing than others (e.g. verb tense is much more obligatory than noun gender in English), and fairly difficult to sacrifice. In Greek, verbal aspect is fully obligatory; there is no way to abandon verbal aspect, since every verbal form (with the exception of the Future [see chapt. 9] and a handful of aspectually vague verbs [see chapt. 10]) has a morphologically-bound aspectual designation. "In the interference of two grammatical patterns," Weinreich says, "it is ordinarily the one which uses relatively free and invariant morphemes in its paradigm--one might say, the more explicit pattern--which serves as the model for imitation" (*Languages*, 30, 42-43, 41). Again, a possible influence of Greek on the Semitic languages can be noted.

(e) Finally, Weinreich notes four standards which new hybrid languages attain, if in fact they become languages (*Languages*, 104-06). (1) A "form palpably different from either stock language." Not excluding Turner's protestations, neither side in the debate argues this is the case. (2) A "certain stability of form after initial fluctuations." A lasting influence of Semitic elements on hellenistic Greek, especially considering the large amount of materials available for examination, cannot be found. (3) "Functions other than those of a workaday vernacular," i.e. the language must not be a pidgin (on pidgins and creoles see Hudson, *Sociolinguistics*, 61-71). Here the table is turned, since the least Semitic Greek is the vulgar or workaday Greek of the papyri, which provide many pertinent parallels to the language of the NT. (4) A "rating among the speakers themselves as a separate language." This is difficult to determine, but on the basis of the vulgar texts and the letters of the NT, especially Paul's many letters to various unvisited hellenistic cities and the little comment that exists, there is little chance anyone thought he was using anything other than the hellenistic Greek of the day.

4. CONCLUSION. To conclude briefly, several important linguistic topics have been discussed. (1) 1st-cent. Palestine was almost certainly a bilingual (Greek and Aramaic) if not trilingual (plus Hebrew) environment for most inhabitants, including Jesus. (2) The Greek of the area was part and parcel of hellenistic Greek, an essentially unitary variety which dominated the entire Mediterranean world. (3) Though several broad language varieties came into heavy and constant contact, in the central matter of verbal aspect, Greek was unaffected by the Semitic languages, except for occasional enhancement of already existing patterns. (4) Whereas no one denies the presence of lexical and syntactical Semitisms in hellenistic Greek, especially the translation Greek of the LXX, these function at the level of text or style, and not of code. (5) Finally, these conclusions comport well with a general theory of multilingualism. In short, no Semitic intervention in NT Greek verbal aspect can be detected.

APPENDIX 3A:
SEMITIC VERBAL SYSTEMS

0. Introduction. A few helpful and suggestive comments may be made about the verbal networks of Biblical Hebrew, Mishnaic Hebrew and Aramaic (see Rabin, "Hebrew and Aramaic").

1. Biblical Hebrew

Previous to G.H.A. von Ewald and S.R. Driver most scholars and students of Hebrew conceived of the Hebrew tenses as strictly temporal, with the suffixed root a past tense, the prefixed root a future tense. Ewald and Driver, however, changed this picture (see McFall, *Enigma*, 1-43, 43-57, 60-77). Driver argued that rather than being concerned with the order of time, the two major stems in Hebrew refer to the kind of time, from a relative or subjective perspective, as either complete or nascent (*Treatise*, 1-6). Ewald (and later Driver) was the first to use the terms "Perfect" and "Imperfect" for these verbal forms, describing them as reflecting complete or incomplete action (*Syntax*, 1-13, esp. 3). Though both continued to use the word "tense" they recognized that Hebrew verbs are not strictly temporal but aspectual (Driver [165-66] distinguishes the Participle from the conjugated tenses [personal forms], though he attributes to it a stative, continuous non-progressive view of action). As Mettinger says of recent research into the topic, "Awareness that the Hebrew conjugations express aspect rather than tense is one of the most exciting features. . ." ("Verb System," 73; cf. Dahood, *Psalms III*, 416-23, for examples [some are questionable]).[1] Though a few have reverted to the pre-Ewald/Driver era and maintain that the only difference between the verbal stems is whether they are preformative or aformative, or that the tenses are strictly temporal, without reference to aspect (e.g. Sperber, *Grammar*; Blake, *Resurvey*), Driver's and Ewald's scheme has held sway with a large number of scholars, though with some modifications (e.g. Craigie, *Psalms*, 110-13; see Moscati, *Introduction*, 131ff.; cf. McFall, *Enigma*, 76-77). The two most noticeable modifications are an increasing awareness of temporal implicature (i.e. Perfect as complete action is often used to refer to a past action and Imperfect as still-to-be-complete a future action) and an adoption of Ewald's opposition of Perfect/Imperfect. (See Clines, *I*, 46-49, who argues for temporal structure of "before" and "after"

---

[1]McFall (*Enigma*, 184-85) says that W. Turner's and the Historical-Comparative solutions provide the most potential for further research. McFall also believes there have been no significant advances in research in this area since 1954. Clearly (1) he does not understand fully the implications of verbal aspect (three of his four sources are grammars of English aspect); (2) he overemphasizes diachronic over synchronic study, hence his emphasis on the historical-comparative solution to describe meaning instead of history; and (3) he maintains a difference between Eastern and Western thought, endorsing solutions which maintain this gap and neglecting "language universals" (cf. Barr, *Semantics*, 8-20, for a critique of this kind of approach). See Lawton, Review.

for Isaiah 53--not on the basis of Hebrew tense forms alone [he recognizes temporal limitations]--but on the basis of the discourse structure.)

Using systemic linguistics, a basic scheme can be devised which reflects, I think, the general tenor of thought on the issue. (It is reasonable to use a formally-based model on Hebrew verbal structure since there is a regular correspondence between form and function [see Ornan, "Grammar," col. 141].)

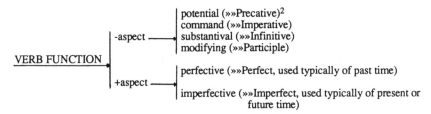

The volatile issue of the nature of the *waw* consecutive in prose narrative cannot be solved here, though a crucial distinction between form and function seems necessary. Perhaps the *waw* affixed to a form changes its aspectual function to its binary opposite, i.e. the simple form plus a *waw* becomes a new form with a definable aspect. (Driver [*Treatise*, 73] and Ewald both considered the consecutive Imperfect to be equivalent to the Greek Aorist, denoting a past complete action [McFall, *Enigma*, 180-81; actually McFall's book focuses on the issue of the Hebrew tenses and their uses of the *waw*].)

de Vries confirms this system for Qumran Hebrew though he notices that the influence of Mishnaic Hebrew is already present ("Syntax"; Kutscher, *History*, 45, cf. 44).

2. Mishnaic Hebrew

As Segal notes, the Hebrew language evolved from the Hebrew of the Bible into the later Mishnaic Hebrew, the language of the Rabbis (400 B.C. to A.D. 200) (*Grammar*, 1-7; supported by Kutscher, "Mishnaic," cols. 1592-93; idem, *History*, 115-20; cf. Ullendorff, "Biblical Hebrew," 10-11; Lapide, "Insights," 485-92; Birkeland, *Language*, 12-16, 18-24; see body of chapt. 3). And while in their main grammatical characteristics the languages are similar, in the use of the verbal tenses they evidence important changes. In Mishnaic Hebrew, the simple tenses have become temporal/aspectual so that the Perfect is used for the past, the Imperfect for the future (and thus for volitive or command clauses) and the Participle usually for the present though also for the future. Analytic tenses with היה and the Participle are used for action seen as repeated (Kutscher, *History*, 131; cf. Segal, 150, 156). The Infinitive has essentially fallen out of use in Mishnaic Hebrew (Segal, 165; Kutscher, *History*, 131. It only appears with ל as the object of a verb), as has the *waw* consecutive (Segal, 72; Black, *Approach*, 80-81). The result, if the Mishnaic Hebrew verbal systems are diagrammed, is different from Biblical Hebrew, since the primary orientation is now temporal rather than aspectual (Rabin, "Hebrew and Aramaic," 1020).

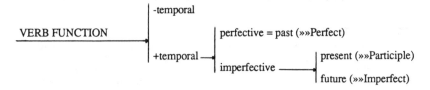

---

[2]Some scholars might question a differentiation of the Precative since it is identical to the Perfect (e.g. Cohen, "Language," 279).

3. Aramaic

Middle Aramaic (300 B.C. to A.D. 200) seems to be a primarily aspectual system, like Biblical Hebrew, but apparently unlike OT Aramaic (Stevenson, *Grammar*, 48, 51, 56-57), which is more like Mishnaic Hebrew. (For a survey of the different periods of Aramaic see Kutscher, "Aramaic," 348ff.; Fitzmyer, "Phases," 60-63; Beyer, *Aramaic Language*.) The main difference is the use in Aramaic of the Participle as imperfective in aspect, though without specific temporal reference (see Stevenson, 56; and Margolis, *Manual*, 78-80, who both note the apparent exception that in narration the Participle may function in continuation of a Perfect). These categories are especially fluid with regard to the Aramaic of the Gospel tradition, since there is still much discussion regarding the linguistic tradition that would have been current in Palestine in the 1st cent. A tentative diagram can be proposed.

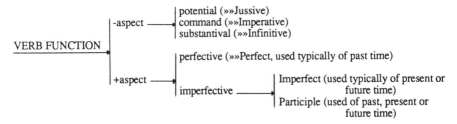

APPENDIX 3B:
MARTIN'S SYNTACTICAL EVIDENCE

Martin (*Evidence* and *Criticism*) has argued, using a statistical method (seventeen grammatical tests), that sixteen small portions of Acts 1-15 are probably translation Greek. Farris (*Hymns*, 31ff.) uses this as the telling evidence that the Lukan hymns are translations of Hebrew sources.

1. Martin's statistical analyses are designed to determine translation versus non-translation Greek; therefore, they cannot by definition be used to determine Semitic influence on Greek documents, since (a) there is no variable for influence; (b) his test produces all or nothing results, best shown in his results for literary and non-literary non-translation Greek texts. Martin classifies Plutarch, Polybius and Josephus as literary koine writers, while non-literary include Epictetus and the papyri. Yet when the results of tests 9-17 are compared among these authors, Epictetus falls further away from the mean than at least one of the literary writers in four tests (12, 14, 16, 17) and the papyri do the same in three tests (13, 14, 17), although Martin (*Criticism*, 138-39) later revised his estimation of Epictetus. Therefore the tests do not reveal style or influence, since one would expect the literary writers to be furthest from the median (fewest elements of non-standard Greek) on a scale of -17 to +17 with the median 0.

2. Martin's data base is not consistent. He does not include any NT texts, like Paul's *Hauptbriefe*, which nobody seriously contends are translated, as a methodological control, though he is testing NT books (Luke-Acts).

3. Admitting in *Evidence* that Josephus (who claims his native language was Aramaic though most of his writing was done in Greek) is of particular interest, Martin determines that Josephus (Antiquities and Against Apion) writes strong non-translation Greek (is this to be expected when he claims to be in some sense a translator? [Ant. 1.5; 10.218]). I checked 192 lines (173 adjusted) in Jewish War (1.431-57), which Josephus claims (1.3) he wrote in Aramaic and had "translated" (μεταβάλλω) into Greek. Thus it is rendered by virtually all standard translators, including Whiston and Thackeray, and supported by many others (Schürer, Goodspeed, Sevenster, Black, Shutt [*Josephus*, 7-8, 21-23]; contra Hata, "Greek Version"; Rajak, *Josephus*, 175-77. Hata's and Rajak's arguments are circular, utilizing their impression that Jewish War has no semitic characteristics). By Martin's test, this section should calculate with the other translation Greek pieces. It does not. In fact, every valid test indicates non-translation Greek (only 13 approaches the median), scoring +14. More surprising is that Jewish War is, of *all* the non-translation texts, furthest or next furthest from the midpoint (least evidence of translation?) in 5 of the 17 tests, and as far away or further from the midpoint than the other Josephus passages in 6 of the 17 tests. Either Josephus's Jewish War is not a translation in any form (even Rajak recognizes that Josephus's Aramaic version probably stands behind the Greek one) from Aramaic as he claims or the test is faulty.

Not trusting my initial results I tested a second portion of 240 lines adjusted (Jew. War 2.405-56) and it scored +16 (one test did not score). Only test 15 approaches the median, with 7 tests furthest or next furthest from the midpoint, and 7 tests as far away as or further than Antiquities. Other results may be of interest: Martin does not analyse Achilles Tatius Introduction (1.1-2; 71 lines adjusted) which scores +15, while the first 203 lines adjusted (1.3-9) of the tale score +10, which tale the author contends was from a Phoenician; Ben Sira Prologue (1-36; 23 lines adjusted) scores +4, in which the grandson of Ben Sira speaks of translating the work from Hebrew, while 1:1-4:31 (111 lines adjusted) scores -11; and Greek Enoch 10.15-15.7 (141 lines adjusted) scores -8. Reiser (*Syntax*, 27-31) discovers correspondingly that several hellenistic Greek works receive scores on individual tests which Martin would ascribe to Semitic influence.

4. Farris provides other valid criticism about the sketchiness of Martin's method, the limited number of criteria, the importance placed on a single item (prepositions), and whether the items selected are the most important. Reiser (*Syntax*, 27-31) also mentions the size of the selections, the issue of linguistic levels, and criteria for establishing categories. Note that there is no test that concerns verbal systems (the test regarding the Participle treats it as an adverb).

5. In Farris's comparison he runs the same tests on Luke 5:12-6:11; 12:13-13:9; Mark 1:40-3:6; Romans 5; Gal 1:11-2:5; all of Paul; Revelation 3; 4:1-5:10; and all of Revelation. The results are intriguing: Paul as a whole and the Lukan passages *in toto* score 0, Mark leans toward non translation (+2) slightly. Luke 12:13-13:9 leans slightly toward translation Greek (-2), while Luke 5:12-6:11 scores 0. (Cf. Martin, *Criticism*, who arrives at very different results for these Gospel passages with the same 'objective' test.) Romans 5 and Galatians 1-2 treated separately are slightly toward non translation (+2, +3), while Revelation is toward translation (-5).

6. Martin's conclusions are highly subjective. In Acts, he decides that some small sub-sections of 8-36 lines (one sentence could skew the results, and Martin is aware that the results change for smaller passages; see Collins, Review, 593) that score +2 or less are translation Greek and others are not. This seems a strange application of the midpoint to data. He justifies his search for translated portions by claiming that Acts 1:11-15:35 (+8) falls between the score of the rest of Acts (+16) and his other Greek texts, and the translation books, thus concluding (*non sequitur*, see 1) that Acts 1:11-15:35 as a whole is not a translation but that subsections are.

7. Conclusion: (a) Martin's test cannot be used to determine the presence of Semitic influence or the degree that intervention or enhancement has occurred. This is seen clearly in the fact that Paul scores a 0, the same as Luke overall, whereas in the former no one contends for translation, and Mark scores a +2, whose Greek is not the same standard of Luke. Besides, what does a 0 indicate? Is Paul less non-translation Greek than Philo (+9), Plutarch (+16), Polybius (+15), Epictetus (+17 for some small passages, and +9 overall), Josephus Antiquities (+16), Jewish War (+14 and +16), or the papyri (+17)? And what do these scores among such widely divergent original Greek selections mean?

(b) It could be argued on the basis of Martin's and Farris's results that the test indicates that the NT is non-translation Greek (possibly excepting Revelation). This shows that this test is highly suspect in its ability to determine translation Greek. Farris wisely limits his use of the test to reinforce scholarly opinion that Luke 1-2 is translation Greek (-16). But is there not an intriguing comparison with Josephus's Jewish War? Both texts are in one language (Greek). One is written by an author capable of standard Greek (Acts 16ff. +16, Acts 1-15 +8, both solidly original Greek), the other by an author claiming his native tongue is Aramaic and that the work was in Aramaic before translation (Luke makes no claim to translation of Luke 1-2). Yet Jewish War scores +14/+16, further from the midpoint than the first half of Acts, while Luke 1-2 scores further from the midpoint in the opposite direction.

CHAPTER 4:
THE AORIST AND PRESENT TENSES
IN THE INDICATIVE MOOD

0. INTRODUCTION. This chapter discusses in more detail several of the categories described in chapt. 2. In part I, the nature of the attitudes (Moods) of Greek are defined, and then criteria for establishing the less heavily marked semantic weight of the Aorist and the more heavily marked semantic weight of the Present are established. In part II, after discussing criteria for differentiating the pragmatic categories of the Aorist and Present/Imperfect, significant examples of the major pragmatic categories are treated, in light of the differentiation of perfective and imperfective aspects.

PART I

1. THE MOODS AND ATTITUDES OF GREEK. a. Assertive attitude (Indicative). The traditional view of the meaning of the Moods is summarized by Humbert, who says the Indicative "exprime les *conditions constitutives de la réalite*" (111), while "Les Anciens avaient défini heureusement le subjonctif et l'optatif en les appelant διαθέσεις ψυχῆς [Apollonius Dyscolus] 'modalités de l'âme.' En opposition avec l'indicatif, qui constate *objectivement*, le subjonctif et l'optatif expriment des dispositions *subjectives*" (113). (See also Brugmann, 555, cf. 571; Chantraine, 2.205; Meillet/Vendryes, *Traité*, 191ff.; Goodwin, *Grammar*, 280; idem, *Syntax*, 76; Smyth, 481; Jannaris, 445ff., 560-67; Moorhouse, 214; Winer, 351-52; Burton, 73ff.; Moule, 20; implied by others: Blass, 205; Moulton, 164-65; Gildersleeve, 143ff.) This widely-held view may be criticized at several points. The most telling objection, as Gonda says, is that:

If the subj. and the opt. are described as being subjective in character or as expressing a subjective disposition, then it must be said that the function of the indicative is similar. The ind. expresses that the person speaking visualizes the process--i.e. the act, action, event, in short any "idea" expressed by a verb--as real or actual. As a rule the speaker is not conscious of this "subjective" character of his statements expressed by means of verbs in the indicative. (*Character*, 3)

For example, in Mark 5:35, 39, a messenger says that the synagogue official's daughter has died (ἡ θυγάτηρ σου ἀπέθανεν), but Jesus says on arrival that τὸ παιδίον οὐκ ἀπέθανεν ἀλλὰ καθεύδει (the child is not dead but is sleeping), at which those observing laugh. Also, a statement made in the Indicative can be incorrect or even an untruth. For example, in Mark 3:22-23 the scribes from Jerusalem say that Jesus Βεελζεβοὺλ ἔχει (has Beelzeboul) and that ἐν τῷ ἄρχοντι τῶν δαιμονίων ἐκβάλλει τὰ δαιμόνια (in the power of the demons he casts out demons). Jesus reportedly calls their assertion into question: πῶς δύναται σατανᾶς σατανᾶν ἐκβάλλειν; (how is Satan able to cast out Satan?).

Thus, although Schwyzer (2.303) says "der Indikativ bezeichnet die Wirklichkeit eines Verbalinhalts," he also says "Aber auch der gewöhnliche Indikativ ist insofern subjektiv, als er nur angibt, was der Sprechende als wirklich aufgefasst wissen will." Kühner/Gerth (1.201) go further: "Aus der gegebenen Bestimmung der *Modusformen* leuchtet ein, dass dieselben einen durchaus *subjektiven* Charakter haben. Sie drücken nie etwas *Objectives* aus, d.h. sie zeigen nie an, wie eine Thätigkeitsäusserung in der *Wirlichkeit* beschaffen sie. Der *Indikativ* drückt an sich nicht etwas Wirkliches . . ." (cf. Jelf, 2.73-74). Both Schwyzer and Kühner/Gerth appear to be aware of the subjective element that runs through use of the various Moods in Greek.

Greek has two distinct sets of inflexional forms, the Indicative and the non-Indicative. Not only are they formally distinct (verbal ambiguity does play a part in certain forms but context virtually always makes the meaning clear; see chapt. 10), but this confirms a perceived distinction between their functional semantics. The traditional analysis, while often recognizing the subjective nature of the non-Indicative Moods, has clearly erred in positing an objective nature for the Indicative Moods. But Gonda's distinction above has rightly been criticized by Collinge for appearing to eliminate objectivity completely ("Reflexions," 80), since the Indicative is the Mood used, for example, in narrative and primarily in description, as well as those contexts where a speaker wants his hearer to believe that he is speaking accurately (e.g. lies). A helpful distinction along slightly different lines than the traditional conception but one in keeping with recent discussion of modality may be made.

Gonda (*Character*, 6) arrives at a helpful formulation (cf. Stahl, 220ff.; Robertson, 914ff.; Zerwick, 100-01; Mandilaras, 241; Rijksbaron, 7; Bers, *Syntax*, 117):

> If we may describe the verbal category of mood (such as it appears in Greek or Sanskrit) as a means of intimating the speaker's view or conception of the relation of the processs expressed by the verb to reality, it will be clear that the main distinction made is between what the speaker puts forward as fact (whether it be true or not) and what he does not regard as such. If he wishes to mention a process which in his opinion is a fact or actuality, he uses the indicative, if he wishes to put forward a process as a contingency the ancient Greek used the optative etc.

This is similar to the formulation put forward by Palmer in his general study of 'mood and modality,' an attempt at a universal typology: "Modality could, that is to say, be defined as the grammaticalization of speakers' (subjective) attitudes and opinions" (*Mood*, 16; esp. 1-50, 96-125, cf. 125-208; de Boel, "Complementizers," 285),[1] and thus relates to what is both factual and not factual on the basis of the speaker's belief (i.e. the Indicative Mood may be used of non-factual processes, and the non-Indicative Moods may be used of factual processes). Thus it is seen that factuality cuts across the two major categories of epistemic [+assertion] and deontic [-assertion] attitudes (Palmer, *Mood*, 18; Lyons, *Semantics*, 736).[2] These are grammaticalized in the Greek verbal network by the Indicative and non-Indicative forms. (Greek does not have modal verbs as traditionally defined [see below on ἄν], and its negative particles do not necessarily correlate with particular attitudes until the hellenistic period, and even then not exactly.) Thus the Indicative is used for

---

[1]Palmer's book has several limitations. (1) There is verbal ambiguity with regard to several of the terms, especially "mood" and "modality," so that sometimes "mood" appears to be a term for what is traditionally called oblique Mood forms, and other times grammaticalized modality. (2) A difficulty with creating a typology for any linguistic category is that it is often difficult to grasp particulars. Thus rarely is an entire language discussed fully, and often there is little specification of how categories exemplified from a certain range of languages relate to another range. This book's best uses appear to be in recounting the state of discussion, describing a number of pertinent categories, and providing a useful framework for further work. Work on a single language, however, must draw on this material where helpful, but must ensure that the conceptual framework is defined in terms of the linguistic particulars of the sample language.

[2]Thus McKay says that the Indicative "is most commonly used for statements of fact (or alleged fact) and intention, both positive and negative, both in independent simple sentences and as the core of clauses whose interdependence may modify its significance to some extent" (148), "The subjunctive mood in independent sentences normally expresses the will of the subject of the verb, and supplements the imperative by replacing it in certain circumstances and by expressing exhortations in the first person. . . . The optative mood in independent sentences normally expresses either a wish . . . a possibility or probability. . . " (149), and "The imperative mood expresses command, including such mild forms of command as advice or entreaty" (148). See also Moulton, 164-65; Abel, 269; Chamberlain, 82-83.

assertive or declarative statements (there is no evidential or judgmental grammatical system), while the non-Indicative forms grammaticalize a variety of related attitudes, having in common that they make no assertion about reality but grammaticalize simply the 'will' of the speaker, and are therefore deontic. Thus the Imperative grammaticalizes [+direction], the Subjunctive grammaticalizes [+projection], and the Optative, marked in relation to the Subjunctive, grammaticalizes [+projection: +contingency] (see chapts. 7 and 8). As the "most frequent mode [i.e. attitude] in all languages," including all types of Greek literature, the Indicative "is the normal mode to use when there is no special reason for employing another mode" (Robertson, 915; cf. McKay, 148) and hence it is less heavily marked in relation to the non-Indicative Moods (Ruijgh, *Autour*, 239: "l'indicatif est le terme neutre de l'opposition." Moorhouse [214] notes that it lacks "the specialization and subjective modifications found in the other moods").

The suggestive possibilities of this discussion are numerous, but within the confines of this work only one of importance is mentioned here: use of ἄν in the Indicative.[3] There has long been discussion of the nature of the particle ἄν, which is often called a "modal particle" (e.g. Liddell/Scott, *Lexicon*, s.v.; Kühner/Gerth, 2.208; Chantraine, 2.221, 311; Schwyzer, 2.305; and Bers, *Syntax*, 117ff., who distinguishes between use of ἄν with the Subjunctive and Optative). The implication is that use of the particle with a particular verb in some way grammatically alters or compromises the attitude of the verb form. This is a misconception. Not only would it argue against morphologically-based attitudinal semantic features, but it directly reflects the view of attitude rejected above, in which there is a distinction between the fundamental viewpoint of the action in the assertive and non-assertive attitudes. Bers (*Syntax*, 125-26), after surveying usage, claims that "the semantic role of ἄν is negligible in the Attic system" and distribution is conjoined to "stereotyped expressions," as opposed to ἄν as a marker of "verbal mood" and as a debasement of Homeric usage. ἄν is better seen as a "conditional" marker (Hulton, "ʹʹAN," esp. 140 n. 1, reflecting a long-standing tradition seen also in Kühner/Gerth, 2.208ff.; Goodwin, *Grammar*, 277-80; idem, *Syntax*, 64-75; Winer, 378; cf. Moorhouse, "AN"; "Reply") or "idealization marker" which indicates "failure to make the existential presuppositon" or presupposes no reference to reality (Lightfoot, *Logic*, 129), much like an assumed conditional clause. McKay ("Action," 37-38) is quick to point out, however, that a Greek speaker would not have necessarily had a conditional statement in mind when using ἄν plus Indicative, claiming that "ἄν in a variety of circumstances is a marker of some kind of generality" (38), although in many instances the conditional is expressed or certainly easily implied (Hulton, 139-40). (According to Blass/Debrunner [¶ 367] and Turner [*Syntax*, 92], in NT and ordinary koine Greek there are no independent main clauses with ἄν and the Indicative Aorist or Imperfect.) No examples of contractions with ἄν (e.g. ὅταν) are included below. This would simply increase the number of examples (see esp. Winer, 378ff.).

---

[3]From what has been said in chapts. 1 and 2, it is considered unnecessary to treat iterative use of ἄν with either perfective or imperfective verbs as a special category of verbal usage, as do many grammars: e.g. Goodwin, *Grammar*, 276-77; Blass/Debrunner, ¶ 367. See also Seaton, "Use," 343-45; cf. untitled, 6 (1892) 201, where he subsumes it under the conditional; and Harrison, untitled, 130, who recognizes "aspectual" differences in iterative ἄν usage.

Thus the Aorist is found in Mark 6:56: ὅσοι ἂν ἥψαντο (whoever would touch, i.e. if someone would touch);[4] Luke 19:23: κἀγὼ ἐλθὼν σὺν τόκῳ ἂν αὐτὸ ἔπραξα (and coming, I would have collected it with interest); par. Matt 25:27: ἐλθὼν ἐγὼ ἐκομισάμην ἂν τὸ ἐμὸν σὺν τόκῳ (coming, I would have received my part with interest); Heb 10:2: ἐπεὶ οὐκ ἂν ἐπαύσαντο προσφερόμεναι (since they would not have ceased offering sacrifices).[5]

The Imperfect is found in Mark 6:56: ὅπου ἂν εἰσεπορεύετο (wherever he would enter); Acts 2:45; 4:35: καθότι ἄν τις χρείαν εἶχεν (in so far as someone would have need); 1 Cor 12:2: ὡς ἂν ἤγεσθε (as you would be led).[6] The Present has no examples in the NT (cf. Rev 14:4: ὅπου ἂν ὑπάγει [where he would go], a variant reading in A C al.).[7]

These examples (see Debrunner, "Nebensatziterativpräteritum," for further examples) illustrate that whereas the particle ἄν may call for a conditional sense, it does not 'weaken the force of the verb itself.' Although the particle ἄν is often used with various Moods, including the Subjunctive and Optative (see below and chapt. 7), the use and meaning of the particle and that of the Moods must be evaluated independently (Hulton, "ʼAN," 139, 140 n. 1). This is particularly important for conditional statements.

b. Non-assertive attitudes (non-Indicative) (see Calboli, "Modi," 235-58, for history of research). Just as the Indicative forms are shown to be non-temporal, so the same may be shown for the non-Indicative Moods (see Schwyzer, 2.304). The major difficulty for grammarians revolves around future reference and the concept of projection. It is shown above that the Indicative Mood is used for assertion, while the non-Indicative Moods are used

---

[4]Cf. Matt 14:36: ὅσοι ἥψαντο. As Winer (384-85) says, "Both expressions are correct, according as the writer conceived the fact as in every respect definite or not. The former [Matt 14:36] must be rendered, *all who* (as many as) *touched him*, of the persons who were surrounding him at that time (ver. 35). Mark's narration does not refer to any particular place (as is shown by ὅπου ἂν εἰσεπορεύετο); he says generally, *all who at any time touched him.*"

[5]For classical parallels see esp. Kühner/Gerth, 2.211-14. Cf. also Th. 1.11.1: τὸ γὰρ ἔρυμα τῷ στρατοπέδῳ οὐκ ἂν ἐτειχίσαντο (for [otherwise] they would not build the defence for the camp); Pl. Symp. 175D: οὐ γὰρ ἂν προαπέστης (for you would not go away before); Rep. 554B: οὐ γὰρ ἂν τυφλὸν ἡγεμόνα τοῦ χοροῦ ἐστήσατο (for he would not establish a blind man as leader of the chorus); X. Anab. 4.2.10: καὶ αὐτοὶ μὲν ἂν ἐπορεύθησαν ᾗπερ οἱ ἄλλοι (and they would have gone in the same way as the others, i.e. if they were able); Lucian Dial. Courtesans 9.2: πρὸς δὲ σὲ οὐκ ἂν (v.l. οὐχ ἃ) εἶπον (I would not speak to you); D L. 2.75: σὺ δ᾽ οὐκ ἂν τριωβόλου ταῦτ᾽ ἐπρίω; (would you not buy this for three obols?); P.Lond. 1394.10, 15 (A.D. 710): εἴ τι δ᾽ ἂν συνῆξας χρυσίον . . . εἴ τι δ᾽ ἂν ἤνυσας . . . (if you would gather some gold . . . and if you would gather . . .).

[6]See esp. Kühner/Gerth, 2.211-14; cf. also Th. 7.55.2: ὃ οὐκ ἂν ᾤοντο (which they would not think of); X. Hell. 1.7.7: τὰς χεῖρας οὐκ ἂν καθεώρων (they would not see the hands); Lys. 3.21: ἐβουλόμην δ᾽ ἄν (and I would wish); Lucian Dial. Dead 10.1: οὐκ ἂν ἐδόξαζον (they would not have thought).

[7]Goodwin (*Syntax*, 65) argues that ἄν is never used with the Present and Perfect Indicative, but that in examples "there is generally a mixture of constructions." E.g. Pl. Laws 712E: ἐγὼ δὲ οὕτω νῦν ἐξαίφνης ἂν ἐρωτηθείς, ὄντως, ὅπερ εἶπον, οὐκ ἔχω διορισάμενος εἰπεῖν τίς τούτων ἐστὶν τῶν πολιτειῶν. Goodwin says ἄν "was used with a view to a following οὐκ ἂν εἴποιμι or some such construction, for which οὐκ ἔχω εἰπεῖν was substituted. The meaning is, *if I should suddenly be asked, I could not say*, etc." Cf. Pl. Meno 72C; Rep. 579D; Arist. Pol. 3.6.1. Perhaps limited use of ἄν with the marked forms is not surprising, but it is questionable whether Goodwin must go to such lengths to eliminate the phenomenon completely.

for non-assertion, i.e. they are used when no claim is made about the state of the world, but some non-existent state is hypothesized or projected, whatever its relationship to the actual world (since this projection is a grammaticalization of a speaker's view of the world). That this is a posited or projected world (deontic attitude) has led a large number of grammarians to argue that the non-Indicative Moods are essentially future tenses (e.g. Hahn, *Subjunctive*, esp. 1-15, 59-122, 138ff.; Jannaris, 560-67 [who gives special treatment to the Moods since Attic times]; Goodwin, *Syntax*, 23, 27; Gildersleeve, 128; cf. idem, "Syntax," 23 [1902] 127; 30 [1909] 1; Kühner/Gerth, 1.217, cf. 1.225; Ruijgh, *Autour*, 241; and recently Lightfoot, *Logic*, 126-32; a view commonly held among NT grammars). As Gonda (*Character*, 7) recognizes, "There is . . . no denying that, if we think in temporal concepts, the processes referred to by a subjunctive [or the other Moods] should they be realized, generally speaking, belong to a time subsequent to the moment of speaking," i.e. if the worlds they project were to come into existence, they in many cases would be future to the time of projection (though this is certainly not always the case), and in this sense the non-Indicative Moods are relative tenses. But this has confused the distinction between temporal reference and the semantics of attitude (the argument concerning historical evolution of forms has also been misleading), misappropriated much of the discussion in the secondary literature, and resulted in implausible interpretations of several types of examples. In defining the semantic qualities of the non-Indicative Moods, two areas must be distinguished.

　　1. Temporal reference. a. Imperative. It can be shown that the Imperative is not to be considered a time-based tense (as Robertson [855] realizes). A command or prohibition can always be rejected, and thus does not refer to a future event but merely a posited one. Jesus reportedly tells the rich ruler in Mark 10:21 (par. Matt 19:21; Luke 18:22): ὕπαγε ὅσα ἔχεις πώλησον καὶ δός [τοῖς] πτωχοῖς, . . . καὶ δεῦρο ἀκολούθει μοι (go, sell what you have and give to the poor . . . and come, follow me), but he went away sad, because he had many possessions. A command or prohibition can refer to an event that in fact cannot be performed, and thus has no relation to the future but only to a projected time and place. The Samaritan woman is told in John 4:16: ὕπαγε φώνησον τὸν ἄνδρα σου καὶ ἐλθὲ ἐνθάδε (go, call your husband and come here). She replies, οὐκ ἔχω ἄνδρα (I don't have a husband). And a command or prohibition can express an assumption, and thus has no necessary relation to a future world. In the Lord's Prayer, the disciples are instructed how to pray in Matt 6:9: πάτερ ἡμῶν ὁ ἐν τοῖς οὐρανοῖς, ἁγιασθήτω τὸ ὄνομά σου (our father who is in heaven, let your name be holy); Paul states in Rom 3:4: γινέσθω δὲ ὁ θεὸς ἀληθής, πᾶς δὲ ἄνθρωπος ψεύστης (let God be true, and every man a liar).[8] The often-made statement that Present Imperatives order

---

[8]Kühner/Gerth (1.236-37) cite among others: Pl. Symp. 201C: ἐγώ, φάναι, ὦ Σώκρατες, σοὶ οὐκ ἂν δυναίμην ἀντιλέγειν, ἀλλ᾽ οὕτως ἐχέτω ὡς σὺ λέγεις (I, clearly, S., would be unable to contradict you, but thus let it be as you say [or McKay, 128: "assume that it is . . . as you say"]); Pl. Phaedr. 246A; Phil. 14A; Th. 2.48.3.

continuation and Aorist Imperatives inception is addressed in chapt. 7 on aspectual usage of the Moods, although the non-temporal basis illustrated above argues strongly against any definitions so based.

b. Subjunctive and Optative. The non-temporal basis of the Subjunctive and Optative is demonstrable as well (see Gonda, *Character*, 68ff.; Collinge, "Reflexions," 91-92; Hulton, "Optatives"; Moorhouse, "Optative," 61). First, use of the word "future" is deceptive. Perhaps this explains Lightfoot's reference (*Logic*, 126-32) to the Subjunctive as a logical future, i.e. where no "existential presupposition" is made the Subjunctive is used. It has been shown that temporal reference in Greek is relative and not absolute; therefore, the temporal point of reference is determined on the basis of each utterance. Thus, when grammarians state that the non-Indicative Moods are future tenses, they mean they are "subsequent" tenses, referring to action subsequent to the point of reference of a given discourse. Some grammarians might think they mean future to the reference point of the speaker, i.e. absolute tense, but this is no solution for several reasons. First, it makes the Greek language heavily repetitious of future-referring forms (a tendency for duplication that runs contrary to many languages, including Greek). Second, it fails to describe adequately the semantic differences grammaticalized by the individual forms. (Donovan ["Subjunctive," 145], responding to Sonnenschein's use of the term "prospective," says, "Futurity--at least relative--will be found in many final, consecutive, causal and conditional clauses, but in distinguishing between these it is the 'special kind of futurity,' not the genus futurity, that will help.") Third, it automatically excludes from consideration several important instances. For example, indirect discourse (see Burton, 130ff.), in which a non-Indicative form is used to characterize something already spoken, illustrates clearly the aspectual rather than temporal basis of Greek verbs, since verbal aspect is maintained, regardless of selection of the Mood of the verb. In hellenistic Greek, apart from Atticizing tendencies, the Indicative or Subjunctive is often used where the Optative would have occurred (on decrease of the Optative see Mandilaras, 277-87; Schwyzer, 2.337-38),[9] although the Infinitive also appears (there are also many instances of direct discourse being retained). It is probable that speakers no longer felt the necessity of differentiating attitude, and followed a general tendency to select the less heavily marked form,[10] i.e. Indicative over Optative.

Examples of the Optative in non future-referring contexts include:[11] Acts 25:16: ἀπεκρίθην ὅτι οὐκ ἔστιν ἔθος Ῥωμαίοις χαρίζεσθαί τινα ἄνθρωπον πρὶν ἢ ὁ κατηγορούμενος κατὰ πρόσωπον ἔχοι τοὺς κατηγόρους τόπον τε ἀπολογίας λάβοι περὶ τοῦ ἐγκλήματος (I answered that it was not the Roman custom to free any man before the one who is accused might have a face to face confrontation with his accusers and might make a defence concerning the charges), possibly the only example in the NT where the Optative in indirect

---

[9]The decrease in the Optative has been disputed by M. Higgins, "Renaissance" (cf. "Why"), who cites numerous examples from papyri to show, he claims, that there was a Standard Late Greek that made use of the Optative. (1) He appears to stereotype and even misconstrue conditional usage in the Attic dialect to create a false argument that the papyri use the Optative for "improbable contingency" ("Renaissance," 54). (2) Schmid (*Atticismus*) argues convincingly that use of the Optative in the hellenistic period had decreased in frequency in significant major authors, and often had become stereotyped in usage. In any case, the Optative is relatively infrequent in the NT. See also Anlauf, *Standard*, 122ff.

[10]Perhaps Gonda (*Character*, 47) is correct that the secondary endings of the Optative are less conspicuous than the primary endings of the Subjunctive, but it does not follow that the Optative is the unmarked form, since other criteria must also be accounted for, such as the lengthened connecting vowel.

[11]Cf. Lys. 13.46: εἰ ἐπ' ἐκείνοις γένοιτο (whether it might come upon them). Sanspeur ("'Potentiel,'" 44) says that Lysias "imagine simplement cette situation. Sur le plan de la réalisation, elle est strictement impossible."

discourse is used for the Subjunctive in direct discourse (contra Jannaris, 52; Boyer, "Classification of Optatives," 137; see below); Luke 8:9: ἐπηρώτων δὲ αὐτὸν οἱ μαθηταὶ αὐτοῦ τίς αὕτη εἴη ἡ παραβολή (his disciples asked him what this parable was). The Optative in indirect questions is the most widespread use of the Optative in the NT in indirect discourse.

Examples of the Subjunctive in non future-referring dependent clauses include: e.g. John 9:2: ῥαββί, τίς ἥμαρτεν, οὗτος ἢ οἱ γονεῖς αὐτοῦ, ἵνα τυφλὸς γεννηθῇ; (rabbi, who sinned, this man or his parents, so that he was born blind?), with the Subjunctive past referring, though relatively future in the sequence of events;[12] Mark 11:28: τίς σοι ἔδωκεν τὴν ἐξουσίαν ταύτην ἵνα ταῦτα ποιῇς (who gave you this authority in order that you might do these things?), with the Subjunctive referring to either Jesus' present or past actions; John 8:56: Ἀβραὰμ ὁ πατὴρ ὑμῶν ἠγαλλιάσατο ἵνα ἴδῃ τὴν ἡμέραν τὴν ἐμήν (A. your father rejoiced in order that he might see my day); John 11:37: οὐκ ἐδύνατο οὗτος ὁ ἀνοίξας τοὺς ὀφθαλμοὺς τοῦ τυφλοῦ ποιῆσαι ἵνα καὶ οὗτος μὴ ἀποθάνῃ; (was this one who opens the eyes of the blind not able to make it so that even this one would not die?), referring to Lazarus. Once this distinction is clarified, it becomes clear that subsequent reference is clearly not the case in many examples. There are many instances where the Subjunctive refers to non-subsequent contexts within its discourse unit, for example in relative clauses. Mark 8:38 par. Luke 9:26: ὃς γὰρ ἐὰν ἐπαισχυνθῇ με καὶ τοὺς ἐμοὺς λόγους ἐν τῇ γενεᾷ ταύτῃ τῇ μοιχαλίδι καὶ ἁμαρτωλῷ, καὶ ὁ υἱὸς τοῦ ἀνθρώπου ἐπαισχυνθήσεται αὐτὸν ὅταν ἔλθῃ ἐν τῇ δόξῃ τοῦ πατρὸς αὐτοῦ μετὰ τῶν ἀγγέλων τῶν ἁγίων (whoever might be ashamed of me and my words in this adulterous and sinful generation, indeed the son of man will be ashamed of him, whenever he might enter in the glory of his father with the holy angels). Examples may be multiplied, although exact determination of temporal reference is often extremely difficult, and in many instances not warranted. This is not only on account of the non-temporal nature of the Greek tense system, and thus the dependence upon deixis, but because it is contended here that the non-Indicative Moods do not grammaticalize a specific conception of a process's status in existence.

2. Semantic features of the Subjunctive, Optative and Future (cf. Moorhouse, 222, who on the basis of pragmatic usage argues that the Subjunctive is both like the Imperative and Future, and the Optative. He is correct in seeing the relationship, though he fails to appreciate individual semantic features).

(a) Projection with no expectation of fulfilment (Subjunctive). Projection with no expectation of fulfilment is realized by the Subjunctive in both independent and dependent usage. There have been two major theories regarding the semantics of the Subjunctive. The temporal

---

[12]See Hom. Il. 10.97-99: δεῦρ' ἐς τοὺς φύλακας καταβήομεν, ὄφρα ἴδωμεν, / μή τοι μὲν καμάτῳ ἀδηκότες ἠδὲ καὶ ὕπνῳ κοιμήσωνται, / ἀτὰρ φυλακῆς ἐπὶ πάγχυ λάθωνται (come, let us go to the guards, so that we may see, lest being already overcome with weariness and drowsiness they might have gone to sleep, and have forgotten about their watch completely); Hom. Od. 13.215-16: ἀλλ' ἄγε δὴ τὰ χρήματ' ἀριθμήσω καὶ ἴδωμαι, / μή τί μοι οἴχωνται κοίλης ἐπὶ νηὸς ἄγοντες ("But now let me count and examine these belongings, for fear they may prove to have gone off with something in their hollow ship" [Stanford, Odyssey, 2.207]); Hom. Od. 24.491: ἐξελθών τις ἴδοι μὴ δὴ σχεδὸν ὦσι κιόντες (someone go out and look lest they might have come near). Cf. Hom. Il. 1.555-56: νῦν δ' αἰνῶς δείδοικα κατὰ φρένα μή σε παρείπῃ / ἀργυρόπεζα Θέτις (but now I am in a fearful state in my heart lest silver-footed T. "'have gained thee over,' i.e. lest she prove to have done so" [Monro, Homer, 1.260] or may win thee over [Goodwin, Syntax, 80]); 10.538. The fact that both understandings are possible within context points to the difficulty of imposing temporal understanding on essentially non-temporal verbal usage.

theory, advocated most forcefully by Goodwin, and later by Smyth, has been treated above. The standard theory, advocated by Brugmann, Delbrück, and others since, is that there are three major uses of the Subjunctive: volitive, deliberative, and prospective. Brugmann (573-78; cf. Bers, *Syntax*, 142ff.) recognizes a single Subjunctive form, but he divides independent usage into these three, while recognizing that firm lines of demarcation between them is not possible, especially with dependent sentences. Examination makes clear that Brugmann has made this division in order to classify three kinds of pragmatic usage, but that he actually is arguing for an underlying conception.

(1) Volitive usage usually occurs in the 1st Person expressing the desire of the speaker, often called the hortatory Subjunctive. E.g. Hom. Od. 23.117: ἡμεῖς δὲ φραζώμεθ' ὅπως ὄχ' ἄριστα γένηται (let us think so that the best results might come about); E. And. 333: Μενάλαε, φέρε δὴ διαπεράνωμεν λόγους (M., come, let us bring these words to an end). Brugmann notes that it only seldom occurs with the Singular verb, as in Hom. Od. 20.296: ἀλλ' ἄγε οἱ καὶ ἐγὼ δῶ ξείνιον (come, let me give a guest's gift), but is used in the NT: Matt 7:4: ἄφες ἐκβάλω τὸ κάρφος ἐκ τοῦ ὀφθαλμοῦ σου (permit me, and let me take out the splinter from your eye). These could be called commands. (He notes that the 2d and 3d Person were unusual in Ionic-Attic, although Aeolic, the LXX [e.g. Ruth 1:9], and several later writers appear to have them.)

When this Subjunctive is negated, Brugmann notes, it may occur in the Aorist or Present 1st Person: e.g. X. Anab. 7.1.29: μὴ πρὸς θεῶν μαινώμεθα μηδ' αἰσχρῶς ἀπολώμεθα (let us not be furious with the gods and let us not shamefully be destroyed). Usually only the Aorist of 2d and 3d Person occurs, and this serves as the prohibition for the Aorist: D. 18.10: μηδὲ φωνὴν ἀνάσχησθε (don't esteem my voice); Th. 3.39.6: καὶ μὴ τοῖς μὲν ὀλίγοις ἡ αἰτία προστεθῆ, τὸν δὲ δῆμον ἀπολύσητε (don't let the accusation be added to the oligarchy and you loose the people). (Brugmann [575] explains this on the basis of Sanskrit. The origin does not concern me.)

This use of the Subjunctive can also express fear or warning: e.g. Pl. Gorg. 462E: μὴ ἀγροικότερον ᾖ τὸ ἀληθὲς εἰπεῖν ("I fear it may be too rude to tell the truth" [Lamb, *Plato 3*, 313; cf. Dodds, *Gorgias*, 224: "I fear it may sound a little crude"]). This usage is very similar to dependent sentences with verbs of fearing, and independent sentences with ὅπως μή: e.g. Pl. Prot. 313C: καὶ ὅπως γε μή, ὦ ἑταῖρε, ὁ σοφιστὴς ἐπαινῶν ἃ πωλεῖ ἐξαπατήσῃ ἡμᾶς (lest, friend, the sophist might deceive us, praising whatever he has to sell). (Brugmann [576] also cites negation with οὐ μή: A. Sev. Thebes 38; X. Anab. 2.2.12; S. Oed. Col. 176.)

(2) The deliberative Subjunctive is used if the speaker postulates what might happen: e.g. Hom. Il. 10.62: αὖθι μένω μετὰ τοῖσι, δεδεγμένος εἰς ὅ κεν ἔλθῃς; (am I then to stay with them, waiting for when you might come?); E. Med. 1271: ποῖ φύγω μητρὸς χέρας; (where shall I flee the hands of my mother?); X. Mem. 1.2.45: πότερον βίαν φῶμεν ἢ μὴ φῶμεν εἶναι; (are we to call that force or are we not?); D. 29.37: τί σοι ποιήσωσιν οἱ μάρτυρες; (what will the witnesses do to you?).

(3) The prospective usage, which Brugmann says can hardly be differentiated from the Future, while possible in independent clauses in Homer (e.g. Hom. Il. 6.459 [Monro (*Homer*, 1.317) calls this the "Subj. of confident prediction"]; Od. 5.465), is confined, apart from a few forms (e.g. πάθω; S. Oed. Col. 216), to dependent clauses in Attic Greek.

Analysis of Brugmann's position is instructive. First, (3) has already been discussed, and it has been shown that the Subjunctive is not essentially future-referring, thus this category is better subsumed under one of the other two. Second, the other two categories are differentiated along functional grounds, although the categories are not precise: (1) is essentially designed to correlate with those functions of the Subjunctive that are similar to commands and prohibitions. It has already been shown that the function of the Imperative is not time-based in Greek, and there is no reason on the basis of the examples Brugmann cites to posit anything different. (2) is labelled deliberative, but it is difficult to see the difference between this and (1). In fact, a number of grammarians refuse to make such a distinction. Thus Humbert (113-16) lists two categories of Subjunctive, the "subjonctif de volonté" and the "subjonctif éventuel," under the former of which he includes independent sentences, such as exhortations, prohibitions, deliberation, and apprehension, and under the latter dependent sentences alone. Whereas Humbert maintains a distinction between these two broad categories, on the basis of what has been shown in usage above they can be unified, since dependent and independent uses are syntactical and not semantic distinctions in this instance.

The semantic feature which unifies this analysis of the Subjunctive is called here "projection." (Collinge ["Reflexions," 90-91] discounts historical speculation on the origin and differentiation of varying values in the Subjunctive and Optative; Bers [*Syntax*, 117ff., esp. 142ff.] shows that presence of ἄν is not a distinguishing factor for dependent or independent usage.) It is selected for several reasons. (1) It is preferable to use this term than any of the terms already used in grammars, since they already have connotations that may limit their usefulness as an overarching term. If, for example, "volition" were used (and in one sense it could be since volition is the essential semantic feature of deontic modality, with the added feature of visualization for the Subjunctive and Optative [the Imperative as grammaticalizing volition is discussed in chapt. 7; see Amigues, "Temps," 228; Kühner/Gerth, 1.236]), those familiar with Brugmann and his stream of thought might think that this category excludes deliberative usage. (2) The language in most grammars revolves around human will. This seems to stem from the dichotomy between the Indicative and non-Indicative Moods as relating to certainty of existence. As noted above, a large number of grammarians--most of the same ones who use language of human directedness in discussing the Subjunctive--posit that the Indicative is used for what in fact exists, whereas the other Moods are used for what either is to come in the future, or can be brought into existence. Thus, since the Indicative is best seen as not grammaticalizing reference to what is but what is asserted to be, this conception itself involves human directedness. (3) The term "projection" seems to capture best the semantic quality involved. Gonda's formulation is helpful (*Character*, 69-70; cf. Moulton, 164, who, while discounting the ability to find a root idea of each Mood, asserts that the oblique Moods "are characterized by a common subjective element, representing an attitude of mind on the part of the speaker"):

> Its general function may . . . have been to indicate that the speaker views the process denoted by the verb as existing in his mind or before his mental eyes, or rather: as not yet having a higher degree of being than mental existence. The subjunctive, in other words, expresses visualization. A process in the subj. represents a mental image on the part of the speaker which, in his opinion is capable of realization, or even awaits realization.

But this formulation has limitations, the major one being that it is too closely tied to creating an actual image of a process in one's mind. Thus in light of recent philosophical discussion of the positing of non-existent worlds, the term "projection" is chosen. (Carson's difficulty [*Fallacies*, 75-77] over the deliberative Subjunctive, the direct-question pseudodeliberative Subjunctive, and the rhetorical pseudodeliberative Subjunctive is a question of pragmatics in relation to audience, not of semantics. The proposal made here should clarify the fundamental difficulty.) The Indicative is used to make an assertion about the way things are, while the non-Indicative Moods make no assertion about the way the world is. The Imperative is used to give direction, while the Subjunctive projects a state of affairs. This formulation is then compatible with the entire range of deictic spheres to which Greek may be used to refer, as well as the general theoretical structure of the Greek verbal network posited in this work (see Schwyzer, 2.303-04; Humbert, 154-59, 177-81; Robertson, 828ff., who recognize that the differences in the forms of the Moods are primarily aspectual; cf. Rijksbaron, 43-48).

(b) **Projection with contingent expectation of fulfilment (Optative).** This category is of limited application to hellenistic Greek (see esp. Jannaris, 450-51, 560-67; Goodwin, *Syntax*, appendix I [371-89]; Mandilaras, 277-87; Schmid, *Atticismus*; Anlauf, *Standard*; contra Higgins, "Renaissance"; "Why"). The standard theory of the Optative is that it has two major semantic qualities, besides use in indirect discourse: wish and potential. (Cf. Schwyzer, 2.320ff.; Sanspeur, "'Potentiel'"; Turner, *Syntax*, 119; Boyer, "Classification of Optatives," 130-39; Bers, *Syntax*, 117ff., who discusses the general Attic use of the potential with ἄν and the wish without ἄν [121], although his treatment of a number of potential uses without ἄν, and admission that such usage is legitimate and in fact on the increase in the hellenistic period [134-35] support Gonda's following analysis. The standard theory apparently originated with Delbrück [*Grundlagen*, 116-17; *Syntax*, 2.369-70], who posited "wish" as the original meaning. Not all agree: Brugmann [578], followed by Schwyzer [2.320], is unable to decide, and Kühner/Gerth [1.201] make no attempt.) As Collinge shows, however, whereas it is difficult (if not impossible) to insist upon internal meaning distinctions of the Optative and of the Subjunctive, the difference between them is clear: Hom. Od. 4.692: ἄλλον κ' ἐχθαίρῃσι βροτῶν, ἄλλον κε φιλοίη (a king might hate someone, but perhaps love another), where "a subtle difference is appreciable between subjunctive and optative, in that one can be somewhat surer of a king's enmity than of his friendship" ("Reflexions," 91). Collinge also uses this example in support of his contention that the Moods of "non-assertion" function "simply as a vehicle of the speaker's opinion," and the example cited "is not a plea and it does not refer to the future."

Virtually every grammar distinguishes between the Subjunctive and Optative, though terminology varies. The Optative may be subsumed under the category of projection, and although the distinction between the semantic features of the Subjunctive and Optative is subtle, [±contingency] seems to be the distinguishing semantic feature of the Optative and Subjunctive. The Optative grammaticalizes [+contingency]: e.g. S. Trach. 903: κρυψασ' ἑαυτὸν ἔνθα μή τις εἰσίδοι (hide yourself in here lest someone might look in) (Bers, *Syntax*, 141); Acts 26:29: εὐξαίμην ἂν τῷ θεῷ καὶ ἐν ὀλίγῳ καὶ ἐν μεγάλῳ οὐ μόνον σὲ ἀλλὰ καὶ πάντας τοὺς ἀκούοντάς μου σήμερον γενέσθαι τοιούτους ὁποῖος καὶ ἐγώ εἰμι παρεκτὸς τῶν δεσμῶν τούτων (I would rejoice to God both in little and in great for not only you but indeed all those hearing me today to become such as I am, apart from these chains). As Gonda (*Character*, 51-52; cf. Prichett, "Sentence," 13-15) says,

> The optative, it would appear to me, enables the speaker to introduce the elements of visualization and contingency, the latter being, in my opinion, the main character of this mood. In using this form the ancient Indo-European took, with regard to the process referred to and which existed in his mind, the possibility of non-occurrence into account; he visualized this process as non-actual: it is possible, or it is wished for, or desirable, or generally advisable or recommended and therefore individually problematic; it may be probable, supposed, hypothetical, or even imaginary, its realization is dependent on a condition or on some event that may or may not happen. This condition or other event may be expressed, be implicit or even be vaguely or generally inherent in the situation. If this hypothesis be correct it becomes also clear why the opt. of wish (cupitive) originally referred to realizable as well as unrealizable wishes. Being the mode of eventuality the optative also renders useful services to those who want to be guarded in what they say. Whether in a particular case an optative is "potential," "general," expressive of some wish or other, depends, to a considerable extent, on the situations or the context, and if such should be resorted to, on other syntactical means (order of words, particles, conjunctions etc.).[13]

On the basis of the significantly less frequent usage, the "distinct vowel system" of the Optative (Mandilaras, 287), the relatively narrow range of syntactical collocations, and the more specific semantic expression, the Optative is the marked form in the Subjunctive/Optative opposition, although its semantic quality is less forceful.

There are approximately 68 instances of the Optative in the NT (including εἰμί).[14] The major distinction in NT usage (and Gonda would argue in all Greek usage) is not the kind of Optative, but the contexts in which they are found, often whether the particle ἄν is present. In the grammars (e.g. Goodwin, *Grammar*, 283-85; Rijksbaron, 39-41), differentiation between wish and potential is often made according to presence of ἄν, although in hellenistic Greek there is a tendency to drop ἄν where it might have been used in classical Greek: e.g. Luke 18:36; Acts 21:33 (Moulton, 198, although Bers [*Syntax*, 128ff.] shows through textual evidence that the so-called potential Optative without ἄν [in independent clauses] is much more widespread than most grammars admit). Besides the lack of formal differentiation, a lack of semantic distinction is seen

---

[13]This calls into question Turner's theory that the Optative declined because "No one can or could quite define its essential function" (*Syntax*, 119; similar to Mandilaras, 287). Allison ("Causes," 354-55) suggests that "phonetic blurring" contributed to the disappearance of the Optative, though as he notes this does not explain Lucian's odd usage of the 1st Person Optative after primary tenses. Moulton (199 n. 2) cites similar examples from the papyri: P.Oxy. 60.9-11 (A.D. 323): ἵν' οὖν εἰδέ/ναι ἔχοιτε [for ἔχητε] καὶ . . . καταστήσηται (˞ε); P.Oxy. 71.17 (A.D. 303): εἴ σοι δοκοῖ for the Subjunctive (or Indicative), although he notes that Thumb dissents (cf. 240). See Mandilaras, 272, for other examples. Harman ("Optative," 11-12) suggests that Semitic speakers used to two tenses did not find the need for Moods, but this does not account for the general decline of the Optative in non-biblical Greek.

[14]Differences in figures revolve around such instances as Eph 1:17 and 2 Tim 2:25, whether δωη is considered a Subjunctive, δώῃ, or an Optative, δῴη. I rely upon my GRAMCORD list, but a published list purporting to be complete is found in Harman ("Optative," 7-10), who does not include Mark 11:14; John 13:24 (the reading with εἴη is surely correct, since it has both Alexandrian and Western attestation, and is given a B rating in UBS³ [Metzger, *Commentary*, 240-41]); 2 Tim 4:16; Jude 9. Cf. Mandilaras, 271-87, for papyric usage.

in the following examples: e.g. Luke 1:62: τὸ τί ἂν θέλοι ("how he would like"), and Acts 21:33: ἐπυνθάνετο τίς εἴη ("who he might be") are difficult to distinguish (Moulton, 194-99, esp. 198). Mark 11:14: μηκέτι εἰς τὸν αἰῶνα ἐκ σοῦ μηδεὶς καρπόν φάγοι (no one will eat fruit from you forever) is labelled as "wish" by many scholars, but is not different from Acts 17:18: τί ἂν θέλοι ὁ σπερμολόγος οὗτος λέγειν; (what will this word-spouter want to say?), apart from the latter being a question. Both project a state of affairs, the first contingent upon the fig tree not bearing fruit and the second upon Paul speaking. See also Phlm 20: ναὶ ἀδελφέ, ἐγώ σου ὀναίμην ἐν κυρίῳ (yes, brother, let me benefit from you in the lord), with a hortatory command; Acts 8:20: τὸ ἀργύριόν σου σὺν σοὶ εἴη εἰς ἀπώλειαν (may your silver be with you unto destruction), with a mild command, contingent upon Simon's persistence in desiring the ability to lay on hands; 2 Tim 4:16: μὴ αὐτοῖς λογισθείη (don't let it be counted against them). As Gonda says, "There is, however, generally speaking no use in attempting to distinguish between a cupitive or a potential function of the mood" (*Character*, 54-55), since the form is always the same, the Optative, regardless of use of ἄν.[15]

Use of γένοιτο seems to express the speaker's projection of someone performing an anticipated yet contingent act (see Lys. 13.46; P.Oxy. 237.31, 39 [A.D. 186]). For example, in Luke 1:38 the Optative is appropriate for the startled Mary to affirm her tentative trust in the angel's message: γένοιτό μοι κατὰ τὸ ῥῆμά σου (may it be to me according to your word). (Cf. X. Hell. 4.1.38: εἴθ', ὦ λῷστε σύ, τοιοῦτος ὢν φίλος ἡμῖν γένοιο [would that you, the best of men, being such a one, would become a friend to us]. This is similar to the "contingent opt., which does not pose the alternative as unequivocally as the subjunctive of deliberation [and] is very suitable to the occasion" [Gonda, *Character*, 56].) With the negative, the opposite is expressed, though it is noteworthy how many contexts actually have clear indications of a "conditional" nature (Gonda, *Character*, 58). Although Acts 8:31 is the only instance of the Optative in the NT with a conditional protasis (a II.c. conditional in the scheme devised in chapt. 6), in both Gal 2:17 and 3:21 μὴ γένοιτο is preceded and followed by εἰ clauses. Every other use of μὴ γένοιτο occurs in response to a rhetorical question and expresses the negative in continuation of the argumentative flow: Rom 3:4, 6, 31; 6:2; 15; 7:7, 13; 9:14; 11:1, 11; 1 Cor 6:15. Instructive is Luke 20:16, where Jesus, at the end of the parable of the vine growers, asks what the lord of the vineyard will do: he will come and kill the wicked farmers. The people respond: μὴ γένοιτο. Their response exemplifies appropriate use of the Optative. They recognize the justice and yet the extremeness of the lord's punishment for people performing such horrible acts.

Use of the Optative is significant for indirect discourse. The ability to retain the verb of direct discourse following secondary forms (with alteration of Person only where necessary), the lack of verbal formal distinction of indirect discourse following primary verbs, and the troublesome nature of distinguishing what qualifies as thought, etc., all point to a problematic distinction between direct and indirect discourse in Greek (cf. e.g. the narrow standards of Jannaris [471-72, 453] to the very broad standards of Goodwin [*Grammar*, 314-22]). More troubling is the statement by grammarians that the Optative in indirect discourse stands for the Indicative or Subjunctive and loses its attitudinal semantics (e.g. Humbert, 158). As mentioned above, there is only one instance in the NT where scholars argue that the Optative replaces the Subjunctive following a secondary form (Acts 25:16), although πρίν (ἤ) is used more frequently with the Optative following a negated clause (Schwyzer, 2.323, 334; cf. Kühner/Gerth, 2.456, who claim that these are all in indirect discourse, although the definition is a wide one: e.g. Hom.

---

[15] It cannot be overlooked that in classical Greek the Optative usually takes μή as its negative, except with ἄν when it takes οὐ. Although this may be a mere convention, it may be that the 'negative of fact' was felt to be more appropriate to counter the conditional force of the particle ἄν.

II. 21.580).[16] There are approximately nineteen other instances of the Optative, and many of these are questionable as indirect discourse. For example, Luke 1:62; 6:11; 9:46; 15:26; John 13:24; Acts 5:24; 10:17 all have ἄν, and follow a pattern found in independent clauses (Blass/Debrunner, ¶ 386[1]). These could be instances of direct discourse. A further result of this, however, is that the remaining examples may also have been in the Optative in direct discourse. The contexts do nothing to argue against this.

For example, in Luke 1:29, Mary may have been debating whether in fact she had had a greeting from the angel. In Luke 3:15, the deliberating people ask themselves whether John might be the Christ. As Winer (374) says of interrogative words in indirect questions, "The optative is used of subjective possibility, of something simply conceived in the mind; and hence this mood is found in narration after a preterite, when some one is introduced with a question which has reference to his own conceptions alone"; see also Luke 8:9; 18:36; 22:23; Acts 17:11. In Acts 20:16, Paul expresses his wish to be able (εἴη) to spend Pentecost in Jerusalem (cf. Phlm 20, where the 1st Person is used); Acts 24:19, Paul tells Felix that it is necessary for the Jews to accuse him directly, if they would be able (ἔχοιεν) to find anything (cf. BGU 969 [i].24 [A.D. 142?]: εἰ δὲ μὴ ἔχοι); see also Acts 27:12, 39. In Acts 25:20, Festus tells Agrippa that he asks Paul whether it would be possible (βούλοιτο) to go to Jerusalem for trial (P.Oxy. 2110.15 [A.D. 370]). Particularly instructive is Acts 21:33: ἐπυνθάνετο τίς εἴη καὶ τί ἐστιν πεποιηκώς (he inquired who he might be and what he has done), where either there is a case of mixed direct and indirect discourse, or, more likely, the full semantic significance of each attitude is preserved. The Optative is used because of the uncertainty by the centurion about who the perpetrator of the crime is, although it is clearly asserted that he has performed such acts (Winer [375] cites X.Eph. 5.12: ἐτεθαυμάκει, τίνες τε ἦσαν καὶ τί βούλοιντο [he marvelled at who they were and what they might be doing], among others). Thus a strong argument can be made that in Greek classification of use of the Optative after secondary tenses as standing in place of another Mood is not entirely correct. In many cases it is clear that an Optative would have been appropriate in direct discourse, and in other cases the semantic value of the Optative is maintained even in indirect discourse.

That attitudinal semantics are to be taken seriously even in instances traditionally called indirect discourse (Schwyzer, 2.333; contra Gildersleeve, "Notes," 205, who calls use of the Optative for the Indicative in indirect discourse a "pseudo-optative") is illustrated by: X. Mem. 1.1.13: ἐθαύμαζε δ᾽ εἰ μὴ φανερὸν αὐτοῖς ἐστιν, ὅτι ταῦτα οὐ δυνατόν ἐστιν ἀνθρώποις εὑρεῖν· ἐπεὶ καὶ τοὺς μέγιστον φρονοῦντας ἐπὶ τῷ περὶ τούτων λέγειν οὐ ταὐτὰ δοξάζειν ἀλλήλοις, ἀλλὰ τοῖς μαινομένοις ὁμοίως διακεῖσθαι πρὸς ἀλλήλους, and 1.2.7: ἐθαύμαζε δ᾽ εἴ τις ἀρετὴν ἐπαγγελλόμενος ἀργύριον πράττοιτο καὶ μὴ νομίζοι τὸ μέγιστον κέρδος ἕξειν φίλον ἀγαθὸν κτησάμενος, ἀλλὰ φοβοῖτο μὴ ὁ γενόμενος καλὸς κἀγαθὸς τῷ τὰ μέγιστα εὐεργετήσαντι μὴ τὴν μεγίστην χάριν ἕξοι. The first is reflection upon Socrates's behaviour in the specific context of going for walks in public areas and responding to the perceived limitations of other professors. Thus the passage appropriately uses the Indicative and may be rendered: "and he marvelled that it was not clear to them, that it is not possible for a man to discover these things, since those who have too presumptuous thoughts on this, when they speak of these things, are not able to hold identical opinions with each other, but like madmen they behave with one another." The other passage, however, is in the context of responding to the charges brought against Socrates, and is thus a response to what the speaker believes to be unfounded charges. The use of the Optative is appropriate, as are the impersonal pronoun and the indefinite substantival Participle: "and he marvelled that someone preaching virtue would earn

---

[16]To the objection that this would reflect a high degree of Attic competence, it may be noted that usage of πρίν with a finite verb is rare anywhere in hellenistic Greek (the Ptolemaic papyri list no examples of πρίν with a finite verb, so Mayser, 2, 1.275, 310). Those who argue that this is an instance of indirect discourse note that the Subjunctive may or may not have had ἄν. "If the ἄν be supposed to have been in the original sentence . . ., it has been dropped in accordance with regular usage in such cases" (Burton, 133), but the sentence is then an instance of a mix of indirect and direct discourse, since ἔστιν is retained (see Winer, 372).

money and not consider creating good friends as having the greatest gain, but he would fear, lest the one becoming good and virtuous would not have the greatest gratitude towards the one who shows him the greatest kindness." A possible explanation for use of the tenses is that the more heavily marked primary forms by their semantic nature do not allow the possibility of altering the strength of the statement (thus the original Mood is preserved), while the less heavily marked secondary forms allow (though they do not require) the speaker to introduce a contingent element. Since the reported speech is asserted by the speaker to have occurred, the Subjunctive, which claims nothing for the reality of the event's coming to fruition, would be inappropriate, while the element of contingency was felt to be appropriate (cf. Robertson, 1030).

Virtually all grammarians are agreed that during the hellenistic period the Optative fell into relative disuse, especially among non-Atticistic writers. From a semantic standpoint (the phonological problems have been recognized above), this development may be read in two ways. The first is that the speakers came to feel that there was no semantic distinction between the Subjunctive and the Optative, i.e. that the Subjunctive was able to do everything that the Optative could and hence subsumed it semantically. The second is that the Optative retained its semantic features but that speakers felt that it was less often necessary to grammaticalize these, with the Subjunctive felt to be sufficient for most purposes (see Turner, *Syntax*, 119; Mandilaras, 287; cf. Higgins, "Renaissance"). The second option appears correct: (1) no new Subjunctive form was invented to reflect the increased semantic weight of incorporating the Optative. (2) The Optative persisted to varying degrees and in varying contexts within hellenistic Greek. Although this usage may not have been according to what might be construed as Attic standards (the question of Attic standards is left aside), there appears to have been a persistence in usage that cannot be explained as simply a formulaic or archaic usage (see de Foucault, *Recherches*, 145-55, esp. 145-46, who discusses persistence of the Optative in Polybius). The analysis suggested above would encompass the theory of Higgins that in fact the Optative continued into the early Byzantine period, although with significantly different usage. (3) The Optative from Homer on was used predominantly in the specific contexts of dependent clauses, unlike the Subjunctive, which thrived in both independent and dependent clauses. Its broader pragmatic range made it more firmly entrenched and thus less easily displaced (this is besides its paradigmatic regularity). This pattern conforms to one, whereby the more heavily marked form decreases in usage in relation to the less heavily marked form (see Schwyzer, 2.337-3). This contrast is particularly acute when seen in relation to classical Greek, which was itself transitional, when a large number of what were later felt to be redundant features were maintained.

(c) **Expectation (Future).** The relation of the Future to the Subjunctive and the Optative is discussed in more detail in chapt. 9, though it is sufficient to state here that the Future is best seen as semantically designating the speaker's expectation [+expectation] that an event is coming about. Since placement of the Future within the Greek verbal network has anomalies (i.e. presence of the Participle and Infinitive, which are difficult to explain in any system of analysis), its semantic character may be seen as reflecting qualities of both attitude and aspectuality; consequently, many traditional grammars appreciate the 'modal' qualities of the Future (e.g. Magnien, *Futur*, v-vii; Humbert, 151-53; Schwyzer, 2.290-94), and several more recent grammars the aspectual (e.g. McKay, 136, 140-41, 147-48; Wilkinson, *"Aspect,"* chapt. 1; Durie, 288, 92). Since it is aspectually vague, formally derived from the Subjunctive, found in parallel usage in, for example, conditional protases, dependent statements such as causal, final, and relative statements, it is often treated functionally in relation to the Subjunctive, where the Future has material, implicational (fewer irregularities of form), and statistical markedness.

2. MARKEDNESS AND THE ASSERTIVE ATTITUDE. In chapt. 2 it is argued on the basis of use of the tense-categories from Homer through to the 2d cent. A.D., and especially of discussion by the earliest grammarians through to the present, that tense-categories are dynamic constructs grammaticalizing aspect in the perfective/imperfective opposition. If an argument were being formulated diachronically alone, it could be argued that there are many cases where the Aorist is the 'older' form, but there would also be significant examples where the Present seems to be 'older' (see e.g. Curtius, *Verb*, 264; Robertson [344-45] dismisses this distinction, arguing for two verb stems originally). The contention here, however, is that the historical argument is far less important than patterns and tendencies in construction of the tense-categories, which reveal that whereas the perfective and imperfective opposition is fundamental, the distinction in markedness is not great. It favours the perfective as the least heavily marked aspect within an equipollent opposition. The major criteria for comparison are the following (see esp. Zwicky, "Markedness," 130-37).

a. Material markedness, i.e. morphological bulk. Though many different categorizations of Greek verbal morphology exist (see e.g. Brugmann, *Flexionslehre*, for one very thorough method), this discussion presents characteristics most noteworthy for a distinction in markedness. (Helpful are Curtius, *Verb*; Brugmann, 312ff.; Goodwin, *Grammar*, 92ff.; Giles, *Manual*, 423ff.; Jannaris, 207ff.; Moulton/Howard, 182ff.; Mayser, 1, 2.113-27, 131-45; Schwyzer, 1.672-737; Robertson, 343ff.; Palmer, *Grammar*, 122-49; Mandilaras, 61ff.; Gignac, 2.255ff. The outline adopted is an adapted version of Goodwin's.)

(1) Stem. Material markedness revolves around what the tense paradigm does to the verb stem. The general rule is that the verb stem may be identical in both the Aorist and the Present, but if they are not the Present usually appears in a strengthened form (Goodwin, *Grammar*, 136), although suppletive verbal paradigms do not conform to this pattern for obvious reasons. It is intriguing that virtually all discussions of tense forms treat the Present before the Aorist and at greater length, since the categories virtually always are spoken of in terms of greater bulk. (a) Verb stem unchanged: λύω/ἔλυσα; γράφω/ἔγραψα; φείδομαι/ἐφεισάμην; φύω/ἔφῡν (ἔφυσαν occurs as early as S. Oed. King 436). Contract verbs--especially in όω and έω--are considered here as well:[17] τιμάω/ἐτίμησα; φιλέω/ἐφίλησα; τελειόω/ἐτελείωσα; περισσεύω/ ἐπερίσσευσα. This is the largest single category of verbs in Greek and presents the relatively strongest evidence for the heavier markedness of the Aorist on the basis of the augment and sigma (σ). The strength of this evidence is reduced when it is realized that: the augment and sigma (with

---

[17]Technically contract verbs, including here ευω (Palmer, *Grammar*, 134), are considered iota verbs (see e.g. Moulton/Howard, 383ff.), but since the verb stem remains unchanged though the connecting vowel is usually lengthened, and the marks of derivation are significantly obscure, they are listed here. Cf. Gignac, 2.365ff.

endings) are paradigm or formal identifiers (the augment, of course, is not present in non-Indicative Moods); and reduplication occurs in several very widely used Present forms in this tense class, thereby increasing their morphological bulk. These include many μι verbs (Robertson [306] thinks they are the oldest Greek verbs): γίνομαι (γίγ[ε]νομαι [synchopated])/ἐγενόμην; τίθημι/ἔθηκα (ἔθηκα replaces ἐτέθην in the NT, and in hellenistic Greek in general); δίδωμι/ἔδωκα. (Most in this class are 2 [strong] Aorists, which are being superceded by 1 [sigmatic/weak] Aorists in hellenistic Greek.) Whereas a number of 2 Aorist verbs (Active and Middle Voice, Infinitive, Subjunctive, and Participle) reduplicate in Homer (Monro, 39; Goodwin, *Grammar*, 128), this has disappeared except for a few instances, such as ἄγω/ἤγαγον (ἤγαγον occurs in the Ptolemaic papyri except for P.Par. 36.12 [163-62 B.C.] with ἀγαγῆσαι. ἦξα predominates in post-Ptolemaic papyri [Mandilaras, 143]). Cf. in classical Greek: ἀλέξω/ἄλαλκον; ἐνίπτω/ἠνίπαπον; ἐρύκω/ἠρύκακον (Goodwin, *Grammar*, 128).
　　(b) Stems which strengthen internal vowels: λείπω/ἔλιπον (ἔλειψα is first attested in 1st cent. B.C. [e.g. κατέλιψα BGU 1141.18 (14-13 B.C.)] and later became regular [Mandilaras, 145]); φεύγω/ἔφυγον. A special class of verbs includes: πλέω/ἔπλευσα (a contract verb? See Palmer, *Grammar*, 125); πνέω/ἔπνευσα; ῥέω/ἐ(ρ)ύην; -χέω/-ἔχεα, which are weak stem verbs in υ. Goodwin (*Grammar*, 137) speculates that "These originally had the strong form in ευ, which became εϝ before a vowel, and finally dropped ϝ, leaving ε." The strengthened internal vowels point to markedness of the Present form.
　　(2) T class. Some labial (π, β, φ) verb stems have τ in the Present: κόπτω/ἔκοψα, -εκόπην; βλάπτω/ἔβλαψα. Whereas the sigma plus consonant forms a double sibilant in the Aorist, the Present retains two consonants.
　　(3) Iota class. There are four subdivisions of iota verbs, formed by the addition of iota and connecting vowel to the verb stem and making the proper emphasis changes. (a) σσω. This ending usually derives from a palatal stem (κ, χ, γ) plus iota: πράσσω/ἔπραξα; ταράσσω/ἐτάραξα; κηρύσσω/ἐκήρυξα; with a few from labial stems: πλάσσω/ἔπλασα. See explanation (2) above.
　　(b) ζω. The Present has the double sibilant, whereas generally the Aorist retains the single root consonant, originally δ or γ (see Goodwin, *Grammar*, 138-39; Moulton/Howard, 404ff.; Palmer, *Grammar*, 137ff.). Many ζω-suffixed verbs, especially with αζω, were formed on analogy, often from αω verbs (cf. ἀμφιέννυσιν [Matt 6:30], which is replaced by ἀμφιέζει [Luke 12:28; v.l. -άζει in B] [Moulton/Howard, 68-69]): ἁρπάζω/ἥρπασα, ἡρπάγην; ἐλπίζω/ἤλπισα; θαυμάζω/ἐθαύμασα; σῴζω/ἔσωσα; σφάζω/ἔσφαξα; κράζω/ἔκραξα (ἀνέκραγον at Luke 23:18, though ἀνέκραξαν a widely attested variant [Tischendorf]; cf. Acts 24:21 with ἐκέκραξα); σαλπίζω/ἐσάλπισα (a new Aorist, the previous form being ἐσάλπιγξα); παίζω/ἔπαιξα.[18]
　　(c) Liquid stems. (1) λι: ἀγγέλλω/ἤγγειλα, -ηγγέλην; βάλλω/ἔβαλον. (2) ανι or αρι, where ι is transposed and then contracted with α to αι: φαίνω/ἔφανα, ἐφάνην; χαίρω/ἐχάρην; -σημαίνω/ἐσήμανα (the papyri prefer ἐσήμηνα, e.g. P.Teb. 743.7 [c. 2d cent. B.C.] [Mayser, 1, 2.133]); αἴρω/ἦρα; καθαίρω/ἐκάθαρα. (3) ενι, ερι, ινι, ιρι, υνι, υπι, where ι drops out and the preceding vowel is lengthened, although in several instances the Aorist form shows a lengthened vowel because of compensatory lengthening for the dropped sigma: κτείνω/-ἔκτεινα; κείρω/ἔκειρα; κρίνω/ἔκρινα; γίνομαι (written as γείνομαι in many manuscripts; Moulton/Howard, 232)/ἐγενήθην; ἐγείρω/ἤγειρα; πλύνω/ἔπλυνα; οἰκτίρω (often spelled οἰκτείρω)/ᾤκτειρα.
　　(d) Stems in αυ (Goodwin [*Grammar*, 140] says the αυ stem became αϝι and then αι; cf. Schwyzer, 1.266. Gignac [2.273 n. 2] notes that κάω never occurs in Attic inscriptions or the NT, but occurs in the papyri and koine authors): καίω/-ἐκάην, ἔκαυσα; κλαίω/ἔκλαυσα.
　　(4) N class. The nasal adds bulk to the Present.

---

[18]παίζω earlier had two forms of the Aorist, ἔπαιξα and ἔπαισα. The number of verbs with alternative Aorist forms (see e.g. Moulton/Howard) shows morphological diversity not found in the Present, and points to the Aorist as the less heavily marked tense form.

(a) Prevocalic ν: κάμνω/ἔκαμον; ⁻τέμνω/ἐτμήθην, ⁻ἔτεμον; ⁻βαίνω/⁻ἔβην; πίνω/ἔπιον; δύνω/ἔδυν, ἔδυσα (cf. the reduplicated form ἐνδιδύσκω in Mark 15:17; Luke 16:19, possibly either a Doricism [Blass/Debrunner, ¶ 73] or the earliest instance of a υν verb transformed into a σκω verb [Palmer, *Grammar*, 18, 148]. On use of both in later Greek see Gignac, 2.279).

(b) αν: ἁμαρτάνω/ἡμάρτησα, ἥμαρτον; αἰσθάνομαι/ἠσθόμην; αὐξάνω/ηὔξησα (in the NT cf. αὔξω/ηὐξήθην in Matt 13:32; Acts 7:17; 2 Cor 9:10; Eph 2:21; 4:15; Col 2:19; 1 Pet 2:2. The Ptolemaic papyri have αὔξω except for αὐξάνεσθα in P.Leid. B, 8 [164 B.C.] [Mandilaras, 89]; cf. Gignac, 2.278). In stems with a short final vowel, a second nasal (μ before a labial, ν before dental, γ before a palatal) is infixed after it: λαμβάνω/ἔλαβον (cf. ἐλήμφθην); λανθάνω/ἔλαθον; τυγχάνω/ἔτυχον.

(c) νε: ⁻ικνέομαι/⁻ικόμην; ⁻κυνέω/⁻εκύνησα.

(d) νυ or ννυ, including νυμι verbs: δείκνυμι[19]/ἔδειξα; σβέννυμι/ἔσβεσα; ζώννυμι/⁻έζωσα; στρώννυμι/ἔστρωσα; ἀποκτέννυμι/ἔκτεινα;[20] ⁻μίγνυμι/ἔμιξα; ⁻όλλυμι/⁻ώλεσα, ⁻ωλόμην.

(e) να: βαίνω/ἔβην. This resembles 4. (c) (2), but inflection in the Aorist is different.

(5) ⁻σκω ending of Present verbs: γηράσκω/ἐγήρασα; εὑρίσκω/εὗρον, εὑρέθην; ἀναλίσκω/ἀνήλωσα (see Gignac, 2.250-51, on reduplication and augment); γι[γ]νώσκω/ἔγνων, ἐγνώσθην; ⁻θνήσκω/⁻έθανον; ἱλάσκομαι/ἱλάσθην; μιμνήσκω (see Gignac, 2.277, for variants)/⁻έμνησα; διδάσκω/ἐδίδαξα; πάσχω (for παθ-σκω)/ἔπαθον; ἀναλίσκω/ἀνήλωσα.

(6) μι verbs with simple stems or often reduplication in Present: ἵστημι/ἔστησα, ἔστην; δύναμαι/ἠδυνήθην; ἐπίσταμαι/ἠπιστήθην; ὀνίνημι/ὠνάμην; πίμπλημι/ἔπλησα.

In general it can be seen that the Present is morphologically bulkier than the Aorist, often evidencing double consonants or lengthened vowels.

b. Implicational markedness. Implicational markedness of verbal categories is shown in two ways. (1) The Present/Imperfect as the more heavily marked form evidences fewer irregularities as a verbal category: e.g. ω forms are overwhelmingly predominant over μι forms, unlike the diversity of weak and strong Aorists; the Aorist, regardlesss of its formation of the Active and Middle Voice, has an irregular formation of the Passive with (θ)ην (see esp. Schwyzer, 1.760-63; Mandilaras, 146-48); and the Aorist of course does not have the augment outside of the Indicative As McKay (223) says, the augment, whatever its origins, was probably an adverbial particle that became part of the Indicative paradigm (see below for discussion of the non-temporal nature of the augment), but its absence in the non-Indicative Moods not only reduces its bulk, but evidences greater irregularity than the more heavily marked Present. (2) The Present/Imperfect shows syncretism, with amalgamation of Middle/Passive Voices, whereas the Aorist realizes all three Voices in separate forms.

---

[19]The NT, like other Greek, shows divided usage with the thematic form.

[20]The classical form is ἀποκτίννυμι, which probably came under the influence of the ε in the Aorist stem κτεν, resulting in ⁻κτέννυμι (⁻κτέννω/κτείνω is probably a thematizing of the μι verb). Cf. Mark 12:5 where ℵ* A B C D read ἀποκτέννοντες and ℵᶜ ἀποκτίννυντες, the older form; and Luke 12:4 where a A read ἀποκτεννόντων and D ἀποκτενόντων (the reading ἀποκτεινόντων in NA²⁶ and UBS³ is late in any case). See Moulton/Howard, 245.

c. Distributional markedness. Questions of tense frequency are often not telling (see Comrie, *Aspect*, 117). Besides, studies of tense frequency in Greek literature are lacking, making investigation of sweeping patterns particularly difficult. But several points may be made. While the numerical figures are not decisive, a case can be made that the Aorist is slightly less heavily marked than the Present/Imperfect. Of approximately 28,110 verbs in the NT, 2600 are aspectually vague (εἰμί, - εἶμι, φημί, κεῖμαι). In the Indicative: 5922 Aorists to 5261 Presents (4086)/Imperfects (1175); Subjunctive: 1393 Aorists to 384 Presents; Optative: 45 Aorists to 11 Presents; Imperative: 763 Aorists to 824 Presents; Infinitive: 1244 Aorists to 845 Presents; and Participle: 2286 Aorists to 3674 Presents; thus 11653 Aorists to 10602 Presents. Several patterns can be observed. In all instances the Aorist exceeds the Present/Imperfect except for the Imperative and Participle. The Imperative is easily explained if it is realized that negated Aorist Subjunctives functioning as prohibitions (note that the Aorist Subjunctive overwhelms the Present) are not included among Aorist Imperatives. The ratio regarding the Participle is noteworthy, since it is the more heavily marked form of the semantic feature [±factive presupposition] in relation to the less heavily marked Infinitive, where the Aorist again predominates. A similar set of patterns is seen in papyri from the 2d-4th cents. A.D., according to the rough statistics of Mandilaras, especially if aspectually vague verbs are considered, although the figures for 2d cent. B.C. to 1st cent. A.D. show predominance of the Present (59; Mandilaras just lists figures, making comparison difficult). Perhaps this can be accounted for by the discourse type of the material, although Plato's dialogues seem to maintain a similar ratio. (Weymouth ["Rendering," 43] gives statistics on Herodotus and Thucydides showing that in both non-narrative and narrative portions the Present/Imperfect surpasses the Aorist; due to his discussion of the historic Present it is possible that these figures only apply to Indicative forms. Schlachter ["Untersuchungen," 22 (1907-08) esp. 229] and Miller ["Imperfect," 142] show that in most major Greek authors from Homer through to Arrian the Aorist exceeds the Imperfect.)

d. Semantic markedness. In chapt. 2, four different analogies are drawn--verbal opposition, conceptual description, planes of discourse, systemic network--to describe the semantic markedness of the individual verb forms. Through each one it can be seen that the Aorist is the less heavily marked verb form in the Present/Imperfect opposition, and the least heavily marked when the Perfect is also considered.

e. Conclusion. In Greek it is best not to see any of the verb forms as unmarked members of a privative opposition. The Aorist and Present/Imperfect instead comprise a bipolar opposition, with the Aorist as the less heavily marked and the Present as the more heavily marked on the basis of material, implicational, distributive, and semantic criteria.

PART II

3. PERFECTIVE ASPECT: RECENT DISCUSSION. a.

Introduction. Chapter 1 argues against the *Aktionsart* theory of kind of action, whereby an objective description of a process is attempted. There it is seen that kind of action cannot be simplistically described as punctiliar, linear, etc. according to any principled grammatical means, and that Greek verb tenses make no such attempt. Chapter 2 defines a model of verb-tense usage using the concept of verbal aspect as opposed to a theory of absolute temporal reference. There it is argued that the tenses in Greek are semantically essentially non-temporal, but that in context of pragmatic usage they have temporal implicature determined by deictic indicators. To guide discussion, pragmatic usage of the tenses is divided into five categories: past, present, future, omnitemporal and timeless reference. The first three provide little difficulty, since the standard conception of the tenses is formulated in these terms. The category of omnitemporal reference is introduced as a means of classifying instances seen to be valid in past, present and future time. Under this category is discussed what is traditionally called 'gnomic' usage, although a more restrictive definition is included. And the fifth category, timeless reference, refers to instances where a statement is not deictically limited, and is perhaps best seen as the closest in meaning to the essentially non-temporal semantic character of the verb itself.

b. Perfective Aspect (Aorist). Two recent articles by NT scholars, one article by a linguist, and one by a classical scholar have taken up some of the challenges posed by these issues. After examining them, it becomes clear that much progress has been made in examining the function of the Aorist, even though many have failed to appreciate the strength and conclusiveness of the arguments offered.

1. In 1972, Stagg published what must now be regarded as a classic article, "The Abused Aorist," in which he argues essentially one point: though the action described by the Aorist "may be momentary, singular, or 'once and for all,' . . . it is not the use of the aorist that makes it such"

(222).[1] After citing a number of abuses of this principle[2] and surveying a representative number of NT grammars (228-31; see my chapt. 1), he cites several crucial examples which illustrate that the traditional conception of the Aorist as punctiliar is unfounded. (He implicitly distinguishes *Aktionsart* from the semantics of the Aorist when he recognizes the distinction "between semantics and the semantic situation" [pragmatics?] [225].)

2 Cor 11:24-25: ὑπὸ Ἰουδαίων πεντάκις τεσσεράκοντα παρὰ μίαν ἔλαβον, τρὶς ἐραβδίσθην, ἄπαξ ἐλιθάσθην, τρὶς ἐναυάγησα. . . (I received forty-nine lashes five times by the Jews, three times I was beaten, once I was stoned, three times I was shipwrecked). As Stagg says, "It would be nonsense to see point action here. These actions were not singular, momentary, or once-for-all" (228). He could have added that even the stoning was not of the character of the "once-for-all" action that many scholars argue regarding the Aorist. See below.

John 2:20: τεσσεράκοντα καὶ ἓξ ἔτεσιν οἰκοδομήθη ὁ ναὸς οὗτος (this temple was built for forty-six years). "The aorist indicative does not here designate a single action in the past" (228). [Cf. Hdt. 1.16.1: Ἄρδυος δὲ βασιλεύσαντος ἑνὸς δέοντα πεντήκοντα ἔτεα . . . καὶ ἐβασίλευσε ἔτεα δυώδεκα (A. reigned for forty-nine years . . . and he ruled twelve years); 1.25.1, 1.84.1, 1.86.1, 1.102.1, 1.107.1, 1.130.1; 1.146.1: οἱ Ἴωνες δυώδεκα πόλιας ἐποιήσαντο (the Ionians made twelve cities); 2.157; Lys. 12.4: ἔτη δὲ τριάκοντα ᾤκησε (he lived there 30 years), followed by statements specifying his actions, using Aorists and the Imperfect, ᾠκοῦμεν; cf. Present, e.g., in Hdt. 1.106.1; 1.18.1: ἐπολέμεε ἔτεα ἕνδεκα (he fought for eleven years).]

Luke 19:13: πραγματεύσασθε ἐν ᾧ ἔρχομαι (carry on business until I come). "The aorist imperative tells nothing of the nature of the action" (228). (See my chapt. 7.)

Although Stagg does not present a rigorous linguistic justification of his thesis, his examples suffice to show that the traditional conception of aoristic action according to the *Aktionsart* theory of punctiliar action is not satisfactory.

This makes more surprising the recent work of Kim (*Origin*, esp. 3-31 [chapt. 1]), where he argues for the centrality of the Damascus road experience in Paul's theology on the basis of use of the Aorist tense. Two quotations suffice: "The aorist ἔλαμψεν [2 Cor 4:6: ὃς [God] ἔλαμψεν ἐν ταῖς καρδίαις ἡμῶν πρὸς φωτισμὸν τῆς γνώσεως τῆς δόξης τοῦ θεοῦ ἐν προσώπῳ [Ἰησοῦ] Χριστοῦ (who shown in our hearts to enlighten the knowledge of the glory of God in the face of [Jesus] Christ] refers back to a definite point of time in the past, the moment of the Damascus event" (7). Not only is the reference suspect, but his characterization of the Aorist neglects recent discussion (cf. 11). A second quotation may be noted:

> There is a series of the aorist forms of the verbs that refer to the call of Paul to apostleship on the Damascus road. It has already been noted that in Rom 12:3; 15:15; 1 Cor 3:10; Gal 2:9; Eph 3:2, 7, 8 Paul uses the formula χάρις + the aorist passive form of the verb δίδωμι + μοι to indicate God's apostolic commission of him on the Damascus road.... A variation of the formula appears in Rom 1:5. Here also the verb (λαμβάνω) is in the aorist

---

[1]Stagg ("Aorist," 222-23) continues: "'Aorist' is one of the few grammatical terms well suited to its purpose. . . . It is 'a-oristic,' i.e., undetermined or undefined. The aorist draws no boundaries. It tells nothing about the nature of the action under consideration. It is 'punctiliar' only in the sense that the act is viewed without reference to duration, interruption, completion, or anything else. . . . The aorist can properly be used to cover any kind of action: single or multiple, momentary or extended, broken or unbroken, completed or open-ended. The aorist simply refrains from describing." In NT study, Stagg was anticipated in some ways by Pistorius ("Remarks") and elucidated by McKay ("Syntax"). His claims are in many ways compatible with the aspectual theory posited in this work.

[2]Culprits (223-28) include Bousset (Rev 2:21; 3:3), Schnackenburg (1 John 5:6), Brown (John 1:5), Dodd (1 John 1:8, 10; cf. 3:6, 9), Wilder (1 John 2:1; cf. 3:6, 9; 5:1), Charles (Rev 4:11), Beare (Phil 2:6-8; 3:10), J.A. Sanders (Phil 2:6-8), Jeremias (Matt 6:11), and Morris (Rev 2:5; 3:3; 5:5, 9; 7:14; 12:11; 20:4). Carson (*Fallacies*, 72) cites others in recent post-Stagg work.

form, indicating a definite point of time where Paul received the apostolic commission. (25-26; cf. 25, 26, 27)

Of his reviewers, apparently only Gardner notes this ("Damascus," 22), although the failure of this part of Kim's argument calls the major support for his entire thesis into question. More importantly it indicates that Stagg has yet to be heard fully.

2. A second article to consider, by Smith, called "Errant Aorist Interpreters" (1981), acknowledging its debt to Stagg, makes five major points.

a. The Aorist does not necessarily refer to past time (207): e.g. Luke 7:35: ἐδικαιώθη ἡ σοφία ἀπὸ πάντων τῶν τέκνων αὐτῆς (wisdom is justified from all her children); cf. Mark 1:1; John 13:31; 15:8; 1 Pet 1:24. See below.

b. The Aorist does not indicate completed action (208): e.g. Rom 5:17: ὁ θάνατος ἐβασίλευσεν διὰ τοῦ ἑνός (death reigned through one). He also cites non-Indicative examples: 1 John 5:21: φυλάξατε ἑαυτὰ ἀπὸ τῶν εἰδώλων (guard yourselves from idols); Eph 2:7: ἐνδείξηται ἐν τοῖς αἰῶσιν τοῖς ἐπερχομένοις τὸ ὑπερβάλλον πλοῦτος τῆς χάριτος αὐτοῦ (he might show in the coming ages the exceeding richness of his grace). Though I note in chapt. 2 that "completed" denotes a temporal dimension not essential to the Aorist, Smith's point here is that the Aorist may be used in contexts where an event is not seen as terminated.

c. The Aorist neither identifies nor views action as punctiliar (209): e.g. Phil 2:12: καθὼς πάντοτε ὑπηκούσατε (as you always obeyed); Acts 28:30: ἐνέμεινεν δὲ διετίαν ὅλην ἐν ἰδίῳ μισθώματι (he remained for two whole years in his own room).

d. The Aorist does not indicate once-for-all action (213): e.g. 1 John 2:24: ὑμεῖς ὃ ἠκούσατε ἀπ᾽ ἀρχῆς (what you heard from the beginning); Acts 10:38: ὃς διῆλθεν εὐεργετῶν (he [Jesus] went about doing good); Matt 22:28: πάντες γὰρ ἔσχον αὐτήν (for all seven men had her); Rev 20:4: καὶ ἔζησαν καὶ ἐβασίλευσαν μετὰ τοῦ Χριστοῦ χίλια ἔτη (and they lived and reigned with Christ for a thousand years); Acts 1:21: ᾧ εἰσῆλθεν καὶ ἐξῆλθεν ἐφ᾽ ἡμᾶς ὁ κύριος Ἰησοῦς (in which the lord Jesus went in and out among us); Matt 27:8: διὸ ἐκλήθη ὁ ἀγρὸς ἐκεῖνος ἀγρὸς αἵματος ἕως τῆς σήμερον (wherefore that field is called "field of blood" until today); Rom 3:23: πάντες γὰρ ἥμαρτον καὶ ὑστεροῦνται τῆς δόξης τοῦ θεοῦ (for all sin and fall short [Present] of the glory of God); cf. John 17:11: τήρησον αὐτοὺς ἐν τῷ ὀνόματί σου (keep them in your name).

e. The Aorist does not occur in classes or kinds (221). Rejecting the common labels for Aorist usage--constative, ingressive, culminative, gnomic, epistolary, and dramatic--Smith makes two potentially contradictory claims. He says "It is hereby affirmed that these labels are wholly unrelated to the concept or function of the aorist tense" and "Most of them are equally applicable to other tenses" (221).

In discussing the Aorist tense in a recent survey of Greek grammar, Carson calls Smith's treatment "linguistically naive" for rejecting the categories listed in e., whereas the meaning of the Aorist in a given passage may be "shaped by the context" to reflect one of these conceptions (*Fallacies*, 73). But Smith further says: "There may be constative, ingressive, or culminative (and etc.) *expressions*, but not constative, ingressive, or culminative aorists" (221). Both Smith and Carson fail to make explicit a crucial distinction between semantics and pragmatics. As argued in chapts. 1 and 2, and as recognized by both scholars above, there is only a single Aorist form, but-- here Smith is in error--it is best seen as delimiting a specific essential semantic quality. Smith is not linguistically naive to make this point clearly, but he is misleading to deny that the Aorist has some essential semantic quality, and to forbid any further descriptive categories which may be used to describe the function of the Aorist in various pragmatic contexts. But these need not be limited to three, six or any set number. Instead a distinction between the meaning of an entire proposition in context and the individual semantic value of its component parts must be made. Because of confusion over the difference between a sentence with, for example, inceptive meaning and the meaning of the individual verb form, it may be better to abandon such descriptive labels.

Smith also makes the challenging assertion that the Aorist does not designate the kind of action (215). Smith is correct, as his examples show, that the Aorist does not designate objectively a particular kind of action, but when he also defines "kind of action" as aspect and claims that "to define the aorist aspect as looking at the action in *any* way is to deny its basic noncommittal significance" (216), he verges on making nonsense. Smith also asserts that the Aorist is not the opposite of the Present, Imperfect, or Perfect (217). The "aorist tense is never in contrast with the other tenses. It cannot be, for it does not assert anything!" (217). Inadvertently Smith endorses a view of the Aorist as an unmarked privative tense, though his failure to treat the tenses systematically (his privative Aorist is in no meaningful opposition) gives no plausible grounds for formulating a theory of tense usage in Greek. Failure to possess an adequate semantic theory of tenses leaves readers of Smith's article with the feeling that though they have a clear idea of what the Aorist cannot mean and some idea of what it can do, its relation to the other verb forms is unsatisfactory. In defining perfectivity, Comrie observes that

> While it is incorrect to say that the basic function of the perfective is to represent an event as momentary or punctual, there is some truth in the view that the perfective, by not giving direct expression to the internal structure of a situation, irrespective of its objective complexity, has the effect of reducing it to a single point. (*Aspect*, 18)

Although Comrie is too dependent upon a theory of *Aktionsart* (see chapt. 1), he raises the problem of an appropriate metalanguage for tense usage. Carson claims that the best grammarians "use the term *punctiliar* much the way a mathematician uses the term *point* in geometry--to refer to a location without magnitude" (the survey of scholars in chapt. 1 makes this assertion dubious). But he also recognizes that "just as the mathematical notion is not intuitively obvious, so also has the notion of punctiliar action been a stumbling block to many interpreters" (*Fallacies*, 70). As seen in the examples cited here and in chapt. 2, however, a mathematical point without magnitude gives a completely wrong impression of the function of the Aorist, since it is used to describe a range of events that in fact do have magnitude, and are seen to have such by the speaker or writer, although he chooses to describe the event from his perspective simply as complete, as John 2:20 clearly illustrates.

 3. In another recent article (1981), D. Armstrong ("Aorist") pushes forward discussion of the aspectual difference between the Aorist and the Present tenses on the basis of collocation with adverbs: "the aorist turns out to be the regular tense with adverbs of cardinal count [ἅπαξ (once), δίς (twice), τρίς (thrice), etc.], and the present with adverbs of frequency count [ἀεί (always), etc.]" (3; Armstrong is open to examination on several issues--most notably his characterization of the Perfect and the history of the evolution of the tenses--but these do not concern me here). As Armstrong says,

> Everyone who has studied Ancient Greek knows that the phrase 'single act' is frequently used to explain the behavior of the aorist stem. Everyone who knows the language well knows that 'twice' and 'three times' and other expressions of definite count commonly take aorist stem, in apparent contradiction of this rule, as do many other adverbs that imply definite limits of repetition. (2)

Armstrong tries to show that every example is tractable in his theory, explaining every apparent exception (see 5-9). Regardless of whether he is convincing, and I will point out those places in relation to the NT where he is not, a general point emerges clearly: while certain kinds of adverbs tend to be used with particular verb stems (and more research needs to be done in this area), the Present and especially the Aorist verb tenses may be used in contexts where the event objectively is anything from singular to multifarious. The speaker's perspective seems to be determinative, governed by the general tendency for collocation with certain kinds of adverbs.

 ἅπαξ: Armstrong uses ἅπαξ as one of his foundational examples to show that adverbs of cardinal count tend to occur with the Aorist (e.g. Hdt. 1.191.1; A. Prom. 750; Zeno B1), but he must then explain the phrase ἅπαξ λεγόμενον (and δίς and τρίς λεγόμενον).[3] In the NT the general pattern is followed, with ἅπαξ occurring with the Aorist in 2 Cor 11:25; Heb 6:4; 9:27, 28; 1 Pet 3:18; Jude 3, 5. But it occurs twice in special contexts: Phil 4:16: ἐν Θεσσαλονίκῃ καὶ ἅπαξ καὶ δὶς εἰς τὴν χρείαν μοι ἐπέμψατε (in T. indeed more than once you sent to me for the purpose of the need); 1 Thess 2:18: διότι ἠθελήσαμεν ἐλθεῖν πρὸς ὑμᾶς, ἐγὼ μὲν Παῦλος καὶ ἅπαξ καὶ δίς (wherefore I wanted to come to you, I Paul indeed more than once). The best translation of ἅπαξ καὶ δίς is probably "more than once" (Morris ["KAI," 207] says it denotes "a plurality of occasions, with no attempt at exact specification"; Armstrong suggests "over and over" for δίς καὶ τρίς [6]: Pl. Phaed. 63E; Gorg. 498E). Although this cardinal adverb occurs with Aorist verbs in the NT (the Present is used in extra-biblical Greek, see e.g. Ar. Peace 1181), it does not necessarily correlate with singular or punctiliar action. The modifiers are best seen as indicators of "indefinite" action. (ἅπαξ occurs twice with the Perfect: Heb 9:26; 10:2. Armstrong notes that both cardinal and frequency adverbs may appear with the Perfect. See the Future in Heb 12:26.)

δίς: Besides the two uses noted above, there are three other examples of δίς with the Aorist: Jude 12: δένδρα φθινοπωρινὰ ἄκαρπα δὶς ἀποθανόντα ἐκριζωθέντα (unfruitful trees in harvest season, twice dead, uprooted); Mark 14:30: ἀμὴν λέγω σοι ὅτι σὺ σήμερον ταύτῃ τῇ νυκτὶ πρὶν ἢ δὶς ἀλέκτορα φωνῆσαι τρίς με ἀπαρνήσῃ (truly I say to you that you today in this night before a cock crows twice will deny me three times); Mark 14:72 (see Mark 14:30); and one with the Present: Luke 18:12: νηστεύω δὶς τοῦ σαββάτου (I fast twice on the sabbath). Armstrong recognizes that "In fifth-century and later Greek *dis* 'twice' co-occurs with present stem in the sense 'again' or 'over again'" (5) (later he says from the mid 6th cent. B.C.). But his example, while showing the acceptability of the construction, is not convincing that this use or meaning of δίς is to be taken frequentatively: Theognis 1009f: δὶς γὰρ ἀνηβᾶν οὐ πέλεται πρὸς θεῶν, which he translates "for to be young (pres.) twice (i.e., again) is not given us by the gods" (6). His explanation of the title of Menander's play, δὶς ἐξαπατῶν (two deceptions), is not better. While he does not give δίς a frequentative meaning, he claims the Aorist Participle must be rejected since it would imply "completed or successful--not, like the present, attempted-- deception" (9) and past action. Neither is the case. His understanding of the relation between action and grammaticalization of description is clearly formulated around *Aktionsart*. But the example of a cardinal count adverb with the Present stands. Two uses of διετίας are also worth noting: Acts 28:30: ἐνέμεινεν δὲ διετίαν ὅλην ἐν ἰδίῳ μισθώματι (he remained for two whole years in his own room), where the Aorist summarizing the action as complete refers to an entire period; Acts 24:27: διετίας δὲ πληρωθείσης ἔλαβεν διάδοχον ὁ Φῆλιξ Πόρκιον Φῆστον (when two years were complete, F. received a successor, P.F.).

τρίς: All uses of τρίς in the NT are with Aorist verbs: Matt 26:34, 75; Mark 14:30, 72; Luke 22:34, 61; John 13:38; Acts 10:16; 11:10; 2 Cor 11:25; 12:8.

πεντάκις: This occurs once in the NT, with the Aorist: 2 Cor 11:24.

---

[3]Armstrong claims that "As the participle is present tense, this seems anomalous till you realize that the literature or the author is conceived of as a permanent entity in which the word is found 'once,' not on one single reading, but as often as anyone looks for it. Such situations of disguished [sic] frequency count occur regularly when what is in question is actions, themselves internally capable of count, that are indefinitely repeated; in such situations it is not the internal count ('doing this three times') but the frequency of the multiple action itself ('always doing this three times,' 'doing this three times every year,' and so on) that dictates the choice of aspect" (8), citing Ar. Frogs 1176ff., Hom. Od. 12.22, Men. Epit. 533f. (?). It is unclear how Hom. Od. 12.21-22 (Σχέτλιοι, οἳ ζώοντες ὑπήλθετε δῶμ᾽ Ἀΐδαο, / δισθανέες, ὅτε τ᾽ ἄλλοι ἅπαξ θνῄσκουσ᾽ ἄνθρωποι [cruel men, who living go down to the house of Hades to die twice, while other men die once]) with the Present confirms this point. Armstrong apparently falls victim to viewing aspect as *Aktionsart* rather than realizing the subjective choice available to the speaker.

ἀεί: This word always occurs with Present verbs: Acts 7:51; 2 Cor 4:11; 6:10; Heb 3:10; 2 Pet 1:12. (Cf. Hom. Il. 21.263: ὡς αἰεὶ Ἀχιλῆα κιχήσατο κῦμα ῥόοιο [as the flowing river always overtook A.].)

πάντοτε: This adverb occurs with the Present in most cases: Matt 26:11; Mark 14:7; John 8:29; 11:42; 12:8; Rom 1:10; 1 Cor 1:4; 15:58; 2 Cor 2:14; 4:10; 5:6; 9:8; Gal 4:18; Eph 5:20; Phil 1:4; 4:4; Col 1:3; 1 Thess 1:2; 2:16; 3:6; 5:15; 2 Thess 1:3, 11; 2:13; 2 Tim 3:7; Phlm 4; Heb 7:25, many in the opening statements of epistles. There are also three instances with the Aorist: John 6:34: κύριε, πάντοτε δὸς ἡμῖν τὸν ἄρτον τοῦτον (lord, always give to us this bread); John 18:20: ἐγὼ πάντοτε ἐδίδαξα ἐν συναγωγῇ καὶ ἐν τῷ ἱερῷ (I always taught in the synagogue and in the temple); Phil 2:12: καθὼς πάντοτε ὑπηκούσατε (as you always obey). Armstrong recognizes that this usage might be exceptional, although he is not willing to grant it unless the meaning of πάντοτε is changed from the sense of "always" (which he claims it means in hellenistic and modern Greek) with Present verbs, to "each (and every) time" with Aorist verbs (6). Armstrong's sense for John 6:34 and 18:20 would obscure Jesus' meaning. Regardless of translational equivalent selected, appearance of πάντοτε with the Aorist is established.

πολλάκις: Armstrong says that it "might be expected" that πολλάκις would occur with either Present or Aorist verbs, depending upon whether it means "often" or "a certain number of times" (3). His generalization does not seem to hold for two significant examples in ancient Greek: X. Mem. 1.1.1: πολλάκις ἐθαύμασα τίσι ποτὲ λόγοις Ἀθηναίους ἔπεισαν οἱ γραψάμενοι Σωκράτην ὡς ἄξιος εἴη θανάτου τῇ πόλει ("I have often wondered by what arguments those who drew up the indictment against Socrates could persuade the Athenians that his life was forfeit to the state" [Marchant/Todd, Xenophon IV, 3]) (cf. Mem. 2.4.7), and App. Civ. Wars 1.1: Ῥωμαίοις ὁ δῆμος καὶ ἡ βουλὴ πολλάκις ἐς ἀλλήλους περί τε νόμων θέσεως καὶ χρεῶν ἀποκοπῆς ἢ γῆς διαδατουμένης ἢ ἐν ἀρχαιρεσίαις ἐστασίασαν ("The plebeians and Senate of Rome were often at strife with each other concerning the enactment of laws, the cancelling of debts, the division of lands, or the election of magistrates" [White, Appian's III, 3]) (cf. Hom. Il. 1.396; 3.232; S. El. 62; Pl. Crito 43B; 49B; Crat. 384C; Lucian Dial. Dead 11.1; 19.2; see Weymouth, "Rendering," 171-72). Neither can be construed easily as reflecting a certain number of times. In the NT, πολλάκις occurs with both the Present/Imperfect (Matt 17:15; Acts 26:11; Phil 3:18; Heb 6:7; 9:25 [see below]; 10:11) and Aorist. Instances of the Aorist include: Mark 9:22: καὶ πολλάκις καὶ εἰς πῦρ αὐτὸν ἔβαλεν καὶ εἰς ὕδατα (often he cast him both into fire and into water); John 18:2: ὅτι πολλάκις συνήχθη Ἰησοῦς ἐκεῖ μετὰ τῶν μαθητῶν αὐτοῦ (because often Jesus gathered there with his disciples); Rom 1:13: ὅτι πολλάκις προεθέμην ἐλθεῖν πρὸς ὑμᾶς (because often I was intending to come to you); 2 Cor 8:22: ὃν ἐδοκιμάσαμεν ἐν πολλοῖς πολλάκις σπουδαῖον ὄντα (whom we have tested in many ways and often as being diligent); 2 Tim 1:16: ὅτι πολλάκις με ἀνέψυξεν (because often he uplifted my spirit); Heb 9:25-26: οὐδ' ἵνα πολλάκις προσφέρῃ ἑαυτόν, ὥσπερ ὁ ἀρχιερεὺς εἰσέρχεται εἰς τὰ ἅγια κατ' ἐνιαυτὸν ἐν αἵματι ἀλλοτρίῳ, ἐπεὶ ἔδει αὐτὸν πολλάκις παθεῖν ἀπὸ καταβολῆς κόσμου (now so that he might offer himself often, as the chief priest enters into the holy places each year with blood not his own, since it was necessary for him to suffer often from the foundation of the world), where πολλάκις occurs with both a Present and an Aorist verb. Whereas the definition of πολλάκις as "a certain number of times" might be possible in Mark 9:22; John 18:2; 2 Cor 8:22, it is highly unlikely in Rom 1:13 and 2 Cor 8:22, and virtually impossible in Heb 9:26. (πολλάκις also occurs with the Perfect: Mark 5:4. See also X. Mem. 3.13.3.)

This brief survey of collocation of adverbs in Greek illustrates at least two points: (1) cardinal count adverbs tend to occur with Aorist verbs, and frequency adverbs tend to occur with Present verbs, although this is only a general principle; (2) contrary to the oft-repeated depiction of the Aorist tense, the findings clearly reinforce the definition offered in chapt. 2 that verbal aspect as the fundamental semantic category of the Greek verb is concerned to show the speaker or author's reasoned grammaticalized conception of the process. Although there is a tendency to utilize certain

188

collocations, the appearance of particular adverbs with the Aorist and Present forms shows that ultimately choice is left with the speaker.[4]

4. A similar thesis to Armstrong's had been argued from a slightly different standpoint earlier by several grammarians, especially Lazzeroni ("L'aspetto"), who discusses adverbs of rapidity in Greek. Their occurrence with imperfective as well as perfective verbs points away from an objective view of action to choice by the speaker in describing his conception of the process. Lazzeroni refers to the subjective choice of aspect as "libertà," or a choice with reason, rather than "liberti," random choice (89, cf. 95 where he defines aspect as "una valutazione non assoluta, ma funzionale e relativistica"). See also Gildersleeve, 88-89; Rose, *Tenses*, 13-14 (who claims that instances with the Imperfect outnumber those with the Aorist in Thucydides approximately three to two); Hultsch, *Zeitformen*, 1.48.

αἰφνίδιος (suddenly): 1 Thess 5:3: τότε αἰφνίδιος αὐτοῖς ἐφίσταται ὄλεθρος (then suddenly destruction comes upon them); cf. Luke 21:34 with Aorist Subjunctive of same verb.

ἐξαίφνης (suddenly): Luke 9:39: καὶ ἐξαίφνης κράζει (and he cries suddenly); cf. Mark 13:36; Luke 2:13; Acts 9:3; 22:6 with Aorists.

εὐθέως (immediately): Luke 12:54: εὐθέως λέγετε ὅτι (immediately you say . . .); Acts 9:20: καὶ εὐθέως ἐν ταῖς συναγωγαῖς ἐκήρυσσεν τὸν Ἰησοῦν (and immediately in the syngagogues he was preaching Jesus); with many found with the Aorist.

παραχρῆμα (immediately): Luke 19:11: ὅτι παραχρῆμα μέλλει ἡ βασιλεία τοῦ θεοῦ ἀναφαίνεσθαι (that immediately the kingdom of God was going to appear); cf. Luke 4:39.

σπουδαίως (urgently), etc.: Luke 7:4: οἱ δὲ παραγενόμενοι πρὸς τὸν Ἰησοῦν παρεκάλουν αὐτὸν σπουδαίως, λέγοντες (those who came to Jesus were beseeching him earnestly, saying); cf. Rom 12:8: ὁ προϊστάμενος ἐν σπουδῇ (the one who leads with diligence); 12:11.

ταχύ (immediately): Matt 5:25: ἴσθι εὐνοῶν τῷ ἀντιδίκῳ σου ταχύ (be making friends with your enemy immediately); Rev 2:16; 3:11; 11:14; 22:7, 12, 20 with a form of ἔρχομαι (come); τάχος (haste): Acts 25:4: ἑαυτὸν δὲ μέλλειν ἐν τάχει ἐκπορεύεσθαι (he himself was about to go out shortly).

5. Conclusion. This brief survey of several noteworthy articles shows two important points: that the critique offered in chapt. 1 and the model outlined in chapt. 2 are in harmony with recent trends in Greek grammar, and that my work advances discussion of several persistent problems by presenting a rigorous defence of verbal aspect over time-based categories as fundamental to the semantics of the Greek verbal network. These articles and the above discussion should lay to rest much confusion over the nature of the Aorist.

4.   PAST-REFERRING IMPERFECTIVE AND PERFECTIVE ASPECTS. a. Introduction. (For a survey of treatments of the narrative tenses see Louw, "Aspek," 15ff.) It need not be justified that the Aorist tense may have past reference, since virtually every Greek grammar or article on the tense form recognizes such usage. The same may be said of the Imperfect. It is also widely recognized that the Present tense

---

[4]Cf. Armstrong, "Aorist," 10-11, who believes the Aorist is marked and the Present unmarked (cf. Haberland, "Note"), partly because of his essentially time-bound definition of tense forms in Greek, as evidenced in his comments on gnomic uses and in spite of his endorsement of Comrie. I question whether his use of Arist. Nic. Eth. 1173A-B actually supports his thesis, or whether it is not a comment upon the concept of pleasure, since Aristotle admits that two Present verbs can be collocated with "quickly."

may also have past reference, in usage often called the 'historic' Present. The fact that three different tense forms (or two tense categories, depending upon treatment of the relation between the Present and Imperfect) may be used for past reference has prompted much discussion. In this section, first, the use of the past-referring Present is discussed; and, second, its usage is compared to that of the Imperfect and Aorist tenses in past contexts. It is claimed here that verbal aspect provides the most convincing explanation of the alternation in tense usage.

b. Past-referring Present ('historic' Present). (See Eriksson, *Präsens*, esp. 1-28; Lilja, *Style*, 101-19, for surveys of usage and research.) The validity of the past-referring Present throughout the history of ancient Greek is illustrated in chapt. 3, where objections on the basis of Semitic influence are shown to be unfounded. This recognized usage of the Present provides important proof for the non-temporal nature of the tense forms in Greek and points to verbal aspect as the distinguishing semantic feature. To do justice to the topic, however, treatment of the four major theories of the 'historic' Present is worth making.

1. The traditional explanation of the historic Present, and the one adopted by most grammarians of Greek, finds its basis in [Longin.] *Sublime* 25:

ὅταν γε μὴν τὰ παρεληλυθότα τοῖς χρόνοις εἰσάγῃς ὡς γινόμενα καὶ παρόντα, οὐ διήγησιν ἔτι τὸν λόγον ἀλλ᾿ ἐναγώνιον πρᾶγμα ποιήσεις. "πεπτωκὼς δέ τις" φησὶν ὁ Ξενοφῶν "ὑπὸ τῷ Κύρου ἵππῳ καὶ πατούμενος παίει τῇ μαχαίρᾳ εἰς τὴν γαστέρα τὸν ἵππον· ὁ δὲ σφαδᾴζων ἀποσείεται τὸν Κῦρον, ὁ δὲ πίπτει." τοιοῦτος ἐν τοῖς πλείστοις ὁ Θουκυδίδης.[5]

Those who follow this analysis often distinguish between two uses of the historic Present: the dramatic, by which "sieht der Sprechende vergangene Ereignisse wie in einem Drama vor sich, indem seine Phantasie durch das Interesse an den Vorgängen lebhaft erregt ist; dadurch wird zugleich beim Hörer 'eine besondere Beachtung desselben veranlasst,'" and the registration or notification use, in which "man erzählt nicht, sondern steht, von dem Zeitverhältnis abstrahierend,

---

[5] "Again, if you introduce circumstances that are past in time as happening at the present moment, you will turn the passage from mere narrative into vivid actuality. 'Someone,' says Xenophon, 'has fallen under Cyrus's horse, and being trampled on, strikes the horse in the belly with his sword. It rears and throws Cyrus, and he falls to the ground.' [X. Cyr. 7.1.37] Thucydides is particularly fond of this device" (Dorsch, *Criticism*, 134).

vor den Tatsachen wie vor einem Bild und beschreibt dieses Bild" (Brugmann, 555, 556).[6] An example from hellenistic Greek that Brugmann cites is Plb. 15.27.10: κατὰ δὲ τὸν καιρὸν τοῦτον προστρέχει τις τῶν ὑπηρετῶν πρὸς τὸν Νικόστρατον, καὶ . . . ἀπηλλάττετο μετὰ σπουδῆς (at this time one of the servants ran up to N. and . . . he left speedily). Besides the difficulty of establishing a formal distinction between these two uses, most NT grammarians contend that the registering Present does not occur in the NT, except possibly in Matt 2:4: συναγαγὼν πάντας τοὺς ἀρχιερεῖς καὶ γραμματεῖς τοῦ λαοῦ ἐπυνθάνετο παρ' αὐτῶν ποῦ ὁ Χριστὸς γεννᾶται (gathering all the chief priests and scribes of the people he inquired of them where the Christ is born) (Robertson, 867).

Several criticisms of this view may be offered. There is (1) difficulty in establishing objective criteria for determining dramatic value in the instances cited, especially when fully half of the instances of the past-referring Present in the NT are verbs of speaking; (2) the clumsiness of shifting temporal spheres with each verb form; (3) over-reliance upon temporal reference of tense forms; and (4) failure to account for tense alteration. An example that illustrates these difficulties is Mark 5:35-42, where a continuous past-referring narrative evidences the following Indicative tense sequence: ἔρχονται (Present), λέγει (Present), ἀφῆκεν (Aorist), ἔρχονται (Present), θεωρεῖ (Present), λέγει (Present), κατεγέλων (Imperfect), παραλαμβάνει (Present), εἰσπορεύεται (Present), λέγει (Present), ἀνέστη (Aorist), περιεπάτει (Present), ἦν (see chapt. 10), and ἐξέστησαν (Aorist).

As Reynolds says,

I believe that no idea of the illusion of actually being present, or of special vividness for certain words can be consistently maintained to explain this interspersing of aorist and imperfect tense forms with the present tense. I do not believe that any explanation saying that verbs of primary importance are put in one tense and verbs of secondary importance in another can be advanced successfully. ("Zero Tense," 70-71)

2. The second view, argued for most stringently by Kiparsky ("Tense," esp. 30-34), claims that the historic Present is the "zero tense" in an instance of tense reduction (see also Levin, "Remarks"; Reynolds, "Zero Tense"; Voelz, "Language," 947-48; Louw, "Aspek," esp. 17ff.; Moorhouse, 187; von Fritz, "Present" [who has points of contact with a. above]). Citing examples like Th. 7.29.3: ἅμα δὲ τῇ ἡμέρᾳ τῇ πόλει προσέκειτο . . . καὶ αἱρεῖ ("at daybreak he attacked the town and takes it") Kiparsky argues that it is "absurd" to seek an explanation for alteration of tenses

semantic differences, however subtle, between aorist and present. But this simply highlights the impossibility of adequately characterizing the so-called historical present on a semantic basis alone. Rather, a syntactic solution is called for. It is beginning to look as if the historical present in early Indo-European is a present tense only in its superficial form [?]. It functions syntactically as a past tense, as shown by sequence of tenses, it is semantically indistinguishable from the past tenses, and it alternates with these in conjoined structures.

---

[6]Although some do not recognize the division between the two uses, virtually every major grammarian takes this position, including: Delbrück, *Grundlagen*, 113; idem, *Syntax*, 2.261-65; Gildersleeve, 85-86; McKay, 142; Humbert, 137-38; Rijksbaron, 22-25; Smyth, 422; Kühner/Gerth, 1.132-34; Goodwin, *Syntax*, 11; idem, *Grammar*, 269; Stahl, 90-92; Jelf, 2.55; Schwyzer, 2.271-73. Other studies worth noting include Wackernagel, *Vorlesungen*, 162-65; Svensson, *Gebrauch*, 91-102, 118-19; Ruipérez, *Estructura*, 97-98, 147-57; Brunel, *L'aspect*, 260, 270-74; Rose, *Tenses*, 27-30. Most NT and hellenistic grammars are included as well: e.g. Winer, 333-34; Blass/Debrunner, ¶ 320; Turner, *Syntax*, 60-62; Robertson, 866-69; Moulton, 120-22, as well as Hultsch, *Zeitformen*, 8.5; 31.1-22; Mayser, 2, 1.131-32 (note use in dream narration); Mandilaras, 108-09; idem, "NT," 38; Ericksson, *Präsens*.

Everything points to its being an underlying past tense, and its conversion into the present tense in the surface structure must be governed by a syntactic rule, evidently some form of conjunction reduction, which optionally reduces repeated occurrences of the same tense to the present. . . .
    The reason that conjunction reduction yields presents and indicatives is evidently that they are the zero or unmarked tense and mood in the sense of Prague School linguistic theory. . . .
        Schematically, then, the sequence ...Past...and...Past... is reduced to ...Past... and... zero..., and since it is the present which is the zero tense, the reduced structure ...Past...and...zero... is realized morphologically as ...Past...and...Present.... ("Tense," 33-34, 34-35)[7]

McKay has set out trenchant criticisms of this view ("Remarks"; he also points out several erroneous and potentially misleading citations by Kiparsky). (1) Kiparsky cannot explain a passage such as Th. 7.43.3-4, with a series of historic Presents without alternation with marked forms:

καὶ ἐπειδὴ ἐγένοντο πρὸς αὐταῖς κατὰ τὸν Εὐρύηλον, ᾗπερ καὶ ἡ προτέρα στρατιὰ τὸ πρῶτον ἀνέβη, λανθάνουσί τε τοὺς φύλακας τῶν Συρακοσίων, καὶ προσβάντες τὸ τείχισμα ὃ ἦν αὐτόθι τῶν Συρακοσίων αἱροῦσι καὶ ἄνδρας τῶν φυλάκων ἀποκτείνουσιν· οἱ δὲ πλείους διαφυγόντες εὐθὺς πρὸς τὰ στρατόπεδα, ἃ ἦν ἐπὶ τῶν Ἐπιπολῶν τρία ἐν προτειχίσμασιν, ἐν μὲν τῶν Συρακοσίων, ἐν δὲ τῶν ἄλλων Σικελιωτῶν, ἐν δὲ τῶν ξυμμάχων, ἀγγέλλουσι τὴν ἔφοδον καὶ τοῖς ἑξακοσίοις τῶν Συρακοσίων, οἳ καὶ πρῶτοι κατὰ τοῦτο τὸ μέρος τῶν Ἐπιπολῶν φύλακες ἦσαν, ἔφραζον.[8]

McKay contends that the traditional view of the historic Present "is more credible at this point then [sic] Kiparsky's theory," as well as explaining the other examples Kiparsky adduces (247). (2) Tense reduction cannot explain X. Anab. 1.1.1, where the discourse begins with a Present form: Δαρείου καὶ Παρυσάτιδος γίγνονται παῖδες δύο, πρεσβύτερος μὲν Ἀρταξέρξης, νεώτερος δὲ Κῦρος (D. and P. had two children, the elder A. and the younger C.),[9] or Reynolds's Mark 5:35-42, which begins with two Present verbs. (3) Kiparsky appears to have a temporal conception of the tense forms which prompts his discussion, and thereby fails to address

---

[7]Kiparsky also states: "The unmarked value of the present and indicative in their respective categories is supported by many grammatical facts apart from those just described concerning conjunction reduction. For example, nominal sentences are normally interpreted as present indicative. Also, while verbs may lack other tenses and moods, no verb lacks a present indicative (though the present tense may be inflected as a perfect in certain verbs, e.g. Gk. *oida* 'know')" ("Tense," 35). Both statements are suspect. See chapt. 10 on nominal sentences, chapt. 5 on οἶδα, and chapt. 10 on verbs, such as εἶπον (say), ἔδραμε (run), εἶδε (see), ἦλθε (go), which lack a Present Indicative apart from supplementation (cf. Levin, "Remarks," 388-89).

[8]"And when they came to them [Epipolae], according to the Euryelian way, which indeed the previous army had gone up first, they were unnoticed by the Syracusan guards and attacking the Syracusan fort which was there they seized it and killed some of the guards; but most, fleeing immediately to the camps which were three upon the Epipolae, one belonging to the Syracusans, one to the other Siceliots, and one to the allies, they announced the attack and informed the six hundred of the Syracusans who were first guards of this portion of the Epipolae."

[9]Levin ("Remarks," 386) argues that the first verb in Greek narrative need not be a past tense, though he does not explain how this accommodates Kiparsky's tense reduction. The registering Present, as McKay realizes, does not explain this use either. It too appears in "uninterrupted series" (247): e.g. Hdt. 1.106.3-107.1. Louw ("Aspek," 21) calls the usage idiomatic, though he seems to argue this in opposition to verbal aspectual categories, and attempts to explain Th. 2.1.1.

adequately the question of verbal aspect in the Indicative. Thus Kiparsky ("Tense," 30-31), after citing the standard theory of the historic Present, says: "the historical present behaves syntactically as a past tense with respect to sequence of tenses. . . . [There is] the propensity of the present for appearing in sentence conjunction after a true past tense in early Indo-European. This alternation of past and present is particulary surprising when it occurs, as frequently happens, in closely parallel structures." But McKay, approaching Th. 7.29.4, treats this kind of passage differently: "αἱρεῖ is followed, after the complex end of the sentence, by details of the capture it introduces, so it can be accepted as signifying an on-going process. Incidentally, within this context it must also be recognized as one of the more emphatic words in the passage" (250). McKay also presents Th. 8.84.4 and 8.102.2, claiming that ἐκβάλλουσιν in the former is the significant word in the passage and that the parallel historic Presents give details of the capture being described.

3. A third explanation, by Buth ("Use") and Levinsohn ("Observations"; followed by Johnson, Study), takes account of recent work in text linguistics in analysing use of the historic Present in Mark (Callow ["Function"] summarizes and analyses their results). Buth, dismissing use of λέγω as "apparently haphazard" (7), analyses the other historic Presents, claiming that "the historical present in Mark has a regular discourse function. It is used in the beginning sentence of a paragraph and describes a change in the geographical setting of participants already on stage, or introduces participants who were off-stage" (13). He admits difficulty in explaining several examples, however. They include the following.

Mark 2:4, where καὶ ἐξορύξαντες χαλῶσι τὸν κράβαττον (and digging out [the roof] they lowered the bed) appears in the middle of the narrative unit; 2:18: καὶ ἔρχονται καὶ λέγουσιν αὐτῷ (and they came and they said to him), where the historic Present follows an introductory sentence; 4:1, where καὶ συνάγεται πρὸς αὐτὸν ὄχλος πλεῖστος (and a large crowd gathered around him) follows the introductory sentence (καὶ πάλιν ἤρξατο διδάσκειν παρὰ τὴν θάλασσαν [and again he began to teach along the sea]); 4:36: καὶ ἀφέντες τὸν ὄχλον παραλαμβάνουσιν αὐτόν (and leaving the crowd they took him along), where the introductory sentence uses the historic Present; 4:38: καὶ ἐγείρουσιν αὐτὸν καὶ λέγουσιν (and they got him up and said to him), where the historic Present occurs mid-narrative; 5:22-23: καὶ ἔρχεται εἷς τῶν ἀρχισυναγώγων . . . καὶ ἰδὼν αὐτὸν πίπτει πρὸς τοὺς πόδας αὐτοῦ καὶ παρακαλεῖ αὐτὸν πολλά (and one of the leaders of the synagogue came . . . and seeing him he fell at his feet and beseeched him many times), where the historic Presents follow the opening verse; 6:1: καὶ ἔρχεται εἰς τὴν πατρίδα αὐτοῦ, καὶ ἀκολουθοῦσιν αὐτῷ οἱ μαθηταὶ αὐτοῦ (and he came into his homeland, and his disciples followed him), following ἐξῆλθεν (he came out); 6:48: περὶ τετάρτην φυλακὴν τῆς νυκτὸς ἔρχεται πρὸς αὐτούς (in the fourth watch of the night he came to them), with the Present in the middle of the section; 8:6: καὶ παραγγέλλει τῷ ὄχλῳ ἀναπεσεῖν ἐπὶ τῆς γῆς (and he instructed the crowd to sit upon the ground); 11:4: καὶ λύουσιν αὐτόν (and they loosed it); 14:13: καὶ ἀποστέλλει δύο τῶν μαθητῶν αὐτοῦ καὶ λέγει αὐτοῖς (and he sent two of his disciples and said to them), where Buth claims the historic Present introduces an "embedded paragraph" (11); 14:51: καὶ κρατοῦσιν αὐτόν (and they seized him), where Buth attributes the Present to "the unexpectedness of the event" (12); 14:53: καὶ συνέρχονται πάντες οἱ ἀρχιερεῖς (and all the chief priests etc. gathered), where the discourse unit opens with ἀπήγαγον (they led away); 15:16-17: καὶ συγκαλοῦσιν ὅλην τὴν σπεῖραν. καὶ ἐνδιδύσκουσιν αὐτὸν πορφύραν καὶ περιτιθέασιν αὐτῷ πλέξαντες ἀκάνθινον στέφανον (and they called together the whole cohort. And they put a purple robe on him and put a crown on him, weaving it from thorns); 15:20: καὶ ἐξάγουσιν αὐτόν (and they led him out), where the historic Present is "paragraph final" (12); 15:24: καὶ σταυροῦσιν αὐτὸν καὶ διαμερίζονται τὰ ἱμάτια αὐτοῦ (and they crucified him and divided his garments), where Buth recognizes that the author is "highlighting the word stauroun 'to crucify,' and he is doing it with the historical present in two ways. (1) There is a dense accumulation of this construction in this episode. (2) He breaks his normal use of the idiom and, in particular, in connection with the word stauroun, which is the theme of the episode" (12). Mark 15:27: καὶ σὺν αὐτῷ σταυροῦσιν δύο λῃστάς (and they crucified two thieves with him), with the historic Present paragraph-final.

Whereas Buth may have described one of the more prominent functions of the historic Present--that of opening a paragraph and describing the setting or introducing participants (he lists many examples, including Mark 1:12, 21; 3:31)--he has not provided a comprehensive theory of this tense usage.

Levinsohn argues two major points for use of the historic Present in Mark: "[1] It is used only in connection with the *interaction* of two participants or groups of participants. . . . [2] Its use is always *cataphoric*, anticipatory, pointing to another action connected with it" ("Observations," 14; cf. Johnson, *Study*, 48-57. Osburn ["Present," 490ff.] uses "cataphoric" indiscriminately). Levinsohn claims that "the historic present establishes the location in which an important interaction will occur" (14), although he must admit that in, for example, 14:32 (καὶ ἔρχονται εἰς χωρίον οὗ τὸ ὄνομα Γεθσημανί ["and they came into a place which is named Gethsemane"]) "the interaction between 'they' (Jesus and His disciples) and Judas does not occur until after the agony scene in the garden (vv 33-42)" (15), with many other historic Present verbs interspersed. And of the historic Present of Mark 1:12, it is misleading to say that "the interaction between Jesus and the devil is described immediately, in v 13" (15), when this consists of no recorded dialogue. In fact, it is highly questionable whether such a formulation with verbs of speaking is helpful, since virtually every verb of speaking is found in a similar context, often followed by direct or indirect discourse. Johnson (*Study*, 48) claims the first point is basically irrelevant: "Since the entire Gospel of Mark is in the form of a series of interactions between Jesus and various participants, this statement does not appear to be saying anything heuristically verifiable" (101 n. 2). Regarding cataphoric reference, Levinsohn never clarifies his brief initial definition, but he seems to be referring to use of the historic Present as "the first half of a couplet, the second half being the action or actions which develop the theme and build upon that event" (16). The term cataphoric--which has proved difficult to define in standard linguistics texts--appears here in an expanded and potentially misleading usage, giving a degree of objective credibility to an ill-defined concept. Also, this definition appears to be unable to explain the paragraph-final uses of the historic Present noted above (cf. also e.g. Matt 4:11; 8:4, 22; 26:35; 28:10; John 1:51; 2:10 [?]; 9:12; 11:27, 44; 13:38; 18:38; 19:5 [?]; 20:18, 29; 21:13). When he analyses Mark 14:12-25, 26-52, 66-72; and 14:53-65; 15:1-16:8, Levinsohn concludes very similarly to the standard definition of the historic Present when he sees the form as "a device to give prominence to the events that lead from and build upon the speech or event so introduced" (27). (Osburn ["Present," 496 n. 30] criticizes Levinsohn for a theory that does not account for several sections where prominent events are treated without the historic Present. This misses the point, since Levinsohn's theory is designed to explain usage, not necessarily account for the phenomenon's absence.) But Levinsohn notes that teaching passages in Matthew are an "apparent exception" to his formulation "in that the punch line frequently is introduced by a quote margin employing the present tense" (27 n. 3): e.g. Matt 13:28b-29; 21:13, 42; 22:21. This would also hold true for many examples in John: e.g. 1:39; 4:7ff.; 4:49-50; 5:6; 7:6, 50; 9:17; 11:23-24; 12:4; 13:25, 27; 18:4-5, 17, 26; 19:14-15; 20:2, 27. Johnson also points out that the marking of prominence as defined by Levinsohn is overly restrictive, and that a variety of features of discourse--location, participants, or even an entire episode--might be marked as prominent (50). Thus, these theories using recent linguistic terminology, while potentially helpful in specific instances, fail to provide a comprehensive theory of use of the historic Present.

4. A fourth view, recently argued by McKay, is that whereas the temporal reference of the verbs may be identical the difference is in verbal aspect (esp. 221; "Remarks," 248-49; cf. Gildersleeve, "Problems," 245). Using Hdt. 1.111.1-3, he says of the historic Presents that

> the first, ἀπικνέεται [arrive], marks the diversion of our attention from the cowherd to his wife, bringing her history up to the same point of time. The second, τίκτει [give birth], is an action parallel to (but not co-terminous with) the process-state of his absence on the journey (οἰχομένου [be away]), τότε [then] referring to a period rather than a point of time. The third, λέγει [say], both introduces a speech and represents the continuation of the wife's effort to win a reprieve for the child. (221)

He argues further that the Present is used mostly in contexts where an Imperfect would have been most appropriate, although the Aorist could also have been used. While McKay is not more explicit on this point, he seems to be distinguishing two factors: temporal reference of the historic Present is similar to that of standard narrative tenses, and the historic Present shares the verbal aspect of the Imperfect.

Three major responses to such a proposal may be made. (1) Brunel (*L'aspect*, 260; cf. 270ff. where he minimizes aspect), with others, claims that the historic Present is equivalent to an Aorist in the intersection of the two oppositions undetermined/determined and durative/momentary (cf. Schwyzer, 2.258; Moorhouse, 184; Winer, 333; Blass, 188; Blass/Debrunner, ¶ 321). This theory, however, is untenable for several reasons. Not only are non-punctual examples able to be posited (Moorhouse, 185; Ruipérez, *Estructura*, 154 [and below]), but Brunel's conception is based upon a theory of *Aktionsart*, which attempts to describe the objective nature of an event.

Citing Pl. *Lach*. 184A, Brunel claims that ἀφίεται is in opposition to ἐφίει (272). But this is not so clear: ἐπεὶ δὲ δὴ παρημείβετο ἡ ναῦς τὴν ναῦν καὶ ἐπέσπα αὐτὸν τοῦ δόρατος ἐχόμενον, ἐφίει τὸ δόρυ διὰ τῆς χειρός, ἕως ἄκρου τοῦ στύρακος ἀντελάβετο. ἦν δὲ γέλως καὶ κρότος ὑπὸ τῶν ἐκ τῆς ὁλκάδος ἐπί τε τῷ σχήματι αὐτοῦ, καὶ ἐπειδὴ βαλόντος τινὸς λίθῳ παρὰ τοὺς πόδας αὐτοῦ ἐπὶ τὸ κατάστρωμα ἀφίεται τοῦ δόρατος (183D-184A). Rather than seeing ἀφίεται as punctual, the movement may be interpreted that Stesilaus let the spear slip through his hand until he was holding onto the end alone, and even then his grip gave way. The gloss would then read: "and since the ship was leaving the side of his ship and driving him on, holding the spear, he was letting the spear through his hand, until he grasped the end of the shaft. And there was laughter and clapping by those from the trading vessel at his appearance, and after someone threw a stone at his feet upon the deck he continued to let the spear go."

Koller ("Praesens," esp. 65ff. and 85ff., cf. 77), followed by Lilja (*Style*, 106), has proposed a similar view, i.e. that the historic Present is used with a set number of verbs with an inceptive-durative *Aktionsart*. Besides Lilja illustrating from early historians that other verbs than those Koller lists are used as historic Presents, as McKay says, Koller's "suggestion of a uniform inceptive meaning is rightly rejected, as this is only one of the possible translation meanings of the Greek imperfective [aspect]" ("Remarks," 250). Many questionable examples could be cited, but one suffices here: Hdt. 5.41.1: χρόνου δὲ οὐ πολλοῦ διελθόντος ἡ ἐσύστερον ἐπελθοῦσα γυνὴ τίκτει τὸν δὴ Κλεομένεα τοῦτον (after not much time had passed, the wife who came later gave birth to this C.). Koller apparently uses ἔτεκε appearing later in the passage as an argument that τίκτει here is equal to an Aorist (93). Besides the fact that these uses are separated by approximately ten lines, Koller clearly neglects other contextual factors: the historic Present introduces the discourse unit, drawing attention to the role of Anaxandrides's second wife in producing a child, Cleomenes; this is a crucial transition away from the discursis on Anaxandrides's problems in producing an heir, and prelude to resuming the incidents surrounding Cleomenes; section 41 goes into more detail about production of an heir; and the later use of the Aorist is hardly parallel, since it is the first of a list of children born. Perhaps a more suitable parallel would be the Imperfect ἔτικτε that closes the section. Koller is clearly working with a view of verbal action formulated around *Aktionsart*, although even here his conception is troublesome, when he claims that verbs such as λείπω (leave), ἵστημι (stand), δίδωμι (give), ἀπικνέομαι (arrive) are inceptive, and verbs such as ἐργάζομαι (accomplish), πνίγω (choke), φθείρω (destroy) are durative (Ruipérez [*Estructura*, 151] makes these criticisms among others).

(2) A second group of scholars argue that the historic Present stands for both Aorist and Imperfect (see esp. Brugmann, 556; Goodwin, *Syntax*, 11; Smyth, 42; Robertson, 867; cf. Rose, *Tenses*, 28-29). This theory need not be considered at length, since its linguistic imprecision is self-evident. Those who argue for this theory have placed temporal reference as primary, and hence confused the ability of the historic Present to appear in past contexts with aspectual synonymity. It is shown both immediately above and in chapt. 2 that temporal similarity implies nothing regarding aspectual similarity, and that supposed substitution for the Aorist is unfounded (see below). More importantly, this theory neglects the fundamental formal opposition of the Present/Aorist in Greek and negates the principle that meaning is choice.

(3) Ruipérez has argued that the historic Present is in fact non-aspectual (*Estructura*, 147-57). When Ruipérez's distinction between transformational and non-transformational verbs and

his use of Brunel's theory of the perfectivizing use of prefixes are eliminated (see chapt. 1, where the theory of the aspectually neutral Present is criticized), his theory has little to commend it. Ruipérez claims to establish the aspectually neutral value of the historic Present by first showing that the historic Present does not have a durative value: he claims that no instance shows development of the action and no historic Present has a conative sense (151-52). Next he claims to show that the historic Present does not have punctual value: although instances of punctual historic Presents exist, non-punctual historic Presents are also found; most historic Presents are transformational verbs, which although they may seem punctual are not to be seen as semantically punctual [?]; non-transformational historic Presents fail to be inceptive; and the historic Present is similar to the punctual Aorist in certain contexts (154). Ruipérez concludes therefore that the historic Present is aspectually neutral. Each of Ruipérez's statements may be questioned, but since he essentially is arguing against various concepts of classification of the historic Present according to *Aktionsart*, his theory sheds little significant light on the aspectual nature of the historic Present. (Even more troublesome is Rose [*Tenses*, 28-29]: "Here [re the historic Present] the important thing is not the kind but the time of the action; the historical present gives no information as to whether the past act which it represents was durative or aoristic, but it is employed to present in a vivid and dramatic manner events which are taken out of the past and reenacted, as it were, before the eyes of the reader.")

Similar difficulty can be seen in von Fritz's treatment, in which he argues that the historic Present is timeless on the basis of: the nature of present time as fleeting (189), a misconception that the historic Present does not occur in earliest Greek literature (189, *passim*; Lilja [*Style*, 101-03] shows not only that the historic Present occurs in the earliest historians but that it appears in Homer: Od. 7.103-31, with textual difficulties; Il. 9.237, among other references), a dubious claim to a distinction in *Aktionsart* between sigmatic and non-sigmatic Aorists (192-93), and the contention that the Present slows down the action into a fixed image (196) (contra Rose, *Tenses*, 28-29). This psychologically-based conceptualization, which also draws heavily upon a temporal definition of tense forms (194: the imperative "necessarily always refers to the future"), despite his positing of an early distinction in verb forms according to kind of action (193), is unhelpful: "the main events are, so to speak, removed from the time coordinate on which the reader occupies a point at the time of reading, or from the actuality of his time and, as the events unfold one after the other like the pictures in a picture book, the pace of the narrative is slackened" (199).

Although each of the major proposals regarding the historic Present may rightly be criticized, this is an instance in Greek grammar where several of the definitions share many helpful points in common (contra Osburn, "Present," 490-500, who endorses three views [essentially a., b., c. above] but fails to show their relationships). Rather than attempting a completely new formulation of the historic Present, it is more important to clarify several of the issues. (1) An aspectual theory of Greek verbal usage provides the most important basis for establishing this formal usage. As Moulton (120) says, "That the Present is not primarily a *tense*, in the usual acceptation of the term, is shown not only by the fact that it can stand for future time, but by its equally well-known use as a past." Since the tense-forms in Greek are essentially aspectually based (and non-temporal), the fact that what is called a Present tense appears in past-referring contexts inherently poses no grammatical problems, merely potentially misleading problems of nomenclature. (2) On the basis of the place of the historic Present within the Greek verbal network, the historic Present is to be considered aspectually imperfective. As seen above, there is no compelling reason to believe that the historic Present has either altered or neutralized its verbal aspect. Rather the historic Present is marked in relation to the Aorist, as well as the Imperfect (see below). In this sense it renders the description of a given event more vivid.[10] (3) Regarding the reasons why the historic Present occurs where it does, the quotation from [Longinus] is perhaps significant. In the example he cites, X. Cyr. 7.1.36-39 has past-referring Presents at several junctures. The Present is used to open the scene (παραγίγνεται [came up]), a usage paralleled in not only other older Greek usage but also in various hellenistic writers, including those of the NT; and to describe the events of Cyrus's fall (see above) and rescue by his aid (ἀναβάλλει [pick up]), examples of selecting particular events within the discourse unit. Within the entire description, the striking of Cyrus's horse by the man on the ground and the horse throwing Cyrus provide dramatic complication, while Cyrus's being picked up appears to be the climax to and resolution of the unit.

To formulate a general theory of the past-referring Present, therefore, the 'historic' Present is used at those places where the author feels that he wishes to draw attention to an event or series of events.[11] This includes the beginning of units of discourse, and thus it is used to highlight possibly the discourse unit itself but certainly the transition to the new unit, often including setting and participants (e.g. Mark 6:1; 9:2 [see Callow, "Function," 11]; John 1:29); events within a discourse unit selected for special significance, such as the climactic turning point (e.g. Mark 5:15; Matt 26:40); dialogue considered as specially pertinent to a discussion (e.g. John 19:9); and final closing events (e.g. Mark 15:20; cf. 2:17; 11:33).[12] This formulation, while limited in its predictive powers, reconciles the major features of the various definitions given above. It accounts for why many scholars, including [Longinus], have seen the vivid quality of the historic Present, without having to postulate an untenable temporal alteration. It explains why the Present form can be used in

---

[10]It is unclear why Levinsohn ("Observations," 27) concludes that "It is inaccurate to say that the historic present is used in Mark's Gospel to give heightened vividness to the narrative. Rather, it is employed as a device to give prominence to the events that lead from and build upon the speech or event so introduced."

[11]It is understandable that Turner (*Syntax*, 61) states that "the hist. pres. is so universal that it is impossible to theorize," although a temporal conception of the tense forms makes his task more difficult.

[12]Examples of these uses in classical Greek may be found in the standard reference grammars. Several representative instances in hellenistic sources not mentioned in Ericksson (*Präsens*) or other reference works include: introductory: Apollod. 1.1.4, 1.2.2; 1.3.1; 1.3.6; 1.6.1 (note transitional clause); 1.7.2, 5; 1.9.3, 4, 6, 7, 8, 10, 11, 13, 17, 18, 21, 26; App. Civ. Wars 1.90; climactic (including verbs of saying): Apollod. 1.1.4, 6; 1.2.1; 1.4.1; 1.5.2; 1.7.2; 1.8.1; 1.9.1, 8, 13, 17, 24, 27, 28; App. Civ. Wars 1.25, 53 (?), 54, 58; Epict. 1.1.30; 1.2.20; 1.29.18 (?), 65, 66; 2.4.2; closing: Apollod. 1.2.1; 1.9.3 (?); App. Civ. Wars 1.4; Epict. 1.26.12.

narrative contexts, without negating its aspectual quality (this would include timeless use in narratives such as parables, where temporal reference is established in relation to the discourse unit; see below). It includes what has been called cataphoric usage by showing that, especially with verbs of speaking but also with other verbs used at significant junctures in discourse, it is to be expected that the series of events being narrated often follows to be dwelt upon. This usage derives from the aspectual (non-temporal) nature of Greek tense forms.

In those instances where it is difficult to establish firm criteria for determining the significance of a given process, there remains the subjective choice of the author to select a particular process (see e.g. Humbert, 137-38; Ruipérez, *Estructura*, 149). Within the possible verbal semantic choices available, the author's subjective choice must not be minimized. Often further analysis of what are held to be arbitrary choices yields appreciation for development of the argument. It is not necessary here to single out instances in Matthew, Mark and John, since they have been used above. Instead, instances in other books are selected for mention (cf. Rom 11:7: ὃ ἐπιζητεῖ Ἰσραήλ [what did Israel seek]).

In Revelation, the Present is used for climactic reference within a discourse unit: 9:17, where the fire coming (ἐκπορεύεται) from the mouth of the angels is the sign of their destructive power (cf. 19:15); 14:3, where the 144,000 sing (ᾄδουσιν) a new song; and 16:21, where the instance, though appearing late in the unit, is apparently climactic. An interesting set of examples is found in 13:11-17, where ποιεῖ (make) is used to mark individual sub-units within the major discourse unit.[13]

In Luke, even with limited instances of the historic Present, a range of uses is displayed: to introduce a unit: 8:49: ἔτι αὐτοῦ λαλοῦντος ἔρχεταί τις παρὰ τοῦ ἀρχισυναγώγου λέγων (while he was speaking someone from the leader of the synagogue came, saying); 11:37: ἐν δὲ τῷ λαλῆσαι ἐρωτᾷ αὐτὸν Φαρισαῖος (while speaking, a P. asked him); 11:45: ἀποκριθεὶς δέ τις τῶν νομικῶν λέγει αὐτῷ (one of the lawyers answered and said to him); 24:36: ταῦτα δὲ αὐτῶν λαλούντων αὐτὸς ἔστη ἐν μέσῳ αὐτῶν καὶ λέγει αὐτοῖς (while they were saying these things, he stood in the midst of them and said to them); to conclude a discourse unit: 24:12:

[13]Similar usage occurs in P.Oxy. 717 (1st cent. B.C.) (mentioned by Moulton, 121). I cite lines 3-9, 12-15: ἀγοράσαντος δέ μου / [αὐτὸ πα]ρέχωι ἔχων τὸν κυβερνήτην καὶ συνβάλλο αὐτὸ κατε- / [.........] εὑρίσκωι αὐτὸ πρὸς τὸ δίλετον, εἰσπορεύομαι εἰς τὴν αὐ- / [... ἔχων α]ὐτὸ καὶ παραλαμβάνωι Ἀσίην τὸν ἀδελφὸν Ἐρασίππου / [.........] . οὖν εἰσπορεύομαι πρὸς τὸν στρατηγὸν ἔχων αὐτὸ καὶ / [συμβάλλω] αὐτὸ πρὸς τὸ χαλκοῦν μέτρον ἐν τῶι συνεδρείωι, εὑρίσ- / [κω αὐτὸ ......] μείζωι δύο ταῖς ἑκατόν. . . . [two Imperfects and an Aorist in narration] β]οώντων δ' αὐτῶν εἰσφέρω τὸ δίλε- / [τον 21 letters] βοῶν καὶ κράζων ὅτι τοῦτο ἔστι [26 letters ἠν]άγκασμαι βοᾶν αυτῶι ὅτι / [28 letters] δὲ οὐκ ἐνβάλλομαι ὧδε ("after I bought it, I brought it, taking the helmsman, and collected it together . . . I found it to be a dileton [as the editors note, the meaning here is obscure], I entered into the . . . taking it and I brought it with me Asia, the brother of Erasipos. . . . Therefore, I entered with the commander, taking it, and I brought it to the copper scale in the council, I found it to be larger than two hundred. . . . while they were shouting, I brought in the dileton . . . shouting and crying that this is . . . I was compelled to cry to him that . . . and I did not involve. . . ."). Note possible confusion over the adscript and subscript iota.

ὁ δὲ Πέτρος . . . βλέπει τὰ ὀθόνια μόνα (and P. saw the linen cloth alone), although a transitional motion clause follows; and to single out climactic incidents or dialogue (see below on timeless usage): 13:8, where the vineyard worker pleads (λέγει) for mercy for the barren fig tree; 16:7, where the steward's instructions to the last debtor (λέγει) immediately precede praise of the master; 16:23, 29, where the Present is used to mark the rich man's seeing (ὁρᾷ) Lazarus in Abraham's bosom, and later when Abraham tells (λέγει) him that his pleading for his family is in vain, since they have Moses and the prophets (note the similarity to the instance from Xenophon above); 19:22, where the Present marks the nobleman's condemnation (λέγει) of the servant who misused his talent. (Acts relies almost exclusively upon φημί; see my chapt. 10 on aspectually vague verbs.)

5. Conclusion. The aspectual distinction between the imperfective and perfective aspects provides a comprehensive theory regarding use of the 'historic' Present, so that the Present may understandably appear in narrative material alongside Aorist and Imperfect, as well as other, verbs.

   c. **Perfective (Aorist) And Remote Imperfective (Imperfect) Narrative Tenses. 1.** Introduction. (Besides standard grammars, several significant articles and monographs may be noted: Blass, "Demosthenische Studien"; Weymouth, "Rendering"; Hultsch, *Zeitformen*; Miller, "Imperfect"; Schlachter, "Untersuchungen"; Hartmann, "Aorist . . . im Griechischen," 316-39, esp. 327-29; Sedgwick, "Uses"; idem, "Use"; Bakker, "Remark." Since virtually every one of these treatments is dependent upon a theory of *Aktionsart*, it is unnecessary to analyse them in detail.) As outlined in chapt. 2 above, the imperfective/perfective opposition is one of two fundamental oppositions in Greek. Whereas the Perfect, the most heavily marked form and part of the stative/non-stative opposition (see chapt. 5 on Perfect), least often enters into narrative contexts (though there are in fact several significant instances of the past-referring [narrative] Perfect in the NT [see chapt. 5] and extra-biblical Greek [see Schwyzer, 2.287]), the Present and Aorist forms comprise the heart of Greek tense usage in such contexts. When a Greek speaker narrated events, the Aorist, used alongside the Imperfect, formed the basis for carrying the narrative, with the historic Present used for selecting processes for emphasis (the most heavily-marked Perfect was available as well). One of the most important uses of the Imperfect is as the imperfective narrative or remote form (concerning the non past-referring use of the Imperfect, see below; cf. McKay, "Action," 23). In this section, several issues are discussed: the semantic difference between the Aorist and Imperfect forms, the semantic difference between the Imperfect and narrative Present, the semantic quality of the past-referring Imperfect, noteworthy uses of the narrative Aorist, and the relation in narrative of the Aorist, Imperfect and narrative Present.

   2. Semantic difference between the Aorist and Imperfect forms. In his lengthy treatment of the Aorist and Imperfect, Hartmann cites Mark 1:31-32, 34; Matt 8:15-16; and Luke 4:39-41, where he notes that, whereas all three use the verb διηκόνει (she was serving) to

describe the activity of Peter's mother-in-law, Mark uses ἔφερον (they were bringing) instead of προσήνεγκαν (they brought) in Matthew and ἤγαγον (they brought) in Luke of people bringing the ill to Jesus, noting "dass der Aorist an diesen Stellen dem Imperfekt der Bedeutung nach sehr nahe steht" ("Aorist," 49 [1920] 2; cf. "Aorist . . . im Griechischen," 327-29).[14] In one sense Hartmann is correct that the meaning of the two forms is similar in that they refer to the same process. But this observation provides little help in formulating a theory of Greek tense usage. Hartmann concludes that the choice of Aorist or Imperfect is one of stylistic preference: "für die historische Darstellung *verschiedene Stilgattungen* zu unterscheiden sind, von denen die eine das Imperfektum, eine andere den Aorist, eine dritte das Präsens bevorzugt" (44). But this does not comport well with his own analysis of the Greek verbal edifice, in which the Aorist is distinguished as the momentary past tense and the Imperfect the durative past tense (this time-based formulation [found in Kühner/Gerth, 1.131] is well-known to discussions of Greek grammar [see my chapt. 1]. Hartmann ["Aorist . . . im Griechischen"] alters his view in accordance with *Aktionsart* to include, for example, punctual Imperfects). Such an analysis--unfortunately adopted by many subsequent grammarians and interpreters--fails on several counts: the analysis itself is self-contradictory, because it cannnot explain the formal difference according to a temporal scheme of analysis; the system of analysis is time-based in the face of much contrary evidence (as Hartmann himself realizes in his survey of the history of Greek tense forms); and this scheme does not recognize the category of verbal aspect, or take seriously kind of action.

In analysis in chapts. 1 and 2, which deals seriously with the weaknesses of the approach outlined above, it is shown that the Aorist and Imperfect forms are best interpreted as realizing different semantic aspectual features. The Aorist as semantically the least heavily marked verb form is aspectually perfective, frequently occurring in past contexts as the background narrative tense. The Imperfect, semantically more heavily marked than the Aorist, is aspectually imperfective (its difference from the Present is discussed directly below), also often occurring in past contexts as the foreground narrative tense.[15] Although many grammars--especially older ones--do not share the exact language used in this description, since they often utilize the language of *Aktionsart* (see chapt. 1), a significant few concur with these findings regarding the Imperfect and Aorist. A representative and well-stated example, which foreshadows the language of aspect, is Goodwin (*Syntax*, 11-13, 16-18), who makes two significant observations: the Imperfect "dwells on the course of an event instead of merely stating its occurrence" (12), as does the Aorist; and "the same event may be looked upon from different points of view by the same person" (16) (cf. also Kühner/Gerth, 1.157 [although emphasis is on the objective nature of the action]; Humbert, 134-35; Winer, 276; Robertson, 837-38; Gildersleeve, "Problems," 250-52). Goodwin cites as examples D. 30.33: τῇ ἀληθείᾳ συνῴκει καὶ οὐδέπω καὶ τήμερον ἀπολέλοιπεν. . . .

---

[14]Hartmann's article ("Aorist," 49 [1920]) is fundamentally flawed in several ways other than those mentioned above: he bases many of his conclusions on comparative study of modern Greek, Slavonic languages, and modern European languages such as German and French to formulate an analysis of Greek, even though he admits "dass die Aktionsartensysteme der einzelnen Sprachen stark von einander abweichen und dass demnach die Abweichungen erst auf ihren Grund untersucht werden müssen" (2); his formulation is heavily dependent upon a reconstruction of the history of Greek and other IE languages. In "Aorist," 48 (1919) 2ff., he surveys previous research, although with several gaps, esp. with reference to English language scholarship. Is it possible also that concentration on problems with εἰμί and φημί, which form the basis for several major analyses, have misled much of the discussion? See my chapt. 10 on vague verbs.

[15]Although the use of statistics must be carefully regulated, Miller ("Imperfect," 142) shows that within narrative contexts, the Aorist generally predominates over the Imperfect (especially when forms of φημί and εἰμί are not counted); Schlachter ("Untersuchungen," 22 [1907-08] 229) evidences similar though less precise figures for a larger list of authors. The figures seem to show that in the hellenistic writers--such as Polybius, Diodorus, Josephus, Plutarch (Them.), and Arrian--the Aorist maintains a clear-cut superiority in frequency. This is also true of NT writers.

ἀλλὰ παρὰ ζῶντος Τιμοκράτους ἐκείνῳ συνῴκησε ("she was his wife in good faith, and has not yet even to this day been divorced; but she went to live with him from Timocrates while T. was still living"), where the use of συνῴκει and συνῴκησε is contrasted. As an example of the second he cites D. 18.71: πότερον ταῦτα ποιῶν ἠδίκει καὶ παρεσπόνδει καὶ ἔλυε τὴν εἰρήνην, ἢ οὔ; ("in doing all these things was he acting unjustly, breaking treaties, and destroying the peace, or not?"), and 73: καὶ μὴν τὴν εἰρήνην γ᾽ ἐκεῖνος ἔλυσε τὰ πλοῖα λαβών ("he broke the peace, taking the boats"). Consequently, Goodwin can assert:

> In all these cases the fundamental distinction of the tenses, which was inherent in the form, remained; only it happened that either of the two distinct forms expressed the meaning which was here needed equally well. It must not be thought, from these occasional examples, that the Greeks of any period were not fully alive to the distinction of the two tenses and could not use it with skill and nicety. But the Greeks, like other workmen, did not care to use their finest tools on every occasion; and it is often necessary to remember this if we would avoid hair-splitting. (17)

He retreats, however, reflecting a view often expressed by those analysing the use of the Imperfect and the Aorist:

> Since the same event may thus be stated by the aorist or the imperfect according to the writer's point of view, it is natural that it should occasionally be a matter of indifference which form is used, especially when the action is of such a nature that it is not important to distinguish its duration from its occurrence. For example, this distinction can seldom be important in such expressions as *he said, he commanded.* . . . (17)

Goodwin allows his theory of *Aktionsart*, and possibly translation, to dictate his analysis at this point.

Several other more recent grammarians have argued to the contrary. In a work which foreshadows discussion of verbal aspect, Rose (*Tenses*, 7), whose work has not received the attention it deserves, disputes the traditional definitions of tense forms, especially regarding such terminology as "point action" or "momentary" for the aorist,

> because the use of this tense or of any other tense is not determined by the length of time consumed by the action. The duration that leads to the use of a durative tense is not in the action itself but in the mind of the speaker or writer. When his mind dwells upon an action long enough to describe it or see it in its development, he uses a durative tense to denote it. On the other hand, if his mind does not dwell upon it nor see it in its development, but views it as a whole, as a single act, then he uses an aorist to denote it, no matter how long a time was consumed by it. One writer, for instance, might relate a series of facts with aorists, another might depict these same facts with imperfects; or the same writer might on one occasion employ aorist tenses, on another occasion durative tenses, to narrate the same story.

Rose faithfully applies his analysis to verbs of saying in Thucydides: "In the same manner are to be explained the imperfect and the aorist of verbs of saying that introduce speeches; that is to say, the aorist sums up and presents the action as a whole; whereas the imperfect describes and stresses the development of the action" (22): Th. 1.53.2; 2.34.8; 3.36.6; 4.84.2; 5.84.3; 6.8.4 with the Imperfect, and 1.53.3; 2.72.1; 4.9.4; 5.112.1; 6.41.1; 7.65.3 with the Aorist. In concurrence are Gonda (*Rgvedic*, 55: "Greek authors also like to refer to chief actions by imperfects, setting forth the subordinate points or the particular instances of the general actions by aorists," e.g. Th. 7.19.3-4) and Bakker ("Remark"), who finds no statistically significant correlation between use of demonstratives with Aorist and Imperfect forms introducing direct speech in Herodotus, and concludes that choice between the Imperfect and Aorist is "so subjective that one always finds too many exceptions" and that the Imperfect and demonstrative pronoun "are easily combined inasmuch as both of them cause a stagnation in the flow of the narrative" (28); and McKay (216), who says "the aorist simply sums up the act of speaking, the pronoun τάδε being sufficient warning that details follow, while the imperfect, equally legitimately, by its stress on process indicates that we are to pause for a fuller account of the speech. These are usually marginal instances, in which even an ancient Greek reader (or hearer) would hardly notice the difference, and the writer might make a purely subjective choice." The same analysis may apply to conclusions of speeches as well. As Rose says, "When a speech is over, it is almost invariably summarized by a complexive aorist indicative, the aorist εἶπον being the usual form. However, there are in Thucydides a few examples of a durative form at the end of a speech" (22). He cites 2.65.1: τοιαῦτα ὁ Περικλῆς λέγων ἐπειρᾶτο τοὺς Ἀθηναίους τῆς . . . ἐς αὐτὸν ὀργῆς παραλύειν ("Pericles, by saying such things as you heard, tried to rid the Athenians of their anger against him"; see 2.90.1; 4.96.1; 7.16.1; 7.78.1).[16] Against those who dispute use of a "durative" tense to end a speech, Rose asserts that "duration must be put where it belongs, 'in the eye of the beholder, in the heart of the sympathizer, and not in the action itself.' So here in the passage under consideration the present participle λέγων indicates that the mind continues to dwell upon the action ('saying as was seen')" (22).

In responding to Winer (337), who in recognizing the difference between the Aorist and Imperfect claims that "It is often left to the writer's choice whether he shall regard the action as transient (momentary) or as lasting," Robertson asks, "Why 'often'? Why not 'always'? The presence of aorist, imperfect and past perfect side by side show how keen the distinction was felt to be" (Robertson, 838, citing the Thayer translation of Winer, 276. The same point is argued by Bakker ["Remark"]).

In the NT, several instances may be cited from the Gospels (cf. Blass/Debrunner, ¶ 329, who give some general patterns of usage in the NT). Matt 3:1 and Mark 1:4: in Matthew, John the Baptist is introduced with the Present παραγίνεται (he came) in contrast to Mark with the Aorist ἐγένετο (he appeared), while Luke 3:2 also uses the Aorist embedded within a context that draws no particular attention to John; cf. also Matt 3:13; Mark 1:9 and Luke 3:21. Matt 3:7 and Luke 3:7: Matthew introduces John's first words with εἶπεν (he said), while Luke uses ἔλεγεν (he was saying). Matt 4:1 (ἀνήχθη [was taken up]) uses the Aorist of Jesus' entry into the desert, while Luke 4:1 (ἤγετο [lead]) and Mark 1:12 (ἐκβάλλει [cast out]) use an Imperfect and a Present. Matt 4:5ff. tends to use the Present for crucial points in the narrative, while Luke continues essentially with the Aorist. Matt 13:54 says Jesus ἐλθών (entering) into his home country ἐδίδασκεν (was teaching) them in their synagogues, while Mark 6:1 says ἐξῆλθεν (he went out) of there and ἔρχεται (entered) into his home country and his disciples ἀκολουθοῦσιν (followed him), and when the Sabbath came (γενομένου σαββάτου) ἤρξατο διδάσκειν (he began to teach) in the synagogue, using the Present in a more detailed narrative transition, with Luke 4:16 using the Aorist throughout; cf. Matt 9:14 and Mark 2:18 with Present and Luke 5:33 with Aorist. When Jesus tells his listeners that a prophet is not without honour, except in his own country, he introduces this with the Aorist εἶπεν in Matt 13:57 and Luke 4:24, but with the Imperfect ἔλεγεν in Mark 6:4; cf. Mark 1:21 and Luke 4:31. In Mark 1:28 and Luke 4:37 the concluding statement about Jesus' healing of a demoniac varies from the Aorist ἐξῆλθεν ἡ ἀκοὴ αὐτοῦ εὐθὺς πανταχοῦ (his fame spread at once everywhere) in Mark to the Imperfect ἐξεπορεύετο ἦχος (a report went out) in Luke; cf. Matt 9:13 and Mark 2:17 with Aorists and Luke 5:32 with a Perfect in

---

[16]Sedgwick ("Uses," 119-20) suggests that Thucydides nowhere uses the Imperfect ἔλεγε to conclude a speech, whereas Herodotus and Xenophon are approximately equal in using it. Sedgwick does not have a theory of aspect which would include other imperfective verbs concluding speeches (besides Rose, see McKay, 215-216). But more importantly, his definition of the Imperfect as expressing "the abiding result of a single past act" (118) fails to explain several instances he himself cites (e.g. Ar. Clouds 49: ταύτην ὅτ᾽ ἐγάμουν συγκατεκλινόμην ἐγώ [when I was married to her I lay with her]) and has received no endorsement from other scholars so far as I am aware.

Jesus' words. Not only is there aspectual variation among authors, even when apparently referring to the same process, but each author chooses occasionally to grammaticalize his conception of a similar kind of process in a different way.

In recognizing the semantic difference between the Aorist and the Imperfect, several grammarians still dispute how the Aorist or the Imperfect forms the backbone of narration. For example, in his recent treatment, Rijksbaron argues that

> Since the imperfect characterizes the action as 'not-completed,' it creates a framework within which other actions may occur, while the aorist indicative characterizes the action as 'completed,' as a mere event. This difference in value between imperfect and aorist indicative is significant for the way in which a story is told. The imperfect creates a certain expectation on the part of the reader/hearer: what else happened?; the aorist indicative, on the other hand, does not have this effect: the action has simply occurred. (12-13)

He cites two examples in support, one (Hdt. 1.114.1-2) where an initial Imperfect begins a story and two actions are enumerated by Aorists; and another (Th. 1.79-85) where an initial Imperfect is elucidated by several Aorists. This analysis may be questioned: Rijksbaron's treatment of these passages is not entirely accurate; and his description does not correlate with his definition. Hdt. 1.114.1-2 states: καὶ ὅτε ἦν δεκαέτης ὁ παῖς, πρῆγμα ἐς αὐτὸν τοιόνδε γενόμενον ἐξέφηνέ μιν. ἔπαιζε ἐν τῇ κώμῃ ταύτῃ ἐν τῇ ἦσαν καὶ αἱ βουκολίαι αὗται, ἔπαιζε δὲ μετ᾽ ἄλλων ἡλίκων ἐν ὁδῷ. καὶ οἱ παῖδες παίζοντες εἵλοντο ἑωυτῶν βασιλέα εἶναι τοῦτον δὴ τὸν τοῦ βουκόλου ἐπίκλησιν παῖδα (now when the boy was ten years old, events revealed him as being who he was. He was playing in this village in which these herdsmen were, and he was playing with others of the same age in the road. And the boys, playing, selected among themselves a king, being the one named son of the cowherd). The scene is actually opened by the Aorist ἐξέφηνε (reveal), followed by two uses of ἔπαιζε (play), apparently stressing that it was during the playing of the game in which he was selected as king that Cyrus revealed his true character, later to be revealed to the king. In Th. 1.79-85, while Rijksbaron gives the impression that the discussion of the situation (ἐβουλεύοντο) is described by the subsequent Aorist verbs, the text seems to indicate otherwise, i.e. the initial discussion ended in a majority opinion that the Athenians were guilty: ἐπειδὴ δὲ τῶν τε ξυμμάχων ἤκουσαν οἱ Λακεδαιμόνιοι τὰ ἐγκλήματα τὰ ἐς τοὺς Ἀθηναίους καὶ τῶν Ἀθηναίων ἃ ἔλεξαν, μεταστησάμενοι πάντας ἐβουλεύοντο κατὰ σφᾶς αὐτοὺς περὶ τῶν παρόντων. καὶ τῶν μὲν πλεόνων ἐπὶ τὸ αὐτὸ αἱ γνῶμαι ἔφερον, ἀδικεῖν τε τοὺς Ἀθηναίους ἤδη καὶ πολεμητέα εἶναι ἐν τάχει· παρελθὼν δὲ Ἀρχίδαμος ὁ βασιλεὺς αὐτῶν, ἀνὴρ καὶ ξυνετὸς δοκῶν εἶναι καὶ σώφρων, ἔλεξε τοιάδε (and when the L.s had heard from the allies the charges against the A.s and from the A.s what they said, sending all away, they were consulting among themselves concerning the present situation. And the opinions of the majority was arriving at the same thing: the A.s were guilty already and there was to be a war without delay. But coming forward, A. their king, a man thought to be intelligent and wise, spoke thus). The two subsequent speeches, both introduced and concluded with Aorists, do not alter this opinion.

A second example worth noting is the work of Ruijgh (*Autour*, esp. 250ff.; "L'emploi," esp. 1-16; Review of Hettrich) and Hettrich (*Kontext*, 20ff.; similar is the scheme of Bakker, *Imperative*, analysed at length in chapt. 7). Providing the basis for Rijksbaron's comments, they formulate a means of relating tense function. For Hettrich, following Ruijgh, these are essentially temporal formulations corresponding to the kind of action depicted by the Aorist and Imperfect tenses. Using temporal particles, he formulates a theory of tense relation by which context is determined by temporal reference of the main clause, with temporal subordinate clauses using the Present/Imperfect verb coincidental and temporal subordinate clauses using the Aorist verb antecedent.[17] Thus in Hdt. 8.116.2: ἐπεὶ δὲ ἀνεχώρησαν ἀσινέες πάντες ἒξ ἐόντες, ἐξώρυξε αὐτῶν ὁ πατὴρ τοὺς ὀφθαλμοὺς διὰ τὴν αἰτίην ταύτην (when all six present departed unsullied, their father plucked out the eyes for this reason), the Aorist ἀνεχώρησαν precedes the main action; and in Hdt 5.20.5: οἱ δέ, ἐπείτε σφέων οἱ Πέρσαι ψαύειν ἐπειρῶντο, διεργάζοντο αὐτούς (and they, since the P.s were attempting to touch them, accomplished these things), the Imperfect ἐπειρῶντο is coincidental with διεργάζοντο.

Hettrich's helpful analysis seems to apply in a number of instances, but it may also be criticized on several counts. (1) Hettrich's scheme is used only of narration and not descriptive material, which both he and Ruijgh realize, although this does not help their analysis present a satisfactory scheme for general tense usage (e.g. the Infinitive) or clauses without temporal subordinators. In a set of examples discussed below from the NT it is shown that the same set of clauses when used in descriptive material fails to provide the same set of temporal relations.

(2) Hettrich admits that there are instances where his scheme has trouble, forcing him to reverse the labels of independent and dependent clauses, an artificial and forced solution. For example, in Hdt. 5.30.2: ὁ γὰρ Ἱστιαῖος . . . ἐτύγχανε τοῦτον τὸν χρόνον ἐὼν ἐν Σούσοισι, ὅτε οἱ Νάξιοι ἦλθον (for H. happened to be in S. at the time when the N.s arrived), Hettrich realizes that the Aorist is used in a dependent clause where there is overlap between the action of the two clauses. Thus the further context compels him to make the alteration. Not only is this in clear disregard of his own rules, but as Rijksbaron points out (Review of Hettrich, 235), it is not appropriate to the context, where the arrival of the Naxians is not related here for the first time, but is a condition previously introduced (5.30.1). Coincidental action appears to be an inevitability. (Hettrich also cites several examples with forms of εἰμί [Hdt. 2.13.1; 7.115.2]; his generalization would not appear to be applicable to an aspectually vague verb.) In hypotactically unclear examples that he cites, a new problem is created by labelling adverbial Participles as secondary independent clauses.

(3) Hettrich's solution clearly does not fit several kinds of process, most noticeably with verbs of speaking, where the process described with a perfective verb does not in fact clearly precede another action, and where imperfective action may precede another process. Hettrich admits that he must expand his definitions for verbs of speaking to include qualities restricted for other verbs (59ff.). This distinction is a lexical one, not a grammatical one. Hettrich also must adopt the distinction by Ruipérez regarding nontransformational verbs, so that he can explain the apparently aoristic characteristics of some Present verbs. E.g. Hdt. 7.4: συνήνεικε αὐτὸν Δαρεῖον, βασιλεύσαντα ἰὰ πάντα ἕξ τε καὶ τριήκοντα ἔτεα, ἀποθανεῖν (it happened to D., reigning all of 36 years, to die), where the Aorist Participle has extension.

(4) Hettrich misapplies several examples. For example, he cites Hdt. 7.4 with a Genitive absolute. But the Genitive absolute by definition (see chapt. 8) is an independent use of the Participle and not grammatically dependent. Examples may be found in contradiction to his rule: Matt 17:22: συστρεφομένων δὲ αὐτῶν ἐν τῇ Γαλιλαίᾳ εἶπεν αὐτοῖς ὁ Ἰησοῦς (when they had come together in G., Jesus said to them), where it is difficult to believe that they were still gathering when he began to speak; Mark 5:21: διαπεράσαντος τοῦ Ἰησοῦ . . . πάλιν εἰς τὸ πέραν συνήχθη ὄχλος πολύς (while Jesus was crossing again to the other side a large crowd gathered), where the events must overlap despite use of the two Aorist verbs. (Cf. App. Civ. Wars 1.12: καὶ ἐνεγίνωσκε καὶ Ὀκταουίου κωλύοντος ἐσιώπα [and he was reading and when O. commanded he was silent]; Th. 1.31.4: καταστάσης δὲ ἐκκλησίας ἐς ἀντιλογίαν ἦλθον

---

[17]Hettrich concludes (Kontext, 31): "Wenn der Sprecher zwei oder mehr Handlungen darstellt und dafür die behandelten syntaktischen Konstruktionen wählt, kann er den TSt [tense stem] des UnV (B-Glied) [dependent clause] nicht nach eigenem, 'subjektivem' Ermessen wählen, sondern ist an die zeitlichen Beziehungen dieser Handlungen innerhalb seines 'concept' . . . gebunden. Liegt dort zwischen zwei dieser Handlungen ein zeitlicher Abstand, so steht das UnV im ASt. Überschneiden sich zwei dieser Handlungen oder löst die im ÜbV [independent clause] dargestellte die des UnV ab (u.a. im Inzidenzschema), so steht letzteres im PSt. Auf den TSt des ÜbV haben diese Beziehungen keinen Einfluss."

[and while the assembly was gathered, they entered into opposing speeches].) He cites Hdt. 7.4; 7.7 where the Participle is the modifier of a headterm in a nominal group and not to be construed as dependent in the way Hettrich is analysing. And finally he cites an adjunctive[S] Present Participle following the main verb, which according to other criteria is probably coincidental, although there are examples of the preceding Present Participle being antecedent (see chapt. 8 on Participle usage). 7.12.1 is interesting: ἐδόκεε ὁ Ξέρξης ἄνδρα οἱ ἐπιστάντα μέγαν τε καὶ εὐειδέα εἰπεῖν (X. thought a large and well-formed man was standing over him, and said), where it is difficult to decide whether the Participle or the Infinitive (as Hettrich selects) is the independent clause. According to semantic weight it appears it should be the Participle (see chapt. 8), although this countermands the categories Hettrich posits.

(5) Hettrich has misconstrued several examples: Hdt. 1.154: ὡς δὲ ἀπήλασε ὁ Κῦρος ἐκ τῶν Σαρδίων, τοὺς Λυδοὺς ἀπέστησε ὁ Πακτύης ἀπό τε Ταβάλου καὶ Κύρου (and as C. went away from S., P. took the L.s away from T. and C.). Hettrich has not noted 1.155.1: πυθόμενος δὲ κατ' ὁδὸν ταῦτα ὁ Κῦρος εἶπε πρὸς Κροῖσον τάδε (learning along the way of these things, C. said to C.), where the author appears to see the trip away from Sardis by Cyrus as a process taking some time, despite his grammaticalization of it as perfective, or else Cyrus could not learn of events happening during it. Hdt. 1.164.1: ὁ δὲ Ἅρπαγος ὡς ἐπήλασε τὴν στρατιήν, ἐπολιόρκεε αὐτούς (H., when he marched against the city, besieged them), where the march cannot be separated from the besiegement, as the first seems to be concerned with the city itself and the second with its citizens. Hdt. 1.160.1: πρὸς ταῦτα ὁ Γέλων, ἐπειδὴ ὥρα ἀπεστραμμένους τοὺς λόγους τοῦ Συάγρου, τὸν τελευταῖόν σφι τόνδε ἐξέφαινε λόγον (to these things G., when he saw the unfriendly words of S., expressed to him this last word), where perception must have preceded his response.

(6) Hettrich has overlooked a very clear pattern, i.e. the subordinate clauses which he cites in many cases precede the independent clause. Also, all four of the significant examples he cites as potentially troublesome, and requiring that he reevaluate which clause constitutes the main and which the dependent, according to their grammatical indicators have the dependent clause following the main clause. This points to a syntactical generalization, in which clauses at least in narrative create their temporal order on the basis of syntactical order. In fact, Hettrich himself states of the examples he uses to establish his pattern that "die . . . Beispiele wurden deshalb so ausgewählt, dass das zeitliche Verhältnis beider Handlungen auch ohne Berücksichtigung der TStt schon aus dem natürlichen Ablauf der beschriebenen Vorgänge ersichtlich wird. Diese Erkenntnisse werden zunächst nicht durch sprachliche Kategorien vermittelt, sondern durch die geschilderte Situation, unabhängig von ihrer sprachlichen Realisierung im einzelnen" (29). This generalization, while valid in a number of instances, should not be pressed as a binding rule, but as one that is compatible with an aspectual theory. (See Grice's formulation regarding order, "Logic"; cf. McKay, 217; and Dahl, *Tense*, 30, who speaks of a "temporal frame," by which one phrase establishes a temporal frame for subsequent narrative; see below.) Since the Aorist is used to grammaticalize perfective aspect its use in contexts where discrete processes are related is understandable, whereas the Present as imperfective is used to depict the process as in progress.

(7) Rijksbaron makes an important case for an expanded concept of context which relies heavily upon the first (often the dependent) clause in a passage, otherwise hanging clauses are the result. As he says, "In general, the subordinate clause precedes the main clause and, thus, comes first in the linear structure of the text. It would seem counterintuitive not to assign a proper value to the tense in the subordinate clause, but to make this value depend upon the presence of an element that still has to come" (230). He cites Hdt. 1.174.1 where there is a long interruption between the initial dependent and main clauses.

(8) Hettrich's scheme is essentially a temporal one and thus fails to provide substantial underpinnings for a comprehensive theory of Greek tense usage, very noticeably in his neglect of the historic Present, which would apparently severely undermine his scheme.

Many NT examples are worth noting (clauses with Subjunctive verbs and their conjunctions are excluded on account of their description of a process as merely posited). Although many conform to the pattern which Hettrich has suggested, a sufficient number of clear exceptions call into question not only the model itself but analysis of the other instances. In each instance analysis of the individual context must be relied upon to see a relation between the processes, with verbal aspect providing the common factor for verbal usage.

Luke 1:34: πῶς ἔσται τοῦτο, ἐπεὶ ἄνδρα οὐ γινώσκω; (how will this be since I do not know a man?), which presents problems for Hettrich's scheme, since (assuming a temporal scheme for the tenses) the main clause would require that the subordinate clause be future, when in fact it is clearly past/present. Mary asserts that she has not been sexually involved with a man. Acts 13:46: ἐπειδὴ ἀπωθεῖσθε αὐτὸν καὶ οὐκ ἀξίους κρίνετε ἑαυτοὺς τῆς αἰωνίου ζωῆς, ἰδοὺ στρεφόμεθα εἰς τὰ ἔθνη (since you reject [the word] and judge yourselves unworthy of eternal life, behold we are turning to the Gentiles), where the narrative sequence indicates a progression from the word being spoken to them, to their rejection, to Paul and Barnabas turning to the Gentiles. Rom 11:6: εἰ δὲ χάριτι, οὐκέτι ἐξ ἔργων, ἐπεὶ ἡ χάρις οὐκέτι γίνεται χάρις (if by grace, then no longer from works, since grace no longer becomes grace), illustrating the difficulty of applying Hettrich's analysis to a descriptive passage (note especially the verbless main clause). 2 Cor 11:18: ἐπεὶ πολλοὶ καυχῶνται κατὰ σάρκα, κἀγὼ καυχήσομαι (since many boast according to the flesh, I too will boast), where the cause and effect relationship, especially with the Future in the apodosis, seems to exclude the kind of overlap Hettrich posits. Heb 4:6: ἐπεὶ οὖν ἀπολείπεται τινὰς εἰσελθεῖν εἰς αὐτήν, καὶ οἱ πρότερον εὐαγγελισθέντες οὐκ εἰσῆλθον δι᾽ ἀπείθειαν (since it is left for certain ones to enter into it, and those previously evangelized do not enter because of disobedience). Heb 9:17: διαθήκη γὰρ ἐπὶ νεκροῖς βεβαία, ἐπεὶ μήποτε ἰσχύει ὅτε ζῇ ὁ διαθέμενος (a covenant is effective upon death, since it is never able when the maker of the covenant is living), where death marks a temporal distinction between the events of the two clauses; cf. Heb 9:26. Heb 10:2: ἐπεὶ οὐκ ἂν ἐπαύσαντο προσφερόμεναι, διὰ τὸ μηδεμίαν ἔχειν ἔτι συνείδησιν ἁμαρτιῶν τοὺς λατρεύοντας ἅπαξ κεκαθαρισμένους; (would they not cease being offered, because those worshipping once purified had still no awareness of sins?), where the process conveyed by the Aorist clearly overlaps with that of the other clause, to say nothing of determining which clause is subordinate. Heb 11:11: πίστει . . . δύναμιν εἰς καταβολὴν σπέρματος ἔλαβεν καὶ παρὰ καιρὸν ἡλικίας, ἐπεὶ πιστὸν ἡγήσατο τὸν ἐπαγγειλάμενον (he received power by faith unto creation of seed and from the time of maturity, since he thought the promise faithful), where to divide belief and works in this instance is to do a serious injustice. Luke 11:6: ἐπειδὴ φίλος μου παρεγένετο ἐξ ὁδοῦ πρός με καὶ οὐκ ἔχω ὃ παραθήσω αὐτῷ (since my friend came to me from a journey and I do not have what I might give him), where within a single dependent clause no clear-cut separation between the friend's coming and the host's possessing bread may be made (clause order appears to be determinative). 1 Cor 1:21: ἐπειδὴ γὰρ ἐν τῇ σοφίᾳ τοῦ θεοῦ οὐκ ἔγνω ὁ κόσμος διὰ τῆς σοφίας τὸν θεόν, εὐδόκησεν ὁ θεὸς διὰ τῆς μωρίας τοῦ κηρύγματος σῶσαι τοὺς πιστεύοντας (since in the wisdom of God the world does [did] not know God through its wisdom, God is [was] pleased through the foolishness of preaching to save those who believe), where it is unreasonable to see no overlap between the knowledge of the world and God's act, especially if this is a timeless use of the Aorist (see below). Matt 12:3: οὐκ ἀνέγνωτε τί ἐποίησεν Δαυὶδ ὅτε ἐπείνασεν καὶ οἱ μετ᾽ αὐτοῦ; (didn't you read what David did when he and those with him were hungry?), where although the hunger preceded David's act, the relation between the two processes is closer than Hettrich's scheme allows; cf. also Mark 2:25 and Luke 6:3. Matt 13:26: ὅτε δὲ ἐβλάστησεν ὁ χόρτος καὶ καρπὸν ἐποίησεν, τότε ἐφάνη καὶ τὰ ζιζάνια (when the grain sprouted and bore fruit, then the weeds appeared), with τότε more a logical than a temporal connective. Matt 21:1: ὅτε ἤγγισαν εἰς Ἰεροσόλυμα καὶ ἦλθον εἰς Βηθφαγὴ εἰς τὸ Ὄρος τῶν Ἐλαιῶν, τότε Ἰησοῦς ἀπέστειλεν δύο μαθητάς (when they came near to J. and came to B. in the Mt. of Olives, then Jesus sent two disciples). ἐγγίζω is a problematic lexical item, since it seems to convey action extended over time. This particular construction provides difficulties for Hettrich's scheme since it would mean that entrance into the region near Jerusalem (and exit from?) occurred distinctly before coming near to Bethphage. A more convincing reading is that the perfective verb is used to speak of the entire set of activities that occurred when Jesus and his group were near to Jerusalem, including the sending of disciples when near to Bethphage. Cf. Mark 11:1: ὅτε ἐγγίζουσιν εἰς Ἰεροσόλυμα εἰς Βηθφαγὴ καὶ

Βηθανίαν πρὸς τὸ Ὄρος τῶν Ἐλαιῶν, ἀποστέλλει δύο τῶν μαθητῶν αὐτοῦ (and when they were approaching J. into B. and B. to the Mt. of Olives, he sent two of his disciples), where in the parallel passage, Mark chooses to depict the same set of events using a different verbal aspect. It is questionable whether Hettrich's scheme can explain the difference without appeal to the subjective choice of the author, i.e. verbal aspect, rather than the objective nature of the events; cf. also Matt 21:34. Luke 4:25: πολλαὶ χῆραι ἦσαν ἐν ταῖς ἡμέραις Ἡλίου ἐν τῷ Ἰσραήλ, ὅτε ἐκλείσθη ὁ οὐρανὸς ἐπὶ ἔτη τρία καὶ μῆνας ἕξ (there were many widows in the days of E. in I., when the heaven was closed for three years and six months), which example, very reminiscent of a pattern in Herodotus (see above), illustrates the use of the perfective aspect to conceptualize a process extending over time. John 19:23: οἱ οὖν στρατιῶται ὅτε ἐσταύρωσαν τὸν Ἰησοῦν ἔλαβον τὰ ἱμάτια αὐτοῦ καὶ ἐποίησαν τέσσαρα μέρη (the soldiers, when they crucified Jesus, took his garment and made four portions), where reference to crucifying Jesus seems to serve as a heading for several other processes, including dividing up his garment, with the syntax establishing the progression (a traditional temporal analysis of the Aorist Participle would cause further difficulty). John 20:24: Θωμᾶς . . . οὐκ ἦν μετ᾽ αὐτῶν ὅτε ἦλθεν Ἰησοῦς (T. was not with them when Jesus came), very similar to the example above that Hettrich recognizes as difficult for his scheme. Acts 27:39: ὅτε δὲ ἡμέρα ἐγένετο, τὴν γῆν οὐκ ἐπεγίνωσκον (when day came, they did not not recognize the land), with the implication being that they saw land before daylight, yet when day came they still did not know its name. Phil 4:15: οἴδατε δὲ καὶ ὑμεῖς, Φιλιππήσιοι, ὅτι ἐν ἀρχῇ τοῦ εὐαγγελίου, ὅτε ἐξῆλθον ἀπὸ Μακεδονίας, οὐδεμία μοι ἐκκλησία ἐκοινώνησεν (you indeed know, P.s, that in the beginning of the gospel, when I went out from M., no church had fellowship with me), with the dependent clause with a verb of motion overlapping with the main clause, since Philippi is part of Macedonia (on why Paul says that the gospel originated in Macedonia see Hawthorne, *Philippians*, 203-04). This is an important example, since it shows that even with verbs of motion, which Hettrich draws upon heavily to establish his model, there are clear examples where the action of the two clauses must overlap. This then suggests reassessment of several other instances: Gal 4:4: ὅτε δὲ ἦλθεν τὸ πλήρωμα τοῦ χρόνου, ἐξαπέστειλεν ὁ θεὸς τὸν υἱὸν αὐτοῦ (when the fulness of time came, God sent his son) and Gal 2:11; 1 Pet 3:19-20: τοῖς ἐν φυλακῇ πνεύμασιν πορευθεὶς ἐκήρυξεν, ἀπειθήσασίν ποτε ὅτε ἀπεξεδέχετο ἡ τοῦ θεοῦ μακροθυμία ἐν ἡμέραις Νῶε κατασκευαζομένης κιβωτοῦ (going to those spirits in prison he preached, to those unpersuaded then when the patience of God waited in the days of N. when an ark was prepared), where the two clauses must overlap if the interpretation of this highly difficult verse is that the spirits in prison were unbelievers in Noah's time (for a defence of this interpretation see Grudem, *Peter, loc. cit.*); Rev 6:1: καὶ εἶδον ὅτε ἤνοιξεν τὸ ἀρνίον μίαν ἐκ τῶν ἑπτὰ σφραγίδων, καὶ ἤκουσα ἑνὸς ἐκ τῶν τεσσάρων ζῴων λέγοντος (and I looked when the lamb opened one of the seven seals, and I heard one of the four living creatures saying), where the Aorist εἶδον appears to function as a headterm for a succession of events. It is difficult to know the discretion of the following events. This makes interpretation of the ὅτε clauses in subsequent verses unclear also: 6:3, 5, 7, 9, 12. To cite further examples would make the point redundantly.

When it is realized that the Aorist and Imperfect tenses are equipollent and not in privative opposition (see chapt. 2), several difficulties regarding apparent significant usage of the Aorist are alleviated. The Aorist provides the backbone for narrative by describing a series of complete events (note e.g. perfective verbs as transition points in change of narrative scene). It is upon this framework that the narrative is built, with the Imperfect providing marked opposition, although the various ways in which individual clauses may relate is varied.

Gildersleeve (91) notes that "The two tenses are often so combined that the general statement is given by the aorist and the details of the action by the imperfect, or the situation is described by the imperfect and isolated points presented by the aorist."[18] As McKay says, the Aorist is the "residual aspect, used when the speaker or writer had no special reason to use any other" ("Syntax," 46; cf. *Grammar*, 138-39, 217-19; Kühner/Gerth, 1.157-58; see also Louw, "Aspek," 23, 1; Peppler, "Durative"; Gonda, *Ṛgvedic*, 55). Examples in the NT include: Luke 6:1ff., where the incident of the plucking and eating of the grain is introduced with two Imperfects. The details of the encounter with the Pharisees are then recorded with Aorists, with the concluding point of the story introduced with the Imperfect (v 5). A similar pattern is found in Luke 24:13ff. In contrast John 10:19ff. records a division that occurs. The fact that there was a schism is recorded with the Aorist, and the details are elucidated with Imperfects. The most common pattern in narrative throughout the NT, and within Greek literature as a whole, is to find an alternation of tenses.

3. Semantic difference between the Imperfect and narrative Present. Having established the semantic difference between the Aorist and Imperfect, it is now possible to distinguish between the Imperfect and Present. (1) There is no aspectual difference: both are aspectually imperfective on the basis of their formal paradigm. Virtually every grammarian who recognizes a category of kind of action holds to this position, although most would argue for a temporal distinction, i.e. the Imperfect is the preterite of the Present. (2) A semantic distinction stems from a functional difference. As McKay has indicated, and as most grammarians have tacitly recognized in analysing the Imperfect, its major usage is in narrative contexts, whereas the Present regularly enters into narrative contexts only as the marked 'historic' Present. Although this has led to the misleading generalization that the Imperfect is strictly a preterite (see below, and where the Imperfect is treated in timeless contexts when used in, e.g., parables), the abundant usage in past-referring contexts in relation to the aspectually identical Present, as well as the need for explanation of the persistence of two aspectually imperfective forms in Greek, points to a contextual distinction. It is at this juncture of usage alone that tense forms in Greek--the Imperfect and the Pluperfect--approach time-based tense forms (contra Moulton, 128: "We turn to the Imperfect, with which we enter the sphere of Tense proper, the idea of past time being definitely brought in by the presence of the augment." See below and chapt. 5).

On the basis of its preponderant use in the unmarked discourse context (narrative), its compatibility with contexts in which the Aorist is found, its restricted range of usage in narrative especially in relation to the formally and functionally marked Present, and its use of the unmarked and morphologically less bulky secondary endings--the Imperfect is best understood as the less heavily marked imperfective form, grammaticalizing [+remoteness], i.e. it is used in contexts where the action is seen as more remote than the action described by the (non-remote) Present. The use of "remote" avoids introduction of temporal terms for discussion of the tense forms (McKay, "Action," 43; cf. Lyons, *Semantics*, 819-20: "It might even be argued that what is customarily treated as being primarily an opposition of tense--past vs. non-past--in English and other languages, should be more properly regarded as a particular case of the distinction remote vs. non-remote ['then' vs. 'now' being a particular case of 'there' vs. 'here']"). Not only does this establish the relation of the Imperfect and the Present along both formal and functional lines, with the Present remaining marked in relation to the Imperfect with which it has identical verbal aspect, but it clarifies the relation of the Imperfect and the Aorist, both of which appear in narrative contexts.

---

[18]He cites esp. Pl. Phaed. 57A; Isoc. 8.99-100; 5.53-54; X. Hell. 2.3.55-56; Th. 4.119.1-3. Other grammarians have suggested: Hom. Il. 23.291 versus 294; Il. 2.106-07 versus 5.165 (Palmer, "Language," 146); Hdt. 3.19; 9.38-39; Th. 7.19.3-4; Ar. Wasps 986-88; Frogs 686-91; Clouds 348-52; Pl. Phaed. 60A.

For example, Mark 3:20-21: καὶ ἔρχεται εἰς οἶκον· καὶ συνέρχεται πάλιν [ὁ] ὄχλος, ὥστε μὴ δύνασθαι αὐτοὺς μηδὲ ἄρτον φαγεῖν. καὶ ἀκούσαντες οἱ παρ᾽ αὐτοῦ ἐξῆλθον κρατῆσαι αὐτόν, ἔλεγον γὰρ ὅτι ἐξέστη (and he entered into a house. And again a crowd gathered, so that they were not able to eat. And hearing, those with him went away to grab him, for they were saying that he was beside himself), with the Present used to introduce the scene and establish the significance of the situation, the Aorist to carry the movement of the narrative, and the Imperfect to record the thoughts of Jesus' followers. Mark 5:22-24: καὶ ἔρχεται εἷς τῶν ἀρχισυναγώγων, ὀνόματι Ἰάϊρος, καὶ ἰδὼν αὐτὸν πίπτει πρὸς τοὺς πόδας αὐτοῦ καὶ παρακαλεῖ αὐτὸν πολλὰ λέγων ὅτι τὸ θυγάτριόν μου ἐσχάτως ἔχει, ἵνα ἐλθὼν ἐπιθῇς τὰς χεῖρας αὐτῇ ἵνα σωθῇ καὶ ζήσῃ. καὶ ἀπῆλθεν μετ᾽ αὐτοῦ. καὶ ἠκολούθει αὐτῷ ὄχλος πολύς, καὶ συνέθλιβον αὐτόν (and one of the leaders of the synagogue came to him, by the name of J., and seeing him he fell at his feet and beseeched him many times saying that "my daughter is dying," so that coming he might lay hands upon her so that she might be saved and live. And he went away with him. And a great crowd was following him, and crushing him). A similar pattern to the above is seen, with the Present introducing the section and highlighting several significant events, the Aorist propelling the narrative forward (cf. v 21 using the Aorist to connect the narrative), and the Imperfect describing several significant features of the narrative in preparation for the next pericope (Emden ["Use," 148] lists these examples in defence of Mark's "skill and accuracy" in use of the Imperfect).

5. INTRODUCTION TO NON PAST-REFERRING TENSES.

a. Introduction. It is almost axiomatic within Greek grammar to assert without argument that the Imperfect and especially the Aorist Indicative are preterites, because of the presence of the augment (e.g. Kühner/Gerth, 1.154; Jannaris, 185; Robertson, 365). Since this is taken to be a fact of Greek grammar, it has coloured subsequent analysis of the two tense forms, i.e. because the augment is a past time indicator, the Imperfect and Aorist must be past-referring, and recognized usage that does not appear conducive to such a scheme must nevertheless be explained from this point of reference.

b. The Augment. The augment is a formal feature of the Aorist and Imperfect Indicatives (McKay, 223), but it has long been disputed what function the augment played in the earliest forms of Greek. (A comprehensive analysis appears in Drewitt, "Augment"; see also Curtius, *Verb*, 72-76; Chantraine, 1.479-84, cf. 2.186; Platt, "Augment," who argues that the augment is not a time indicator even though he interprets the tense forms temporally. Several scholars argue that the augment is a reality marker: e.g. Wackernagel, *Vorlesungen*, 181; Schwyzer, 2.285; and Friedrich, "Theory," S16; Wilkinson ["*Aspect*," 83] points out that this terminology is imprecise [does it imply that the Present is unreal?].) Summarizing the accepted facts about the augment in Homer, Drewitt argues that the augment is "purely scansional" (45) on the basis of the following factors.

(1) "True present-aorists, such as are seen in the similes and gnomes, take the augment *idiomatically.* In the whole of the similes there are only sixteen unaugmented aorists; three of the instances are difficult [Il. 3.4; 4.279; 15.682], but the rest could be emended by slight changes" (Chantraine [1.484] cites also Od. 4.791; 8.481; 22.386; Il. 17.99; 22.140 as examples of 'gnomic' Aorists without augment [in Il. 22.140, οἴμησε (swoops down) does not have an augmented temporal form attested]). (2) "Iteratives do not take the augment; [Od. 20.7] is the only certain exception." (3) "In the narrative proper both the aorist and the imperfect are relatively much

less often augmented than they are in speeches." (4) Within the speeches, Drewitt notices a "curious difference of treatment." (a) What he calls the "present-reference aorist . . . nearly always takes the augment. For example, the aorist with νῦν shows hardly any unaugmented forms except such as βουλεύσατο or ἱκόμην." (b) "True preterite aorists (i.e. aorists which have a plain past sense) can very well dispense with the augment even in speeches." Thus Drewitt concludes: "These points suggest one thing clearly enough. It is not the augment that creates or emphasizes the past meaning in any tense. The iterative, a purely narrative tense, does not admit the augment. The present-aorist, a typically non-narrative tense, can hardly exist without it" (44). Whereas the clarity of his conclusion is refreshing, the fact that approximately ten percent of the similes admit of non-augmented verbal forms (with several that cannot be explained on other grounds [contra e.g. Rijksbaron, 30, who posits that the Homeric similes must occur with the augment]) both reinforces the non-temporal and scansional nature of the augment and illustrates, as Drewitt recognizes, the importance of deictic indicators for determining temporal reference in Greek. Whether Drewitt is right or not that the augment originally was a 'present' indicator, there is reason to believe that augmented tenses were originally avoided in narrative, with the augment being a later insertion (46-47, cf. also 48, 49-50). As McKay (223) says, "it is quite clear that by the classical period it was simply a formal feature of the imperfect, aorist and pluperfect indicative. By the Hellenistic period it was so devoid of special significance that it ceased to be attached to the pluperfect, and in later centuries it disappeared altogether except when accented."

    c. The Imperfect. (See Mateos/Alepuz, "Perfecto," for list of Imperfects in the NT.) Despite its widespread use in narrative, which statistically reinforces the preponderance of occurrences with past-time reference (see above on remoteness), the Imperfect is no exception to the theory that the tenses in Greek are not time-based, since the Imperfect can be used in a number of non past-time contexts,[19] as a few grammarians recognize (esp. McKay, "Action," who cites examples from earlier Greek). These uses include appearance in the protasis of I.b. conditionals with present reference (see chapt. 6), and appearance in present contexts withᾰν (see above). Some grammarians have been hesitant, however, to recognize the use of the Imperfect in other less-formally established non-past contexts, e.g., use in such timeless narratives as parables.

    For example, Kühner/Gerth (1.145) state, "Das *Imperfekt* scheint bisweilen *statt des Präsens* zu stehen, indem die durch dasselbe ausgedrückte Handlung in der Gegenwart fortbesteht. Der Redende nimmt alsdann keine Rücksicht auf das Fortbestehen der Handlung in der Gegenwart, sondern versetzt sich in den Zeitpunkt der Vergangenheit zurück, in welchem er dieselbe erkannte oder von ihr die Rede war" (cf. Schwyzer, 2.280). Goodwin (*Syntax*, 13) calls this the philosophic Imperfect, followed by Law ("Note"), although he bases much of his

---

[19]The remote Indicative form of εἰμί is used in two Homeric similes: Il. 15.273-74: τὸν μέν τ᾽ ἠλίβατος πέτρη καὶ δάσκιος ὕλη / εἰρύσατ᾽, οὐδ᾽ ἄρα τέ σφι κιχήμεναι αἴσιμον ἦεν (and a sheer rock and thick forest save him, nor is it fated to find him); 21.493-95: ὥς τε πέλεια, / ἥ ῥά θ᾽ ὑπ᾽ ἴρηκος κοίλην εἰσέπτατο πέτρην, / χηραμόν· οὐδ᾽ ἄρα τῇ γε ἁλώμεναι αἴσιμον ἦεν (and as a dove, which flies under a hawk into a hollow rock, a cleft; it is not fated to be caught). Supporting non-past use here of ἦεν are McKay, "Action," 46; Drewitt, "Augment," 49; against Wilkinson, *"Aspect,"* 179ff. (Ruipérez [*Estructura*, 166] considers ἦεν a gnomic Aorist.) On εἰμί as aspectually vague, see chapt. 10. McKay (42-45) and Goodwin (*Syntax*, 13) cite several significant examples of the remote Indicative of εἰμί in non-past contexts. NT examples include: Matt 26:24; Luke 1:66; 2 Pet 2:21; Rev 3:15; beside conditionals, such as John 8:42 (I.b. conditional). Hellenistic examples include Paus. 1.4.3.

argument on forms of -ἥκω. (I tentatively believe that this verb is part of the Perfect paradigm.) Kühner/Gerth cite Pl. Crito 47D, claiming that διαφθεροῦμεν ἐκεῖνο καὶ λωβησόμεθα, ὃ τῷ μὲν δικαίῳ βέλτιον ἐγίγνετο, τῷ δὲ ἀδίκῳ ἀπώλλυτο (we will destroy and injure that which becomes better by justice and is destroyed by injustice) stands for τῷ μὲν δικ. βέλτιον γίγνεσθαι, τῷ δὲ ἀδ. ἀπόλλυσθαι ἐλέγετο ἑκάστοτε ὑφ' ἡμῶν περὶ τῶν τοιούτων διαλεγομένων (it was said always by us as we discussed such matters that such a thing becomes better by justice and is made worse by injustice). It must be questioned whether such an explanation is possible, especially since there is no intimation within the dialogue that the speaker is referring to a past occasion. Crito has entered and begun talking to Socrates about his impending death, urging Socrates to make an attempt to escape. Socrates and Crito have just begun their philosophical discussion, and it is in this speech that Socrates seriously addresses the question of right and wrong (περὶ ὧν νῦν ἡ βουλὴ ἡμῖν ἐστιν [which our discussion is now about]) (cf. McKay, "Action," 44).[20] Further, Imperfect verbs are constituents of complements in apodoses of II.c. conditional statements, and thus in the realm of hypothetical and not time-based discussion. Thus this example is better explained along the lines that, within the hypothetical conditional, Socrates says that if there were one worthy of being followed, injury surely is the result to that which is in progress being made better by justice and made worse by injustice. The question is why the remote imperfective is used as opposed to the non-remote. The imperfective aspect was apparently felt to capture the process best, but the author wished to create a greater contrast between the two apodoses, and thus used the remote form.

Once it is seen that the time-based conception of the Imperfect is not only unnecessary but potentially misleading, other examples present themselves, especially in the NT. (Virtually every grammar lists several examples of the Imperfect found to be intractable without an appeal to present time reference: e.g. Winer, 352-54; Blass/Debrunner, ¶ 358; Robertson, 885-87.)

John 11:8: λέγουσιν αὐτῷ οἱ μαθηταί, 'Ραββί, νῦν ἐζήτουν σε λιθάσαι οἱ 'Ιουδαῖοι, καὶ πάλιν ὑπάγεις ἐκεῖ; (the disciples said to him, "Rabbi, the Jews are now seeking to stone you, and again you are going there?"), with the non-remote imperfective (Present) being stressed over the remote imperfective, and the deictic indicator (νῦν) establishing the temporal sphere of reference. Acts 25:22: 'Αγρίππας δὲ πρὸς τὸν Φῆστον, ἐβουλόμην καὶ αὐτὸς τοῦ ἀνθρώπου ἀκοῦσαι (A. to F., I myself am wanting to hear the man), where the less heavily semantically marked remote imperfective seems appropriate to Agrippa's expressing reticent curiosity about the fellow Jew Paul (1 Tim 2:8; Titus 3:8, with the Present; cf. 2 Cor 1:15: καὶ ταύτῃ τῇ πεποιθήσει ἐβουλόμην πρότερον πρὸς ὑμᾶς ἐλθεῖν [and with this confidence I was wanting previously to come to you] with the deictic indicator establishing past reference). Rom 9:3: ηὐχόμην γὰρ ἀνάθεμα εἶναι αὐτὸς ἐγὼ ἀπὸ τοῦ Χριστοῦ ὑπὲρ τῶν ἀδελφῶν μου (I indeed pray to be anathema from Christ on behalf of my brothers), probably with timeless use of the Imperfect (in contrast to more marked use of the Present in v 1 with reference to Christ) establishing Paul's attitude toward his own people, although an 'epistolary' Imperfect is also possible. 2 Cor 11:1: ὄφελον ἀνείχεσθέ μου μικρόν τι ἀφροσύνης· ἀλλὰ καὶ ἀνέχεσθέ μου (would that you would be patient with my foolishness for a little while; but indeed you are patient with me), where Paul expresses his current wish that the Corinthians would be patient with him, while acknowledging that in fact they are patient with him. 2 Cor 12:11: ἐγὼ γὰρ ὤφειλον ὑφ' ὑμῶν συνίστασθαι (for I am obligated to be commended by you), where the timeless context of 12:9-12 contains Paul's personal reflection upon his relation to Christ and the Corinthians. Gal 4:20: ἤθελον δὲ παρεῖναι πρὸς ὑμᾶς ἄρτι (and I want to be present with you now), with ἄρτι establishing present reference (cf. Epict. 1.19.18: ἤθελον αὐτὸν ἀποβληθῆναι τοῦ κοπρῶνος [I want him to be cast out of the dunghill], where this timeless use of the Imperfect occurs within the context of rhetorical questions). Phlm 13: ὃν ἐγὼ ἐβουλόμην πρὸς ἐμαυτὸν κατέχειν (whom I myself want to retain for myself), where Paul uses four parallel relative clauses, the first being past in reference (v 10), but the subsequent three present (the second and fourth verbs are

---

[20] Cf. Paus. 1 4.5; ἄγκυρα δέ . . . ἦν ἔτι καὶ ἐς ἐμὲ ἐν ἱεφῷ (and the anchor is still in my time in the temple).

Aorists). (Cf. 2 John 12: πολλὰ ἔχων ὑμῖν γράφειν οὐκ ἐβουλήθην διὰ χάρτου καὶ μέλανος, ἀλλὰ ἐλπίζω γενέσθαι πρὸς ὑμᾶς [having many things for you I am not wanting to write through paper and ink, but I hope to come to you], where the less heavily marked Aorist contrasts the stronger hope conveyed through the Present.)

Several grammarians recognize catenative constructions (see appendix 10B) with the non past-referring Imperfect: Matt 23:23: ταῦτα [δὲ] ἔδει ποιῆσαι κἀκεῖνα μὴ ἀφιέναι (it is necessary to do these things and not to neglect the others), with omnitemporal reference; Luke 15:32: εὐφρανθῆναι δὲ καὶ χαρῆναι ἔδει (it is necessary to rejoice and be glad), since the party is currently being held; Luke 24:26: οὐχὶ ταῦτα ἔδει παθεῖν τὸν Χριστὸν καὶ εἰσελθεῖν εἰς τὴν δόξαν αὐτοῦ; (are these things not necessary, i.e. for the Christ to suffer and to enter into his glory?), with a timeless use of ἔδει in the mouth of the risen Jesus. (Cf. Heb 9:26: ἐπεὶ ἔδει αὐτὸν πολλάκις παθεῖν ἀπὸ καταβολῆς κόσμου· νυνὶ δὲ ἅπαξ ἐπὶ συντελείᾳ τῶν αἰώνων εἰς ἀθέτησιν [τῆς] ἁμαρτίας διὰ τῆς θυσίας αὐτοῦ πεφανέρωται [since it was necessary for him to suffer many times from the foundation of the world; but now once upon the end of the age for removal of sin through his sacrifice he is made manifest], where temporal indicators are difficult.) Acts 1:16: ἄνδρες ἀδελφοί, ἔδει πληρωθῆναι τὴν γραφὴν ἣν προεῖπεν τὸ πνεῦμα τὸ ἅγιον διὰ στόματος Δαυὶδ (brothers, it is necessary to fulfil the scripture which the holy spirit spoke through the mouth of D.), with present reference to beginning the process of filling Judas's place among the disciples; Acts 24:19: τινὲς δὲ ἀπὸ τῆς Ἀσίας Ἰουδαῖοι, οὓς ἔδει ἐπὶ σοῦ παρεῖναι καὶ κατηγορεῖν εἴ τι ἔχοιεν πρὸς ἐμέ (certain Jews from A., for whom it is necessary to come before you and to make accusation if they might have something against me), with present reference indicated by the clause using the Imperative in v 20; 2 Cor 2:3: καὶ ἔγραψα τοῦτο αὐτὸ ἵνα μὴ ἐλθὼν λύπην σχῶ ἀφ᾽ ὧν ἔδει με χαίρειν (and I write this so that, coming, I might not have grief from whom it is necessary to make me rejoice), with the use of the Subjunctive establishing a timeless context (note present use of the Aorist). Cf. Rom 1:27, in a timeless context.

Three important observations may now be made: (1) showing the augment not to be a temporal indicator eliminates one of the most widely noted points of support for assertions about the essential temporal nature of at least the so-called preterite Indicatives in Greek; (2) the emphasis shifts from explaining apparent aberrations in the temporal scheme (see below), to an emphasis upon the non-temporal nature of Greek verbal usage, thus making prima facie a strong case for the approach used in this work: to analyse the range of usage and to formulate a synthetic analysis which is faithful to the formal evidence of the language; and (3) the predominant usage of the Imperfect within narrative contexts must not be minimized, although the use of the tense form must be seen as semantically contrastive to other available verb tenses for speaker use, grammaticalizing the semantic feature of [+remoteness].

6. NON PAST-REFERRING PERFECTIVE AND IMPERFECTIVE ASPECTS. a. Introduction. As seen in chapt. 1, the non past-referring Aorist--while recognized as a category by many grammarians--is often treated either as still explainable in terms of past reference, or as a recognizable but essentially semantically unimportant aberration from standard usage.

b. Recent Discussion. That this idea persists is particularly surprising in light of work by Péristérakis (*Essai* [1962]), in which he argues that the intemporal Aorist is a recognizable and relatively widespread usage, in many instances parallel to that of the Present. However, none of the Greek grammars completed since 1962 and with possible access to Péristérakis mentions his work (e.g. McKay, Blass/Debrunner/Rehkopf, Moorhouse, Rijksbaron, Brooks/Winbery, Hoffmann/Siebenthal). His thesis is a simple one. In departing from widespread research on the 'gnomic' Aorist (see below for discussion of various theories), Péristérakis relies upon three primary criteria to establish the intemporal use of the Aorist: context, in which "La place de chaque forme verbale dans le texte ordonne sa fonction" (v); synonymous expressions, in which a clear expression is used to clarify another expression (this is similar to the criterion of substitution; see my chapt. 2); and verbal aspect (vi, cf. 10), distinguishing between the Aorist representing a fact and the Present a process in evolution.

It is in his discussion of verbal aspect that Péristérakis shows one of the two major weaknesses of his study, since he is content to accept one of the standard explanations of the tense forms. Although he believes that "L'aoriste n'est pas originellement un 'prétérit.' La nuance qui distingue l'aoriste du présent n'est pas toujours temporelle" (3), he also believes, following Meillet/Vendryes (*Traité*, 198), that the tripartite temporal structure is "un fait de civilisation" (3).[21] His resolution shows his failure to reconcile these two elements in a principled linguistic fashion:

> En effet, lorsqu'un auteur s'exprime d'une façon générale, fait des réflexions qui n'ont aucun rapport avec des événements concrets, qu'il crée avec sa fantaisie un monde, un tableau, ou qu'il décrit une idée, une vérité ou même une coutume, alors il se place en dehors de tout temps réel parce que ce qu'il dit est ou doit être valable et réalisable dans tous les temps. Alors ces expressions verbales non seulement n'ont pas besoin de marquer le temps, mais sont plus justes et plus expressives, si elles sont dépourvues de toute valeur temporelle. Et c'est là justement la valeur et l'importance des procédés dont le grec dispose, à savoir les formes verbales intemporelles; cela s'observe surtout au présent et à l'aoriste de l'indicatif. Ces représentations générales, de même que les comparaisons, appartiennent à la réalité, elles ont rapport à ce qui existe et que chacun peut saisir par son intelligence ou par ses sens. (5)

---

[21]Péristérakis also accepts Brunel's theory (*L'aspect*) on use of the prefix to make an undetermined verb form a determined one, e.g. ἀπέβη in Pl. Symp. 197A (56); see appendix 1A for critique.

While Péristérakis's formulation helpfully shows that, for example, habitual (5) and instantaneous uses[22] of a tense are matters of syntax and not verb form, and he places value upon individual syntactical constructions, he too sees the non past-referring Aorist as a special though widespread case for expression of general or gnomic-like statements. In fact he defines the intemporal Aorist in comparison with previous discussion of the 'gnomic' Aorist, seeing its appropriateness for moral statements, comparisons, and descriptions of natural phenomena (6-11).

It is not necessary to summarize every nuance of Péristérakis's work, but he does marshal a large number of examples from poetry and prose, both early and late but virtually all pre-hellenistic, which show that the Greek Aorist is capable of non-past reference in a variety of contexts. His discussion divides the examples into essentially three categories: those which are found in conditional or conditional-like statements (following Participles, relative clauses, etc.) (28-117), those which are found in clauses related by μέν-δέ (118-23), and those which are found in clauses apart from the above but which still indicate non-past reference (125-63) (the book includes much more besides). The second limitation is readily apparent: because he begins with a view that sees the tenses at least in the Indicative as predominantly time-bound (despite their origins in aspectual categories) he seems to overemphasize the role of the syntactical construction to point clearly to an intemporal use, rather than beginning from the non-temporal basis of all tense usage and looking to the discourse features to establish temporal reference. Analysis of two areas-- tense substitution and aspectual analysis--are important here.

In constructions that use Aorist and Present tenses in similar circumstances (synonymous usage), Péristérakis asks what the difference in tense forms is if it is not temporal distinction. For example, Th. 2.11.4: ἄδηλα γὰρ τὰ τῶν πολέμων, καὶ ἐξ ὀλίγου τὰ πολλὰ καὶ δι' ὀργῆς αἱ ἐπιχειρήσεις γίγνονται· πολλάκις τε τὸ ἔλασσον πλῆθος δεδιὸς ἄμεινον ἠμύνατο τοὺς πλέονας διὰ τὸ καταφρονοῦντας ἀπαρασκεύους γενέσθαι (unclear are the things of wars, and the attacks become many from little reason and through anger; and many times the less in number fearing worse defends against the many because the contemptuous are unprepared). In response to Moller (*Phil.* 8 [1853] 124), who claims that the 'gnomic' use of the Aorist refers to a past experience and the Present to reality, Péristérakis says: "Mais nous considérons l'aoriste . . .

---

[22]E.g. Pl. Phaed. 73D: οὐκοῦν οἶσθα ὅτι οἱ ἐρασταί, ὅταν ἴδωσιν λύραν ἢ ἱμάτιον ἢ ἄλλο τι, οἷς τὰ παιδικὰ αὐτῶν εἴωθε χρῆσθαι, πάσχουσι τοῦτο· ἔγνωσάν τε τὴν λύραν καὶ ἐν τῇ διανοίᾳ ἔλαβον τὸ εἶδος τοῦ παιδός, οὗ ἦν ἡ λύρα; τοῦτο δέ ἐστιν ἀνάμνησις (do you not know that the lovers, whenever they might see a lyre or a garment or any other thing, which their lover is permitted to make use of, they suffer this, and they know the lyre and in their mind they receive the image of the lover, where the lyre was? This is recollection), where Péristérakis says: "Il est vrai que le contexte nous autorise ici à attribuer aux aoristes ἔγνωσαν, ἔλαβον une valeur d'instantanéité. . . . Mais ce ne sont pas les aoristes qui comportent originellement cette valeur. C'est la nature de l'esprit humain, dont il s'agit dans cet exemple de Platon, qui est ainsi capable de reconnaître instantanément et de relier deux images qui ont un rapport quelconque entre elles" (34-35).

comme intemporel, et nous nous demandons si la phrase de Thucydide est correcte et exprime la même idée si nous remplaçons l'aoriste ἡμύνατο par le présent ἀμύνεται. Il y a certainement une différence. L'aoriste marque l'événement dans sa γένεσις. Il n'exprime pas, au moins ici, une loi générale. Au point de vue du 'temps' il ne diffère pas du présent" (69). Although his explanation of the aspectual differences of the tenses is open to question (see below), the principle of substitution points clearly to the non time-based nature of the tense forms.

Several examples which Péristérakis cites to illustrate aspectual contrast are worth examination (especially since his aspectual theory posits that the Present tense represents a general law, while the Aorist tense marks a resultant fact). D. 1.11: ἄν μὲν γάρ, ὅσ' ἄν τις λάβῃ, καὶ σώσῃ, μεγάλην ἔχει τῇ τύχῃ τὴν χάριν, ἄν δ' ἀναλώσας λάθῃ, συνανήλωσε καὶ τὸ μεμνῆσθαι [τὴν χάριν] (for whoever obtains and saves, he has great joy in his fortune, but whoever loses through squandering, he loses with it the remembrance of fortune). Péristérakis says "L'aoriste συνανήλωσε s'oppose au présent (μεγάλην) ἔχει . . . τὴν χάριν. L'un exprime ce qui reste et dure, c'est une conséquence qui se prolonge; l'autre, l'aoriste, marque la conséquence inéluctable d'une action qui ne dure pas" (25). Besides the fact that another reading might be given--that the one who obtains is only grateful for the one act of fortune but that one who loses never remembers again--the tense opposition points to use of marking of aspects. In his speech Demosthenes contrasts the fortunes and misfortunes of cities, exhorting the Athenians to restore their prosperity. Cf. Arist. Ath. Const. 63.5: ἐπειδὰν δὲ ὁ θεσμοθέτης [v.l. νομοθέτης in Péristérakis] ἐπικληρώσῃ τὰ γράμματα ἃ δεῖ προσπαρατίθεσθαι τοῖς δικαστηρίοις, ἐπέθηκε φέρων ὁ ὑπηρέτης ἐφ' ἕκαστον τὸ δικαστήριον τὸ γράμμα τὸ λαχόν (whenever the law-giver assigns the letters which must be distributed to the courts, the servant, taking them, gives to each court the assigned letter), where Péristérakis claims that "L'aoriste exprime le fait connu de tous, qui se réalise sans aucun doute dès que le thesmothète tire au sort les lettres. C'est un fait certain que tout le monde attend en vertu de la législation athénienne" (45). The facts may be true, but this interpretation appears not only to make the Aorist bear too much weight, but to contradict what is claimed for the Aorist in D. 1.11 above. The point is not that the action is of no duration but that it is seen by the author as the ongoing procedure, the accepted state of affairs.

Pl. Laws 854D-E: οὐ γὰρ ἐπὶ κακῷ δίκη γίγνεται οὐδεμία γενομένη κατὰ νόμον, δυοῖν δὲ θάτερον ἀπεργάζεται σχεδόν· ἢ γὰρ βελτίονα ἢ μοχθηρότερον ἧττον ἐξηργάσατο τὸν τὴν δίκην παρασχόντα (justice brings about nothing for evil, coming into being according to the law, but it accomplishes usually two things. Either better or less villainous it makes the one who suffers the punishment). Péristérakis is correct in noting the alternation in Present and Aorist tense forms (although he stresses the role of the contrasting prefixes too much). Péristérakis is also correct that the difference lies in aspect, but not with the Present envisioning "un accomplissement d'une transformation qui n'est pas arrivée dans sa conclusion finale" and the Aorist as "une forte expression verbale du fait final de cette transformation menée à son terme" (162). In this instance the Present marks the assertion that there are two results. In a sentence with inverted word order to draw attention to the complements (βελτίονα . . . μοχθηρότερον ἧττον) and not the predicate, the suitable use of the less heavily marked Aorist implies nothing of a stronger degree of accomplishment but specifies the two characteristics. The next sentence introduces the consequence of such an act, by way of a conditional-like sentence. Similar is Pl. Rep. 551B: ταῦτα δὲ ἢ βίᾳ μεθ' ὅπλων διαπράττονται, ἢ καὶ πρὸ τούτου φοβήσαντες κατεστήσαντο τὴν τοιαύτην πολιτείαν (these things either they accomplish by violence with soldiers, or indeed before this by causing fear they establish such a government). Péristérakis claims that "Si nous admettons que la première est générale et qu'elle est utilisée plus souvent que la seconde--ce qui n'est pas loin de la réalité--nous avons une explication du présent διαπράττονται et de l'aoriste κατεστήσαντο. Plus souvent, en effet, un régime s'impose par la force et par les armes que par une simple intimidation. Le dernier cas est rare; c'est un fait particulier" (92). This explanation relies less on verbal aspect than Péristérakis imagines: there is no textual indication that the first event is general and more frequent than the second; there is no reason to connect a rare instance with a particular instance, or a general one with a more frequent one; and he has overlooked the temporal indicator πρὸ τούτου. A more plausible reading is that the author draws attention to the force of arms as the more noteworthy and perhaps dangerous situation, seen as a last resort after intimidation has failed.

Th. 1.120.5: πολλὰ γὰρ κακῶς γνωσθέντα ἀβουλοτέρων τῶν ἐναντίων τυχόντα κατωρθώθη, καὶ ἔτι πλείω καλῶς δοκοῦντα βουλευθῆναι ἐς τοὐναντίον αἰσχρῶς περιέστη· ἐνθυμεῖται γὰρ οὐδεὶς ὁμοία τῇ πίστει καὶ ἔργῳ ἐπεξέρχεται, ἀλλὰ μετ᾽ ἀσφαλείας μὲν δοξάζομεν, μετὰ δέους δὲ ἐν τῷ ἔργῳ ἐλλείπομεν (many badly-considered things having the lack of consideration of their opponents succeed, and still more, things thought to be well advised turn out shamefully for the opposite. For no one in the same way plans in faith and accomplishes in work, but on the one hand we think with confidence, but we fall short in the work with fear). Of these omnitemporal uses of the Aorist and Present, Péristérakis says that the Aorist "marquent les faits consécutifs à des circonstances particulières exprimées par κακῶς γνωσθέντα ἀβουλουτέρων τῶν ἐναντίων τυχόντα. Ils s'opposent aux présents du passage qui désignent des lois générales" (69). Péristérakis's contrast can be refined. It is not between sequence and general laws, but between negative considerations expressed with the Aorist and positive considerations expressed with the Present, reinforcing the more heavily marked semantic weight of the Present.

Hdt. 4.60.1-2: τὸ μὲν ἱρήιον αὐτὸ ἐμπεποδισμένον τοὺς ἐμπροσθίους πόδας ἕστηκε, ὁ δὲ θύων ὄπισθε τοῦ κτήνεος ἑστεὼς σπάσας τὴν ἀρχὴν τοῦ στρόφου καταβάλλει μιν, πίπτοντος δὲ τοῦ ἱρηίου ἐπικαλέει τὸν θεὸν τῷ ἂν θύῃ καὶ ἔπειτα βρόχῳ περὶ ὧν ἔβαλε τὸν αὐχένα, σκυταλίδα δὲ ἐμβαλὼν περιάγει καὶ ἀποπνίγει, οὔτε πῦρ ἀνακαύσας οὔτε καταρξάμενος οὔτ᾽ ἐπισπείσας (the victim itself, bound by its front feet, stands, and the one sacrificing, standing behind the beast, casts it down, pulling the end of the rope, and as the victim falls, he calls upon the god to whom he sacrifices and then he throws the noose around the neck, and thrusting in the stick he twists and strangles it, neither lighting a fire nor offering firstfruits nor pouring a libation). Péristérakis has difficulty explaining use of the Aorist ἔβαλε here (How/Wells [*Commentary*, 1.185] note that Herodotus "often uses this tmesis of the empiric aorist, in describing customs"; see also 1.194.4; 2.40.2; cf. Péristérakis, 144ff.). He claims it should describe "le fait résultat final de toutes les opérations qui précèdent" (151), a role taken by the Present καταβάλλει. This example illustrates use of the less heavily marked Aorist serving as a transition between significant events marked by the Present and Perfect tenses. The discourse itself points to this in its use of Aorist Participles to specify what the sacrificer does not do, while the two Present verbs (περιάγει and ἀποπνίγει) mark his procedure. The same pattern is found in the following sentence: ἀποπνίξας δὲ καὶ ἀποδείρας τράπεται πρὸς ἕψησιν (having strangled and flayed it up he prepares it for cooking), where the Aorist Participles recapitulate. (Cf. also Hdt. 2.96.2; 4.196; 7.10.e [145-48] and Hdt. 2.47.3, where Péristérakis is correct that καὶ ἔπειτα καταγίζει πυρί [and then he burns it with fire] "est la partie la plus intéressante du sacrifice" but incorrect that this is because "C'est une action qui dure . . . et qui est consécutive aux faits préparatoires" [110].)

Isoc. 1.46-47: ἐν μὲν γὰρ τῷ ῥαθυμεῖν καὶ τὰς πλησμονὰς ἀγαπᾶν εὐθὺς αἱ λῦπαι ταῖς ἡδοναῖς παραπεπήγασι, τὸ δὲ περὶ τὴν ἀρετὴν φιλοπονεῖν καὶ σωφρόνως τὸν αὐτοῦ βίον οἰκονομεῖν ἀεὶ τὰς τέρψεις εἰλικρινεῖς καὶ βεβαιοτέρας ἀποδίδωσι· κἀκεῖ μὲν πρότερον ἡσθέντες ὕστερον ἐλυπήθησαν [v.l. ˉθημεν], ἐνταῦθα δὲ μετὰ τὰς λύπας τὰς ἡδονὰς ἔχομεν (for when being idle and loving satiety, immediately griefs plant themselves alongside pleasures, on the other hand the love of virtue and building up of one's life wisely always yields pure and constant pleasure; on the one hand, in the former, having previously enjoyed pleasure, they grieve later, on the other hand, in the latter, after the grief we have pleasures). As Péristérakis notes "nous avons un très bon exemple de l'emploi de l'aoriste, du parfait et du présent dans les phrases de sens général" (72). But his explanation of the Perfect showing result, the Present signifying prolonged duration of the act (a law), and the Aorist specifying an inceptive act (72-73) is less convincing. The Perfect is not best interpreted as resultive (see my chapt. 5), although the temporal sphere appears to be contemporaneous with that described with the following Present and Aorist verbs. But his contrast in kind of action of the Aorist and Present cannot be sustained at either the level of semantic explanation or pragmatic usage here. The distinction between fact and law cannot be maintained, since there is no indicator of this by way of either tense form or context, and in fact the context clearly indicates a timeless situation in which all three verbs function. The first sentence appears to contrast the unexpected state resulting from pursuit of pleasure, grammaticalized by the Perfect, with the less striking though still important description of pleasures resulting from well-considered acts, using the less heavily marked Present. The second sentence details the results. The Aorist does not dwell on the results of seeking pleasure, but the Present signals the gains once grief is past. (Cf. also Isoc. 1.33 [121-22; 135-36]; 1.6, where Péristérakis says the text is abbreviated.)

Péristérakis provides a very important collection and analysis of examples which clearly illustrate significant and widespread usage of the Aorist and Present (and Perfect) tenses in temporally identical contexts, which includes non-past reference for the Aorist. Although his explanations are not always persuasive (due in part to his description of verbal action), his analysis provides valuable insight for further work, including noting parallel contextual usage and aspectual function.

In light of Péristérakis's work, it is significant to note that one of the most persistent generalizations is that the Aorist may be used in a present context when it stands for a brusque or quick process, often an expression of sudden emotion in dialogue (e.g. Kühner/Gerth, 1.163-65; Goodwin, *Syntax*, 18; Smyth, 432; Humbert, 144-45; idem, "L'aoriste," 188-89; Schwyzer, 2.281-82; Moorhouse, 195-96; Rijksbaron, 28-29; see below). This analysis is not adequate to explain several important though often overlooked examples: e.g. Pl. Phaedr. 244-256 (see appendix 4A), where Socrates discusses love in light of his hearers' questions. The selection contains a significant number of Aorist and Present verbs throughout. A similar pattern occurs in hellenistic usage, as clearly seen in Polybius 6 (see appendix 4A), where the historian discusses the Roman military, particularly selection of centurions. This selection, using the Aorist predominantly, appears between two major sections which use the Present predominantly, with no deictic indicators to signify a shift in temporal reference, and with very similar contexts (Walbank [*Commentary*, 1.706ff.] does not comment upon the use of the Aorist in this description, although he does make comments upon tense changes elsewhere [e.g. 675 on 6.11.13]). The selection of examples marshalled not only illustrates use of the Aorist without past reference in isolated usage (which many grammarians recognize, see below), but it well illustrates that the Aorist could be used in sustained discourse without past reference. (Weymouth ["Rendering," 179-80] recognized in 1890 the distinction between the narrative or past-referring Aorist and the non-narrative Aorist ["wholly indefinite in time"], finding this pattern in reading Lucian Dialogue of Gods, confirmed in Herodotus, Thucydides and Xenophon.)

It is difficult to label each usage of the Aorist in the extended examples, but two points emerge: the Aorist can be used in clearly non past-referring contexts in Greek. Gildersleeve (113) calls such usage the "AORIST IN GENERAL DESCRIPTIONS." This term is helpful in bringing to mind that the Aorist can and does appear in non-narrative contexts in Greek, though this is not to be considered non-standard usage. Although I have labelled more specifically the usage in the example from Plato (Phaedr. 244-56), and recognize that the examples in Polybius are timeless, omnitemporal or present-referring, depending upon how the author's presentation is construed, the fact emerges clearly that the Aorist, semantically the least heavily marked, is an appropriate tense to be used in non-past or descriptive contexts alongside other verb forms such as the Present (as well as the Imperfect).

    c.   **Temporal Implicatures of the Non Past-Referring Perfective and Imperfective Aspects.** For convenience, usage of the Aorist and Present forms in non past-referring contexts is discussed under four categories. It must be remembered, however, that in every instance the Aorist or the Present is formally unchanged, and that its relational semantic function at the level of code is stable throughout its range of pragmatic implicatures.

    1.   **Omnitemporal reference ('gnomic' use of tenses).**[23] In Greek language study (see chapt. 1), the gnomic use of tenses has proved notoriously difficult. The difficulty for most grammarians stems from two factors: the concept of the gnomic is one of continuous or regularly repeated action (hence the consideration of such usage as omnitemporal), which seems to contradict the generally accepted nature of at least the Aorist tense, if not the Present as well. There is also the problem, especially with the Aorist, of translation into English. Distinction between the semantic category of verbal aspect and pragmatic usage, however, provides a means through the difficulty surrounding gnomic use of the tenses. At the pragmatic level usage may be analysed according to various temporal categories, the first discussed above being past reference. The non-past sphere is here divided into four areas, the first omnitemporal reference. Lyons defines an omnitemporal proposition as "one that says that something has been, is and always will be so: it is a proposition whose truth-value is constant for all values of t_i, in a finite or infinite set of time-points or time-intervals, $[t_1, t_2, t_3, \ldots, t_n]$. . . .

---

[23]Gnomic uses do not appear to have been commented on by the ancient grammarians, so Obata, "Aorist," 61. The closest statement is perhaps found in Aristotle (Rhet. 1394A): ἔστι δὲ γνώμη ἀπόφανσις, οὐ μέντοι περὶ τῶν καθ᾽ ἕκαστον, οἷον ποῖός τις Ἰφικράτης, ἀλλὰ καθόλου· καὶ οὐ περὶ πάντων καθόλου, οἷον ὅτι τὸ εὐθὺ τῷ καμπύλῳ ἐναντίον, ἀλλὰ περὶ ὅσων αἱ πράξεις εἰσί, καὶ αἱρετὰ ἢ φευκτά ἐστι πρὸς τὸ πράττειν. ὥστ᾽ ἐπεὶ τὰ ἐνθυμήματα ὁ περὶ τούτων συλλογισμός ἐστι σχεδόν, τά τε συμπεράσματα τῶν ἐνθυμημάτων καὶ αἱ ἀρχαὶ ἀφαιρεθέντος τοῦ συλλογισμοῦ γνῶμαί εἰσι (a maxim is a statement, not therefore concerning the things of each, such as of what sort a certain I. is, but of the whole; and not concerning the whole of all things, such as that the straight is opposite to the crooked, but concerning such things as actions are, and choice or rejection in practicing them. Thus as enthymemes are the syllogism pertinent to these things, the conclusions of enthymemes indeed are the principal maxims of unstated syllogisms).

Omnitemporal propositions are one subclass of time-bound propositions: they are time-bound, but temporally-unrestricted" (*Semantics*, 680). Lyons suggests one reason that tense forms in relation to temporal categories in Greek have posed problems for speakers of English:

> In English and many other languages, both timeless and omnitemporal propositions are expressed characteristically be sentences in the so-called present tense: cf. "God is just," "The sun rises every day." It is important to realize, however, that there is no intrinsic connexion between the grammatical category of tense, and still less between any particular tense, and the expression of either timeless or omnitemporal propositions.

It is in this category that discussion of what is traditionally called gnomic tense usage in Greek is placed, although the two are not fully contiguous.

The label 'omnitemporal' is used in this work because it is more precise as a linguistic category. The term gnomic seems to imply a value-structure beyond that of temporal reference and is thus out of character not only with the categories for discussion in this work but with other categories used in more traditional grammatical discussion. As Lyons observes,

> Linguists frequently employ the term gnomic to refer to such so-called general truths as "It never rains but it pours," "Corruption starts at the top." Many of these truths (if they are truths) are expressed in the proverbs and aphorisms that are passed on in all cultures, from generation to generation. The temporal status of the propositions embodied in gnomic utterances is extremely diverse: some are timeless and others are omnitemporal; but many of them could hardly be said to describe anything more than tendencies, generalities and assumed regularities. (*Semantics*, 681)

Among major grammatical discussions, which usually focus upon the Aorist because it at first sight appears to provide the difficult 'exceptions,' at least the following explanations have been put forward (for a history of discussion see Kravar, "Autour," 33-40; Obata, "Aorist," 61ff.).

a. A few grammarians claim that at least within the NT there is no such thing as a gnomic Aorist. As Winer states categorically, "In no passage of the N.T. does the aorist express a habitual act. . ." (346; see also Radermacher, 152). As he admits, however,

> With more reason might Jas 1:11, ἀνέτειλεν ὁ ἥλιος σὺν τῷ καύσωνι καὶ ἐξήρανεν τὸν χόρτον κ.τ.λ. [the sun rises with its heat and withers the grass], be considered an example of this use of the aorist (compare 1 Pet 1:24) . . . these aorists however simply narrate (as describing an actual event), and all taken together they mark the rapid succession of the events, *the sun rose, and* (immediately) *withered*, etc.,--scarcely had the sun risen when the flower withered.--Such passages as Eph 5:29 exhibit the transition to this use of the aorist [to express an habitual act], which easily follows from the primary meaning of the tense. . . . In Jas 1:24, κατενόησεν ἑαυτὸν καὶ ἀπελήλυθεν καὶ εὐθέως ἐπελάθετο ὁποῖος ἦν [he observes himself and goes away and immediately forgets what he is like], neither aorist nor perfect is used for the present, but the case mentioned in v 23 by way of example is taken as actual fact, and the apostle falls into the tone of narration. (346-47)

This strikes me as special pleading. (1) Winer's conception of the tense forms as time-based constitutes the basis for his assertion that the Aorist and the Perfect in Jas 1:24 do not stand for the Present. Elsewhere it has been shown that this formulation is misguided. (2) Winer's use of Eph 5:29 (οὐδεὶς γάρ ποτε τὴν ἑαυτοῦ σάρκα ἐμίσησεν, ἀλλὰ ἐκτρέφει καὶ θάλπει αὐτήν [for no one ever hates his own flesh, but feeds and takes care of it]) is far from clear. (3) His explanation of Jas 1:11 is apparently confused, because he overlooks how the Aorist is able to be used as if it were describing an actual event and shifts to an unnecessary punctiliar description of the action (he seems to be followed here by Moule [12-13], who finds more plausible explanations, such as narrative Aorists [10-11]; and Zerwick [256], who claims that examples cited present unsolvable difficulties).

　　b. van Gronigen attempts to explain the gnomic Aorist on the basis that the Aorist Indicative expresses reference to past time, as well as a particular aspect (although he does not define this) ("Considérations"; see also Brugmann [564], who traces the origin to the mind of the oriental; Elmer ["Note"], who depicts the gnomic Aorist as a preterite used of present time with the idea of progress left out). Rejecting the source of the gnomic Aorist in the empiric, historic or present Aorist, van Gronigen turns to "psychologie" (51). "Ces trois groupes correspondent en principe aux trois tranches que l'esprit humain distingue spontanément dans le courant chronologique: l'avenir, le présent, le passé" (52). This temporal grid provides the basis for his solution. Whereas the Present is reserved for immediate, direct experience, the Imperfect and Aorist are used for the past. "L'aoriste est donc le temps verbal qui exprime p. ex. les points saillants d'une narration, les moments décisifs. . . . L'aoriste est le temps de la certitude objective dans le passé que nous connaissons" (53). Since Greeks were supposedly concerned with why things are as they are, the Aorist stands behind such questions and uses narration to relate the myths which give certitude to man regarding God. When what is recounted with the Present becomes established, it is past, and then established and eternal. In the eyes of the Greek, narration is related to facts, and thus to the distant, the ideal and the general truth. For example, Pi. Ol. 7.43-44: ἐν δ' ἀρετὰν / ἔβαλεν καὶ χάρματ᾿ ἀνθρώποισι Προμαθέος Αἰδώς (Reverence, daughter of Forethought, places virtue and joy in men) is supposedly the personification of a myth. Thus the gnomic Aorist

> raconte une chose passée--et voilà pourquoi même dans Homère il a toujours l'augment---; il raconte un fait certain ou considéré comme tel, un fait important et définitif qui décide une fois pour toutes de tous les cas analogues présents et à venir. Il ne nous engage pas à l'examiner à loisir comme cas particulier, quoiqu'il le présente comme tel, mais il l'impose comme loi générale. L'aoriste gnomique sert donc à formuler cette loi, non pas malgré son caractère de prétért, mais de par ce caractère. (57)

　　This description must be rejected. (1) van Gronigen is overly dependent upon a temporal conception of Greek tense forms, so much so that he creates an entire reconstruction of the Greek mind on the basis of this concept. (2) van Gronigen engages in a mythology of his own in his depiction of the Greek. It cannot be denied that language is to some extent a product of the mind, yet van Gronigen's presuppositions regarding the Greek mind--besides being broad generalizations with little fact to endorse them--make the Greek look unique, and thus imply that the gnomic tense could not be found in another culture, or certainly not in one not nearly so reflective as the Greek one. van Gronigen has left linguistic discussion behind. (3) His supposition of the gnomic Aorist residing in myth is highly questionable, since most examples of the gnomic Aorist cited in grammars in fact have no myth standing behind them (see Wilkinson, "Aspect," 80).

　　c. A similar view--and the most popular--is taken by scholars who posit that behind the gnomic Aorist lies a specific past action. (E.g. Humbert, 145-46; cf. idem, "L'aoriste," 187-91; Kühner/Gerth, 1.158-60; Stahl, 131-33; Blass/Debrunner, ¶ 333: "An act which is valid for all time . . . either because the aorist indicative serves for a non-existent perfective present . . . or because [originally at least] the author had a specific case in mind in which the act had been realized. . ."; Goodwin, Syntax, 53-54; Smyth, 431-32; Moulton, 135 [citing Goodwin]; Jannaris, 436; Kravar, "Autour" [in comparison with Slavonic languages]; de Foucault, Recherches, 131-

32; Rijksbaron, 30-32.)[24] This position is usually argued for on the basis of a supposed distinction between empiric and gnomic Aorists. For example, Humbert argues that the former is truly past, but modified by an adverb which shows that it represents a *"vérité d'expérience"* (145), and the latter expresses a recognized truth. But the two examples Humbert cites do not necessarily prove his distinction: Hes. Works 240: πολλάκι καὶ ξύμπασα πόλις κακοῦ ἀνδρὸς ἀπηύρα (often an entire city receives ill treatment from an evil man), which he labels as an Aorist of experience, and Hom. Il. 9.320: κάτθαν᾽ ὁμῶς ὅ τ᾽ ἀεργὸς ἀνὴρ ὅ τε πολλὰ ἐοργώς (he dies alike, the idle man and the man accomplishing much), which he labels gnomic. Why is the analysis not the reverse? In fact, Goodwin advances a specific group of examples of gnomic Aorists which are modified by adverbs such as πολλάκις, ἤδη, and οὔπω. Also it is clear that the pastness of the Aorist is given priority in analysis. (Wackernagel [*Vorlesungen*, 179] disputes the correlation between the two kinds of Aorists, but his objection that Imperfects and Perfects cannot be used as gnomic tenses as well [180] is unfounded.)

d. Several grammarians recognize what they call a timeless use of the Aorist in the gnomic Aorist. Robertson (836) asserts that the "real 'gnomic' aorist is a universal or timeless aorist and probably represents the original timelessness of the aorist indicative." In debating examples, however, Robertson makes a distinction that is untenable according to his own definition: he classifies some examples as gnomic and others as timeless, debating over for example John 15:6, 8. Turner claims the gnomic Aorist is "a timeless and almost futuristic aorist, expressing axioms which avail for all time" (*Syntax*, 73). After this throwing together of three distinguishable temporal spheres, he claims that "the present stem in Greek being linear, it would not be suitable for expressing generalities" (73), giving no reason why what he calls the "instantaneous" or *"punctiliar"* Aorist (59) would be better (he rejects reference to a specific act as the basis for gnomic usage [73]). After his elaborate explanation of the augment as the temporal indicator (distinct from the aspectual indicator), this seems a forced conclusion. He recognizes that the augment cannot be "jettisoned," but "we must look rather to the stem than the augment" (73). Turner (73) also asserts that the Aorist is sometimes "noncommittal" on aspect, regarding the action as "a whole without respect to duration."

e. These several views have been persistent in the secondary literature for a number of years, thus making a new proposal regarding the gnomic Aorist welcome. Such has been made by Obata ("Aorist"). Relying on the work of Benveniste (*Problème de linguistique générale* [Paris, 1966] 151-67), Obata looks first to the noun phrase to explain the gnomic Aorist. Whereas the verbal phrase belongs to narration, the noun phrase belongs to discourse, presenting something absolutely (it insists or proves or refers), often for persuasive purposes. Since tense, Person or situation are not required, noun sentences are suitable for proverbs or general truths. The gnomic Aorist therefore replaces a noun clause, with the verb only indicating the lexical meaning, Person and Voice, excluding aspect, tense, and Mood. Defining aspect as a grammatical category, Obata recognizes that all verb forms indicate aspect at the centre of the verb, i.e. the stem, with the Aorist as unlimited (Meillet). Obata does not distinguish Mood from tense in Greek, separating off two kinds of Indicative: (1) for the here and now and (2) for the past. He uses this distinction to show that Mood/tense does not have limitation, since a non-augmented form (Optative) may be found in Indicative 2. This is also found with such forms as the Imperfect and Aorist, which lack augments in Homer (he claims it is much older, appearing in Mycenean as well). He infers that these are the older forms, used for past reference, while the unaugmented forms, not used for past reference,

---

[24]A variation on this view is that the gnomic Aorist has common origin with the Homeric simile, extending a specific or typical situation (see Schwyzer, esp. 2.284-86): e.g. Hom. Il. 4.141: ὡς δ᾽ ὅτε τίς τ᾽ ἐλέφαντα γυνὴ φοίνικι μιήνῃ / Μῃονὶς ἠὲ Κάειρα, παρήϊον ἔμμεναι ἵππων (as when a certain woman stains an elephant tusk with scarlet, a M. or C., to make a sidecloth for horses). This view may be criticized for relying upon a temporal conception of the tense forms, positing as innovative a phenomenon apparently already assumed as established usage in Homer, and not having explanatory power for other gnomic statements in Greek, even in Homer. For criticism see Wackernagel, *Vorlesungen*, 179-80; Humbert, 146; Wilkinson, *"Aspect,"* 83.

derive from the injunctive. Latest opinion, he claims, treats the injunctive as a morphologically simple form with the least modal limitation, indicating only lexical meaning, aspect, Person, Voice, and *Erwähnung* (mention). Thus in Indo-Iranian the injunctive used for general truths and proverbs coincides almost completely with the use of the gnomic Aorist. Obata infers that the gnomic Aorist in Greek is the formalization of the Aorist injunctive. Whereas most uses of the injunctive were absorbed by the Imperative, Subjunctive and Indicative 2, the injunctive remained only in non-temporal descriptions of general truths. Since injunctives were absorbed by their nearest Mood/tense, and the Present Indicative 1 had a form used in the present, the Aorist injunctive was absorbed into the Aorist Indicative. Later users, not knowing of this formal assimilation, were careful to attach the augment, thinking it was a temporal indicator.

Obata's speculative theory, like many discussions of the gnomic tenses, does not rely upon a large number of examples to illustrate the model's viability. It might legitimately be asked how examples would help Obata's treatment, since he appears less concerned to describe the function of the gnomic tenses than to explain their origin, two separate questions. It is difficult to evaluate his reconstruction of proto-Greek regarding the injunctive, but several other points are worth raising. (1) Obata seems to know in advance how the gnomic Aorist functions, otherwise he would not be able to make his two major correlations between the noun clause and the injunctive (these two strands to his argument are not well-connected). (2) Not only does this reinforce that his discussion is an historical and not a functional one, but it means that he begs several questions regarding tense, Mood and aspect. He begins with a temporal understanding of the tense forms in Greek, hence his conflation of Mood and tense and his concern to correlate the injunctive with the Aorist Indicative. He overlooks the distinctive features of the individual Moods, conflating their functions with temporal uses and then tense categories. (The clearly non-temporal basis of the non-Indicative Moods might call into serious question both his analysis and his historical reconstruction of the injunctive in relation to the Indicative Mood/tenses, since this revolves around a temporal grid.) And (3) he presents no substantive argument for his definition of the aspect represented by the Aorist apart from appeal to Meillet's definition. Obata's theory, while renewing discussion of the gnomic tenses, does not present a significant way forward.

f. Omnitemporal usage. None of the proposals above provides compelling evidence to overthrow the main contention of this work, i.e. tense usage in Greek even within the Indicative is based upon verbal aspect and not temporal reference. The concerted discussion over the years (only a representative sample of scholars has been cited) attests that the non past-referring Aorist Indicative is a matter of serious concern since its usage is a fact that cannot be denied. To summarize those who find gnomic tenses in Greek, two common features emerge from their definitions: (1) temporal reference is a point of confusion, since especially for the Aorist there is felt to be a conflict between the Aorist tense and the general character of the truth expressed; (2) the gnomic use often refers to an example or typical case (cf. Hom. Il. 3.23-26: ὥς τε λέων ἐχάρη [as a lion rejoices]). I add that (3) much terminological confusion revolves around the distinction between form and function. Two strands of thought from the above discussion are compatible with usage of the Aorist in 'gnomic' contexts. Those who refer to a past event appear to be correct that the gnomic tenses do have a close correlation with observed processes, although it is better to see them more narrowly defined in terms of recurring natural processes. As Lyons says, "We can base our assertion of a general truth upon the evidence of our past experience" (*Semantics*, 681; cf. A. Buttmann, 201-03). This in no way attempts to reintroduce a past-temporal conception of the Aorist, since the contexts in which it is used seem to indicate, as scholars realize, not only past reference but some sort of present reality, and the implication of continued or future relevance. The second strand therefore is that a set temporal framework for the use of the tense cannot be established. On the basis of the characterization proposed above it is worthwhile to separate timeless from omnitemporal usage, with the former used to describe processes for which there is no deictic limitation on when the process may occur and the latter used to describe processes for which the deictic limitation is that they may occur at any time, hence the correlation with natural processes. Omnitemporal usage may occur with all the tense forms, as examples in the grammars indicate.

One reason that the Present has not been analysed so much as the Aorist is translational value. In English, as in some other languages, omnitemporal processes are often referred to with present tenses (the Present appears to be the 'unmarked' tense in English and is thus suited to such usage), as Lyons (*Semantics*, 681) and Burton (21: "the Aorist is used in proverbs and comparisons where the English commonly uses a General Present") recognize. Hence there is a tacit acceptance of the omnitemporal Present, possibly without realizing what constitutes the usage. A major factor cited by grammars to distinguish gnomic use of the Aorist is collocation with the Present form of the verb (e.g. Schwyzer, 2.285; Rijksbaron, 31-32), as well as non-Indicative (primarily Subjunctive) forms of the Aorist (Kravar, "Autour," 45-46). Several examples of omnitemporal Aorist and Present tenses may be cited in the NT. The distinction between the two is not temporal reference but use of verbal aspect, with the Aorist grammaticalizing the omnitemporal process as complete and the Present grammaticalizing the omnitemporal process as in progress. (Gildersleeve [109-10] recognizes the difference in kind of action, although he categorizes the gnomic Aorist as a "universal present"; Elmer ["Note," lxii] asks: "Now the present indicative necessarily involves the idea of progress. . . . is it not likely that the Greek and the Latin would have sought some means by which an act in the *present* also might be presented, with the idea of progress left out?" His temporal dependence is unfortunate.)

At least the following omnitemporal Aorists in the NT are worth noting.

John 15:6a, 8: ἐὰν μή τις μένῃ ἐν ἐμοί, ἐβλήθη ἔξω ὡς τὸ κλῆμα καὶ ἐξηράνθη. . . . ἐν τούτῳ ἐδοξάσθη ὁ πατήρ μου. . . . (If anyone does not remain in me, he is cast out as a branch and burned . . . in this my father is glorified). In v 6, Jesus, in reference to himself as the true vine, makes a general reference to any who are not abiding to remain with him. Although the Subjunctive conditional (II.a.) is a construction with timeless deictic implicature, here the apodosis seems to establish a general rule of nature, the "inevitable accompaniment of the separation" (Westcott, *John*, 218), with the Aorist depicting the event as complete.[25] If v 8 appeared in a narrative context, probably no question would arise as to whether it constituted a gnomic Aorist: it could easily be construed as a simple past use of the Aorist Indicative or even a timeless Aorist. But, in context, the utterance seems to formulate the conclusion to Jesus' extended metaphor on his disciples as branches of his vine. The ἐν τούτῳ refers back to the series of events of vv 6-7 and shows the "necessary consequence" of abiding in him (Westcott, 219), making ἐδοξάσθη a summary term used by Jesus regarding God's action.

Rom 3:23 (cf. 2:12; 5:12): πάντες γὰρ ἥμαρτον καὶ ὑστεροῦνται τῆς δόξης τοῦ θεοῦ (for all sin and fall short of God's glory). In the midst of a timeless discussion, Paul uses πάντες apparently to make his statement an omnitemporal generalization. There is a possibility that he has the first sin of Adam in mind here, although he does not specify it until 5:12ff. More probable is that this verse arises out of his observation of human nature (cf. Burton, 28). In accordance with extra-biblical Greek patterns noted above, this statement has parallel Aorist and Present tense forms. Cf. Rom 9:30: ἔθνη τὰ μὴ διώκοντα δικαιοσύνην κατέλαβεν δικαιοσύνην (nations not pursuing justification receive justification), where Paul questions the truthfulness of this omnitemporal statement referring to some Gentile nations (Cranfield, *Romans*, 2.506).

Eph 5:29: οὐδεὶς γάρ ποτε τὴν ἑαυτοῦ σάρκα ἐμίσησεν (for no one ever hates his own body). After a brief discussion of Christ and the church (vv 25b-27), v 28 returns to the subject of men and women's relations, proceeding toward the passage's climax in v 31. No matter one's view of Paul's advice for men and women, his argument appeals to a general principle of human nature: no one is able to hate his own body but he feeds and takes care of it. As Mitton states, "The basic self-concern of every human being is here accepted quite bluntly" (*Ephesians*, 205). Sampley's study of this passage neglects to mention use of the omnitemporal Aorist.

---

[25]Morris (*John*, 671 n. 16) claims "the aorist ἐβλήθη views the action as completed," and (672 n. 21) calls the verbal action of v 8 "complete." Comrie (*Aspect*, 18-19) discusses the important distinction between "complete" and "completed," the first reflecting a non time-bound and the second a time-bound understanding of verbal usage.

Instead he notes that vv 25bff. consistently use Aorist verbs, but v 29b switches to the Present: "The nourishing and cherishing of one's own flesh is no punctiliar, completed action, but is a continuing action" ('*And the Two*,' 143). It appears that he has misconstrued the Aorist both in its omnitemporal use and in its aspectual function.

1 Tim 6:7: οὐδὲν γὰρ εἰσηνέγκαμεν εἰς τὸν κόσμον, ὅτι οὐδὲ ἐξενεγκεῖν τι δυνάμεθα (we do not bring anything into the world, because we are not able to take anything out). The truth of this statement is not dependent upon a theological understanding but the simple observation of individuals in relation to material wealth.

1 Pet 1:24-25: πᾶσα σὰρξ ὡς χόρτος, καὶ πᾶσα δόξα αὐτῆς ὡς ἄνθος χόρτου· ἐξηράνθη ὁ χόρτος, καὶ τὸ ἄνθος ἐξέπεσεν· τὸ δὲ ῥῆμα κυρίου μένει εἰς τὸν αἰῶνα (all flesh is as grass, and all of its glory is as the flower of the field; the grass withers and the flower falls, but the word of the lord abides forever). In his quotation of Isa 40:6-8 (LXX, with minor, non-verbal variations), Peter seems to be using an event associated with the course of nature (reflecting human life?) as an ineluctable proof about the word of the lord. First he sets up a parallel between human bodies and vegetation (note that the first two clauses are verbless), including its more glorious expression (the blossom of the flower), in order to draw a fundamental conclusion: as vegetation dries up and flowers fall off, so individual human life also passes away. Peter's final statement is that the lord's word abides and remains (Present) forever. As Spicq says, "Cette Parole divine n'est pas une abstraction, c'est un message concret de salut que Dieu addresse dans tout l'universe é ses élus" (*Pierre*, 76).

Jas 1:11: ἀνέτειλεν γὰρ ὁ ἥλιος σὺν τῷ καύσωνι καὶ ἐξήρανεν τὸν χόρτον, καὶ τὸ ἄνθος αὐτοῦ ἐξέπεσεν καὶ ἡ εὐπρέπεια τοῦ προσώπου αὐτοῦ ἀπώλετο (for the sun rises with its heat and withers the grass, and its flower falls and the beauty of its face is destroyed). This verse verbally echoes the previous citation (although they use the Isaiah passage differently [Dibelius, *James*, 86]) and makes even clearer the cycle of nature and its apparent consistency. Mitton (*James*, 41) claims James uses the gnomic Aorist because "it stood in the Septuagint from which he quotes." There is more to it than that. In v 10 James uses the Future tense, παρελεύσεται (he will pass away), throwing the following verse (v 11) into a hypothetical orientation. Having said that he expects the flower of the grass to pass away (v 10), James then gives the reason (γάρ): the sun comes up, scorching and drying up the grass.[26] Probably no more assured event can be cited than the sun's dawning. James then expands his proverb for emphasis, saying that the flower falls off and its beauty is destroyed, D. Brown calling this a "*law* in the vegetable kingdom" ("Aorist," 76). James closes the verse by applying this aphorism (οὕτως) to the rich, using the Future tense once more (μαρανθήσεται [shall wither]).

The omnitemporal Aorist, therefore, should be recognized as a non-past use of the Aorist Indicative. Aspect is predominant in Greek verbal systems, and this is the case with the omnitemporal Aorist. The writer conceives of the situation as complete, extending as far as the eternal rising of the sun, but still viewed as a whole event. This does not mean that the omnitemporal Aorist is to be treated as a Present or Future Indicative, though that may be the best translation in English. Instead the Aorist grammaticalizes perfective aspect. The omnitemporal Aorist, therefore, is time-bound in the sense of being omnitemporal (as the examples above show), yet not tense bound, as tense is normally conceived.

A comparison with omnitemporal Present constructions helps confirm what has been said above. At least the following are relevant (cf. also Rom 3:23; 1 Tim 6:7 above).

Matt 6:2: ὥσπερ οἱ ὑποκριταὶ ποιοῦσιν ἐν ταῖς συναγωγαῖς καὶ ἐν ταῖς ῥύμαις (as the hypocrites do in their synagogues and streets). Whereas it is possible that only Jewish hypocrites are referred to, it is more likely that within the timeless context of the temporal clause a generalization is made about what is typical of all hypocrites.

Matt 6:26: the birds οὐ σπείρουσιν οὐδὲ θερίζουσιν οὐδὲ συνάγουσιν εἰς ἀποθήκας, καὶ ὁ πατὴρ ὑμῶν ὁ οὐράνιος τρέφει αὐτά (do not sow nor harvest nor gather into

---

[26]Davids (*James*, 78) argues that καύσωνι may refer to (1) burning heat or (2) a sirocco, the probable reference to the latter pointing to the proverbial nature of the phrase.

storehouses, and our heavenly father feeds them). Whereas the second main clause may be timeless, the first major clause draws upon observation in nature to assert an omnitemporal truth.

Matt 7:17-18: οὕτως πᾶν δένδρον ἀγαθὸν καρποὺς καλοὺς ποιεῖ, τὸ δὲ σαπρὸν δένδρον καρποὺς πονηροὺς ποιεῖ· οὐ δύναται δένδρον ἀγαθὸν καρποὺς πονηροὺς ποιεῖν, οὐδὲ δένδρον σαπρὸν καρποὺς καλοὺς ποιεῖν (thus every good tree bears good fruit, but the bad tree bears bad fruit; a good tree is not able to bear bad fruit, nor a bad tree to bear good fruit). After describing the false prophets and pointing to their expected coming (ἐπιγνώσεσθε [v 16]), Jesus makes a general statement that, while applicable here, has an extended pertinence in establishing a standard for deciding the worth of anything: a good thing produces good products (v 17). He then reverses this affirmation in v 18, using Present Infinitives (ποιεῖν) besides the Present Indicative.

Mark 2:22: οὐδεὶς βάλλει οἶνον νέον εἰς ἀσκοὺς παλαιούς--εἰ δὲ μή, ῥήξει ὁ οἶνος τοὺς ἀσκούς, καὶ ὁ οἶνος ἀπόλλυται καὶ οἱ ἀσκοί--ἀλλὰ οἶνον νέον εἰς ἀσκοὺς καινούς (no one puts new wine in old skins--unless, the wine will tear the skins, and the wine is lost and the skins--but new wine in new skins), with an omnitemporal use of the Present as well (see chapt. 9).

Mark 4:28: αὐτομάτη ἡ γῆ καρποφορεῖ (automatically the earth bears fruit), where the use is prototypically omnitemporal, even though it occurs within the context of a timeless parable. See similarly John 3:8: τὸ πνεῦμα ὅπου θέλει πνεῖ, καὶ τὴν φωνὴν αὐτοῦ ἀκούεις (the wind blows there it wills and you hear its sound).

John 7:52b: ἐκ τῆς Γαλιλαίας προφήτης οὐκ ἐγείρεται (a prophet does not rise up from G.). This verse has generated much discussion. Several scholars have noted that, in fact, many prophets arose from Galilee (e.g. Westcott [*John*, 125] cites Jonah, Hoshea, Nahum, and perhaps Elijah, Elisha, and Amos). How is it that the Pharisees can tell Nicodemus to search (ἐραύνησον) and see (ἴδε) the scriptures to confirm that no prophet comes from Galilee? Several answers have been suggested. (1) "A prophet" should be interpreted as "the prophet" or Messiah (Schnackenburg, *John*, 2.161. There is no significant textual variant with the article). (2) The Pharisees were clearly in error: "It is not true, to be sure, but this was not the only error of the Sanhedrin" (Robertson, 866). (3) The verb should be taken to mean "arises as a rule." Abbott claims this last solution is forced and would expose the Pharisees to the charge of impiety, and therefore the text is inexplicable (358). The Pharisees seem to be overreacting to the situation and therefore rhetorically ask Nicodemus to search the scriptures. Whether the Pharisees are right or wrong, the omnitemporal Present views the coming of prophets as a habitual process in progress, and is suitable to the context. The Pharisees, faced with news of the "new" upstart, Jesus, tell Nicodemus, an apparent sympathizer, to search the scriptures, because he will see that "habitually prophets do not arise out of Galilee."

Jas 3:3-12: in perhaps the largest section of omnitemporal Present usage in the NT, James draws a comparison between the tongue and processes found in nature: horses are led (μετάγομεν) by bridles, ships are steered (μετάγεται) by rudders, and the animal kingdom is being subdued (δαμάζεται; cf. omnitemporal Perfect δεδάμασται) by humankind. But no one is able (δύναται) to control the tongue of man. These examples select several uses of the Present out of many in this section with omnitemporal reference (cf. Davids, *James*, 135ff., who recognizes the proverbial nature of much of the material in this passage).

Robertson is not as precise as he might be in calling the gnomic Present "the aorist present that is timeless in reality, true of all time" (866; cf. Moulton, 135). Even more so than with the omnitemporal Aorist, however, the nature of the omnitemporal Present emerges less clearly defined in translation, because of use of the English Present tense. To be more precise, the Present here seems to refer to a recurring situation without specific delimitation of its temporal location; therefore, it is omnitemporal.

The omnitemporal Present grammaticalizes a different aspect than does the omnitemporal Aorist. Robertson therefore mistakes the aspectual differentiation between Present and Aorist when he cites the gnomic Present as "the aorist present" (cf. Elmer, "Note," lxii). Again, this differentiation is clouded by use of the English Present tense translation for both aspects. But this seems inevitable due to the unmarkedness of the simple English Present. Each aspect describes a different perceived relation between process time and reference time, and they are not to be merged. The omnitemporal Aorist grammaticalizes conception of the process as complete, without reference to internal time; the omnitemporal Present grammaticalizes conception of the process as in progress, with attention paid to the internal, phasal structure.

Since the imperfective in relation to the perfective is semantically more heavily marked in Greek, special attention should be paid to use of the omnitemporal Present in contrast to the omnitemporal Aorist. Nothing makes a process better suited intrinsically to the Aorist or to the Present, since the author chooses to grammaticalize his conception of it. The semantic features grammaticalized by the form, however, become an important part of the context, which is reflected in the examples cited. For example, the casting out and burning of branches, the sinfulness of human nature, the complete act of God's glorification, grass scorching and the flower falling, all are seen as very different from the earth bearing fruit, a tree being in progress bearing fruit, prophets rising up out of Galilee, hypocrites continuing their behaviour, and the struggle with horses, ships and the tongue. The examples chosen by the authors reinforce the selection of aspect, though this is not to say that the other aspect could not have been used. In that case, however, the semantic meaning would be altered. So the omnitemporal Aorist and Present, though different, are different for specific reasons on the basis of verbal aspect. Other examples could be cited, but this list is sufficient to justify the definition of the category along aspectual lines.

2. Present reference. a. Introduction. It is commonly asserted by virtually all grammars that the Present is a present-referring form. This certainly is one of several major uses of this form; therefore, it is not necessary to justify this usage. (Grammarians [e.g. Robertson, 864ff.] recognize that present reference may include action that objectively is "punctiliar," e.g. Acts 16:18: παραγγέλλω [I command]; extended, e.g. Matt 23:3: the Pharisees λέγουσιν γὰρ καὶ οὐ ποιοῦσιν [they say and do not do]; or iterative, Luke 9:39, where the actions of the boy with an unclean spirit are described.) On the basis of the evidence presented elsewhere this cannot be seen as the essential meaning of this tense form, and many instances cited as present-referring by grammars may in fact have deictic implicatures of another temporal sphere. Verbal aspect explains and allows this range of usage.

b. The Aorist as present-referring. That the Aorist may be present-referring has not always been accepted by a large number of grammarians. Two responses are common. The first argues that in no instance can the Aorist be interpreted as anything but past-referring in its traditional sense (see chapt. 1 for representative proponents, Winer being one of the most prominent). Sufficient evidence has already been given to show that this assertion cannot be sustained. The second allows that the Aorist may be used in present-referring contexts, but argues that this is possible for a variety of reasons which take this usage beyond the bounds of regular usage (e.g. Kühner/Gerth, 1.160-65; Smyth, 432 [although he denigrates it]; Chantraine, 2.184). Several of the categories invoked to justify this usage include the following.

(1) Ancient usage from proto IE or Sanskrit. Robertson refers to the dramatic Aorist as similar to the common use in Sanskrit "to express what has just taken place" (841). As might be expected, this usage is found in Homer: e.g. Od. 10.64: πῶς ἦλθες, Ὀδυσεῦ; (how have you arrived, O.?), as well as later writers: X. Hell. 1.7.16: τὰ μὲν κατηγορήσων . . . ἀνέβην ἐνθάδε (I have come up here, partly making accusations). Moulton (134), followed by Robertson (842-43), finds at least the following instances in Matthew alone: 5:28: ἤδη ἐμοίχευσεν (he has already committed adultery); 9:18: ἡ θυγάτηρ μου ἄρτι ἐτελεύτησεν (my daughter is now dead); 14:15: ἡ ὥρα ἤδη παρῆλθεν (the hour has already come); 17:12: Ἡλίας ἤδη ἦλθεν (E. has already come); 6:12: ὡς καὶ ἡμεῖς ἀφήκαμεν (as we forgive; see chapt. 3); 14:2: αὐτὸς ἠγέρθη (he is raised); 16:17: σὰρξ καὶ αἷμα οὐκ ἀπεκάλυψεν (flesh and blood have not revealed); 20:12: ἴσους ἡμῖν αὐτοὺς ἐποίησας (you have made us equal to them); 26:10: ἔργον γὰρ καλὸν ἠργάσατο (she has done a good work); 26:13: ὃ ἐποίησεν (what she has done); 26:65: ἐβλασφήμησεν . . . νῦν ἠκούσατε (he has blasphemed . . . now you have heard); 26:25, 64: σὺ εἶπας (you say); 27:19: πολλὰ γὰρ ἔπαθον σήμερον (for I have suffered many things today); 27:46: ἱνατί με ἐγκατέλιπες (why have you forsaken me?) (LXX quotation of Ps 21:2); 28:18: ἐδόθη μοι πᾶσα ἐξουσία (all authority is given to me); and perhaps 21:42: οὐδέποτε ἀνέγνωτε (have you never read?). Robertson also includes: Mark 16:6: ἠγέρθη (he is raised); Luke 7:16: προφήτης μέγας ἠγέρθη . . . ἐπεσκέψατο ὁ θεός (a great prophet is raised up . . . God has visited); Luke 24:34: ἠγέρθη . . . ὤφθη (he is raised . . . has appeared); Luke 14:18-20: ἀγρὸν ἠγόρασα καὶ ἔχω ἀνάγκην. . . . ἠγόρασα . . . πορεύομαι. . . . ἔγημα . . . οὐ δύναμαι (I have bought a field and have an obligation. . . . I have bought . . . I am going. . . . I have married . . . and am not able [cf. tense alteration and discussion below under timeless reference]); Luke 15:32: ἔζησεν . . . εὑρέθη (he is alive . . . and is found) (cf. v 24); Luke 19:42: νῦν . . . ἐκρύβη (now it is hidden); John 11:41: ἤκουσάς μου (you hear me); John 12:19: ἴδε ὁ κόσμος ὀπίσω αὐτοῦ ἀπῆλθεν (behold the world is going after him); John 12:27: διὰ τοῦτο ἦλθον (because of this I have come); John 13:1: ἦλθεν αὐτοῦ ἡ ὥρα (his hour has come); John 21:10: ἐπιάσατε νῦν (you have now caught); 1 Cor 9:19-20, 22: πᾶσιν ἐμαυτὸν ἐδούλωσα . . . καὶ ἐγενόμην τοῖς Ἰουδαίοις . . . ἐγενόμην τοῖς ἀσθενέσιν (I enslave myself to all . . . and I become to Jews . . . I become to the weak); Rev 14:8; 18:2: ἔπεσεν ἔπεσεν (it has fallen). The examples cited above illustrate that resorting to proto IE or Sanskrit use is only necessary if one begins with a temporal conception of the tense forms in Greek (the historical argument regarding Sanskrit or proto IE also fails because speakers or listeners could not be expected to know the historical relation). If verbal aspect is seen to be the governing semantic category, present reference of the Aorist is understandable. It is shown in chapt. 2 (and is argued by many grammarians, from the Greeks to Robertson and McKay) that the present moment is not simply a simple point (otherwise much use of the Present tense would fail to be present-referring as well), but one of the temporal grids imposed upon reality. The Aorist may be used to grammaticalize reference to present time if that process is seen as a complete process in its entirety. According to this definition, many of the examples above are present-referring Aorists.

(2) Certain kinds of verbs, especially those of emotion or of action of short duration. Hom. Il. 3.415. ὡς νῦν ἔκπαγλ' ἐφίλησα (as now I love you / how I love you wondrously); E. Helen 673-74: κατεδάκρυσα καὶ βλέφαρον ὑγραίνω / δάκρυσιν (I cry and wet my eyes with tears); Alc. 391: ἀπωλόμην τάλας (I, a wretch, am destroyed); Ar. Knights 696-97: ἤσθην

ἀπειλαῖς· ἐγέλασα ψολοκομπίαις· / ἀπεπυδάρισα μόθωνα· περιεκόκκυσα (I am delighted with threats; I laugh at empty noises; I dance a rude dance; I cry cuckoo); Luke 16:4: ἔγνων τί ποιήσω (I know what I shall do) (see below). This category is widely recognized in extra-biblical Greek, although some grammarians resort to special pleading to explain it. For example, Rijksbaron (28-29) says that "this use of the aorist indicative usually indicates that the speaker had begun to feel the emotion concerned before his interlocutor finished speaking [ingressive use of the aorist indicative . . .]," citing Ar. Peace 1066. Regarding verbs of understanding, knowing, etc., he continues: "The use of the aorist indicative signifies that the understanding, etc. was completed while the other was speaking," citing E. And. 918-19: συνῆκα· ταρβεῖς τοῖς δεδραμένοις πόσιν ("I understand: because of what happened, you are afraid of a husband"). This explanation is unconvincing (cf. Green, 17). See also Hes. Works 218; A. Choeph. 887; S. El. 668, 1478; Aj. 536.

(3) Sentences with particular adverbs, such as νῦν (see above also). Hom. Il. 2.114: νῦν δὲ κακὴν ἀπάτην βουλεύσατο καί με κελεύει (he now plans an evil trick and commands me); Pl. Symp. 193A: νυνὶ δὲ διὰ τὴν ἀδικίαν διῳκίσθημεν ὑπὸ τοῦ θεοῦ (but now because of injustice we are dispersed by God); Isoc. Letter 7.10; Plb. 6.4.11: οἷα δὴ νῦν εἶπον (of what I now speak); John 13:31: νῦν ἐδοξάσθη ὁ υἱὸς τοῦ ἀνθρώπου, καὶ ὁ θεὸς ἐδοξάσθη ἐν αὐτῷ (now the son of man is glorified, and God is glorified in him), although this example may be future-referring (see below); John 21:14: τοῦτο ἤδη τρίτον ἐφανερώθη (this is already the third time he was manifested); Rev 12:10: ἄρτι ἐγένετο ἡ σωτηρία καὶ ἡ δύναμις (now comes the saviour and the power);[27] cf. Phil 3:23 with ἤδη and parallel Perfect verb. Cf. Rev 17:7 with διὰ τί.

(4) Appeal is also made to the apodoses of conditional statements (see chapt. 6 and below, where these are better classified as logical constructions, at least in the first instance).

Whereas each of these explanations may have some descriptive power (apart from appeal to proto IE, which is a question of historical reconstruction and not of usage), each contradicts the other. For example, there are instances where the verb used is one of emotion or of action of short duration, but examples referring to continuous action are found with verbs of motion. All of the above--plus a large number of other examples intractable in the above schemes--can only be accounted for by verbal aspect. As McKay (223) says, "The circumstances in which aoristic completeness in a temporally present action is important are rare in literature, but when they do occur the verb is used in the aorist." While the temporal basis of McKay's analysis might be questioned, his essential point is accurate (see also Humbert, "L'aoriste").

It is often stated that the present use of the Aorist occurs mostly in poetic sources. What is to be noted is that the usage often (though not always) occurs in dialogue, which often is recorded in poetic sources. But it appears that preconceptions have dictated discovery of the phenomenon, however, since it is also well known in prose.

Matt 23:23: the Pharisees tithe (ἀποδεκατοῦτε) and ἀφήκατε (you disregard) the weightier matters of the law; Matt 25:24: ἔγνων σε (I know you); Mark 3:21: they were saying of Jesus that ἐξέστη (he is out of his mind); Luke 2:30-31: Simeon says that now (νῦν) you are releasing your servant, God, ὅτι εἶδον οἱ ὀφθαλμοί μου τὸ σωτήριόν σου ὃ ἡτοίμασας κατὰ πρόσωπον πάντων τῶν λαῶν (because my eyes see our salvation which you prepare before the face of all the people); Luke 4:34: ἦλθες ἀπολέσαι ἡμᾶς; (have you come to destroy us?); Luke 8:46: ἐγὼ γὰρ ἔγνων δύναμιν ἐξεληλυθυῖαν ἀπ᾽ ἐμοῦ (I know that power has gone out from me); Luke 8:52: οὐ γὰρ ἀπέθανεν ἀλλὰ καθεύδει (she is not dead but sleeping), where the difference in verbal aspect is clearly seen; the author contrasts the condition of deadness with her being in progress sleeping, with stress falling on the latter. John 7:48: μή τις ἐκ τῶν ἀρχόντων ἐπίστευσεν εἰς αὐτὸν ἢ ἐκ τῶν Φαρισαίων; (it is not that anyone from the rulers or P.s believes in him, is it?); John 11:14: Λάζαρος ἀπέθανεν (L. is dead); John 13:34: καθὼς ἠγάπησα ὑμᾶς (as I love you); John 16:30: ἀπὸ θεοῦ ἐξῆλθες (you are come from God); Acts 7:52: οὐ νῦν

---

[27]See H[ort], untitled, for discussion of temporal and logical senses of νῦν; cf. Conybeare, "Use," 223-24.

ὑμεῖς προδόται καὶ φονεῖς ἐγένεσθε (of whom now you have become traitors and murderers); Acts 26:16: εἰς τοῦτο γὰρ ὤφθην σοι (for this I am appearing to you); Rom 5:11: δι' οὗ νῦν τὴν καταλλαγὴν ἐλάβομεν (through whom now we have reconciliation), where the 1st Person verbs indicate a present descriptive use (cf. anonymous, "Translation," 388, who recognizes present reference); 1 Cor 4:18: ὡς μὴ ἐρχομένου δέ μου πρὸς ὑμᾶς ἐφυσιώθησάν τινες (since I have not come, many are arrogant toward us); 2 Cor 4:4: the God of this age ἐτύφλωσεν (blinds) the understanding of unbelievers, although timeless or even past reference is possible; 2 Cor 5:13: ἐξέστημεν (we are out of our mind), cf. Present verb following; Phlm 7: χαρὰν γὰρ πολλὴν ἔσχον (for I have much joy), in a section of thanksgiving; Jas 2:6: ὑμεῖς δὲ ἠτιμάσατε τὸν πτωχόν (you treat the poor shamefully), followed by two Present verbs; Rev 5:5: ἰδοὺ ἐνίκησεν ὁ λέων (behold the lion stands victorious).

c. A usage meriting brief mention is the so-called epistolary Aorist. Levinson, describing the standard analysis of this usage, labels the epistolary tense as an instance where deictic simultaneity, i.e. the assumption that speaker and hearer share the same temporal sphere, is violated, so that the coding time of the letter is different from receiving time (*Pragmatics*, 73-74; similar to most grammars: e.g. Burton, 21). But this is not a necessary assumption if tense forms are not temporally based. Instead what appears to occur is that the author composes the letter within his own coding time, and at junctures he may refer to coincidental processes using the Aorist, with the close of a letter a noteworthy point to refer to the process of composition or some related process. The reader then interprets the letter from the same perspective as the author, beginning from an understanding of the coding-time implicatures implied by the author's use of temporal deictic indicators (within a given letter the temporal deixis may shift according to other indicators).

The phenomenon is discussed in the secondary literature (see esp. Robertson, 845-46; Schwyzer, 2.279-80; Mandilaras, 166-68; Mayser, 2, 1.143-45, cf. 138. Add P.Louvre. 18.3-5 [2d/3d cent. A.D.]: ἔπεμψά σοι τὸ σῶμα Σενύριος / τῆς μητρός μου κεκηδευ/μένος [I send to you the body of S. my mother mummified]. Gildersleeve [128] attributes usage in the NT to Latin influence. But this is unlikely on account of its being found in earlier Greek as well as the papyri; thus Blass/Debrunner, ¶ 334. What is said here applies to the epistolary Imperfect as well.) Classical examples exist, although they are not abundant. Th. 1.129.3: ἀλλὰ μετ' Ἀρταβάζου ἀνδρὸς ἀγαθοῦ, ὅν σοι ἔπεμψα, πρᾶσσε θαρσῶν καὶ τὰ ἐμὰ καὶ τὰ σά (but with A. a good man, whom I send to you, conduct confidently my and your affairs); Mnesiergus epistle lines 1-4: Μνησίεργος / ἐπέστελε τοῖς οἴκοι / χαίρεν καὶ ὑγιαίνεν / καὶ αὐτὸς οὕτως ἔφασ[κ]ε [ἔχεν] (M. sends to those at home greetings and health and thus he says he is) (Deissmann, *Light*, 151; this is the oldest Greek letter known, according to Deissmann, dating from the 4th cent. B.C.).

In the NT see: Rom 15:15 (?); Acts 23:30; 1 Cor 5:9 (?), 11; 9:15; 2 Cor 2:3, 4, 9 (?); 7:12; 8:17-18, 22; 9:5; Eph 6:22; Phil 2:25, 28; Col 4:8; Phlm 12; Heb 13:22; 1 Pet 5:12; 1 John 2:21, 26; 5:13; 2 John 12 (cf. Eph 3:3 where Paul refers to what he has written above), several of which conform to the papyric pattern of following the epistolary Aorist with a purpose clause: 2 Cor 9:3: ἔπεμψα δὲ τοὺς ἀδελφούς, ἵνα μὴ τὸ καύχημα ἡμῶν τὸ ὑπὲρ ὑμῶν κενωθῇ ἐν τῷ μέρει τούτῳ (I send the brethren, so that your boasting on behalf of us might not be in vain in this regard); P.Oxy. 1156:12-14 (3d cent. A.D.): [ἐπε]μψα οὖν αὐτὸν πρὸς / [σέ, ἵ]να τοκοῦν σοι μετ' αὐ/τοῦ [π]οιή[ση]ς (I send him to you, so that you might do with him as you please). The usual tense is the Present: 1 Cor 4:14; 14:37; 2 Cor 13:10; 2 Pet 3:1 (cf. BGU 827 [2d/3d cent. A.D.]). The papyri make use of the Aorist in a comparable way to the NT, often including passages similar to Gal 6:11 (ἴδετε πηλίκοις ὑμῖν γράμμασιν ἔγραψα τῇ ἐμῇ χειρί [see how large are the letters I write to you in my hand]) and Phlm 19 (ἐγὼ Παῦλος ἔγραψα τῇ ἐμῇ χειρί [I P. write in my hand]) with a note made that someone has written a letter in place of another. See e.g. P.Hamb. 4.14-15 (A.D. 87): ἔγραψεν ὑπὲρ αὐτοῦ φαμένου / μὴ εἰδέναι γράμματα Ἰσίδωρος νομογράφος (I., a scribe, writes on behalf of him claiming not to be literate); BGU 1579.27-28 (A.D. 118/19).

1 John 2:11-14. Of this well-known passage, in which three Present Indicatives are followed by three Aorist Indicatives, Moule states, "No really convincing explanation is known to me" (12). Perhaps this problem has been overcome in the recent thorough treatment of the passage in Brown's commentary (*Epistles*, 294-301, esp. 294-97, for proponents of various views; cf. Smalley, *John*, 76-78). The issue of the tenses can be separated from the two other pressing issues in this passage: the groups of people mentioned, and the interpretation of ὅτι. There are two major schools of thought on the use of the tenses: those who claim two writings are referred to and those who claim one writing is referred to.

Those who claim that two writings are referred to assert that the Present tenses refer to 1 John and the Aorist tenses may refer to: the Gospel of John, 2 John, a lost letter, or the epistle's source. As Brown states, "the appeal to a lost letter is a desperate hypothesis that is quite unverifiable" (295) as is appeal to a supposed source. Efforts to find parallels to 2 John find at best only superficial points of comparison (295). Points of comparison between the Gospel and the epistle are slightly more prevalent but not certain (296).[28] Brown also recognizes a problem in referring to the previous letter after the current one, especially since the content of the Present tense clauses is virtually the same as that of the Aorist tense clauses. There is the further problem that these proposals all seem predicated upon justifying a temporal use of the tense forms, illustrating how temporal criteria still form the basis for much analysis of tense usage in NT Greek. Once this assumption is removed the above proposals are seen to be virtually without merit, especially in light of use of the lexical item γράφω in letters.

Those who claim that one writing is referred to assert that the Aorists refer either to what the author has written above in 1 John or to the entire epistle. Brown shows that the first proposal has little to offer because the points of correlation are few (296).[29] Besides the problem mentioned above of the order of the tense usage when the content is parallel, there is again the underlying supposition of this position that an Aorist verb must be past-referring. When this is eliminated the last vestige of this argument's strength disappears.

The proposal that the Aorist tenses refer to the entire letter is the most plausible. As seen above, the use of the 'epistolary' Aorist is not because of a shift in viewpoint of the author and audience, but because one of the temporal spheres of reference of the Aorist is present time. The points of support are as follows. (1) The author of 1 John refers to his own letter or the content of the letter using both the Present (1:4, 5 [?]; 2:1, 7, 8, cf. 3:11) and Aorist (2:21, 26; 5:13) tenses, without apparent difference in temporal reference. (2) Within this epistle the author uses the Present form of γράφω before 2:12 and the Aorist after 2:14. This points to 2:12-14 as significant to the developing argument of the epistle. Smalley notes that the Present form of γράφω usually introduces statements, and the Aorist form usually introduces discussion about statements (*John*, 78). Thus in the first half of the epistle he is possibly asserting (or re-asserting) truths which he then later uses as assumptions for further teaching. The tense alteration however does not indicate, as Brown, followed by others (e.g. Turner, *Syntax*, 73), asserts, that the shift in verb tenses represents merely a "stylistic variant" (296) "with no significant difference of meaning" (297). Betraying his dependence upon temporal categories to give verb tenses meaning, Brown and those he represents fail to appreciate aspectual differences. (3) Brown argues that the Aorist verbs of

---

[28]E.g. reference to children (John 13:33; 21:5); the one true God (17:3) and father (8:19; 14:7; 16:3); the beginning (1:1; 8:25); strength (14:27; 16:1); the word of God abiding (15:7; 5:38); victory and conquest (16:33; 12:31; 17:15).

[29]E.g. child (1 John 2:1); "I know him" (2:4); beginning (1:1); keeping the word (2:5), but nothing correlates with the idea of being strong and conquering the evil one.

2:14 are "slightly more emphatic than the present[s] of 2:12-13, chiefly because the author is repeating himself--whence my 'Yes, I have been writing'" (296). Brown conflates two issues here. The first is the difference in the individual meanings of the verb tenses, and the other is the weight that should be placed upon the content that is repeated. He is perhaps correct to indicate that the repetition of the content makes the same points more forcefully, but the verbal network of Greek does not necessarily aid this. On the basis of the Present being the more heavily marked tense, another interpretation of the tense movement might be suggested. The author of the epistle-- like Shakespeare in *Lear*, in which he says everything twice--introduces a set of assertions with Present verbs to his three-fold audience (the ὅτι clauses in 2:12-14 use the most heavily marked Perfect to summarize the entire theology of the epistle). Rather than using the more heavily marked Present to re-introduce his repeated assertions the author uses the less heavily marked Aorist in the second set so as not to detract emphasis from the message itself.

    3. Future reference. Discussion of future-referring Present and Aorist tenses begins with the fact that the Greek language appears to be a bi-temporal language, i.e. its major concern is with the present and the past, and that it does not grammaticalize future reference (the closest it comes to grammaticalizing temporal reference is [+remoteness] forms). Its non-Indicative forms grammaticalize projection or in the case of the Future grammaticalize expectation. In some instances this may resemble reference to the future, and in actual instances may require future fulfilment, but speakers did not grammaticalize this conception in tense forms (see chapt. 9 on the Future as well). The Present and Aorist tenses are used occasionally in contexts where the author seems to imply that he is speaking of the future. Similar temporal reference does not imply that the future-referring Present and the Future grammaticalize the same semantic features. As Moulton (120) recognizes in part, "we may define the futural present as differing from the future tense mainly in the tone of assurance which is imparted," alluding to aspectual and attitudinal differences.

    The future-referring capacity of the Present is still under scrutiny in the eyes of some grammarians. Some grammarians claim the Present "is used for the future in appearance only, when an action still future is to be represented as being as good as already present, either because it is already firmly resolved on, or because it must ensue in virtue of some unalterable law" (Winer, 331), which reveals over-reliance upon a temporal definition of tense forms. Others speculate that this is a late development of hellenistic Greek, possibly under Semitic influence (e.g. Thompson, *Apocalypse*, 29-35). Thompson says that "a point of biblical Greek grammar not yet adequately explained by grammarians is the strange yet obvious future sense expressed by certain present indicative Greek verbs" (29). This seems to present a problem if the grammarian fails (as does Thompson) to make the formal/functional distinction between the label attached to a verb form and its functional capabilities (see Porter, Review). Examples of future-referring Presents are found in several different contexts. Well-known is the Present in the apodosis of a conditional or conditional-like statement (e.g. Th. 6.91.3; Hdt. 1.109.10; P.Oxy. 1291.11 [A.D. 30]; cf. Th. 6.40.2 in protasis; see chapt. 6 on conditionals), but these are not listed here since the future reference is better treated as a logical future reference on the basis of the syntactic pattern of the conditional statement. The Present has the capability of future reference on the basis of its verbal aspect. As Robertson (881-82) says, "Since the pres. ind. occurs for past, present and future time it is clear that 'time' is secondary even in the ind." The speaker conceives of the process as in progress and this progress may very well carry over into what he sees as the future. This would also explain the preponderance of usage with verbs of motion (Blass/Debrunner, ¶ 323[3]; A. Buttmann [204] finds two kinds of future-referring Presents: those whose lexical items have a future sense [e.g. verbs of motion], and those which derive their future reference from context).

Many of the examples cited by grammarians are not to be seen as clearly future-referring, since the imperfective aspect lends itself to this interpretation (see e.g. Matt 2:4; 24:43; John 8:14; 10:32; 13:6, 27; 21:3; Rom 15:25; 1 Cor 15:2; 2 Cor 13:1). Several examples worth noting in this regard occur in Revelation, where Present and Future verbs appear side by side (see Charles, *Revelation*, 1.cxxiii; Mussies, *Morphology*, 333-36): Rev 1:7: ἰδοὺ ἔρχεται μετὰ τῶν νεφελῶν, καὶ ὄψεται αὐτὸν πᾶς ὀφθαλμός (behold he is in progress coming with the clouds and every eye will see him), where the speaker in his first song praising Jesus Christ asserts that he is coming, with the expectation that every eye then will see him. There is no need to make both verbs refer temporally to the same sphere when an attitudinal difference seems to be the major difference. Cf. Rev 17:12-14, where there is a clear distinction between assertion about the state of affairs (vv 12-13) and the expected course of events (v 14).[30] Excluded also is 1 Cor 3:13, which functions like the apodosis of a conditional.

Sufficient examples of the future-referring Present in extra-biblical Greek may be found in the grammars. (See esp. Brugmann, 557-58; Kühner/Gerth, 1.138-39; Stahl, 92-95; Wackernagel, *Vorlesungen*, 161-62; Schwyzer, 2.273; Gildersleeve, 83-84; Mayser, 2, 1.133-34; Mandilaras, 102-05, who claims it is "quite frequent" in classical Greek. Mahlow ["Futurgebrauch," 601-03] provides examples, but his theoretical basis is deficient, since he posits that the future use of the Present is to provide durative *Aktionsart*. This is followed by Brugmann.)

Examples from NT Greek might include the following, although examples must be understood in the first instance in terms of imperfective verbal aspect (see esp. Winer, 331-33; Blass/Debrunner, ¶ 332; Robertson, 869-70). Matt 17:11: Ἠλίας μὲν ἔρχεται καὶ ἀποκαταστήσει πάντα (E. is coming and will restore all things); Matt 26:2: after two days τὸ πάσχα γίνεται, καὶ ὁ υἱὸς τοῦ ἀνθρώπου παραδίδοται εἰς τὸ σταυρωθῆναι (the passover comes about, and the son of man is betrayed to be crucified), cf. Matt 26:45 and Mark 9:31; Matt 26:18: with you, ποιῶ (I make) the passover; Matt 27:63: μετὰ τρεῖς ἡμέρας ἐγείρομαι (after

---

[30]This pattern is found in extra-biblical Greek as well: e.g. Hdt. 7.140.2-3: οὔτε γὰρ ἡ κεφαλὴ μένει ἔμπεδον οὔτε τὸ σῶμα, / οὔτε πόδες νέατοι οὔτ᾽ ὦν χέρες, οὔτε τι μέσσης / λείπεται, ἀλλ᾽ ἄζηλα πέλει· κατὰ γάρ μιν ἐρείπει / πῦρ τε καὶ ὀξὺς Ἄρης, Συριηγενὲς ἅρμα διώκων. / πολλὰ δὲ κἄλλ᾽ ἀπολεῖ πυργώματα κοὐ τὸ σὸν οἶον· / πολλοὺς δ᾽ ἀθανάτων νηοὺς μαλερῷ πυρὶ δώσει (neither is the head going to remain in its place nor the body, neither are the lowly feet nor hands, neither any in between is going to be left, but it is miserable; fire and the fierceness of A. are going to bring it to destruction, driver of chariots of S. Many other fortresses are being destroyed and not you alone; but many temples of gods he will give to raging fire), where the Present verbs appear to be future-referring.

three days I am raised); Mark 10:33: ἀναβαίνομεν εἰς Ἱεροσόλυμα, καὶ ὁ υἱὸς τοῦ ἀνθρώπου παραδοθήσεται (we are going up to J., and the son of man will be betrayed); Luke 13:32: ἐκβάλλω δαιμόνια καὶ ἰάσεις ἀποτελῶ σήμερον καὶ αὔριον, καὶ τῇ τρίτῃ τελειοῦμαι (I am casting out demons and accomplishing healings today and tomorrow, and on the third I reach my goal); Luke 19:8: Zacchaeus says δίδωμι (I am giving) half my possessions to the poor; John 3:36: the one who believes in the son ἔχει (has) eternal life but the one unpersuaded by the son οὐκ ὄψεται (will not see) life, but the wrath of God μένει (abides) upon him; John 4:21: ἔρχεται ὥρα (an hour is coming), cf. John 16:2 and 17:11; John 4:35: ἔτι τετράμηνός ἐστιν καὶ ὁ θερισμὸς ἔρχεται (still it is four months and the harvest comes); John 10:15: τίθημι (I lay down) my life for the sheep; John 14:3: ὅπου [ἐγὼ] ὑπάγω (where I am going) you do not know; John 16:16, 17: in a little while οὐκέτι θεωρεῖτε (you no longer see) me and again in a little while ὄψεσθε (you will see) me; John 21:23: ἐξῆλθεν οὖν οὗτος ὁ λόγος εἰς τοὺς ἀδελφοὺς ὅτι ὁ μαθητὴς ἐκεῖνος οὐκ ἀποθνῄσκει (this word went out to the brothers that that disciple is not dying), where one's critical theory of the book's composition probably dictates interpretation of temporal reference; 1 Cor 15:26: ἔσχατος ἐχθρὸς καταργεῖται ὁ θάνατος (death the last enemy is destroyed); 1 Cor 16:5: διέρχομαι (I am passing through) Macedonia; Eph 5:5: any evil οὐκ ἔχει κληρονομίαν ἐν τῇ βασιλείᾳ τοῦ Χριστοῦ καὶ θεοῦ (does not have an inheritance in the kingdom of Christ and God); Col 3:6: δι' ἃ ἔρχεται ἡ ὀργὴ τοῦ θεοῦ (on account of which the anger of God comes); Heb 4:3: εἰσερχόμεθα γὰρ εἰς [τὴν] κατάπαυσιν οἱ πιστεύσαντες (those who believe are entering into the rest); Rev 9:6: ἐπιθυμήσουσιν ἀποθανεῖν καὶ φεύγει ὁ θάνατος ἀπ' αὐτῶν (they will desire to die and death flees from them). (For apostolic Greek examples see Jannaris, 434.)

Stahl (94) notes that prophets make noteworthy use of the future-referring Present. Because of the often prophetic nature of the NT, perhaps this accounts for what some posit as an expansion of the use of the Present in future contexts in the NT (see Hdt. 7.140.2-3 above; cf. Blass/Debrunner, ¶ 323[1]; Turner, *Syntax*, 63; Mandilaras, 105).

The Aorist may be used with future reference as well. Again verbal aspect provides the basis for this usage. Robertson (846) claims that future reference of the Aorist "is a vivid transference of the action to the future by the timeless aorist," but Mandilaras (168 n. 1) is right to question this definition: "It is inconsistent, however, to say that the aorist referring to the future is vivid, and at the same time, that the aorist is timeless. If the aorist were timeless, there would be nothing remarkable, and so nothing vivid, in its reference to the future" (Mandilaras is incorrect however to claim that the use is vivid and that the Aorist is a past tense). In some instances the speaker seems to conceive of a future process as complete and he uses the Aorist for this conception. Most of the examples cited by grammarians are the apodoses of conditional or conditional-like statements (e.g. Hom. Il. 9.412-13; 4.160-61; S. Ant. 303; E. Alc. 386; Med. 77; Th. 6.80.2) and are better treated as logical future-referring statements (see chapt. 6), but several other instances are found as well.

There are constructions with τί οὖν (see esp. Kühner/Gerth, 1.165-66; Rijksbaron, 29-30). Many grammarians treat these as examples of the present-referring Aorist, but since the action is asserted still to be completed, future reference is more plausible. For example, Pl. Prot. 317D: τί οὖν, ἔφην ἐγώ, οὐ καὶ Πρόδικον καὶ Ἱππίαν ἐκαλέσαμεν καὶ τοὺς μετ' αὐτῶν, ἵνα ἐπακούσωσιν ἡμῶν; (I said, why don't we call P. and H. and those with them, so that they might listen to us?).

Other uses might be cited, although this usage is not widespread, for reasons already suggested: Hdt. 8.102.2: οἱ γὰρ σοὶ δοῦλοι κατεργάσαντο (for your servants are going to accomplish it), where this independent sentence follows a conditional statement (see Wackernagel, *Vorlesungen*, 176-78). (Gonda [*Rgvedic*, 67] cites a Dorian inscription [Heraclea 122; 143] with κατεδικάσθεν, where judgment is certain.)

Apart from timeless instances found in the apodoses of conditional or conditional-like statements (e.g. Matt 12:26, 28; 18:15; 1 Cor 7:28, Epict. 4.1.39; 4.10.27, which are only logically future and often require a present-referring translation), there are a few possible instances in NT Greek also (on the papyri see Mandilaras, 168-69): John 13:31: νῦν ἐδοξάσθη ὁ υἱὸς τοῦ ἀνθρώπου, καὶ ὁ θεὸς ἐδοξάσθη ἐν αὐτῷ (now the son of man is to be glorified, and God is to be glorified in him), if νῦν is taken not as a temporal deictic indicator but a logical one: now it is to be the case that the son . . . . In support of the future reference is v 32: [εἰ ὁ θεὸς ἐδοξάσθη ἐν αὐτῷ] καὶ ὁ θεὸς δοξάσει αὐτὸν ἐν αὐτῷ, καὶ εὐθὺς δοξάσει αὐτόν ([if God is glorifed in him][31] indeed God will glorify him in him, and immediately will glorify him); John 17:18: καθὼς ἐμὲ ἀπέστειλας εἰς τὸν κόσμον, κἀγὼ ἀπέστειλα αὐτοὺς εἰς τὸν κόσμον (as you sent me into the world, I send them into the world); Jude 14: ἰδοὺ ἦλθεν κύριος ἐν ἁγίαις μυριάσιν αὐτοῦ (behold the lord is coming with his many saints).

There is sufficient proof in the diversity of syntactical constructions in which future reference may be found that although this usage is not widespread it is a category of usage which cannot be ignored. It cannot be adequately explained on the basis of a time-based conception of the tenses, but is fully commensurate with an aspectual model.

4. Timeless reference. A useful distinction is made in chapt. 2 and again above between omnitemporal and timeless propositions. Lyons defines a timeless proposition as "one for which the question of time-reference (whether deictic or non-deictic) simply does not arise: the situation, or state-of-affairs, that it describes is outside time altogether. Obvious examples of timeless propositions are the so-called eternal truths of mathematics and theology" (*Semantics*, 680). Considering Lyons's observation, it is surprising that grammarians of NT Greek--in light of the subject matter of the corpus--do not discuss this category more vigorously. (Cf. Hom. Il. 17.177-78: ὅς τε καὶ ἄλκιμον ἄνδρα φοβεῖ καὶ ἀφείλετο νίκην / ῥηϊδίως [(Zeus) terrifies even brave men and snatches victory away easily]. Is this similar to the "mythological Aorist"? See Kühner/Gerth, 1.161.) Lyons does not clarify the relation between statements for which temporal reference does not arise and those that lie outside time altogether, but a helpful means of viewing this is that the author does not appear to choose to limit his sphere of temporal reference, whether this is because the process referred to does not tangibly exist (the time frame of fiction is timeless in this sense) or because it refers to a realm beyond the sphere of time (truths of God's nature). Timeless use encompasses both, unified around the concept of the events not being limited to the temporal constraints of this world (see Dahl, *Tense*, 30). Thus the time-frame may be timeless even though processes referred to within the frame may be organized

---

[31]Although this clause receives a C rating in UBS[3], the textual evidence seems fairly clearly against its inclusion.

temporally, e.g. narrative progression within a story conveying timeless truth. It is argued here that Greek tense structure is fundamentally non-temporal, i.e. Greek tenses do not grammaticalize absolute temporal reference, but that they are aspectually based. Tense is a deictic category whereas verbal aspect is not. Therefore, it logically follows that the timeless use of the tenses (not deictically limited) is the closest to their essential semantic meaning. Examples of timeless usage could legitimately include every Greek verb, since semantically Greek tenses are not deictically specified, although pragmatically most Greek verbs are deictically limited within their respective discourse units. Under the category of timeless usage are listed Aorist and Present tense forms used self-consciously within discourse without deictic specification.

1. Aorist. It has been seen above in reference to Péristérakis, as well as extended examples from extra-biblical Greek (see appendix 4A), that timeless use of the Aorist is not uncommon in Greek, both in certain established syntactical patterns such as the conditional and in other constructions.[32] In NT Greek the following examples may be cited (conditional statements, to be included here, are treated at length in chapt. 6).

a. In chapt. 3 several examples are cited that might best be interpreted as timeless uses of Aorist tense forms: e.g. Matt 3:17; Mark 1:11; Luke 3:22; Matt 17:5; 2 Pet 1:17 with εὐδόκησα (I am pleased); ὡμοιώθη (it is like) with reference to the kingdom of God in Matt 13:24; 18:23; 22:2; and ἀφήκαμεν (we forgive) in Matt 6:12. These have already been discussed and need not be discussed further.

b. Parables and other exemplary literary units. Dahl's concept of "temporal frame" is particularly helpful at this point. He argues that certain clauses establish the time-frame in which other events are narrated (Dahl, *Tense*, 30). Parables and similar literary units fit well within this analysis. The narrative is proceeding chronologically, but then a discourse marker indicates that the narrative is shifting from the linear relation of events to another sphere of reference, sometimes narrative and sometimes descriptive. But neither appears to be temporally limited; the nature of the discourse indicates timeless reference, because the story is for didactic or instructional purposes. Thus the story does not pretend to be a story about what has happened or what is happening, or even a story about what always happens, but it is a story with no specific temporal reference (though internal chronological sequence, and hence temporal relations may be established, using

---

[32]When the category called gnomic Aorist is investigated in many grammars, the examples that are cited there are often better seen as timeless: e.g. Isoc. 1.6: ῥώμη δὲ μετὰ μὲν φρονήσεως ὠφέλησεν, ἄνευ δὲ ταύτης πλείω τοὺς ἔχοντας ἔβλαψε, καὶ τὰ μὲν σώματα τῶν ἀσκούντων ἐκόσμησε, ταῖς δὲ τῆς ψυχῆς ἐπιμελείαις ἐπεσκότησεν (strength with wisdom is of profit, but apart from it it harms more those who possess it, and it adorns the bodies of those who train, but it obscures the concerns of the soul) (Gildersleeve, 109), where no deictic indicator implicates specific reference for such an observation; and D. 2.10: ἀλλὰ τὰ τοιαῦτ᾽ εἰς μὲν ἅπαξ καὶ βραχὺν χρόνον ἀντέχει, καὶ σφόδρα γ᾽ ἤνθησεν ἐπὶ ταῖς ἐλπίσιν, ἂν τύχῃ, τῷ χρόνῳ δὲ φωρᾶται καὶ περὶ αὐτὰ καταρρεῖ (but such [evils] once and a short time prevail, and immediately blossom on hopes, if possible, but in time they are detected and all is destroyed around them) (Goodwin, *Syntax*, 54). Cf. D. 2.9: ὅταν δ᾽ ἐκ πλεονεξίας καὶ πονηρίας τις ὥσπερ οὗτος ἰσχύσῃ, ἡ πρώτη πρόφασις καὶ μικρὸν πταῖσμ᾽ ἅπαντ᾽ ἀνεχαίτισε καὶ διέλυσεν (whenever from deception and evil someone as he gains power, the first pretext, even a small blunder, overthrows and destroys everything) (Gildersleeve, 109-10).

discourse deictic indicators). This pattern can be found in extra-biblical Greek as well: Pl. Phaedr. 244ff.; Epict. 1.2.25ff.; Philostr. Life Apoll. 2.30 (other examples are to be found with the Present and Imperfect). In the NT, several examples worth noting.

Matt 7:24-27: after a conditional-like statement, the Aorist is used of a hypothetical man who ᾠκοδόμησεν (builds) his house upon a rock and the rain κατέβη (comes down) and the rivers ἦλθεν (come) and the winds ἔπνευσαν (blow) and προσέπεσαν (strike) the house and οὐκ ἔπεσεν (it does not fall), for he has built (τεθεμελίωτο [most heavily marked Perfect]) the foundation upon rock. The same story is then told using the Aorist of an unwise man.

Matt 13:24ff.: in the parable of the weeds and wheat (introduced by ὡμοιώθη; see chapt. 3), while the sowers are sleeping (καθεύδειν) the enemy ἦλθεν (comes) and sows (ἐπέσπειρεν) weeds and ἀπῆλθεν (goes away). When the grain ἐβλάστησεν (sprouts) and ἐποίησεν (bears) fruit, then the weeds ἐφάνη (are revealed). The narrative continues, using the Aorist to propel the narrative, but including several uses of the Present (v 27 ἔχει [have]; λέγουσιν [say; 'historic' Present], cf. φησιν; θέλεις [you want]). This parable, although internally it makes use of the Greek tenses as might be expected in narrative, is best interpreted as timeless, since there is no attempt to establish temporal implicature of the series of events. See also Matt 18:23ff.; 22:2ff., both parables introduced by ὡμοιώθη and using the timeless Aorist. Cf. Matt 13:3-9, the parable of the sower, where the nature of the event described, as well as the articular "sower," makes omnitemporal understanding more likely.

Matt 13:44: the kingdom is like a man who, finding (εὑρών) a treasure in a field, ἔκρυψεν (hides it) and because of his joy ὑπάγει (goes) and πωλεῖ (sells) all that he has and ἀγοράζει (buys) that field. Cf. 13:46 with Perfect; and 13:48ff. with Aorists. Luke 13:19: the kingdom is like a mustard seed which a man ἔβαλεν (casts) into his garden and ηὔξησεν (it grows) and ἐγένετο (becomes) a tree and the birds κατεσκήνωσεν (nest) in its branches; cf. Luke 13:21 in the parable of leaven.

Luke 14:16-23: in the parable of the great banquet the narrative is told using the Aorist after an initial Imperfect to set the stage. Several times Aorist and Present verbs are juxtaposed in dialogue: v 18: ἀγρὸν ἠγόρασα καὶ ἔχω ἀνάγκην (I have bought a field and have responsibility); v 19: ζεύγη βοῶν ἠγόρασα πέντε καὶ πορεύομαι δοκιμάσαι αὐτά (I have bought a team of five oxen and I am going to examine them); v 20: γυναῖκα ἔγημα καὶ διὰ τοῦτο οὐ δύναμαι ἐλθεῖν (I have married a woman and because of this I am unable to come). Whereas a temporal opposition may be present (this is not so clear since the process referred to by the Present verb could imply that the process referred to by the Aorist is still underway) the verbal aspectual opposition is clear. The respondent uses the perfective aspect to describe a complete process, and then makes his excuse using the imperfective aspect. The climax of the parable uses the Perfect (v 22): γέγονεν ὃ ἐπέταξας (what you ordered has come about).

Luke 15:11-32: the parable of the forgiving father relies almost entirely upon the Aorist. This example perhaps more than any other illustrates the timeless character of Greek verbs, since the context of speaking does not intend to limit the story's application to a particular temporal realm.

Luke 20:9ff.: the narrative is conveyed by the Aorist, speaking of the vineyard owner sending (ἀπέστειλεν) his servants to the tenants. Each time the messenger is abused and sent away. When the owner sends his son, the farmers διελογίζοντο (discuss) with each other, λέγοντες (saying) that this is the heir. They then kill him. Significantly the parable closes (vv 15ff.) with a series of Future forms used in questions to the hearers regarding the expected actions of the owner.

Use of the Aorist in the telling of parables also points to the primacy of the narrative function in use of the perfective aspect.

c. Doctrinal passages, where theological truths are conveyed. The prophecy of Zecharias (Luke 1:68-79) may be cited here. Mary's hymn appears to make specific reference to the circumstances she has experienced, and past implicature is entirely plausible (see chapt. 3), but Zacharias's is not so certain. The hymn begins with a verbless clause giving praise to the God of Israel, because ἐπεσκέψατο καὶ ἐποίησεν (he cares for and makes) redemption to his people (v 68), and ἤγειρεν (raises) a horn of salvation to us (v 69). Past implicature may be appropriate

(Farris, *Hymns*, 135),[33] although the redemption he anticipates appears to be current; a present sense (Fitzmyer, *Luke*, 1.383), referring to God's current salvific action, excludes much of God's work; and omnitemporal implicature appears inappropriate since the point is not that God is always performing this redeeming act. The parallel of this passage with others noted above with future reference makes future use of the Aorist a possibility, with the author grammaticalizing his reference to the complete care and redemptive action of God still to come. The example is placed under timeless reference, however, since the opening lines of the hymn seem to be definitional, elucidating who is the God of Israel (see Marshall, *Luke*, 90). He is the God of care and redemption. The author then recounts specific instances in support of this analysis: God ἐλάλησεν (spoke) through the mouths of the saints (v 70), God ὤμοσεν (swore) an oath with Abraham (v 73), and he projects a function for a child, probably John (v 76). (See Farris, esp. 133, for helpful outline of the text.)

Particularly significant here are the epistles of Paul, especially Romans. For example, Rom 1:18ff.: Paul begins with the timeless statement that the wrath of God ἀποκαλύπτεται (is revealed) on all ungodliness and injustice of men, since the knowledge of God is manifest in all men. God, he says, ἐφανέρωσεν (makes it clear) to them (v 19). From the foundation of the world his unseen attributes, etc., καθορᾶται (are perceived) (v 20). Then he shifts to the Aorist to specify the nature of this revelation, maintaining the timeless implicature. Although they know (γνόντες) God, οὐχ ὡς θεὸν ἐδόξασαν ἢ ηὐχαρίστησαν, ἀλλ' ἐματαιώθησαν (they do not glorify or give thanks to him as God, but make foolishness) in their discussions and their heart ἐσκοτίσθη (is darkened) (v 21). Saying to be wise ἐμωράνθησαν καὶ ἤλλαξαν (they are foolish and exchange) the glory of the uncorrupt God (vv 22-23). The result is that God παρέδωκεν (gives them over) to their desires (v 24), those who μετήλλαξαν (exchange) the truth of God for a lie and ἐσεβάσθησαν καὶ ἐλάτρευσαν (worship and serve) the creation rather than the creator (vv 24-25). Women μετήλλαξαν (transform) natural desires and men likewise ἐξεκαύθησαν (are lustful) (vv 26-27). And as they οὐκ ἐδοκίμασαν (do not see fit) to know God, he παρέδωκεν (hands them over) to untrained minds (v 28), etc. Paul concludes by saying that those who know (ἐπιγνόντες) but more importantly practice (πράσσοντες [imperfective aspect]) are worthy of death, they not only ποιοῦσιν (do) these things but συνευδοκοῦσιν (approve) those who do (v 32). Several times perfective and imperfective Participles and Infinitives are used within the passage, but the movement is clear and forceful, with the imperfective Present Indicative setting the stage and concluding, and the perfective Aorist Indicative specifying details.

The visions of Revelation are to be noted as well. Whereas they are related in narrative tenses, often the Aorist, they by nature are timeless or possibly future. For example, Rev 11:1ff. tells of the two witnesses. The narrative proceeds with a series of Future verbs and conditionals, then shifts to Present verbs, and then to Aorists (vv 11ff.), while the sphere of temporal reference remains the same. A plausible explanation is that the Future and conditional statements are used to establish the vision-quality of the narrative, and once this is established certain assertions are made about the two witnesses. In any case temporal reference cannot be the deciding factor in tense usage of these verbs.

d. Individual uses of the timeless Aorist may be cited as well: e.g. Mark 11:24: πιστεύετε ὅτι ἐλάβετε, καὶ ἔσται ὑμῖν (believe that you receive, and it will be to you), with no specification of the time of receipt;[34] Luke 7:35: ἐδικαιώθη ἡ σοφία ἀπὸ πάντων τῶν τέκνων αὐτῆς (wisdom is justified from all her children); Luke 12:32: ὅτι εὐδόκησεν ὁ πατὴρ ὑμῶν δοῦναι ὑμῖν τὴν βασιλείαν (our father is well pleased to give to you the kingdom); Luke 18:14: the tax collector κατέβη (goes down) justified; Luke 12:48: παντὶ δὲ ᾧ ἐδόθη πολύ, πολὺ ζητηθήσεται παρ' αὐτοῦ, καὶ ᾧ παρέθεντο πολύ, περισσότερον αἰτήσουσιν αὐτόν (to

---

[33]Farris (*Hymns*, 135) says, "The verb is aorist and ought to be interpreted in its normal sense [!] as referring to something which has happened in the past."

[34]The textual variant with λαμβάνετε is rightly dismissed, with the Aorist receiving an A rating in UBS[3].

everyone to whom much is given, much shall be required from him, and to whom much is entrusted, they will request much of him); John 1:18: after stating (using the most heavily marked Perfect) that no one has ever seen God, the author states that the only begotten God ἐξηγήσατο (makes known). It appears that the preceding negative clause excludes an omnitemporal reference, leaving the timeless reference the most plausible, i.e. God is the revealer. John 6:27: τοῦτον γὰρ ὁ πατὴρ ἐσφράγισεν ὁ θεός (this the father, God, seals); Acts 28:4: ἡ δίκη ζῆν οὐκ εἴασεν (justice does not permit to live), where the speaker appears to appeal to a concept of justice; Rom 2:12: ὅσοι γὰρ ἀνόμως ἥμαρτον, ἀνόμως καὶ ἀπολοῦνται· καὶ ὅσοι ἐν νόμῳ ἥμαρτον, διὰ νόμου κριθήσονται (whoever sins lawlessly, they will be destroyed lawlessly; and whoever sins in law, through law they will be judged), with 5:12; cf. Rom 3:23. Demio ("Translation," 388) correctly notes that ἥμαρτον need not be rendered identical to the preceding Aorist verbs, since it is not parallel. The understanding depends upon reference of the sinful act. A timeless implicature is most likely. Rom 8:29-30: ὅτι οὓς προέγνω, καὶ προώρισεν συμμόρφους τῆς εἰκόνος τοῦ υἱοῦ αὐτοῦ, εἰς τὸ εἶναι αὐτὸν πρωτότοκον ἐν πολλοῖς ἀδελφοῖς· οὓς δὲ προώρισεν, τούτους καὶ ἐκάλεσεν· καὶ οὓς ἐκάλεσεν, τούτους καὶ ἐδικαίωσεν· οὓς δὲ ἐδικαίωσεν, τούτους καὶ ἐδόξασεν (because whom he foreknows, indeed he sets apart having the same form as that of his son, in order for him to be the first born among many brothers; whom he sets apart, these indeed he calls; and whom he calls, these indeed he justifies; and whom he justifies, these indeed he glorifies) (D. Brown, "Aorist," 77). 1 Cor 1:20-21: does not God ἐμώρανεν (make foolish) the wisdom of the world? For since in his wisdom the world οὐκ ἔγνω (does not know) God, through wisdom God εὐδόκησεν (is pleased) through the foolishness of preaching to save those who believe (τοὺς πιστεύοντας); cf. Col 1:19: ἐν αὐτῷ εὐδόκησεν πᾶν τὸ πλήρωμα κατοικῆσαι (in him all the fulness is pleased to live). 1 Cor 1:27-28: God ἐξελέξατο (elects) the foolish, weak, and inferior to accomplish his purposes; 1 Cor 12:18: νυνὶ δὲ ὁ θεὸς ἔθετο τὰ μέλη . . . ἐν τῷ σώματι καθὼς ἠθέλησεν (now God puts the members in the body as he wants), with νυνί forming a logical transition from the rhetorical questions to a timeless description (cf. 1 Cor 15:38), including use of the Present in vv 21, 23, 24 and the Aorist in 12:24: God συνεκέρασεν (unites) the body. Gal 2:19: I through the law ἀπέθανον (die) to the law, following a conditional clause; Eph 2:4: God is rich in mercy according to the love ἣν ἠγάπησεν ἡμᾶς (which he loves us); 1 Thess 4:7: οὐ γὰρ ἐκάλεσεν ἡμᾶς ὁ θεὸς ἐπὶ ἀκαθαρσίᾳ ἀλλ᾽ ἐν ἁγιασμῷ (for God does not call us in uncleanness but in holiness), where the object may make this past referring; Heb 4:10: ὁ γὰρ εἰσελθὼν εἰς τὴν κατάπαυσιν αὐτοῦ καὶ αὐτὸς κατέπαυσεν ἀπὸ τῶν ἔργων αὐτοῦ (for one who enters into his rest indeed he himself rests from his work), where the author appears to be stating a definitional tautology; Jas 2:5: after a series of commands and conditional statements, the author instructs his hearers to listen: οὐχ ὁ θεὸς ἐξελέξατο (does not God elect) the poor in faith and rich in faith and heirs of the kingdom which ἐπηγγείλατο (he announces) to those who love him? 2 Pet 1:21: prophecy οὐ . . . ἠνέχθη ποτέ (is not ever brought) from the will of man, but men carried by the holy spirit ἐλάλησαν (speak) from God, a definition of prophetic utterances; 1 John 2:11: ἡ σκοτία ἐτύφλωσεν (the darkness blinds) his eyes; 1 John 4:8: ὁ μὴ ἀγαπῶν οὐκ ἔγνω τὸν θεόν (the one who does not love does not know God), because God is love; 1 John 5:11: God ἔδωκεν (gives) us eternal life. 1 John contains several definitional uses of the timeless Aorist. (Rom 11:34; 1 Cor 2:16; 2 Tim 2:19 in quotations of OT.)

2. **The timeless Present** is recognized by grammarians, since the phenomenon is readily evidenced in Greek literature, although the language used to discuss the particular usage is confused with other categories used for present reference, often the gnomic (e.g. Robertson, 866; Péristérakis, *Essai*, 188-201).

a. For parables and other exemplary literary units, and doctrinal passages, see above also. Mark 4:13-20 and Luke 8:11-15: the parable of the sower is explained using the imperfective aspect. This is a good illustration of the distinction made in chapt. 2 about types of discourse, where it is noted that perfective aspect is often found in narrative but that imperfective aspect is found in description. Jesus is cited as explaining the various aspects of the narrative, but an absolute temporal reference is not possible. While relative present reference is possible here, this is discounted since he is not relating a series of present events but merely providing definitions of the various characters in the parable. See also Luke 8:16-18, where in the parable of the light under a vessel the imperfective aspect is used to define the state of affairs, not give a narrative progression.

Luke 6:39ff.: μήτι δύναται (it is not possible) for a blind man to lead a blindman, is it? A disciple is (ἔστιν) not greater than his teacher. Why βλέπεις (do you see) the speck in your brother's eye but οὐ κατανοεῖς (do not consider) the log in your own? How δύνασαι (are you able) to speak to your brother?

Luke 13:6-9: in the parable of the barren fig tree a man εἶχεν (has) a tree and ἦλθεν (he comes) seeking fruit which οὐχ εὗρεν (he does not find). εἶπεν (he says) to the tender, for three years ἔρχομαι (I have been coming) seeking fruit οὐχ εὑρίσκω (I have not found): cut it down. The tender protests (λέγει). After the initial Imperfect to set the stage, the Aorist is used to propel the narrative, until the climactic dialogue, which uses the Present. The parable closes with Subjunctives and the Future. Cf. Luke 16:19 with Imperfect.

Luke 15:4-7: the parable of the lost sheep uses the Present tense to carry the narrative and report Jesus' moral, with the Aorist used in the dialogue. Verbal aspect draws attention to the fact that it is the progress of events regarding finding the lost sheep that lies at the heart of this parable.

Rom 2:1-8: whereas the use of the timeless perfective Aorist in Rom 1:18ff. to specify the sinful nature of man is cited above, the imperfective Present is used in 2:1-8 to explain the righteous judgment of God. The contrast of verbal aspect appears intentional. After recapitulation in 2:1 using the Present, Paul states that οἴδαμεν (we know) that the judgment of God is true. He then uses the Present to structure his exposition: λογίζῃ (you consider), καταφρονεῖς (you despise); ἄγει (it leads); θησαυρίζεις (you store up), until he begins to specify those he is addressing, with personal deictic indicators in vv 9ff.

b. Individual uses. Matt 5:14-15 par. Luke 8:16: οὐ δύναται πόλις κρυβῆναι ἐπάνω ὄρους κειμένη· οὐδὲ καίουσιν λύχνον καὶ τιθέασιν αὐτὸν ὑπὸ τὸν μόδιον ἀλλ' ἐπὶ τὴν λυχνίαν, καὶ λάμπει πᾶσιν τοῖς ἐν τῇ οἰκίᾳ (a city is not able to be hidden sitting upon a mountain; neither do they light a lamp and put it under the basket but upon the lamp stand and it burns for all in the house); cf. Mark 4:21-23, where the same parable is told using the Subjunctive. Mark 4:25: ὃς γὰρ ἔχει . . . καὶ ὃς οὐκ ἔχει, καὶ ὃ ἔχει (whoever has . . . and whoever does not have and what he has), cf. Luke 8:18 with Subjunctives. Luke 7:47: ᾧ δὲ ὀλίγον ἀφίεται, ὀλίγον ἀγαπᾷ (to whom little is forgiven, he loves little); John 3:18: ὁ πιστεύων εἰς αὐτὸν οὐ κρίνεται (the one who believes in him is not judged), cf. following clause with Perfect Indicative. John 5:23b: ὁ μὴ τιμῶν τὸν υἱὸν οὐ τιμᾷ τὸν πατέρα τὸν πέμψαντα αὐτόν (the one who does not honour the son does not honour the father who sent him), echoing a Subjunctive clause in v 23a; Rom 2:21: ὁ οὖν διδάσκων ἕτερον σεαυτὸν οὐ διδάσκεις; ὁ κηρύσσων μὴ κλέπτειν κλέπτεις; (do you who teaches another teach yourself? Do you who preaches not to steal steal?); Rom 3:9: προεχόμεθα; (are we excusable?), cf. Aorist in same verse. Rom 8:24: who ἐλπίζει (hopes) for what βλέπει (he sees)?; Rom 8:26-27: the spirit συναντιλαμβάνεται (helps in our weakness) . . . but the same spirit ὑπερεντυγχάνει (intercedes). The one who examines hearts knows (οἶδεν) the thought of the spirit because according to God ἐντυγχάνει (he intercedes) on behalf of the saints, where a noticeable shift occurs between timeless and deictically specific statements, on the basis of person deixis. 1 Cor 12:21, 23, 24: the eye οὐ δύναται (is not able) to speak. . . . and what δοκοῦμεν (we consider) less honourable, περιτίθεμεν (we bestow) more honour on them and our private parts ἔχει (have) more attractiveness and our presentable parts οὐ . . . ἔχει (do not have) a need; 2 Cor 9:7: Paul justifies his request for the offering by making a theological statement: ἱλαρὸν γὰρ δότην ἀγαπᾷ ὁ θεός (for God loves a joyful giver); Jas 1:13: ὁ γὰρ θεὸς ἀπείραστός ἐστιν κακῶν, πειράζει δὲ αὐτὸς οὐδένα (for God is untempted of evil, and he himself tempts no one), where James uses the imperfective aspect to describe God's character; Jas 4:11: following a command the author says ὁ καταλαλῶν ἀδελφοῦ ἢ κρίνων τὸν ἀδελφὸν αὐτοῦ καταλαλεῖ νόμου καὶ κρίνει νόμον (the one who speaks against a brother or judges his brother speaks against the law and judges the law), followed by a conditional clause.

7. CONCLUSION. Three major points are made in this chapter. (1) A working definition of the attitudes grammaticalized by the Moods is posited, and this allows for a differentiation of the two major attitudes of Greek, [±assertion]. This chapter concentrates upon the assertive attitude as grammaticalized in the Indicative Mood. (2) Through citing a number of examples it is clear what is meant by verbal aspect. Verbal aspect is the essential semantic category grammaticalized by Greek verb tenses. In this chapter the Present/Imperfect and Aorist tense forms are discussed in light of their grammaticalizing imperfective and perfective aspect. Several patterns of usage are explored, although it is difficult to limit the configurations since verbal aspect is predicated upon reasoned subjective choice by the speaker or author, not temporal reference. The examples cited explore several of the possible underlying reasons. Although several of the examples may be questioned, an explanation according to the traditional methods of interpretation certainly fails to be satisfactory. This reinforces the point being made, that deictic reference in Greek is not a matter of tense-form usage, since the same form may refer to several different deictic spheres. The constant factor is the tense form itself, which grammaticalizes the speaker's conception of the process. (3) A range of deictic categories to which the verb tenses may be applied is discussed, illustrating that the individual tense forms are compatible with a number of different deictic categories established by discourse features, and at the same time reinforcing the contention that Greek verb forms are not absolutely temporally referring. An attempt is made to expand the categories suggested by the individual grammars, showing that instances often treated as anomalies must be integrated by an adequate explanatory theory of verb tenses, and that verbal aspect provides such an explanatory semantic category.

APPENDIX 4A:
Pl. PHAEDR. 244-56 AND PLB. 6.24-25

Pl. Phaedr. 244-56:[1] After several conditional and conditional-like statements, Socrates appeals to ancient practice. "Therefore it is worthy to note that those of old who gave names did not consider madness shameful or reproachful. For to the most beautiful art form, by which that which is coming about is judged, they would not call [οὐ . . . ἂν . . . ἐκάλεσαν] madness, affixing to it the same name. . . ." ὅταν θείᾳ μοίρᾳ γίγνηται . . . οἱ δὲ νῦν ἀπειροκάλως τὸ ταῦ ἐπεμβάλλοντες μαντικὴν ἐκάλεσαν (present use of Aorist; whenever it might come by divine gift . . . they now call it mantic, vulgarly inserting the T). The subsequent sentence is parallel, but with νῦν . . . καλοῦσιν (now they call) in the 'apodosis.' (244B-C) ἀλλὰ μὴν νόσων γε καὶ πόνων τῶν μεγίστων, ἃ δὴ παλαιῶν ἐκ μηνιμάτων ποθὲν ἔν τισι τῶν γενῶν ἡ μανία ἐγγενομένη καὶ προφητεύσασα, οἷς ἔδει ἀπαλλαγὴν ηὕρετο, καταφυγοῦσα πρὸς θεῶν εὐχάς τε καὶ λατρείας, ὅθεν δὴ καθαρμῶν τε καὶ τελετῶν τυχοῦσα ἐξάντη ἐποίησε τὸν [ἑαυτῆς] ἔχοντα πρός τε τὸν παρόντα καὶ τὸν ἔπειτα χρόνον (but from the diseases and greatest troubles, which are from an ancient cause of wrath somewhere to certain of the families, mania, entering and interpreting, finds [omnitemporal use of Aorist?] relief for whom it is necessary [non-past use of the Imperfect], offering refuge by prayers and acts of service to the gods, by which means, obtaining purification and ritual rites, makes [omnitemporal use of Aorist] well the one who possesses it for the present and later time). (244D-E) . . . ὃς δ' ἂν ἄνευ μανίας Μουσῶν ἐπὶ ποιητικὰς θύρας ἀφίκηται, πεισθεὶς ὡς ἄρα ἐκ τέχνης ἱκανὸς ποιητὴς ἐσόμενος, ἀτελὴς αὐτός τε καὶ ἡ ποίησις ὑπὸ τῆς τῶν μαινομένων ἡ τοῦ σωφρονοῦντος ἠφανίσθη (whoever might arrive without the madness of the Muses at the door of poetry, persuaded that by skill he will be a sufficient poet, he is immature and the poetry by the sane man is made to vanish [timeless use of Aorist] by that of the madman). (245A) The conditional-like statement is a fitting close to this section.

After a discussion of the immortality of the soul (245C-246A), Socrates likens the soul to a pair of winged horses and a charioteer.[2] πῇ δὴ οὖν θνητόν τε καὶ ἀθάνατον ζῷον ἐκλήθη πειρατέον εἰπεῖν (an attempt is made to say in what way a living being is called [timeless, or perhaps omnitemporal, use of Aorist] mortal and immortal). (246B) Since there is no discussion of living beings before this, the Aorist cannot refer to the immediately preceding discussion, but is used as part of discussion of a new subject. ἡ δὲ πτερορρυήσασα φέρεται ἕως ἂν στερεοῦ τινος ἀντιλάβηται, οὗ κατοικισθεῖσα, σῶμα γήϊνον λαβοῦσα, αὐτὸ αὑτὸ δοκοῦν κινεῖν διὰ τὴν ἐκείνης δύναμιν, ζῷον τὸ σύμπαν ἐκλήθη, ψυχὴ καὶ σῶμα παγέν, θνητόν τ' ἔσχεν ἐπωνυμίαν (and the wingless soul is borne until it might grasp something solid, which inhabiting,

---

[1]The context that Socrates sets is a theoretical discussion of love with consideration of practical questions of his hearers.

[2]A. Buttmann (201) refers to 246ff. as "ideal pictures."

taking an earthly body, itself seen to move because of the power of that soul; the whole is called [timeless use of Aorist] a living being, joining soul and body, and takes [timeless use of Aorist] the name of mortal). (246C)

Using omnitemporal Perfects regarding the inherent function of the wing (246D-E), Socrates introduces the heavenly court, including Zeus and his army of gods. τῶν δὲ ἄλλων ὅσοι ἐν τῷ τῶν δώδεκα ἀριθμῷ τεταγμένοι θεοὶ ἄρχοντες ἡγοῦνται κατὰ τάξιν ἣν ἕκαστος ἐτάχθη (and of the others those gods who are placed in the twelve and are leaders, they lead according to the order in which each is placed [omnitemporal use of Aorist, though possibly past use]). . . . αἱ μὲν γὰρ ἀθάνατοι καλούμεναι, ἡνίκ᾽ ἂν πρὸς ἄκρῳ γένωνται, ἔξω πορευθεῖσαι ἔστησαν ἐπὶ τῷ τοῦ οὐρανοῦ νώτῳ, στάσας δὲ αὐτὰς περιάγει ἡ περιφορά, αἱ δὲ θεωροῦσι τὰ ἔξω τοῦ οὐρανοῦ (for those called immortal, because they might come to the top, going out they stand [timeless use of Aorist] upon the edge of heaven, and the revolution carries around [timeless use of Present to select further events] those who are standing, and they see [timeless use of Present] the things outside of heaven). (247A-C)

After a past use of the Aorist (ὕμνησε [sing]), established by the deictic indicator πω (yet, ever, to this point), Socrates makes a series of timeless statements about the divine. καὶ τἆλλα ὡσαύτως τὰ ὄντα ὄντως θεασαμένη καὶ ἑστιαθεῖσα, δῦσα πάλιν εἰς τὸ εἴσω τοῦ οὐρανοῦ, οἴκαδε ἦλθεν. ἐλθούσης δὲ αὐτῆς ὁ ἡνίοχος πρὸς τὴν φάτνην τοὺς ἵππους στήσας παρέβαλεν ἀμβροσίαν τε καὶ ἐπ᾽ αὐτῇ νέκταρ ἐπότισεν (and likewise seeing and eating the other realities, entering again into the inside of heaven, [the divine intelligence) goes home [timeless use of Aorist]. After this comes about, the charioteer, placing the horses at the manger, gives [timeless use of Aorist] them ambrosia and in addition to it waters [timeless use of Aorist] them with nectar). (247E)

Socrates continues with a description of other souls. ἡ μὲν ἄριστα θεῷ ἑπομένη καὶ εἰκασμένη ὑπερῆρεν εἰς τὸν ἔξω τόπον τὴν τοῦ ἡνιόχου κεφαλήν, καὶ συμπεριηνέχθη τὴν περιφοράν, θορυβουμένη ὑπὸ τῶν ἵππων καὶ μόγις καθορῶσα τὰ ὄντα· ἡ δὲ τοτὲ μὲν ἦρεν, τοτὲ δ᾽ ἔδυ, βιαζομένων δὲ τῶν ἵππων τὰ μὲν εἶδεν, τὰ δ᾽ οὔ (the [soul], following best and most like god, raises up into the outer region the head of the charioteer, and he is carried around the revolution, being troubled by the horses and hardly seeing the realities; and another then rises, and then sinks, and because the horses are violent, it sees some things and not others). (248A) Plato continues this discussion with a series of timeless Present verbs, including a number of conditional and conditional-like statements. The souls of those who live philosophically for three periods of a thousand years become winged, Socrates says. αἱ δὲ ἄλλαι, ὅταν τὸν πρῶτον βίον τελευτήσωσιν, κρίσεως ἔτυχον, κριθεῖσαι δὲ αἱ μὲν εἰς τὰ ὑπὸ γῆς δικαιωτήρια ἐλθοῦσαι δίκην ἐκτίνουσιν, αἱ δ᾽ εἰς τοὐρανοῦ τινα τόπον ὑπὸ τῆς Δίκης κουφισθεῖσαι διάγουσιν ἀξίως οὗ ἐν ἀνθρώπου εἴδει ἐβίωσαν βίου (but others, whenever they might complete the first life, obtain [timeless use of Aorist] judgment: and after being judged, some, going to the places of judgment under the earth, pay [timeless use of Present] the full penalty, and others, being raised up into a heavenly place by Justice, live [timeless use of Present] worthy of the way they lived in the form of a human). (249A) Plato uses the timeless Aorist to describe the complete event, while two Present verbs specify the details. According to discourse and time deictic indicators, the relative clause appears to have past reference, although an omnitemporal use depicting the human way of life is also possible.[3] Perhaps this helps to analyse the following: καθάπερ γὰρ εἴρηται, πᾶσα μὲν ἀνθρώπου ψυχὴ φύσει τεθέαται τὰ ὄντα, ἢ οὐκ ἂν ἦλθεν εἰς τόδε τὸ ζῷον· ἀναμιμνήσκεσθαι δὲ ἐκ τῶνδε ἐκεῖνα οὐ ῥάδιον ἁπάσῃ, οὔτε ὅσαι βραχέως εἶδον τότε τἀκεῖ, οὔθ᾽ αἱ δεῦρο πεσοῦσαι ἐδυστύχησαν, ὥστε ὑπό τινων ὁμιλιῶν ἐπὶ τὸ ἄδικον τραπόμεναι λήθην ὧν τότε εἶδον ἱερῶν ἔχειν. ὀλίγαι δὴ

---

[3]Contrast 249C: τοῦτο δ᾽ ἐστιν ἀνάμνησις ἐκείνων ἅ ποτ᾽εἶδεν ἡμῶν ἡ ψυχὴ συμπορευθεῖσα θεῷ καὶ ὑπεριδοῦσα ἃ νῦν εἶναί φαμεν, καὶ ἀνακύψασα εἰς τὸ ὂν ὄντως (this is a remembrance of those things which our soul then saw, traveling with god and overlooking things we now say exist and rising up to real being), where the time deictic indicators establish past and present reference.

λείπονται αἷς τὸ τῆς μνήμης ἱκανῶς πάρεστιν (for as it has been said, every soul of man by nature sees the realities, or it would not enter [omnitemporal Aorist] into the living being; but it is not easy for those realities to be remembered by them in all things, neither those who see [omnitemporal Aorist] them briefly there, nor those who, falling, are unlucky [omnitemporal Aorist], so as to be turned toward injustice by certain communications and to have forgotten the holy things they then see [omnitemporal Aorist?]. Few then are left [omnitemporal Present] with whom the memory sufficiently remains). (249E-250A) Although past reference is probable in some parts within this section since it recapitulates previous discussion, as well as includes time deictic indicators (e.g. τότε) within the unit, the nature of the description concerning what happens to all souls warrants consideration of the omnitemporal use of the Aorist and Present. Cf. 250B where a contrast of previous and subsequent events is related.

Socrates turns to discussion of beauty, spoken of earlier (εἴπομεν [we said]). After a description of beauty (this section may rely on a timeless use of ἔλαμπεν [shining], κατειλήφαμεν [find], and ἔρχεται [come]), the speaker says νῦν δὲ κάλλος μόνον ταύτην ἔσχε μοῖραν, ὥστ᾽ ἐκφανέστατον εἶναι καὶ ἐρασμιώτατον (and now beauty has [timeless use of Aorist] this privilege alone, that it is most clearly seen and loveliest). . . . ὁ δὲ ἀρτιτελής, ὁ τῶν τότε πολυθεάμων, ὅταν θεοειδὲς πρόσωπον ἴδῃ κάλλος εὖ μεμιμημένον ἤ τινα σώματος ἰδέαν, πρῶτον μὲν ἔφριξε καί τι τῶν τότε ὑπῆλθεν αὐτὸν δειμάτων, εἶτα προσορῶν ὡς θεὸν σέβεται (and the newly initiated, who has then seen many of them, whenever he might see a god-like face or certain form of body well imitating beauty, first he shudders [timeless use of Aorist] and then something of the awe-inspiring comes over [timeless use of Aorist] him, then, seeing, he reveres it as a god). . . . δεξάμενος γὰρ τοῦ κάλλους τὴν ἀπορροὴν διὰ τῶν ὀμμάτων ἐθερμάνθη ᾗ ἡ τοῦ πτεροῦ φύσις ἄρδεται, θερμανθέντος δὲ ἐτάκη τὰ περὶ τὴν ἔκφυσιν, ἃ πάλαι ὑπὸ σκληρότητος συμμεμυκότα εἶργε μὴ βλαστάνειν, ἐπιρρυείσης δὲ τῆς τροφῆς ᾤδησέ τε καὶ ὥρμησε φύεσθαι ἀπὸ τῆς ῥίζης ὁ τοῦ πτεροῦ καυλός (having received the emanation of the good through the eyes, he is on fire [timeless use of Aorist], by which the growth of the feather is watered [timeless use of Present], and being on fire, he melts [timeless use of Aorist] the things concerning the growth, which things previously being shut up tight were hindering [Imperfect] sprouting, but as the nourishment flows, the shaft of the feather both swells [timeless use of Aorist] and begins [timeless use of Aorist] to grow from the root). (250C-251B)

Having moved to the subject of love, Socrates describes the relationship of the soul to love. He closes a lengthy section using the analogy of the two horses and the charioteer: καὶ πρὸς αὐτῷ τ᾽ ἐγένοντο καὶ εἶδον τὴν ὄψιν τὴν τῶν παιδικῶν ἀστράπτουσαν (and to him they come [timeless use of Aorist] and see [timeless use of Aorist] the shining vision of the lover). The next section is dominated with non past-referring Aorist verbs: ἡ μνήμη πρὸς τὴν τοῦ κάλλους φύσιν ἠνέχθη, καὶ πάλιν εἶδεν αὐτὴν μετὰ σωφροσύνης ἐν ἁγνῷ βάθρῳ βεβῶσαν· ἰδοῦσα δὲ ἔδεισέ τε καὶ σεφθεῖσα ἀνέπεσεν ὑπτία, καὶ ἅμα ἠναγκάσθη εἰς τοὐπίσω ἑλκύσαι τὰς ἡνίας οὕτω σφόδρα. . . . ἀπελθόντε δὲ ἀπωτέρω, ὁ μὲν ὑπ᾽ αἰσχύνης τε καὶ θάμβους ἱδρῶτι πᾶσαν ἔβρεξε τὴν ψυχήν, ὁ δὲ λήξας τῆς ὀδύνης, ἣν ὑπὸ τοῦ χαλινοῦ τε ἔσχεν καὶ τοῦ πτώματος, μόγις ἐξαναπνεύσας ἐλοιδόρησεν ὀργῇ. . . . καὶ πάλιν οὐκ ἐθέλοντας προσιέναι ἀναγκάζων μόγις συνεχώρησεν δεομένων εἰς αὖθις ὑπερβαλέσθαι. . . . ἕλκων ἠνάγκασεν αὖ προσελθεῖν τοῖς παιδικοῖς ἐπὶ τοὺς αὐτοὺς λόγους, καὶ ἐπειδὴ ἐγγὺς ἦσαν. . . . τήν τε κακηγόρον γλῶτταν καὶ τὰς γνάθους καθῆμαξεν καὶ τὰ σκέλη τε καὶ τὰ ἰσχία πρὸς τὴν γῆν ἐρείσας ὀδύναις ἔδωκεν. . . . (the memory is brought [timeless use of Aorist] to the nature of the good, and again he sees [timeless use of Aorist] it with modesty placed upon a pure pillar; seeing it, he is afraid [timeless use of Aorist], and revering it, he falls back [timeless use of Aorist], and he is at once required [timeless use of Aorist] to pull backwards the reins violently. . . . the two having gone further off, one, because of shame and wonder, moistens [timeless use of Aorist] the entire soul with sweat, and the other, ceasing from pain, which he has on account of the bridle and the fall, having hardly taken a breath, reviles [timeless use of Aorist] with anger. . . . and again, compelling the animals not wanting to go forward, he hardly yields [timeless use of Aorist], being begged to give way again. . . . willingly he compels [timeless use of Aorist] them again with the same words to approach the boy, and when they are [timeless use of ἦσαν] near. . . . and the evil tongue and the jaws he drenches with blood [timeless use of Aorist], and the bones and haunches hurling to the ground, he inflicts pain [timeless use of Aorist]). (254B-E)

Interwoven with several conditional and conditional-like statements, Socrates continues: προϊόντος δὲ ἤδη τοῦ χρόνου ἤ τε ἡλικία καὶ τὸ χρεὼν ἤγαγεν εἰς τὸ προσέσθαι αὐτὸν εἰς ὁμιλίαν (as time is passing, both his age and fate lead him to enter into community). (255A) After a conditional-like statement using person deixis to establish past temporal reference (ὃν ἵμερον Ζεὺς Γανυμήδους ἐρῶν ὠνόμασε [which Zeus, loving Ganymede, named desire]), Plato once again uses the non past-referring Aorist: καὶ οἷον πνεῦμα ἤ τις ἠχὼ ἀπὸ λείων τε καὶ στερεῶν ἀλλομένη πάλιν ὅθεν ὡρμήθη φέρεται. . . . τὰς διόδους τῶν πτερῶν ἄρδει τε καὶ ὥρμησε πτεροφυεῖν τε καὶ τὴν τοῦ ἐρωμένου αὖ ψυχὴν ἔρωτος ἐνέπλησεν (and as a spirit or some echo rebounding from a lion and a stone is brought back [omnitemporal use of Present] again from whence it begins [omnitemporal use of Aorist]. . . . the passages of the wings [the flow of beauty] waters [timeless use of Present] and begins [timeless use of Aorist] to grow feathers, and fills up [timeless use of Aorist] the soul of the beloved with love). (255C-D) The noteworthy juxtaposition of the Present and Aorist verbs well illustrates the non-temporal nature of each.

In one of the concluding sections of his soliloquy, Socrates uses several conditional and conditional-like statements. One uses a non past-referring Imperfect in the apodosis: ἐὰν μὲν δὴ οὖν εἰς τεταγμένην τε δίαιταν καὶ φιλοσοφίαν νικήσῃ τὰ βελτίω τῆς διανοίας ἀγαγόντα, μακάριον μὲν καὶ ὁμονοητικὸν τὸν ἐνθάδε βίον διάγουσιν, ἐγκρατεῖς αὐτῶν καὶ κόσμιοι ὄντες, δουλωσάμενοι μὲν ᾧ κακία ψυχῆς ἐνεγίγνετο, ἐλευθερώσαντες δὲ ᾧ ἀρετή (if therefore the better things of the mind, leading unto the ordered way of life and philosophy, might be victorious, they live a blessed and well-balanced life here, being in control of himself and being orderly, subjecting that which brings [timeless use of Imperfect] evil of the soul, and giving liberation to virtue).   And another uses non past-referring Aorists: ἐὰν δὲ δὴ διαίτῃ φορτικωτέρᾳ τε καὶ ἀφιλοσόφῳ, φιλοτίμῳ δὲ χρήσωνται, τάχ' ἄν που ἐν μέθαις ἤ τινι ἄλλῃ ἀμελείᾳ τὼ ἀκολάστω αὐτοῖν ὑποζυγίω λαβόντε τὰς ψυχὰς ἀφρούρους, συναγαγόντε εἰς ταὐτόν, τὴν ὑπὸ τῶν πολλῶν μακαριστὴν αἵρεσιν εἱλέσθην τε καὶ διεπραξάσθην (if indeed with common cause and without philosophy, they might be possessed of love of honour, probably when in drunkenness or some other careless condition the unruly pair, taking the unguarded spirit, gathering them together, seize [timeless use of Aorist] and accomplish [timeless use of Aorist] that considered blissful by the many). (256A-C)

Plb. 6.24-25:[4] ἐξ ἑκάστου δὲ τῶν προειρημένων γενῶν πλὴν τῶν νεωτάτων ἐξέλεξαν ταξιάρχους ἀριστίνδην δέκα. μετὰ δὲ τούτους ἑτέραν ἐκλογὴν ἄλλων δέκα ποιοῦνται. καὶ τούτους μὲν ἅπαντας προσηγόρευσαν ταξιάρχους, ὧν ὁ πρῶτος αἱρεθεὶς καὶ συνεδρίου κοινωνεῖ· προσελέγονται δ' οὗτοι πάλιν αὐτοὶ τοὺς ἴσους οὐραγούς. ἑξῆς δὲ τούτοις μετὰ τῶν ταξιάρχων διεῖλον τὰς ἡλικίας, ἑκάστην εἰς δέκα μέρη, πλὴν τῶν γροσφομάχων· καὶ προσένειμαν ἑκάστῳ μέρει τῶν ἐκλεχθέντων ἀνδρῶν δύ' ἡγεμόνας καὶ δύ'οὐραγούς. τῶν δὲ γροσφομάχων τοὺς ἐπιβάλλοντας κατὰ τὸ πλῆθος ἴσους ἐπὶ πάντα τὰ μέρη διένειμαν. καὶ τὸ μὲν μέρος ἕκαστον ἐκάλεσαν καὶ τάγμα καὶ σπεῖραν καὶ σημαίαν, τοὺς δ' ἡγεμόνας κεντυρίωνας καὶ ταξιάρχους. οὗτοι δὲ καθ' ἑκάστην σπεῖραν ἐκ τῶν καταλειπομένων ἐξέλεξαν αὐτοὶ δύο τοὺς ἀκμαιοτάτους καὶ γενναιοτάτους ἄνδρας σημαιαφόρους. [6.24.1-6] ... παραπλησίως δὲ καὶ τοὺς ἱππεῖς εἰς ἴλας δέκα διεῖλον, ἐξ ἑκάστης δὲ τρεῖς προκρίνουσιν ἰλάρχας, οὗτοι δ' αὐτοὶ τρεῖς προσέλαβον οὐραγούς. [6.25.1] ... τοὺς δὲ λοιποὺς διεῖλον εἰς δύο μέρη, καὶ καλοῦσι τὸ μὲν δεξιόν, τὸ δ' εὐώνυμον κέρας. [6.26.9] (From each of the appointed groups apart from the youngest they select [Aorist] ten taxiarchs according to merit. With these they make another selection of ten others [Present]. And all of these they name [Aorist] taxiarchs, of whom the first

---

[4]The context is a description of the Roman military (6.19ff.), more particularly selection of the centurions, which arises out of a general discussion of government, a discussion which Polybius realizes might be subject to criticism (6.11).

selected participates [Present] in the council; and these themselves select [Present] equal numbers of rearguard officers. Next, with the taxiarchs they divide up [Aorist] the group, each into ten groups, apart from the javelin throwers; and they place [Aorist] with each portion two leaders and two rearguard officers from the selected men. And from the javelin throwers they assign [Aorist] equal portions according to number to each group. And they call [Aorist] each portion tagma and speiran and semaian, and the leaders centurions and taxiarchs. And they themselves appoint [Aorist] from those remaining according to each speiran two of the strongest and noblest men as standard bearers. . . . Likewise the cavalry they divide [Aorist] into ten squadrons, and from each they choose [Present] three squadron leaders, and they themselves appoint [Aorist] three rearguard officers. . . . And the rest they divide [Aorist] into two groups, and they call [Present] them the right and the left wings.)

CHAPTER 5:
THE STATIVE ASPECT AND PERFECT TENSE

0. INTRODUCTION. A reasonably large amount of material has been published of late on the Perfect tense, so much that one might legitimately wonder whether much of significance remains to be said. An initial glimpse shows that virtually all of the standard grammars are in agreement about both the tense's function and significance. Whereas there is a significant amount of agreement (see Dahl, *Tense*, 129ff., for recent discussion), several crucial issues still await satisfactory resolution. This chapter attempts a systemic explication of the opposition between the stative and non-stative aspectual systems in the Greek verbal network; a definition of the stative aspect, emphasizing its non-temporal character and orientation to the subject; a catalogue of its major contextual uses; an analysis of recent discussion that discounts viability of the tense in hellenistic Greek, supporting its continued semantic distinction; a brief examination of οἶδα and γινώσκω, defending the stative aspect of οἶδα; and a proposal regarding the Pluperfect. Examination of the non-Indicative Moods, Participles and Infinitives occurs in chapts. 7 and 8.

1. MARKEDNESSS AND THE STATIVE ASPECT. Greek realizes three aspectual choices as the result of two fundamental binary oppositions in its verbal network: the [+perfective] / [-perfective] (see chapts. 2 and 4), and the [+imperfective] / [+stative]. The first is broader, opposing the Aorist to the non-Aorist forms. On the basis of frequency of use, stem formation, history of the Greek verbal network, and most importantly aspectual meaning, the [+stative] can be established as the most heavily marked aspect (see Ruipérez, *Estructura*, 45-65; Lyons, *Introduction*, 314-15; Comrie,

Aspect, esp. 127, although their models seem to make the [+stative] / [-stative] opposition a broader choice).

a. Distributional markedness. The Perfect/Pluperfect forms display the least frequency of usage of the three tense forms. (Statistics alone are not a reliable method for determining markedness [Comrie, *Aspect*, 116-17], though in Greek, a language with clearly differentiated formal/morphological categories, they can serve as one of several criteria.) Trotter (*Use*, 34-49, esp. 45) has shown that a representative sampling from Greek writers evidences that Paul and the writer of Hebrews use the Perfect in terms of forms per line of text on a close par with Plato, while Luke displays very similar usage to that of Josephus and in some ways Thucydides.[1] A perusal of these classical and hellenistic writers confirms that the Perfect is clearly the least frequent of the tense forms. No argument for stylistic similarities is made here, except to assert that the range of usage of the Perfect in the NT falls generally within the same very broad parameters of usage as displayed by extra-biblical writers. Mandilaras (59-60) has shown from a slightly different perspective that the Perfect is quite clearly the least frequent of the tense forms in the papyri.

b. Material markedness. The Perfect has the most morphological bulk of all the tenses, because of its unthematic root, endings and reduplication. The unthematic root, without connecting vowel, already proved clumsy in pre-Homeric Greek and faded before the thematic root in all tenses except the Perfect. In the Perfect paradigm it remained, resulting in direct affixation of endings without a connecting vowel (Moulton/Howard, 183, 187-88, 220ff.). This is the bulkier and less smooth means of suffixed verb formation. Reduplication is not unique to the Perfect (cf. Present γιγνώσκω; Aorist ἤγαγον) but it is only in the Perfect that reduplication is integrally part of the

---

[1]Trotter's statistics reveal for example that Thucydides uses the Perfect approximately once every four lines of text sampled, while Plato once every sixteen lines. As Gildersleeve ("Stahl's Syntax," 395) says, "The perfect belongs to the drama, to the orators, to the dialogues of Plato" (see also Jelf, 2.60), thus perhaps accounting for Paul's and the writer of Hebrews's relative frequency of use in persuasive material, and the relative scarcity in the Gospel writers, who at least *prima facie* appear to be historical writers. This does not explain the comparatively frequent use of the Perfect in John's writings, especially the Gospel and 1 John, which do not conform to the statistics of classical or Septuagintal usage. This does not necessarily point to Semitic influence or even indirect Septuagintal influence (so Abbott, 325-27). See Chantraine, *Histoire*, 229-32, on the subjective nature of the Perfect and hence its suitability in rhetorical writing, including John. As Barr (*Semantics*, 240 n. 3) indicates, the aspectual meaning of the Perfect (as distinct from that of the Aorist) could only be approximated in Hebrew by "much circumlocution." For a discussion of the Perfect in John see Enslin ("Perfect Tense"), who claims that the Perfect is used aspectually correctly, though many Perfects were inserted later as "theological perfects." This latter claim is unsupportable. More reasonable is the claim by Chantraine (230) that John's style is "sontenus et solonnels" or "expressive."

stem (except for, e.g., οἶδα and ἥκω). The Perfect displays both major types of reduplication: reduplication of the entire syllable (e.g. ἀκήκοα, ἐλήλυθα, ἀπόλωλα, etc.) and reduplication of the initial consonant with ε (e.g. λέλοιπα, τέθεικα, ἔσχηκα; with variations on the rule for aspirates, rough breathing and other phenomena) (see Robertson, 362-64). A distinction is not made here between reduplication of the initial consonant with ι or ε as two separate types of reduplication.

    c. Implicational markedness. 1. Irregularities. The Perfect maintains a morphological regularity unknown in the other tenses. Whereas the Aorist and Present forms contend with thematic and nonthematic roots, with various kinds of augmentation or reduplication and suffixes, the Perfect simply affixes its endings to the very regular verb stem. (See Curtius, *Verb*, 354-436 [who specifically notes the formal distinctions between the Present/Aorist and Perfect tenses]; Brugmann, 372-80; Schwyzer, 1.764-79; Giles, *Philology*, 403ff., esp. 449-51, for discussion of the Perfect stem; and Goodwin, *Grammar*, 153-55, on morphological regularity of Pluperfect endings.) These endings have remained consistent regardless of whether the form is considered a 1 (κ) or 2 Perfect, except for reasonably slight variations such as the shift from the Attic endings of οἶδα (2d Person Singular οἶσθα and the Plurals ἴσμεν, ἴστε, ἴσασι[ν]), the adoption beginning in the 2d cent. B.C. of ‾αν as the 3d Person Plural Active ending following the Aorist (e.g. Acts 16:36; Rom 16:7; Luke 9:36; Col 2:1; Rev 21:6; 19:3; 18:3; John 17:6, 7; Moulton/Howard, 221; cf. also Jas 5:4 [B P] as a possibility; Mandilaras, 212-13; idem, "Confusion," 13-14; Mayser, 1, 2.84-85), and a few cases where the 2d Person Singular endings were changed to ‾ες (e.g. Rev 2:3; Moulton/Howard [221] also suggest Rev 2:5; 11:17; John 8:57; Acts 21:22; Mandilaras [210-11] claims to show evidence of "numerical superiority" for ‾ες in the papyri, though Mayser [1, 2.81-82] shows less evidence).

    2. Defectivation. The failure to maintain a full range of forms attests to the markedness of the Perfect. In the NT, the Perfect Subjunctive is only found ten times, the Imperative four times, and the Optative not at all. And the Pluperfect occurs only 86 times (see discussions below). The loss of the Optative is in keeping with the development of hellenistic Greek (contra Harry, "Perfect Forms," 55-57, but his figures are skewed by his method of analysis), but the Subjunctive and Imperative are also lacking. This is true of classical Greek as well, in which the Perfect Subjunctive Active was "rarely formed," more commonly occurring periphrastically, and the Middle/Passive was "almost always" realized by the periphrastic (the same can be said of the Perfect Optative). The Perfect Imperative Active is also "very rare" except in a few instances of μι verbs, again using periphrasis (Goodwin, *Grammar*, 159, 161, 163; Harry, "Perfect Subjunctive," 19 [1905] 347ff., 20 [1906] 100ff.; idem, "Perfect Forms," 53ff.; see my chapt. 10).

    d. Semantic markedness. The above morphological evidence points clearly to the Perfect as the most heavily marked form of the Greek verb, and clearly the more heavily marked in the [+imperfective] / [+stative] opposition.

As strong as this evidence is, it can be supplemented by functional evidence as well.

A surprisingly large degree of consistency can be found in definitions of the meaning of the Greek Perfect, i.e. definitions of its aspectual function. Before these are analysed more closely, it is helpful to turn to Ruipérez's reasons for distinguishing the Perfect as the marked term. He argues that the aspect expressed by this form is that of "resultant state," which he conveniently diagrams:

$$A \quad\underline{\quad\quad} B \ldots\ldots\ldots C \ldots\ldots$$

The Perfect, he claims, expresses state C resulting from action AB. The resultant state is different from the action itself, and in fact does not consider the event itself (*Estructura*, 45), no matter whether it is conceived of as perfective or imperfective. In a distinct way, therefore, the stative aspect is more complex than the other aspects, since it in effect subsumes either, or both, of the Present and Aorist, which again points to its markedness. E.g. X. Mem. 3.5.26: τί δέ; ἐκεῖνο ἀκήκοας. . . . τοῦτό γ', ἔφη, ἀκούω. . .(what is this? *Have you heard* that. . . . Indeed, he said, I have heard this).

Many scholars have claimed that as a result the Present and Aorist can be used where objectively the Perfect could be used. (See Ruipérez, *Estructura*, 45-47; Goodwin, *Syntax*, 5-6, on Present; 25, on Aorist; Schwyzer, 2.274-75, 287-88 [where he sees confusion between the Aorist and Perfect as a hellenistic development]; Gildersleeve, 87-88; 107-08 [where he posits this on the basis that many verbs do not have Perfect forms]; Jelf, 2.55-56, 63; Kühner/Gerth, 1.135-36, 167-68; Jannaris, 435, 437; Humbert, 135, on Present; Blass/Debrunner, ¶ 322, on Present; Burton, 9-10, 22; Turner, *Syntax*, 62, 72; Robertson, 881 [cf. 843-45, where he disagrees that an Aorist can substitute for a Perfect]; Moule, 13-15, on Aorist; Mayser, 2, 1.142-43.)[2] (1) Most scholars making such a claim, however, do so on the basis of *Aktionsart*, by which they interpret the lexical meaning of a given verb, especially one in the Present, as compatible with their idea of the Perfect meaning. As discussed in the introduction and chapt. 2, substitution does not entail complete synonymy, especially where substitution is from a different verbal paradigm. Hence this analysis neglects synthetic verbal aspect as a morphologically-based category, and provides no formal criteria for evaluation. (2) Later scholars argue this on the presupposition that the Perfect is declining in importance, especially in relation to the Aorist where the two are becoming virtually synonymous. This analysis is open to serious question, as is argued below.

In dealing with marked and unmarked categories of aspect, in some languages the unmarked terms have no specified semantic value (they exist in privative opposition with their marked terms) and are used both when there is no need for expression of an aspectual value and often in place of other expressed aspectual values. Such is not the case in Greek, however, where each aspect has distinct value, and markedness is a means of signifying semantic difference (see Zwicky, "On Markedness," esp. 140). However, a pattern does emerge where the less heavily

---

[2]Mandilaras (99-102, 162-65) seems to recognize the conflict between aspect and *Aktionsart*, though he opts for the latter cautiously; Moulton (141-48) is very cautious, recognizing with Mandilaras that only a few verbs--ἔχω, γίνομαι, λαμβάνω in Revelation--could possibly function as Perfects; and Winer (344) says baldly, "There is no passage in which it can be certainly proved that the aorist stands for the perfect." He does not entertain substitution for the Present either.

marked verbal form often follows the more heavily marked form in a parallel syntagmatic unit. There are several examples worth considering.

X. Mem. 3.5.26: τί δέ; ἐκεῖνο ἀκήκοας, ὅτι Μυσοὶ καὶ Πισίδαι ἐν τῇ βασιλέως χώρᾳ κατέχοντες ἐρυμνὰ πάνυ χωρία καὶ κούφως ὡπλισμένοι δύνανται . . . αὐτοὶ δὲ ζῆν ἐλεύθεροι; καὶ τοῦτό γ', ἔφη, ἀκούω (What? Have you heard that, that the M.s and P.s are able to live as freemen, possessing in the land of the king an entire fortified area? Indeed, he said, I have heard this), where the larger context makes a clear distinction between the more heavily marked Perfect being used by the questioner, and the less heavily marked Present by the answerer; cf. 3.5.25. Pl. Gorg. 503C: Θεμιστοκλέα οὐκ ἀκούεις ἄνδρα ἀγαθὸν γεγονότα . . . καὶ Περικλέα τουτονὶ τὸν νεωστὶ τετελευτηκότα, οὗ καὶ σὺ ἀκήκοας; (are you not in progress learning of T. who was a good man . . . and P. who has died recently in this way, whom indeed you have heard), where the Perfect emphasizes the state of Socrates being a personal auditor of Pericles; Plu. Marc. Cato 23.1: ταῦτα δ' οὐχ . . . Καρνεάδῃ δυσχεράνας ἔπραξεν, ἀλλ' ὅλως φιλοσοφίᾳ προσκεκρουκὼς καὶ πᾶσαν Ἑλληνικὴν μοῦσαν καὶ παιδείαν ὑπὸ φιλοτιμίας προπηλακίζων (he did these things not as personally ill-tempered things against C., but striking out wholly against philosophy and smearing all Greek culture and training on account of honour), where the second forms a sub-set of the first category; cf. 26.2. P.Teb. 56.5-8 (2d cent. B.C.): γείν[ωσ]κε δὲ / περὶ τοῦ κατακεκλῦσθαι τὸ πεδίον / ὑμῶν καὶ οὐκ ἔχομεν ἕως τῆς / τροφῆς τῶν κτηνῶν ἡμῶν (know that our plain stands flooded and we are not possessing so much as food for our cattle), where the plain's being flooded is the necessary precondition for not possessing any food (although the non-parallel use of the verb forms points away from substitution).[3]

In the NT see: Matt 8:14: Peter's mother in law is βεβλημένην καὶ πυρέσσουσαν (thrown down [on a bed] and feverish), with the more heavily marked preceding the less heavily marked tense; Luke 13:25: people shut out of the kingdom began ἑστάναι καὶ κρούειν (to stand and knock at) the door, with the more heavily marked Perfect used to describe the people's position and the less heavily marked their behaviour; John 3:29: the friend of the bridegroom is ὁ ἑστηκὼς καὶ ἀκούων αὐτοῦ (the one who stands and hears him) (Barrett [John, 223] contrasts attitude and action); John 6:36: ἑωράκατέ [με] καὶ οὐ πιστεύετε (you have seen [me] but not believed), where seeing is the auditor's state but believing is not what they are involved in; Acts 5:25: an informer tells the Jewish authorities that the men are ἑστῶτες καὶ διδάσκοντες (standing and teaching) in the temple, with it unclear why "standing" is here marked, unless it is part of the emphasis within this series of events upon the apostles standing on their own (v 20), defying the authorities and imprisonment (v 23, with the state of imprisonment contrasted). Col 1:23: Paul tells his readers to remain τεθεμελιωμένοι (grounded), steadfast, and not μετακινούμενοι (moved), where an adjective falls between Perfect and Present Participles; Col 2:6-7: Paul again tells his readers ἐν αὐτῷ περιπατεῖτε, ἐρριζωμένοι καὶ ἐποικοδομούμενοι ἐν αὐτῷ καὶ βεβαιούμενοι τῇ πίστει καθὼς ἐδιδάχθητε, περισσεύοντες ἐν εὐχαριστίᾳ (walk in him [Christ], being rooted and built up in him and established in the faith as you were taught, being rich in thanksgiving), where the Perfect Participle seems to serve as a headterm (the question of whether the Participles here are functioning like commands is a pragmatic and not a semantic one); 1 Tim 5:9: let widows be enrolled γεγονυῖα (being) 60 years of age and μαρτυρουμένη (being borne witness to) by good works, where age is the primary requirement; Titus 3:11: the author tells Titus that a man is divisive because he ἐξέστραπται (is perverted) and ἁμαρτάνει (sins), where perverted behaviour is seen to cause sin; 1 John 1:2: John says we ἑωράκαμεν (have seen) and μαρτυροῦμεν (bear witness) and ἀπαγγέλλομεν (announce) eternal life, with first-hand witness forming the basis for subsequent attestation (cf. 1 John 4:14). Smalley (John, 9) says the Participles "express in order the three ideas of experience, attestation and evangelism which form part of any genuine and lasting response to the gospel. Using again the theologically

---

[3]Cited by Mandilaras, 98; cf. "Confusion," 18, with examples, refuted by McKay, "Perfect . . . Non-Literary Papyri," 31-32. Few of the examples Mandilaras cites display the kind of opposition examined here, since he lets lexical meaning dictate verbal aspect.

significant notion of 'seeing,' as in v 1, with a similarly 'personal' implication, John stresses the reality of God's revelation in Christ." (Brown [*Epistles*, 167] imposes a time-based scheme on the Participles.) Rev 3:17: the message to Laodicea quotes them as saying "εἰμι (I am) rich, i.e. I πεπλούτηκα (have grown rich) and ἔχω (have) a need for nothing," where the Perfect and Present explain the initial statement. Cf. Lys. 12.100: ἀκηκόατε, ἑωράκατε, πεπόνθατε, ἔχετε (you have heard, you have seen, you have suffered, you have received [the accusations]). Rev 3:20: ἰδοὺ ἔστηκα ἐπὶ τὴν θύραν καὶ κρούω (behold I stand at the door and am knocking), with the Perfect taking the modifier; Rev 7:1: John says he saw four messengers ἑστῶτας (standing) upon the four corners of the earth and κρατοῦντας (grasping) the four winds. The existence of the Aorist Participle of ἵστημι (e.g. John 8:3) argues for the heavy markedness of the Perfect Participle.

The same opposition between more heavily marked and less heavily marked forms can be found between the Perfect and Aorist, though to a lesser degree, probably because the Aorist as the least heavily marked form is not so closely related semantically to the Perfect as is the Present. (This is not to be confused with what is often called the "perfective, effective or eggressive Aorist," a lexical/syntactical interpretation of use of a particular lexical item, which distorts the aspectual nature of the perfective aspect.)

Pl. Apol. 17A: Socrates says ὅ τι μὲν ὑμεῖς, ὦ ἄνδρες Ἀθηναῖοι, πεπόνθατε ὑπὸ τῶν ἐμῶν κατηγόρων, οὐκ οἶδα· ἐγὼ δ' οὖν καὶ αὐτὸς ὑπ' αὐτῶν ὀλίγου ἐμαυτοῦ ἐπελαθόμην· οὕτω πιθανῶς ἔλεγον. καίτοι ἀληθές γε ὡς ἔπος εἰπεῖν οὐδὲν εἰρήκασιν (in what way you, A. men, are/were affected by my accusers, I do not know, but I myself was made to forget by them for a little while; so persuasively were they speaking. And yet to state it plainly they spoke nothing of the truth), where the Perfects draw attention to the state of Socrates's auditors in relation to the charges brought, with the Aorist used of himself; Epict. 1.8.10: οὐχὶ δὲ πάντας τοὺς λόγους τούτους καταπατήσας ἐπηρμένος ἡμῖν καὶ πεφυσημένος περιπατεῖ μηδ' ἀνεχόμενος (does he not live, trampling down all these words, being suitably appointed for us and prideful, not being submissive), with the Aorist Participle referring to a specific response, while the Perfect Participles describe his state of appointment, and the negated Present Participle draws attention to a short-coming. Syntax as well as formal differences serves to distinguish the use of the tenses. P.Oxy. 1295.16-18 (2d/3d cent. A.D.): καὶ δήλωσόν μοι / πόσου χαλκοῦ δέδωκες αὐτῶι / καὶ εἰ ἐκομίσω τὸ ἱμάτιον (let me know how much money you have given him and whether you purchased the cloak), where in the context of the mother's letter to her son's guardian the receipt of the funds is the dominant concern (cited in Mandilaras, 162).

In the NT see: Mark 5:19: Jesus reportedly tells the demoniac to return and tell others of the things the lord σοι πεποίηκεν καὶ ἠλέησέν σε (has done for you and has been merciful to you), with the Perfect encompassing all of Jesus' acts, including his mercy. Taylor (*Mark*, 284) sees a deliberate change of form indicating that the distinction between the tenses was preserved in hellenistic Greek; cf. Moulton, 143. But on the basis of there being no evidence of a Perfect form of ἐλέω, Cranfield (*Mark*, 181-82) suggests similar reference of the Perfect and Aorist. Cranfield's is a difficult argument to support on the basis of the limited evidence available. John 3:32: John says that the one coming after him bears witness (μαρτυρεῖ) to ὃ ἑώρακεν καὶ ἤκουσεν (what he has seen and heard), with the Perfect used to describe the most significant process in relation to one coming from heaven (v 31) (see Blass/Debrunner, ¶ 342[2]; McKay, "Perfect . . . NT Greek," 319; contra Barrett, *John*, 225); cf. 1 John 1:3. John 8:38: "What I ἑώρακα (have seen) from the father I am speaking (λαλῶ); and therefore what you ἠκούσατε (have heard) from the father you are doing (ποιεῖτε)";[4] Acts 22:15: Paul, telling of his conversion, says that the voice told him he would be a witness to all men of the things you ἑώρακας καὶ ἤκουσας (have seen and heard). This use of the marked Perfect may be surprising in light of Paul's call to ministry by Christ, unless the author is emphasizing Paul's subsequent first-hand

---

[4]Barrett (*John*, 347) contrasts "the difference between the direct seeing of supernatural things which Jesus enjoys, and the hearing which is possible for men" as accounting for the minor textual variant of ἑώρακα for ἠκούσατε (p66 ℵ* D etc.).

acquaintance by sight with events surrounding testifying to Christ. Heb 2:14: the author says that since the children κεκοινώνηκεν (shared) in blood and flesh, Jesus likewise μετέσχεν (shared) in them, with the Perfect used to emphasize the common state of Christ and his followers; 2 Pet 2:21: Peter says it was better for some μὴ ἐπεγνωκέναι (not to understand) the way of righteousness than ὑποστρέψαι (to depart) from the holy commandment, with the Perfect used of the less desired state; 1 John 4:10: John says love is not that we ἠγαπήκαμεν (loved) God but that he ἠγάπησεν (loved)[5] us and ἀπέστειλεν (sent) his son as a ransom, again with the Perfect marking the process to be discounted (note use of contrasting pronouns); Rev 3:3: the message to Sardis is to remember how you εἴληφας καὶ ἤκουσας (received and heard) the message, cf. also Rev 5:7 and 8:5 (Chantraine, *Histoire*, 239: "Ces deux exemples sont particulièrement claire"); 11:17 (see Moulton, esp. 142-43; Robertson, 901, for instructive discussions; cf. Swete, *Apocalypse, loc. cit.*; and Thompson, *Apocalypse*, 44, who sees Semitic influence).

This is not a complete list but presents a number of the more important examples in confirmation of the Perfect as the marked member of the [+stative] / [-stative] opposition. Several lexical items recur in this list, indicating further that the distinction is one of lexis and not verbal semantics, since virtually every verb had a range of forms available; and the most convincing examples virtually always have the more heavily marked form preceding the less heavily marked, reinforcing the scheme of markedness according to the semantic hierarchy of tense forms. This is an understandable progression whereby the less heavily marked form is used in support of the more heavily marked. In no case is it convincing that the less heavily marked form causes the neutralization of the verbal aspect of the the more heavily marked form, as some grammarians posit (much of their argument is based on the traditional definition of the semantic meaning of the Perfect, discussed below). Neither formal criteria nor semantic criteria (often invoked on the basis of lexical or translational value) provide evidence for this. Although in certain cases the less heavily marked member of an opposition is able to function parallel to its more heavily marked member, the marked member virtually always serves as a focal item, with a few possible exceptions (see John 5:14; 2 Cor 3:12; Heb 2:14; Luke 9:45; John 1:32).

2. THE PERFECT AS STATIVE ASPECT. To formulate a more precise definition of the aspectual category realized by the Perfect, two definitions must be examined.

a. The first definition--by far the most widely known--usually entails a correlation of the Aorist and Present tenses or their conception of the action with a temporal assignment, and (though it need not) often introduces the difference between the subjective and resultative Perfect (see below). A well-formulated expression of this position is found in Turner (*Syntax*, 81ff.). In essential agreement are virtually all grammars (e.g. Jannaris, 438; Jelf, 2.59;

---

[5]Cf. textual variants with Perfect in B and some miniscules. It is to be rejected; contra Brown, *Epistles*, 518.

Kühner/Gerth, 1.146-50; Brugmann, 550-52; Schwyzer, 2.286-87; Stahl, 107; Goodwin, *Syntax*, 18; Smyth, 434-35; Gildersleeve, 98; Humbert, 147; Friedrich, "Theory," S16-17; Ruipérez, *Estructura*, esp. 62; Rijksbaron, 34; Mayser, 2, 1.176-77; Mandilaras, 221-28; Winer, 338; Moulton, 141; Blass/Debrunner, ¶ 340; Abel, 257; Moule, 13; Dana/Mantey, 200; Nunn, 70; Zerwick, ¶ 285).[6] Turner states:

> The *Aktionsart* belonging properly to the [Perfect] tense is either fulfilment in the present of a process begun in the past or else the contemplation of an event having taken place in the past with an interval intervening. . . . It is therefore a combining of the *Aktionsarten* of aorist and present. Originally it had no resultative force but simply expressed the subject's state; this had been arrived at by some previous activity, but the state arrived at was represented by the perfect as so permanent that the perfect can be said from long before the NT period to have present meaning. . . . the old intrans. perfect was giving way before the active, transitive and resultative pf. . . . and its meaning is difficult to distinguish from the aorist. (81-82, 83)

Not all grammars express the position in such detail, but resemble Blass/Debrunner, who say, "The perfect combines in itself, so to speak, the present and the aorist in that it denotes the *continuance* of *completed action*" (¶ 340).

(1) A response to this definition may be made at several levels. (a) It is argued throughout this work (see esp. chapts. 2 and 4) that Greek tenses are not primarily temporally-based. Therefore any theory of the semantics of the Perfect that depends upon the Aorist and Present as time-referring, or that posits a temporal scheme dependent upon posited temporal features, to establish a temporal framework for the Perfect cannot be formulated by definition. The major problem remaining for a theory of aspect of the Perfect is to account for uses of the Perfect in at least past and present-referring contexts, both of which are recognized by virtually all the grammarians cited above.

(b) When the aspectual model posited above is examined it becomes clear that there are significant examples it cannot explain adequately (see Louw, "Waarde," esp. 23-24). Blass/Debrunner argue that "a perfect like πεπληρώκατε Acts 5:28 may be resolved into ἐπληρώσατε καὶ νῦν πλήρης ἐστίν" (¶ 340), in which the state that arises continues on the object. (Blass/Debrunner [¶ 340] also claim that "before the form καθέστακα [I have placed] arose, the same idea was expressed by ἔχω [present] καταστήσας [aorist] [D. 19.288]"; see my chapt. 10.) This definition or a variant of it is contained in most grammars noted above. But the issue is clouded by imprecision. For example, Goodwin cites the example of γέγραφα: "I have written," that is "my writing is now finished" (*Syntax*, 18). Though he fails to distinguish whether the finished action resides with the subject or object, his example (though perhaps not as precise as possible) clearly indicates the object, certainly not the subject.

---

[6]Cf. Robertson, 892-902; and Burton, 37-38, who suggest this as the "usual force" (Robertson, 893) or "most frequent use" (Burton, 37) of the tense, though they describe several others as well, Robertson claiming, "No single graph for the perfect can therefore be made" (893). Briggs (*Significance*, 12-29) and Trotter (*Use*, 69-84) follow Robertson closely. A survey of the grammars above illustrates well Louw's point ("Waarde," 23) that the treatment of the Perfect in most grammars never goes beyond tabulation of the most frequently used contextual varieties of usage, with a traditional choice of a sort of basic meaning. Humbert (146-47) recognizes this difficulty, although he does the same.

As Louw indicates, this model may apply in certain contexts with a small number of lexical items, but certain kinds of verbs are not adequately treated. A significant example is the verb οἶδα. Moulton argues that οἶδα means "'I discovered (εἶδον) and still enjoy the results,' *i.e.* 'I know'" (109; cf. Brugmann, 551: "ich habe ausfindig gemacht und weiss nun"). But this is not the same as translating it as "I discovered x and now x is discovered," as Blass/Debrunner imply. In fact this translation makes nonsense of a good number of uses of οἶδα, where, as Louw argues, οἶδα means "I know," clearly indicating a state for the subject and the subject only.

Smyth (434) attempts to circumvent this difficulty by noting that "The effects of a completed action are seen in the resulting present state. The state may be that of the subject or of the object." But closer analysis of his examples supports the subjective interpretation: Aeschin. 2.4: ἐφοβήθην μὲν γάρ, καὶ ἔτι καὶ νῦν τεθορύβημαι, translated "I was struck with fear, and even at the present moment am still in a state of agitation." But the translation would better read "I was frightened and even now am agitated," retaining the passive sense, where it is clear that the state referred to is not that of the cause of fear but of the grammatical subject of the Passive verb, the agent being the cause of fear with "I" as its object (cf. other Perfect verbs in the section). See also Th. 1.144.1. The example from Aeschines informs X. Anab. 3.2.10: οἱ δὲ πολέμιοι . . . τὰς σπονδὰς . . . λελύκασιν, which Smyth translates "the enemy have broken the truce (which is now broken)," but is better glossed "the enemy have broken the truce and stand as truce-breakers." The inaccurate objective translation sheds no light on the subjective use Smyth posits. Two other examples are more problematic: X. Econ. 9.2: τὰ οἰκήματα ᾠκοδόμηται, is translated "the rooms have been constructed (their construction is finished)," but this is like the examples above, with the emphasis on the grammatical subject of the verb (object of the action), the rooms, with the agent not focused upon. D. 9.26: τὰς πόλεις αὐτῶν παρήρηται, is rightly translated "he has taken away (and still holds) their cities," which Smyth would call an objective case, although his translation rightly indicates emphasis upon the subject. His use of Pl. Charm. 176C (τί βουλεύεσθον ποιεῖν; οὐδέν, ἔφη ὁ Χαρμίδης, ἀλλὰ βεβουλεύμεθα) is again what he would call an objective use, although his translation is left ambiguous ("we have already conspired"), but the context reinforces that the subject is of interest, not the resulting conspiracy. The intransitive examples are consigned to the categories of "Perfect with Present Meaning" and "'Intensive' Perfect" (see [2] below).

Several illustrative examples with οἶδα in the NT include: Matt 21:27: the Jewish leaders are asked whether John the Baptist's authority was from heaven or earth and they answer οὐκ οἴδαμεν (we do not know), where emphasis is clearly upon the subjects, not their knowledge; cf. Matt 20:22. Matt 9:6: when the scribes question Jesus' healing of a paralytic he is quoted saying he has told them so that "εἰδῆτε [you might know] that the son of man has authority to forgive sins"; John 13:7: when Peter questions Jesus for washing his feet Jesus reportedly says, "What I am doing you οὐκ οἶδας ἄρτι [do not know now]"; John 16:30: Jesus' disciples are relieved because he is no longer teaching in parables, since they "are confident that now already, before the death and exaltation of Jesus, before the coming of the Spirit, they have reached the moment of knowledge" (Barrett, *John*, 497): νῦν οἴδαμεν ὅτι οἶδας πάντα (now we know that you know everything), with a contrast in the knowing subjects; Eph 1:18: Paul speaks of God enlightening his audience in order for them εἰδέναι [to know] the hope of their calling; cf. 1 Thess 5:12.

A significant example is the verb ἐλπίζω. ἤλπικα never indicates a state for an object, so the state referred to must continue on the subject and be translated "I have set my hope on = I hope." For example, in John 5:45 Jesus' adversaries are told that the one who accuses them is Moses, in whom ὑμεῖς ἠλπίκατε (you yourselves hope), with the pronoun reinforcing the subjective orientation; cf. 1 Cor 15:19 (see my chapt. 10). 2 Cor 1:10: Paul speaks of God unto whom ἠλπίκαμεν (we hope) that he still will rescue us; cf. 1 Tim 4:10; 5:5. 1 Tim 6:17: the author warns Timothy not to be proud (ὑψηλοφρονεῖν) nor ἠλπικέναι (to hope) upon the uncertainty of wealth. As a result of recognizing these difficulties some grammarians thus introduce a category of verbs called "present Perfects" or "intensive Perfects" that are so intractable for them that these verbs can never be understood according to the definition above indicating a state of the object as the result of a completed action, or even of an equivalent state of the subject. They are treated as being like Present verbs. (See e.g. Wackernagel, *Studien*; Schwyzer, 2.263;

Brugmann, 550; Stahl, 107-09; Kühner/Gerth, 1.148-49; Smyth, 434-35; Gildersleeve, 100-01; de Foucault, *Recherches*, 133. Some of the terminology differs here: e.g. Goodwin [*Syntax*, 15] includes under present Perfects verbs with continuing effect, regardless of whether a past event can be referred to, whereas others distinguish those verbs without reference to a past event.) Examples found in NT and other Greek include the following (many others may be cited from the grammars).

γέγονα (be, become): Matt 1:22; Luke 14:22; John 1:3, 15; 14:22; Rom 16:7; 2 Cor 1:19; Heb 11:3; Rev 16:17; D.S. 16.1.6; Str. 2.5.35; P.Oxy. 743.41 (2 B.C.); P.Cairo Zen. 59426.2-3 (260-50 B.C.) (Edgar/Hunt 91); P.Lond. 405.6 (A.D. 346).

δέδεκα (receive): Acts 8:14: the Jerusalem apostles heard that the Samaritans δέδεκται (received) the word of God; Hom Od. 7.72; Il. 4.4, 107; 5.228; 8.296; 10.62; A. Eum. 894; Theoc. 25.228.

ἔγνωκα (know): John 5:42; 6:69, cf. πεπιστεύκαμεν (we believe); 1 John 4:16; John 8:52: where the Jews say to Jesus, νῦν ἐγνώκαμεν (now we know) that you have a demon; John 17:7; 8:55; 1 Cor 2:8, 11, cf. οἶδα; 8:2; 1 John 2:3-4, 13-14; 3:6, cf. ἑώρακεν (he has seen), 16; 2 John 1.

εἴωθα (be accustomed): Matt 27:15; Mark 10:1; Luke 4:16; Acts 17:2; Hom. Il. 5.766; 8.408; Ar. Eccl. 282; P.Giess. 80.6 (2d cent. A.D.) (Edgar/Hunt 116).

ἔοικα (be like): Jas 1:6, 23: in two timeless statements James says that: the one who doubts ἔοικεν (is like) the wave of the sea; and one who hears but does not do ἔοικεν (is like) a man who sees his face in a mirror but forgets it when turning away; Hom. Il. 11.613; Od. 1.208; 17.500; Pl. Lach. 193D; Rep. 584D; Crat. 437A; Phaed. 62D; D. 2.1; J. Ag. Ap. 2.124, 173; Jew. War 1.392 *passim* (ὡς ἔοικεν); Plu. Marc. Cato 23.3; P.Oxy. 899.18 (A.D. 200).

ἑστάναι (stand): e.g. Matt 6:5: those who pray are not to be like hypocrites who love to pray ἑστῶτες (standing); Luke 1:11: while Zacharias was in the temple an angel of the Lord appeared (ὤφθη) to him ἑστώς (standing) on the right side of the altar; cf. Heb 10:11. Luke 13:25; Acts 25:10: Paul claims his right as a Roman citizen to stand (ἑστώς εἰμι) upon Caesar's judgment; among many others.

ἥγημαι (think): Acts 26:2: Paul tells Agrippa that he considers (ἥγημαι) himself fortunate to be giving his defence before him (Blass/Debrunner, ¶ 341; contra Bruce, *Acts*, 440); Phil 3:7; Hdt. 1.126.6; 2.40.1; 2.115.6; Pl. Tim. 19E.

κέκραγα (shout):[7] John 1:15: John bore witness concerning the logos and κέκραγεν (cried) saying that he was the one he spoke of;[8] Aeschin. 3.218; Ar. Wasps 415; S. Fr. 208; Aj. 1236; A. Prom. 743; D. 18.199; Men. Samia 11; Epict. 1.16.11.

κέκρικα (judge): John 16:11; Acts 16:15; 20:16; 1 Cor 5:3; 7:37; Titus 3:12; Ar. Birds 1521; Hom. Il. 10.417; Od. 13.182; Pi. Nem. 4.1; E. Supp. 969; Hdt. 3.31.3; 7.16.a.

μέμνημαι (remember): 1 Cor 11:2; 2 Tim 1:4: Paul says he remembers (μεμνημένος) Timothy's tears.

---

[7]Louw ("Waarde," 23-24) also cites βέβρυχε (bellow) in Hom. Od. 12.242 (some texts have the Pluperfect ἐβέβρυχει); cf. also Il. 17.264; Od. 5.412; S. Trach. 1072.

[8]Contra McKay, "Perfect . . . NT Greek," 328: "The single occurrence in John 1:15 of κέκραγεν is insignificant in relation to the use of the perfect generally in the NT: it is a survival of what was already a rare and anomalous survival in Homeric times, and the problem it poses is simply why this archaism should be used at this point." But the persistence of the form, as well as others with similar usage, makes it more than an anomaly. Cf. Barrett's (*John*, 167) enigmatic comments: "The tenses are remarkable. The perfect κέκραγεν is used with the force of a present. . . ." With Present forms (κράζω, etc.) in use, it is difficult to argue that κέκραγεν is a 'historic' Present (Blass/Debrunner, ¶ 321), in spite of the reduplicated Aorist ἐκέκραξα (Acts 24:21; cf. ¶¶ 75, 101). There appears to be confusion over form and function (¶ 341).

μέμυκα (initiate): Phil 4:12: in a series of clauses with Perfect verbs, Paul says μεμύημαι (I know the secret) of being well fed and hungry, of being rich and lacking; Hes. Works 508; Ar. Frogs 158, 456; Hdt. 2.51.2; Pl. Gorg. 497C.

πεπαλαίωκα (make old): Heb 8:13: when saying "new," it πεπαλαίωκεν (renders obsolete) the first (covenant), cf. Present; Hp. Art. 7; SB 5827.11 (69 B.C.).

πέποιθα (trust): Matt 27:43; Luke 20:6; Rom 2:19; 8:38; 14:14; 2 Cor 1:9; 10:7; Gal 5:10; Phil 2:24; 2 Thess 3:4; Heb 6:9.

σεσίγηκα (be still): Rom 16:25: Paul speaks of the μυστεηρίου χρόνοις αἰωνίοις σεσιγημένου (mystery silent in ages past).

τέθνηκα (be dead): Matt 2:20; Mark 15:44; Luke 7:12; 8:49; John 11:44: Lazarus, ὁ τεθνηκώς (the one dead), came out of the tomb; John 19:33; Acts 14:19; Acts 25:19: Festus explains that Paul was accused of something concerning Ἰησοῦ τεθνηκότος, ὃν ἔφασκεν ὁ Παῦλος ζῆν (dead Jesus, whom Paul said was alive); 1 Tim 5:6.

This list could be expanded but the point is well enough made if it is stressed that the standard definition of the aspectual function of the Perfect leaves large numbers of Greek verbs inadequately explained and hence forces grammars to introduce inadequate descriptive categories. Many grammarians admit to these examples, recognizing that they lack evidence of a continuum between event and result. (See e.g. Mandilaras, 222, 224-27; Schwyzer, 2.286-88; Jannaris, 438; Humbert, 148; Goodwin, *Syntax*, 19; Winer, 342-43; Burton, 37, 39-40; Moulton, 143-48; Robertson, 894-95, 898-902; Blass/Debrunner, ¶¶ 341, 343; Abel, 257-58. Others dispute this: e.g. Jelf, 2.60-61.) Most of these grammarians also claim that certain verbs always function in this way. For example, Turner (*Syntax*, 82) lists οἶδα, ἕστηκα, πέποιθα, κεῖμαι, μέμνημαι, τέθνηκα, πέπεισμαι, ἤλπικα, ἤγημαι, κέκραγα, ὄλωλα, πέφηνα, εἴωθα in the NT and papyri (Jannaris [438] gives a similar list for classical Greek).

Unfortunately this is not an adequate explanation for two reasons. (1) It does not explain the semantic category grammaticalized by the Greek Perfect. (2) There are many other examples of verbs that do not seem to show result: e.g. John 11:27: when Jesus asks Martha if she believes (πιστεύεις [v 26]), she answers ἐγὼ πεπίστευκα (I indeed believe) that you are the Christ (Kühner/Gerth [149] cite πεπιστευκότα in D. 37.48). Cf. John 6:69, where Barrett (*John*, 306), calling John's use of πεπίστευκα "characteristic," renders the verbs "we are in a state of faith and knowledge; we have recognized the truth and hold it." The second half is unnecessary. John 14:29: Jesus reportedly warns his disciples that he is leaving and says, "νυν εἰρηκα [now I tell] you before it happens." It could be argued that this refers to a recent past event: "Now I have told you," but the point would not appear to be the one being made in this context (cf. Plb. 6.4.6); cf. John 16:1, 4, 6 with λελάληκα. Rev 19:3: the narrator describes several voices calling out and in v 3 the second εἴρηκαν (speaks) a message (the first and third are introduced with Present Participles). John 20:17: Jesus tells Mary at the tomb that οὔπω . . . ἀναβέβηκα [I am not ascended] to the father (cf. P.Oxy. 1155.3-4 [A.D. 104] with ἐπιβέβη/κα); Acts 7:56: Stephen looks up and exclaims that he sees τοὺς οὐρανοὺς διηνοιγμένους (the open heavens); Acts 14:16: Paul proclaims that God permitted all the nations to go their own way ἐν ταῖς παρῳχημέναις γενεαῖς (in the past generations) (Bruce [*Acts*, 283] cites a parallel in J. Ant. 8.12.3); 2 Cor 7:14: εἴ τι αὐτῷ ὑπὲρ ὑμῶν κεκαύχημαι οὐ κατῃσχύνθην (if I boast in anything to him on behalf of you I am not ashamed); Gal 5:11: after dismissing charges that he is preaching circumcision, Paul affirms that in this way the scandal of the cross κατήργηται (stands abolished). Betz (*Galatians*, 269) says that v 11b is the "end and conclusion to the discussion on circumcision (5:2-12)," making the Perfect appropriate as a marked summary term. Heb 7:6: Melchizedek, the author says, δεδεκάτωκεν (tithed) Abraham, though he was not genealogically related and εὐλόγηκεν (blessed) the one possessing the promise; cf. v 10 (see Weymouth, "Rendering," 168). Heb 8:5: when Moses was intending to build the temple, he κεχρημάτισται (was instructed) to follow a particular pattern; Heb 11:17: by faith Abraham προσενήνοχεν (offered up) Isaac as a sacrifice. Matt 3:2 par. Mark 1:15; Matt 4:17; 10:7; Luke 10:9, 11: all these passages speak of the kingdom coming near (ἤγγικεν); Matt 26:45, 46 par. Mark 14:42: Jesus tells his sleeping disciples that his hour/betrayer ἤγγικεν (is come); cf. Luke 21:8. Rom 13:12: Paul says that the night is cut short and the day ἤγγικεν (is come), so put away works of darkness; Jas 5:8: James tells his readers that the coming of the lord ἤγγικεν (has arrived) (Adamson [*James*, 191] claims that the "tense of the verb indicates that the coming is near." Does he not mean the lexical meaning of the verb?).

(c) Many Perfect forms do not conform to the temporal pattern referred to by grammarians, but seem to be used contextually in a variety of ways: including past, future, omnitemporal and timeless, besides present, reference. A list of examples is given below. Several grammarians recognize that the standard conception of the Perfect tense as temporally based is not an adequate model in all instances and have offered varying explanations. For example, Winer (341-43) recognizes an overlap between the Perfect and Aorist usage, noting that both can in certain instances have present reference, but he disputes heavily any future reference of the Perfect except in conditional statements (see below and chapt. 6), disputing John 5:24; 17:10; 14:7 in particular. A second response, made by scholars like Mandilaras (222-28), Robertson (892ff.), and Burton (37ff.), is to cite the standard definition as the predominant use but then to refer to other uses-- stative, past, future, timeless, iterative--as unusual or ancient/original uses. It is commendable that these grammarians recognize the diversity of usage of the Perfect, but unfortunate that they do not push their categories further. The third response, by Turner (*Syntax*, esp. 81, 85), is to minimize the perseverance of the Perfect and its aspectual function in the NT era, except for a few stereotyped forms. Turner raises here an issue of great importance, since the ancient Perfect has in fact become obsolete in modern Greek (see below).

b. From discussion above, several facts become evident. (1) Any conception of the Perfect function cannot be essentially temporally based, not only since the analogy of the Aorist and Present tenses cannot hold (see chapts. 2 and 4), but since the Perfect itself functions in a variety of temporal contexts (see below). Robertson ponders the question of temporal reference of the Perfect, but he begins with the assumption that it is present-referring, though he admits this cannot be the case with the Subjunctive, Imperative, Infinitive and Participle. He concludes, "Perhaps at first it was just the perfect tense . . . and was timeless" (894).

(2) Since the time-based conception has inadequate explanatory powers, another proposal must be found which not only is able to encompass the range of pragmatic contextual usage but which unifies these at the level of semantics. Whereas some uses of the Perfect may seem to depict the result of a past act, others seem to convey only that of the state or condition without its antecedent event. Burton describes this as "when the attention is directed wholly to the present resulting state, the past action of which it is the result being left out of thought." He cites Matt 27:43; 1 Cor 11:2; Luke 24:46; Rev 19:13 (37), several of which are cited above. One must wonder, however, how many of the examples so often cited as clear indicators of the traditional understanding are not based upon the interpreter's wanting to see such a conception on the basis of a preconceived definition.

(3) The Perfect itself gives no formal criteria for distinguishing these several temporal and conceptual differences. Burton recognizes this when he says,

> There is no sharp line of distinction between the Perfect of completed Action and the Perfect of Existing State. To the latter head are to be assigned those instances in which the

past act is practically dropped from thought, and the other turned wholly to the existing result; while under the former head are to be placed those instances in which it is evidenced that the writer had in mind both the past act and the present result. (38)

Though he overstates the case, the essence of his argument is sound: the differentiation of Perfect uses is not formal but pragmatic, on the basis of temporal implicature and lexis.

On the basis of these factors, several grammarians have posited a conception of the Perfect that they claim is able to unify these several functions into a conceptual whole. Chantraine says, "Les grammarians anciens ont bien défini la valeur originale du parfait. Ce thème exprime 'τὸ παρακείμενον.' Le rôle propre du parfait est d'exprimer l'*état*" (*Histoire*, 4 and *passim* [he quotes Dionysius Thrax, Uhlig ed., 53]; later he emphasizes that this state is present [13, 16-20, 20]). McKay clarifies this (146), his definition forming the basis for discussion in his several articles on the Perfect (see bibliography; cf. Louw, "Waarde," 31):

The perfect tense expresses the state or condition of the subject of the verb mostly in present time, but also without specific time reference, and in some circumstances . . . with an added strong reference to a past event. In fact, it applies the state principle of the perfect aspect . . . to present time, timeless situations, extensions from past to present, and the implications of future reference. . . .

Hence the Perfect is best described as the stative aspect.

Several issues must be clarified. (1) The temporal functions described by McKay are very similar to those of the imperfective aspect and perfective aspect, as McKay recognizes. As established already, however, the verbal system in Greek is not essentially temporally based, i.e. many different forms can be used in similar temporal contexts, so this overlap does not neutralize differences among the aspects, but in fact the use of discrete forms with similar temporal reference points to a distinction in verbal aspect, in which the Perfect is the most heavily marked formally and semantically. Zerwick (¶ 288) summarizes this nicely: "It is to be noted that the choice between aorist and perfect is not determined by the objective facts, but by the writer's wish to connote the special nuance of the perfect; if this be not required, the aorist will be used."

(2) The Perfect grammaticalizes the speaker's conception of the verbal process as a state or condition. Louw, using formal data that he claims show that the Present and Aorist are similar but distinct from the Perfect, argues that this formal distancing (this evidence is not unambiguous) is related to a functional aspectual distancing (see also Collinge, "Reflexions," 95-96). The formulation of the aspect shows that the stative is distanced from the action

itself in its conception of the event, unlike the perfective and imperfective. This distancing of action from the "sprecksituasie" ("conversation situation," as he calls it) brings the verbal aspect into focus as the one concerned with an entire state. The result is that the Perfect gives "the appearance of something precisely more emphatic than the aorist. The perfect awakes therefore the impression as though it were more pertinent" ("Waarde," 27, 29). As Louw says,

> Die Griekse Perfektum, wat ook morfonolgies skerp van die ander sg. tempora afwyk, distansieer hom nie net van die spreeksituasie alleen nie, maar ook van die gebeure self soos sy aspek, wat tradisioneel *toestand* genoem word, maar wat juister met die term *statief* omskryf kan word, duidelik na vore bring. Met *statief* word bedoel dat *nie die gebeure' nie, maar die 'saak' as voldonge gestel word*. Hier lê die eintlike verskil t.o.v. die tradisionele definisie nl. voortduur van 'n afgehandelde *handeling*. In die begrip *statief* wat dui op die saak wat as voldonge gestel word, lê die kern van die Perfektum se semantiese vlak, en taalentiteite moet immers semanties gedefinieer word. Hierdie vlak dui op die *betekenis-inhoud*; en dit is nie dieselfde as die *betekenisgebruik* nie. (27)[9]

In Luke 8:49, a servant says to the leader of the synagogue, τέθνηκεν ἡ θυγάτηρ σου (your daughter is in a state of death). This is to be contrasted with e.g. Luke 8:42, where Jairus reportedly asks Jesus to heal his daughter, whom the author says ἀπέθνῃσκεν (was dying), and 1 Thess 4:14, where Paul says Jesus ἀπέθανεν (died) and rose (ἀνέστη), and Mark 5:35 (parallel) with the Aorist also. (Fitzmyer [*Luke*, 1.748] says that Luke improves Mark's Greek by using the Perfect instead of the Aorist. Is this true?) Likewise in 2 Cor 2:13 Paul says οὐκ ἔσχηκα ἄνεσιν τῷ πνεύματί μου (I was not in the state of having, i.e. possessing, rest in my spirit), while I was not able to find Titus (cited by many grammarians as illustrating the aoristic Perfect: Blass/Debrunner, ¶ 343[2]; Moulton, 145; Moule, 14; Burton, 39; contra Robertson, 900-01). In contrast, see 2 Cor 6:10, where after a startling display of contrasts using imperfective verbs, Paul sees his progress ὡς λυπούμενοι ἀεὶ δὲ χαίροντες, ὡς πτωχοὶ πολλοὺς δὲ πλουτίζοντες, ὡς μηδὲν ἔχοντες καὶ πάντα κατέχοντες (as mourning but always rejoicing, as obtaining nothing but securing all things); and Gal 4:22, where Paul says Ἀβραὰμ δύο υἱοὺς ἔσχεν (A. had two sons).

The Perfect is used to grammaticalize a state of affairs, the Present a process in progress, and the Aorist a process seen as complete, with the Perfect the most heavily marked. As Louw ("Waarde," 29) states: "Die dien veral om

---

[9]"The Greek Perfect, which also differs sharply morphologically from the other so-called tempora, does not simply distance it from the conversation situation but also from the events themselves so that it brings aspect, which is traditionally called *state*, but which could better be described by the term *stative*, clearly to the fore. By *stative* I mean that *not the events but the whole affair is established as completed*. Here lies the essential difference with regard to the traditional definition, namely continuance of a completed *action*. In the concept *stative* which points to the whole affair, established as complete, there lies the nucleus of the semantic level of the perfect, and linguistic entities must of course be defined semantically. This level points to the *semantic content*; and this is never the same as the *meaning usage*." A similar conclusion is reached by Collinge ("Reflexions," 95-96) in his historical reconstruction of the evolution of the tense forms in Greek, when he says that "The perfect (set apart by stem metaphony and internal apophony and special endings) denoted simple state, but presupposed a completed process, as against the uncompleted process of the present."

die Perfektum die skyn van iets net amfatieser as die Aoristus te gee" (This serves first and foremost to give the Perfect the appearance of something precisely more emphatic than the aorist).

(3) While there may be reference to a previous act that results in a state or condition, this is a matter of lexis in context. The aspect itself merely represents the state or condition of the grammatical subject, as conceptualized by the speaker or writer. Several authors have been concerned to differentiate the major lexical categories of Greek verbs. For example, Ruipérez designates transformational and non-transformational semantemes on the basis of whether there is modification in the state (*Estructura*, 49-59). He argues that the transformational semantemes evidence the resultive use of the Perfect and the non-transformational the purely stative. This is unhelpful. (i) Ruipérez claims that whether a verb is transformational or non-transformational can only be determined by its use in the Present Indicative, the neutral aspect. But the Present is not aspectually neutral (see chaps. 1 and 2). (ii) He admits that a single verb can present different meanings belonging to different categories on the basis of the conceptual content of the semanteme. In other words an individual verb, despite its one form, may really be several different semantemes. This is undoubtedly true, but this is not a grammatical but purely lexical distinction that cannot be made on principled linguistic grounds, since all verbal meanings are realized by the same form. (See chapt. 1 for further comments.) Rijksbaron, McKay and Wilkinson differentiate what they call dynamic/terminative/action verbs and stative verbs. Rijksbaron claims the former display what might be called resultive qualities while the latter are pure states or intensive Perfects (34-36; Ruipérez [*Estructura*, 51] is correct that reference to the intensive Perfect is purely subjective on the part of the interpreter). On the other hand McKay and Wilkinson assert the opposite, that the stative verbs "denote a state consequent on the aoristic action of the verb" (McKay, 139-40; Wilkinson, *"Aspect,"* chapt. 1). This differentiation also appears to be based on lexis and not formal grammatical categories.

c.   **Conclusion.** It is appropriate to reassert that the Perfect grammaticalizes the state or condition of the grammatical subject as conceived by the speaker. Whether a previous event is alluded to or exists at all is a matter of lexis in context and not part of aspectual semantics. Such a determination is in effect concerned with the objective nature of an event (*Aktionsart*--see chapt. 1), but aspect is concerned with the subjective conception of a process. Therefore, the objective nature of the event itself-- whether it has durative, punctiliar, or iterative value--does not come into semantic consideration. (See Ruipérez, *Estructura*, 47, and 62, 63, for diagrams that illustrate the relation of aspect to objective events.

3. PRAGMATIC USAGE OF THE STATIVE ASPECT. The configuration of pragmatic usage is very similar to that suggested for the perfective/imperfective verbal aspects. The two major categories are those that are deictically limited and not-limited. Under the deictically not-limited is included timeless usage, which includes various sub-categories (e.g. conditional sentences, see chapt. 6). These are noted only where appropriate. Deictically limited usage includes omnitemporal and temporal categories, the latter including past, present and future reference. All of these categories are represented in extra-biblical Greek (see esp. Schwyzer, 2.287-88; Kühner/Gerth, 1.147ff.; Goodwin, *Syntax*, 53-54 [esp. 'gnomic' usage]; Gildersleeve, 98ff.; Stahl, 108ff.). This eliminates one of Chantraine's (*Histoire*, 13, *passim*) major arguments for the decline of the Perfect in later Greek, i.e. that it only refers to a present state, although he recognizes the narrative use in the NT (239; see below).

a. Past.[10] Since the Perfect is often called a present-referring tense form, it is beneficial to concentrate first upon past usage. The Perfect may be used in a past context, often parallel with other past-referring verb forms. In the historical books a number of examples of past implicature may be cited. These quite often appear in narrative or with clear person deixis. Winer notes specifically that the simple Perfect, therefore, may function in an identical context as the Pluperfect, the remote form (342, paralleled in all periods of ancient Greek usage). Since the Pluperfect is the more heavily marked form of the two this is understandable. A representative number of the more important examples is cited, though other examples may be posited, since temporal reference in Greek is by implicature on the basis of deixis, not tense form. (See Papanikolaou, "Narrative Perfect," who argues for synonymy between the Aorist and Perfect. This is unconvincing, simply because of the co-existence of the two [plus others, such as the Imperfect] past-referring tenses over the course of several centuries. Aspectual reasons, however, can account for their difference; cf. A. Buttmann, 196-97.) Besides several of the examples cited above, the following may be cited.

---

[10]E.g. Isoc. 8.19: ὁ . . . πόλεμος ἁπάντων ἡμᾶς τῶν εἰρημένων ἀπεστέρηκεν· καὶ γὰρ πενεστέρους πεποίηκε καὶ πολλοὺς κινδύνους ὑπομένειν ἠνάγκασε καὶ πρὸς τοὺς Ἕλληνας διαβέβληκε καὶ πάντας τρόπους τεταλαιπώρηκεν ἡμᾶς (the war has robbed us of all the things spoken of; for it has made us poorer and compelled us to endure many dangers and it slandered us to the Greeks and it made us humbler in all ways); X. Anab. 1.4.8: ἀπολελοίπασιν ἡμᾶς Ξενίας καὶ Πασίων (X. and P. have deserted us); Plb. 3.1.1: τρίτῃ . . . ταύτης ἀνώτερον βύβλῳ δεδηλώκαμεν (in the third book before this one we made clear; cf. 4.1.1 with ἐδηλώσαμεν [Hultsch (*Zeitformen*, 460) recognizes a distinction between the Aorist and Perfect in Polybius]); 3.111.3ff.; 12.25 for extended narration; Arr. 1.23.5: τὰς ἄκρας ἃς οἵ τε Πέρσαι καὶ οἱ μισθοφόροι κατειλήφεσαν (the heights which the P.s and the mercenaries had seized); Plu. Marc. Cato 10.4: ὅσα πέπωκεν ἢ βέβρωκε (whatever he drank or ate). See below also.

Matt 19:8, where Jesus reportedly asks if ἀπ' ἀρχῆς . . . οὐ γέγονεν οὕτως (it was not thus from the beginning) with the Jews (cf. Plu. Marc. Cato 8.5: σωφροσύνη γεγόνασι μεγάλοι [by self-control they became great]); 21:4; 26:56.

Mark 5:33: Mark narrates that the woman healed of her flow of blood knew ὃ γέγονεν αὐτῇ (what had happened to her); cf. Mark 9:21, where any other than past implicature makes nonsense of the question, "at what time was (ἐστίν) it ὡς τοῦτο γέγονεν αὐτῷ;" (that this occurred to him?). Mark 16:4: when the two Marys arrived at the tomb they saw (θεωροῦσιν) that the stone ἀποκεκύλισται (had been rolled away). Taylor (Mark, 605) calls the use "vivid." The Perfect is clearly marked. Mark 15:44: Pilate marvelled (ἐθαύμασεν) that Jesus ἤδη τέθνηκεν (was already dead) and asked (ἐπηρώτησεν) a centurion if Jesus had died (ἀπέθανεν) long ago. This example could qualify as one where the unmarked Aorist is used parallel to a Perfect (contra e.g. Cranfield, Mark, 462; Taylor, Mark, 600, who contrast the tenses according to traditional differentiation).

Luke 1:22: when Zacharias emerged from performing his ritual, the people immediately recognized that he ἑώρακεν (had seen) a vision in the temple. This example serves well to illustrate both past implicature of the Perfect, and its stative verbal aspect emphasizing a state or condition regardless of its preceding act. Zacharias was in the state then (there is no need to posit a continuing result of seeing) of having seen the vision; cf. Luke 9:36. Luke 17:10: this example illustrates the importance of context in determining temporal implicature. If the response of the servants is purely hypothetical then a timeless descriptive use is the most convincing interpretation. If the response is seen as the servants' direct response to a set of events hypothesized as now accomplished, then past reference may be implicated: ὃ ὠφείλομεν ποιῆσαι πεποιήκαμεν (what we were obligated to do we have done); cf. John 13:12. Luke 24:29: the two travellers to Emmaus beg Jesus to stay with them, since κέκλικεν ἤδη ἡ ἡμέρα (the day was already set).

John 1:3, 15: in his syntactically simple prologue, John uses the Greek tenses masterfully. In v 3 he shifts from reference to the act of creation (ἐγένετο, cf. vv 1, 2) to the state of creation (γέγονεν) (on whether ὃ γέγονεν is best linked with v 3 or v 4 see Schnackenburg [John, 1.239-40]). In v 15 temporal implicature is clearer on the basis of more explicit deicitic indicators. John the Baptist says that the word which became flesh (v 14) was the one he spoke/speaks of: the one who came after existed (γέγονεν) before him (ἔμπροσθέν μου); cf. John 1:30. John 1:32: John again testifies; τεθέαμαι (I saw) the spirit descending on Jesus; John 2:10: the steward calls to the groom at the wedding of Cana and makes first a timeless statement that every man serves the good wine first but that you (person deixis) τετήρηκας (have kept) the good wine ἕως ἄρτι (until now), with the implication that the keeping was in the past but the serving of it is present. John 3:26: John's disciples came to him and asked about the one ᾧ σὺ μεμαρτύρηκας (to whom you bore witness). While this may have present implicature, its context in discussion of what John had done previously on the other side of the Jordan points to past reference. This is confirmed in the disciples' surprise that this one from the past is now so active; cf. John 5:33. John 6:32: Jesus responds to the multitude by denying that Moses οὐ . . . δέδωκεν (did not give) to them the bread from heaven. The following descriptive statements might implicate timeless use, especially in a negative sentence, but the person deixis seems to implicate reference to the past state. Brown (John, 1.262) treats the Perfect here as a past tense; contra Barrett, John, 290. Cf. John 7:19, 22. Cf. Apollod. 1.1.7: Ῥέα δὲ λίθον σπαργανώσασα δέδωκε Κρόνῳ καταπιεῖν (but R., wrapping a stone in swaddling clothes, gave it to C. to swallow); 1.9.12: Melampus ἐπὶ ἡμέρας δέκα δέδωκε πιεῖν (gave it for ten days to drink). John 8:57: the Jews question Jesus' reference to Abraham rejoicing when he saw Jesus' day, establishing temporal reference through person deixis and saying πεντήκοντα ἔτη οὔπω ἔχεις καὶ Ἀβραὰμ ἑώρακας; (you are not 40 and you saw Abraham?). This text consciously exploits verbal aspect. The fact that the Jews question whether Jesus could see Abraham, using the Perfect, shows that they do not treat it as having continuing results. They are concerned with the apparent historical discrepancy between Jesus and Abraham in age; cf. John 9:29; 20:18, 25. John 11:34: in the narrative, Jesus asks ποῦ τεθείκατε αὐτόν; (where did you put him?). Jesus is not inquiring about any continuing effect on Mary and Martha but about the place where they laid the body. John 12:29: when the voice came from heaven the crowd standing there (ἑστώς) were of mixed feelings on its origins (cf. ἀκούσας [heard]). Some claimed βροντὴν γεγονέναι (thunder clapped) and others that an angel λελάληκεν (spoke). In either case the narrative has past implicature. John 16:28: whereas many comparisons between Jesus and his father cannot be temporally constricted (e.g. John 18:37), in this instance a profitable contrast is made between Jesus' coming from the father (ἐξῆλθον) with his entrance into the world (ἐλήλυθα εἰς τὸν κόσμον), with the marked Perfect used of his entrance. John 19:28: Jesus, εἰδώς (in a state of knowledge) that ἤδη πάντα τετέλεσται (everything was already fulfilled), reportedly said that he was thirsty, with the Perfect Indicative capturing the state of fulfilment that preceded and allowed Jesus' death.

Acts 6:11: in a concerted effort to convict Stephen, men were brought to make false charges, claiming ἀκηκόαμεν (we heard) him saying blasphemous words against Moses and God; cf. Acts 6:14. Acts 7:35: Stephen, in giving his accusers a brief history lesson, speaks of Moses, Israel's leader and redeemer, as one whom God ἀπέσταλκεν (sent). Moulton (144) debates how to understand this Perfect, but a past sense seems appropriate. Acts 8:14: the apostles, when they heard (ἀκούσαντες preceding the main Aorist verb) that the Samarians δέδεκται (had received) the word of God, sent Peter to them; Acts 9:17: Ananias tells Paul that God ἀπέσταλκεν (had sent) him, referring back to vv 10ff.; Acts 10:45: all the Jewish Christians were astonished because the gift of the holy spirit ἐκκέχυται (had been poured out) on Gentiles. The astonishment, described using an Aorist (ἐξέστησαν), is overshadowed by the cause, using the more heavily marked Perfect. Acts 13:33: Paul says ὅτι ταύτην ὁ θεὸς ἐκπεπλήρωκεν τοῖς τέκνοις [αὐτῶν] ἡμῖν ἀναστήσας Ἰησοῦν. This may be a present use of the Perfect, in which case the sentence should be translated "that God is fulfilling this (gospel) to our children after raising Jesus." But the placement of the Aorist Participle seems to argue against a strictly temporal sequence (see chapt. 8). Perhaps a better rendering sees the Perfect and Aorist as referring to the same act and hence both having past implicature: "God fulfilled this (Gospel) to our children when he raised/by raising Jesus." Acts 16:10: this verse is complicated by shift to a "we section." The verse is best understood as continuing the narrative of Paul's vision and call to Macedonia. "They" concluded that God προσκέκληται (had selected) them to preach the Gospel to the Macedonians.

Rom 16:7: in his closing words Paul admonishes his readers to greet several fellow Christians, who are well-known among the apostles and who γέγοναν (came into a state of being = were) in Christ before him (πρὸ ἐμοῦ). Past implicature is established through temporal deixis.

1 Cor 9:1: Paul appears to refer to his Damascus Road experience of seeing the risen Jesus, when he asks rhetorically of his audience, "ἑώρακα[11] (did I not see) Jesus our lord?" Kim (Origin, 3) notes that this is one of the standard references cited for Paul's vision of Jesus, though the text itself does not specify it as the "risen Christ" (7; on this as a rhetorical question see 29). 1 Cor 15:3-4: this well-known Pauline summary of the Gospel says that Christ died (ἀπέθανεν) on behalf of sins, and that he was buried (ἐτάφη), ἐγήγερται τῇ ἡμέρᾳ τῇ τρίτῃ (he was raised on the third day) and that he was seen (ὤφθη) by Cephas and the twelve. Many commentators extrapolate an unhealthy amount of exegetical insight from the Perfect (e.g. Robertson/Plummer, First Corinthians, 334; Orr/Walthers, I Corinthians, 317), claiming that it means that Christ was raised and the results of his being raised continue. This may be good theology, but it cannot be argued for solely on the basis of the stative aspect. In this context temporal deixis (τῇ ἡμέρᾳ τῇ τρίτῃ) specifically limits the temporal implicature to the state of raisedness that was in existence three days after the burial (see McKay, "Points," 330). Cf. 1 Cor 15:12, 13, 14, where this specific past state is referred to, twice in conditional sentences. Cf. P.Goodspeed 10.3 (A.D. 180): διαγ(εγρ)ά(φηκεν) (he paid).

2 Cor 1:9: in recounting his trials to the Corinthians Paul refers to a past time when ἐσχήκαμεν (we possessed) the sentence of death (Furnish [II Corinthians, 113] supports narrative use of the Perfect here). Cf. 2 Cor 1:10 with ἠλπίκαμεν (we were in a state of hopefulness); 2 Cor 2:13, with use very similar to that of the Pluperfect; 7:5. 2 Cor 13:2: Paul sets his remarks in

---

[11]ἑόρακα is the usual Attic form, though ἑώρακα is well known. See Moulton/Howard, 193, for textual evidence here.

the context of his two previous trips to Corinth. During the second trip (ὡς παρὼν τὸ δεύτερον καὶ ἀπὼν νῦν [with you the second time and away now]), he says προείρηκα καὶ προλέγω to those who were in a state of sin (προημαρτηκόσιν). The Perfect seems best linked to the second trip and thus has past implicature, while the Present is more difficult. If it is linked to Paul now that he is away present implicature would be possible. On the other hand it may also be past-referring.

Gal 1:9: in a conscious use of verbal aspect, Paul contrasts his state of having spoken before (προειρήκαμεν) with his being in progress speaking now again (ἄρτι πάλιν λέγω). Bruce (*Galatians*, 84) suggests that the previous reference is to v 8. Cf. Plb. 3.107.10: καθά που καὶ πρότερον εἰρήκαμεν (as indeed we previously stated). Gal 3:18: Paul says that God κεχάρισται (was gracious) to Abraham through the promise. This whole complex of ideas is linked specifically to past events by person and place deixis.

Gal 3:19; 24: Paul asks rhetorically "what about the law?" (Betz, *Galatians*, 162) in a section where he anticipates at every point objections to his view that the promise to Abraham came by faith, that the law which came 430 years later had no place in Abraham's inheritance and that the law is wholly without function (3:15-18). He attacks directly, though his thought is not entirely clear at every point. Paul seems to progress *seriatim*. First he states that the law, probably the Mosaic law given at Sinai with its commands and requirements and apart from the promise fulfilled in Christ, was "added" (the Aorist refers to a specific process here, but that is because of the process, not the Aorist itself) by God (divine Passive?) on account of or for the purpose of transgressions,[12] until the seed which ἐπήγγελται (had been promised) might come. This marks the *terminus ad quem* of the law's function: the coming of the seed, Christ (3:16), to whom the promise was given by God. Verses 24-25, as a concluding section to 3:19-25, further elucidate this relationship by specifying that the result was that the law served (γέγονεν) as a παιδαγωγός (protector) until Christ (see Lightfoot, *Galatians*, 148-49, on telic use of εἰς).

Col 1:16: Paul says that in Christ all things were created (ἐκτίσθη), and then after listing the dimensions of this creation he concludes by stressing that all things through him and unto him ἔκτισται (were created); Col 2:14: in a highly imagistic passage apparently drawing upon Greco-Roman war parades, the author speaks in an almost violent manner of Christ's work on the cross. God left the debt against us behind, and he ἦρκεν (took) it from our midst and nailed it (προσηλώσας, Aorist Participle following main verb; see chapt. 8) to the cross.

1 Thess 2:1, 4: following a present use of οἶδα, reassuring the Thessalonians of the knowledgeable state they are in (Bruce [*Thessalonians*, 24] disputes that this is part of a "disclosure formula"), he proceeds to recount that his coming to them οὐ κενὴ γέγονεν (had not been in vain). He then describes briefly his troubles in Philippi, justifying his message that, as he and his companions δεδοκιμάσμεθα (had been approved) by God, thus they were speaking (λαλοῦμεν, 'historic' Present?).

1 Tim 2:14: in persuading Timothy not to let women have power over men Paul claims that whereas Adam was created first it was not he but Eve who was deceived and γέγονεν (entered) into transgression.

Heb 1:4: the use of πάλαι in v 1 establishes past implicature of vv 1-4 (in v 5 ποτε calls for a shift to timeless implicature). Thus the author says in v 4 that the one who was seated at the right hand of the majesty in the heights also became (γενόμενος) greater than the angels and κεκληρονόμηκεν (inherited) a name greater than theirs. In this progression the marked Perfect stands at the climax to the section (cf. v 2) by drawing attention to the state of inheritance as the crowning glory of this act of enthronement (see Dunn, *Christology*, 207-08, on inheritance). Heb 2:18: the author, dwelling on the past human life of Jesus, states that while πέπονθεν αὐτός (he

---

[12]χάριν may be either telic (Titus 1:5, 11; Jude 16) or causal (Luke 7:47; 1 John 3:12). There have been several major interpretations of the phrase τῆς παραβάσεως χάριν. It seems best to see the law as multiplying transgressions, whether by bringing men to full knowledge of them or even causing them directly (cf. Burton, *Galatians*, 188; Mussner, *Galaterbrief*, 245-46; Schlier, *Galaterbrief*, 152-54).

himself suffered), being tempted, he was able (δύναται, 'historic' Present?) to help those who were tempted. While the second clause is unclear deictically and may best be interpreted as simply descriptive, the first clause implicates past reference to Christ's earthly suffering. Heb 7:6, 9: 7:1ff. contain an extended description of Melchizedek. In v 6 the author says that the one who was without a genealogy (μὴ γενεαλογούμενος) δεδεκάτωκεν (received a tithe) from Abraham and εὐλόγηκεν (blessed) him. The Perfect verbs with past implicature emphasize the importance in this reversal of roles. Melchizedek--one outside the line of descent--was both tithed and blessed by Abraham. By extension, the author says, even Levi, who received tithes as priest, δεδεκάτωται (paid tithes), since he was in the loins of Abraham. Heb 7:11: within the author's rhetorical conditional sentence, he reiterates the fact that the Levitical priesthood was significant at one stage (cf. v 12), for the people νενομοθέτηται (were given the law) through it; Heb 7:14: the one spoken of came from a tribe that never offered sacrifices, for it is clear that our lord ἀνατέταλκεν (rose up) from Judah. Heb 7:22: reference to "Jesus" gives this sentence past implicature, since the author often refers to Christ as lord. It was Jesus, he says, who γέγονεν (became) the guarantee of a greater covenant. Heb 8:5: those who worship on earth do so according to the law, serving as a copy and a shadow of the heavenly things, just as Moses κεκρημάτισται (was instructed) when he was intending to finish the tabernacle. Heb 9:18: in affirming the place of death in establishing a covenant, the author says that not even the first convenant (ἡ πρώτη) ἐγκεκαίνισται (was inaugurated) apart from blood. Temporal deixis gives past implicature, while the structure and use of emphatic negation reinforces the emphasis of the marked Perfect. Heb 10:14: in contrast to the priests whose sacrifices were never able to take away sin, with one offering Jesus Christ (cf. v 10) τετελείωκεν (perfected) for all time those who are pure. Heb 11:5: Enoch was transformed (μετετέθη) so that he would not see death, and he was not found (ηὑρίσκετο) because God μετέθηκεν (transformed) him. The use of verbal aspect is transparent. The simple fact of Enoch's transformation is recorded with the Aorist, but the Perfect is used of God himself bringing about the state of transformation. Heb 11:17, 28: in the catalogue of the faithful, the author says that by faith Abraham προσενήνοχεν (offered) Isaac when he was tempted (Present Participle); in v 28, the author says that Moses πεποίηκεν (made) the passover. The only uses of the Perfect Indicative in Hebrews 11, they draw attention to two of the pivotal events in Israel's history (see McKay, "Perfect . . . NT Greek," 318).

1 John 1:1-3, 5: in the epistle's preface, the author establishes past reference using the remote form of εἰμί and the temporal deictic indicator ἀπ᾽ ἀρχῆς (from the beginning). Using ἀκηκόαμεν (we have seen) and ἑωράκαμεν (we have heard) both in the Perfect, and in various combinations and orders, he emphasizes that the message that he has passed on to them is founded not upon simple hypothesis or second-hand information, but comes from the condition of first-hand attestation (cf. Lys. 12.100 above). "What is from the beginning, what we were in a state of having heard and seen with our eyes, what we saw (Aorist, reiterating the above as transition to next section) and our hands grasped concerning the word of life---and the life was manifested, and we were in a state of having seen it and were testifying and announcing it to you . . . .--what we have seen and heard, we were announcing to you. . . ." Apparent reference to the letter itself breaks the temporal flow so that v 4 has present implicature. Verse 5 with ἀκηκόαμεν probably has past implicature on the basis of its repetition of vv 1-3, though it may also be used timelessly in conjunction with vv 6-10. Louw ("Aspect," 101) is right in not reducing the force of the Perfect (cf. 98-99), although he believes the Aorist is unmarked. He translates the Perfects with full emphasis on the "state of affairs": "I have heard; it is true that I have heard, no doubt!" (It does not follow that there is "exegetically no distinction in meaning . . . between the perfects and aorists in 1 John 1:1. They all have the semantic value of the perfect tense.") 1 John 4:9, 10, 14: verse 9 consciously breaks from a timeless resume of one's obligation to love God, by referring to God's tangible manifestation of his love in his son, whom he ἀπέσταλκεν (sent) into the world. The ἵνα clause then shifts the flow of the argument back to the hypothetical, though the writer implicates past reference again in vv 10, 14.

Rev 5:7; 8:5; 11:17, cf. 3:3: with εἴληφεν/ς, in which the narrator depicts an object being taken up. Schwyzer (2.187-88), followed by Louw ("Waarde," 28-29) and others (Blass/Debrunner, ¶ 343[1]; Thompson, Apocalypse, 44), argues that the Perfect in Rev 5:7 is equivalent to an Aorist. But the presence of an Aorist form λαβ in Greek and in Revelation (e.g. 5:8; 10:10; 17:12; 20:4; see also Subjunctive [3:11; 18:4]; Imperative [10:8, 9; 22:17]; and Infinitive [4:11; 5:9, 12; 6:4]), and the presence of the Perfect form elsewhere in Revelation not juxtaposed directly to the Aorist argue clearly against this. Failure to make a translational distinction does not minimize semantic value or contrast. (In support of the distinction see Swete, *Apocalypse*, 78; Charles, *Revelation*, 1.cxxiv-cxxvi.) Rev 7:14: within the larger narrative frame of the dream-vision, the author/seer was addressed by one of the elders, and then answered (εἴρηκα) (see below). Cf. Rev 19:3; see also 12:4; 13:8; 14:8.

This decisive and yet only representative number of past-referring uses of the Perfect is sufficient to dispel the traditional conception of the Perfect as representing the present result of a past event and establish further the essentially non temporally-based nature of this tense as grammaticalizing stative aspect.

b. Present. Present usage of the Perfect tense is the most commonly accepted category in the standard grammars and need not be exemplified from extra-biblical Greek. It can be questioned whether nearly so many examples as is often assumed actually fit this category; nevertheless, clear cases with deictic indicators can be found.

Matt 21:27: the Jewish leaders, asked whether John the Baptist's authority was from heaven or earth, answer οὐκ οἴδαμεν (we do not know). Cf. Matt 20:22. Matt 24:25: in the midst of a discourse about the end times Jesus reportedly informs his disciples ἰδοὺ προείρηκα ὑμῖν (I am telling you beforehand); cf. Mark 13:23. Mark 6:14: Herod says: Ἰωάννης ὁ βαπτίζων ἐγήγερται ἐκ νεκρῶν (John the Baptizer is raised from the dead). Whether or not this is indirect speech, Herod is concerned with John being alive now. Cf. Pl. Phaedr. 227D: ἐπιτεθύμηκα ἀκοῦσαι (I desire to hear). Mark 7:29: when the persistent woman is told that the demon ἐξελήλυθεν (has come out) of her daughter, the point seems to be more than a mere description but is linked to her present persistence and faith. Luke 16:26: between them χάσμα μέγα ἐστήρικται (a great chasm is fixed), where no antecedent act is stated or implied. Cf. P.Gen. 36.27, 28: σεσημείωμαι (I sign).

John 1:26: μέσος ὑμῶν ἕστηκεν ὃν ὑμεῖς οὐκ οἴδατε (in the midst of you he whom you do not know stands). This sentence implicates present use of the Perfect, in which the general state of knowing is compared to the crowd's present position. John 1:41: Andrew runs to Simon and reportedly proclaims εὑρήκαμεν (we have found) the messiah. The act of finding quite clearly is prior, but Andrew is declaring the state he is in at the time of addressing Peter. John 5:14: ἴδε ὑγιὴς γέγονας (behold you are well). The healed man is informed of his present condition before being commanded about his lifestyle (μὴ ἁμάρτανε [don't sin]). John 8:52: νῦν ἐγνώκαμεν ὅτι δαιμόνιον ἔχεις (now we know that you have a demon), a state of knowledge the Jews have acquired from the repartee. Cf. John 11:22; 16:30; 17:7; Acts 12:11; 20:25; 26:6; Rom 11:5 (ἐν τῷ νῦν καιρῷ [in this present age]); 2 Thess 2:6; Heb 12:26 (τότε / the voice of God νῦν . . . ἐπήγγελται [now promises]); John 13:7 (οἶδας ἄρτι). John 9:37: after healing the man blind from birth, and hearing of his "excommunication" (ἐξέβαλον αὐτὸν ἔξω [v 35]), Jesus reportedly asks him whether he believes in the son of man. When he inquires further Jesus says, ἑώρακας αὐτὸν καὶ ὁ λαλῶν μετὰ σοῦ ἐκεῖνός ἐστιν (you are looking at him and the one who is speaking with you is that one). John 12:23: ἐλήλυθεν ἡ ὥρα (the hour is come). This use interprets the present as a broad span of time, including the entire passion, yet it is more than a description--it implicates the present period as bearing upon the hour's coming. John 14:9: Jesus asks Philip, τοσούτῳ χρόνῳ μεθ᾽ ὑμῶν εἰμι καὶ οὐκ ἔγνωκάς με; (I am with you for such a time and you do not know me?); John 14:25: Jesus says λελάληκα (I am speaking) to you about these things, i.e. keeping his word, παρ᾽ ὑμῖν μένων (while abiding with you); John 20:29: ὅτι ἑώρακάς με πεπίστευκας; (because you see me do you believe?). Jesus asks Thomas this immediately after his confession of Jesus as God (Brown [*John*, 2.1027] takes it as an affirmation).

Acts 4:10: Peter, when interrogated by the Jewish officials, answers their question about his authority for healing by speaking of Jesus, finishing with the statement that because of him ὃν ὑμεῖς ἐσταυρώσατε, ὃν ὁ θεὸς ἤγειρεν ἐκ νεκρῶν, ἐν τούτῳ οὗτος παρέστηκεν ἐνώπιον ὑμῶν ὑγιής (whom you crucified, whom God raised from the dead, by him/this this one stands before you well), though it is not until v 14 that the reader is informed that the man is in fact present; Acts 15:27: in the letter from the Jerusalem church to Christians in Syria and Cilicia, the apostles and elders inform the recipients that they are not only sending Paul and Barnabas but others committed to Jesus Christ. Therefore ἀπεστάλκαμεν (we are in a state of sending) Judas and Silas. This emphatic use of the Perfect singles out these men as ministers of the Jerusalem church. (Bruce [*Acts*, 303] claims that this is an epistolary Perfect. As discussed in chapt. 4, the category of epistolary tenses arises out of a need to see Indicative tense forms--commonly postulated as referring to absolute time--from a relative temporal standpoint; see Mandilaras, 237-38, on epistolary Perfect.)

1 Cor 1:16: Paul in remembering those he baptized says οὐκ οἶδα (I do not know) if there are any others; Phil 4:18: Paul acknowledges the Philippians' generosity (ἀπέχω . . . πάντα καὶ περισσεύω [I acknowledge receipt of all things and have more than enough]), saying πεπλήρωμαι (I am fulfilled), having received the things from them through Epaphroditus. Hawthorne (*Philippians*, 206) rightly notes that πεπλήρωμαι "repeats and intensifies the idea expressed in περισσεύω." 2 Thess 2:2: Paul asks the Thessalonians not to be upset with regard to Jesus Christ's parousia, as if the day of the lord ἐνέστηκεν (is present). Bruce (*Thessalonians*, 165) cites parallels (Rom 8:38; 1 Cor 3:22; 7:26; Gal 1:4; Heb 9:9) in support of the rendering "is present," although he is willing to entertain that the temporal implicature may be either present reality or imminence (= future?). 2 Tim 4:6: At the end of his life apparently, the author warns his readers about the times ahead (4:1ff.). He evaluates his own position as one already poured out (ἤδη σπένδομαι), and the time of his release (?) ἐφέστηκεν (is upon him).

1 John 2:18: John instructs his readers that rot only is this the last hour (ἐσχάτη ὥρα) and the antichrist is in progress coming, but νῦν ἀντίχριστοι πολλοὶ γεγόνασιν (now many antichrists are present). Smalley (*John*, 98) says that the verb refers "to the sudden materialization of antichrists in time," in contrast with ἦν.

Several significant examples of present implicature of the stative aspect can be cited in the NT. Surely there are many more depending upon interpretation of individual contexts, although the number seems to be larger in the Gospels and Acts within their active dialogues than in the discursive rhetoric of the epistles.

c. **Future.**[13] As posited above (and further supported in chapt. 9), Greek is best described as a bi-temporal language, in which speakers are accustomed to making assertions about that which is present or past, rather than that which is future. Their reticence seems to be connected to the way in which time is viewed, with the future as a realm not as firm and definite as that which is past or present. Therefore there are only a few uses of the Perfect with future implicature, and even these are not altogether clear. The examples in the NT where the Perfect has future reference apparently take the place of the now obsolete Future Perfect (Gildersleeve, 101; see chapt. 9).

---

[13]E.g. S. El. 674: οἳ ᾽γὼ τάλαιν᾽, ὄλωλα τῇδ᾽ ἐν ἡμέρᾳ (poor me, I am going to be destroyed in this day).

Matt 20:23 = Mark 10:40:   the mother of the sons of Zebedee reportedly asks Jesus for special places for her sons in the kingdom. Jesus asks the two if they are able (δύνασθε, v 22) to drink the cup he is going to drink (ὃ ἐγὼ μέλλω πίνειν). Jesus' response to their affirmative answer is that "you can expect to drink (πίεσθε [Future]), but to give places is not my affair, but for whom ἡτοίμασται (it is going to be prepared) by my father." A timeless sense is plausible, though future implicature seems implied by reference to a state of affairs not yet in effect. John 5:24: Jesus says that the one who hears his word and believes the one who sent him has (ἔχει [or is going to have?]) eternal life and is not going to come (ἔρχεται) into judgment, but μεταβέβηκεν (is going to pass) from death to life. This may be present-referring, though the allusion to life and death appears to have future implicature (cf. 1 John 3:14). Bultmann (*John*, 257-58) and Barrett (*John*, 261) recognize the tension in this verse regarding the future. John 17:22: κἀγὼ τὴν δόξαν ἣν δέδωκάς μοι δέδωκα αὐτοῖς (and I am going to give to them the glory which you give me), so that they might be (ὦσιν) one as he and his father are one. The first Perfect may be present or past-referring, although an allusion to future glorification is a distinct possibility. Acts 22:10: in recounting his Damascus conversion Paul says that he responded to the voice with "what shall I do?" (ποιήσω). The lord responded, "Go in Damascus κἀκεῖ σοι λαληθήσεται περὶ πάντων ὧν τέτακταί σοι ποιῆσαι" (and it will be told you concerning all the things which are appointed for you to do). NASB translates this "you will be told of all that has been appointed for you to do." This might be correct, except that there is no clear deictic indicator of past reference. Perhaps the Perfect should be seen as parallel to the Future, and the sentence glossed "it will be told you concerning all the things which are going to be assigned to you to do." Jas 5:2-3: James sets the context as describing ταῖς ἐπερχομέναις (the things going to happen) to the rich. He says their riches σέσηπεν (are going to rust) and their garments γέγονεν (are going to become) moth food (cf. ἔσται and φάγεται, both Future forms, in v 3). The use might be omnitemporal, but reference to the last days (v 3b) implicates future reference. As Davids (*James*, 175) says, "This anticipatory sense is maintained as the author brings out the first reason for weeping: 'your wealth is temporal' (using a perfect in all three verbs as a prophetic anticipation of the event. . .)."

d.   Omnitemporal.[14]   In contrast to the three temporal uses just specified, there are instances where the Perfect is used in a context with omnitemporal implicature, i.e. the so-called gnomic use. These appear to be fairly rare in all periods of Greek usage.

Luke 12:7: αἱ τρίχες τῆς κεφαλῆς ὑμῶν πᾶσαι ἠρίθμηνται (all of the hairs of our head are numbered). Marshall (*Luke*, 514) calls reference to hair "proverbial." The use of the marked term highlights the comparison between great and small. If God knows of every sparrow that falls and if he even has numbered every hair (note fronting of reference to hair), then his followers have no grounds for fear.

John 3:8: Nicodemus is told that the spirit/wind blows where it wants and one hears its sound, but you οὐκ οἶδας (do not know) from where it comes or goes. While use of οἶδα may here be timeless, the 2d Person appears to make the reference general. (See Schnackenburg, *John*, 1.373-74, on whether this is a short parable.) A fitting conclusion to the analogy is provided by the ambiguous οὕτως ἐστὶν πᾶς ὁ γεγεννημένος ἐκ τοῦ πνεύματος (thus is everyone who is in a state of being begotten by the spirit).

Rom 7:2: ἡ γὰρ ὕπανδρος γυνὴ τῷ ζῶντι ἀνδρὶ δέδεται νόμῳ (the married woman stands bound to her living husband by law). Whether this clause is omnitemporal depends upon

---

[14]E.g. Hdt. 7.130.1: ὄρεσι γὰρ περιεστεφάνωται πᾶσα Θεσσαλίη (all T. is crowned with mountains); Epict. 1.7.13: ἔστιν ἐφ' ὧν δεδώκαμεν ὑγιῶς τὰ λήμματα καὶ συμβαίνει τουτὶ ἐξ αὐτῶν (this is the place upon which we soundly give the premises and this comes from them); cf. 4.8.34; Epict. 2.13.22: ἱππεὺς οὖν ὢν εἰς πεδίον ἐληλυθὼς πρὸς πεζὸν ἀγωνιᾷς, ὅπου σὺ μεμελέτηκας, ἐκεῖνος δ' ἀμελέτητός ἐστιν; (being on horseback, having come into a plain against a man on foot, are you anxious, whereas you are in a state of preparation, and he is unprepared?).

the sense of νόμος. If it refers to the Mosaic law, then the usage is probably present. If it is natural law, then a case can be made for an omnitemporal use. (See Cranfield, *Romans*, 1.333-35: does he mean "omnitemporal" when he calls this "an illustration of the principle stated in the ὅτι-clause of v 1" [335]?) Cf. 1 Cor 7:14, where husbands and wives are spoken of as sanctifying (ἡγίασται) each other; 1 Cor 7:34-39: in 7:39 the clause γυνὴ δέδεται ἐφ᾽ ὅσον χρόνον ζῇ ὁ ἀνὴρ αὐτῆς (the woman is bound for such a time as her husband lives) does not specify whether this follows any sort of law.

Jas 3:7: πᾶσα γὰρ φύσις θηρίων τε καὶ πετεινῶν ἑρπετῶν τε καὶ ἐναλίων δαμάζεται καὶ δεδάμασται τῇ φύσει τῇ ἀνθρωπίνῃ (for every kind of beast and bird and reptile and fish is subdued and in a state of subjection to human nature). James's use of the same lexeme (cf. also v 8) with different verbal aspects appears conscious, referring back to the orders of creation found in Genesis 1. (Davids [*James*, 144] calls this an "analogy from nature"; he interprets the Perfect and Present verbs as past and present referring.) See also under omnitemporal Present. 2 Pet 2:19: ᾧ γάρ τις ἥττηται, τούτῳ δεδούλωται (for by what someone is overcome, by this he is enslaved).

e. Timeless.[15] Since the verb forms in Greek are essentially non-temporal, timeless implicature is closer to the semantic essence of the tense form. In one sense any analysis of verbal usage, therefore, should assume a timeless use unless contextual factors indicate otherwise. But pragmatic usage is often deictically limited and thus the timeless category need not constitute the largest category of usage. Since this discussion is not so interested in formulating statistical comparisons as analysing the range of usage, only a representative number of uses of the Perfect with timeless usage is mentioned. One particular grammatical construction meriting special discussion is the conditional statement (see chapt. 6).

Matt 7:11 = Luke 11:13: if you who are evil οἴδατε (are in the state of knowledge) about giving good gifts to your children, then how much more the father in heaven intends to give (δώσει) good things to those who are asking him, with the Perfect in the protasis of the conditional. To see deictic limitation of the conditional, or to posit a temporal scheme between the protasis and apodosis, is to miss the point. Matt 13:46: the man who finds the pearl goes and πέπρακεν (sells) all that he has. In the immediate context of narrative progression but the larger context of a parable, the reference is timeless, with the Perfect drawing attention to the significance of the reaction. Luke 11:44: the Pharisees are likened to the unseen tombs, and men who walk over them οὐκ οἴδασιν (are not knowledgeable) of it (perhaps τὰ μνημεῖα τὰ ἄδηλα refers to a τάφοις κεκονιαμένοις [adorned grave], hence it is not recognized as a tomb [Matt 23:27] [Marshall, *Luke*, 499]).

Rom 6:5: Paul poses the simple condition that if we γεγόναμεν (become) planted together in the likeness of his death, then the consequence is being "of his resurrection." In Paul's opposition to antinomism he makes a number of conditional and conditional-like statements (Harris [*Immortal*, 172] recognizes the conditional nature), often with descriptive Aorists. In v 5 he uses the marked Perfect as a peroration of his numerous comparisons to assert the condition of the posited resurrection. 2 Cor 2:5, 10: "εἰ δέ τις λελύπηκεν, οὐκ ἐμὲ λελύπηκεν (if anyone causes

---

[15]E.g. S. Phil. 74-75: εἴ με τόξων ἐγκρατὴς αἰσθήσεται / ὄλωλα καὶ σὲ προσδιαφθερῶ ξυνών (if he, carrying a bow, will meet me, I am lost and I will destroy you also); X. Anab. 1.8.12: κἂν τοῦτ᾽. . . νικῶμεν, πάνθ᾽ ἡμῖν πεποίηται (if we might be victorious in this, our entire task is accomplished); Epict. 1.1.27: εἰ δ᾽ ὡς κουφότερον, τίς σοι δέδωκεν; (and if as the lighter, who gives to you [choice]?); 1.4.22: εἰ δ᾽ ἐπὶ τὴν . . . ἕξιν τέταται καὶ ἐκπονεῖ καὶ ἐπὶ τοῦτο ἐκδεδήμηκε (if he is appointed upon this frame of mind and is in progress working upon this and travels toward this), I say for him immediately to go home; cf. 3.22.14.

any grief, he does not cause grief to me), but to a degree--so that I may not be burdensome--to all of you. . . . ὃ κεχάρισμαι, εἴ τι κεχάρισμαι (what I have forgiven, if I have forgiven anything), was because of them and in the face of Christ." If specific individuals are in mind (Furnish, *II Corinthians*, 154) then these clauses are deictically limited, but if these verses are indefinite and hypothetical, then timeless reference is a distinct possibility (see Plummer, *Second Corinthians*, 55, 62, who recognizes that "The hypothetical statement [in v 10] is exactly parallel to εἴ τις λελύπηκεν. . ."). 2 Cor 10:7: Paul in justifying himself tells the Corinthians that εἴ τις πέποιθεν (if anyone persuades) himself that he is of Christ, then let him think again for himself, that as he is of Christ, thus we are as well." 1 Tim 3:5: the author asks rhetorically that if one οὐκ οἶδεν (does not know) how to govern his own house, how would he take care of the church of God?

Several cases may also be cited where the Perfect appears in the apodosis of a conditional sentence (see chapt. 6).

John 3:18: two conditional-like statements state that the one who believes (ὁ πιστεύων) in Jesus is not judged (οὐ κρίνεται), but the one who does not believe (ὁ . . . μὴ πιστεύων) ἤδη κέκριται (is already judged), with the emphatic Perfect stressing the doomed state of the unbeliever. See Rom 14:23 (Sanday/Headlam [*Romans*, 393] call this a maxim).

Rom 4:14: in saying that the promise did not come through the law, Paul reinforces the fact that the law is a dead-end: if one is from the law, κεκένωται ἡ πίστις καὶ κατήργηται ἡ ἐπαγγελία (faith stands empty and the promise stands nullified). 1 Cor 8:3: in discussing things sacrificed to idols, Paul recapitulates a few basic points about knowledge, using two conditional statements. If anyone thinks he knows (ἐγνωκέναι) anything, he does not yet know (ἔγνω) as it is necessary to know. And if anyone loves God, ἔγνωσται (he is in a state of being known) by him. The chiastic structure of the two conditionals is reinforced by use of the more heavily marked Perfect (personal reference of the second apodosis is unclear; see Robertson/Plummer, *First Corinthians*, 165).

Heb 3:14: the author draws a timeless conclusion from his speaking of the rest of God's people, saying that μέτοχοι γὰρ τοῦ Χριστοῦ γεγόναμεν (we are become sharers of Christ), if we might hold (κατάσχωμεν) firmly to our beginning confidence until the end (cf. Heb 3:6). Carson (*Fallacies*, 88) is correct that the Perfect "reveals an extra ingredient in the verse," although it does not necessarily reveal the present result of a past act. Jas 2:10-11: James uses a number of conditional and conditional-like statements. In v 10 he says that whoever might keep the whole law but might stumble in one thing, γέγονεν πάντων ἔνοχος (he becomes guilty of all); and in v 11, he says that if you do not commit adultery but kill, γέγονας παραβάτης νόμου (you are a law-breaker). Here the result of a I class conditional is stressed. 1 John 2:5: whoever might keep his word (Nominative absolute?), truly the love of God τετελείωται (is complete) in him; cf. v 3 with ἐγνώκαμεν (know).

Several other timeless uses are worth mentioning briefly, besides use of γέγραπται (it stands written), which appears frequently in the NT: e.g. Matt 4:4, 6, 10; 21:13; Luke 2:23; Acts 1:20; Rom 1:17; 1 Cor 2:9.[16]

John 1:18: θεὸν οὐδεὶς ἑώρακεν πώποτε (no one sees God ever). It would be difficult to posit temporal implicature (for this state, since the discourse indicates that this state applies to no temporal sphere in particular (πώποτε). 1 John 4:12: using a different lexeme, the author makes the same timeless assertion: θεὸν οὐδεὶς πώποτε τεθέαται (no one has ever seen God), followed by a conditional statement with a Perfect Participle in the apodosis.

---

[16]Cf. Plu. Marc. Cato 2.3: words οἷς κέχρηται καὶ Πλάτων (which indeed P. made use of); 12.3: ὡς ἐν τοῖς περὶ ἐκείνου γέγραπται (as it is written in the things concerning him); 15.5: ὡς λέλεκται (as it is said); cf. 24.6: μέμνηται μὲν αὐτοῦ πολλάκις ἐν τοῖς βιβλίοις ὁ Κάτων (C. remembers him often in his books). Perhaps one of the most well-known uses of γέγραπται is Th. 2.1.1: γέγραπται ἑξῆς ὡς ἕκαστα ἐγίγνετο κατὰ θέρος καὶ χειμῶνα ([an account of the war] stands written in order as each was occurring, each summer and winter); cf. 1.9.3: ὡς Ὅμηρος τοῦτο δεδήλωκεν (as H. clarifies this); 1.10.1: οἳ . . . ποιηταὶ εἰρήκασι (the poets say).

Rom 5:5: ἡ ἀγάπη τοῦ θεοῦ ἐκκέχυται ἐν ταῖς καρδίαις ἡμῶν (the love of God is poured out in our hearts), making a timeless theological point about God's nature and activity; Rom 6:7: ὁ γὰρ ἀποθανὼν δεδικαίωται ἀπὸ τῆς ἁμαρτίας (the one who dies is justified from sin), reflecting a theological principle; 1 Cor 7:18 (cf. v 15): Paul, in establishing that each should be content in his circumstances, poses two conditional-like statements. Those called in circumcision should not be uncircumcised and those called in uncircumcision (i.e. if one is called in uncircumcision; κέκληται) let him not be circumcised. The use of the Perfect seems to suite Paul's purposes well, since he is arguing against comformity to the Jewish law but for a sense of Christian freedom.

1 John 5:1: anyone who believes that Jesus is the Christ γεγέννηται (is in a state of begottenness) from God, and the one who loves the one who begets (τὸν γεννήσαντα) loves the one who is in a state of begottenness (γεγεννημένον) from him. This example may also be considered a conditional-like statement.

f. Conclusion. This extended list, although not pretending to be complete (especially since temporal reference in Greek is a matter of pragmatic interpretation), provides a selection of examples that illustrate the range of usage of the Perfect in the Greek of the NT. Not only does it show further evidence that the traditional conception lacks explanatory power, but it reinforces the definition of the Perfect tense as grammaticalizing the author's stative conception of a process.

4. VIABILITY OF THE PERFECT FORM DURING THE HELLENISTIC PERIOD. The question must be asked whether the Perfect was a viable tense form during the hellenistic period. It is commonly conceded that the Perfect form attained the peak of its development during the 5th-3d cents. B.C. (e.g. Chantraine, *Histoire*, 87ff.), though this is according to extant sources only. The Perfect tense possibly attained a high level of usage at a much earlier time but these forms were not preserved in the extant texts of today (McKay, "Use," 2-3, who makes important comments about the reliability of the various available literary sources, including papyri and ostraca). In any case, this section surveys recent work which discusses whether the Perfect continued to be a viable form after its period of peak development, i.e. to express its particular verbal aspect in relation to the others available through to the post NT era, or whether this distinction was lost.

a. Introduction. Several groundrules must be asserted. (1) "No single linguistic phenomenon can be studied in isolation" (McKay, "Use," 3). As McKay makes clear, an aspect is only distinct in relation to other aspects (this is what is meant by networking), so that confusion or evolution in one verbal category requires an examination of the others as well. (2) "[M]ost language systems admit variant possibilities, so if one distinction (e.g. of time) is suppressed in a particular context in order to permit the expression of another distinction (e.g. of aspect) important in that context, there is no confusion" (Mandilaras, "Confusion," 11; similar to Collinge, "Reflexions," 99-100, 100 n. 1). As already seen, the use of the historic Present in past contexts, and the Imperfect and Aorist in similar narrative contexts does not argue against aspectual distinctions. In fact, the "mere fact of the use of aorists and perfects side by side does not prove confusion of tenses. It rather argues the other way" (Robertson, 901). Or as Louw ("Waarde," 31) says, "'n Subtiele nuance moet nie verontagsaam Word net ondat dit vir ons logiese DENKE nic al te duidelik of Sinvol is nie" (a subtle nuance must not be lost sight of simply because this is not very clear or meaningful to our logical THINKING). (3) It becomes possible to speak of "confusion or substitution of tenses only where a particular instance contravenes the regular usage of the period in which it occurs as established by a sufficient number of examples" (Mandilaras, "Confusion," 14; cf. Collinge, 83). (4) The presence of a Perfect form in distinction from the Aorist in a significant number of cases would provide a strong argument for the Perfect persisting in its unique semantic function. (5) That translation of two tenses may be identical is no indication whether the forms involved convey identical semantic values (McKay, "Syntax," e.g. 52-53). Often an additional gloss is required to clarify the difference.

b. Arguments against viability of the Perfect. Those who argue for confusion between the Perfect and other, especially the Aorist, tenses rely upon the following arguments.

(1) Turner argues that the Perfect "extended its sphere to cover the functions of the aorist," thus the Perfect tended to be confused with the Aorist and eventually to disappear (*Syntax*, 81; cf. Abel, 258-59; Chantraine, *Histoire*, 240ff.; de Foucault, *Recherches*, esp. 135, for supposed papyric evidence). Turner's argument seems to be an understated assumption in Chantraine as well, since he claims the Perfect is present-referring but then in later Greek appears in past contexts, though his emphasis on subjective/objective orientation is more important (see below). Turner apparently means by this that the Perfect extended its use away from a strictly present-referring subjective emphasis to a past-referring resultive emphasis as well.

It has been shown in this chapter that the Perfect throughout its history has been compatible with past-referring contexts and, below, further support is given that speakers never developed Turner's posited resultive Perfect. This eliminates much of the force of Turner's argument. Mandilaras further clarifies several factors in this regard. (a) In "sentences where aorist and perfects are used side by side," they "must be treated with caution, because the writer may be indicating a special meaning rather than coincidence of the two tenses" ("Confusion," 17; cf. *Verb*, 225). He cites P.Oxy. 1295.16-18 (2d/3d cent. A.D.): δήλωσόν μοι / πόσου χαλκοῦ δέδωκες αὐτῶι / καὶ εἰ ἐκομίσω τὸ ἱμάτιον (let me know how much money you gave to him and whether you received the cloak), with probably greater emphasis on the payment than purchase of the garment. (b) When the Perfect is linked syntactically to an Aorist, or just because there is past implicature, this does not negate an aspectual difference (18; he includes another consideration--contexts with no distinct temporal reference--which he considers uncertain because of the abbreviated contexts in the papyri). Many forms in Greek may be used in identical temporal contexts without being identical in semantic meaning: e.g. Aorist, Imperfect and historic Present. (c) The past reference of the Perfect is, as Mandilaras admits ("Confusion," 16-18; *Verb*, 224-25), a known feature of extra-biblical Greek (see previous section):

Pl. Crito 44A: τεκμαίρομαι δὲ ἔκ τινος ἐνυπνίου ὃ ἑώρακα ὀλίγον πρότερον ταύτης τῆς νυκτός (I am judging from a particular dream which I saw a little while earlier this very night); Isoc. Letter 6.7: ὧν πρότερον ἠκηκόατε (which you heard previously); Aeschin. 1.9: τῶν οἰκετῶν οὐδένα κατέλιπεν, ἀλλ᾽ ἅπαντας πέπρακε (he left behind none of the servants but tended to all of them); P.Petrie ii 2(2).5 (221 B.C.): ἀπέσταλκα αὐτὸν πρὸς σέ (I sent him to you); P.Par. 65.18-19 (146 B.C.): ἡ τὲ ἐντολὴ / ἐγδέδοται ἡμῖν (the order was given to you); P.Teb. 49.6-8 (113 B.C.): ἐγλύοντος / τ[ὰ] ἐν τῆι ἑαυτοῦ γῆι ὕδατα / κατακέκλυκεν ([he], releasing the water in his own land, flooded); P.Teb. 238.8-10 (93 or 60 B.C.): ἐξε/λήλυθεν ἐπὶ τὴν μητέρα . . . δέδωκα αὐτῆι πληγὰς / πλήους (it came upon my mother [and] gave her many diseases); P.Oxy. 1295.16-18 (see above); P.Oxy. 1676.11-12, 15-17 (3d cent. A.D.): οὐ παρεγένου ἱς τὰ γενέσια / τοῦ παιδίου μου. . . . ἀλλὰ πάντως κρείττο/να εἶχες· διὰ τοῦτο ὑπερη/φάνηκας ἡμᾶς (you did not come to the celebration of my child. . . . but you always had better things; because of this you shamed us).

Turner claims there is a tendency to favour the Perfect tense in the less cultured papyri and hence to emphasize the connection of past and present action (*Syntax*, 81-82). Turner's point is not entirely clear here, since it may mean nothing more than that the supposed less-cultured writers found the Perfect particularly suitable to their linguistic purposes. In any case, Eakin argued as early as 1916 that the Aorist and Perfect tenses in the papyri and the NT were used in a "uniformly accurate" ("Aorists," 266) way.[17]

This analysis by Turner actually argues against the Perfect disappearing. It is typical of the less heavily marked tense to display a wide range of functions. The growth of the Perfect should have led to the disappearance of the Aorist. According to Mandilaras, such a tendency can be seen but only briefly. Taking into account a number of letters, private documents, public documents, and various official documents he shows that in the 2d and 1st cent. B.C. the Perfect did rival the Aorist for dominance because of repetition of common forms (ἀπέσταλκα, γέγονα, γέγραφα, δέδωκα, εἴληφα, εἴρηκα, ἐνήνοχα, ἕστηχα, ἔσχηκα, πέπρακα, τέθεικα). The Perfect showed particular strength in private letters from 3d cent. B.C. on, until in the 1st cent. A.D. a rather dramatic growth in strength of the Aorist can be seen, though the Perfect maintained a corresponding viability until at least the 3d-4th cent. A.D., when the Aorist began to squeeze the Perfect out (Mandilaras, 218-20; Eakin, "Aorists," 272-73; McKay, "Use," 17; Louw, "Waarde," 30). Even if it could be maintained that the Perfect assumed an aoristic function, another explanation must be found for the resurgence of the Aorist. As McKay says, "Linguistic change does not proceed at a constant rate." Although there may have been confusion between Aorist and Perfect just before the Perfect's disappearance it does not necessarily mean that this confusion was "the culmination of a long slow evolution spread over the whole period or the evidence available" ("Use," 4). In fact the evidence as marshalled by Eakin, Mandilaras and McKay seems to indicate otherwise.

(2) Turner posits that the weak endings of the Aorist were introduced into the Perfect paradigm (Syntax, 81). It is true that -αν tended to replace -ασι as the 3d Person Plural Perfect Indicative ending, beginning in the papyri around 2d cent. B.C. and in the inscriptional evidence from around 3d cent. B.C. (Mandilaras, 212). It is not to be written off as a mere Alexandrianism (Blass, 46, following Buresch [RhM (1891) 193ff.]; cf. Blass/Debrunner, ¶ 83[1]). Mandilaras points out that statements about the -αν termination by Sextus Empiricus "misled some modern grammarians into disputing the genuineness of the termination -αν in the text of the New Testament but the appearance of it in other localities besides Egypt and its frequent occurrence in the papyri permit us to accept that it was widespread in the Greek language" ("Confusion," 13-14), and it is not a "vulgarism due to the occasional lapse of an early scribe" (Moulton, 52). But neither is it a convincing argument for confusion of the Aorist and Perfect tenses because: (a) this seems to be an analogical development to bring the 3d Person Plural ending of the Perfect into line with the other endings which already were identical to the 1 Aorist, a form much more common than the Perfect. Some common Aorist forms already contained a κ instead of an σ and thus the -καν ending. (b) The 1 Aorist endings were encroaching upon those of the 2 Aorist. As McKay points out, the wonder is that -ασι survived so long. There are other morphological changes, as well. For example, the substitution of -ασι for -αν appears to be a forced attempt at correctness (McKay, "Perfect . . . Non-Literary Papyri," 24; idem, "Syntax," 43-44; Mandilaras, 212, idem, "Confusion," 13; Mayser, 1, 2.84-85; Jannaris, 200; Schwyzer, 1.666; Gignac, 2.354-55; cf. Robertson, 336-37), and -ες for -ας, appearing in late 1st cent. B.C., may have been an attempt to

---

[17]Eakin, "Aorists." Eakin, in support of Winer, notes that Moulton, Blass and Robertson find exception with εἴληφα, εἴρηκα, ἔσχηκα, and γέγονα. Eakin only takes exception with εἴρηκα and εἴληφα in a few instances in the the papyri, but even here if he had a less temporally-based conception of the tenses and took appropriate account of lexical meaning, these too probably would not be exceptions. For example, in P.Oxy. 278.16-18 (A.D. 17): καὶ μετὰ τὸν χρόνον / ἀποκαταστησάτωι ὁ μάνης τὸν μύλον / ὑγιῆι καὶ ἀσινῆι, οἶον καὶ παρείληφεν ("And at the end of the time the servant [?] shall restore the mill safe and uninjured in the condition in which he received it"), he disputes the Perfect force because it does not have the sense of "let him restore the mill in the condition in which it was and still is." But this meaning of the Perfect is not required and in fact has been argued against in this chapter. The other examples he cites are susceptible to this reanalysis.

standardize secondary endings, though this is not widespread in the Ptolemaic papyri and only somewhat more frequent in the Roman (Gignac, 2.353-54; Blass/Debrunner, ¶ 83[2]).

(3) Turner argues further that during the hellenistic period the Perfect Middle Participle crystalized in usage and assumed "the strength of an adjective" (*Syntax*, 81; cf. Aerts, *Periphrastica*, 5-15). This argument has little force, since one of the most common uses of the Participle in Greek, from Homeric through to hellenistic times, has been as a modifier. Indeed, many became lexicalized as adjectives in their own right (e.g. πεπνυμένος [wise]) (Jelf, 2.8). This has no bearing on whether its verbal aspect was neutralized.

(4) Turner concludes lastly that in hellenistic Greek a "periphrastic conjugation becomes established" (*Syntax*, 81). This point hardly warrants address, since, as McKay says in summarizing what is stated in most grammars, the "use of the perfect participle with forms of εἶναι was already well established in classical literature, and in fact had almost completely replaced some of the simple inflexions [e.g. Perfect Subjunctive, Optative, Imperative and even Indicative[18]--a natural development in view of the use of the perfect to express a meaning akin to that of εἶναι with an adjective" (McKay, "Perfect . . . Non-Literary Papyri," 25; cf. "Perfect . . . NT Greek," 291; "Syntax," 42-43). Aerts, in his monograph devoted entirely to periphrasis, finds that in hellenistic Greek the "construction of εἶναι + perfect participle is in principle the same as in ancient Greek" (*Periphrastica*, 96; see my chapt. 10 on periphrastics).

While other, less important reasons might be cited to argue for confusion between the Aorist and Perfect,[19] these are the strongest. Turner concludes that by the 1st cent. A.D., as the NT reveals, the number of Perfect forms had decreased, being "limited to only a few verbs," and "its meaning is difficult to distinguish from the Aorist" (*Syntax*, 83). It may be true that the NT uses a limited number of individual words (perhaps because of the relatively limited subject matter?), but Mandilaras notes that a number of new Perfects can be seen to have developed in the papyri (208-10, cf. 219-21; see McKay, "Perfect . . . Non-Literary Papyri," 24, for necessary reservations regarding use of statistics). Turner's analysis would be hard-pressed to explain this phenomenon, and must in general be dismissed.

c. Subjective vs. objective nature of the Perfect. The semantic force of the Perfect also is much clearer than Turner posits. Whereas the Perfect did eventually lose its semantic value and disappear (does it follow that because many new Perfects developed, they could be used where classical writers would have used the Aorist and thus this was its swan song before disappearing? See Mandilaras, 210), probably because of its morphological bulk, its semantic complexity and its continued use in narrative contexts where simpler forms existed, this did not occur until at least the 4th-5th cent. A.D. Moreover, the Perfect tense realizes a distinct semantic value in contrast to that realized by the Aorist and Present tenses, an aspectual value very much in line

---

[18]Harry ("Perfect Subjunctive" 19 [1905]) argues that periphrasis accounts for all these forms and uses, but his method of computation, in which he excludes certain Perfect forms on the basis of his estimation of their lexical semantic meaning, renders his findings suspect.

[19]Mandilaras ("Confusion," 12-13) argues that defective writings (e.g. ἐμισθώκαμεν in P.Gen. 70.18-19 [A.D. 381] for either ἐμισθώσαμεν or μεμισθώκαμεν) show confusion of the tenses. But McKay ("Perfect . . . Non-Literary Papyri," 24) says instances like this are no more common than other accidental errors (e.g. ἔραψεν and ἔγρψεν for ἔγραψεν in P.Mich. 304.10; 305.22). Mandilaras (111, 427) provides another plausible solution: the writers may have dropped the augment or reduplication (according to the tendency of the time), since the endings were thought sufficient to recognize a form.

with the mainstream of previous Greek usage: stative aspect of the grammatical subject expressed by the speaker or writer.

(1) Most standard grammars, both classical and hellenistic, state that the object receives the verbal action of a transitive verb (e.g. Jelf, 2.60; Schwyzer, 2.287; Humbert, 148-49; Mandilaras, 222; Robertson, 895-96; Blass/Debrunner, ¶ 342[4]; Turner, *Syntax*, 83-84. See McKay, "Use," 1ff., for review of the literature and critique). This classification grows out of work begun by Malden, continued by Wackernagel and brought to its fullest statement by Chantraine (for an overview of morphology see Curtius, *Verb*, 354-436).

Malden ("Perfect Tenses") claimed to establish that the Perfect tense had grown and developed from the time of Homer, as evidenced in the formation of κα Perfects, only found previously on stems ending in a vowel (e.g. βάλλω, βέβληκα; κάμνω, κέκμηκα). This change in morphology, he contended, was reflected in a change of meaning, from a present subjective to a resultive use, with many transitive verbs found only in the Passive (e.g. θάπτω, τέθαπται but no *τέταφα ever; δάκνω, δέδηγμαι but rare δέδηχα), and with many transitive Active verbs having passive meaning (e.g. ἄγνυμι [I break]; ἔαγα [I am broken]; σβέννυμι [I extinguish]; ἐσήβηκα [I am extinguished]). Consequently κα Perfects expanded in later use as objective resultive Perfects (e.g. ἐγείρω, ἐγήγερκα in Dio Cassius; ὄλλυμι, ὀλώλεκα in Thucydides).

Wackernagel (*Studien*) gives essentially the same account (without reference to Malden) with greater detail, claiming that construction of new forms was aided by the language of comedy (12). He accounts for the development of Active forms by showing their origins in Aorist endings placed on Passive stems, ablauts, and 1 Aorists. He is in disagreement with Malden, however, contending not that the Perfect has widened its use but that the objective resultive Perfect, originally present in only a few verbs, developed in many verbs only relatively late.

Chantraine (*Histoire*) takes a different tack in his work. Starting from the premise that the Perfect functions as an aspect (4-20) he argues that the original form of the Perfect was intransitive, and had Active endings (-α, -θα, -ε [the endings are from IE]), as well as sense, as in βέβηκα, εἰλήλουθα, δέδρομε, etc. (21-46). The Perfect Middle (even if the Present was deponent, e.g. βούλομαι/βέβουλα) was introduced through the Participle and Pluperfect, and became strongly productive in Homeric times. The sense (except for a few archaic forms [47-54]) was similar to the relationship that the Present Middle maintained with its intransitive use and it thus became passive in meaning (47-70). The intransitive/subjective sense continued to flourish in the Attic period (4th-3d cents. B.C.) (71-73 provide a list from Thucydides and Demosthenes), while the Middle form even became active in meaning in several instances, along with several Active forms from Homer disappearing (71-86). In conjunction with the firm establishment of the Perfect Middle in the 5th cent. B.C., the development of the Perfect reached its height in the 4th-3d cents. B.C., when the resultive/objective sense developed in the Active (αἰτιᾶσθαι), taking an Accusative object (87-118). Chantraine sees the development of the κα Perfect on the basis of the Aorist Passive as contributing to this shift (see 123ff.). Thus the Perfect, previously precarious in its relation to the other tenses, came to follow the same model as the others (e.g. sigmatic infix in Aorist) (119-45; see list of Perfect resultive forms, 130ff.). But the rich increase in forms was also the beginning of its downfall. Since it functioned in conjunction with the Aorist and Present, partaking of both in effect, and thus having lost its original distinctive character, it was eventually eliminated as superfluous, primarily because of its resultive/transitive sense which, because of past reference, was very near that of the Aorist. In Plato the tendency to abandon the strictly present state of the Perfect, Chantraine thinks, is especially noteworthy, although he cites many other examples (146-90).

The NT (Chantraine argues strongly against any Semitic influence on use of the Perfect in the NT [215]), Chantraine argues, already shows a decrease in the number of Perfects, most of which reflect the subjective/stative use (often with Middle endings), over the resultive/transitive objective use, with the Johannine writings containing the largest number of resultive Perfects (215-25, 229-40), although Chantraine admits that a number are used with their "ancient value" (234). He contends that other hellenistic literature, both literary and non-literary, evidences a wide use of the resultive/transitive Perfect (225-29, 240-45). (And he believes that the Participle has increased in usage in periphrastic constructions [246-52]; see his conclusion, 253-56; cf. T.A.S., Review.) (2) Though this position has had a significant impact on treatment of the Perfect, being adopted by many grammarians, especially of the NT, there remains much question about whether in fact it is correct. (a) The question of literary evidence arises. The sources for Homeric and pre-Homeric Greek are so sparse that to posit the lack of a particular form runs the risk of being an argument from silence (McKenzie, "Greek Perfect," 184; McKay, "Use," 2). McKay points out several times where pronouncements about lacking forms have been disproved later by increased evidence.

(b) Chantraine argues that once the Perfect is used to emphasize the effect on the object it becomes like a narrative Aorist and thus loses its distinct aspectual value (164-67). This is the criterion he often invokes when he says that he finds no distinction between the Perfect and the Aorist (esp. 234ff.). Several issues are at stake here, one being the relation between form and function. While it is true that the Perfect may function like a narrative Aorist, and in fact the Perfect did fade from use eventually under pressure from the Aorist, because two tenses are found in identical temporal contexts does not mean their aspectual values are equal, nor does it follow that confusion between the two immediately results. In fact, if the individual forms are maintained, the strong probability is that the forms are used distinctly, as with the historic Present in narrative contexts (McKay, "Use," 2). This illustrates also Chantraine's tendency throughout to evaluate tense meaning on temporal grounds, despite his claim to use aspectual categories.

(c) The change Wackernagel and Chantraine advocate is fundamental, as Chantraine admits (189-90). Virtually all grammarians are agreed that originally the Perfect's aspectual value (however specified) resided on the subject. The aspectual value then is supposed to have shifted to a condition whereby subjective and objective values were both maintained. It could be argued that the κα forms of the Perfect are used with the latter sense, though this is not entirely plausible since it destroys a unified aspectual conception, the linguistic evidence is limited with serious uncertainty regarding forms available in pre-Attic Greek (Markey ["Deixis," 279] believes with McKay that the κα Perfect developed early), several κα Perfects clearly do not derive from Aorist Passives (e.g. πέφυκα), and the distinction that κα Perfects are all transitive and the others are not just does not hold: e.g. ἕστηκα is intransitive, and οἶδα, claimed by Chantraine to be an ancient Perfect, is transitive (he also claims that the transitive use was picked up by the ancient non-κα forms, e.g. ἔφθορα is used transitively like ἔφθαρκα, as is τέτροφεν in S. Oed. Col. 186 [121]).

Regardless of whether Chantraine's historical reconstruction is accurate, the only way to evaluate Chantraine's hypothesis is to examine the specific examples he cites, to see if in fact they evidence the shift in aspectual value. McKay has undertaken in a detailed way such a task. After examining use of the Perfect in e.g. C.I.A. ii. 403 (I.G.II² pp. 191ff.) 37ff. (3d cent. B.C.); Pl. Ion 541C; S. Trach. 486-87; Pi. Isth. 4; Pl. Alc. 1.123Eff., he makes a convincing case against the use of the transitive Perfect as resultive/objective. Since the κ and non-κ forms overlap in their functions, and since he cannot find any compelling textual reason to endorse an objective, resultive meaning, McKay concludes: "Whatever their pre-Greek development, the different perfect formations within historical Greek do not appear to correspond to different senses" ("Use," 11, cf. 17). McKay has extended his study to the Greek papyri as well, where he argues similarly for such likely instances as P.Mich. 367.9ff. (c. A.D. 169); P.Grenf. ii 14(b) (3d cent. B.C.); P.Mich. 206.4ff., 17f. (2d cent. A.D.); and P.Mich. 473.20 (2d cent. A.D.) with an impersonal subject and personal object; and P.Col. Zen. 95 (3d cent. B.C.); 83 (245/44 B.C.) ("Perfect . . . Non-Literary Papyri," 32-34; cf. 26-28 on subjective perspective).

(3) Several significant examples in the NT are cited by Turner, who in following Chantraine argues most vociferously for the resultive/objective sense (*Syntax*, 83-84; cf. Chantraine, *Histoire*, 229, and pages following for discussion). In analysing these examples, several points must be remembered: (a) the distinction cannot be made on form alone, as Chantraine himself admits. (b) Aspect is subjectively oriented by definition (and the Perfect itself is subjective historically) so the burden of proof lies with those arguing for an objective sense to show that such is clearly the case in context. (c) It need not be proved that intransitive and Passive

verbs are subject-oriented (see McKay, "Perfect . . . Non-Literary Papyri," 33; "Perfect . . . NT Greek," 310, for similar guidelines; cf. Chantraine, *Histoire*). McKay performs a similar analysis as the one below ("Perfect . . . NT Greek," 309-14), using examples of his own choosing, and concluding that

> There appears to be no compelling need to explain these, or any of the other transitive perfects, other than as expressing the state of the subject, any more than there is in the language of the papyri or elsewhere in ancient Greek, and the most scientific approach would be to adopt the single explanation which covers all the examples rather than assume a different explanation for a minority. (314)

John 2:8-9: at Canaan, the servants are told to fill up the water pots, then to draw some off (ἀντλήσατε) and take it to the steward. When he tasted it he did not know where it came from, but the servants, οἱ ἠντληκότες τὸ ὕδωρ (they who drew off the water), knew. Several factors are at work here. While it is true that the water was now wine, even more important is the contrast between the steward and the servants. The latter's role is emphasized by the subjective Participle. As McKay ("Perfect . . . NT Greek," 311) says "equally clearly, although with less emphasis, the state of the servants described by the participle is being signalled, and not that of the water."

Luke 4:18-20: the spirit of the Lord has anointed Jesus to preach to the poor and ἀπέσταλκεν (sent) him to preach freedom to captives and restoration of sight to the blind. A Passive form could have been used (cf. v 21: πεπλήρωται ἡ γραφὴ αὕτη [this scripture is fulfilled]), but choice of the Active places emphasis on the spirit of the Lord, who commissions. The passage begins with this direct statement and the crowds become angry with Jesus not because he is the one selected but because he sees himself as selected by God.[20] John 5:36: the author stresses that Jesus' testimony is greater than John's. The works which the father δέδωκεν (gave) him bear witness that the father ἀπέσταλκεν (sent) him. Throughout the passage the emphasis is clearly on the father as origin of what the son possesses (Westcott, *John*, 90). Cf. John 20:21, where Jesus reportedly equates his sending of the disciples with God's sending of him (ἀπέσταλκέν με ὁ πατήρ); Acts 9:17; 10:17. 1 John 4:9: the author says that in this the love of God was manifested that God ἀπέσταλκεν (sent) his only begotten son into the world. Throughout this passage (vv 7-10), John emphasizes that love and God are interrelated. This relationship is founded upon the fact that God himself sent his son. See also 1 John 4:14.

John 4:42: those who return with the Samaritan woman tell her that they no longer believe because of her telling them but because ἀκηκόαμεν καὶ οἴδαμεν (we have heard and known) that Jesus is saviour of the world, with the pronoun reinforcing subjective emphasis. John 5:37: Jesus reaffirms that the father has borne witness to him, but that those around him οὔτε . . . πώποτε ἀκηκόατε (never even have heard) his voice nor ἑωράκατε (have seen) his image. Though the objects are emphatically placed, it is not God's voice or image that is focused upon but that the audience had never heard or seen them. 1 John 1:1ff.: a series of 1st Person Plural verbs links the object of the action (ὅ) with its transmission. At first the reader only knows that whatever it is that we have heard (ὅ ἀκηκόαμεν), seen (ἑωράκαμεν) with our eyes, etc., we are announcing to others. And this is the announcement which we heard (ἣν ἀκηκόαμεν) and are announcing, etc. Though the message is certainly crucial, the narrative makes excellent use of the subjectively focused verbs. McKay ("Perfect . . . NT Greek," 319-20) finds in the "rather full and repetitive" style a progression: "One could reduce this introduction to a brief and unrepetitive statement with but one or two perfects, but given the author's chosen style one can recognize the suitability of using perfects for both the seeing and the hearing in the transition from establishing the competence of the witness to the passing on of the message received." See also 1 John 2:1; and John 3:11.

---

[20]Chantraine (*Histoire*, 237) cites Luke 7:19-20, but the textual evidence clearly indicates the Aorist ἀπέστειλον not the Perfect ἀπέσταλκεν.

John 13:2: John says that when passover came, the devil had already βεβληκότος (entered) into the heart of Judas. It seems evident that the devil is the point of emphasis in this statement, giving a reason for Judas's betrayal. (The sentence is not strictly transitive.)

John 5:42: Jesus reportedly says that he does not receive glory from men, but "I know you" (ἔγνωκα ὑμᾶς), that you do not have the love of God within you. Throughout this section of exhortation (vv 19ff.) Jesus stresses his role in relation to others. See also John 6:69 and 1 John 4:16 with emphatic ἡμεῖς. John 8:52, 55: the Jews open the discussion confident of their position (οὐ καλῶς λέγομεν ἡμεῖς ὅτι). Jesus' response is equally confident (ἐγώ, etc.), giving rise to the Jews' confident rejoinder: νῦν ἐγνώκαμεν ὅτι διαμόνιον ἔχεις (now we know that you have a demon). Jesus concludes that in reality they do not know his God (οὐκ ἐγνώκατε) but he does (ἐγὼ δὲ οἶδα αὐτόν). The orientation in all instances is toward the subject. 1 Cor 2:8: Paul tells the Corinthians he is speaking of the wisdom of God hidden in a mystery, a wisdom which God designated before eternity and which no one of the leaders of this age ἔγνωκεν (knows). The contrast appears to be between the God who acts and the ignorant of this age. 1 Cor 8:2: Paul says that if anyone thinks he knows (ἐγνωκέναι) anything, he does not yet know as he should. The emphasis seems to be not what one knows but that someone knows, and how inadequate his knowledge is. 2 Cor 5:16: in a precise use of aspect, Paul contrasts the state and process of knowing: if ἐγνώκαμεν (we are in the state of knowing) Christ according to the flesh, now we are no longer in progress knowing. The emphasis is not on Christ but on the status of those who know; cf. 1 John 2:3 for the reversed pattern. 1 John 2:13: the author tells fathers he is writing them because they have known (ἐγνώκατε) from the beginning. Any posited resultive sense does not affect the clear emphasis on the subject. 1 John 3:6: John contrasts those who are abiding in Christ and not sinning with those who are sinning as not having seen (ἑώρακεν) or known (ἔγνωκεν) him, emphasis being on the subjects representing contrasting life-styles; 1 John 3:16: ἐν τούτῳ ἐγνώκαμεν τὴν ἀγάπην (in this we know love), could at first sight appear objective/resultive, except that the context (vv 13ff.) is addressed to "us." In the immediate context, the emphasis on "we" and not love is seen in the next clause where "we" are called upon to lay down our lives.

John 19:22: this verse contains the only Perfect Active form of γράφω in the NT. When the Jews came to protest Pilate's inscription placed above Jesus' head, Pilate responded ὃ γέγραφα, γέγραφα (what I have written I have written). McKay ("Perfect . . . NT Greek," 317-18 n. 68) renders this "I accept responsibility for what I have written." The author stresses repeatedly that Pilate had the inscription put above Jesus' head, and thus took responsibility for his action. In contrast, the Passive appears in a large number of instances, allowing emphasis to fall on the thing written. Especially noteworthy is γέγραπται/γεγραμμένον for quotations of OT passages, much like classical use of the Perfect by historians quoting authoritative sources (see above).

John 3:35: the father loves the son and δέδωκεν (has put) all things in his hands. From v 34, God is depicted as sending (the clause has an unexpressed antecedent, thus emphasizing the subject of the clause further?) and giving (δίδωσιν). As a result of God's loving he has created the state of having given all things (v 35; cf. John 3:27, with Passive Participles emphasizing the thing given). See also John 5:36; 17:4, 6, 7, 9, 14, 24; 6:39; 10:29; 18:9. John 17:22: Jesus, speaking to God, says that κἀγώ . . . δέδωκα (I am going to give [with emphatic pronoun]) to his followers the glory which δέδωκας (you [God] give) to him. As noted above, emphasis falls on the two subjects, God passing on to Jesus who passes on to his followers, whenever this may occur (this verse is treated above as future-referring).

John 5:45: it is said that not Jesus but Moses is the one who accuses his listeners, the Moses in whom they themselves place their hope (εἰς ὃν ὑμεῖς ἠλπίκατε). The irony is telling.

John 1:41, 45: when Andrew finds Peter he tells him εὑρήκαμεν τὸν Μεσσίαν (we have found the M.). While Jesus' messiahship is of significance here, it is perhaps more likely (with a Passive form available) that in this context John is capturing the excitement of Andrew, who, having left John the Baptist and followed Jesus, is excited to tell his brother of his long-awaited discovery (cf. McKay, "Perfect . . . NT Greek," 312; Westcott, John, 26: "This form of the sentence . . . seems to imply that Philip and Nathanael had often dwelt on the Old Testament portraiture of Messiah"). Verse 45 reinforces this subjective understanding with an independent Nominative: οἱ προφῆται εὑρήκαμεν. Rom 4:1: Paul asks whether we shall say that Abraham εὑρηκέναι (was found)[21] as our forefather[22] according to the flesh. It is Abraham, not the issue of being a forefather, that is pursued in the following verses.

Mark 5:15: when the swine herders returned they saw the demoniac sitting clothed, τὸν ἐσχηκότα τὸν λεγιῶνα ("the one who had had [but no longer had] the legion" [McKay, "Perfect . . . NT Greek," 312]), with emphasis upon the man who was now composed, not the legion that once was in him; 2 Cor 1:9: Paul, recounting his despair during his visit to Corinth, reminds his readers that he and his group αὐτοὶ ἐν ἑαυτοῖς . . . ἐσχήκαμεν (possessed within ourselves) the sentence of death. Though the "sentence" is important, Paul is emphasizing the knowledge that motivated his action, with the prepositional group marking the reflexive sense. 2 Cor 7:5: Paul says that in Macedonia their flesh ἔσχηκεν (possessed) no relief at all but was persecuted in every way, externally and internally. Though the object is emphatic, it seems to contrast with the even greater emphasis on what was happening to their flesh. (ἔσχηκα is debated heavily in the grammars; see Moulton, 145; Robertson, 900-01.)

Matt 22:4: the king tells his servant to tell the reluctant guests that he has the feast prepared (ἡτοίμακα). The focus throughout the parable is upon the king and his various acts and reactions, with the crucial point being not that there was a feast but that the king prepared it. As Carson ("Matthew," 456) notes on vv 4-5, "The king not only graciously repeats his invitation but describes the feast's greatness in order to provide an incentive to attend it. . . ." The independent Nominative shows the author's (belated?) recognition of the semantic value of the Perfect.

Phil 3:7: Paul has just finished repeating his Jewish heritage and, after the strong adversative, ἀλλά, states that whatever things that were gain (using an inclusive indefinite pronoun), ταῦτα ἥγημαι . . . ζημίαν (I consider these things to be worthless). Paul seems to have used the semantics and syntax very consciously so that the movement is from "things" in the former clause to his subjective evaluation in the latter (see Hawthorne, *Philippians*, 135). (The deponent verb is treated here for the sake of inclusiveness.)

1 Cor 7:15: after teaching on separation of husband and wife, Paul affirms that κέκληκεν ὑμᾶς ὁ θεός (God calls us) in peace, focusing on the fact that their place as Christians is not dictated by personal but divine choice; cf. 7:17 similarly.

Acts 20:16: in recounting the travel itinerary Luke gives the reason for the sailing by Samos to Miletus. κέκρικει . . . ὁ Παῦλος (Paul determined) to bypass Ephesus, directly attributing responsibility to Paul's wishes. See also 1 Cor 5:3; 7:37, where pronouns and word order show clear emphasis on the subject.

John 6:63: Jesus, contrasting the spiritual and earthly realms, reportedly says that the words ἃ ἐγὼ λελάληκα (which I speak) are the ones that are spirit and life. The personal pronoun emphasizes what is already clear from use of the Perfect, that not just any words but the ones Jesus speaks are of particular value (see Westcott, *John*, 110). John 8:40: Jesus reportedly rhetorically asks the Jews νῦν δὲ ζητεῖτέ με ἀποκτεῖναι, ἄνθρωπον ὃς τὴν ἀλήθειαν ὑμῖν λελάληκα ἣν ἤκουσα παρα τοῦ θεοῦ (are you now seeking to kill me, a man who tells you the truth which I hear from God). In contrast to the Jews' intentions, Jesus is the clear focus of the section as the one who hears and speaks God's message.

John 4:18: repeating back the Samaritan woman's marital situation, Jesus is quoted as concluding τοῦτο ἀληθὲς εἴρηκας (you have spoken this correctly); cf. her use of the Aorist (v 17). If the author had wished to stress the correctness of the statement over the honesty of the speaker, he could have used the Passive (cf. Luke 4:12). Heb 1:13: the author asks rhetorically to which of the angels did God εἴρηκεν (say) that he could sit at his right hand. Though the introductory section of Hebrews is devoted to an exaltation of his son, the author makes it clear throughout that God's action lies behind this status. See also Heb 4:3, 4; 10:9, 15; 13:5, where

---

[21]Lightfoot (*Notes*, 276-77) seriously considers omitting εὑρηκέναι. His evidence is weak.

[22]See Moeller/Kramer, "Pattern," 28, on determining the subject and predicate in such an Infinitive construction.

rather than a Passive verb the Active Voice is used to introduce a quotation, calling upon God's (spirit's) authority to lie behind the words. Rev 7:14; 19:3: Moulton argues that uses of εἴρηκα here are to be considered "actual aorists in the writer's view" since they are without apparent reduplication (Moulton, 145, followed tentatively by Robertson, 902). This may have been true, except that the author knows the suppletive Aorist form (7:14; 22:7) and a Perfect with past reference is just one of its possible pragmatic implicatures. Rather, the author uses the Perfect because of its emphasis on the stative condition of the subject. In 7:9ff. the several speeches by others are introduced by imperfective verbs, until the narrator is asked who those clothed in white robes are, to which he emphatically replies with the Perfect εἴρηκα. Apparently caught unaware, he states: κύριέ μου, σὺ οἶδας (my lord, you know), using a Perfect verb as well. The interrogator then closes the passage with a lengthy explanation introduced by an unobtrusive Aorist, εἶπεν. A similar pattern can be seen in 19:1ff., in which what is stated as heard uses the imperfective and that which is directly attributed to the source uses the stative.

John 15:18: a I class conditional quotes Jesus saying that if the world is hating you, γινώσκετε ὅτι ἐμέ πρῶτον ὑμῶν μεμίσηκεν (know that it is in the state of hatred first toward me before you). While the contrast between "you" and Jesus is certainly important (hatred of the latter in effect is responsible for hatred of the former), the apodosis in the next verse shows that this passage is concerned with the world's hatred of Jesus' followers.

John 1:34: John says κἀγὼ ἑώρακα, καὶ μεμαρτύρηκα (I have seen and borne witness) that Jesus is the son of God. Verses 29ff. are John's testimony to Jesus, and it is appropriate that the climax of the passage has John attesting emphatically. Cf. v 32, where similar verbs are used, though in narration. (Chantraine [*Histoire*, 237] calls the explanation that sight is essential "un peu subtile.") See also John 3:26; 5:33. Similarly John 5:37 stresses the father (ὁ πέμψας με πατήρ) as witness to Jesus; 1 John 5:9. John 19:35: the narrator interjects in the crucifixion narrative his solemn testimony that what he saw really occurred: καὶ ὁ ἑωρακὼς μεμαρτύρηκεν (indeed the one who has seen is bearing witness); John 1:18: John tells his readers that no one ever (πώποτε) has seen God, with the importance resting on any who would attempt to see him; John 6:46 contrasts the fact that no one has seen the father (a rhetorical question is used) with the son who has. In John 14:9 the sentences are combined into one statement: ὁ ἑωρακὼς ἐμὲ ἑώρακεν τὸν πατέρα (the one who has seen me has seen the father), emphasizing Jesus' subjective role. Ironically, John 14:7 stresses that if one knows Jesus he will know the father, and this is tantamount to seeing (ἑωράκατε) him. The entire verse stresses the progression that "you" may make to see God (a conditional clause is used). See also 1 John 3:6 with ἑώρακεν and ἔγνωκεν. John 6:36: Jesus tells his listeners that they are indeed (emphatic καί) in a state of having seen him (ἑωράκατε) but they are not believing. The stative aspect implies the audience's responsibility. John 20:18: Mary Magdalene comes to the disciple and says she has seen (ἑώρακα) the lord and he spoke to her. While seeing the lord is crucial in the resurrection narrative, here the stress seems to fall on Mary as the one who sees and bears witness, particularly crucial in a social context where a woman's testimony was not legally admissible. See also 1 Cor 9:1; John 8:57; 8:38 with personal pronoun; 4:45; Col 2:18; Luke 1:22. John 3:32: ὃ ἑώρακεν καὶ ἤκουσεν τοῦτο μαρτυρεῖ (what he has seen and heard, this he bears witness to). McKay says that "the reliability of the witness is being strongly asserted, the verb of seeing comes first and, especially in the circumstances, must be the more significant" ("Perfect . . . NT Greek," 319). Acts 22:15: Paul answers his audience that they not only know his will but are witnesses to all men of the things they have seen (ἑώρακας) and heard (ἤκουσας). The less heavily marked Aorist reinforces the subjective aspectual nature of the Perfect, "where Paul's commissioning as a witness is the topic" (McKay, "Perfect . . . NT Greek," 319). See also Luke 9:36; and Col 2:1; 1 John 4:20, which stress the emphasis on the subject through the pattern of discourse and anaphoric reference.

Phil 1:6: in his opening thanksgiving, Paul emphasizes his gratitude to God, πεποιθὼς αὐτὸ τοῦτο (being persuaded of this same thing), that the one who began a good work will bring it to completion. Though Paul continues in Philippians to stress the role of Christ, at this point he is introducing the idea as a result of his persuasion about the Philippians. See also Rom 2:19; 2 Cor 10:7 with reflexive pronouns; Gal 5:10 with a personal pronoun; and 2 Cor 2:3; Phil 2:24; 2

Thess 3:4 with ὅτι clauses. Phil 1:14 has an Infinitive as complement, clearly stressing, with much modification, the subjective role of τούς . . . πεποιθότας (those who trust).

Acts 5:28: the chief priest asks Peter rhetorically if it is not true that the Sanhedrin asked them not to teach (παρηγγείλαμεν) but now πεπληρώκατε (you have filled) Jerusalem with their teaching. The contrast of "we" and "you" is clear, as is the presence of a Passive form to emphasize the object (cf. John 7:8).

Luke 17:10: Jesus mocks the attitude of his listeners by comparing them to slaves. If a slave does as he is commanded there is no room for boasting or claiming that ὃ ὠφείλομεν ποιῆσαι πεποιήκαμεν (what we are obliged to do we have done). Jesus is pointing at his listeners, not at their responsibilities. The possible use of a Passive form further supports this understanding.

Matt 9:22: Jesus reportedly says to the woman who touches his robe that ἡ πίστις σου σέσωκέν σε (your faith has healed you). The emphasis on faith is seen in contrast to her superstitious preoccupation with touching him (v 21). See the Passive verb in v 22b.

Jude 6: the author recounts God's treatment of those who are disobedient. He has destroyed unfaithful peoples, and even disobedient angels he τετήρηκεν (has kept) unto judgment (cf. Aorist in the same verse).

2 Pet 2:6: Peter recounts the history of God's destruction of evil upon the earth, starting with the angels. He says of Sodom and Gomorrah that God condemned them (τεθεικώς) then as an example for those intending evil. See also Acts 13:47; Rom 4:17 with OT quotations.

Rev 11:9: the narrator sees two bodies lying in the street for three and a half days, and the nations and peoples watching οὐκ ἀφίουσιν τεθῆναι (do not give permission to bury) the bodies. The bodies are not the point of interest, since bodies are normally put in graves, but the people who do not allow burial.

John 12:40: John explains why people did not believe in Jesus by quoting Isa 6:10: God τεφτύφλωκεν (has blinded) their eyes and hardened (ἐπώρωσεν) their heart. Though God is not mentioned by name the emphasis appears to be upon him as agent in such a stark act, since blindness is after all normally associated with eyes. Chantraine (*Histoire*, 138) claims the values of the Aorist and Perfect here are identical and that use of the Perfect is arbitrary, but that is unlikely.

John 16:27: Jesus explains the dynamics of the relation among God, Jesus and his disciples, saying that the father himself is loving them because ὑμεῖς ἐμὲ πεφιλήκατε καὶ πεπιστεύκατε (you love me and believe) that he has come from God. Each group is given its role, emphasized by nouns or pronouns as well as syntax.

d. Conclusion. In the overwhelming majority of cases where the transitive Perfect occurs the emphasis appears to be on the subject. In several marginal cases the balance is tipped in favour of a subjective view by presence of a Passive form which could have been used if emphasis upon the object were sought. As Rijksbaron points out, citing Th. 5.26.1: γέγραφε δὲ καὶ ταῦτα ὁ αὐτὸς Θουκυδίδης Ἀθηναῖος (the same T. of Athens wrote these things) and Th. 5.24.2: ταῦτα δὲ τὰ δέκα ἔτη ὁ πρῶτος πόλεμος ξυνεχῶς γενόμενος γέγραπται (the first war stands written, being unceasing for these ten years), the object/resultive Perfect is "untenable" because the two examples

> would convey the same information: in both cases the emphasis would be on the state of ταῦτα. This is, given the availability of two different constructions, a priori improbable. In other words: if Thucydides' intention was to stress the state of ταῦτα, he should not have used [5.26.1], a construction with an explicit Agent, but a construction like [5.24.2], in which no Agent at all occurs, so that all attention would have been directed towards ταῦτα. (36, examples on 35)

In either case, whether an Active or a Passive verb is used, the state of the grammatical subject is conceived of by the speaker. In the Active Voice the agents and subjects are typically the same. In the Passive Voice, the so-called object of the action is typically made the grammatical subject and consequently receives emphasis, since a Passive verb has no 'direct object' which could be considered to have emphasis placed upon its state (see Rijksbaron, 34-35).

5. Οἶδα AND γινώσκω. a. Introduction. A discussion of the Perfect cannot avoid treatment, however brief, of use of οἶδα and γινώσκω. I do not presume to say much new at this point but to clarify several issues in the discussion. Debate has traditionally divided over whether the distinction between οἶδα and γινώσκω posited for classical Greek is maintained in hellenistic Greek. Liddell/Scott define this as the difference between γινώσκω meaning "come to know, perceive," and οἶδα "know by reflection" (*Lexicon*, γινώσκω). In NT studies thought on this has moved in roughly two directions. Generally, 'older' scholars posit that the classical distinction holds in NT Greek, while 'younger' commentators tend to argue that the words no longer maintain this distinction, i.e. that they are synonymous.[23]

Discussion of word-relations in linguistics is a challenging area (the latest summary is Cruse, *Semantics*). Even among those debating usage in modern languages with native speakers capable of giving intuitive judgments, there is surprisingly little consensus in discussion of individual examples. But several general points agreed upon by linguists form the basis of discussion of synonymy in an ancient language. (1) A profitable distinction can be made between words that may enter into synonymous relations and words that enter into contiguous meaning relations, i.e. improper synonymy (see Silva, *Words*, 119-29, esp. 125-26). When Silva lists words of "knowing," he is including terms within the very broad semantic field of words related to the concept of "to know" ("Style," 189ff.).[24] As he admits for "fuller verbal expressions," they are only roughly equivalent, i.e. they enter into contiguous meaning relations. (2) There are few absolute synonyms in any language, i.e. words that are interchangeable in any context, though there may be cases of partial synonymy, i.e. words that can be interchanged in a specific context at a give time when the difference is neutralized. (This language is dependent upon Ullmann, *Semantics*, 141-42; cf. also idem, *Principles*, 108-09; Lyons, *Introduction*, 446-53; idem, *Language and Linguistics*, 148-49; Cruse, *Semantics*, esp. 84-95, 265-94.) (3) Levels of synonymy must be distinguished (see Lyons, *Introduction*, 448). Many words may have identical reference, a good number may have similar denotation, but few if any have the same sense (see Lyons, *Semantics*, 197-206). These terms are much more helpful than concepts such as connotation and style (used by Ullmann, *Semantics*,

---

[23]Representatives of the 'older' school include Westcott, Lightfoot, Cremer, Godet, E.A. Abbott, Swete, Lohmeyer, Taylor, Law, Plummer, Brooke, A. Robertson, A.T. Robertson, Vincent, C.H. Turner, and Lenski, among others; the 'younger' school Bernard, Dodd, Barrett, Blass/Debrunner, Bultmann, Seesemann, N. Turner and Morris. See the historical summaries by de la Potterie, "Οἶδα," 709-10 nn. 1, 2; and Burdick, "Οἶδα," 345-46.

[24]E.g. ἀκούω, ἀνακρίνω, ἀρνέομαι, αὐγάζω, βλέπω, δέχομαι, διακρίνω, δοκιμάζω, εὑρίσκω, καταλαμβάνω, κρίνω, μιμνήσκομαι, μνημονεύω, παρακολουθέω, παραλαμβάνω, πέποιθα, προακούω, καθοράομαι, μωραίνομαι, τύφομαι, μυέω.

151-52; Silva, *Words*, 159-60). The distinction among sense, reference and denotation harkens back to the fundamental presupposition of meaning implying choice. The converse is that choice implies a difference of meaning. As Bloomfield says, "If the forms are phonemically different, we suppose that their meanings also are different. . ." (*Language*, 145; cf. Palmer, *Semantics*, [2d ed.] 89; Ullmann, *Semantics*, 142; Cruse, *Semantics*, 270). (4) Various tests have been devised to determine synonymy. They generally revolve around whether one word or another can be used in the same construction without any change of 'meaning.' Ullmann (*Principles*, 109) calls this the test of substitution, Lyons (*Structural Semantics*, esp. 176-225) the test of distribution in various environments, and Kempson (*Theory*, 40; cf. Lyons, *Introduction*, 450) the question of mutual entailment where the two sentences' truth conditions are identical.[25] These three tests are not capable of capturing sense relations. In fact, all three tests only address the level of reference or denotation. It seems best to posit that the formalist criterion of each form containing a different sense is the firmest standard, especially for an epigraphic language, from which to begin analysis. (Lyons [*Structural Semantics*, 216 n. 1] recognizes some basis for such a distinction; McKay ["Style," 320-23] applies similar criteria to distinguishing ἀγαπάω and φιλέω esp. in John 21:15-17.)

b. Recent discussion of οἶδα and γινώσκω in the Greek of the NT.

1. Several recent attempts to argue for the semantic distinction between οἶδα and γινώσκω tend to overstate the differences.

a. de la Potterie, treating the Gospel of John, falls victim to illegitimate totality transfer on several occasions. For example, in discussing John 10:14, the allegory of the good shepherd, he says that for John union with Christ is not something passive and inert, but a vital reality which seems to imply a veritable progress. Therefore if John uses the present, it is precisely to mark this character of continual development ("Οἶδα," 721, citing in support E.A. Abbott, *Johannine Vocabulary* [London, 1905] nn. 1626-27). He continues in this vein with treatment of 17:3 on knowing the true God: "Eternal life in St. John is not so much salvation realized in the next world, but the gift brought by Christ and already possessed down here. The knowledge this text talks about is not that of the vision face to face, but that of the believers: 'It doesn't exist so much in the possession of a completed knowledge as in the effort of a knowledge in progress'" (721).[26] As Erickson so aptly states, "de la Potterie appears already to have made up his mind before considering the evidence. . . . he forces some evidence, ignores other, and more than once completely begs the question at issue in order to make his point" ("OIDA," 111).

b. The second major treatment is by Burdick, who considers Pauline use of οἶδα and γινώσκω. His method is virtually unprincipled, since he relies upon his subjective evaluation of each instance: "In each instance the question asked was: Does this passage more naturally support the classical meaning of the verb used . . . or does it more naturally indicate that the verbs were used interchangeably?" ("Οἶδα," 346). Though he does concentrate on instances where the verbs appear in proximity and those with similar syntax, this lacks the linguistic rigour demanded. He

---

[25]Lyons (*Structural Semantics*, 206) argues that the distinction Liddell/Scott make between οἶδα and γινώσκω does not seem to hold in Plato, for instance where the verb governs indirect speech. Standard examples used to support the distinction provide difficulty (206ff.): e.g. Pl. Phaed. 75D: τὸ γὰρ εἰδέναι τοῦτ᾽ ἔστιν, λαβόντα τοῦ ἐπιστήμην ἔχειν καὶ μὴ ἀπολωλεκέναι (this is knowledge: to have understanding and not to lose it); Arist. Anal. Post. 76A: χαλεπὸν δ᾽ ἐστὶ τὸ γνῶναι εἰ οἶδεν ἢ μή. χαλεπὸν γὰρ τὸ γνῶναι εἰ ἐκ τῶν ἑκάστου ἀρχῶν ἴσμεν ἢ μή. ὅπερ ἐστὶ τὸ εἰδέναι (it is harder to know if one knows or not, for it is harder to know if we know from the beginning of something or not. Such is it to know). One factor Lyons does not take into full consideration is the difference in verbal aspect as defined here.

[26]He cites Westcott, *John*, 239, whose original reads: "It is not an acquaintance with facts as external, nor an intellectual conviction of their reality, but an appropriation of them (so to speak) as an influencing power into the very being of him who 'knows' them."

concludes that in 90 of 103 instances Paul uses οἶδα in its classical sense with five usages equivocal and eight used with the same meaning as γινώσκω; and in 32 of 50 instances he uses γινώσκω according to classical standards, with eight equivocal and ten with the same meaning as οἶδα.

For example, in Gal 4:8-9, Burdick argues for a "nice distinction" in which the initial εἰδότες "describes the time when the Galatians were without knowledge of God. They did not possess such knowledge. It is not stated that they had not yet come to know God, but simply that they did not know him. Verse 9 indicates that now a change has occurred. Whereas once they did not know God, now they know him," thus warranting the switch from εἰδότες to γνόντες. "To give a more complete explanation of what had occurred, the apostle added the words 'or rather are known [γνωσθέντες] by God.' The use of γινώσκω to describe God's knowledge may be questioned. . . . The answer is that he is not describing knowledge of facts but of persons" (351-52; cf. also McKay, "Perfect . . . NT Greek," 307-08). As Silva points out, however, Burdick's fretting is for naught: "Burdick wonders why, if God knows directly without the process of observation, Paul should imply this verb when referring to divine knowledge. The question is almost meaningless, however, since εἰδέναι, not being used in the passive, was not a choice available to Paul" ("Style," 202).

c. Silva himself follows a method similar to that of Lyons in his treatment of Plato's vocabulary, describing syntactical patterns. On the basis of his analysis of verbs of "knowledge" (see above), he selects several patterns worthy of note. Though οἶδα occurs twice as often as γινώσκω in Paul it governs a direct object in only 23 instances, as opposed to 33 for γινώσκω. οἶδα also appears 56 times with ὅτι clauses as opposed to eight with γινώσκω ὅτι. "The inference seems inescapable that the combination εἰδέναι ὅτι, being largely predictable, should not be pressed." Thus in Rom 8:28 and 1 Cor 15:58, "It seems more reasonable to suggest that the choice of the verb in these and similar cases was dictated by stylistic, rather than semantic, reasons" (201). Silva's findings, though instructive, do not seem to fulfil the purpose he designates for them, however. His attempt is to explicate "lexical" stylistics, and though his findings are applicable, his conclusions are more restricted to what he calls "syntactical stylistics," since he tends to suggest both that similarity of syntax negates lexical distinction and that syntactical predictability negates lexical choice.

2. Discussion of lexical semantics is beyond the scope of this work, but the issue of verbal aspect has been widely neglected in discussion of the semantics of οἶδα and γινώσκω. a. οἶδα is an interesting lexical item in Greek. Some might argue that it is aspectually vague (see chapt. 10) since it does not appear to offer a paradigmatic choice of forms. Others treat it as a Present since its translation into English often has present implicature and it appears to lack reference to past event with present results that traditionally typifies definition of the Perfect (e.g. Liddell/Scott, Lexicon, οἶδα; Bauer, Lexicon, οἶδα; and many grammars: e.g. Goodwin, Syntax, 20, Moulton, 176; Robertson, 881; Turner, Syntax, 82). (1) It seems evident that Greeks considered οἶδα, an unreduplicated form and probably one of the oldest Perfects, to be part of a paradigm of *ειδω, with εἶδον as its Aorist opposition. Though οἶδα is often translated "know" as mental perception, its origin is surely in knowing as being in the state of mental "seeing" (Cope, "γίγνεσθαι," 79-80). So εἶδον and οἶδα, though they developed clear semantic distinctions, such that εἶδον formed contiguous semantic linkage with verbs like ὁράω, βλέπω, etc., continued to be seen as paradigmatically related. (On the morphology of οἶδα see Goodwin, Grammar, 183; Giles, Manual, 449-50; Wackernagel, Vorlesungen, 169; Wright, Grammar, 318, 321-22, 323.) οἶδα therefore is to be treated as a genuine Perfect. (The major objection that its conception of the action is out of harmony with the traditional semantic analysis of the Perfect is eliminated by the model endorsed in this chapter.) As McKay states, "There appears to have been no doubt in the minds of

Greeks from the time of Homer to well beyond the time of the NT that οἶδα was in every respect a perfect," and one of the most frequently used (McKay, "Perfect . . . NT Greek," 298-99; cf. idem, "Perfect . . . Non-Literary Papyri," 26; Mandilaras, 222; Winer, 395). (2) The criterion of translation proves deceptive to understanding the Greek verb, since, as substantiated previously, identical temporal implicature in no way determines aspect.

b. Leaving aside other verbs of knowing, which may enter into lexical relations with οἶδα and γινώσκω, though most seem to be fairly distinct (see McKay, "Perfect . . . NT Greek," 298; cf. Lyons, *Structural Semantics*), several factors warrant comment. (1) οἶδα offers no semantic choice in the Passive. As surprising and perhaps unaccountable as it may seen, Greek speakers never seem to have developed a Middle/Passive form throughout the ancient language's history. Intriguing proof of this is found in several mid 2d cent. A.D. inscriptions from the Corpus Monumentorum Religionis Dei Menis in Lydia:

Ἀρτεμίδωρο/ς Διοδότου καὶ Ἀμιὰς / μετὰ τῶν συγγενῶν ἐξ ἰδό/των καὶ μὴ ἰδότων λύτρ/ον κατ᾽ ἐπιταγὴν Μηνὶ / Τυράννῳ καὶ Διὶ Ὀγμην/ῷ καὶ τοῖς σὺν αὐτῷ θεοῖς (Artemidoros son of Diodotos and Amias with their relatives, both those who are aware and those who are not [?], a ransom, in accordance with an injunction, to Men Tyrannos and Zeus Ogmenos and the gods in his company) New Docs 1977, 58.1-7 (CMRDM 1.61) (translation adapted).

Μῆνα ἐγ Διοδότου / Ἀλέξανδρος Θαλού/σης μετὰ Ἰουλίου καὶ / τῆς ἀδελφῆς ἐλυτρώ/σαντο τὸν θεὸν ἐξ εἰδότ/των καὶ μὴ εἰδότων (Alexander son of Thalouse with Julius and his sister paid to the god Men of Diodotos a ransom for things known and not known) New Docs 1978, 46.1-6 (CMRDM 1.66)

The editor comments that "the phrase ἐξ ἰδότων καὶ μὴ ἰδότων is very difficult to understand." The original editor of the text claims, "the only proper explanation, however difficult it may be even in the strange Greek of this area to take ἰδότων as passive, is that we have people paying a λύτρον to secure their release from witting and unwitting sin" (Horsley, *New Documents 3*, 72, quotation is from E.N. Lane, ed., *Corpus Monumentorum Religionum Dei Menis*, 4 vols. [EPRO: Leiden, 1971-78] 3.22). Horsley calls Lane's explanation a "desperate strait." These examples illustrate several facts. No Passive form of οἶδα seems to have existed by the 2d cent. A.D.; even non-native speakers did not feel free to invent such a form (this is a subtle argument against non-lexical foreign influence on Greek); and the Active did not serve well or widely as passive in meaning (this is confirmed for all uses of οἶδα in Josephus as well, by my reckoning). Therefore to push for a distinction in the Passive Voice between οἶδα and γινώσκω is fruitless, as Silva warns.

(2) Verbal aspect provides a vital and significant semantic component, even though this is often not captured in English translation. Therefore, when οἶδα and γινώσκω appear in the Perfect it is legitimate to posit a lexical semantic difference. Erickson, following Lyons, has distorted this relationship by adopting a definition of verbal aspect that is clearly dependent upon *Aktionsart*. Therefore, on the basis of his understanding of the kind of action described by οἶδα and γινώσκω he posits the following scheme (120):

Imperfective Aspect	Aorist Aspect	Perfective Aspect
gnōnai	gnōnai	egnōkenai/ginōskein
"to come to know"	"to know"	"to know"
-----	-----	eidenai
		"to know"
idein?	idein	blepein?
		eidenai?!
"to come to see/	"to see"	"to see, to have come to
perceive"		see = know?"

This scheme has little to offer rigorous analysis of verbal aspect, and is highly suspect for lexis. McKay has put forward a far more useful analysis. He redefines the difference in meaning between γινώσκω and οἶδα as the difference between "states of knowledge with and without reference to its acquisition" (McKay, "Perfect . . . NT Greek," 300 n. 23; cf. "Syntax," 53; see also "Perfect . . . Non-Literary Papyri," 26). McKay introduces an important factor into the discussion by eliminating the traditional disjunction. The two verbs are better seen in hyponymous relation (see Silva, *Words*, 126-29; Lyons, *Stuctural Semantics*, 69-71; idem, *Introduction*, 453-55; idem, *Semantics*, 291-95; Cruse, *Semantics*, 88-92), in which γινώσκω--the superordinate term--is used of knowledge whether gained by acquisition or not, with two hyponyms: οἶδα of knowledge specifically without reference to acquisition, and γινώσκω of knowledge with reference to acquisition. This incorporates the non-contiguous availability of verbal aspect in the tenses, includes both terms within the sphere of verbs of knowing, distinguishes them along the lines of whether reference is made to the means of acquisition, and is able to handle contexts both where reference to acquisition of knowledge is referred to (using γινώσκω) and where it is not (using γινώσκω or οἶδα). This provides a convincing explanation of for example 1 Cor 8:1-4, where οἶδα in vv 1, 4 refers to "common knowledge," while ἐγνωκέναι (v 2) "adds a suggestion of its acquisition, which is then taken up by the aorists ἔγνων and γνῶναι: these refer entirely to an event (or events) of knowing which logically must be the acquisition of knowledge" (McKay, "Perfect . . . NT Greek," 301). McKay (301) notes that if several verbs were switched for other tenses "the meaning would still be essentially the same, but it would not come across so neatly and effectively."

In use of the Present and Aorist the same aspectual semantic opposition does not hold, since οἶδα does not have a Present and the Aorist (εἶδον) in its paradigm seems to be used in a different set of contexts, referring essentially to physical seeing. (γινώσκω may form oppositions to other lexical items, but that does not concern me here.) As McKay states above, however, there seems to be a place to posit that in certain contexts where οἶδα and γινώσκω appear together logical implications can be made on the basis of syntax and context, though McKay seems to overstate his case by drawing out implications of the opposition of Perfect forms in his discussion of imperfective and perfective aspect, where he treats several instances in which οἶδα does not present an aspectual choice.

There is no formal criterion for making a distinction in John 21:17: κύριε, πάντα σὺ οἶδας, σὺ γινώσκεις ὅτι φιλῶ σε (lord, you know everything, you know that I love you). John writes that "you are in a state of knowledge without reference to its acquisition," and he elucidates this with a specification introduced by a contrastive, less heavily marked aspect, "you are in progress knowing that I love you." Although γινώσκω may simply be used stylistically to avoid repetition or to allow emphasis to fall on the ὅτι clause, the context seems to indicate another reason for its use. Whereas the lord's knowledge with reference to the cosmos is seen as unlimited and not requiring reference to its acquisition, the second clause specifies knowledge that the lord has regarding Peter, acquired through Peter's being a follower. As McKay ("Perfect . . . NT Greek," 304) suggests, "Even if γινώσκεις is introduced as a stylistic variation to avoid a repetition of οἶδας (although this writer is not normally averse to repeating a word), it does not follow that there is no variation of meaning."

Rom 6:6, 9: τοῦτο γινώσκοντες ὅτι (knowing this that) our old man is crucified, so that (v 6). . . . If we die with Christ, we believe that we will be raised with him εἰδότες ὅτι (knowing that) Christ, raised from the dead, is no longer dying (v 9). While an argument might be made that γινώσκω does not denote knowledge by acquisition, and is identical to the Perfect Participle clause (Burdick, "Οἶδα," 350), this is not the only possible analysis. A second is that Paul is making steady progress in his argument by using conditional statements. If the γινώσκω Participle clause forms the protasis of a conditional-like statement, it could refer to knowlege that must be acquired, especially since the subject matter is in relation to the experiential realm of the Christian, while the οἶδα clause, following an apodosis, reminds the reader of what he must know by faith, i.e. without reference to acquisition (cf. Barrett, *Romans*, 120, who sees the structure in a similar way; contra Cranfield, *Romans*, 1.313).

Rom 7:7: Paul says he did not know (ἔγνων) sin unless through the law, for he did not know (ᾔδειν) desire unless the law said. . . . This theologically difficult verse introduces (7:7-25) the Pauline "autobiography." In the ἔγνων clause Paul specifically lists the means of acquisition, the law. In the clause using the Pluperfect, understanding the negation is crucial. He in effect says that he was not in a state of knowledge of desire, without reference to his acquisition of it (ᾔδειν).[27] In fact he knew with the help of the law (this restatement would require a form of γινώσκω). Most commentators who treat the two verbs as synonymous fail to consider the role of negation here (e.g. Cranfield, *Romans*, 1.348). The two verbs are not synonyms here or the parallelism would break down. (Sanday/Headlam [*Romans*, 179] maintain the classical distinction; contra Burdick ["Οἶδα," 350-51] who claims οἶδα is used with the classical sense of γινώσκω.)

2 Cor 5:16: Paul says that from now on οὐδένα οἴδαμεν (we know nothing) according to the flesh. If ἐγνώκαμεν (we know) Christ according to the flesh, νῦν οὐκέτι γινώσκομεν (we are now no longer knowing) him in this way. The contrast of the Perfect forms is clear, with the negative pronoun modified by the prepositional group (see Rom 6:9 above; Burdick, "Οἶδα," 351), but what is debated is the sense of the Present Indicative. The negation points to negation of the meaning that we know by acquisition, hence the distinction between οἶδα and γινώσκω may logically be inferred here (McKay, "Syntax," 53).

Eph 5:5: τοῦτο γὰρ ἴστε γινώσκοντες, ὅτι. . . . If the Participle is adjunctive in relation to the verb ἴστε the difference between the two may be imperceptible and hence probably emphatic. If the Present Participle is substantive, meaning "you who are knowing know this," or even if it is conditional-like, meaning "if you are knowing this," a provocative distinction may be established between knowledge with reference to acquisition forming the basis of a knowing state. There is also the possibility that ἴστε is an Imperative. (On these issues see Moulton, 245; Barth, *Ephesians*, 2.563.) (Anarthrous Participles in subjects are rare, though known in the NT: e.g. Luke 5:17.)

Eph 6:21-22: so that εἰδῆτε (you might know) the things against me, Paul says, I made known to you Tychicus, whom I send to you, so that γνῶτε (you might know) the things concerning us. The verbs appear to be used lexically synonymously, without reference to the acquisition of knowledge, in parallel purpose clauses, unless Paul uses the first verb merely to set the stage, and the second to establish Tychicus as the means of acquisition.

John 7:27: the Jerusalemites say they know (οἴδαμεν) where Jesus is from, without reference to how they acquired their knowledge. But they also say that no one knows (γινώσκει)

---

[27] It is regrettable that Dunn misconstrues the Pluperfect, claiming it has an "imperfect sense" describing "the beginning of a continuing experience; he still experiences lust." Even if the sense of the Pluperfect were as an Imperfect (which it does not appear to be), the Imperfect would not of itself imply continuing action. Unfortunately this is not Dunn's only misconstrual of the tenses in these verses: "The change of tense occurs between vv 7-13 and 14ff. In 7:7-13 Paul speaks in the past tense [sic] of a stage of experience which was behind him. In vv 14ff. he speaks in the present tense--that is, of his present experience as a Christian." See Dunn, "Rom 7:14-25," 261, 262-63; and other commentators.

where the Christ is from. The two verbs may be used lexically synonymously, although the author may be saying more. There is no need to mention the means of acquisition of knowledge about the man Jesus, the author is saying, but even if one were to seek the means one could not find the origin of the Christ. In any case the contrast in verbal aspect is to be noted.

1 John 2:29: the author posits, if εἰδῆτε (you might know) that Christ is just, then γινώσκετε (you know) that . . . . The author posits the protasis without reference to acquisition. There seems to be a distinction semantically between the two verbs, however, with γινώσκομεν as the superordinate term including in its process of acquisition the knowledge that the protasis gives, as well as grammaticalizing the less heavily marked aspect.

c. Conclusion. This section has concentrated upon the relation between οἶδα and γινώσκω, focusing specifically on use of οἶδα as a Perfect verb form. It is argued that οἶδα was a viable Perfect form during the hellenistic period and that it enters into a hyponymous lexical semantic relationship as a hyponym of γινώσκω, a superordinate/hyponymous term. When this relationship is understood, interpretation of several problematic verses is possible. In any case, much of the discussion of these lexical items has neglected to consider the Voice of οἶδα, which offers no formal choice, and its verbal aspect, which has restricted choice. When these limitations are considered, several problems of interpreting the relationship between οἶδα and γινώσκω are reduced.

6. THE PLUPERFECT. a. Introduction. The Pluperfect is traditionally defined in terms similar to that of the Perfect, i.e. "The pluperfect equals the aorist plus the imperfect" (Blass/Debrunner, ¶ 347[1]; cf. Turner, *Syntax*, 86; Robertson, 903-06; Mandilaras, 234; Abel, 259; Kühner/Gerth, 1.151; Gildersleeve, 102-03; Humbert, 150-51). Not only does this definition present problems in relation to previous discussion in this work regarding the non-temporal nature of the tense forms, including the proposed semantic analysis of the Perfect, but grammarians themselves admit that many times this definition does not conform to instances of use of the Pluperfect. Blass/Debrunner stress that the aorist meaning predominates, although "generally there is no encroachment upon the territory of the aorist in the NT" (¶ 347[3]). This explanation is not particularly helpful for several kinds of examples.

b. Difficulties. 1. There are several instances where the aoristic past act is not of importance (see Robertson, 904).[28] Mark 1:34: Jesus did not permit the demons to speak, ὅτι ᾔδεισαν αὐτόν (because they did not know him); Mark 9:6: Peter asks Jesus at the transfiguration whether he wants him to build three shelters, for οὐ . . . ᾔδει τί ἀποκριθῇ (he did not know what he asked); cf. Mark 14:40. Mark 10:1: a crowd gathered around Jesus and ὡς εἰώθει (as he was accustomed) he was teaching them again; Luke 11:22: ἐπὰν δὲ ἰσχυρότερος αὐτοῦ ἐπελθὼν νικήσῃ αὐτόν, τὴν πανοπλίαν αὐτοῦ αἴρει ἐφ' ᾗ ἐπεποίθει (whenever one stronger than he comes and conquers him, he takes his armour upon which he relies), where the Pluperfect is clearly part of a timeless context; John 6:17: darkness had come and Jesus οὔπω ἐληλύθει (had not come) to them; cf. John 7:30. John 7:37: on the last day of the feast Jesus εἱστήκει (stood) and cried (ἔκραξεν); John 19:25: several people εἱστήκεισαν (stood) around the cross of Jesus; Acts 1:10: as Jesus' followers were looking into heaven two men παρειστήκεισαν (stood) by them in white clothing. Several of these verbs are similar to those cited above in disputing the traditional conception of the aspect of the Perfect.

2. There are several instances where result is lacking:[29] John 11:13: Jesus εἰρήκει (spoke) concerning his death; John 18:16: Peter εἱστήκει (stood) outside the door; John 21:4: the disciples οὐ . . . ᾔδεισαν (did not recognize) Jesus; Acts 23:5: Paul says οὐκ ᾔδειν (I did not know) that the man was the chief priest.

3. There are instances where the context is not past-referring:[30] Matt 12:7: εἰ δὲ ἐγνώκειτε τί ἐστιν . . ., οὐκ ἂν κατεδικάσατε τοὺς ἀναιτίους (if you knew what is . . ., you would not condemn those who are not guilty); Matt 24:43 par. Luke 12:39: εἰ ᾔδει ὁ οἰκοδεσπότης ποίᾳ φυλακῇ ὁ κλέπτης ἔρχεται, ἐγρηγόρησεν ἄν (if the householder knew in which watch the thief comes, he would watch); John 8:19: εἰ ἐμὲ ᾔδειτε, καὶ τὸν πατέρα μου ἂν ᾔδειτε (if you knew me, indeed you would know my father) (see below); 1 John 2:19: εἰ γὰρ ἐξ ἡμῶν ἦσαν, μεμενήκεισαν ἂν μεθ' ἡμῶν (if they were from us, they would remain with us); John 4:10: εἰ ᾔδεις τὴν δωρεὰν τοῦ θεοῦ . . . σὺ ἂν ᾔτησας αὐτόν (if you knew the gift of God you would ask him), which is strictly hypothetical. (McKay ["Perfect . . . NT Greek," 323] refers to Acts 26:32: Agrippa says to Festus of Paul that εἰ μὴ ἐπεκέκλητο Καίσαρα [if he had not appealed to C.] he could have been released, with McKay claiming that "the emphasis is not on the making of the appeal, but on his now being subject to the obligations of the appeal." This seems to put too much emphasis on finding the result of a previous action, where the person deixis seems to implicate Paul's past act.)

---

[28]Gildersleeve (103) and Smyth (435) cite classical parallels: e.g. D. 19.148: κακῶν Ἰλιὰς περιειστήκει Θηβαίους (an Iliad of evils surrounded the T.s); Th. 4.47.1: ὡς δὲ ἔπεισαν . . . τὸ πλοῖον ἐκπλέοντες ἐλήφθησαν, ἐλέλυντό τε αἱ σπονδαί ("and when they were [persuaded and, sailing away the boat,] captured, the truce was [already] at an end" [Smyth, who also notes that in "subordinate clauses the pluperfect is rarely used to mark an action as anterior to an action already past"]); X. Cyr. 6.2.9: ἦλθον οἱ Ἰνδοὶ ἐκ τῶν πολεμίων οὓς ἐπεπόμφει Κῦρος ἐπὶ κατασκοπήν ("the Indians returned whom Cyrus had sent to get news of the enemy" [Smyth]); and Mandilaras (234-35) cites papyri: e.g. P.Lille ii 42.7 (221 B.C.): ἕως τοῦ {τὸ} ἐγδῦσαί με ὁ περιεβεβλήμην ἱμάτιον ("the cloak, which I had put on and was wearing"), although this translation is debatable.

[29]E.g. Isoc. 12.233: ἀλλ' εὐθὺς παρεκέκληντο μὲν οὓς εἶπον (but immediately they called those I mentioned); Schwyzer, 2.288-89; Mandilaras, 235; de Foucault, *Recherches*, 142, list more examples.

[30]E.g. Th. 6.29.1: καὶ εἰ μὲν τούτων τι εἴργαστο, δίκην δοῦναι (and if he did any of them, to pay the penalty); P.Oxy. 939.21-23 (4th cent. A.D.): εἰ μὴ ἐπινόσως ἐσχήκει τὸ σωμάτιον / τότε ὁ υἱὸς Ἀθανάσιος αὐτὸν ἂν ἀπέστειλα πρὸς σὲ / ἅμα Πλουτάρχῳ (if my son A. had not then been ill, I would have sent him to you with P.).

4. The traditional model has difficulty with certain examples: e.g. Luke 8:29: πολλοῖς γὰρ χρόνοις συνηρπάκει αὐτόν (for many times it seized him). As Moulton (148) says (referring to the traditional definition of the Pluperfect), "it must be admitted that the extension of this [the "perfect of broken continuity"] to the pluperfect is complex, and if there is a simple alternative we should take it."[31] (See in chapt. 4 on adverb collocation.)

c. The Pluperfect as [+remoteness] stative aspect. Morphologically the Pluperfect form is particularly unwieldy (accounting for its demise and periphrastic substitutes; see chapt. 10), often with an augment besides Perfect reduplication (although this augment is often dropped in hellenistic Greek) and primary endings with ει (or η) thematic vowels attached to the Perfect stem (on morphology of the Pluperfect see Mandilaras, esp. 229ff.). These morphological features and the predominant use of the Pluperfect in narrative or past-referring contexts points to the Pluperfect as grammaticalizing [+stative: +remoteness] aspect. The Perfect grammaticalizes [-remoteness], since it shares the same aspectual semantics but appears more readily in a variety of contexts. The Pluperfect is not past-bound but appears predominantly in contexts with this implicature, although also in remote contexts such as I.b. conditionals (cf. McKay, 147; idem, "Perfect . . . NT Greek," 322; idem, "Perfect . . . Non-Literary Papyri," 34-35; Rijksbaron, 36-37). In the NT, the Pluperfect only appears three times (Rom 7:7; 1 John 2:19; Rev 7:11) outside of the Gospels and Acts, in which it is virtually always in narrative in its immediate context, even if used within teaching material such as a parable. A final example illustrates this: John 8:19-20: in discussion with the Pharisees the question of knowledge arises, with Jesus speaking of himself as knowing and the Pharisees as not knowing (cf. v 14 with οἶδα) his origins and purpose. This includes reference to Jesus' father, and the Pharisees ask where his father is. Jesus reportedly answers that they do not know (οἴδατε) him or his father: εἰ ἐμὲ ἤδειτε, καὶ τὸν πατέρα μου ἂν ἤδειτε (if you knew me, indeed you would know my father), with the Pluperfect used in the I.b. conditional statement (see chapt. 6) as a fitting summary statement to the dialogue. The narrator then says that Jesus said these things while teaching in the temple, and no one seized (ἐπίασεν) him, ὅτι οὔπω ἐληλύθει ἡ ὥρα αὐτοῦ (because his hour had not yet come), with the Pluperfect closing the entire narrative pericope.[32]

7. CONCLUSION. This chapter attempts to do several things. (1) It argues rigorously for a little-known proposal for the aspectual semantic features grammaticalized by the Greek Perfect tense. This has been labelled the stative aspect, and it is the most heavily marked of the Greek aspects. Like the implicatures of the other aspects, its temporal implicatures can be categorized as past, present, future, omnitemporal and timeless reference. (2) The concept of verbal aspect proves helpful in reestablishing firm evidence of the viability of the Perfect form and its subjective orientation by the speaker

---

[31]Mandilaras (237) cites a possible parallel in PSI 435.11-13 (258 B.C.): ἐνεχείρησεν οἰκοδομεῖν Σαραπιεῖον. . . καὶ προσ/αγηγόχει λίθους· ὕστερον δὲ ἀπεῖπεν αὐτῶι ὁ θεὸς μὴ οἰκοδομεῖν κἀκεῖνος / ἀπηλλάγη (he undertook to build S.. . . and "he was bringing stones, but then God forbade him" to build and he went away), although as he admits the understanding might also be "had (already) collected stones."

[32]Besides examples listed in the classical grammars, examples abound in hellenistic literature: e.g. App. Civ. Wars 1.3: ἐκ πολλοῦ διελελοίπεσαν (they were abandoned for a long time); Apollod. 1.1: οἳ μεγέθει τε ἀνυπέρβλητοι καὶ δυνάμει καθειστήκεσαν (they stood unsurpassed in size and power); Plu. Marc. Cato 27.5: ταύτην μὲν οὖν τὴν ἀπόφασιν ταχὺ δι' ἔργων ἐβεβαίωσεν ὁ Σκηπίων (S. confirmed quickly this account through deeds); Arr. 1.1.10: ἃς μάλιστα ἐδεδίεσαν (which they feared greatly), cf. Aorist verbs; P.Fay. 12.18-19 (c. 103 B.C.): ἐδέξυσαν ὃ περ[ιε]/βεβλήμην ἱμάτιον (they stripped the garment which I was wearing).

toward the process to which it refers, in support of McKay and against the well-established tradition of Chantraine. (3) The semantic difference between οἶδα and γινώσκω is treated briefly using the category of hyponymy from recent lexical semantics. And (4) the Pluperfect is analysed as grammaticalizing remoteness. In chapts. 7 and 8, the stative aspect of the Perfect is illustrated in the non-Indicative Moods, Infinitive and Participle.

CHAPTER 6:
CONDITIONAL STATEMENTS

0. INTRODUCTION. An important area for applying the theory of the Moods and tense forms put forward in this work is conditional statements, since so much discussion revolves around their sphere of temporal reference![1]

1. MAJOR VIEWS. Although conditional statements have been categorized according to several different criteria: form of the protasis, form of the apodosis, function, and temporal reference, among others, currently there are two major schools of thought on the nature of conditional statements. **a.** Perhaps the most widely held view was developed by Goodwin ("Classification"), from which the basic terminology and examples (few are strictly conditionals!) are taken, although in light of subsequent revision in his grammar and syntax (cf. *Grammar*, 295-304; *Syntax*, 135ff.). Among grammars he has been followed by many: e.g. Smyth (512-37); Stahl (382-413); McKay (196-200); Burton (101-12); Nunn (116-19); Zerwick (101-13). (See also Hahn, *Subjunctive*; Greenberg, "Realis-Irrealis"; Wakker, "Potential." Two other means of classifying proposed earlier were by Horton-Smith [*Theory*], rightly rejected by Sonnenschein ["Horton-Smith's"] for among other things its lack of theoretical rigour; and by Sonnenschein himself,

---

[1] Involved debate on this topic occurred in the late 19th cent.: Pritchett ("Sentence") and Roberts ("Aspects") survey the major works; Jannaris (462-65) provides a concise history of the construction. It is fair to concur with Blass/Debrunner (¶ 371) that discussion in the secondary literature is confusing. Thus the analysis here focuses on formally established conditionals, although other constructions may be categorized according to the following scheme. Most noteworthy is the indefinite relative clause with ὅς or ὅστις (see esp. Kühner/Gerth, 2.421-27; Robertson, 953-62), as well as Participle constructions, although contextual factors must be determinative here. Cf. also Wooten, "Nature," 81ff. (and Robertson, 977), who suggests πρίν + finite verb forms as forming conditional clauses. An approach using transformational grammar is Houben, *Sentence*.

criticized by Donovan ["Sonnenschein's"].) Goodwin argues for four conditional statements:

I: "Present and past . . . conditions implying nothing as to fulfillment." This occurs in two forms: particular, with εἰ + Indicative (including the Future) in the protasis and any verb in the apodosis, e.g. Pl. Apol. 21D: ἃ μὴ οἶδα οὐδὲ οἴομαι εἰδέναι (what I do not know I do not think I know); or general, either present with ἐάν + Subjunctive in the protasis and Present Indicative in the apodosis, e.g. D. 4.6: συμμαχεῖν καὶ προσέχειν τὸν νοῦν τούτοις ἐθέλουσιν ἅπαντες, οὓς ἂν ὁρῶσι παρεσκευασμένους καὶ πράττειν ἐθέλοντας ἃ χρή (all want to fight with and have regard for those whom they see preparing and wanting to accomplish what is necessary), or past with εἰ + Optative in the protasis and Imperfect in the apodosis, e.g. X. Cyr. 5.3.55: οὓς . . . ἴδοι εὐτάκτως καὶ σιωπῇ ἰόντας, προσελαύνων αὐτοῖς τίνες τε εἶεν ἠρώτα καὶ ἐπεὶ πύθοιτο ἐπήνει (which [ranks] he saw marching in silence in order; coming to them he questioned those who were there and when he would inquire, he approved). II: "Present and past conditions implying non-fulfillment." This occurs with εἰ + past form Indicative in the protasis and ἄν + past form Indicative in the apodosis, e.g. Pl. Charm. 171E: οὔτε γὰρ ἂν αὐτοὶ ἐπεχειροῦμεν πράττειν ἃ μὴ ἠπιστάμεθα (we did not undertake to accomplish what we did not understand). III: "Future conditions (more vivid form)." This occurs with ἐάν + Subjunctive (sometimes εἰ + Future) in the protasis and any future (i.e. modal) form in the apodosis, e.g. S. Ant. 91: ὅταν δὴ μὴ σθένω, πεπαύσομαι (whenever I shall be weak, I shall cease). IV: "Future conditions (less vivid form)." This occurs with εἰ + Optative in the protasis and ἄν + Optative in the apodosis, e.g. X. Mem. 2.1.18: ὁ μὲν ἑκὼν πεινῶν φάγοι ἂν ὁπότε βούλοιτο (the one who was hungry would eat whenever he wanted).

Several criticisms of this scheme may be made. (1) It fails to consider the role of verbal aspect (or kind of action) in distinguishing conditional statements within the same category. In the scheme exemplified below, verbal aspect constitutes one of the fundamental pillars for understanding conditional sentences.

(2) This scheme--overlooking important differentiations of form and function--fails to appreciate the role of attitude, since Goodwin's time-based scheme both places different forms within the same temporal category (Future, Subjunctive and Optative as future conditions), and places similar forms within different temporal categories (Subjunctive and Future) (cf. Chambers, "Classification," 293, cf. 294). This separation of tense form from temporal reference points away from time as the essential factor in distinguishing conditional statements.

(3) The distinction between particular and general conditionals on the basis of form is untenable. For example, of Aeschin. 3.196 (εἴ τις ἐν δημοκρατίᾳ τετιμημένος . . . τολμᾷ βοηθεῖν τοῖς παράνομα γράφουσι, καταλύει τὴν πολιτείαν ὑφ᾽ ἧς τετίμηται [if someone being honoured by the government dares to come to the rescue of those accused of proposing unconstitutional measures, he destroys the system by which he is honoured]), a specific conditional in Goodwin's scheme, Gildersleeve says, "I am unable to see why such a gnomic sentence should not be generic" ("On εἰ," 6-7;[2] Smyth [515, 517] realizes some of the difficulties). The same may be said of formally generic conditionals: X. Cyr. 5.3.27: ἐὰν οὖν ἴῃς νῦν, πότε ἔσῃ οἴκοι; (if you are going now, when might you be home?); D. 4.50: κἂν μὴ νῦν ἐθέλωμεν ἐκεῖ πολεμεῖν αὐτῷ, ἐνθάδ᾽ ἴσως ἀναγκασθησόμεθα τοῦτο ποιεῖν, ἂν ταῦτ᾽ εἰδῶμεν, καὶ τὰ δέοντ᾽ ἐσόμεθ᾽ ἐγνωκότες καὶ λόγων ματαίων ἀπηλλαγμένοι (and if we do not want to fight him there now, we perhaps shall be required to do it here; if we know these things, we shall know what is required and put away foolish words). As Zerwick (111) concludes, "The distinction . . ., though certain grammarians make it, is not a linguistic or grammatical one, but a purely extrinsic one based on the subject-matter (and on an analysis according to the speech-habits of some other language than Greek)," citing as examples: John 14:15 and 23: ἐὰν ἀγαπᾶτέ με, τὰς ἐντολὰς . . . τηρήσετε. . . . ἐάν τις ἀγαπᾷ με τὸν λόγον μου τηρήσει (if you love me,

---

[2]He also cites X. Econ. 11.24; Pl. Laws 865A-B; D. 23.54; see also E. Fr. 294; Pl. Apol. 25B.

keep my commandments. . . . if someone loves me, he will keep my word); and John 8:31; 1 John 1:9 (Boyer ["Third . . . Class Conditions," 172-75] concurs).

(4) The distinction between the Subjunctive and Optative on the criterion of vividness has been strongly criticized on the grounds that in a given example the Subjunctive or Optative might appear to be equally vivid in describing the event.[3] For example, D. 4.11-12: καὶ γὰρ ἂν οὗτός τι πάθῃ, ταχέως ὑμεῖς ἕτερον Φίλιππον ποιήσετε. . . . καίτοι καὶ τοῦτο. εἴ τι πάθοι καὶ τὰ τῆς τύχης ἡμῖν . . . καὶ τοῦτ᾽ ἐξεργάσαιτο (for if this one were to suffer anything [Subjunctive], immediately you would create another P.. . . .and indeed even this; if he might suffer anything [Optative] indeed our fortune . . . might accomplish this). (Cf. D. 18.147-48, with two Subjunctive and two Optative protases in a section of indirect discourse. Goodwin defends his interpretation of this passage in *Demosthenes*, 110.)

(5) Goodwin's scheme has difficulty categorizing the Subjunctive, Optative or Future. The examples cited are found in Goodwin's various discussions, without necessarily endorsing his categories, especially those used of future reference. Greenberg ("Realis-Irrealis," 252), reocgnizing the problem, attempts to avoid it by dividing the Subjunctive and Future into separate categories.

The Future may express a present intention (Ar. Birds 759: αἶρε πλῆκτρον, εἰ μαχεῖ [raise your spur, if you will fight]), or be used like the Subjunctive (E. Fr. 5: εἰ μὴ καθέξεις γλῶσσαν, ἔσται σοι κακά [if you will not hold your tongue, you will have trouble]). The Optative may express a future condition (A. Prom. 979: εἴης φορητὸς οὐκ ἄν, εἰ πράσσοις καλῶς ["you would not be endurable, if you should be in prosperity" (Goodwin, *Grammar*, 301)]) or a past general condition (Th. 8.66.2: εἰ δέ τις καὶ ἀντείποι, εὐθὺς ἐκ τρόπου τινὸς ἐπιτηδείου ἐτεθνήκει [if anyone objected, immediately he was killed from a certain designated place]). And the Subjunctive may express a future condition (X. Anab. 7.3.11: ἂν δέ τις ἀνθιστῆται, σὺν ὑμῖν πειρασόμεθα χειροῦσθαι [if someone will stand against us, we shall attempt to overcome with you]) or a present general condition (E. Alc. 671-72: ἢν δ᾽ ἐγγὺς ἔλθῃ θάνατος, οὐδεὶς βούλεται / θνῄσκειν [if death comes near, no one wants to die]).

(6) The II class conditional, in which the Imperfect refers to present (or past) time, is out of character with his temporal scheme. Thus Goodwin's analysis, primarily because of its overriding dependence upon a temporal method of classification, proves inadequate.[4]

b. The second major conditional scheme--appreciating use of the Moods--was promoted by Gildersleeve first in his Latin grammar, and for Greek first by C. Morris ("Forms," 46; Gildersleeve applied this scheme to Greek in esp. "On εἰ," 6-14; "Syntax," 435-37). Grammars using similar schemes include: Winer (363-70); Robertson (1004-27); Blass (213-25); Blass/Debrunner (¶¶ 371-73); Kühner/Gerth (2.463-88); Jelf (2.525-42);

---

[3]As will be seen below, much of this criticism has been misdirected by wanting to find objective characterizations of events. Actually, Goodwin and his critics are in fundamental agreement that the Subjunctive and Optative are used distinctively, but they have trouble expressing what this difference is. Besides the grammars, see esp. Sewall, "Distinction"; C. Morris, "Forms"; and a response in Goodwin, "'Shall.'"

[4]The recent treatment by Wakker ("Potential") is vitiated by dependence upon a temporal criterion, even though he realizes this is not satisfying (225). His translations of examples confirm this: e.g. Ar. Ach. 476: κάκιστ᾽ ἀπολοίμην, εἴ τί σ᾽ αἰτήσαιμ᾽ ἔτι ("may I perish miserably, if I asked you anything else") he cites as an example of "clear" future reference (225), and S. Oed. Col. 991-94: ἐν γὰρ μ᾽ ἄμειψαι μοῦνον ὧν σ᾽ ἀνιστορῶ. / εἴ τίς σε . . . αὐτίκ᾽ ἐνθάδε κτείνοι . . ., πότερα / πυνθάνοι᾽ ἂν εἰ / πατήρ σ᾽ ὁ καίνων ἢ τίνοι᾽ ἂν εὐθέως; ("I ask you to answer one thing only; if, here and now, someone were to attempt to kill you, would you ask if the killer was your father or would you take vengeance immediately?") as present (227).

Schwyzer (2.682-88); Rijksbaron (68-74). By using Gildersleeve's Mood-oriented analysis, along with the significant contribution of verbal aspect, a sizable step forward can be taken in understanding conditional statements. (See Gonda, *Character*, 171ff., who discounting a temporal scheme formulates a theory on the basis of attitude and aspect; this is suggested by Schwyzer [2.686]; and Zerwick [107] for the "unreal" conditional.) This scheme essentially combines a formal analysis of the protasis with the semantics of attitudinal function (see chapt. 2; Greenberg ["Realis-Irrealis," esp. 248] also defends a formal analysis, focusing upon the protasis). The result is two major categories of conditional statements, those of assertion and those of projection, differentiated along the lines of attitude. Within the first category there is one major category, that of assertion for the sake of argument, with a sub-category, that of assertion to the contrary. Within the second category there are three sub-categories, that of projection with no reference to fulfilment, that of projection with contingency for fulfilment, and that of expectation of fulfilment. Within these five sub-categories (except the last), verbal aspect differentiates usage.

From a linguistic standpoint, on the basis of tense form and Mood function in Greek and in the discourse context, the protasis is best described as "non-factive," i.e. "its utterance commits the speaker to neither the truth nor the falsity of the proposition expressed. . ." (Lyons, *Semantics*, 796). Therefore, it is inappropriate in the first instance to ask questions of temporal reference of the conditional itself in either protasis or apodosis (apart from deictic indicators, as in chapt. 2), since as seen above, these questions are matters of reference to the real world, not the possible world of the conditional statement. As Palmer (*Mood*, 189) says, "Neither [the protasis or apodosis] indicates that an event has occurred (or is occurring or will occur); the sentence merely indicates the dependence of the truth of one proposition upon the truth of another."

2. NEW PROPOSAL.

I. Assertion. Within this category all examples that utilize the Indicative Mood are found (of course excluding the Future per above and chapt. 9).

a. Assertion for the sake of argument. The general form of this conditional is εἰ + Indicative. Goodwin's categorial description is more accurate than Gildersleeve's at this point, since Goodwin, followed by Gonda, specifies that this category implies nothing of completion. As Braunlich points out ("Goodwin," 181-82), calling this category "logical," as do Gildersleeve and others (e.g. Pritchett, "Sentence," 5ff.; Boyer, "First Class," 81-82), is unhelpful, since there is nothing more logical about this category than any other. In fact, there are several instances in which it is difficult to see what the logical connection between the protasis and apodosis is: E. Iph. Taur. 1288:[5] τί δ᾽ ἔστιν, εἰ χρὴ μὴ κελευσθεῖσαν λέγειν; (what is it, if it is possible to speak not being commanded?); Rom 11:18: εἰ δὲ κατακαυχᾶσαι, οὐ σὺ τὴν ῥίζαν βαστάζεις ἀλλὰ ἡ ῥίζα σέ (but if you are boasting, you are not bearing the root but the root you).

Despite much work on the Moods, there is still the persistent belief among certain grammarians that this category of conditional asserts a fact (this belief seems to be more widespread among NT grammars than classical grammars: e.g. Winer, 364; Turner, *Syntax*, 115; Blass/Debrunner, ¶¶ 371-72),[6] or is at least believed to be fulfilled (Robertson, 1006). This may be disproved through citation of parallel conditionals in opposition: Matt 26:39, 42: Πάτερ μου, εἰ δυνατόν ἐστιν, παρελθάτω ἀπ᾽ ἐμοῦ τὸ ποτήριον τοῦτο . . . Πάτερ μου, εἰ οὐ δύναται τοῦτο παρελθεῖν ἐὰν μὴ αὐτὸ πίω, γενηθήτω τὸ θέλημά σου (my father, if it is possible, let this cup pass from me . . . my father, if it is not possible for this to pass by unless I might drink it, let your will come to pass); John 10:37-38: εἰ οὐ ποιῶ τὰ ἔργα τοῦ πατρός μου, μὴ πιστεύετέ μοι· εἰ δὲ ποιῶ, κἂν ἐμοὶ μὴ πιστεύητε, τοῖς ἔργοις πιστεύετε (if I do not do the works of my father, don't believe me; but if I do, and if you might not believe me, believe my works); John 14:7, 11.

A comparable study of classical Greek is still awaited (although the same categorization applies), but Boyer has analysed the 300+ examples of this construction in the NT, and has concluded that (1) 37% have conditions "obviously true," (2) 12% "obviously false," and (3) 51% "undetermined" ("First Class," 76). Thus fully 63% of NT examples do not show that this conditional asserts a fact as true. The best description is non-factive, though attitudinally asserted.

Examples of (2), obviously false conditionals, include: Matt 12:27: εἰ ἐγὼ ἐν Βεελζεβοὺλ ἐκβάλλω τὰ δαιμόνια, οἱ υἱοὶ ὑμῶν ἐν τίνι ἐκβάλλουσιν; (if I cast out the demons by Beelzeboul, by whom do your sons cast out?); John 10:37: (see above); John 18:23: εἰ κακῶς ἐλάλησα, μαρτύρησον περὶ τοῦ κακοῦ (if I speak evily, testify concerning the evil); John 20:15: εἰ σὺ ἐβάστασας αὐτόν, εἰπέ μοι ποῦ ἔθηκας αὐτόν (if you took him, tell me where you put him); 1 Cor 15:13-14: εἰ δὲ ἀνάστασις νεκρῶν οὐκ ἔστιν, οὐδὲ Χριστὸς ἐγήγερται· εἰ δὲ Χριστὸς οὐκ ἐγήγερται, κενὸν ἄρα [καὶ] τὸ κήρυγμα ἡμῶν (if there is no resurrection from the dead, Christ was not raised; and if Christ was not raised, our preaching is empty).[7]

It is appropriate to include here also examples that are usually classified as II.b. (unreal) conditionals without ἄν in the apodosis, since formally the protasis is identical (Boyer, "Second Class," 85). See for example: Matt 26:24 (cf. Mark 14:21): καλὸν ἦν αὐτῷ εἰ οὐκ ἐγεννήθη ὁ ἄνθρωπος ἐκεῖνος (it is better for him if that man was not born); John 9:33: εἰ μὴ ἦν οὗτος παρὰ θεοῦ, οὐκ ἠδύνατο ποιεῖν οὐδέν (if this one is not from God, he is not able to do anything); John 15:22, 24: εἰ μὴ ἦλθον καὶ ἐλάλησα αὐτοῖς, ἁμαρτίαν οὐκ εἴχοσαν. . . . εἰ τὰ ἔργα μὴ ἐποίησα ἐν αὐτοῖς ἃ οὐδεὶς ἄλλος ἐποίησεν, ἁμαρτίαν οὐκ εἴχοσαν (if I do not come and speak to them, they have no sin. . . . if I do not do works among them which no one

---

[5]Braunlich also cites E. El. 1086-87: εἰ δ᾽, ὡς λέγεις, σὴν θυγατέρ᾽ ἔκτεινεν πατήρ, / ἐγὼ τί σ᾽ ἠδίκης᾽ ἐμός τε σύγγονος; (and if, as you say, my father killed your daughter, how was I unjust to you, and to my own brother?).

[6]Voelz ("Language," 944), following Kruger (*Conditional*, 15), claims that the I class conditional in NT Greek is used exclusively for facts, as opposed to classical Greek usage. They seem to confuse this with the fact that in hellenistic Greek εἰ is no longer widespread with the Subjunctive, as well as with the forms of negation (see below).

[7]E.g. Pl. Apol. 34D: εἰ δή τις ὑμῶν οὕτως ἔχει--οὐκ ἀξιῶ μὲν γὰρ ἔγωγε, εἰ δ᾽ οὖν--ἐπιεικῆ ἄν μοι δοκῶ πρὸς τοῦτον λέγειν λέγων ὅτι . . . (if anyone of you is thus--for I myself do not think this, but if so--I would be thinking fairly to say to this one, saying that); D. 18.12: τῶν μέντοι κατηγοριῶν καὶ τῶν αἰτιῶν τῶν εἰρημένων, εἴπερ ἦσαν ἀληθεῖς, οὐκ ἔνι τῇ πόλει δίκην ἀξίαν λαβεῖν, οὐδ᾽ ἐγγύς (of the accusations and spoken charges, if they are true, there is no way for the city to receive adequate justice, nor a way near). Many more examples might be cited.

else does, they have no sin); Acts 26:32: ἀπολελύσθαι ἐδύνατο ὁ ἄνθρωπος οὗτος εἰ μὴ ἐπεκέκλητο Καίσαρα (if he did not appeal to C., this man was able to be released). Particularly instructive here is John 19:11: οὐκ εἶχες ἐξουσίαν κατ᾽ ἐμοῦ οὐδεμίαν εἰ μὴ ἦν δεδομένον σοι ἄνωθεν (you do not have any authority over me unless it is given to you from above), to illustrate that it is the context of the argument that establishes whether the conditional is treated by the author or speaker as unreal, not necessarily the form of the conditional (Smyth, 515; see e.g. D. 27.37: τοῦτο τοίνυν, εἰ καὶ τἆλλα πάντ᾽ ἀποστεροῦσιν ἀρνούμενοι μὴ ἔχειν, ἀποδοῦναι προσῆκεν [even if they take away all the other things, denying that they have them, it is proper to give back this]). These examples are best classified as I.a.[8]

The question of the relation of οὐ and μή must be entertained here (see e.g. Kühner/Gerth, 2.189; Wackernagel, *Vorlesungen*, 279; Goodwin, *Syntax*, 138; Schwyzer, 2.593; Humbert, 351-52). Koppers (*Sentences*, esp. 34-48, 77-78, 113-26), following Goodwin, argues convincingly that selection of the negative is according to the feeling of the speaker (38), with, as Moorhouse terms it, οὐ the negation of the "concrete or actual," and μή the negation of the "notional or ideal" (*Studies*, 40 n. 1), with both οὐ and μή occurring in so-called 1 class conditionals. The situation in hellenistic Greek is complicated by expansion of μή, so that it virtually dominates the non-Indicative Moods, while οὐ predominates in the Indicative (Blass's canon [253]; see also Gildersleeve, "Encroachment"; Green, "Μή for οὐ"; cf. Gonda, *Character*, 203 n. 1: "If we are right in the opinion that μή essentially served to reject the realization of a process, it involved an element of emotion and subjectiveness [cf. also Stahl, p. 233] which being foreign to the more intellectual οὐ, has no doubt contributed to its spread"). Moulton (170-71) notes that only in four instances--1 Cor 15:2; 2 Cor 13:5; Gal 1:7; 1 Tim 6:3--of 31 negative 1 class conditionals is οὐ μή used, while οὐ μή in unfulfilled conditionals is in all but Mark 14:21 par. Matt 26:24. But this classification is skewed, since it appears that the negation, as well as the construction of the apodosis with ἄν, has been used to establish the categories. Once Koppers's thesis is taken into account, as well as construction of the apodosis, a far larger number of 1 class conditionals is seen to be negated with μή (cf. Koppers, 77-78, for classical examples). Perhaps the difference is between negating the simple supposition (e.g. S. Aj. 1131: εἰ τοὺς θανόντας οὐκ ἐᾷς θάπτειν [if you do not permit burying the dead]; John 5:47: εἰ δὲ τοῖς ἐκείνου γράμμασιν οὐ πιστεύετε [if you do not believe his writings]) and negating the more subjective or notional supposition (e.g. Pl. Apol. 27B: εἰ μὴ σὺ βούλει ἀποκρίνεσθαι [if you do not want to answer]; 1 Cor 15:2: ἐκτὸς εἰ μὴ εἰκῇ ἐπιστεύσατε [except if you did not believe in vain]), although this is difficult to determine.

Examples of (3), undetermined conditionals, include: Matt 5:29, 30: εἰ δὲ ὁ ὀφθαλμός σου ὁ δεξιὸς σκανδαλίζει σε, ἔξελε αὐτὸν καὶ βάλε ἀπὸ σοῦ. . . . καὶ εἰ ἡ δεξιά σου χεὶρ σκανδαλίζει σε, ἔκκοψον αὐτὴν καὶ βάλε ἀπὸ σοῦ (if your right eye causes you to stumble, pluck it out and cast it from you. . . . and if your right hand causes you to stumble, cut it off and cast it from you); Matt 17:4: εἰ θέλεις, ποιήσω ὧδε τρεῖς σκηνάς (if you want, I will make here three tents); Matt 26:39, 42: εἰ δυνατόν ἐστιν, παρελθάτω ἀπ᾽ ἐμοῦ τὸ ποτήριον τοῦτο. . . . εἰ οὐ δύναται τοῦτο παρελθεῖν ἐὰν μὴ αὐτὸ πίω, γενηθήτω τὸ θέλημά σου (if it is possible, let this cup pass from me. . . . if it is not possible for this to pass by unless I drink it, let your will come to pass), cited above also; Acts 5:39: εἰ δὲ ἐκ θεοῦ ἐστιν, οὐ δυνήσεσθε καταλῦσαι αὐτούς (if this is from God, you will not be able to destroy them); Rom 8:9-11: ὑμεῖς δὲ οὐκ

---

[8] See also Luke 19:42, an elliptical construction; Gal 4:15, with a verbless protasis; and 1 Cor 12:17, 19: εἰ ὅλον τὸ σῶμα ὀφθαλμός, ποῦ ἡ ἀκοή; εἰ ὅλον ἀκοή, ποῦ ἡ ὄσφρησις; . . . εἰ δὲ ἦν τὰ πάντα ἓν μέλος, ποῦ τὸ σῶμα; (if the whole body is an eye, where is the hearing? if the whole is hearing, where is the smelling? . . . if the whole is one part, where is the body?). Though the verbless protasis, as well as this method of classification, makes the point moot, 1 Cor 12:17, 19 is usually classified as an unreal conditional.

ἐστὲ ἐν σαρκὶ ἀλλὰ ἐν πνεύματι, εἴπερ πνεῦμα θεοῦ οἰκεῖ ἐν ὑμῖν. εἰ δέ τις⁹ πνεῦμα Χριστοῦ οὐκ ἔχει, οὗτος οὐκ ἔστιν αὐτοῦ. εἰ δὲ Χριστὸς ἐν ὑμῖν, τὸ μὲν σῶμα νεκρὸν διὰ ἀμαρτίαν, τὸ δὲ πνεῦμα ζωὴ διὰ δικαιοσύνην. εἰ δὲ τὸ πνεῦμα τοῦ ἐγείραντος τὸν Ἰησοῦν ἐκ νεκρῶν οἰκεῖ ἐν ὑμῖν, ὁ ἐγείρας Χριστὸν ἐκ νεκρῶν ζωοποιήσει καὶ τὰ θνητὰ σώματα ὑμῶν διὰ τοῦ ἐνοικοῦντος αὐτοῦ πνεύματος ἐν ὑμῖν (you are not in the flesh but in the spirit, if the spirit of God dwells in you. And if someone does not have the spirit of Christ, he is not of him. And if Christ is in you, the body is dead on account of sin, but the spirit is life on account of righteousness. And if the spirit of the one who raised Jesus from the dead lives in you, the one who raised Christ from the dead will make alive indeed your mortal body through his indwelling spirit in you); 1 Cor 7:12-13, 15: εἴ τις ἀδελφὸς γυναῖκα ἔχει ἄπιστον, καὶ αὕτη συνευδοκεῖ οἰκεῖν μετ᾽ αὐτοῦ, μὴ ἀφιέτω αὐτήν· καὶ γυνὴ εἴ τις ἔχει ἄνδρα ἄπιστον, καὶ οὗτος συνευδοκεῖ οἰκεῖν μετ᾽ αὐτῆς, μὴ ἀφιέτω τὸν ἄνδρα. . . . εἰ δὲ ὁ ἄπιστος χωρίζεται, χωριέσθω (if some brother has an unbelieving wife, and she agrees to live with him, let him not divorce her; and if some woman has an unbelieving husband, and he agrees to live with her, let her not divorce him. . . . And if the unbeliever departs, let him depart); 1 Cor 9:17: εἰ γὰρ ἑκὼν τοῦτο πράσσω, μισθὸν ἔχω· εἰ δὲ ἄκων, οἰκονομίαν πεπίστευμαι (for if I do this willingly, I have a reward; and if unwillingly, I am faithful to my responsibility); 2 Cor 1:6: εἴτε δὲ θλιβόμεθα, ὑπὲρ τῆς ὑμῶν παρακλήσεως καὶ σωτηρίας· εἴτε παρακαλούμεθα, ὑπὲρ τῆς ὑμῶν παρακλήσεως τῆς ἐνεργουμένης ἐν ὑπομονῇ τῶν αὐτῶν παθημάτων (if we are persecuted, it is on behalf of our comfort and salvation; and if we are comforted, it is on behalf of your comfort which is effective in patience of the same sufferings).[10]

A common distinction in this class of conditional is that the Aorist and Imperfect are past-referring and the Present is present-referring.[11] Rarely is mention made of the Perfect. As argued in chapt. 2, since it has been shown that the tense forms are not essentially time-based, it is inappropriate first to ask questions of temporal reference of verbal usage in Greek. In any case, temporal distinctions simply do not hold if determined along the lines of tense form (although it is not the case that in every instance a tense form can be shown to depart from the standard conception). Enough clear examples exist to prove the standard rule inadequate and force subsequent examination to approach verbal usage from a non-temporal perspective.

---

[9]Beyer (Syntax, 226-28) claims that εἴ τις/ἐάν τις may be Semitic. Although he admits that the protasis following the apodosis is Greek (e.g. Pl. Apol. 27E), other examples that call his analysis into question may also be cited. Pl. Apol. 33B: εἰ δέ τίς φησι παρ᾽ ἐμοῦ πώποτέ τι μαθεῖν . . . εὖ ἴστε ὅτι (if anyone says of me that I ever suffered anything . . . you well know that); Epict. 1.3.1: εἴ τις τῷ δόγματι τούτῳ συμπαθῆσαι κατ᾽ ἀξίαν δύναιτο . . . οἶμαι . . . (if anyone might be able to be convinced by this doctrine according to its worthiness . . . I think).

[10]E.g. Pl. Apol. 27B: εἰ μὴ σὺ βούλει ἀποκρίνεσθαι, ἐγὼ σοὶ λέγω καὶ τοῖς ἄλλοις τουτοισί (if you do not want to answer, I am going to tell you such things); Antipho 5.85: εἰ δὲ δύο ἐξ ἑνὸς ἀγῶνος γεγένησθαι, οὐκ ἐγὼ αἴτιος, ἀλλ᾽ οἱ κατήγοροι (if two [trials] have come about from one trial, I am not the cause, but the accusers); X. Anab. 4.6.10: εἰ μὲν ἀνάγκη ἐστὶ μάχεσθαι, τοῦτο δεῖ παρασκευάσασθαι ὅπως ὡς κράτιστα μαχούμεθα· εἰ δὲ βουλόμεθα ὡς ῥᾷστα ὑπερβάλλειν, τοῦτό μοι δοκεῖ σκεπτέον εἶναι ὅπως ὡς ἐλάχιστα μὲν τραύματα λάβωμεν, ὡς ἐλάχιστα δὲ σώματα ἀνδρῶν ἀποβάλωμεν (if it is a necessity to fight, it is necessary to be prepared so that we might fight most strongly; but if we want to excel most easily, this seems to me to be the matter for consideration, that we might receive the least injuries, and we might lose the fewest men). Many more examples might be cited.

[11]Of this class of conditional in the NT approximately 7% use a form of εἰμί, and 13% are verbless. Particularly noteworthy is the fact that virtually all conditionals about Jesus' divinity use εἰμί: e.g. Matt 4:3, 6; 27:40; Luke 12:28; 22:67; 23:35, 37; John 1:25; 10:24.

Thus, the Aorist in several cases is not past-referring (of course this does not mean that it must be present-referring).[12]

John 15:20: εἰ ἐμὲ ἐδίωξαν, καὶ ὑμᾶς διώξουσιν· εἰ τὸν λόγον μου ἐτήρησαν, καὶ τὸν ὑμέτερον τηρήσουσιν (if they persecute me, indeed they will persecute you; if they keep my word, indeed they will keep yours). Embedded in a series of conditional statements, these two conditionals with Aorist verbs in the protasis illustrate that to press temporal distinctions on the basis of verb tense is to run the risk of making nonsense. This section (vv 18ff.) begins with the words of Jesus: εἰ ὁ κόσμος ὑμᾶς μισεῖ, γινώσκετε ὅτι ἐμὲ πρῶτον ὑμῶν μεμίσηκεν (if the world hates you, know that it is in a state of hating me first before you. Brown (*John*, 2.686) says, "Grammatically this is a real condition [?]; the world does hate the disciples" (cf. on v 19; cf. 1 John 3:13), but there is little if any substantial evidence in the Gospel to this point that Jesus, much less the disciples, is hated by the world, having just experienced his triumphal entry into Jerusalem (John 12:12ff.). This indicates a timeless or perhaps future use of the verb, in the non-factive conditional, with this section being embedded in a lengthy section of teaching by Jesus (14:1ff). Verse 19 confirms this with a non-past use of ἦτε in a contrary assertion reinforced by an assertion assumed for argument. If temporal reference must be established, the protasis in v 20 may be future-referring, alluding to Jesus' death (contra Barrett [*John*, 480], who treats these verses as part of the Johannine church's experience). This is fairly well assured for the second conditional, where past reference would make little sense of the flow of the argument (if the sentence is past-referring the implication would be that this is the protasis of a contrary assertion, although the apodosis does not conform to the usual form), since whatever teaching Jesus refers to (temporal reference of v 20a--τοῦ λόγου οὗ ἐγὼ εἶπον ὑμῖν [the word which I speak to you]--is not clear) has had virtually no chance to be tested.[13]

Gal 2:17: εἰ δὲ ζητοῦντες δικαιωθῆναι ἐν Χριστῷ εὑρέθημεν καὶ αὐτοὶ ἁμαρτωλοί, ἆρα[14] Χριστὸς ἁμαρτίας διάκονος; (if seeking to be justified in Christ we are found to be sinners, Christ is then a servant of sin?). Cf. v 18 with timeless Present. Betz (*Galatians*, 119-20), in deciding whether v 17 is a real or unreal conditional (note his potentially misleading language), decides that it is a real conditional, while v 18 is an unreal.

Matt 10:25b: εἰ τὸν οἰκοδεσπότην Βεελζεβοὺλ ἐπεκάλεσαν, πόσῳ μᾶλλον τοὺς οἰκιακοὺς αὐτοῦ (if they call the householder Beelzeboul, how much more the members of his household). A series of timeless statements about the relations of teachers and disciples (10:24-25a) is rounded off with a conditional statement. If the conditional has personal deictic reference to

---

[12]E.g. E. Iph. Aul. 1395-96: εἰ δ᾽ ἐβουλήθη τὸ σῶμα τοὐμὸν Ἄρτεμις λαβεῖν, / ἐμποδὼν γενήσομαι 'γὼ θνητὸς οὖσα τῇ θεῷ; (if A. wants to take my body, will I be able being mortal to impede the goddess?); Pl. Apol. 33D: εἰ γὰρ δὴ ἔγωγε τῶν νέων τοὺς μὲν διαφθείρω τοὺς δὲ διέφθαρκα, χρῆν δήπου, εἴτε τινὲς αὐτῶν πρεσβύτεροι γενόμενοι ἔγνωσαν ὅτι νέοις οὖσιν αὐτοῖς ἐγὼ κακὸν πώποτέ τι ξυνεβούλευσα, νυνὶ αὐτοὺς ἀναβαίνοντας ἐμοῦ κατηγορεῖν καὶ τιμωρεῖσθαι (for if I was corrupting some of the youth and corrupted others [note contrast in aspect], it is doubtless required, if any of them, having become older, *know* that there are youths among them to which I ever gave bad advice, now that they are grown to accuse and rebuke me); cf. following Imperfect, ἤθελον (they want). Epict. 1.25.32: εἴ τις ἀπείρῳ τῶν ἰατρικῶν τοῦτο εἶπεν, οὐκ ἂν κατεγέλα τοῦ λέγοντος; (if anyone says he is untested of the doctors, would he not laugh at the one speaking?); P.Oxy. 1291.5-8 (A.D. 30): ἡ (= εἰ) ἔπεμ/ψας διὰ Κολλούθου / ἐπιστολήν, εἰδοὺ ἀρ/τάβηι σοι γίνεται (if you send a letter through K., behold the artabe is going to come to you), with following (lines 8-12) ἐὰν / δὲ θέρῃς (= θέλῃς) εἰς Ἀλεξάν/δρεαν ἀπελθεῖν, Ἀπολ/λῶς Θέωνος ὑπάγει / αὔριον (if you might want to go away to Alexandrea, A. T. is going tomorrow).

[13]Cf. John 13:32, with εἰ ὁ θεὸς ἐδοξάσθη ἐν αὐτῷ (A^c ℵ^c C^2 K f^13). But this receives only a C rating in UBS^3. On the strength of the textual evidence against its inclusion (p^66 ℵ* B C* D L W X f^1 etc.) it should probably be rejected. See Metzger, *Commentary*, 242.

[14]See Bruce, *Galatians*, 141, on ἆρα as an inferential particle.

Jesus, it might refer to a previous event, but this is not required, since Jesus appears to have been accused of being a demon on various occasions: e.g. Matt 9:34; 12:22ff. (Carson, "Matthew," 254). The statement is kept on the general and non-temporal level to coordinate it with the previous generalizations. The verbless apodosis reinforces this understanding.

Mark 3:26 (cf. Luke 11:18): εἰ ὁ σατανᾶς ἀνέστη ἐφ' ἑαυτὸν καὶ ἐμερίσθη, οὐ δύναται στῆναι ἀλλὰ τέλος ἔχει (if Satan rises up against himself and is divided, he is not able to stand but has attained his end). When seen in light of two previous projected conditionals (with no reference to fulfilment), this parallel conditional is clearly seen as timeless. The scribes were accusing Jesus of being Beelzeboul, and claiming that he was casting out demons in his power. Jesus replies, first with a general question: πῶς δύναται σατανᾶς σατανᾶν ἐκβάλλειν; (how is Satan able to cast out Satan?) (v 23). Two hypothetical possibilities are given: ἐὰν βασιλεία ἐφ' ἑαυτὴν μερισθῇ, οὐ δύναται σταθῆναι ἡ βασιλεία ἐκείνη· καὶ ἐὰν οἰκία ἐφ' ἑαυτὴν μερισθῇ, οὐ δυνήσεται ἡ οἰκία ἐκείνη σταθῆναι (if a kingdom is divided upon itself, that kingdom is not able to stand; and if a house is divided upon itself, that house will not be able to stand). Jesus' response to his critics substitutes portions of his original question into various conditional statements, and is extended in v 27. The same pattern can be seen in Luke 11:18, with one interesting further observation. In v 18a the protasis is 3d Person, the unmarked Person, and probably timeless. But in v 18b, the person shifts to 2d Person and then 1st Person, so that v 19 (cf. v 20) reads: εἰ δὲ ἐγὼ ἐν Βεελζεβοὺλ ἐκβάλλω τὰ διαιμόνια, οἱ υἱοὶ ὑμῶν ἐν τίνι ἐκβάλλουσιν; (if I cast out the demons by Beelzeboul, by whom do your sons cast out?). It is worth considering whether the person deixis grounds this conditional in present reference, although timeless use is likely. Matt 12:26-28 illustrates the same shift in Person, although all of the verbs in protases are Present forms.

Rom 3:3, 7: τί γὰρ εἰ ἠπίστησάν τινες;[15] . . . εἰ δὲ ἡ ἀλήθεια τοῦ θεοῦ ἐν τῷ ἐμῷ ψεύσματι ἐπερίσσευσεν εἰς τὴν δόξαν αὐτοῦ, τί ἔτι κἀγὼ ὡς ἁμαρτωλὸς κρίνομαι; (what if certain ones don't believe?. . . If the truth of God multiplies into his glory in my lie, why am I still judged as a sinner?). From 2:17ff. Paul is engaged in a theoretical discussion of what it means to be a Jew. This discussion is conducted with few deictic indicators apart from reference to the law, and includes several hypothetical conditional statements (2:25, 26). Paul is clearly concerned to establish principles, thus he asks rhetorically what the advantage of being a Jew is (3:1). Much in every way, he says, for the words (λόγια) of God are believed. He then asks, τί γὰρ εἰ ἠπίστησάν τινες; While this may refer to a previous period in Jewish history, Paul's subsequent question points away from this: μὴ ἡ ἀπιστία αὐτῶν τὴν πίστιν τοῦ θεοῦ καταργήσει; (their unfaithfulness will not establish the faithfulness of God, will it?). μὴ γένοιτο. Paul now reflects briefly on God's nature. It is here that he includes two parallel conditional statements: 3:5 (εἰ δὲ ἡ ἀδικία ἡμῶν θεοῦ δικαιοσύνην συνίστησιν, τί ἐροῦμεν; [if our injustice is demonstrating the righteousness of God, what will we say?]) and 3:7. He restates 3:5a in a less favourable light: μὴ ἄδικος ὁ θεὸς ὁ ἐπιφέρων τὴν ὀργήν; (it's not that the God who brings wrath is unjust, is it?). μὴ γένοιτο, since God would be unable to judge the world. Paul then asks the question of 3:7. In response to those who reportedly say that Paul teaches that people should do bad so that good comes, he says that their condemnation is just. Quite clearly, a temporal scheme would ruin the impact of the crescendo Paul is building. First he says that man's unfaithfulness does not establish God's faithfulness, since God's character is faithful independent of man. Having said this, Paul then uses the two parallel conditions. If the first were taken to be temporally referential on the basis of the Present verb, it would undermine what Paul has just said regarding God's character. It is making a timeless assertion for the sake of argument, and one that warrants a strong negative. The parallel conditional in 3:7, if it were to be taken as past-referring, would lead the argument even further afield.

Of the approximately 53 Aorist conditionals of this type, the vast majority have no specific deictic indicators: e.g. Rom 6:8 (cf. 2 Tim 2:11): εἰ δὲ ἀπεθάνομεν σὺν Χριστῷ, πιστεύομεν ὅτι καὶ συζήσομεν αὐτῷ (if we die with Christ, we believe that we will live with him). The

---

[15]Cf. Cranfield, *Romans*, 1.179-80, for alternative punctuation: τί γάρ; εἰ. . . .

complexity of temporal determination can be seen in this example. 6:2ff. use several different metaphors to describe events of Christian experience, such as dying to sin (v 2), being baptized into Christ or his death (vv 3, 4), and being buried with him (v 4). On the one hand, although they cannot be taken literally, they could refer to various past experiences that Christians share in. On the other, the timeless statement of v 7 (ὁ γὰρ ἀποθανὼν δεδικαίωται ἀπὸ τῆς ἁμαρτίας [the one who dies is justified from sin]) is obviously alluded to in v 8, which picks up the Aorist tense and lexical item in the protasis. In line with the non-factive character of the conditional, it is best to begin from non-temporal reference in this instance. Cf. Col 2:20: εἰ ἀπεθάνετε σὺν Χριστῷ ἀπὸ τῶν στοιχείων τοῦ κόσμου, τί ὡς ζῶντες ἐν κόσμῳ δογματίζεσθε; (if you die with Christ from the elementary principles of the world, why, as living in the world, are you bound by rules?), where this timeless statement illustrates antecedent action in the protasis, grounding the conditional in a previous situation of general Christian experience. (Lightfoot [*Colossians*, 200] claims that the Aorist is used to refer to "one absolute *crisis*.") It seems that the non-temporal nature of the tense forms is in full accord with the temporally non-determinative nature of non-factive conditional statements, but that temporal distinctions can be made on the basis of deictic indicators.

Conditionals that are past-referring virtually always have clear temporal deixis: e.g. Luke 16:11 (discourse deixis); 19:8 (time deixis); John 20:15 (discourse deixis); Rom 4:2 (person deixis); 11:17, 18, 21, 24 (person deixis); 1 Cor 15:32 (time deixis); 2 Cor 7:8 (time and discourse deixis); 2 Pet 2:4-9 (person and time deixis); Rev 20:15 (discourse deixis).

Unlike classical and other hellenistic Greek, there are no instances in the NT of an Imperfect verb in the protasis of this class of conditional (apart from assertions to the contrary; see below), although a similar argument could be made for the various temporal uses (see chapt. 4 for discussion of the Present and Imperfect, both imperfective in aspect).[16] There are, however, instances of the Present, the most widely used verb tense in this class of conditional, used in clearly non present-referring contexts (this is not to say that examples not mentioned or those not clearly non present-referring are present-referring).[17]

Matt 5:29, 30; 18:8, 9 (timeless; see above). Matt 8:31 (future-referring): the Gadarene demons beseech Jesus, saying εἰ ἐκβάλλεις ἡμᾶς, ἀπόστειλον ἡμᾶς εἰς τὴν ἀγέλην τῶν χοίρων (if you are going to cast us out, send us into the herd of swine). Mark 9:42: ὃς ἂν σκανδαλίσῃ ἕνα τῶν μικρῶν τούτων τῶν πιστευόντων [εἰς ἐμέ], καλόν ἐστιν αὐτῷ μᾶλλον εἰ περίκειται μύλος ὀνικὸς περὶ τὸν τράχηλον αὐτοῦ καὶ βέβληται εἰς τὴν θάλασσαν (whoever causes the least of these who believe [in me] to stumble, it is better for him if a mill stone is tied around his neck and he is cast into the sea), with the indefinite relative with Subjunctive verb in a conditional-like statement setting the hypothetical tone for the conditional. Luke 16:31 (past): in the parable of the rich man and Lazarus, Abraham tells the rich man of his brothers that εἰ Μωϋσέως καὶ τῶν προφητῶν οὐκ ἀκούουσιν, οὐδ᾽ ἐάν τις ἐκ νεκρῶν ἀναστῇ πεισθήσονται (if they did not listen to M. and the prophets, they will not be convinced if someone might rise from the dead), with the person and discourse deixis establishing past reference. (It is difficult to see how Cranfield [*Mark*, 638] can justify treating these conditionals as

---

[16]E.g. Pl. Apol. 33D: εἰ δὲ μὴ αὐτοὶ ἤθελον, τῶν οἰκείων τινὰς τῶν ἐκείνων . . . εἴπερ ὑπ᾽ ἐμοῦ τι κακὸν ἐπεπόνθεσαν αὐτῶν οἱ οἰκεῖοι, νῦν μεμνῆσθαι καὶ τιμωρεῖσθαι (if they do not want to, certain ones of their household . . . if their household stands persuaded of something evil by me, ought now to remember and to punish), following a conditional with a Present Indicative; Epict. 1.4.13: καθάπερ εἰ ἀθλητῇ διελεγόμην "δεῖξόν μοι τοὺς ὤμους," εἶτα ἔλεγεν ἐκεῖνος "ἴδε μου τοὺς ἀλτῆρας" (just as if I say to an athlete, "Show me your shoulders," then he says, "See my jumping-weights").

[17]Pl. Phaed. 78C: εἰ δέ τι τυγχάνει ὂν ἀσύνθετον, τούτῳ μόνῳ προσήκει μὴ πάσχειν ταῦτα, εἴπερ τῳ ἄλλῳ; (if there is something which is uncompounded, in this way only does it come not to suffer these things, if anything?); cf. Phaed. 76C. See also PGM 4.1510-19 (4th cent. A.D.) with a string of timeless conditionals in a hypothetical context.

present and future-referring, apart from a standard conception of the tenses.) John 7:23 (timeless): εἰ περιτομὴν λαμβάνει ἄνθρωπος ἐν σαββάτῳ ἵνα μὴ λυθῇ ὁ νόμος Μωϋσέως, ἐμοὶ χολᾶτε ὅτι ὅλον ἄνθρωπον ὑγιῆ ἐποίησα ἐν σαββάτῳ; (if a man receives circumcision on the sabbath so that the law of M. is broken, are you mad at me because I make the man well on the sabbath?), in which there is no possible referential event mentioned. As Barrett (*John*, 320) claims this is a "customary fact which can be assumed as protasis to the argument."

1 Cor 3:12-14 (timeless): εἰ δέ τις ἐποικοδομεῖ ἐπὶ τὸν θεμέλιον χρυσόν, . . . ἑκάστου τὸ ἔργον φανερὸν γενήσεται. . . . εἴ τινος τὸ ἔργον μένει ὃ ἐποικοδόμησεν, μισθὸν λήμψεται (if someone builds upon the foundation with gold . . . his work will become clear. . . . if the work which he builds endures, he will receive a reward). Robertson/Plummer (*First Corinthians*, 64) note that whether the conditionals are present or future-referring (and the forms are either Presents or Futures) is "not very important." (The timeless use may point to the forms being Futures.) Whereas reference to the Corinthian church may be found in 3:10, the shift in v 12 to the conditional speaking of building with gold, etc., reinforces the strictly hypothetical nature of Paul's subsequent conditional assertions. Significant is Paul's use in 1 Cor 3:15 of the conditional with Future in the protasis (see below), which emphasizes the shift to the destructive potential of others' work. Verse 16 uses 2d Person deictic reference to ground the verse in the present church situation, leading to the timeless conditional in v 17: εἴ τις τὸν ναὸν τοῦ θεοῦ φθείρει, φθερεῖ τοῦτον ὁ θεός (if someone corrupts the temple of God, God will destroy him). 1 Cor 6:2 (future?): εἰ ἐν ὑμῖν κρίνεται ὁ κόσμος, ἀνάξιοί ἐστε κριτηρίων ἐλαχίστων; (if the world is going to be judged by you, are you unworthy of the most trivial matters?). Temporal reference of this conditional is directly dependent upon one's interpretation of v 2a: ἢ οὐκ οἴδατε ὅτι οἱ ἅγιοι τὸν κόσμον κρινοῦσιν; (don't you know that the saints are going to judge the world?), a theological rather than grammatical decision (see my chapt. 4 on future reference of the Present). 1 Cor 8:2-3 (timeless): εἴ τις δοκεῖ ἐγνωκέναι τι, οὔπω ἔγνω καθὼς δεῖ γνῶναι· εἰ δέ τις ἀγαπᾷ τὸν θεόν, οὗτος ἔγνωσται ὑπ᾽ αὐτοῦ (if someone thinks he knows anything, he does not yet know as it is necessary to know; and if someone loves God, he is known by him). (Orr/Walthers [*I Corinthians*, 226] claim that "the past aorist [in the apodosis] defies the translator." But is it a past Aorist? It does not appear so.) While reference to the Corinthian church situation is possible (v 1), the conditional with τις following the general statements of v 1a seem to indicate two general conditional statements. (τις/τι as subject is used in every conditional of this type in 1 Timothy: 1:10; 3:1, 5; 5:4, 8, 16; 6:3, 4, except 5.9-10, where the case of widows is specified. τις/τι appears in slightly over 20% of NT conditionals of this type.) 1 Cor 15:15-17, 19, 29, 32, 44: because ἐμαρτυρήσαμεν (we bear witness [Orr/Walthers (324-25) entertain the future (and aoristic?) use of the verb]) against God that he raised (ἤγειρεν) Christ, whom he did not raise (οὐκ ἤγειρεν) εἴπερ ἄρα νεκροὶ οὐκ ἐγείρονται. εἰ γὰρ νεκροὶ οὐκ ἐγείρονται, οὐδὲ Χριστὸς ἐγήγερται· εἰ δὲ Χριστὸς οὐκ ἐγήγερται, ματαία ἡ πίστις ὑμῶν (if dead men [note generic anarthrous noun] are not raised. For if dead men are not raised, neither was Christ raised; and if Christ was not raised, our faith is useless). . . . εἰ ἐν τῇ ζωῇ ταύτῃ ἐν Χριστῷ ἠλπικότες ἐσμὲν μόνον, ἐλεεινότεροι πάντων ἀνθρώπων ἐσμέν (if we have placed our hope in Christ in this life only, we are of all men the most pitiable). . . . εἰ ὅλως νεκροὶ οὐκ ἐγείρονται, τί καὶ βαπτίζονται ὑπὲρ αὐτῶν; (if dead men are wholly unraised, why do some get baptized for the dead [temporal reference here is unclear]?). . . . εἰ κατὰ ἄνθρωπον ἐθηριομάχησα ἐν Ἐφέσῳ, τί μοι τὸ ὄφελος; εἰ νεκροὶ οὐκ ἐγείρονται, φάγωμεν καὶ πίωμεν (if as a man I fought beasts in Ephesus, what good is it to me? If dead men are not raised, let us eat and drink). . . . εἰ ἔστιν σῶμα ψυχικόν, ἔστιν καὶ πνευματικόν (if a physical body exists, there is also a spiritual one). This series of conditional statements illustrates the importance of interpreting each in its proper context. The repeated timeless protasis (εἰ γὰρ νεκροὶ οὐκ ἐγείρονται) comprises a point of beginning for repeated non-factive suppositions that Paul uses to push forward his overall argument.

Jas 2:11 (timeless): εἰ δὲ οὐ μοιχεύεις, φονεύεις δέ, γέγονας παραβάτης νόμου (if you are not committing adultery, but you are killing, you are a breaker of the law). Even though James has referred to statements by Jesus in v 11a, the contrast which encompasses a range of sins serves to reinforce the timeless nature of Jesus' commandments. 1 Pet 2:19-20 (timeless or omnitemporal?): τοῦτο γὰρ χάρις εἰ διὰ συνείδησιν θεοῦ ὑποφέρει τις λύπας πάσχων ἀδίκως. ποῖον γὰρ κλέος εἰ ἁμαρτάνοντες καὶ κολαφιζόμενοι ὑπομενεῖτε; ἀλλ᾽ εἰ ἀγαθοποιοῦντες καὶ πάσχοντες ὑπομενεῖτε, τοῦτο χάρις παρὰ θεῷ (this is grace: if on account of conscience for God someone bears pain, suffering unjustly. For what kind of a report is it, if you endure when doing wrong and being struck for it? But if when doing good and suffering you endure, this is grace from God). This definition uses conditionals to establish a principle. The first, using τις, is not deictically centred, and although the second conditional could use person deixis, it appears in light of the final clause echoing the first that even the 2d Person reference is non-specific. Rev 13:9-10 (omnitemporal): εἴ τις ἔχει οὖς ἀκουσάτω (if any one has ears, let him hear). This obviously omnitemporal conditional, referring to something characteristic of humankind at all times, is followed by two timeless conditionals, using verbless protases: εἴ τις εἰς αἰχμαλωσίαν, εἰς αἰχμαλωσίαν ὑπάγει· εἴ τις ἐν μαχαίρῃ ἀποκτανθῆναι, αὐτὸν ἐν μαχαίρῃ ἀποκτανθῆναι (if someone [goes] unto captivity, unto captivity he goes; if someone [is] to be killed with the sword, he is to be killed with the sword),[18] referring to something that could happen at any time, but does not happen as a course of regular occurrence. To insist upon the present reference of this clause (or to try to interject finite verbs into the second and third) is to impose an unnecessary grid upon the language. Cf. variants on this phrase: Rev 2:7, 11, 17, 29; 3:6, 13, 22.

There are also several examples of the Perfect in this class of conditional, not usually cited by grammarians. The low number is in keeping with other ancient Greek usage.[19] Timeless reference is usual, thus not supporting traditional analysis of conditionals. (It is possible that the traditional time-based definition of the Perfect is responsible for its lack of treatment in the grammars.) For more detailed treatment of the range of temporal spheres of the Perfect see chapt 5. Below is a representative set of examples.

John 11:12 (present reference): κεκοίμηται (he sleeps), with person deixis to Lazarus; John 13:17 (present reference [Brown, *John*, 2.553]): οἴδατε, with 2d Person deictic reference reinforced by v 18 (οὐ περὶ πάντων ὑμῶν λέγω [I do not say this concerning all of you]); John 14:7 (timeless) (Brown [2.621] debates whether this is a real or contrary to fact conditional); Acts 16:15 (past or present?): κεκρίκατε (you judge), illustrating the importance of aspect over temporal reference in Greek, since it is the state of judgment, not when it was made, that is important; 1 Cor 15:14, 17, 19 (timeless; see above); 2 Cor 2:5, 10 (timeless): τις λελύπηκεν (someone grieves), κεχάρισμαι (I rejoice) with Paul using the same verb in the apodosis; 2 Cor 5:16 (timeless), where Plummer (*Second Corinthians*, 62) says that Paul "is not suggesting a doubt as to whether he has granted forgiveness, but he puts the fact of there being something for him to forgive as a mere hypothesis" (see chapt. 5); 2 Cor 10:7 (timeless): πέποιθεν (anyone persuades), with τις reinforcing timeless reference; 1 Tim 3:5 (timeless): τις . . . οἴδεν (someone knows), with the conditional introducing a timeless statement about government of one's family.

Discussion of ἄν above, and the realization that ἐάν is probably a combination of εἰ + ἄν (this has been questioned by some on the basis of accentuation; see Lightfoot, *Logic*, 127 n. 28)

---

[18]Textual variants attest to the difficulty of this verse, primarily by addition of verbs in the protasis of the first conditional. Charles's supposition that the pronoun should be αὐτός is groundless (*Revelation*, 1.355-56). See also Thompson, *Apocalypse*, 33, 63, 120.

[19]E.g. X. Mem. 2.2.7: ἀλλά τοι εἰ καὶ πάντα ταῦτα πεποίηκε καὶ ἄλλα τούτων πολλαπλάσια, οὐδεὶς ἂν δύναιτο αὐτῆς ἀνασχέσθαι τὴν χαλεπότητα (but indeed if she does all these things and many other things than these, no one would be able to bear her bad temper); Epict. 1.2.34: διὰ τί οὖν, εἰ πρὸς τοῦτο πεφύκαμεν, οὐ πάντες ἢ πολλοὶ γίνονται τοιοῦτοι; (why, therefore, if we are naturally endowed for this, do not all or many become such?).

allows the following examples to be noted, which might otherwise be considered aberrant,[20] since the determining factor is Mood: 1 John 5:15: ἐὰν οἴδαμεν ὅτι ἀκούει ἡμῶν ὅ ἐὰν αἰτώμεθα, οἴδαμεν ὅτι . . . (if we know that he hears us whatever we ask, we know that), contra Brown, *Epistles*, 610, who says it differs little from ἐὰν + Subjunctive; 1 Thess 3:8: νῦν ζῶμεν ἐὰν ὑμεῖς στήκετε ἐν κυρίῳ (now we know if you stand in the lord), where Marshall (*Thessalonians*, 96) claims that the construction "emphasises its factuality." (John 5:31 and 1 Cor 13:2 are almost assuredly not to be included here.) As noted in several examples above, several alterations of the conditional pattern, with εἰ μή, etc., may be included in the proper conditional categories, since classification is on the basis of Mood of the verb. See Boyer, "Other Conditional," for NT examples. These categories are treated by classical grammars as well: e.g. Kühner/Gerth, 2.481-88.

Three further examples will serve to illustrate clearly the difference in verbal aspect denoted by this class of conditional: John 3:12: εἰ τὰ ἐπίγεια εἶπον ὑμῖν καὶ οὐ πιστεύετε, πῶς ἐὰν εἴπω ὑμῖν τὰ ἐπουράνια πιστεύσετε; (if I speak to you of earthly things and you do not believe, how will you believe if I speak to you of heavenly things?). While a traditional view of tenses might make a plausible case for the Aorist referring to Jesus' previous speech (3:5-8) (Westcott, *John*, 52; Bultmann, *John*, 147) and the Present to Nicodemus's current situation, the discourse and person deixis rather seems to indicate present reference, although Schnackenburg (*John*, 1.377) claims with plausibility that this is a hypothetical conditional construction, and translates it "If I speak of earthly things." As present-referring, Jesus expresses surprise that Nicodemus fails to grasp the impact of the this-worldly things he is discussing with him. (The Subjunctive in the apodosis projects the possibility of discussion on a different level.) The Aorist describes the entire conversation, while the Present selects and marks the point of decision. Acts 25:11: εἰ μὲν οὖν ἀδικῶ καὶ ἄξιον θανάτου πέπραχά τι, οὐ παραιτοῦμαι τὸ ἀποθανεῖν (if therefore I have done anything wrong and accomplished anything worthy of death, I am not asking to escape death). When Festus asks Paul if he would consent to be judged in Jerusalem Paul appeals to Caesar, insisting that he has done nothing unjust (οὐδὲν ἠδίκησα). He then reformulates this in a conditional statement. While ἀδικῶ might alternatively be translated "I am guilty," the discourse seems to indicate past temporal reference for both verbs, since Paul bases the apodosis on having actually done something worthy of death, although use of the Aorist and Present of ἀδικέω reinforces the non-temporal nature of the Greek tenses (they have similar deictic reference). It also well illustrates their aspectual basis. Paul insists that he has done nothing wrong, though he would be willing to pay the suitable punishment if he had. καί in the protasis may be explanatory, with the rendering "if I have done something wrong, i.e. I have done something worthy of death. . . ." The verbal aspects are complementary, with the Present referring to his being involved in wrong-doing and the Perfect capturing the state of affairs of one who has done such things. Rom 2:17-21: εἰ δὲ σὺ Ἰουδαῖος ἐπονομάζῃ καὶ ἐπαναπαύῃ νόμῳ καὶ καυχᾶσαι ἐν θεῷ καὶ γινώσκεις τὸ θέλημα καὶ δοκιμάζεις τὰ διαφέροντα κατηχούμενος ἐκ τοῦ νόμου, πέποιθάς τε σεαυτὸν ὁδηγὸν εἶναι τυφλῶν, . . . ὁ οὖν διδάσκων ἕτερον σεαυτὸν οὐ διδάσκεις; (if you call yourself a Jew and rely upon the law and boast in God and know his will and examine the differences, teaching from the law, and you persuade yourself to be a guide of the blind . . . you, therefore, who teaches another, do you not teach yourself?). Addressed to a hypothetical Jew (the letter is addressed to more than one), this clearly timeless conditional statement uses Present verbs to build to a single use of the Perfect. The Jew is said to name, rely, boast, know, and examine, and the result is that he persuades himself that he is a reliable guide of the blind. The stative aspect

---

[20]Cf. [Lucian] Demos. 37: εἰ τοῦτον τὸν ἄνθρωπον ὅπλων ἀπέφηναν καὶ νεῶν καὶ στρατοπέδων ⟨καὶ⟩ δὴ καὶ καιρῶν καὶ χρημάτων κύριον, ὀκνῶ μὴ περὶ τῆς Μακεδονίας ἂν κατέστησέ μοι τὸν λόγον (if they sent away this man of the hoplites and commander of the youth and foot-soldiers and ⟨indeed⟩ times and goods, I am concerned, lest he might give me an order concerning M.). See Blass/Debrunner, ¶ 372(1)(a); cf. Turner, *Syntax*, 115-16, who contends that this use is "perhaps a half-way-house of actuality" between the Subjunctive and Indicative.

introduces the long list of condemning qualities that prompt the question by Paul of whether in fact the Jew ever learns from himself.

b. Assertion to the contrary. Sometimes called the irrealis or unreal condition, scholars have debated whether this conditional in and of itself expresses a contrary to fact situation or whether outside information is required.[21] But since this conditional can be used where wrong information is asserted as contrary to fact, as in Luke 7:39, where the Pharisee says: οὗτος εἰ ἦν προφήτης, ἐγίνωσκεν ἂν τίς καὶ ποταπὴ ἡ γυνὴ ἥτις ἅπτεται αὐτοῦ (this one, if he were a prophet, would know what sort of woman it is who is touching him); and John 18:30, where the Jewish leaders say to Pilate of Jesus: εἰ μὴ ἦν οὗτος κακὸν ποιῶν, οὐκ ἂν σοι παρεδώκαμεν αὐτόν (if this one were not doing evil, we would not have brought him to you), it is best to view this conditional as a non-factive put in the form of a contra-factive, i.e. the speaker posits the information as if it were unreal, whether in fact what he may say is true or false. Like all conditionals, this one requires context to establish its relation to the world.[22] The use of μή as the negative of this conditional confirms this analysis, since the notional or ideal negative is used with what is asserted as contra-factive. (On negation in conditionals in earlier Greek see Koppers, *Sentences*, esp. 113ff. on irrealis; cf. Pritchett, "Sentence," 13 n. 49.) Since the protasis qualifies as I.a., this conditional is a subcategory of I.a., the difference being that the apodosis is considered as well. The distinguishing feature of this conditional statement is εἰ + Imperfect, Aorist, or Pluperfect in the protasis,[23] and ἄν with the same in the apodosis (c. 36 instances in the NT) (Zerwick, 107 [cf. 109]; contra most other grammarians who include examples without ἄν in the apodosis). Although most grammarians claim that use of ἄν is becoming looser in the NT era (e.g. Boyer, "Second Class," 81-88; Schwyzer, 2.353, who includes the following example [X. Anab. 7.6.16], without quoting the entire context), it is better to distinguish examples with and without ἄν. Particularly helpful is X. Anab. 7.6.16-17:

ἀλλ᾽ εἴποιτ᾽ ἂν ὅτι ἔξεστι καὶ τὰ ὑμέτερα ἔχοντα παρὰ Σεύθου τεχνάζειν. οὐκοῦν δῆλον τοῦτό γέ ἐστιν, εἴπερ ἐμοὶ ἐτέλει τι Σεύθης, οὐχ οὕτως ἐτέλει δήπου ὡς ὧν τε ἐμοὶ δοίη στέροιτο καὶ ἄλλα ὑμῖν ἀποτείσειεν, ἀλλ᾽ οἶμαι, εἰ ἐδίδου, ἐπὶ τούτῳ ἂν (v.l. δὴ) ἐδίδου ὅπως ἐμοὶ δοὺς μεῖον μὴ ἀποδοίη ὑμῖν τὸ πλέον. εἰ τοίνυν οὕτως ἔχειν οἴεσθε, ἔξεστιν ὑμῖν αὐτίκα μάλα ματαίαν ταύτην τὴν πρᾶξιν ἀμφοτέροις ἡμῖν ποιῆσαι, ἐὰν πράττητε αὐτὸν τὰ χρήματα. δῆλον γὰρ ὅτι

---

[21]Bayfield ("On Conditional Sentences," 201) says, "Indeed no Conditional Sentence can *of itself* convey any implication either as to the facts or the speaker's impression of the facts. The hearer knows (if he knows at all) whether the condition is or is not fulfilled, by independent information already in his possession," citing E. Ion 354; Pl. Meno 93E, 94D; X. Hell. 3.4.18; and S. Oed. King 220. See idem, "Conditional Sentences," 90-92, citing D. 28.5; 29.47; 25.69; 23.96.

[22]Respondents to Bayfield include Sonnenschein, "Bayfield," 199-200 ("I thought it was now generally admitted that no conditional sentence implies fact" [199]); Harrison, "Remarks," 297-98 ("The rule holds: the unreality, though a secondary acquisition, has become inherent; and the hearer knows from the mere formula that the supposition is, and is designed to be, contrary to the facts assumed and asserted by the speaker" [297]); Seaton, untitled, 6 (1892) 201, citing Th. 6.31.5; Clapp, "Bayfield," 397-99 ("In interpreting any formula of language the proper test is not the external fact, but the intention of the writer; the form in which he chooses to present his thought" [397]), who responds directly to Bayfield's examples. Boyer ("Second Class," 83) notes that Jesus is never in error using this conditional. Greenberg ("Realis-Irrealis," 258) recognizes the closeness between my I.a. and b. (his I and III) class conditionals.

[23]See Lyons, *Semantics*, 818, who says that "in many languages, including English, the grammatical category of past tense is regularly used to convert a non-factive into a contra-factive utterance." This view is taken by virtually all grammars, including Goodwin (*Grammar*, 298-300) and more recent literature, e.g. Pritchett ("Sentence," 8-9), Boyer ("Second Class," 83-84).

Σεύθης, εἰ ἔχω τι παρ' αὐτοῦ, ἀπαιτήσει με, καὶ ἀπαιτήσει μέντοι δικαίως, ἐὰν μή βεβαιῶ τὴν πρᾶξιν αὐτῷ ἐφ' ᾗ ἐδωροδόκουν.[24]

There is no reason, or means apart from the narrative, to classify the first underlined conditional as unreal. In fact the simple assertion seems in character with the speech, and thus gives good reason for the I.b. conditional to be used once the argument has progressed further. The third conditional with a hypothetical apodosis moves the discussion into the realm of events yet to transpire.

The failure to distinguish the referential world from what the conditional conveys through its form appears to be Winger's difficulty ("Conditions"; on use of the 'unreal' condition as an important intellectual tool in ancient Greek writing see Krischer, "Rolle"). He poses the problem of "two similar conditional sentences with a curious difference in form" (110): Gal 2:21 (εἰ γὰρ διὰ νόμου δικαιοσύνη, ἄρα Χριστὸς δωρεὰν ἀπέθανεν [for if justification (is) through law, then Christ died freely]) and 3:21 (εἰ γὰρ ἐδόθη νόμος ὁ δυνάμενος ζῳοποιῆσαι, ὄντως ἐκ νόμου ἂν ἦν ἡ δικαιοσύνη [for if a law were given able to make alive, righteousness would indeed have been by law]). Winger implicitly acknowledges that every unreal condition must have ἄν in the apodosis (111 n. 6), although he fails to realize that verbless clauses pose their own difficulties. But Winger wants to argue further on the basis of whether the condition is in actual fact unfulfilled. Hence he singles out eighteen examples where he claims Paul regards the condition as "unfulfilled in fact" (111), and classifies them as improbable hypotheses (1 Cor 12:17a, b, 19; Gal 1:10), past conditions (Rom 7:7e; 9:29; 1 Cor 2:8; Gal 4:15), and those which others claim are fulfilled (Gal 2:21; 3:21; Rom 4:2, 14; Gal 3:18; 1 Cor 15:13, 14, 15, 16, 17, 19, 29b, 32b; Gal 5:11). He concludes that Paul "uses ἄν in the apodosis of conditions that otherwise would seem plausible" (112), since the improbability of other unreal conditions is evident from context. Although Winger is correct about the use of context, and has perceived that I.b. conditionals are used to make explicit the assertion of something believed to be contrary to fact, he has misconstrued the I.b. form. It has already been shown that numerous instances of "unreal" propositions are conveyed through I.a. conditional forms, with the primary concern not being plausibility but its contribution to the argument (see Zerwick, 106-07).

In contradistinction to the general rule found in the grammars, the difference in verb forms within the I.b. conditional relates to their verbal aspect, not temporal reference. (Boyer ["Second Class," 85-86] makes this distinction, though his treatment is clearly time-based. Gonda [*Character*, 179] notes the difficulty in temporal reference with any hypothetical statement, especially with contra factives.)

Although Boyer claims that every instance of the Aorist is past-referring, several examples are worth reconsidering.[25] Mark 13:20, cf. Matt 24:22: εἰ μὴ ἐκολόβωσεν κύριος τὰς ἡμέρας, οὐκ ἂν ἐσώθη πᾶσα σάρξ (if the lord were not going to cut short the days, all flesh would not be saved), in which reference to the great tribulation is clearly future (Zerwick, 108; Taylor, *Mark*, 514; cf. Cranfield, *Mark*, 404-05, who speaks of fulfilment being past, present and future); Luke

---

[24]"But you might say that it is possible indeed to have procured through cunning your possessions from S. Then this is clear, *if S. has paid to me anything, doubtless he thus has not paid* as if he might lose what he might have given me and other things he might pay out to you, but I think, *if he were giving, he was giving* in this way so that giving to me worse he might give to you the better. If therefore you think this is the case, it is possible for you immediately to make this act worthless for both of us, if you take his possessions. For it is clear that S., *if I have anything from him, he will demand it from me*, and he will demand justice, unless I fulfil the deed for him for which I was accepting his gifts."

[25]E.g. Pl. Apol. 20A: εἰ μέν σου τὼ ὑεῖ πώλω ἢ μόσχω ἐγενέσθην, εἴχομεν ἂν αὐτοῖν ἐπιστάτην λαβεῖν καὶ μισθώσασθαι . . . (if your two sons were two colts or calves, we would be able to get and pay an overseer for them); cf. following νῦν δ' ἐπειδὴ ἀνθρώπω ἐστόν, τίνα αὐτοῖν ἐν νῷ ἔχεις ἐπιστάτην λαβεῖν; (but now since they are men, what sort of overseer do you have in mind for them?) (20B).

19:42: εἰ ἔγνως ἐν τῇ ἡμέρᾳ ταύτῃ καὶ σὺ τὰ πρὸς εἰρήνην (if you indeed would know in this day the things toward peace), where there is agreement that this is an instance of aposiopesis (Blass/Debrunner, ¶ 482; endorsed by Fitzmyer, *Luke*, 2.1258, claiming an understood "it would please me"; and Marshall, *Luke*, 718, who says this is the "protasis of a present, unfulfilled condition"), although the deictic reference of ταύτῃ seems determinative of whether it is present or past-referring; cf. Rom 9:29: εἰ μὴ κύριος Σαβαὼθ ἐγκατέλιπεν ἡμῖν σπέρμα, ὡς Σόδομα ἂν ἐγενήθημεν καὶ ὡς Γόμορρα ἂν ὡμοιώθημεν (if the lord of Sabaoth had not left a seed for us, we would become as S. and be like G.), where quotation of Isa 1:9 complicates deictic reference, depending upon whether Jesus or the remnant is envisioned; Gal 3:21: εἰ γὰρ ἐδόθη νόμος ὁ δυνάμενος ζῳοποιῆσαι, ὄντως ἐκ νόμου ἂν ἦν ἡ δικαιοσύνη (if a law were given, one able to make alive, indeed justification would be by law), where anarthrous νόμος (cf. ὁ νόμος in v 20) points away from the OT law to a general treatment of law. Burton (*Galatians*, 194) observes that although this is contrary to fact by form, this is not proved until later in the epistle. (Cf. Betz, *Galatians*, 173, who says that Paul "proposes another hypothetical case. This case, however, is not really hypothetical at all, but is identical with one of the fundamental ideas of Judaism." Has he confused grammar and theology?)

Those examples which are past-referring often have strong deictic indicators: e.g. Matt 11:21, 23; Luke 10:13, with reference to Tyre, Sidon, and Sodom; 1 Cor 2:8, with Christ's crucifixion in the apodosis; Heb 4:8, with reference to Jesus (i.e. Joshua).

Examples with the Imperfect of present reference need not be discussed, but probably include: Luke 7:39; Gal 1:10 (ἔτι). Examples of the Imperfect of non-present reference probably include at least:[26] John 5:46 (past): ἐπιστεύετε (you had believed), with reference to Moses; 1 Cor 11:31 (timeless): διεκρίνομεν (we would judge), with 1st Person deixis not specifying any temporal sphere (or perhaps to soften the impact, so Robertson/Plummer, *First Corinthians*, 254).

In the several uses of the Pluperfect, a range of temporal implicature is illustrated. Matt 12:7: εἰ δὲ ἐγνώκειτε τί ἐστιν, ἔλεος θέλω καὶ οὐ θυσίαν, οὐκ ἂν κατεδικάσατε τοὺς ἀναιτίους (if you knew what this is, "I want mercy and not sacrifice," you would not condemn those who are not guilty), which although it may have past reference to former Israelite persecution (Hos 6:6 is quoted and David has just been referred to), present reference to Jesus' disciples plucking grain on the Sabbath is more likely; Matt 24:43 par. Luke 12:39 (timeless): ᾔδει (he were in a knowledgeable state), referring to the parable of the householder (surely this is not equivalent to an Aorist [?], as Marshall [*Luke*, 538] states); John 4:10 (present): ᾔδεις (you were in . . .), referring to the present condition of the Samaritan woman; John 8:19 (timeless): ᾔδεις (you were in . . .), following οἴδατε, with both himself and his father as complements, Jesus using a conditional to refer to a timeless principle about his father (Bultmann [*John*, 283] suggests for this verse and 19:11 that ἂν be omitted).[27]

II. Projection.

As noted above, there is much debate about the difference in meaning of the individual verb forms within this category. Two misunderstandings must be laid aside before proceeding to more precise

---

[26]E.g. Pl. Apol. 32E (past): ἆρ᾽ οὖν ἄν με οἴεσθε τοσάδε ἔτη διαγενέσθαι εἰ ἔπραττον τὰ δημόσια, καὶ πράττων ἀξίως ἀνδρὸς ἀγαθοῦ ἐβοήθουν τοῖς δικαίοις καὶ ὥσπερ χρὴ τοῦτο περὶ πλείστου ἐποιούμην; (would you think I could live so many years if I had lived a public life and, acting worthily of a good man, I had given aid to what was just and, as was necessary, I had done this concerning the highest good?); Epict. 1.2.27 (timeless): ἄλλος δὲ κἂν τὸν τράχηλον ἀπετμήθη, εἰ ζῆν ἠδύνατο δίχα τοῦ τραχήλου (but another would cut off his neck, if he were able to live without his neck). Cf. Gonda, *Character*, 187.

[27]A number of conditionals of this class have a form of εἰμί in the protasis: Matt 23:30; John 8:42; 9:41; 11:21, 32; 15:19; 18:30 (not periphrastic), 36; Acts 18:14; Heb 8:4, 7; 1 John 2:19; and one verbless: John 14:2. Since εἰμί is aspectually vague, no further discussion of its role is necessary here.

definition. First, Goodwin and others are correct in placing the Subjunctive, Optative and Future forms together (although characterization according to future reference is surely misleading), since all three refer to projection by the speaker of a non-factive process. At this level they have similar meaning. Second, Morris, Gildersleeve, and others are correct in claiming that, for example, the Future and the Subjunctive, and the Subjunctive and the Optative, cannot be substituted for each other within the same sentence without in some way, however slight, changing the meaning, since each of these three forms grammaticalizes attitude in a slightly different way. As Gonda says,

> Those scholars who deny the existence of any perceptible difference between a "prospective" subj. and a future or are at least convinced that these categories are "particularly close" [Hahn, *Subjunctive*, 80] run the far from imaginary risk of blurring out subtle distinctions which may always be found to exist when a language possesses two apparently synonymous categories. (*Character*, 74, cf. 173ff.; see also Koppers, *Sentences*, 89ff.)

The simple fact that from Homer through to the hellenistic period all three forms existed (though in varying frequencies) indicates that while their essential semantic meaning may have been similar, the three forms were still semantically distinct. In fact, virtually every grammarian recognizes such a distinction, however he may choose to define it (usually in terms of the Subjunctive/Optative opposition): more or less vivid (Goodwin, etc.), anticipatory or ideal (Gildersleeve, etc.), eventual or potential (Schwyzer, Humbert), more probability or less probability (Burton), pure conception or uncertainty/contingency (Sewall), projection or contingency (Gonda).

II.a. This class of conditional, the most numerous of the II class, has ἐάν + Subjunctive in the protasis, and is the unmarked conditional protasis (Gildersleeve ["On εἰ," 9] suggests this, though he claims it is because of a "greater temporal exactness"). The II.a. class conditional occurs approximately 277 times in the NT, with 107 Present, 205 Aorist, and six Perfect Subjunctives (Boyer, "Third . . . Class Conditions," 163ff.; cf. Palmer, "Language," 162-65, on the varieties of forms in Homeric Greek), with as many as 300+ conditional-like statements. An analysis of the use of the formally-exact instances, as well as examples from earlier Greek, shows that it conforms to general usage of the Subjunctive Mood to express projection without any statement of the probability of its coming to pass (see Greenberg, "Realis-Irrealis," 254-55, who characterizes the difference between I and II class conditionals as definite versus indefinite, since he realizes that there are instances of his I class conditionals where existence cannot be substantiated [e.g. S. Trach. 943-45 speaking of counting on tomorrow]).[28]

Boyer is to be commended for attempting to calculate the degree of probability implied for each protasis, according to which calculations only 7% are certain of fulfilment, 23% are probable, but 43% have no indication and 2.5% are certain not to be fulfilled.[29] But closer examination reveals interesting anomalies in Boyer's analysis. He may be correct in considering John 12:32; 14:3; 16:7; 1 Cor 6:4; Col 4:10 and even 2 Cor 5:1 as certain of fulfilment, but this is on the basis of either seeing later fulfilment or having observed the course of human affairs. It is not clear why 1 John 2:28; 3:2; Rom 9:27; and 1 Cor 9:16 should be considered as certain, since the events projected have not in fact occurred, and the strength of their fulfilment rests on theological and not grammatical suppositions. Other doubtful cases include Mark 4:22; John 5:31; 8:14, 16; 1 John 2:29. Two examples illustrate the point: Mark 10:29-30: οὐδείς ἐστιν ὃς ἀφῆκεν οἰκίαν . . . ἕνεκεν ἐμοῦ καὶ ἕνεκεν τοῦ εὐαγγελίου, ἐὰν μὴ λάβῃ ἑκατονταπλασίονα νῦν ἐν τῷ καιρῷ τούτῳ οἰκίας καὶ ἀδελφοὺς καὶ ἀδελφὰς καὶ μητέρας καὶ τέκνα (there is no one who gives up house . . . on account of me and on account of the gospel, unless he might receive one hundred times more houses and brothers and sisters and mothers and children in this present time), where the evidence of any present certain fulfilment is completely lacking; and Rom 2:25: περιτομὴ μὲν γὰρ ὠφελεῖ ἐὰν νόμον πράσσῃς· ἐὰν δὲ παραβάτης νόμου ᾖς, ἡ περιτομή σου ἀκροβυστία γέγονεν (circumcision is obligated if you practice the law; but if you are a violator of the law, your circumcision becomes uncircumcision), where perhaps Paul knows his audience--or human nature--well enough that the statement is certain, although Boyer himself admits that 2:26 (ἐὰν οὖν ἡ ἀκροβυστία τὰ δικαιώματα τοῦ νόμου φυλάσσῃ, οὐχ ἡ ἀκροβυστία αὐτοῦ εἰς

---

[28]Boyer ("Third . . . Class Conditions," 16) appears confused at this point, trying to juggle all the various grammars: "it seems to me that the use of the subjunctive points essentially to the condition expressed by the protasis as being doubtful, uncertain, undetermined (because it has not yet been determined). The term *potential* is accurate. It is 'not yet.' It may be, if. . . . Perhaps the term *contingent* would be even clearer. It depends on any number of factors. In any case, the common denominator is futurity."

[29]It is difficult to compare statistics from other Greek, but the same categories appear to hold: e.g. D. 1.11: ἂν μὲν γάρ, ὅσ' ἂν τις λάβῃ, καὶ σῴζῃ, μεγάλην ἔχει τῇ τύχῃ τὴν χάριν, ἂν δ' ἀναλώσας λάθῃ, συνανήλωσε καὶ τὸ μεμνῆσθαι [τὴν χάριν] (if whoever might receive indeed might save, he has great gratitude in his fortune, but if, squandering it, he might lose it, he loses along with it memory of his gratitude) (Greenberg ["Realis-Irrealis," 255] articulates what has long been known--the relative conditional may replace the true conditional, especially common in II class conditionals); Pl. Rep. 473C-D: ἐὰν μή . . . ἢ οἱ φιλόσοφοι βασιλεύσωσιν ἐν ταῖς πόλεσιν ἢ οἱ βασιλῆς τε νῦν λεγόμενοι καὶ δυνάσται φιλοσοφήσωσι γνησίως τε καὶ ἱκανῶς, καὶ τοῦτο εἰς ταὐτὸν συμπέσῃ . . . τῶν δὲ νῦν πορευομένων χωρὶς ἐφ' ἑκάτερον αἱ πολλαὶ φύσεις ἐξ ἀνάγκης ἀποκλεισθῶσιν, οὐκ ἔστι κακῶν παῦλα (unless either the philosophers might rule in the cities or those who are called kings and rulers might philosophize wisely and sufficiently, and this might join these things . . . and of those who now come upon each apart from the other, the many natures might of necessity be shut out, there is not going to be a cessation of evils); P.Sel. 111.13-14 (2d cent. A.D.): εἴ τινα ἐὰν εὕρω, γράφω / σοι (if I might find someone, I am going to write to you), where the occasional nature of the papyri makes fulfilment extremely difficult to determine (cf. e.g. P.Goodspeed Chicago 3 [1st cent. A.D.], where the Subjunctive is used for mathematical suppositions); Epict. 1.17.5, 7: ἀλλ' ἄν μοι λέγῃς ὅτι . . . κἄν τι κατ' ἀμφίβολον φωνὴν εἴπω καὶ λέγῃς μοι . . . οὐκ ἔτι ἀνέξομαί σου, ἀλλ' ἐρῶ σοι. . . . ἂν δὲ μὴ διαλάβωμεν πρῶτον τί ἐστι μόδιος μηδὲ διαλάβωμεν πρῶτον τί ἐστι ζυγός, πῶς ἔτι μετρῆσαί τι ἢ στῆσαι δυνησόμεθα; (but if you might say to me that . . . and if I might say something according to an ambiguous term and you might say to me . . . I shall not still bear with you but will tell you. . . . But if we do not grasp first what a modus is and do not grasp first what a scale is, how shall we be able to measure or weigh anything?).

περιτομὴν λογισθήσεται; [if therefore the uncircumcision guards the requirements of the law, is not his uncircumcision counted as circumcision?]) is only conceivable of fulfilment, although it is more likely that Paul's rhetorical flow is not dependent upon such a category. As Boyer later rightly admits, "all these 'degree of probability' terms are derived from the *context*; they all are simply ἐάν + subjunctive conditions" (Boyer, "Third. . . Class Conditions," 169. This comports well with previous analysis of the function of the Subjunctive).

The appropriateness of this form of conditional for mere projection is seen in a number of instances where both sides of contingent circumstances are cited: e.g. Matt 6:14-15: ἐάν . . . ἀφῆτε τοῖς ἀνθρώποις τὰ παραπτώματα αὐτῶν. . . . ἐάν . . . μὴ ἀφῆτε τοῖς ἀνθρώποις. . . . (if you forgive men their sins. . . . if you do not forgive men. . . .); Matt 18:15-16; John 11:9-10; cf. Matt 10:13; 6:22-23; Rom 14:8. (Cf. Pl. Apol. 25B: πάντως δήπου, ἐάντε σὺ καὶ Ἄνυτος οὐ φῆτε ἐάντε φῆτε [surely it is, if you and A. deny and if you admit it]; D. 21.205. Of course, since no Mood necessarily grammaticalizes absolute facts, the I class conditional may be used in this way as well; see above.)

Also to be included here are examples of εἰ + Subjunctive. Some grammarians consider this a vulgarism (Radermacher, 175), although it is well-known in hellenistic Greek,[30] and even found in classical Greek sources, including Homer and Pindar.[31] Since classification in this scheme is on the basis of Mood, it is appropriate to place this form here: Luke 9:13: εἰ μήτι προευθέντες ἡμεῖς ἀγοράσωμεν εἰς πάντα τὸν λαὸν τοῦτον βρώματα (if we don't go and purchase food for all the people); 1 Cor 14:5: ἐκτὸς εἰ μὴ διερμηνεύῃ (apart from if someone interprets); Phil 3:12: εἰ καὶ καταλάβω (if indeed I might catch); Rev. 11:5: εἴ τις θελήσῃ αὐτοὺς ἀδικῆσαι (if someone might want them to be unjust; cf. I.a. conditional in v 5a); cf. Rom 11:14; 1 Thess 5:10: ἵνα εἴτε γρηγορῶμεν εἴτε καθεύδωμεν ἅμα σὺν αὐτῷ (if either we may watch or sit with him), possibly with Subjunctives. (The list is from Robertson, 1017. For a different interpretation of several examples see Burton [105], who admits that εἰ + Subjunctive is probably semantically equivalent to ἐάν + Subjunctive; Moulton, 187; cf. Winer, 368.)

Several examples illustrate the attitudinal difference between Subjunctive and Indicative conditionals.

Luke 16:31: εἰ Μωϋσέως καὶ τῶν προφητῶν οὐκ ἀκούουσιν, οὐδ᾽ ἐάν τις ἐκ νεκρῶν ἀναστῇ πεισθήσονται (if they did not listen to M. and the prophets, neither if someone might rise from the dead will they be convinced). The first protasis, using the Indicative, is the unmarked of the two hypotheses, asserting for the sake of argument an event that is within the realm of possibility (and quite possibly of past reference), and perhaps within the experience of the rich man's brothers' knowledge. The second protasis, using the Subjunctive, projects an event not only beyond the realm of the brothers' experience, but an event beyond the expected, with no comment on whether in fact it could occur (contra Fitzmyer, *Luke*, 2.1134, who calls this the Subjunctive of "emphatic future" [?]). The conclusion for each hypothesis is the same. The rich man's brothers would not believe what they could already investigate, much less that which was beyond their experience.

---

[30]Radermacher (199) cites the following, among others: Epict. 2.18.11; Paus. 2.35.3 (the best texts read an Optative). See also P.Oxy. 496.11 (A.D. 127): εἰ δὲ ἦν (= ᾖ) [ὁ] γαμῶν πρότερος [τ]ετελ[ε]υτηκ[ὼ]ς ἐχέτω ἡ γαμουμένη . . . (and if there might be the male marriage partner, dying first, let the female marriage partner have); and an inscription of Mopsuestia in Cilicia: ἐκτὸς εἰ μὴ [ἐ]ὰν Μάγνα μόνη θε[λή]σῃ (apart from if Magna alone might want) (Deissmann, *Studies*, 118 = Waddington, 3.2, 1499); and Mayser, 2, 3.54. Jannaris (464) claims it is frequent in many later prose writers.

[31]E.g. Th. 6.21.1; Pl. Laws 761C; 958D; D. 19.221 (Jannaris, 464), although many of the texts cited have variants in standard editions, some including and others excising the particle. This may very well be because of textual regularizing. A clear case seems to be X. Cyr. 8.4.16. See also Chantraine, 2.279ff.; Kühner/Gerth, 1.221-22; Gildersleeve, "Studies," 8; Capp, "Sentences," 49.

Mark 3:24-27: ἐὰν βασιλεία ἐφ' ἑαυτὴν μερισθῇ, οὐ δύναται σταθῆναι ἡ βασιλεία ἐκείνη· καὶ ἐὰν οἰκία ἐφ' ἑαυτὴν μερισθῇ, οὐ δυνήσεται ἡ οἰκία ἐκείνη σταθῆναι. καὶ εἰ ὁ σατανᾶς ἀνέστη ἐφ' ἑαυτὸν καὶ ἐμερίσθη (v.l. μεμέρισται), οὐ δύναται στῆναι ἀλλὰ τέλος ἔχει. ἀλλ' οὐ δύναται οὐδεὶς εἰς τὴν οἰκίαν τοῦ ἰσχυροῦ εἰσελθὼν τὰ σκεύη αὐτοῦ διαρπάσαι ἐὰν μὴ πρῶτον τὸν ἰσχυρὸν δήσῃ, καὶ τότε τὴν οἰκίαν αὐτοῦ διαρπάσει (if a kingdom might be divided upon itself, that kingdom is not able to stand; and if a house is divided upon itself, that house will not be able to stand. And if Satan stands against himself and is divided, he is not able to stand but he has his end. But no one is able, entering into the house of the strong man, to seize his goods, unless he might bind the strong man first, and then he will seize his house). In the four conditional statements, two projections are made, each referring to a hypothetical state of affairs. In the third, Jesus reportedly uses the I.a. conditional to make an assertion about the specific situation of address (note non-temporal use of the Aorist Indicative), before concluding with another general hypothesis. (Cranfield [*Mark*, 138] claims that δήσῃ implies that Satan is already bound, but this reads too much into the Aorist.) It might appear that the third conditional should be the marked one, but another way of viewing this is that the two clear and forceful suppositions make the specific assertion a foregone conclusion.

Acts 5:38-39: ἐὰν ᾖ ἐξ ἀνθρώπων ἡ βουλὴ αὕτη ᾖ τὸ ἔργον τοῦτο, καταλυθήσεται· εἰ δὲ ἐκ θεοῦ ἐστιν, οὐ δυνήσεσθε καταλῦσαι αὐτούς, μήποτε καὶ θεομάχοι εὑρεθῆτε (if this plan or this work might be from man, it will be destroyed, but if it is from God, you will not be able to destroy them, lest indeed you might be found fighting with God). Although Radermacher believes that the conditionals reveal the author's editing, since Gamaliel would have formulated it oppositely (176: "εἰ mit dem Indikativ zum Ausdruck der objektiv gegebenen Bedingung" [174]), there is at least one other way to view the two conditionals. The II.a. conditional expresses what Gamaliel projects. Though the form does not carry this implication it is clear from the context that this is what he hopes to be true, and this form of the conditional is appropriate in this context. The I.a. conditional makes a mere assertion, clearly one that he hopes is not true, although he chooses not to use the I.b. form, possibly because of his own uncertainty. Not only do the conditionals seem appropriate for the author of Acts, but also for Gamaliel himself. (Bruce [*Acts*, 149] says it is a "rare construction for an open condition referring to the present," with the possible translation "If it thus ought to be." He recognizes that in εἰ + Present Luke uses a less remote construction.)

John 13:17: εἰ ταῦτα οἴδατε, μακάριοί ἐστε ἐὰν ποιῆτε αὐτά (if you know these things, you are blessed if you do them), where the marked projection is the fundamental condition for blessedness, not merely knowing. Cf. 1 Cor 7:36: εἰ δέ τις ἀσχημονεῖν ἐπὶ τὴν παρθένον αὐτοῦ νομίζει ἐὰν ᾖ ὑπέρακμος καὶ οὕτως ὀφείλει γίνεσθαι, ὃ θέλει ποιείτω (if someone thinks he is acting unseemingly toward his virgin, if she might be of mature age, and thus it ought to be, let him do what he wants), where primary attention is drawn to the fact that the virgin is of mature age, and secondary to the man who acts in an inappropriate way (contra Orr/Walthers, *I Corinthians*, 222, who say that the "general condition with the subjunctive . . . is dependent upon the preceding first class [simple] condition").

The major distinction within this category of usage, however, is verbal aspect. The Aorist, the least heavily marked tense, is predominant, serving well the role of projection with no regard for whether in fact it will ever occur, as illustrates 2 Tim 2:5: ἐὰν δὲ καὶ ἀθλῇ τις, οὐ στεφανοῦται ἐὰν μὴ νομίμως ἀθλήσῃ (and if someone competes, he will not receive a crown if he does not compete by the rules). The protasis with the Aorist, with the less heavily marked form reinforced by the indefinite τις, projects the realm in which the condition obtains, regardless of whether a real competition is envisioned. The protasis with the Present, the more heavily marked Subjunctive, narrows the focus by projecting a second hypothesis--someone not competing by the rules. Within the realm of competition, if someone does not compete by the rules, then the result is that he does not receive the prize for winning.

1 Cor 13:2-3: ἐὰν ἔχω προφητείαν καὶ εἰδῶ τὰ μυστήρια πάντα καὶ πᾶσαν τὴν γνῶσιν, καὶ ἐὰν ἔχω πᾶσαν τὴν πίστιν ὥστε ὄρη μεθιστάναι, ἀγάπην δὲ μὴ ἔχω, οὐθέν εἰμι (and if I have prophecy and I am in a state of knowing all mysteries and all knowledge and if I have all faith so that I remove a mountain, and I do not have love, I am nothing). Though some

dispute whether οἶδα has stative aspect in every Mood (see chapt. 5), in this instance the case for οἶδα maintaining its stative force seems clear, since not only was a form of γινώσκω available, but Paul in his writings usually uses a form of γινώσκω when speaking of mysteries (Rom 11:25; Eph 1:9; 3:3; 6:19; Col 2:2). In a series of projections well-suited to the rapturous tone of the love passage in 1 Corinthians, Paul here selects knowledge of all mysteries for special emphasis,[32] although the imperfective aspect of the other protases (and v 1) is also significant. Interestingly, v 3 has Aorist Subjunctives, used possibly when the author refers to the human person instead of divine gifts, except in v 3c, where possession seems to be emphasized.

1 John 1:6-10: ἐὰν εἴπωμεν (if we might say) that we are having fellowship with him and περιπατῶμεν (we might walk) in darkness, we are liars and not doing the truth. ἐὰν . . . περιπατῶμεν in light as he is in the light, we are having fellowship with each other and the blood of Jesus his son cleanses us from all sin. ἐὰν εἴπωμεν that we are not having sin, we are deceiving ourselves and the truth is not in us. ἐὰν ὁμολογῶμεν (if we might confess) our sins, he forgives us and cleanses us from all unrighteousness. ἐὰν εἴπωμεν that we do not sin (οὐχ ἡμαρτήκαμεν [note the heavily marked Perfect used peroratively]) we lie and his word is not in us. In his contrast between saying and doing, the author uses the Aorist for stating and the Present for doing, usually with the former used negatively and the latter positively.

Luke 6:33-34: ἐὰν ἀγαθοποιῆτε τοὺς ἀγαθοποιοῦντας ὑμᾶς (if you might do good to those who do good to you), what gain is it to you? and ἐὰν δανίσητε παρ' ὧν ἐλπίζετε λαβεῖν (if you might lend [to those] from whom you hope to receive), what gain is it to you? Temporal distinction does not clarify use of the tenses in this instance since they appear to be concurrent. The author conceives of the process of doing good as an event well worth progressing with; thus he uses the Present, while money-lending, a pertinent example to support his point, is simply stated using the Aorist. See also John 15:6ff.

II.b. In earlier Greek, as well as other hellenistic Greek, the protasis of εἰ + Optative is found, usually followed by ἄν + Optative in the apodosis, e.g. Epict. Fr. 34: εἴ τις ὑπερβάλλοι τὸ μέτριον, τὰ ἐπιτερπέστατα ἀτερπέστατα ἂν γίνοιτο (v.l. γένοιτο) (if someone might exceed the mean, the most pleasing things might become the least pleasing things). See Turner, *Syntax*, 125-28; cf. Mandilaras, 283-86; de Foucault, *Recherches*, 192-93; Higgins, "Renaissance," 51-79; Boyer, "Classification of Optatives," 135-36. In classical Greek negation is with οὐ, which Greenberg ("Realis-Irrealis," 261) suggests is because of its similarity to the apodosis, which takes οὐ (as opposed to protases with μή). There is no example of this exact form of the conditional in the NT, although there are several others meriting note. In each instance the contingent nature of the projection is evidenced (contra Sewall, "Distinction"). Acts 24:19: οὓς ἔδει ἐπὶ σοῦ παρεῖναι καὶ κατηγορεῖν εἴ τι ἔχοιεν πρὸς ἐμέ (it is necessary for them to come and make accusation before you if they might have anything against me), with an apodosis more often found in I class conditionals, stressing the necessity in Paul's mind of his accusers' presence. (Haenchen [*Acts*, 656 n. 1] calls this "classically incorrect," but as Jannaris [462] indicates, "The form of the apodosis is not always fixed by the form of the protasis, but depends on the individual conception or intention of the speaker.") 1 Pet 3:14: ἀλλ' εἰ καὶ πάσχοιτε διὰ δικαιοσύνην, μακάριοι (but if you suffer because of righteousness, [you are?] blessed), with a verbless apodosis; 1 Pet 3:17: κρεῖττον γὰρ ἀγαθοποιοῦντας, εἰ θέλοι τὸ θέλημα τοῦ θεοῦ, πάσχειν ἢ κακοποιοῦντας ([it is] better doing good, if he might want the will of God, to suffer than doing evil), with a verbless apodosis. Several seem to contain stereotyped protases. Boyer ("Third . . . Class Conditions," 170 n. 41) suggests these are relics surviving the construction becoming archaic. Acts 20:16: ἔσπευδεν γὰρ εἰ δυνατὸν εἴη αὐτῷ τὴν ἡμέραν τῆς πεντηκοστῆς γενέσθαι εἰς Ἱεροσόλυμα (for he desired, if it might be possible, to be in J. for P.), probably in indirect discourse (cf. Lucian Nav. 44: εἰ δέ τις ἐχθρὸς εἴη. . . . καὶ μὴν εἴ τις ὑπερόπτης εἴη. . . . καὶ εἰ δόξειέ μοι [and if someone might be an enemy . . . and if someone might be haughty . . . and if he might think me]); Acts 27:12: εἴ πως δύναιντο καταντήσαντες

---

[32]Whenever the hiddenness of the "mystery" is spoken of by Paul, the Perfect is also used: Rom 16:25; Eph 3:9; Col 1:26.

εἰς Φοίνικα παραχειμάσαι λιμένα τῆς Κρήτης βλέποντα κατὰ λίβα καὶ κατὰ χῶρον (if somehow they might be able, arriving in P., a harbour of C., facing Southwest and Northwest, to spend the winter [Bruce, *Acts*, 457]), possibly with implied indirect discourse; Acts 27:39: εἰς ὃν ἐβουλεύοντο εἰ δύναιντο ἐξῶσαι τὸ πλοῖον (unto which [island] they determined to land their boat, if they were able), possibly indirect discourse; 1 Cor 14:10: τοσαῦτα εἰ τύχοι γένη φωνῶν εἰσιν ἐν κόσμῳ καὶ οὐδὲν ἄφωνον (if it happens to be, there are such sources of noise in the world and none is insignificant); 1 Cor 15:37: ἀλλὰ γυμνὸν κόκκον εἰ τύχοι σίτου ἤ τινος τῶν λοιπῶν (but a bare kernel, if it happens to be of wheat or of something else), although these two Pauline examples might better be placed above as true examples (see Moulton, 196; cf. Lucian Tox. 4: καὶ ταῦτα καπήλους καὶ ταριχοπώλας, εἰ τύχοι, τοὺς πολλοὺς αὐτῶν ὄντας [and these salesmen and fishmongers, if it so happens, there being many of them]); Acts 17:27: ζητεῖν τὸν θεόν, εἰ ἄρα γε ψηλαφήσειαν αὐτὸν καὶ εὕροιεν, καί γε οὐ μακρὰν ἀπὸ ἑνὸς ἑκάστου ἡμῶν ὑπάρχοντα (to seek God, if perhaps they might grope after and find him, indeed being not far from each one of us). Haenchen (*Acts*, 524) says that the condition indicates that "the finding cannot be taken for granted." (One example of εἰ + Optative appears in an indirect question: Acts 25:20: ἔλεγον εἰ βούλοιτο πορεύεσθαι εἰς Ἱεροσόλυμα κἀκεῖ κρίνεσθαι περὶ τούτων [I was saying whether he might want to go to J. and be judged there concerning these things]).

II.c. Expectation.

The protasis with εἰ + Future is best placed in this category on the basis of its place in the Greek verbal network (see above and chapt. 9). Grammarians on both sides of the debate regarding conditionals recognize the connection between the Future and the Subjunctive, with Goodwin actually placing the two together (*Grammar*, 300; cf. Smyth, 525: "**Emotional Future Conditions.**--When the protasis expresses strong feeling the future indicative with εἰ is commonly used instead of ἐάν with the subjunctive. . ."), while Gildersleeve says,

> In future relations, εἰ with the future indicative may be dissected into ἐάν with the present subjunctive and ἐάν with the aorist subjunctive; and hence, whenever it is important to distinguish continued from concentrated action, whenever it is important to distinguish overlapping from priority, ἐάν with the subjunctive is preferred, not only in general sentences but in particular sentences. . . ("Forms," 9),

finding the Future well-suited for more marked contexts than the Subjunctive. (Gildersleeve ["Forms," 9] also says: "The fact then is patent enough to every one who will be at the pains to count, that for model Greek prose ἐάν with the subjunctive is preferred to εἰ with the future indicative," although the reason he gives--greater temporal precision of the Subjunctive--seems to be misguided; cf. 10-11, where he ascribes characteristics of markedness to the Future.)

Approximately twelve examples occur in the NT (see below for those in contrast to II.a. conditionals). (Cf. Epict. 1 intro 5-8, where four conditional protases appear, the first with the Future, the second with the Optative, the third verbless, and the fourth with the Indicative.)

Luke 11:8: εἰ καὶ οὐ δώσει αὐτῷ ἀναστὰς διὰ τὸ εἶναι φίλον αὐτοῦ, διά γε τὴν ἀναίδειαν αὐτοῦ ἐγερθεὶς δώσει αὐτῷ ὅσων χρῄζει (if, getting up, he will not give to him because he is his friend, indeed because of his shamelessness,[33] getting up, he will give to him what he needs), used in a timeless context. Rom 11:13-14: τὴν διακονίαν μου δοξάζω, εἴ πως παραζηλώσω μου τὴν σάρκα καὶ σώσω τινὰς ἐξ αὐτῶν (I glorify my service, if somehow I might make my flesh jealous and save some of them), in which the verbs are probably Futures. (The fact that εἰ strengthened by πως may take the Subjunctive complicates analysis [cf. Phil 3:11-12]; see Blass/Debrunner, ¶ 375.) Paul either projects a vision of his determination for or expects

---

[33]The meaning of ἀναίδειαν and whose it is has been discussed widely. See Bailey, *Poet*, 19-33. Fitzmyer (*Luke*, 2.912) opts for the one who is asking, while Marshall (*Luke*, 465) selects the one being asked.

the Jews to be saved. Paul follows this conditional with three verbless conditionals (they should probably be categorized as I.a. if for no other reason than that is the unmarked conditional) making analogies with the experience of the Jews, and rounds off the section in v 17 with a I.a. conditional with ἐξεκλάσθησαν (cut away). 1 Cor 3:15: εἴ τινος τὸ ἔργον κατακαήσεται, ζημιωθήσεται, αὐτὸς δὲ σωθήσεται (if the work of some will be burned up, it will be lost, but he will be saved). This conditional appears in a series of conditionals Paul uses to characterize metaphorically the work of Christian ministry. In the first set he speaks of the testing of the foundations, concluding that (v 14) εἴ τινος τὸ ἔργον μένει ὃ ἐποικοδόμησεν, μισθὸν λήμψεται (if someone's work which he builds abides, he will receive a reward). Paul contrasts the use of the I.a. conditional with the Present tense (or are these Futures as well?) for the logical outcome of successful building, with the stark and startling image of projected failure. The image of a giant conflagration, using the marked Future, is sure to stick in the reader's mind. 1 Cor 9:11: εἰ ἡμεῖς ὑμῖν τὰ πνευματικὰ ἐσπείραμεν, μέγα εἰ ἡμεῖς ὑμῶν τὰ σαρκικὰ θερίσομεν; (if we sow spiritual things with you, [is it] great, if we shall reap your fleshly things?), in which Paul uses the marked Future to project the result he would abhor to receive, and the I.a. protasis to assert the fundamental supposition.

2 Tim 2:11-13: εἰ γὰρ συναπεθάνομεν, καὶ συζήσομεν· εἰ ὑπομένομεν, καὶ συμβασιλεύσομεν· εἰ ἀρνησόμεθα, κἀκεῖνος ἀρνήσεται ἡμᾶς·[34] εἰ ἀπιστοῦμεν, ἐκεῖνος πιστὸς μένει, ἀρνήσασθαι γὰρ ἑαυτὸν οὐ δύναται (if we die, indeed we shall live; if we abide, indeed he will reign; if we shall deny, indeed that one will deny us; if we are unfaithful, that one remains faithful, for it is impossible for him to deny himself), contains a number of conditional sentences, the first two and the last being I.a., and the third II.c. The obvious parallelism of this passage--two positive and two negative units, use of καί introducing the first three apodoses, use of the prefix σύν--while perhaps not indicating an early Christian hymn, certainly points to a well-reasoned construction (see Knight, *Sayings*, 112-37, although he both pushes the temporal nature of the tenses much too far and at places denies this: e.g. συζήσομεν in comparison with Rom 6:8 [118-19]). This is confirmed in the use of the tenses in the protases of the conditional statements. The first two protases make assertions about the state of affairs of Christian experience, and hence the Indicative Mood is appropriate. The third statement, in contrast, is by far the most potentially devastating, both in act and consequence. The author uses the Future to create expectation of the event of denial that if performed would lead to exclusion from God's kingdom. The fourth conditional returns to the Indicative Mood. Since it too posits a negative event, it may seem surprising that this protasis does not use the Future as well. The author had this as a choice, but chose otherwise for good reason. The verb ἀπιστεύω may be rendered "not believe" or "be unfaithful." The use of the Indicative, as well as the apodosis--ἐκεῖνος πιστὸς μένει (that one remains faithful)--seems to confirm the latter interpretation. Unfaithfulness, but not unbelief, is part of Christian failure to live up to the standards set by Christ himself. In the apodosis of this conditional the author changes his tack slightly (probably accounting for the lack of καί), by asserting not a consequence of the protasis but an adversative state of affairs (see Kruger, *Conditionals*, 112). The final clause clarifies this in relation to God's nature. Throughout the section use of verbal aspect reinforces the progression, with the least heavily marked Aorist referring to the fundamental condition of Christian experience giving way to the more heavily

---

[34]Cf. Matt 10:33: ὅστις δ' ἂν ἀρνήσηταί με ἔμπροσθεν τῶν ἀνθρώπων, ἀρνήσομαι κἀγὼ αὐτὸν ἔμπροσθεν τοῦ πατρός μου τοῦ ἐν [τοῖς] οὐρανοῖς (whoever might deny me before men, I shall deny him before my father in heaven); Luke 12:9: ὁ δὲ ἀρνησάμενός με ἐνώπιον τῶν ἀνθρώπων ἀπαρνηθήσεται ἐνώπιον τῶν ἀγγέλων τοῦ θεοῦ (the one who denies me before men will be denied before the angels of God). These parallel passages use two conditional-like constructions, the first a relative with a Subjunctive in the protasis, and the second a Participle.

marked Present referring to what the author sees as a more emphatic concept. The Present in the fourth conditional markedly depicts failure as well.[35]

Examples of ἐάν + Future also occur, but these present no problem for classification, although ἄν with the Future is noteworthy. (Cf. Moorhouse, "AN"; Hulton, "᾿AN," for discussion of instances in classical Greek. Moorhouse is convincing that many of these must be accepted as original and semantically plausible.) Luke 19:40: ἐὰν οὗτοι σιωπήσουσιν, οἱ λίθοι κράξουσιν. Marshall (*Luke*, 716) suggests four options on translating this verse, the most plausible being: "if the disciples keep silent, the stones will be found to proclaim the mighty acts of God instead of them." Acts 8:31: πῶς γὰρ ἂν δυναίμην ἐὰν μή τις ὁδηγήσει με; (how should I be able unless someone will lead me?). As Moulton (198-99) notes, this is the only Lukan example of ἄν + Optative in an apodosis with a protasis (he also observes that the presence or absence of ἄν often does not affect the meaning of the clause). Plausible readings are also found in Rev 2:22.

In several examples above a contrast with I.a. conditionals has been seen. Several examples of II.c. and II.a. conditionals complete this section. Gildersleeve claims that only rarely are the Subjunctive and Future used in antithesis, but that when they are generally the Future is the harsher or more solemn ("On εἰ," 11; cf. "Conditional Forms," where he distinguishes minatory [warning, threat] conditional protases with the Future and non-minatory with the Subjunctive. Greenberg ["Realis-Irrealis," 252-53] uses this and Clapp's ["Conditional Sentences"] libidinal use to justify his distinction between the two).[36]

X. Cyr. 4.1.15: ἦν μὲν τοίνυν . . . σωφρόνως διαφυλάττωμεν αὐτήν, ἴσως δυναίμεθ᾿ ἂν ἀκινδύνως εὐδαιμονοῦντες γηρᾶν· εἰ δ᾿ ἀπλήστως χρώμενοι ταύτῃ ἄλλην καὶ ἄλλην πειρασόμεθα διώκειν, ὁρᾶτε μὴ πάθωμεν (if therefore . . . we might be able to watch over it wisely, equally we might be able to grow old without danger, being accounted happy; but if being insatiate in this we will be tempted to pursue more and more, watch out lest we might suffer); Isoc. 6.107: ἦν μὲν γὰρ ἐθέλωμεν ἀποθνήσκειν ὑπὲρ τῶν δικαίων, οὐ μόνον εὐδοκιμήσομεν. . . . εἰ δὲ φοβησόμεθα τοὺς κινδύνους, εἰς πολλὰς ταραχὰς καταστήσομεν ἡμᾶς αὐτούς (for if we might want to die on behalf of the just, we will not only be well esteemed. . . . but if we will fear the dangers, we will plunge ourselves into many troubles) (cf. Rom 5:7). Cf. Hdt. 1.71.3: εἰ νικήσεις, τί σφέας ἀπαιρήσεαι . . . ; τοῦτο δέ, ἢν νικηθῇς, μάθε ὅσα ἀγαθὰ ἀποβαλεῖς (if you will be victorious, what will you carry away from them. . .? and indeed, if you might be conquered, notice what good things you are losing), where Gildersleeve claims "both alternatives are unfavorable." (Gildersleeve also cites D. 27.20; 8.17; Isoc. 15.130; 12.237; Lys. 27.7; Ar. Clouds 586, 591; D. 21.22; Isoc. 17.9; and Hdt. 6.11.2; 3.36.5 [not 3.36.3]. The last, he claims, seems to reverse the usual emphasis, although the texts are so uncertain whether to read Subjunctive or Future forms that any conclusion is tentative. See also Pritchett, "Sentence," 7.)

---

[35]εἰ + Future is used to introduce direct discourse in: Mark 8:12: ἀμὴν λέγω ὑμῖν, εἰ δοθήσεται τῇ γενεᾷ ταύτῃ σημεῖον (truly I say to you that a sign will be given to this generation); Heb 3:11; 4:3, 5: (ὡς ὤμοσα ἐν τῇ ὀργῇ μου,) εἰ εἰσελεύσονται εἰς τὴν κατάπαυσίν μου (as I swore in my wrath that they will enter into my rest).

[36]Dover ("Inscriptions," 13) cites an interesting Athenian inscription: I.G. I² 16.15-19 (= SEG 10.16) (c. 450 B.C.): ἐὰν δέ τ[ις ἄλλη τῶ(?)]ν ἀρχῶν δέξηται δ/[ίκην κατὰ] Φασηλιτῶν τινος /[........, ε]ἰ μὲν καταδικάσο/[.., ἡ καταδίκ]η ἄκυρος ἔστω (if any [other (contract)] of the leaders receives judgment against any of the P.s . . ., if it will be/might be annulled, let the annulment be invalid). He says: "are we to say (i) that εἰ + subjunctive (εἰ καταδικάσῃι) was acceptable in Attic prose usage as late as 460, or (ii) that εἰ + future (εἰ καταδικάσει) was a normal alternative to ἐάν + subjunctive, without the undertone of conjecture, hope, fear or threat which is detectable in the literary examples? Or are we to postulate a readiness on the part of the corpora either to 'stretch' εἰ + future semantically or to adopt a poetic construction, εἰ + subjunctive, for the sake of stylistic variation. . . . avoiding ἐὰν . . . δέξηται . . . ἐὰν καταδικάσῃ?" Cf. Bers, *Syntax*, 147, who argues for the Subjunctive, because of parallel Subjunctives and Ionic influence.

315

In the NT, several examples are significant. Matt 26:33 par. Mark 14:29: εἰ (καὶ [Mark]) πάντες σκανδαλισθήσονται ἐν σοί, ἐγὼ οὐδέποτε σκανδαλισθήσομαι (if [although (Mark)[37]] all will be made to stumble by you, I shall never be made to stumble), good evidence of the expectative quality of the Future. Despite Peter's categorical pronouncement, he soon betrays Jesus. A note of irony might be found in this verse, which uses the marked Future, the specific pronouns πάντες and ἐγώ, and the emphatic negative οὐδέποτε for a promise so quickly denied. Cf. Matt 26:35: κἂν δέῃ με σὺν σοὶ ἀποθανεῖν, οὐ μή σε ἀπαρνήσομαι (even if [Gundry, Matthew, 531] it might be necessary for me to die with you, I shall not deny you), with the Subjunctive in the protasis. After Jesus' words about coming disaster, Peter vigorously denies that he will fall away, no matter what else others will do. But Jesus rebukes him gently by stating matter-of-factly that in that very night Peter will deny Jesus three times. The question is why Peter's response uses the Subjunctive instead of the Future. It could be argued that v 35 is the stronger statement, with Peter vowing to follow Jesus to death. But a second possibility is that Jesus' straightforward response to Peter's first denial of failure has suddenly made Peter retreat slightly from his previous bold stance. He cannot take back his words, but instead he phrases it in a way that reveals less confidence, using the auxiliary verb δέω.

2 Cor 5:1-3: οἴδαμεν γὰρ ὅτι ἐὰν ἡ ἐπίγειος ἡμῶν οἰκία τοῦ σκήνους καταλυθῇ, οἰκοδομὴν ἐκ θεοῦ ἔχομεν οἰκίαν ἀχειροποίητον αἰώνιον ἐν τοῖς οὐρανοῖς. καὶ γὰρ ἐν τούτῳ στενάζομεν, τὸ οἰκητήριον ἡμῶν τὸ ἐξ οὐρανοῦ ἐπενδύσασθαι ἐπιποθοῦντες, εἴ γε[38] καὶ ἐνδυσάμενοι[39] οὐ γυμνοὶ εὑρεθησόμεθα (for we know that if our earthly house of this tent might be destroyed, we have a habitation from God, a house not made with hands, eternal in the heavens. For indeed in this we groan, longing to put on [over] our heavenly habitation, if indeed we, being clothed, shall not be found naked). 2 Cor 5:1-10 is a complex passage, with commentators usually focusing on the possible contradiction between vv 1-5 and 6-10. These problems do not affect the first three verses, which at least grammatically are fairly straightforward. Paul begins by projecting the hypothesis that our earthly house might be destroyed. Bultmann (Corinthians, 131-32) suggests several times for this loosing to occur, including the moment of dying, the parousia (assuming one is not dead before it occurs), and a process of dying. If our earthly house might be destroyed, Paul says, we have a special house from God. Attempts by various commentators to establish the exact temporal referent of ἔχομεν are often misled by the supposition that a Present verb must have present reference. Examples include Harris, "2 Corinthians," loc. cit.; Furnish, II Corinthians, loc. cit; cf. Bultmann, Corinthians, 131-32, who claims that ἔχομεν = ἕξομεν, and that the Present is not a true Present

---

[37]Burton (113) claims that the concessive "generally introduces a supposition conceived of as actually fulfilled or likely to be fulfilled." This cannot be determined on grammatical grounds, since the "concessive" configuration is a subset of the conditional statement. See Blass/Debrunner, ¶ 374; Robertson, 1026-27, who recognize the concessive as a "subspecies" of the conditional.

[38]There is a textual variant here, with εἴπερ the reading in p46 B D F G 33 1175, and the text in ℵ C K L P. There is debate whether the sense of the connective is one of assurance or doubt, though εἴπερ probably indicates a positive later understanding. See Thrall, Particles, 86-91, who finally decides for a positive sense followed by most commentators: "At any rate if we shall not be found to be disembodied--as I am sure we shall not" (91). Cf. Epict. 3.1.4: οὐκ οὖν ὅπερ κύνα ποιεῖ καλόν, τοῦτο ἵππον αἰσχρόν, ὅπερ δ᾽ ἵππον καλόν, τοῦτο κύνα αἰσχρόν, εἴ γε διάφοροι αἱ φύσεις εἰσὶν αὐτῶν (does not whatever makes a dog beautiful, this makes a horse ugly, and whatever makes a horse beautiful, this makes a dog ugly, if indeed their natures are different?).

[39]There is a textual variant here, with ἐκδυσάμενοι the reading in D* ℵ f c, and the text in p46 ℵ B C D2 etc. It is highly dubious that NA26 and UBS3 select the variant (UBS3 does not discuss it). See Metzger, Commentary, 579-80, who discusses the committee's decision, although he personally opts for ἐνδυσάμενοι. He is followed by most commentators: Plummer, Barrett, Bruce, Harris, Martin, Furnish (Bultmann being the notable exception), and most translations, including NIV, NEB, RSV, NASB.

(n. 117). Bultmann appears to have confused verbal form and function, a confusion found in grammars as well: e.g. Robertson, 1019. All that Paul seems to state here is that the fulfilled condition is possession of a new house. In vv 2-3 Paul expands this comparison, inverting the sentence order in the second conditional, with the result that the protasis and apodosis are only loosely connected. Paul says that in fact we long to put on our heavenly clothing, so that we will not be found naked. The second conditional clearly carries the weight not only of the logical argument but of the emotional appeal as well for Paul.

3. APODOSIS. To this point discussion has focused almost exclusively upon the protasis of the conditional statement. A few brief comments may now be made about apodoses. On the basis of what has been said above regarding tense forms, attitude, and aspect, and the importance of the conditional statement as a sub-discourse unit, these comments need not be long. It appears that in apodoses the verb forms function in the same way as in other contexts, i.e. their semantic weight is the result of aspectual and attitudinal choices, with temporal reference determined by deictic indicators within the context of the discourse unit. From what has been noted in previous discussion, however, it is not surprising to see that a sizable number of scholars posit that the apodosis of a conditional functions in relation to the protasis in a temporal relation, on the basis of the tense form of the verb (this issue was of concern to Stoic philosophers as well: e.g. S.E. Out. of Pyrrh. 110-12).

a. Two Major Analyses. 1. The first is by Goodwin (*Syntax*, 170-72; *Grammar*, 298-300), followed by Smyth (527-29), who in an ambiguous exposition argues with regard to what he calls general conditions that the apodosis is present or past in absolute tense terms according to the tense form. (For a critique of general conditions see above; whereas there is the implication that such a scheme holds for other classes of conditional, no explicit statement is made; see the following section for an analysis that would hold for such an instance in any case.)

This is untenable on several grounds. (a) It is argued elsewhere that there is no semantic category of absolute tense in Greek, only relative tense, dependent upon clear deictic indicators. (b) If the Subjunctive is prospective in its semantic meaning (as there is good grounds for arguing, in part endorsed by Goodwin in his treatment of future-referring conditionals), then this makes nonsense of Goodwin's own scheme, since he would have apodoses being fulfilled before a projected protasis comes to pass. (c) This neglects other possible (non-temporal) relationships between the protasis and the apodosis. (d) The division between past and present neglects the semantic value of various verb forms which may share the same temporal reference. And (e) there are clear examples where this scheme does not aid interpretation: e.g. S. Ant. 755: εἰ μὴ πατήρ ἦσθ', εἶπον ἄν σ' οὐκ εὖ φρονεῖν (if you were not my father, I would say you were not thinking correctly). Gonda (*Character*, 188), citing this as a non past-referring Aorist, says it "points to a mere fact dependent on a condition. . . ." E. Alc. 386: ἀπωλόμην ἄρ', εἴ με δὴ λείψεις, γύναι (I am lost, if you will leave me, woman); also E. Med. 77-78. Hdt. 2.29.2: ἢν δὲ ἀπορραγῇ, τὸ πλοῖον οἴχεται φερόμενον ὑπὸ ἰσχύος τοῦ ῥόου (and if it [the rope] might break, the boat, being carried by the strength of the current, is carried away), where the sequence of the rope breaking and the boat being taken down river is clearly the emphasis; Euc. Ax. 2: ἐὰν ἴσοις ἴσα προστεθῇ, τὰ ὅλα ἐστὶν ἴσα (if equal parts might be added to equal parts, the wholes are equal), where the conclusion can only hold true "of anytime or of all time" if the protasis is fulfilled (Smyth, 528); Th. 8.66.2: εἰ δέ τις καὶ ἀντείποι, εὐθὺς ἐκ τρόπου τινὸς ἐπιτηδείου ἐτεθνήκει (if anyone objected, immediately he was killed from a specially designated place), with the Pluperfect. The explanation is sufficiently ambiguous--for example in including instances of the 'gnomic' Aorist under the heading of present condition, e.g. X. Cyr. 1.2.2: ἦν δέ τις τούτων τι παραβαίνῃ, ζημίαν αὐτοῖς ἐπέθεσαν (if one of them might transgress any [law], they punish them)--and not applied to other forms of conditional, that this theory does not bear upon what is proposed here.

2. The second scheme, proposed in different ways by Rijksbaron and Carson, claims that the tense form of one clause is determinative in relation to the other clause. a. Rijksbaron (68-74; cf. Gonda, *Character*, 175) argues that the tense-form of the protasis in relation to the apodosis can be either concurrent or antecedent, depending upon whether the verb is Present or Aorist (he applies this to all categories but the I class, granting that these are indeterminate).

Whereas emphasis upon relative tense in relation to context is to be welcomed, adherence to traditional tense-categories renders this scheme less useful: e.g. Hom. Il. 2.364-65: εἰ δέ κεν ὣς ἔρξῃς καί τοι πείθωνται Ἀχαιοί, / γνώσῃ ἔπειθ' ὅς θ' ἡγεμόνων κακὸς ὅς τέ νυ λαῶν (if you might accomplish [this] and the A.s might be persuaded, you might know then who of the leaders is bad and who of the people). Whereas the order of events might follow syntactical order, there is the strong possibility that persuading the Achaeans (Present Subjunctive) is seen to precede division of the troops according to tribes (Aorist Subjunctive). In either case, both precede the action of the apodosis. X. Cyr. 5.5.13: ἐὰν γάρ τί σε φανῶ κακὸν πεποιηκώς, ὁμολογῶ ἀδικεῖν· ἐὰν μέντοι μηδὲν φαίνωμαι κακὸν πεποιηκὼς μηδὲ βουληθείς, οὐ καὶ σὺ αὖ ὁμολογήσεις μηδὲν ὑπ' ἐμοῦ ἀδικεῖσθαι; (if I might appear to you, having done anything evil, I confess to being wrong; but if I might appear, having done nothing evil nor having planned it, will you not confess that no wrong was done by me?), where the instances of revelation appear to be within the same temporal sphere, and both antecedent to the apodosis.

Pertinent NT examples that show Rijksbaron's theory to be ill-founded include: Luke 13:3, 5: ἐὰν μὴ μετανοῆτε πάντες ὁμοίως ἀπολεῖσθε. . . . ἐὰν μὴ μετανοῆτε πάντες ὡσαύτως ἀπολεῖσθε (unless you repent all likewise will be destroyed. . . . unless you repent all likewise will be destroyed), where the Present verb appears to be antecedent to the action of the apodosis; John 5:19: οὐ δύναται ὁ υἱὸς ποιεῖν ἀφ' ἑαυτοῦ οὐδὲν ἐὰν μή τι βλέπῃ τὸν πατέρα ποιοῦντα (the son is not able to do anything by himself unless he sees something the father does); John 8:55: κἂν εἴπω ὅτι οὐκ οἶδα αὐτόν, ἔσομαι ὅμοιος ὑμῖν ψεύστης (if I say that I do not know him, I will likewise be a liar to you), where the two events seem contemporaneous.

b. Carson (*Fallacies*, 81-82), with particular reference to traditionally-labelled third class conditions (ἐάν + Subjunctive) in the NT, argues on the basis of the apodosis that the Present Indicative is concurrent, the Future is subsequent, and οὐ μή + Subjunctive is subsequent. Although he does not mention them it is logical to infer from what he does say that the Aorist Indicative is antecedent, and that the Subjunctive and Imperative are future (his scheme for the Perfect remains unclear).

Whereas Boyer argues that every apodosis is future-referring, since from the perspective of the speaker every conditional of this sort is future-referring, Carson is right in criticizing Boyer and attempting to interpret the relation between the clauses of the conditional instead. But Carson's scheme remains time-based, and on the basis of what has been discussed above reveals inadequate explanatory powers for a number of examples.

Examples with Aorist verbs in the apodosis prove particularly difficult. Boyer ("Third . . . Class Conditions," 175) explains these as "expressive of 'discovered resulting action,'" unhelpful terminology. Matt 18:15: ἐάν σου ἀκούσῃ, ἐκέρδησας τὸν ἀδελφόν σου (if he hears you, you gain your brother), where use of the Aorist Indicative is better explained according to a theory of attitude than time. In a section on the brother who sins, five projections are made regarding the proper procedure for treating the difficulty. In the second, the least heavily marked Aorist Indicative describes the benefit of the brother's positive response. Several grammarians note the use of the Aorist in this kind of condition (II.a.), calling it timeless (Moulton, 134; Radermacher, 152; Robertson, 146-47); futuristic (Zerwick, 84-85; Blass/Debrunner, ¶ 333[1]; Carson, "Matthew," 404); or gnomic (Robertson, 836-37). Such an idiom is found in ancient Greek outside the NT (see also chapt. 4): Epict. 4.1.39: ἂν μὲν στρατεύσωμαι, ἀπηλλάγην πάντων τῶν κακῶν (if I serve as a solidier, I am relieved of all troubles; Moulton, 247; followed by Robertson, 1019-20); 4.10.27: ὅταν θέλῃς, ἐξῆλθες καὶ οὐ καπνίζῃ (whenever you want, you go out and do not choke [see just above with Aorist Infinitive in apodosis]; Barrett, *John*, 474-75, who calls this a timeless Aorist). But the main emphasis of the passage is on what to do if he continues disobediently, and hence the Imperative is used.

John 15:6: ἐὰν μή τις μένῃ ἐν ἐμοί, ἐβλήθη ἔξω ὡς τὸ κλῆμα καὶ ἐξηράνθη, καὶ συνάγουσιν αὐτὰ καὶ εἰς τὸ πῦρ βάλλουσιν καὶ καίεται (if someone does not remain in me, he is cast out as the branches and is burned, and they gather them and throw them into the fire and they are burned). This use of the omnitemporal Aorist (see my chapt. 4) is best explained as use of the less heavily marked Aorist to mark the result of a condition, with the following Present Indicative verbs marking the final result of apostacy (cf. 15:8 with Aorist Indicative). 1 Cor 7:28: ἐὰν δὲ καὶ γαμήσῃς, οὐχ ἥμαρτες; καὶ ἐὰν γήμῃ ἡ παρθένος, οὐχ ἥμαρτεν (if you might marry, you do not sin; and if the virgin might marry, she does not sin). Although this verse is obscure at several points, it is clear that whether the estimation of sinfulness comes concurrently or subsequently to the act of marrying, it does not come antecedently (see comments on John 15:6 above; cf. Matt 19:9, where the Present Indicative is used in the apodosis of a II.a. conditional-like clause).

Jas 2:2-4: ἐὰν γὰρ εἰσέλθῃ εἰς συναγωγὴν ὑμῶν ἀνὴρ χρυσοδακτύλιος ἐν ἐσθῆτι λαμπρᾷ εἰσέλθῃ δὲ καὶ πτωχὸς ἐν ῥυπαρᾷ ἐσθῆτι, ἐπιβλέψητε δὲ ἐπὶ τὸν φοροῦντα τὴν ἐσθῆτα τὴν λαμπρὰν καὶ εἴπητε, Σὺ κάθου ὧδε καλῶς, καὶ τῷ πτωχῷ εἴπητε, Σὺ στῆθι ἐκεῖ ἢ κάθου ὑπὸ τὸ ὑποπόδιόν μου, οὐ διεκρίθητε ἐν ἑαυτοῖς καὶ ἐγένεσθε κριταὶ διαλογισμῶν πονηρῶν; (if a man might enter into your synagogue wearing a gold ring and in shiny clothing, and a poor man might enter in shabby clothing, you might look upon the one dressed in the shiny clothing and say, you sit here in a good place, and to the poor man say, you stand here or sit under my footstool, do you not judge among yourselves and become judges of evil reasoning?). Whereas a relative past interpretation is possible (Boyer renders it "*have* you not *discriminated* and *become* judges" ["Third . . . Class Conditions," 175]), the act of judging is inextricably linked to the events depicted in the protasis, thus indicating non-antecedent reference (cf. Dibelius/Greeven, *James* , 130-31).

Several examples with various other tense forms in the apodosis of conditionals also provide problems for this temporal perspective: Mark 3:24-25: ἐὰν βασιλεία ἐφ' ἑαυτὴν μερισθῇ, οὐ δύναται σταθῆναι ἡ βασιλεία ἐκείνη· καὶ ἐὰν οἰκία ἐφ' ἑαυτὴν μερισθῇ, οὐ δυνήσεται ἡ οἰκία ἐκείνη σταθῆναι (if a kingdom might be divided upon itself, that kingdom is not able to stand; and if a house is divided upon itself, that house will not be able to stand), where an attitudinal distinction rather than a temporal distinction is more plausible. Jesus is not saying that whereas a divided kingdom is currently unable to stand a house will only fall in the future. Instead he uses the marked Future to emphasize that whereas talk of a kingdom may be true and the result simply stated, in the practical sphere of his hearers (cf. v 20--ἔρχεται εἰς οἶκον [he came into a house]) the projected result of divisiveness is catastrophe. John 14:3: ἐὰν πορευθῶ καὶ ἑτοιμάσω τόπον ὑμῖν, πάλιν ἔρχομαι καὶ παραλήμψομαι ὑμᾶς πρὸς ἐμαυτόν; (if I might go and prepare a place for you, I am going to come again and will receive you to myself). Although it is possible that Jesus refers to a present coming, i.e. he is in progress even as he speaks, the subsequent-referring Present parallel to the emphatic Future stressing being received by him is more plausible. Whereas Schnackenburg (*John*, 3.410 n. 92; cf. Brown, *John*, 2.620) claims ἐὰν = ὅταν and the clause is temporal, Westcott (*John*, 201) perceives the structure of the conditional:

"This departure is itself the condition of the return." Rom 7:2-3: ἐὰν δὲ ἀποθάνῃ ὁ ἀνήρ, κατήργηται ἀπὸ τοῦ νόμου τοῦ ἀνδρός. . . . ἐὰν δὲ ἀποθάνῃ ὁ ἀνήρ, ἐλευθέρα ἐστὶν ἀπὸ τοῦ νόμου (if the husband might die, she might be freed from the law of the husband. . . . but if the husband might die, she is free from the law), where the temporal reference of the Subjunctive and Indicative appears to be identical. Perhaps the marked Subjunctive is used because of the emotional attachments still present in the woman's relation to the dead husband, whereas the Indicative asserts her changed legal status (cf. v 3a with Future in apodosis). Other examples of the Present in the apodosis worth noting include: Matt 18:13: ἐὰν γένηται εὑρεῖν αὐτό, ἀμὴν λέγω ὑμῖν ὅτι χαίρει ἐπ᾽ αὐτῷ μᾶλλον ἢ ἐπὶ τοῖς ἐνενήκοντα ἐννέα τοῖς μὴ πεπλανημένοις (if he might be able to find it, truly I say to you that he rejoices more over it than upon the 99 that did not wander away), where the apodosis refers to subsequent action (cf. v 12, with Future, also describing subsequent action); and John 7:51: μὴ ὁ νόμος ἡμῶν κρίνει τὸν ἄνθρωπον ἐὰν μὴ ἀκούσῃ πρῶτον παρ᾽ αὐτοῦ καὶ γνῷ τί ποιεῖ; (our law does not judge the man, unless it first might hear from him and might know what he has done, does it?), where Nicodemus makes the point that judgment under the law comes after hearing the facts first. Whereas it is to be expected that use of non-Indicative Moods would usually implicate subsequent action, an instance is worth noting of the Imperative in 1 Cor 14:28: ἐὰν δὲ μὴ ᾖ διερμηνευτής, σιγάτω ἐν ἐκκλσίᾳ, ἑαυτῷ δὲ λαλείτω καὶ τῷ θεῷ (if there might not be an interpreter, let him be silent in church, and let him speak to himself and to God), where the silence commanded seems to be coincident with the absence of the interpreter. (Conzelmann [*Corinthians*, 244-45] suggests an alternative translation of the protasis: "But if he is not an interpreter. . . ." This would seem to ensure coincident action.). An instance of the Future is found in Mark 14:31 par. Matt 26:35: ἐὰν δέῃ με συναποθανεῖν σοι, οὐ μή σε ἀπαρνήσομαι (if it might be necessary for me to die with you, I will never deny you), where a future reference of the apodosis to the protasis is difficult. Whereas most analyses of the individual statements of conditionals focus upon temporal relations, it is shown above that such a correlation cannot be made on the basis of tense forms.

b. Nutting/Kruger.

Pursuing a different line of analysis, Nutting, in a series of articles on conditional statements, argues that different kinds of logical relations hold between the protases and apodoses of conditional statements. After analysis of conditionals using English and Latin, he formulates four possible relations: cause and effect, ground and inference, relation of equivalence, and unreal conditional periods ("Order," 25-39, 149-62, and esp. "Modes," the last of which outlines the relations designated above. He cites examples from older Greek). This scheme is adopted and applied to conditional statements of the NT by Kruger (*Conditionals*). His analysis provides a significant step forward in understanding some of the kinds of relations that obtain, without resorting to problematic temporal categories.

Among other instances the following are worth noting. Cause and effect: Rev 20:15: εἴ τις οὐχ εὑρέθη ἐν τῇ βίβλῳ τῆς ζωῆς γεγραμμένος ἐβλήθη εἰς τὴν λίμνην τοῦ πυρός (if someone was not found, being written in the book of life, he was cast into the lake of fire). See also Matt 4:3; 9:21; 15:14; Mark 8:3; John 11:48; Acts 4:9; 1 Cor 3:17; 8:10 (Kruger, 101-05). Ground and Inference: Heb 9:13: εἰ γὰρ τὸ αἷμα τράγων καὶ ταύρων καὶ σποδὸς δαμάλεως ῥαντίζουσα τοὺς κεκοινωμένους ἁγιάζει πρὸς τὴν τῆς σαρκὸς καθαρότητα, πόσῳ μᾶλλον τὸ αἷμα τοῦ Χριστοῦ (if the blood of goats and bulls and ashes of a heifer sprinkling those who are defiled purifies to the cleansing of the flesh, how much more the blood of Christ). See also Matt 11:23; Rom 11:16; 1 Cor 11:31 (or cause and effect?); 15:13; Gal 4:7; Heb 4:8; 1 Pet 4:18 (Kruger, 106-08). Relation of equivalence, or the defining period: Jas 1:23: εἴ τις ἀκροατὴς λόγου ἐστὶν καὶ οὐ ποιητής, οὗτος ἔοικεν ἀνδρὶ κατανοοῦντι τὸ πρόσωπον τῆς γενέσεως αὐτοῦ ἐν ἐσόπτρῳ (if someone is a hearer of the word and not a doer, he is like a man recognizing his natural face in a mirror). See also Matt 26:24 par. Mark 14:21; 1 Cor 7:8; 11:14-

15; 15:19; 1 Tim 3:1; 1 John 4:20 (Kruger, 108-111). Adversative, or conditional-concessive periods: 2 Cor 4:16: εἰ καὶ ὁ ἔξω ἡμῶν ἄνθρωπος διαφθείρεται, ἀλλ' ὁ ἔσω ἡμῶν ἀνακαινοῦται ἡμέρᾳ καὶ ἡμέρᾳ (if our outer man is being decayed [contra Plummer, *Second Corinthians*, 135; Furnish, *II Corinthians*, 261, who consider the concessive construction as being actually the case or fulfilled], but our inner man is being renewed day by day). See also Matt 16:26; 26:33; Mark 14:31; Luke 11:8; 16:31; 18:4-5; 22:67b, 68; John 1:25 (or is this ground and inference?); Acts 13:41; Rom 11:17; 1 Cor 4:15; 8:2, 5; 9:2, 16a; 12:15; 2 Cor 5:16; 7:8, 12; 12:15; Phil 2:17; Col 2:5; 2 Tim 2:13; Jas 2:14; 1 Pet 3:1 (Kruger, 111-15).

Whereas it is clear that these categories are appropriate for discussing a significant number of conditional statements, there are both a number of examples that could be categorized differently and a number to which these categories do not seem to apply. For example, is John 4:10 (εἰ ᾔδεις τὴν δωρεὰν τοῦ θεοῦ καὶ τίς ἐστιν ὁ λέγων σοι, Δός μοι πεῖν, σὺ ἂν ᾔτησας αὐτὸν καὶ ἔδωκεν ἄν σοι ὕδωρ ζῶν [if you knew the gift of God and who the one is saying to you, give me to drink, you would ask him and he would give to you living water]) cause and effect or better ground and inference? And is John 8:36 (ἐὰν οὖν ὁ υἱὸς ὑμᾶς ἐλευθερώσῃ, ὄντως ἐλεύθεροι ἔσεσθε [if the son might make you free, you will be free indeed]) equivalence or better cause and effect? Schnackenburg (*John*, 2.490 n. 80) seems to see a causal relation between the two. Few examples can be decided with any degree of certainty. Does any of the categories adequately explain John 21:22-23: ἐὰν αὐτὸν θέλω μένειν ἕως ἔρχομαι, τί πρὸς σέ; σύ μοι ἀκολούθει. . . . ἐὰν αὐτὸν θέλω μένειν ἕως ἔρχομαι [, τί πρὸς σέ]; (if I want him to remain until I come, what is that to you. . . ?)? Kruger categorizes it as adversative (112), but the lines are tenuous at best. None of the other categories seems satisfactory either. Other examples could be cited as well, but the point appears to be that the conditional establishes a relation between protasis and apodosis. Although this relationship is not specified on the basis of tense form as a temporal relationship, several different logical means of analysis may apply.

4. CONCLUSION. There probably will never be a scheme for conditionals that will meet with the approval of all grammarians, but formal criteria utilizing attitudinal and aspectual semantics provide a helpful basis for advancing discussion of the protasis. Establishing the exact relation between protasis and apodosis is more difficult, since there are no firm criteria by which such an analysis may be made. The conditional is a construction that functions in the realm of pragmatic usage, linking two smaller units within one larger discourse unit. Whereas the items that make up the individual clauses can be semantically defined in many instances with high degree of specificity, the relation between the clauses is beyond the scope of semantically secure formal criteria. Hence it is better to recognize that the conditional statement posits a relation between the protasis and the apodosis, and that some of these may be described as cause and effect, ground and inference, equative, and adversative, depending upon the context of situation, although these are not the only pragmatic categories that may be invoked.

CHAPTER 7:
THE AORIST, PRESENT AND PERFECT
IN THE NON-INDICATIVE MOODS

0. INTRODUCTION. In the above chapters (esp. 2 and 4), it is argued that Greek tense forms grammaticalize the speaker's conception of a process (verbal aspect), and not temporal reference. Verbal aspect provides the controlling category for understanding Greek tense usage, although other pragmatic factors--such as deictic indicators and implicature--have pertinence in limiting temporal reference of the aspect. In discussing the non-Indicative Moods in Greek, it is again important to stress the relevance of verbal aspect, despite repeated insistence by some that the tenses are primarily future-referring (e.g. Hahn, *Subjunctive*), although several of the more recent expositions argue for the non time-based nature of non-Indicative verbs (e.g. McKay, esp. 148-49). (On the nature of the attitudes realized by the Moods see chapt. 4.) Many issues concerning the range of usage of these various verbal elements go beyond the concern of this work; consequently, these issues must be passed by, though warranting further investigation. The Present and Aorist Subjunctive/Optative and then Imperative are treated first, since they constitute the largest category of usage. Then the few instances of the Perfect are surveyed.

1. THE SUBJUNCTIVE AND OPTATIVE. a. Introduction. "Modality could, that is to say, be defined as the grammaticalization of speakers' (subjective) attitudes and opinions" (Palmer, *Mood*, 16; cf. de Boel, "Complementizers," 285), and thus relates to what is both factual and not factual on the basis of the speaker's belief. Thus it is seen above that the issue of factuality cuts across the two major categories of epistemic [+assertion] and deontic [-assertion] attitudes (see Palmer, *Mood*, 18; Lyons, *Semantics*, 736).

These are grammaticalized in the Greek verbal network by the Indicative and non-Indicative forms. (Greek does not have modal verbs as traditionally defined, and its negative particles do not necessarily correlate with particular attitudes until the hellenistic period, and even then not exactly.) Thus the Indicative is used to grammaticalize assertive or declarative statements, while the non-Indicative forms grammaticalize a variety of related attitudes, having in common that they make no assertion about reality but grammaticalize the volition of the speaker, and are therefore deontic. Thus, in more traditional terms, McKay says the Indicative "is most commonly used for statements of fact (or alleged fact) and intention, both positive and negative, both in independent simple sentences and as the core of clauses whose interdependence may modify its significance to some extent" (148), "The subjunctive mood in independent sentences normally expresses the will of the subject of the verb, and supplements the imperative by replacing it in certain circumstances and by expressing exhortations in the first person. . . . The optative mood in independent sentences normally expresses either a wish . . . a possibility or probability. . . " (149), and "The imperative mood expresses command, including such mild forms of command as advice or entreaty" (148; see also Moulton, 164-65; Abel, 269; Chamberlain, 82-83). Avoiding the language of volition (because of its connotations in the grammatical tradition) the non-Indicative forms appear to grammaticalize the following semantic features: the Imperative grammaticalizes [+direction] (volition toward a process), the Subjunctive grammaticalizes [+projection] (volition with a visualization), and the Optative, marked in relation to the Subjunctive, grammaticalizes [+projection: +contingency].

  b. Aspectual usage. 1. Non-temporal nature of attitude. (See also Brugmann, 573; Schwyzer, esp. 2.304; Goodwin, *Grammar*, 272; Blass, 194; Burton, 46ff.; contra Kühner/Gerth, 1.217; Goodwin, *Syntax*, 371-87, 23-28, although his examples certainly do not prove that the tenses are future-referring [cf. 2-4]; Winer, esp. 355ff.; Moulton, 186; Blass/Debrunner, ¶¶ 357ff.; Abel, 270-71; Robertson, 848, who is confusing at this point.) In discussion of individual examples below, the non-temporal nature of the Subjunctive and the Optative (proposed in chapt. 4) is further confirmed. It has already been seen above that the Subjunctive and Optative are not time-based, and hence may be used in a variety of contexts, some with specific temporal reference and others without. The syntactical constructions in which they are often found have captured the attention of most grammarians.[1] The varied implicatures support the non-temporal basis of their usage to grammaticalize [+projection] of a process. Already cited in chapt. 4 for the Subjunctive are indirect discourse (e.g. Matt 6:25: μὴ μεριμνᾶτε τῇ ψυχῇ ὑμῶν τί φάγητε [don't trouble your soul with what you might eat]) and relative clauses (Matt 5:21: ὃς δ' ἂν φονεύσῃ, ἔνοχος ἔσται τῇ κρίσει [whoever might commit murder, he shall be liable to

---

[1]See the grammars cited above for reference to various uses. One issue heavily debated in the secondary literature is the so-called deliberative relative. See e.g. Goodwin, "Extent"; Hale, "'Extended'"; Earie, "Subjunctive of Purpose"; idem, "Subjunctive in Relative"; idem, "Notes"; J.D., "Remote Deliberative"; Sidgwick, "Remote Deliberative." Cf. Naylor, "Optative."

judgment]; cf. 5:21ff. with Aorist and Present Subjunctives). This is reinforced by a variety of other uses. For example, the Subjunctive is used in hortatory, commanding or prohibiting situations (see Roberts, "Subjunctive"), where a projected event with no necessary fulfilment is referred to (Gal 5:26: μὴ γινώμεθα κενόδοξοι [let us not be vainglorious]); final or resultive clauses (John 17:21: ἵνα ὁ κόσμος πιστεύῃ [so that the world might believe]); deliberative clauses (Mark 12:14: δῶμεν ἢ μὴ δῶμεν; [should we give or not?]); and conditional and conditional-like clauses (Matt 5:46-47: ἐὰν γὰρ ἀγαπήσητε τοὺς ἀγαπῶντας ὑμᾶς, τίνα μισθὸν ἔχετε; . . . καὶ ἐὰν ἀσπάσησθε τοὺς ἀδελφοὺς ὑμῶν μόνον, τί περισσὸν ποιεῖτε; [if you might love those who love you, do you have a certain reward . . . and if you might greet your brothers only, what more do you do?]; contra Moulton, 186; see my chapt. 6 on conditionals). In response to the hypothesis that the Subjunctive is future-referring, reference to present and past contexts (1 Cor 15:32: φάγωμεν καὶ πίωμεν, αὔριον γὰρ ἀποθνήσκομεν [let us eat and drink, for tomorrow we die]; 1 Tim 1:20: οὓς παρέδωκα τῷ σατανᾷ ἵνα παιδευθῶσιν μὴ βλασφημεῖν [whom I handed over to Satan, so that they might be taught not to blaspheme]; Titus 1:5) are problematic. A similar range of uses may be cited for the Optative: μὴ γένοιτο (may it never be), which may deny any sphere of temporal implicature; conditionals (see chapt. 6); timeless and omnitemporal reference (Acts 17:27: εἰ ἄρα γε ψηλαφήσειαν αὐτὸν καὶ εὕροιεν [if he might seek after and might find him]; Acts 25:16: ὁ κατηγορούμενος κατὰ πρόσωπον ἔχοι τοὺς κατηγόρους τόπον τε ἀπολογίας λάβοι [(the Roman custom is that) the one accused might face his accusers and might have a chance at a defence]). Hulton's conclusion for the Optative is also pertinent for the Subjunctive:

> the most convenient supposition--one that may be held to explain all such instances in the same way, in place of the varying explanations commonly given, and at the same time to make them accord with a general theory--is that the optative [and Subjunctive] as such [have] no temporal reference at all, as indeed might be expected, since moods, after all, are not tenses; it simply supplies the notion of potentiality and may be fitted into *any* temporal context, and in this way given a "temporal application"--but it takes on such temporal colouring as it has by reflection from its surroundings rather than possessing it in its own right. ("Optatives," 140)

2. Subjunctive. What has been stated above in chapts. 2 and 4 regarding verbal aspect need not be repeated here. The Aorist is clearly the least heavily marked in the Subjunctive and Optative in comparison with the Present (and certainly the Perfect Subjunctive), and this on all counts: materially, where the sigmatic Aorist is compensated for by the morphological variety of the root (of course, there is no augment to the Aorist); distributionally, where the Aorist is found at a ratio of over 3:1 to the Present, with the Perfect numerically relatively insignificant; implicationally, with the Aorist showing a less regular paradigm; and semantically (see chapt. 2 and below). Thus as Robertson says, "The aorist is used as a matter of course here unless durative action [?] is to be expressed" (889). Chantraine ("Remarques," 76) observes that this has been the case with the Subjunctive and the Optative in Greek from the Homeric period through to the papyri. In justifying an "aspectual" approach to the verb forms he claims that "L'emploi du présent apparaît rare, il comporte volontiers une valeur expressive et pittoresque" (74). Perhaps the large number of Aorist Subjunctives in the NT (as well as other hellenistic Greek) explains the relative neglect by the grammarians of verbal aspect in the

Subjunctive. But significant enough numbers of Present Subjunctives are used in the NT to warrant comment. Two kinds of examples of the Subjunctive are cited here. First, a set of examples from extra-biblical Greek is put forward to illustrate the contrast in aspectual semantics when the two appear in similar or parallel contexts. Then pertinent NT Greek examples cited roughly book-by-book are analysed according to verbal aspect to shed light on the semantic contribution to the given proposition.

a. Extra-biblical Greek (see esp. Goodwin, *Syntax*, 25-26): E. Ion 758: εἴπωμεν ἢ σιγῶμεν; (should we speak or remain silent?), where no necessary correlation exists between the events referred to and the tense used. Rather, the more heavily marked Present is used for the speaker's desired option (cf. following Future: δράσομεν [what shall we do?]). Aeschin. 1.73: βούλεσθε οὖν τὸ ὅλον πρᾶγμα ἀφῶμεν καὶ μὴ ζητῶμεν; (do you desire that we let the whole matter drop and not be in progress on our investigation?); X. Anab. 7.1.29: μὴ πρὸς θεῶν μαινώμεθα μηδ᾽ αἰσχρῶς ἀπολώμεθα πολέμιοι ὄντες καὶ ταῖς πατρίσι καὶ τοῖς ἡμετέροις αὐτῶν φίλοις τε καὶ οἰκείοις (let us not be acting mad toward the gods and let us not die shamefully, being enemies to our homeland and to our friends and kinsmen); D. 21.34: χρὴ δ᾽, ὅταν μὲν τιθῆσθε τοὺς νόμους, ὁποῖοί τινές εἰσι σκοπεῖν, ἐπειδὰν δὲ θῆσθε, φυλάττειν καὶ χρῆσθαι (it is necessary, whenever you might be in progress putting forward laws, to observe what kind they are, but when after you enact, to guard and make use of them), with a clear contrast being made between diligence during the legal process, and once the laws are established, their profitable use (cf. D. 9.69; 57.16); Isoc. 6.101: ἁπάντων οὖν τούτων ἀναμνησθέντες ἐρρωμενέστερον ἀντιλαβώμεθα τοῦ πολέμου, καὶ μὴ περιμένωμεν ὡς ἄλλων τινῶν τὰς παρούσας ἀτυχίας ἰασομένων (remembering all these things, let us take up the war more vigorously and not remain as if certain others would aid the present misfortune), where the tenses used do not correlate with expectations, drawing attention to the more heavily marked Present referring to the process to be shunned.[2]

b. NT Greek (proper conditional statements are not treated here; see chapt. 6): Matt 7:12 πάντα οὖν ὅσα ἐὰν θέλητε ἵνα ποιῶσιν ὑμῖν οἱ ἄνθρωποι, οὕτως καὶ ὑμεῖς ποιεῖτε αὐτοῖς (all such things which you might want that men might do for you, thus you do to them), with a doubly marked protasis. Although the Present of θέλω predominates in the NT, the Aorist is used including in the Subjunctive (e.g. 1 Cor 4:19; Gal 5:17), calling attention to those statements (often conditional-like) which stress one's desire. See also Matt 20:26-27 par. Mark 10:43-44: ὃς ἐὰν θέλῃ ἐν ὑμῖν μέγας γενέσθαι ἔσται ὑμῶν διάκονος, καὶ ὃς ἂν θέλῃ ἐν ὑμῖν εἶναι πρῶτος ἔσται ὑμῶν δοῦλος (whoever might want to be great among you shall be your servant, and whoever might want to be first among you shall be your servant); Mark 6:22: Herod, impressed with his daughter's dancing, tells her, αἴτησόν με ὃ ἐὰν[3] θέλῃς, καὶ δώσω σοι (ask of me whatever you might want, and I will give it to you), with the least marked portion of the sentence

---

[2]Inscr. Magnesia of Meander 1.10-12: ὅπως οἱ οἰκονόμοι οἱ ἐνεστηκότες ἀγοράσωσιν ταῦρον, καὶ οἱ ἀεὶ καθισταμένοι ἀγοράζωσιν ταῦρον ὡς κάλλιστον (so that the acting stewards might buy a bull, and the present appointees might be in progress purchasing the most beautiful bull possible), cited in Chantraine, "Questions," 42-43, from O. Kern, *Inscr. Magn.* 98 = Sokolowski, *Lois sacrées d'Asie Mineure* 32. Is the Present used "Lorsque la répétition ou la durée sont envisagées" (43)? More likely, the Aorist states the simple transaction, and the more heavily marked Present the more important purchase. There is no indication that either repetition or duration applies to either set of events. Cf. an inscription from Priene, 18.32 (270 B.C.): ὅπως στήλη τε κατασκευασθῆι καὶ ἀναγραφῆι (so that a stele might be prepared and inscribed), cited in de Foucault, *Recherches*, 185.

[3]On ἐάν for ἄν see Rydbeck, *Fachprosa*, 119ff.; cf. Langdon, "History"; Moulton, "Characteristics," 9 (1904) 359-60.

with the Aorist Imperative, the more heavily stressed with the Present Subjunctive, and the most heavily marked with the Future; Mark 8:35: after an initial I.a. conditional, the Present Subjunctive (ὃς γὰρ ἐὰν θέλη τὴν ψυχὴν αὐτοῦ σῶσαι [whoever might want to save his soul]) forms the protasis of a conditional-like statement (II.a.), with a Future in the apodosis, repeated in the protasis of the following conditional-like statement (II.c.).

Matt 15:2: Pharisees complain to Jesus that his disciples do not wash their hands ὅταν ἄρτον ἐσθίωσιν (whenever they might eat bread). The use of the Aorist Subjunctive in unmarked contexts (Mark 8:1; 14:12) reinforces the strength of the usage in the Pharisees' complaint. Matt 26:46: ἐγείρεσθε, ἄγωμεν (get up, let us go), with the hortatory Present Subjunctive parallel to the Present Imperative. The common non-assertive feature (related to volition) appears to be the factor that allows the Imperative and Subjunctive (as well as the Optative) to be used by speakers in similar commanding and prohibiting contexts.

Mark 4:12, cf. John 9:39: ἵνα βλέποντες βλέπωσιν καὶ μὴ ἴδωσιν, καὶ ἀκούοντες ἀκούωσιν καὶ μὴ συνιῶσιν, μήποτε ἐπιστρέψωσιν καὶ ἀφεθῇ αὐτοῖς (so that having seen they might be in progress of seeing and not see, and having heard they might be in progress of hearing and not understand, lest they might repent and it be forgiven to them). One of the most problematic verses of the entire NT, two issues are suggested. (1) Scholars have disagreed over how to interpret the ἵνα clause, although most recent commentators have returned to the traditional resultive sense, often because of the force of the parallel μήποτε.[4] (2) More important here is use of the Subjunctives. An altered quotation of Isa 6:9-10 (Evans ["Isaiah," 126-27] fails to note that the LXX has the Future forms ἀκούσετε and βλέψετε instead of the Subjunctives, although he does note the change from ἰάσοναι to ἀφεθῇ), the author's restructuring is aspectually significant. Essentially he reverses the first two lines and appends the altered third directly after excising intermediate material. Thus he uses the marked cognate Present Participle and Present Subjunctive in contrast with another verb of visual perception, a negated Aorist Subjunctive. He then uses the same technique in the climactic second line, placing a negated Present Subjunctive as the most damning judgment of the entire unit--that the audience of the parables hears but does not understand. The final line closes with two Aorist Subjunctives. Cf. Mark 4:21-22, where after the introductory phrase the entire parable is told using the Aorist, especially Subjunctives. The climactic final statement of v 23 (εἴ τις ἔχει ὦτα ἀκούειν ἀκουέτω [if someone has ears to hear let him hear]) closes with three Presents.

Mark 4:26-29 in contrast uses Present, Aorist and Perfect verbs: Jesus is quoted as saying (ἔλεγεν) that the kingdom of God is like a man who might oast (βάλῃ) seed upon the earth and he is going to sleep (καθεύδῃ) and getting up (ἐγείρηται) night and day, and the seed is sprouting (βλαστᾷ) and growing (μηκύνηται) in a way that he does not know (οἶδεν). Automatically the earth is growing fruit (καρποφορεῖ). Whenever the fruit is ripe (παραδοῖ), immediately he sends in (ἀποστέλλει) the sickle, because the harvest is at hand (παρέστηκεν). Not only does this use of the tense forms reinforce their aspectual nature by running contrary to traditional temporal criteria (e.g. ἄνθρωπος βάλῃ τὸν σπόρον [timeless, not futuristic as Moulton, 185]; εὐθὺς ἀποστέλλει; ὅταν . . . παραδοῖ ὁ καρπός), but aspectual usage is self-conscious. The parable is constructed in two sections (vv 26-27, 28-29), each beginning with a Present form, moving to an Aorist, and then concluding with at least one Present and a climactic Perfect; the first section focusing upon the activities of the man and the second on the growth of the seed (cf. Mark 13:28:

---

[4]See esp. Evans, "Isaiah." The five major views are: it is inauthentic or misrepresents Jesus' original teaching; fulfilment = ἵνα πληρωθῇ; causal; consecutive = ὥστε; and final; cf. Holzmeister, "Verstockungszweck," 358-62; Gnilka, Verstockung, 45-50. A recent commentator is Marcus, Mystery, esp. 119-21; see also Cranfield, Mark, 155-56; Taylor, Mark, 257; contra Lane, Mark, 159 n. 34, who implies both final and fulfilment. Pertinent though widely varying grammatical discussions are to be found in Jannaris, 408-09 (causal); Robertson, "Causal Use" (rejecting any causal use in the NT); Winer, 576-77 (fulfilment); Blass/Debrunner, ¶ 369(1) (final); Moule, 142-43 (Semitic); Zerwick, 140-41, 146-47 (causal, though Semitic); and Black, Approach, 211-16 (Aramaic dᵉ).

ἐκφύῃ τὰ φύλλα [the foliage grows]); the first concluding with the man not knowing how these natural events occur, and the second with the harvest in a ready state; the first speaking of a hypothetical man, using the Subjunctive, and the second the process of nature, using the Indicative (cf. the Aorist Subjunctive in 4:29 which forms a basic assumption).

Mark 6:8: the twelve were told that they might take nothing (μηδὲν αἴρωσιν) on their journey except. . . (cf. Mark 15:21 par. Matt 27:32 with Aorist Subjunctive). Cf. vv 10ff., where Aorist Subjunctives are used in the protases of conditional and conditional-like clauses (cf. Luke 9:5; 10:8, 10 with Present Subjunctives), until v 12, speaking of the purpose of the disciples' preaching: ἵνα μετανοῶσιν (so that they might repent). (A profitable contrast is made with use of the Aorist Subjunctive in Rev 2:5, 21. In 2:5 the II.a. protasis is simply recapitulative. 2:21 is parallel to Mark 6:12, occurring in a ἵνα clause, parallel to an Aorist Infinitive of the same verb.) Mark 6:41 and 8:6: the author draws attention to the distribution of the bread (ἵνα παρατιθῶσιν [so that they might distribute]), par. Luke 9:16 with Aorist Infinitive. Two points are worth noting here. (1) These are the only two uses of the Present Subjunctive of this verb in the NT; (2) in Mark 8:6 the Aorist Indicative of the same verb is used referring to the same process, illustrating that the objective conception of the process is not primarily at issue in selection of verbal aspect.

Mark 9:37: ὃς ἂν ἐν τῶν τοιούτων παιδίων δέξηται ἐπὶ τῷ ὀνόματί μου, ἐμὲ δέχεται· καὶ ὃς ἂν ἐμὲ δέχηται, οὐκ ἐμὲ δέχεται ἀλλὰ τὸν ἀποστείλαντά με (whoever might receive one of these children in my name, he receives me; and whoever might be receiving me, he does not receive me but the one who sent me), with a striking contrast between the Aorist Subjunctive and Present Subjunctive, with the Present Subjunctive stressing the greater importance of receiving Jesus; Mark 9:42ff.: a similar contrast is seen in these verses, in which the initial conditional-like statement uses the Aorist Subjunctive, but then in a series of parallel II.a. conditionals the Present Subjunctive is used when applied to the individual (ἐὰν σκανδαλίζῃ σε [if x might be causing you to stumble]); cf. Matt 18:8, 9, with Present Indicative. Mark 13:11: ὅταν ἄγωσιν ὑμᾶς παραδιδόντες (whenever they might take you, arresting you), reflecting not only a possible interest of a church under persecution, but a tendency of Mark to use the Present Subjunctive when the issue personally affects those present, i.e. the hortatory Present Subjunctive (1:38; 14:42); Mark 13:34: the doorkeeper is specifically told to watch (ἵνα γρηγορῇ) for the lord of the house, with the Present Subjunctive forming the turning point in the story (cf. 1 Thess 5:10), continued with a Present Imperative γρηγορεῖτε.

Mark 12:7 and 14:1: in the parable of the vineyard, the farmers say δεῦτε ἀποκτείνωμεν (come let us kill) the owner's son, and the chief priests and scribes are reported to have been seeking πῶς αὐτὸν ἐν δόλῳ κρατήσαντες ἀποκτείνωσιν (how, catching [Jesus] in treachery they might kill him). While it may be coincidental that the deaths of the two are plotted against using the same verb in the same verbal aspect, the use of the more heavily marked aspect is not. Mark 14:25: Jesus is reported telling his disciples that οὐκέτι οὐ μὴ πίω ἐκ τοῦ γενήματος τῆς ἀμπέλου ἕως τῆς ἡμέρας ἐκείνης ὅταν αὐτὸ πίνω καινὸν ἐν τῇ βασιλείᾳ τοῦ θεοῦ (no longer might I drink from the fruit of the vine until that day whenever I might be drinking it new in the kingdom of God), with a self-conscious contrast between the negated Aorist Subjunctive and the Present Subjunctive for the new and desired state.

Luke 6:31: the new rule of retribution is stated using Present verbs (cf. Isoc. 1.14; 3.61; cf. 2.24, 38; and Hdt. 3.142.3): καθὼς θέλετε ἵνα ποιῶσιν ὑμῖν οἱ ἄνθρωποι, ποιεῖτε αὐτοῖς ὁμοίως (as you are wanting so that men might be doing to you, do likewise to them); cf. John 13:34-35. Luke 8:18: ὃς ἂν γὰρ ἔχῃ, δοθήσεται αὐτῷ, καὶ ὃς ἂν μὴ ἔχῃ, καὶ ὃ δοκεῖ ἔχειν ἀρθήσεται ἀπ' αὐτοῦ (whoever might be having, it shall be given to him, and whoever might not be having, indeed what he thinks he has shall be taken away from him), with the Present Subjunctive used affirmatively and negatively as the protasis of two II.a. conditional-like statements, with Future verbs in the apodoses; cf. Matt 13:12; Mark 4:25, with Present Indicatives in the protasis of I.a. conditionals. Luke 11:2: Luke introduces the Lord's Prayer with the imperfective aspect, ὅταν προσεύχησθε, λέγετε (whever you might be praying, say); cf. Matt 6:9 with Present Indicative/Imperative, although both prayers utilize the Aorist throughout (except Luke 11:3); and Matt 6:5, 6.

Luke 11:21-22: the author contrasts the strongman who guards (φυλάσση) his own house, and it is safe, with when the strongman is overpowered (νικήση) and his possessions are taken (αἴρει). One might expect the aspects to be reversed (both sets of forms are found in the NT), except for two factors: (1) v 23 indicates that the point of the saying revolves around being with Jesus and prepared, thus reinforcing the need for watchfulness; (2) in v 22, the focus is not upon the conquest itself, but that once the conquest occurs the armed man may be stripped of his possessions, thus warranting the Present Indicative in the apodosis. Luke 16:26ff.: the chasm between heaven and hell is so wide, the parable says, ὅπως οἱ θέλοντες διαβῆναι ἔνθεν πρὸς ὑμᾶς μὴ δύνωνται, μηδὲ ἐκεῖθεν πρὸς ἡμᾶς διαπερῶσιν (so that those who want to cross over from here to you might not be able to, and neither might they cross over from there to us). The rich man replies that he wants Lazarus ὅπως διαμαρτύρηται (so that he might bear witness to) his brothers, with the Present Subjunctives drawing attention to two significant points in the narrative. Luke 22:30: in the dispute about greatness, Jesus is reported to have said that he would give to his disciples as was given to him ἵνα ἔσθητε καὶ πίνητε ἐπὶ τῆς τραπέζης μου ἐν τῇ βασιλείᾳ μου, καὶ καθήσεσθε ἐπὶ θρόνων τὰς δώδεκα φυλὰς κρίνοντες τοῦ Ἰσραήλ (so that you might be eating and drinking at my table in my kingdom, and you will sit upon thrones judging the twelve tribes of I.), where the semantic weight of the marked Present Subjunctives is exceeded by the semantic weight of the Future form, with the movement from projection to expectation.

John 3:16-17: God loved the world so that he gave his son, ἵνα πᾶς ὁ πιστεύων εἰς αὐτὸν μὴ ἀπόληται ἀλλ᾽ ἔχῃ ζωὴν αἰώνιον (so that everyone who believes in him might not perish but have eternal life; cf. John 6:40; 8:6; 17:13), for he did not send his son into the world ἵνα κρίνῃ τὸν κόσμον, ἀλλ᾽ ἵνα σωθῇ ὁ κόσμος δι᾽ αὐτοῦ (so that he might judge the world but so that the world might be saved through him). The contrast between the Aorist and Present Subjunctives in the first clause marks reference to death, but the second set of clauses is more difficult. κρίνῃ may be a Present Subjunctive in contrast to the Aorist Subjunctive in chiastic structure, or they may both be Aorist Subjunctives, following as result clauses of the negated major clause to clarify what God has not done. John 4:15: the woman at the well is reported to have told Jesus: δός μοι τοῦτο τὸ ὕδωρ, ἵνα μὴ διψῶ μηδὲ διέρχωμαι ἐνθάδε ἀντλεῖν (give me this water, so that I might not be thirsting and not be passing through here to draw water), where the Future verbs Jesus used (διψήσει and γενήσεται [v 14]) are changed to Present Subjunctives, retaining the stress upon her desire to share in this living water, but not detracting from the expectation of fulfilment of Jesus' own words. Similar patterns may be found in John 4:36; 5:20; 6:38; 11:15; 12:47; 14:31; 15:2; 16:30. John 5:23: amidst a series of oppositions, the author says the father judges no one but gives judgment to the son, ἵνα πάντες τιμῶσι τὸν υἱὸν καθὼς τιμῶσι τὸν πατέρα (so that all might honour the son as they honour the father), with a conscious alteration of attitude between the projected result and the asserted state of affairs (the only use of the Present Subjunctive of this verb in the NT); John 6:28-29: the crowd asks Jesus τί ποιῶμεν ἵνα ἐργαζώμεθα τὰ ἔργα τοῦ θεοῦ; (what might we be doing in order to accomplish the works of God?). And Jesus reportedly answers ἵνα πιστεύητε εἰς ὃν ἀπέστειλεν ἐκεῖνος (that you might be believing in whom [God] sent). In v 30 Jesus' questioners follow up their first question with a second, using the Aorist Subjunctive when recapitulating Jesus' answer. This contradicts Barrett's (John, 287) characterization of the first Present Subjunctive as referring to a "life of faith" rather than an "act of faith." John 8:44: ὅταν λαλῇ τὸ ψεῦδος, ἐκ τῶν ἰδίων λαλεῖ (whenever he might speak the lie, he speaks from his own), with the marked Present Subjunctive projecting a timeless state of affairs; John 10:10: John contrasts the thief who does not come εἰ μὴ ἵνα κλέψῃ καὶ θύσῃ καὶ ἀπολέσῃ (unless so that he might steal and kill and destroy), characterized by Westcott (John, 153) as a universal truth, with his own coming ἵνα ζωὴν ἔχωσιν καὶ περισσὸν ἔχωσιν (so that they might have life and might have abundantly). The three negated Aorist Subjunctives stand in contrast with Jesus' marked projection about himself.

John 10:37-38 (cf. John 9:31): εἰ οὐ ποιῶ τὰ ἔργα τοῦ πατρός μου, μὴ πιστεύετέ μοι· εἰ δὲ ποιῶ, κἂν ἐμοὶ μὴ πιστεύητε, τοῖς ἔργοις πιστεύετε, ἵνα γνῶτε καὶ γινώσκητε[5] ὅτι ἐν ἐμοὶ ὁ πατὴρ κἀγὼ ἐν τῷ πατρί (if I am not doing the works of my father, don't be believing me; but if I am doing [them], and if you might not be believing *me*, believe the works, so that you might know and you might understand [translation based on Westcott, *John*, 161] that in me is the father and I am in the father). These verses illustrate well the aspectual and non-temporal basis of Greek tense usage. (1) The parallel Aorist and Present Subjunctives refer to the same process of belief that results from fulfilment of belief in the works of Jesus, and do not have either future reference (there is no necessary correlation with the future, only with result) or past reference (the argument only works if the results are not in existence but solely projected). (2) The aspectual contrast is made between the act of knowing and continuing progress in understanding. John emphasizes the importance of belief: see John 6:29; 13:19; 17:21; 19:35; 20:31 (cf. parallel ἔχητε [have]),[6] where ἵνα with Present Subjunctive is either used by the evangelist of Jesus or put into the mouth of Jesus. Cf. John 17:3: amidst a series of ἵνα clauses in vv 2-5, the Present Subjunctive is used in Jesus' definition of eternal life, ἵνα γινώσκωσιν σὲ τὸν μόνον ἀληθινὸν θεόν (so that they might know you the only true God).

John 13:15: ἵνα καθὼς ἐγὼ ἐποίησα ὑμῖν καὶ ὑμεῖς ποιῆτε (so that as I do for you, you might do), where Jesus' assertion of his action is contrasted with his hearers' projected action; John 15:12, 17: the author encloses this paragraph with the phrase ἵνα ἀγαπᾶτε ἀλλήλους (so that you might love one another), the first used definitionally (v 12c follows with καθὼς ἠγάπησα ὑμᾶς [as I love/d you]) and the second resultively; John 15:16: Jesus is reported to say that he elected his followers ἵνα ὑμεῖς ὑπάγητε καὶ καρπὸν φέρητε καὶ ὁ καρπὸς ὑμῶν μένῃ, ἵνα ὅ τι ἂν αἰτήσητε τὸν πατέρα ἐν τῷ ὀνόματί μου δῷ ὑμῖν (so that you might go and bear fruit and your fruit might remain, so that whatever you might ask the father in my name he might give to you), where the author contrasts primary qualities with what he sees as a subordinate series of processes. Although ὑπάγω and φέρω appear only in the Present form in the Subjunctive in the NT, their full aspectual value should not be overlooked, since -άγω is used as part of the Aorist paradigm, as is the suppletive Aorist ἤνεγκα. John 16:4: Jesus reportedly tells his disciples ἵνα ὅταν ἔλθῃ ἡ ὥρα αὐτῶν μνημονεύητε αὐτῶν ὅτι ἐγὼ εἶπον ὑμῖν (so that whenever their hour might come you might remember that I said them to you), in which remembering is stressed over coming; John 17:21, 23, 24: in a series of ἵνα clauses with forms of aspectually vague εἰμί, Jesus reportedly prays ἵνα ὁ κόσμος πιστεύῃ . . . ἵνα γινώσκῃ ὁ κόσμος . . . ἵνα θεωρῶσιν τὴν δόξαν τὴν ἐμήν (so that the world might believe . . . so that the world might know . . . so that they might see my glory); cf. John 8:51 with the negated Aorist Subjunctive.

Acts has relatively few Subjunctives, with only a few Present Subjunctives (several in conditional clauses: e.g. Acts 13:41; 26:5). Acts 8:19: as both the apodosis of a II.a. conditional and as a result clause, Simon reportedly asks to be given the holy spirit ἵνα ᾧ ἐὰν ἐπιθῶ τὰς χεῖρας λαμβάνῃ πνεῦμα ἅγιον (so that by it if I lay on hands he might receive the holy spirit). Acts 24:4: the rhetor Tertullus begs Felix to hear him, ἵνα . . . μὴ ἐπὶ πλεῖόν σε ἐγκόπτω (so that I might not detain you overly long). Is there irony here, or is Tertullus merely beginning his rhetorical flourishes? Acts 27:42: the plan of the soldiers was ἵνα τοὺς δεσμώτας ἀποκτείνωσιν (so that they might kill the prisoners), with the ἵνα introducing indirect discourse (temporal reference is strictly past, although the attitudinal orientation of projection is significant). Cf. Matt 26:4; Mark 12:8; 14:1.

---

[5] A textual variant with an added καὶ πιστεύσητε receives only a C rating in UBS[3]. See Metzger, *Commentary*, 233.

[6] There is some question whether the Subjunctives in John 19:35 and 20:31 are Present or Aorist. On the basis of the most difficult reading they should probably be read as Present Subjunctives, although there is only a C reading for UBS[3] at 20:31. See Carson, "Purpose," 640-41; cf. Riesenfeld, "ἵνα-Sätzen."

Rom 2:14: Paul uses the ὅταν clause with Present Subjunctive as a transition from the lawlessness of men to those who without the law still do (ποιῶσιν) the things of the law; Rom 6:1: after his significant section on the work of Adam and Christ (5:12-21), speaking of Christ's righteousness overcoming sin, the question presents itself: what shall we say (ἐροῦμεν)? ἐπιμένωμεν (should we abide) in sin, ἵνα ἡ χάρις πλεονάσῃ (so that grace may abound)? Paul uses the most heavily marked Future to mark the shift in discussion, and then the more heavily marked Present Subjunctive to pose the unwelcome situation (cf. v 2 with μὴ γένοιτο [may it not be]), and the less heavily marked Aorist Subjunctive in the purpose clause (contra Lightfoot, *Notes*, 295, who argues that the "conjunctives are stronger than the futures, and represent the indignant rejoinder of some objector. . ."). Rom 15:4, 6: Paul says he writes for the Romans' instruction, ἵνα through the patience and comfort of his writings τὴν ἐλπίδα ἔχωμεν (we might have hope [v 4]), and so that with one accord δοξάζητε (you might glorify [v 6]) the God and father of our lord Jesus Christ, clearly as one of the significant affirmations of the epistle; cf. Rom 5:1: most commentators believe the Present Indicative should be read here, but the overwhelming textual support and the parallel make the hortatory Subjunctive ἔχωμεν likely;[7] Rom 15:20: Paul says he fulfilled (Perfect Infinitive) the gospel of Christ all the way to Illyricum (v 19), so that (ἵνα) he might not build (οἰκοδομῶ) upon another's foundation, with Paul stressing the independence of his missionary commission.

1 Corinthians has the largest number of both Aorist and Present Subjunctives of all the Pauline letters (including the Pastorals). Several examples are worth noting. 1 Cor 1:10: Paul at the outset beseeches the church ἵνα you all might τὸ αὐτὸ λέγητε (be at peace/make up differences [a classical idiom: Th. 4.20.4; 5.31.6; Arist. Pol. 2.3.3; Plb. 2.62.4; 5.104.1, so Lightfoot, *Notes*, 151]), followed by two Subjunctives of εἰμί specifying what this entails. Cf. 1 Cor 3:4, where Paul introduces his refutation of divisiveness with the Present Subjunctive also. 1 Cor 1:27: in parallel clauses Paul says that God chooses the foolish and the weak so that ἵνα καταισχύνῃ (he might shame) the wise and strong, followed by two Aorist Subjunctive clauses, καταργήσῃ (he might condemn [v 28]), καυχήσηται (he might boast [v 29]). It is difficult to understand why Paul has chosen the tense forms he has (cf. 2 Cor 9:4, where he uses the Aorist Subjunctive with reference to his own shame), but two factors might be noted. (1) Each Present Subjunctive follows its own 'election' clause, while the Aorist Subjunctives are both in fulfilment of a single 'election' clause. (2) Within this section God's election of the wise/foolish, powerful/weak and high/low-born figures prominently (v 26), with each being treated in turn. 1 Cor 7:5. Paul strongly forbids his readers to deny sexual relations to their partners, unless for an agreed-upon time, ἵνα σχολάσητε τῇ προσευχῇ καὶ πάλιν ἐπὶ τὸ αὐτὸ ἦτε, ἵνα μὴ πειράζῃ ὑμᾶς ὁ σατανᾶς (so that you might devote yourself to prayer and again might be together, so that Satan might not tempt you), with Paul following up his stated reason for the separation (Aorist Subjunctive) with the reason why the separation should be for only a short period. The grammatical connection of the second ἵνα clause is not clear, although it probably is dependent upon the Imperative, ἀποστερεῖτε (deny) (see Orr/Walther, *I Corinthians*, 206). 1 Cor 10:8-9: Paul exhorts his readers not to be (γίνεσθε) idolatrous (v 7), and then shifts to the hortatory Present Subjunctive: μηδὲ πορνεύωμεν . . . μηδὲ ἐκπειράζωμεν τὸν Χριστόν (let us not commit sexual immorality . . . let us not tempt Christ). In light of the emphasis upon morality in

---

[7]Arguments for the Indicative in Rom 5:1 include: the Subjunctive yields a supposedly unsuitabale sense because the author is entering a doctrinal section, in which exhortation is out of place, especially since Indicative verbs follow (Meyer, *Romans*, 179); the Subjunctive does not go with οὐ μόνον δέ (not only that [v 3]). Arguments for the Subjunctive include: Paul passes elsewhere from argument to exhortation (Sanday/Headlam [*Romans*, 120] cite 6:(1), 12, (15); 8:12), possibly reflecting diatribe style; the Subjunctive sense is appropriate (contra Moule, 15, who looks for a "perfect" meaning); and the context of previous enmity (now peace) allows for the implication that Paul is saying Christians should no longer fight against God but cultivate their privilege (Lightfoot, *Notes*, 284; cf. Bruce, *Romans*, 122-23). Cf. Metzger, *Commentary*, 511, for textual discussion.

this epistle, it is not surprising to see emphatic commands against immorality made, here equating sexual immorality with idolatry (reflecting OT background, as do the examples Paul selects [see Robertson/Plummer, *First Corinthians*, 204-05]). What is more noteworthy is the shift from 2d Person to 1st Person prohibition, with Paul becoming more inclusive as he moves to the most important and wide-ranging command. 1 Cor 11:27: after temporal conditional statements in vv 25, 26, using Present Subjunctives in the protases, Paul presents the opposite case in a conditional-like statement, saying that ὃς ἂν ἐσθίῃ τὸν ἄρτον ἢ πίνῃ τὸ ποτήριον τοῦ κυρίου ἀναξίως (whoever might eat the bread or drink the cup of the lord unworthily), he will be guilty of the body and the blood of the lord. Paul's use of Present verbs regarding the institution of the 'Lord's supper' is significant. 1 Cor 12:25: God is said to unite the body, giving abundant honour to the least, ἵνα there might not be a schism, ἀλλὰ τὸ αὐτὸ ὑπὲρ ἀλλήλων μεριμνῶσιν τὰ μέλη (but the members might care about each other the same way), with the aspectually marked Present Subjunctive, following in emphatic contrast to the aspectually vague ᾖ. This is the only occurrence of the Present Subjunctive of μεριμνάω in the NT; the Aorist Subjunctive is found in the Gospels: e.g. Matt 6:31, 34; 10:19. 1 Cor 14:1, 5: one should pursue and seek the spiritual things (Present Imperatives), μᾶλλον δὲ ἵνα προφητεύητε (especially so that you might prophesy), elucidated in the rest of the section, and repeated in v 5. The one who prophesies is better than the one who speaks in tongues (Present Participles), since he builds up the church rather than himself, unless (ἐκτὸς εἰ μὴ) διερμηνεύῃ, ἵνα ἡ ἐκκλησία οἰκοδομὴν λάβῃ (he might interpret, so that the church might have edification), with final stress upon the importance of the interpreter. Cf. 1 Cor 14:12: seeking the building up of the church is commanded ἵνα περισσεύητε (so that you might abound); 2 Cor 8:7.[8] 1 Cor 14:23, 26: Paul develops the theme of building up the church, using the Aorist Subjunctive in v 23 (ἐὰν . . . συνέλθῃ) in a similar syntactical environment to the Present Subjunctive in v 26. Paul says that ὅταν συνέρχησθε (whenever you might come together), each has (Present Indicative) something to contribute; cf. 1 Cor 11:34. The semantic difference is that in v 26 the gathering is stressed because it is then that each makes a contribution, while in v 23 the question is if the whole church gathers, with instructions being given to regulate its meetings. 1 Cor 14:31: all are able to prophesy, ἵνα πάντες μανθάνωσιν καὶ πάντες παρακαλῶνται (so that all might learn and all might exhort); 1 Cor 16:2: the Corinthians are told to store up ὅ τι ἐὰν εὐοδῶται, ἵνα μὴ ὅταν ἔλθω τότε λογεῖαι γίνωνται (whatever might be prospered, so that whenever I might come then the collections might be known). The markedness of the Present Subjunctive is appropriate not only to theological passages but also narrative or descriptive ones, with Paul commending present stewardship, so that a hasty future effort may be avoided (note that the Present Subjunctive may have present or future reference, though neither is an essential meaning of the form). See also 1 Cor 16:16; 2 Cor 9:4.

2 Cor 3:15: ἕως σήμερον ἡνίκα ἂν ἀναγινώσκηται Μωϋσῆς κάλυμμα ἐπὶ τὴν καρδίαν αὐτῶν κεῖται (up until today whenever M. is read a veil lies over their hearts), with the importance of Moses (reference here is apparently to the Torah) being recognized, although the irony is appreciable: it does does not lead to enlightenment but veiled understanding. The Present Subjunctive has at least partly past reference. 2 Cor 12:7: Paul says that the thorn in his flesh was given to him, ἵνα μὴ ὑπεραίρωμαι (so that I might not be puffed up), a messenger of Satan, ἵνα με κολαφίζῃ, ἵνα μὴ ὑπεραίρωμαι (so that he might trouble me, so that I might not be puffed up). The use of the Present Subjunctive, forming an inclusio (or chiasm) (Furnish, *II Corinthians* , 528), focuses strongly upon the results of the thorn, which provide the basis for Paul's important words from the lord that his grace is sufficient (introduced with a Perfect Indicative). This is reinforced by use of ὑπεραίρωμαι twice (although some texts omit the second use [Metzger,

---

[8]On imperatival ἵνα see Cadoux, "Use"; Meecham, "Use"; contra George, "Use," who attempts to refute every instance, often by appealing to ellision but also understanding the ἵνα-clause as content. Deer ("Still more") presents a 'complete' list of 38 examples of 'imperatival ἵνα.' See also Morrice, "Imperatival ἵνα"; Deer, "More"; Radermacher, 138; Doudna, *Greek*, 49-51; Winer, 396, for extra-biblical examples. See also discussion of Phil 1:9 below.

Commentary, 585]). Cf. 2 Cor 12:10, which encapsulates the paradox Paul has learned from his trial: ὅταν γὰρ ἀσθενῶ (whenever I am weak), then I am strong; 2 Cor 13:9. 2 Co 13:7: Paul rejoices that his readers do not do evil, οὐχ ἵνα ἡμεῖς δόκιμοι φανῶμεν, ἀλλ᾽ ἵνα ὑμεῖς τὸ καλὸν ποιῆτε (not so that we might appear approved, but so that you might do good) and we might be as unapproved. In contrastive purpose clauses Paul presents the preferred option with the imperfective aspect.

Gal 2:10: in an independent ἵνα clause of indirect speech, Paul recounts that the Jerusalem apostles gave him the right hand of fellowship, commending him and Barnabas μόνον τῶν πτωχῶν ἵνα μνημονεύωμεν (only that we might remember the poor), which he says he desired to do anyway, emphasizing the importance of the commendation; Gal 5:25: in the apodosis of a I class conditional, Paul says εἰ ζῶμεν πνεύματι, πνεύματι καὶ στοιχῶμεν (if we live in the spirit, let us indeed conduct our lives in the spirit), with the Present Indicative grammaticalizing the simple assertion and the Present Subjunctive grammaticalizing the projected response. (Bruce [*Galatians*, 257] says Paul "does not suggest that it is possible to do the former [live by the Spirit] without also doing the latter [keep in step with the Spirit]." This is a theological and not a grammatical point.) Gal 6:9-10: τὸ . . . καλὸν ποιοῦντες μὴ ἐγκακῶμεν, καιρῷ γὰρ ἰδίῳ θερίσομεν μὴ ἐκλυόμενοι. ἄρα οὖν ὡς καιρὸν ἔχομεν, ἐργαζώμεθα τὸ ἀγαθὸν πρὸς πάντας (doing good, let us not become cowardly, for in its time we shall harvest, not giving up. Therefore as we have time, let us accomplish the good for all); Gal 6:12: part of Paul's final warning to the Galatians is that anyone who compels circumcision does so only ἵνα τῷ σταυρῷ τοῦ Χριστοῦ μὴ διώκωνται (in order that they might not be persecuted for the cross of Christ), a serious charge.

Eph 4:28: the reader is encouraged to work with his own hands, ἵνα ἔχῃ (so that he might have) to share with the one who has a need; Eph 5:33: the author says, let each one love (ἀγαπάτω) his own wife as himself, and the wife ἵνα φοβῆται (so that she might fear) her husband, with the Present Imperative and Subjunctive parallel (see Cadoux, "Use," 167; George, "Use," 58); Phil 1:9: Paul is praying for this, that (ἵνα)[9] our love more and more περισσεύῃ (might grow [a favourite Pauline word, so Hawthorne, *Philippians*, 26]) in knowledge and all insight, with the Present Subjunctive grammaticalizing the author's view of the action as in progress (note modifiers, ἔτι μᾶλλον καὶ μᾶλλον); cf. Phil 1:26. Phil 1:27: using the strong Present command (πολιτεύεσθε), Paul tells the Philippians to live ἵνα εἴτε ἐλθὼν καὶ ἰδὼν ὑμᾶς εἴτε ἀπὼν ἀκούω τὰ περὶ ὑμῶν (so that coming and seeing you or being away I might hear of the things concerning you), i.e. that they are standing firm (Present Indicative) in one spirit. Paul contrasts his being aware of the Philippians' situation with his physical location. Phil 2:2: Paul requests that the Philippians fill up his joy ἵνα τὸ αὐτὸ φρονῆτε (so that you might think the same way). This verse is difficult syntactically, with the clause either describing the content of filling up his joy, or serving functionally as a command (cf. 2 Cor 13:11) (see Moule, 145 n. 3; Turner, *Syntax*, 94-95). Col 3:21: fathers, μὴ ἐρεθίζετε τὰ τέκνα ὑμῶν, ἵνα μὴ ἀθυμῶσιν (don't make your children bitter, so that they might not lose spirit). Although the only Present Subjunctive in this *Haustafeln* section of Colossians, it is one of several imperfective verbs stressing moral actions. Col 4:17: the author commands his readers to tell Archipus to be watchful

---

[9]Hawthorne (*Philippians*, 25) proposes that this is a content clause; Cadoux ("Use," 172) a commanding clause for Phil 1:10; George ("Use," 60) a purpose clause. This example illustrates two points: (1) there is terminological confusion when, for example, Cadoux (166) says, "the ἵνα-clause virtually became as much a main sentence as if the plain imperative had been used." There is no basis for positing that the clause became confused with an independent form, but the issue is whether the speaker could use the clause to make commands. All indications are that this is possible (see Mandilaras, 262-64), regardless of whether the origin of this phenomenon is ellipsis. (2) The various functional distinctions of the ἵνα clause (result, purpose, temporal [= where], commanding, and causal) are according to pragmatic usage. The form remains the same. See above discussion under 2 Cor 8:7.

(βλέπε) of his service, ἵνα αὐτὴν πληροῖς (so that you might fulfil it), with the Present Subjunctive being used as a command in parallel with the Present Imperative.

1 Thessalonians and Philemon are the only Pauline epistles where Present Subjunctives exceed Aorist Subjunctives. Considering the overall ratio in the Greek of the NT, this is significant, but when the practical moral urgency of the epistles is appreciated, the use of imperfective verbs is understandable. 1 Thess 4:1: Paul beseeches (ἐρωτῶμεν . . . παρακαλοῦμεν) his listeners, ἵνα as they received (παρελάβετε) from him how it was necessary to walk and please God, as they walk, ἵνα περισσεύητε μᾶλλον (so that you might grow more), with contrasting καθώς clauses, one with the perfective describing their receipt and the other their progress through life; cf. Phil 1:9. 1 Thess 4:12: Paul shifts the argument, repeating that he beseeches (παρακαλοῦμεν [v 10]) his audience to grow more (περισσεύειν μᾶλλον [v 10]), to aim to live quietly, to mind their own affairs, and to work with their own hands, ἵνα περιπατῆτε (so that you might live) appropriately with those outside and μηδενὸς χρείαν ἔχητε (might have need of no one/thing). Whereas above the emphasis was on the object of growing more, here this is expressed through the Infinitive [-factual presupposition] (see chapt. 8), with the result clause stressing appropriate behaviour. Cf. 1 Thess 4:13; 5:3. 1 Thess 5:6, 10: ἄρα οὖν μὴ καθεύδωμεν ὡς οἱ λοιποί, ἀλλὰ γρηγορῶμεν καὶ νήφωμεν (therefore let us not sleep as the rest, but let us be watching and be sober), with three hortatory Present Subjunctives in a row. Bruce notes that ἄρα οὖν is "a common collocation in Paul, introducing a further stage in an argument or a summing up" (*Thessalonians*, 111). The further argument in 1 Thess 5:7ff. stresses being adequately prepared for Christ's return, repeating the call to sobriety (νήφωμεν) and concluding in v 10: ἵνα εἴτε γρηγορῶμεν εἴτε καθεύδωμεν ἅμα σὺν αὐτῷ ζήσωμεν (so that if we might watch or sleep, then with him we might live). As important as living with Christ is (Aorist Subjunctive), the stress in this passage is upon right behaviour leading to the conclusion of life with Christ. (Note the number of Present Imperatives in 1 Thessalonians 5.) 2 Thess 3:1: the Thessalonians are told to pray ἵνα the word of the lord τρέχῃ καὶ δοξάζηται (might run and be glorified), reflecting again Paul's concern for the progress of the gospel; 2 Thess 3:12: reflecting a dispute over idleness in Thessalonica, Paul says that if someone does not want to work, do not let him eat (v 10), but he beseeches them in the lord ἵνα having worked in silence τὸν ἑαυτῶν ἄρτον ἐσθίωσιν (they might eat their own bread), with imperfective verbs throughout this section drawing attention to the urgency of the situation.

1 Tim 1:18: Timothy has this announcement made to him, that (ἵνα) στρατεύῃ (he might fight) the good fight; cf. 1 Tim 2:2: the author beseeches Timothy to pray, that (ἵνα) διάγωμεν (we might lead) a peaceful and quiet life; 1 Tim 5:20: after outlining procedures for making accusations toward elders, the author turns to those who continue sinning, saying that they should be rebuked (ἔλεγχε), ἵνα the rest ἔχωσιν (might have) fear; cf. Titus 1:13: after quoting Epimenides as a true statement, the author says to rebuke (ἔλεγχε) them severely, ἵνα ὑγιαίνωσιν ἐν τῇ πίστει (so that they might be purified in the faith); 1 Tim 6:1: the ἵνα clause after the conditional-like statement is syntactically difficult, with either a compound subject or a simple subject with a complement after a Passive verb. The latter is probably correct: "that indeed the teaching might not be blasphemed (βλασφημῆται) regarding the name of God" (cf. Luke 7:29; see Goodwin, *Grammar*, 266). Titus 2:4, 5, 10: the author commends men and then women to proper behaviour, ἵνα σωφρονίζωσιν (so that they might act wisely) towards all ages, ἵνα μὴ ὁ λόγος τοῦ θεοῦ βλασφημῆται (so that the word of God might not be blasphemed). An intervening ἵνα clause regarding those hostile to the gospel uses an Aorist Subjunctive, but then when commending the faithful again the author closes the section with the Present Subjunctive: so that (ἵνα) κοσμῶσιν (they might keep in order) the teaching of our saviour God.

Phlm 13, 15, 19: Paul tells Philemon he wanted Onesimus with him so that διακονῇ (he might) serve him instead of Philemon; he then hypothesizes that perhaps Onesimus was separated from him for a short time so that (ἵνα) ἀπέχῃς (he might have) him forever; and then Paul, in clinching his argument with Philemon that he should welcome back Onesimus, says he will repay the debt: ἵνα μὴ λέγω σοι ὅτι καὶ σεαυτόν μοι προσοφείλεις (that I might not say to you that indeed you owe yourself to me [see Robertson, 1199; Cadoux, "Use," 172]). Verse 19 plays strategic importance in Paul's argument (Petersen, *Paul*, esp. 165-66, 264).

Heb 4:16: προσερχώμεθα (let us come) with boldness to the throne of grace, so that λάβωμεν (we might receive) mercy and εὑρωμεν (we might find) grace as a suitable help, with the imperfective projection suitable for a bold approach to God, and the perfective aspect specifying the projected results; cf. Heb 4:14. Heb 13:13, 15: τοίνυν ἐξερχώμεθα πρὸς αὐτὸν ἔξω τῆς παρεμβολῆς. . . δι᾽ αὐτοῦ [οὖν] ἀναφέρωμεν θυσίαν αἰνέσεως (therefore let us come out to him from the camp . . . through him therefore let us offer up a sacrifice of praise); Heb 5:1: the purpose of the human priest is specified: προσφέρῃ δῶρά τε καὶ θυσίας (he might offer gifts and sacrifices); cf. Heb 6:1. Heb 10:22, 23, 24: in vv 19-25, all three finite verbs are hortatory Present Subjunctives. The author, after recapitulating his argument, says προσερχώμεθα (let us draw near) in fulness of faith, κατέχωμεν (let us hold fast) to the confession of hope, and κατανοῶμεν (let us consider) others. Cf. Heb 12:1; Heb 12:28, where the Present Subjunctives bring the argument to a conclusion (διό [wherefore]). Heb 12:15: μή τις ῥίζα πικρίας ἄνω φύουσα ἐνοχλῇ καὶ δι᾽ αὐτῆς μιανθῶσιν πολλοί (lest a certain bitter root, growing up, might cause trouble and through it many might be defiled), with the imperfective aspect used of the instigating process, and the perfective aspect of the result.

1 Pet 4:11: ἵνα ἐν πᾶσιν δοξάζηται ὁ θεὸς διὰ Ἰησοῦ Χριστοῦ (so that in all things God might be glorified through Jesus Christ). One of several doxologies in the NT, it is difficult to know why it is placed here. Perhaps Selwyn is correct that authors tended to use them when they sprang to mind (*Peter*, 220), but in this epistle there appears to be another function. The author has just told his audience to be wise and sober-minded, and the praise to God then precedes a section where these qualities are put to the test through suffering.

1 John 1:3: the authors say that they bear witness of what they have seen and heard (Perfect Indicative), ἵνα καὶ ὑμεῖς κοινωνίαν ἔχητε μεθ᾽ ἡμῶν (so that indeed you might have fellowship with us). The stative aspect is used self-consciously to open the epistle, but the Present Subjunctive also appears deliberate, making a connection from the 'evidence' to the effect; cf. 1 John 4:17. 1 John 2:5: ὃς δ᾽ ἂν τηρῇ αὐτοῦ τὸν λόγον (whoever might keep his word), truly in him the love of God is made complete (τετελείωται), with the imperfective aspect used in a general statement (Smalley, *John*, 48) to refer to being in progress keeping Christ's word, although the stative aspect of the apodosis receives paramount emphasis in this anacoluthon; cf. 1 John 5:3. 1 John 3:17-18: ὃς δ᾽ ἂν ἔχῃ τὸν βίον . . . καὶ θεωρῇ τὸν ἀδελφὸν . . . καὶ κλείσῃ τὰ σπλάγχνα αὐτοῦ (whoever might have life and might see his brother and might close his compassion) how does the love of God abide in him? τεκνία, μή ἀγαπῶμεν λόγῳ μηδὲ τῇ γλώσσῃ (children, let us not love in word and tongue) but in work and truth, in which the imperfective aspect is used to grammaticalize the author's depiction of one who is securely possessing and observing, and the perfective aspect to depict the process of singularly closing off concern. The author then issues a call to unhypocritical action using the imperfective. 1 John 3:23: the author states the command of God, that πιστεύσωμεν (we might believe) in the name of his son and ἀγαπῶμεν (we might love) each other. The alteration in verb tenses is noteworthy (see Brown, *Epistles*, 462ff., for a survey of scholarly opinion). Although the author only uses the Present Subjunctive of ἀγαπάω, he uses the Aorist and Perfect of it in other Moods, as he does πιστεύω, so one must look elsewhere for reasons for the alteration. Whereas the author links belief with the Christian life here, throughout this section (3:10-24) the clear stress has been upon love, with the theme stated in v 11: the commandment of God is that ἀγαπῶμεν (we might love) one another (Smalley, *John*, 209; cf. Brown, *Epistles*, 665-666). Verses 11 and 24 form a chiasm: commandment/love, love/commandment. Cf. 1 John 4:7, 19. 2 John 5, 6: having stated that the new commandment is that ἀγαπῶμεν (we might love) each other, the author defines love: ἵνα περιπατῶμεν (that we might walk) according to the commandments; and the commandment is this: that περιπατῆτε (you might walk) in it, where a demonstration of love is called for. 3 John 4: the author says he has no greater joy than that ἀκούω (I might hear) of my children walking in the truth. As Smalley says, "In this v the writer underlines and expands the point of v 3. The presbyter rejoices greatly in the knowledge that those for whom he is responsible . . . are committed to the truth of the Christian gospel, and are daily advancing in that truth" (*John*, 347-48); cf. 3 John 8.

Rev 3:18: the message to the church at Laodicea is that they buy gold ἵνα πλουτήσῃς (so that you might be rich) and white garments ἵνα περιβάλῃ (so that you might be clothed) and ἵνα the shame of your nakedness μὴ φανερωθῇ (might not be evident), and to anoint your eyes with salve ἵνα βλέπῃς (so that you might see), with the perfective aspect used in response to the Laodicean's complaints about their physical problems but the imperfective aspect used of metaphorical seeing, i.e. spiritual insight that they seem to lack. That the use of the imperfective is conscious is reinforced by Rev 21:23: ἵνα φαίνωσιν αὐτῇ (that they might appear to her). Cf. Rev 16:15: one is commended for watching and keeping his garments, ἵνα μὴ γυμνὸς περιπατῇ καὶ βλέπωσιν τὴν ἀσχημοσύνην αὐτοῦ (so that he might not walk naked and they might see his shame); Rev 7:1: the angels are grasping the four winds of the earth, ἵνα μὴ πνέῃ ἄνεμος (so that the wind might not blow) upon the land or upon the sea or upon any tree; Rev 19:7: in a song to God, the voices of many call out blessings to God because he reigns (timeless Aorist), χαίρωμεν καὶ ἀγαλλιῶμεν, καὶ δώσομεν τὴν δόξαν αὐτῷ (let us rejoice and be glad, and let us give[10] him glory), where imperfective hortatory Subjunctives help build climactically to the Future Indicative, ascribing glory to God.[11]

3. **Optative** (see Robertson, 935-40). As noted in chapt. 4, there are only approximately eleven instances of the Present Optative in the NT. The Optative has already been discussed under attitude, since several of its oddities in relation to its limited usage warrant exploration of its attitudinal semantics. The Present Optatives found in the NT use only a few lexical items, and virtually all in Acts. Despite this, Robertson insists that the distinctions in the tenses still apply, although it appears he is more concerned for things like inceptive and eggressive action (854). Usage of the Present Subjunctive includes Luke 1:62; Acts 17:18; 1 Pet 3:17 with θέλοι (want); Acts 8:31; 27:12, 39 with δυναίμην (be able); and Acts 17:11; 24:19; 25:16 with ἔχοι (have), all of which are only found with the Present and not the Aorist Optative form in the NT. Two examples are particularly interesting: Acts 25:20: in indirect discourse the Present βούλοιτο (he might want) is used by Festus to describe his attempt to get Paul to stand trial in Jerusalem, the use of a classical idiom that was quickly fading from hellenistic Greek (Turner [Syntax, 131-33] speculates on the construction); 1 Pet 3:14: εἰ καὶ πάσχοιτε διὰ δικαιοσύνην, μακάριοι (although you might suffer because of righteousness [you are] blessed) (see my chapt. 6). As Winer says, "here the πάσχειν is not represented as something which will occur in the future, but is simply conceived in the mind as something which may very possibly take place, without any reference to determinate time (and as often as it may take place)" (367).

c. **Conclusion.** Although the imperfective aspect of the non-assertive attitude has been restricted in its use in the hellenistic period, especially the language of the NT, this does not indicate that its semantic features have been

---

[10]The text is very uncertain at this point, with the best choice lying with either δώσωμεν, an irregular Aorist Subjunctive (the choice of the UBS³ text and read in P 2081 2344), or δώσομεν, a Future (their second choice and read in ℵ^a A 2042 2053 2065 2432). Metzger (*Commentary*, 762) calls the Future "intolerable" after two hortatory Subjunctives, but the textual evidence clearly lies with this reading, and is chosen here. Cf. E. Ion 758, where two Subjunctives are followed by a Future.

[11]An interesting shift occurs in use of the hortatory particle with the Subjunctive, from a Present form in earlier Greek, such as ἄγε (Hom. Il. 20.296) or φέρε (E. And. 333; Hdt. 7.103) to an Aorist form in the hellenistic period. For example: Luke 6:42: ἀδελφέ, ἄφες ἐκβάλω τὸ κάρφος τὸ ἐν τῷ ὀφθαλμῷ σου; cf. Mark 15:36: ἄφετε ἴδωμεν; Matt 27:49 with Plural main verb following Singular ἄφες. See also Plb. 1.9.15; 1.15.7; 2.18.24.

neutralized. The semantics of the Subjunctive Mood, in the Aorist and Present tense forms, have already been established by a variety of means. In the above discussion, on the basis of paradigmatic distinctions reflected in the semantic structure of the language, an attempt has been made to explicate contextual reasons why the more heavily marked Present Subjunctive might have been chosen by a given author. Many of the explanations are clear and confirm the major thesis of this work. Several of the explanations are recognizably less convincing. As has already been argued, however, verbal aspect is a matter of reasoned subjective choice by the speaker. Therefore, failure to perceive the aspectual difference (by means of translation or gloss?) in no way minimizes the significance of the distinction within the language itself. The theory of verbal aspect, as well as the clear cases of exposition, provides impetus for formulating more convincing reasons for the more difficult cases. The Optative has clearly fallen on difficult times, such that the more heavily marked Present Optative is virtually extinct except in what appear to be several set forms. The loss of marked forms and the slight retention of less heavily marked forms is what would be expected, since speakers obviously did not feel the need to express [+projection: +contingency] as often, and [+imperfective] as opposed to [+perfective] hardly at all.

2. **THE IMPERATIVE: COMMANDS AND PROHIBITIONS. a. Direction as attitude.** It has been indicated above (chaps. 2 and 4) in discussing attitude that the Subjunctive grammaticalizes [+projection] (= +volition, +visualization) and the Imperative [+direction] (= volition, but this terminology is avoided because of use by grammarians for one kind of Subjunctive [e.g. Amigues, "Temps," 228; Kühner/Gerth, 1.236]). As Dana/Mantey (174) state, "The imperative is the mood of command or entreaty--the mood of *volition*. . . . It expresses neither probability nor possibility, but only intention, and is therefore, the furthest removed from reality." One of the most common uses of the Imperative is in commands, although it is also used for, for example, general assumptions (McKay, 128; Gildersleeve, 158ff.), as well as other instances where the Imperative is not future-referring. The command attitudinally grammaticalizes the speaker's desire to give direction to a process. In many languages--and Greek is no exception--Imperative forms are some of the least morphologically marked in the language, often with very simple personal endings attached to roots that are not expanded, for example, with augments (see Curtius, *Verb*, 296; cf. Greenberg, *Universals*, chapt. 2). There have been two major issues that persistently have been broached in discussion of NT Greek and commands. (In this section both the Imperative in its many forms and the negated Aorist Subjunctive are treated. See d. below for suggestions about why the negated

Aorist Subjunctive is used in this way. The so-called hortatory Subjunctive is treated under the Subjunctive.) The first concerns the aspectual nature of commands, especially in relation to verbal and objective action, with it being commonly asserted that the Aorist refers to point action and hence to a particular act to be performed or not to be begun, and the Present refers to continuous action and hence to continuation or cessation of an ongoing action. The second concerns the Aorist in prayers to gods.

b. Verbal aspect and the Greek Command. 1. Introduction. There has been much recent discussion of the aspectual nature of the command in Greek. Attention is first paid to recent discussion of aspect, then two issues often introduced are treated through a survey of several significant articles: kind of action and objective action, and temporal schemes and the command. These three streams of thought illustrate that some of the supposed pressing issues of grammatical discussion regarding the command and prohibition have already been thoroughly discussed. These discussions are a suitable prelude to exemplification of an aspectual theory of commands and prohibitions in NT Greek, including prayers and general usage.

2. Verbal aspect. Many grammarians in their treatment of Greek commands and prohibitions, even those who endorse a theory of verbal aspect, seem to endorse the position of Humbert, who recognizes that verb choice has nothing to do with time: "Dans la théorie comme dans la pratique, la justification des temps à l'impératif constitue la question la plus délicate de la syntaxe du verbe." This reflection stems from the fact that "dans un certain nombre d'exemples, la différence entre le présent et l'aoriste finit par devenir *imperceptible*, du moins pour nous" (177). He cites as an example the use of verbs of speaking and reading in the orators. Post put forward much earlier the assertion that while "it has long been generally agreed that the kind of action (*Aktionsart*) described is in Greek an important factor, often the sole factor, in determining choice of tense. . . . I shall surprise some by my statement that the aspect theory does not adequately explain the use of tenses in the imperative" ("Uses," 31). In support he cites S. Oed. King 622: ἢ με γῆς ἔξω βαλεῖν; / ἥκιστα· θνῆσκειν οὐ φυγεῖν σε βούλομαι. He says of this example:

> Oedipus in Sophocles' play . . . is asked by Creon, whom he is accusing, "do you want to expel me from the land?" "Not at all," he replies, "death, not exile, is my wish for you" (θνῆσκειν οὐ φυγεῖν). The contrast between the heavy penalty of death and the light penalty of exile is underlined by the use of present and aorist. Both of the verbs have heavier stems in the present than in the aorist. (34)

Perhaps grammarians have been looking for the wrong thing in their analysis of the Imperative (it is shown throughout this work that such is often the case). In fact a better support than Post's for pursuing an aspectual theory for explaining use of the Imperative could not be asked for. (Post classifies use of the Imperative according to its dramatic uses. This interesting and detailed study does not pertain directly to discussion of verbal aspect, except in several of his conclusions. For example, he contends that "in general the present may for most verbs replace the aorist for dramatic reasons; it often happens that the present is not so replaceable by the aorist for any reason" [36].)

Three recent authors have devoted significant work to developing an aspectual theory of the Imperative, besides McKay ("Aspect," 201ff.; "Aspects"), who adapts the theory he has endorsed elsewhere (his conclusion ["Aspects," 55] depends upon differentiation between stative and action verbs, analysed in my chapt. 1). The first is Louw ("Prohibitions"; assessed by McKay, "Aspects," 45-47), who begins his treatment with a re-evaluation of Apollonius Dyscolus's view of the Imperative (45-46):[12]

ἀλλὰ καὶ εἴπομεν ὡς ἃ μὲν προστάσσεται αὐτῶν εἰς παράτασιν. ὁ γὰρ ἀποφαινόμενος οὕτω· γράφε, σάρου [= σαῖρε?], σκάπτε, ἐν παρατάσει τῆς διαθέσεως τὴν πρόσταξιν ποιεῖται, ὡς ἔχει καὶ τὸ βάλλ᾽ οὕτως, αἴ κέν τι φόως Δαναοῖσι γένηαι· φησὶ γὰρ ἐν τῷ πολέμῳ καταγίνου εἰς τὸ βάλλειν. ὅ γε μὴν λέγων κατὰ τὴν τοῦ παρῳχημένου προφορὰν γράψον, σκάψον, οὐ μόνον τὸ μὴ γινόμενον προστάσσει, ἀλλὰ καὶ τὸ γινόμενον ἐν παρατάσει ἀπαγορεύει, εἴ γε καὶ τοῖς γράφουσιν ἐν πλείονι χρόνῳ προσφωνοῦμεν τὸ γράψον, τοιοῦτόν τι φάσκοντες, μὴ ἐμμένειν τῇ παρατάσει ἀνύσαι δὲ τὸ γράφειν. (περὶ συντάξεως, p.

---

[12]Louw follows Poutsma, "Tempora." Although Poutsma begins from Apollonius Dyscolus, and takes a view very similar to Louw, that "the speaker, in using the Present Imperative, conceives of the action as taking place with παράτασις, i.e. as in progress; in using the Aorist, as attaining συντελείωσις, i.e. accomplishment or achievement" (69), his actual discussion is in terms of *Aktionsart*, thus reinforcing Headlam's view (see below). To reconcile his definition with his objective classification of the action, he includes such categories as the Present for events already begun, "inchoative-durative Present," "durative-finite Present," "iterative Present." He also discusses the Aorist in terms of confusion with the Perfect and vice versa. That Poutsma's treatment of Apollonius Dyscolus is not a precise theory of aspect is seen in this statement: "Very often the context is of such a nature that παρατάσεως as well as συντελειώσεως ἔνοια is in harmony with the matter described, so that to a modern reader both Present and Aorist would appear to be suitable. Why the writer has chosen the tense which actually we find in the text, is frequently far from evident; various causes may have been of influence, e.g. the kind of diction (prose or verse, metre, rhythm), tradition or fashion, the person's idiosyncrasy. In not a few cases the choice may have been a matter of mere chance, some one tense being unavoidable and a plurality of tenses being impossible" (73).

253, 6 sqq. Bkk.) εἰς τὸ γίνεσθαι οὖν ἢ γενέσθαι ἡ πρόσταξις γίνεται, εἰς μὲν παράτασιν σκαπτέτω, εἰς δὲ συντελείωσιν σκαψάτω. (περὶ συντάξεως, p. 70)[13]

Louw's treatment, valuable as it is, exemplifies several shortcomings: (i) the Greek grammarians themselves were not the most faithful descriptive linguists. Apollonius fails to account for, for example, instances where the Aorist command is given while the action is underway but where there is no reference to its proceeding too slowly; instances where the Present command is given while the action is not underway; and commands given when no relation to the action is implied. At best it appears that Apollonius has described tendencies (McKay ["Aspects," 46] calls it a cursory treatment). (It is not clear how Ruijgh ["L'emploi"], who believes that the Aorist Indicative indicates antecedent action and the Present Indicative concurrent action [following Hettrich], can claim Apollonius Dyscolus for support of the Present Imperative as imminent [24] and the Aorist Imperative in terms of "l'ordre d'exécute une action qui inert pas encore en cours" [26].) (ii) Louw's translation obscures several of the issues involved. First is translation of παράτασις and συντελείωσις. Louw's translations "duration" and "terminating point" give the reading a temporal basis that is unjustified (see chapt. 1 where the Greek grammarians are discussed). Second, he attempts to ground the conception of the action in objective reality by relating it to actual completion or duration (he uses the term *Aktionsart* [50]). If translation is necessary, the opposition is better seen as between "incomplete/durative/in progress" and "complete" (McKay, "Aspect," 216; Bakker, *Imperative*, 39). (iii) Louw's translation of several of the other words is unnecessarily time-based. (iv) While the first part describes tense usage, the second merely makes a comment on tense correlation, not the thorough statement that Louw claims. A better rendering might be (cf. McKay, "Aspects," 46-47):

But we have seen how some of them point to "incompletion." For the one who specifies: γράφε, σάρου, σκάπτε, makes the command with "incompletion" of the attitude [?] .... For he says "in war be in progress toward striking." The one saying according to the previous discussion γράψον, σκάψον, not only that which is not occurring, but indeed forbids its occurring in incompleteness; that is to say, if to those writing for a long time we call out γράψον, we are saying such: don't remain in incompletion but make an end of writing. . . . the command becomes γίνεσθαι or γενέσθαι, either for the purpose of παράτασις, σκαπτέτω, or for συντελείωσις, σκαψάτω.

This rendering leaves Apollonius not only essentially in agreement with earlier grammarians already discussed (use of συντελείωσις to describe the action of the Perfect in the Stoic grammarians and for the Aorist in Apollonius Dyscolus provides an interesting reinforcement of

---

[13]Louw's translation of Apollonius Dyscolus is as follows (45-46): p. 253: "But we have also shown how some of them are enjoined to indicate the παράτασις (*the duration*). For he who declares thus: γράφε, σάρου, σκάπτε, gives the command with reference to the παράτασις (duration) of the διάθεσις (verbal form??), e.g. βάλλ᾽ οὕτως, αἴ κέν τι φόως Δαναοῖσι γένηαι (Strike thus, if any good [lit. light] is to come to the Danaeans). He *uses* βάλλε for he wishes to say: Busy yourself with striking (βάλλειν) in the battle. He who according to the argument we have just discussed [lit. the utterance of the foregoing] says: γράψον, σκάψον, not only commands what (at the time of speaking) is not (yet) taking place, but also prohibits the παράτασις (duration) of what is occurring (already commenced), e.g. if we say to persons writing slowly: γράψον, we say something of the following nature, viz.: Do not remain in παράτασις (in the duration of the occurrence), but complete your writing (make an end of your writing)." p. 70: "Therefore the order (command) concerns either the γίνεσθαι (duration) or the γενέσθαι (the single event), that is to say: if the command refers to the παράτασις (duration) of an action, we use σκαπτέτω and, on the other hand, if the command refers to the συντελείωσις (the terminating point) of the action, we use σκαψάτω."

the analysis of the Perfect provided in my chapt. 6), but with his scheme reinforcing at least in part the aspectual scheme promoted in this work.

This aspectual understanding is able to make better sense of several of the passages which Louw mentions, although in his exposition of Apollonius Dyscolus Louw extrapolates further than the text as *he* renders it allows, for example, claiming that the Aorist may prohibit "incomplete" events, forgetting that Apollonius applies this only to events that have gone on too long. This helps Louw to explain S. Phil. 1275: παῦε, μὴ λέξῃς πέρα ("Stop, do not speak any more" [48]), where the adverb of duration is important (McKay, "Aspects,"47); or Ar. Wasps 652: παῦσαι καὶ μὴ πατέριζε (stop and don't call "father"). My rendering above allows these examples to be accounted for without reference to Louw's reading of Apollonius (Louw also assumes a future understanding of all commands [48]).

S. Phil. 1400: μὴ βράδυνε μηδ᾽ ἐπιμνησθῇς ἔτι / Τροίας (don't be tarrying and don't remember still T.). Louw says

> the present describes the παράτασις: Do not tarry (any longer), following the promise of Neoptolemos (already in line 524sqq.) to take Philoctetes home (311), and the aorist (μηδ᾽ ἐπιμνησθῇς ἔτι) "do not recall Troy to mind any more," demands the συντελείωσις: "Get done with remembering Troy"; the present views the whole act of tarrying in its occurrence, as process (παράτασις). The context suggests that the tone of the aorist is stronger, more decisive. The aorist does not allow one to look on at leisure and in comfort. Here is no rooom for παράτασις, it states the action and directs the mind to the effective aspect. (49)

This explanation reveals several difficulties. (i) It is based on the objective nature of the event, equating the Present tense with the act of tarrying. (ii) It equates the action with a temporal scheme, failing to consider verbal aspect sufficiently. (iii) Louw seems to confuse his analysis by introducing the question of tone. Although he admits that tone is contextually dictated (with reference to Post's article [49 n. 29, cf. 50]), what he appears to mean is that in this context reference to remembrance of Troy is more decisive (this in itself is questionable). His statement is easily interpreted to mean the Aorist itself here is stronger, although he admits that the converse-- that if the Aorist is used the action is emphatic--is not true (51). Louw has failed to consider the issue of marking, although his translation of Apollonius hints at understanding the Aorist as the less heavily marked of the two. A more convincing reading recognizes that the Aorist and Present in commands may be referring to the same state of affairs--whether the action is current or only anticipated--and have no necessary correlation with the process described. Thus the more heavily marked Present is used to highlight a persistent point, being conceived by the writer as a further possible delay, while the less heavily marked Aorist is used for any persistent or remaining remembrance of Troy (contra McKay, "Aspects," 45, though he recognizes the role of aspect).

Louw discusses several examples that show his own rendering of συντελείωσις to be inaccurate, especially when he mentions ingressive use of the Aorist, in line with Apollonius's reference to commands for processes not yet taking place: e.g. S. Oed. Col. 731: μήτ᾽ ὀκνεῖτε μήτ᾽ ἀφῆτ᾽ (don't hesitate, don't permit); A. Prom. 783: μηδ᾽ ἀτιμάσῃς (don't rebuke); S. Ant. 546: μή . . . θάνῃς (don't die); Phil. 1181: μή . . . ἔλθῃς (don't go). Thus in a footnote (52 n. 37) Louw indicates that the Aorist *Aktionsart* describes the action as undefined, and is suitable for ingressive usage. He must conclude, however, that συντελείωσις is "therefore not the only aspect conveyed by the aorist in prohibitions" (53). The conative Present prohibition undermines Louw's scheme as well: A. Prom. 684-85: μηδέ μ᾽ οἰκτίσας / σύνθαλπε μύθοις ψευδέσιν (don't, having pity on me, cheer me up with false stories), leaving his explanation unsatisfactory for describing Aorist or Present usage. The ingressive Aorist and conative Present are pragmatic uses on the basis of lexis in context. A systemic view of aspect sees the supposed ingressive uses not only as an internal inconsistency within Louw's system, but as grammatically unprincipled. A semantic view of the action as complete or in progress is fully satisfactory and consistent.

The most complete study of Greek commands to date is by Bakker (*Imperative*; followed by Moorhouse, 218-19; analysed by McKay, "Aspects," 48ff.).[14] He begins from the premise that there "is general agreement now, one might say, on what aspect actually is: aspect denotes the speaker's point of view of the action. But no agreement has been reached yet as to the structure of the aspect system of the Greek verb" (19). Relying heavily upon Ruipérez (*Estructura*) and Seiler (*L'aspect*) he adopts the French school's definition of the Aorist as "l'action pur et simple" (e.g. Meillet, Chantraine, Péristérakis) and Seiler's definition of the Present as "coincidence." By this he means that the imperfect is compared "with a line[,] one of the points of which coincides with another occurrence" (24), whether at the beginning, middle or end. It is worth examining this definition. (1) This definition is predicated upon an understanding of aspect in modern Greek. To read this understanding back into ancient Greek poses a clear problem, especially since it is recognized that Greek verbal aspect changed during and after the Byzantine period (Humbert, "Aspect"; McKay, "Aspect," 201-02 n. 2, among other works). (2) More importantly, Bakker's definition is closer to a theory of *Aktionsart*, in that the process is seen not according to the conception of the event (per his own definition above, see also 27), but according to the action of the event itself. (3) He tries to maintain that the Aorist represents the "absolute fact, the mere process" (27), but this does not comport well with its principal aspectual characteristics (see my chapts. 2 and 4).

(4) Most importantly, Bakker's examples are often unconvincing. Hdt. 8.64.1: ἡμέρη τε ἐγίνετο καὶ ἅμα τῷ ἡλίῳ ἀνιόντι σεισμὸς ἐγένετο, which Bakker translates "day was breaking, and just as the sun rose the shock of an earthquake was felt," with the Imperfect ἐγίνετο coinciding with the Aorist ἐγένετο. Another translation might be "day came, and just as the sun rose an earthquake struck." The only overlap of events is between the sun rising and the earthquake striking, but this is established by the temporal Dative group, not verbal aspect. (This understanding seems to be reflected by de Sélincourt [*Herodotus*, 544]: "Day broke; just as the sun rose the shock of an earthquake was felt. . . ." Cf. Godley [*Herodotus*]: "At sunrise on the next day there was an earthquake . . ." where the two events are treated as complete and overlapping.) Hom. Od. 11.321-24: Ἀριάδνην / . . . ἥν ποτε Θησεὺς / ἐκ Κρήτης ἐς γουνὸν Ἀθηνάων ἱεράων / ἦγε μέν, οὐδ᾽ ἀπόνητο· πάρος δέ μιν Ἄρτεμις ἔκτα, which Bakker translates "Ariadne . . . who was once taken by Theseus from Crete to the holy hills of Athens; he did not enjoy her, though, for Artemis killed her." This makes it the more perplexing when he says that "the imperfect ἦγε coincides with ἔκτα. But in this case the 'point' of the aorist is not somewhere on the line formed by ἦγε, but brings it to an abrupt end" (25). This does not

---

[14]Voelz (*Use*) takes a similar view to Bakker, seeing on the basis of 1 Pet 1:13-4:11 versus 4:12ff. (108ff.) that the Aorist Imperative has an absolute use, and the Present one of connection between the process and those involved in the context. Criticisms of Bakker's scheme apply, but several criticisms of Voelz's scheme may be made also. (1) Voelz's 1977 work shows a complete unawareness of modern aspectual theory (though his later work, "Grammar," makes a correlation with the work of McKay; see my chapt. 1). (2) Consequently, he argues against the traditional theory of *Aktionsart*, which he rightly criticizes, although two results emerge: (a) his own view has similarities to *Aktionsart* since he places emphasis upon an objective characterization of the action; (b) his scheme has inconsistencies, so that he is forced to admit with Poutsma ("Tempora," 73) that verbal usage may appear arbitrary (118). (3) Voelz states that since Aorist and Present Imperatives may appear in similar contexts, and in violation of the traditional definitions of action according to *Aktionsart*, the logical conclusion is that there is absolutely no correlative semantic relationship between the verb tense and its meaning (102). (4) Voelz claims to be making a totally inductive study of Imperatival usage, but he begins with a distinction between policy (= general) and specific commands, into which he fits all of his examples, although it is difficult to determine why, e.g., 1 Cor 16:13-14 is general rather than specific. The fact that Present Imperatives are often used in policy commands is circular and does not explain exceptions. (5) The concept of connectedness, especially formulated around 1 Pet 4:11, 12, is beyond grammatical analysis, but attempts to ground verbal usage in ontology.

seem to be an accurate assessment. Luke 8:51-52: ἐλθὼν δὲ εἰς τὴν οἰκίαν οὐκ ἀφῆκεν, εἰσελθεῖν τινα σὺν αὐτῷ . . . ἔκλαιον δὲ πάντες καὶ ἐκόπτοντο αὐτήν ("arriving at the house he did not let anybody enter with him . . . and all were mourning and wailing over her" [25]), where Bakker says "the two imperfects clearly coincide with an implied 'the moment he entered'" (25). In other words, the first half of the quotation is completely unnecessary, since Bakker must posit a non-existent Aorist. Hom. Od. 13.281: ἀλλ' αὕτως ἀποβάντες ἐκείμεθα νηὸς ἅπαντες ("when all of us, just as we were, had left the ship, we lay down" [25]). Bakker argues that "the imperfect often coincides with an occurrence which is situated at the beginning of the action" (25), but these two events do not overlap at all, since it would be difficult to lie down before or during exit from the ship, but only after it; in fact the use of the tenses is reversed, since according to his scheme one would expect the Participle to be in the Present and the main verb in the Aorist. The same applies to Hom. Od. 6.252: εἵματ' ἄρα πτύξασα τίθει καλῆς ἐπ' ἀπήνης ("after folding the clothes, she put them in the beautiful car . . .") (25). Hom. Il. 9.478: φεῦγον ἔπειτ' ἀπάνευθε δι' Ἑλλάδος εὐρυχόροιο ("after that I fled [I started fleeing] far away through spacious Greece") (25) is incomprehensible to me. Bakker says that "there is a close connection between ὑπέρθορον [lept] in 476 and the imperfect φεῦγον" (25), but the grammatical connection is with the following ἄναχθ' (arrived [line 480]), which renders the example questionable. Th. 3.49.1: ῥηθεισῶν δὲ τῶν γνωμῶν τούτων . . . οἱ Ἀθηναῖοι ἦλθον μὲν ἐς ἀγῶνα ὅμως τῆς δόξης . . . ἐκράτησε δὲ ἡ τοῦ Διοδότου. καὶ τριήρη εὐθὺς ἄλλην ἀπέστελλον κατὰ σπουδήν. Bakker translates this "'when these motions had been put forward . . . the Athenians still held conflicting opinions. . . the motion of Diodotus, however, was passed. Immediately another trireme was sent out in all haste. . . .'" Here εὐθύς helps to indicate where ἐκράτησε and ἀπέστελλον coincide" (25). Bakker is misleading, since εὐθύς indicates that the two processes do not overlap. Hdt. 3.19.1: Καμβύσῃ δὲ ὡς ἔδοξε πέμπειν τοὺς κατασκόπους, αὐτίκα μετεπέμπετο . . . τοὺς ἐπισταμένους τὴν Αἰθιοπίδα γλῶσσαν ("having decided that the spies should go, Cambyses immediately sent for some men who were acquainted with the Ethiopian language" [25]). As Bakker admits, "it gives us a great deal of trouble to conceive this μετεπέμπετο as durative, but Herodotus uses an imperfect all the same. He apparently wants to express a close connection between Cambyses' decision and this 'sending for.' With the decision as his starting-point he views the process of 'sending for' in its perspective" (25-26). This shows that Bakker's theory, dependent upon Aktionsart, does not provide an adequate explanation. Mark 1:31: καὶ ἀφῆκεν αὐτὴν ὁ πυρετός, καὶ διηκόνει αὐτοῖς ("and the fever left her, and [from that moment on] she was serving them"). Bakker says "there is a very close connection between ἀφῆκεν and διηκόνει. Here the relationship between the two parts of the sentence seems to be a temporal one, but a causal relationship is also easily discernible" (26). The relationship is close, but does not seem to be the one he has defined as aspectual. And the causal relationship is unclear. Several other examples he cites are equally problematic for the causal connection and its relation to aspect: Hom. Il. 1.33: ἔδεισεν δ' ὁ γέρων καὶ ἐπείθετο μύθῳ ("the old man seized by fear immediately started [for that reason] carrying out the order" [26]), where the fearing has to have some objective durative meaning; and Hom. Od. 6.71: ὡς εἰπὼν δμώεσσιν ἐκέκλετο, τοὶ δ' ἐπίθοντο ("after these words he gave his orders to the slaves, and they obeyed" [26]), where the Aorist and Imperfect do not necessarily overlap.

Although Bakker has definite opinions in his theoretical section on the nature of "connection," he does not pursue his definition of aspect rigorously, but instead often interprets individual instances in ways compatible with the language of markedness. Hence, his actual analysis contains much language that is reminiscent of recent aspectual theory (42; see also McKay, 136ff.; idem, "Aspect," 203-04; Chantraine, "Questions," 42; Humbert, 177; Amigues, "Temps," 22):

the only constant that may be defined with a high degree of certainty and will hold good in every dramatic situation is the aspectual content of the verbal forms. The aorist stem is, and always will be an aorist stem, and the aspectual characteristics it has will always be the same. This, of course, also applies to the present stem. When speaking (or writing) a Greek uses these constant characteristics as he likes, for he determines the context and the intonation. . . . Whether the speaker chooses the present stem or the aorist stem does not depend on a general rule, but only on the state of mind of the speaker. He visualizes the situation and the action ordered in some way or other, and he makes his choice accordingly.

While his last few statements, reminiscent of Poutsma, overstate the arbitrariness of choice by failing to consider markedness and contextual factors, his general point is well made.

The third and final analysis of aspect in relation to commands and prohibitions is put forward by Amigues, who, specifically concerned with analysis of the commands of orators, notes that "une interprétation superficielle des temps rencontrés dans les ordres de l'orateur au greffier s'inspire de l'opinion courante que le présent est duratif ou itératif, l'aoriste, ponctuel ou semelfactif" ("Temps," 224; see my chapt. 1 and several grammars: Goodwin, *Syntax*, 22; Kühner/Gerth, 1.189; Gildersleeve, 164). She concentrates on the opposition between ἀναγίγνωσκε (which is comparatively rare) and ἀνάγνωθι, which frequently occur in the same syntactical patterns: e.g. D. 56.36: ἀνάγνωθι δέ μοι πάλιν τὴν συγγραφήν (read to me again the agreement); and D. 35.37: καί μοι ἀναγίγνωσκε τὴν συγγραφήν πάλιν (read to me the agreement again). From this verbal opposition, accepting the work of Chantraine that choice of verb form is subjective and citing a clear aspectual difference in And. Ag. Midios 107-08 (λαβὲ δή μοι τὸν περὶ τῶν δώρων νόμον. ἐν ὅσῳ δὲ τὸν νόμον, ὦ ἄνδρες Ἀθηναῖοι, λαμβάνει, βούλομαι μικρὰ πρὸς ὑμᾶς εἰπεῖν ["*Prends*-moi donc la loi sur les pots-de-vin. . . . Pendant qu'il *tâche de mettre la main sur* cette loi, Athéniens, je veux vous parler un peu"; 229]), she argues for an opposition between the Present grammaticalizing "le fait qu'aux yeux du locuteur--et nous retrouverions ici la subjectivité reconnue de l'aspect--l'ordre de lire *prolonge* en quelque sorte l'annonce précédente de la lecture" and the Aorist as grammaticalizing "un simple fait de vocabulaire qui n'affecte pas l'idée sous-jacente de communication orale" (226). Thus Amigues characterizes the difference between the Aorist and Present Imperative as follows: "On peut supposer que le jeu des aspects permet d'énoncer simplement un ordre (impératif aoriste correspondant au schéma: volonté + action), ou de mettre l'accent sur son exécution (imperatif présent = volonté + ACTION)" (228).[15] From what has been argued above (esp. chapts. 2 and 4), this correlates well with the theory propounded in this work.[16]

3. Kind of action and objective action.

In 1895 Donovan published an article on the Greek jussive ("Jussives"), starting from two consensus opinions: "In all moods, except the indicative, *i.e.* the infin., imper., opt., subj., the present and aorist have a *common difference* . . . . This common difference is not a *time*-distinction, as Buttmann put it, as far back as 1854:--'Dahingegen bezeichnen die Modi des Praesens und Aorists *durchaus keine Zeit*'" (145). (Brugmann [587] misses the essential point, and cites Donovan in support of his contention that use of the Imperative relates to the differing *Aktionsarten* of the verbal stems.) Previous discussion in this work illustrates the firm linguistic basis for both of these assertions. Donovan proceeds to make one simple and major point: that Aorist and Present Imperatives are found in identical contexts, and are used of action which objectively may be variously described.

Examples include: Pl. Charm. 155B: παῖ κάλει Χαρμίδην (child, call C.); and Ar. Peace 195: ἴθι νῦν κάλεσόν μοι τὸν Δί᾽ (now call to me Zeus), where "in neither case is there a trace of habitual or repeated action. Objectively one is not more continuous than the other" (147). Pl. Gorg. 448D: ἀλλὰ σύ, εἰ βούλει, ἐροῦ αὐτόν (but you, if you want, interrogate him);[17] 462B:

---

[15]Amigues (231ff.) further argues that λέγε is aspectually neutralized in the orators because the Aorist does not appear with the sense of "read." (1) The suppletive paradigm is complete in these and other authors, thus it does not properly qualify as aspectually neutral or vague. (2) This formulation is apparently based primarily upon lexical meaning. (3) As McKay ("Aspects," 53) says, "While there may be a formulaic element in the way these verbs are used, the choice of aspect in each case is not without appropriate significance. The function of the clerk is to speak the evidence, so the use of the imperfective to instruct him to proceed with his duty is to be expected, whether λέγε is the final word before the evidence or is followed by further instruction or explanation. The activities of taking up the documents or reading them are more specific auxiliaries to the speaking, so it is appropriate for them to be specified as complete actions, although reading overlaps with speaking sufficiently to be substituted for it sometimes in the imperfective."

[16]Contra Ruijgh, "L'emploi." How can he reconcile the following examples? D. 23.22: λαβὲ δὴ τοὺς νόμους αὐτοὺς καὶ λέγε (take these laws and read), where he says the act of accepting the laws precedes their reading; D. 24.32: ἀνάγνωθι δέ μοι λαβὼν τουτονὶ πρῶτον τὸν νόμον, ὃς διαρρήδην οὐκ ἐᾷ νόμον οὐδέν᾽ ἐναντίον εἰσφέρειν, ἐὰν δέ τις εἰσφέρῃ, γράφεσθαι κελεύει. ἀναγίγνωσκε (read to me, taking this first law, which does not permit introducing a contradictory law, but if someone might enter one, it commands him to be indicted. Read), where he claims that "au moment où l'orateur prononce cette phrase, le greffier n'est pas encore tout à fait prêt à lire. . . . ce n'est qu'après cette lecture que l'orateur pourra continue son discours en renvoyant à ce texte. Après que l'orateur a prononcé cette phrase, le greffier a pris en mains le document en question et est donc prêt à lire. A ce moment, l'orateur lui dit: ἀναγίγνωσκε . . .," en lui faisant ainsi signe de commencer la lecture" (31), with D. 18.289: λέγε δ᾽ αὐτῷ τουτὶ τὸ ἐπίγραμμα, ὃ δημοσίᾳ προείλεθ᾽ ἡ πόλις αὐτοῖς ἐπιγράψαι, ἵν᾽ εἰδῇς, Αἰσχίνη, καὶ ἐν αὐτῷ τούτῳ σαυτὸν ἀγνώμονα καὶ συκοφάντην ὄντα καὶ μιαρόν. λέγε (read the epitaph for him, which the city voted to inscribe for them, so that you might know, A., indeed by this what is your own callousness and sychophancy and brutality. Speak) (34). See also Ar. Ach. 812; Knights 102; Clouds 200 (35).

[17]Examples in Plato's Gorgias provide suitable examples for the point made in 4. below.

καὶ νῦν δὴ τούτων ὁπότερον βούλει ποίει· ἐρώτα ἢ ἀποκρίνου (now do whichever of these things you want: ask or answer); Gorg. 449D: ἴθι δή μοι ἀπόκριναι οὕτω καὶ περὶ τῆς ῥητορικῆς (indeed answer me thus concerning rhetoric); 475D: μὴ ὄκνει ἀποκρίνασθαι, ὦ Πῶλε . . . ἀλλὰ γενναίως τῷ λόγῳ ὥσπερ ἰατρῷ παρέχων ἀποκρίνου, καὶ ἢ φάθι ἢ μὴ ἃ ἐρωτῶ (don't hesitate to answer, P. . . . but paying attention exactly to the word, as to a doctor, answer either yes or no to what I say); Gorg. 506C: λέγε, ὦ 'γαθέ, αὐτὸς καὶ πέραινε (speak, good man, complete this); 522E: ἀλλ' ἐπείπερ γε καὶ τἄλλα ἐπέρανας, καὶ τοῦτο πέρανον (but since your have completed the other things, complete this); Gorg. 506C: ἄκουε δὴ ἐξ ἀρχῆς ἐμοῦ ἀναλαβόντος τὸν λόγον (listen then, while I take up the account from the beginning); 453A: ἄκουσον δή, ὦ Γοργία (listen, G.), in which "none of the foregoing refer either to habitual or repeated action" (147); Th. 1.86.5: ψηφίζεσθε οὖν . . . ἀξίως τῆς Σπάρτης τὸν πόλεμον (vote for a war worthy of S.); 1.124.2: ἀλλὰ νομίσαντες ἐς ἀνάγκην ἀφῖχθαι, ὦ ἄνδρες ξύμμαχοι . . . ψηφίσασθε τὸν πόλεμον (but considering having reached a state of necessity, fellow allies, vote for the war); Ar. Knights 106: σπονδὴν[18] λαβὲ δὴ καὶ σπεῖσον Ἀγαθοῦ Δαίμονος (take a libation and pour to good fortune); 221: ἀλλὰ στεφανοῦ καὶ σπένδε τῷ Κοαλέμῳ (but crown yourself and pour a libation to K.); Th. 6.80.5: σκοπεῖτε οὖν καὶ αἱρεῖσθε ἤδη (think therefore and choose now); 1.143.5: σκέψασθε δέ (just think); Pl. Gorg. 482A: μὴ θαύμαζε ὅτι ἐγὼ ταῦτα λέγω (don't marvel that I say these things); Tim. 29C: ἐὰν οὖν . . . μὴ δυνατοὶ γιγνώμεθα πάντῃ πάντως . . . λόγους . . . ἀποδοῦναι μὴ θαυμάσῃς (if therefore we who are capable might not know in every way always the words to say, don't marvel); Th. 4.118.9: ἰόντες ἐς Λακεδαίμονα διδάσκετε (go into L. and teach); Pl. Euth. 6E: ταύτην τοίνυν με αὐτὴν δίδαξον τὴν ἰδέαν (now teach me this particular idea); Gorg. 482A: νόμιζε τοίνυν καὶ παρ' ἐμοῦ χρῆναι ἕτερα τοιαῦτα ἀκούειν (think now that from me it is necessary to hear other such things); Th. 1.82.4: μὴ γὰρ ἄλλο τι νομίσητε τὴν γῆν (don't think of their land as any other thing); Th. 7.63.4: ἀμύνασθε αὐτοὺς καὶ δείξατε (avenge them and show); Ar. Knights 246: ἀλλ' ἀμύνου καὶ δίωκε καὶ τροπὴν αὐτοῦ ποιοῦ (but avenge and pursue and make him flee); Th. 1.85.2: πρὸς τοὺς Ἀθηναίους πέμπετε μὲν . . . πέμπετε δέ (send to the A.s and send); E. And. 923: πέμψον με χώρας τῆσδ' ὅποι προσωτάτω (send me to a land far far away); Th. 7.77.4: χωρεῖτε (advance); 4.95.3: χωρήσατε οὖν ἀξίως ἐς αὐτοὺς τῆς τε πόλεως . . . καὶ τῶν πατέρων (depart quickly to them of the city and of their fathers). There is a final set of instances where the Present and Aorist "occur side by side in the same sentence, referring to the same particular occasion and sometimes even to the same action" (148): E. Med. 1258-60: ἀλλά νιν, ὦ φάος διογενές, κάτειρ/γε, κατάπαυσον, ἔξελ' οἴκων τάλαι/ναν (but then, divinely begotten light, stop her, hinder her, take away the wretch from homes); Ar. Peace 516: μὴ νῦν ἀνῶμεν ἀλλ' ἐπεντείνωμεν (don't let up now but press on); Th. 1.42.1: νεώτερός τις . . . ἀξιούτω . . . καὶ μὴ νομίσῃ (let any youth be worthy and not think); Pl. Lach. 190C: μὴ τοίνυν . . . περὶ ὅλης ἀρετῆς εὐθέως σκοπώμεθα . . . ἀλλὰ μέρους τινὸς πέρι πρῶτον ἴδωμεν (let us not seek concerning the entire virtue immediately but let us know portions of it at the first).

Donovan clearly proves (in advance of Amigues [above] and McKay ["Aspects," esp. 44]) that Aorist and Present Imperatives do not have a necessary correlation to the objective kind of action depicted, since the Aorist and Present may be found with reference to the same kind of event and even with reference to the same event, in similar syntactical and larger contexts. This is an important finding, unfortunately one often overlooked in discussion of verbal function of the command in NT Greek (see below for examples).

4. Temporal schemes and the command. Discussion in this century can be marked from a brief note by Headlam ("Passages," 295), who regarding prohibitions claimed that

---

[18]Most texts place this word with the above speaker.

the negated Aorist Subjunctive means "'see that you do not do this' at whatever future time" and that the negated Present Imperative means "do not do as you are doing," "do not continue doing so," "cease to do so." In support he cites Theoc. 5.31: μὴ σπεῦδε, which elicits the response ἀλλ' οὔτι σπεύδω; S. El. 395: μή μ' ἐκδίδασκε, which elicits ἀλλ' οὐ διδάσκω. And S. El. 830: μηδὲν μέγ' εἴπης and μηδὲν μέγ'αὔσης, he claims, "are interruptions in anticipation."[19] He took his hint from Jackson ("Prohibition," 263), who cited Pl. Apol. 20E: μὴ θορυβήσητε, and 21A: μὴ θορυβεῖτε, claiming that the first is used before the clamour begins and the second when it has begun ("don't disturb" and "don't keep disturbing"). Headlam's position is widely held: e.g. Smyth, 411; Rose, *Tenses*, 38-39; Moulton, 122; Blass/Debrunner, ¶¶ 335-37 (Headlam's analysis of the Present was suggested by Humphreys ["Negative Commands," 48], citing D. 40.29: μὴ ἐπιτρέπετε [don't allow]; 21.28: μὴ . . . ἐᾶτε [don't permit]; Pl. Rep. 338A: μὴ . . . ἄλλως ποίει [don't be contrary]).

This prompted two responses. Seaton ("Prohibition," 438) questioned Jackson's example, claiming that it only works if the rule is established, but it does not establish the rule. In fact, he claims, the context here indicates otherwise. "Socrates says, please do not make a clamour if in what I am about to say you think I say something boastful (τι μέγα). Before however he actually does say anything that could be considered boastful he says again καί, ὅπερ λέγω, μὴ θορυβεῖτε," thus indicating that either command was possible before the process began. (Cf. Pl. Apol. 30C: μέλλω γὰρ οὖν ἄττα ὑμῖν ἐρεῖν καὶ ἄλλα ἐφ' οἷς ἴσως βοήσεσθε· ἀλλὰ μηδαμῶς ποιεῖτε τοῦτο [I am going to speak to you of these and other things, about which you will possibly cry out; but never do this].)

The second response came from Naylor ("Prohibitions," 26-30), who made a complete study of the tragedians, concluding that there is evidence both for (e.g. E. Ion 766-70; S. Ant. 546; A. Eum. 800; S. Phil. 574) and against Headlam and Jackson's proposal: E. And. 87-88: ὀρᾶς; ἀπαυδᾶς ἐν κακοῖς φίλοισι σοῖς // οὐ δῆτα· μηδὲν τοῦτ' ὀνειδίσῃς ἐμοί (you see? you deny your evil friends. Not a word; don't rebuke me for this), where Headlam's scheme would require the Present; E. Hec. 1180-84: ἄπαντα ταῦτα συντεμὼν ἐγὼ φράσω· / γένος γὰρ οὔτε πόντος οὔτε γῆ τρέφει / τοιόνδ', ὁ δ' ἀεὶ ξυντυχὼν ἐπίσταται. // μηδὲν θρασύνου, μηδὲ τοῖς σαυτοῦ κακοῖς / τὸ θῆλυ συνθεὶς ὧδε πᾶν μέμψῃ γένος (cutting short all these things I will speak; for neither sea nor earth feeds such a breed; but the one who is with them always understands. Don't be bold, and don't here, cursing women, blame for your own evils the entire breed); E. Helen 1255-59: προσφάζεται μὲν αἷμα πρῶτα νερτέροις· // τίνος; σύ μοι σήμαινε, πείσομαι δ' ἐγώ. // αὐτὸς σὺ γίγνωσκ'· ἀρκέσει γὰρ αν διδῷς. // ἐν βαρβάροις μὲν ἵππον ἢ ταῦρον νόμος. // διδούς γε μὲν δὴ δυσγενὲς μηδὲν δίδου (first blood is a sacrifice to the gods of the underworld. Of whom? Indicate to me, and I will obey. You yourself decide; for what you might give is pleasing. Among barbarians a horse or a bull is the rule. Don't give mean sacrifices); E. Hec. 385-87: τήνδε μὲν μὴ κτείνετε, / ἡμᾶς δ' ἄγοντες πρὸς πυρὰν Ἀχιλλέως / κεντεῖτε, μὴ φείδεσθ' (which don't kill, but leading us to the doors of A., kill, don't spare), where "we here have κεντεῖτε--present looking to a future act--lying between two negatived presents which are supposed to mean 'cease killing,' 'cease sparing'" (28). He also cites A. Prom. 683, 807; E. Helen 1427; E. Alc. 690; E. Med. 61, 90; E. Phoen. Maid. 1072; D. 21.40; 39.35; Ar. Birds 1532-34; Frogs 618-22. Naylor includes as well several

---

[19]Translations in the spirit of what he is advocating would be: "don't continue desiring," answered by "but I am not still desiring"; "don't continue teaching me," answered by "but I am not teaching"; and "don't begin to shout loudly."

instances where either meaning is acceptable, often because particles seem to make the distinction Headlam draws slight.[20]

Naylor is compelled to admit, therefore, that in many instances there is not a difference between the Present and Aorist Imperatives. As far as the distinction which Headlam makes, Naylor's point has strength.

Headlam's response is interesting for making three points. (1) He admits that there are exceptions to his rule ("Prohibitions," 33), but stresses that the majority usage should be focused upon (and lists more examples to support his case). But this is unhelpful, since it leaves a significant area of usage without adequate explanation, while only providing a generalization for the majority of usage. (2) He claims that he knows of no instance where a Present Indicative follows μή + Aorist Subjunctive. But this does not affect the issue, since a syntactical tense sequence pattern may be in effect. The clear instances where the tenses are not used according to his rule still must be explained. Some he explains as colloquial usage, but the number and variety of exceptions seems too large to eliminate the need for discussion. The explanation is that in fact the tense forms of the Imperative (like all Moods) have no necessary correlation to the actual character of the process referred to. (3) Headlam cites examples where an Aorist interrupts another person speaking: Pl. Gorg. 521B (cited as 321B): K. ὡς εἰ μὴ ταὐτά γε ποιήσεις. Σ. μὴ εἴπῃς ὃ πολλάκις εἴρηκας (unless you will do these things. Don't say what you have said many times); Ach.Tat. 8.6.15-7.1: εἰ δὲ μή, αὐτοὶ γὰρ ἴστε οἷα εἰκὸς ἐν τοσαύταις αὐτὴν ἐπιβουλαῖς γενομένην ἄκουσαν-- καὶ εὐθὺς ἡ Λευκίππη, πρὶν τὸν ἱερέα εἰπεῖν τὸν ἑξῆς λόγον· ὥς γέ μοι δοκεῖ, μηδὲ εἴπῃς (but if not, for you know that unwillingly in such trials which befell her learning--and immediately L., before the priest could speak the entire sentence: as it seems to me, don't speak). Headlam admits that a Present Imperative could be used in this kind of context as well: Ar. Wasps 919: πρὸς τῶν θεῶν, μὴ προκαταγίγνωσκ', ὦ πάτερ, πρὶν ἂν γ' ἀκούσῃς ἀμφοτέρων (by the gods, don't decide against us, father, before you might hear both sides). McKay ("Aspects," 54) notes that the reading of evidence in orations is never interrupted by the imperfective but usually by the perfective and occasionally the stative (D. 24.64) aspects.

Although few grammars show cognizance of this discussion, these results have been accepted and expanded upon in several important articles. For example, Poutsma ("Tempora," 30-35 on the Present; 35-41 on the Aorist), although he believes that the Present Imperative essentially depicts a process as in progress, recognizes examples where the Present is used in contexts which are incompatible with progress, such as X. Anab. 7.4.9: παῖε . . ., εἰ κελεύει ὁ παῖς καὶ μέλλει χάριν εἰδέναι (strike, if the boy commands and he is going to see freely); and where the Aorist is used in contexts which are incompatible with completion, such as Pl. Symp. 214D: ἀλλ' οὕτω ποίει, φάναι τὸν Ἐρυξίμαχον, εἰ βούλει· Σωκράτη ἐπαίνεσον (but do that, said E., if you want; praise S.). And Chantraine ("Questions"), following Humbert (134), looks to context to establish the difference between the Aorist and the Present Imperative, since each may be equally possible in a context.

5. Conclusion. This survey shows that the theory of verbal aspect argued in this work--supported especially by the work of Donovan and Naylor--also holds for a troublesome area of Greek verbal usage, commands and prohibitions. Thus verbal aspectual choice of the command or prohibition involves the author's subjective choice to grammaticalize a process as

---

[20]Naylor ("Prohibitions") makes two further assertions: he introduces a "conative" Imperative, so that παῦε παῦε, a common use of the Present Imperative in Greek drama, and an obvious problem for Headlam's proposal, means "be for ceasing," and is "merely less preemptory than παῦσον" (27); second, he argues that all Imperatives or prohibitions "refer in sense to the future" (28), in that the Imperative "looks to an action [the not-coming] which lies in the future" (28). See also Naylor, "More," 348.

perfective or imperfective, and these categories may apply to action however it is objectively conceived and however it is depicted in relation to the time of commanding.

c. The Aorist Imperative and prayer to gods. Prayers to gods qualifies as an important usage of the Imperative and deserves special attention. Recent discussion of this issue begins with Mozley's treatment of Present and Aorist Imperatives ("Notes," esp. 280), in which he argues that in the Greek of the NT and LXX God is addressed only with the Aorist. The exceptions he notes are very few, the most noteworthy being Luke 11:3: τὸν ἄρτον ἡμῶν τὸν ἐπιούσιον δίδου ἡμῖν τὸ καθ' ἡμέραν (give to us our daily bread each day), where Matt 6:11 has the Aorist (see also 3 Kgdms 3:9, 10; Job 10:2; 13:21; 14:15; Sir 33:11). Kieckers confirmed this general tendency in his study of 2d Person Imperatives in the Iliad, Odyssey, Hesiod, Sappho, Aeschylus, Sophocles, Euripides, and Aristophanes, where in each author instances of the Aorist in prayers of men to gods exceed instances of the Present. A noteworthy exception is Pindar, where he counts twelve Presents to seven Aorists. Thus Kieckers notes that "Mir scheint vielmehr der gebrauch, welcher im biblischen Griechisch anzutreffen ist, hier nicht willkürlich und plötzlich entstanden zu sein, sondern nur die konsequenteste Durchführung eines im Prinzipe Jahrhunderte lang bestehenden Sprachgebrauchs zu repräsentieren" ("Zum Gebrauch," 17). (Gildersleeve ["Brief Mention," 30 (1909)] believes Pindar uses the tenses in recalcitrancy against Homer, as well as in his personification of new deities, noting also that Homer addresses the Muse in the Present in Od. 1.1. See also Meltzer, Review, 612, who sees the Aorist as a pressing form, and the Present by implication more deferential; Scott, "Prohibitives.") Poutsma, however, later analysed Pindar, Bacchylides, and the Homeric Hymns, concluding that in all of these the Present Imperative occurs more often than the Aorist in prayers addressed to gods ("Tempora," 64-68). Kieckers's explanation of the tendency for the Aorist to be used in address of gods is that, "wie mir scheint, eine Feinheit der griechsichen Sprache zum Ausdruck. Nicht das durative Präsens, sondern der perfektive Aorist is in der Regel die Aktionsart, in der der endlich beschränkte Mensch die unendliche Gottheit anrufen dar" (17). Grassi notes that if this is correct, it does not explain how the Aorist can be used of another human being ("Imperativo," 187). And Kretschmer argues in response, "man würde eher erwarten, dass den Handlungen, die von den Göttern erbeten werden, Dauer zugeschrieben und daher der Imperativ des Präsens gewählt worden wäre" ("Imperativus," 120; cf. "Literaturbericht," 342; followed by Post, "Use," 34 n. 7). Kieckers's et al. view is based on a concept of Aktionsart that sees the Aorist as instantaneous or momentary; and there is the serious question of why men are more insistent towards gods and more deferential to their fellow men (see Grassi, 187-88). Beschewliew takes a similar view (first in Kritik der bisherigen Ansichten über den Gebrauch des Imperativs und Optativs im griechischen Gebet [Diss. Würzburg 1925], summarized in "Gebrauch"). Criticizing his predecessors for relying overly much upon statistics rather than usage (and claiming to have found some 300 examples of Present Imperatives addressed to gods), he concludes that the difference in usage can be accounted for according to Aktionsart: the Aorist is used in concrete prayers to refer to a single, certain case in daily life, while the Present is used for general, repeated or unfounded requests. Beschlewiew's view is based upon both a misleading concept of verbal action (= Aktionsart, see criticism above [Bakker (Imperative, 14-15) inaccurately characterizes Beschlewiew's view as one of verbal aspect]) and a mentalistic concept which equates action with life. In response, first, it cannot be concluded that the Aorist is reserved for address by humans toward deity, but that this is only a tendency, perhaps strengthened in the biblical material. Another explanation must be found, although this view has an influential following: e.g. Moulton 173; Mayser, 2, 1.146; Blass/Debrunner, ¶ 337; Robertson, 947-48; Chamberlain, 86-87; Chantraine, 2.196; Humbert, 181. Second, explanations which appeal to human nature are more mentalistic than grammatical. Third, viability of the contrasting verb tenses within similar general contexts (see discussion above) reinforces a semantic difference between the tense forms themselves. Thus further exploration of the concept of verbal aspect is in order.

There have been at least two studies that have applied discussion of verbal aspect to the question of prayers to gods. The first account is by Grassi ("Imperativo"). He begins from the assumption that aspect is independent of the material duration of the action, with the imperfective indicating the evolution of an action, and the perfective the result or completion of the action. Thus ἀναγίγνωσκε is not equivalent to ἀνάγνωθι, even though they both mean "read," with nothing more modest about the former or peremptory about the latter.

Grassi then appears to contradict himself, however, claiming that semantically durative verbs tend to prevail in the imperfective aspect, and punctual or momentary verbs tend to prevail in the perfective aspect. He cites λαμβάνω and δίδωμι as momentary where the Aorist predominates in such authors as Euripides, Demosthenes, Lysias, Thucydides and Homer; μάχομαι, ἔπομαι, and διώκω, as durative where the Present predominates in the same authors; and ὀρᾶν/ἰδεῖν, ἀκούειν/ἀκοῦσαι, and ποιεῖν/ποιῆσαι, where the verbs may be either durative or punctual and the statistical usage is approximately similar (189-94). Thus, Grassi concludes, the preponderance of the Aorist over the Present Imperative in prayers to gods (this is not universal; Grassi admits that in Pindar the ratio is equal [197]) occurs principally, if not exclusively, in verbs which speak of the ultimate or final stage. This occurs for two reasons: (i) prayers to gods have a certain affinity of psychological situation with desires formulated with the Optative (especially introduced by εἴθε, εἰ γάρ, etc.); and (ii) the Present Imperative is used for indicating an action in progress or a condition of indeterminate duration. Thus, since prayer is not the normal condition for man, but a request for divine favour in difficulty, the Aorist over the Present Imperative is chosen.

Grassi's scheme, despite beginning from an aspectual basis, has several difficulties. (1) He is as psychologically dependent as his predecessors, with the result that he in fact "does not prove that and why instantaneous verbs occur more frequently in prayer than in orders and prohibitions directed by men to their fellow-men" (Bakker, *Imperative*, 15). (2) His definition of verbal aspect is clearly inadequate, not only definitionally but practically (see below). (3) His categorization of durative and punctiliar verbs is untenable (see chapt. 1): e.g. Pi. Ol. 1.85: τὺ δὲ πρᾶξιν φίλαν δίδοι (you, do a friendly deed), where the Present may not be punctual as his definition seems to require (nor is it an Aorist). And (4) he has difficulty within his scheme of explaining several important examples. For example, he admits that in Hom. Od. 3.380 the Present Imperative of δίδωμι is used in a prayer (cf. Od. 1.1).

The most complete study to date is by Bakker (*Imperative*), already treated above (followed by Moorhouse, 218-19; Voelz, *Use*). Bakker does not pursue his definition of aspect rigorously, but often interprets individual instances in ways compatible with the language of markedness. When discussing prayers, however, he introduces a new set of categories related to a posited three situations in which humans pray: cases of actual distress, in which deity is addressed emotionally; wishes dependent upon an existing situation; and general wishes (99).

This analysis has two major disadvantages: Bakker's reasoning is circular, since he moves between the categories dictating the kind of situation, and then reads this situation back into the tense usage; and many examples cannot fit adequately within his scheme. Since these categories appear to be impertinent to the language of the NT for the most part, extended discussion is not necessary. (1) In situations of actual distress, Bakker posits that Aorist Imperatives are the rule, since "a human being who is in such straitened circumstances that he cannot do much about them, does not usually try to create an understanding between himself and the deity" (100-101). It has already been shown that this definition of aspect (note the subtle shift from connectedness of events to connectedness between speaker and recipient) is inadequate.

(2) According to Bakker, the Present Imperative calls for immediate action. However, this analysis creates inconsistencies when he cites examples. Of A. Prom. 582-85: πυρί ⟨με⟩ φλέξον, ἢ χθονὶ κάλυψον, ἢ / ποντίοις δάκεσι δὸς βοράν, / μηδέ μοι φθονήσῃς / εὐγμάτων, ἄναξ (consume me with fire, or bury with dirt, or give to the animals in the sea as food, don't refuse my prayers, lord), Bakker says that Io, though tormented by the horse-fly, "leaves the decision to the deity to whom she directs her supplication" to "decide whether he will react, and if so, when" (101). In context this is implausible, especially considering Bakker's immediately preceding discussion. Bakker also admits exceptions (103): e.g. Hom. Il. 15.375-76: τῶν μνῆσαι καὶ ἄμυνον, Ὀλύμπιε, νηλεὲς ἦμαρ, / μηδ' οὕτω Τρώεσσιν ἔα δάμνασθαι Ἀχαιούς (remember

and ward off, O., the ruthless day, don't permit the T.s to destroy the A.s); also Od. 8.242-44; Sapph. 1.1, although he claims there are mitigating circumstances for use of the Present Imperative. But this does not explain A. Pers. 645-46: πέμπετε δ' ἄνω οἷον οὔπω / Πέρσις αἶ' ἐκάλυψεν (send above such a one that P. land never buried), where earlier (line 630) the cry was with the Aorist πέμψατε, although Bakker claims that "this is a cry of distress, not a supplication" (105). See also A. Supp. 900; E. El. 671-73. A more convincing explanation for the examples he cites is found in his treatment of S. Trach. 1031-33: ἰὼ παῖ, / τὸν φύσαντ' οἴκτιρ',[21] ἀνεπίφθονον εἴρυσον ἔγχος, / παῖσον ἐμᾶς ὑπὸ κλῆδος, ἀκοῦ δ' ἄχος (child, have mercy on the one who begat you, draw a reproachless spear, strike me by the beam, and hear my cry), where he says "after compelling his son to have pity on him, he tells him by means of aorist imperatives . . . what kind of actions he wants his son to use to show his pity. But then, letting himself go, he lapses into a cry of distress. . ." (106).

(3) Not only are the particular examples problematic, but Bakker fails to reconcile his other two situations, contending that the Aorist Imperative may also be used in wishes where there is a lack of emotion. Instances with the Present are noteworthy: Pi. Ol. 1.85 (see above); A. Ag. 973: Ζεῦ Ζεῦ τέλειε, τὰς ἐμὰς εὐχὰς τέλει (Z., Z. the perfect, answer my prayers); and Men. Epit. 379-80 (K Fr. 981; Loeb 556-57): φίλη Πειθοῖ, παροῦσα σύμμαχος / πόει κατορθοῦν τοὺς λόγους οὓς ἂν λέγω (dear Persuasion, being an ally, make the words which I may speak to succeed). (See also Ar. Peace 987ff.; A. Eum. 235-36.) He therefore is compelled to introduce a category of hortatory Present Imperative (112ff.)

Bakker's categories regarding prayer, therefore, are not viable. The attempt to describe the situations and then to plot aspectual usage is full of inconsistencies. The situational context (if this is important in the terms Bakker describes) and the use of a particular tense form must be distinguished. While statistics may indicate the predominance of the Aorist Imperative, this does not of itself describe individual verbal function in which the verb itself exercises a prominent part in creating the context. The perfective command or prohibition appears to be the less heavily marked and the imperfective the more heavily marked verbal aspect. The correlation that Bakker speaks of regarding emotion of usage--that the Aorist Imperative is used in conversational situations where the process is "viewed and expressed as abstract facts" (119) and the Present Imperative "when the tone is beseeching" (121)--reinforces that the Present Imperative is semantically more heavily marked, although the point is better made with regard to the Greek verbal network itself than by appeal to a reader's interpretation of a situation. Although throughout his discussion Bakker reiterates (often imprecisely) the contrasting nature of the Aorist as the unattached form and the Present as the form that is used when there is some sort of emotional crisis, exceptional contexts are still to be found. His conclusion regarding the use of the Aorist for prayers is thus that, first, "in most cases the present imperative in question so typically belongs to the human sphere of daily conversation that it is very difficult to imagine that such an expression could ever be used in prayer; secondly, some uses of this imperative are imbued with such strong emotion that even a Greek felt that it would be improper to use them in addressing the gods" (126), although since "he does not always regard the deity as a distant, invisible being, but sometimes as an assistant, an ally who stands beside him and supports him in all his actions" (127), the Present may also be used.

Another explanation worth considering is that use of the command in prayers is essentially the same as use in other contexts, i.e. dictated by aspectual factors. The Aorist is the form usually utilized unless there is a reason for the speaker to use the more heavily marked Present. The reasons may not always be clear to the interpreter, but as is seen above, verbal aspect is not a matter of the subjective choice of the interpreter but of the speaker. The formal opposition of the [+direction] feature, as part of the entire Greek aspectual network, points to a semantic distinction. Such a distinction is made occasionally by Bakker and can go far in treating the examples he cites, as well as eliminating the major problem of accounting for exceptional emotional contexts. Several examples in NT Greek may be cited in support of this.

---

[21]Jebb reads τὸν φύτορ' ὀκτίρας (have mercy on your begetter) here (Davies, *Trachiniae*).

The classic example is Luke 11:3. All of the commands in Matthew's version (6:9-13) of the Lord's Prayer are forms of the Aorist. In Luke's shorter version of the same prayer, four of the commands are Aorists: ἁγιασθήτω (sanctify); ἐλθέτω (let come); ἄφες (forgive) and μὴ εἰσενέγκης (don't lead), as most grammars note. The middle command, in v 3, has the Present: τὸν ἄρτον ἡμῶν τὸν ἐπιούσιον δίδου ἡμῖν τὸ καθ' ἡμέραν (give our daily bread to us each day). A standard explanation of use of the Aorist in Matthew is that σήμερον (today) makes the request specific and of use of the Present is that the following phrase-- τὸ καθ' ἡμέραν--calls for use of the Present to make the sense iterative (e.g. Turner, *Syntax*, 77). But as McKay points out, "the aorist could have been used to signal the completeness of each act of giving requested" ("Aspect," 211). A more important contextual feature has been overlooked however, and that is that the Lukan version is followed by the story of the man who implores his friend for bread at midnight (Luke 11:5ff.). The story concludes (v 8), εἰ καὶ οὐ δώσει αὐτῷ ἀναστὰς διὰ τὸ εἶναι φίλον αὐτοῦ, διά γε τὴν ἀναίδειαν αὐτοῦ ἐγερθεὶς δώσει αὐτῷ ὅσων χρῄζει (if he will not give to him, getting up, because he is his friend, because of his persistence [?], getting up, he will give to him what he needs). Then Jesus reportedly ties the prayer into the story (vv 9-10; cf. Matt 7:7-8): αἰτεῖτε, καὶ δοθήσεται ὑμῖν· ζητεῖτε, καὶ εὑρήσετε· κρούετε, καὶ ἀνοιγήσεται ὑμῖν. πᾶς γὰρ ὁ αἰτῶν λαμβάνει, καὶ ὁ ζητῶν εὑρίσκει, καὶ τῷ κρούοντι ἀνοιγήσεται (ask and it will be given to you; seek and you shall find; knock and it will be opened to you. For everyone who asks receives, and the one who seeks finds, and to the one who knocks it shall be opened), with the Imperatives and Participles in restatement in the Present tense. The entire unit is closed by saying that if those who are evil know how to give good gifts to their children (v 13), πόσῳ μᾶλλον ὁ πατὴρ [ὁ] ἐξ οὐρανοῦ δώσει πνεῦμα ἅγιον τοῖς αἰτοῦσιν αὐτόν (how much more the father from heaven will give a holy spirit to those who ask him). The Present Imperative in the prayer appears to be a self-conscious use of the marked Present to draw attention to a theme that is pursued in the following material.

In Luke 22:42, Jesus prays to God: Πάτερ, εἰ βούλει παρένεγκε τοῦτο τὸ ποτήριον ἀπ' ἐμοῦ· πλὴν μὴ τὸ θέλημά μου ἀλλὰ τὸ σὸν γινέσθω (father, if you want, take away this cup from me; nevertheless, let not my will but yours be done). Luke uses the Present Imperative in a rhetorically balanced sentence to draw attention to Jesus' choice of destiny. As McKay ("Aspect," 214) says, "the comparison of the two wills leads to greater emphasis on the process" (cf. Mark 14:36, with θέλω [I want], Present Indicative). Voelz (*Use*, 46) calls the use emphatic. He lists these two as the only instances in the NT where prayers to God use the Present form.

While most of the requests made to Jesus in the Gospels use Aorists, there are a few in which Presents are used. (Bakker [*Imperative*, 138] lists examples with the Aorist.)

Matt 15:25: a Canaanite woman approaches Jesus and says Κύριε, βοήθει μοι (lord, help me). It is possible that one indicator of her faith, which Jesus reportedly commends in v 28, is her use of the Present. Mark 9:24: the father of the boy with an unclean spirit first says to Jesus εἴ τι δύνη, βοήθησον ἡμῖν σπλαγχνισθεὶς ἐφ' ἡμᾶς (if something might be possible, help us, having compassion upon us) (v 22). Jesus is quoted as mildly rebuking the father, telling him that all things are possible to those who believe. The father responds: πιστεύω· βοήθει μου τῇ ἀπιστίᾳ (I believe; help my unbelief), where the Present is apparently consciously used to show his attempt at increased faith. Luke 7:6: when Jesus approaches the house of the centurion to heal his servant, he tells Jesus, Κύριε, μὴ σκύλλου, οὐ γὰρ ἱκανός εἰμι ἵνα ὑπὸ τὴν στέγην μου εἰσέλθης (lord, don't trouble, for I am not worthy that you might enter under my roof), then explaining the military chain of command (cf. v 8 with Aorist and Present Imperatives). He is commended as the most faithful man in Israel (v 10), possibly with the Present Imperative a primary indicator of this man's belief that Jesus need only speak a word to heal his servant.

Rev 22:20: λέγει ὁ μαρτυρῶν ταῦτα, Ναί, ἔρχομαι ταχύ. ἀμήν, ἔρχου, κύριε Ἰησοῦ (the witness says these things, Yes, I am coming immediately. Amen, come, lord Jesus). Bakker explains this use as concerning "not so much a prayer as a conversational situation: John is able to respond to Christ's words at once and may, therefore, express a connection. Such a connection cannot usually be expressed in prayer" (134). Perhaps a more plausible explanation is that this verse comes as the final climactic statement to John's entire vision of future events. He uses the marked Present Imperative to express his keen desire for such things to transpire.

d. NT Examples. Before analysing use of commands in the NT, two observations warrant comment. (1) Through a treatment of a number of examples cited by other earlier scholars, as well as an analysis of Apollonius Dyscolus's description of commands, it has been shown above, first, that temporal categories are unsatisfactory for analysis of commands. As McKay says, "Time is even less important in the imperative than in other moods; logically it cannot be past or present, and it makes no difference to the aspect whether immediate or distant future, or actual or general time is implied" ("Aspect," 207; cf. Blass, 194, who, though he distinguishes between general and individual cases, admits there are many exceptions [194-96]). Second, it has been shown that the aspectual semantic system defined above (see esp. chapts. 2 and 4) is confirmed as well for commands, and thus it appears that the general tense usage of the command is consistent from classical through to hellenistic Greek (see McKay, "Aspect," esp. 201; Blass/Debrunner, ¶ 387; Robertson, 946; contra Bakker, *Imperative*, esp. 85). The Aorist is the less heavily marked form and normally used when a command is made, treating it as a complete process, with the negated Aorist Subjunctive used for prohibitions when the process is treated as a whole; and the Present is the more heavily marked Imperative and used when the speaker wishes to in some way specify this command, treating it as in progress, or to deny this process as being in progress. On this basis the artificial distinction between a general and a specific command is circumvented. Both tenses may be used for each, as examples below indicate. That "aspect" within context is the deciding factor has been confirmed by Voelz (*Use*, 49-54) also, when he argues that verbal objects; the destinations of verbs of motion; limitations; and adverbs, conjunctions, and particles do not have a bearing upon command usage. (See McKay, "Aspect," 203-04, 206-07, 216-17, whose article is the most thorough treatment of commands in the Greek of the NT; also Bakker, *Imperative*, 78-87; W. Martin, "1 Cor 11:2-16"; Heidt, "Translating," 253-56, who although his definition of the tenses is incorrect is concerned to show their difference when translating; Morrice, "Translating," 131-34; Boyer, "Classification of Imperatives.")

(2) Several of the issues still raised in NT grammars are issues that have been discussed thoroughly many years previously, and the value of many of these studies has only been enhanced by later research. For example, of the common assertion that the Present Imperative exhorts continuing action and the Aorist Imperative beginning action, Donovan, followed by others such as Naylor and consummated in the extensive lists of Poutsma, Louw and Bakker, shows clearly that such is not the case. Thus it is of concern when Turner (*Syntax*, 74-75) repeats the accepted axiom, and refers nowhere in his work to

the articles by Donovan, Naylor, Poutsma or Louw. Turner admits that e.g. 2 Cor 13:11-12 does not conform, but he uses this to draw the following conclusion: "The problem of the *Aktionsarten* of the tenses is by no means solved as yet for the NT, and possibly John gives a clue when he seems to vary the tense according to the verb he is using. Why is the same prohibition, however, μὴ ὀμόσῃς in Matt 5:36 and μὴ ὀμνύετε in Jas 5:12?" (75; cf. also Winer, 393-95, although he must admit that "many cases" depend "entirely on the writer's preference" [395]; Moulton, 122-26; Moule, 135-36; Blass/Debrunner, ¶¶ 336-37, although Blass/Debrunner/Rehkopf [¶¶ 335(2), 336(3)] are more cautious). Responding to those who indicate that μή + Present Imperative means "stop doing something already being done," Boyer has calculated that 100 of the 174 uses of this construction in the NT give no indication of time. Further, 32 examples illustrate that previous action is denied in context, and only 38 examples have probable or explicit reference to previous action ("Classification of Imperatives," esp. 43-44). Verbal aspect is able to explain this usage. The rest of this section, therefore, treats specific examples in the NT, including Imperative and negated Aorist Subjunctive forms. Various substitutes for commands and prohibitions--e.g. Participle, Future--are treated under their proper formal category where pertinent (see e.g. Robertson, 942-46; and Zilliacus, "Notes," for classical Greek).

Matt 2:20, where the angel tells Joseph to get up (ἐγερθείς), take (παράλαβε) the child and πορεύου (go) into Israel, followed by the Perfect to explain why: those seeking the child τεθνήκασιν (are dead). Matt 25:9: the foolish maidens are told to go (πορεύεσθε) and buy (ἀγοράσατε) their own oil. The Present Imperative may be used to stress the urgency of the situation or the hardship the maidens face by being compelled to go, or, with a twist of irony, to draw attention to the wise maidens' knowledge that to leave is to risk the bridegroom coming. Verbs of motion are often used at the beginning of a commanding sequence. McKay ("Aspect," 213) claims that the Present may be transitional, but this is unlikely, since imperfective verbs of motion may be found with destinations stated: Acts 22:10; Luke 5:24 (see Blass/Debrunner, ¶ 336[1]; cf. Epict. 1.25.10: πορεύου πρὸς τὸν Ἀχιλλέα καὶ ἀπόσπασον τὴν Βρισηίδα [go to A. and drag away B.]). The more heavily marked form appears to serve as a comprehensive term or to provide the motivating force for the individual complete processes referred to. See e.g. Mark 14:13: ὑπάγετε . . . ἀκολουθήσατε αὐτῷ (go . . . follow him), where the objective nature of the action is clearly not referred to by the verb.

John 1:46: Philip tells Nathaniel: ἔρχου καὶ ἴδε (come and see), with the Present used of action not yet begun. Turner (*Syntax*, 75) opposes Matt 6:10 (ἐλθέτω ἡ βασιλεία σου) to the Johannine usage, contrasting "the Kingdom being present already as a grain of seed" with "continue to come." This is unnecessary theologizing. Since the verbs in John are connected with καί, possibly the first "contains the condition or supposition upon which the action indicated by the second will take place" (Winer, 391). Cf. John 7:52: ἐραύνησον καὶ ἴδε (search and see).

Several grammarians (e.g. Robertson, 948-49; Blass/Debrunner, ¶ 387[1, 2]; Boyer, "Classification of Imperatives," 38-40) note the possible conditional use of the Imperative: e.g. Eph 4:26: ὀργίζεσθε καὶ μὴ ἁμαρτάνετε (be angry and do not sin), or as Winer glosses it: "if ye are angry, do not sin, do not fall into sin"; John 2:19: λύσατε τὸν ναὸν τοῦτον καὶ ἐν τρισὶν ἡμέραις ἐγερῶ αὐτόν (destroy this temple and in three days I will raise it) (Barrett, *John*, 199; Morris, *John*, 199); 2 Cor 12:16. First, Dodd (*Interpretation*, 302 n. 1), for example, says that an Imperative in the protasis of a conditional is a "well-known Hebrew idiom" (cf. Beyer,

Syntax, 252), but it has approximate parallels in extra-biblical Greek: e.g. D. 18.112: εἰ δέ φησιν οὗτος, δειξάτω, κἀγὼ στέρξω καὶ σιωπήσομαι (if he speaks, let him prove it, and I will be satisified and be silent; see Rijksbaron, 42-43). Second, it is not surprising to find the Imperative syntactically linked to the Future Indicative (John 2:19), on the basis of their semantic features and pragmatic implicatures (see chapt. 9). Third, there is potential for confusion if it is said that the Imperative is anything other than an Imperative. Contextually the first verb may express a condition or supposition for the second process, but formally the Imperative is nothing but an Imperative and its [+direction] semantic force is present. Thus the question of usage is a pragmatic and not a grammatical one. The opposite sequence is found in the following, where the verb of motion follows another command: Luke 5:24: the paralytic is told ἔγειρε (get up), take (ἄρας) your bed and πορεύου (go) home; Luke 18:22: the rich ruler is told πώλησον (sell) and διάδος (give away), and when this is done then ἀκολούθει (follow) him; Matt 16:24: the disciples are told by Jesus that if someone wants to follow him, ἀπαρνησάσθω ἑαυτὸν καὶ ἀράτω τὸν σταυρὸν αὐτοῦ καὶ ἀκολουθείτω μοι (let him deny himself and take up his cross and follow me). Cf. Acts 22:10: Jesus told Paul ἀναστὰς πορεύου (get up and go) into Damascus. Here the Present verb emphasizes what should get underway, contra Turner who says "the rule demands aor." (*Syntax*, 75). But his citation of Matt 8:9 (πορεύθητι, καὶ πορεύεται [go and he goes]) as correct is difficult in light of v 9b: ἔρχου, καὶ ἔρχεται . . . ποίησον τοῦτο, καὶ ποιεῖ (come and he comes . . . do this and he does it).

Matt 5:24: Jesus' listeners who may have been angry with others are told that they should leave (ἄφες) their gift, go (ὕπαγε), be reconciled (διαλλάγηθι) to their brother, and then come (ἐλθών) and offer (πρόσφερε) their gift. A clear sequence of events is established, but this is on the basis of not the verb tenses but the narrative order (contra Turner, *Syntax*, 75; *Insights*, 30, who translates this verse: "First be reconciled once and for all [aorist] to your brother, and then come and offer as many gifts as you like [present]"). The first Aorist provides a pivoting point in the action, turning it from the altar. The Present then impels motion toward the new goal of being reconciled before one is able to offer the gift. The second Present Imperative reiterates the Present Subjunctive in the protasis of v 23, focusing upon the necessity of a pure life before participating in this sacramental act. Cf. Matt 8:4, where the Aorist Imperative is used, since here the focus is not on the sacrifice but, first, seeing that no one is told, and then going to show the priest.

Matt 5:36: μήτε ἐν τῇ κεφαλῇ σου ὀμόσῃς (don't swear on your head); Jas 5:12: μὴ ὀμνύετε (don't swear). James appears to be a verbal echo of the words of Jesus. Not only does this indicate the subjective aspectual nature of verbal choice in Greek, but it shows how this factor helps to mould context. In Matt 5:33-37 all the commands use the Aorist, treating them as complete processes, while in Jas 5:7ff. the Aorist predominates as well, until v 12. The author says πρὸ πάντων (above all), followed by the Present Imperative, with an extended modifying phrase.

Matt 5:39-42; Luke 6:29-30: in Matthew Jesus is recorded as saying that whoever strikes (ῥαπίζει), στρέψον (turn) to him the other cheek; to the one who wants (τῷ θέλοντι) to sue and take your coat, ἄφες (give) to him; and whoever will force (ἀγγαρεύσει) you one mile, ὕπαγε (go) two; to the one who asks (τῷ αἰτοῦντι) δός (give); and to the one who wants (τὸν θέλοντα), μὴ ἀποστραφῇς (don't deny). In Luke Jesus is recorded as saying to the one who strikes (τῷ τύπτοντι) you, πάρεχε (give) the other cheek, and from the one who asks (τοῦ αἴροντος) μὴ κωλύσῃς (don't hold back), to everyone who asks (αἰτοῦντι) δίδου (give), and from the one who asks (τοῦ αἴροντος) μὴ ἀπαίτει (don't demand) in return. There is a conscious structure to these commands in the Gospels. In all the pairs in Matthew the one who instigates the process is referred to with the Present, except in Matt 5:42 with the Future. Every response uses the Aorist except in v 42 with the Present. The contrast for Matthew therefore is between a more heavily marked aspect in the request and a less heavily marked aspect in the response. In Luke every request is in the Present, as are the responses except in 6:29 with the negated Aorist Subjunctive. Turner explains the difference between δός and δίδου as the difference between a "definite occasion and person," and "anyone who asks" (*Syntax*, 76). This may be true, but it is not because of the verb tenses but because of other contextual indicators, such as the conditional-like protasis and use of the modifier παντί. More likely is the difference between seeing giving as a complete process and as a process in progress. Turner uses his same logic to explain καταμάθετε (consider) in Matt 6:28 as "a command now, once and for all, to look at the lilies, probably during a walk in the fields" (76). Cf. Jas 5:7-8: μακροθυμήσατε . . . ἕως τῆς παρουσίας τοῦ κυρίου (be patient until the coming of the lord). . . . μακροθυμήσατε καὶ ὑμεῖς, στηρίξατε τὰς καρδίας ὑμῶν (be patient, strengthen your hearts), where such reasoning makes nonsense of the verse. The Aorist grammaticalizes reference to the process as a whole, and thus is appropriate for an extended length of time. (Turner [77] lists the following as Aorists used for precepts referring to the lord's coming: Matt 5:39; 6:6; 1 Tim 6:12, 14, 20; 2 Tim 4:2, 5; 1:14; 2:2, 3, 15; 1 Pet 1:13, 17, 22; 2:17; 5:2; 1 John 5:21.) See also Rev 2:25: πλὴν ὃ ἔχετε κρατήσατε ἄχρι[ς] οὗ ἂν ἥξω (therefore what you have hold onto until when I might come); 2 Thess 2:15: στήκετε, καὶ κρατεῖτε τὰς παραδόσεις (stand and grasp the traditions).

Matt 6:25-34: Jesus is reported to have told his listeners μὴ μεριμνᾶτε (don't trouble yourselves) over the necessities of life. Then he asks them to consider several examples, using the Aorist Imperative: ἐμβλέψατε (look at) the birds (v 26); καταμάθετε (consider) the flowers (v 27), each followed with a question regarding God's nature. In v 31 he repeats the command not to be concerned (μὴ . . . μεριμνήσητε) about what they might eat, drink or wear (all Aorist Subjunctives), possibly using the Aorist in parallel with the previous Aorists, although more likely as a summary statement and turning point for the words that follow. One should not be troubled, for their heavenly father knows (οἶδεν) that they need (χρῄζετε) all these things (v 32). ζητεῖτε (seek) first the kingdom of God and they will be given to you (v 33). He closes with the Aorist Subjunctive again (μὴ . . . μεριμνήσητε) (v 34). Whereas worrying and seeking may be equally time-consuming Jesus seems to be saying here that rather than do the former (grammatically referred to with the less heavily marked Aorist used of a complete process), they are directed to do the latter (with the more heavily marked Present). All this is predicated upon the father knowing what they need, with the most heavily marked Perfect Indicative used. Cf. Luke 12:29-32, which uses the same essential argument, except that Luke reveals a greater concern for worrying, in v 29 telling his readers μὴ ζητεῖτε (don't seek) and μὴ μετεωρίζεσθε (don't worry), with the Present Imperative.

Mark 1:15: it is theologically tendentious to understand μετανοεῖτε καὶ πιστεύετε (repent and believe) as in any sense objectively continuous, since the scheme occurs at the beginning of Jesus' ministry, perhaps to highlight his call throughout it. Cf. Mark 5:36, where Jesus tells Jairus μὴ φοβοῦ, μόνον πίστευε (don't fear, only believe), with Luke 8:50, where the Aorist Imperative πίστευσον is used. This alteration appears to be a further proof of the subjective nature of verbal aspect, since the same process may be grammatically described with contrasting verb tenses (contra Turner, *Syntax*, 75). Cf. Mark 6:50; Matt 14:27; John 6:20, where Jesus commands his disciples μὴ φοβεῖσθε (don't be fearing), where contextual indicators suggest that the disciples are already frightened (the Aorist could have been used, except that in each instance these are Jesus' first words to his disciples, clearly semantically marked). Matt 1:20: the angel tells Joseph μὴ φοβηθῇς (don't fear) to take Mary as his wife. Verse 19 shows Joseph was already afraid. Similar marked usage is clear in Luke 1:13, 30; 2:10, where the words open an angelic communication. Cf. Matt 10:26-31, where the initial negated Aorist Subjunctive, possibly "resumptive, summing up the lesson of the preceding section, and appropriately making this a total prohibition" (McKay, "Aspect," 218), is followed by three Present Imperatives of φοβέω, with the first and last forming an inclusio which moves from fearing of men and their actions on a human sphere to fearing in relation to God; Acts 18:9: μὴ φοβοῦ, ἀλλὰ λάλει καὶ μὴ σιωπήσῃς (don't fear, but speak and don't be silent), where both sides of the issue are referred to. Paul is not to fear but speak. Unfortunately Louw puts this contrast in temporally-based terms: "The Jews opposed Paul who was preaching that Jesus was the Christ. μὴ φοβοῦ refers to Paul's fear: 'Cease to fear, for I am with you and no man shall harm you.' Following the assurance, a command (positive and negative) is given: μὴ σιωπήσῃς (a thing which he has not yet done) i.e.: 'Fear no more, but keep on speaking (λάλει) and do not hold your peace' (in future)" ("Prohibitions," 53).

Mark 4:39: Jesus is recorded telling the sea: σιώπα, πεφίμωσο (be silent, be still). The use of Present and Perfect Imperatives appears self-conscious, since this is one of the few non-formulaic uses of the Perfect Imperative in the NT. The reported results speak for themselves. Mark 14:34; and Matt 26:38: μείνατε ὧδε καὶ γρηγορεῖτε μετ᾽ ἐμοῦ (remain here and watch with me). The contrasting tense usage illustrates the aspectual difference. Jesus surely does not mean for the disciples to remain momentarily but to remain and watch, with the stress being laid upon their watching. Cf. Mark 14:42: ἐγείρεσθε ἄγωμεν (get up and let's go), where the Present Imperative is used of a single event (cf. Blass/Debrunner/Rehkopf, ¶ 336[3], who cite examples of the Present Imperative for certain single events).

Luke 3:11: ὁ ἔχων δύο χιτῶνας μεταδότω τῷ μὴ ἔχοντι, καὶ ὁ ἔχων βρώματα ὁμοίως ποιείτω (let the one who has two chitons share with one who does not have, and one who has food let him do likewise). This passage argues for an aspectual distinction between the Aorist and Present Imperative not formulated around criteria of objective kind of action or temporal relation. The progression in the author's mind proceeds from an easy to a more difficult case, from simply sharing one of two chitons (one would be sufficient anyway), to a situation where something more important and more difficult to judge is at stake, food. The more heavily marked aspect is used for the more difficult decision (contra Martin, "1 Cor 11:2-16," 236, who makes a category mistake, claiming that for a "specific article [one coat] . . . we find the aorist . . . but for a recurring action in a possible everyday situation, the present imperative [ποιείτω "let him do"] is used").

Luke 9:23: εἴ τις θέλει ὀπίσω μου ἔρχεσθαι, ἀρνησάσθω ἑαυτὸν καὶ ἀράτω τὸν σταυρὸν αὐτοῦ καθ᾽ ἡμέραν, καὶ ἀκολουθείτω μοι (if someone wants to come after me, let him deny himself and take up his cross each day, and follow me), where the Aorist Imperative is used to refer to the daily taking up of the cross as a complete event, but where more importantly the use of imperfective aspect draws attention to the process of going and following Jesus (contra Turner, *Syntax*, 76, who claims self-denial is a "once and for all" decision, but following is continuous). Mark 8:34 has ἀκολουθεῖν for ἔρχεσθαι; Matt 16:24, by contrast, has the Aorist ἐλθεῖν, and both exclude καθ᾽ ἡμέραν. The use of the tenses in this way reinforces their aspectual and non-temporal nature. Cf. Matt 8:21-22: a follower reportedly says to Jesus: ἐπίτρεψόν μοι πρῶτον ἀπελθεῖν καὶ θάψαι τὸν πατέρα μου (permit me first to go and bury my father), all with the Aorist, but Jesus says, ἀκολούθει μοι, καὶ ἄφες τοὺς νεκροὺς θάψαι τοὺς ἑαυτῶν νεκρούς (follow me, and let the dead bury their own dead), with the emphatic Present Imperative in contrast to the surrounding Aorists. Acts 12:8: the angel tells Peter, ζῶσαι καὶ ὑπόδησαι (dress and tie) your shoes. When he had done (ἐποίησεν) this, the angel said (λέγει), περιβαλοῦ (put on your cloak) and ἀκολούθει (follow me) me. And he went out (ἐξελθών) and followed (ἠκολούθει). The historic Present singles out the angel's following words as significant. There is a possible verbal allusion here to the original call of Jesus to his disciples.

Luke 10:35-37: the innkeeper is told by the Samaritan ἐπιμελήθητι (take care) of the injured man until he return. In applying the story to his listeners, Jesus tells them πορεύου καὶ σὺ ποίει ὁμοίως (go and do likewise).

Luke 12:19: the rich man in thinking he has so much says ἀναπαύου, φάγε, πίε, εὐφραίνου (rest, eat, drink, celebrate). Whereas it is difficult to understand the reason for the alteration in verbal aspect, their spheres of reference seem to be identical.

Luke 14:17, 21, 23: the initial Present Imperative ἔρχεσθε (come) is followed by Aorists in the following commands: ἔξελθε (go out), εἰσάγαγε (bring in), ἔξελθε, ἀνάγκασον (urge).

Luke 15:22-23: the forgiving father tells his servants immediately ἐξενέγκατε (bring out) a robe and ἐνδύσατε (clothe) his son, and δότε (put) a ring on his finger and φέρετε (bring) the fatted calf, and θύσατε (kill) it, concluded with a hortatory Subjunctive. Not only do these verses argue against a stereotyped use of φέρετε (contra Turner, *Syntax*, 75), but they confirm an aspectual distinction between the forms of the verb. This is reinforced in the following section vv 25ff., where the object of discussion is the fatted calf that the father has killed for the son.

Luke 17:8: Moule (135) claims that these verses conform to the rule of Imperative usage, with ἑτοίμασον (prepare) as specific and διακόνει (serve) as continued action. This may be an accurate characterization of the particular processes but it does not provide a basis for generalizing on tense usage, as the following clauses attest: ἕως φάγω καὶ πίω (while I might eat and drink). The Present Imperative of supposed continued action appears to overlap exactly with the action characterized by the two Aorist Subjunctives for eating and drinking. Thus a tense form does not refer in and of itself to the objective nature of a process but grammaticalizes the speaker's conception.

Luke 23:18, 21: the crowd yells αἶρε (take) Jesus, but ἀπόλυσον (release) Barabbas. No passage could be clearer in illustrating self-conscious aspectual contrast and choice, since both verbs are found in their Imperative forms in both tenses in the NT. The crowd's sympathies are clear: they want Jesus taken away! And they want Barabbas released. (Cf. also Acts 21:36; 22:22; 21:28.) The crowd's demand is confirmed in v 21, when it demands σταύρου, σταύρου αὐτόν (crucify, crucify him), repeating the Present command; cf. Mark 15:13: σταύρωσον αὐτόν (crucify him); Matt 27:23: σταυρωθήτω (let him be crucified). As McKay says, "as Luke makes more of Pilate's reluctance to order the execution his imperfective better suits the dramatic situation (*go on with what you should be doing and stop obstructing*), and its effect is heightened by the repetition." He continues, however, "The aorist would have been appropriate enough, even if in this context it seemed stylistically weaker: in the context of Mark's narrative there is less to choose between the two aspects. In the more indirect approach of Matt 27:22 . . . there seems to be no reason to signal anything but the complete action" ("Aspect," 212; cf. Bakker, *Imperative*, 83, who stresses the emotion).

John 2:5-8: amidst a series of Aorist Imperatives--ποιήσατε (do); γεμίσατε (fill), ἀντλήσατε (draw)--there appears the Present φέρετε. The perfective commands chronicle the sequence of complete events leading up to the presenting of the wine steward with the new wine (contra Robertson, 855, although he recognizes that the Present has semantic significance).

John 3:7: μὴ θαυμάσῃς ὅτι εἶπόν σοι (don't marvel that I said to you), where the disciples are already marvelling. Cf. Mark 1:44: ὅρα μηδενὶ μηδὲν εἴπῃς, ἀλλὰ ὕπαγε (see that you say nothing to no one, but go). John 15:4: μείνατε ἐν ἐμοί (remain in me); cf. 1 John 2:28: μένετε ἐν αὐτῷ (remain in him), where the same lexical item refers to the same objective action in similar contexts but with differing verbal aspects (contra Morrice, "Translating," 130, who claims the distinction in the tenses is disregarded in the Johannine examples).

John 20:17: the accepted interpretation of this clause, μή μου ἅπτου, is that Jesus says to Mary Magdalene "don't keep on touching me" (Roby, "Imperative," 229: "Do not keep clinging to me, i.e. you need not cling to me, for I have not yet ascended to my father, i.e. I am still here on earth and the time for ascension is not yet come." See also Brown, *John*, 2.992; Barrett, *John*, 565-66; Morris, *John*, 840). This interpretation is probably dictated in part by reference to Matt 28:9, which says that the women grasped Jesus' feet, and the traditional interpretation of the Present prohibition as referring to a durative event. The difficulty is that whereas in this verse Jesus says that Mary should not touch him because he has not "ascended" to the father, in John 20:27 Jesus instructs Thomas to put his finger in his hands and side, although he does not yet appear to have ascended. While it is certain that the prohibition itself need not refer to an ongoing event, the parallel makes it at least plausible, although that cannot be established grammatically in this passage (Fowler ["Meaning," 16-25] argues along literary grounds for the older rendering, "touch me not"). A recent proposal by McGehee warranting consideration is that the following γάρ clause is not causal but an anticipatory conjunction meaning "since," dependent not on the prohibition but on the following command. Besides the evidence McGehee cites--that no satisfactory explanation of the γάρ clause as it stands has been proposed, that many solutions are overly complex (e.g. Brown's equation of the resurrection with the ascension), and that the usual understanding of the γάρ clause cannot be understood literally ("Reading," 299-302)--a fourth factor is the use of verbal aspect. Jesus is reported to say οὔπω . . . ἀναβέβηκα (I have not yet reached a state of ascension) but tell the disciples that ἀναβαίνω (I am in progress ascending). The implied contrast between seeing the process as a state of affairs not yet attained and the process as in progress further links the two clauses, thus leaving the prohibition standing on its own.

Paul uses the negated Present Imperative frequently in his epistles (Moulton, 125; followed by Voelz, *Use*, 25; Turner, *Syntax*, 77). Grammarians often posit that he is commanding his readers not to continue their practice. This may be the case, but this cannot be established grammatically, only contextually. The grammatical analysis is that Paul uses the more heavily marked form. The reasons for this may vary but one seems to be to impress upon his readers the urgency of the situation and his strong desire that they take his advice. As Moulton (126) says, "What has been said will make it clear that such commands were very practical indeed,--that the apostles were not tilting at windmills, but uttering urgent warnings against sins which were sure to reappear in the Christian community, or were as yet only imperfectly expelled." For example, Rom 6:12-13: Paul says μή . . . βασιλευέτω ἡ ἁμαρτία (let not sin reign) in your mortal bodies, μηδὲ παριστάνετε (do not offer) your members as instruments of unrighteousness, but παραστήσατε (offer) yourselves to God. Although it is possible that the Romans were presently slaves to sin and Paul is calling for them to start offering themselves to God, this is a theological and not a grammatical point. Rather Paul tells the Romans not to be involved in the events that cause sin to reign (whenever they may be confronted), using the more heavily marked Present, and reiterates what they already know (offer yourselves to God), using the less heavily marked Aorist. Eph 5:18: μὴ μεθύσκεσθε οἴνῳ (don't be drunk with wine), where the author contrasts this with πληροῦσθε ἐν πνεύματι (be filled in the spirit). A temporal scheme makes little sense of this marked contrast between depictions of ways of Christian life. Cf. Col 3:9: μὴ ψεύδεσθε (don't lie).

1 Cor 7:9, 11: Paul says that if they are not able to exercise self control γαμησάτωσαν (let them marry), but if a woman might be separated, μενέτω (let her remain) unmarried or καταλλαγήτω (let her be reconciled) to her husband. As the logical results of conditional clauses, these verbs are clearly timeless, the difference lying in their verbal aspect. The traditional definition is of καταλλαγήτω as punctiliar or momentary (see Morris, *Apostolic Preaching* , 232), but it may also refer to the process of laying aside of anger and persuading the antagonistic party to do the same (Rom 5:9-11; 2 Cor 5:18-20) (see Marshall, "Meaning," 121; cf. Bruce, *Corinthians*, 210; Schlier, *Römerbrief*, 156). Thus the distinction in this verse is not between an abiding state and a point of transformation, even if characterizing the process in itself. The distinction is between one being enjoined to be in progress staying single, unless one undertakes to be reconciled with one's mate. Paul apparently sees remaining single as the more pressing problem.

1 Cor 7:21: δοῦλος ἐκλήθης; μή σοι μελέτω· ἀλλ' εἰ καὶ δύνασαι ἐλεύθερος γενέσθαι, μᾶλλον χρῆσαι. This verse has been variously interpreted, with the major views and opinions summarized well in Bartchy's recent monograph (*Slavery*, esp. 6-7, for a list of exponents of the two major positions). The two major opinions have traditionally been to translate it "were you called as a slave? Don't let it bother you; but although you are able to become free, rather make use of your slavery," supplying a reference to slavery (e.g. Barrett, *First Corinthians*, 170-71); or to translate it "were you called as a slave? Don't let it bother you; but if indeed you are able to become free, rather make use of your freedom," supplying a reference to freedom (most grammarians, including Turner [*Syntax*, 76], Moule [167 n. 3], Moulton [174], Thrall [*Particles*, 81], and Robertson/Plummer [*First Corinthians*, 147]). Three factors appear to be important for making a decision. (1) The change in verbal aspect. Turner, among others, says, "important for exegesis is the aor. imper. in 1 Cor 7:21 μᾶλλον χρῆσαι; the Corinthian Christians are urged to make use once and for all of the opportunity to be free; only with a pres. imper. ought the interpretation to be *use your present state* to the glory of God." This grammatical analysis fails on two counts: it is a misrepresentation of the semantics of the individual verb tenses, and a misrepresentation of their temporal reference. (2) The strength of the word group ἀλλ' εἰ καί. It may be interpreted either as an adversative-concessive ("but even though") or as a strengthened adversative ("but if indeed"). (3) The word to be supplied in v 21c. An extension of the second alternative, argued for by Bartchy, is to supply the words "God's calling" as the object of the verb χράομαι, which he interprets to mean "to live according to/to keep [the laws of God]/to follow [a way of life]" (179). The use of the verb tenses alone will not prove which side is correct in this instance. Context is important, and here Bartchy must be considered on the issue of manumission. But several grammatical issues are important. First, the Present Imperative μελέτω must receive emphasis over the Aorist Imperative in this verse. Paul's overriding concern appears to be to "Stop being concerned about [being a slave]" (Bartchy [175] notes the emphatic force of the

Present Imperative).[22] Paul also uses the Present Indicative δύνασαι, which reinforces ἀλλ' εἰ καί as a strong adversative. Manumission did not reside with the slave but with the owner and the use of the Present seems to stress that the opportunity for freedom must be seized upon when it comes. Second, those who argue that the word "in slavery" be supplied must not only take εἰ καί as fully concessive but must minimize the adversative force of ἀλλά. There is also a misunderstanding of εἰ καί as concessive: it is an extension of the conditional εἰ (1 Cor 4:7; 7:11-12; 7:27-28; 2 Cor 4:2-3; 7:8b-9; 11:5-6), not necessarily a negation of it (as in 2 Cor 4:16; 7:8a; 7:8c; 12:11). There are no instances of concessive εἰ καί in 1 Corinthians (see Bartchy, 178; also Thrall, *Particles*, 79-81; Denniston, *Particles*, 3-11, 303). Thus 1 Cor 7:21 should probably be rendered with Bartchy, "Were you a slave when you were called? Don't worry about it. But if, indeed, you become manumitted, by all means [as a freedman] live according to God's calling" (183; cf. Moulton/Howard, 165).

1 Cor 7:36: εἰ δέ τις ἀσχημονεῖν ἐπὶ τὴν παρθένον αὐτοῦ νομίζει ἐὰν ἦ ὑπέρακμος, καὶ οὕτως ὀφείλει γίνεσθαι, ὃ θέλει ποιείτω (if someone thinks to behave improperly toward his virgin, if she might be of age, and thus he is obligated to, let him do what he wants), where Paul is not necessarily permitting someone to continue what he is already doing, but emphasizing the course of events that should come about if the protasis is fulfilled (note two following Present verbs).

1 Cor 11:6: εἰ γὰρ οὐ κατακαλύπτεται γυνή, καὶ κειράσθω· εἰ δὲ αἰσχρὸν γυναικὶ τὸ κείρασθαι ἢ ξυρᾶσθαι, κατακαλυπτέσθω (for if a woman is not in the progress of being covered, indeed let her be shorn; but if it is shameful for a woman to be shaved or shorn, let her be covered). Martin interprets this such that the Aorist Imperative has "cessative force, referring to a particular situation," and the Present Imperative refers to "a non-terminative, inchoative action" ("1 Cor 11:2-16," 239). But this is reminiscent of the contrast between punctiliar and durative action. The use of the aspectual contrast here places emphasis upon the woman being covered. The structure forms an inclusio, in which the Present verb reinforces the desired condition of the woman being covered, with the Aorist used of the alternative not to be sought.

2 Cor 13:11-12: Paul tells his fellow Christians χαίρετε, καταρτίζεσθε, παρακαλεῖσθε, τὸ αὐτὸ φρονεῖτε, εἰρηνεύετε . . . ἀσπάσασθε ἀλλήλους ἐν ἁγίῳ φιλήματι (rejoice, be perfect, be comforted, think the same thing, be peaceful . . . greet each other with a holy kiss). Turner argues that "we find the aor. ἀσπάσασθε without being aware of anything significant in the change" (*Syntax*, 75). He overlooks that the more heavily marked Present Imperatives, standing unsupported in a concluding statement after a forceful letter, are followed by the Aorist, which is then elucidated by the Present Indicative: ἀσπάζονται ὑμᾶς οἱ ἅγιοι πάντες (for all the saints greet you). Cf. Rom 16:3-16, where in Paul's list of greetings each is begun with the Aorist Imperative, including v 16a with instructions to greet each other with a holy kiss. He then closes with a clause using the Present Indicative ἀσπάζονται. Similar patterns of closing epistles are found in 1 Cor 16:19-20; Phil 4:21-22; 1 Thess 5:26; 2 Tim 4:21; Titus 3:15; Phlm 23; Heb 13:24; 1 Pet 5:14; 2 John 13. 3 John 15 closes with ἀσπάζου τοὺς φίλους κατ' ὄνομα (greet the friends by name), where it may be distributive but is more likely parallel with the preceding phrase ἀσπάζονταί σε οἱ φίλοι (the friends greet you). (Similar patterns of closing are found in personal letters: P.Oxy. 1296 [3d cent. A.D.]; P.Oxy. 1676 [3d cent. A.D.]; BGU 385 [2d/3d cent. A.D.];

---

[22]Cf. 1 Tim 4:14, where in the context of 1 Tim 4:11ff., the author, using a series of Present Imperatives instructs Timothy to proclaim and teach, let no one look down on his youth, pay attention to his work and μὴ ἀμέλει (disregard not) the charismata among you. Moulton (125) poses the question: "But does μὴ ἀμέλει in 1 Tim 4:14 require us to believe that Timothy was 'neglecting' his 'charism' . . . ?" The answer is no, as it is for 1 Tim 5:22, where Timothy is directed μηδενὶ ἐπιτίθει and μηδὲ κοινώνει (don't lay hands on and don't have fellowship). Moulton himself invents explanations to avoid the difficulty. Cf. BGU 624.12, 17 (A.D. 184-305): μὴ ἀμελήσῃς . . . μὴ ἀμέλει (don't be negligent/unconcerned); BGU 822.3 (2d/3d cent. A.D.): μὴ μελησάτω σοι (let it not be of concern to you).

P.Lond. 951 verso [3d cent. A.D.]; PSI 299 [3d cent. A.D.]; P.Merton 83 [2d cent. A.D.]; SB 7572 [2d cent. A.D.]; SB 6823 [c. A.D. 40].)

Eph 6:10-20: the author enjoins his readers ἐνδυναμοῦσθε (empower) themselves in the lord and his strength, using the Present Imperative. Then he specifies what this entails: ἐνδύσασθε (put on) the armour of God to stand against the devil (v 11); ἀναλάβετε (take on) the armour of God to stand in the day of evil (v 13), followed by a number of Aorist Participles; and δέξασθε (receive) the helmet of salvation (v 17). See Jas 5:13-14: two Present Imperatives are followed by two Aorist Imperatives.

1 Tim 6:11-12: the author commands the man of God, φεῦγε (flee) false teachings (anaphoric reference), but δίωκε (pursue) righteousness, etc. ἀγωνίζου (agonize) over the good works of faith, ἐπιλαβοῦ (put on) eternal life. The perfective aspect is used here not as the goal of these actions but as the fundamental or underlying "substance of the striving" (Winer, 392).

2 Tim 2:14-16: ταῦτα ὑπομίμνῃσκε, διαμαρτυρόμενος ἐνώπιον τοῦ θεοῦ μὴ λογομαχεῖν, ἐπ᾽ οὐδὲν χρήσιμον, ἐπὶ καταστροφῇ τῶν ἀκουόντων. σπούδασον σεαυτὸν δόκιμον παραστῆσαι τῷ θεῷ, ἐργάτην ἀνεπαίσχυντον, ὀρθοτομοῦντα τὸν λόγον τῆς ἀληθείας . τὰς δὲ βεβήλους κενοφωνίας περιΐστασο (remember these things, bearing witness before God not to fight for the profit of none, for a catastrophe of hearers. Desire to establish yourself as respectful to God, a workman without shame, dividing the word of truth. And avoid godless chatter). Voelz says that the alteration of the tenses in this passage is arbitrary (*Use*, 24). In light of his later admission, following Poutsma, that there are several factors to consider, many of which are not understood by later interpreters, this is presumptuous. Also, he is judging their arbitrariness according to the standard definition of *Aktionsart*. But his solution that the Present Imperative depicts connection and the Aorist the abstract fact provides no way forward. The second sentence by his criteria should have the Present Participle because it is a personal application. Contextually, ταῦτα refers anaphorically to vv 11-13, with the Present Imperative stressing their importance in bearing witness before God to avoid those things that are worthless and lead to disaster. The Present Imperative is used again in v 16 in this same way, while the Aorist Imperative is used for the positive command.

Phlm 17, 22: Paul uses the Aorist προσλαβοῦ (receive) in the apodosis of a I.a. conditional as the logical outcome of his protasis, that if Philemon has fellowship with him (ἔχεις), he will receive Onesimus. In v 22, Paul uses the Present in instructing Philemon: ἑτοίμαζέ μοι ξενίαν (prepare for me a room). Moule has difficulty understanding why the Present is used here (135). Throughout Paul's letter he has used a subtle argumentation in writing to Philemon, showing that in fact Philemon owes his very (Christian) life to Paul, and that Paul has refrained from collecting on this debt. He uses this as leverage in requesting Onesimus's safe return to Philemon. What sort of a check can Paul have? He himself hopes (ἐλπίζω) to return.

Jas 1:5-7: if someone lacks wisdom, αἰτείτω (let him ask) from God. αἰτείτω (let him ask) in faith, for μή . . . οἰέσθω ὁ ἄνθρωπος ἐκεῖνος (let not that man think) that he will receive if he is double-minded. The Present Imperative as the apodosis of the conditional is linked by lexeme to directives regarding a general situation.

1 Pet 1:13-4:11: it is often noted by scholars that this section is overloaded with Aorist Imperatives. On the basis of what he perceives to be a pronounced shift from the Aorist Imperatives of 1:13-4:11 to the Present Imperatives of 4:12ff. Voelz argues for his theory of the "connectedness" of the Present over the "absolute" emphasis of the Aorist Imperative (*Use*, esp. 108). As seen elsewhere, however, this theory of verbal usage cannot stand. Whatever may be true of the origin of this section (i.e. that it is a paschal liturgy [Cross, *1 Peter*], or a baptismal sermon or liturgy [Beare, *Peter*, 6ff.], comment must be made on the use of the verb tenses. First, it is more an appearance than a reality that this section is so heavily dominated by one particular verb tense. Virtually every Mood and tense is found. Considering the recognizable skill of the writer of the epistle, it would be unlikely that his manipulation of tenses was without conscious reason. Second, an explanation for the apparently abundant use of the Aorist Imperative may be found in the nature of his admonitions. In 1:13-4:11 the writer is making general commands in relation to the Christian life, hence the Aorist Imperative is appropriate. In 4:12-19 a sense of urgency is introduced when he begins to speak of a πυρώσει (fiery ordeal), as well as various

forms of persecution. The Present Imperative is appropriate to mark these references: μὴ ξενίζεσθε (don't be surprised), χαίρετε (rejoice), μὴ . . . πασχέτω (don't let anyone suffer), μὴ αἰσχυνέσθω (let him not be ashamed), δοξαζέτω (let him praise), παρατιθέσθωσαν (let them offer). Third, in 5:2, 5, 6, 8, 9, the Aorist Imperative is used again.

1 Pet 2:17: πάντας τιμήσατε, τὴν ἀδελφότητα ἀγαπᾶτε, τὸν θεὸν φοβεῖσθε, τὸν βασιλέα τιμᾶτε (honour all, love the brethren, fear God, honour the king). There have been several proposals put forward for this verse. Most involve seeing some form of parallelism (Bammel ["Commands," 279-81] summarizes the major opinions), although Voelz follows the NEB in its rendering: "give due honour to everyone: love to the brotherhood, reverence to God, honour to the sovereign" (Voelz [*Use*, 58] classifies this use as one tense defining another). Those who see parallelism are unable to incorporate the use of the initial Aorist with the three following Present Imperatives. Within its context (see above), the Aorist Imperative is merely descriptive, here followed by a general object. Then the marked Present is used with three specific objects, probably marking specific instances of the general concept of honouring all things. Thus the NEB has rendered the passage correctly. (Bammel's objections [280] that "it is improbable that fear of God was thought of as an explanation and intensification of the general τιμᾶν" and that "it is also very questionable whether the force of the imperative aorist in the first clause is properly rendered by the use of 'due' and a colon. And where remain the pagans in the explanation, who surely are included in the πάντας?" are special pleading which do not take the grammatical questions seriously. Contra also Neal, "Greek," 12-13.)

e. The negated Aorist Subjunctive as prohibition in 2d Person. Within this section the negated Aorist Subjunctive has been treated with the Imperative for commands and prohibitions. There is debate about the origin of the Imperative in relation to the negated Subjunctive. Some believe that the negated Subjunctive was an early feature of the language and that the more recent Imperative never was able to dislodge it (Robertson, 941. Although no examples are found in NT Greek, there are a few instances of negated Aorist Imperatives in earlier Greek. See Chantraine, 2.230-31; Louw, "Prohibitions," 43; Moorhouse, 221). Music contends that the negation of an event conceived of perfectively makes no sense, since it has no beginning and ending, especially in a prohibition of an event in progress ("Zum Gebrauche," 209-10. This is unconvincing since the perfective aspect would still be negated in the Subjunctive). Some argue that the Imperative came first but was reserved exclusively for commands and that the negated Subjunctive was later drafted to serve in this capacity, possibly being the negated injunctive which was formally identical to the Subjunctive, although explanations of the negated Present Imperative are not as convincing (it was later replaced by the negated Present Subjunctive) (Miller, "Imperative," 418-24. There are other debatable issues as well, such as whether the Aorist or Present Imperative developed first. Other proponents of this view include e.g. Brugmann, 587; Schwyzer, 2.341; Delbrück, *Grundlagen*, 120; Stahl, 232; Wackernagel, *Vorlesungen*, 214-15). And Stephens proposes an origin in commanding sigmatic Futures, later re-analysed as Aorists ("Origins," esp. 76-78). The chronological development is not important here, because the system as treated above seems to have been intact throughout the larger period of discussion of this work. It has been seen that the forms grammaticalizing [-assertive] attitude have in common deontic attitude, in distinction from the [+assertive] attitudes. The major attitudinal choice for the [-assertive] attitude is between projection and direction. These are closely related, with the first grammaticalizing a projected visualization by the speaker, and the latter grammaticalizing simply the speaker's direction of his audience toward a process. The former is visual/volitional [+projection], while the latter is solely volitional [+direction]. If the injunctive was formally identical to the Subjunctive this further establishes the semantic relation between the Imperative and the Subjunctive. Even though the injunctive was lost from Greek, the use of the negated injunctive now Subjunctive as the Aorist prohibition continued. Origin in the Future would also help to explain the Future's tendency toward volitional semantic weight. In any case, aspect is the same in the Aorist Imperative and Subjunctive: perfective. The Aorist remains the less heavily marked form, even though the form is morphologically bulkier (see Robertson, 943). Not only does the negated Aorist Subjunctive serve as the 2d and occasionally the 3d Person prohibition, but the 1st Person command was throughout this period provided by the so-called hortatory Subjunctive (discussed under the Subjunctive). Although generally speaking the Imperative is the least morphologically and semantically weighted form of the non-Indicative forms (see Curtius, *Verb*, 296; Greenberg, *Universals*, 37), eventually the Subjunctive seems to have replaced it.

    3. THE PERFECT IN THE NON-INDICATIVE MOODS. Many scholars have shown that the number of simple non-Indicative forms of the Perfect is rather small in number in the hellenistic period, especially Harry ("Perfect Forms," esp. 54-68; cf. "Perfect Subjunctive," 19 [1905]). Harry's work, however, is vitiated by a failure to distinguish form and function; consequently, although he recognizes certain verbs as Perfect in form he excludes them from his computation because their translational value does not conform to his conception of the tense. (Sonnenschein ["Perfect . . . Greek," 155-56; "Perfect . . . Reply," 439-40] points this out. Harry responds in "Perfect Subjunctive," 20 [1906]). The same is true of the Greek of the NT (see chapt. 8 on Participles), with periphrastics widely used instead, especially in the Middle and Passive Voice (see chapt. 10; and Robertson, 907-10; McKay, "Perfect . . . NT Greek," 323-25; Mayser, 2, 1.242; Mandilaras; Kühner/Gerth, 1.182-200; Goodwin, *Syntax*, 31-35).

    a. Subjunctive. The Subjunctive occurs ten times in the Greek of the NT (the Optative is completely absent in the Perfect), all of them forms of οἶδα. They confirm analysis in chapts. 4 and above that the Subjunctive is not merely a future tense, since the uses here are distributed between purpose clauses and conditional statements (see chapt. 6 on conditionals). (McKay ["Perfect . . . Non-Literary Papyri," 36] sees similar patterns in the papyri.)

Mark 2:10 par. Matt 9:6 and Luke 5:24; Eph 6:21 (cf. v 22 with ἵνα γνῶτε τὰ περὶ ἡμῶν καὶ παρακαλέσῃ τὰς καρδίας ὑμῶν [so that you might know the things concerning us and he might comfort your hearts]); 1 John 5:13 (cf. v 15): ἵνα (δὲ) εἰδῆτε (ὅτι) (so that you might know); 1 Cor 2:12 (cf. v 11): ἵνα εἰδῶμεν τὰ ὑπὸ τοῦ θεοῦ χαρισθέντα ὑμῖν (so that we might know the things given to you by God); 1 Tim 3:15: ἐὰν δὲ βραδύνω, ἵνα εἰδῇς πῶς δεῖ ἐν οἴκῳ θεοῦ ἀναστρέφεσθαι (if I might delay, so that you might know how it is necessary to behave in the house of God).

1 Cor 13:2: ἐὰν ἔχω προφητείαν καὶ εἰδῶ τὰ μυστήρια πάντα καὶ πᾶσαν τὴν γνῶσιν καὶ ἐὰν ἔχω πᾶσαν τὴν πίστιν . . . οὐθέν εἰμι (if I might have prophecy and I might know all mysteries and all knowledge and if I might have all faith . . . I am nothing). It is difficult to explain use of the Perfect in the midst of many Present and a few Aorist Subjunctive verb forms, but it appears conscious since other verbs of knowing could have been used in the Subjunctive (e.g. γνῶ / γινώσκω). Further, Paul's use of γινώσκω when speaking of the mysteries of God makes this use more noteworthy. 1 Cor 14:11: ἐὰν οὖν μὴ εἰδῶ τὴν δύναμιν τῆς φωνῆς, ἔσομαι τῷ λαλοῦντι βάρβαρος καὶ ὁ λαλῶν ἐν ἐμοὶ βάρβαρος (if therefore I might not know the power of the voice, I will be in speaking a barbarian and one who speaks a barbarian to me); 1 John 2:29 (cf. v 28, 3:1): ἐὰν εἰδῆτε ὅτι δίκαιός ἐστιν, γινώσκετε ὅτι καὶ πᾶς ὁ ποιῶν τὴν δικαιοσύνην ἐξ αὐτοῦ γεγέννηται (if you might know that he is just, know/you know that indeed everyone who does righteousness might be begotten from him), with chiastic structure drawing attention to the Perfect Subjunctives.

b. Imperative. The Perfect Imperative occurs four times. In classical Greek the Perfect Imperative was rare, especially in the Active and Middle Voices. The 3d Person Passive is more frequent though not numerous (Gildersleeve, 160-62, see 158; cf. Goodwin, *Syntax*, 19-20; Moulton, 176; Robertson, 908. For examples in papyri see Mayser, 2, 1.185; McKay, "Perfect . . . Non-Literary Papyri," 36).

Mark 4:39: πεφίμωσο (be in a silent state), with the Imperative obviously marked in relation to the Present Imperative σιώπα (be silent).

Acts 15:29: ἔρρωσθε (farewell).[23] Cf. P.Oxy. 269 (ii).14 (A.D. 57); 1295.21 (2d/3d cent. A.D.); 1296.20 (3d cent. A.D.); 1676.40 (3d cent. A.D.); PSI 333.18 (256 B.C.); P.Jews. 1912.109 (A.D. 41). See also P.Cairo Zen.59192.11 (255 B.C.) (Edgar/Hunt 92); 59251.11 (252 B.C.) (Edgar/Hunt 93); P.Flor. 338.19 (3d cent. A.D.); (Edgar/Hunt 212); P.Hal. 1.185 (3d cent. B.C.) (Edgar/Hunt 207), and many others, including X. Cyr. 4.5.33. See Exler, *Form*, 69-77; cf. White, *Light*, 198-202.

Eph 5:5: ἴστε (be in a knowledgeable state) (see Gignac, 2.411-12); Jas 1:19: ἴστε. This may be Indicative: cf. Heb 12:17.

The first two forms persisted long after the Perfect Imperative faded from general use, the first possibly as a "solemn stereotyped phrase used in adjurations" (Turner, *Syntax*, 85), although its contextual use seems to retain its aspectual meaning, and the second as a suitable salutation to close letters. The fact that ἴστε persisted attests to the wide use of οἶδα in all Greek until the close of the hellenistic age.

4. CONCLUSION. The verbal aspectual model of the Greek tenses proposed in this work proves profitable for analysis of several recurring problems of understanding non-Indicative usage in NT Greek, e.g. the relation

---

[23]Cf. Acts 23:30 in S E H L P, according to Turner, *Syntax*, 85.

of the command to the objective and extra-textual referent of the process involved. Many grammarians have long recognized that the use of the verb in the non-Indicative Moods is not temporally-based but their attempts to apply a theory of kind of action often have resulted in temporal categories being reimposed. Especially with the Subjunctive, they have failed to illustrate that the difference in forms is not simply between punctiliar or durative action. A list of examples illustrates how verbal aspect provides a satisfactory analysis of non-Indicative Greek verbal usage.

CHAPTER 8:
THE AORIST, PRESENT AND PERFECT PARTICIPLES AND INFINITIVES

0. INTRODUCTION. The Participle and Infinitive may be treated together at the outset, since they are in many ways functionally related. Standard histories of the two forms state that the Participle is related to the adjective and the Infinitive is related to the noun, while retaining verbal characteristics.[1] While this may be true, their functional usage and grammatical relations in Greek allow for several other observations to be made. (This discussion does not intend to be inclusive since so much has already been written on both, but to illustrate certain constructions that reinforce aspectual analysis of the Greek verbal network and hence to account more satisfactorily for specific semantic features of the Greek Infinitive and Participle.) The first section concentrates on analysis of the Present and the Aorist Participle and Infinitive, both since they provide the basis for most discussion in the grammars, and since they are the most active and widely used forms in Greek, including that of the NT. The second section, utilizing the observations from the first section, focuses upon the Perfect, providing material about a form that is much neglected in the grammars and interpreting it in light of the new model of its semantic value posited in chapt. 5.

---

[1]The problems of classification apparently were already realized by the ancient Greek grammarians. See Dionysius Thrax sect. 19: μετοχή ἐστι λέξις μετέχουσα τῆς τῶν ῥημάτων καὶ τῆς τῶν ὀνομάτων ἰδιότητος. παρέπεται δὲ αὐτῇ ταῦτά ἃ καὶ τῷ ῥήματι καὶ τῷ ὀνόματι, δίχα προ[σ]ώπων τε καὶ ἐγκλίσεων (the Participle is a word sharing the characteristic of the verb and the noun. These things which are of the verb and the noun follow side by side, unlike Person and Voice) (Bekker, *Anecdota Graeca*, 2.639). For treatments of the history of the Infinitive see Jannaris, 568-80; Aalto, *Studien*, 7ff.; Brugière, *Histoire*, esp. 23-28; Kurzová, *Struktur*, 13ff. On the Participle see Jannaris, 504-06.

1. THE AORIST AND PRESENT PARTICIPLES AND INFINITIVES. a. Analysis. 1. The Participle.[2]

The Participle is an element both in the class of verbal group, i.e. it grammaticalizes choice of verbal aspect (filling predicate structure); and in the class of noun group, i.e. it grammaticalizes Case, Gender and Number, and at the rank of clause acts as an element in subjects, complements and adjuncts. At the rank of group, the Participle may fill the slot of either a headterm or a modifier, of a completive, or of a verb. For example, in Luke 16:18, πᾶς ὁ ἀπολύων (everyone who divorces), the Participle is the headterm with two preceding modifiers; and in Gal 5:3, παντὶ ἀνθρώπῳ περιτεμνομένῳ (to every circumcised man), the Participle is the following modifier of the headterm, also preceded by a modifier. While the Participle most often occurs in attributive constructions when filling the place of the modifier in a headterm/modifier structure (e.g. John 4:10: ὕδωρ ζῶν [living water]; Titus 2:1: τῇ ὑγιαινούσῃ διδασκαλίᾳ [the sound teaching]; Phil 4:7: ἡ εἰρήνη τοῦ θεοῦ ἡ ὑπερέχουσα πάντα νοῦν [the peace of God surpassing all understanding]); Mark 14:4: ἦσαν . . . τινες ἀγανακτοῦντες [there were certain ones who were disputing]), several variations also occur. The Participle modifier may be non-attributive with an articular headterm:[3] Rom 2:27: ἡ ἐκ φύσεως ἀκροβυστία τὸν νόμον τελοῦσα (the circumcision of nature completing the law). Boyer ("Classification of Participle," 166-67) lists twenty instances in the NT: Matt 6:30 twice; 27:37; Mark 6:2; Luke 11:21; 12:28 twice; 16:14; John 2:9; 4:39; 8:9; 14:10; Acts 13:32; 1 Cor 8:12; 2 Cor 4:15; Eph 2:4; 5:27; Heb 3:2; 1 Pet 3:20; 4:12. Or the Participle modifier may be attributive with an anarthrous headterm: 1 Pet 1:7: χρυσίου τοῦ ἀπολλυμένου (gold which is destroyable); Jas 4:12: σὺ δὲ τίς εἶ, ὁ κρίνων τὸν πλησίον (who are you, one who judges the neighbour?); Acts 4:12: οὐδὲ γὰρ ὄνομά ἐστιν ἕτερον ὑπὸ τὸν οὐρανὸν τὸ δεδομένον ἐν ἀνθρώποις (there is not another name under heaven which is given among men). (See below for discussion of the temporal reference of the Participle and discussion of what is traditionally called the adverbial or circumstantial Participle.) Often the Participle is involved in rankshifting. For example: in Gal 6:6: κοινωνείτω δὲ ὁ κατηχούμενος τὸν λόγον τῷ κατηχοῦντι ἐν πᾶσιν ἀγαθοῖς (let the one who is taught the word share with the one who is teaching in all good things) illustrates this phenomenon twice. ὁ κατηχούμενος τὸν λόγον consists of a predicate and complement rankshifted to subject, and τῷ κατηχοῦντι ἐν πᾶσιν ἀγαθοῖς consists of a predicate and adjunct rankshifted to complement.

The traditional terminology for defining the functional uses of the Participle often fails to make explicit the intricacies of Participle use. The dispute is essentially over whether there is a threefold division of attributive, circumstantial and supplementary, or a two fold division of adjectival and adverbial use. It is unnecessary to debate the merits of the traditional classification,

---

[2]Helpful is Stevens, "Use." Wide-ranging accounts may be found in the grammars, esp. Kühner/Gerth, 2.46-113; Goodwin, *Syntax*, 329-67; Smyth, 454-79; Gildersleeve, 138-43; Schwyzer, 2.385-409; and most recently Oguse, *Participe*. On NT and hellenistic Greek see esp. Winer, 427-47; Blass/Debrunner, ¶¶ 339ff.; Blass, 242-53; Mayser, 2, 1.339-57; Boyer, "Classification of Participles." An early and in many ways satisfying application of linguistic methodology to the Participle is Jones, *Ab urbe condita*. A disappointing treatment from a Harrisian linguistic perspective is Karleen, *Syntax*. All of the following categories may be paralleled in earlier Greek, although the categories used are unique to this work, using language adapted from Berry, *Introduction*, 1.62ff.; Fawcett, *Linguistics*, 47ff. (the distinction between modifiers and qualifiers is unnecessary).

[3]Cf. Th. 7.29.3: ἅμα δὲ τῇ ἡμέρᾳ τῇ πόλει προσέκειτο οὔσῃ οὐ μεγάλῃ (then in daylight he attacked the city which was not large); X. Hell. 4.5.12: ὁ . . . πολέμαρχος σὺν τοῖς ὁπλίταις οὖσιν ὡς ἑξακοσίοις ἀπῄει πάλιν (the polemen went away again with the hoplites who were about 600).

since the only item of significant dispute is over use of the terminology of circumstantial or adverbial, the first a description of its relation to the event and the second to its syntax.

Before clarifying analysis of so-called adverbial usage, several other classificatory schemes must be examined. The Participle fills the place of the completive of a preposition in approximately 135 instances (including nineteen where the Participle is modified by a form of πᾶς; examples with Perfect Participles are included below), functioning as an adjunct[A] at the rank of clause (this is labelled adjunct[A], for adverbial, to distinguish it from adjunct[S], for substantival; see below).[4] It is surprising that grammars do not introduce this significant usage. Mandilaras (357), although claiming the phenomenon occurs in the papyri, cites potentially misleading examples.[5] The majority of instances have the Participle articularly modified: Matt 5:44: προσεύχεσθε ὑπὲρ τῶν διωκόντων ὑμᾶς (pray on behalf of those who pursue you), here with rankshifting, a relatively common occurrence; Mark 6:26: διὰ τοὺς ὅρκους καὶ τοὺς ἀνακειμένους (because of the oath and those sitting at table) par. Matt 14:9; Matt 23:21: ἐν αὐτῷ καὶ ἐν τῷ κατοικοῦντι αὐτόν (by him and the one who inhabits it); Matt 24:14: ἐν ὅλῃ τῇ οἰκουμένῃ (in the whole inhabited earth); cf. Acts 11:28; Heb 1:6; and Rev 3:10. Luke 19:26: ἀπὸ δὲ τοῦ μὴ ἔχοντος (but from the one who does not have); Rom 5:14: ἐπὶ τοὺς μὴ ἁμαρτήσαντας (upon those who do not sin); Heb 11:7: περὶ τῶν μηδέπω βλεπομένων (concerning things never seen). (Other examples include: Matt 10:28 par. Luke 12:4; Matt 23:22; 24:47 par. Luke 12:44; Matt 24:49; 25:9; Luke 2:18, 33; 6:28, 29, 30; 14:7; 21:35; John 6:2; 7:33; 12:44; 16:5; 12:2, 20; 17:20; Acts 3:2; 5:5, 11; 10:44; 15:33; 17:17; 19:4, 12, 13; 20:32; 22:11; 24:5; Rom 1:25; 2:2; 3:22; 4:5, 24; 8:20, 37; 9:12; 10:12, 20 with textual variant; 11:22; 15:31; 1 Cor 1:2; 3:11; 2 Cor 2:15 twice; 4:3; 5:12; 10:2; Gal 1:6; 2:6; 5:8; Eph 1:6; 6:24; Phil 1:28; 4:13; 1 Thess 4:13; 2 Thess 1:10; 1 Tim 2:2; 2 Tim 2:22; Heb 1:14; 5:7; 7:21; 8:1; Jas 2:3; 1 Pet 1:12; 1 John 2:26; Rev 2:9; 6:10; 10:6; 11:11; 14:6; 19:19. Should John 19:17: εἰς τὸν λεγόμενον Κρανίου Τόπον be placed here? The capitalization in both NA[26] and UBS[3] indicates that this is their understanding [to the one called Place of the Skull], although εἰς τὸν λεγόμενον Κρανίου τόπον is also possible [to the place called Skull].) This usage is not in and of itself surprising, since it resembles use described above for the subject and complement.

One important variant occurs when the Participle is Neuter, used for an abstract concept: Matt 12:32: ἐν τούτῳ τῷ αἰῶνι οὔτε ἐν τῷ μέλλοντι (neither in the present age nor in the coming one); Luke 13:9: εἰς τὸ μέλλον (unto the coming time); Phil 3:8: διὰ τὸ ὑπερέχον τῆς γνώσεως Χριστοῦ Ἰησοῦ (because of the exceeding of the knowledge of Christ Jesus); Heb 12:10 (twice): οἱ μὲν γὰρ πρὸς ὀλίγας ἡμέρας κατὰ τὸ δοκοῦν αὐτοῖς ἐπαίδευον, ὁ δὲ ἐπὶ τὸ συμφέρον εἰς τὸ μεταλαβεῖν τῆς ἁγιότητος αὐτοῦ (for they teach for a little while according to what appears to them, but he for our improving in order to receive his holiness). (See also Mark 12:44 par. Luke 21:4; Luke 8:3; 12:15; 15:4; 16:21; 22:22; Eph 1:21; 1 Tim 6:19.) And several occur after what are called improper prepositions: Acts 8:32: ἐναντίον τοῦ

---

[4] This is found in earlier Greek as well: e.g. Hdt. 1.15: ἐπὶ . . . τούτου τυραννεύοντος Σαρδίων (in his reign of S.); Th. 1.142.8: ἐν τῷ μὴ μελετῶντι (in not practicing); 5.102.1: μετὰ . . . τοῦ δρωμένου (with action); Pl. Symp. 198B: μετὰ καλὸν οὕτω καὶ παντοδαπὸν λόγον ῥηθέντα (after speaking such a fine and manifold statement). Goodwin (Syntax, 331-32) notes that an Infinitive construction could be used for each of the above; cf. Carter, "Uses," 6; Stevens, "Use," 54, citing D. 19.100.

[5] P.Lond. 42.14-20 (168 B.C.): ἀηδίζομαι ἕνεκα τοῦ ἐκ τοῦ τοιούτου / καιροῦ ἐμαυτήν τε καὶ τὸ παιδίον σου / διακεκυβερνηκυῖα καὶ εἰς πᾶν τι / ἐληλυθυῖα διὰ τὴν τοῦ σίτου τιμὴν / καὶ δοκοῦσα νῦν γε σοῦ παραγενομένου / τεύξεσθαί τινος ἀναψυχῆς, σὲ δὲ / μηδ᾽ ἐντεθυμῆσθαι τοῦ παραγενέσθαι (I am uneasy, on account of such that from this time, having governed both myself and your child and gone through every such thing because of the price of wheat and considered that now, since you are present, to create some rest, but you are not concerned to be present); and P.Lips. 108.5-6 (2d/3d cent. A.D.): καὶ οὐκ ἠδυνήθην διὰ τὸ ἐμὲ / μετρείως ἔχοντα (and I was not able on account of my possessing in due measure).

κείραντος αὐτόν (before the one who sheers him). (See also Luke 14:10; 1 Cor 15:27; 2 Cor 7:12 [twice] followed by an Infinitive as completive of a preposition; Rev 4:10.)

Perhaps the most important set of examples is those in which the Participle is anarthrous: Rom 5:16: δι᾽ ἑνὸς ἁμαρτήσαντος (through one who sinned), if the numeral is a modifier; Rom 10:14: χωρὶς κηρύσσοντος (apart from preaching); Rom 12:15 (twice): χαίρειν μετὰ χαιρόντων, κλαίειν μετὰ κλαιόντων (to rejoice with rejoicers, to cry with criers); Heb 11:3: εἰς τὸ μὴ ἐκ φαινομένων τὸ βλεπόμενον γεγονέναι (so that that which is seen did not come about from the visible); Heb 11:20: περὶ μελλόντων (concerning coming things); 1 Pet 3:12: ἐπὶ ποιοῦντας κακά (upon doers of evil). This last category resembles closely use of the Infinitive. Parallel usage of the Participle and Infinitive is discussed below when determining their semantic difference. (See below on verbal use of the Participle in Genitive absolute clauses, as well as discussion of the Participle as Imperative. The Participle fills the place of the verb element in what are called periphrastic constructions [complex word]: see chapt. 10.)

As seen above, at the rank of clause the Participle may fill the structure of a subject, complement, or adjunct. The question is how to categorize the following examples: Acts 25:2-3: παρεκάλουν αὐτὸν αἰτούμενοι χάριν κατ᾽ αὐτοῦ (they were beseeching him, requesting a favour from him); Acts 21:2: εὑρόντες πλοῖον διαπερῶν εἰς Φοινίκην ἐπιβάντες ἀνήχθημεν (finding a boat crossing into P. [and] getting aboard we were taken across). Most grammarians-- whether they call the use here circumstantial or adverbial--posit a relationship in which the Participle is the equivalent of a dependent clause or in some way is related to the predicate. Thus the Participle group would be classified at the level of clause as adjunctive. This appears to overlook one major factor in evaluating the role of the Participle, however, and that is that in this construction it is in grammatical agreement with either a stated or implied element (headterm at the rank of noun group) of the subject. Traditional analysis often overlooks the nominal elements of the Participle, since the Participle appears always to be a modifier of a stated or implied (if even within the monolectic verb) head. (Greenlee ["Participles," 100] recognizes this. Berry [*Introduction*, 1.92] classifies as clause "whistling merrily," in "whistling merrily, he cycled down the road." This is unacceptable in Greek, where a grammatical relation exists which makes clause reduction an unacceptable explanation and seems to emphasize the modifying function. See Matthews, *Syntax*, 175-79, for a helpful discussion.) 1 Cor 11:4 illustrates: πᾶς ἀνὴρ προσευχόμενος ἢ προφητεύων κατὰ κεφαλῆς ἔχων καταισχύνει τὴν κεφαλὴν αὐτοῦ. This might be analysed at the rank of clause as either a subject consisting of a noun group with a headterm with one preceding and several modifiers following, or a subject with one or more adjunctive Participles following, focusing on the difficulty of determining how ἔχων relates to the subject and the other Participles. In the analysis here presented this tension is alleviated, since syntactically at the rank of group all the Participles are modifiers of ἀνήρ (rankshifting of the Participles is to be noted, in which the predicate is preceded by the adjunct). The fact that many of the Participles in these constructions are anarthrous and their headterms are articular poses no problem. On the one hand traditional grammar recognizes that the Participle must be in appropriate agreement with its stated or implied headterm, and on the other hand it is noted above that in Greek concordance of the article is not a necessity in Participle structures. For classificatory purposes the term modifier is used when discussing the use of a Participle at the rank of group in relation to a headterm, and the terms subject, complement and adjunct[S] are used at the rank of clause, remembering that the Participle in adjunct[S] structure also modifies a stated or implied headterm (see Stevens, "Use," 52).

2. Infinitive.[6] At the rank of group, the Infinitive may fill the slot of either a headterm or a modifier, of a completive, or of a verb. For example, in Mark 9:10: τὸ ἐκ νεκρῶν ἀναστῆναι (to be raised from the dead), the Infinitive is the headterm with two preceding modifiers (one is the article and the other is a rankshifted prepositional group); and in Rom 14:13: τοῦτο κρίνατε μᾶλλον, τὸ μὴ τιθέναι πρόσκομμα (but instead determine this, not to be a cause of stumbling), the Infinitive is the following modifier of the headterm (this is also called an appositional or epexegetic Infinitive, categories often distinguished by grammarians, though they serve no useful purpose here); Matt 3:14: χρείαν . . . βαπτισθῆναι (need to be baptized); Acts 27:20: ἐλπὶς πᾶσα τοῦ σώζεσθαι ἡμᾶς (all hope for us to be saved); Luke 15:19: ἄξιος κληθῆναι (worthy to be called); Luke 24:25: βραδεῖς . . . τοῦ πιστεύειν (difficult to believe). The Infinitive also is involved in rankshifting. For example, in Jas 1:26: εἰ τις δοκεῖ θρησκὸς εἶναι (if anyone thinks that he is religious), where the Infinitive in a (subject)-complement-predicate structure is rankshifted to complement (common in indirect discourse). This usage is well known to occur with impersonal verbs: e.g. Acts 27:24: Καίσαρί σε δεῖ παραστῆναι (that you stand before C. is necessary), where the Infinitive in a complement-subject-predicate structure is rankshifted to subject. The Infinitive as an element of clause structure may also be rankshifted to complement: e.g. Phil 2:6: οὐχ ἁρπαγμὸν ἡγήσατο τὸ εἶναι ἴσα θεῷ (he did not consider being equal with God as a prize); Matt 5:17: ἦλθον καταλῦσαι (I came to destroy). The relationship with the predicate is often governed by a preposition (this often involves rankshifting): e.g. 1 Thess 3:5: ἔπεμψα εἰς τὸ γνῶναι τὴν πίστιν ὑμῶν (I sent in order to know your faith).

The so-called 'subject' of the Infinitive must be discussed here. Usually it is treated as an Accusative of reference, or the like (see Robertson, 1082-85). But on the basis of use of the Nominative as subject of the Infinitive in earlier Greek, the dependency of the Infinitive upon the unstated subject in clauses that do not state the subject (e.g. Acts 25:11: οὐ παραιτοῦμαι τὸ ἀποθανεῖν [I do not refuse to die]), it is better to see use of the Accusative as a means of distinguishing the subject. Thus rankshifting exists, in which the Infinitive at the rank of clause, with subject in the Accusative Case, fills lesser structures. For example, in Rom 6:6: τοῦ μηκέτι δουλεύειν ἡμᾶς τῇ ἁμαρτίᾳ (we serve sin no longer), the Infinitive clause is an element in the adjunct stucture; Rom 1:11: εἰς τὸ στηριχθῆναι ὑμᾶς (in order that you are strengthened), where the Infinitive is completive of a preposition; and Matt 19:14: μὴ κωλύετε αὐτὰ ἐλθεῖν πρός με (don't prevent that they come to me). The traditional terminology for defining the functional uses of the Infinitive, as with the Participle, often fails to make explicit the intricacies of their use.

In use of the Infinitive, Moulton says, "only one classical development failed to maintain itself, viz. the rare employment of the infin. as a full noun, capable of a dependent genitive" (215, citing from Demosthenes τό γ᾽ εὖ φρονεῖν αὐτῶν ["their good sense"] or from Plato διὰ παντὸς τοῦ εἶναι). The only instance is Heb 2:15: διὰ παντὸς τοῦ ζῆν (through all life).

[6]See besides the monographs listed above Stork, *Usage*, esp. 1-50 (cf. bibliography for earlier individual studies); Kühner/Gerth, 2.3-46; Gildersleeve, 132-38; Goodwin, *Syntax*, 197-328; Smyth, 437-54; Schwyzer, 2.356-84; and for NT and hellenistic Greek esp. Robertson, 1050ff.; Winer, 399-427; Blass, 221-42; Mayser, 2, 1.297-339; Boyer, "Classification of Infinitives." This language is adapted from Berry, *Introduction*, 1.62ff.; Fawcett, *Linguistics*, 48ff. (the distinction between modifiers and qualifiers is unnecessary). The issue of the anarthrous versus articular Infinitive is not discussed here, since it does not appear to affect the issues raised. The rise of the articular Infinitive did not affect significantly either its range of uses beyond the natural expansion of some (e.g. completive of preposition) or its semantic usage, especially regarding verbal aspect. On the articular Infinitive see Gildersleeve, "Contributions"; "Articular Infinitive"; "Articular Infinitive Again." Various articles have been written on individual authors: e.g. Vendryes, "L'infinitif"; Hewlett, "Articular Infinitive." A summary for hellenistic usage is found in Moulton, 213-20; Boyer, 24-26.

b. Use of the Participle and the Infinitive as predicate. 1. Participle (see Kühner/Gerth, 2.110-13; cf. Goodwin, *Syntax*, 337-40; Schwyzer, 2.398-402). a. Absolute: Genitive (see Spieker, "Genitive Absolute"; Argyle, "Genitive Absolute"), Accusative (e.g. 1 Cor 16:6; Acts 26:3, according to Robertson, 490-91; see Acts 26:3 [γνώστην ὄντα σε (you might be knowledgeable)]), and Dative. (There is debate whether the Accusative and Dative absolute appear in NT Greek: Matt 14:6: γενεσίοις δὲ γενομένοις τοῦ Ἡρῴδου [the birthday party of H. came about]. Hartman [*Constructions*, 11] believes it does not, following Blass/Debrunner, ¶ 200[3].) In the Genitive absolute the Participle functions as an element of the predicate at the rank of clause. On the basis of there being significant instances in earlier Greek where the subject is in some form repeated in the main clause, a significant difference in use of the Genitive absolute from earlier to hellenistic Greek cannot be posited (see Spieker, 322, who notes especially examples where the 'subject' of the construction is referred to in the clause with a finite predicate; Goodwin, *Syntax*, 338; and Doudna, *Greek*, 58, on the papyri). It is noteworthy that whereas usually the Genitive absolute has a stated subject, this is not always the case and hence is apparently not necessary. Whether this is explained as ellipsis of an implied subject or whether the Participle is to be considered monolectic is immaterial here. The point is that there is at least implied grammatical agreement between the Participle as predicate and its subject. Instances of the Accusative and Dative absolute are much fewer, but the principle is the same.

The difference between the Aorist and Present absolute is one of verbal aspect. Matt 18:24-25: ἀρξαμένου δὲ αὐτοῦ συναίρειν προσηνέχθη αὐτῷ εἷς ὀφειλέτης μυρίων ταλάντων. μὴ ἔχοντος δὲ αὐτοῦ ἀποδοῦναι ἐκέλευσεν αὐτὸν ὁ κύριος πραθῆναι καὶ τὴν γυναῖκα καὶ τὰ τέκνα καὶ πάντα ὅσα ἔχει, καὶ ἀποδοθῆναι (when he began to settle accounts one debtor of countless talents was brought to him. When he did not have by which to pay back, the master ordered him to sell both his wife and children and all that he had, and to be repayed), with the Aorist and Present Participles having the same temporal relation to the main clause, the difference being between the Aorist introducing the situation, and the Present used as a marked transition recounting the desperateness of the debtor's affairs. Luke 2:42-43: ἀναβαινόντων αὐτῶν κατὰ τὸ ἔθος τῆς ἑορτῆς καὶ τελειωσάντων τὰς ἡμέρας (they went up according to the custom of the feast and completed the days), where traditional temporal determinations on the basis of tense form make nonsense of the passage. The difference is that the Present is used of the entire trip as one in progress, while the Aorist is used as a transition to summarize the event as complete. As in extra-biblical Greek, the Genitive absolute is often used transitionally, as well as in the midst of narrative: Acts 1:8: ἐπελθόντος τοῦ ἁγίου πνεύματος ἐφ᾽ ὑμᾶς (when the holy spirit comes upon you); Acts 4:37: ὑπάρχοντος αὐτῷ ἀγροῦ (a field belonged to him).

b. Independent Participle. A lengthy and at times heated debate has been conducted in the secondary literature over whether in hellenistic Greek there exists an imperatival Participle. The three major proposals are: (1) the imperatival Participle, while not found in classical Greek, is a phenomenon attested in hellenistic Greek if only sporadically; (2) any example of the imperatival Participle can be explained as anacoluthon or some other less grammatically regular usage; and (3) the imperatival Participle results from the influence of Semitic languages. This discussion may be recounted.

(1) Moulton (180-83, 223-25), later followed by grammarians such as Robertson (944-46 [who finds P.Teb. 59 uncontestable]) and Turner (*Syntax*, 343; cf. idem, *Insights*, 167-68; Zerwick, 129-30; Blass/Debrunner, ¶ 968), argues that the papyri establish "beyond question" (180) that the Participle can substitute for the Imperative. After citing examples where the Participle can be used for the Indicative (222-23, this is returned to below), he cites two kinds of imperatival uses of the Participle from the papyri (223; more of the text is given in several instances): (a) P.Grenf. i 35.7-9 (99 B.C.): ἑαυτῶν δὲ ἐπιμελό/μενοι ἵν᾽ ὑγιαίνητε. ἔσμεν ἐν Πτολεμαΐδι. / ἔρρωσθε (take care of yourself so that you might be well. We are in P. Keep well.); P.Par. 63.18ff. (164 B.C.); P.Grenf. i 30.9-11 (102 B.C.); Path P 1.11f. (?); P.Teb. 12.12-13 (118 B.C.) (all without intervening clause), etc.; and (b) P.Fay. 112.8-14 (103 B.C.: τῶν ὤγμον τῆς / ᾽Απιάδος ἕως σήμερον οὐ ἐθέρ[ι]σας ἀλλ᾽ ἡμέ/ληκας αὐτοῦ καὶ μέχρι τούτου τὼ ἥμυ/συ αὐτοῦ ἐθέρισας, ἐπέχον (=-ων) τῷ δακ/τυλιστῇ Ζωίλωι καὶ εἵνα αὐτὸν μὴ δυσω/πήσῃς· ἀθέριστον αὐτὸν ἕως σήμερον ἀφί/κας· διὼ μένφομαί σαι μεγάλως (the field of A. until today you have not harvested but you did not take care of it and up to now you have harvested the half of it. "Attend to [the measurer?] Z. and don't look askance at him" [Moulton, 178]. You have left it unharvested until today, wherefore I blame you greatly); P.Teb. 59.8-12 (99 B.C.): ἐν οἷς ἐὰν προσδέησθέ / μου ἐπιτάσσοντές μοι προθυ/μότερον διὰ τὸ ἄνωθεν φοβεῖσθαι / καὶ σέβεσθαι τὸ ἱερόν, / ἔρρωσθε (among which if you might need me, govern my service on account of my previous reverence and worship of the temple. Keep well); and P.Petrie ii 19 (1a).1-9 (3d cent. B.C.): ἀξιῶ / σε μετὰ δεήσεος καὶ ἱκετείας οὔνε/κα τοῦ θεοῦ καὶ τοῦ καλῶς ἔχοντος / δοὺς τὰ πιστὰ Μηζάκωι [Moulton's reading; the edition has μηζα ? κωι] μηθέν με / εἰρηκέναι σοι καθ᾽ αὐτοῦ μηδέποτε / ἄτοπον ὅπερ καὶ ἀληθινὸν ἐστιν καὶ / ὡς ἂν τοῦτο ποιήσηις ἀξιώσας αὐτὸν / με]ταπέμψασθαί με καὶ δίεσθαι / ἀπὸ τῆς φυλακῆς (I request of you with requests and prayers on account of the god indeed who is good, give faithful assurances to M. that I never said anything inappropriate to you against him on account of what is true and if you do this, request of him to send for me and to release me from prison). Thus he concludes that "Though fairly certain, [the imperatival Participle] was not very common" (223), possibly facilitated by lack of the Imperative ἐστέ in the NT (180).

Moulton's position was enhanced by others. Meecham ("Use") elucidates two further examples: P.Grenf. i 30.6-11 (cited erroneously as P.Amh. ii 39.16ff.): ἐφ᾽ οἷς ἂν οὖν ὑμῶν προσδέωνται / ἀντιλαμβανόμενοι καὶ ὑμῖν (=ἡμῖν?) δὲ γράφοντας (=-ητες?) / ὑπὲρ ὧν αἵρεσθε [Meecham reads αἱρεῖσθε] ὡς πᾶν προθυμότερον μελεω/θησόμενον. ἐπιμελόμενοι δὲ καὶ ἑαυτῶν / ἵν᾽ ὑνιαίνητε. ἔρρωσθε (for which things they might need of you, be of assistance and write to us, on behalf of which you choose, as ever desire being filled, and take care of yourselves so that you might be well, remain well); and P.Fay. 109.10-11 (1st cent. A.D.): καὶ νῦν παρακληθεὶς νομίσας ὅτι κιχρᾶς μοι / [αὐτούς] μὴ κατάσχης Κλέωνα κτλ. (now being advised, consider that you are lending to me [the money], don't hold up K.). He admits that the evidence is slim, but claims that a "variant formula which employs two imperatives seems to support this equivalence" (208), citing F. Bilabel, *Griechische Papyri* No. 35: ἔρροσο, πρὸ πάντων σατοῦ ἐπιμελοῦ, ἵνα ὑγιαίνης (keep well, above all watch out for yourself, so that you might remain healthy); No. 41: ἔρρωσο ἐπιμέλου σεαυτῶ (keep well, take care of yourself); P.Teb. 55.9-11 (2d cent. B.C.): τὰ δὲ ἄλλα ἐ[πι]μέλου σαυτοῦ / ἵν᾽ ὑγιαίνης. / ἔρρωσο (watch out for yourself regarding these other things, so that you might be healthy; keep well) (207-08). He also supports Moulton's citations of P.Grenf. i 35 and P.Teb. 59.

Salom ("Use"), besides adding examples of the formulaic ἐπιμελόμενοι ἵν᾽ ὑγιαίνητε (P.Teb. 19.14-15 [not line 19 as listed] [114 B.C.]; 20.10 [113 B.C.]; P.Lond. 42.32 [168 B.C.]) adds two examples: P.Cairo Zen. 59154.1-3 (256 B.C.): τῶν ξηρῶν ξύλων / ἐμβαλόμενος εἰς πλοῖον κορμοὺς ὅτι πλείστους καὶ / παχυτάτους ἀπόστειλον τὴν ταχίστην εἰς ᾿Αλεξάνδρειαν ("From the dry wood put on board a boat as many of the thickest logs as possible and send them immediately to Alexandria" [48]); and P.Cairo Zen. 59251.6-7 (252 B.C.): τὴν δὲ τιμὴν ἀπὸ τοῦ σησάμου καὶ τοῦ κροτῶνος δοὺς εἰς ταῦτα, καὶ τῆς οἰκίας δὲ τῆς ἐν Φιλαδελφείαι / ἐπιμελόμενος ("and pay the cost of them out of the produce of the sesame and croton, and also see to the house in Philadelphia" [48]). (Salom also cites P.Amh. ii 39.16 [?] and P.Fay. 109.10, without citing Meecham's article.)

(2) In responding to those who claim that the Participle substitutes for a finite verb, already Winer argued that this was infrequent and then only for "simple tense and mood forms," proceeding to explain every instance as either a regular use of the Participle or anacoluthon (esp. 442. Of course he does not treat the papyri). Mayser (2, 1.196-97 n. 3, 340-41), responding directly to Moulton, argues, for example, that in P.Grenf. i 35.7, ἐσμὲν ἐν Πτολεμαΐδι is parenthetical, with ἐπιμελόμενοι dependent upon ἔρρωσθε. He argues similarly for the other examples, such as P.Par. 63, where no intervening clause causes difficulty (1.196-97 n. 3). Besides responding to Moulton's use of P.Petrie ii 19.1ff. by noting Moulton's acknowledgement (in the German edition) of the possibility of anacoluthon and that in similar contexts authors often use καλῶς ποιήσεις or χαριεῖ μοι instead of the ἀξιῶ σε that was used here, he attempts to refute several other examples: P.Hib. 78.6-13 (244-43 B.C.): ἔτι οὖν καὶ νῦν / ἐπιμελὲς σοι ἔστω ἀπολύ/ειν αὐτοὺς τῆς νῦν εἰς ᾿Αλα/βάστρων πόλιν λειτουργίας / διὰ τὸ μὴ ἐκπεσ[εῖ]ν αὐτοῖς τὸ / νῦν λειτουργῆσαι, καὶ ἐὰν / ἐκ τοῦ ᾿Οξυρυγχίτου ἐπιλέ/γωνται Ζωΐλον ἀπολύσας (now, therefore, let there be concern by you to release them from service now in the city of A. because it does not fall to them to serve now, and if they might choose from the O., release Z.), where, expecting an Imperative or Infinitive for ἀπολύσας, analocuthon occurs as if ἐπιμέλου were written above; P.Hal. 7.2-3 (A.D. 232): ἀποδοὺς οὖν καὶ ὡς ἂν ᾿Απολλώνιον [ἐ]ξαποστείληις πρὸς ἡμᾶς / κομίζοντα τὰ προγεγραμμένα σοι, διασάφησον ἡμῖν παραχρῆμα (send away therefore [the letter] and if you might send A. to us bearing the things written to you make it clear to us immediately), where the Participle--in parallel structure with the following Imperative and connected by καί--has no independent imperatival force; and P.Eleph. 10.1-6 (A.D. 223): ὡς ἂν ἀναγνῶις τὴν ἐπιστολήν, ἐπιλαβὼν / παρὰ τῶν τραπεζιτῶν τῶν ἐν τοῖς ἱεροῖς τὰ πεπτωκ[ό]τα εἰς τὸ ἐν ᾿Απόλλωνος / πόλει τῆι μεγάληι ἱερὸν ὁμοίως δὲ καὶ τοῦ εἰσμεμετρημένου σίτου παρὰ τῶν / πρὸς τοῖς θησαυροῖς ἀπὸ τοῦ πρωτίστου χρόνου ἕως τοῦ ἐνεστῶτος κατὰ μῆνα / καὶ καθ᾿ ἔτος, διεστάλθω δὲ εἰς ἃ πέπτωκεν ἔτη, καὶ τοῦ[το ποιή]σας ἐπιμελῶς / ἀπόστειλ[ο]ν ἡμῖν (if you might read the letter, take it from the tables where things are sold in the temples to the great temple in the city of A., and likewise of the measurements of the wheat from those with storehouses from the earliest time until the present each month and each year, determine the years in which it sold and do this; send acknowledgement to us), where if διεστάλθω is replaced by διεσταλκώς (perhaps διαστείλας is possible) and τοῦ[το ποιή]σας κτλ. by τοὺς ἄνδρας ἐπιμελῶς ἀπόστειλον, the problem is corrected. Mayser's conclusions, rather than weakening the case that Moulton and others make, however, helps it by his special pleading against arguably strong examples, especially since he abbreviates his examples to make the Participle appear closer in proximity to a finite verb. This confusion may be predicated upon an error that Mayser makes in failing to distinguish between the Participle as a finite verb and the Participle instead of a finite verb. His argument, while refuting the former, endorses the latter (see Frisk, "Participium," 58, 56).

(3) Those who argue for Semitic influence upon the imperatival Participle have been numerous as well. The major arguments come from Daube ("Note"; NT, 90-97; see also Barrett, "Participle"; Moule, 179-80. Daube's arguments were picked up and disseminated by Talbert, "Tradition," so that most major commentators on Romans follow him: e.g. Cranfield, Romans, esp. 2.629 n. 4; Black, Romans, 153-54; Michel, Römerbrief, 381-82; Wilckens, Brief . . . Römer, 3. loc. cit.). He questions Moulton's analysis, claiming that in the formulaic use of ἐπιμελόμενοι the Participle can be connected to the final greeting, as it can in P.Teb. 59. Of P.Fay. 112 he suggests several ways of understanding ἐπέχου: in light of the author's atrocious spelling and grammar, Daube suggests, ἐπέχον might be "some aorist imperative; or, if it represents ἐπέχων, Gemellus may have connected it, as a proper participle, with ἐθέρισας even

though speaking of an action to be performed by the addressee in the future. (Gemellus was fond of carousing with his friends; he may have written this when he had not recovered from one of his bouts.)" [Can this last statement be taken seriously in an article of this sort?] Daube also suggests an Accusative absolute, thus giving the rendering "according to" or "to judge by the report of"; an "unattached participle" if Moulton's correction is accepted; or a Participle "instead of the indicative" ("Note," 469). Barrett ("Participle," 165) cites a larger context to establish that an earlier use of νομίσας is not imperatival but parallel to δός in P.Fay. 109.2-6 (1st cent. A.D.): καὶ νῦν / παρακληθεὶς τοὺς τρεῖς στατῆρες οὓς εἴρηκέ / σοι Σέλευκος δῶναί μοι ἤδη δὸς Κλέωνι, νομί/σας ὅτι κιχρᾷς μοι αὐτούς, ἐὰν σε δ⟨έ⟩η τὸ εἱμάτιόν / σου θεῖναι ἐνέχυρον (and now, please, give to K. the three staters which S. told you to give to me already, thinking that you owe them to me, if he might require you to give your garment as a pledge). Thus in line 10 νομίσας is constructed with κατάχης, with the rendering: "And now, please, having borne in mind the fact that it is (in view of my generosity on other occasions--see line 2) only a loan you are making, don't keep Cleon waiting" (165). (Barrett could have noted that P.Fay. 109.11-13 continues: καὶ συνπροσ/[γενοῦ Κ]λέωνι καὶ αἴτησον Σάραν τὰς τοῦ (δραχμὰς) ιβ. / [μὴ οὖν ἄ]λλως ποιή[σ]ης [and go to K. and ask S. for the twelve drachmas. Don't do otherwise].) Barrett also argues for P.Grenf. i 30.6 that all three Participles "may certainly be constructed with ἔρρωσθε; and the καὶ ὑμῖν (ἡμῖν lgd.), καὶ ἑαυτῶν seem to bind all three together and so to link them with the final imperative" (165).

Having dismissed the evidence of the papyri, Daube argues further that "Even if the evidence from the papyri were valid in itself, it would yet be inapplicable to the cases from the NT that it is sought to explain, for three reasons" ("Note," 470): (a) in the NT the Participle appears side-by-side with adjectives, but not in the papyri; (b) the supposed imperatival Participle in the NT never expresses a command to a specific person but a rule, and the papyri so far offer no examples; and (c) against Moulton's claim that the imperatival Participle was a genuine hellenistic Greek development, it only occurs in *Haustafeln* and similar sections in the NT. Thus it is more than merely careless usage, but not hellenistic Greek.

Daube suggests "the participles in question may be due to Hebrew or (though less probably) Aramaic influence" (471): "In Tannaitic Hebrew, though not yet in Biblical, the participle, equivalent to our present or future tense, is common in rules of conduct and even in actual religious precepts. In fact, it is by far the most frequent for of the laws of *Mishnah*, *Tosefta* and *Baraita*" (472). For example *m. Ber.* 2.4: "Craftsmen may recite (the Shema) on the top of a tree" (472). Not infrequently the Participle appears next to an Imperative. For example *m. Sabb.* 1.3: "Rightly they have said, The schoolmaster may look [Participle] where the children read . . . but he himself may not read [Imperfect]" (473). While the two are often synonymous, there are contexts in which the Participle cannot occur, indicating that it never loses its function "as denoting a custom" (474).

Daube thus argues "that the imperative participles of the New Testament may be translations of the Tannaitic ones" (476): unlike those in the papyri, the Tannaitic and NT Participles are unattached; unlike those in the papyri, the Tannaitic Participles occur frequently throughout their works; the Tannaitic Participles can explain the "imperative adjectives" (476) of the NT as translational equivalents; the Tannaitic and NT Participles are confined to rules. Daube proceeds further to show an overlap in teachings between the Tannaitic and NT material. Daube then analyses the NT instances (see below), and thus concludes that the writers of the epistles drew upon a set of moral codes.

Before formulating a counterproposal to the issue of the imperatival Participle, several comments may be made in response to Daube and his followers. (a) Most of the parallels that he uses are at best roughly contemporary with the NT, but more likely later. Rabbinic scholarship since the time of his and Davies's writing has come to recognize the significance of several factors: the compilation of the Mishnah around A.D. 200; the problems of dating Tannaitic material; and the crucial significance of the fall of Jerusalem in A.D. 70, thus rendering reference to the rabbis as anachronistic (several of these issues are discussed in Neusner, "'Judaism'"; idem, "Problems," 61-81; P. Alexander, "Judaism"; Chilton, *Rabbi*, 13-35). Daube suggests a parallel in the Qumran Manual of Discipline, which he dates from 2d cent. B.C. to 2d cent. A.D., but he does not say whether it makes use of the Participle. Kanjuparambil ("Participles") has recently suggested parallels between Rom 12:9ff. and the Manual of Discipline (1QS), which is generally acknowledged to predate Romans.[7] But the points of difference between the two documents override the rather slender similarities: Romans is in 2d Person Plural, while 1QS is in 3d Person Singular and Plural. Rom 12:9-15 is an exhortation, but 1QS 5:1-7 "has diverse determinations and explanations" (287). And the "spirit" animating the writers and their communities is different.

(b) Daube admits that the imperatival use of the Participle is a Mishnaic Hebrew phenomenon unknown in earlier or Biblical Hebrew. Thus this phenomenon had to be introduced into the language. On the basis of the issues of dating the parallel material suggested above, it may just as well be possible for hellenistic Greek to have influenced Hebrew. A more likely explanation is independent development.

(c) Daube's use of parallels is open to question. On the basis of the questions regarding dating, the parallels he cites--though interesting--can in no way be seen as determinative for the NT. Even if the two bodies of material are contemporary a cause and effect relationship has not been established. When examined closely, the individual exhortations are different in many respects (see Furnish, *Theology*, 38-42; Davies, *Paul*, 135, who admits to the difficulty of establishing a precise source for Paul's material). This points to the necessity of separating the grammatical from the exegetical at this point, a point that Kanjuparambil misses. In conjunction with this, N. Turner believes that, since C.L. Mitton has shown that 1 Peter is "indebted" to Ephesians, in particular that 1 Pet 2:18 with the Participle is dependent upon Eph 6:5 with the Imperative, there is another explanation than Daube's that Peter and Paul were translating the Hebrew Participles in moral codes in different ways. "This may be cited as evidence that a participle could be used to express the meaning of an imperative" (C.L. Mitton, *The Epistle to the Ephesians* [Oxford, 1951], 193, cited in Turner, *Insights*, 167-68; Talbert's ["Tradition," 93-94 n. 6] citation of Kümmel in support of Peter and Paul as dependent upon common catechetical material misses Turner's point. Turner's suggestion that Semitic influence could have come via a Jewish Greek [168] does not solve any of the difficulties involved here). Salom argues further that the supposed imperatival Participle occurs in several passages in the NT that are not *Haustafeln*, such as Eph 4:2-3; 1 Pet 1:14; and Luke 24:47f. (43). Thus Daube's argument does not hold that the confinement of the Participle to one specific kind of context in the NT points to a Semitic source.

(d) Salom suggests a fourth objection: "the idea in Hebrew expressed by the participle is that of necessity or obligation and not a true command" (44). If these had been translated into Greek, δεῖ or ἐάω would probably have been used, not the Participle. Besides there appears to have been a heavy amount of editorial activity performed, since the Tannaitic material is quite lengthy in comparison with the supposed parallel NT material.

(4) Examination of the imperatival Participle is now in order. (a) A distinction must be made between the Participle as grammaticalizing an essential semantic feature and its pragmatic usage. The Participle is always a Participle by form, with its concomitant semantic meaning. Much discussion of the issue of the imperatival Participle appears to have been confused over a failure to distinguish form and function. No matter what the function of the Participle, it is never more or less than a Participle serving in the structures of several different units (see above), one of which is the predicate. As Frisk ("Participium," 56) says, "Das Participium ist immer als Partizipium aufgefasst worden. Das Problem lautet also night: das Participium als Verbum finitum (so Mayser a.a. O.), sondern: das Participium statt eines Verbum finitum." Some of the language used in discussing the imperatival Participle implies that language-users considered the Participle actually to be a finite verb (e.g. Blass/Debrunner, ¶ 468[2]: "It appears as if Paul considered the

---

[7]The shared characteristics are: (1) Nominative clauses announcing the theme in both; (2) the stated need to turn away from evil and to cling to God's will; (3) enumeration of virtues and vices; (4) a variety of forms used imperatively; and (5) a distinction by both writers between Imperatives to express God's inviolable laws and imperatival Participles and Infinitives to express secondary or derivative laws.

descriptive ptcp. to be the equivalent of the impera."). There is no evidence to support this. Indicative and Imperative are formal designations, not functional ones. The confusion arises when analysis is reduced to asking whether the Participle is an Imperative or an Indicative. Then extrapolations about the Participle are implied on the basis of the nature of the, for example, Imperative, failing to realize that the Participle remains a Participle. The Indicative and Imperative in Greek grammaticalize different attitudinal features which are proper to see in distinction. But this distinction is inappropriate when discussing the Participle, which formally and semantically is outside the ATTITUDE system. Thus a category mistake is made. The analysis is better formulated as stating that the Participle may appear in contexts where the Indicative or Imperative might be expected, without stating anything about any supposed alteration of the Participle. Since the Participle forms its grammatical relationship with a headterm, the question perhaps should not be why no finite verb is present with independent Participles, but what is the implied or stated headterm that the Participle modifies. Supposed uses of the Participle for a finite verb may be accounted for in this way.

(b) As stated above and as noted by grammarians in discussing the Genitive absolute, the Participle in Greek may function as a predicate at the rank of clause. Traditional grammarians have recognized the category of the independent Participle. For example, extra-biblical Greek uses the independent Participle (see esp. Kühner/Gerth, 2.105-07; Schwyzer, 2.403-04): Hdt. 4.185.2: ἔστι δὲ ἁλός τε μέταλλον ἐν αὐτῇ διὰ δέκα ἡμερέων ὁδοῦ καὶ ἄνθρωποι οἰκέοντες (and there is a salt mine in this [ridge] every ten days journey and men live there); Th. 1.42.1: ὦν ἐνθυμηθέντες καὶ νεώτερός τις παρὰ πρεσβυτέρου αὐτὰ μαθὼν ἀξιούτω τοῖς ὁμοίοις ἡμᾶς ἀμύνεσθαι, καὶ μὴ νομίσῃ δίκαια μὲν τάδε λέγεσθαι, ξύμφορα δέ, εἰ πολεμήσει, ἄλλα εἶναι (consider these things and let every youth, learning these things from an elder, consider it worthy for us to be defended in like ways, and let him not think that these just things are to be spoken of, but that they are to be of another kind of profit, if he will go to war); with an example of a commanding Participle; Th. 1.25.4: οὔτε γὰρ ἐν πανηγύρεσι ταῖς κοιναῖς διδόντες γέρα τὰ νομιζόμενα οὔτε Κορινθίῳ ἀνδρὶ προκαταρχόμενοι τῶν ἱερῶν ὥσπερ αἱ ἄλλαι ἀποικίαι, περιφρονοῦντες δὲ αὐτοὺς καὶ χρημάτων δυνάμει ὄντες κατ᾽ ἐκεῖνον τὸν χρόνον ὁμοῖα τοῖς Ἑλλήνων πλουσιωτάτοις καὶ τῇ ἐς πόλεμον παρασκευῇ δυνατώτεροι, ναυτικῷ δὲ καὶ πολὺ προύχειν ἔστιν ὅτε ἐπαιρόμενοι καὶ κατὰ τὴν Φαιάκων προενοίκησιν τῆς Κερκύρας κλέος ἐχόντων τὰ περὶ τὰς ναῦς (for neither in common public assemblies did they give common privileges nor did they offer to a C. man the first sacrifice of the temple as the other colonies, but they treated them with contempt and were at that time, in the power of their weath, equal to the richest of the Greeks and more powerful in preparation for war, and for the navy there was much to commend it, when boasting, regarding the previous occupation of C. of the P.s who had fame for their ships); Pl. Laws 686D: ἀποβλέψας γὰρ πρὸς τοῦτον τὸν στόλον οὐ πέρι διαλεγόμεθα, ἔδοξέ μοι πάγκαλός τε εἶναι καὶ θαυμαστὸν κτῆμα παραπεσεῖν τοῖς Ἕλλησιν, ὅπερ εἶπον, εἴ τις ἄρα αὐτῷ τότε καλῶς ἐχρήσατο (look at [?] this robe concerning which we are speaking; it seems to me to be an all-beautiful and marvelous creation to offer to the Greeks, which I said, unless someone then makes good use of it), with asyndeton of the second clause possibly arguing for the commanding use of the Participle.

Hellenistic writers use the independent Participle as well: App. Civ. Wars 1.29: προσέκειτο δέ, εἰ κυρώσειε τὸν νόμον ὁ δῆμος, τὴν βουλὴν πένθ᾽ ἡμέραις ἐπομόσαι πεισθήσεσθαι τῷ νόμῳ, ἢ τὸν οὐκ ὀμόσαντα μήτε βουλεύειν καὶ ὀφλεῖν τῷ δήμῳ τάλαντα εἴκοσιν, ὑπονοοῦντες οὕτως ἄλλους τε τῶν δυσχεραινόντων ἀμυνεῖσθαι καὶ Μέτελλον ὑπὸ φρονήματος οὐκ ἐνδώσοντα ἐς τὸν ὅρκον (it was put forward, if the people might enact the law, for the council to swear within five days to be obedient to the law, or to advise the one who does not swear indeed to incur a fine of 20 talents to the people, they were thinking thus to avenge others of the malcontents and M. who because of high-spiritedness was not giving in to the oath); Plu. Marc. Cato 4.4: ἐπίβλημα δὲ τῶν ποικίλων Βαβυλώνιον ἐκ κληρονομίας κτησάμενος εὐθὺς ἀποδόσθαι (he gained possession of a B. robe of many colours from an inheritance which was put away immediately) (the text continues: τῶν δὲ ἐπαύλεων αὐτοῦ μηδεμίαν εἶναι κεκονιαμένην, οὐδένα δὲ πώποτε πρίασθαι δοῦλον ὑπὲρ τὰς χιλίας δραχμὰς καὶ πεντακοσίας [of his residences none was plastered, and no servant ever was purchased for more than 1500 drachmas], with Infinitives parallel to the independent Participle). In the papyri (see esp. Moulton, 223; Mandilaras, 372. Mayser [2, 1.340-46] again tries to explain the examples as anacoluthon): P.Teb. 14.12-14 (114 B.C.): τῶι οὖν σημαινομένωι Ἡράτι / παρηγγελκότες ἐνώπιον τῆι ιδ / τοῦ ὑποκειμένου μηνός (we gave notice before the so-called H. on the 14th of the current month); P.Teb. 42.5-6 (114 B.C.): ἠδικημένος καθ'ὑπερ/βολὴν ὑπὸ Ἁρμιύσιος συναλλαγματογράφου / τῆς αὐτῆς (I have been treated very unjustly by A., the writer of contracts of [the village]);[8] P.Fay. 113.10-12 (A.D. 100): εὖ οὖν πυή/σας ἐξαυτῆς πέμσις αὐτὸν / ἐξαυτῆς (I ask urgently, send him at once); cf. P.Fay. 114.3-5 (A.D. 100); P.Fay. 116.3 (A.D. 104) all from the same writer; P.Giss. Univ.-Bibl. 21.3-5 (2d cent. A.D.): παρακληθείς, κύριε, μνήσ/θητί μου τῆς δεήσεως ἧς / κατ᾽ ὄψιν σοι πεποίημαι (I beseech you, lord, remember my prayer which I made before your face); P.Oxy. 2351.58-63 (A.D. 112): ἐὰν δὲ ἀδωσιτικῶσι ἐν τῇ ἀποδόσι τῶν / προκειμένων ὡς ἐπάνω δεδήλωται ἔξον/τος τῷ Φατρῇ ἐντὸς τοῦ χρόνου ἑτέροις / μεταμισθοῖν καὶ ἐκπράσσειν αὐτοὺς / τὰ ὅλα ὀφειλόμενα διὰ τὸ ἐπὶ τούτοις / ἑστάσθαι (if they might fail in the payment of the obligations set forth as made clear above, it will be lawful to P. within the time to release to others and to require of them the entire obligation on account of being set with them); BGU 1676.6-10 (2d cent. A.D.): καὶ οἱ με/σῖται ἀκούσαντες ἀπὸ τῶν ἀντι/δίκων σου, ὅτι τὸ πρᾶγμα ὅλον ἱς σαὶ / ἔβαλλειν, ἔδωκα ἐνγύην τῷ μα/χεροφόρῳ (and the arbiters heard from your opponents, because the entire deed was put upon you, I gave surety to the police). (Frisk ["Participium"] cites several later papyri, as well as several examples from Josesphus: Ant. 4.181; 17.128f., all of which he refutes. He claims that there is no "reinen Nominalsatz, wo das prädikat aus einem adjektivischen Partizipium besteht" [64].)

(c) There are several examples cited above of the commanding Participle used in a context that is not part of a closing formula: e.g. P.Fay. 112.8; P.Petrie ii 19.1ff.; P.Hib. 78.6; P.Cairo Zen. 59251.6; 59154.2; P.Fay. 109.10. While anacoluthon may serve as a possible explanation for some of them, this is not convincing for all. In fact, the terms of discussion must be shifted. It has been established that the independent Participle is an acceptable use of the Participle in Greek. The question is not whether these examples may qualify as such, but whether they pragmatically are used as commands. Whereas pragmatic categories by their very nature appear susceptible to endless dispute, there is nothing grammatically which stands in the way of the commanding Participle as a description of one of the uses of the Participle in Greek. (Barrett ["Participle," 166] notes that Pol. Phil. 4-6 has "Perhaps the longest list of imperatival participles *and adjectives*." Cf. also Did. 5.1ff.) Thus the use of the commanding Participle in hellenistic Greek is not a radical shift in verbal usage, but simply an extension of capabilities implicitly present in usage of the Participle from earliest times.

(d) Daube objects to several of the examples cited on the basis of their being formulaic uses. He inadvertently endorses the category of the commanding Participle with this assertion, however. Idioms of a language by nature are set patterns of accepted usage, often quite old. The fact that the closing patterns of the papyri are so similar points to this being an acceptable idiom of hellenistic Greek, possibly dating to a much earlier period. (Mandilaras [373], following Mayser, claims that there is an understood καλῶς ποιήσεις (-σετε) in the closing formulas, but as Turner [*Insights*, 167] states, "however one accounts for it, the idiom is there.")

Examples of a Participle serving in place of an Indicative might include: Acts 24:5; Rom 5:11; 2 Cor 4:13; 5:6, 12; 6:3; 7:5; 8:20; 9:11, 13; 10:4, 15; 11:6; Eph 5:21; 2 Thess 3:8; Heb 6:8; 7:2; 10:8, 16; 1 Pet 3:1; 5:7; 2 Pet 1:17; 2:1; 3:5; Rev 10:2; 21:12, 14, among others. (Winer [440-44] explains all examples as either grammatically dependent or anacoluthon.) Examples of a Participle serving in place of an Imperative might include: Rom 12:9-19; 13:11; 2 Cor 6:3-10;

---

[8]P.Teb. 24.7-11 (117 B.C.) reads: ὁ γὰρ ἐγκ[α]λούμενος ἐν τῷ αὐτῷ / συνείπαντος Θρακίδα Ἀπολλωνίου τῶν / ἐκ τῆς αὐτῆς, ἐν γὰρ τῷι ἐνεστῶτι ἔτει / Θωὺθ ἐθέμην μίσθωσιν τῆς ὑπαρχ[ού]σης μοι / περὶ τὴν αὐτὴν βασιλικῆς γῆς (for the accused in the same way conspired with T. son of A., from the same [village], for in the present year T., I made payment for my possession of royal land around the village).

8:24; 9:11, 13; Eph 3:17-18; 4:2; 5:16-22; Phil 1:30; Col 2:2; 3:16ff.; 4:11; Heb 13:5; 1 Pet 2:12, 18; 3:1, 7, 9; 4:8ff.; 2 Pet 3:3; and Luke 24:47, among others. It is unnecessary to dispute which ones are better seen as within an Indicative-like context or which ones are better seen as within an Imperative-like context. The implications of such distinctions are not semantically but pragmatically based.

2. **Independent Infinitive.** This usage has long been recognized in both earlier and later ancient Greek (see e.g. Goodwin, *Syntax*, 310-13; Stork, *Usage*, 89ff.): X. Hell. 1.4.16: ὑπάρχειν γὰρ ἐκ τοῦ δήμου αὐτῷ μὲν τῶν τε ἡλικιωτῶν πλέον ἔχειν τῶν τε πρεσβυτέρων μὴ ἐλαττοῦσθαι, τοῖς δ' αὐτοῦ ἐχθροῖς τοιούτοις δοκεῖν εἶναι οἷόσπερ πρότερον, ὕστερον δὲ δυνασθεῖσιν ἀπολλύναι τοὺς βελτίστους, αὐτοὺς δὲ μόνους λειφθέντας δι' αὐτὸ τοῦτο ἀγαπᾶσθαι ὑπὸ τῶν πολιτῶν ὅτι ἑτέροις βελτίοσιν οὐκ εἶχον χρῆσθαι (for under the democracy it was for him to be better than his peers and not less than the elders, but with his enemies it appeared to be such as before, but later being able to destroy the best men, but leaving themselves only on account of this they were loved by the citizens because they did not have other better men to make use of); Epict. 4.10.18: ἵνα δὲ ταῦτα γένηται, οὐ μικρὰ δέξασθαι οὐδὲ μικρῶν ἀποτυχεῖν (so that these things might occur, one must receive no small things and must miss no small things). To translate the language into the appropriate category, the Infinitive group may fill the paradigmatic slot of predicate at the rank of clause, whether the pragmatic function be defined here as asserting or commanding. Examples in the NT include the classical phrase ὡς ἔπος εἰπεῖν (as to say a word) found in Heb 7:9 (see Mandilaras, 322, for the few recorded instances in the papyri) and the Infinitive in greetings: Acts 15:23; 23:26; Jas 1:1. (This is extraordinarily common in the papyri: e.g. P.Teb. 10.1; 12.1, 2; 13.1; 14.2; 15.1; 16.2; 17.1; 18.1; 19.2; 20.1; 21.1; 22.2; 23.1; 27.2; 28.1; 30.2; 31.2; 32.1, 5; 33.1; 34.2; 35.3; 36.2; 37.2, just in the official correspondence [nos. 8-37, all from 201-73 B.C.]. For a comparison between NT and other epistles see most recently Lieu, "'Grace,'" esp. 162-63, 167ff.) Commanding uses might include (see Kühner/Gerth, 2.19-24; Moulton, 179; Robertson, 1092-93; Burton, 146; Mandilaras, 316-19; Mayser, 2, 1.303-05): Phil 3:16: τῷ αὐτῷ στοιχεῖν (live the same way); Rom 12:15: χαίρειν μετὰ χαιρόντων, κλαίειν μετὰ κλαιόντων (rejoice with those rejoicing, cry with those crying); Luke 9:3: μήτε [ἀνὰ] δύο χιτῶνας ἔχειν (don't have two chitons); and Titus 2:2-10 (Winer [397] and Moulton [179] argue for the Infinitive dependent on the verb of speaking). (Significant examples from the papyri include: P.Mich. Zen. 89.3-5 [3d cent. B.C.]: εἴ σοι / δοκεῖ, δ[οῦναί] μοί τι ὀψώνιον [if you are able, give to me some provisions]; P.Teb. 34.3-4 [c. 100 B.C.]: ἅμα τῷ σε λαβῖν τὸ ἐπιστόλιν / συνελθεῖν Ὥρῳ [then when you receive the letter go to H.]; P.Oxy. 1929.3-4 [4th/5th cent. A.D.]: φροντίσαι οὖν τουτω / πάραυτα ῥωῆσαι [?] [consider helping in this immediately] [this last is by a person of marginal literacy].) And strictly independent: Rev 12:7: ὁ Μιχαὴλ καὶ οἱ ἄγγελοι αὐτοῦ τοῦ πολεμῆσαι μετὰ τοῦ δράκοντος (M. and his angels to fight with the dragon). (Not to be included are 1 Thess 3:11; 2 Thess 2:17; 3:5, since these are Optatives.)

c. Relative temporal reference of the Participle and the Infinitive, with reference to syntax and aspect. 1. Participle. a. Discussion of the Greek Participle has been surrounded by much terminological confusion,[9] much stemming from an insistence on the one hand that the tense forms function according to a supposed temporal scheme, and recognition on the other hand that the numerous exceptions to such a temporal scheme provide insurmountable difficulties (e.g. Ballantine, "Aorist

---

[9]A classic example is the dispute between Carter and Whitelaw over the "instrumentality" and temporal relation of the Participle, much of which confusion stems from a category mistake: Carter, "Uses"; Humphreys, untitled; Whitelaw, "Uses"; Carter, untitled.

Participles"; "Predicative Participles"). Recently it has been recognized by Hettrich--who argues stringently for a temporal relation between the Imperfect and Aorist tenses in the Indicative--that the Participle, whether Present or Aorist, may be antecedent or coincidental (*Kontext*, 77-83, although he still attempts to impose his temporal scheme [see my chapt. 4]). Those who recognize (to varying degrees) the 'timelessness' of the Participle include Seymour ("Use"); Platt ("Participles"); Campbell (untitled); Oguse (*Recherches*, esp. 26, whose work is hampered by failure to consider kind of action or aspect); Rose (*Tenses*, 34-35); Burton (54 and ff.); McKay (esp. 219-20); and Robertson, who says, "It may be said at once that the participle has tense in the same sense that the subjunctive, optative and imperative have, giving the state of the action as punctiliar, linear, completed. In the beginning this was all that tense meant in the participle. The participle was timeless. Indeed the participle in itself continued timeless, as is well shown by the articular participle" (1111). On the basis of the argumentation presented above (esp. chapts. 2 and 4), it is clear that the essential semantic feature of Greek verbal structure is certainly not absolute temporal reference (relative temporal reference may be established from context) but verbal aspect. That the Participle is not temporally-based is seen in a number of examples which defy the traditional temporal conception.[10]

Matt 10:39-40: ὁ εὑρὼν τὴν ψυχὴν αὐτοῦ ἀπολέσει αὐτήν, καὶ ὁ ἀπολέσας τὴν ψυχὴν αὐτοῦ ἕνεκεν ἐμοῦ εὑρήσει αὐτήν. ὁ δεχόμενος ὑμᾶς ἐμὲ δέχεται, καὶ ὁ ἐμὲ δεχόμενος δέχεται τὸν ἀποστείλαντά με (the one who finds his soul will lose it, and the one who loses his soul on account of me will find it. The one who receives you receives me, and the one who receives me receives the one who sent [?] me), where the perpetrator of a negative act is described using the Aorist, and the perpetrator of a positive act with the Present. Matt 10:4 versus 26:25 and 27:3: Judas is referred to in the first as ὁ . . . παραδούς and in the second two as ὁ παραδιδούς (the betrayer); Matt 16:28, Acts 9:12, and Mark 9:1: ἂν ἴδωσιν τὸν υἱὸν τοῦ ἀνθρώπου ἐρχόμενον (he might see the son of man coming), εἶδεν ἄνδρα Ἀνανίαν ὀνόματι εἰσελθόντα καὶ ἐπιθέντα αὐτῷ (he saw a man by the name of A. enter and put on him), and ἂν

---

[10]For classical examples see e.g. Th. 1.69.1: ὁ δουλωσάμενος . . . ὁ δυνάμενος . . . παῦσαι, περιορῶν ([the state] which enslaves . . . which is able to cease, looking on); D. 21.178: Χαρικλείδου, τοῦ ἄρξαντος (C., the archon); Lys. 30.12: οἱ καταλύοντες τὸν δῆμον . . . οἱ τῶν τριάκοντα γενόμενοι (those who were destroying the democracy . . . those who were members of the thirty); cf. Winer, 427ff., and those cited above.

ἴδωσιν τὴν βασιλείαν τοῦ θεοῦ ἐληλυθυῖαν (they might see the kingdom of God coming).[11] Other examples of the Aorist include: Matt 25:16, 18, 20 and 24: ὁ λαβών and ὁ εἰληφώς (the possessor) are temporally identical, with the perfective aspect grammaticalizing simple reference to one who possesses (Louw, "Waarde," 29), but the stative aspect used of the one who misused his master's trust; Matt 21:44:[12] ὁ πεσών (the one who falls) upon this stone, parallel to a conditional-like relative protasis; Matt 23:20-22: ὁ ὁμόσας (the swearer); Luke 12:9: ὁ . . . ἀρνησάμενος (the denier) parallel with a relative conditional in v 8; John 3:33: ὁ λαβών (the one who receives) his testimony certifies that God is true; John 5:29: ἐκπορεύσονται, οἱ τὰ ἀγαθὰ ποιήσαντες εἰς ἀνάστασιν ζωῆς, οἱ δὲ τὰ φαῦλα πράξαντες εἰς ἀνάστασιν κρίσεως (they will go out, those who do good to resurrection of life, and those who do evil to resurrection of judgment); John 16:2: πᾶς ὁ ἀποκτείνας (every killer); Acts 10:3: Peter saw in a vision an ἄγγελον τοῦ θεοῦ εἰσελθόντα (an angel of God coming) to him; cf. 11:13: Peter relates the same incident telling of an ἄγγελον . . . σταθέντα καὶ εἰπόντα (angel standing and saying); 2 Cor 7:12: εἰ καὶ ἔγραψα ὑμῖν, οὐχ ἕνεκεν τοῦ ἀδικήσαντος, οὐδὲ ἕνεκεν τοῦ ἀδικηθέντος, ἀλλ' ἕνεκεν τοῦ φανερωθῆναι τὴν σπουδὴν ὑμῶν (if I write to you, it is not on account of the one acting unjustly, nor on account of the one being treated unjustly, but on account of your desire being made known). Other examples of the Present include (see Meecham, "Participle," 285-86): Matt 2:20: Joseph is told that οἱ ζητοῦντες (those who were seeking) the child are dead; Matt 5:22: πᾶς ὁ ὀργιζόμενος (everyone who swears), with this pattern quite common: Luke 6:47; John 3:15, 16; 8:34; 11:26; 12:46; 19:12; 1 John 3:4, 15; 5:1; Rom 10:11; Rev 22:15; John 9:8: οἱ θεωροῦντες αὐτὸν τὸ πρότερον (those who saw him previously); Acts 3:10: ὁ πρὸς τὴν ἐλεημοσύνην καθήμενος (the one who was sitting for alms); Acts 10:7: ὁ ἄγγελος ὁ λαλῶν αὐτῷ (the angel who spoke to him); Gal 1:23: ὁ διώκων ἡμᾶς ποτε νῦν εὐαγγελίζεται τὴν πίστιν ἥν ποτε ἐπόρθει (the one who was then persecuting us is now proclaiming the faith which he then was destroying); Heb 10:14: τοὺς ἁγιαζομένους (those sanctified). (Timeless use of the Present is very common with the Participle. Examples not cited above [since the translation in English is similar to the traditional conception] but certainly to be included are: Luke 23:49; Eph 4:28; 1 Pet 3:5.)

Participles as elements in subject, predicate, complement, or adjunct structures establish temporal reference from context. Several grammarians persist, however, in claiming that the Participle is temporally based in what is traditionally called adverbial usage (adjunctive[s]). On the basis of the general theory being presented here, as well as the examples using the Participle cited above, and other examples cited below, this can be seen to be a false hypothesis. For example, the common phrase ἀποκριθεὶς εἶπεν (answering he said) is intractable (e.g. Matt 19:27; Acts 4:19; but cf. explanation below) (Ballantine, "Predicative Participles," 787-88). A second set of examples difficult to

---

[11]This section, as well as discussion by earlier grammatical studies, makes the statement by Lieu (*Epistles*, 84) on 2 John 7 quite surprising: "The present participle **'Jesus Christ** *coming* **in (the) flesh'** ('Ιησοῦν Χριστὸν ἐρχόμενον ἐν σαρκί), instead of the perfect of 1 John 4:2, 'having come' (ἐληλυθότα), *grammatically* makes a reference to the past fact of the incarnation improbable. Since in the Greek of the New Testament period the future of 'to come' (ἰέναι) was not frequently used and the present could be used with future meaning, the most natural translation *grammatically* would be a reference to a future coming 'in the flesh.'" This judgment is questionable. (1) It is not a grammatical statement. (2) It is contradictory to the evidence. (3) It reflects an inadequate estimation of tense function in Greek. Cf. Th. 4.81.1: ἐξῆλθε πλείστου ἄξιον Λακεδαιμονίοις γενόμενον (he went away, becoming valuable to the L.s).

[12]Some manuscripts omit this verse: D 33 etc. It receives a C rating in UBS[3].

explain in this model is Aorist Participles which are clearly coincidental (see e.g. Burton, 64-65).

Matt 27:4: ἥμαρτον παραδοὺς αἷμα ἀθῷον (I sinned, betraying innocent blood); Acts 7:36: God ἐξήγαγεν (led them out), ποιήσας (performing) wonders and signs in the land of Egypt and in the Reed Sea and in the desert for 40 years (Bruce's comments [Acts, 171] about the "ordinary force" of the Participle are special pleading); Acts 10:33: σύ τε καλῶς ἐποίησας παραγενόμενος (you did well, coming); Acts 11:30: ὃ καὶ ἐποίησαν ἀποστείλαντες (which indeed they did, sending); Acts 12:25: Barnabas and Saul ὑπέστρεψαν εἰς Ἰερουσαλήμ πληρώσαντες τὴν διακονίαν, συμπαραλαβόντες Ἰωάννην τὸν ἐπικληθέντα Μᾶρκον (returned to J., fulfilling their ministry, taking with them John the one called Mark), with the major question being whether εἰς Ἰερουσαλήμ is to be taken with the following Participle (see Bruce, Acts, 251-52); Acts 15:8; Acts 19:2: εἰ πνεῦμα ἅγιον ἐλάβετε πιστεύσαντες; (whether you received the holy spirit upon believing?), in a verse which has proved crucial in recent debate about the holy spirit (see Dunn, Baptism, 86-87; Ervin, Conversion, 62, both following Burton, 59-60); Acts 22:24: the chiliarch ἐκέλευσεν (ordered) Paul to be taken into the barracks, εἴπας (saying) for him to be examined by whipping; Acts 24:22: Felix ἀνεβάλετο (adjourned) Paul and his accusers, εἴπας (saying) . . . ; Acts 27:3: φιλανθρώπως τε ὁ Ἰούλιος τῷ Παύλῳ χρησάμενος ἐπέτρεψεν πρὸς τοὺς φίλους πορευθέντι ἐπιμελείας τυχεῖν (J., treating Paul well, permitted him to receive care by going to his friends); Rom 4:19-21: Abraham, μὴ ἀσθενήσας (not being weak) in faith, κατενόησεν (considered) his own body as dead, being (ὑπάρχων) almost 80 . . . but the promise of God he οὐ διεκρίθη (did not doubt) in unbelief but ἐνεδυναμώθη (was empowered) by faith, δούς (giving) glory to God and πληροφορηθείς (being convinced) that what was promised was possible; Heb 7:27: τοῦτο γὰρ ἐποίησεν ἐφάπαξ ἑαυτὸν ἐνενέγκας (he did this once, offering up himself).

A third set of examples difficult to explain is Present Participles which are clearly antecedent: Luke 9:5-6: ἐξερχόμενοι (going out) from an inhospitable city, ἀποτινάσσετε (shake off) the dust from your feet as a testimony. ἐξερχόμενοι δὲ διήρχοντο (going out, pass through) each village, εὐαγγελιζόμενοι καὶ θεραπεύοντες (proclaiming good news and healing); Acts 4:34: πωλοῦντες ἔφερον τὰς τιμὰς τῶν πιπρασκομένων (having sold, they brought the proceeds of the sales); cf. v 37: πωλήσας ἤνεγκεν τὸ χρῆμα (having sold he brought the money).

b. Despite this evidence, in many instances the Aorist Participle is antecedent and the Present coincidental. Rather than this residing with the Participle itself, however, verbal aspect and syntax must be taken into consideration. (1) Since verbal aspect provides the essential semantic feature of Greek verbal usage, and since as seen above the aspects may implicate a range of temporal spheres, there is no reason to believe that the Participle would not be used in this way as well. In fact, it would be surprising if the Participle were not used in this way. (2) Although it is difficult to establish clear statistics for NT Greek, much less for extra-biblical Greek, it appears that the Aorist Participle tends to precede the finite verb of the clause and that the Present Participle tends to follow the finite verb of the clause (there are many potential ambiguities in calculating the adjunctive[s] category) (see Hartman, Constructions, passim, for some statistics on this. Many examples are syntactically ambiguous, whether the Participle is an element in an adjunct[s] or subject structure). From this an alternative explanation may be posited. It has already been shown that a strictly temporal conception (whether absolute or relative) of Greek verb tenses, including the Participle, does not explain large numbers of examples. To determine temporal reference of the Participle strictly in terms of relation to the main verb neglects the grammatical relation of the Participle being in concord with its stated or implied headterm. Instead, the Participle modifies this headterm, but the syntactical pattern appears to be used to make relative statements about when the process is seen to have occurred (this recognizes the artificiality of imposing temporal criteria upon Participle usage, since pragmatically a range of relations, such as causal, concessive, conditional, commanding, etc., may be possible). Thus when the Participle is placed before the main verb, there is a tendency for the action to be depicted as antecedent, and when the Participle is placed after the main verb, there is a tendency for the action to be seen as concurrent or subsequent (see Grice, "Logic." This syntactical analysis conforms to Grice's maxim of manner, in which conversation must be orderly). This is not a binding classification but appears to function in a large enough number of cases to warrant the generalization (the rule seems to hold for extra-biblical Greek also, although much work needs to be done here). As a general syntactical rule it still requires that each context be analysed to establish temporal reference of the particular usage (this kind of a syntactic rule has been recognized at least in part by e.g. Moulton, 130-31; Rose, *Tenses*, 34; Robertson, 1113; Blass, 197). It also helps to explain how the traditional estimation of the temporal relations of the Participles emerged out of a syntactical tendency. As Blass/Debrunner (¶ 339) say,

> Participles originally had no temporal function, but denoted only the *Aktionsart*, their temporal relation to the finite verb was derived from the context. Since, however, a participle expressing the notion of completion often preceded the finite verb . . . so that the sequence normally was: the completion of the action denoted by the participle, then the action of the finite verb, the idea of relative past time became associated to a certain degree with the aorist participle. . .

(see Rijksbaron, Review, 248: "I still think that the aorist participle has its proper value: while not expressing anteriority, in the strict, temporal sense, it *does* refer to a completed action. . . . We might say, then, that the action of the participle is logically prior to that of the main verb, not temporally," but cf. *Syntax*, 114ff.).

Two recently gathered sets of data from GRAMCORD bear out this generalization. (1) Of approximately 85 instances in the NT where a Present and Aorist Participle modify the same main verb, in approximately 75 of the instances the Aorist precedes and the Present follows. (References are from Knorr, "Aorist." Analysis is my own.)[13]

Instances where the Aorist precedes and the Present follows an Aorist main verb that conform to the pattern above include the following (see also Matt 8:25; 14:30b [cf. v 30a: βλέπων (seeing) the wind ἐφοβήθη (they were afraid)]; 15:22; 16:22; 19:22; 21:20; 25:20; 26:8, 42; 27:29b [cf. v 29a]; 28:13, 18; Mark 6:25; 10:22 [?]; 14:60; Luke 1:63; 5:8, 13; 7:18-19, 39; 8:24, 54; 24:23; Acts 3:26; 5:22-23 [cf. v 22a]; 12:7; 22:26): Matt 8:3: Jesus ἐκτείνας (stretched out) his hand, ἥψατο (touched) the leper, λέγων (saying). This is a common pattern, in which two processes are described in their completeness and then a statement is made that in some way grows out of this series of events. Matt 14:26: Jesus' disciples ἰδόντες (seeing) him walking (περιπατοῦντα) upon the sea, ἐταράχθησαν (were troubled) λέγοντες (saying); Matt 26:27: λαβὼν ποτήριον καὶ εὐχαριστήσας ἔδωκεν αὐτοῖς λέγων (taking the cup and giving thanks he gave it to them, saying); Matt 26:39: προελθὼν μικρὸν ἔπεσεν ἐπὶ πρόσωπον αὐτοῦ προσευχόμενος καὶ λέγων (going ahead a little he fell upon his face, praying and saying); Matt 27:3-4: τότε ἰδὼν Ἰούδας ὁ παραδιδοὺς αὐτὸν ὅτι κατεκρίθη μεταμεληθεὶς ἔστρεψεν τὰ τριάκοντα ἀργύρια τοῖς ἀρχιερεῦσιν καὶ πρεσβυτέροις λέγων (then J., his betrayer, seeing that he was condemned, being regretful, returned the 30 silvers to the chief priests and elders, saying), where a traditional temporal conception of the tense forms makes nonsense of this verse; Matt 27:35: σταυρώσαντες (having crucified him) διεμερίσαντο (they divided) his garments βάλλοντες (casting) lots; Mark 9:25: ἰδὼν δὲ ὁ Ἰησοῦς ὅτι ἐπισυντρέχει ὄχλος ἐπετίμησεν τῷ πνεύματι τῷ ἀκαθάρτῳ λέγων (Jesus, seeing that a crowd was accompanying him, rebuked the unclean spirit, saying), where the historic Present does not alter the syntactical patterning; Luke 2:45: καὶ μὴ εὑρόντες ὑπέστρεψαν εἰς Ἰερουσαλὴμ ἀναζητοῦντες αὐτόν (not finding him, they returned to J., seeking him), where the Present Participle may indicate subsequent action; Luke 5:12: ἰδὼν (seeing) Jesus, πεσὼν (falling) upon his face, ἐδεήθη (he begged) him λέγων (saying); Luke 10:34: προσελθὼν (approaching) κατέδησεν (he bound) his wounds, ἐπιχέων (pouring on) olive oil and wine (is there a chance that the olive oil and wine were poured over the bound wound?); Luke 22:19: λαβὼν ἄρτον εὐχαριστήσας ἔκλασεν καὶ ἔδωκεν αὐτοῖς λέγων (taking bread, blessing it, he broke it and gave it to them, saying); Acts 13:12: τότε ἰδὼν ὁ ἀνθύπατος τὸ γεγονὸς ἐπίστευσεν ἐκπλησσόμενος ἐπὶ τῇ διδαχῇ τοῦ κυρίου (then seeing the state of affairs, the proconsul believed, being amazed at the teaching of the lord), where it is questionable whether the process grammaticalized by the Present Participle is antecedent or concurrent.

---

[13]In extra-biblical Greek: Th. 1.63.1: παρῆλθε παρὰ τὴν χηλὴν διὰ τῆς θαλάσσης βαλλόμενός τε καὶ χαλεπῶς, ὀλίγους μέν τινας ἀποβαλών, τοὺς δὲ πλείους σώσας (he passed along the breakwater through the sea, being attacked fiercely, losing a few men, and saving others); Th. 2.29.1: οἱ Ἀθηναῖοι πρότερον πολέμιον νομίζοντες πρόξενον ἐποιήσαντο καὶ μετεπέμψαντο, βουλόμενοι (the A.s, having previously considered him an enemy, made proxenus and summoned, wanting); Plb. 2.8.3: οἱ δὲ Ῥωμαῖοι, παρακούοντες τὸν πρὸ τοῦ χρόνον τῶν ἐγκαλούντων τοῖς Ἰλλυριοῖς . . . κατέστησαν πρεσβευτάς (the R.s, having previously ignored the complaints against the I.s, appointed envoys); Arr. 1.16.1: καὶ οἱ Πέρσαι παιόμενοί τε πανταχόθεν ἤδη ἐς τὰ πρόσωπα αὐτοί τε καὶ οἱ ἵπποι τοῖς ξυστοῖς καὶ πρὸς τῶν ἱππέων ἐξωθούμενοι, πολλὰ δὲ καὶ πρὸς τῶν ψιλῶν ἀναμεμιγμένων τοῖς ἱππεῦσι βλαπτόμενοι, ἐγκλίνουσι (the P.s, from all quarters already they and their horses having been struck in the faces with lances, and been driven by the cavalry, and been hit hard many times even by the light troops who became mixed up with the cavalry, they gave way to this); App. Civ. Wars 1.25: καὶ αὐτὸν οὕτως ἔχοντα θορύβου κατιδὼν δημότης ἀνὴρ Ἀντύλλος ἐν τῇ στοᾷ θύων, ἐμβαλὼν τὴν χεῖρα, εἴτε τι πυθόμενος ἢ ὑποπτεύων ἢ ἄλλως ἐς τὸν λόγον ὑπαχθείς (a plebian A. saw him thus having a look of distress, sacrificing in the portico, put his hand on him, either having learned something or being suspicious or being moved to words by another reason).

Instances of the Aorist preceding and the Present following an Imperfect main verb conforming to the pattern include (see also Matt 9:18; 15:23, 25 [?]; 16:13; 18:26, 28b [cf. v 28a], 29; 20:11-12; Mark 14:57 [?]; Luke 19:7; 22:41-42; Acts 4:15; 23:9; 26:31; 27:38): Matt 5:2: ἀνοίξας (opening) his mouth ἐδίδασκεν (he was teaching) them λέγων (saying); Mark 9:20: πεσὼν ἐπὶ τῆς γῆς ἐκυλίετο ἀφρίζων (falling upon the earth he was rolling around having a fit); Mark 10:16: ἐναγκαλισάμενος αὐτὰ κατευλόγει τιθεὶς τὰς χεῖρας ἐπ᾽ αὐτά (taking them in his arms he was blessing them putting hands upon them); Luke 22:64: περικαλύψαντες αὐτὸν ἐπηρώτων λέγοντες (blindfolding him they were asking him saying); Acts 19:8: εἰσελθών (entering) into the synagogue ἐπαρρησιάζετο (they were bold) for three months, διαλεγόμενος καὶ πείθων (discussing and persuading) concerning the kingdom of God, where the Aorist is certainly not punctiliar but serves as a transition by summarizing the repeated process as a complete event; Acts 19:28: ἀκούσαντες (hearing) and γενόμενοι (becoming) full of anger ἔκραζον λέγοντες (he was crying out saying).

Instances with a Present Indicative as the main verb are also consistent (see also Luke 15:9): Luke 15:5: εὑρὼν ἐπιτίθησιν ἐπὶ τοὺς ὤμους αὐτοῦ χαίρων (finding [the sheep] he puts it upon his shoulders, rejoicing).

Instances where both Participles precede the main verb include: Matt 16:1: προσελθόντες οἱ Φαρισαῖοι καὶ Σαδδουκαῖοι πειράζοντες ἐπηρώτησαν αὐτόν (coming out, the P.s and S.s, testing, asked him); where the Present Participle may well be antecedent; Luke 7:37-38 (cf. v 39): ἐπιγνοῦσα ὅτι κατάκειται ἐν τῇ οἰκίᾳ τοῦ Φαρισαίου, κομίσασα ἀλάβαστρον μύρου καὶ στᾶσα ὀπίσω παρὰ τοὺς πόδας αὐτοῦ κλαίουσα, τοῖς δάκρυσιν ἤρξατο βρέχειν τοὺς πόδας αὐτοῦ καὶ ταῖς θριξὶν τῆς κεφαλῆς αὐτῆς ἐξέμασσεν (learning that he was reclining in the house of a P., buying a vial of perfume and standing behind, crying at his feet, she began with her tears to wash his feet and with her hair she wiped his head), where the sequence of Aorist and Present Participles is clearly antecedent (she could not begin to use the tears before she cried them); Acts 5:5: ἀκούων δὲ ὁ Ἀνανίας τοὺς λόγους τούτους πεσὼν ἐξέψυξεν (A., hearing these words, falling, expired), where the syntax as well as logical course of events indicates that the processes grammaticalized by the Participles are antecedent to that of the main verb (see also 2 Cor 11:9, where the first Participle is παρών [from πάρειμι]; cf. chapt. 10 on aspectually vague verbs).

An instance where both Participles follow the main verb includes: Matt 10:5: ἀπέστειλεν ὁ Ἰησοῦς παραγγείλας αὐτοῖς λέγων (Jesus sent [the twelve], ordering them saying), where both subordinate processes are probably coincidental to the main process. Luke 8:47: ἰδοῦσα δὲ ἡ γυνὴ ὅτι οὐκ ἔλαθεν τρέμουσα ἦλθεν καὶ προσπεσοῦσα αὐτῷ (the woman, seeing that she did not escape notice, trembling, she came and fell at his feet) is particularly instructive. Whether the second Aorist Participle is taken as coincidental or subsequent, in any case the Participles are relatively temporally determined on the basis of syntax.

Exceptions to this syntactic rule are few, but might include: Matt 22:1: ἀποκριθείς (answering), Jesus again εἶπεν (spoke) in parables to them λέγων (saying), although there is another possible explanation. The quite evident repetition of verbs of speaking indicates *prima facie* a distinction in the processes referred to. Whereas they might be coincidental, it is possible that the author is saying something like, "when he answered this time (answering seen as a complete process to introduce the section), Jesus again spoke in parables (complete process referring to the way in which he answered), saying (with the imperfective aspect marking the particular parable used)." (Ballantine ["Predicative Participles," 794] recognizes this as a "glaring exception" to his time-based rules.) See also Luke 14:3; Luke 23:40: ἀποκριθεὶς δὲ ὁ ἕτερος ἐπιτιμῶν αὐτῷ ἔφη (answering, the other, rebuking him, said), where the aspectually vague verb may have an influence; Acts 11:4: ἀρξάμενος δὲ Πέτρος ἐξετίθετο αὐτοῖς καθεξῆς λέγων (beginning, P. was explaining to them in order, saying), although it appears that the placing of ἀρξάμενος first syntactically reinforces the orderliness of the explanation.

(2) The second GRAMCORD study is of the Aorist Participle in Paul, in which it is concluded that of the approximately 120 Aorist Participles found in relation to a main verb, approximately 78 precede and 42 follow the main

verb, with those preceding showing a definite tendency toward antecedent action and those following showing a definite tendency toward coincidental action. (See Taylor, "Sequence," for list of examples. Analysis is my own.)[14]

Examples of those preceding need not be cited, since this has not only already been explained but conforms to the traditional analysis of tense form function. But several examples of those following are worth noting (see also 1 Cor 12:24; Gal 3:19; Phil 2:7, 8, 30; 4:14; Col 2:14, 15; with aspectually vague verbs see Eph 2:10, 14-15, 20): Rom 4:20-21: Paul says of the promise of God Abraham οὐ διεκρίθη τῇ ἀπιστίᾳ ἀλλ' ἐνεδυναμώθη τῇ πίστει, δοὺς δόξαν τῷ θεῷ καὶ πληροφορηθείς (did not doubt in unbelief but was empowered by faith, giving glory to God and being convinced); 2 Cor 5:19: God was reconciling the world in Christ (see chapt. 10 on the periphrasis), μὴ λογιζόμενος (not counting) their sins against them, and θέμενος (putting) among us the word of reconciliation; Gal 2:1: after fourteen years ἀνέβην (I went up) again to Jerusalem with Barnabas, συμπαραλαβών (taking with) me Titus; Gal 3:13: Christ ἐξηγόρασεν (redeemed) us from the curse of the law, γενόμενος (becoming) a curse on behalf of us (although there is a possibility the main verb is timeless); Eph 1:4-5: God ἐξελέξατο (elected) us in him before the foundation of the world, προορίσας (foreordaining) us to sonship, see also Eph 1:9, 11; Eph 1:20: ἐνήργησεν ἐν τῷ Χριστῷ ἐγείρας αὐτὸν ἐκ νεκρῶν, καὶ καθίσας ([God] acted in Christ raising him from the dead and seating him); Eph 2:16: ἀποκαταλλάξῃ (he might reconcile [this double compound is probably a Paulinism, so Büchsel, TDNT, 1.258]) the both in one body to God through the cross, ἀποκτείνας (killing) the enemy in it/him [?]), cf. Col 1:20; Eph 5:26: ἁγιάσῃ καθαρίσας (he might sanctify [the church], purifying it); Col 2:2: their hearts παρακληθῶσιν (might be comforted), συμβιβασθέντες (being united) in love, where reference of the Participle depends upon whether their previous unity or (better) the unity that is concomitant with their comfort is being spoken of; Col 2:13: συνεζωοποίησεν (he makes/made alive) us with him, χαρισάμενος (forgiving) us all our transgressions, where the syntax makes it difficult to distinguish the two processes temporally; 1 Tim 1:12: God πιστόν με ἡγήσατο θέμενος (considered me faithful putting me) into service, where the following clause refers to previous existence; 2 Tim 4:10: Demos με ἐγκατέλιπεν ἀγαπήσας (left me, loving) the present age.

Several disputable instances include: Rom 7:6: νυνὶ δὲ κατηργήθημεν ἀπὸ τοῦ νόμου, ἀποθανόντες ἐν ᾧ κατειχόμεθα (but now we are released from the law, dead by what we were possessed), depending upon whether dying refers to a previous or coincidental process; Eph 6:14-16: the author says στῆτε (stand) therefore περιζωσάμενοι (wrap around) your waist in truth, and ἐνδυσάμενοι (put on) the breastplate of righteousness, and ὑποδησάμενοι (tie on) the sandles, in everything ἀναλαβόντες (take up) the shield of faith. These Participles are probably coincidental on the basis of v 17, which commands the reader δέξασθε (receive) the helmet of

---

[14]In extra-biblical Greek: S. Ant. 171-72: λοντο παίσαντές τε καὶ / πληγέντες (they were killed, being tormented and struck), doubted by Whitelaw, "Uses," 248, who does cite S. Oed. King 707-08; Th. 1.71.4: βοηθήσατε κατὰ τάχος ἐσβαλόντες ἐς τὴν Ἀττικήν (help, invading immediately into A.); Th. 1.101.3: ὡμολόγησαν Ἀθηναίοις τεῖχός τε καθελόντες καὶ ναῦς παραδόντες, χρήματά τε ὅσα ἔδει ἀποδοῦναι αὐτίκα ταξάμενοι καὶ τὸ λοιπὸν φέρειν (they came to terms with the A.s, both pulling down the walls and handing over the ships, and agreeing to hand over whatever possessions were necessary and to pay tribute for the remainder); D. 19.50: εὐφημότατ' ἀνθρώπων τούτοις παραδοῦναι γέγραφε τὸ ἱερὸν γράψας τοῖς Ἀμφικτύοσι παραδοῦναι (he wrote kindly to give the temple to those men, writing to give to the A.s); Pl. Phaed. 60C: εὖ γ' ἐποίησας ἀναμνήσας με (you did well, reminding me), cited by Curtius, Elucidations, 217; cf. Hdt. 5.24.4: εὖ γὰρ ἐποίησας ἀπικόμενος (you did well, coming); X. Cyr. 1.4.13: ὡς βουλεύομαί γε ὅπως σε ἀποδρῶ λαβὼν τοὺς ἡλικιώτας ἐπὶ θήραν. . . . καλῶς . . . ἐποίησας προειπών (for I am planning so that I might flee from you, taking my comrades on a hunt . . . you did well, telling me in advance); Arr. 1.19.10: πέμπει ἐπ' αὐτὰς κατὰ σπουδήν, ἐμβάλλειν ἀντιπρώρους κελεύσας (he sent them upon them with haste, ordering them to ram).

salvation; cf. 1 Tim 5:8. Phil 2:19: εὐψυχῶ γνούς (I might take courage knowing) the things concerning you, depending on whether the things known are past, present or even possibly future depending upon Timothy's journey; Col 1:3-4: εὐχαριστοῦμεν (we give thanks) to God, praying (προσευχόμενοι) for you always, ἀκούσαντες (hearing of) your faith, where the process of hearing is probably past, although placement after the main verb and the Present Participle is noteworthy; Col 3:9-10: μὴ ψεύδεσθε (don't lie) to each other, ἀπεκδυσάμενοι (putting off) the old man with his practices and ἐνδυσάμενοι (putting on) the new, where again the reference of the Participle may be to a previous or coincidental process.

The point need not be belaboured that the Participle in Greek is not temporally-based, but that differentiation according to verbal aspect allows for a range of temporal reference determined on the basis of context. Syntactic features appear to be important in this but are not a substitute for analysis of individual instances.

c. Since this is the case, it is surprising that a continuing point of contention is whether the Aorist Participle is ever 'future-referring.' As has been seen, there is nothing inherent in the Participle that forbids its reference to subsequent action in relation to the main verb of the sentence. In fact it would appear that the perfective aspect of the Aorist, since it grammaticalizes an event as a complete process, would be suitable not only for antecedent and coincidental reference but for subsequent reference as well. There is good evidence that this is the case.

In extra-biblical Greek, the following examples may be cited. (Lee ["Aorist Participle"; "Parallels"] provides the most complete list, with "Past Participle," 199, where he cites a parallel from Pliny *Natural History* 8.185. Cf. Platt, "Participles"; Harding, "Action," who also cites the less clear Pi. Ol. 7.5; Wifstrand, "Apostelgeschichte," 134-36, who cites parallel examples down to the 10th cent. A.D., including D.S. 22.13 with a Genitive absolute.) Hom. Il. 5.368-69: ἔνθ' ἵππους ἔστησε ποδήνεμος ὠκέα Ἶρις / λύσασ' ἐξ ὀχέων (there wind-swift, quick I. stayed the horses, [then] loosing them from their fastenings); Il. 13.34-35: same as above; Il. 1.139-40 (see under Present); Od. 2.2-3: ὄρνυτ' ἄρ' ἐξ εὐνῆφιν Ὀδυσσῆος φίλος υἱός, / εἵματα ἑσσάμενος (then the beloved son of O. rose from bed, putting on his clothes); Od. 4.307-08: same as above; Od. 20.124-25: Τηλέμαχος δ' εὐνῆθεν ἀνίστατο, ἰσόθεος φώς, / εἵματα ἑσσάμενος (T., a godlike light, got up from bed, [then] putting on his clothes);[15] Il. 16.852-54: ἀλλά τοι ἤδη / ἄγχι παρέστηκεν θάνατος καὶ μοῖρα κραταιή, / χερσὶ δαμέντ' Ἀχιλῆος

---

[15]Scott ("Participle," 245-46) argues that Hom. Od. 1.437 (ἕζετο δ' ἐν λέκτρῳ, μαλακὸν δ' ἔκδυνε χιτῶνα [he was sitting on the bed, and he took off his soft chiton]) explains the above uses: "The thing is perfectly plain; Telemachus did not undress until he had reached his bed, while in the morning the process was reversed, for he did not leave his bed until he had slipped on his chiton." Thus, he claims, the Aorist Participle is appropriate to antecedent action. Scott, however, has apparently overlooked two factors. (1) A distinction should here be made between χιτῶνα and εἵματα. (2) All three contexts go on to say: περὶ δὲ ξίφος ὀξὺ θέτ' ὤμῳ, / ποσσὶ δ' ὑπὸ λιπαροῖσιν ἐδήσατο καλὰ πέδιλα (and he put around his shoulder a sharp sword, and under his shining feet he bound on good sandals). When he dresses in the morning, εἵματα seems to include at least his χιτῶνα and possibly more. In any case, understanding the Participle as subsequent makes better sense of the progression of events: he gets up, and then puts on his clothes, sword and sandals. Hom. Il. 2.42-43 (ἕζετο δ' ὀρθωθείς, μαλακὸν δ' ἔνδυνε χιτῶνα, / . . . περὶ δὲ μέγα βάλλετο φᾶρος [he sat upright, and he put on his soft chiton . . . around him he threw his large cloak]) would not help Scott's case, since the narrative never states when he stood up, yet he is down by the ships by 2.47. See also Platt, "Participles," 128.

ἀμύμονος Αἰακίδαο (but already, indeed, death stands near, and mighty fate, being killed by the hands of A., unequalled son of A.); Pi. Pyth. 4.189: λέξατο πάντας ἐπαινήσαις Ἰάσων (J. gathered, [then] praising all); E. Phoen. Maid. 1505-07: τὰς ἀγρίας ὅτε / δυσξύνετον ξυνετὸς μέλος ἔγνω / Σφιγγὸς ἀοιδοῦ σῶμα φονεύσας (when the intelligent [Oedipus] recognized the difficult song of the songstress S., [then] killing the body of the savage); Lyc. 277-78: καὶ θῆλυν ἀμφὶ σῶμα τλήσεται πέπλον / δῦναι, παρ' ἱστοῖς κερκίδος ψαύσας κρότων (and he will take to put on the feminine robe around his body, [then] handling the shuttle alongside the web looms with their noises); Babr. 143.1-4: ἐχιν γεωργὸς ἐκπνέοντ' ὑπὸ ψύχους / λαβὼν ἔθαλπεν· ἀλλ' ἐκεῖνος ἡπλώθη / τῇ χειρὶ προσφύς , καὶ δακὼν ἀνιήτως / ἔκτεινεν [αὐτὸν τὸν θέλοντ' ἀναστῆσαι] (a farmer, taking up a viper dying from cold, warmed it; but it stretched out, [then] fastening to his hand, and biting without relenting, it killed him who was wanting to restore him); Memn. 13(21) (Jacoby, *Fragmente*, III B 347-48): πολλὰ δὲ οἱ τῆς Καλλατίδος ὑπὸ τῶν πολεμίων παθόντες, / ὕστερον εἰς διαλύσεις ἦλθον, ἀπὸ ταύτης τῆς συμφορᾶς οὐκέτι σχεδὸν ἀναλαβεῖν αὐτοὺς δυνηθέντες (but many times those who suffered from the wars of C. entered later into a cessation of hostilities, hardly ever being able after this agreement to recover themselves); D.L. 5.58: σχολαρχεῖν . . . ἤρξατο τῇ τρίτῃ καὶ εἰκοστῇ καὶ ἑκατοστῇ Ὀλυμπιάδι, τῆς σχολῆς ἀφηγησάμενος ἔτη ὀκτωκαίδεκα (he began to take life easy in the 123d Olympiad, telling of the retirement for 18 years); Apollod. 3.5.9: παραγενόμενος δὲ σὺν Ἀντιγόνῃ τῆς Ἀττικῆς εἰς Κολωνόν . . . καθίζει ἱκέτης, προσδεχθεὶς ὑπὸ Θησέως (entering with A. of A. into C. the suppliant sat, being received by T.); Plu. Phil. 20.3: ἐξέπιε καὶ πάλιν αὐτὸν ἀπέκλινεν, οὐ πολλὰ πράγματα τῷ φαρμάκῳ παρασχών, ἀλλ' ἀποσβεσθεὶς ταχὺ διὰ τὴν ἀσθένειαν (he drank up and again lay himself down, not having much trouble with the drug, but dying immediately because of sickness). In the papyri (cited in Howard, "Use," 404, who cites other examples, but in these the Participle is the modifier of an explicit headterm): P.Goodspeed 14.8-14 (A.D. 343): καὶ ταῦτα κομίσωσι ἐπὶ τὴν/ λαμπροτάτην / Νέαν Πόλιν καὶ παραδώσωσιν εἰς τοὺς δημοσίους / τῆς Νέας Πόλεως ἐποίσαντες ἐπ' ὀνομα/[τος τὰ διπλ(Howard)]οματα τῆς παραδόσεως τοῦ προκειμένου / μέτρου σίτου καὶ προσκομίσαντες / . . . .] τῆς γενομένης ὑπ' αὐτῶν παραδόσεως (they might carry these things to the famous N. P. and deliver to the officials of N. P., making invoices for the delivery of the aforesaid measure of grain and conveying [a receipt] for that delivered by them). It is significant that in these instances the Participle follows the main verb. This need not always be the case, but the proportion of instances must not be overlooked.

Regarding the NT, scholarly opinion generally runs against the Aorist Participle of subsequent action. (See e.g. Moulton, 132-34; Robertson, 861-63, 1113; idem, "Participle." Chambers ["Use"], accepting his analysis, interprets several Aorist Participles, including 2 Macc 9:36; 4 Macc 3:13; Acts 12:25; 25:13; Heb 9:12, as Participles of purpose [he also cites several where textual variants exist for the Aorist over the Future Participle (186)]; cf. Howard, "Use.") The following examples, however, may be noted: Luke 1:9: ἔλαχε τοῦ θυμιᾶσαι εἰσελθὼν εἰς τὸν ναόν (he chose lots, [then] entered into the temple to make sacrifices); Acts 16:6: διῆλθον δὲ τὴν Φρυγίαν καὶ Γαλατικὴν χώραν, κωλυθέντες ὑπὸ τοῦ ἁγίου πνεύματος λαλῆσαι τὸν λόγον ἐν τῇ Ἀσίᾳ (they passed through the P. and G. region, [then] being forbidden by the holy spirit to speak the word in A.), with the Aorist Participle in v 7 (ἐλθόντες [coming]) preceding the Imperfect (ἐπείραζον [were attempting]), conforming to the expected order of events. Moulton's objection that "we really have nothing to show *when* the Divine monition was given" (133) is to be taken seriously, although syntactical order seems to establish narrative order here (Moulton is followed by Bruce, *Acts*, 309-10). Acts 17:26: ἐποίησέν τε ἐξ ἑνὸς πᾶν ἔθνος ἀνθρώπων κατοικεῖν ἐπὶ παντὸς προσώπου τῆς γῆς, ὁρίσας προστεταγμένους καιροὺς καὶ τὰς ὁροθεσίας τῆς κατοικίας αὐτῶν (he made from one every nation of men to live upon the entire face of the earth, establishing the appointed times and the boundaries of their dwelling), where although the establishment of man's home may have preceded his creation (so Moulton, 133), this may rely more on theology than grammar; Acts 23:27: τὸν ἄνδρα τοῦτον συλλημφθέντα . . . ἐπιστὰς σὺν τῷ στρατεύματι ἐξειλάμην, μαθὼν ὅτι Ῥωμαῖός ἐστιν (learning that this man was captured by the Jews . . . I rescued him with the guard, [then] learning that he was a Roman), where commentators are often quick to point out that "the tribune twists the truth slightly in his own favour in the last phrase in the verse: it was not till after the arrest and the attempt to scourge him that the tribune learned that Paul was a Roman citizen" (Marshall, *Acts*, 371; also Bruce, *Acts*, 418). Haenchen [*Acts*, 648] attributes the supposed change to Luke's desire to provide "the reader with the image which he is to retain: the general impression that the Roman State respected Paul's Roman citizenship from the beginning"). The grammatical explanation offered here indicates that the tribune is describing the circumstances in the same order as the events recorded earlier, with the syntax in full support. Acts 23:35: Felix ἔφη (said) he would hear Paul when his accusers arrived, κελεύσας ἐν τῷ πραιτωρίῳ τοῦ Ἡρῴδου φυλάσσεσθαι αὐτόν (ordering him to be guarded in the praetorium of H.), where the syntax seems to indicate subsequent action (coincident seems logically excluded); Acts 25:13: Ἀγρίππας ὁ βασιλεὺς καὶ Βερνίκη κατήντησαν εἰς Καισάρειαν ἀσπασάμενοι[16] τὸν Φῆστον (A. the king and B. arrived in C., [then] greeting F.), where despite efforts by several grammarians to argue otherwise the syntax is clearly in support of the logical order of events;[17] Phil 2:7: ἀλλὰ ἑαυτὸν ἐκένωσεν μορφὴν δούλου λαβών, ἐν ὁμοιώματι ἀνθρώπων γενόμενος (but he emptied himself, [then] taking the form of a servant, [and?] being in the likeness of men), where the parallel Aorist and Perfect Participles, regardless of their temporal relationship, appear subsequent to the action of the main verb. Also worth citing are Heb 9:12: εἰσῆλθεν ἐφάπαξ εἰς τὰ ἅγια, αἰωνίαν λύτρωσιν εὑράμενος (he entered once into the holy places, [then] finding eternal redemption), although this--like so many examples in theological contexts--depends upon the reference of the process of finding. As McNeile ("Note," 402) says, "the meaning of 'obtain redemption' must decide the grammar." And 1 Pet 3:18: Χριστὸς ἅπαξ περὶ ἁμαρτιῶν ἔπαθεν . . . ἵνα ὑμᾶς προσαγάγῃ τῷ θεῷ θανατωθεὶς μὲν σαρκὶ ζωοποιηθεὶς δὲ πνεύματι (Christ died once for sins . . . so that he might lead us to God, being put to death in flesh and made alive in spirit), where there is controversy over whether being "made alive in spirit" occurred at the resurrection, i.e. after Christ's death (see Selwyn, *Peter*, 197).

In every one of the examples above the Aorist Participle follows the finite verb. The evidence is compelling that the subsequent reference of the Aorist Participle must be recognized.

d. Several instances of the future-referring Present Participle may be cited as well. Extra-biblical examples might include (see Harding, "Action," xxxix; Gildersleeve, 140): Hom. Od. 1.139-40: σῖτον δ᾽ αἰδοίη ταμίη παρέθηκε φέρουσα, / εἴδατα πόλλ᾽ ἐπιθεῖσα, χαριζομένη παρεόντων (the modest housewife brought bread, offering it, putting down many edibles, giving freely of her possessions); X. Hell. 2.1.29: αὐτὸς μὲν ὀκτὼ ναυσὶν ἀπέπλευσε παρ᾽ Εὐαγόραν εἰς Κύπρον, ἡ δὲ Πάραλος εἰς τὰς Ἀθήνας, ἀπαγγελλοῦσα τὰ γεγονότα (he sailed away with eight ships with E. to C., and P. to A. announcing what had happened).

NT examples may also be found (see O'Rourke, "Participle," 116-18, who makes the category mistake of confusing future reference with Future form, hence asking whether future-referring Present Participles are Participles of purpose; Zerwick, 96). Matt 20:20: τότε προσῆλθεν (then came) to him the mother of the sons of Zebedee προσκυνοῦσα καὶ αἰτοῦσα

---

[16]A textual variant of a Future Participle is found in a few late MSS, but the Aorist Participle is supported by both external (p⁷⁴ ℵ A B C etc.) and internal criteria, and thus warrants a B rating in the UBS³ text. Blass's (197) assertion that "the reading of the majority of the MSS. . . . is not Greek" cannot be supported.

[17]The example of coincident action Moulton (238) cites (OGIS 219.43-46 [3d cent. B.C.]: ἑλέσθαι δὲ καὶ πρεσβευτὰς . . . [οἵτινες] / ἀσπασάμενοι αὐτὸν παρὰ τ[οῦ δήμου πρῶτον μὲν κελεύσουσιν ὑ]/γιαίνειν . . / . [ἔπειτα δ᾽ ἀπαγγελοῦσιν αὐτῶι τὴν τι]μήν [ambassadors were elected . . . who, greeting him from the people, first wished him health and then announced to him the honour]) is interesting though not exactly parallel.

(worshipping and asking); Matt 22:16: ἀποστέλλουσιν (they sent) to him their disciples with those of the Herodians λέγοντες (saying), where an *ad sensum* Participle may be used; Luke 2:45 (see above); Luke 10:25: ἀνέστη ἐκπειράζων αὐτὸν λέγων ([a certain lawyer] got up, testing him, saying), where the Participles may be coincidental; Acts 18:23: ποιήσας χρόνον τινὰ ἐξῆλθεν, διερχόμενος καθεξῆς τὴν Γαλατικὴν χώραν καὶ Φρυγίαν, ἐπιστηρίζων πάντας τοὺς μαθητάς (finishing a certain time he went away, passing through from place to place the land of G. and P., strengthening all the disciples), which is to be contrasted with Acts 14:21-22, where the action is coincidental; and possibly Rom 15:25: πορεύομαι (I am going) to Jerusalem διακονῶν (serving) the saints.

2. **Infinitive.** It is recognized that the Infinitive does not express temporal relations, except, so it is often posited, when used in indirect discourse (e.g. Robertson, 1091; Stork, *Usage*, esp. 11ff.; Rijksbaron, 102).[18] Relative temporal reference must be established by context, and one of the significant deictic indicators is the preposition.

πρίν (ἤ), πρὸ τοῦ for antecedent, ἐν τῷ for coincidental, and μετὰ τό for subsequent action. In Acts 8:40, ἕως τοῦ ἐλθεῖν αὐτόν (until he come) is used prospectively. πρίν (ἤ) always occurs with the Aorist Infinitive (Matt 1:18; 26:34, 75; Mark 14:30; Luke 22:61; John 4:49; 8:58; 14:29; Acts 7:2). πρὸ τό however occurs with both the Aorist (Luke 2:21; John 1:48; 13:19; Acts 23:15; Gal 2:12; 3:23) and the Present (Luke 22:15). ἐν τῷ occurs with the Aorist (Luke 2:27; 3:21; 11:37; Acts 11:15; 1 Cor 11:21) and the Present (Mark 2:23; 6:48; Luke 1:8; 1:21; 2:43; 10:35; 11:27; 17:11, 14; 24:4; Acts 2:1; 8:6; 9:3) as well. μετὰ τό occurs with the Aorist (Matt 26:32; Mark 1:14; 14:28; 16:19; Luke 12:5; 22:20; Acts 1:3; 7:4; 10:41; 15:13; 19:21; 20:1; 1 Cor 11:25; Heb 10:26) and the Perfect (Heb 10:15). This evidence shows that the Infinitive itself cannot be temporally based if it can appear in opposite (antecedent and subsequent) temporal contexts, and if Present and Aorist Infinitives can appear in identical syntactical and contextual (temporal) environments.

Stork claims rightly that in Hdt. 8.34: ἔσωζον δὲ τῇδε, δῆλον βουλόμενοι ποιέειν Ξέρξῃ ὅτι τὰ Μήδων Βοιωτοὶ φρονέοιεν (they were safeguarding it, wanting to make clear to X. that the B.s might think on the things of the M.s) and Hdt. 1.174.3: ὤρυσσον οἱ Κνίδιοι ἐν ὅσῳ Ἄρπαγος τὴν Ἰωνίην κατεστρέφετο, βουλόμενοι νῆσον τὴν χώρην ποιῆσαι (the K.s dug a trench while A. was conquering the I.s, wanting to make their land an island) that "the difference between the [Present Infinitive] ποιέειν ... and the [Aorist Infinitive] ποιῆσαι ... is an exclusively *aspectual* difference" (11). See also Isoc. 4.95: ἡγοῦντο ... ἀλλ' ὥσπερ τῶν ἀνδρῶν τοῖς καλοῖς κἀγαθοῖς αἱρετώτερόν ἐστι καλῶς ἀποθανεῖν ἢ ζῆν αἰσχρῶς, οὕτω καὶ τῶν πόλεων ταῖς ὑπερεχούσαις λυσιτελεῖν ἐξ ἀνθρώπων ἀφανισθῆναι μᾶλλον ἢ δούλαις ὀφθῆναι γενομέναις (they think that just as with the good deeds of men to die well rather than to live shamefully is preferable, thus with the illustrious of cities, to be blotted out to not be seen by men rather than to be seen being slaves). (Pernée ["Aspect," 297-300] perceives the role of aspect, though defining it with categories from *Aktionsart*, without raising the question of indirect discourse, citing esp. Thphr. Char. 11, 3; Lys. 14.15; X. Hell. 2.3.6.) Stork cites then Hdt. 4.194: τούτων δὲ Γύζαντες ἔχονται, ἐν τοῖσι μέλι πολλὸν μὲν μέλισσαι κατεργάζονται, πολλῷ δ' ἔτι πλέον λέγεται δημιουργοὺς ἄνδρας ποιέειν (G.s possess these

---

[18]See also M. Higgins, "Clauses," on result clauses with the Infinitive in the NT, which he argues conform to classical usage by emphasizing the quantity or quality of the action expressed. The non-temporal nature of such usage is not in wide dispute. Contra Ruijgh, "L'emploi," 40ff., who cites Pl. Rep. 390C: καὶ οὕτως ἐκπλαγέντα ἰδόντα τὴν Ἥραν, ὥστε μηδ' εἰς τὸ δωμάτιον ἐθέλειν ἐλθεῖν, ἀλλ' αὐτοῦ βουλόμενον χαμαὶ συγγίγνεσθαι ([Zeus], struck with excitement seeing H., did not want to enter into his house, but wanted to lie with her on the ground) as proof that the Present Infinitive is inceptive and the Aorist Infinitive neutral. The opposite seems to be the case, if *Aktionsart* is pressed.

areas, in which bees produce much honey, and it is said that the workmen produce still much more), and Hdt. 1.75.4: ἀπορέοντος γὰρ Κροίσου ὅκως οἱ διαβήσεται τὸν ποταμὸν ὁ στρατός . . . λέγεται παρεόντα τὸν Θαλῆν ἐν τῷ στρατοπέδῳ <u>ποιῆσαι</u> αὐτῷ τὸν ποταμὸν ἐξ ἀριστερῆς χειρὸς ῥέοντα τοῦ στρατοῦ καὶ ἐκ δεξιῆς ῥέειν, <u>ποιῆσαι</u> δὲ ὧδε (since K. was at a loss how the army would pass over the river . . . it is said that T., being in the camp, made for him the river flowing on the left side of the camp to flow from the right, and he did it thus), claiming that the difference between the examples "is an exclusively temporal difference, viz. non-past *vs.* past" (13).[19] But another example he cites undermines his argument: Hdt. 7.129.3: τὸ δὲ παλαιὸν λέγεται, οὐκ ἐόντος κω τοῦ αὐλῶνος καὶ διεκρόου τούτου, τοὺς ποταμοὺς τούτους καὶ πρὸς τοῖσι ποταμοῖσι τούτοισι τὴν Βοιβηίδα λίμνην οὔτε ὀνομάζεσθαι κατά περ νῦν ῥέειν τε οὐδὲν ἧσσον ἢ νῦν, ῥέοντας δὲ ποιέειν τὴν Θεσσαλίην πᾶσαν πέλαγος (it was said long ago, when there was not the ravine and this channel, these rivers and with them those rivers not named the B. lake, according to flow was not less than now, but the flowing made all T. a sea). Stork claims that the "context makes clear (τὸ παλαιόν) that the situation referred to in the statement of fact (ῥέοντας ποιέειν τὴν Θεσσαλίην πᾶσαν πέλαγος) is conceived of as being anterior to the act of speaking" (13). This sentence is a record of the Imperfect with past reference. But if this is the case, then Stork has proved nothing more than that indirect discourse follows aspect and not temporal reference, since the imperfective Infinitive is used for imperfective verbs, regardless of temporal reference. As he admits, context must be the deciding factor for temporal reference. Thus he has no explanation with his analysis of non-Indicative forms in indirect discourse: e.g. Acts 21:12: παρεκαλοῦμεν ἡμεῖς τε καὶ οἱ ἐντόπιοι τοῦ μὴ ἀναβαίνειν αὐτόν (we and those with us were beseeching him not to go) up to Jerusalem, where a Present Imperative was probably found in the original statement. (Pernée ["Aspect," 297] cites Pl. Ep. 7.338A: Διονύσιος μὲν ἔφη μεταπέμψασθαι Δίωνα καὶ ἐμὲ πάλιν [D. said to send D. and me again], although the Oxford text reads the Future Infinitive.) This provides another argument against the temporal basis of the Infinitive (this was already used as a basis for comments on the Participle by Seymour, "Use," 90). If the Infinitive can be used in catenative constructions with verbs of volition (with no necessary connection to completion) and in statements of indirect discourse which may represent assertive and non-assertive attitude, not only is the Infinitive without attitudinal indication but it must of necessity be without temporal indication as well (Lightfoot [*Logic*, 39] says "there is no logical or semantic basis for this distinction and it is ridiculous to specify two types of infinitives for βούλομαι ἀπιέναι and βούλομαί σε ἀπιέναι" i.e. prolate and complement Infinitives).

The Present Infinitive is more heavily marked. As Robertson says, "In general, as with the subj., opt. and imper., the aorist inf. came to be the natural one unless some reason for the present or perf. or fut. existed" (1080; he recognizes there is "no time-element in the inf." [1080] except [he claims] for the Future; see my chapt. 9). Only a few examples are necessary: Matt 14:22: Jesus required his disciples ἐμβῆναι εἰς τὸ πλοῖον καὶ προάγειν αὐτὸν εἰς τὸ πέραν (to get in the boat and to take him to the other side); Acts 15:37-38: Barnabas ἐβούλετο συμπαραλαβεῖν (wanted to take) John Mark, but Paul ἠξίου . . . μὴ συμπαραλαμβάνειν τοῦτον (was thinking not to take him), who had left them in Pamphilia and not accompanied them in the work (cf.

---

[19]This is the distinction often now made between the dynamic and the declarative Infinitive. See Kurzová, *Struktur* (who says next to nothing about the role of verbal aspect); "Entstehung." It is beyond the scope of this work to trace the origin or the nature of the declarative Infinitive in relation to the dynamic. See also Moorhouse, "Origin"; Rijksbaron, 99-105, who rightly criticizes the terminology (101), although his new choice of "virtual" versus "factual" is no better, since the Infinitive in indirect speech does not state the actual words used (and certainly does not indicate attitude), only the aspect used. The semantics of the Infinitive appear to be consistent, but its function may vary according to its syntactic context. Burton (53) contends that in the NT the Aorist Infinitive in indirect discourse is not used for the Aorist. But here he appears to have fallen victim to a purely temporal conception of use of the Infinitive, since Luke 24:46; 2:26; Acts 3:18, which he cites, would appear to be instances.

Metzger, "Grammars," 482);[20] Epict. 4.10.18: ἵνα δὲ ταῦτα γένηται, οὐ μικρὰ δέξασθαι οὐδὲ μικρῶν ἀποτυχεῖν (but so that these things might occur one must not accept small things and not miss small things). The parallel use of the Infinitives is clearly not possible on temporal grounds but only on aspectual ones.

d. The semantic relation between the Participle and the Infinitive.

This work--primarily concerned with the issue of verbal aspect-- has established the relevance of verbal aspect both positively, i.e. by defining the nature of verbal aspect, and negatively, i.e. by showing that traditional analysis of the tense categories as temporally based provides an unviable conceptual model. To complete the analysis, however, a brief word must be said about the semantic values of the Participle and the Infinitive. Although much more work may be done in this area, several important studies on complementation in Greek provide a useful starting point for positing a fundamental semantic distinction. (The following discussion is dependent upon Lightfoot, *Logic*, 25-48, esp. 36-43; Horrocks, Review; de Boel, "Complementizers," esp. 289-99; Schmidt, "Study," 36-38.)

Analysis begins with verbs which may take an Infinitive or a Participle (see Smyth, 474-76).

ἀκούω: 1 Cor 11:18: ἀκούω σχίσματα ἐν ὑμῖν ὑπάρχειν (I hear there are schisms among you) with the Infinitive; and Acts 14:9: οὗτος ἤκουσεν τε Παύλου λαλοῦντος (he was hearing P. speaking); Acts 6:11; 10:46; 15:7 with the Participle.

γινώσκω: Matt 16:3: τὸ . . . πρόσωπον τοῦ οὐρανοῦ γινώσκετε διακρίνειν (you know to judge the face of heaven) with the Infinitive; and Luke 8:46: ἔγνων δύναμιν ἐξεληλυθυῖαν ἀπ᾽ ἐμοῦ (I know power has gone out from me); Luke 24:18: οὐκ ἔγνως τὰ γενόμενα ἐν αὐτῇ (you do not know the things that have happened in [the city]?) with the Participle.

δοκιμάζω: Rom 1:28: οὐκ ἐδοκίμασαν τὸν θεὸν ἔχειν ἐν ἐπιγνώσει (they did not see fit to have God in understanding); 1 Thess 2:4: δεδοκιμάσμεθα ὑπὸ τοῦ θεοῦ πιστευθῆναι τὸ εὐαγγέλιον (we had been approved by God for the gospel to be believed) with the Infinitive; and Rom 2:18: δοκιμάζεις τὸ διαφέροντα κατηχούμενος ἐκ τοῦ νόμου (you proved what is right, being taught from the law); 2 Cor 8:22: ὃν ἐδοκιμάσαμεν ἐν πολλοῖς πολλάκις σπουδαῖον ὄντα (whom we proved in many ways being diligent) with the Participle.

ἐπιτρέπω: Matt 8:21: ἐπίτρεψόν μοι πρῶτον ἀπελθεῖν καὶ θάψαι (permit me first to go away and to bury); Matt 19:8; Luke 8:32; Acts 21:39; 26:1 with the Infinitive; and Luke 9:59: ἐπίτρεψόν μοι ἀπελθόντι πρῶτον θάψαι (permit me first going away to bury) with the Participle.

εὑρίσκω: Luke 6:7: ἵνα εὕρωσιν κατηγορεῖν αὐτοῦ (that they might find to accuse him); Rev 5:4: οὐδεὶς ἄξιος εὑρέθη ἀνοῖξαι τὸ βιβλίον (no one worthy was found to open the book?) with the Infinitive; and Matt 20:6: εὗρεν ἄλλους ἑστῶτας (he found others standing); Matt 12:44; 21:2; 24:46; 26:40, 43; Mark 7:30; 11:2, 4; 13:36; 14:37, 40; Luke 2:12; 7:10; 8:35; 11:25; 12:37, 43; 15:6; 19:30; 23:2; 24:2, 33; John 2:14; 9:35; Acts 5:23; 23:29; 24:12-13; 2 Cor 9:4; Rev 3:2 with the Participle.

οἶδα: Matt 7:11: οἴδατε δόματα ἀγαθὰ διδόναι (you know how to give good gifts); Luke 11:13; 12:56; Phil 4:12; 1 Thess 4:4; 1 Tim 3:5; Jas 4:17; 1 Pet 5:9; 2 Pet 2:9 with the Infinitive; and Acts 20:22: τὰ ἐν αὐτῇ συναντήσοντά μοι μὴ εἰδώς (not knowing the things to be met by me in it) with the Participle.

---

[20]John 13:36-37 has a significant textual variant (unnoted in the UBS[3] text) which has the Present Infinitive in Peter's response to Jesus.

ὁμολογέω: Matt 14:7: μεθ᾽ ὅρκου ὡμολόγησεν αὐτῇ δοῦναι (he swore with an oath to give to her) with the Infinitive; and 1 John 4:2: πᾶν πνεῦμα ὃ ὁμολογεῖ Ἰησοῦν Χριστὸν ἐν σαρκὶ ἐληλυθότα (every spirit which confesses Jesus Christ come in the flesh) with the Participle.

(αἰσχύνομαι [be ashamed; Luke 16:3]; ἄρχομαι [begin; numerous examples]; δεικνύω [show; Acts 10:28]; ἐπιλανθάνομαι [forget; Matt 16:5; Mark 8:14]; μανθάνω [learn; 1 Cor 14:31; Phil 4:11]; παύω [stop; 1 Cor 13:8]; ποιέω [make, represent; Matt 5:32; Mark 1:17; 7:37; John 6:10]; καθίζω [sit; 1 Cor 10:7]; νομίζω (think; Luke 2:44; Acts 7:25; 8:20; 14:19; 16:13, 27; 1 Cor 7:26, 36; 1 Tim 6:5]; τίθημι [put; Acts 27:12] may also be included, although they do not have an example in the NT with a Participle; ἀνέχομαι [endure; 1 Cor 4:12]; ὑπομένω [endure; 1 Pet 2:20]; ἔοικα [appear; Jas 1:6] may also be included, although they do not have an example in the NT with an Infinitive.)

Lightfoot (*Logic*, 41-42), followed by Schmidt ("Study," 37), suggests that the means of accounting for the difference between the use of the Participle and Infinitive with the same verb is that "use of a participle construction indicates that the author of the sentence presupposes and wishes the hearer to think that he presupposes that the complement reflects a real, actual, existing state of affairs." It is clear that both the Infinitive and the Participle do not grammaticalize attitude, yet there is a persistent and distinct semantic difference between the two when used in similar syntactical configurations. Lightfoot, Schmidt, and de Boel argue that this is an existential or factual presupposition for the Participle. This analysis seems to hold to the untenable presupposition that the Indicative Mood grammaticalizes reference to facts, a distinction automatically excluded when the Participle and Infinitive are used with non-Indicative Moods, except that Lightfoot (*Logic*, 43ff.), de Boel ("Complementizers," 292), and probably Schmidt believe that the non-Indicative Moods grammaticalize future reference, another untenable presupposition. Thus it is better to characterize the difference between the Participle and the Infinitive as the Participle grammaticalizing a factive presupposition, i.e. it presupposes that the "speaker is committed to the truth of the proposition. . . . It is not concerned with statements of fact, but with presupposition. . ." (Palmer, *Mood*, 18, cf. 140-41), while the Infinitive does not grammaticalize such a presupposition (this makes no comment on whether one could make such a presupposition, thus the Infinitive is used in indirect discourse and as, e.g., the complement of volitional verbs). An instructive example is 2 Cor 7:12: Paul says that if I write to you οὐχ ἕνεκεν τοῦ ἀδικήσαντος, οὐδὲ ἕνεκεν τοῦ ἀδικηθέντος, ἀλλ᾽ ἕνεκεν τοῦ φανερωθῆναι τὴν σπουδὴν ὑμῶν τὴν ὑπὲρ ἡμῶν (not on account of the one acting unjustly, nor on account of the one being treated unjustly, but on account of your desire on behalf of us being made known). The parallel of the Participles and Infinitives is conspicuous, especially if the third ἕνεκεν is redundant (Furnish [*II Corinthians*, 390] thinks that the causal sense of the articular Infinitive suffices; see Blass/Debrunner, ¶ 216[1]). Paul appears to presuppose at least for the argument one who acts/acted unjustly and one wronged, in this instance probably referring to actual individuals who figure in the Corinthian correspondence, while he merely refers to their manifested desire, not presupposing anything about it. The negation is significant in this regard, with nexal negation of both of the Participle groups more emphatically denying the grounds for his writing. (See D.Chr. 12.13: οὐδὲν γὰρ δεῖ οὔτε τροφὴν προβάλλειν οὔτε φωνὴν μιμεῖσθαι, μόνον δ᾽ ἐπιδεικνύντα τὴν γλαῦκα πολὺ πλῆθος ἔχειν ὀρνέων [(the fowler) has no need to throw out food nor to imitate a call, but only show the owl to have more than enough birds].)

At the beginning of this section it is shown that the Participle and the Infinitive share virtually an identical set of syntactical configurations, and thus on the basis of this and the semantic unity of a given form, the semantic distinction [±factive presupposition] appears to hold for the Participle and Infinitive throughout their range of usage, and is thus a necessary semantic feature in analysis.

2. THE PERFECT INFINITIVE AND PARTICIPLE. a.

Infinitive. The Perfect Infinitive appears approximately 49 times in NT Greek. A traditional time-based understanding of the Greek Perfect has difficulty with the following example: Mark 5:4: of the Gerasene demoniac it is said that no one was ever able to bind (δῆσαι) him, διὰ τὸ αὐτὸν πολλάκις πέδαις καὶ ἁλύσεσιν δεδέσθαι καὶ διεσπάσθαι ὑπ᾽ αὐτοῦ τὰς ἁλύσεις καὶ τὰς πέδας συντετρῖφθαι (because he many times was bound with shackles and chains and the chains were torn apart by him and the shackles were shattered). The author stresses the state of violence in which the demoniac lived, using the Perfect as the narrative label as well as in the supporting description. In chapt. 5 a new assessment of the verbal aspect grammaticalized by the Perfect tense is offered. There is little discussion of the Perfect in grammars (most discussion focuses upon the Aorist and Present tenses), thus it is warranted to illustrate the usage of the Participle and Infinitive over its range of uses.[21]

Luke 13:25: Jesus says that those locked out of the narrow gate might begin ἑστάναι καὶ κρούειν (to stand and knock) at the door. It is unlikely that the verbal aspects are undifferentiated since the Present form of ἵστημι was available. Rather the Perfect precedes the Present as in many pairs in which the first term establishes the tenor which the second less heavily marked term reinforces. Luke 20:7: when Jesus asks whether the baptism of John was from heaven or from men, the Jewish leaders, knowing that the people were persuaded (πεπεισμένος) that John was a prophet, answered μὴ εἰδέναι πόθεν ([they] did not know whence), with the Perfect Participle used to mark the significant state of belief of the crowd that leads to an answer with the marked Perfect Infinitive; Luke 24:23: on the road to Emmaus the disciples explain to their fellow traveller that some women came to the tomb and did not find the body, instead saying καὶ ὀπτασίαν ἀγγέλων ἑωρακέναι (indeed to have seen a vision of angels), who said that he was alive (ζῆν), with the Perfect Infinitive, reinforced by καί, used to establish the authority of the reports of Jesus' resurrection. The Perfect is often used in the NT with reference to Jesus Christ (e.g. 1 John 1:1ff.).

John 12:18: the crowd met Jesus upon his entry into Jerusalem because they had heard that he πεποιηκέναι (accomplished) the sign of raising Lazarus, marking this event as a chief motivating force in the crowd's interest; John 12:29: when a voice from heaven was heard, some of the crowd (ὁ ἑστὼς καὶ ἀκούσας) was saying βροντὴν γεγονέναι (it was thunder), while others were saying an angel spoke (λελάληκεν) to him. The series of Perfect verbs, including the Infinitive in indirect discourse, highlights reflection by the crowd on the state of affairs surrounding the voice. The Perfect Infinitive is used reasonably often in indirect discourse (see Robertson, 1081; also Acts 12:14; 16:27; 18:2 [see below]).

Acts 8:11: the people had regard for Simon because ἐξεστακέναι αὐτούς (they were astonished) at his magical acts, with the Perfect well illustrating use of verbal aspect as the subjective conception of an event; Acts 14:19: Jews from Antioch and Iconia persuaded the crowds to stone Paul and drag him outside the city, thinking αὐτὸν τεθνηκέναι (he was in a dead state). Luke contrasts Paul's apparent state of death with the unlawful and brutal failed attempt to

---

[21]In other hellenistic Greek see e.g.: Plb. 12.4a.5: δεῖ τὸν Ἔφορον ὑπερβεβηκέναι τῇ μωρίᾳ (it is necessary for E. to surpass in stupidity); Plu. Marc. Cato 13.1: τὸν πόλεμον ἐκκεκλεικέναι νομίζων (thinking to shut out the war); Str. 2.4.1: τὸ μὲν οὖν τῷ πλεύμονι ἐοικὸς αὐτὸς ἑωρακέναι τἆλλα δὲ λέγειν ἐξ ἀκοῆς (the likeness of the sea bugs he saw himself, but the other things he speaks of from hearing).

kill him. Acts 18:2: Paul stayed with Aquila and Priscilla, who had come recently from Italy because διατετάχεναι Κλαύδιον χωρίζεσθαι πάντας τοὺς Ἰουδαίους ἀπὸ τῆς Ῥώμης (C. had ordered all the Jews to depart from R.). Whereas one expects the discourse to draw attention to the departure rather than the command, the author stresses Claudius's involvement in the order. Acts 25:25: Festus says that he discovered nothing worthy of death that Paul πεπραχέναι (accomplished). The Perfect Infinitive in the mouth of the Roman governor is used by Luke to emphasize one of his major themes in Acts, that never was Paul found guilty of violating the law in his preaching of Christ; see Acts 26:32: Agrippa says to Festus that Paul was able ἀπολελύσθαι (to depart), except for his appeal to Caesar (ἐπεκέκλητο), where again the authorities--this time the Jewish king--endorse Paul's innocence. Acts 27:9: reference to the fast already παρεληλυθέναι (being past), indicates that the sea voyage had entered into its most potentially dangerous period with regard to the weather (c. October 5 [Bruce, Acts, 455-56]); Acts 27:13: just when they thought τῆς προθέσεως κεκρατηκέναι (to be in a condition of grasping their plan), the violent storm struck, the Perfect Infinitive contrasting their sense of assurance with their soon dangerous physical predicament.

Rom 4:1: in his discussion of righteousness, Paul introduces the crucial example of Abraham, asking whether εὑρηκέναι Ἀβραὰμ τὸν προπάτορα ἡμῶν κατὰ σάρκα (A. was found our forefather according to the flesh); Rom 15:8: in concluding his epistles, Paul recapitulates his position on the relation of the gospel to Jews and Gentiles, stressing that Χριστὸν διάκονον γεγενῆσθαι περιτομῆς ὑπὲρ ἀληθείας θεοῦ (Christ became a servant of circumcision on behalf of the truth of God); Rom 15:19: again, in concluding his epistle regarding his commission as a missionary, Paul stresses that from Jerusalem all the way to Illyricum he πεπληρωκέναι τὸ εὐαγγέλιον τοῦ Χριστοῦ (fulfilled the gospel of Christ).

1 Cor 2:2: Paul in placing himself in relation to the gospel of Christ says that he determined not τι εἰδέναι ἐν ὑμῖν εἰ μὴ Ἰησοῦν Χριστὸν καὶ τοῦτον ἐσταυρωμένον (to know anything among you unless Jesus Christ and him crucified), with the Perfect Infinitive stressing the content of his state of knowledge, and the Perfect Participle stressing the state of the crucified Christ which forms the basis of his message (note that the traditional aspectual definition of the Perfect has difficulty with this use of the Participle); 1 Cor 8:2: if someone thinks ἐγνωκέναι τι (to know anything), he does not yet know as it is necessary to know. Regardless of one's view of the relation between γινώσκω and οἶδα (the use of the Perfect Infinitive of γινώσκω with an Infinitive of οἶδα available endorses a lexical semantic difference) the Perfect Infinitive stresses one's confidence in being in a knowledgeable state.

Paul often says that he wants (θέλω) his readers εἰδέναι (to know): 1 Cor 11:3; Col 2:1; 1 Thess 4:4. Mullins notes that hellenistic epistolary writing evidences a formulaic disclosure formula, with a form of θέλω, a noetic verb in the Infinitive, a person-address, and information conveyed. The above instances in which Paul uses the Perfect Infinitive apparently stress the state of knowledge, since use of the Perfect in other hellenistic literature appears not to be widespread. Mullins ("Disclosure") only cites one example: P.Oxy. 1670.16-20 (3d cent. A.D.): εἰδέναι σε θέλω ὅτι / εἰσήλθαμεν εἰς Ἀλε/ξάνδρειαν ὁλοκλη/ροῦντες τῇ εἰκάδι / Ἐπείφ (I want you to know that we arrived safely in A. on the 20th of E.); cf. P.Oxy. 1155.3-4 (A.D. 104) with the Perfect in the information clause. Mandilaras (342-43) cites an expression with variations worth noting: ἔγραψεν ὑπὲρ αὐτοῦ . . . διὰ τὸ μὴ εἰδέναι αὐτὸν γράμματα [someone writes on behalf of him . . . because he does not know how to write]). Other examples in Paul, using Present Infinitives, include Rom 1:13; 11:25; 1 Cor 10:1; 12:1; 2 Cor 1:8. Paul shows a greater flexibility in the construction of the discourse unit, as opposed to the rigidity of the papyri. Cf. Eph 1:18: Paul requests that God might give to them a spirit of understanding and enlightened (πεφωτισμένους) eyes of their heart in order εἰδέναι (to know) what is the hope of Christ's calling; Col 4:6; 1 Thess 5:12.

2 Cor 5:11: Paul uses the Perfect verb form in chapt. 5 to stress knowledge of the human condition (see 5:1, 6). In 5:11 he says that knowing (εἰδότες) the fear of the lord we persuade men but are in a manifest state (πεφανερώμεθα) to God; and we hope indeed πεφανερῶσθαι (to be in a manifest state) in our consciences. Heb 9:8: in discussing the earthly and heavenly sanctuaries, the author says that the the second sanctuary, the way of the saints, in contrast to the

first, μήπω πεφανερῶσθαι (has not yet been manifested); 2 Cor 11:5: in Paul's apparent conflict with competing apostles he stresses that μηδὲν ὑστερηκέναι τῶν ὑπερλίαν ἀποστόλων (he lacks nothing of the outstanding apostles), using the Perfect Infinitive in the climax of the discourse unit; cf. Heb 4:1.

Phil 3:4: Paul challenges his readers that if someone thinks πεποιθέναι ἐν σαρκί (to be in a confident state in the flesh [cf. v 3 with Perfect Participle πεποιθότες]), he much more so. Paul then lists his Jewish pedigree. Cf. Phil 3:13: Paul says that he himself is still pressing toward the goal: it is not that he has already received or already is complete (τετελείωμαι) (v 12); ἐγὼ ἐμαυτὸν οὐ λογίζομαι κατειληφέναι (I do not consider myself to have attained).

1 Tim 6:17: to those rich in the present age Paul encourages his readers to instruct them μὴ ὑψηλοφρονεῖν μηδὲ ἠλπικέναι (not to be proud nor to hope) upon uncertain riches, but upon God. The Present Infinitive precedes the Perfect Infinitive, with the Perfect governing the following contrasting phrases. 2 Tim 2:18: the heretical belief of Hymenaeus and Philetus is said to be that they say that the resurrection ἤδη γεγονέναι (has already occurred).

Heb 11:3: before recounting the feats of faith the author introduces the section (vv 1-2) with two general statements, concluding that by faith the ages were established by the word of God, so that μὴ ἐκ φαινομένων τὸ βλεπόμενον γεγονέναι (that which is seen did not come from the visible); Heb 11:5: Enoch was translated by God because he bore witness (μεμαρτύρηται) εὐαρεστηκέναι (to please) God.

1 Pet 4:3: the author says that the ὁ παρεληλυθὼς χρόνος (the past [?] time) is sufficient κατειργάσθαι (to establish) the will of the nations. In light of his concern for right living the Perfect well describes the deplorable state of the unholy. 2 Pet 2:21: the author says it is better for those who are corrupted μὴ ἐπεγνωκέναι (not to understand) the way of righteousness than to turn from (ὑποστρέψαι) the holy commandment given to them, with the Perfect marking the preferred state.

b. Participle. There are approximately 673 Perfect Participles in the NT, with approximately 70 of these in periphrastic constructions (see chapt. 10).[22] The Perfect Participle displays a range of usage, functioning as an element of the predicate at the rank of clause, and as an element of the subject or adjunct (of several kinds), often including rankshifting. It is generally recognized that the Perfect Participle is temporally relative (e.g Robertson, 909 [he discusses where the past event occurs in relation to the main verb, but this is predicated upon the traditional definition of the meaning of the tense form]; see also Burton, 54; Kühner/Gerth, 1.182; Mandilaras, 359ff.); therefore, it is not necessary to argue for such here, but rather to indicate several noteworthy uses in relation to verbal aspect, tense and syntax.

---

[22]Semantically the Participle may retain its modifying function when used with a verb such as εἰμί. See for example Acts 22:3; Rom 15:14. Also of interest are verbless clauses and *ad sensum* constructions: 2 Cor 1:7: ἡ ἐλπὶς ἡμῶν βεβαία ὑπὲρ ὑμῶν, εἰδότες ὅτι (our hope is effective on behalf of you, knowing that); Col 4:6: ὁ λόγος ὑμῶν πάντοτε ἐν χάριτι, ἅλατι ἠρτυμένος (our word is always in grace, seasoned with salt); Eph 3:17: ἐν ἀγάπη ἐρριζωμένοι καὶ τεθεμελιωμένοι (being rooted and grounded in love), where the contrasting verbal aspects depict both the progress and state of Christian experience; Rev 7:4: ἐσφραγισμένοι (being sealed), cf. vv 5, 8; Rev 7:9.

1. The Perfect Participle may function as an element of the predicate at the rank of clause in the Genitive absolute:[23] Matt 22:41; 27:17; Acts 20:7 with συνηγμένων (gather); John 12:37 with πεποιηκότος (accomplish); John 20:19 with κεκλεισμένων (closed); Acts 9:8; 2 Cor 2:12 with ἀνεῳγμένων/ης (opened); Heb 9:6 with κατεσκευασμένων (prepared); 2 Pet 1:3 with δεδωρημένης (give). All have subjects expressed and are past in reference because of use in narrative contexts, except 2 Pet 1:3. Whereas most serve as transitional clauses, Acts 9:8 is significant for falling within a discourse unit. When Saul got up from the ground after seeing the flashing light from heaven, the author says ἐνεῳγμένων δὲ τῶν ὀφθαλμῶν αὐτοῦ οὐδὲν ἔβλεπεν (although his eyes were in an open state, he was seeing nothing), emphasizing the contrast between eyes being open but incapable of seeing.

2. The Perfect Participle filling the slot of headterm or modifier functions without reference to the temporal sphere in most instances.[24] Matt 8:14: Jesus saw τὴν πενθερὰν αὐτοῦ βεβλημένην καὶ πυρέσσουσαν ([Peter's] mother in law thrown down and feverish), where the Perfect Participle is parallel to a Present Participle, distinguishing by aspect her state of reclining and her being feverish; cf. Matt 9:2. The articular noun is followed by anarthrous Participles (cf. Matt 24:15; John 20:1; Rev 3:2; 14:1; 15:2), not unknown in classical Greek (see above). Matt 10:6: Jesus came to τὰ πρόβατα τὰ ἀπολωλότα (the sheep in a lost state) of the house of Israel; Matt 11:8: ἄνθρωπον . . . ἠμφιεσμένον (a man clothed); John 1:6: ἐγένετο ἄνθρωπος ἀπεσταλμένος (there came a man in the state of being sent) from God, which may be part of an adjunctive structure; Matt 25:41: Jesus says he will send some to τὸ πῦρ τὸ αἰώνιον τὸ ἡτοιμασμένον (the eternal, prepared fire), possibly with past but more likely with timeless reference. Mark 5:15: θεωροῦσιν τὸν δαιμονιζόμενον καθήμενον ἱματισμένον καὶ σωφρονοῦντα, τὸν ἐσχηκότα τὸν λεγιῶνα (they saw the demoniac, sitting, clothed and sane, the one who had the demon). Robertson (1117) calls this passage "most instructive," since not only do the historic Present and Aorist Indicative occur together, but the "attributive and the predicate participles appear side by side. The present and the perfect participles come together. Of the two perfect participles, one ἱματισμένον, is still true (punctiliar plus linear [sic]) and describes the man's present state; the other, τὸν ἐσχηκότα, is no longer true and describes the state of the man before Jesus cast out the demon, which casting-out is itself in the past." Mark 11:2, 4: Jesus tells his disciples they will find πῶλον δεδεμένον (a bound colt), with the Participle describing its condition, without reference to absolute time; Luke 1:1: Luke says he has undertaken to compile an account περὶ τῶν πεπληροφορημένων ἐν ἡμῖν πραγμάτων (concerning the events that are in a state of accomplishment among us); John 11:39: ἡ ἀδελφὴ τοῦ τετελευτηκότος Μάρθα (M., the sister of the dead man) spoke to Jesus, with the Participle describing Lazarus's state; cf. John 11:44: ἐξῆλθεν ὁ τεθνηκὼς δεδεμένος (the dead man came out, bound), with the juxtaposed Perfect Participles having different spheres of temporal reference, although both describe his condition. (Robertson [1117] says, "Here δεδεμένος is still true, though τεθνηκὼς is not. Lazarus had been dead, but is not now." He fails to grasp the aspectual strength of the Perfect, concentrating instead upon reference to a specific event.) John 19:38: Joseph of Arimathia ἠρώτησεν (asked) Pilate for the body of Jesus, ὢν μαθητὴς τοῦ Ἰησοῦ κεκρυμμένος δὲ διὰ τὸν φόβον (being a disciple of Jesus and being in a hidden state because of fear) of the

---

[23]See e.g. Plb. 3.34.7: προσπεπτωκότων δὲ προσφάτως αὐτῷ καὶ τῶν ἐκ τῆς Καρχηδόνος (the things from C. had come to him lately); App. Civ. Wars 1.34: τῆς ὑπατείας αὐτῷ δεδαπανημένης (his consulship expired), used transitionally.

[24]Cf. Plb. 3.21.2: ταύτας ἔφασαν ἤδη συνωμολογημένας (they said these things were already agreed); App. Civ. Wars 1.36: μαχαίριον ἐμπεπηγμένον (a knife thrust in); Epict. 1.6.37: παρασκευὴν ἐκ σοῦ μοι δεδομένην (resources given from you to me); 1.9.6: ταῦτα . . . κατὰ τὸν λόγον ἐπιπεπλεγμένα (these things . . . intertwined according to reason), with the Participle and the demonstrative separated; P.Fay. 91.28-29 (A.D. 99): κατὰ τὰ προ/γεγραμμένα (the above written items); BGU 1591.6-7 (A.D. 123): ὑπὲρ τοῦ διεληλυθότος ἑβδόμου ἔτους / ἀργυρίου (payment of the seventh year's money); P.Wisc. II 52.3, 8, 12 (A.D. 32).

Jews (note placement of adjuncts). Rom 16:25-26: κατὰ ἀποκάλυψιν μυστηρίου χρόνοις αἰωνίοις σεσιγημένου φανερωθέντος δὲ νῦν διά τε γραφῶν (according to the revelation of the mystery kept silent for ages but now manifest through writings), where the Perfect Participle is given past reference by temporal and discourse deixis, and the Aorist Participle is present. As Robertson (1117) says, "the long silence is now expressly said to be broken. Note the sharp contrast in the aorist participle with νῦν. This distinction between the perfect and aorist participle is often clearly drawn. . . . The same act may be looked at from either standpoint." See also 2 Cor 12:21: τῶν προημαρτηκότων καὶ μὴ μετανοησάντων (those who are in a state of sin and not repentant); 1 Pet 2:10: οἱ οὐκ ἠλεημένοι νῦν δὲ ἐλεηθέντες (those who are not in a merciful state but now are being shown mercy). 1 Cor 2:2: Paul says he knows (εἰδέναι) nothing but Jesus Christ and τοῦτον ἐσταυρωμένον (this crucified one), with reference not to the act of crucifixion but to Jesus as the man who is distinguished by the state of one crucified; Heb 7:26: several adjectives and two Participles--κεχωρισμένος (stand separate) and γενόμενος (be)--modify ἀρχιερεύς (chief priest); 1 Pet 1:4: Peter speaks of ἐλπίδα ζῶσαν (v 3) . . . τετηρημένην (living hope . . . kept) in heaven for us, where the Participle may be timeless, possibly with future reference; Rev 7:9: περιβεβλημένους στολὰς λευκάς (clothed in white robes).

3. The Perfect Participle as an element of the subject, as in earlier Greek, in virtually every instance is articular,[25] except in 1 Cor 3:22, where it is parallel to several nouns (ἐνεστῶτα [standing]). In many instances the subjective use of the Perfect Participle is timeless, or at least difficult to reconcile with the standard definition of the tense form: Matt 5:10: οἱ δεδιωγμένοι (those in a state of persecution) are blessed; Matt 11:28: Jesus calls to himself πάντες οἱ κοπιῶντες καὶ πεφορτισμένοι (all who are in progress working and in a state of being burdened); 2 Tim 3:8: ἄνθρωποι κατεφθαρμένοι τὸν νοῦν (men corrupt in their understanding); Rom 13:2: ὁ ἀντιτασσόμενος τῇ ἐξουσίᾳ τῇ τοῦ θεοῦ διαταγῇ ἀνθέστηκεν, οἱ δὲ ἀνθεστηκότες ἑαυτοῖς κρίμα λήμψονται (the one who is resisting the authority is in a state of standing against the commandment of God, and those who are in this state will receive judgment on themselves), with Paul using the more heavily marked Perfect to emphasize the serious nature of such a state of rebellion. Coincidental reference is also apparent: Matt 26:73 (cf. Mark 14:70): οἱ ἑστῶτες (those standing) spoke to Peter; Mark 12:15: ὁ . . . εἰδώς (the one who knew) their hypocrisy spoke; John 14:9: ὁ ἑωρακώς (the one who is in a state of seeing) me has seen the father, Jesus says, possibly with present reference to his time on earth, although omnitemporal implicature is likely.

Several instances of the Perfect Participle in complement structures reflect similar semantics.[26] The Participle describes the state of the object or person referred to: Matt 5:32: Jesus says that whoever might marry ἀπολελυμένην (one who is in a divorced state) commits

---

[25]Cf. Plb. 5.26.9: ἧκε πρὸς τὸν αὐλὴν ὁ προειρημένος εὐθέως ἐκ πορείας (the one spoken of went immediately to the court from his journey); App. Civ. Wars 1.19: ὁ . . . ἐς τοὺς πολέμους αὐτοῖς κεχρημένος (the one who made use of them in the wars), although this may be adjunctive use preceding an Aorist verb (ὤκνησε [shirked from]); Epict. 1.9.4, 6: ὁ τοίνυν τῇ διοικήσει τοῦ κόσμου παρηκολουθηκὼς καὶ μεμαθηκώς . . . εἴπη (one who follows the administration of the world and is learned . . . might say), with the Participles possibly functioning as adjunctives preceding the Aorist Subjunctive. Also the distance between the Participles and the finite verb makes the Participles virtually independent. Philostr. Life Apoll. 1.22: ἐβόων τε οἱ ἐκ τῆς κώμης συνερρυηκότες (those rushing from the village were yelling).

[26]Cf. Plb. 3.29.6: καὶ τοῖς οὖσι τότε καὶ τοῖς μετὰ ταῦτα προσληφθησομένοις (both those who were existing then and those who took sides after these things), cf. 3.103.6; Epict. 1.6.7: τῆς κατασκευῆς τῶν ἐπιτετελεσμένων (the preparation of all fashioned things); 1.7.15: οὐχ ὑγιῶς παρεχώρησα τὰ ὡμολογημένα (not wisely I gave place to the things granted); 1.9.7: παρέχειν (enable) men who are living (διάγοντας) in security and without presumption (ἀκαταφρονήτους) and δεδοικότας (fearful) of nothing; Apollod. 1.5.1: καταλαβοῦσα εἰς πῦρ ἐγκεκρυμμένον ἀνεβόησε (having discovered the one buried in the fire she called out).

adultery; Matt 7:14: τεθλιμμένη ἡ ὁδὸς ἡ ἀπάγουσα (in a narrow state is the way leading) to life, cf. Matt 23:39 par. Luke 13:35, and Luke 1:42; 19:38; Luke 2:36: αὕτη προβεβηκυῖα ἐν ἡμέραις πολλαῖς (she [Sarah] was greatly advanced in years), with the Participle describing her state; Luke 14:7: Jesus was speaking a parable πρὸς τοὺς κεκλημένους (to those in an elect or called state); Luke 18:9: Jesus spoke πρός τινας τοὺς πεποιθότας (to certain ones persuaded or confident) in themselves; Luke 22:37: τοῦτο τὸ γεγραμμένον (this writing) must be accomplished among you, followed by an OT quotation (cf. Acts 24:14), cf. Acts 2:16; 13:40 with τὸ εἰρημένον (the thing spoken); Luke 24:12: Peter marvelled at τὸ γεγονός (the event), with temporal reference unspecified, but probably including the event that left Jesus' tomb empty; cf. Acts 4:21. John 6:13: the disciples gathered the remains from τοῖς βεβρωκόσιν (those eating), possibly with past reference, although this is not to be pressed.

4. Adjunctive^A (completive of a preposition). In all of the instances the Participle as headterm has an article as modifier: Luke 2:24, 27 (κατὰ τὸ εἰθισμένον [according to the custom]); 3:13; 4:16; 18:9 (see above under complement structure); 22:52; 24:14; John 8:31; Acts 3:10; 4:21; 17:2; 23:31; 26:18; Rom 4:18; 2 Cor 4:13; Rev 20:12.

5. Adjunctive^S. The most important category is use of the Participle in adjunctive structures. (1) Not all uses of the Participle in this construction establish temporal relation with the governing verb (most grammars discuss a variety of configurations, including such categories as causal, concessive, etc.). In any scheme of analysis the verbal forms involved remain identical (i.e. there is no, for example, causal marker attached to the Participle) and rarely is a specific word introduced into the syntax that unambiguously establishes the relationship. It is at the level of syntactical relation that such discussion must be carried out. (2) The adjunctive use of the Perfect Participle enters into a variety of configurations with its main verb.

The Perfect Participle precedes a Perfect main verb in Phil 1:25: πεποιθὼς οἶδα ὅτι (being persuaded I know that), with the Participle providing a summary statement that leads to Paul's conclusion, i.e. he knows, etc.; and follows in John 7:15: the Jews asked how Jesus γράμματα οἶδεν μὴ μεμαθηκώς (knows the scriptures, not being educated), with reference to Jesus' state of education, not the process he supposedly missed out on. In two instances the Perfect Participle follows the Pluperfect: Luke 16:20: Lazarus ἐβέβλητο (was thrown down) at the rich man's gate εἱλκωμένος (in a sore-covered state), with the Participle possibly subsequent, if not coincidental; John 18:18a: the servants and the slaves εἱστήκεισαν (stood) πεποιηκότες (making) a coal fire, where a likely possibility is that they were standing at the site before making the fire (cf, v 18b). (Cf. Arr. 1.12.6: διαβεβηκυῖα . . . ἐστρατοπεδεύκει [having passed through (the Hellispont) he made camp]).

The Perfect Participle precedes the Present Indicative: John 6:19: ἐληλακότες (having rowed) a distance the disciples θεωροῦσιν (saw) Jesus walking (περιπατοῦντα) on the sea, with the Participle describing the state or condition that caused the distance to be covered, and thus being antecedent to the action of the historic Present; Acts 20:22: Paul says δεδεμένος (being bound) by the spirit πορεύομαι (I went) to Jerusalem, μὴ εἰδώς (not knowing) the things to be met with there (τά . . . συναντήσοντα), with the condition of boundness apparently providing the compelling reason for the action of the main verb, and with the negation nullifying any sense of specific knowledge. Not only does the negative apparently negate the assertion with the stative aspect but it may negate the sense of antecedent action as well. 2 Cor 5:6 with parallel Present Participle; 2 Cor 5:11: εἰδότες (knowing) the fear of the lord πείθομεν (we persuade) men, but πεφανερώμεθα (we are manifest) to God, where the Participle is probably coincidental. Antecedent action is possible, however, especially if knowing the fear of the lord constitutes the basis for the state of being made manifest to God, in light of the opposition of the two finite verb clauses.

The Perfect Participle follows the Present Indicative: Matt 6:5: hypocrites, Jesus says, φιλοῦσιν . . . ἑστῶτες προσεύχεσθαι (love . . . standing to pray), with the verbal action coincidental (also instrumental?); Matt 12:44: the unclean spirit εὑρίσκει (finds) the empty house, and σεσαρωμένον καὶ κεκοσμημένον (sweeps and decorates), with the Participles subsequent to the action of the main verb; Matt 22:29: πλανᾶσθε μὴ εἰδότες τὰς γραφάς (you are mistaken, not knowing the scriptures), with the instrumental use probably coincidental (cf. Mark 12:15); Rom 6:8-9: πιστεύομεν (we believe) that we will live with him, εἰδότες (knowing) that Christ no longer dies, with the Participle probably coincidental with the timeless use of the main verb in the apodosis of a conditional statement; cf. 2 Cor 4:13-14; 1 Thess 1:3-4; 2 Pet 1:13-14. 1 Cor 7:25: δίδωμι (I give) knowledge ὡς ἠλεημένος (as being shown mercy) by the lord, where temporal reference depends upon whether Paul refers to a specific act or to the state of his life as a follower of Christ. The latter is more likely. Phil 1:6: Paul says εὐχαριστῶ (I give thanks) to God for his readers (v 3), making (ποιούμενος) prayers (v 4) and πεποιθώς (being convinced) of this, etc.; Col 1:23: if ἐπιμένετε (you remain) in the faith, τεθεμελιωμένοι (grounded) and steadfast and not shaken (μετακινούμενοι), with the coincidental Participles contrasting their verbal aspect; 2 Tim 1:4: ἐπιποθῶν (I desire) to see you, μεμνημένος (being in a state of remembrance of) your tears.

The Perfect Participle precedes the Present Subjunctive once: Luke 11:21: the strong man καθωπλισμένος φυλάσσῃ (being fully armed, guards) his own house, where the state of the Participle despite its placement appears to be coincidental, unless the act of arming is stressed. It follows twice: 1 Tim 1:8-9; and Heb 10:22: προσερχώμεθα (let us come) with true hearts in certainness of faith, ῥεραντισμένοι (having sprinkled) hearts from an evil conscience and λελουσμένοι (standing washed) in our bodies with pure water. Although the Participles may be antecedent, they seem to refer to coincidental conditions. The Perfect Participle follows the Imperative: 1 Cor 15:58: ἑδραῖοι γίνεσθε (be firm), steadfast, abounding (περισσεύοντες) in the work of the lord always, εἰδότες (knowing) that your work is not in vain in the lord, with both contrasting Participles, parallel to an adjective, describing what it means to stand firm; Eph 6:8, 9, with parallel Present Participles, apparently coincidental; Col 2:6-7: περιπατεῖτε, ἐρριζωμένοι καὶ ἐποικοδομούμενοι (walk, being rooted and built up) in him and βεβαιούμενοι (established) in the faith, abounding (περισσεύοντες) in thanksgiving, with the Perfect Participle introducing a series of less heavily marked Present Participles, all coincidental; 1 Tim 5:9: καταλεγέσθω (let be enrolled) widows γεγονυῖα (being) not less than 60 years, with the Participle defining the category of widow; 2 Tim 3:14: μένε . . . εἰδώς (remain . . . knowing); 1 Pet 5:9: ἀντίστητε . . . εἰδότες (stand firm . . . knowing); Heb 13:3: μιμνῄσκεσθε . . . ὡς συνδεδεμένοι (remember [the prisoners] as being bound with them).

The Perfect Participle precedes the Imperfect: Luke 18:13: the tax-collector μακρόθεν ἑστὼς οὐκ ἤθελεν (standing at a distance did not want) to lift up his eyes, with the action probably coincidental, unless the Perfect Participle describes the publican's physical position even before he begins his act of humiliation (cf. v 14) (the Participle may serve as a modifier in the nominal group; John 4:6: Jesus κεκοπιακώς (being tired) from his journey ἐκαθέζετο (was sitting down), with the Participle describing antecedent causal action; Acts 8:16b: βεβαπτισμένοι ὑπῆρχονεἰς τὸ ὄνομα τοῦ κυρίου Ἰησοῦ (in a state of baptism into the name of the lord Jesus, they were), where the processes are apparently coincidental (cf. v 16a). The Perfect Participle follows the Imperfect: Mark 6:20, cf. Luke 8:53: the disciples κατεγέλων (were laughing) at Jesus, εἰδότες ὅτι ἀπέθανεν (knowing that [Jairus's daughter] was dead), where laughing occurs apparently because of their state of knowledge, not the death itself; Mark 14:51: a certain youth συνηκολούθει αὐτῷ περιβεβλημένος (was following [Jesus], clothed), where the Participle may be a modifier of νεανίσκος; John 11:56: the Jews ἔλεγον (were speaking) with each other ἑστηκότες (standing) in the temple, with the Participle describing concurrent action; John 21:12: none of the disciples ἐτόλμα (was daring) to ask Jesus who he was, εἰδότες (knowing) that he was the lord, with an ad sensum construction; Rev 19:14: the soldiers ἠκολούθει (were following) him, ἐνδεδυμένοι (clothed) in pure white linen. (Cf. App. Civ. Wars 1.18: the owners μετετίθεντο [were transferred], οὐδὲ . . . ἀκριβῆ πεποιημένοι [having not done carefully] the land survey on the captured lands; Epict. 1.6.33: ἐντετυλιγμένος ἂν ἐκάθευδεν [being rolled up he would be sleeping]; Plu. Marc. Cato 23.3: ἀκηκοώς [having heard] the reply ἔλεγε [he was saying] there was a common oath among physicians.)

The Perfect Participle precedes the Aorist Indicative: Matt 12:25: εἰδώς . . . εἶπεν (knowing . . . he said), where although the verbal acts are to some extent coincidental, the emphasis appears to be upon Jesus' knowing prompting his verbal response; Mark 5:33: the healed woman, εἰδυῖα ὃ γέγονεν αὐτῇ, ἦλθεν (knowing what happened to her, came), where again the Perfect Participle seems to impel her action; Luke 9:47: Jesus εἰδὼς τὸν διαλογισμὸν τῆς καρδίας αὐτῶν ἐπιλαβόμενος παιδίον ἔστησεν αὐτὸ παρ' ἑαυτῷ (knowing the dissension of their hearts, taking up the child, stood it alongside himself), where the three verbs form a chronological progression, with the Perfect marking the governing state that determines Jesus' action; John 13:1: Jesus, before (πρό) the passover feast, εἰδὼς (knowing) that his hour had come and loving (ἀγαπήσας) his own in the world, ἠγάπησεν (he loved) them to the end, where the temporal deictic indicators establish a clear progression for the Participles, with the Perfect and the Aorist antecedent to the main verb (cf. v 3); Acts 2:30-31: being (ὑπάρχων) a prophet and εἰδὼς (knowing) that God swore to him, προϊδὼν ἐλάλησεν (knowing beforehand, he said) concerning Christ's resurrection, where the order of the Participles as well as the temporal indicators indicates the process described in the Participles as preceding the prophet's pronouncement about Christ; 1 Cor 7:18: περιτετμημένος τις ἐκλήθη; (in a circumcised state was anyone called?), with the emphasis in this section on one remaining as he was called, and thus the Participle is used coincidentally (cf. v 25); 2 Cor 3:7: if the ministry of death ἐντετυπωμένη (inscribed) on stones in writing ἐγενήθη (came) in glory, with the Participle probably coincidental; Eph 4:19: ἀπηλγηκότες ἑαυτοὺς παρέδωκαν (being without feelings they gave themselves) to ungodliness, where it is not clear whether the state of affairs led to abandonment or whether it accompanied it; Phlm 21: πεποιθὼς τῇ ὑπακοῇ σου ἔγραψά σοι, εἰδὼς ὅτι (being persuaded of your reputation I write to you, knowing that), with the contrasting placement of the two Perfect Participles indicating a temporal distinction. Paul says that knowledge of Philemon's reputation precedes his writing in confidence that he would respond. 2 Pet 2:6: God, having reduced them to ashes (τεφρώσας), κατέκρινεν (judged) Sodom and Gomorrah, τεθεικὼς (making) a sign of that coming to the ungodly, where the Aorist Participle describes coincidental action, as does the Perfect. (Arr. 1.8.1: Perdiccas, προτεταγμένος [being commander] of the camp of foot soldiers with his own group and ἀφεστηκὼς [lying down] not far from the palisades of the enemies, waiting [προσμείνας] not for the agreed-upon signal for battle from Alexander, προσέμιξε [attacked] first; 1.27.4: Alexander, seeing [ἰδών] the strong land and himself not παρεσκευασμένος [prepared] for a long siege, οὐδὲ . . . ξυνέβη [did not agree] with them on terms.)

The Perfect Participle follows the Aorist Indicative: Luke 1:11: an angel ὤφθη (was seen) by Zacharias, ἑστώς (standing) by the right side of the altar, with emphasis apparently on the state of the angel, not his coming; Luke 18·14· the publican κατέβη . . . δεδικαιωμένος (went down, in a justified state), with the Perfect describing the coincidental state as the man departed; John 4:45: the Galileans ἐδέξαντο (received) Jesus, ἑωρακότες (seeing) all the things which he did in Jerusalem during the feast, where the following Participle apparently describes antecedent action; John 11:44: see above; Acts 11:11: three men ἐπέστησαν (stood) before the house, ἀπεσταλμένοι (being sent) from Caesarea, where the temporal relation depends upon whether the act of sending or the state of the men as emissaries is stressed. The syntax argues for the latter. Acts 15:5: certain ones of the Pharisees ἐξανέστησαν (marvelled), πεπιστευκότες, λέγοντες ὅτι (believing, saying that), with the Perfect Participle describing the Pharisees' state and the Present Participle introducing their words; Acts 16:34: ἠγαλλιάσατο (he rejoiced) with his entire household πεπιστευκὼς (believing) in God, with the causal Participle probably stressing the coincidental state, although an antecedent reference is possible; Acts 24:22: Felix ἀνεβάλετο (adjourned) them, εἰδὼς (knowing) more strictly things concerning the way and saying (εἴπας), where the two Participles probably share coincidental temporal reference, the first describing his state at adjournment and the second the means by which he adjourned (see above on Aorist Participle); 2 Cor 2:3: Paul says ἔγραψα (I write) so that, coming, I might not have (μὴ ἐλθὼν . . . σχῶ) grief from you, πεποιθὼς (standing persuaded) by all of you, with the coincidental Perfect Participle modifying the Aorist Indicative; Gal 3:1: Jesus Christ προεγράφη ἐσταυρωμένος (was displayed crucified), with temporal reference depending upon whether the Participle is causal and hence antecedent, or more likely, instrumental and hence coincidental; Rev 15:6: the seven angels ἐξῆλθον (came out), ἐνδεδυμένοι (clothed) in pure bright linen and περιεζωσμένοι (wrapped about) with gold belts, with the Participles describing the angels' condition upon appearance; Rev 20:15: if someone οὐχ εὑρέθη (was not found) γεγραμμένος (being written) in the book of life, he was cast out. As with finite forms of γράφω in the Perfect, the scheme of reference is difficult. The author seems to be saying that if at the time of examination of the book one's name is not found, then that person is cast out. Thus the Participle is coincidental, although possibly referring to an antecedent act. (Plb. 1.6.6: the Romans, ὑφ᾽ αὐτοὺς πεποιημένοι [put under them] the Etruscans and Samnites, and νενικηκότες [conquered] the Italian Celts in many battles, ὥρμησαν [they attacked] then for the first time the rest of Italy, not as against foreigners, but for the most part making war [πολεμήσοντες] as against that which was rightfully already their own, γεγονότες [becoming] truly masters of the works of war from their struggles with the Samnites and Celts. The pattern of preceding Participles being antecedent and following Participles coincidental seems to hold here.)

The Perfect Participle follows the Aorist Subjunctive: Rom 15:16: Paul wants his readers to serve as priests of the gospel, so that the offering of the nations γένηται (might be) well-pleasing, ἡγιασμένη (made holy) by the holy spirit, with the Participle defining what it is to be well-pleasing to God; Col 4:12: σταθῆτε (you might stand) mature, καὶ πεπληροφορημένοι (accomplished) in the entire will of God, with either the Participle parallel to the adjective, or better with καί serving as an epexegetic conjunction; 2 Tim 2:26: ἀνανήψωσιν (they might return to their senses) from the grasp of the devil, ἐζωγρημένοι (being caught) by him, with the Participle probably referring to their current state (and hence functioning coincidentally) and not some previous act of entrapment. The Perfect Participle precedes and follows the Aorist Imperative once: 1 Pet 1:22-23: ἡγνικότες (having kept pure) your souls in the obedience of the truth, ἀγαπήσατε (love) one another, ἀναγεγεννημένοι (being born again) not from a corrupt seed but incorrupt, with the first Participle probably functioning as a command, and with the second Participle probably antecedent to the time of the main verb.

c. Conclusion. Because of the stative verbal aspect grammaticalized by the Perfect, describing a state of affairs removed from direct reference to the verbal process itself, temporal reference of the form is particularly broad and consequently difficult to define. Although the same general trends established for the Present and Aorist obtain--when the Participle precedes the main verb the action is usually antecedent to that of the main verb, and when the Participle follows the main verb the action usually is coincidental or subsequent to that of the main verb--this cannot be pressed in many instances, where the state grammaticalized by the Perfect overlaps with the process described by the finite verb.

3. CONCLUSION. There is much that can be said about the Infinitive and the Participle. This chapter does not attempt to address every issue, especially those issues where there is a wide range of consensus about the nature and range of functions the forms may perform (e.g. the various 'modal' uses of the Participle). Instead several significant issues are treated, in order to clarify the terminology by which the function of the Participle and the Infinitive may be discussed, to explore the range of their temporal reference including subsequent use of the Aorist Participle, and to illustrate use of the widely neglected Perfect Participle and Infinitive. The results for the Aorist and the Present are sure to be discussed in the future, if for no other reason than there appears to be a great deal of emotional attachment to particular positions. It is possible that the Perfect provides the most provocative place for exploring the use of the Participle in relation to syntax, since its temporal reference is difficult to establish because of its verbal aspect. The stative aspect distances itself from the process itself, referring to the state of the represented process. Because of this ambiguity the role of syntax probably must play a greater role than heretofore recognized in establishing temporal implicature for discourse.

CHAPTER 9:
THE FUTURE FORM:
TENSE, ASPECT, OR MOOD?

0. INTRODUCTION. The Future tense raises important questions for grammarians and theologians alike. For grammarians, the Future is often treated as clearly future-time referring (e.g. Stahl [140] says, "Das Futurum . . . bezeichnet die Zukunft"), while for biblical theologians, the Future tense seems to promise a firm foothold to ground biblical prophecy and eschatology. For example, Jeremias, in his discussion of the parable of the Pharisee and publican (Luke 18:9-14), asserts matter-of-factly of ταπεινωθήσεται and ὑψωθήσεται (v 14) that "the future [form] is eschatological" (*Parables*, 142 n. 54). But what if the Future form does not refer to future time in quite the straightforward way that seems to be assumed *a priori*? This chapter argues that the Future form--an anomaly in the Greek verbal network--grammaticalizes the semantic feature of [+expectation], being neither fully aspectual nor an attitude.

    1. BRIEF HISTORY OF THE FUTURE FORM. Discussion of the Future form may begin with brief mention of its place in the evolution of the Greek language, though conclusions are not based solely on this piece of linguistic history; instead it is used to elucidate and support other findings. (Gonda [*Character*, 3-4, 68] warns against trying to reconstruct a primitive IE language; Sears [*Use*, 33-46] does this very thing.)

    Most historians of Greek are fairly well decided that in its earliest stages Greek, like other IE languages, had a form (Indicative?) used for both present and future reference that later developed a lengthened form (athematic » e/o; thematic » ē/ō [Buck, *Grammar*, 298-99]) or Present Subjunctive form (e.g. Kurylowicz, *Categories*, 136; Hahn, *Subjunctive*, 59ff.). The origin of the Aorist Subjunctive is more difficult to trace. One theory is that it developed from the sigmatic Aorist Indicative (e.g. Hahn, *Subjunctive*, 60-61), though Kurylowicz objects on the semantic ground that there is no direct link between the values of these two verbal categories (114). A second theory is that IE had a sigmatic desiderative form which became the functional equivalent of the Aorist Subjunctive (Kurylowicz, 111-14; Mandilaras, 171). Some are content to note that, at the earliest stages that can be substantiated, Greek had a distinct form for the Subjunctive, and probably for the Optative as well (Buck, 298, among many others; Hahn [34-35, 50-51] notes that H. Pedersen holds that IE had no Subjunctive but only the Optative. This does not concern me here), though whether this constituted a proper tense (Hahn [2] posits that these forms were originally tenses or even aspects, though she does not pursue the latter topic [2 n. 3]) or a non-Indicative Mood is open to question (Gonda, *Character*, 68ff., cf. 4; see Gildersleeve, 115).

The Greek Future was, by common opinion, a later development within Greek itself, evident by the time of Homer though not without some risk of confusion with the Aorist Subjunctive (Mandilaras [242] notes this confusion due to phonology, see 245-48; cf. Jannaris, 561; Wilkinson, *"Aspect,"* 135-51; Turner, *Syntax*, 115). Some have proposed that the Greek Future (even without the intervocalic sigma) was modelled after the IE (Sanskrit) *sie/o* Future, while others have argued that the sigmatic Aorist Subjunctive is responsible.[1] Kurylowicz argues that, on the basis of the origin of the sigmatic Future, a decision between the two need not be made, since the sigmatic Future goes back to an athematic Subjunctive form to which the thematic vowel was added. As he says, "this only proves the relative lateness and independence of the future-formations in the different languages" (*Categories*, 115. Brugmann [552] combines the two solutions). The Future continued in use through the hellenistic period until, under competition from other forms with apparently similar functions, most notably the Subjunctive, it retreated significantly and eventually disappeared. (See Jannaris, 441-44, 552-59, 560-67, for a history of the Future, both as a form and in relation to the Moods.)

2. FUTURE AS TENSE AND ASPECT.

In discussing the function of the Greek Future, and in keeping with the major emphasis of this work, two separate issues must be discussed: the functions of the Future as a tense or Mood, and the Future in relation to verbal aspect. The Greek grammars have various things to say about each.

a. Future as tense. 1. One group of grammarians argue quite forcefully that the Future form is an absolute tense serving as its name suggests, to describe events that are to take place in the future, i.e. subsequent to the present standpoint of the speaker (i.e. absolute tense)[2] As Kühner/Gerth say, "Das *Futur* (im Indikative) bezeichnet eine *zukünftige* Handlung, d.h. eine vom Standpunkte des Redenden aus in der Zukunft eintretende" (1.170; Jannaris [441] calls the Future "nothing else than the present transferred to a time to come"). Several NT grammarians argue similarly. Turner for example claims the Future "is the one tense which . . . simply states the time of action relative to the speaker" (*Syntax*, 86; cf. also Burton, 31, 70). Blass/Debrunner are even more forceful, arguing, "In meaning, time is practically the only significance of the future (even in the optative, infinitive and participle)" (¶ 318). And they, like Burton, imply that whereas the non-Indicative Moods convey relative time only, with temporal relation determined by "something else appearing

---

[1]See Robertson, 354; Kurylowicz, *Categories*, 115; Buck, *Grammar*, 278-79; Meillet/Vendryes, *Traité*, 210, who argue for the former; while Schwyzer, 1.779-87; Pariente, "Sobre los Futuros"; Wright, *Grammar*, 303; Moulton, 148-49 (though recognizing the possibility of mixed origin); Giles, *Philology*, 446, argue for the latter. Magnien (*Futur*, 288) argues that the Future is based directly on the sigmatic desiderative form; and Sears (*Use*, 34) calls it "self-evident" that the Future was "originally a mood."

[2]E.g. Jannaris, 441-42; Brugmann, 552-54; Stahl, 140-43; Kühner/Gerth, 1.170-79; Jelf, 2.68-70 (who distinguishes the Present expressing futurity and will "viewed as futurity"), cf. 75-76; Goodwin, *Grammar*, 268; idem, *Syntax*, 36; Gildersleeve, 115; Smyth, 427-28 (with acknowledgment that "the action is future according to the opinion, expectation, hope, fear, or purpose of the speaker or agent" [427]); Lightfoot, *Logic*, 126-32, although he recognizes a generic non-future referring use.

in the speech or narrative" (¶ 318), the Future, like other Indicative forms, conveys a more absolute sense of time (i.e. it is a proper tense) (Lyons, *Semantics*, 681. Burton [36] says the gnomic Future is used "to state what will customarily happen when occasion offers." Is he consistent here?). This analysis warrants further examination.

Blass/Debrunner cite a gnomic use of the Future in Rom 5:7 (scarcely would anyone ἀποθανεῖται [die] on behalf of a righteous man) "to express that which is expected under certain circumstances" (¶ 349[1]). Though they do not define what is meant by gnomic, it usually includes at minimum a definition by which past circumstances form the pattern for future occurrences (see Lyons, *Introduction*, 304-06, on omnitemporality); this is hardly absolute time but only expected. They also cite a relative use of the Future after verbs of believing to denote time subsequent to the acquisition of belief: in Matt 20:10, the parable of the labourers, with use of λήμψονται (they thought that they would receive more), and John 21:19, where John comments that Jesus "said this to signal by which death [Peter] would δοξάσει (glorify) God." After acknowledging a relative time value for the Infinitive (¶ 350), Blass/Debrunner must admit that the Participle may be used "as a supplement to the main verb (to express purpose)" (¶ 351[1]) (see below). They also refer to "modal functions of the fut. indic." (¶ 349[2]), listing the use of the Future in injunctions and prohibitions in OT quotations (¶ 362). Though they make no temporal claims for commands, it is difficult to see a future sense in the context of many of these, since the discussion focuses more on general, timeless principles: e.g. in Matt 4:7, Jesus reportedly quotes scripture saying "you will not ἐκπειράσεις [tempt] the lord your God" after his temptation by Satan; cf. also Matt 5:21ff.; examples abound. Though Blass/Debrunner cite the οὐ μή construction as "the most negative form of negation regarding the Future" (¶ 365), it is difficult to see a clear future sense in the conditional-like statement of Matt 15:6 (whoever says . . . he does not honour [οὐ μή τιμήσει] his father); and in Luke 21:33, to press that Jesus is claiming his words will not pass away in the future (οὐ μή παρελεύσονται) leaves them to fend for themselves today. And Blass/Debrunner admit that τί ἐροῦμεν (what shall we say) in Rom 3:5; 4:1 "at least approaches the deliberative meaning" (¶ 366).[3] Blass/Debrunner also cite the final or purpose use of the Future with ἵνα and μή (¶ 369), for example in Gal 2:4 (Paul warns that false brothers might enter ἵνα . . . καταδουλώσουσιν [to enslave them]), where the Future verb refers to an event probably past to the speaker, though strict temporal reference, it seems, is eliminated by definition in this kind of clause (see e.g. 1 Cor 9:15: ἵνα οὕτως γένηται ἐν ἐμοί [so that it might be this way with me]). Blass/Debrunner note as well that the Future may be used in "expressions of expectation which accompany the action" (¶ 375). Their example of Acts 8:22 (pray [δεήθητι] to the lord whether the intent of your heart ἀφεθήσεται [will be forgiven]) is problematic, since the εἰ clause is linked to an Imperative, thus the Future form is coincidental with a relative verbal act, hardly future except by implicature and certainly not absolute. And use of the Future in Luke 11:6 in what Blass/Debrunner call a "qualitative-consecutive relative clause" (¶ 379) misses the point if a temporal sense is pressed (the host says he does not have anything that he could possibly offer [ὃ παραθήσω], since he has already looked). And "conditional relative clauses," Blass/Debrunner state outright, "usually make no assertions about concrete realities" (¶ 380; see Matt 10:32; 18:4). In fact, they cite an example where the Future "can also be equal to a present with ἄν": Luke 17:31, a clearly hypothetical reference to one who may be upon his roof (ὃς ἔσται). And finally, the Future in protases of 1 class conditionals (according to traditional terminology) reveals difficulty for those positing a strictly future sense. Even if Boyer's estimation of the 1 class conditional as strictly logical--with no temporal implicature (Boyer, "First Class," 75ff.; see my chapt. 6)--is put aside, Blass/Debrunner posit that this conditional either has reference to present reality bordering on a causal sense (¶ 372[1]), with present, past or future

---

[3]Burton has a special category of deliberative Future for forms used "in questions of deliberation, asking not what will happen, but what can or ought to be done" (36), as in Luke 22:49 and John 6:68, the former where the disciples ask εἰ πατάξομεν ἐν μαχαίρῃ (whether we should strike with our sword) and the latter where they ask Jesus πρὸς τίνα ἀπελευσόμεθα; (to whom should we go?).

verbs, or when non-causal a logical sense. (Citing Matt 26:33 [par. Mark 14:29] Blass/Debrunner note the element of prediction involved, when Peter says, "if all are ashamed with you [σκανδαλισθήσονται], I shall never be ashamed [σκανδαλισθήσομαι].)

These examples, from the most detailed discussion of the Future in any of the NT grammars, show that Blass/Debrunner's position--that the Future is essentially an absolute future-referring tense form--must die the death of innumerable qualifications (the analysis could have been made with a number of other grammars, including those of classical Greek: e.g. Goodwin, *Syntax*, 18-20). Certainly there are instances where the Future appears to have future implicature, but since the Future Participle and Infinitive have only relative temporal value indicated by deixis, and the finite Future forms may be found in relative contexts like those where the Subjunctive is so common, the implication is that the Future too has only relative temporal reference. In any case, if a unifying factor for use of this tense is being sought (as Blass/Debrunner and virtually all other grammarians claim) absolute future temporal reference does not seem to be that common factor.

2. A smaller group of grammarians argue that the temporal function of the Future is divided between those functions normally ascribed to the Indicative Mood and those of the non-Indicative Moods.[4] Mandilaras, like McKay and Wilkinson, claims that the temporal element of the Future is clearly seen "when it refers to events or acts which, by natural sequence, will take place in future time, or when it states a piece of information the effect of which comes into force in the future" (182). But this is certainly not a stringent enough criterion, since certain uses of the Present, Perfect and Aorist function similarly. Mandilaras also claims that the Future, "although formally a tense, approximates in usage to a mood, on a par with the subjunctive and imperative," listing a volitive use as "unquestionably modal in character" (184),[5] an imperatival use (188-90),[6] a deliberative use (190-91),[7] and an admittedly rare gnomic use (191). Most grammarians in this camp, therefore, place their temporal and modal functions side by side, admitting though not fully realizing the inherent difficulties in such a procedure.

---

[4]Mandilaras, 181-91; Robertson, 872-76 (cf. 876, where he says that in the Moods the Future "has always the element of time"); Ruipérez, *Estructura*, 91-94; McKay, 147-48; Wilkinson, *"Aspect,"* 148-50; Winer, 348-51; and Gildersleeve, 115ff., who recognizes the original modal nature of the Future and its modal use in dependent clauses, but claims this is "more or less effaced" in principle clauses. Wackernagel (*Vorlesungen*, 192-206) goes much further when he argues that, while the other tenses in Greek say nothing in and of themselves about time, the Future mediates temporal reference through the form itself (199), though he also asserts the primary and enduring modal sense (204-06); Zerwick (93-95) deliberates this seriously; Moulton (148-51) seems to assume a future reference though he clearly ties the form to its modal background and uses.
[5]E.g. P.Oxy. 743.38-40 (2 B.C.): καὶ σὺ / δὲ ὑπὲρ ὧν ἐὰν θέλῃς γράφε μοι, καὶ ἀνό/κνως ποήσω (and you write me about what you want and I will do it without hesitation); P.Petrie iii 42.8-10 (3d cent. B.C.); P.Lips. 105.6-7 (1st/2d cent. A.D.); P.Oxy. 498.28-29 (2d cent. A.D.).
[6]E.g. P.Oxy. 1482.17 (2d cent. A.D.): γράψις μοι περὶ τούτων (write to me concerning these things); P.Oxy. 1760.10-11 (2d cent. A.D.): πέ[μ]ψεις οὖν ἡμεῖν ἐπιστό/λιον (send to us the letter).
[7]E.g. P.Teb. 289.5-8 (A.D. 23): οὕτως γὰρ γνώσομαι / πότερον ἐπὶ τόπων σε ἐάσω / πράττοντά τι ἢ μεταπεμψάμε(νος) / πέμψωι τῶι ἡγεμόνι (for thus I shall make known whether I should leave you working in this place or sending for you for you should send you [to the prefect]).

(1) To call the Future both a tense and a Mood is to commit what Ryle calls a category mistake (*Concept*, 16-18). Grammarians must speak in terms of either temporal relation (traditional parlance uses Aorist for past, Present for present and Future for future) or attitude (Indicative, Subjunctive, Imperative, Optative), which are not on equal planes. Most grammarians would argue they are speaking of a form that has functions similar to those of the non-Indicative Moods, hence it is 'modal.' Thus they argue that a form they call the Indicative functions often like a Subjunctive and Imperative, and when it does so it often no longer functions as a Future. In any case, they are left without either a clear morphologically-based category, which is evidenced by the other tenses (i.e. there is no firm basis for distinguishing which Mood is represented), or a corresponding essential verbal function, again which the other tenses display. A purely temporal scheme is not sufficient, as the grammarians in this group admit. Tense in language has to do with the relation between an event and the placement of a speaker or writer. According to this definition (see chapts. 2 and 4) there is no formal category of (absolute) tense in Greek, and no reason to posit an exception for the Future. (The logical implications of this are great, i.e. the tense form is probably misnamed, but since the concern here is with form and function as separate issues the name, while perhaps inconvenient, will remain as a label.)

(2) Semantically speaking there are no formal criteria for making a choice between these essentially different definitions of the Future function; these choices, if they are to be made at all, must be differentiated pragmatically in some way. Therefore, whereas it is clear that future time is not at the heart of the Future's function, and neither is a mixed conception of time and Mood, the unifying principle all grammarians seek has not yet been determined.

3. A very small group of grammarians argue for the purely modal character of the Greek Future.[8] Magnien assumes that "Comme les thèmes (temporels) des verbes indoeuropéens, les thèmes (temporels) du grec n'expriment pas proprement le temps. . . . Pas plus que les autres thèmes dits temporels, le futur n'est vraiment un temps. . . . Il indique essentiellement la volonté, le désir. . ." (*Futur*, v). Humbert argues similarly that the Future is not an objective (or absolute) tense but a "virtual" tense which indicates that an event is trying to come to pass. Consequently, he claims, the Future participates more in the subjectivity of the non-Indicative Moods. Though Humbert, like Magnien, claims that the virtuality of the future leads to a temporal use (so that the "temporal future" becomes a legitimate description of one of its uses), he claims that practically the temporal and desiderative uses complement each other, though they often must be distinguished. Rijksbaron adds, "It is clear . . . that 'fact' and 'future' are hardly compatible. . . . Hence the future indicative expresses at best a more or less reliable prediction" (33).

While this proposal is very attractive, it fails to account for the formal characteristics of the Future, i.e. the Future has a single finite form in the hellenistic period, as well as a Participle and an Infinitive, fails to distinguish verb stems, and fails to account for the Indicative-like contexts in which the Future appears.

b. **Aspect.** In discussion of aspect or kind of action (most of the older grammarians refer to *Aktionsart*), three major positions have been maintained.

---

[8]Magnien, *Futur*, v-vii; Schwyzer, 2.290-94; Humbert, 151-53; Palmer, "Language," 153; Rijksbaron, 33, though he hesitates a bit, cf. 4-6; cf. Moule, 21-23. I frankly was surprised that though Magnien is often cited in bibliographies, his position, assumed in his preface, is largely ignored.

1. The largest group of exponents claim that a distinction can be made between "durative" and "punctiliar" kinds of action.[9] The argument is made along various lines. Brugmann argues that the kind of action is determined by the meaning of the verbal root (i.e. ὄψομαι may mean either "I will look at" or "I will glimpse," the one non-punctual and the other punctual). Kühner/Gerth claim that only in those cases where a double form exists can it be argued that the Future displays a difference in the kind of action (i.e. ἔχω has durative [ἕξω] and punctiliar [σχήσω] forms [cf. Hauri, *Kontrahiertes*, 196-98]; contra Hartmann, "Frage," who proposes that double forms are remnants of development from the Aorist Subjunctive [127]). Smyth argues both, and Moulton recognizes the possibility of both in classical Greek, though he makes clear that hellenistic Greek "generally got rid of alternative forms," so that such a distinction plays no real part in NT Greek (150). Jannaris maintains that in certain instances Attic Greek did discriminate kinds of action on the basis of Voice, citing approximately 50 verbs in which, he claims, the Passive served as the effective (punctiliar) form and the Middle as the durative passive (i.e. ἀχθήσομαι and ἄξομαι from ἄγω), though he admits this distinction was not carried out systematically and that by hellenistic times, owing to the retreat of the Middle, such a formulation cannot be imposed. (He claims periphrasis is the later substitute.)

2. A smaller number have argued that the Future, rather than constituting either a temporal category or differentiating the traditional categories of kind of action or aspect, constitutes a verbal aspect in its own right. (McKay, 136, 140-41, 147-48; Wilkinson, *"Aspect,"* chapt. 1; Durie, 288, 92.) McKay claims that the Future, being anomalous in the Greek verbal system in that it lacks what are usually called Moods (and sees very limited use in classical Greek of its Infinitive and Optative) should be regarded as an aspect "expressing intention" (136). Though he argues elsewhere that certain statements of futurity appear "to have little or no direct relevance" to intention (147), he sees this as a consequence of the intentional idea. Durie makes the claim that the Future does not refer to a real event, thus it lacks analogy with various tenses used of the past and present (292).

Though this is a commendable attempt, this group is compelled to define aspect on different criteria than used elsewhere. Instead of formulating a category around the idea of internal constituency or paradigmatic choice, this definition is a hotchpotch of intentional and external temporal features, and hence fails to be fully convincing.

3. A last group of scholars contend that the Future form expresses no grammatical aspect, though an individual verbal usage, on the basis of lexis in context, may be interpreted as either punctiliar or durative, or the like.[10] Like Mandilaras, Burton notes that the Future "does not mark the distinction

---

[9]Kühner/Gerth, 1.170-71; Brugmann, 552-54; Jannaris, 441-42; Goodwin, *Grammar*, 269; idem, *Syntax*, 36; Gildersleeve, 115; Smyth, 427-28; Moulton, 149-50; Nunn, 77; Robertson, 870-72 (though his discussion is confusing); Sears, *Use*, 31-32. See Rose, *Tenses*, 30-32, for discussion. Wackernagel (*Vorlesungen*, 200-04) and Magnien (*Futur*, 279-80) offer a critique of these kinds of proposals.

[10]Stahl, 120-42; Mandilaras, 181-82; Humbert, 151; Schwyzer, 2.264-66; Rose, *Tenses*, 32; Magnien, *Futur*, 278-82; Rijksbaron, 33; Turner, *Syntax*, 86, though somewhat ambivalent; Burton, 31-37; Zerwick, 93, though he entertains the idea that the Future may constitute its own aspect; Blass/Debrunner, ¶ 178; cf. Hartmann, "Frage," who concludes similarly on the basis of evolution of the forms and contextual meaning.

between action in progress and action conceived of indefinitely without reference to its progress; it may be either aoristic or progressive" (32), though it "may be doubted whether any of the distinctions indicated . . . are justified from the point of view of pure grammar" (33). (Dana/Mantey [191] argue that since the Future and Aorist forms are similar and the future is uncertain all Futures are punctiliar. Moule [10] argues likewise.) As seen here, there is clear divergence of opinion on both whether the Future constitutes an aspect (i.e. whether aspect can be so defined to include the Future tense) and whether the Future maintains any of the traditional aspectual categories.

3. SEMANTIC DEFINITION OF THE FUTURE FORM. a. Upon observation of the formal paradigm of the Future, whether in classical or NT Greek, several facts emerge. As already noted, an overwhelming majority of grammarians categorize the Future (obviously apart from the Infinitive and Participle) as an Indicative form. 1. Since the Future has only one set of forms it is problematic to categorize. If it is considered an Indicative--which it morphologically resembles (i.e. the Present with sigma and short theme vowel, except in liquid stems with compensatory lengthening; see Curtius, *Verb*, 467)--it does not offer a contrast, as the Aorist, Present, and Perfect do, with its Subjunctive, Optative, and Imperative forms. And if it is treated as a non-Indicative Mood there is no Indicative choice. The three Indicative forms--Aorist, Present, and Perfect--each offer a complete set of Moods (of course, the paradigm is complete to varying degrees, with varying frequencies of usage), while the Future has essentially a single form. In any case the Future is unusual, thus warranting close analysis. (Wilkinson ["*Aspect*," 149] claims that because the Future has a Participle and an Infinitive it cannot be a non-Indicative Mood alone.)

2. The Future developed two short-lived forms worth noting. a. The Future Optative appeared first in Pindar (e.g. Pyth. 9.126; 5th cent. B.C.) and was rare even in Attic Greek, to which it is peculiar. It is found in indirect discourse only after a secondary tense or the historic present and served as a substitute for the simple Future.[11] The simple Future, however, was often retained (Goodwin, *Syntax*, 44). The Future Optative does not occur in the NT. b. The Future Perfect (many consider it a Perfect), a form essentially peculiar to Attic Greek, was more common in the Passive Voice but was formed periphrastically in the Active construction (Jannaris, 444). Many grammarians define this as a Perfect "transferred to the future" (e.g. Goodwin, *Syntax*, 21; cf. Schwyzer, 2.289). When it is noted that many of these same grammarians define the use of the non-Indicative Moods as in essence future-referring it becomes probable that the Future Perfect grew up in the Perfect paradigm by analogy of form and function, as a substitute for a lacking Perfect Subjunctive and as a complement to the Pluperfect (to make the scheme resemble the Aorist and Present) (see Goodwin, *Grammar*, 159, on the rare Perfect Subjunctive). By NT times the form had virtually disapppeared; in the NT there is no instance except for an inferior reading of κεκράξονται (cry) in Luke 19:4 and possibly εἰδήσουσιν (know) in Heb 8:11 (see Blass/Debrunner, ¶ 62[2]; Robertson, 906-07; cf. Mandilaras, 240; idem, "NT," 49, where he cites one example: PSI 441.9-10 [3d cent. B.C.]: προ/εστήξομαι). Moulton (151)

---

[11]See Keith, "Uses," 122-26, who attempts to give it new life. Jannaris (452) claims that in Greco-Roman and Byzantine Greek it became comparatively more common but he doubts it derives directly from the Attic form, being rather a creation by analogy on the part of fastidious scribes in place of the Subjunctive. Hahn (*Subjunctive*, 3 n. 6) claims that the Attic form was created analogically to balance the simple Future, while Magnien (*Futur*, 126) posits that it may be an ancient form that saw more development in Homeric than Attic Greek.

summarizes the nature of both these temporary incursions very well when he notes, "the moods of the Future have in Hellenistic Greek receded mostly into their original non-existence, as experiments that proved failures." This leaves the Future throughout most of its history, and certainly during its period of widest usage the hellenistic, with a simple form plus the Infinitive and Participle. (Magnien [*Futur*, 1-4] notes the "Imperfect Future" and "Imperative Future," claiming that their very rare usage, almost exclusively in Homer, points to their being pre-hellenic in use.)

Since the Future comprises a single paradigmatic edifice, and is morphologically undifferentiated (though it may have done this at one time with duplicate forms, and allows for an objective interpretation of an individual act [*Aktionsart*]), the Future offers no clear aspectual choice in establishing an author's conception of the constituency of a process. In one sense Mandilaras is right in asserting that the Future is merely concerned with the facticity of a process (181; cf. Burton, 32-34), though it is preferable to say the Future form is *aspectually vague* (on ambiguity and vagueness see Kempson, *Theory*, 123-38; and my chapt. 10).

b. Linguists recognize that grammatical forms and their concomitant functions do not necessarily correlate with the temporal distinctions speakers are able to make, otherwise there would be an endless number of verbal forms. Instead, a language system provides a framework for speaking about time. For example, English only has Past and Present simple forms and a periphrastic modal-volitional Future, though speakers believe they are able to posit events that they believe will occur, though they have not yet transpired. The reason for this breakdown seems to be in the way time is perceived. A speaker can make assertions about the present since he is experiencing it or has access to it. Likewise, he is able to speak of the past since it is a matter of (known) events that have transpired previously. But reference to future time is different. He could say "It will rain tomorrow, I just know it," but even with the highest certainty on his part, he will have to wait and see. And if he says, "The world will end tomorrow," or "The last judgment will come next Friday," whether he is wrong cannot be known until tomorrow or Friday are past. As Rijksbaron says (33), "whether or not the action concerned will be a fact, 'only future can tell.'" This is the important distinction Entwistle makes between "facts and notions" (*Aspects*, 184; cf. Rijksbaron, 33, who says, "It is clear . . . that 'fact' and 'future' are hardly compatible"; and Jespersen, *Philosophy*, 260), when he says:

> Among notions we must include the future. In the most concrete sense the future is remote from the present just like the past, and the chronological series consists of *then-now-then*. But the past has been a fact, whereas the future is a mere notion associated variously with desire, will, obligation, emotion, and incompletion. These are modes of activity.

Greek has Moods to grammaticalize such conceptions of action.

I am aware of the Whorfian linguistic approach, in which a language is said to reflect and dictate the mental state of its users (see Whorf, *Language*, esp. his essays "The Punctual and Segmentative Aspects of Verbs in Hopi" [51-56]; "An American Indian Model of the Universe" [57-64]; and "A Linguistic Consideration of Thinking in Primitive Communities" [65-86]), and am in essential agreement with Barr's criticism of the excesses of this approach (*Semantics*, esp. 8-106), especially as evidenced in Boman's work. Most linguists take the position that whereas language does not dictate thought, and whereas virtually any language can be made to handle any subject matter, certain languages make treatment of certain concepts easier than others. (See Thiselton, *Two Horizons*, 133-39, esp. 137; Spence, "Review Article"; Lyons, *Language and Linguistics*, 303-12. If I were arguing along Bomanian/Whorfian lines I would claim that the

Greeks had difficulty conceiving of future time, which is thus seen in use of a Future form that limited their ability to conceive of and express future reference. Neither appears to be the case.) It is often implied and usually assumed that the past, present and future time distinctions speakers are able to make are "essential to the notion of tense" and could theoretically be grammaticalized in similar ways (e.g. Jespersen [*Philosophy*, 254-57] describes different logical schemes of temporal relation, although acknowledging that none fits the way a language actually functions). However, this is rarely the case, partly because, as Lyons says, "the future is not like the past from the point of view of our experience and conceptualization of time" (*Semantics*, 677; see Palmer, *Modality*, 5-6, for a discussion of the relation between modality and time).

In theory, a language could treat futurity or the prospective view as grammatically parallel to statements about the past and present. This is in fact what most grammarians of Greek believe they see. But most are forced to admit, as the examples cited above reveal, that at least in some sentences future time is not referred to by sentences with Future verbs. Those who posit a mixed use of the tense require that it function both assertively and non-assertively, thus destroying any unified conception of the formal category of the Future tense, and eliminating any principled linguistic grounds for meaningful choice of the form.

c. The Future is recognizably used in distinctly non-future contexts (gnomically [Rom 5:7; 7:3], as a command [Matt 21:3], as a supposition in conditional and conditional-like statements [Mark 14:29; Matt 10:32], and as parallel in function to various uses of the Subjunctive, like the relative clause), as even the most stringently time-based grammars admit. (See Blass/Debrunner [see above]; Rijksbaron, 64ff.; Goodwin, *Syntax*, esp. 137-42; Keith, "Uses," 121-22.) Several grammarians over the years have argued that the non-Indicative Moods are essentially "Future tenses" as well (e.g. Hahn, *Subjunctive*, 2ff.; Lightfoot, *Logic*, 133ff., with notable caveats regarding "illogical" Futures that do not conform; Moulton, 164ff.; Goodwin, *Grammar*, 281ff.; Gildersleeve, 128; Smyth, 415ff. Other grammarians recognize the *modus irrealis* of the non-Indicative Moods, esp. Gonda, *Character*, 1ff.; see my chapts. 4 and 7). They are right in the sense that all processes that are merely hypothesized, if they were to occur, would have to occur in some time future to the present. But this is not what is meant by tense in language and does not solve the problem of whether the Future should be considered as an Indicative in function, since no one wants to argue that all the non-Indicative Moods are after all actually Indicatives, and still does not deal with the question of the function of the non-Indicative Moods. Besides, this imposition of temporal values would eliminate the fine degrees of distinction between the various non-assertive functions in Greek.

d. Usage in apparently prospective statements (non-Indicative Moods display this ability) reveals that references to future time are qualitatively different from references to the present and past, and that the degree of certainty is of a different kind. This points rather to Greek as a bi-temporal language (past-present)--as are most IE languages--rather than tri-temporal (Lyons, *Introduction*, 304-06; *Semantics*, 677-78). Temporal reference in Greek, not grammaticalized in any of the tense forms, is an implicature derived from deictic indicators, hence the Future can have as one of its subordinate uses future temporal reference, though this is one of many possible pragmatic interpretations of the form's function.

e. The history of the language shows that the Future was a rather late development growing out of the Subjunctive and or desiderative forms, thus indicating its origin not as an Indicative but as a non-Indicative form, thus in some way related to or extending the Subjunctive meaning (see chapts. 4 and 7). Most grammarians recognize that Homeric Greek still had a tendency to confuse the two forms (Monro, 297-98; Goodwin, *Grammar*, 288-89. This formal difficulty is still present in the NT to some extent. Magnien [*Futur*, 5] claims, "Rien ne permet d'affirmer que le subjonctif du futur ait jamais existé en grec").

f. There are functions and constructions that the Future shares with Indicative verbs and there are functions and constructions that the Future shares with non-Indicative Moods. Usage in independent, relative, and conditional-like clauses does not demonstrate conclusively the similarity of the Future with either the Indicative or non-Indicative Moods, although several other uses--such as in commands, in relative and conditional-like clauses, and with τί (all exemplifed by Blass/Debrunner above, as well as other reference grammars)--illustrate affinity with the non-Indicative Moods. Several other syntactical considerations are worth noting. (1) The Future tends to follow εἰ without ἄν in conditional protases, whereas the Subjunctive is accompanied by ἐάν. (Magnien [*Futur*, 147] says that εἰ + Future is not notably different from ἐάν + Subjunctive in NT Greek, see also 193-213; cf. Rijksbaron, 69. On whether ἐάν results from εἰ + ἄν see Lightfoot, *Logic*, 127 n. 28.) This evidence is not unequivocal.[12] As Moorhouse ("AN"; "Reply") and Hulton ("'AN") argue (see also Richards, "'Αν"), there are several clear instances in classical Greek of ἄν + Future,[13] and in the NT the Future appears with ἐάν in Acts 8:31. The Optative appears with εἰ, and occasionally Indicative verbs appear with ἐάν. Thus criteria of εἰ and ἄν do not establish the place of the Future in the Mood paradigm. (2) The Future tends to be negated with οὐ, while non-Indicative Moods with μή. (Blass's canon makes this statement for NT Greek [253]; cf. Moulton, 170-71; Robertson, 1155-75; Blass/Debrunner, ¶¶ 426-33; Turner, *Syntax*, 281-87; and esp. Moorhouse, *Studies*, the most wide-ranging study of negation in Greek.) This has not always been so clear. The negative μή, though originally used only with independent clauses, was eventually used with all instances of the Subjunctive, Optative, and Imperative (in Homer οὐ was used as the negative of certain Subjunctives: e.g. Hom. Il. 1.262; 6.459; see Goodwin, *Grammar*, 288). As the Future became more distinct from the Subjunctive it seems to have taken οὐ with it,

---

[12]Primarily on the basis of collocation with ἐάν and use in conditional statements, Lightfoot (*Logic*, 132, 133-34) defines the Subjunctive and Future as kinds of futures, the one "logical" and the other "existential" or "illogical" (it is ambiguous whether he is speaking formally or functionally), though he admits, "all future tenses must be modal to some extent and not as totally objective as a present or past tense since the future is not in the realm of undeniable, objective fact. Any reference to the future must be modal and imply some kind of colouring, an intention, prediction, promise, order, guess, hope, expectation" (17). He also admits that his view of the Future as "future-generic," trying to include both temporal and modal functions, "solves nothing" except preventing interpreters "from taking a simplistic and non-modal view of the future 'tense'" (131). See de Boel, "Complementizers," 285-86; and Horrocks, Review, esp. 81-83.

[13]In Homer as well, where there is still morphological confusion between the Subjunctive and Future, ἄν occurs with the Future. Hom. Il. 4.176; 1.174; cf. Pl. Apol. 29C. Goodwin, *Grammar*, 277-78.

with οὐ dropping from use with the Subjunctive (Robertson, 1160), quite possibly to distinguish the forms further, but also possibly in line with the general distinction between μή as the notional and οὐ as the concrete negative, reflecting a degree of semantic markedness (see Moorhouse, *Studies*, 40; Gonda, *Character*, 203 n. 1; cf. Pritchett, "MH," 392 n. 1). A closer correlation between οὐ and μή remained than might have been expected, and this makes more understandable the steady increase of μή the stronger negative at the expense of οὐ (Moulton, 169),[14] so that in NT Greek there are examples of the Future with μή (e.g. Matt 7:6; Col 2:8; Acts 8:31; Heb 3:12; and possibly Rom 11:21, rare in classical Greek as well), as well as οὐ μή (e.g. Mark 13:31 par. Luke 21:33; Mark 14:31 par. Matt 26:35; Matt 15:6; 16:22; John 4:14; 6:35; 10:5; [20:25?;] Gal 4:30; Heb 10:17; Rev. 3:5; 9:6; 18:14). Instances of μή with the Indicative, apart from questions and I.b. class conditionals, include John 3:18; Rom 4:19. Moulton (192-93) cites μή with the Indicative meaning "perhaps" as well: Luke 11:35; Col 2:8; Heb 3:12; Gal 4:11; and P.Par. 49.30-31 (160 B.C.); P.Gen. 17 (3d cent. A.D.); P.Teb. 333.11 (A.D. 216); cf. Epict. 4.5.9 (ὅτι μὴ ἔπληξεν); 4.10.34 (ὅτι μὴ ἔχεις . . .). (On οὐ μή as a negative see esp. Goodwin, *Syntax*, 389-97; Whitelaw, "Construction"; Moorhouse, *Studies*.) (3) While the Future is often placed in the category of 1 class conditionals according to traditional classification (Goodwin [*Syntax*, 163] and Smyth [525] place the Future with the Subjunctive for intensive usage), the Future appears regularly in the apodosis of so-called 3 class conditionals ('future' conditions, often with Subjunctive in protasis), along with Subjunctives, Imperatives, Optatives, and Infinitives (see Goodwin, *Syntax*, 164-65). (4) Purpose clauses following ἵνα (and ὅπως, etc.) are not confined to the non-Indicative Moods (see Winer, 360-61; Magnien, *Futur*, 239ff.): e.g. X. Anab. 3.1.18: ὅπως τοι μὴ ἐπʼ ἐκείνῳ γενησόμεθα πάντα ποιητέον (so that we shall not become all possessed by that one). While ὅπως + Future, etc., does not occur in the NT (it is fairly common in classical Greek, being used in dependent clauses instead of the Subjunctive apart from rare negated instances [note replacement of the final relative clause with the Subjunctive by the Future in Attic Greek]), ἵνα + Future--an apparent replacement--appears in, for example, Gal 2:4; 1 Pet 3:1; Rev 22:14; 3:9; 6:4, 11; 14:13 (cf. also S. Oed. Col. 621-22; Ar. Frogs 1231; Homer, with ἵνα + Future).

g. Conclusion. 1. Definition.

It appears that much of the problem regarding the Future is that grammarians have attempted to place it within already-established categories; thus, some argue that the Future is strictly a tense (= Indicative), while others argue it is modal, while still others posit that it is an aspect. Each side has some evidence in support of its case, but none is wholly satisfactory. It is proposed here that on the basis of its distinctive yet tense-related morphological features, the Future constitutes part of the Greek verbal system that results in full aspectual choices, but as seen above, it is not fully aspectual (no paradigmatic choice is offered). This system is labelled ASPECTUALITY. Therefore the Future is compatible with environments where full aspectual choice is made, but it does not grammaticalize such choice itself (it is aspectually vague).

The question of the terminal semantic feature of the Future must still be answered. It has been noted that the Future is found in environments where the non-Indicative Moods are used (deliberative or purpose clauses, commands,

---

[14]See Gildersleeve, "Encroachment," with many examples from classical writers; Green "Μή for οὐ." Moorhouse ("Negating Greek Participles," esp. 40) cites fifteen examples, mostly in Sophocles, Euripides, and Thucydidies, where μή evidences expansion in negating Participles; see also Pritchett, "MH"; Braunlich, "Euripides"; P. Wallace, "MH," esp. 321-23.

etc.). Grammarians are agreed, reinforced by the recent work of D. Lightfoot, that where a choice is offered between the Subjunctive and the Future, the Future is the more heavily marked semantically (see esp. Gonda, *Character*, 76-77; Rijksbaron, 33; Sears, *Use*, 128; cf. Gildersleeve, "Forms," 9). For example, of Isoc. 6.107: ἢν μὲν γὰρ ἐθέλωμεν ἀποθνήσκειν ὑπὲρ τῶν δικαίων, οὐ μόνον εὐδοκιμήσομεν, . . . εἰ δὲ φοβησόμεθα τοὺς κινδύνους, εἰς πολλὰς ταραχὰς καταστήσομεν ἡμᾶς αὐτούς (for if we might want to die on behalf of the just, we will not only be well esteemed. . . . but if we will fear the dangers, we will plunge ourselves into many troubles), Goodwin says, "Here what is feared is expressed by the emphatic future as a warning, while the alternative that is preferred has the subjunctive" (*Syntax*, 166). In chapt. 4 it is posited that the semantic feature which best characterizes the Subjunctive and Optative is [+projection] (see Gonda, *Character*, 47-116, esp. 51-52, 69-71),[15] derived from the volitional sense (wording avoided because of terminological confusion) it shares with the other non-Indicative Moods. The Future does not grammaticalize [-assertion] since it does not offer paradigmatic choice, yet it appears to be semantically compatible in many instances. A review of the opinions expressed by grammarians on the semantics of the Future reveals much the same thing, although they place these statements under various categories. At essence they believe similarly that (those who posit a strict temporal analysis have been clearly enough disproved to disregard their assertion, especially since they themselves must qualify it) the Future expresses a volition, a desire, an aim toward a goal, a prediction, an intention, an expectation. Not only the tension of classification but the tension of labelling can be relieved if this conceptual similarity is reduced to the single label of [+expectation] (Arist. Rhet. 1393A; Humbert [151] notes the role of the Future in Greek in forming a relation between virtuality and reality). The Future is thus a unique form in Greek, similar both to the aspects and to the attitudes, but fully neither, and realizing not a temporal conception but a marked and emphatic expectation toward a process.[16]

It is difficult to gloss this important semantic feature for every Future form, though difficulty in translation does not necessarily reduce its value as a feature (see Gleason, *Introduction*, 77, who points out how "translation is a very inadequate means of expressing meanings. . ."). The problems dissolve

---

[15]Cf. Moulton, 164, who, while discounting the ability to find a root idea of each mood, asserts that the non-Indicative Moods "are characterized by a common subjective element, representing an attitude of mind on the part of the speaker"; Winer, 351; Robertson, 848ff. *passim*; Schwyzer, 2.303-04; McKay, 148-49.

[16]Lightfoot (*Logic*, 32) concludes that the Future makes an "existential presupposition." His discussion is confusing at this point, since he seems to be referring to existential and factive presupposition (see Allwood *et al.*, *Logic*, 150-51).

somewhat, however, if the roles of the speaker and agent of the process are distinguished. Since they are correlated in 1st Person, the 1st Person should be understood as "I or we expect that it very well could occur, that I . . ." 2d Person seems best read as "the speaker expects that you . . ," i.e. "it can be expected that you. . . ." 3d Person is the most problematic, especially with inanimate subjects. But since the emphasis is on the speaker's expectation of the process, the grammatical subject's perspective is of relatively little consequence: "the speaker expects that he/it . . ," i.e. "it can be expected that he. . . ." The traditional language of volition or intention is often coincident with this understanding of the role of the speaker's expectation of a process, and it is very often possible to include this implicature in translation. (My language here is helped by Wilkinson, *"Aspect,"* 148-49; McKay, "Aspects," 56; cf. Magnien, *Futur*, v, vii. Appropriate adjustments of the glosses must be made for the Participle and Infinitive according to speaker and agent.)

2. Examples. Before looking more closely at the range of pragmatic implicature of the Future, examination of several instances where a Future form is used parallel to a Subjunctive is warranted. This is a feature well-known in classical literature: e.g. E. Ion 758: εἴπωμεν ἤ σιγῶμεν ἤ τί δράσομεν; (should we speak or be silent or do something?), with Aorist and Present Subjunctives and Future; S. Trach. 973: τί πάθω; τί δὲ μήσομαι; (what is to happen to me? What am I to do?); A. Sev. Thebes 1057. On the basis of the semantic distinction from the Moods, it should be possible to establish a difference (if only subtle) between the Future and Subjunctive, though their presence in parallel syntactical constructions and like immediate contexts shows an inherently close relation (see Blass/Debrunner, ¶¶ 369, 378; Turner, *Syntax*, 100, who notes confusion of Future and Aorist Subjunctive forms in the various texts [is this because of formal confusion alone, or because of functional similarity also?]; Robertson, 960-61, on classical parallels to these constructions).

In relative clauses, the Future has a sense of expectation missing from the Subjunctive: e.g. Mark 1:2 (par. Matt 11:10; Luke 7:27) has a sense of urgency suitable to the strategic use of the quotation of Mal 3:1/Exod 23:20 to reinforce John the Baptist's role of preparing for Christ. And Matt 18:4 affirms strongly the greatness of one who will humble himslf (see also Matt 21:41; 24:2 [par. Luke 21:6]; Acts 7:40 [Exod 32:1]). In ἵνα or μή clauses, in Luke 20:10 the vineyard owner sends a servant for the express (and expected) purpose of bringing his portion back, highlighted by the tenants' refusal of him; Luke 14:10 says that if you sit in the wrong place, you can expect to be asked to move up; and in Acts 21:24, after Paul pays the four Jews' expenses, they can expect to shave their heads and people can be expected to know Paul's devotion. Paul himself in 1 Cor 9:15 is emphatic when he claims no one can expect to bankrupt his boasting. (See also John 7:4; Gal 2:4; Eph 6:3; 1 Pet 3:1; and Rev 3:9; 6:4, 11; 8:3; 9:4, 5, 20; 13:12; 14:13; 22:14; cf. P.Sitzungsber. Preuss. Ak. 1911, p.79b.22-26 [A.D. 19] [Edgar/Hunt 211]; P.Oxy. 275.17-18 [A.D. 66]: ἐφ' ᾧ / δώσει αὐτῷ κατὰ μῆνα ὁ Πτολεμαῖος [on condition that P. is expected to give to him each month].)

Several examples where Future and Subjunctive forms are found in close proximity are also helpful (e.g. Matt 13:15, John 12:40 [Isa 6:9-10]; Rom 3:4 [Ps 116:11], in OT quotations).

Matt 5:25: "Your enemy might hand you over to the judge (παραδῷ) and you can expect to be thrown (βληθήσῃ) into prison." Matthew says that if one is arrested, though this is in no way a certain event but merely a projection, then the chance of being thrown into prison becomes a very real expectation. See also Luke 12:58.

Mark 6:37: "Let us go and buy (ἀγοράσωμεν) bread and give it (δώσομεν) to them to eat." Here Mark places two commands in parallel, expressed by an Aorist Subjunctive and a

Future. The speaker says that if we buy bread then we can expect to be able (the pre-condition is met) to give it out to eat. (Cranfield [*Mark*, 217] calls the use of the Future "very harsh," though he recognizes the use of the deliberative Subjunctive. Taylor [*Mark*, 322] opts for a Subjunctive reading.)

Matt 7:6: Jesus reportedly instructs his listeners not to cast pearls before pigs, lest they can be expected to trample (καταπατήσουσιν) the pearls under their feet and then may turn on them and tear them up. Jesus implies by his use of the Future that whereas it is likely the pigs will trample the pearls, they may not necessarily attack the men.

Luke 8:17: "It is not hidden what will not be revealed (οὐ . . . γενήσεται) nor revealed what might not be known (οὐ μὴ γνωσθῇ) and come into appearance (ἔλθῃ)." Here the difference between the Future and Aorist Subjunctive is slight. The Future, stating that the speaker believes that what has the possibility of being revealed is not expected, is followed by the Subjunctive in two parallel clauses (Marshall, *Luke*, 330).

John 6:35: "The one who comes to me," Jesus reportedly says, "may never hunger (οὐ μὴ πεινάσῃ) and the one who believes in me can expect never ever to thirst (οὐ μὴ διψήσει)." Though Jesus could be making commands to those who follow and believe in him, more likely he is saying that he does not see any hungering or thirsting (figurative?) while they are in relationship with him. The difference between the Subjunctive and Future is reinforced by the adverb πώποτε (ever), emphasizing (with the double negative) that belief eliminates lacking. (Barrett [*John*, 293] calls this a correct Subjunctive and "incorrect" Indicative: "John seems quite careless in handling this construction"; cf. Morris, *John*, 366 n. 94, who, noting the change, says there does not seem to be significance in it.)

John 10:28: "I am giving them eternal life and they may never perish (οὐ μὴ ἀπόλωνται) and no one can expect to seize (οὐχ ἁρπάσει) them from my hand." Jesus makes an assertion about the process he is undertaking, and then visualizes the results. The Aorist Subjunctive gives the result from the recipients' standpoint--he never perishes--while the Future form is used to stress that no one should entertain the hope of wresting them from his hand.

Rom 9:15: "I will have mercy (ἐλεήσω) on whomever I might have mercy (ἐλεῶ) and will have compassion (οἰκτιρήσω) on whomever I might have compassion (οἰκτίρω)." In this quotation of Exod 33:19, Paul quotes God as saying that he expects to have mercy on anyone he might select (expectation does not enter into account). The Future describes God's capability, while the Aorist Subjunctive describes God's act without constraint. This is a rewording of a II.a. class conditional-like statement, with the Aorist Subjunctive in the protasis. Cf. Matt 23:12 with Future in the protasis and apodosis.

4. PRAGMATIC IMPLICATURE OF THE FUTURE FORM.

Several uses of the Future are worthy of note (since these are not grammatically or morphologically differentiated, many of the examples are open to question). Not every example can be cited, since there are over 1600 instances of the Future in the NT, but representative examples are treated. There are essentially two uses of the Future, those directly related to the temporal state of affairs perceived by the speaker and those that are not, i.e. those that are deictically *limited* or *not limited*. Those that are not deictically limited may implicate timeless usage or commands. Futures used as commands (or prohibitions) have already been mentioned, and timeless usage is often found in conditional or logical statements, very often overlapping with use of the Subjunctive. Those that are deictically limited may be described as either omnitemporal Futures or not, the non-omnitemporal being either deliberative or prospective. Deixis binds the particular usage to the world of time, so that an event may be seen as occurring regularly in time, as a matter of deliberation, or as anticipated in the future (prospective).[17]

a. Participle and Infinitive. Before treating the simple forms, a look at the Participle and Infinitive is warranted. (See Magnien,*Futur*, 6-58, on the Participle; 59-124, on the Infinitive; and Papanicolau, "Development," who suggests alternative constructions employed in the NT: Infinitive, Present or Aorist Participle, Indicative Future, ἵνα + Subjunctive. All of these may be used with 'modal' qualities.)

In classical Greek the Future Participle was used to express volition by the agent and was considered a "final participle" (Jannaris, 503; Goodwin, *Syntax*, 207; Magnien, *Futur*, 7; Keith, "Uses"), though [+expectation] is preferred since it distinguishes the Future from fully aspectual/attitudinal forms. Though Moulton (230 n. 1), Zerwick (¶ 282) and to some extent Robertson (877-78) and Blass/Debrunner (¶¶ 348, 351) seem to recognize this, Turner (*Syntax*, 86-87) and Burton (71) assert a purely temporal use. While it is true that some uses may refer to future time, it seems rather that the NT uses the Future Participle according to the classical model, though its frequency of usage, as in much hellenistic writing, is very low compared to previous periods (see Magnien, *Futur*, 6-7, esp. 11 on verbs of movement; Thackeray, 194; Mandilaras, 52. Examples with verbs of motion conform to the general rule of appearing in the Nominative Case; see Paley, "Peculiarities").

Adjunctive[S] Participle usage: Matt 27:49: the crowd, hearing Jesus' cry on the cross, say, ἄφες ἴδωμεν εἰ ἔρχεται Ἡλίας σώσων αὐτόν (wait! Let us see whether Elias is coming to save him). σώσων, embedded in a conditional clause and following the Present ἔρχεται, is grammatically linked to Elias and probably refers to the same (hence coincidental) act of his coming, with the expectation of salvation. The implicature is not clearly either present or future. The dependent concurrent Participle refers to the expected purpose of Elias's coming (Gundry, *Matthew*, 574).

Acts 8:27; 24:11: the Ethiopian Eunuch and Paul both went to Jerusalem expecting to worship (προσκυνήσων). Again there is correlation between the act of going and the expected purpose for going (Bruce, *Acts*, 191, 424; de Zwaan, "Use," 33), though the two acts need not be thought of as identical. Acts 22:5: Paul, in recounting his conversion, says, "I received letters from the officials in Jerusalem and was on my way to the brothers in Damascus, in order to lead (ἄξων) those who were captive there to Jerusalem." Since Paul never reached Jerusalem for this purpose, his use of ἄξων can only indicate his expectation (Bruce, *Acts*, 401). Acts 24:17: Paul continues his defence before Felix, saying that after many years ἐλεημοσύνας ποιήσων εἰς τὸ ἔθνος μου παρεγενόμην καὶ προσφοράς (I came to bring alms and offerings to my nation). Clearly the two verbal processes--coming and bringing alms--are coincidental (and past in actual time) and point to Paul's expected purpose for coming--to bring gifts to the Jerusalem Christians (Bruce, *Acts*, 424, 425; de Zwaan, "Use," 33). In any case, the Participle is of relative temporal value, not absolute value, even in direct speech.

Heb 13:17: the author of Hebrews exhorts his readers to be obedient to their leaders, for they take care of them ὡς λόγον ἀποδώσοντες (as if giving an account). This hypothetical clause, very similar to the classical idiom with the emphatic ὡς, not meant to be interpreted temporally, refers metaphorically to the leaders of the church as stewards who are called upon to

---

[17]All of these uses are discussed in the grammars: e.g. Gildersleeve, 111-12, 115-17; idem, "Problems," 259; McKay, 147-48; Schwyzer, 2.290-93; Smyth, 427-29; Goodwin, *Syntax*, 36-38; Robertson, 873-76, 888-89; Blass/Debrunner, ¶¶ 348-49; Burton, 31-37. Magnien (*Futur*) binds his definition too closely to volition, so he is not able to include as many diverse uses without positing exceptions; see esp. 150ff. *passim*. See also Dahl, *Tense*, 108, on issues of linguistic typology.

show the tangible results of their labours. (Cf. Plb. 2.9.3: εἰσελθόντες ἐν αὐτοῖς τοῖς περιζώμασιν ὡς ὑδρευσόμενοι [entering with those clothed as for the expected purpose of watering]. See Magnien, *Futur*, 33-42; Papanicolau ["Development," 630 n. 2] claims the ὡς occurs because the main verb "has no meaning of movement.")

Subject, complement usage (Robertson [878] claims, "The future participle with the article is futuristic, not volitive." But see Magnien, *Futur*, 45-57; Sears, *Use*, 85, contra 129). Luke 22:49: those around Jesus, seeing τὸ ἐσόμενον (what they expected to happen), spoke to him. Here, in a past narrative context, there is a close alliance between evaluation of a situation to see its logical outcome and the sense of 'knowing' the future. The disciples' reactions show that they really only knew what they expected Judas and the crowd were about. (Magnien [*Futur*, 49] says of Participles as objects of verbs, "Le sens volontatif ou final du participe dans cette construction est d'ordinaire très clair"; cf. 52.)

John 6:64: John, interjecting commentary into his narrative, says Jesus knew from the beginning there were some who did not believe and who was ὁ παραδώσων (the one expecting to betray him).[18] The fact that Jesus is described as foretelling his own betrayal (cf. Matt 26:21ff.; Mark 14:18ff.; John 19:11; possibly Matt 17:22 and the like) probably colours understanding of verbal usage here. This Participle, as well as the Present Participle (οἱ . . . πιστεύοντες [those believing]), must have relative temporal value, since the narrator at the deictic centre is describing a past utterance by Jesus referring to an event subsequent to the utterance itself, yet antecedent to present time.

Acts 20:22: Paul tells the gathered Ephesian elders that he is going to Jerusalem, not knowing τὰ . . . συναντήσοντα (what to expect might happen) to him there. The problem of negation in Greek has not yet been fully explored with regard to presuppositions in a sentence, but at the least, while the phrase here is future in the context of the entire sentence (though past in terms of the entire narrative), this is an implicature derived from his expectation, since the point is that Paul is unsure of what might happen.

Rom 8:34: Paul asks, who is ὁ κατακρινῶν (the one we expect will judge)? 8:31ff. have a number of Future forms, so this one may be as well (the form is identical with a Present). While the judgment may be seen as still future (see Michel, *Römer*, 216: "Es ist wahrscheinlich, dass Pls an eine zukünftige Gerichtsituation denkt. . ."), the context here is better seen as one of hypothetical question-and-answer (or forensic?) (Bruce, *Romans*, 179) regarding Christian status (see vv 31a, 32b, 33a, 35). 1 Cor 15:37: Paul uses an agricultural metaphor stating that when one plants seeds, one does not plant τὸ σῶμα τὸ γενησόμενον (the expected mature plant) but the bare seed (cf. Th. 2.13.1: ὡς ἔγνω τὴν ἐσβολὴν ἐσομένην [he knew of the expected invasion]). In this omnitemporal statement, a logical temporal sequence is established, since the mature plant only comes after planting (see v 36 with gnomic Present). (Barrett [*First Corinthians*, 370] notes the lack of particularization.) But an absolute temporal framework misses the point.

Heb 3:5: Moses is commended by the author as a faithful servant and witness τῶν λαληθησομένων (of the things he expected to be spoken). The only Passive Future Participle in the NT cannot have an absolute future reference here since the things spoken of were already revealed at the time of narration (actual past reference), but does have relative reference to Moses, theoretically allowing a Present or Aorist Participle as well, except for the sense of expectation. A volitional pragmatic implicature makes sense of a context in which Moses was a witness of the things expected to be spoken by God. 1 Pet 3:13: in a II.a. class conditional, Peter posits that if you are zealots of the good, "Who could do you evil (ὁ κακώσων)?" The hypothetical conditional has volitional implicature reinforced by sense, since Peter is asking, who would expect to do you evil, if you are so enthusiastic for good. (Cf. Selwyn, *Peter*, 191: "It is still . . . a contingency rather than a universal fact"; Goppelt, *Petrusbrief*, 233; Beare, *Peter*, 136: "The question is

---

[18]D reads a Present Participle in John 6:64 according to Turner (*Syntax*, 86), and p⁶⁶ ℵ* read ὁ μέλλων αὐτὸν παραδιδόναι. The first tries to align the two Participles, while the second probably shows the copyist's (correct) interpretation of the text. See Metzger, *Commentary*, 215.

obviously rhetorical; he is asserting boldly [and somewhat naively], that if their lives are wholly devoted to goodness, no one will do them harm"; Spicq, *Pierre*, 130.)

The Future Participle conveys in a number of cases a sense of an expected or intended result, with relative temporal value, in line with the essential nature of the tense function and the function of Participles in general.

The Future Infinitive has almost disappeared from the NT. Magnien (*Futur*, 59) notes that in classical Greek the Infinitive was more frequent than the Participle, both of which virtually disappeared in hellenistic Greek. He cites approximately ten possible instances of the Future Infinitive in the LXX. Several examples in the NT with textual variants include Acts 26:7; John 21:25. Of the five undoubted instances, four are with ἔσεσθαι (Acts 11:28; 23:30; 24:15; 27:10) and three of these follow a form of μέλλω (all except Acts 23:30). Since εἰμί conveys the lexical meaning of "existence," its appearance after μέλλω reinforces an intentional implicature for the form in this context.[19] In Heb 3:18 (τίσιν δὲ ὤμοσεν μὴ εἰσελεύσεσθαι εἰς τὴν κατάπαυσιν αὐτοῦ εἰ μὴ τοῖς ἀπειθήσασιν; [to whom did he swear not to enter into his rest unless to the disobedient?] the timeless sentence, removed completely from external temporal reference, refers to an impossible state of affairs (though UBS[3] lists this as a quotation from the OT, there are no verbal parallels of concern).

b. Temporal implicature of finite forms. Whereas some Future Participles may share the implicature of future temporal reference in context, the sense of an expected process is the only semantic feature that seems to unify the verbal function in all contexts. This is certainly true of the finite forms.

1. Commanding (see McKay, "Aspect," 219-20; Mandilaras, 188-90). A great number are prohibitions in quotations of the OT (LXX):

Matt 4:7, Luke 4:12 (Deut 6:16; cf. 1 Cor 10:9 with hortatory Present Subjunctive); Matt 4:10, Luke 4:8 (Deut 6:13); Matt 5:21 (Exod 20:13; Deut 5:17); 5:27 (Exod 20:14); 5:33 (?Lev 19:12; Num 30:2; Deut 23:21); 5:43, Mark 12:31, Gal 5:14, Jas 2:8 (Lev 19:18); Matt 22:37, 39, Luke 10:27, Mark 12:30 (Deut 6:5-6); Matt 19:5, Mark 10:7-8, Eph 5:31 (Gen 2:24); Matt 19:18-19 (cf. τίμα in positive command), Rom 13:9 (Exod 20:12-16; Deut 5:16-20; Lev 19:18--the parallels in Mark 10:19 and Luke 18:20, as well as Jas 2:11, have the Aorist Subjunctive);[20] Gal 4:30 (cf. Aorist Imperative; Gen 21:9); Rom 7:7 (Exod 20:17; Deut 5:21); Matt 21:13, Mark 11:17, Luke 19:46 (Isa 56:7), Acts 2:17, 21 (Joel 2:28ff.); Acts 23:5 (Exod 22:28); 1 Cor 9:9, 1 Tim 5:18 (Deut 25:4); Heb 1:5 (Ps 2:7); 8:5 (cf. Present Imperative; Exod 25:40); 1 Pet 1:16 (Lev 11:44, 45; 19:2; 20:7); Rev 7:16 (Isa 48:10?).

There is no question of Semitic interference here (though there may be LXX enhancement), as some have suggested (Burton, 35; Moule, 178-79; Turner, *Syntax*, 86; Zerwick, ¶¶ 279-80; Mandilaras, "NT," 25 [contra idem, 188-89]; cf. Blass/Debrunner, ¶ 362; Abel, 271; Thackeray, 194). The command (or prohibition) with the Future is known in classical Greek (e.g. Hom. Od. 1.124; Pl. Gorg. 505C; Ar. Clouds 1352, and most standard grammars), often with οὐ μή as its negative particle in strong denials or prohibitions (e.g. Ar. Frogs 462: οὐ μὴ διατρίψεις, ἀλλὰ γεῦσαι τῆς θύρας [don't delay, but taste the door]; Wasps 397; Clouds 505; E. Bacc. 343; see

---

[19]Cf. Hom. Od. 6.165; Arist. Poet. 1459A33; cf. Plb. 1.29.6; Plu. Alex. 4.5. Stanford (*Homer*, 225) says μέλλω indicates likelihood, not futurity (see my chapt. 10). Bruce (*Acts*, 419) calls μέλλειν ἔσεσθαι a "set phrase." Cf. Blass/Debrunner, ¶ 424; Jannaris, 443; and Magnien, *Futur*, 60, who (99-100) debates various translations and interpretations of μέλλω + Infinitive, concluding, "c'est la chose qui n'existe pas, mais qui existera parce qu'elle a actuellement les déterminations necessaires pour exister," and is thus similar in translational meaning to the use of the simple Future form. This construction is classified as catenative; see my chapt. 10.

[20]Sander (*Ethics*, 51-52) notes Paul's and Matthew's use of the Future against Mark's and Luke's use of the Aorist Subjunctive, calling the latter "better Greek" (52).

Gildersleeve, "Οὐ μή," 204-05, for examples).[21] And οὐ appears in questions that serve as positive commands (e.g. D. 4.44: οὐκ ἐμβησόμεθα; οὐκ ἔξιμεν αὐτοὶ . . .; οὐκ ἐπὶ τὴν ἐκείνου πλευσόμεθα; [shall we not man the ship? Shall we not go out ourselves . . .? Shall we not sail against his land?]; 6.25), though οὐ also serves in prohibitions (e.g. E. Med. 1320; X. Anab. 1.3.5 [οὔποτε ἐρεῖ οὐδείς (never will anyone say)]; Cyr. 3.3.3; see McKay, 155; Rijksbaron, 33; Mandilaras, 188-89), as does μή (e.g. E. Med. 822 [N.B. λέξεις is a textual variant in the Oxford text, being replaced by λέξῃς, though clearly the more difficult reading]; D. 19.92. Goodwin [Syntax, 19-20] lists D. 23.117; Lys. 29.13; Men. Mon. 397; and A. Sev. Thebes 250; cf. Whitelaw, "On μή," 322-23).

The NT, like other ancient Greek, uses the Future as a command (or prohibition with οὐ, μή or οὐ μή) in a variety of contexts. As Gildersleeve says, "The future is sometimes used where an imperative might be expected": e.g. X. Cyr. 3.2.29; Pl. Gorg. 505C. But it is not equivalent in functional significance, as Gildersleeve asserts (116 [he continues: "It is not a milder form of imperative"]; contra Goodwin, Syntax, 37, who calls it "a mild form of imperative"; Winer, 396-97; McKay, 155). The commanding Future is a stronger command, on the basis of its formal and semantic distinctions, and the unmarked character of the Imperative (see Gonda, Character, 80; Greenberg, Universals, 47; Sears, Use, 132; cf. Jannaris, 443, who says it "expresses a peremptory or absolute command, when the speaker feels certain that his order will be carried out"). Thus the Future is entirely appropriate in marked moral contexts.

Many Future commands are 2d Person, e.g. Matt 1:21; 6:5; 7:7; 21:3 and Luke 19:31 (cf. Aorist Imperative in Mark 11:3); Matt 27:4 (σὺ ὄψῃ [you see to it]),[22] 24; 28:7; Luke 13:9, parallel to Aorist Imperative in v 7 (McKay, "Aspect," 219); 17:4, parallel to Aorist Imperatives in v 3; 17:8, parallel to Aorist Imperatives in vv 7, 8a respectively; 1:31; 22:11, parallel to Aorist Imperative in v 10; John 1:39, 42 (McKay ["Aspect," 214] says this is the only such usage in John); 13:7; 21:6; Acts 18:15;[23] P.Oxy. 1482.16-17 (2d cent A.D.); Lucian Zeus Cat. 1 (with οὐ).

Some are 1st Person, e.g. Matt 11:28; Luke 20:3; 1 Tim 6:8; Lucian Zeus Rants 7; Plb. 1.13.9; Lucian Zeus Cat. 2.

Some significant examples are in 3d Person, e.g. Matt 4:4, Luke 4:4 (Deut 8:3); Matt 15:6 (with οὐ μή); 10:39; Mark 3:28[24] (following λέγω) and Matt 12:31; Luke 10:6; 11:29; 17:21 (with οὐδὲ ἐροῦσιν); John 9:21; 10:28 (cf. Aorist Subjunctive); Acts 19:39; Gal 6:5; Phil 4:7; 1 John 5:16 (αἰτήσει--let him ask); Rev 9:4 (with μή); P.Jews. 1912.34-38 (A.D. 41); BGU 197.14 (A.D. 17) (with μή); P.Rev. Laws 54.18-19 (259-58 B.C.) (with Future and Imperative).

It appears that εἰμί is used fairly regularly as a commmand in its Future form, e.g. Matt 5:21, 48; 6:5; 16:22; 19:30; 20:16, 26-27; 23:11; Mark 9:35; 10:31; Luke 1:32-33; 15:7 (following λέγω); 10:14 (cf. Matt 10:15); Acts 22:15; Jas 1:25; Rev 21:3-4.

This evidence confirms that simple Future forms are able to function as commands and prohibitions.

---

[21]Ballantine ("Futures") and Moulton (187-92) posit on the basis of Semitic influence that οὐ μή has lost its place in the NT as an emphatic negative, especially in the words of Jesus. Since there is no Semitic equivalent, and on the basis of analysis of the NT texts, this seems unlikely; cf. McKay, "Aspects," 15-16; J. Lee, "Features," 18-23. On whether οὐ μή is a negative question see Whitelaw, "οὐ μή," 239-41.

[22]Moulton (177) says this Future has "the tone of absolute indifference," while Gildersleeve (116 n. 1) calls it an "idiomatic colloquial expression," denying it as a Hebraism.

[23]Bruce (Acts, 347-48) calls the use "colloquial," but describes Gallionas as "directing" the Jews to take their complaint to their own authorities.

[24]Lane (Mark, 145) calls it a "solemn warning."

2. Timeless. Like commands, timeless Futures are not specific in their deictic reference but implicate general, conditional or logical expected processes. (This contrasts with omnitemporal use, see chapts. 2 and 4.)

Future verbs are used in conditionals, either in the protasis (see chapt. 6) or the apodosis (e.g. Pl. Rep. 376C; Lys. 1.36: εἰ δὲ μή, τοιαύτην ἄδειαν τοῖς μοιχοῖς ποιήσετε [otherwise, you will give pleasure to adulterers]); Epict. 1.1.20; 3.1.10; P.Sel. 260.20-21 [A.D. 173?]). NT examples with the Future in the apodosis of true conditionals include: Matt 6:14, 15; 15:14; 17:20; 19:21; 24:28; 26:33; Mark 5:28; 8:3; 11:31; Luke 11:8, 18; 13:3, 5; 19:40; 16:30; 20:5, 6; John 11:12, 40, 48; 14:3, 7, 14, 15, 23; 15:10; 16:7; Acts 3:23; 5:38; Rom 6:5; 11:21; 1 Cor 3:14-17; 1 Pet 3:1; 4:18; 1 John 2:24; 5:16. While there would be some dispute regarding individual examples, whether some are not more specific and realize another pragmatic choice than the one indicated (there are several conditionals that may be more deliberative in meaning), the point is well enough made if it is admitted that these examples show that, in character with the conditional, the action is not temporally based but only relative to the argument of the conditional itself (hence virtually any verb form may be said to have future reference in the apodosis of a conditional statement by virtue of implicature, not grammar or tense).

Other examples of timeless use of the Future include the following.

Matt 6:33, 34: Jesus commands his listeners to seek (ζητεῖτε) first the kingdom of God and his righteousness, and ταῦτα πάντα προστεθήσεται ὑμῖν (all these things can be expected to be be added) to you. Its conditional force and the placement of the Future verb in relation to the Imperative leave this example outside the sphere of temporal reference and in that of logical connection. (Beyer [Syntax, 238-55, esp. 252] claims Semitic influence for this construction. Cf. Kühner/Gerth, 2.236-37, who recognize use of the Imperative in conditional sentences; and Black, Approach, 90-91, who discounts Semitic influence.) Jesus continues by enjoining his listeners not to worry about today (μὴ . . . μεριμνήσητε) because today μεριμνήσει ἑαυτῆς (will worry about itself). This Future may well have present or omnitemporal reference, perhaps as in a "wisdom-like " statement (Schweizer, Matthew, 166). Cf. Matt 7:5, where Schweizer (169) speaks in terms of a general statement; Wis 1:4: ὅτι εἰς κακότεχνον ψυχὴν οὐκ εἰσελεύσεται σοφία οὐδὲ κατοικήσει ἐν σώματι κατάχρεῳ ἁμαρτίας (wisdom will not enter into an evily constructed soul and it will not inhabit an abused body of sin).

Matt 9:15: in his description of a bridegroom, Jesus asks whether the friends of the bridegroom fast while he is with them ἐλεύσονται . . . ἡμέραι (days are expected to come) when the bridegroom may be taken away from them, and τότε νηστεύσουσιν (then they expect to fast). Clearly reflecting a hypothetical situation, almost conditional in structure ("If the bridegroom . . ."), even if Jesus speaks of himself, or is meant by the author (Hill, Matthew, 176-77; cf. McNeile, Matthew, 121), the sentence describes the logical result of a situation, though an omnitemporal sense is also possible. There could be a day when the bridegroom is not present, and Jesus says that such a day is expected. That is the day for fasting. Matt 10:41: ὁ δεχόμενος προφήτην (the one who receives a prophet) in the name of a prophet μισθὸν προφήτου λήμψεται (he can expect to receive the reward of a prophet), and ὁ δεχόμενος δίκαιον (the one who receives a just man) in the name of justice μισθὸν δικαίου λήμψεται (he can expect to receive a just reward). These conditional-like sentences are quite clearly hypothetical in their implicature. Matt 5:41: ὅστις σε ἀγγαρεύσει (whoever compels you) to go a mile go with him two. The Future serves similarly to the protasis of a II.c. class conditional-like statement, again clearly descriptive and non-temporal (cf. Arr. l. P3: ὅστις δὲ θαυμάσεται . . . [whoever will marvel]). Cf. Mark 8:35, where Lane (Mark, 308) speaks of Jesus' words as envisioning men before a court. Matt 10:39; 16:25; John 12:25 all use relative conditional sentences, with the Future serving as equivalent to the protasis of a II.a. class conditional (cf. Luke 9:24 with Aorist Subjunctive). Matt 18:12: Jesus poses a question through a II.a. conditional. If a man might have 100 sheep and lose one, οὐχὶ ἀφήσει (is he not expected to leave) the 99 and, going, ζητεῖ (seek) the lost one?

Luke 1:37: the angel tells Mary that οὐκ ἀδυνατήσει (nothing can be expected to be impossible) for God. Even though this appears in the context of the past act of making Elizabeth pregnant, this possibly omnitemporal statement is apparently meant by the angel as a statement of God's timeless character, a common theme in biblical texts (so Marshall, *Luke*, 72). This kind of statement distinguishes timeless statements as well (Lyons, *Semantics*, 680). Luke 6:39 (cf. Matt 5:14 and *Gos. Thom.* 34 with conditional sentences [Marshall, *Luke*, 268]): Jesus asks regarding two hypothetical blindmen on a walk whether they both ἐμπεσοῦνται (can expect to fall) into a ditch. This question in a hypothetical context refers to a possible logical result, not a necessary future event. Luke 7:42: after finishing his story of the two forgiven debtors, Jesus asks who ἀγαπήσει (could be expected to love) the lord more. The context is a story told with the narrative Aorist, and Jesus uses the Future to draw attention to human desire and expectation. Though the narrative Aorist may be translated as past-referring in English, this is not necessarily the understanding in Greek. To push a temporal understanding with either tense misses the point. Luke 11:5: Jesus reportedly asks, "Which one of you ἕξει (expects to have) a friend who would come and say, 'Friend I need three loaves of bread'?" Some future time is not contemplated but rather any person who may (already?) have a friend. The opening words, rather than being specific words of address, ask "Can anyone of you imagine that. . .?" (Marshall, *Luke*, 463; contra his conclusion regarding Semitic influence). Note also the parallel use of the Aorist Subjunctive--εἴπη (he might say), prompting Magnien (*Futur*, 147) to cite this as an instance where a Subjunctive replaces a Future (cf. Matt 23:33; 26:54; Rom 10:14); contra Schweizer, *Luke*, 192, who calls the Future "not-quite-accurate" (?), since it may "suggest future situations in which Jesus' disciples will be making similar requests." Robertson (875), seeing deliberative use, admits "future [reference] is . . . doubtful from the nature of the case." Future and Subjunctive forms were both used in deliberative statements in hellenistic Greek. Cf. Matt 12:11 with the same introductory phrase and alternation with the Aorist Subjunctive.

John 3:36: ὁ . . . ἀπειθῶν (the one who is disobedient) ὄψεται (cannot expect to see) life. In this conditional-like statement, conspicuous is the use of μένει (abides) in the next clause. John says that the disobedient person's actions reveal that he cannot expect to see life, but rather he is in the position of God's wrath resting upon him (cf. Schnackenburg, *John*, 1.391 n. 119, who recognizes both logical and temporal senses of the Future). Cf. John 5:43, where Schnackenburg (*John*, 2.128) says, "the conditional clause . . . does not envision any real event"; and Brown (*John*, 1.226) translates: "let someone else come in his own name."

Acts 8:22: Peter commands Simon the Magician to repent so that, if he would, the intention of his heart ἀφεθήσεται (can be expected to be forgiven). The clause with the Future is clearly bound to the Imperatives (μετανόησον and δεήθητι--repent and pray). The conditional clause, referring then to the same discourse context, emphasizes that the logical result of repentance is forgiveness.

Rom 1:10: Paul expresses his desire to see the Romans, saying εἴ πως ἤδη ποτέ εὐοδωθήσομαι (if somehow already I can expect to have been blessed) by the will of God in order to come to them. Paul's intention to make his oft-planned visit to Rome shows, though the prospect is left uncertain in the passage, Paul not knowing the future and possibly being anxious about his visit to Jerusalem (Black, *Romans*, 41). The adverbs ἤδη ποτέ possibly have past/present implicature (Sanday/Headlam, *Romans*, 20), with the Future referring to Paul's expectation of God's desire to bless him. This is reinforced by the prepositional group of intention, ἐν τῷ θελήματι τοῦ θεοῦ. "The thought of an actual journey is not present in the verb," however, "which is used here metaphorically" (Cranfield, *Romans*, 1.78). Rom 5:7: Paul says perhaps τις ἀποθανεῖται (someone can be expected to die) for a just man. Many grammarians see this as an omnitemporal Future (Burton, 36; Blass/Debrunner, ¶ 349[1], who also say it is equal to a conditional; Turner, *Syntax*, 86), but the implicature is not that this is an omnitemporal event but rather a timeless one. It cannot be counted upon to occur (μόλις [perhaps]) but is an ideal to seek.

Rom 6:5, 8: these two verses are often cited as evidence for a future resurrection. While that may be an implicature in terms of a theological model, all that can be posited here grammatically is that being or living with Christ is the logical result (I class conditional) of a posited event: if we are planted in the likeness of his death, ἐσόμεθα (we can expect to be) of his resurrection. . . . If we die/died with Christ, we believe that συζήσομεν (we can expect to live) with him, without reference at the grammatical level to when either the protasis or apodosis necessarily occurs. To the contrary, it seems rather that if the condition is granted, the result is already in effect. The use in v 8 is reinforced by dependence on the verb of belief. Tannehill (*Dying*, 10-12, 88) argues against the logical sense of the Future, neglecting the conditional construction (see Boyer, "First Class," 75ff.). While Harris (*Raised Immortal*, 172-73) recognizes the conditional nature of resurrection, he does not see the dependence of the theological construction (a saving relation with Christ) on the grammatical construction (conditional statement), hence he assumes a future sense of the resurrection on the basis of the tenses (he even uses the vague and possibly misleading subheading "The tenses of the resurrection") and must find Paul relating future and present resurrection in one passage (Rom 6:1-11) because of them. The syntactical evidence can be used in fact to argue just the opposite, that Paul sees the "resurrection" of the believer already present once he is "planted" in or "dead" to Christ. (Barrett [*Romans*, 123-24] entertains the logical sense in v 5 though he opts for the future sense on the basis of v 8; Cranfield [*Romans*, 1.308] argues firmly for the future sense in each, discounting the influence of "believe that" in v 8 on the meaning of the future; cf. Leenhardt, *Romans*, 141, Schlier, "Taufe," 58, who argue for logical Futures.)

Rom 8:35, 39: τίς ἡμᾶς χωρίσει (who can expect to separate us) from the love of God? This possibly deliberative or more likely rhetorical question (Barrett, *Romans*, 173) alludes to the desire of others to separate Christians from the love of God, an impossible hypothesis according to Paul (v 35b). In other words Paul contrasts the logical "can" with the empirical "can." Verse 39 says neither height nor depth nor any other creation δυνήσεται (is able) to separate mankind from God's love.

1 Cor 7:37: Paul says that if one has decided to keep his own virgin (?) καλῶς ποιήσει (he will do well). This conditional-like sentence, perhaps following on from the conditional clause in v 36, is a reference not to some future action or intrinsic capability but the good intention of one so decided. Cf. Rom 13:2 with a conditional-like clause with a Participle and "no reference here to eternal punishment" (Sanday/Headlam, *Romans*, 367); 1 Cor 15:28 with τότε establishing logical progression (Conzelmann, *Corinthians*, 274-75; contra Barrett, *First Corinthians*, 360); 2 Cor 9:6 using emphatic τοῦτο to draw attention to a "well-established and important law" (Plummer, *Second Corinthians*, 258; cf. Héring, *Corinthians*, 66-67, who implies omnitemporal use; Windisch, *Korintherbrief*, 275, who labels it gnomic and eschatological; Barrett, *Second Corinthians*, 235-36, who says it "has the appearance of a proverb"); and Gal 6:16 with a relative conditional, though the classical construction would be ὅσοι ἄν + Subjunctive (Bruce, *Galatians*, 273). Gal 2:16: Paul, speaking of justification, says that no man is justified by works of the law but only by faith, and those who believe in Christ may see themselves as justified by faith, because no flesh can be expected to be justified (δικαιωθήσεται) by works (cf. Ps 143:2). In the context of Paul's discussion, this justification is timeless (contra Betz, *Galatians*, 119). Col 3:25: ὁ . . . ἀδικῶν κομίσεται (the one who is acting unjustly, whether slave or master, can expect to receive) what he does with no favouritism. In this conditional-like statement, or possibly "general maxim" (Abbott, *Ephesians*, 275), Paul displays a conscious focus upon aspectuality, exploiting the timeless nature of both the Future and Aorist. The "inviolable law" (Lohse, *Colossians*, 161) seems to be that one who is involved in unjust acts is envisaged by Paul as receiving back the same kind of treatment.

3. Omnitemporal. In certain contexts, the author refers not to a hypothetical or conditional world but specifically to a process in this world that "will customarily happen when occasion offers" (Burton, 36), i.e. the omnitemporal use of the Future. There are several examples worth noting.

In extra-biblical Greek see: Hdt. 1.173.4; Men. Mon. 45 (ἀνὴρ ὁ φεύγων καὶ πάλιν μαχήσεται [a man who flees expects to fight again (or is this deliberative?), cited in Goodwin, *Syntax*, 19]); Epict. 1.7.3-4; Wis 2:4.

Matt 10:29: καὶ ἓν ἐξ αὐτῶν οὐ πεσεῖται ἐπὶ τὴν γῆν ἄνευ τοῦ πατρὸς ὑμῶν (one of [the sparrows] cannot be expected to fall to the earth apart from your father). An occurrence in the natural world, part of the "inexorable and apparently cruel, laws of nature" (McNeile, *Matthew*, 146), is used to illustrate a point, apart from whether this event is occurring in the past, present or future; it applies to all three.

Matt 5:13: Jesus equates his listeners with salt, saying that if the salt loses its flavour, ἐν τίνι ἁλισθήσεται (how can it be expected to be salty)? This conditional statement (thus hypothetical to some degree) creates an inner logic between the protasis and apodosis, apart from direct temporal reference, recalling the importance of salt in Middle Eastern life (cf. Hill, *Matthew*, 115; Schweizer, *Matthew*, 101-02, on this as a wisdom saying).

Mark 2:22 (and Luke 5:37; Matthew uses the Indicative): using a series of Future verbs, Jesus concludes with a brief statement from everyday life about wine. No one puts new wine in old skins because ῥήξει ὁ οἶνος τοὺς ἀσκούς (the new wine can be expected to rip the skins), and the wine and the skins are then lost. (Luke has a second Future--καὶ αὐτὸς ἐκχυθήσεται [and it will pour out].) This verse illustrates well the inherently relative temporal value of verbs in Greek; if a strict temporal progression were followed (absolute tense), the wine and skins would be lost before the new wine burst the skin, since ἀπόλλυται (lost) is a Present. Cf. Epict. 1.2.8-10.

Rom 7:3: Paul is laying down the rules (νόμον--v 1) of marriage, and includes the statement that, while her husband is living a woman μοιχαλὶς χρηματίσει (can be expected to be called an adulteress) if she marries another man. Paul seems to be endorsing a law he believes obtains for all time, that if a woman remarries she brings upon herself the title of adulteress (see Burton, 36; cf. Cranfield, *Romans*, 1.333 n. 4; Sanday/Headlam, *Romans*, 173), although it may simply be timeless descriptive use.

4. Deliberative.
In deictically-determined contexts the Future verb may be used to ascribe intention directly to a personal agent. This is most easily seen in the 1st Person: e.g. Pl. Apol. 29E; Ar. Ach. 203; S. Oed. Col. 1289; J. Jew. War 1.18; Philostr. Life Apoll. 1.13 with ὡς . . . μοι δυνατόν; Plb. 3.2.1ff., cf. 1.5.1; Epict. 1.1.23-24 (the above examples often use words like πειράσομαι to describe the author's intention), but it is also apparent in 2d Person: e.g. S. Phil. 1233; Philostr. Life Apoll. 1.11; Epict. 1.1.23: τὸ σκέλος μου δήσεις (you intend to bind my leg), and 3d Person: e.g. Th. 4.118.10; D. 5.18: ἔτι δ' ἐχθροτέρως σχήσουσιν (still they intend to have animosity); P.Jews. 1912.71-72 (A.D. 41). (This usage is not confined to questions [see Robertson, 875-76].)

Matt 21:37 (cf. Mark 12:9): in Jesus' parable of the wicked tenants, the landowner thinks that he will send his son, saying ἐντραπήσονται τὸν υἱόν μου (they can be expected to welcome my son). This cannot be a future statement on a par with use of the assertive attitude, but is the father's projected expectation (it verges on a command), which the tenants are quite able to disregard. Matt 21:43: Jesus reportedly says, ἀρθήσεται ἀφ' ὑμῶν ἡ βασιλεία τοῦ θεοῦ καὶ δοθήσεται ἔθνει ποιοῦντι τοὺς καρποὺς αὐτῆς (the kingdom of God will be taken from you and it will be given to a nation producing its fruits). This statement may implicate a future time (McNeile, *Matthew*, 312) but that is more because of the context and knowledge of Jesus' and Paul's ministry than of the grammar. The Passive softens the attribution of intention behind this possibly timeless description. Whether God or Christ is the expected subject is of little importance; what is significant is that the expectation is to remove the kingdom and give it to another people.

Luke 9:57: someone reportedly comes up to Jesus along the road and says, ἀκολουθήσω σοι ὅπου ἐὰν ἀπέρχῃ (I expect to follow you wherever you go) (cf. v 61). Jesus tells him to follow, but the man gives certain stipulations before he can come, implying that he actually never follows. Is this man a liar? Only in the sense that if one says it will rain tomorrow and it does not he is a liar. Perception of the future is different from that of present and past, and Greek uses the Future tense to grammaticalize one's expectation of a possible course of events. The man who met Jesus expected to follow (Marshall, *Luke*, 410), but nothing more. Luke 11:24 (cf. Matt 12:43-45): by contrast, the homeless spirit says, ὑποστρέψω εἰς τὸν οἶκον μου ὅθεν ἐξῆλθον (I expect to return to the house I came from). This statement, grammatically parallel to the ones in Luke 9:57, 61, is fulfilled (v 26), the difference not lying in the verb, which merely projects an expected course of events, but the entire story (discourse deixis). Luke 22:49: similarly, the

425

disciples at Jesus' arrest ask him, πατάξομεν ἐν μαχαίρῃ (should we strike with a sword)? The question refers less to future events (as if Jesus were seen as a fortune-teller) and more to the disciples' own motives (contra Marshall, *Luke*, 836-37). Cf. Epict. 1.6.25. Luke 23:16: Pilate's initial verdict on Jesus is παιδεύσας . . . αὐτὸν ἀπολύσω (after whipping him I expect to release him). Pilate expects that Jesus is to be released, but his intentions are altered by the Jewish leaders.

John 4:23: Jesus says an hour has come (νῦν [its temporal reference encompasses a broad span, from the immediate moment to a large stretch of time; Bauer, *Lexicon*, νῦν]) when the true worshippers προσκυνήσουσιν (expect to worship) in spirit and in truth. If the hour is present, the worship that occurs (ὅτε) probably should be seen as present also. But the expectation of the worshippers is the point of emphasis. (Barrett [*John*, 237] and Brown [*John*, 1.172] both try to understand present and future reference here.)

John 11:22-26: Martha tells Jesus that she knows now that whatever he might ask for δώσει σοι ὁ θεός (God can be expected to give you). Jesus reportedly answers, ἀναστήσεται ὁ ἀδελφός σου (your brother can expect to be raised). Martha responds that she knows that ἀναστήσεται ἐν τῇ ἀναστάσει ἐν τῇ ἐσχάτῃ ἡμέρᾳ (he can expect to be raised in the resurrection in the last day). Jesus informs her that he is the resurrection and that for the one who believes in him, even if he should die, ζήσεται (he'll live), and everyone who believes in him will not die (οὐ μὴ ἀποθάνῃ--Aorist Subjunctive) forever. Several things in these verses should be noted. Several pragmatic functions of the Future verb are displayed, and the word-play seems to revolve around this to a large extent. Martha's use of δώσει forms the apodosis of a conditional-like statement thus making a timeless statement, apparently about God's character, though it may refer to her expectation about what Jesus could have done had he been in Bethany earlier (Morris, *John*, 549). Jesus responds in essence that it is his or God's will that her brother is resurrected (Barrett [*John*, 395] calls it a "general truth"; Schnackenburg [*John*, 2.330] sees possible ambiguity), with no reference to when. Martha automatically equates this with the last day, a legitimate use of the Future (Morris, 549, see also 549 n. 49). But Jesus then clarifies to her that the resurrection he is speaking of is present (Morris, 550; Barrett, 396; Schnackenburg, 2.330), using two conditional-like statements (the first using the Future, v 25b, and the second using the Aorist Subjunctive parallel to the Future, v 26a). Both uses of the Future are appropriate, but the context shows that a Future verb need not necessarily implicate future reference. Rather, Jesus seems to be using it as an emphatic contrast to the Aorist Subjunctive.

John 13:36-38: when Peter asks Jesus where he is going, Jesus reportedly tells him he is not able to follow now but ἀκολουθήσεις . . . ὕστερον (you can expect to follow later). Peter questions the first, not the second statement, pronouncing solemnly, τὴν ψυχήν μου ὑπὲρ σοῦ θήσω (I expect to lay down my life for you). Jesus, taking Peter's statement and turning it into a deliberative question ("you will lay down your life for me?") then tells Peter that truly a rooster will not crow until ἀρνήσῃ (you can expect to deny) him three times. This dialogue is an exceptionally good illustration of verbal usage. The first Future is given temporal implicature through the deictic indicators νῦν (now) and ὕστερον (later). Peter's response that he would lay down his life for Jesus is not true (see Barrett, *John*, 453), though Peter fully expected this as what he would do. Jesus formulates the statement into a question, apparently to contrast Peter's intention with what he knows the case to be. Then Jesus is quoted as foretelling the future, using the Future (cf. Matt 26:75).

Acts 21:11: Agabus comes to Paul in Caesarea and "prophesies" of him that δήσουσιν ἐν Ἰερουσαλήμ οἱ Ἰουδαῖοι καὶ παραδώσουσιν εἰς χεῖρας ἐθνῶν (the Jews can be expected to take you captive in J. and hand you over into the hands of the Gentiles). Agabus may have thought the Jews intended this, and in fact they certainly intended to seize Paul (Acts 21:27ff.), but the second part of the projection is not correct. Until the Roman commander intervened, the Jews intended to kill Paul. So Agabus is merely saying what he expects to happen to Paul. Acts 17:32: at the end of Paul's speech to the Athenians, he mentions the resurrection, whereby the Athenians laugh and tell Paul ἀκουσόμεθά σου περὶ τούτου καὶ πάλιν (we expect to hear you on this again). Admittedly, it is difficult to see any true volition in this use of the verb, but it is even more difficult to see the strictly future sense. Discounting the likely ironic tone, the philosophers seem to be saying, "we can probably expect to hear you again," and they could have, but it never came to pass according to the records.

1 Cor 4:17, 19: Paul tells the Corinthians that Timothy is coming to them ὃς ὑμᾶς ἀναμνήσει τὰς ὁδούς μου τὰς ἐν Χριστῷ (who expects to remind you of my ways concerning Christ). Paul then says ἐλεύσομαι (I expect to come) quickly, if the lord wills, and γνώσομαι (make known) the word. Of course Paul cannot compel his audience to remember but is rather telling of his plan for Timothy in going to Corinth (Barrett [*First Corinthians*, 117] cites a final use of the Greek Future; cf. Robertson, 960, 989), just as Paul intended to go to Corinth, if the lord would will it (Subjunctive; he could never be sure). 1 Cor 15:35: Paul says ἐρεῖ τις (who will ask, or, but it may be asked [Conzelmann, *Corinthians*, 280 n. 4]) regarding the resurrection. Anticipating the question that his audience intends to ask, Paul uses this fairly frequent rhetorical phrase (see Rom 3:5; 6:1; 9:14, 19; 11:19; 1 Cor 14:7, 9 [with πῶς γνωσθήσεται], 16), possibly part of the diatribe style (Bruce, *Corinthians*, 151). 1 Cor 15:49, 51: in comparing the earthly to the heavenly man, Paul says that just as we put on the image of the earthly, φορέσομεν (we expect to put on)[25] the image of the heavenly. He follows by describing a mystery, that πάντες οὐ[26] κοιμηθησόμεθα, πάντες δὲ ἀλλαγησόμεθα (we all do not expect to sleep but we all expect to be changed). Paul's vision contrasts the earthly and heavenly realms, the first Christians are experiencing and the second only anticipating. In this logical sense the events must be future but this is an implicature on the basis of time and spatial deixis.

2 Cor 1:10: Paul states first that God rescued (ἐρρύσατο) us from death and ῥύσεται (can be expected to rescue) us, but he then clarifies his use of the Future with εἰς ὃν ἠλπίκαμεν ὅτι καὶ ἔτι ῥύσεται (unto whom we have hope that indeed he will rescue us). Paul betrays his understanding of the Future with the auxiliary sentence conveying his confidence as hope (Plummer, *Second Corinthians*, 19). Cf. Gal 5:10, 12 where he uses similar auxiliary words to define his understanding of the future: πέποιθα (persuaded) and ὄφελον (would that). Phil 1:6: Paul reassures the Philippian church that he is persuaded (see above) and confident that God, who has already begun the work of salvation, ἐπιτελέσει (expects to complete it) until (ἄχρι) the day of Christ Jesus (cf. Beare, *Philippians*, 53; Martin, *Philippians*, 66). The reference to the day of Christ seems to have future implicature, especially if ἄχρι has in mind the goal of the action (cf. Rom 1:13). But if ἄχρι has its more usual sense of "until" as interval (Matt 24:38; esp. Phil 1:5), the work of salvation and its completion are then depicted as two overlapping events--once the good work has begun it is being completed, so that the Future refers to past, present and future events, but even more than that, to Paul's expectation of them.

Heb 9:14: the author says that Christ's blood καθαριεῖ (can be expected to cleanse) the conscience from dead works in order to serve a living God. Though in the form of a conditional sentence (and so possibly better treated above), the emphasis appears to be on an expected result.

5. Prospective. The final category of usage of the Future needs no justification, since it is commonly held to represent the overriding and unifying semantic feature of the Future tense. But future temporal implicature is dependent upon deictic indicators and grows naturally out of the semantic function of expectation.

Why is it then that so many examples of the Future used in the NT (and cited by the grammars) are often construed as having future reference? (1) Its semantic meaning is well-suited

---

[25]Bruce (*Corinthians*, 153) notes the textual variants with the Aorist Subjunctive in p[46] ℵ A C D etc., though he opts for a future statement rather than exhortative. Orr/Walther (*I Corinthians*, 344) claim the textual evidence is better for an Aorist Subjunctive with hortatory sense, but opt for the Future because of editorial and theological reasons. They seem to see an inherent temporal sense in the Future, wanting it to affirm the centrality of future events. Conzelmann (*Corinthians*, 288) sees it as clearly eschatological.

[26]N.B. the textual variants for placement of the negative; cf. Metzger, *Commentary*, 569.

to situations where it is firmly believed that expected (and heretofore hypothetical) events are to occur. (2) The most convincing examples that are cited (not all examples are equally persuasive) to show prospective value have temporal deictic indicators: e.g. Matt 7:22; 12:36; 22:28; Luke 10:12; 14:14; Gal 5:21; 1 Thess 4:14-17; 1 Tim 4:1; 2 Tim 3:1, with reference to "that day," the "day of judgment," the "kingdom," or the "resurrection." Luke 21:7; John 16:16; Epict. 1.18.16 use temporal adverbs; and John 8:21; Acts 1:8; 9:6; 11:14; 2 Cor 13:4; 3 John 14 have discourse deictic indicators. Cf. P.Teb. 58.58-60 (3d cent. B.C.); BGU 1107.27-29 (13 B.C.); P.Fay. 93.15-17 (A.D. 161). (3) Many of the examples that seem best-suited to temporal reference have inanimate objects as their subject, making it difficult to articulate the concept of expectation. A more detailed analysis is given of several examples in the next section.

5. PROSPECTIVE USE OF THE FUTURE FORM. a. Introduction.

There exists a form in Greek called the Future. That this is a legitimate formal designation is not in dispute. What is under discussion is the function of that form. In any discussion of a formal category in Greek, grammarians seek to elucidate a semantic feature at the level of code that is able to unify their conception of that form's function in texts. On the basis of the various uses of the Future in NT Greek (reinforced by examination of classical and other hellenistic Greek), the perception of time in language, especially Greek, and the element of choice in determination of morphological aspect, it is posited that the Future functions uniquely in the Greek verbal network, grammaticalizing [+expectation]. This provides a powerful explanatory model.

What are the benefits or consequences of such a model? The most obvious is that it is now possible to understand better a traditional trouble-spot in characterization of the Greek tenses. Many grammarians have vacillated among several different estimations of the form's function, unable to find a central function, though they do attempt to characterize it in these terms. Though the analysis put forward here may at first seem radical, it logically concludes from the data presented by a linguistic estimation of tense function, the various comments of the grammarians, and the evidence of Greek itself. This understanding of the Future form aids in better understanding the entire Greek language, both synchronically and diachronically. The origin of the Future form in the Subjunctive or desiderative makes better sense when the Future is seen grammaticalizing expectation. Also this discussion helps to define more precisely the function of the Imperative and Subjunctive (and even Optative) in relation to the Future. Thus a more elegant description of the entire Greek verbal network is created, with inclusion of the Future system representing a particular function, similar to some but yet distinct from others.

b. These several benefits should be enough to warrant an investigation of this sort, except for one important fact. The Future form occurs in relatively high proportion in passages in the NT which are often cited as eschatological or prophetic. What is to be made of these, if they are dependent upon a tense form that is not in fact a conveyor of future reference at the semantic level? Of course, pragmatically the Future--like other forms--may implicate future time, though this is a possible function at the textual level and not its essential meaning at the level of code. It is striking that in several major works on eschatological texts (e.g. Kümmel, *Promise*; Jeremias, *Parables*; Chilton, *God*, among others), there is a lack of recourse to invoking the Future form. Either these theological constructs of the eschatology of the NT may not in fact be based to any large degree upon the tense usage of the NT at a semantic level, but rather upon pragmatic indicators of time or extra-grammatical features; or NT theologians assume the temporal nature of the tenses in the NT and thus cite passages tacitly understanding that a Future form refers to future time. Rather than determine which is the case, however, a discussion of several verses cited as characteristic of NT prophecy and eschatology is warranted. (I rely upon examples cited by Aune, *Prophecy*.) Tentative conclusions will be drawn regarding prophecy in the NT on the basis of grammar.

1. Passages cited as suggesting the imminent coming of the kingdom of God. Several of the more important passages referred to concerning the imminence of the kingdom do not use the Future form but the Subjunctive (e.g. Mark 9:1; Luke 9:27; Matt 16:28; 10:23) or the Indicative (e.g. Mark 1:15; Matt 10:7-8a). On the basis of previous discussion, other texts using Future forms may warrant citation as referring to the imminence of the kingdom (or like theological concepts) if the issue of futurity is not bound to the verb form.

2. Predictions of the destruction of the temple and of Jerusalem. Mark 14:58 (cf. Matt 26:61): Jesus is accused of saying, ἐγὼ καταλύσω (I expect to destroy) this temple made with hands and after three days οἰκοδομήσω (I expect to build) another not made with hands. It is immaterial to discussion (throughout this section) whether this is an authentic quotation of Jesus or whether it was fulfilled exactly as stated. At minimum it must be recognized that Jesus expected the temple to be destroyed and rebuilt, though an internal future sense seems implicated by time deixis (the interval of three days). Once the initial expected event occurs, the second is expected three days hence. The accusers do not believe that the utterance of a Future is to be treated as established with certainty, otherwise they would not presumably be attempting to kill Jesus to forestall the act. Since the temple was still standing, any destruction would of necessity have come in the future, but this is of secondary importance to their belief in Jesus' intention. (In Mark 15:29, those who taunt Jesus use the Present Participle rather than the Future in their mocking, displaying that they believe not in the temporal assertion of a Future form but that it reveals an expectation that may still be frustrated.) If Mark 13:2 (par. Matt 24:2; Luke 21:6) is the source of Mark 14:58, as some scholars posit (Aune, *Prophecy*, 174; contra Cranfield, *Mark*, 441-42; Taylor, *Mark*, 66-67), the Subjunctive may help explain the use and meaning of the Future in 14:58.

John 2:19: destroy this temple (λύσατε τὸν ναὸν τοῦτον) and in three days ἐγερῶ (I expect to raise) it. Here Jesus is actually quoted as making a statement regarding the temple. He claims in what may be a conditional-like statement (see my chapts. 6 and 7) that if this temple is destroyed, he expects to raise it in three days, or after a short time (Schnackenburg, *John*, 1.349). Whether this temple refers only to his body (cf. v 21) or not (some think it may be a later addition), the verse grammatically makes no absolute claim to Jesus' destruction of the temple, only a logical temporal implicature relating the two events, as in Mark 14:58 (above).

Luke 13:35 (par. Matt 23:39 without Future): you won't see me, Jesus reportedly says, until ἥξει (it will come)[27] when you may say. . . . The variant reading, even if not original, reinforces the conditional-like sense. Future reference may be introduced by ἕως in the "protasis" but the syntax instead seems to emphasize a logical argument (Aorist Subjunctive in the apodosis), referring to an event which is expected. (Aune [*Prophecy*, 175] apparently treats the entire statement as future referring, but he does not say how he arrives at this.) The Matthean version has clearer implicature of future time because of time deixis (ἀπ' ἄρτι).

Luke 19:43-44: ἥξουσιν ἡμέραι (days can be expected to come) upon you, and παρεμβαλοῦσιν οἱ ἐχθροί σου (your enemies will set up against you) barracades, and περικυκλώσουσίν σε καὶ συνέξουσίν σε πάντοθεν (they will surround you and completely encircle you), and ἐδαφιοῦσιν (they will completely destroy) you and your children with you, and ἀφήσουσιν (they will not leave) stone upon stone with you. These verses display two distinct uses of the Future. The first seems prospective with the impersonal subject and reference to "days" not yet present (though it may be a command), while the others seem to function deliberatively with personal subjects. Syntactically and pragmatically the verse thus posits a series of expected subsequent events, predicated upon the "days" coming, though even here Jesus may merely be saying he expects days to come. (See Ellis, *Luke*, 226, who recognizes the difficulty of chronology in relating events of the NT, whether historical or eschatological.) Cf. Luke 23:29-31 with "days are coming" (Present Indicative) (Marshall [*Luke*, 225] calls "days are coming" a stereotyped phrase) and the *qal wahomer* conditional statement with the deliberative Aorist Subjunctive (Aune, *Prophecy*, 177; see Blass/Debrunner, ¶ 316[1]; Turner, *Syntax*, 99) used omnitemporally in v 31.

3. Statements of death and resurrection.

Mark 10:33-34 (par. Matt 20:18-19; Luke 18:32-33) and 9:31, cf. 8:31: ὁ υἱὸς τοῦ ἀνθρώπου παραδοθήσεται (the son of man can expect to be betrayed) to the chief priests and scribes and κατακρινοῦσιν (they can be expected to condemn) him to death and παραδώσουσιν (to hand him over) to the Gentiles. And ἐμπαίξουσιν αὐτῷ καὶ ἐμπτύσουσιν αὐτῷ καὶ μαστιγώσουσιν αὐτὸν καὶ ἀποκτενοῦσιν (they can be expected to humiliate him and spit on him and beat him and kill him), and after three days ἀναστήσεται (he can be expected to rise up). This is the most precise statement that corresponds to Jesus' actual death, though the order of events is different from 15:15-20 (see Lane, *Mark*, 374-75). Referring to the son of man with the Passive 3d Person verb, which distances the grammatical subject from himself (see below on the son of man), Jesus says that he expects betrayal, etc., on the basis of his knowledge of his opponents' character and behaviour, and the fate of other prophets before him. Though Mark 8:31 uses Indicative and Infinitive verbs to refer to the anticipated action, Mark 9:31 uses the Indicative παραδίδοται for an assertion of action seen as in progress, followed by two Futures referring to that which is expected as the consequence--death and resurrection. All three of Mark's passion predictions refer to the three day interval, and this time deixis establishes a temporal implicature reinforced by the discourse itself, which gives a logical order to the events. A clear differentiation of code from textual usage enables the role of each to be seen more clearly.

4. Judgment statements.

Matt 11:22, 24; 10:15 (par. Luke 10:12): Jesus says it would be better (ἀνεκτότερον ἔσται) for certain cities in "day of judgment" than for certain people around him. The reference to "day of judgment" may give the entire sentence prospective implicature if it refers to a specific day (Hebraic influence?), though the anarthrous noun may mean "any day of judgment" (see Blass/Debrunner, ¶ 259; Goodwin, *Grammar*, 206), in which case Jesus is projecting an expected result (cf. 11:21 with conditional).

---

[27]Text: D certainty of the reading in UBS[3], with D; ἄν A W etc. The shorter text is obviously the more difficult, though its textual attestation is not strong. Good textual evidence also exists for deleting the Future: א B K L X p[75] f[13], etc. See Metzger, *Commentary*, 163.

Matt 11:23 (par. Luke 10:15): σύ, Καφαρναούμ, μὴ ἕως οὐρανοῦ ὑψωθήσῃ; ἕως ᾅδου καταβήσῃ (C., you cannot expect to be elevated to heaven, can you? You can expect to descend to hades). This conditional-like statement (if you will not be elevated, you will descend) seems to be best interpreted as an expected hypothetical scenario.

Matt 8:11-12 (par. Luke 13:28-29): Jesus says to those around him (λέγω) that he expects many from the East and West ἥξουσιν (will come) and ἀνακλιθήσονται (will be seated) with Abraham and Isaac and Jacob in the kingdom of heaven. But the sons of the kingdom ἐκβληθήσονται (will be thrown out) into the outer darkness where the wailing and gnashing of teeth ἔσται (will be). These remarks, made after witnessing the faith of the centurion, stand out for their lack of deictic reference in the context, whatever the reason (Chilton [God, 179-201] discusses redaction of this passage). Jesus expects a banquet where Gentiles who come from East and West are seated together with Jews (although some are excluded), not specifying here whether the events are symbolic or literal (see Beasley-Murray, Jesus, 172-74). The image may be of the apocalyptic last banquet, in which case temporal deixis gives a clear future implicature, but since the exact temporal reference of Jesus' kingdom is uncertain, it is not clear. As Dodd says, "the saying does not answer the question whether Jesus expected any further 'coming' of the Kingdom of God beyond that which was already taking place in his own ministry" (Parables, 55). (What is certain is Jesus' teaching of great agony for those who are excluded. Matthew refers to wailing and gnashing of teeth also in 13:42, 50; 22:13; 24:51; 25:30.) Chilton says with reference to ἀνακλίνω that it is used in a 'modal' sense, though he need not posit that it translates a Semitic Imperfect (God, 200, following Jeremias, Promise, 55 n. 3).

5. Son of man sayings.[28]

Mark 8:38 (cf. Matt 16:27; par. Luke 9:26): Jesus reportedly says that if someone is ashamed of him and his words in this adulterous and sinful generation, ὁ υἱὸς τοῦ ἀνθρώπου ἐπαισχυνθήσεται (the son of man will be ashamed) of him, whenever he might come in the glory of his father with the holy angels. Parallel to 8:35 (Lane, Mark, 310), this conditional-like sentence (cf. Luke 12:8, 9), grounded by deictic indicators to this generation, is concerned with the logical response by the son of man to those who are ashamed of Jesus (cf. Matt 10:32, 33). Käsemann has argued that this is an example of a sentence of holy law, on the pattern of early Christian prophetic speech. But Berger has shown more recently that in conditional-like sentences dealing with reward and punishment the hortatory purpose renders any reference to future time as relatively less essential.[29] The fulfilment could occur at any time, though the concluding temporal clause with the Aorist Subjunctive, while projecting such an event, does not necessarily posit a temporal

---

[28]There is a wealth of material on the son of man question (see bibliography), since the issues are obviously complex. Reference to origin, source, redaction, and authenticity is avoided. Instead, each saying is treated in its biblical final form to grasp the grammatical structure.

[29]Käsemann ("Sentences") distinguishes five characteristics of sentences of prophetic Christian holy law: chiasmus; use of the same verb in both sections of the statement; God's eschatological activity referred to often in the Passive Voice; divine retribution; and conditional protasis with apodictic apodosis. Berger ("Sätzen," 16-18) distinguishes four kinds of conditional-like sentences treating reward and punishment ([1] ὃς ἐάν or ὃς ἄν in protasis, [2] πᾶς ὁ + Present Participle in protasis, [3] ὅταν in the protasis with an Imperative or a demand in the apodosis, and [4] ἐάν in the protasis with a demand in the apodosis) to prove that these sentences are based in parenetic wisdom-like rather than Christian prophetic material. Though he puts too much emphasis on the temporal implications of verbs in the apodosis of conditionals and neglects the classical origins of these conditional and conditional-like statements (cf. Beyer, Syntax, 75ff., who cites classical parallels for virtually every conditional construction), Berger does realize the gnomic use of the Future and that apodoses with Future forms may speak of the goal of an action (see 26, 33), rather than mere futurity. Hill ("Evidence," 270-74) claims that Käsemann's theory is pure assertion without argument, and that there is not evidence of Christian prophets speaking in the name of the risen Lord; cf. Aune, Prophecy, 237-40; Hill, NT Prophecy, 170-74, for summary and critique of Berger.

scheme. The use of the 3d Person, clearly the unmarked Person in Greek, distances the reference from Jesus, since there is no direct grammatical linkage (see Hooker, *Son*, 120-22; Tödt, *Son*, 57; Higgins, *Jesus*, 60; Beasley-Murray, *Jesus*, 226-29, on identity of the son of man; cf. Lindars, "New Look," 437ff.). Though the reference to the son of man is the climax of this pericope (Mark 8:34ff.) (see Hooker, 116-22, esp. 116-17), nothing of his time of coming is asserted (contra Kümmel, *Promise*, 44-46; cf. Tödt, 47; Lindars, *Jesus*, 50-57).

Luke 12:8-9 (par. Matt 10:32): Jesus is reported to say that whoever confesses him before men, ὁ υἱὸς τοῦ ἀνθρώπου ὁμολογήσει[30] (the son of man is expected to confess) him before the angels of God, and whoever denies him before men ἀπαρνηθήσεται (is expected to be denied) before the angels of God. Often cited as being related in form and content to Mark 8:38 (see Aune, *Prophecy*, 182; but cf. Hahn, *Titles*, 30), this conditional-like statement clearly makes no specific time reference but sets up a logical argument related to earthly confession and confession before God (Marshall, *Luke*, 514). There is a noticeable lack of grammatical correlation between the speaker, Jesus, and the son of man, who seems (v 9) to be a functionary of God (see Hahn, 35-36; Aune, 181, cf. 181-82; Lindars, *Jesus*, 49). The use of the son of man in 3d Person is well-suited to hypothetical statements and would function as hypothetical even if Jesus is referring to himself (cf. Schweizer, *Luke*, 205), since the grammatical disassociation would be conscious. As Perrin says, "this is still not necessarily a reference to the 'coming' Son of man. . . . If we take the saying by itself, then the reference is only a general one to the imagery of Dan 7:13, this imagery being used as a symbol for vindication." He says further that Jesus could have made a general reference to Dan 7:13 in terms of the 'coming' one, but "such a reference would still only be a general assurance of vindication; it would say nothing about the form or time of that vindication" (*Rediscovering*, 191, believing, however, that Mark 8:38 does have the specific reference he here mentions, though his treatment of Daniel may be questioned. Cf. Kümmel, *Promise*, 44-46, who imposes a rigid temporal scheme).

Luke 17:22-24, 26, 30 (par. Matt 24:27, 37, 39): ἐλεύσονται ἡμέραι ὅτε ἐπιθυμήσετε (days will come when you will desire) to see one of the days of the son of man but οὐκ ὄψεσθε (you will not see). And ἐροῦσιν (they will say) to you. . . . thus the son of man will be (ἔσται) in his day. And as it came about in Noah's days, thus it will be (ἔσται) in the days of the son of man. . . . in the same way it will be (ἔσται) in the day the son of man is revealed. Hahn calls this an "announcement of a sudden advent of the Son of man, visible to all men, clothed in a tersely figurative formula. . ." (*Titles*, 31). But deciphering the specificity of the many figures is difficult. Besides the problems of redaction, questions arise regarding the nature of the "day," whether it has the same meaning in the Singular and Plural or whether it means the same as parousia in Matthew 24. While it is reasonable that parousia in Matthew 24 is to be understood as future-referring (see esp. Higgins, *Jesus*, 87; cf. Gundry, *Matthew*, 486), the 'gnomic' comparisons in Matthew and Luke militate against this. In Luke 17, however, the argument is more complex. The use of "day" may have either present or future reference (Kümmel, *Promise*, 44-46). Jesus may be saying that he expects the last days, or he may be describing the current days which will have certain characteristics, since he addresses events pertinent to those standing with him who will be frustrated in their desire (v 22) (see Beasley-Murray, *Jesus*, 314-15). Verse 23 need not have specific temporal reference since it is conditional-like, and v 24 (so Marshall, *Luke*, 659) uses another omnitemporal comparison to emphasize the suddenness of the coming (see Higgins, *Son*, 5; Beasley-Murray, 318), not clarified by the reference to "his day." The logical enumerator, πρῶτον (v 25), may be construed as implicating an internal or logical temporal framework, but it does not clarify vv 22ff. The comparisons with Noah and Lot show that the day or days may be concurrent with the days of the son of man, so that v 30, if it refers to Jesus, could mean the present day. In any case, temporal reference is unclear on grammatical grounds and to impose a future temporal conception upon the Future form does not clarify the issues (see Beasley-Murray, 317-18, for appropriate warnings).

---

[30]ὁμολογέω ἐν may be Semitic; see Moulton, 104.

Luke 18:8b: when/if the son of man comes (ἐλθών) εὑρήσει (will he find) faith on the earth?, Jesus asks. A deliberative use of the Future poses the question of whether, whenever the son of man comes (conditional-like use of the Aorist Participle), he can expect to be able to discover faith. This supplements, though shifting the emphasis from God to man, the timeless conclusion regarding the divine nature of God suggested in vv 7-8a (see Tödt, *Son*, 99-100; Jeremias, *Parables*, 84). Though Higgins notes the discussion of whether the time is present or future on the basis of identification of the son of man with Jesus, the syntax leaves the question intentionally vague. What seems more assured is that the son of man will be looking for faith in Jesus (Higgins, *Jesus*, 91-92. This is the only place in the Gospels that associates the son of man with faith).

Matt 13:41-43: the son of man ἀποστελεῖ (will send). . . . and συλλέξουσιν (gather). . . . and βαλοῦσιν (throw them). . . . and there will be (ἔσται). . . . Then the righteous ἐκλάμψουσιν (will shine forth). This expectation of a future time, on the basis of temporal deixis in v 40, says that, just as the tares are gathered and thrown into the fire, thus the end of the age is visualized. Note the contrasting timeless description of the sower as the son of man.

Matt 12:32 (par. Luke 12:10; cf. Mark 3:28-29 and Matt 19:28; 25:31): whoever might say a word against the son of man ἀφεθήσεται αὐτῷ (can expect to be forgiven him); whoever might say anything against the holy spirit οὐκ ἀφεθήσεται αὐτῷ (it will not be forgiven him) neither in this age nor the one that is coming (μέλλοντι). All of these statements are conditional-like, with Matt 12:32 providing a clear example of use of the Future. (Gundry [*Matthew*, 237] claims the Future corresponds to the Aramaic Imperfect, which has a "virtual rather than future meaning," hence it should be translated "can be forgiven.") This statement is not temporally bound but establishes two general precepts regarding deprecatory statements and forgiveness (see Käsemann, "Sentences," 66-81), with temporal implicature established by reference to this age and the age that is coming (μέλλοντι). Temporal deixis occurs in Matt 19:28 with reference to the παλιγγενεσίᾳ, though future implicature with the Participle is not firm.

Luke 11:30-32 (cf. Matt 12:40-42; 16:4; Mark 8:12): Jonah, Jesus says, became a sign to the Ninevites, thus the son of man shall be (ἔσται) in this generation. This comparison of characters-- Jonah and the son of man--is made upon the temporal conception that each is a sign to his generation. Deixis limits the temporal implicature of ἔσται (cf. v 29) so that the comparison is with the expected condition of the current generation, a condition which will not be known in the same way as Jonah's until after the fact (hence the use of the Indicative). This solves Lindars's dilemma whether the Future is "logical," conveying the "intended" time in relation to the "past example of Jonah," or translation of an Aramaic Imperfect used modally. It may be the latter but it is certainly acceptable Greek as the former (Lindars, *Jesus*, 41-42). Marshall (*Luke*, 484-85) recognizes that though most scholars understand ἔσται as a "real future" [sic], it may be understood as a logical Future, though he does not take it as such. The addition of the reference to three days in Matthew 12 does not establish external temporal relation but only internal reference, though this is probably significant retrospectively when compared to Jesus' time in the tomb (Perrin, *Rediscovering*, 193-94; cf. Beasley-Murray, *Jesus*, 257, who notes that Luke does not mention the parousia but probably refers to Jesus' impending death). Temporal implicature is instead established here by reference to judgment. But reference to judgment (in both passages) contrasts present time (ὧδε [here] and τῇ γενεᾷ ταύτῃ [this generation]) with one where the Ninevites, the queen from the South and "this generation" are to be gathered, and shows that the Future form can refer prospectively with proper deictic indicators (see Higgins, *Jesus*, 133-40). As Perrin says, "it says nothing about the form of this future moment, nor about the time element involved, beyond the fact that it is future" (*Rediscovering*, 195. Perhaps the word "fact" is too strong).

John 8:28 (cf. 3:14): Jesus reportedly said, whenever you might lift up the son of man, τότε γνώσεσθε (then you can expect to know) that I am. This conditional-like statement makes no reference to time but to theological outcome (τότε) of a projected event. The protasis of this conditional sentence is fulfilled in the crucifixion, or so it can be posited retrospectively, though the apodosis's fulfilment, the meaning of "I am," and the relation of Jesus to the son of man are open to debate (Maddox, "Function," 198; Higgins [*Son*, 168] interprets ὑψόω as "crucify." There is possibly a change in reference of the 2d Person subjects of the two clauses, thus distinguishing between two different groups involved; see Borsch, *Son*, 303). This theological scheme, however, should not be used to dictate the semantic understanding of the verbs.

John 1:51: ὄψεσθε (you will see) the heavens open and the angels of God ascending and descending upon the son of man. Preceded by the affirmation of "truly, truly I say to you" (see Moloney, *Johannine Son*, 25; Lindars, *Jesus*, 148), this Future may be used as a command, as in 1:50 (Casey [*Son*, 197] says ὄψεσθε may be a catchword to illustrate use of ὄψῃ in v 50). The change from Singular to Plural reinforces the conception of the verb as a general statement to the entire group; cf. John 3:7 where the same shift occurs (Moloney, *Johannine Son*, 25-26; Westcott, *John*, 51).

John 6:27 (cf. vv 53, 62): Jesus says don't work for the destructible food but the food that lasts forever, which the son of man δώσει (will give) you. Since the son of man will give food that lasts forever there is a temporal implicature (Borsch, *Son*, 295, cf. 296-98), though the time of giving is not specified. The verbal semantics point to the final clause as referring to the son of man's action as expected by the speaker. Though one may want to push the temporal scheme by claiming that, since one would have to receive the "food" in one's lifetime while one is able to work, there is present temporal reference (as opposed to the age to come), the general character of the exhortation does not demand this.

6. Mark 13 (and pars. Matt 24:1-36; Luke 21:5-33).

Much material has been written on Mark 13 (see e.g. Wenham, *Rediscovery*). Regardless of the authenticity of the various statements and the genre of the unit, this discourse "constitutes the longest and most concentrated section of the synoptic gospels devoted exclusively to the description of the events surrounding the end of the age" (Aune, *Prophecy*, 184). The major question for discussion is how this is conveyed. One important feature of the language of the chapter is its hortatory nature (Beasley-Murray, *Mark 13*, 18; idem, *Jesus*, 212-16; Lane, *Mark*, 445-48), evidenced in the comparatively large number of Imperatives (nineteen) and Subjunctives (seven). This creates a framework that helps explain the pragmatics of the Future form.

Watch out so that . . . (Aorist Subjunctive) (v 5b)
    Reasons: Many will come (ἐλεύσονται). . . and deceive (πλανήσουσιν) (v 6)
Don't be upset whenever . . . (Aorist Subjunctive) (v 7)
    Reasons: They are necessary (δεῖ) but then the end (τέλος). Nation will be raised
      up (ἐγερθήσεται) (vv 7-8)
Watch out (v 9a)
    Reasons: They will hand you over (παραδώσουσιν). . . drag you (δαρήσεσθε) .
    . . stand you (σταθήσεσθε). . . . It is necessary (δεῖ) to preach the gospel
    first (vv 9b-10)
Don't worry what to say (Aorist Subjunctive), whenever . . . (Aorist Subjunctive), but
    speak (v 11a)
    Reasons: You are not going to be (ἐστε !) (v 11b)
    Reasons (in vv 12-17 the order is reversed): Brother will betray brother
      (παραδώσει), children will turn against parents (ἐπαναστήσονται) and
      you will be (ἔσεσθε) hated (vv 12-13a)
He will be saved (σωθήσεται) if he has endured to the end (v 13b)
Let the one who reads beware, whenever . . . (Aorist Subjunctive). Then let those in
    Jerusalem flee (vv 14-17)
Pray that (ἵνα--Aorist Subjunctive) . . . (v 18)
    Reasons: These days will be unparalleled (ἔσονται). . . and may never occur
      (Aorist Subjunctive) (vv 19-20)
Don't believe if . . . (Aorist Subjunctive) (v 21)
    Reasons: False Christs and prophets will be raised up (ἐγερθήσονται) and will
      perform (δώσουσιν) signs and wonders (v 22)
Watch out (v 23)

Reasons: I am telling you the results of all these things. But in those days after (μετά) that tribulation, the sun will be darkened (σκοτισθήσεται), the moon will not give light (δώσει), the stars will be falling (ἔσονται . . . πίπτοντες) from heaven, the powers in heaven will be shaken (σαλευθήσονται). (vv 24-25) Then (τότε) they will see (ὄψονται) the son of man coming in clouds with great and glorious power (v 26; par. Matt 24:30; Luke 21:27; cf. Mark 14:62) and then (τότε) he will send (ἀποστελεῖ) the angels and will gather (ἐπισυνάξει) his elect (v 27)

Learn from the fig tree (vv 28-29)

Truly I tell you (Aorist Subjunctive) (v 30)

Reasons: Heaven and earth will pass away (παρελεύσονται) but my words will not ever pass away (παρελεύσονται) (v 31) (But no one knows when, v 32)

Watch out

Reasons: You don't know when the time will be (ἐστιν). (v 33) Parable (vv 34-36)

Conclusion: What I am telling you, I am telling all--watch out! (v 37)

This discourse in Mark 13 (and essentially the same in Matthew 24 and Luke 21) has a quite obvious structure as an exhortatory or parenetic address, as is seen in the work of Lambrecht (*Redaktion*, 9ff.), Pesch (*Naherwartungen*, esp. 15-18), Lane (*Mark*, esp. 446), Rousseau ("Structure," 157-62), Grayston ("Study," 376, 383-84), and Beasley-Murray (*Jesus*, 322-37), all of whom construct a somewhat similar outline around the Imperatives (with varying emphasis on temporal relation), usually making the following groupings: vv 5-6, 7-8, 9-13, 14-20, 21-23, 24-27, 28-32, 33-36, 37 (cf. Aune, *Prophecy*, 185, who reverses the order and puts apocalyptic prediction before parenesis). It follows the pattern of exhortation (whether warning or comfort) followed by reasons for the warning, ending with a last admonition (see Gaston, *Stone*, 52). Jesus quite probably is referring to the end times, but this address does so on the basis of: (1) the order of the argument, in which Jesus follows an admonition with what necessitates the warning (Gaston [*Stone*, 52] notes that γάρ should be read in vv 6, 7b, 8, 9b, 11b, 19, 22, 33, 35 as providing the ground for the parenetic material). In one sense, the entire address has future reference since Jesus is talking about a period not yet present, but that is on the basis of the nature of time and events (and the reference to the parousia in v 3?), not tenses alone, since Indicative Presents and Aorists, as well as Imperatives, Subjunctives, Futures, and Participles are used. Rather the future reference comes as a logical result of the entire argument (discourse deixis). (2) The internal deictic modifiers, like τότε, μετά, πρῶτον, οὔπω, τέλος, coordinate the internal movement of the argument, though this is not to be conveyed as a strict chronological sequence, since each unit of admonition-and-reason is somewhat independent. (Kümmel [*Promise*, 97-98] emphasizes the sequential order. But vv 23-27 make it clear this is not intended to be strict or throughout.) (3) A tentative or even general view of the future is given, even in vv 24-27 with their cataclysms (see Grayston, "Study," 383-86; cf. 379-81, where he discounts apocalyptic elements). Commands by nature do not have to be obeyed, neither do Subjunctives and Futures refer necessarily to future events in the way that other verbal forms may be used to refer to the past and present. For example, many of the warnings are qualified (vv 5b, 7, 11, 13, 14, 18, 21, 30), and the reasons, given often with the Future but also with the Subjunctive and even Indicative, are hypothetical in nature--6 with subject "many," v 10 with "they," vv 12-13 referring to family betrayal, v 25 with οὐ μὴ γένηται, vv 24-25 with obvious OT language concerning changes in the universe (Mark quotes a variety of passages, from Isa 13:10; 34:4; Joel 2:10; 3:4, 15; Hos 12:26), and vv 28-29 with the Aorist Subjunctive.

The Future is used for a variety of functions in this passage, including description (vv 6, 9), command (v 31), omnitemporal statements (v 8), deliberation (vv 22, 27), and prospection (vv 24-25). All however express expectations of completion, on the basis of OT prophecy, logical outcome, or possibly the simple fact that Jesus is recorded to have stated them. The Future, therefore, is used to encourage the reader that no matter how bad the world becomes, the end is assured. No other usage could do this so well. As Lane says, the "primary function of Ch. 13 is not to disclose esoteric information but to promote faith and obedience in a time of distress and upheaval" (*Mark*, 446).

7. Pauline material.

1 Cor 15:51-52: πάντες οὐ[31] κοιμηθησόμεθα, πάντες δὲ ἀλλαγησόμεθα (all of us do not expect to sleep, but all can expect to be changed), in a flash, in the blink of an eye, in the last trumpet. For σαλπίσει . . . καὶ οἱ νεκροὶ ἐγερθήσονται ἄφθαρτοι, καὶ ἡμεῖς ἀλλαγησόμεθα (it will sound and the dead will be raised incorruptible and we will be changed). Paul begins this section (vv 50ff.) after he contrasts the earthly state of humans with his expectation of the heavenly. He says, speaking generally, that flesh and blood are not able to inherit the kingdom of God (omnitemporal or timeless Presents?). He continues by sharing a mystery (see Aune, *Prophecy*, 250-51, on oracular character of this section). In a timeless description Paul contrasts his expectation of instant transformation with that of sleeping. Though the last trumpet possibly refers to the end times (Conzelmann, *Corinthians*, 291), it may serve as a metaphor for suddenness, on the basis of parallelism with the two other temporal expressions emphasizing quickness. At this moment the dead are raised and those left are changed. The use of the 1st Person, while not as natural as the 3d Person in general statements, is known in Paul (e.g. 1 Cor 6:14). As Moore says, "Paul probably means Christians generally," and includes himself "as one who awaits the Parousia as an event which might occur at any moment" (*Parousia*, 118-19. He argues that Paul does not include himself in the "we" reference; cf. Aune, *Prophecy*, 251, who contends the oracle was originally in the 3d Person). Verse 53 continues the timeless description with the metaphor of putting on immortality. Though the verbal semantics in this context describe an expected situation, future implicature is possible on the basis of time deixis (τότε [v 54]). And the application of all these verses to the end times could be made on the basis of discourse deixis, though the lack of specific temporal indications in vv 35ff. makes this questionable. Paul is grammatically expressing his expectation of an event (on the basis of God's action?).

Rom 11:26: οὕτως πᾶς Ἰσραὴλ σωθήσεται (thus all Israel expects to be saved). Paul, revealing another mystery, says that a hardening of Israel has come until (ἄχρι) the fullness of the Gentiles may come (εἰσέλθη [Aorist Subjunctive]) and in this way Israel will be saved (v 25). οὕτως more likely refers back to the previous clause, though it may refer to what is written in the OT (Isa 59:20-21) (cf. Bauer, *Lexicon*, οὕτως). In the logic of the argument here, Paul claims that the hardness has come and will last until such time when the fulness of the Gentiles may come (Aorist Subjunctive) and only then will Israel be saved. The Future form is used parallel to the Subjunctive, here designating a logically subsequent event in relation to another projected event (another Subjunctive could have served equally well grammatically), with the added assurance that if the fullness of the Gentiles enters then the salvation of Israel is expected (cf. Cranfield, *Romans*, 2.574-76, who divides the verse into three sections, though a conditional sense still seems plausible). The use of "mystery" and temporal use of οὕτως (Bruce, *Romans*, 222) may be deictic indicators with specific reference to a future state. Aune further argues that the OT quotation must constitute the second strophe of the oracle, with the first constituting an "unconditional announcement of salvation" and the second positing the reasons for this. Though it has deixis of place (Zion [Aune (*Prophecy*), 252] claims that "from Zion" is an addition (midrash pesher?)]) the event is not placed temporally. It only states that the saviour intends to come from Zion but that this covenant is dependent upon whenever (ὅταν) their sins might be taken away (Aorist Subjunctive).

1 Thess 4:14-17: if we believe that Jesus died and rose, thus God ἄξει (is expected to lead) with him through Jesus Christ those who sleep. For we are saying this to you in a word of the lord, because we, the living who are left unto the parousia of the lord, may in no way precede (φθάσωμεν [Aorist Subjunctive]) those asleep. Because the lord himself, in a command, in a voice of an archangel, and in a trumpet of God, καταβήσεται (he will descend) from heaven and

---

[31]Turner (*Syntax*, 286-87) and Moule (168) claim that the negative must mean οὐ πάντες. But is this correct? Robertson (753) thinks not. Cf. Blass/Debrunner, ¶ 433(2).

the dead in Christ ἀναστήσονται (will rise) first, then we, the living who are left, ἁρπαγησόμεθα (will be grabbed) with him in a cloud toward a meeting in the air. (And thus we will be [ἐσόμεθα] always with the lord.) The passage begins with a I class conditional sentence which establishes the hypothetical foundation for the following description,[32] i.e. all that follows seems predicated upon this condition. In his word of the lord Paul stresses we will *not* precede those who are dead (Aorist Subjunctive). The reason is that Paul sees the lord descending from heaven, the dead in Christ being taken up first and those who are alive being second. The logic of the argument, though on the basis of a conditional foundation, establishes an internal temporal frame through discourse and internal time deixis (πρῶτον [v 10], ἔπειτα [v 17]), which point to events future to the first events. This is not necessarily externally temporally grounded, but is a pragmatic application of verbal semantics, as is evidenced by the use of indicators (πάντοτε) in v 17. Though deixis of Person is 1st Person (cf. 1 Cor 15:51-52 above), it does not seem to colour the hypothetical nature of the statement. Moore (*Parousia*, 109-10) defends the general use on five other grounds as well: (1) there is an impersonal contrast between those living and dead; (2) time is of concern in 1 Thess 5:1-11 (not here), where he says it comes suddenly; (3) in 4:15, 17 "we" is expanded to a rather broad undefined group; (4) Paul's personal experience surely taught him not to include himself among those who would be alive; and (5) this dual hope of the coming and living is found elsewhere in Paul, e.g. 2 Cor 5:9. Thus, all that can be asserted with regard to the Future verbs is that Paul expects the situation to unfold in this way. It has yet to be verified.

Gal 5:21b: those who practice such things, Paul says, οὐ κληρονομήσουσιν (cannot expect to inherit) the kingdom of God. Paul seems to be stating that whoever practices such sins as murder, drunkenness, etc. (vv 19-21) is expected not to inherit the kingdom of God, possibly with the commanding Future used. The concept of kingdom of God does not provide a firm deictic indicator for temporal implicature of this statement. (Aune [*Prophecy*, 258] recognizes this conditional-like structure, though he seems to posit a clear external future temporal reference.) And his use of προλέγω (predict [5:21a]) shows that Paul recognizes that his statement about what has not yet appeared is qualitatively different from that which has been accomplished (see Betz, *Galatians*, 284-85).

8. Other passages.

Acts 18:10: οὐδεὶς ἐπιθήσεταί σοι τοῦ κακῶσαί σε (no one can be expected to put a hand on you to harm you). The lord's promise to Paul, following several commands, gives the reasons or logical result of God's promise for Paul's security--the lord is/will be with him and no one will harm him, because he has people in that city (cf. Aune, *Prophecy*, 267, for a slightly different view of the structure). The parallel sentences are instructive. Since the argument is that Paul can feel secure since God not only is with him now but can be expected to continue to be with him, present and future implicature is likely for the two διότι clauses, of which the first includes the Future. Cf. Acts 13:11: in these two clauses the first (verbless) has present implicature (reinforced by νῦν), along with the pronouncement of judgment, though the second seems to be stressing the expected logical result of the first. This expected event becomes a realization in v 11b, where blindness comes upon the magician (παραχρῆμα [immediately]).

---

[32]Contra Best, *Thessalonians*, 187, who misses the point of the distinction between semantics and pragmatics when he writes, "There is nothing hypothetical about *if*; it is a fact that the church believes that Jesus died and rose"; and Morris, *Thessalonians*, 139, who says the conditional "is not to be taken as indicating any uncertainty. The implication of this type of conditional clause is that the condition has been fulfilled." Here they are wrong. See Boyer, "First Class," 75-76, who argues that only 37% of NT 1 class conditionals make a claim to be fact. See my chapt. 6.

9. Revelation.[33]

Seven letters to the churches--2:5, 7, 10 (cf. 2:11 with Aorist Subjunctive), 16, 17, 23, 25, 26-28; 3:3-4, 5, 9-10, 12 (cf. Aorist Subjunctive), 20, 21. The seven letters contain several uses of the Future tense in conditional or conditional-like sentences (see Caird, *Revelation*, 32, also 49-50; Sweet, *Revelation*, 82, who note this especially for verbs of "coming"). One is as the apodosis of conditional sentences enumerating results of previous incidences of disobedience. Another expresses God's expected intention to give "rewards" to those who fulfil certain conditions.

Rev 1:7a: ὄψεται αὐτὸν πᾶς ὀφθαλμός (every eye expects to see him). The first clause in 1:7 says the lord is coming with the clouds, not indicating when. Neither does it say when their eyes are to see him, though a case can be made for subsequence on the basis of logical order and the conditional-like statements of 1:7b. Cf. 1:8 using Present Participle with future implicature.

Rev 14:13 (cf. 6:11): the spirit says, yes, ἵνα (v.l. ὅτι p[47]) ἀναπαήσονται (they expect to cease) from their works. The ἵνα + Future form may be relative, causal, final, or commanding.[34] Though it is not entirely certain, the command sense seems more likely on the basis of the parallel usage with the verbless clause, the use of ναί, and the following γάρ clause. None of these has an inherent temporal value: the causal sense implicates a timeless statement which describes the reason for the blessing at death, whenever it may occur; the final clause describes the result of their blessedness; and the command instructs them. A prospective sense might be found, but the grammar does not demand this. (Aune [*Prophecy*, 283] reads a future sense because he wants to equate those addressed with those who will face martyrdom in the future. This theological construct may be true, but it does not impinge upon the semantics of the verb itself.)

Rev 18:21: οὕτως ὁρμήματι βληθήσεται Βαβυλὼν ἡ μεγάλη πόλις (thus B. the great city will be cast down with violence). Interpreting the imagery of Revelation is particularly difficult, but here the use of the Future seems inextricably bound to the expectation of the sure destruction of the new Babylon (Rome?) along the same lines as the destruction of the old (cf. vv 2-3). The entire action (not just v 21a) is apparently meant symbolically. The parallel Subjunctives in emphatic negative statements about the same event confirm the usage. Cf. Rev 21:3-4, 5-8 with similar visions.

Rev 22:18-19: if anyone might add (ἐπιθῇ [Aorist Subjunctive]) to them, ἐπιθήσει ὁ θεός (God can be expected to add) to him the plagues which stand written in this book, and if anyone may take away ἀφέλῃ [Aorist Subjunctive]) from the words of the book of this prophecy, ἀφελεῖ ὁ θεός (God can be expected to take away) his portion from the tree of life. . . . This II.a. class conditional use of the descriptive Future lists the logical results of a hypothetical event, making no reference to specific time (cf. Aune, *Prophecy*, 288, who discusses briefly the two conditional curse formulas). This kind of warning is found elsewhere (Sweet [*Revelation*, 318] cites e.g. Deut 4:2ff.). Cf. Rev 3:20 with a II.a. class conditional.

Regarding prophecy in the NT, three apparent facts emerge. (1) Of the one hundred plus examples Aune cites as prophetic, fewer than half contain Future verbs. This reveals that prophecy (or prospective reference) need not

---

[33]Charles (*Revelation*, l.cxxiii-iv) notes that use of the Present and the Future in Revelation is not arbitrary. The Future is used in so-called prophetic contexts like 7:16ff.; 14:10; 17:14f.; and in clauses with a "frequentative sense," e.g. 4:9-10. Charles contends the Present would be better here, but on the basis of the conditional construction this is not altogether certain. Thompson (*Apocalypse*, 45-47), on the other hand, posits an underlying Semitic Imperfect for the Future in Rev 4:9-10; 5:10; 11:15; 17:8; 18:8. See my chapt. 3.

[34]See Blass/Debrunner, ¶ 369(2); Turner, *Syntax*, 100, cf. 102; Zerwick, ¶¶ 414, 415; Magnien, *Futur*, 253-55; Morrice, "Imperatival ἵνα," 329-30; Moulton, 248; Radermacher, 178; Cadoux, "Use," 171; Meecham, "Use," 180; Robertson, *Studies*, 54-55. In classical Greek a Future may follow ὅπως, ὄφρα, ὡς, ἐπεί, ὥστε, μή, and ἵνα. See Magnien (230-60) for examples. See also P.Teb. 56.11-15 (2d cent. B.C.) with ὡς; PSI 1100.28-29 (A.D. 161) with ἵνα.

be related to a particular tense form. If prophecy can be made apart from a particular tense form, and not every use of a particular tense, i.e. the Future, is necessarily prophetic, it reinforces the earlier evaluation that the Future is not essentially time oriented but focuses on some other semantic feature (this is not a necessary argument in and of itself). (2) Not enough attention is paid to the use and meaning of the tenses in Greek in relation to temporal theological schemes. If the Future is not necessarily future-referring, then this undermines many unexpressed assumptions regarding the nature of NT language, and certain interpretations of particular passages. (3) The role of deictic indicators in prospective language must be recognized. Two are worth mentioning. Person deixis with Paul or Jesus as the speaker takes on new importance. It seems unavoidable that certain theological assumptions regarding these two speakers are inherent in interpretation of their utterances, i.e. that they necessarily knew and expressed more than their language (or at least the language their words are expressed in) could express in simple forms. If in fact they did, then attention must be paid to the role of deixis rather than to a particular verbal form alone as the basis of understanding their utterances. In other words, prophecy is not firmly entrenched in the future realm because of a tense form, but attribution of future reference must be made on the basis of a mixture of factors, including especially person deixis. Time deixis is also very important, perhaps as one of the few relatively sure indicators of temporal relation in the Greek language. Without clear future temporal deixis the interpreter is hard-pressed to establish clear temporal relations of any statement.

6. CONCLUSION. Three important propositions appear to be true regarding the Greek Future. (1) NT Greek evidences such a form and uses it actively. (2) This form is best understood as grammaticalizing a unique semantic feature [+expectation]. (3) The Future is not fully aspectual and is thus aspectually vague, since it offers no morphologically-based choice between forms. These three conclusions best harmonize three kinds of data. (a) The synchronic data are displayed as an elegant network of verbal dependence in that this semantic feature of the tenses unifies most easily the various functional, pragmatic uses found in NT Greek, as well as displaying use of this form in relation to others. (b) The diachronic data are clarified since the reason for the late emergence of the Future form as well as its paradigmatic peculiarities is explained. (c) The data found in the discussions of the major grammars are unified. Virtually all grammarians of Greek (rightly) seek a unity of tense functions, and whereas the Future has posed an especially acute problem because of the supposition of a strictly-temporal function this difficulty is now alleviated.

What are the implications of these findings? (1) As mentioned in the previous section, these findings do nothing to alter belief in the role or function of prophecy in the NT, but only heighten awareness of the importance of close reading of specific texts. (2) This discussion forces interpreters to view the Future as speaking of events in a different way, not making assertions about that which is claimed to exist but grammaticalizing expectation regarding the not yet in existence. (3) Understanding of all the tenses must be shifted to accommodate this semantic function of the Future, realizing that the Greek verbal network is above all one of interdependence and interrelationship. (4) Perhaps the greatest benefit of this discussion of verbal forms is to oblige interperters to pay closer attention to the many factors in language usage, and to be aware of grammar's interpretative limitations. (5) This evaluation of the Greek Future is compatible with recent findings in linguistic typology. For example, Ultan ("Nature") concludes the same for a cross-section of the world's languages: the Future usually derives from modal forms and has predominantly a volitional or desiderative, rather than strictly future, sense (cf. Dahl, *Tense*, 103-11).

CHAPTER 10:
VAGUE VERBS
AND PERIPHRASTICS:
'EXCEPTIONS THAT
PROVE THE RULE'

0. INTRODUCTION. To some it may seem too programmatic to argue that every verb in Greek allows selection from at least one set of aspectual meaning choices. One of the most compelling reasons for such an analysis, however, is that there is a handful of verbs in the Greek language that appear quite clearly not to realize paradigmatic opposition in their tense forms. This chapter argues three points. (1) A surprisingly small number of verbs in Greek that do not realize formal choices in verb tenses do not differentiate aspect. The concept of verbal aspectual vagueness (defined in opposition to ambiguity) provides a helpful metalanguage for discussing this set of verbs. (2) The verb εἰμί, because of its aspectual vagueness and its important lexical meaning forms a significant part of periphrastic constructions. (3) Formal criteria for determining periphrasis can be established, and the consequence for interpretation of individual passages is considered. In the body of the chapter a representative number of instances of periphrastic constructions is treated, often at length. In appendix 10A a further number is treated that should together with those in the main chapter form a virtually complete list of examples of periphrasis in the NT. Appendix 10B treats briefly pseudo-periphrastic--or preferably catenative--constructions. The level of discussion is warranted on the basis of the virtual absence of treatment of these issues in the secondary literature regarding Greek of the NT. Thus the significance of the argument stands out the more.

1. DEFINITION OF ASPECTUAL VAGUENESS. (This section depends upon Porter/Gotteri, "Ambiguity.") **a.** To discuss vagueness in the Greek verbal network, a distinction must first be drawn between ambiguity and vagueness (see Ullmann, *Semantics*, 116-28, 156-75). In principle, at least, the distinction is straightforward: a piece of language is ambiguous if it has more than one discrete interpretation, whereas if it is simply open to a variety of interpretations because it is unspecific, i.e. it does not have a plurality of discrete interpretations, it is vague. Ambiguity is probably much easier illustrated than vagueness, though it often goes unnoticed because one particular meaning appears quite obviously to be much more likely or appropriate than other theoretically possible meanings. For example, in John 21:15, Peter says to Jesus, "you know that φιλῶ you." Whereas φιλῶ may have the meaning of "kiss" (Mark 14:44) besides the emotional sense of "love," here the context makes clear that the latter is the likely interpretation.

Vagueness however can be surprisingly difficult to explain and exemplify. Some might argue that vagueness is what a speaker is tempted to describe as ambiguity until he realizes that the meanings are not discrete but are subsumed under one overall meaning. Kempson defines four types of vagueness (*Theory*, 123-38; cf. Cruse, *Semantics*, 48ff.). (1) Referential vagueness occurs when, even if a speaker can agree on the difference between two categories, he has trouble placing an item in one or the other. In John 6:44, ἀναστήσω may be either a Future Indicative or an Aorist Subjunctive. (2) Indeterminacy of meaning occurs when the kind of relationship specified by a grammatical construction is unclear. In Rom 1:17 Paul speaks of the δικαιοσύνη . . . θεοῦ. Does this refer to righteousness toward God (so-called objective Genitive), God's acting out of righteousness (subjective Genitive), divine righteousness (qualitative Genitive), God's own righteousness (possessive Genitive), or what? With identical formal realizations differentiation is difficult (this is opposed to the Genitive of time which has discrete semantic features). (3) Lack of specification in meaning is found for example in the English verbs *go* and *do*, and the Greek γίνομαι. And (4) the disjunction of different interpretations occurs when it is possible for one interpretation to be true simultaneously with, or to the exclusion of, others. The particle δέ evidences this vague quality.

By looking at some of these matters more systemically the distinction between ambiguity and vagueness can be clarified. Essentially, if an item realizes or is capable of realizing more than one set of meaning choices, i.e. more than one selection expression from a network, then it is ambiguous, if not, then any doubts about its interpretation may be put down to vagueness.

It is well known that in Greek a number of different semantic verbal choices is realized in identical formal expressions.[1] The number of more common instances shows the potential for confusion that exists, though in actual fact these rarely present a problem for ascertaining the proper semantic choice underlying a given realization, since the immediate and/or broader context usually makes the proper choice clear. There are exceptions, of course, like ιαται (Present--ίαται; Perfect--ίαται) in Acts 9:34; Mark 5:29 (Cadbury, "Perfect," 57-58). But despite occasional difficulties these cases represent legitimate instances of verbal ambiguity in Greek.

b. A greater problem is found, however, in certain irregular μι verbs, where the resultant paradigms for what might be called the Imperfect and 2 Aorist forms are identical, the only clear difference with many (e.g. τίθημι, δίδωμι) being the formative prefix of the Present stem (Giles, *Philology*, 479). The μι verbs are possibly the oldest verb forms in the Greek language. (Some speculate that at one time every verb was a μι verb [e.g. λέγομι » λέγω]: Robertson, 306. They are certainly the simplest [Curtius, *Verb*, 96].) Attestation exists for only about 50 in all, however. By the time of Homer μι verbs are beginning to retreat before the superior formative powers of the ω verbs. By the time of Herodotus, Plato and Xenophon the retreat is fully evident. The μι verbs contained neither complete nor systematic paradigms and borrowed early on from the ω conjugation. The more well-ordered ω forms either usurped the μι forms (e.g. δείκνυμι » δεικνύω; ίστημι » ιστάω, ιστάνω; πίμπλημι » πιμπλάω; τίθημι » τίθω; συνίημι » συνίω; δίδωμι » δίδω; ἀπόλλυμι » ἀπολλύω; είμί » εἶμαι) or substituted completely different verbs (e.g. φημί » λέγω, εἶπεν; είμί » ὑπάρχω). Though μι verbs continued in use during the classical through to the hellenistic periods, for the most part in a limited number of stereotyped forms, in modern Greek only εἶμαι remains of the μι class of verbs. (For overviews of the history of the μι verb see Jannaris, 234-35; Robertson, 306-20.)

In ancient Greek είμί (I am), εἶμι (I go), κεῖμαι (I lie), φημί (I say), ἦμαι (I sit) and νέομαι (I go), the first four found in the NT, are aspectually vague. (Other verbs in Greek do not have complete paradigms, but it is argued here that for a certain category of verb the paradigm does not suggest aspectual choice.) This can be argued from two perspectives: lack of differentiation of an Aorist/Imperfect dichotomy in the Indicative (i.e. a perfective/imperfective opposition), and a single set of forms for the non-Indicative Moods, including the Participle and Infinitive.

Whereas είμί exemplifies aspectual vagueness clearly[2] (and it serves to explain periphrastic constructions below), the verb φημί presents special problems worth discussing. 1. It is the only

---

[1]E.g. 1st, 2d, 3d Person Singular and 1st Plural of Present Active Indicative and Subjunctive of all alpha contract verbs (τιμάω » τιμῶ, τιμᾶς, τιμᾷ, τιμῶμεν) and 1st Person Singular Present Active Subjunctive and Indicative of all contract verbs (φιλέω » φιλῶ; δηλόω » δηλῶ), 2d Person Plural Present Indicative and Imperative (λύω » λύετε), certain Future and Present Active Indicative liquid verbs (μένω » μενω, μενεις, μενει), 1st Person Singular and 3d Plural 2 Aorist and Imperfect Indicatives (ἔβαλον, ἔλεγον), the Neuter Nominative and Accusative Singular and Plural Participles (λύον, λύα), 3d Person Plural Present Active Indicative and Masculine Dative Plural Present Active Participle (λύουσι), among others.

[2]On είμί see Curtius, *Verb*, esp. 101-03; Goodwin, *Grammar*, 177-78; Robertson, 312-13; Mandilaras, 76-80; Mayser, 1, 2.127; Gignac, 2.400-08. Changes in its paradigm are easily explained: e.g. ἤμην to avoid confusion between ἦ and ἦν. είμί as a copulative has other distinguishing characteristics as well. See McGaughy, *Analysis*, 1-10 (though this treatment depends upon English translation and transformational grammar), and below.

two syllable nonthematic verb beginning with a consonant known in Greek (Buttmann, *Catalogue*, 254), from the root φα, often cited as punctiliar by comparative philologists (e.g. Brugmann, 543), but whether such a distinction can be made must be examined further. 2. φημί is well-attested in Homeric and pre-Homeric Greek, where it originally had augmented forms in the Active and Middle Voice, labelled the Imperfect or 2 Aorist (ἔφην, etc.; ἐφάμην, etc.) (Debrunner, "Aorist"). By classical times, however, speakers developed a 1 Aorist form for φημί (ἔφησα, etc.), though not apparently for the other verbs labelled as aspectually vague, but this form was only used sporadically in the Indicative or non-Indicative Moods (Schwyzer, 1.673, 640; Jacquinod, "L'evolution," 9.12-19; see e.g. Gignac, 2.400-14, for comments on the similarity of the hellenistic verbal paradigms to those of the classical period). Although the Aorist was occasionally used in the hellenistic period (the 1 Aorist does not occur in the NT; see Mayser, 1, 2.200), φημί itself was retreating quickly before other verbs of saying, like λέγω, εἶπεν. 3. φάσκω may have been considered a suppletive verb of φημί, since in some cases the Participle, Infinitive and non-Indicative Moods of φάσκω may have been used for φημί, and in the Indicative, ἔφασκον may have served as the Imperfect for the Aorist ἔφην (Jacquinod, 9.12-19; Liddell/Scott, *Lexicon*, φημί, cf. φάσκω).

If it is true that speakers considered ἔφην to be the Aorist of φημί, or if they considered φάσκω to complete the verbal paradigm of φημί, then φημί may be categorized as a fully aspectual suppletive verb. But several facts argue against this. (a) The Aorist form of φάσκω, developed in the Attic period, was never particularly common, and seems to have decreased significantly during the hellenistic period. The few instances cited by Mayser (Mandilaras cites no instance) could have been formed by analogy with the long α found in the singular paradigm, plus the sigma in 2d Person (ἔφησθα). (Jacquinod ["L'evolution," 9.14-15] admits that the Aorist was an attempt at alignment with the 1 Aorist paradigm.) (b) Most grammarians do not treat φάσκω as suppletive, since its intrusion is minimal outside of the Participle and Infinitive (e.g. Schwyzer, 2.261-62, cf. 1.641; Jannaris, ¶ 975; Smyth, 251; see Robertson, 319, who cites Acts 24:9; Rom 1:22 for use of φάσκω as a Participle in the NT). Jacquinod's argument that the lack of a Present Indicative of φάσκω in Demosthenes supports its suppletive use since it is used for the Imperfect (two Present Indicative forms, besides being redundant, would point away from suppletive use) loses force in the hellenistic period during which the Present Indicative is used. (The possibility exists for classical Greek that textual evidence is incomplete or that instances have been regularized: e.g. Pl. Phaed. 113C v.l. [Veitch, *Verbs*, 675]. See Liddell/Scott, *Lexicon*, φημί, besides grammars of the papyri; contra Ruipérez, *Estructura*, 112-13, who dates emergence to the 3d cent. A.D. Another possibility is that φάσκω, from a class of σκ verbs that do not have complete paradigms, might itself be ambiguous; see Schwyzer, 1.707.)

The point of discussion turns on the fact that Greek has a few unreduplicated (Present) roots which besides being able to form Imperfects can also function as Aorist stems. For example, βα functions as the Present root for βαίνω (I go), but it also serves as the Aorist root for ἔβην, etc., with the same exact endings and vowel lengthening as with ἔφην, etc. (cf. βιόω [I live], ἁλίσκομαι [I am caught], δύω [I sink]; see Goodwin, *Grammar*, 175). ἔφην has been singled out for particular discussion since grammarians of Greek have had difficulty in describing the function of this form. They are fairly well, yet somewhat arbitrarily, decided that the form is an Imperfect, but they have had much trouble reconciling this with its formal and functional similarity to an Aorist (instances of the 1 Aorist of φημί are vanishingly infrequent overall, as mentioned above, and do not occur in the NT, thus ἔφην appears to be the only narrative form of φημί in consistent use in Greek through to hellenistic times).

There seem to be three solutions to this conflict of opinion. The following categories could apply to defining any aspectually vague verb. Application to εἰμί is obvious (despite what is often said by grammarians about εἰμί, in part dependent upon prevailing considerations mentioned above), but discussion continues with φημί because of its interesting treatment by grammarians.

1. ἔφην amalgamates realizations of two selection expressions in one form and is therefore ambiguous. (Though they do not use this exact terminology see Smyth, ¶ 785; Goodwin/Gulick,

¶ 519; Gildersleeve, 92; Schwyzer, 1.640, but cf. 2.261; and H. Fournier, *Les verbes "dire" en grec ancien* [1946] 46ff. [cited by Ruipérez, *Estructura*, 112].)

Many classical Greek grammars argue, therefore, that the form ἔφην may function either perfectively (on the basis of the supposed punctiliar root φα and parallels with other perfective verbal functions) or imperfectively (on the basis of context and a supposed paradigmatic correlation with the Present φημί). Examples of perfective use in classical Greek might include Lys. 16.13; Pl. Prot. 317D; Hom. Il. 22.280,[3] while imperfective use might include Ar. Clouds 70; X. Econ. 17.10; and S. Oed. King 350. In NT Greek, without a strictly recognizable Aorist form available, it is not surprising to hear arguments made for ἔφην as both perfective (or functioning like an Aorist) and imperfective (or functioning like an Imperfect) (e.g. Blass, 50; Robertson, 310 n. 6). Perfective uses might include, e.g., Matt 8:8; Luke 23:3, 40; Acts 17:22; and 23:17, since main verbs of saying following Participles often occur in the Aorist; and Matt 13:28; 26:61; 27:11, 23; Mark 9:12; 10:20; 14:29; Luke 22:58; John 9:38; Acts 10:30; 22:27, 28, since subject-predicate-complement structures with verbs of saying occur very frequently in the Aorist. On the other hand, an equally strong argument might be made that, e.g., Matt 4:7 (contra Robertson, 311); 17:26; 21:27; 25:21, 23; 26:34; 27:65; Mark 9:38; 12:24, are imperfective because the predicate-complement-subject-complement structure occurs often with imperfective verbs.

In differentiating perfective and imperfective functions in this work, more rigorous linguistic criteria are applied than the highly subjective *Aktionsart*-type judgment apparently utilized by most grammarians discussing this issue. But even then, the criterion of context is slippery at best, and difficulty in judging examples becomes apparent. To take one classical example, in X. Cyr. 4.1.23 the narrator says, "Thus taking the man, he went out (ἔξῄει). When they had gone out (Aorist), Cyrus said (εἶπε [Aorist]), Now you will clarify if you were saying the truth (ἔλεγες [Imperfect]), when ἔφης you like looking at me." The question is whether ἔφης has as its parallel εἶπε, an Aorist, or ἔλεγες, an Imperfect. The syntagmatic structures are identical. In the NT similar instances can be found. Responding to the devil's temptation: in Matt 4:4 Jesus uses εἶπεν, in 4:7 ἔφη, and in 4:10 λέγει (he said, Present). Is ἔφη here to be treated as an Aorist or an Imperfect? (See also Matt 8:8.) The situation in Greek is not clear-cut. (Some verbs are thought actually to have switched paradigmatic categories in the course of their evolution. For example, some grammarians suspect that ἔτεκον and ἐγενόμην were once Imperfect forms of the lost verbs τέκω and γένομαι but were later treated as Aorists in the paradigms of τίκτω [I give birth] and γίγνομαι [I become]; see Wright, *Grammar*, ¶ 503.)

2. A possible solution not based exclusively on formal features is that ἔφην expresses a clear semantic choice one way or the other, on the basis of position in the verbal paradigm. (See e.g. Giles, *Philology*, 479; Schwyzer, 1.673, 640, cf. 2.261; Curtius, *Verb*, 126. Moulton [128] recognizes an Imperfect form with aoristic meaning.)

Debrunner argues that in its augmented form φημί, like other verbs, differentiates aspect according to its Voice, with the Active ἔφην, etc., being an Imperfect, and the Middle ἐφάμην, etc., being an Aorist, citing Homeric usage in which the Middle is used in past contexts (Od. 6.200; 10.562; 13.131; Il. 12.125, 165). The past contexts show, he claims, that the usage does not confine the augmented Middle to non past-referring contexts. He also applies this to non-Indicative forms, finding the Aorist compatible with the contexts ("Aorist," 74-79). Not only are the two major instances he cites (Od. 6.200; 10.562) highly debatable (Murray and Sandford render them as present-referring), but the Middle Indicative form seems to have been lost in post-Homeric including hellenistic Greek, and certainly is not found in NT Greek, leaving such a distinction problematic.

Schwyzer recognizes that there are Present roots that appear to form Aorist stems as well, but he argues that generally there is a clear differentiation of Imperfect and Aorist forms on the basis of vowel length and/or accent (e.g. λειπε/ο--λιπε/ο; φευγε/ο--φυγε/ο; γλύφειν--γλύφων;

---

[3]Wackernagel (*Vorlesungen*, 173) claims that an imperfective use in the Homer example would be unthinkable, as would use in Pythagoras's phrase αὐτὸς ἔφα, but is he not evaluating according to a theory of *Aktionsart*?

φυγεῖν--φυγών), as well as place in the verbal paradigm. He argues therefore that ἔφην is Imperfect since it is formed from the same exact stem as the Present, φημί. ἔβην is clearly Aorist, however, even though its vowel and endings are identical with ἔφην, since the Present is βαίνω and the Imperfect ἔβαινον. Somewhat the same occurs with ἔστην (from στα), in which the Aorist has similar formal features as ἔφην, though the Present is ἵστημι and the Imperfect ἵστην. If Schwyzer is right in assuming on such grounds that ἔφην is an Imperfect, then all contexts in which it occurs would include the conception of the action by the speaker as in progress. Further confirmation would be found in those texts where ἔφην is used parallel with other 'durative' verbs, as in X. Econ. 17.10; Ar. Clouds 70; S. Oed. King 349-50; Lys. 13.50 (cf. e.g. Pl. Gorg. 466E, 496, where φημί might be argued for as clearly durative). In the NT imperfective use of ἔφην could be evidenced by correlations with the use of λέγω and other durative verbs of speaking, including historic Present, to highlight significant utterances as opposed to the less heavily marked narrative use of the Aorist εἶπεν. Significant examples could include Acts 22:27-28, where Paul answers with ἔφη when the Roman tribune uses εἶπεν; and Acts 23:35, where ἔφη is used as an interjection in discourse as in much classical Greek writing. (Giles [*Philology*, 479] says ἔφην and ἔλεγον frequently are found in the same constructions as are Aorists of verbs to speak.)

Brugmann (543, 558), on the other hand, feels obliged by what he sees as a punctiliar root to classify ἔφην along with other punctiliar preterites (this formulation is in terms of *Aktionsart*) as an Aorist, like ἔφυγον (I fled), ἐβλήμην (I struck), ἔτλην (I bore, took upon myself), ἔφυν (I grew) (cf. Jannaris, ¶ 977; Buttmann, *Catalogue*, 254; Svensson, *Gebrauch*, 64; Liddell/Scott, *Lexicon*, s.v.). Wackernagel argues further that the preterite of any verb must be an Aorist, i.e. that there was never a special Aorist form built for a verb, so that ἔφην as the preterite of φημί must be considered an Aorist (*Vorlesungen*, 173). (The case for εἰμί would be slightly different, since the ες root is considered to be durative [Kahn, *Verb 'Be,'* 196-97].) Many of the arguments by comparative philologists, however, are based on the supposed 'punctual' nature of the root φα (hence the claim that φημί is aoristic as well), claims about the nature of speaking, and conception of such through translation. (N.J.C. Gotteri [personal correspondence] suggests that German philologists may have tended to this position because German requires fewer semantic choices in past temporal reference than for example English.)

3. A possible resolution of the conflict is that Greek neither allows nor pre-empts the choice between Aorist and Imperfect in the case of such verbs as φημί, εἰμί, εἶμι, κεῖμαι, and the like. (See e.g. Veitch, *Verbs*, 675-76; Ruipérez, *Estructura*, 111-13; and Jacquinod, "L'evolution," 9.08-09, in Homer; cf. Schwyzer, 2.261, who here opts for "aspektlose" use.) Most grammarians do not recognize this category and hence push to decide for a specific resolution to the problem.

The choice, in other words, stops at a relatively less specific point; the form concerned is vague. Whereas a significant number of verbs in Greek do not evidence all possible paradigmatic expressions, most of these either complete their tense-form paradigms with suppletive forms, or are part of a paradigm that a speaker could have drawn on for a suitable formal expression: e.g. ἔρχομαι/ἦλθον; ἐσθίω/ἔφαγον; λέγω/εἶπεν; ὁράω/εἶδεν etc. (see Strunk, "Überlegungen," 16-19; Stork, *Usage*, 402-03). There are a small number of verbs, however, that quite clearly show a limited number of forms, confined to one tense category, especially εἰμί, -εῖμι, φημί, κεῖμαι in the NT, but also apparently ἦμαι and νέομαι. Without trying to reconstruct the proto-history of Greek, it may be said that some of the oldest surviving Greek verb forms (including the μι verbs) may have been living relics of an earlier stage where certain aspectual or tense differentiations were not developed, or at least were not developed fully by speakers. It is quite possible that, since the verbs concerned refer to very common processes (being, coming/going, staying, saying, etc.) and hence were fairly widely used in a variety of contexts, language users felt no need for a more precise aspectual-semantic choice. The age of the form did not preclude further development, since for example ἵημι though irregular developed a complete verbal paradigm, as did τίθημι, δίδωμι, etc., to say nothing of the great majority of verbs. Rather, frequent occurrence allowed certain μι verbs to survive as living relics of an earlier stage in the language, while the overwhelming tendency of the language early on was to develop morphologically-contrastive aspectual forms.

Whereas εἰμί, ⁻εἶμι, φημί and κεῖμαι, like other μι verbs, have a number of Indicatives that may be called Present and Imperfect for formal purposes, there seems to have been a resultant attempt to determine their aspectual values. But the non-Indicative forms only maintain a single set of forms for the Subjunctive, Optative, Imperative, as well as Participle and Infinitive, forms.[4] This failure to realize a formal choice confirms the interpretation of not only the Indicative, including the Present, as aspectually vague, but the entire paradigm as well. (Ruipérez [*Estructura*, 113-14] recognizes the aspectual neutrality of εἰμί, and that it does not form a verbal opposition to γίνομαι, as some grammarians suggest.) If this solution is adopted, then attempts to press the formal classification of, for example, ἤμην, etc., in terms of Aorist and/or Imperfect are misguided, and efforts to decipher the aspectual value of any form are also doomed to frustration. Since no choice is offered, formally or semantically (this does not deny semantic value to other formal differentiations in the paradigm, like Indicative versus Subjunctive), ἤμην is in this sense aspectually vague rather than ambiguous, sufficiently vague to be able to appear in what some have argued (to their frustration) are typically Aorist or typically Imperfect contexts.

2. PERIPHRASTIC CONSTRUCTIONS IN THE SECONDARY LITERATURE. In this century there have been several significant studies of periphrastic constructions in Greek. (Aerts [*Periphrastica*, esp. 5-7, 12-17] surveys the major theorists.)

In roughly chronological order, W. Alexander ("Periphrases"), though he does not refer to NT Greek specifically, has been very influential, claiming that in periphrastic constructions the Participle takes on an adjectival quality when combined with the copulative verb. He distinguishes two forms of periphrastic. Those with the order λύων ἐστι, which periphrastic form asserts the existence of a certain quality in the subject, have three categories of usage: substitutes for verbs with no adjective forms, conceptions of verbal qualities, and Participles that show no adjectival qualities but are used in this particular syntactic pattern. The second form (ἐστι λύων), with εἰμί emphatic and not copulative, does not qualify as a periphrastic. It has three uses as well: true periphrastics which appear in this syntax incidentally, uses of εἰμί meaning "is really, actually," and independent εἰμί meaning "exists" with a Participle of circumstance. Alexander concentrates on the Present Participle, explaining the lack of Aorist Participles in periphrastics along the lines that since the Aorist refers to a specific act it is not easily compatible with representing adjectival qualities. On the other hand, the Perfect abounds (Alexander does not treat the Perfect) since its description of the action has a qualitative sense inherently. Alexander's theory, though containing several important points about the kind of action represented by the Participle, does not define suitable formal criteria for distinguishing a periphrastic. For example, the second form, first usage, begs the question of what constitutes a periphrastic, and does not define a suitable functional standard for differentiating the meanings of εἰμί, since he admits that placement either before or after the Participle is not decisive.

---

[4]Jacquinod ("L'evolution," 9.12-19) claims that for φημί in Demosthenes Aorist and Present forms of the Participle (φήσας; φήσων), 3d Person Singular and Plural Aorist Subjunctive (φήσῃ 3x, φήσωσι 1x) and a complete set of Aorist Optatives are found. Unfortunately he cites no references and other reference sources do not cite these categories.

Regard (*Phrase*, esp. 109-89) follows Alexander at several points, defining the periphrastic as any formal combination of a Participle (or for that matter adjective) with a copulative verb, used to emphasize the movement of the action, which he characterizes in the traditional terms of *Aktionsart* (developing, durative, continuous, habitual, etc.). He differentiates three classes: proper periphrastics, those assimilable to adjectives, and those which are not true combinations, though he does not set down firm criteria for determining how to distinguish these categories. In contrast to Alexander, he claims that in true periphrastics the copulative is rarely after the Participle but normally occurs just before.

The second major theory has been argued by Björck (*HN ΔΙΔΑΣΚΩΝ*), who limits himself to the Present Participle with reference to the Aorist (he excludes the Perfect Participle). He differentiates two classes of periphrastic construction. The first is adjectival periphrasis, where the Participle functioning like an adjective appears with εἰμί to supply a verbal quality or to substitute for a simple form that is either unavailable or would disturb the sense or form of the sentence. The second, true periphrasis, includes the progressive periphrasis, equivalent to English *to be -ing*; various Aorist Participle periphrastics, often substituting for the Pluperfect; and Future periphrastics. Though Björck gives a list of Participles that are solidified as adjectives (dependent on Alexander), he does not fully explain how to determine the completeness of this list, how to differentiate an adjectival periphrastic functioning in place of a finite verb form and true periphrastic substituting for a finite verb form, or why his progressive periphrastic must be accepted as the sole explanation in Greek when the construction is so varied in English.

Rosén and Gonda take a third approach. Rosén ("'Zweiten' Tempora") asserts that every simple finite verb form can be substituted for by periphrasis but that periphrasis is only employed for a particular kind of emphasis. That is, when the author wishes to draw attention not to the action conveyed by the verb but to other items in the sentence, like the subject, complement, adjunct, etc. Gonda ("Remark") has offered a critique of Rosén and Björck at some length while asserting his own theory of periphrastics. He asserts that periphrastics are semi-nominal constructions used instead of sentences with finite verbs, the former directing the reader's attention to "what is" rather than the latter's "what happens." The periphrastic, thus in contrast to the finite form, retards the action of the sentence, maintaining the sense of the auxiliary as "there is/was" while throwing the Participle phrase, possibly with its complements or adjuncts, into relief.

Aerts (*Periphrastica*, esp. 12, 17) has attempted a synthesis of the major positions proposed above, taking especially seriously the work of Björck. After sifting the evidence he concludes that periphrasis of εἰμί with a Present Participle (this really constitutes an introductory definitive section for all Participle forms) does not occur when εἰμί is used independently meaning "to exist," with a Dative of possession or location, where εἰμί is suggested as emphatic, or when the Participle is completely adjectivised. Everything remaining can be considered periphrastic, with generally a situational-describing, intransitive nature, though Aerts realizes that this is not altogether clear.

Kahn (*Verb 'Be,'* esp. 126-48), in the latest major treatment of the subject, departs significantly from the traditional approaches above and uses Z. Harris's pre-Chomskyan transformational syntax to define periphrasis. He specifically criticizes Aerts as representative of most who have approached the question and shows that they have mixed formal and functional criteria (his terms are "syntactical" and "stylistic" / "lexico-semantic"). The syntactical criteria are that εἰμί (and/or ἔχω) appears with a Participle to express some sort of verbal unit, though there are a wide number of opinions regarding the placement of the individual items in this syntactical structure. The semantic criteria include an interpretation of what sense the auxiliary verb has, whether it maintains a full or emphatic force, has a weakened sense, etc. Kahn decides that formal criteria alone must be used to define periphrastics: "I propose a syntactic definition of the following sort: the occurrence of εἰμί + *participle* in a given sentence is periphrastic whenever there is only one kernel sentence underlying both forms in the transformational source of the given sentence" (127). This definition, however, is problematic. Kahn, in using transformational grammar and the theory of kernel sentences, has already unfortunately adopted an illusory theory of meaning, one grounded in translation. Therefore, he seems to beg the question by positing that he can decide on structural grounds alone whether a periphrastic construction transforms into one kernel and hence is a true periphrastic or transforms into two (or more) kernels and thus is non-periphrastic. In other words, the essential question once more is how to recognize a periphrastic.[5]

3. Εἰμί AS GREEK AUXILIARY VERB IN PERIPHRASTICS.

The importance of the two elements of the periphrastic construction, the auxiliary verb and the Participle, must be recognized. As Aerts says, "on the whole . . . the discussions on the constructions εἶναι + participle bestow too little attention to [sic] the fact that the periphrasis is made up of two components. . ." (7). Previous chapters in this work discuss the Participle, appreciating that each form of the Participle--the Aorist, Present, and Perfect--grammaticalizes verbal aspect. It has been noted that the Participle, like the Infinitive, a vital part of the verbal paradigm, functions in a variety of ways, i.e. as subject, adjunct, complement, or predicate. In this chapter, the nature of aspectually vague verbs, including εἰμί, is discussed, and it is posited that εἰμί is compatible with any aspectual context. The question becomes why εἰμί is used in periphrastics and other aspectually vague verbs are not. There are a number of constructions in Greek that grammarians call periphrastic (see below), but εἰμί is by far the most common auxiliary; surely its use in periphrastics has to do with its aspectual vagueness and its lexical meaning. This is not intended as a study of particular lexical items, but εἰμί warrants some discussion.

The traditional view holds that IE ες was just like any verb, with the meaning of existence or some other concrete meaning. At this stage the nominal sentence and use of predicate opposition served instead of the copulative verb. The verb ες was used in such contexts (as were other verbs like πέλω, τελέθω), but apparently its concrete meaning faded to that of only a copulative without an established content when emphasis was placed on the subject or predicate. As a result the verb ες could be used in a variety of contexts to link nouns and adjectives (see e.g. Brugmann, 656-57; idem, *Kurze . . . Grammatik*, 3.626-93; Delbrück, *Syntax*, 3.10-18, 117-21; Gildersleeve, 41ff.; Kühner/Gerth, 1.3, 40-44; Schwyzer, 2.623-24; cf. Shields, "Speculations").

Kahn claims instead that since the nominal sentence in Greek usually occurs in a limited context reflecting the ellision of 3d Person Indicative, the theory of its being the original form is suspect (*Verb 'Be ,'* 199-200). He posits instead an original copulative use of εἰμί, claiming that only this scheme can account for both predicative and existential functions performed by a single linguistic sign. Though Kahn accepts much of the work of comparative philology--agreeing that a locative-spatial meaning probably predates metaphorical usage (see Kahn, "Verb," esp. 257ff.; Lyons, "Note," esp. 390)--he argues that the original locative-copulative use, already rare in Homer, gave way to a strictly copulative use. He distinguishes two major levels, copulative and non-copulative uses. First order uses of εἰμί include the elementary uses as nominal copula (e.g. Hom. Il. 2.485; 9.25; A. Prom. 771), including periphrasis (e.g. Hom. Il. 1.388), adverbial

---

[5]Cf. Karleen, *Syntax*, 113-36, who treats the periphrastic. His treatment need not be analysed since it is limited by three important factors: (1) he is more concerned with the synchronic generation of a periphrastic as "a re-introduction of an adjectival participle into the predicate" (115; cf. 115-18; he too uses Harris's model, 16-24); (2) he accepts and works with the definitions of periphrasis given by especially Aerts and Gonda; and (3) his view of aspect is closer to that of *Aktionsart* (see esp. 123ff.). Thus he does not probe the essential question--what is a periphrastic--but merely tries to explain using transformational grammar where the examples agreed upon by others came from.

copula (e.g. E. Hec. 532), locative copula (e.g. Hom. Il. 8.16), locative-existential copula (X. Anab. 1.2.7), and impersonal copula (e.g. Hom. Od. 3.180). Second order or derived uses of εἰμί include existential sentences (e.g. Hdt. 1.201), existential sentences with an abstract noun as subject (Hom. Od. 11.605), possessive constructions (e.g. X. Anab. 1.9.14), potential constructions (e.g. Hom. Il. 21.193), and veridical uses (e.g. Pl. Great. Hipp. 282A). Kahn singles out the copulative, existential and veridical functions as the most important functions which any theory of "to be" must unify. He does not argue that they are "univocal," but that "the verb has a number of distinct uses or meanings that are all systematically related to one fundamental use" (401), i.e. predication or the copulative use. This primary function, he claims, makes use of the same lexeme for speaking of truth and existence, in that there is an implicit truth claim in the declarative (or assertive) use of the copula sentence. In veridical usage this truth claim is made explicit, though Kahn is careful to assure his readers that the veridical use is not derived from the copulative use. Concerning the existential category, Kahn notes that the major difference from the copulative is the initial position of the verb, often with an indefinite pronoun and attributive form for the predicate. This use is a direct extension of the copulative use.[6]

Kahn's scheme gives the impression of trying to make too much out of usage of a single lexical item. In a lengthy review, Ruijgh has not only criticized Kahn but put forward a more plausible explanation of εἰμί. (Ruijgh summarizes Kahn's position on 44-55. Ruijgh's criticism of Kahn begins with observations about Kahn's dependence upon Harris, Kahn's projection of philosophical ideas, the selective use of evidence, and most importantly the essential differences between Greek and English syntax [55-56].)

Ruijgh claims that Kahn's method is not rigorous enough and that he has, despite his effort to find a unity in the function of εἰμί, defined it as a homonymous term, not polysemous. Ruijgh believes that it is possible "considérer la valeur locale de εἶναι ('être présent, être là') comme fondamentale, tout en reconnaissant la place centrale de la construction copulative dans l'emploi de εἶναι" (55). He defines the "valeur fondamentale" as its value in a neutral context and situation (56). On the basis of Hom. Il. 23.420 (ῥωχμὸς ἔην γαίης [there was a rift in the ground]), Hdt. 1.183.3 (ἔστι δὲ καὶ ἴδια ἀναθήματα πολλά [and there are many other private offerings]), Pl. Prot. 315E (τοῦτό τ᾽ ἦν τὸ μειράκιον [the youth was there]), I.G. II/III² 2.1.1533.1-2 (στέφανος ἀργυροῦς, ὃν Δίων ἀνέθη[κ]εν, [οὐ]/κ ἔστιν [a crown of silver . . . is not there]), and P.Ber. I 121.17 (ἔστιν δὲ καὶ ὁ συναποδεδρακὼς αὐτῷ Βίων [there is the B. who escaped with him]), all absolute uses that Kahn would consider existential (though he does not treat such cases) but which are as neutral as Ruijgh claims can be found, Ruijgh shows that the fundamental use of εἰμί is the local or "présentielle" sense (57-59; cf. Halliday, "Structure," 154-55). (van Bennekom ["Existential"] questions Ruijgh's analysis; Ruijgh successfully counters in "Valeur.") This coordinates well with the wide use of παρεῖναι, and other prefixed forms, where the prefix gives a specific locale to the otherwise unspecified locative sense of εἰμί (60). This "présentielle" sense is then compatible with the many different functional contexts in which εἰμί can be found, including the copulative (61-62), though it is not easy to differentiate these uses (e.g. Hdt. 2.181.5 [ἄγαλμα ἀπέπεμψε ἐς Κυρήνην, τὸ ἔτι καὶ ἐς ἐμὲ ἦν σόον] is susceptible to two interpretations: "she sent a statue to C., which was intact there in my time" [copulative] or "which was there, intact, in my time" [absolute with the adjective functioning in apposition]).

When the subject is human, or when presence in the world must be expressed, εἰμί is able to carry a sense of "existence," which is a special application of the fundamental locative sense: e.g. in Ar. Clouds 1470ff.: Φ: Ζεὺς γάρ τις ἔστιν; (Does Z. exist?) Σ: ἔστιν. (He exists.) Φ:

---

[6]Kahn (196-97, 217-22) discusses what he calls the "aspect" of εἰμί. He assumes that εἰμί has only durative forms (Present and Imperfect), and, using Lyons's scheme of contrasting static and kinetic verbs (*Introduction*, 390-97), concludes that εἰμί is static, as opposed to verbs of becoming (γίγνομαι, φύω, τρέφω, τελέθω, τέλω, τεύχω and occasionally τυγχάνω), which are kinetic. Though Kahn recognizes synthetic aspect (196-97 n. 17), he is defining the meaning of individual verbs on the basis of lexis, not morphological or grammatical categories, hence his claim that the above verbs, as well as ἧμαι, κεῖμαι and ἵσταμαι, are "be" replacers in Homer.

οὐκ ἔστ' οὐκ, ἐπεὶ Δῖνος Βασιλεύει τὸν Δί' ἐξεληλακώς. (He does not exist, no, since D. rules, having banished Z.). Zeus's existence is directly related to his being present, but since his banishment he is no longer there (62). The same is true of a generic notion (e.g. Pl. Laws 676B). Use with concrete (ὕδωρ [water]), impersonal (φῶς [light]) or abstract subjects (κλαγγή [noise]), or in a veridical context is treated by this model. The former (the line between concrete and abstract is a tenuous one) is clearly related to a locative sense (e.g. X. Anab. 2.2.19: δοῦπος ἦν [there was a noise]), and the latter is an extension of the locative use in that something that is there may be abstracted to something that is true (63-65). Coordination of two clauses also is handled well by this theory (e.g. Ar. Knights 1037: ἔστι γυνή, τέξει δὲ λέονθ' [there is a woman, she will give birth to a lion], which thus explains complex clauses like ἔστι γυνὴ ἡ [τις] τέξει λέοντα) (63).

The final major category Ruijgh treats is the locative copula, although he is careful to recognize that much of the differentiation lies in matters of intonation (which are largely unrecoverable) and punctuation. An initial position of the verb seems to emphasize "présentielle" meaning (e.g. Pl. Prot. 315C-D: ἐπεδήμει γὰρ ἄρα καὶ Πρόδικος. . . ., ἦν δὲ ἐν οἰκήματί τινι, ᾧ. . . [P. was returning home. . . . and he was in a certain room]), though Hom. Il. 6.152 (ἔστι πόλις Ἐφύρη μυχῷ Ἄργεος [there is a city, E., in the heart of A.]) has a locative sense even without the parenthetic phrase of location (μυχῷ Ἄργεος), while in 6.153 (ἔνθα δὲ Σίσυφος ἔσκεν [S. lived there]) the locative is necessary to convey the sense of specification. An adjective may be used to specify location as well (e.g. Hom. Il. 23.480: ἵπποι δ' αὐταὶ ἔασι παροίτεραι [the same horses are in the front]). Ruijgh concludes, "le verbe εἶναι lui-même se prête facilement à des emplois étendus, métaphoriques ou abstraits, qui s'expliquent tous à partir de la valeur fondamentalement locale du verbe" (67).

Returning to the suitability of εἰμί for periphrastics, Ruijgh asks why εἰμί is so well suited to copulative usage, answering with an explanation of the nominal clause. (1) εἰμί "est le verbe le moins marqué sémantiquement de la langue" (67). It is thus particularly well-suited for use with the Nominative Case, which is the unmarked Case in Greek (68) (see Bers, *Syntax*, 195; cf. 193-96, where he surveys discussion of nominal versus verbal expressions). (2) Ruijgh argues convincingly that the theory that nominal clauses have ellipsis of the verb "to be" simply is not the case (Robertson, 395; contra Schwyzer, 2.623: "In klassischer und späterer Zeit wurde der reine Nominalsatz als Ellipse empfunden"). (This excepts instances of secondary ellision, e.g. Rom 2:28-29.) Exclamations are not inherent in the nominal clause, yet they can be created apart from a verb (e.g. X. Anab. 4.7.24: θάλαττα θάλαττα), and a simple word such as Σωκράτης can be paraphrased as "There's Socrates," "Socrates is there," "That is Socrates who is before my eyes," or as Σωκράτης ἐστί, further reinforcing the relation between the "présentielle" meaning and copulative use (68-69). Ruijgh disagrees further with Kahn that cumulative Nominatives, e.g. Βασιλεὺς Ἀλέξανδρος, must be seen as elliptical copulative usage, since such a phrase may mean "The King: Alexander," "King Alexander," "The King, Alexander," or even "The king is Alexander" (69-70). (3) Ruijgh posits rightly that the Greek verb is monolectic, in that it includes reference to a subject. This is not a separable morphological bit or a suppressed transformation. The 1st and 2d Persons are more heavily deictically marked than the 3d Person, thus a verb form with a subject expressed is not simply used of a non-emphatic reference but a combination of a nominal phrase and a verbal phrase that becomes a verbal phrase with an external subject. (4) When a form of εἰμί and a Nominative are used, e.g. κύων ἐστί, the resulting phrase is very similar to a simple nominal phrase--it expresses existence and location before the eyes of the speaker, no matter whether the subject is primary or secondary in Kahn's scheme--with the added semantic feature of person designated (71-72).[7]

---

[7]Ruijgh includes an application of his formulation to several troublesome areas, such as use of the demonstrative pronoun, where Ar. Birds 1029 (ἔστιν δ' ὁ μισθὸς οὑτοσί) is understood as "here is the salary" (72). Impersonal subjects pose no problem either, since a locative sense can account for various ambiguities of interpretation, e.g. whether νύξ ἐστί may best be translated "it is night" (74).

Ruijgh concludes, "la valeur fondamentale de ἐσ- en grec ancien est 'être présent, être là' sans spécification ultérieure et qu'il est facile d'expliquer tant diachroniquement que synchroniquement l'emploi copulatif à partir de dette valeur" (78). Thus the lexically vague semantic meaning of εἰμί, revolving around the central meaning of "being present," is apparently ideally suited to serving as an auxiliary in periphrastic constructions.

4. DEFINITION OF PERIPHRASIS IN GREEK. Various treatments of periphrastic constructions show that the criteria for determining the nature and function of periphrastics have not been standardized. (Dover [Review, 87] suggests that periphrastics have been of "marginal interest" for scholars since they do not contribute to what most consider important areas of language.) For example, Turner seems to list virtually every clause in the NT with a form of εἰμί and an anarthrous Participle in agreement as periphrasis (*Syntax*, 87-89, including verbal adjectives; see Regard, *Phrase*, 111ff.; Dietrich, "Verbalaspekt," 206). Aerts on the other hand has a much shorter list since he eliminates those clauses where εἰμί is "used independently (εἶναι = to exist, εἶναι with dative of possession or (in)commodi, weaker εἶναι in a position in the sentence where emphasis is at least suggested--associative emphasis)" or where the "participle is completely adjectivised" (17). These criteria are a step forward, but the practical result is that virtually identical constructions are one time periphrastic, the other not (e.g. X. Anab. 4.7.2; Luke 23:55 [Aerts, *Periphrastica*, 46-47; cf. Burton, 168-69; Doudna, *Greek*, 42-47]), because of the subjectivity of such criteria as the emphasis and independence attributed to εἰμί. Part of Aerts's difficulty also lies in the fact that "periphrastic" is a slippery term, which he, like many others, including Björck and Rydbeck, uses to mean "true" periphrastics, substantival periphrasis, adjectival periphrasis, pseudo-periphrasis with independent εἰμί, as well as an umbrella term for all combinations of εἰμί and a Participle. Even Kahn, though he believes he can account for periphrastics along the lines of transformational grammar, merely transfers the problem to the realm of English translation when he imports the idea of kernel sentences. Some do not seem concerned to define periphrasis at all (so most grammars: e.g. Kühner/Gerth, Stahl, Schwyzer, Mayser, Winer, Moulton, Blass, Robertson, Moule, etc).

On the basis of the discussion above and a survey of many supposed instances of the phenomenon, periphrasis may be defined as follows. (This does not mean to produce definitive criteria, but attempts to establish along formal lines a set of grammatical features evidenced in Greek itself.)

a. A periphrastic construction must contain (1) an aspectually vague auxiliary verb and (2) a Participle in agreement with its referent. The auxiliary verb must be aspectually vague to avoid aspectual conflict with the Participle, otherwise a catenative verbal construction results (see appendix

10B). This means that in Greek εἰμί + Participle, the minimum formal unit of a periphrastic construction, forms a single grammatical unit (complex word), in which the auxiliary establishes attitude, Person, and relation to discourse (εἰμί is unmarked, ἦν is the [+remoteness] form), while the Participle determines verbal aspect (see Regard, *Phrase*, 112-13, who tries to appreciate the role of aspect; contra McGaughy, *Analysis*, 7, who argues that εἰμί "contributes to tense as aspect in periphrastic constructions" (?), cf. 80-82).

b. The Participle not only must be grammatically in suitable agreement with the auxiliary but must be adjacent to it, either before or after (contra Alexander, "Periphrases," esp. 293, 300). Except for connectives, εἰμί and the Participle may be separated only by adjuncts or complements of the Participle as predicate, otherwise the Participle is considered not to form a periphrastic construction. Insertion of elements modifying or specifying the auxiliary (e.g. subject) between the auxiliary and Participle is seen as a formal means of establishing the independence of the auxiliary, whereby a complement or adjunct of the Participle is fully compatible with its verbal use and draws no special attention. One point of potential difficulty occurs when a locative or temporal group falls between the auxiliary and Participle. In these instances it is often difficult to determine whether there is periphrasis. Greek word order is flexible enough that the placement of completive elements must be seen as of particular importance.

c. A common question to ask of periphrastics is whether they can substitute for simple verbal forms. This is difficult to answer, but several approaches can be clarified. It is argued here that periphrasis, in terms akin to Gonda's formulation, is best seen as a construction that draws attention to the Participle and its modifiers, i.e. the predicate plus its complements and adjuncts (this is hinted at by Winer, 438; Jannaris, ¶ 687; Jelf, 2.31, though other grammarians occasionally see emphatic usage). In those places in the verbal paradigm where simple forms have passed out of use (because of unwieldy morphological bulk, such as reduplication, long connecting vowels, secondary endings, large stems, etc.) the periphrastic could be called a substitute form. It is unmarked, since there is no other formal choice available (Gildersleeve [122] notes there is a "certain indifference" in such cases), although choice of verbal aspect is still meaningful. In those cases where a periphrastic can be constructed alongside a simple form, the concept of synonymity becomes very important.

Aerts (*Periphrastica*, esp. 2-3), Björck (*HN ΔΙΔΑΣΚΩΝ*, 9) and others (e.g. Rosén, "'Zweiten' Tempora," 133; Kühner/Gerth, 1.38) state that a periphrastic expresses "an elementary verbal conception, e.g. Koine ἦν διδάσκων = ἐδίδασκεν" (Aerts, 2), implying absolute synonymy. Why would the language support two different forms with identical meanings? It is better to say that the two are synonymous denotationally, in the sense that they may on occasion be compatible with the same context, but not with regard to sense, i.e. they are cognitive synonyms, not absolute. For example, if two people are talking in the room next door, one might turn to a companion and say "That's Dennis and Helen talking," or "Dennis and Helen are talking next door," or any number of other sentences that refer to the same event (the truth-conditions are identical), have generally the same sense, and yet would not be synonymous in all contexts, and in fact can be distinguished in this context (see Ullmann, *Principles*, 108-13; Cruse, *Semantics*, 265ff.). The same is true of periphrastics in Greek. In answer to the question of whether they serve as substitutes for simple forms, they do often occur in similar contexts, though the periphrastic itself contributes a certain marked semantic meaning on the basis of its construction.

d. Regarding delimitation of periphrasis on the basis of adjectivisation of the Participle, such a distinction must be dismissed. Depending upon Alexander ("Periphrases," 295), and followed by many other grammarians, like Aerts and Blass/Debrunner, Björck has made the most detailed case for adjectivised Participles not constituting true periphrastics. He argues that certain impersonal, durative verbs in the Present Participle form have lost their emphasis on the kind of action and cannot be used as substitutes for the simple form of the verb without an alteration of the sense (*HN ΔΙΔΑΣΚΩΝ* , 84-35), though there might be occasion when such a Participle will have to take the place of a non-existent simple form (30-31). The impersonal form, with the adjectivised Participle (36), emphasizes a state by asserting a quality of the subject, with εἰμί as a copulative, and any verbal quality is merely incidental (28-29). Two criteria used for determination of this phenomenon are the usual lack of attachments of objects (20) and parallel use with true adjectives (32).

Björck (*HN ΔΙΔΑΣΚΩΝ*, 17-18) and Aerts (*Periphrastica*, 12-13) appreciate the difficulty of determining when a Participle has become adjectivised. For example, Aerts cites the English sentences "the results are disappointing" and "he is lazy and disappointing to his parents"; "her manner of dress is startling" and "her dress is startling because of....."; and "he is living/dying" (13). These show that translation into English (or German) does not provide a suitable criterion for determining adjectivisation, since similar phenomena appear equally problematic in English. Neither does parallel use of the Participle with 'true' adjectives seem helpful. A speaker may refer to a "seeing man" or a "blind man" without being able to determine whether "seeing" is adjectivised (cf. "he is seeing her off on the train"). In Greek the same occurs, as Björck notes (25). In Acts 9:9, the author says Saul ἦν ἡμέρας τρεῖς μὴ βλέπων, καὶ οὐκ ἔφαγεν οὐδὲ ἔπιεν (was not seeing for three days, and he did not eat or drink). Rather than the Participle being adjectivised, it seems that the periphrastic ἦν . . . βλέπων here 'substitutes' for the Imperfect ἔβλεπε in marked contrast to the two Aorists (cf. Ar. Plut. 15: οἱ γὰρ βλέποντες τοῖς τυφλοῖς ἡγούμεθα [for we who are seeing are leading the blind]).

Björck's reasoning that impersonal intransitive verbs tend toward adjectivisation does not seem to exclude their asserting aspectual value, however. For example, Matt 3:15, οὕτως γὰρ πρέπον ἐστὶν ἡμῖν πληρῶσαι πᾶσαν δικαιοσύνην, shows how translation can colour interpretation. If the sentence is translated as "thus it is fitting for you to fulfil every righteous thing" the Participle may seem wholly adjectival, but if it is glossed as "it is becoming to/suiting us," or the like, the periphrastic structure is emphasized (cf. Lys. 19.59: νῦν δὲ πρέπον ἐστὶ καὶ ὑμᾶς ἀκοῦσαί μου [now it is suiting you to hear me]. Björck, *HN ΔΙΔΑΣΚΩΝ*, 21).

Gildersleeve (124, 122, 81-82), while recognizing the tendency for adjectivisation of Participles, still treats them as suitable for periphrastic constructions, since he recognizes that the Participle, especially the Perfect Participle, asserts a verbal aspect that is in some ways inherently 'adjectival' in character. One of many possible functions of the Participle is as a modifier (see chapt. 8). The argument for rejecting the distinction between adjectival Participles and periphrasis is compelling. It seems rather that while a Participle may function like an adjective, in periphrasis (as elsewhere) it still asserts its verbal aspect.

5.   FORMAL CATEGORIES OF PERIPHRASIS IN NT GREEK. As Gildersleeve says, "The Greek language has ample facilities for a large number of periphrastic tenses" (122). The various periphrastic forms available in NT Greek are now categorized according to verbal aspect of the Participle and form of the auxiliary. The classification focuses upon periphrastics according to the previously established formal criteria, though comparison with other constructions is made as well (cf. Turner, *Syntax*, 87-89, for a reasonably complete list, though with errors). The translations provided are to be treated as glosses to bring out the semantic and pragmatic values of a particular usage. The danger of interpretation through translation, especially with a dead language, has been emphasized before, but it is still wise to remember that an attempt must be made to treat the Greek language in terms of its own verbal network, and not according to English translation.

1. Present Participle

a. [-remoteness] form of εἰμί + Present Participle

The use of εἰμί + Present Participle is acknowledged by virtually all grammarians as present in ancient Greek from the classical period through to the hellenistic (e.g. Gildersleeve, 81-82). Though it does not occur frequently in Homer,[8] the tragedians show increased usage,[9] which continued through the historians and beyond.[10] In the NT several examples are worth noting.

Matt 1:23; Mark 5:41; 15:22, 34; Acts 4:36: ὅ ἐστιν μεθερμηνευόμενον (which is [being] translated); cf. John 9:7. The timeless use of εἰμί with the Participle,[11] probably emphasizing the translated words, appears with OT phrases in Matthew (Isa 8:8) and Mark 15:34 (Ps 22:1); with

---

[8]Possibly except for Hom. Od. 4.807 (οὐ μὲν γάρ τι θεοῖς ἀλιτήμενός ἐστι [for he is not sinning in any way in relation to the gods]) if the Participle from ἀλιταίνω is not an Aorist (see Aerts, *Periphrastica*, 14) and Il. 2.295 (ἡμῖν δ᾽ εἴνατός ἐστι περιτροπέων ἐνιαυτός [for us the ninth year is changing]) (Dietrich, "Verbalaspekt," 202).

[9]E.g. S. Aj. 1320: οὐ γὰρ κλύοντές ἐσμεν αἰσχίστους λόγους . . .; (are/were we not hearing shameful words . . .?); Phil. 419-20: ἀλλὰ καὶ μέγα / θάλλοντές εἰσι νῦν ἐν Ἀργείων στρατῷ (but indeed great men are flourishing now in the army of the A.); E. Hec. 668: δέσποιν᾽, ὄλωλας οὐκέτ᾽ εἶ βλέπουσα φῶς (woman, you are destroyed, you are no longer seeing light/are no longer alive).

[10]E.g. Hdt. 3.133.2: δεήσεσθαι δὲ οὐδενὸς τῶν ὅσα ἐς αἰσχύνην ἐστὶ φέροντα (to be bound by none of the things which are bringing into shame); 2.99.1: μέχρι μὲν τούτου ὄψις τε ἐμὴ καὶ γνώμη καὶ ἱστορίη ταῦτα λέγουσά ἐστι (thus far my observation, knowledge and history, they are speaking. . . .); Th. 1.38.4: εἰ τοῖς πλέοσιν ἀρέσκοντές ἐσμεν (we are pleased with most); X. Anab. 4.1.3: καὶ τοῦ Εὐφράτου δὲ τὰς πηγὰς ἐλέγετο οὐ πρόσω τοῦ Τίγρητος εἶναι, καὶ ἔστιν οὕτως ἔχον (and it is said the source of the E. is not far from the T., and it is indeed thus [possessing such]); 3.3.2: καὶ ἐνθάδε δ᾽ εἰμὶ σὺν πολλῷ φόβῳ διάγων (and here I am living with great fear). See also Pl. Euth. 10B: οὐκ ἄρα διότι ὁρώμενόν γέ ἐστιν, διὰ τοῦτο ὁρᾶται (wherefore it is not that a thing exists as being seen, because it is being seen) (Gildersleeve [81] notes that "here the difference between predication and action is insisted on"); Ar. Eccl. 1093-94: ἐγγὺς ἤδη τῆς θύρας / ἑλκόμενός εἰμ᾽ (I am already near wounding the door); cf. Frogs 36: βαδίζων εἰμί (I am striking) (Gildersleeve ["Mention," 22 (1902) 110] objects to this example, citing Pl. Meno 84A as well); P.Hamb. 27.18 (250-49 B.C.): ἐνοχλούμενος πρὸς τῶι σπόρωι εἰμί (I am involved in sowing). See esp. Gonda, "Remark"; Aerts, *Periphrastica*, 5-26; Gildersleeve, 81-82, for examples.

[11]McNeile (*Matthew*, 10) claims that the earliest use of the Participle form is the prologue to Ben Sira.

Aramaic phrases in Mark 5:41; 15:22; and with a proper name in Acts 4:36 (contra Aerts, *Periphrastica*, 72, who claims these are either strictly adjectival or display independent use of εἰμί; cf. Malalas 26.2: Πάρθοι, ὅ ἐστιν ἑρμηνευόμενον Περσικῇ διαλέκτῳ Σκύθαι [Aerts, 73]; and Moule, 17, who translates: "which means [lit. is, when said or translated] Skull Place. . ."). Matt 27:33 (ὅ ἐστιν Κρανίου Τόπος λεγόμενος) is very similar (cf. Matt 15:22) except that the complement of the Participle falls between the auxiliary and the Participle. (Cf. Paus. 2.3.9: ἔπη δὲ ἔστιν ἐν Ἕλλησι Ναυπάκτια ὀνομαζόμενα [it is called N. in Greek].)

Matt 3:15; 1 Cor 11:13. Matthew says, οὕτως γὰρ πρέπον ἐστὶν ἡμῖν πληρῶσαι πᾶσαν δικαιοσύνην (for thus it is becoming to us to fulfil all righteousness). Though the Participle is often seen as adjectivised on the basis of its impersonal usage, this does not necessarily minimize its aspectual nature (see above). In this case it conveys the sense of John being in progress performing a fitting act (cf. Isoc. Letter 5.3). 1 Cor 11:13 makes this aspectual emphasis clear when Paul asks, πρέπον ἐστὶν γυναῖκα ἀκατακάλυπτον τῷ θεῷ προσεύχεσθαι; (is it fitting for a woman to pray to God uncovered?). (Contra Aerts, *Periphrastica*, 53, who calls them "pseudo-periphrasis.") Cf. Lys. 19.59; Pl. Lach. 188D; P.Oxy. 1121.11 (A.D. 295), where the aspectual nature of πρέποντα is even clearer. πρέπω in Greek displays a full range of Present and Aorist forms, but not a Perfect. Though it is not aspectually vague, the fact that its use is stereotyped may reduce its semantic force. See also E. Hec. 1179: ἡ νῦν λέγων ἔστιν τις (or now someone is speaking), another example occasionally cited as having an adjectivised Participle.

Acts 5:25: οἱ ἄνδρες . . . εἰσὶν ἐν τῷ ἱερῷ ἑστῶτες καὶ διδάσκοντες τὸν λαόν. This periphrasis is ambiguous, since it may be interpreted either with ἐν τῷ ἱερῷ modifying εἰσίν, in which case "the men are there in the temple, standing and teaching" (cf. Björck, *HN ΔΙΔΑΣΚΩΝ*, 51), or as is more likely, with the locative group completing the Perfect Participle, "the men are standing in the temple and teaching the people" (cf. Regard, *Phrase*, 119). The parallelism of the Perfect (ἑστῶτες) and Present (διδάσκοντες) Participles displays a well-judged use of verbal aspect, since the first gives the author's view of the apostles' condition or state, while the second the progress they are making.

Gal 4:24: ἅτινά ἐστιν ἀλληγορούμενα (such things are being expressed allegorically). This passage more than most shows the problem of grammatical evaluation by translational equivalent, since the common rendering reads "these are allegorical" (Aerts [*Periphrastica*, 72] falls victim here, as do most commentators, such as Burton, *Galatians*, 253). The imperfective aspect is wholly appropriate, since although Paul has made his contrast between Hagar and Sarah his allegory is not complete: he has now to make explicit the allegorical implications regarding covenant.

Col 2:5: ἀλλὰ τῷ πνεύματι σὺν ἡμῖν εἰμι χαίρων καὶ βλέπων ὑμῶν τὴν τάξιν καὶ τὸ στερέωμα τῆς εἰς Χριστὸν πίστεως ὑμῶν. UBS³, NA²⁶, and Souter all place a comma after εἰμι, thus indicating a reading such as, "but I am with you in the spirit, rejoicing and seeing. . . ." This reading has strong force on the basis of parallelism with the immediately preceding clause (so most commentators: e.g. O'Brien, *Colossians*, 73, 75). But another possibility is to omit the comma and thus create two periphrastics, to be rendered, "but in spirit (modifying either εἰμι or χαίρων) I am rejoicing with you and seeing your order/discipline and the steadfastness of your faith in Christ." This transfers the emphasis away from the aspectually vague verbs describing Paul's whereabouts to his strong feelings for the Colossians.

Col 3:1: οὗ ὁ Χριστός ἐστιν ἐν δεξιᾷ τοῦ θεοῦ καθήμενος. This clause is ambiguous, since the locative group either may modify the auxiliary and be rendered, "where Christ, seated, is at the right hand of God," with the Participle modifying Christ (cf. O'Brien, *Colossians*, 161-62; Regard, *Phrase*, 121), or may complete the Participle, thus forming a periphrastic: "where Christ is sitting at the right hand of God." (Lohse [*Colossians*, 132] suggests: "where Christ is, sitting at the right hand of God," possibly reflecting Ps 110:1.) In the first rendering a point of continuity is formed around Christ as the one raised and now above, whereas the periphrastic emphasizes Christ as the one sitting at God's right hand. (Cf. E. Or. 60-61: ἔστιν δ' ἔσω / κλαίουσ' ἀδελφήν [she is-inside-weeping her sister]; Paus. 1.3.1: πρώτη δέ ἐστιν ἐν δεξιᾷ καλουμένη στοᾷ βασίλειος [first on the right is called the Royal porch (?)]; cf. 2.3.4.)

Jas 1:17: πᾶσα δόσις ἀγαθὴ καὶ πᾶν δώρημα τέλειον ἄνωθέν ἐστιν καταβαῖνον ἀπὸ τοῦ πατρὸς τῶν φώτων (every good gift and every mature gift is descending from above from the father of lights). Though Souter and UBS³ place a comma after ἐστιν (Mussner [*Jakobusbrief*, 90-91] and Davids [*James*, 86] discount periphrasis), it is entirely possible that the comma should be omitted (see NA²⁶) to form a periphrastic (Dibelius, *James*, 100). The double locative reference, while it may seem to support the first reading (Aerts [*Periphrastica*, 70] calls it "an ugly pleonasm" and opts for a non-periphrastic construction; contra Regard, *Phrase*, 118-19), may just as likely provide a greater emphasis on the point of origin of the descending gift in keeping with a timeless use of the auxiliary (Davids, 86) and emphasis on the Participle in the periphrastic (cf. Jas 3:15, where the intervening subject makes periphrasis highly unlikely).

2 Pet 3:7: οἱ δὲ νῦν οὐρανοὶ καὶ ἡ γῆ τῷ αὐτῷ λόγῳ τεθησαυρισμένοι εἰσὶν πυρὶ τηρούμενοι εἰς ἡμέραν κρίσεως. . .[12] (the present heaven and earth by the same word are in a state of having stored up fire [and] are in the process of keeping it for the day of judgment). As noted above, the rationale for use of Perfect and Present Participles can often be discerned in context. Responding to criticism about the lord's coming, Peter states that the heavens and earth were formed by the word of God (v 5). The Perfect Participle looks to the state of the world because of God's creative act, implying that fire is a part of its condition or character (see Bauckham, *Jude*, 299-301, who claims the Perfect Participle is surprising here), while the Present Participle looks to its activity, preparing for judgment.

b. [+remoteness] form of εἰμί + Present Participle

Björck argues that the narrative form of εἰμί + Present Participle forms what he calls a "progressive" periphrastic, claiming that it not only serves as a durative form but as a backdrop for positing a punctual event (*HN ΔΙΔΑΣΚΩΝ*, esp. 41-42; he finds copula-Participle-adjunct the normal word order, but his definition of periphrasis does not follow my work). Whereas Björck resists arguing for Semitic influence on the basis that Luke is the main user of this form when he is not following Mark (68), Aerts reassesses the evidence. Most grammarians have suggested at the least an Aramaic background to the phrase on the basis of the posited frequency of the periphrastic where an underlying Aramaic source may be suggested (e.g. Blass, 202-03; Blass/Debrunner, ¶ 353[1]; Thumb, *Sprache*, 132; Moulton, 226-27; Moulton/Howard, 451-52; Abel, 266-68; Moule, 16). Aerts himself discounts this, especially on the basis of Luke's usage even in Acts 16ff. and its widespread use in the LXX (*Periphrastica*, 61-62; 63-64, Jonah 1:10; 2 Kgdms 3:6), arguing instead for a more general Semitic influence (see 56-58, 60ff.). Much of Aerts's argument grows out of his conviction that the "progressive" periphrastic is virtually non-existent in classical Greek (52-53). This does not seem to be the case, however (Gonda, "Remark," 105-06; cf. Dietrich, "Verbalaspekt," 200-01, who notes the importance of clarifying questions of Semitic influence on Greek). Aerts has an over-restrictive definition of what constitutes a periphrastic construction in this instance and makes a false opposition (unsupportable formally and only possible lexically) between situation-fixing and progressive periphrasis, both predicated on what seems to be translation of the construction. [+remoteness] εἰμί + Present Participle is clearly found in Homeric and classical Greek (see Kühner/Gerth, 1.38-39; followed by Rydbeck, "Bemerkungen," 200; Moulton, 226, who is cautious; Karleen, *Syntax*, 124; Dietrich, 202-03, for examples, though not all examples listed by these authors qualify here).

Hom. Od. 10.156; 12.368: ἀλλ᾽ ὅτε δὴ σχεδὸν ἦα κιὼν νεὸς ἀμφιελίσσης (but when I was in progress going near a rowing ship).

Hdt. 8.137.4: ἐνθαῦτα ὁ βασιλεὺς τοῦ μισθοῦ πέρι ἀκούσας, ἦν γὰρ κατὰ τὴν καπνοδόκην ἐς τὸν οἶκον ἐσέχων ὁ ἥλιος, εἶπε. . . . (the king having heard concerning the payment, for (while) the sun was coming through the smoke-hole into the house, said. . .). de Sélincourt (*Herodotus*, 571) translates "was shining," while Aerts (*Periphrastica*, 53) "fell" (see

---

[12] I omit the comma after πυρί in UBS³, following NA²⁶.

Rydbeck, "Bemerkungen," 192-94). Hdt. 2.134.2: κατὰ Ἄμασιν βασιλεύοντα ἦν ἀκμάζουσα Ῥοδῶπις (R. was flourishing while A. was ruling); cf. 3.57.1 with simple form (Gonda, "Remark," 98); 7.179: ἔνθα ἦσαν προφυλάσσουσαι νέες τρεῖς Ἑλληνίδες (three Greek ships were standing guard here); 8.136.1: Μαρδόνιος δὲ ἐπιλεξάμενος ὅ τι δὴ λέγοντα ἦν τὰ χρηστήρια. . . (M., having considered what the oracles were saying) (Aerts [52] translates this "taking into consideration what the oracles meant," obscuring the conscious contrast of verbal aspect). Th. 7.50.4: καὶ ὁ Νικίας (ἦν γάρ τι καὶ ἄγαν θειασμῷ τε καὶ τῷ τοιούτῳ προσκείμενος) οὐδ' ἂν διαβουλεύσασθαι ἔτι ἔφη. . . (and N. [for he was inclining himself too much to divination and such] was still refusing to deliberate. . .); 3.2.2: καὶ ἃ μεταπεμπόμενοι ἦσαν (which were being sent for); X. Anab. 4.5.15: καὶ ἐτετήκει διὰ κρήνην τινὰ ἣ πλησίον ἦν ἀτμίζουσα ἐν νάπῃ (and it [the snow] stood melted because of a certain spring which was steaming in a glen nearby); X. Hell. 3.5.20: ὡς δὲ ἄνω ἤδη ἦσαν διώκοντες καὶ δυσχωρία τε καὶ στενοπορία (as previously they were pursuing already both the difficult ground and the narrow passes); S. Trach. 22-23: ἀλλ' ὅστις ἦν / θακῶν ἀταρβὴς τῆς θέας (but whoever was sitting fearless of the sight); E. Iph. Taur. 1368: πυγμαὶ δ' ἦσαν ἐγκροτούμεναι (blows were being struck); Isoc. 5.110: ἥ περ ἦν προσήκουσα (Aorist) μὲν καὶ πρέπουσα τοῖς προειρημένοις, τὸν δὲ καιρὸν ἔχουσα μάλιστα σύμμετρον τοῖς νῦν λεγομένοις (which was heard and fitting to the things spoken before, and having the length proportionate to the things being spoken currently).

Several instances in the NT may be cited.[13]

Matt 7:29[14] = Mark 1:22[15] = Luke 4:31; 5:17; 13:10; 19:47: ἦν διδάσκων (he was teaching); cf. Luke 4:44: ἦν κηρύσσων (he was preaching). The classic example of this periphrastic construction, and the only place where both Matthew and Luke retain a Markan periphrastic (C. Turner, "Usage," 28 [1957] 349), has provoked extended discussion by Björck (HN ΔΙΔΑΣΚΩΝ, esp. 44-45) and other grammarians and commentators. Though it often occurs in a context with other narrative imperfective verbs (cf. Matt 7:20; Mark 1:21-22; Luke 4:32; 19:47), it serves to emphasize the teaching function of Jesus (cf. Fitzmyer, Luke, 1.544, 580; contra Hartman, Constructions, 26), hence use of the periphrastic to open (Luke 4:31; 5:17; 13:10; 19:47[?]) and close (Matt 7:29) pericope, as well as elicit a sense of amazement in Matt 7:29 and Mark 1:22. (Aerts [Periphrastica, 53 n. 1] calls use in Luke 5:17 "situation-fixing," which resembles an aspectual analysis, as well as "adjectival"; contra Moulton, 227, on Matt 7:29.)

Matt 24:38: ὡς γὰρ ἦσαν ἐν ταῖς ἡμέραις [ἐκείναις] ταῖς πρὸ τοῦ κατακλυσμοῦ τρώγοντες και πίνοντες, γαμοῦντες καὶ γαμίζοντες. This sentence may be construed as periphrastic, with the temporal group completing the Participles (as they were eating and drinking in the days before the flood) or, more likely, the temporal group emphasizes the independent

---

[13]N. Turner (Syntax, 88) is misleading in his emphasis upon Mark's usage, while C. Turner's theory ("Usage," 28 [1957] 351) that the Markan periphrastic with narrative auxiliary is used "to give the continuous sense of the imperfect" reveals a misconception of the aspect of the Imperfect, as well as failure to note the contexts in which the periphrastic occurs. Pryke (Style, 103-06) notes that Luke has a higher percentage of periphrastics than Mark and that they are to be regarded as nothing (?) more than a sign of non-literary Greek in an author influenced by the LXX, not as Semitisms; contra Doudna, Greek, 110. Black (Approach, 83) cites Luke 5:17 as translation of an Aramaic circumstantial Participle; contra Fitzmyer, Luke, 1.122. See also Taylor, Mark, 172-73, cf. 45, 62-63, on Semitic influence.

[14]The following phrase (ὡς ἐξουσίαν ἔχων) is probably best seen as parallel to ὡς οἱ γραμματεῖς αὐτῶν, despite lack of an article.

[15]Mark 1:39 has ἦν instead of ἦλθεν in A C D K f¹ f¹³ etc., with the accepted reading (ἦλθεν κηρύσσων) receiving a C rating in UBS³. Pryke (Style, 67-68) draws attention to the following ἐκβάλλων (v 39), παρακαλῶν, γονυπετῶν, and λέγων (v 40).

existential use of ἦσαν, with the Participles parallel (in the days before the flood they were there, eating and drinking. . .).

Mark 4:38: καὶ αὐτὸς ἦν ἐν τῇ πρύμνῃ ἐπὶ τὸ προσκεφάλαιον καθεύδων. This sentence may be periphrastic (he was sleeping in the stern upon the cushion [so Cranfield, *Mark*, 173; Taylor, *Mark*, 275]) or, more likely, ἦν is strictly locative (he was in the stern--upon the cushion--sleeping), reinforced by the emphatic personal pronoun. (Aerts [*Periphrastica*, 53] views this as an adjectival Participle. He also notes, "It is striking that when εἶναι is linked with an adjective of place, the latter comes between the form of εἰμί and the participle.")

Mark 9:4: καὶ ἦσαν συλλαλοῦντες τῷ Ἰησοῦ (and they were speaking with Jesus). In each of the Synoptic Gospels the transfiguration plays a crucial role in making Jesus known to his disciples. Though Matt 17:3 (Participle) and Luke 9:30 (Imperfect) do not use periphrastic constructions, the periphrasis in Mark seems well-suited to his narrative. After Jesus' recorded instruction about his death and resurrection (Mark 8:31ff.), he takes Peter, James and John up into the mountains, where he is transformed and is seen with Elias and Moses. The narrator says, in fact, they were *speaking with Jesus* (contra Hartman, *Constructions*, 23). This, the turning point of the story, prompts Peter's desire to build three tents. (Cf. Plb. 22.17.4: οἵπερ ἦσαν ἔτι διασῳζόμενοι τῶν δυναστῶν [who of the kings were still preserved].)

Mark 10:32: ἦσαν δὲ ἐν τῇ ὁδῷ ἀναβαίνοντες εἰς Ἰεροσόλυμα, καὶ ἦν προάγων αὐτοὺς ὁ Ἰησοῦς (they were travelling on the road to J. and Jesus was going before them). Though the first clause may not be periphrastic, position at the beginning of the pericope and parallel use with the second periphrastic and the subsequent Imperfect verbs point to an initial periphrastic construction (see Taylor, *Mark*, 437). Two points are made in this context: travel up to Jerusalem is being stressed (cf. v 33) and Jesus' role as literal and symbolic leader is emphasized (cf. v 32c, d, where the disciples are said to be amazed and fearful as they follow Jesus). See also Luke 9:53: τὸ πρόσωπον αὐτοῦ ἦν πορευόμενον εἰς Ἰερουσαλήμ. The Samaritans reject Jesus because, literally, his face was going toward Jerusalem (Marshall [*Luke*, 406] calls this Semitic; cf. Hdt 6.103.4: ὁ . . . πρεσβύτερος . . . Στησαγόρης ἦν τηνικαῦτα παρὰ τῷ πάτρῳ Μιλτιάδῃ τρεφόμενος ἐν τῇ Χερσονήσῳ [the elder son S. was being reared at this time in C. with his uncle M.]).

Mark 14:54: καὶ ἦν συγκαθήμενος μετὰ τῶν ὑπηρετῶν καὶ θερμαινόνεμος πρὸς τὸ φῶς (he was sitting together with the servants and warming himself at the fire). Though Matthew (26:58) and Luke (22:55) are content to use the simple Imperfect, ἐκάθητο (the only time they make the same change in Mark's periphrastic [so Turner, "Usage," 28 (1957) 350]), Mark uses the marked periphrastic to refer to Peter's activity in the courtyard of the chief priest: after he followed from a distance (Aorist), Peter . . . . John, by contrast, while referring to Peter standing and warming himself, uses existential ἦν (18:18).

Luke 1:22: καὶ αὐτὸς ἦν διανεύων αὐτοῖς (and he was making signs to them). When Zacharias came from the temple, he was unable to speak (Imperfect) and the people recognized that he had seen (Perfect) a vision, hence his signalling. The use of the tenses seems oriented to Zacharias's transformation, especially seen in the fact that he had to resort to sign language while remaining dumb (Imperfect).

Luke 2:51: καὶ ἦν ὑποτασσόμενος αὐτοῖς (and he was being obedient to them). This story of Jesus' growing self-consciousness is fraught with Christological difficulties. Plummer says, "this sums up the condition of the Messiah during the next seventeen years. The analytical tense gives prominence to the continuance of the subjection" (*Luke*, 78; cf. Fitzmyer, *Luke*, 1.445). This may be true, but the imperfective aspect in v 51 seems only to emphasize that once Jesus went back to Nazareth with his parents (two less heavily marked Aorist verbs), he was being obedient to them (so Regard, *Phrase*, 133; contra Aerts, *Periphrastica*, 54, who sees an adjectival Participle. Zerwick [360] claims the Participle is more effective than an adjective phrase like ἦν ὑπήκοος).

Luke 4:20: καὶ πάντων οἱ ὀφθαλμοὶ ἐν τῇ συναγωγῇ ἦσαν ἀτενίζοντες αὐτῷ (and the eyes of everyone in the synagogue were focusing on him). This scene contrasts Jesus' pronouncement of his mission and the crowd's response to him (see v 29). After Jesus entered and read, he closed the book and sat down (two Aorists). The periphrastic introduces the expectant people (Fitzmyer, *Luke*, 1.533), apparently anticipating their heated response to his words. Acts 1:10 uses a similar construction, but with the Participle preceding the auxiliary: ὡς ἀτενίζοντες ἦσαν εἰς τὸν οὐρανόν (as they were looking into heaven), with Bruce (*Acts*, 71) noting the classical origins of this periphrastic (cf. Haenchen, *Acts*, 149 n. 7, who follows Björck; see Rydbeck, "Bemerkungen," 195, citing examples from Hippocrates).

Luke 5:29: οἳ ἦσαν μετ᾽ αὐτῶν κατακείμενοι. Although this clause is roughly parallel with the clause above (ἦν ὄχλος πολὺς τελωνῶν κτλ.) and thus possibly not periphrastic (who were there with them, reclining), the accompaniment clause seems more likely to modify the Participle (who were reclining with them [Fitzmyer, *Luke*, 1.591]), stressing the reclining together of the tax-collectors and others, in violation of Pharisaic standards of cleanliness (cf. Matt 9:10 = Mark 2:15). (Cf. D.S. 14.48.2: ἡ πόλις ἦν ἐπί τινος νήσου κειμένη [the city was situated upon a certain island].)

Luke 15:1: ἦσαν δὲ αὐτῷ ἐγγίζοντες πάντες οἱ τελῶναι καὶ οἱ ἁμαρτωλοὶ ἀκούειν αὐτοῦ (the tax collectors and sinners were drawing near to him to hear him). Whether this refers to a single occasion or an on-going practice by the sinners (cf. Marshall, *Luke*, 1.599; Plummer, *Luke*, 367-68), it elicits a complaint from the Pharisees and scribes. Luke uses the marked periphrastic to open the pericope and emphasize the setting for the parable of the lost sheep (contra Sparks, "Semitisms . . . Gospel," 131, who calls this periphrastic "characteristically Aramaic").

Luke 24:53: καὶ ἦσαν διὰ παντὸς ἐν τῷ ἱερῷ εὐλογοῦντες[16] τὸν θεόν. Though the locative and temporal groups may modify ἦσαν (they were always in the temple, blessing God), placement at the end of the pericope as well as the entire book, and apparent emphasis on their ongoing activity (cf. v 52 with Aorist verbs referring to the return to Jerusalem), make a periphrastic construction likely (they were always blessing God in the temple).

John 13:23: ἦν ἀνακείμενος εἷς ἐκ τῶν μαθητῶν αὐτοῦ ἐν τῷ κόλπῳ τοῦ Ἰησοῦ (one of his disciples was lying in the bosom of Jesus). It is perhaps significant that the only periphrastic of this type in John's Gospel[17] is used to refer to the position in which the beloved disciple was situated when he asked Jesus about his betrayer.

Acts 1:14: οὗτοι πάντες ἦσαν προσκαρτεροῦντες ὁμοθυμαδὸν τῇ προσευχῇ (they all were devoting themselves to prayer with one accord). The pericope closes with a periphrastic, not specifying whether this is a regular routine or a single occasion, though the former is hinted at by the narrative (v 15). The author uses the marked construction to draw attention to the unity of purpose found in the post-ascension group. Cf. Acts 2:42 (ἦσαν δὲ προσκαρτεροῦντες τῇ διδαχῇ τῶν ἀποστόλων καὶ τῇ κοινωνίᾳ [they were devoting themselves to the teaching of the apostles and fellowship]), which periphrastic serves an identical function.

Acts 8:1: Σαῦλος δὲ ἦν συνευδοκῶν τῇ ἀναιρέσει αὐτοῦ (S. was agreeing with his death). This tactfully placed clause brings the Stephen story to a close while introducing a new character into the drama of the early church. The periphrastic construction pushes the narrative forward, foreshadowing the importance of this new figure. In Acts 22:20 (καὶ αὐτὸς ἤμην

---

[16]Regardless of whether εὐλογοῦντες (p[75] א B C* L) or αἰνοῦντες (D) is the correct reading (both is surely a conflation), the construction remains the same; see Metzger, *Commentary*, 190-91.

[17]All the other possible periphrastic constructions in John place the subject between the auxiliary and the Participle: e.g. 1:9, 28; 2:6; 3:23; 5:5; 10:40; 18:18, 25, 30. See Bultmann, *John*, 481 n. 5; 93 n. 2. Virtually all of these examples are locative or existential use of εἰμί + modifying Participle on the basis of not only syntactical order but other clear indicators (e.g. ὅπου, ἐκεῖ, reference to place, etc.) (Dover [Review, 87] recognizes the plausibility of this explanation for John 3:23; 10:40). John 1:9 is the only example that presents potential problems, since there are no explicit existential or locative elements in support of the intervening subject-isolating use of ἦν. Several other considerations might be noted, however: locative use of ἦν in v 10 and fronting of ἦν in support of locative/existential use, according to Ruijgh. Incidentally this instance is not cited as periphrastic in Dietrich's full list of examples from the NT (even though he lists all the others listed above in this note), nor in Aerts's treatment.

ἐφεστὼς καὶ συνευδοκῶν καὶ φυλάσσων τὰ ἱμάτια [I myself was standing by and approving and watching the coats]) Paul recounts, using marked periphrastics (cf. Björck, *HN ΔΙΔΑΣΚΩΝ*, 45; Haenchen, *Acts*, 627), his involvement in the stoning of Stephen, supplementing it with a more detailed, interwoven account using three periphrastic Participles sharing the same auxiliary. The Perfect Participle seems to establish Paul's state or condition as one of being physically present (contra Regard, *Phrase*, 144, who claims it equals the Present Participle), while the two Present Participles explore his attitude and involvement. And in Acts 22:19 (ἐγὼ ἤμην φυλακίζων καὶ δέρων κατὰ τὰς συναγωγὰς τοὺς πιστεύοντας ἐπὶ σέ [I was imprisoning and beating in every synagogue those who were believing in you]) Paul speaks animatedly of his pre-conversion activities. (Bruce [*Acts*, 405] claims that since Acts 22:19, 20 are "in a speech translated from Aram. we may reasonably regard the periphrasis as an Aramaism." This does not necessarily follow.)

Acts 8:13: καὶ βαπτισθεὶς ἦν προσκαρτερῶν τῷ Φιλίππῳ. This sentence has managed to avoid commentary by any of the major NT grammars, though it potentially presents problems: is it a periphrastic with the Aorist Participle or the Present Participle, or possibly both? The results would vary the emphasis: "and he was baptized, devoting himself to P."; "having been baptized, he was devoting . . ."; or "he was baptized and devoting himself to P." The fact that this kind of construction only appears twice in the NT (see Acts 20:13 below) seems to argue against two periphrastics, and the infrequency of Aorist periphrastics argues against the first option, while the number of narrative periphrastics with the Present Participle in Acts argues strongly for its use here. In any case, the meaning seems clear: Simon believed, was baptized, and was devoting himself to Philip.

Acts 20:13: οὕτως γὰρ διατεταγμένος ἦν μέλλων αὐτὸς πεζεύειν. This is the second passage which has potential for confusion because of two Participles flanking a single auxiliary. The D codex includes ὡς before μέλλων (Blass/Debrunner, ¶ 425[3]), and thus allows for understanding the Perfect Middle Participle to be periphrastic followed by the adjunctive Participle (thus he had arranged it, since he was going to travel by foot), though this is certainly not the only interpretation. (A similar construction appears in Plb. 21.29.11: ἄλλως δὲ πρᾶξιν ἔχων νεανικὴν ἦν μάλιστα παρὰ τῷ στρατηγῷ πιστευόμενος. Should it be interpreted as a periphrastic with adjunctive Participle [above all he was performing youthful deeds, especially since he was being trusted by the consul] or two periphrastics [above all he was performing youthful deeds and being especially trusted by the consul]?)

Acts 8:28: ἦν τε ὑποστρέφων καὶ καθήμενος ἐπὶ τοῦ ἅρματος (he was returning and sitting in his chariot). It is difficult to understand the marked function of the periphrastic in comparison with v 28c, which uses an Imperfect (ἀνεγίνωσκεν) to introduce Isaiah, a major focus of the section. Haenchen, following Björck, claims the first periphrastic is "A piece of general scene-setting," against which "background the special feature that 'he was reading' stands out" (*Acts*, 311 n. 1). Another explanation lies in the transition from the Eunuch's stated purpose in going to Jerusalem (v 27) to the fact that he is now returning, with the author not referring to events in Jerusalem, itself. A subtle irony is contained in the fact that it is while returning through a desert place (biblical history is full of significant desert experiences) that he is confronted by God's message.

Acts 9:28: καὶ ἦν μετ᾽ αὐτῶν εἰσπορευόμενος καὶ ἐκπορευόμενος εἰς Ἰερουσαλήμ, παρρησιαζόμενος ἐν τῷ ὀνόματι τοῦ κυρίου. Two questions are to be asked of this verse: whether the prepositional group modifies ἦν (he was with them, going in and out of J.) or completes the Participles and thus is periphrastic (he was going in and out of J. with them) (Haenchen [*Acts*, 332] claims a durative sense, but it seems rather to be iterative); and whether παρρησιαζόμενος ἐν τῷ ὀνόματι τοῦ κυρίου (speaking boldly in the name of the lord) constitutes an independent or periphrastic use of the Participle. In the flow of the discourse (vv 26ff.) it seems likely that v 28 has two periphrastic constructions built around the single ἦν, serving as a marked peroration of Paul and the apostles' activities in Jerusalem, though the lack of a connective with παρρησιαζόμενος may argue against this. (Bruce [*Acts*, 79] claims that "going in and out" is a common OT Semitism: Deut 31:2; 2 Sam 3:25; Ps 121:8.) Acts 10:24 (ὁ δὲ Κορνήλιος ἦν προσδοκῶν αὐτούς, συγκαλεσάμενος τοὺς συγγενεῖς αὐτοῦ [C. was expecting them (and) called together his relatives]) is susceptible to similar analysis as παρρησιαζόμενος . . . except συγκαλεσάμενος is an Aorist Participle.

2 Cor 5:19: ὡς ὅτι θεὸς ἦν ἐν Χριστῷ κόσμον καταλλάσσων ἑαυτῷ, μὴ λογιζόμενος αὐτοῖς τὰ παραπτώματα αὐτῶν, καὶ θέμενος ἐν ἡμῖν τὸν λόγον τῆς καταλλαγῆς. In a theologically rich passage, one of just a handful in the NT that uses the verb καταλλάσσω (see also Rom 5:10-11; 1 Cor 7:11), Paul discusses the complex relationship among God, man and Christ (see Martin, *Reconciliation*, esp. 90-110; Furnish, "Ministry"; contra Käsemann, "Some Thoughts," who minimizes the importance of the theme of reconciliation in Paul). Within Paul's "great digression" (2:14-7:1) in 2 Corinthians, 5:18-20 comes as a climax to a series of contrasts (Martin, *Corinthians*, 137-38). Paul's teaching is opposed to an understanding of the Christian message which focuses upon Moses as law-giver (3:1-18), a reliance on worldly success and lordly power as validation of its preachers (4:1-15), and an eschatological teaching which denies the future hope of resurrection in its focus upon the present (4:16-5:10). Paul answers by appealing to Christ's love (5:14-15) and proclaiming what God does/has done through Christ (5:18-21) as a correct interpretation of the coming of the new age (5:17) (see Furnish, *II Corinthians*, 321; cf. Martin, *Reconciliation*, 92-93). In 5:18-20, he uses the verb καταλλάσσω three times and the noun καταλλαγή two times. In v 18 Paul says that God reconciles/ed us to himself, i.e. God takes/has taken the initiative in reconciliation, through Christ (see 5:14-15). Three major options can be considered for the clause θεὸς . . . ἑαυτῷ in v 19. (1) If ἦν is completely independent with "God" as a complement (intensive), it might be rendered "There was God, in Christ reconciling the world to himself," though this is an awkward and formally indefensible interpretation. (2) If the locative prepositional group ἐν Χριστῷ (in Christ) is used to specify the locative/existential use of ἦν, the sentence might be construed as "God was in Christ, reconciling the world to himself." Harris ("Appendix," 1192-93) argues this on the basis of the two components of a periphrasis rarely being separated by up to three words and the placement of the διά prepositional group outside the verb and its complement in sentences using καταλλάσσω (he admits that κόσμον remains a problem). Though a possibility, this is probably not the best understanding, since the attributive or appositional use of the Participle seems to imply an incarnational theology not at issue in this passage (Bultmann [*Corinthians*, 161] calls it "inconceivable"). (3) The best choice is a periphrastic rendering (so Regard, *Phrase*, 134; Bultmann, 161, among others; contra Moulton, 227): "God was reconciling the world to himself." The group "in Christ" could be understood to modify "the world," but surely it is not "the world in Christ" that needs reconciliation. More probably, ἐν Χριστῷ is functionally parallel to διὰ Χριστοῦ in v 18,[18] and perhaps translated "in Christ, God was reconciling the world to himself" (Plummer [*Second Corinthians*, 183]; Furnish [*II Corinthians*, 318]; Martin [*Corinthians*, 153-54] rehearse the major options, selecting periphrasis). The emphatic periphrastic form is apparently used by Paul to affirm that God is/was in world-reconciling activity, rather than referring to the simple fact that God reconciles/ed the world (Aorist in v 18), though both have reference to Christ's work on the cross (see Meyer, *Corinthians*, 536; contra Furnish, *II Corinthians*, 319). The two subsequent Participles appear to form a further elucidation (see under Aorist Participle in this chapter). In v 20, Paul concludes by begging his readers to be reconciled (καταλλάγητε) to God. (καταλλάγητε may be deponent, with reference to man reconciling himself, but it is best understood passively, in which case a man puts himself into the position of those whom God has reconciled [Marshall, "Meaning," 123-24].)

Gal 1:22-23: ἤμην δὲ ἀγνοούμενος τῷ προσώπῳ ταῖς ἐκκλησίαις . . . μόνον δὲ ἀκούοντες ἦσαν ὅτι (I was *entirely* unknown by sight in the churches . . . but they[19] were *hearing* only that . . . [translation based on Moulton, 227]). In a summary-like statement of his travels to Jerusalem and to the regions of Syria and Cilicia (note the predominant use of Aorist

---

[18]ἐν Χριστῷ may be a stylistic variation for διὰ Χριστοῦ (Martin, *Reconciliation*, 105), or more likely a means of emphasizing how completely God is at work in Christ (Bruce, *Corinthians*, 209).

[19]Burton (*Galatians*, 64) suggests the members of the churches as the logical subject here, thus the Participle is *ad sensum* (Bruce, *Galatians*, 104).

verbs), Paul concludes by saying that throughout this trip he was not being recognized (or he remained unknown) but that the churches were hearing rumours about him (Burton [*Galatians*, 62-63] notes the emphasis; followed in translation by Betz, *Galatians*, 80; and Bruce, *Galatians*, 103, 104, who notes the emphasis on "continuity of the state or action" [103]).

Phil 2:26: ἐπειδὴ ἐπιποθῶν ἦν πάντας ὑμᾶς καὶ ἀδημονῶν. This sentence may be interpreted as consisting of a periphrastic with adjunctive Participle (since he was longing for all of you, being distressed [UBS³]) or of two periphrastic constructions (since he was longing for you and was being distressed [NA²⁶]). The latter is more likely (contra Moulton, 227, who finds the Participles "decidedly adjectival") since the two Participles are not repetitious but supplemental, emphasizing that Paul's reason for sending Epaphroditus was both his longing and his being deeply distressed at the Philippians' concern for him.

Rev 17:4: καὶ ἡ γυνὴ ἦν περιβεβλημένη . . . καὶ κεχρυσωμένη . . . ἔχουσα ποτήριον χρυσοῦν (the woman was clothed . . . and gilded . . . having a gold cup). Though the Present Participle following the two Perfect periphrastics may be adjunctive because of its separation from the auxiliary and its lack of a connective, it is probably periphrastic. The narrator sees the woman and her state as one of being clothed in certain coloured gowns and being adorned with precious metals,[20] while in her hand she is holding a cup, possibly the one from which she is drinking the blood of the saints and martyrs (v 6, with Present Participle).

[+remoteness] εἰμί + Present Participle is fairly well known in the LXX (e.g. Gen 4:2; 13:10; 14:12; Exod 3:1; 1 Kgdms 2:18; 3:1; 14:26; 2 Kgdms 3:6; Dan 8:5 B; 10:2; Jonah 1:10; see Aerts, *Periphrastica*, 62ff.; Dietrich, "Verbalaspekt," 205), but the above survey shows that Semitic intervention in the NT must be rejected. Rosén, however, argues that of NT usage, 20% are suppletives, 60% according to classical usage of periphrastics, 12% parallel to an adjective with copula, and 20% under influence of the parallel Aramaic construction ("Ἦν διδάσκων," xxiii-xxiv. The statistics exceed 100%). On this basis Semitic enhancement might be claimed. But on the basis of the form's use in Homeric, classical and hellenistic Greek (Dietrich [203] characterizes it as "lebendig und jederzeit möglich"; see Rydbeck, "Bemerkungen," 194-905, for other examples), and its widest use in Luke-Acts in the NT (as well as later Patristic Greek [Dietrich, 207-09], the most that can be claimed is Septuagintal enhancement (see Rydbeck, 196-98, 200). Dietrich (204) notes that, though in hellenistic Greek the examples are relatively few (although they are fairly widespread in distribution), most of the examples occur in factual or somewhat Atticistic artistic prose. The NT, he posits, was a new form of hellenistic literature that exploited the possibilities of the construction.

c. [+expectation] form of εἰμί + Present Participle

Aerts (*Periphrastica*, 59) claims that the Future form of εἰμί + Present Participle is only found in one disputed passage in ancient Greek, X. Hiero

---

[20] Thompson (*Apocalypse*, 72) claims on the basis of 1 Chr 21:16, where περιβεβλημένοι translates a Hebrew pual Participle, and Exod 26:32, where κεχρυσωμένων translates a Hebrew pual Participle, that Rev 17:4 uses the Greek Perfect to represent the Hebrew Participle (see also Rev 10:1; 11:3; 18:16; 19:13, for similar patterns). Despite the sparse evidence he marshals, this can be rejected as a significant indication of Semitic influence on the basis of Thompson's own admission that such constructions are "acceptable Greek" (71) and the implausibility of the Greek Perfect falling under Semitic influence when indicating stative aspect (see Barr, *Semantics*, 240 n. 3). Thompson's problems in part stem from his viewing the Greek Participle as time-bound (73), categorizing all uses of the Perfect Passive Participle as "attributive" (71, 85), and, though he admits Turner's classification of Rev 17:4 as periphrastic, discounting the construction itself on the basis of the *textus receptus* reading of ἡ γυνὴ ἡ περιβεβλημένη over the accepted reading with א A 046 *al* (51-52).

11.7: εὖ ἔσῃ νικῶν (you will be conquering successfully [miscited as 2.7])[21] and thus argues that since this construction "only occurs to any extent in the LXX and the New Testament" (59), the LXX accounts for NT usage. He claims further that other hellenistic literature lacks the construction as well (Björck [*HN ΔΙΔΑΣΚΩΝ*, 87] lists a few hellenistic examples; and Aerts [60] adds several others from religious texts). It must be admitted that the Future of εἰμί with Present Participle is rare, but it is rare in all forms of Greek literature. Aerts also has apparently slighted the ancient Greek literature.

S. Oed. Col. 1432-33: ἀλλ' ἐμοὶ μὲν ἥδ' ὁδὸς / ἔσται μέλουσα δύσποτμός τε καὶ κακή (but my road, miserable and evil, will be causing concern [Stahl, 145. Or is the Participle a modifier of the adjective?]).

Hdt. 3.134.4: καὶ ταῦτα ὀλίγου χρόνου ἔσται τελεύμενα (these things will be coming to completion in a little while).

Lycurg. 27: ῥᾳθυμότατοι ἔσεσθε καὶ ἥκιστα ἐπὶ τοῖς δεινοῖς ὀργιζόμενοι (you will be most relaxed and getting least enraged at awful things). (Gildersleeve [125] classifies this as a periphrastic where the Participle is parallel with an adjective.)

Examples in the NT are few as well.

Matt 10:22; 24:9 = Mark 13:13 = Luke 21:17: ἔσεσθε μισούμενοι ὑπὸ πάντων διὰ τὸ ὄνομά μου (you will be in progress being hated by all because of my name). See chapt. 9 on Mark 13 for discussion of the hypothetical nature of Future forms, and the overall structure of these eschatological discourses. In context, discourse establishes apparent future reference, with the periphrastic used as a fitting climax to the various kinds of trouble followers of Jesus will encounter from other humans. (Regard [*Phrase*, 136] calls the appearance of a periphrastic alongside two simple forms "remarquable"; Aerts [*Periphrastica*, 58-59] posits an independent use of the Participle though he admits the possibiliity of periphrasis.)

Luke 5:10: ἀπὸ τοῦ νῦν ἀνθρώπους ἔσῃ ζωγρῶν (from now on you will be fishing for men). This marked, commanding (?) use of the Future of εἰμί in periphrasis emphasizes Jesus' mission for his followers (Björck [*HN ΔΙΔΑΣΚΩΝ*, 86-87] discounts substantive use of the Participle here, though Aerts [*Periphrastica*, 59] calls it "defining"). They will no longer be fishing for fish but for men. Cf. Matt 4:19; Mark 1:17, with δεῦτε and simple Future verbs.

1 Cor 14:9: ἔσεσθε γὰρ εἰς ἀέρα λαλοῦντες (you will be speaking into air). Paul answers a rhetorical conditional-like question[22] with this pronouncement. If you, Paul says, do not give an intelligible word, how will what you are saying be understood? The result will be that of *speaking* (so Regard, *Phrase*, 135) words into the air. Or as Robertson/Plummer (*First Corinthians*, 310) say, "The periphrastic tense indicates the lasting condition to which the unintelligible speaker is reduced."

---

[21]There is much textual uncertainty here, with the best texts reading κηρυχθήσῃ (cf. X. Symp. 8.37), and with variants εὖ ἔσῃ and οὖ ἔσει, etc.

[22]Beyer (*Syntax*, 82) notes the distinctively Greek formulation here, with two protases.

465

d. [+projection] form of εἰμί + Present Participle

The Subjunctive of εἰμί + Present Participle is known in classical literature, though it does not seem abundant.[23] Instances with the Optative might also be noted.[24] Only a single possible example of the Subjunctive with the Present Participle is found in the NT.

Jas 1:4: ἵνα ἦτε τέλειοι καὶ ὁλόκληροι, ἐν μηδενὶ λειπόμενοι (so that you might be mature and whole, lacking in nothing). This construction is arguably not periphrastic (Aerts [*Periphrastica*, 73] calls it "explicative"), since the Participle is parallel to two adjectives. This construction is susceptible to analysis as periphrastic, however, for the basic reason that the author does not use a third adjective, although one was available. James apparently uses a verbal construction to emphasize the hypothesis that the result of testing is not only maturity or wholeness but even more importantly a maturity that lacks nothing. (This differs from Eph 4:14, where a noun intervenes between the auxiliary and Participle; contra Regard, *Phrase*, 178.)

The Present Participle, though more heavily marked in opposition to the Aorist, does not occur in the NT with the Subjunctive auxiliary for two possible reasons: the simple Subjunctive form is active in ancient Greek as the less heavily marked non-assertive form and thus does not readily need a periphrastic substitute, and there is apparently something inherently odd about such a form appearing in a periphrastic (this helps explain the lack of periphrastics with the Aorist Participle).

e. [+direction] form of εἰμί + Present Participle

The Imperative of εἰμί + Present Participle is found very infrequently in ancient Greek, though it is not unknown,[25] thus discounting possible Semitic influence (Moulton, 226, citing Wellhausen). Two examples are found in the NT.[26]

Matt 5:25: ἴσθι εὐνοῶν τῷ ἀντιδίκῳ σου ταχύ (be making friends with your enemy quickly). Jesus, teaching about anger, reportedly instructs his followers about their attitudes towards others. In his final set of instructions (v 25), he makes an emphatic opening statement about one's relationships to adversaries. The imperfective verbal aspect as a subjective conception is not in conflict with the adverb ταχύ, since aspect does not refer to objective action (see my chapt. 4).

Luke 19:17: ἴσθι ἐξουσίαν ἔχων ἐπάνω δέκα πόλεων (be having authority over ten cities). In the parable of the ten measures, the nobleman commends the first servant using a periphrastic, giving him authority over ten cities (cf. v 19, where he commends the second servant with a Present Imperative). As Marshall says, the periphrastic seems "unmotivated," unless to

---

[23]E.g. S. Oed. King 580: ἂν ᾖ θέλουσα πάντ᾽ ἐμοῦ κομίζεται (all of what she might be wanting of mine is being provided); Pl. Phil. 37E: ἂν δέ γε ἁμαρτανόμενον τὸ δοξαζόμενον ᾖ (the glorified thing/thing of good repute might be isolated); possibly E. Cyc. 381: πῶς ... ἦτε πάσχοντες τάδε; (how might you be suffering here?); P.Grenf. ii 14(a).4-5 (270/233 B.C.): ἐὰν ἐνδεχόμενον / ᾖ (if it might be possible); P.Lille 1.20-21 (A.D. 259/60): ἐὰν [τις] κατὰ φύσιν / τῶν χωμάτων κειμένη ᾖ (if it might be lying according to the nature of the embankments); P.Teb. 72.197 (114-13 B.C.): κἂν ἦι / ἐν ὑπολόγωι ἀναφερομένη (if [the earth] might be taken into account [corrected from ἀναφέρηται]); PSI 530.7-8 (3d cent. A.D.): ἐὰν ᾖ σχολά/ζον (if it [beast of burden] might be resting); P.Rev. Laws 19.8 (259 B.C.): ἐὰν ᾖ περιγινόμενόν ἐκ τῶν / ἄλλων ὠνῶν (whether it might be exceeding the other farms).
[24]E.g. S. Phil. 544; Aj. 1330; Hdt. 1.86.3; J. Jew. War 1.503. No NT instances occur.
[25]E.g. Pl. Laws 881B: ἔστω δὴ λεγόμενον τὸ μετὰ τοῦτο τῇδε (let this next [law] be spoken).
[26]Eph 5:5 has ἔστε instead of ἴστε (from οἶδα) in a few manuscripts (D E K L).

emphasize the disproportionate size of the reward (*Luke*, 706. His explanation that it "may be meant as a sign of eternal reward" is unconvincing).

(The Infinitive or Participle of εἰμί + Present Participle as periphrasis is not found in the NT. Both are found in ancient Greek: see Kühner/Gerth, 1.39; Dietrich, "Verbalaspekt," 205, 209; Mayser, 2, 1.224.)

2. Perfect Participle

The Perfect Participle with εἰμί forming a periphrastic has long been recognized (for a brief summary see Chantraine, *Histoire*, 246-60). Its continued use probably is due to (1) an aspectual meaning that is conducive to a modifying function (Karleen, *Syntax*, 113), (2) double markedness in its aspectual opposition to both the Present and Aorist forms, and (3) the extreme cumbersomeness of several simple Perfect forms, several of which virtually dropped from the language and were thus replaced by periphrasis (e.g. Future Perfect; the Imperative, Subjunctive and Optative Perfect in simple and periphrastic forms persisted in hellenistic Greek, though in very infrequent use: see Harry, "Perfect Forms"). Much of the discussion of Perfect periphrasis is coloured by the view that the Perfect shifted semantically in the period from Homer through to the classical period from an intransitive subjective use to a transitive objective use and then to semantic equality with the Aorist. On the basis of what is stated in chapt. 5 it is only necessary to repeat here that the Perfect (whether Indicative, Participle, etc.) continued to maintain its subjective aspectually-stative meaning from the Homeric through to the hellenistic period, and this meaning is displayed in periphrastics as well (Karleen [*Syntax*, 131-32] uses the supposed shift in orientation in defence of the continued stative quality of the verb form).

From around the 4th cent. B.C. the Perfect Participle is used in increasing numbers in the 3d Person Plural in Middle/Passive Voice, especially with verbs ending in a consonant or adding σ, often in place of a simple form (Aerts, *Periphrastica*, 41; Gildersleeve, 122; Mandilaras, 216, 232; Mussies, *Morphology*, 302-03. Problems of documentation must be considered). Only a few possible examples occur in the NT: Rom 13:1 (αἱ δὲ οὖσαι ὑπὸ θεοῦ τεταγμέναι εἰσίν [those who are commanded by God]) and Acts 13:48 (ἐπίστευσεν ὅσοι ἦσαν τεταγμένοι εἰς ζωὴν αἰώνιον [those who were in a state of appointment to eternal life believed], in a rare construction with the periphrastic forming a relative clause),[27] and possibly Matt 9:36 (ὅτι ἦσαν ἐσκυλμένοι καὶ ἐρριμμένοι ὡσεὶ πρόβατα [they were in a state of being worried and helpless as sheep]); Luke 8:2 (γυναῖκές τινες αἳ ἦσαν τεθεραπευμέναι ἀπὸ πνευμάτων πονηρῶν [certain women who were healed from evil spirits; cf. Pluperfect ἐξεληλύθει in loose parallel]); John 1:24 (ἀπεσταλμένοι ἦσαν ἐκ τῶν Φαρισαίων [they were in a state of being sent from the P.s]);[28] and Acts 2:13 (ὅτι Γλεύκους μεμεστωμένοι εἰσίν [they are drunk with sweet wine]). The form is still periphrastic, but it lacks markedness due to a lack of formal choice. More importantly, though the Perfect periphrasis may be "of a situation-fixing character" (Aerts, 51), there is no reason to

---

[27]Cf. P.Petr. ii 45(iii).12-13 (c. 246 B.C.): ὅσοι οὐκ ἦ[σ]αν τ[εταγμένοι] (Mandilaras [234] reconstructs the reading, though doubtful). Moeris 196.29 (c. 200 A.D.) includes the stereotyped simple 3d Person Plural Perfect: ἐτετάχατο Ἀττικῶς, τεταγμένοι ἦσαν Ἑλληνικῶς (Mandilaras, 232 n. 2; cf. ¶ 453[3]).

[28]Cf. P.Teb. 89(i).5 (113 B.C.): [ἐσπαρ]μέναι ἦ[σαν] (they were sown).

posit that the Perfect has altered its subjective emphasis, even if the periphrastic construction marks the nominal part of a periphrastic construction.

a. [-remoteness] form of εἰμί + Perfect Participle

The Present form of εἰμί + Perfect Participle is fairly common in ancient Greek from Homer through to the hellenistic period.[29] In the NT, there are several important examples, as there are in other hellenistic writings[30]

Matt 10:30: αἱ τρίχες τῆς κεφαλῆς πᾶσαι ἠριθμημέναι εἰσίν (all the hairs of your head are in a state of being numbered). This timeless use of the auxiliary brings a pericope on fear to a close, stressing that God's concern extends even to knowledge of the hairs on people's heads (contra Aerts, *Periphrastica*, 93) (v 31 seems anti-climactic in contrast; cf. Luke 12:7 with ἠρίθμηνται).

Matt 10:26: οὐδὲν γάρ ἐστιν κεκαλυμμένον = Luke 12:2: οὐδὲν δὲ συγκεκαλυμμένον ἐστὶν ὃ οὐκ ἀποκαλυφθήσεται (nothing is hidden which shall not be revealed). Jesus reportedly warns his disciples of hypocrisy, especially that of the Pharisees, with this proverbial statement stressing the contrast between the state of hidden things and revelation of them. That which is hidden is destined for revelation. (The implication may be that the time of revelation is the judgment [so Marshall, *Luke*, 512], but this is not a grammatical conclusion.)

Luke 12:6: καὶ ἓν ἐξ αὐτῶν οὐκ ἔστιν ἐπιλελησμένον ἐνώπιον τοῦ θεοῦ; (and is it not true that one of them is not overlooked before God?) In a statement not included in the Matthean version (see 10:30 above), Luke shifts the emphasis of the pericope slightly by stressing not God's intimate knowledge so much as his oversight of the broad expanse of the world.

John 2:17; 6:31, 45; 10:34; 12:14; 20:30: ἔστιν γεγραμμένον. Of the Gospel writers, John uses this phrase exclusively, perhaps as a periphrastic substitute for the simple form (so Aerts, *Periphrastica*, 93; Regard, *Phrase*, 140-41), but more likely as a means of stressing that the OT quotation that follows has direct application to the case the Evangelist is making for Jesus. (Cf. also Paus. 1.1.2: ἐν ᾗ Θεμιστοκλῆς ἐστι γεγραμμένος [on which is written (depicted) T.]; 1.3.4; contra 1.5.5; and D. 22.73: ἐπιγέγραπται· . . . τούτου τοὔνομ᾽ ἐν τοῖς ἱεροῖς ἐπὶ τῶν φιαλῶν γεγραμμένον ἐστίν [stands written upon it. . . . of this one the name stands written on the pillars in the holy places].)

Acts 21:33: καὶ ἐπυνθάνετο τίς εἴη καὶ τί ἐστιν πεποιηκώς (and the centurion enquired who he might be and what he has done). In an interesting contrast of attitude the author of Acts relates the centurion's enquiry about Paul's identity in the Optative (classical usage) and about what he has been doing in the Present Perfect periphrasis. Aerts calls this "avoidance of the oblique optative in the perfect" a "striking feature," attributing it to the fact that in the NT "the optative is practically always used to express a wish" (*Periphrastica*, 92). But Bruce explains it along these

---

[29]Hom. Il. 5.873-74: αἰεί τοι ῥίγιστα θεοὶ τετληότες εἰμὲν / ἀλλήλων ἰότητι (we gods are always in a state of bearing the plans of others) (cf. 3.309); Od. 5.90: εἰ δύναμαι τελέσαι γε καὶ εἰ τετελεσμένον ἐστίν (if I am in progress fulfilling it [Hermes's request] and if it is in a state of fulfilment); A. Pers. 759-60: τοιγάρ σφιν ἔργον ἐστὶν ἐξειργασμένον / μέγιστον (therefore a work is in a state of accomplishment for them) (cf. Hdt. 9.75); Hdt. 9.27.5: ἡμῖν δὲ εἰ μηδὲν ἄλλο ἐστὶ ἀποδεδεγμένον (if nothing else is pointed out to us) (cf. 4.22.2); Th. 3.68.1: ἀγαθὸν ἐν τῷ πολέμῳ δεδρακότες εἰσίν (they are in a state of accomplishment of something good in the war); D. 21.104: ἐγὼ τὸ πρᾶγμ᾽ εἰμὶ τοῦτο δεδρακώς (I am in a state of accomplishing this deed); Lys. 22.2: εἰσιν . . . εἰργασμένοι (they are in a state of accomplishment); X. Hell. 3.2.14: πάλιν πεπερακότες εἰσὶ τὸν Μαίανδρον (they were in a state of having passed through the M. again); Cyr. 8.6.9: οἱ χιλίαρχοι . . . εἰσὶ καθεστηκότες καὶ παρὰ βασιλεῖ ἀπογεγραμμένοι (the centurions are appointed and have registered with the king); Pl. Symp. 191E: ἀλλὰ μᾶλλον πρὸς τὰς γυναῖκας τετραμμέναι εἰσί (but they are rather in a state of meeting with women).

[30]E.g. Paus. 2.1.9: εἰσιν ἐπειργασμένοι τῷ βάθρῳ καὶ οἱ Τυνδάρεω παῖδες (the children of T. are depicted on the base); P.Hib. 127.3-5 (250 B.C.). See esp. Mayser, 2, 2.224-25; Mandilaras, 116-17.

lines: "the optative in τίς εἴη was appropriate as the prisoner was quite unknown; . . . the indicative is retained as the tribune was quite sure that he had done something or other" (*Acts*, 397; cf. Regard, *Phrase*, 138, who notes the expressive value of the periphrastic). See also P.Hib. 127.3-5 (250 B.C.): ἐπεὶ οὐκ ὀλί/γον ἀργύριον ἀφηρπακότες εἶ / σύ (since you are in a state of possessing by seizure some silver).

Acts 26:26: οὐ γάρ ἐστιν ἐν γωνίᾳ πεπραγμένον τοῦτο (for this is/was not accomplished in a corner). Whereas there might be some question whether this is a periphrasis because of the locative group (the writer uses a classical proverbial phrase, ἐν γωνίᾳ; cf. Pl. Gorg. 485D; Epict. 2.12.17 [Bruce, *Acts*, 448-49]), the displacement of the subject helps establish it as periphrastic. Paul uses the periphrasis here when he wants to stress the objectivity of his account.

1 Cor 15:19: εἰ ἐν τῇ ζωῇ ταύτῃ ἐν Χριστῷ ἠλπικότες ἐσμὲν μόνον (if we are in a state of having hope in Christ in this life only[31]. . .). Paul concludes his brief argument for the resurrection from the dead (vv 12-19) by saying that if the dead are not raised then Christ is not raised; if Christ is not raised, our faith is useless, we are still in our sins and we are destroyed. Therefore if we put hope in a Christ who is merely confined to this world, we are the most pitiable of all (on possible embarrassment of this argument see Conzelmann, *Corinthians*, 267). As Regard says, this "comporte d'une manière propante la nuánce de caractère et l'expression de l'état" (*Phrase*, 138).

2 Cor 4:3: εἰ δὲ καὶ ἔστιν κεκαλυμμένον τὸ εὐαγγέλιον ἡμῶν, ἐν τοῖς ἀπολλυμένοις ἐστὶν κεκαλυμμένον (if our gospel is hidden, it is hidden to those who are being destroyed). In a I class conditional sentence, Paul answers an objection that might arise from 3:5, where he says that a veil rests upon the hearts of Jews when Moses is read. Paul answers that if the gospel is hidden, it is only hidden to those in the state of destruction. According to Lias, this "is not the language of logic, but of deep and strong conviction, resting, not in logic, but on something beyond it" (2 *Corinthians*, 59; Moule [18] doubts the periphrasis).

Eph 2:5, 8: (τῇ γὰρ) χάριτί ἐστε σεσῳσμένοι (διὰ πίστεως) (by grace you are in a state of salvation [through faith] [Regard (*Phrase*, 142) debates whether these verses should be translated "you are saved" or "you have been saved"; cf. Moule, 19, who seeks a temporal sense for the Participle]). In this brief section, 2:1-10, the author of Ephesians recounts the transformation from being dead in sin to alive in Christ. In v 5, he interjects a periphrastic construction, apparently emphasizing that the state of salvation comes as a gift of God. In v 8, after completing the progression that sees believers seated in the heavenly places with Christ, he theologizes upon the basis for such a transformation by repeating and expanding the periphrasis.

Heb 7:20, 23: οἱ μὲν γὰρ χωρὶς ὀρκωμοσίας εἰσὶν ἱερεῖς γεγονότες (they have become priests without an oath [v 20]). In discussing the orders of priesthood, the author of Hebrews separates them along different lines. In an "elegant periphrasis" (Bruce, *Hebrews*, 149 n. 62), the Levitical priesthood is said to have become a priesthood without an oath (v 20), whereas Jesus received an oath (v 21). The former priesthood existed in greater numbers (οἱ μὲν πλείονές εἰσιν γεγονότες ἱερεῖς [v 23]) because they were prevented by death from continuing.

Heb 10:10: ἐν ᾧ θελήματι ἡγιασμένοι ἐσμὲν διὰ τῆς προσφορᾶς (by the will [of God] we are sanctified through the offering . . .). Christ is quoted as saying he has come to do God's will, and the author says that it is by this will and through his offering of his body that we are sanctified. Bruce notes that this act of sacrifice is "once for all," though he notes also that this is expressed by a Perfect form (*Hebrews*, 236 and n. 54).

1 John 4:12: ἡ ἀγάπη αὐτοῦ ἐν ἡμῖν τετελειωμένη ἐστίν. If the locative group modifies the subject, the understanding is that God abides in us and "his love in us" is in a state of completion. If the locative completes the Participle and the construction is periphrastic, it means that God abides in us and his love is in a state of completion in us. (Cf. P.Petr. ii 32[1].12-14 [3d cent. B.C.]: καὶ πρότερον ἐν / τοῖς ἐπάνω χρόνοις τοῦθ᾽ ἡμῖν κεχωρη/μένον ἐστίν [this is

---

[31]μόνον may modify any number of items in this sentence. I follow the NASB. See Barrett, *First Corinthians*, 349-50.

in a state of having been permitted to us in a previous time], where the preceding action is brought into account by a temporal phrase.)

b. [+remoteness] form of εἰμί + Perfect Participle

The narrative form of εἰμί + Perfect Participle is widely attested in both pre-hellenistic[32] and hellenistic Greek,[33] surely because of the weakness of the Pluperfect. As seen in chapt. 5, the unwieldy morphological bulk of the Pluperfect never allowed it to develop into wide usage, hence it was often substituted for by the simple Perfect or a narrative auxiliary and Perfect Participle, depending upon whether emphasis was sought. In the NT the periphrastic Perfect with narrative auxiliary is fairly common as well.

Luke 4:16: οὗ ἦν τεθραμμένος (where he was brought up).[34] In opening the narrative of Jesus' rejection (see Fitzmyer, *Luke*, 1.525-40; Marshall, *Luke*, 175-90), Luke says Jesus went (Aorist) to Nazareth, a city of little importance, except that it was where Jesus was reared. The marked periphrastic is highlighted further by the reaction against Jesus in v 22 (Marshall, 181) and Jesus' own remark in v 24 that no prophet is accepted in his own country (see Fitzmyer, 1.527-28, for parallels, discussed by Anderson, "Horizons," esp. 264-65). Cf. also P.Teb. 16.7-8 (114 B.C.): ὡς ἦν ὑβρισμένος οὐ μετρίως / ὑπὸ Ἀπολλοδώρου καὶ [τοῦ] τούτου υἱοῦ (as he was treated very badly by A. and his son).

Luke 4:17: οὗ ἦν γεγραμμένον (where it was written). See above on John 2:17 etc., the difference being that the narrative auxiliary reflects the narrative context: Jesus took the book (Aorist), unrolled it (Aorist), and found (Aorist) the place where it stood written, etc., and then closed the book (Aorist), etc. The OT quotation from Isa 61:1-2 and 58:6 is duly emphasized by the periphrastic construction in the midst of narrative Aorists. See also John 12:16; 19:19, 20; 20:30 (Karleen [*Syntax*, 133] cites the following finite simplex verb [γέγραπται (v 31)] in support of periphrasis in v 30).

Luke 5:17: καὶ ἦσαν καθήμενοι Φαρισαῖοι καὶ νομοδιδάσκαλοι οἳ ἦσαν ἐληλυθότες ἐκ πάσης κώμης (and P.s and law teachers were seated, who were in a state of having come from every village). Luke shows a subtle use of verbal aspect in describing Jesus' ministry. Verse 17 begins by saying that Jesus was in progress teaching (periphrasis with Present Participle), in contrast to the state of his observers (Aerts, *Periphrastica*, 92). This contrast sets the scene for the conflict of the entire pericope: Jesus' healing on the Sabbath. (Marshall [*Luke*, 212] claims that the reading οἳ ἦσαν ἐληλυθότες "implies that every village had its quota of Phrarisees. . . ." Is

---

[32]E.g. Hom. Od. 1.18: οὐδ' ἔνθα πεφυγμένος ἦεν ἀέθλων (neither was he in a state of having fled from trouble there); A. Pers. 381: ὡς ἕκαστος ἦν τεταγμένος (as each [captain] was in a state of being ordered); S. Phil. 435: χοῦτος τεθνηκὼς ἦν (he was in a state of being dead); Hdt. 7.212.2: οἱ δὲ Ἕλληνες . . . κεκοσμημένοι ἦσαν καὶ ἐν μέρεϊ ἕκαστοι ἐμάχοντο (and the Greeks . . . were in a state of arrangement and they were fighting in portions) (cf. 7.65; 4.78.3); 3.89.3: ἦν κατεστηκὸς οὐδὲν φόρου πέρι, ἀλλὰ δῶρα ἀγίνεον ([Cyrus] was in a state of having established nothing [no law] concerning tribute, but he was accepting gifts) (cf. 3.93.3); Th. 3.3.1: ἦσαν γὰρ τεταλαιπωρημένοι ὑπό τε τῆς νόσου (for [the Athenians] were in a state of being distressed by the disease); X. Anab. 4.7.2: συνεληλυθότες δ' ἦσαν αὐτόσε (they [men, women, etc.] were gathered in the same place) (cf. 6.1.6); Isoc. 12.233: ἐφ' ἃ συνεληλυθότες ἦσαν (about which they were gathered); D. 6.29: ἦν πολὺ τούτων ἀφεστηκότα τὰ τότε λεγόμενα (he was standing much aloof from the things he had then spoken); 48.16: ὅσον μὴ ἦν ἀνηλωμένον (which [money] was not lost/spent).

[33]See e.g. Arr. 2.8.3; 2.12.3; 2.13.3; 2.15.2; 2.19.4; 2.20.7; 2.21.1.

[34]Sparks ("Semitisms . . . Gospel," 136) claims "one possible indication of Aramaic influence" on Luke's Gospel is ἦν ἀνατεθραμμένος (he cites the variant found in א L W Y f¹³ *al*; the accepted reading is found in A B etc.), though he admits to classical Greek and LXX parallels.

this because of the periphrasis or the prepositional group following? There is no basis for arguing this on the basis of the periphrastic alone.) In Luke 5:18 (see also Acts 9:33) the paralytic himself is described as one ὃς ἦν παραλελυμένος (who was paralysed). Cf. Luke 23:55.

Luke 15:24, 32: ἦν ἀπολωλὼς καὶ εὑρέθη (he was in a state of destruction and he was found). In the climactic statement of the parable of the forgiving father (or lost son), attributed first to the father and then to Jesus, the author uses two parallel oppositions to force home the point of the story. The father says: my son/your brother was (ἦν) dead and he came to life (Aorist), he was destroyed (Perfect) and he was found (Aorist). The emphasis falls on the second and third terms, in which the first Aorist is in emphatic contrast to the aspectually (and lexically) vague εἰμί, and the Perfect is emphasized in relation to the Aorist (contra Aerts, *Periphrastica*, 91, who considers both adjectival). (Cf. P.Teb. 15.20, 22 [114 B.C.]: μετὰ τὸ προσανενεγκεῖν . . . ὡς ἦν ἐξηγμένος [after bringing it up . . . it was explained. . .] [note Infinitive and Participle].)

John 19:11: εἰ μὴ ἦν δεδομένον σοι ἄνωθεν (unless [authority] is/was given to you from above. (Barrett [*John*, 543] notes that ἐξουσία and δεδομένον are not in agreement. Thus he translates: "Unless it had been granted you to have authority"). The protasis of a conditional (see my chapt. 6) is placed in inverted order to its apodosis to emphasize that, as Jesus says, unless God has given someone authority over him, no one may exercise it against him (Aerts [*Periphrastica*, 93] calls it a periphrastic Pluperfect).

Acts 14:26: ὅθεν ἦσαν παραδεδομένοι τῇ χάριτι τοῦ θεοῦ εἰς τὸ ἔργον ὃ ἐπλήρωσαν (from whence [Antioch] they were handed over by the grace of God into the work which they completed). The order of discourse must be relied upon to give a proper understanding of the tenses (Acts 13:1-3). The meaning seems to be that the narrator says that Paul and Barnabus returned to the place where they had been placed under commission before beginning their subsequent and now complete trip. Cf. Acts 18:25.

Gal 2:11: ὅτι κατεγνωσμένος ἦν (because he stood condemned [NASB]). In Paul's description of his confrontation with Peter, Paul says that when Peter came to Antioch (Aorist), he opposed him (Aorist), because he was in a state of condemnation (already?). The periphrasis stresses the condition Peter was in at the time of the confrontation itself (contra Mussner, *Galaterbrief*, 137; Schlier, *Galaterbrief*, 82 n. 2, who view the Participle as adjectival). Implicature of the state already existing might be supported by the periphrasis, but not derived from it. (Cf. Arr. 2.4.3: ὅσοι βαρύτερον ὡπλισμένοι ἦσαν [who were heavily equipped].)

Eph 2:12: ἦτε τῷ καιρῷ ἐκείνῳ χωρὶς Χριστοῦ ἀπηλλοτριωμένοι τῆς πολιτείας τοῦ Ἰσραήλ. UBS³ and NA²⁶ both place commas after Χριστοῦ, giving the rendering "you were apart from Christ in that time, a stranger of the citizenship of I." An alternative is to view this as a periphrastic, glossed "in that time apart from Christ you were in a state of alienation from the citizenship of I." Temporal deixis seems to eliminate a possible Subjunctive interpretation of ἦτε.

Rev 17:4: see above under Present Participle.

c. [+expectation] form of εἰμί + Perfect Participle.

The Future Perfect periphrasis is not widely used in ancient Greek, but it can be found.[35]

Matt 16:19: καὶ ὃ ἐὰν δήσῃς ἐπὶ τῆς γῆς ἔσται δεδεμένον ἐν τοῖς οὐρανοῖς, καὶ ὃ ἐὰν λύσῃς ἐπὶ τῆς γῆς ἔσται λελυμένον ἐν τοῖς οὐρανοῖς (whatever you might bind upon the earth can be expected to be in a state of boundness in heaven; and whatever you might loose upon the earth can be expected to be in a state of loosedness in heaven); Matt 18:18: ὅσα ἐὰν δήσητε ἐπὶ τῆς γῆς ἔσται δεδεμένα ἐν οὐρανῷ καὶ ὅσα ἐὰν λύσητε ἐπὶ τῆς γῆς ἔσται λελυμένα ἐν οὐρανῷ.

Few passages with periphrastics have generated as much discussion as Matt 16:17-19 (18:18 is treated in conjunction with it).[36] Virtually every discussion of these verses seems to arrive sooner or later at a discussion of the periphrastic constructions in v 19. As Aerts (*Periphrastica*, 96) says, Matt 16:19 contains "pregnant examples." There have been several analyses of the structure of v 19, all of which affirm the unity of at least the two conditional clauses (e.g. Burney, *Poetry*, 115; Brown et al., *Peter*, 95; Jeremias, κλείς, *TDNT*, 3.749-50, who posits a high Semitic influence). Verse 19a continues Jesus' instruction to Peter, saying that his intention is to give him the keys of the kingdom of heaven (or plural, heavens). Carson notes the shift of metaphor from Peter being the foundation to being the gatekeeper (cf. Rev 9:1-6; 20:1-3; Carson, "Matthew," 370), though Jeremias may be correct in emphasizing that in biblical and Jewish usage handling the keys implies full authority (cf. Isa 22:22; Rev 1:18; 3:7; Jeremias, 3.750).

There are two major competing opinions on the meaning of the periphrastic constructions in Matt 16:19.

1. Since his article ("Mistranslation") in the 1939 issue of *JBL*, and again in 1973 ("Evidence," where he depends heavily on a Th.D. thesis by his student W.T. Dayton), Mantey has been a strong proponent that the future auxiliary and Perfect Passive Participle should be translated as an English Future Perfect Passive: i.e. "shall have been bound/loosed," where a future event is the result of a first event which has occurred before the time of speaking or writing (he is followed by Turner, *Insights*, 80-82; Albright/Mann, *Matthew*, 197; Gundry, *Matthew*, 335; and tentatively Carson, "Matthew," 370-72). He argues this along four main lines. (a) A number of Greek grammarians state that the Perfect tense refers to the continuing results of a past action (Kühner, Smyth, Hadley and Allen, Goodwin, Jelf, Burton, and Robertson). (b) Though not all Perfect verbs maintain this temporal construct (some refer to past time, others refer to the present,

---

[35]Hom. Il. 1.212; 2.257; 8.286, 401; 9.310; 22.410; 23.672; Od. 2.187; 17.229; 18.82; 19.487: τετελεσμένον ἔσται (it will be in a state of accomplishment) (this set phrase virtually always follows a simple Future of speaking, establishing a scene in which the speaker posits that he will speak and then the thing spoken of will come to pass); Hdt. 1.112.3: οὔτε ἡμῖν κακῶς βεβουλευμένα ἔσται (neither shall it be in the state of giving evil to us); X. Anab. 3.2.31: οἱ πολέμιοι πλεῖστον ἐψευσμένοι ἔσονται (the cities shall be in a state of being deceived greatly) (cf. Cyr. 7.2.13); 7.6.36: ἴστε ὅτι ἄνδρα κατακεκονότες ἔσεσθε (know that you will be in a state of having killed a man . . .); Hell. 5.2.27: σὺ κατεστραμμένος ἔσει Θήβας (you will be in a state of having overthrown T.) (implicature of a past act, of which this state is a result, can be posited, but it is still future from the point of speaking; cf. 7.2.20); Pl. Gorg. 469D: κατεαγὼς ἔσται αὐτίκα μάλα . . . διεσχισμένον ἔσται (he shall be in a state of being smashed immediately . . . it [his head] shall be in a state of being split in two) (see Dodds, *Gorgias*, 240: "the right state for the victim is having his skull smashed"; cf. Meno 86A); D. 4.50: τὰ δέοντ᾽ ἐσόμεθ᾽ ἐγνωκότες καὶ λόγων ματαίων ἀπηλλαγμένοι (we shall be in a state of knowledge of what is required and put away foolish words). Mandilaras (240; "NT," 49) claims a single example of the simple form is found in the papyri: PSI 441.9-10 (3d cent. B.C.): προ/εστήξομαι.

[36]For an insightful history of interpretation and bibliography see Burgess, *History*; cf. also Cullmann, *Peter*, 164-76; Wilcox, "Peter," 73 n. 1; Meyer, *Aims*, 185-96. There are no significant textual issues of concern: Schmidt, ἐκκλησία, *TDNT*, 3.519-20.

while some may even refer to the future), he claims that "sound exegesis requires that the regular usage of tenses be given the benefit of the doubt . . ." ("Mistranslation," 245). (c) Several grammars reinforce his view that the Future Perfect refers to an action to be completed in future time. (d) A number of passages in the NT support this interpretation (Luke 5:20, 23; 7:47; 1 John 2:12; esp. John 20:23), as well as other Greek writings (see below). Using a rough-and-ready definition of periphrasis, in which the Participle and εἰμί are "unquestionably" periphrastic when side-by-side but non-periphrastic when they have one or more words between them (248), he argues that in Matt 16:19 and 18:18 (as well as John 20:23) instead of a simple Future Passive ("will be bound/loosed" [so Moule, 18; Maier, *Matthäus-Evangelium*, 1.573; Beare, *Matthew*, 351; Derrett, "Binding," 112]) the Future Perfect Passive shows that Christ was elevating his disciples to the rank of scribes who were to interpret God's will to men: "This passage does not teach that God concurs in men's conclusions; but rather it teaches that those who live in accordance with Christ's directions will decide to do just what God has already decided should be done" (246). In other words, men will ratify decisions already made in heaven.

2. Cadbury, responding to Mantey in the same 1939 issue of *JBL* ("Meaning"), admits that the Perfect usually indicates a "situation already existent at some time contemplated in the sentence" (251), but disputes Mantey's assertion that the time referent is the same as that of the other verbs in the sentence, since the major examples are found in the "apodosis of a general condition" (251), a conditional sentence which is difficult to evaluate temporally. Citing several examples (1 John 2:5; Jas 2:10; Rom 14:23; 13:8), as well as referring to major grammarians (Blass/Debrunner, Moulton, Robertson, Burton, and Winer), Cadbury claims that this type of conditional construction *may* refer to future action (he cites John 20:23; Rom 7:2; 1 Cor 7:39; X. Anab. 1.8.12) but does *not* do so here. He concludes that Matt 16:19 and 18:18 "seem to imply a permanent condition rather than a condition prior to the time of the relative clause" (252), and thus should be translated "shall be once for all" (253, in contrast to John 20:23, "shall be at once"). He concludes by showing that several examples in the NT (Mark 2:5ff.; Luke 7:47, etc.) make impossible Mantey's reading of a Perfect as referring to a past action preceding the time of speaking.

Matt 16:19 is problematic for interpretation whichever view is adopted. The following understanding is suggested.

a. The construction is clearly periphrastic, since it consists of a Future form of εἰμί and a Perfect Passive Participle in the configuration defined above (Mckay ["Perfect . . . NT Greek," 325] treats it as a "future perfect"). In Matt 16:19 and 18:18 the semantics are of expectation of fulfilment of a hypothetical event, that is binding and loosing. Attempts to establish future temporal implicature on the basis of the Future verb form alone are not acceptable (so Turner, *Insights*, 80), since the Future in Greek is best understood as semantically conveying expectation (Bonnard [*L'évangile*, 245] recognizes a modal sense akin to the Subjunctive).

b. The Perfect Passive Participle is best understood as aspectually designating the state or condition of being bound or loosed (see Louw, "Waarde"), without implicature of either the temporal construct that Mantey and many grammarians posit, or the strictly adjectival sense that Moule (18) suggests. Even if a Perfect Participle is used "adjectivally," one of the common functions of a Participle, especially with the stative aspectual semantic feature, its verbal aspect is not neutralized. This is further confirmed by the fact that δέω and λύω are both found with relatively complete sets of forms in the NT.[37] Thus Turner's view of the Perfect in its original sense as being stative agrees with the understanding of the periphrastic posited here, glossed "can be expected to be in a state of being bound or having boundness," without explicit reference to by verb form alone to when this event might occur. Not only is any presupposition of a rigid temporal scheme unsupportable, but any undue emphasis on the permanence of the state (i.e. "once for all") cannot be posited here on the basis of the Participle alone (contra Allen, *Matthew*, 177;

---

[37]δέω is only found in the NT in the Present stem in the stereotyped forms δεῖ, etc., and δέον, though other conjugations of the Present were current in hellenistic Greek. See Liddell/Scott, *Lexicon*, s.v.; Carson, "Matthew," 372.

apparently followed by Cadbury, "Meaning," 253). The state is in effect, without alluding to the time of its inception or termination.

    c. Cadbury is correct in emphasizing the importance of the conditional or conditional-like statement for determining temporal implicature. The II.a. class conditional--usually with the Subjunctive and ἐάν or its equivalent in the protasis and almost any verb in the apodosis--posits a hypothetical situation and specifies its logical fulfilment. An internal logical order is all that can be posited for the conditional or conditional-like statement apart from temporal deictic indicators. Jesus in essence states, "if something might be bound (Subjunctive) upon the earth, then the consequence is a state of boundness in heaven, and if something might be loosed on earth, then the consequence is a state of loosedness in heaven."[38]

    Jeremias argues that the Passive Voice of the Perfect Participles is a substitute for the divine name, with Jesus following the custom of the time in speaking of God's action by means of circumlocutions (*Theology*, 1.9; curiously he only lists δέω in 16:19; 18:18 as unique to Matthew as divine Passive, not λύω [11]). Thus he renders the verse, "What you bind on earth God will recognize to be bound (at the Last Judgment), and what you loose on earth God will recognize to be loosed (at the Last Judgment)" (κλείς, *TDNT*, 3.751. In *Theology*, 1.9, he renders ἐν τοῖς οὐρανοῖς as "with God," which could be interpreted quite differently). Jeremias not only imposes a rigorous temporal framework on the statements (presumably on the basis of the Future verbs) but he has neglected the obvious non-temporal contrast between heaven and earth. A temporal scheme might be posited, but a *stringent* scheme referring to the judgment is made unlikely not only by the use of the Future verb but by the conditional-like construction that links the two concepts. A second possibility, and probably a better one, is that "heaven" and "earth" refer to spheres of existence. The contrast is found elsewhere in Matthew, e.g. 5:34-35; 6:10; 6:19-20, which use the singular form of heaven, like 18:18 (Thompson [*Advice*, 189] observes that the compound phrase "heaven and earth"--e.g. Matt 5:18; 11:25; 24:35; 28:18--signifies a totality), and stresses the opposition between the two realms (ἐπί with γῆ and ἐν with οὐρανός follow the general pattern, except 5:34-35; cf. Allen, *Matthew*, 177, who claims the opposition is "merely literary"). Debate over the inauguration of the kingdom falls outside the concern of this passage, since Jesus asserts no more than that the assured consequence of an act of binding or loosing in the earthly realm, the realm of the church, if such an act might occur, is the state of boundness or loosedness in the heavenly sphere. In the sense that heaven is God's realm the Participle may be a divine Passive, though the agent does not appear to be nearly so important as the state that results. But the possibility must be recognized that the Passive is used with Peter *et al.* as the agents. The arguments for this are two. (1) Jesus addresses the words to Peter and by implication the other disciples, and there is no indication in the text of another agent. (2) This may be seen as a more natural reading and thus explanation of why the Passive is used: to avoid the clumsiness of the four Active Voice verbs.

    d. An examination of the parallel examples cited by Mantey is in order. (Cf. also e.g. Epict. 2.22.37, where the periphrasis is parallel to simple Future forms. See also Mayser, 2, 1.225; Gignac, 2.307.) He contends that they endorse his position, though he argues this essentially by assertion. They are more reasonably interpreted according to the explanation of periphrasis given above.

---

[38]There are at least five current solutions to the question of what binding and loosing mean: (1) in Rabbinic thought, (a) banning or acquitting members of the community (*Tg. Mo'ed Qatan* 16a) (Strack/Billerbeck, *Mätthaus*, 1.739; Jeremias, κλείς, *TDNT* 3.751); (b) prohibiting or permitting in conduct (cf. *m. Yebam* 1.4) (Strack/ Billerbeck, 1.738-41, esp. 739, 740); (2) opposition of antithetical elements as a comprehensive statement, i.e. all power (Lambert, "Lier-délier"; J. Hoffmann, "Zum Wesen"); (3) dependence upon Isa 22:22 (MT) (Emerton, "Binding"; cf. Díez Macho, "Palestinian Targum"; Vermes, "Versions," 109); (4) exorcism (Heirs, "'Binding'"); (5) opening or closing the kingdom (Luke 11:52; cf. Matt 23:13; J. Jew. War 1.111; Carson, "Matthew," 373; cf. Brown *et al.*, *Peter*, 97). See Thompson, *Advice*, 89-93, for survey; and Burgess, *History*, 62-64, for historical overview.

Lys. 22.19: ἐὰν δ᾽ ἀζημίους ἀφῆτε, πολλὴν ἄδειαν αὐτοῖς ἐψηφισμένοι ἔσεσθε ποιεῖν ὅ τι ἂν βούλωνται. This more likely means, "if you might free them unpunished, then you will be in a state of having voted them freedom to do whatever they might want," rather than that they were given freedom before their remission. Note the II.a. class conditional construction, which merely posits a hypothetical event.

Lys. 12.100: ὅσοι μὲν ἂν τούτων ἀποψηφίσησθε, αὐτῶν θάνατον κατεψηφισμένους ἔσεσθαι (whoever of you would vote [to acquit] them, they [re the condemned] will be in a state of being condemned [by vote] to their death). In this conditional-like statement, the logical consequence of acquittal is said to be condemnation to death, with no indication of a previous event of condemnation contemplated.

Lucian Phal. 1.1: καὶ τοῖς ἄλλοις ἅπασι δι᾽ ὑμῶν ἀπολελογημένος ἔσεσθαι. In context the message of Phalaris, conveyed by messenger, is that he feels that if (II.b. class conditional) he clears himself he will stand cleared through the Delphians and before all the other Greeks. Surely, it does not mean that if he clears himself he will be ratifying a decision to be cleared before he actually undertakes his effort to exonerate himself.

BGU 596.11, 13 (1st-2d cent. A.D.?): τοῦτο οὖν ποιή/σας ἔσῃ μοι μεγάλην / χάριταν κατ[α]τεθειμ[έ]νος (if/when/after you do this, you will be in a state of having bestowed on me a great favour). The same interpretation holds for this sentence, where the Aorist Participle may be interpreted as forming the protasis of a conditional-like statement.

P.Par. 14.49-50 (2d cent. B.C.): τούτου δὲ γενο/μένου ἔσομαι βεβοηθημένος (if/when/after this happens I will be in a state of being helped); 8.22-24 (129 B.C.): τούτου δὲ / γενομένου ἔσομαι τετευχυῖα τῆς / παρά σου ἀντιλήψεως (if/when/after this happens I will be in a state of reception of help from you). Both of these constructions close letters, and as above, use the Aorist Participle to set up a conditional-like statement. Even if the Aorist Participles refer to previous events, the logic of the conditional establishes any continuing sense, not the Perfect Participle alone.

e. Care must be taken not to formulate conception of Greek tenses on the basis of translation into English. Mantey, to some extent Cadbury, and others, seem to believe implicitly that an English Future Perfect conceives of a future event that comes about as the result of an event prior to the point of speaking or writing. This is highly questionable. Comrie, in his recent work on tense, has argued forcefully that the English Future Perfect is an absolute/relative tense. This means that there is an absolute reference to future time in relation to the speaker but a relative reference to the event that precedes this future event (*Tense*, 69ff.). Thus "I will have arrived next Tuesday, and I am leaving tomorrow" is a legitimate use of the English Future Perfect which does not require reference to a past event with future result. Matt 16:19 could, even with Mantey's interpretation, be construed such that earth dictates to heaven, since the act of heaven binding/loosing could be placed subsequent to earthly binding/loosing. English translation, therefore, as is so often the case, is not necessarily a reliable guide to the understanding of Greek tenses.

Heb 2:13: ἐγὼ ἔσομαι πεποιθὼς ἐπ᾽ αὐτῷ (I will trust in him). A quotation of Isa 8:17 (καὶ πεποιθὼς ἔσομαι ἐπ᾽ αὐτῷ [LXX]), the author of Hebrews places these words in Christ's mouth as a testimony to God.

d. [+projection] form of εἰμί + Perfect Participle

In classical Greek the Subjunctive form of εἰμί + Perfect Participle occurs, but is not frequent (see Harry, "Perfect Subjunctive," 19 [1905] 350-51; "Perfect Forms," 60), perhaps because of the mixing of the relatively unmarked attitude of the auxiliary with the strongly marked aspectual nature of the Participle (see Aerts, *Periphrastica*, esp. 40-41, 48-50).[39] The Optative with Perfect Participle appears relatively more frequently,[40] though few appear in the papyri (see Gignac, 2.306) and none occurs in the NT. In the NT, there are several examples of the Subjunctive auxiliary with the Perfect Participle (the periphrastic clearly rivals the simple form, since no verb apart from οἶδα appears in the simple Subjunctive in the NT [see chapt. 7]).

John 3:27: ἐὰν μὴ ᾖ δεδομένον αὐτῷ ἐκ τοῦ οὐρανοῦ (lest it might be given to him from heaven) (see McKay, "Perfect . . . in NT Greek," 324; Barrett [*John*, 222] recognizes the Perfect Subjunctive and translates it: "unless it has been given," stressing God's initiative). In the protasis of an inverted II.a. class conditional, John the Baptist poses to Jesus the hypothetical case (Bultmann [*John*, 172] calls it a maxim) that if one is not the recipient of something from heaven (by God?[41]) then he is not able to receive anything. (Morris [*John*, 240] claims that the Perfect verb has the idea of a "permanent gift," but this surely misses the point.) Cf. 6:65: ἡ δεδομένον. (Cf. P.Oxy. 2342.32 [A.D. 102]: ἵν' ὣ βεβοηθημένος ἐπὶ τοῦ . . . [so that I might be helped by the]. This is a standard closing remark: see also P.Oxy. 488.33 [2d/3d cent. A.D.].)

2 Cor 1:9: ἵνα μὴ πεποιθότες ὦμεν ἐφ' ἑαυτοῖς (so that we might not stand convinced in ourselves). Paul uses two Perfect verbs in this complex sentence. With the first he says that he and his companions housed (Perfect) the sentence of death in themselves, with the result/purpose that they might not put their confidence in themselves but in God. The periphrasis is probably used to maintain the emphatic nature of the sentence and Paul's denigration of his own human condition. (Barrett [*Second Corinthians* , 65] entertains the idea that the periphrasis "suggests the discontinuance of an existing condition.") (Cf. P.Lond. 363.9 [1st/2d cent. A.D.]: ἵν' ὦμεν ὑπὸ σοῦ εὐεργ[ετημένοι [so that we might be shown kindness by you] [reconstructed]; P.Oxy. 486.36 [A.D. 131]; 1117.18 [c. A.D. 178]; 2234.24-25 [A.D. 31]; 2411.37-38 [c. A.D. 173]; P.Lond. 177.26 [A.D. 40-41]. See Gignac, 2.305.)

e. Participle of εἰμί + Perfect Participle

In the NT there are two examples.

Eph 4:18: ἐσκοτωμένοι τῇ διανοίᾳ ὄντες ἀπηλλοτριωμένοι τῆς ζωῆς τοῦ θεοῦ. Cf. Col 1:21· ἡμᾶς , , , ὄντας ἀπηλλοτριωμένους καὶ ἐχθροὺς τῇ διανοίᾳ. The Ephesians passage is complicated by two factors. (1) Use of ὄντες appears to be *ad sensum*, using the Accusative ὑμᾶς (v 17) as its antecedent, although an independent use of the Participle may also be plausible here. Barth (*Ephesians*, 2.500) claims ὄντες "is added to the perfect participle 'blocked out' for good measure." This unlikely view does little to clarify the grammar. (2) The construction may be taken as a single periphrasis with the first Participle and a modifying use of the second (see punctuation in NA[26], "you are darkened in mind, being strangers of the life of God"; Abbott [*Ephesians*, 129] argues that each Participle phrase forms an emphatic unit); vice versa (being darkened in mind, you are strangers [Barth, 2.500]); or a double periphrasis sharing ὄντες (you are darkened in mind and are strangers). In Colossians the periphrasis is clear, though parallelism with the noun ἐχθρούς is to be noted.

---

[39]E.g Pl. Rep. 601D: πρὸς ἣν ἂν ἕκαστον ἢ πεποιημένον ἢ πεφυκός (to which each might be in a state of being made or being so by nature); Gorg. 502B: ἐάν τι αὐτοῖς ἡδὺ μὲν ᾖ καὶ κεχαρισμένον (if something might be indeed in a state of being pleasing to them).

[40]E.g. Hom. Il. 5.873-74 (?); Hdt. 1.45.1; 3.28.1; X. Anab. 4.8.26; Hell. 1.1.11; Pl. Euthyd. 280C. See Gildersleeve, 123-24, for classical examples; Harry, "Perfect Subjunctive," 19 (1905) 351-53, for discussion; idem, "Perfect Forms," 61-62, for hellenistic examples.

[41]See Haenchen, *John 1*, 210; Schnackenburg, *John*, 1.415; Bultmann, *John*, 172; Barrett, *John*, 222; Dalman, *Words*, 217-20.

(The Imperative and Infinitive forms of εἰμί + Perfect Participle in periphrasis are not found in the NT.[42])

3. Aorist Participle

As Gildersleeve states (125), "Periphrases with the aorist participle are rare." And debate exists whether the Aorist periphrasis has the sense of a Perfect or of an Aorist. Björck argues that the narrative auxiliary and Aorist Participle is equivalent to a Latin Pluperfect (*HN ΔIΔAΣKΩN*, 74; it is debatable whether the Latin Pluperfect is not itself ambiguous), while Gildersleeve (125), along with Björck and others, posits that the Aorist periphrasis "may be regarded as the shorthand of the perfect" (Gildersleeve continues that it may also be adjective-like or quasi-substantive; Björck, 84; Blass/Debrunner, ¶ 355). This formulation is not convincing for several reasons. (1) The Perfect has its own set of periphrastic forms, used for emphatic contrast or in place of obsolete simple forms, thus under this theory leaving the Aorist without an equivalent periphrasis and the Perfect with an unnecessary duplicate set of forms to serve the same function. This is an even more unlikely hypothesis if it is further posited that the Perfect periphrasis serves as substitute for the simple Aorist (see above in chapt. 5 on the integrity of the Perfect and its aspectual semantics). (2) The argument that the Perfect never developed certain Participle forms and thus needed the Aorist periphrasis does not find linguistic suppport, since (a) a complete record of all verbal forms in ancient Greek simply does not exist, and (b) the periphrastic functions at the rank of complex word and not lexical rank. Speakers of Greek seem to have distinguished the grammatical categories outlined above, and if a Perfect form were missing in a paradigm, it must not have been needed by them (the language user's ability to create new lexical items when needed must be recognized) and certainly does not argue that another construction filled this supposed gap. (3) Such formulations seem to be constructed along translational lines (as Björck above), a very poor criterion for formally differentiating aspectual semantics.

Aerts argues, on the other hand, on the basis of the verbal aspect of the Aorist that the Aorist periphrastic is distinct from Present and Perfect periphrastics and should be viewed as roughly equivalent to a timeless, unaugmented simple Aorist Indicative (*Periphrastica*, 27, though it is not clear what he means that "one expects a factual meaning that establishes action instead of a static, situation-fixing meaning"; 35). Despite Aerts's apparent confusion about the relation of the augment to temporal reference and his time-bound conception of tense forms, his characterization of the Aorist periphrasis is essentially correct. The reason for its recognized infrequency in

---

[42]These forms occur in extra-biblical Greek: e.g. Imperative: Hom. Il. 8.524; Infinitive: Hom. Od. 9.455; Pl. Laws 814B.

ancient Greek through to the hellenistic period may be bound up closely with the less heavily marked nature of its verbal aspect when used in a marked periphrastic construction. Present and Perfect periphrastics are used to mark the semantic meaning of an already more heavily marked form (or the periphasis is the marked term of the simple/periphrasis opposition), while speakers of Greek do not seem to have required often a marked form of the least heavily marked verbal aspect, though the presence of the Aorist periphrasis attests further to the great flexibility of Greek that where such a form is needed it can be provided.

In ancient Greek the Aorist periphrasis may be found in a number of authors, with a number of different forms of the auxiliary,[43] although the narrative form of the auxiliary is the only form found in the NT.[44] In the NT three possible examples can be cited.

Luke 23:19: ὅστις ἦν διὰ στάσιν τινὰ γενομένην ἐν τῇ πόλει καὶ φόνον βληθεὶς[45] ἐν τῇ φυλακῇ. While Aerts claims that the size of the group of words between the auxiliary and Participle is "striking" and thus periphrasis is "doubtful," and the sentence should be rendered "that was someone who, because of . . ., (at that time) was thrown into prison" (*Periphrastica*, 81-82, cf. 116), this is not entirely certain. The intervening distance is larger than usual, but the causal clause is probably best seen as modifying the Participle. An acceptable periphrasis results (Regard [*Phrase*, 151] calls it an unassailable example): "he was thrown into prison because a certain rebellion and murder had occurred in the city." In v 25 a different construction is used, but the periphrasis is appropriate for emphatic introduction by the narrator of Barabbas, the man released instead of Jesus. (Cf. possibly Th. 5.32.5: αἳ ἦσαν Ἀθηναίοις καὶ Βοιωτοῖς πρὸς ἀλλήλους οὐ πολλῷ ὕστερον γενόμεναι αὐτῶν τῶν πεντηκοντουτίδων σπονδῶν [which had come about not much later than the A.s' and B.s' 50 years' treaty with each other].)

2 Cor 5:19: see under Present Participle. If the Present Participle is seen as periphrastic, it is entirely possible to accept the parallel Present and Aorist Participles as periphrastic as well. A possible interpretation is to see καταλλάσσων as a head-periphrastic with two elucidating or epexegetic periphrastics following. God was reconciling the world, i.e. he was not counting their

---

[43]E.g. Present form of the auxiliary: Hom. Il. 5.177; S. Oed. King 90; Hdt. 2.10.3; Epict. 3.22.23; Optative: S. Oed. King 970; E. Alc. 465-66; Future: S. Oed. King 1146; Oed. Col. 816; Ant. 1067. See Aerts, *Periphrastica*, 27-35; Gildersleeve, 125-26; Stahl, 145-46; Kühner/Gerth, 1.38-39.

[44]E.g. Hom. Il. 4.210-11: Μενέλαος / βλήμενος ἦν (M. was cast); Hdt. 5.69.2: ἦν τε τὸν δῆμον προσθέμενος πολλῷ κατύπερθε τῶν ἀντιστασιωτέων (he had gained the support of the crowd much more than his rivals); Lys. 20.1: οἱ μὲν γὰρ ἐπιβουλεύσαντες ἦσαν αὐτῶν (for some of them had laid plans); Epict. 1 intro 2: οἷόν τε ἦν γραψάμενος ὑπομνήματα (such was written down as a memorial); Arr. 7.7.2: αἱ δὲ ἄλλαι αὐτῷ νῆες ἀνακομισθεῖσαι κατὰ τὸν Εὔλαιον ἔστε (and the rest of the ships are/were sailed upstream along the E.); Plb. 10.45.3: καὶ μὴν οὐδ' αὐτῶν τῶν ἐν τῇ βακτηρίᾳ γεγραμμένων οὐδέν ἐστιν ὡρισμένον (and indeed none of the things written on the rod is defined); P.Jews.1914.35-36 (A.D. 335): ἐπιδὴ ἐπὶ συκοφαντίᾳ καὶ δινὰ [δεινά] ἦσαν γράψαν/τες κατὰ Ἡραείσκου (they had written such a thing in slander against H.); P.Teb. 423.18 (3d cent. A.D.): ἐὰν οὖν μὴ ἧς λαβὼν τὰ πρόβα/τα (if therefore you might not have taken the sheep); P.Lond. Inv. No. 1575.16-17 (3d cent. A.D.): ἡ (= εἰ) ἧς μετ' ἐμοῦ ἀναβάς, πάλε / ἤμην διδαχθείς (if you had come up with me, I should have been taught long ago) (Mandilaras, 239) (see Björck, ΗΝ ΔΙΔΑΣΚΩΝ, 81, for other examples of Aorist periphrasis in conditionals).

[45]See NA[26] for textual variants. Björck (ΗΝ ΔΙΔΑΣΚΩΝ, 77) selects the variant βεβλημένος.

sins against them but was putting the word of reconciliation among men (see Martin, *Corinthians*, 154). The Present Participle (λογιζόμενος) is probably best understood as an emphatic contrast to the initial Participle (καταλλάσσων), while the Aorist Participle (θέμενος), is less heavily marked in opposition to the Present, recapitulating the initial reference to reconciliation (for a different view see Furnish, *II Corinthians*, 319-20). The use of καταλλαγή further rounds off the sentence.

Acts 8:13: βαπτισθεὶς ἦν προσκαρτερῶν. See under Present Participle. (Cf. Arr. 2.6.4: ὅ τι περ ἥδιστον ἦν δοξασθέν [whichever (opinion) was considered really agreeable].)

6. CONCLUSION. Two conclusions may be drawn from this survey. (1) All uses of periphrastics in the NT are found in other ancient Greek literature of both the pre-hellenistic (including often Homeric) and hellenistic periods. This includes the so-called progressive periphrasis of Björck, which (a) is a rather dubious category to define grammatically since it displays no formal criteria to differentiate it from the normal Present periphrasis, and (b) is apparently formulated along lexical and translational and not aspectual lines, the last of which is seen to be one of the crucial factors in distinguishing the meaning and importance of periphrastic constructions (so Aerts,*Periphrastica*, 30, except for his endorsement of Björck). (2) Semitic intervention into periphrastic constructions in the NT cannot be supported. Whereas perhaps the use of the Present periphrasis is aided by Septuagintal precedent (Septuagintal enhancement) the fact that this construction is found throughout ancient Greek literature mitigates the argument.

APPENDIX 10A:
PERIPHRASTIC CONSTRUCTIONS

1. Present Participle
a. [-remoteness] form of εἰμί + Present Participle

Acts 19:36: δέον ἐστὶν ὑμᾶς κατεσταλμένους ὑπάρχειν (it is binding for you to be prepared). This gloss attempts to capture the sense of the Ephesian town scribe instructing the people in their responsibilities, trying to keep them calm to avoid a riot. (Cf. P.Oxy. 727.19 [A.D. 154] and 1061.13 [22 B.C.]: δέον ἦν; Epict. 2.7.4: τί γὰρ ἐστι συμφέρον οἶδεν; [why, does he know it is expedient?]. Blass [204] says periphrases with impersonal verbs "must be given a place to themselves, since they are not only common in Hellenistic Greek . . ., but are also found previously in Attic [ἐστὶ προσῆκον D. 3.24].")

Rom 13:6: λειτουργοὶ γὰρ θεοῦ εἰσιν εἰς αὐτὸ τοῦτο προσκαρτεροῦντες (for servants of God are devoting themselves to this same thing, or with this end in view). (See Cranfield, *Romans*, 2.669; contra Sanday/Headlam, *Romans*, 368, who view the Participle as absolute.) In speaking of obedience to rulers, Paul posits that it is obligatory to be subordinate not only for fear of wrath but out of conscience. This gives a reason for taxes, since God's servants are involved.

1 Cor 8:5: καὶ γὰρ εἴπερ εἰσὶν λεγόμενοι θεοὶ εἴτε ἐν οὐρανῷ εἴτε ἐπὶ γῆς. Though it is likely λεγόμενοι is an anarthrous Participle serving as a modifier of θεοί (see Robertson/Plummer, *First Corinthians*, 167, Bruce, *Corinthians*, 80; Barrett, *First Corinthians*, 191-92), it could be construed as a periphrastic to be rendered either "even if or though they are called 'gods' either in heaven or on earth," or, less likely, "even if gods are called/spoken of either in heaven or on earth." Either is a possibility in Paul's hypothetical argument about the nature of the divine, followed by his ὥσπερ clause. (Cf. Paus. 1.5.1: Θόλος ἐστὶ καλουμένη [is called T.]; Str. 1.1.9: Ἵππαρχος δ᾽ οὐ πιθανός ἐστιν ἀντιλέγων τῇ δόξῃ ταύτῃ [H. is not convincing, contradicting this view. . .]. See Jones, *Geography*, 1.19, who translates "Hipparchus is not convincing when he contradicts this view. . . .")

2 Cor 9:12: ἡ διακονία τῆς λειτουργίας ταύτης οὐ μόνον ἐστὶν προσαναπληροῦσα τὰ ὑστερήματα τῶν ἁγίων, ἀλλὰ καὶ περισσεύουσα διὰ πολλῶν εὐχαριστιῶν τῷ θεῷ (the service[1] of this worship not only is filling up the lackings of the saints but indeed abounding through many blessings to God[2]). Paul commends the Corinthians' generosity, emphasizing not only its very important function of meeting physical needs but the even more important function of reflecting their spiritual attitude.

---

[1]Barrett (*Second Corinthians*, 239-40) argues the translation should read "execution"; see Martin, *Corinthians*, 292-93.

[2]"To God" may be linked with either the Participle or the Genitive group; see Plummer, *Second Corinthians*, 265.

Col 1:6: καθὼς καὶ ἐν παντὶ τῷ κόσμῳ ἐστὶν καρποφορούμενον καὶ αὐξανόμενον καθὼς καὶ ἐν ὑμῖν (as indeed in the whole world it is bearing fruit and growing as indeed in you). The locative groups seem best interpreted as completive elements of the two Present Participles, since Paul is relating to the Colossians his thanks to God for the productivity of the gospel both in the world at large and among them (the Middle form of the Participles appears to have an active sense; see Moule, *Colossians*, 50. On the oddness of the logic of using these two verbs in this order see Schweizer, *Colossians*, 36). (Cf. Plb. 5.19.7: ἥτις ἐστὶν ὡς πρὸς μέρος θεωρουμένη πλείστη [which is seen as great as to portion].)

Rev 1:18: ἰδοὺ ζῶν εἰμι εἰς τοὺς αἰῶνας τῶν αἰώνων (behold I am living forever). Thompson is right that this is periphrastic in accord with Greek usage (*Apocalypse*, 51; see also Aerts, *Periphrastica*, 69-70; Regard, *Phrase*, 118). The visionary speaker is contrasting the fact that he was dead (ἐγενόμην) with the even more important statement (ἰδού?) that he is in progress of living forever. The contrast does not refer to the "essential life of God" (ὁ ζῶν). (Cf. S. Oed. King 1045: ἦ κἄστ᾽ ἔτι ζῶν οὗτος; [and is this one still living?].)

b. [+remoteness] form of εἰμί + Present Participle

Luke 21:37: ἦν δὲ τὰς ἡμέρας ἐν τῷ ἱερῷ διδάσκων, may be rendered either with the temporal and locative groups functioning in relation to the auxiliary (he was in the temple during the day, teaching) or with the temporal and locative groups functioning as completive elements of the Participle (he was teaching in the temple during the day) (a third possibility, the Accusative of time modifying the auxiliary and the locative group completing the Participle, is rather unlikely). Perhaps the periphrastic interpretation is more likely, on the basis of parallelism with the following clause (Marshall [*Luke*, 784] treats it as reflecting 19:47).[3]

Matt 12:4: ὃ οὐκ ἐξὸν ἦν αὐτῷ φαγεῖν (which was not legal [being legally possible] for him to eat) (cf. Mark 2:26 = Luke 6:4). David's entrance into the house of God to eat the showbread was emphatically not legal.

Matt 19:22 = Mark 10:22: ἦν γὰρ ἔχων κτήματα πολλά (for he was in progress possessing many things). Matthew and Mark conclude their story of the rich man with the reason for this potential follower's grief at Jesus' requirements. This is the only Gospel story which records that a command to follow Jesus is tacitly refused (so Taylor, *Mark*, 430). Björck (*HN ΔΙΔΑΣΚΩΝ*, 114) considers this progressive periphrasis, though use of an adjective in the Lukan parallel (18:23) might argue otherwise. Hartman (*Constructions*, 25) hypothesizes that the Participle was ambiguous and Luke thus avoided the expression. (Blass/Debrunner [¶ 62(2)] claim Aramaic influence, contra Moulton, 227; Tabachovitz, *Septuaginta*, 44-45.)

Mark 1:13: ἦν ἐν τῇ ἐρήμῳ τεσσεράκοντα ἡμέρας πειραζόμενος ὑπὸ τοῦ σατανᾶ. Though this construction may be periphrastic (he was being tempted in the desert by S. for 40 days) (Regard, *Phrase*, 134), the Participle is probably solely adjunctive (he was in the desert--for forty days--being tempted by S.) on the basis of the abundance of modifying elements and the locative function of ἦν in the next clause (the Accusative of time does not occur often with εἰμί, though it is not unknown, e.g. John 7:33).

Mark 5:5: ἦν κράζων καὶ κατακόπτων ἑαυτὸν λίθοις (he was in progress crying and cutting himself with stones). Though preceded by a series of temporal and locative phrases, this combination of the narrative auxiliary and Present Participle emphasizes the histrionics in which the demoniac was involved.

Mark 15:43: ὃς καὶ αὐτὸς ἦν προσδεχόμενος τὴν βασιλείαν τοῦ θεοῦ (who himself was expecting the kingdom of God). Despite the redundant personal pronoun, this relative clause provides a marked emphasis upon what the author considers the most important quality of Joseph. He may have been from Arimathea but his expectation of the kingdom set him apart. (Björck [*HN ΔΙΔΑΣΚΩΝ*, 54] debates whether it is adjectival or progressive.)

---

[3]Cf. Mark 14:49 (καθ᾽ ἡμέραν ἤμην πρὸς ὑμᾶς ἐν τῷ ἱερῷ διδάσκων [each day I was with you-in the temple-teaching]), where ἤμην has two modifiers that virtually insure its independent usage (Aerts, *Periphrastica*, 58), though ἐν τῷ ἱερῷ is ambiguous.

Luke 2:8: καὶ ποιμένες ἦσαν ἐν τῇ χώρᾳ τῇ αὐτῇ ἀγραυλοῦντες καὶ φυλάσσοντες φυλακάς. Though this sentence opening a pericope may be periphrastic (shepherds were living outdoors in the same country and keeping guard), the locative group is ambiguous and probably emphasizes an existential sense of the auxiliary (shepherds were in the same country, living outdoors and keeping guard), as posit Aerts (*Periphrastica*, 53) and Moule (17), contra Karleen (*Syntax*, 130), who claims it is progressive periphrasis on the basis of the following verse (καὶ ἄγγελος κυρίου ἐπέστη αὐτοῖς [and an angel of the Lord stood before them] [v 9]). (Cf. J. Jew. War 1.503: εἰ μή τινες ἦσαν ἀναπείθοντες καὶ τὸ τῆς ἡλικίας εὔκολον ἐπὶ κακῷ μεταχειριζόμενοι [unless they were misleading him and leading the goodness of youth to evil].)

Luke 4:38: πενθερὰ δὲ τοῦ Σίμωνος ἦν συνεχομένη πυρετῷ μεγάλῳ (the mother-in-law of Simon was being distressed by a high fever). When Jesus came up from the synagogue and entered Simon's house (two Aorists), Simon's mother-in-law was suffering from her high fever.

Luke 5:16: αὐτὸς δὲ ἦν ὑποχωρῶν ἐν ταῖς ἐρήμοις καὶ προσευχόμενος (as a habit he was withdrawing in the desert and praying). This double periphrastic, joining two pericope on healing, indicates a process Jesus was regularly involved in throughout his ministry. (Fitzmyer [*Luke*, 1.575] stresses the iterative *Aktionsart*; while Marshall [*Luke*, 210] and Plummer [*Luke*, 151] emphasize the durative.) The marked emphasis on withdrawing to pray helps explain Jesus' success in performing healings. Cf. Luke 5:17, which resumes the narrative with several periphrastics. See also Luke 6:12, where Jesus is said to have gone out to pray on the mountain, and was in progress passing the night in prayer (ἦν διανυκτερεύων ἐν τῇ προσευχῇ).

Luke 11:14: καὶ ἦν ἐκβάλλων δαιμόνιον (and he was in progress casting out demons). At the beginning of the Beelzeboul controversy the author sets the tone of the pericope with the introductory, though "slightly odd" (Marshall, *Luke*, 472), periphrasis which leads directly past the event itself (especially if the textual variant is accepted[4]) to the rationale for it.

Luke 13:11: καὶ ἦν συγκύπτουσα καὶ μὴ δυναμένη ἀνακύψαι (and she was already bending over and not being able to straighten up or raise her head). The incident begins with the periphrasis in v 10 introducing Jesus as teacher, and is continued with an introduction of the second character, the woman, who is suffering from a debilitating illness such that, the author emphasizes, she both is bent over and cannot raise up.

Luke 14:1: καὶ αὐτοὶ ἦσαν παρατηρούμενοι αὐτόν (and they were watching him closely). Jesus had already caused several stirs on the sabbath (Luke 6:2ff; 13:14ff.), including plucking grain, so when he entered a leader's house (of the Pharisees, or synagogue?) they (the people or other Pharisees?) were actively in progress observing him. (Plummer [*Luke*, 354] calls it an "error" if any translation does not treat this as periphrastic; cf. Karleen, *Syntax*, 129, who claims the example is progressive).

Luke 23:8: ἦν γὰρ ἐξ ἱκανῶν χρόνων θέλων ἰδεῖν αὐτόν (for a long time he was wanting to see him). Verse 8 contrasts Herod's great joy at seeing Jesus (Aorist), with the even more important reason for that joy: he had long had the desire to meet him. (Cf. Plb. 20.4.1: ὅτι Βοιωτοὶ ἐκ πολλῶν ἤδη χρόνων καχεκτοῦντες ἦσαν [B. for many years was a dead state]; cf. Plb. 20.7.4; 1.68.10; 28.17.12.)

Luke 24:13: δύο . . . ἦσαν πορευόμενοι εἰς κώμην[5] (two were going to a village). The pericope about the two disciples' walk to Emmaus opens with a periphrastic description of their being on the journey. This narrative is continued by other imperfective verbs.

Luke 24:32: οὐχὶ ἡ καρδία ἡμῶν καιομένη[6] ἦν [ἐν ἡμῖν] (our heart was burning within us, wasn't it?). Once Jesus made himself known to the disciples in Emmaus he disappeared from

---

[4][καὶ αὐτὸ ἦν] κωφόν, accepted by A^c C D f^13 but rejected by p^74 75 ℵ* B f^1, a D reading in UBS^3. See Metzger, *Commentary*, 158.

[5]The textual variant does not affect this interpretation.

[6]Note the textual uncertainties here, prompting various theories of underlying Semitic substrata; see Black, *Approach*, 254-55.

them (v 31, Aorist verbs), leaving them to wonder to themselves about the strange feelings (Regard [*Phrase*, 131] sees emphasis on "burning") generated by their meeting the risen Jesus. Plummer (*Luke*, 557-58) is probably mistaken in asserting that the periphrastic is used to emphasize the "continuance of the emotion," rather than the author's conception of the action itself.

Acts 1:13: οὐ ἦσαν καταμένοντες (where they were living). The author contrasts the act of the disciples' going into the upstairs room for a particular occasion with the fact that this is where they regularly lived. Haenchen (*Acts*, 153) says the periphrasis "implies permanent residence," but this may be overstating the case. Cf. as well Acts 2:2 (οὐ ἦσαν καθήμενοι [where they were sitting]) and 18:7 (οὗ ἡ οἰκία ἦν συνομοροῦσα τῇ συναγωγῇ [where the house was sitting next door to the synagogue]). Bruce (*Acts*, 345) observes that periphrastics are fewer in the second half of Acts.

Acts 2:5: ἦσαν δὲ εἰς Ἰερουσαλήμ κατοικοῦντες Ἰουδαῖοι (Jews were living in J.). Though this phrase might be locative use of ἦσαν[7] (Jews were in J., living there), the periphrastic interpretation seems more likely, especially since the subject is dislocated from the auxiliary and the syntactical unit seems to propel the narrative forward at the beginning of the pericope. (Cf. Lys. 2.75: οἷοίπερ ἐκεῖνοι ζῶντες ἦσαν [such as when they were living].)

Acts 9:9: καὶ ἦν ἡμέρας τρεῖς μὴ βλέπων (and he was not seeing for three days). Though a non-periphrastic construction is possible ("and he was three days without sight" [AV, NASB; cf. Aerts, *Periphrastica*, 53; Bruce, *Acts*, 200]), the periphrastic rendering draws attention to the seriousness of Paul's experience on the Damascus road. The fact that he did not eat or drink (two Aorists) for the same length of time is apparently of secondary importance to the author. Acts 10:30 (ἤμην τὴν ἐνάτην προσευχόμενος ἐν τῷ οἴκῳ μου) is less clear since the Accusative of time might make an existential use of ἤμην explicit (I was there in the ninth hour, praying in my room), though, more likely, it constitutes a periphrastic (I was praying in my room during the ninth hour) (so Regard, *Phrase*, 123). The same problem is found in Acts 11:5 (ἐγὼ ἤμην ἐν πόλει Ἰόππῃ προσευχόμενος) with the locative group "in the city of Joppa" (Regard [130] translates the sentence "j'étais en train de prier dans . . .") and Acts 16:12 (ἦμεν δὲ ἐν ταύτῃ τῇ πόλει διατρίβοντες ἡμέρας τινάς [and we were--in this city--waiting for several days]) (see Björck, *HN ΔΙΔΑΣΚΩΝ*, 52).

Acts 12:5: προσευχὴ δὲ ἦν ἐκτενῶς γινομένη ὑπὸ τῆς ἐκκλησίας ("prayer was being made fervently for him by the Church" [NASB]). In this unusual passive use of the deponent verb γίνομαι, the author closes his pericope about Peter's imprisonment by shifting from Peter's condition in prison to the church's fervent activity during this time. As Bruce (*Acts*, 245) says, "if it differs from ἐγίνετο, it must be as laying special emphasis on the continuousness of the praying," though Haenchen (*Acts*, 353 n. 2) claims ἐκτενῶς does not indicate only duration. (Cf. Plb. 10.41.7: ὃ δὴ τότε μάλιστα συνιδεῖν ἦν γινόμενον ὑπὸ τοῦ Φιλίππου [which then was becoming known by P. (his actions)].)

Acts 12:20: ἦν δὲ θυμομαχῶν Τυρίοις καὶ Σιδωνίοις (and he was in progress being very angry with the residents of T. and S.). Herod is a focal point in chapt. 12 (see e.g. vv 1, 6, 19, 21), and this use of the narrative periphrastic opens the third major section of the chapter by propelling the narrative to the time when Herod dies.

Acts 14:7: κἀκεῖ εὐαγγελιζόμενοι ἦσαν (and they were spreading the good news there). This periphrastic construction rounds off Paul and Barnabus's time at Iconium by showing them resuming their ministry in Lystra and Derbe after fleeing Iconium.

Acts 16:9: τις ἦν ἑστὼς καὶ παρακαλῶν αὐτὸν καὶ λέγων (a certain man was standing and beseeching him and saying . . .). The author's apparently conscious use of the tenses contrasts the man from Macedonia's state as one of standing (Perfect Participle), with the activity he is in progress performing (Present Participle), beseeching Paul. The use of καί to connect the 'redundant' λέγων implies a third periphrastic. (Cf. D.H. Rom. Ant. 5.33.2: ὁ Ταρκύνιος ἦν

---

[7]εἰς with εἰμί is rare in the NT, though not unknown, e.g. Luke 11:7; Acts 8:20. Regard (*Phrase*, 127) recognizes the possibility of a copulative or an absolute use of εἰμί.

ἐπιορκίαν τε καὶ ἀπιστίαν τοῖς 'Ρωμαίοις ἐγκαλῶν καὶ τὸν βασιλέα παροξύνων [T. was calling out oaths and disbelief of the R.s and imitating/goading the king].)

c. [+expectation] form of εἰμί + Present Participle

Luke 21:24: καὶ 'Ιερουσαλὴμ ἔσται πατουμένη ὑπὸ ἐθνῶν (J. shall be being trampled by nations). In an extended conditional-like pericope the author posits (Aorist Subjunctive) that Jerusalem may be destroyed. When this happens, he asserts, certain consequences can be expected, including being trampled under foot.

Mark 13:25: καὶ οἱ ἀστέρες ἔσονται ἐκ τοῦ οὐρανοῦ πίπτοντες (the stars shall be falling from heaven). The locative group seems clearly to complete the Participle. This clause lies third in a series of four clauses about events after the days of tribulation. It is difficult to interpret the marked quality, unless this construction draws attention to the fact that this is the only stiche that speaks of a transformation of a heavenly body (Aerts [*Periphrastica*, 59] calls it an "expressive periphrasis"). Otherwise the periphrastic is parallel to a simple form (Taylor [*Mark*, 518] claims that it may be an Aramaism [though this does not explain why it stands alone] but is more probably a "vernacular variant" that Matt 24:29 corrects).

Luke 1:20: ἔσῃ σιωπῶν καὶ μὴ δυνάμενος λαλῆσαι ἄχρι (you will be in progress being silent and unable to speak until . . .). The angel tells Zacharias that because he has not believed the news of a child he will no longer be able to speak. The auxiliary might be interpreted as a command but in any case the selection of tense conveys the expectation of the angel's message. Despite some thought that the Present Participle is adjectivised (Aerts, *Periphrastica*, 59; cf. Johannes Moschos 143.37.51), the context seems to demand an aspectual analysis.

2. Perfect Participle

a. [-remoteness] form of εἰμί + Perfect Participle

Luke 20:6: πεπεισμένος γάρ ἐστιν 'Ιωάννην προφήτην εἶναι (for the crowd is persuaded that John was a prophet). While the scribes are deliberating Jesus' question about John's baptism, they stress their knowledge that the crowd was fully persuaded that John was a prophet (contra Moule, 18, who because he cannot see a temporal sense in the Participle posits an adjectival use).

Luke 23:15: οὐδὲν ἄξιον θανάτου ἐστὶν πεπραγμένον αὐτῷ (nothing worthy of death is being practiced by him[8]). Pilate stresses to the chief priests and rulers that after his and Herod's deliberation both concur that nothing calling for the death sentence was committed by Jesus. (Moulton/Howard [459], contra Wellhausen, reject this construction as an Aramaism, citing examples from Kühner/Gerth, 1.422: Th. 1.51, 118; Hdt. 6.123; Isoc. 4.4; Lys. 24.4; X. Anab. 1.8.12; 7.6.32; Cyr. 7.2.15; and D. 29.1: δεῖ διδάξαι διηγήσασθαι τὰ τούτῳ πεπραγμένα περὶ ἡμῶν [it is necessary to instruct in and discuss the things done by him concerning us].)

Luke 24:38: τί τεταραγμένοι ἐστέ; (why are you terrified?). Appearing to the shocked disciples, Jesus asks why they are in a frightened state, stressing that they of all people should have expected his return.

John 3:21: ὅτι ἐν θεῷ ἐστιν εἰργασμένα (that in God [his works] are accomplished). In his mini-theology for Nicodemus, Jesus reportedly stresses the contrast of light and dark, concluding grandly that, whereas those who are practicing evil hate the light, those who have done the truth come to the light, which shows that their works are accomplished in God.

John 3:28: ὅτι 'Απεσταλμένος εἰμὶ ἔμπροσθεν ἐκείνου (I am sent before him). John quiets the jealousy of his disciples by pointing out two things to them: he is not the Christ, but he *is the one sent before* the Christ.

Acts 25:10: ἐπὶ τοῦ βήματος Καίσαρος[9] ἑστώς εἰμι (I stand on the bema-seat of C.). When Festus threatens to take Paul to Jerusalem for trial, Paul solemnly pronounces the words above (Bruce, *Acts*, 431; contra Regard, *Phrase*, 138, who claims that the sense of ἑστώς is close

---

[8]Blass/Debrunner (¶ 191) claim that this is perhaps the only genuine example in the NT of the Dative of agent with a Passive verb. Manuscripts D N G f[13] *al* provide ἐν before αὐτῷ, though Blass/Debrunner suggest the correct reading may omit the Participle; cf. Acts 25:5.

[9]Note repetition of ἑστώς in B.

to a Present Participle), explaining to Festus that while he is willing to suffer a just punishment, he would prefer that it be given by Caesar. (Cf. P.Petr. ii 4[10].2-3 [260 B.C.]: τεῖχος μέρος μέν τι αὐτοῦ / πεπτώκος ἐστιν [a certain portion of wall is dilapidated].)

Acts 25:14: ἀνήρ τίς ἐστιν καταλελειμμένος ὑπὸ Φήλικος δέσμιος (a certain man, a prisoner, is left by F.). Festus relates to Agrippa the circumstances of Paul's imprisonment. He begins by stressing that this is a problem left over from his predecessor.

1 Cor 5:2: καὶ ὑμεῖς πεφυσιωμένοι ἐστέ (you are puffed up). After citing a specific offense of which certain Corinthians are guilty (incest), Paul generalizes on their condition as one of arrogance. Bruce contends that the offence of arrogance was much worse than incest (*Corinthians*, 54), perhaps further justifying the periphrasis.

1 Cor 7:29: ὁ καιρὸς συνεσταλμένος ἐστίν (the time is shortened). With a due preface for emphasis (τοῦτο δέ φημι [I am saying this]) Paul gives the clinching reason for his stringent view of marriage--the time stands shortened because the world is passing away (v 31). (Cf. P.Lille 26.2-3 [3d cent. B.C.]: αὐτή μὲν οὖν ἐστιν παντελῶς ἀπηρ/γμένη [it (the land) is fully cut off].)

Col 2:10: καὶ ἐστὲ ἐν αὐτῷ πεπληρωμένοι (you are fulfilled in him/it). The locative group is better seen as referring to the state of being fulfilled, which takes place in or through him/it (periphrastic) (Schweizer, *Colossians*, 139-40); rather than as referring to being in him/it, resulting in the state of being fulfilled.

Heb 4:2: καὶ γάρ ἐσμεν εὐηγγελισμένοι καθάπερ κάκεῖνοι (for we are in a state of having the gospel[10] preached, as they are). In a passage abounding in Perfect verbs the author is making a statement about the condition that people are found in on the basis of having heard the good news proclaimed. The author claims that while both groups have had the good news proclaimed to them, for some it has been to profit and for others not. (Cf. PSI 424.15-16 [3d cent. B.C.]: ἐστιν δὲ πεπαιδευμέ/νος πᾶσαν παιδείαν [he is in a state of having educated all the children].)

2 Pet 3:7: see above in main text under Present Participle.

b. [+remoteness] form of εἰμί + Perfect Participle

Mark 15:46: ὃ ἦν λελατομημένον ἐκ πέτρας (which was in a state of being carved from rock). Though the lexis seems to demand implicature of a previous act of carving, the emphasis in use of the Perfect Participle is that it stood as a carved tomb. Cf. Matt 27:60 with ἐλατόμησεν.

Luke 1:7: καὶ ἀμφότεροι προβεβηκότες ἐν ταῖς ἡμέραις αὐτῶν ἦσαν (both were in a state of old age). The idiom προβαίνω ἐν ταῖς ἡμέραις is conducive to the stative aspect, either in simple or periphrastic form, to capture the condition of those who have lived many years.[11] Luke (ironically?) describes Zacharias and his wife (vv 5-6) as righteous people who were childless, because Elizabeth was sterile and both were advanced in age. (Cf. BGU 5.61 [2d cent. A.D.]: ἐὰν ὁ ἀπελευθερούμενος ὑπὲρ τριάκοντα ἔτη ἦν γεγονώς [if the one who is set free has become more than 30 years old].)

Luke 2:26: καὶ ἦν αὐτῷ κεχρηματισμένον ὑπὸ τοῦ πνεύματος τοῦ ἁγίου (and it was revealed to him by the holy spirit). Simeon is described as a just and devout man expecting the salvation of Israel. The holy spirit in fact had revealed to him that he would not see death before he would see the Christ, and it was in this state that he lived.

Luke 5:1: αὐτὸς ἦν ἑστὼς παρὰ τήν λίμνην (he himself was in a state of standing alongside the lake). In a subtle use of aspect the author, after introductory comments to set the stage, says Jesus was standing along the lake of Genaseret, and two boats were standing (Perfect) there as well. From his meeting with the owners of these two boats come Jesus' first disciples (Marshall [*Luke*, 201], following Black [*Approach*, 83] and Beyer [*Syntax*, 31], sees the clause as circumstantial). Cf. Acts 16:9 (see above); 22:20 (see above); contra John 18:18, 25.

---

[10]This may simply mean "good news," or, as Bruce (*Hebrews*, 72 n. 16) suggests: "we have been evangelized."

[11]Plummer (*Luke*, 10) notes that classical Greek would have τῇ ἡλικίᾳ.

Luke 9:45: ἦν παρακεκαλυμμένον ἀπ' αὐτῶν (it was hidden from them). See 2 Cor 4:3, considering the narrative context of Luke 9.

Luke 23:51: οὗτος οὐκ ἦν συγκατατεθειμένος τῇ βουλῇ (he was not in agreement with the decision). Luke wants to clarify parenthetically and yet emphatically that though Joseph was a member of the sanhedrin, he had not stood in agreement with their decision to kill Jesus (cf. Hartman, *Constructions*, 27). Cf. Mark 15:43 above, where a different author chooses to note a different fact about Joseph's character.

John 3:24: οὔπω γὰρ ἦν βεβλημένος εἰς τὴν φυλακήν (John was not yet thrown into prison). The author, interjecting one of his parenthetical comments, stresses that John was continuing to baptize in Aenon near Salin, because he was not yet imprisoned.

John 13:5: ᾧ ἦν διεζωσμένος[12] (in which he was clothed). It is not readily apparent why the author chooses to emphasize that Jesus used the towel in which he was wrapped to wipe off the disciples' feet, unless it is to stress further the degree of humility displayed, i.e. he used the very cloth that he stood wrapped in. Cf. John 19:41, drawing attention to the cave as previously unoccupied; Acts 4:31, emphasizing that the shaking at Pentecost focused on their gathering. (Cf. P.Oxy. 285.10-11 [A.D. 50]: ὃν ἤμην / ἐνδεδυμένος χιτῶνα [which chiton I was clothed in].)

Acts 1:17: ὅτι κατηριθμημένος ἦν ἐν ἡμῖν (because he was in a state of being counted among us). Peter tells his fellow apostles that Judas was part of the fulfilment of the scriptures, that he was an actual member of them and received the reward of that service, but that he went astray and suffered dire and well-known consequences. Perhaps the periphrastic is used here to stress a fact that could be overlooked, that Judas had been one of them (for a purpose) at one time. (Cf. Απ. 2.2.3: οὐδὲ . . . τοσαύτη ξυνηγμένη ἦν ὡς δι' ὀλίγου προσδοκᾶν ἔσεσθαι ἄν σφισι παρ' αὐτοῦ τινὰ ὠφέλειαν [a sufficient (fleet) was not gathered as to expect any immediate help would come from him (Alexander) to them].)

Acts 8:16: οὐδέπω γὰρ ἦν ἐπ' οὐδενὶ αὐτῶν ἐπιπεπτωκός. The locative group may be interpreted as either modifying the auxiliary (the holy spirit never was upon any of them, having fallen/when it fell) or completing the Participle (the holy spirit never was in a state of having fallen upon any of them). The periphrastic construction seems likely, especially in view of the stress on sending the apostles Peter and John to guarantee that the Samarians receive proper spiritual experience.

Acts 20:13: διατεταγμένος ἦν μέλλων. See above in main text under Present Participle.

Acts 21:29: ἦσαν γὰρ προεωρακότες Τρόφιμον . . . ἐν τῇ πόλει σὺν αὐτῷ (for they were in a state of having seen beforehand T in the city with him). The author relates Paul's arrest in the temple precinct by the Jews, who accused him of taking a Greek into the temple and thus defiling it. He then interjects the important reason for their spirited act: they had seen Trophimus, the Ephesian Gentile, in the city.

Acts 22:29: ὅτι αὐτὸν ἦν δεδεκώς (that he was in a state of having beaten him). The centurion grows worried when he discovers Paul's Roman citizenship and realizes that he has beaten him. The pericope is well constructed to draw attention to this violation of Roman law: it ends with an emphatic periphrasis, with the complement, referring to Paul, displaced to the front of the clause. (Aerts [*Periphrastica*, 92] argues strongly that the Perfect Participle expresses a "temporary circumstance," while the Present expresses a "permanent quality." The grounds for his reasoning are unclear.)

Gal 4:3: ὑπὸ τὰ στοιχεῖα τοῦ κόσμου ἤμεθα δεδουλωμένοι (we were enslaved by the elementary principles of the world). Though Paul uses parallel clauses with an adjective (we were children [childish]), this does not discount the aspectual nature of the Perfect Participle. Instead it provides an emphatic contrast: when we were children we were . . . . As Bruce says (*Galatians*, 193), the periphrastic "emphasizes the state in which 'we' were 'when we were infants,'" more so than the simple form. (Cf. P.Petr. ii 4[7].3 [255-54 B.C.]: ἐπεὶ (= ἐπὶ, Mandilaras, 234) τῶν ἔργων τεθλιμμένοι ἤμεθα [by the works we were confined]; P.Mich. 512.4-5 [3d cent. A.D.]:

---

[12]This is not an Aorist as per Morris, *John*, 616 n. 17.

εἰ μὴ ὅτι συνεζήτηκα / τῷ Πτολεμαίῳ πάλαι ἂν ἀπηλλαγμένοι ἦσμεν [except that I am in a state of dispute with P., we would be set free for a long time].)

d. [+projection] form of εἰμί + Perfect Participle

Luke 14:8: μήποτε ἐντιμότερός σου ᾖ κεκλημένος ὑπ᾽ αὐτοῦ (lest one more esteemed than you might be invited by him). In a lesson in humility, Jesus reportedly posits the hypothetical situation that when invited to a marriage feast one might seat himself too highly and then be forced to move down, because one of higher station might be invited (Marshall [*Luke*, 582] gives the sense of "has [already] been invited"). The periphrastic reinforces the extreme sense of embarrassment should this happen (contra Aerts, *Periphrastica*, 95, who says ᾖ tends to be independent). (Cf. Plb. 12.25a.2: καὶ τοῦτο γεγονὸς ᾖ κατὰ προαίρεσιν [and this might come about according to plan].)

John 16:24: ἵνα ἡ χαρὰ ὑμῶν ᾖ πεπληρωμένη (so that your joy might stand fulfilled). Jesus reportedly instructs his followers to ask (Present Imperative) and receive (Future, used as a command or sure consequence?), with the result that their joy may be complete. While emphasis surely rests on the Future verb for the outcome of asking, the periphrasis draws attention to the state of completeness of such a joy. As Barrett (*John*, 495) says, the joy is "more closely defined; it consists in the access to God which is described as asking and receiving" (cf. McKay, "Perfect . . . NT Greek," 324). Cf. Phil 1:10-11, where the auxiliary is separated from the Participle by two parallel adjectives; and 1 John 1:4: ἵνα ἡ χαρὰ ἡμῶν ᾖ πεπληρωμένη (so that your joy might be fulfilled).

John 17:23: ἵνα ὦσιν τετελειωμένοι εἰς ἕν (so that they might be matured into one). In a prayer to God, an especially large number of Subjunctives (vv 20ff.) and the phrase ἕν . . . ὦσιν (vv 21, 22) are used. In v 23 attention is drawn to more than just "being one" but the state of being mature or made into one group (see Morris, *John*, 735; Bultmann, *John*, 516 n. 3, who sees an eschatological sense). (Cf. Plb. 6.19.5: ἐὰν μὴ δέκα στρατείας ἐνιαυσίους ᾖ τετελεκώς [unless ten years of service might be complete].)

1 Cor 1:10: ἦτε δὲ κατηρτισμένοι ἐν τῷ αὐτῷ νοΐ (you might be united in the same mind). The marked sense here is difficult to see unless it is the climactic result--a state of unity of mind and knowledge--of Paul's exhortation. Cf. 2 Cor 9:3: ἵνα . . . παρεσκευασμένοι ἦτε (so that you might be prepared). (Cf. SB 7987.10-11 [A.D. 81-96]: ἐὰν . . . ᾖς περισπασμένος [if you might be stripped]; P.Oxy. 1583.8-9 [2d cent. A.D.]: αἰὰν [1. ἐὰν] ᾖς εἰληφὼς / παρὰ Φαριτῶν τὴν δερματικὴν [1. δαλματικὴν] [if you might receive from P. the leather goods].)

Jas 5:15: κἂν ἁμαρτίας ᾖ πεποιηκώς (and if he might have committed sins). In the protasis of a II.a. class conditional, James continues his statements about the effectiveness of prayer for healing the sick, by extending it to sin. If this man has sinned, it will be forgiven (Future) him. (Cf. BGU 5.45 [2d cent. A.D.]: ἐὰν δὲ ἦν (=ᾖ) προτετεκνωκώς [if she might have borne children previously].)

APPENDIX 10B:
CATENATIVE CONSTRUCTIONS

0. INTRODUCTION. A brief word must be said about what might most appropriately be called catenative constructions in Greek (Matthews, *Syntax*, 183-86, 192-93). A periphrastic construction in Greek consists of the aspectually vague verb εἰμί and a Participle in agreement, linked in certain fairly specific configurations. It has long been recognized that in Greek Participles (and Infinitives) may function variously in sentences. It has also long been recognized that certain verbs have a greater tendency to collocation with Participles (and Infinitives) and thus in some sense may be said to serve as auxiliaries. These form catenative constructions, in which two verbs have a tendency to be linked together but the finite verb form contributes verbal aspect to the verbal semantics of the given clause. Although these constructions are often listed as periphrastics, they do not qualify in my narrow definition, since the auxiliary inherently maintains its integrity as an independent contributor to the semantics of the clause. Whereas these constructions are potentially very interesting, what has been stated previously about verbal aspect allows nothing more than a list of several of these catenative constructions (the list is not complete, since in one sense virtually any two verbs may be combined in some form) with a brief explanation of a few examples.

1. Verbs of capability, desire, etc. (δύναμαι, θέλω, δεῖ, μέλλω, βούλομαι, etc.)
These verbs might be described as 'modal' verbs: see Palmer, *Mood*, esp. 51-125. Since attitude is grammaticalized in Greek (Palmer, 3-7), modal verbs do not technically exist. Many of these verbs are cited by grammarians as substitutes for the Future (e.g. Stahl, 147; Robertson, 878-79; Turner, *Syntax*, 89; and esp. Dietrich, "Verbalaspekt"), but this is not to be mistaken for a formal substitution. Whereas the Future is semantically aspectually vague, grammaticalizing expectation (and thus similar in function to non-assertive forms), these catenative verbs are attitudinally specified with a volitional lexical meaning that points toward anticipated or posited action.

a. δύναμαι. This verb usually grammaticalizes imperfective aspect (exceptions include Matt 17:16) with an Aorist Infinitive[1] but also with a limited number of the Present Infinitive, mostly in the Johannine writings,[2] and a rare instance of εἶναι (e.g. Luke 14:26). A gloss of Matt 7:18 (οὐ δύναται δένδρον ἀγαθὸν καρποὺς πονηροὺς ποιεῖν, οὐδὲ δένδρον σαπρὸν καρποὺς καλοὺς ποιεῖν) might state that "you don't see good trees producing bad fruit," and

---

[1]E.g. Matt 3:9; 8:2 (Mark 1:40; Luke 5:12); 9:28; 17:16, 19 (Mark 9:28, 29); 19:25 (Mark 10:26; Luke 18:26; cf. Acts 15:1); 20:22 (cf. μέλλω + Present Infinitive; Mark 10:38); 26:61; 27:42 (Mark 15:31); Mark 2:7 (Luke 5:21); 3:20 (cf. v 23), 24, 25, 26; 6:5; Luke 20:36; John 3:3, 5; 5:44; 6:44; 7:34; 10:21; 11:37; Acts 20:32; Rom 16:25; 1 Cor 10:13; 12:3; Gal 3:21; Eph 3:20; 6:11; Phil 3:21; Heb 2:18; 10:1, 11; Jas 4:12; Rev 13:4. See C. Turner, "Usage," 28 (1927) 354-55, on Mark. Cf. P.Wisc. II 55.45 (2d cent. A.D.).

[2]Mark 4:33; Luke 6:42; John 3:2; 5:19; 6:60; 8:43; 9:4, 16, 33; 10:29; 12:39; 15:5; 16:12; 1 John 3:9.

488

likewise "you don't see a bad tree producing good fruit." The main verb and the Infinitive are imperfective. In Matt 9:28 (πιστεύετε ὅτι δύναμαι τοῦτο ποιῆσαι;), Jesus asks the blind men if they are in progress believing that he is able to perform the simple act of healing them, using an Aorist Infinitive.

   b. θέλω. This verb virtually always grammaticalizes imperfective aspect with an almost equal number of Aorist Infinitives[3] and Present Infinitives,[4] and a couple of instances with εἶναι.[5] Sentences using the aspectually vague εἶναι appear to stress more strongly the aspect of the major verb. For example in 1 Cor 7:32 (θέλω δὲ ὑμᾶς ἀμερίμνους εἶναι), Paul says he is very much wanting the Corinthians to exist undivided by strife (Conzelmann [Corinthians, 134] notes that μεριμνάω forms a catchword to link vv 32-34).

   c. δεῖ. Though it might be argued that δεῖ should be considered aspectually vague because of its limited number of forms in the NT, it seems better to say that it forms part of the paradigm of the verb δέω (a complete paradigm exists in hellenistic Greek), though in a stereotyped form in the Present (Imperfect, Subjunctive, Participle). The verb is usually completed by the Aorist Infinitive, though a sizable number of Present Infinitives[6] and several uses of εἶναι[7] occur. Matt 16:21 with δεῖ and an Aorist Infinitive (δεῖ αὐτὸν εἰς Ἱεροσόλυμα ἀπελθεῖν καὶ πολλὰ παθεῖν ἀπὸ τῶν πρεσβυτέρων. . . καὶ ἀποκτανθῆναι καὶ τῇ τρίτῃ ἡμέρᾳ ἐγερθῆναι) might be glossed as meaning that the author sees it as a necessary process for Jesus to go to Jerusalem, suffer many things from the elders, etc., to be killed and to be raised in three days, all conceived of as complete acts, while with the Present Participle in Luke 13:14 (ἐξ ἡμέραι εἰσὶν ἐν αἷς δεῖ ἐργάζεσθαι), the chief priest says it is a necessity to be in progress accomplishing things on the six non-sabbath days.

   d. μέλλω. Much debate has been generated by μέλλω, with most grammarians arguing that it is readily used as a substitute for the Future (e.g. Kühner/Gerth, 1.177-79; Stahl, 144; Rijksbaron, 33-34; Goodwin, Syntax, 38; Blass, 204-05; Blass/Debrunner, ¶ 356). On the basis of the nature of the Future and verbal aspect, it appears to function similarly to other catenative verbs. Semerényi's theory has been the most convincing, in which he argues that the essential meaning of the verb is "go" and is thus used in potential statements very similar to uses of the Future, but with the determination of verbal aspect ("Greek μέλλω," esp. 361, which corrects the view of Platt, "ΜΕΛΛΩ," besides those of the grammars; Burton [36, cf. 71] hints at this understanding; Bassett [Les emplois] is too tied to Guillaume). There is a difference of opinion which configurations are the most common, but instances can be found where the Imperfect of μέλλω is completed by a Future Infinitive[8] but also occasionally by a Present[9] or Aorist[10] Infinitive, and also where the Present of μέλλω is followed by the Present,[11] Future,[12] or Aorist[13]

---

[3]E.g. Matt 11:14; 16:24, 25 (Mark 8:35; Luke 9:24); 22:3; 19:17; 20:14, 26; 23:37; 27:34; Mark 7:24; Luke 10:24; John 5:6, 40; Rom 9:22; 1 Cor 11:3; 2 Cor 5:4; Col 1:27; 2:1; 1 Tim 2:4; Rev 2:21.
[4]E.g. Mark 8:34; Luke 9:23; John 6:67; 7:17; 21:23; Rom 1:13; 7:21; 11:25; 13:3; 1 Cor 10:1; 12:1; 2 Cor 1:8; Gal 4:9; 1 Thess 4:13; 2 Thess 3:10; 1 Pet 3:10.
[5]E.g. 1 Cor 7:32; 1 Tim 1:7.
[6]E.g. Luke 13:14, 33; 18:1; 22:7; John 3:30; 4:4, 20; 9:4; Acts 5:29; 9:6; 15:5; 16:30; 19:36; 20:35; 24:19; 25:10; Rom 12:3; 1 Cor 15:25; 2 Cor 2:3; 11:30; 1 Thess 4:1; 2 Thess 3:7; 1 Tim 3:7, 15; 2 Tim 2:6, 24; Titus 1:11; Heb 2:1; 2 Pet 3:11.
[7]E.g. Luke 2:49; 1 Cor 11:19; 2 Tim 2:24; Titus 1:7.
[8]E.g. Hom Il. 11.700-01; Od. 2.156; 8.510; Ar. Clouds 1301; Th. 3.115.5; 5.116.1.
[9]E.g. Hom Il. 2.36.
[10]E.g. Hom. Il. 18.98; Od. 9.475-76.
[11]E.g. Hom. Od. 18.19; Pl. Rep. 412A; D. 8.2.
[12]E.g. Pl. Apol. 21B; X. Cyr. 1.6.17.
[13]E.g. Hom. Od. 1.232-33; 4.377-78; Il. 13.776-77; E. Phoen. Maid. 300.

Infinitive. Rarer uses include forms of the Aorist[14] of μέλλω, as well as the Optative[15] and Participle.[16]

In the NT, the predominant form of μέλλω is the Present (e.g. Luke 19:11), but the Imperfect (John 6:71), Present Participle (Heb 1:14), Present Infinitive (Acts 24:15), Present Subjunctive (Mark 13:4), and Future (Matt 24:6) also occur. Virtually all are completed by the Present Infinitive, with only a few Aorist Infinitives found in this catenation (Rom 8:18; Gal 3:23; Rev 1:19; 3:2), as well as three uses of the Future Infinitive of εἶναι (Acts 11:28; 24:15; 27:10). The use of "go" in a gloss helps capture the meaning of this catenative construction. For example, 1 Thess 3:4 (ὅτι μέλλομεν θλίβεσθαι) says we are going (in progress going) to be persecuted. As Best (*Thessalonians*, 136) recognizes, this is not simply a substitute for a Future: "**We were to** . . . is more than a round-about way of writing a future; it involves necessity, as in v 3b" (Marshall [*Thessalonians*, 92] translates this: "we are going to suffer affliction"). Rev 3:2 (ἃ ἔμελλον ἀποθανεῖν) says the rest were going (ἔμελλον) to (simply) die (Aorist [see Blass, 197]).

e. βούλομαι. βούλομαι occurs relatively fewer times than other catenative verbs, but the same pattern is generally found. The verb most often grammaticalizes imperfective aspect (except e.g. Jas 1:18 without Infinitive), followed by approximately even numbers of Aorist[17] and Present[18] Infinitives.

2. ἔχω

ἔχω is often cited by grammarians as a verb that comprises part of a periphrastic construction (e.g. Gildersleeve, 126-27; Goodwin, *Syntax*, 229; Kühner/Gerth, 2.61-62; Jelf, 2.359-60; Chantraine, *Histoire*, 250-51). Even Aerts, however, in his definitive study of the construction (he devotes one-third of his book to ἔχω; *Periphrastica*, 128-67), admits that in classical Greek not only are the instances fewer in number than with εἰμί, but he finds that only in approximately 60% of these instances can he find a periphrastic sense (only one-third of total instances cited). This is usually on the basis of positing the construction as a substitute for a little or late-known form of the Perfect, since ἔχω, found virtually always with an Aorist Participle (he cites one example of the Perfect: X. Anab. 1.3.14. See also Pl. Thaeat. 200A; S. Phil. 600), occurs mainly before the 5th cent. B.C. (see his conclusions, 159-60).

A full discussion of this construction in classical Greek cannot be attempted here, but several important observations can be made. (1) As noted above, Aerts does not provide suitable formal criteria to distinguish a periphrastic from a non-periphrastic construction, but relies heavily on translational interpretations (e.g. Aerts [150] refers to "all sorts of nominal and verbal periphrases, for example with εἶναι, ποιεῖν, ποιεῖσθαι, μελλειν, ερχεσθαι, ἰέναι, etc."). This results in a very loose definition of periphrasis.

(2) Aerts contends that "this periphrasis almost always has the meaning of a transitive perfect resultative" (159) and "can be looked upon as a phenomenon concomitant to the development of the monolectic resultative perfect active in -κα" (160). If McKay is correct in arguing against Chantraine's claim that κα Perfects are resultive (i.e. transfer the emphasis to the object of the verb), or that the Perfect was anything other than subjective until after the hellenistic period (my chapt. 5 argues that both are correct), then Aerts's argument falters. It may be the case that ἔχω + Aorist Participle formed a periphrasis at one time (it seems, on Aerts's admission, to have been short-lived), though it is doubtful it has a close connection to the development of the Perfect (Dietrich ["Verbalaspekt," 210] claims to have found only one example in classical Greek: E. Troad. 315-17, though he cites several from later Greek as well). Besides the fact that perfective aspect is compatible with virtually every aspectual context, the conception of the stative

---

[14]E.g. Th. 1.134.4.

[15]E.g. Hdt. 1.158.1; X. Hell. 3.3.7.

[16]E.g. Th. 1.134.1, 3; Pl. Rep. 614B; E. El. 17.

[17]E.g. Matt 11:27; Luke 10:22; Acts 5:28; 17:20; Heb 6:17; 2 Pet 3:9. Cf. P.Wisc. II 54.12-13 (A.D. 116).

[18]E.g. Phil 1:12; 1 Tim 2:8; 5:14; 6:9; Titus 3:8.

verbal aspect of the Perfect posited in this work is quite different from that held by most scholars, such as Aerts (Gildersleeve [127], in arguing that the periphrasis is "equivalent" to the Perfect, claims "the double nature of [the periphrasis] is thus analyzed, ἔχω representing one end, the participle the other"). Another factor to consider is that lack of textual attestation or supposed later appearance of a form does not necessarily prove its lateness in development (because of a closed corpus of texts), or its exact equivalence to another form found in similar contexts. In fact, the situation may be interpreted differently. At one point speakers of Greek may have thought it sufficient to use ἔχω with an adjunctive Aorist Participle to refer to certain kinds of processes, but they found that this was insufficient to capture the stative sense that already existent Perfect forms conveyed, and hence they developed (or increased usage of) necessary simple Perfect forms.

(3) While Aerts argues that "in combination with the aorist participle, the verb ἔχειν is usually weakened to auxiliary verb" (159), he does not consider verbal aspect of the auxiliary. While ἔχω appears in the Present form in most instances Aerts cites (Indicative including Imperfect, Subjunctive, Optative, Imperative, Infinitive, Participle), it also appears in the Aorist (e.g. Hdt. 1.75.1), making it not only difficult to grasp the relation between the auxiliary and periphrastic but to see in what sense the auxiliary is, as Aerts says, "weakened" when a marked form predominates.

(4) Aerts's highly subjective interpretation of particular instances is clearly formulated along translational lines. For example, he contends that Pl. Phaedr. 257C (τὸν λόγον δέ σου . . . θαυμάσας ἔχω) is periphrastic, meaning "I am surprised at your discourse" (156, cf. 135), while X. Anab. 1.3.14 (οἱ Κίλικες . . . ὧν πολλοὺς καὶ πολλὰ χρήματα ἔχομεν ἀνηρπακότες)[19] is not periphrastic but means "of whom we have taken many prisoner [sic] and have stolen many possessions" (158). It is not clear why, by Aerts's own criteria, the first could not be rendered "I am grasping your statement, and am surprised," thus eliminating the need for reference to periphrasis. The same argument could be made for virtually every example Aerts cites. He recognizes the variety of meanings of ἔχω (Aerts, 166: "The use of ἔχειν in the sense of *to be, to exist, to find oneself*, etc., occurs in both ancient and modern Greek. Whether or not this verb is accompanied by a qualifying participle makes no difference to the meaning"), but he has failed to consider adequately the lexical ambiguity of ἔχω (see Earle, "Notes," 94), in which its lexical meaning has a number of specific meanings (have, know, be able, etc.) suitable to a variety of uses in both transitive and intransitive contexts. Thus it is linguistically implausible to posit the use of ἔχω in periphrastic constructions in classical Greek.

Aerts is in agreement regarding the hellenistic period, since "this construction begins to disappear from every-day language in the first half of the fourth century B.C." (160). Aerts cites two constructions that may be interpreted as retaining their periphrastic character. The first is ἔχω + object + Perfect Participle. It is puzzling that this is included as periphrastic, since the examples appear to be simple instances of the modifying Participle. Aerts himself admits that in most instances the Participle is appositive,[20] though several he claims are "more periphrastic in character" (161), e.g. Luke 13:6 (συκῆν εἶχέν τις πεφυτευμένην ἐν τῷ ἀμπελῶνι αὐτοῦ), though "here again it would seem more correct to look upon the participle as appositive and ἔχειν to have the meaning *to possess*" (162). Aerts is undoubtedly correct since ἔχω + Participle does not form a periphrasis with intervening τις as subject and the Participle in the Accusative Case. The Participle must be seen as in some sense modifying the object συκῆν (Feminine Accusative Singular also): "someone was possessing a fig tree which was growing in his vineyard." The same applies also to Luke 19:20 (see Aerts, 162-64, for other examples from hellenistic literature).

The second construction Aerts refers to is ἔχω + adjunct of time (often in the Accusative) + Participle, though he cites no examples from the NT.[21] On the basis of work by Tabachovitz,

---

[19]This is a Perfect Participle, but Aerts (158) contends it is "only a variation" of the normal use of the Aorist Participle.

[20]Mark 3:1; 8:17; Luke 14:18, 19; John 17:13; Rev 14:1; 19:12, 16; 21:12.

[21]Aerts (164) cites John 5:5 as an instance where the Participle is replaced by another means of expression.

Aerts argues that "the adjunct of time is the object of the verb ἔχειν and that the participle fulfils an explicative function" (164, cf. 164-66). He then interprets examples along these lines. As noted in discussion of periphrasis with εἰμί, when the temporal phrase modifies the auxiliary the construction is not periphrastic.

3. γίνομαι

Several grammarians cite instances of γίνομαι + Participle as forming periphrastic constructions (e.g. Kühner/Gerth, 1.39 [with ὑπάρχω]; contra Winer, 440, who categorically denies this construction as periphrastic), apparently viewing γίνομαι as synonymous with εἰμί on the basis of lexical similarity. Much of what is said under ἔχω above applies in this instance as well. γίνομαι appears to be the aspectually marked lexical equivalent of the lexically vague εἰμί, and thus its vague meaning is suitable to any number of contexts, while still contributing an aspectual semantic component. In the NT, the following instances are noted (see Turner, *Syntax*, 89, except Rev 1:18).

Mark 9:3: καὶ τὰ ἱμάτια αὐτοῦ ἐγένετο στίλβοντα λευκὰ λίαν.[22] This account of Jesus at the transfiguration is best translated "his garments became gleaming exceedingly white" (see Winer, 440) with the anarthrous Participle modifying the anarthrous complement, rather than e.g. "his garments became radiant and exceedingly white" (NASB).

Mark 9:7: καὶ ἐγένετο νεφέλη ἐπισκιάζουσα αὐτοῖς (a cloud came, and was in progress enveloping them [Cranfield, *Mark*, 292]). Here the anarthrous Participle modifies the headterm in the nominal group.

2 Cor 6:14: μὴ γίνεσθε ἑτεροζυγοῦντες ἀπίστοις. Here the Participle serves as the complement of the verb γίνεσθε: "don't become those who are in progress being mismatched with others" (contra Blass/Debrunner, ¶ 354, who treat this as periphrasis: "do not lend yourselves to . . .").

Col 1:18c: ἵνα γένηται ἐν πᾶσιν αὐτὸς πρωτεύων (so that he might become one who is above everything else in every way).[23] The anarthrous Participle πρωτεύων is best interpreted as modifying the pronoun αὐτός (Moule [*Colossians*, 69] translates the pronoun "himself alone," and the whole clause "that he might be alone supreme among all" [70]), though it is possibly the complement of γένηται.

Heb 5:12: καὶ γεγόνατε χρείαν ἔχοντες γάλακτος, [καὶ] οὐ στερεᾶς τροφῆς (and you are [become] in a state of having a need for milk, [and] not of solid meat) (Winer [440] translates: "ye have become persons needing, etc."). The author of Hebrews uses the Perfect γεγόνατε to describe the state of his readers, in which they are seen as in progress requiring milk, not solid food, since they have been lazy.

Rev 3:2: γίνου γρηγορῶν (become one who is watchful). The Present Participle appears to function as the element of the subject of the clause with the Present Imperative in its predicate (see McKay, "Future," 224 n. 60). "It has been pointed out that it is especially suitable in an address to the Church at Sardis; twice during the history of that city the acropolis had fallen into the hands of an enemy through want of vigilance on the part of its citizens (viz. in B.C. 549, 218; . . .); and a similar disaster now threatened the church of Sardis from a similar cause" (Swete, *Apocalypse*, 48).

Rev 16:10: καὶ ἐγένετο ἡ βασιλεία αὐτοῦ ἐσκοτωμένη (and his kingdom became darkened) (Sweet, *Revelation*, 248: lit. "was put into darkness," noting the Perfect Participle). The author apparently juxtaposes the articular subject (kingdom) with the anarthrous Perfect Participle serving as element of the complement: his kingdom entered into a state of darkness, possibly foreboding death (Swete, *Apocalypse*, 201).

Other grammarians cite other instances of what they call periphrastic constructions in the NT, but these are best subsumed under normal use of the Participle, even though English

---

[22]Streeter (*Four Gospels*, 315-16) argues that our text was shortened from an original: καὶ ἐγένετο στίλβον τὸ πρόσωπον, καὶ τὸ ἱμάτια αὐτοῦ λευκὰ λίαν, which included reference to Jesus' face.

[23]Lohse (*Colossians*, 56) argues for Neuter form here; cf. O'Brien, *Colossians*, 51.

translation may indicate a meaning close to that of a proper periphrasis (cf. e.g. Dietrich, "Verbalaspekt," 209-10, who treats τυγχάνω + Participle [no instances in NT]; ἕστηκα + Present Participle [Mark 11:25; Luke 23:10; Acts 1:11; 26:22]; and Blass/Debrunner, ¶ 414, who suggest certain supplementary constructions with Participles: e.g. ὑπάρχω, ἄρχομαι, etc.

BIBLIOGRAPHY

Aalto, P. *Studien zur Geschichte des Infinitivs im Griechischen.* Annales Academiae Scientarium Fennicae B 80, 2. Helsinki: n.p., 1953.

Abbott, E.A. *Johannine Grammar.* London: Adam and Charles Black, 1906.

Abbott, T.K. *A Critical and Exegetical Commentary on the Epistles to the Ephesians and to the Colossians.* International Critical Commentary. Edinburgh: T. and T. Clark, 1897.

_____. *Essays, Chiefly on the Original Texts of the Old and New Testaments.* London: Longmans, Green, 1891.

Abbott, W.G. "Did Jesus Speak Aramaic?" *Expository Times* 56 (1944-45) 305.

Abel, F.-M. *Grammaire du grec biblique: Suivie d'un choix de papyrus.* Etudes bibliques. Paris: Gabalda, 1927.

Abrahams, I. *Studies in Pharisaism and the Gospels.* 2d Series. Cambridge: UP, 1924.

Adams, D.Q. Review of Mussies, *Morphology. Lingua* 33 (1974) 190-97.

Adamson, J.B. *The Epistle of James.* New International Commentary. Grand Rapids: Eerdmans, 1976.

Adrados, F.R. "El método estructural y el aspecto verbal griego." *Emerita* 22 (1954) 258-70.

_____. "Observaciones sobre el aspecto verbal." *Estudios clasicos* 1 (1950) 11-25.

Aejmelaeus, A. *Parataxis in the Septuagint: A Study of the Renderings of the Hebrew Coordinate Clauses in the Greek Pentateuch.* Annales Academiae Scientarum Fennicae Dissertationes Humanarum Litterarum 31. Helsinki: Snomalainen Tiedeakatemia, 1982.

Aerts, W.J. *Periphrastica: An Investigation into the Use of εἶναι and ἔχειν as Auxiliaries or Pseudo-Auxiliaries in Greek from Homer up to the Present Day.* Amsterdam: Hakkert, 1965.

Albright, W.F., and C.S. Mann. *Matthew.* Anchor Bible 26. Garden City, New York: Doubleday, 1971.

Alexander, L.C.A. *Luke-Acts in its Contemporary Setting with Special Reference to the Prefaces (Luke 1:1-4 and Acts 1:1).* D.Phil. thesis, Univ. of Oxford, 1977.

_____. "Luke's Preface in the Context of Greek Preface-Writing." *Novum Testamentum* 28 (1986) 48-74.

Alexander, P.S. "Rabbinic Judaism and the NT." *Zeitschrift für die neutestamentliche Wissenschaft* 74 (1983) 237-46.

Alexander, W.J. "Participial Periphrases in Attic Prose." *American Journal of Philology* 4 (1883) 291-308.

Allen, E.L. "On this Rock." *Journal of Theological Studies* NS 5 (1954) 59-62.

Allen, L.C. *The Greek Chronicles: The Relation of the Septuagint of I and II Chronicles to the Massoretic Text.* Part 1: The Translator's Craft. Supplements to Vetus Testamentum 25. Leiden: Brill, 1974.

Allen, W.C. "The Aramaic Element in St. Mark." *Expository Times* 13 (1901-02) 328-30.

494

_____. *A Critical and Exegetical Commentary on the Gospel According to S. Matthew*. International Critical Commentary. 3d ed. Edinburgh: T. and T. Clark, 1912.

Allison, F.G. "On Causes Contributory to the Loss of the Optative etc. in later Greek." *Studies in Honor of B.L. Gildersleeve*. Baltimore: Johns Hopkins Press, 1902: 353-56.

Allwood, J., L.-G. Andersson, and Ö. Dahl. *Logic in Linguistics*. Cambridge Textbooks in Linguistics. Cambridge: UP, 1977.

Amigues, S. "Les temps de l'impératif dans les ordres de l'orateur au greffier." *Revue des études grecques* 90 (1977) 223-38.

Anderson, H. "Broadening Horizons: The Rejection at Nazareth Pericope of Luke 4:16-30 in Light of Recent Critical Trends." *Interpretation* 18 (1964) 259-75.

Anderson, J. *An Essay Concerning Aspect: Some Considerations of a General Character Arising from the Abbé Darrigol's Analysis of the Basque Verb*. Janua Linguarum. The Hague: Mouton, 1973.

Anderson, L.B. "The 'Perfect' as a Universal and as a Language-Specific Category." *Tense-Aspect: Between Semantics and Pragmatics*. Ed. P.J. Hopper. Amsterdam: Benjamins, 1982: 227-64.

Angus, S. "The Koiné. The Language of the NT." *Princeton Theological Review* 8 (1910) 44-96.

Anlauf, G. *Standard Late Greek oder Attizismus? Eine Studie zum Optativgebrauch im nachklassischen Griechisch*. Ph.D. thesis, Univ. of Cologne, 1960.

Anonymous. "Review of Weymouth on Perfect." *Classical Review* 5 (1891) 267-69.

Anscombe, G.E.M. *Intention*. Oxford: Blackwell, 1958.

_____. *An Introduction to Wittgenstein's Tractatus*. London: Hutchinson, 1959.

Arabski, J. *Errors as Indications of the Development of Interlanguage*. Katowice: Uniwersytet Slaski, 1979.

Argyle, A.W. "The Accounts of the Temptations of Jesus in Relation to the Q Hypothesis." *Expository Times* 64 (1952-53) 382.

_____. "Did Jesus Speak Greek?" *Expository Times* 67 (1955-56) 92-93; 383.

_____. "The Genitive Absolute in Biblical Greek." *Expository Times* 69 (1957-58) 285.

_____. "Greek Among the Jews of Palestine in NT Times." *NT Studies* 20 (1974) 87-89.

Armstrong, D. "The Ancient Greek Aorist as the Aspect of Countable Action." *Syntax and Semantics 14: Tense and Aspect*. Ed. P. Tedeschi and A. Zaenen. New York: Academic, 1981: 1-11.

Armstrong, P.B. "The Conflict of Interpretations and the Limits of Pluralism." *Publications of the Modern Language Association* 98 (1983) 341-52.

von Arnim, J., ed. *Stoicorum veterum fragmenta*. Vol. 1: Zeno et Zenonis discipuli. Leipsig: Teubner, 1905.

Atkinson, B.F.C. *The Greek Language*. London: Faber and Faber, 1931.

Atkinson, M., D. Kilby, and I. Roca. *Foundations of General Linguistics*. London: George Allen and Unwin, 1982.

Aune, D.E. *Prophecy in Early Christianity and the Ancient Mediterranean World*. Grand Rapids: Eerdmans, 1983.

_____. "The Significance of the Delay of the Parousia for Early Christianity." *Current Issues in Biblical and Patristic Interpretation*. Ed. G.F. Hawthorne. Grand Rapids: Eerdmans, 1974: 87-109.

Bache, C. "Aspect and Aktionsart: Towards a Semantic Distinction." *Journal of Linguistics* 18 (1982) 57-72.

_____. *Verbal Aspect: A General Theory and its Application to Present-Day English*. Odense Univ. Studies in English 8. Odense: UP, 1985.

Bader, F. "Parfait et moyen en grec." *Mélanges de linguistique et de philologie grecques*. Paris: Klincksieck, 1972: 1-21.

Baetens Beardsmore, H. *Bilingualism: Basic Principles*. 2d ed. Clevedon, England: Multilingual Matters, 1987.

495

Bailey, K.E. *Poet and Peasant: A Literary Cultural Approach to the Parables in Luke.* Grand Rapids: Eerdmans, 1976.

Bakker, W.F. *The Greek Imperative: An Investigation into the Aspectual Differences between the Present and Aorist Imperatives in Greek Prayer from Homer up to the Present Day.* Amsterdam: Hakkert, 1966.

_____. "A Remark on the Use of the Imperfect and Aorist in Herodotus." *Mnemosyne* Series 4, 21 (1968) 22-28.

Ballantine, W.G. "Attributive Aorist Participles in Protasis, in the NT." *Bibliotheca Sacra* 46 (1889) 342-50.

_____. "Negative Futures in the Greek NT." *American Journal of Philology* 18 (1897) 453-59.

_____. "Predicative Participles with Verbs in the Aorist." *Bibliotheca Sacra* 41 (1884) 787-99.

Bammel, E. "The Commands in 1 Pet 2:17." *NT Studies* 11 (1964-65) 279-81.

Barber, E.J.W. "Voice--Beyond the Passive." *Proceedings of the First Annual Meeting of the Berkeley Linguistics Society, February 1975.* Berkeley: Berkeley Linguistics Society, 1975: 16-24.

Barclay, W. "The NT and the Papyri." *The NT in Historical and Contemporary Perspective.* Ed. H. Anderson and W. Barclay. Oxford: Blackwell, 1965: 57-81.

Bardy, G. *La question des langues dans l'église ancienne.* Vol. 1 Etudes de théologie historique. Paris: Beauchesne et ses fils, 1948.

Barnes, O.L. *A New Approach to the Problem of the Hebrew Tenses and its Solution without Recourse to Waw-Consecutive.* Oxford: Thornton and Son, [1965].

Barnes, W.E. Review of Burney, *Aramaic Origin. Journal of Theological Studies* 23 (1921-22) 419-21.

Barr, J. *Biblical Words for Time.* Studies in Biblical Theology. 2d ed. London: SCM, 1969.

_____. "Common Sense and Biblical Language." *Biblica* 49 (1968) 377-87.

_____. *Comparative Philology and the Text of the OT.* Oxford: Clarendon, 1968.

_____. "Hypostatization of Linguistic Phenomena in Modern Theological Interpretation." *Journal of Semitic Studies* 7 (1962) 85-94.

_____. *The Semantics of Biblical Language.* Oxford: UP, 1961.

_____. *The Typology of Literalism in Ancient Biblical Translations.* Nachrichten der Akademie der Wissenschaften in Göttingen I. Philologisch- Historische Klasse. Mitteilungen des Septuaginta-Unternehmens (MSU) 15. Göttingen: Vandenhoeck und Ruprecht, 1979.

_____. "Which Language did Jesus Speak?--Some Remarks of a Semitist." *Bulletin of John Rylands Library* 53 (1970) 9-29.

_____. "Words for Love in Biblical Greek." *The Glory of Christ in the NT.* Ed. L.D. Hurst and N.T. Wright. Oxford: Clarendon, 1987: 3-18.

Barrett, C.K. "Biblical Classics: IV. J.H. Moulton: A Grammar of NT Greek: Prolegomena." *Expository Times* 90 (1978-79) 68-71.

_____. *A Commentary on the Epistle to the Romans.* Black's NT Commentaries. London: Adam and Charles Black, 1962.

_____. *A Commentary on the First Epistle to the Corinthians.* Black's NT Commentaries. London: Adam and Charles Black, 1968.

_____. *A Commentary on the Second Epistle to the Corinthians.* Black's NT Commentaries. London: Adam and Charles Black, 1973.

_____. "The Eschatology of the Epistle to the Hebrews." *The Background of the NT and its Eschatology.* Ed. W.D. Davies and D. Daube. Cambridge: UP, 1956: 363-93.

_____. *The Gospel According to St. John: An Introduction with Commentary and Notes on the Greek Text.* 2d ed. London: SPCK, 1978.

_____. "The Imperatival Participle." *Expository Times* 59 (1947-48) 165-66.

Bartchy, S.S. *First-Century Slavery and 1 Cor 7:21.* Society for Biblical Literature Dissertation Series 11. N.p.: SBL, 1973.

Barth, M. *Ephesians*. 2 vols. Anchor Bible 34. Garden City, New York: Doubleday, 1974.

Basilius, H. "Neo-Humboldtian Ethnolinguistics." *Word* 8 (1952) 95-105.

Basset, L. *Les emplois périphrastiques du verbe grec μέλλειν: Etude de linguistique grecque et essai de linguistique générale*. Collection de la Maison de l'Orient Mediterranean Ancien 7.1. Lyon: Maison de l'Orient, 1979.

Bauckham, R.J. *Jude, 2 Peter*. Word Biblical Commentary 50. Waco, Texas: Word, 1983.

Bauer, W. *A Greek-English Lexicon of the NT and Other Early Christian Literature*. Trans. W.F. Arndt and F.W. Gingrich. Rev. F.W. Gingrich and F.W. Danker. 2d ed. Chicago: U of Chicago P, 1979.

Bayer, H.F. *Jesus' Predictions of Vindication and Resurrection: The Provenance, Meaning and Correlation of the Synoptic Predictions*. Wissenschaftliche Untersuchungen zum Neuen Testament 2. Reihe 20. Tübingen: J.C.B. Mohr (Paul Siebeck), 1986.

Bayfield, M.A. "Conditional Sentences in Greek and Latin:--Indefinite Sentences in Greek." *Classical Review* 6 (1892) 90-92.

_____. "On Conditional Sentences in Greek and Latin, and Indefinite Sentences in Greek." *Classical Review* 4 (1890) 200-03.

_____. Report of paper to Cambridge Philological Society. *Classical Review* 3 (1889) 276-77.

Bazell, C.[E.] *Linguistic Form*. Istanbul: n.p., 1953.

_____. Review of Lyons, *Introduction*. *Archivum Linguisticum* NS 2 (1971) 151-54.

Beare, F.W. *A Commentary on the Epistle to the Philippians*. Black's NT Commentaries. London: Adam and Charles Black, 1959.

_____. *The First Epistle of Peter: The Greek Text with Introduction and Notes*. Oxford: Blackwell, 1958.

_____. *The Gospel According to Matthew: A Commentary*. Oxford: Blackwell, 1981.

Beasley-Murray, G.R. *A Commentary on Mark Thirteen*. London: Macmillan, 1957.

_____. *Jesus and the Future: An Examination of the Criticism of the Eschatological Discourse, Mark 13 with Special Reference to the Little Apocalypse Theory*. London: Macmillan, 1954.

_____. *Jesus and the Kingdom of God*. Grand Rapids: Eerdmans, 1986.

_____. "Second Thoughts on the Composition of Mark 13." *NT Studies* 29 (1983) 414-20.

Beet, J.E. "The Greek Aorist, as Used in the NT." *Expositor* First Series 11 (1880) 191-201; 296-308; 372-85.

Bekker, I. *Anecdota Graeca*. Vol. 2. Berlin: G. Reimer, 1816; rpt. Graz, Austria: Akademische Druck- und Verlaganstalt, 1965.

van Bennekom, R. "Existential and other Sentences in Ancient Greek." *Mnemosyne* Series 4, 37 (1984) 257-63.

Bennett, M., and B. Partee. *Toward the Logic of Tense and Aspect in English*. Bloomington, Indiana: Indiana Univ. Linguistics Club, 1978.

Berger, K. "Hellenistische Gattungen im NT." *Aufstieg und Niedergang der römischen Welt*. II.25.2. Ed. W. Haase. Berlin: de Gruyter, 1984: 1031-43.

_____. "Zu den sogennanten Sätzen heiligen Rechts." *NT Studies* 17 (1970-71) 10-40.

Berlin, A. *The Dynamics of Biblical Parallelism*. Bloomington: Indiana UP, 1985.

Berrettoni, P. "Per un'analisa delle categorie del verbo greco." *Studi e Saggi Linguistici* 13 (1973) 120-32.

Berry, M. *An Introduction to Systemic Linguistics. Vol. 1: Structures and Systems*. London: Batsford, 1975; *Vol. 2: Levels and Links*. London: Batsford, 1977.

_____. "Is teacher an unanalysed concept?" *New Developments in Systemic Linguistics. Vol. 1: Theory and Description*. Ed. M.A.K. Halliday and R.P. Fawcett. London: Pinter, 1987: 41-63.

Bers, V. *Greek Poetic Syntax in the Classical Age*. Yale Classical Monographs 5. New Haven: Yale UP, 1984.

Bertocchi, A. "Some Problems about Verbal Aspect." *Papers on Grammar I*. Ed. Gualtiero Calboli. Consiglio Nazionale delle Ricerche, Università di Bologna Instituto di Filologia Latina e Medioevale. Bologna: CLUEB, 1980: 141-62.

Beschewliew, W. "Der Gebrauch des Imperativus aoristi und praesentis im altgriechischen Gebet." *Annuaire de la Istoriki- Filologischeski Fakultet*, Sofia 23 (1927) 27-32.

Best, E. *A Commentary on the First and Second Epistles to the Thessalonians*. Black's NT Commentaries. London: Adam and Charles Black, 1972.

_____. *The Temptation and the Passion: The Markan Soteriology*. Society for NT Studies Monograph Series 2. Cambridge: UP, 1965.

Betz, H.D. *Galatians*. Hermeneia. Philadelphia: Fortress, 1979.

Betz, O. "Felsenmann und Felsengemeinde (Eine Parallele zu Matt 16:17-19 in den Qumranpsalmen)." *Zeitschrift für die neutestamentliche Wissenschaft* 48 (1957) 49-77.

Beyer, K. *The Aramaic Language: Its Distribution and Subdivisions*. Göttingen: Vandenhoeck und Ruprecht, 1986.

_____. *Die aramäische Texte vom Toten Meer*. Göttingen: Vandenhoeck und Ruprecht, 1984.

_____. *Semitische Syntax im NT*. Vol. 1. 2d ed. Göttingen: Vandenhoeck und Ruprecht, 1968.

Bickerman, E. "The Septuagint as a Translation." *Studies in Jewish and Christian History*. Part 1. Arbeiten zur Geschichte des antiker Judentums und des Urchristentums 9. Leiden: Brill, 1976: 167-200.

Birkeland, H. *The Language of Jesus*. Avhandlinger utgitt av Det Norske Videnskaps-Akademi I. II. Historish-Filosofisk Klasse I. Oslo: Dybwad, 1954.

_____. "Some Reflexions on Semitic and Structural Linguistics." *For Roman Jakobson: Essays on the Occasion of his Sixtieth Birthday. 11 October 1956*. Ed. M. Halle *et al*. The Hague: Mouton, 1956: 44-51.

Bizos, M. *Syntaxe grecque*. 7th ed. Paris: Vuibert, 1961.

Björck, G. *HN ΔIΔΑΣKΩN: Die periphrastischen Konstruktionen im Griechischen*. Skrifter utgivna av K. Humanistiska Vetenskops- Samfundet i Uppsala 32.2. Uppsala: Almquist and Wiksells, 1940.

Black, Matthew. *An Aramaic Approach to the Gospels and Acts*. 3d ed. Oxford: Clarendon, 1967.

_____. "Aramaic Studies and the Language of Jesus." *In Memoriam P. Kahle*. Ed. M. Black and G. Fohrer. Berlin: Töpelmann, 1968: 17-28.

_____. "The Biblical Languages." *The Cambridge History of the Bible. Vol. 1: From the Beginnings to Jerome*. Ed. P.R. Ackroyd and C.F. Evans. Cambridge: UP, 1970: 1-11.

_____. "Jesus and the Son of Man." *Journal for the Study of the NT* 1 (1978) 4-18.

_____. "The Recovery of the Language of Jesus." *NT Studies* 3 (1956-57) 305-13.

_____. *Romans*. New Century Bible. London: Oliphants, 1973.

_____. "Second Thoughts--IX. The Semitic Element in the NT." *Expository Times* 77 (1965) 20-23.

Black, Max. *A Companion to Wittgenstein's 'Tractatus.'* Cambridge: UP, 1964.

_____. *Models and Metaphors: Studies in Language and Philosophy*. Ithaca, New York: Cornell UP, 1962.

Blake, F.R. "The Hebrew Waw Conversive." *Journal of Biblical Literature* 63 (1944) 271-95.

_____. *A Resurvey of Hebrew Tenses: with an Appendix, Hebrew Influence on Biblical Aramaic*. Rome: Pontificium Institutum Biblicum, 1951.

Blakeney, E.H. "Note on Tense-Translation in the NT." *Expository Times* 8 (1896-97) 381-82.

Blass, F. "Demosthenische Studien. III. (Aorist und Imperfekt.)." *Rheinische Museum* 44 (1889) 406-30.

_____. *Grammar of NT Greek*. Trans. H.St.J. Thackeray. 2d ed. London: Macmillan, 1911.

Blass, F., and A. Debrunner. *Grammatik des neutestamentlichen Griechisch*. 15th ed. Ed. F. Rehkopf. Göttingen: Vandenhoeck und Ruprecht, 1979.

_____. *A Greek Grammar of the NT and Other Early Christian Literature.* Trans. R.W. Funk. Chicago: U of Chicago P, 1961.

Blau, J. "Zum Hebräisch der Übersetzer des AT." *Vetus Testamentum* 6 (1956) 97-99.

Bloomfield, L. *Language.* London: George Allen and Unwin, 1935.

de Boel, G. "Aspekt, Aktionsart und Transitivität." *Indogermanische Forschungen* 92 (1987) 33-57.

_____. "Towards a Theory of the Meaning of Complementizers in Classical Attic." *Lingua* 52 (1980) 285-304.

Bohm, D. "Science as Perception-Communication." *The Structure of Scientific Theories.* 2d ed. Urbana: U of Illinois P, 1977: 374-91.

Bolinger, D.L. *Aspects of Language.* 2d ed. New York: Harcourt, Brace, Jovanovich, 1975.

_____. *Meaning and Form.* London: Longman, 1977.

Bolling, G.M. "The Participle in Apollonius Rhodius." *Studies in Honor of B.L. Gildersleeve.* Baltimore: Johns Hopkins Press, 1902: 449-70.

_____. "The Teaching of the 'Tenses' in Greek." *Classical Journal* 13 (1917-18) 104-10.

Boman, T. Review of Barr, *Semantics* and *Biblical Words.* *Scottish Journal of Theology* 15 (1962) 319-23.

Bonnard, P. *L'évangile selon Saint Matthieu.* Commentaire du NT. 2d ed. Neuchatel: Delachaux et Niestlé, 1970.

Bonsirven, J. "Les aramaïsmes de S. Jean l'Evangéliste?" *Biblica* 30 (1949) 405-32.

Bornkamm, G. "The Authority to 'Bind' and 'Loose' in the Church in Matthew's Gospel: The Problem of Sources in Matthew's Gospel." *Jesus and Man's Hope.* Festival on the Gospels. Vol. 1. Pittsburgh: Pittsburgh Theological Seminary, 1970: 37-50.

Borsch, F.H. *The Son of Man in Myth and History.* NT Library. London: SCM, 1967.

Botha, J.E. "Research Report: The Meanings of pisteuō in the Greek NT: A Semantic-Lexicographical Study." *Neotestamentica* 21 (1987) 225-40.

Bowersock, G.W., ed. *Approaches to the Second Sophistic.* Univ. Park Pennsylvania: n.p., 1974.

Bowker, J. "The Son of Man." *Journal of Theological Studies* NS 28 (1977) 19-48.

_____. *The Targums and Rabbinic Literature: An Introduction to Jewish Interpretations of Scripture.* Cambridge: UP, 1969.

Boyer, J.L. "A Classification of Imperatives: A Statistical Study." *Grace Theological Journal* 8 (1987) 35-54.

_____. "The Classification of Infinitives: A Statistical Study." *Grace Theological Journal* 6 (1985) 3-27.

_____. "The Classification of Optatives: A Statistical Study." *Grace Theological Journal* 9 (1988) 129-40.

_____. "The Classification of Participles: A Statistical Study." *Grace Theological Journal* 5 (1984) 163-79.

_____. "The Classification of Subjunctives: A Statistical Study." *Grace Theological Journal* 7 (1986) 3-19.

_____. "First Class Conditions: What Do They Mean?" *Grace Theological Journal* 2 (1981) 75-114.

_____. "Other Conditional Elements in NT Greek." *Grace Theological Journal* 4 (1983) 173-88.

_____. "Second Class Conditions in NT Greek." *Grace Theological Journal* 3 (1982) 81-88.

_____. "Third (and Fourth) Class Conditions." *Grace Theological Journal* 3 (1982) 163-75.

Braunlich, A.F. "Euripides, *Medea*, 239 and 815: μή with the Causal Participle." *American Journal of Philology* 77 (1956) 415-18.

_____. "Goodwin or Gildersleeve?" *American Journal of Philology* 77 (1956) 181-84.

Bréal, M. *Semantics: Studies in the Science of Meaning (Essai de sémantique,* 1897). Trans. Mrs. H. Cust. Preface J.P. Postgate. London: Heinemann, 1900.

Brennan, P.W. *The Structure of Koine Greek Narrative.* Ph.D. thesis, The Hartford Seminary Foundation, Connecticut, 1968.

Bretscher, P.G. "Exod 4:22-23 and the Voice from Heaven." *Journal of Biblical Literature* 87 (1968) 301-11.

Briggs, R.C. *The Exegetical Significance of the Perfect Tense in the Book of Hebrews.* Th.D. thesis, Southern Baptist Theological Seminary, Louisville, Kentucky, 1946.

Brock, S.P. "Aspects of Translation Technique in Antiquity." *Greek, Roman, and Byzantine Studies* 20 (1979) 69-87.

_____. "The Phenomenon of the Septuagint." *The Witness of Tradition.* Ed. A.S. van der Woude. Oudtestamentische Studiën 17. Leiden: Brill, 1972: 11-36.

_____. Review of Black, *Aramaic Approach,* 3d ed. *Journal of Theological Studies* NS 20 (1969) 274-78.

Bröndal, V. "Structure et variabilité des systèmes morphologiques." *Scientia* (1935) 109-19.

Brooke, G.J. *Exegesis at Qumran: 4QFlorilegium in its Jewish Context.* Journal for the Study of the OT Supplement Series 29. Sheffield: JSOT, 1985.

Brooks, J.A., and C.L. Winbery. *Syntax of NT Greek.* Washington: UP of America, 1979.

Brown, D. "The Aorist in the Greek Testament." *Expository Times* 7 (1895-96) 75-77.

Brown, R.E. *The Birth of the Messiah: A Commentary on the Infancy Narrative in Matthew and Luke.* London: Geoffrey Chapman, 1977.

_____. *The Epistles of John.* Anchor Bible 30. Garden City, New York: Doubleday, 1982.

_____. *The Gospel According to John.* 2 vols. Anchor Bible 29, 29A. Garden City, New York: Doubleday, 1966.

Brown, R.E. *et al.,* ed. *Peter in the NT.* London: Geoffrey Chapman, 1973.

Brown, S. "Biblical Philology, Linguistics and the Problem of Method." *Heythrop Journal* 20 (1979) 295-98.

_____. "From Burney to Black: The Fourth Gospel and the Aramaic Question." *Catholic Biblical Quarterly* 26 (1964) 323-39.

Browning, R. *Medieval and Modern Greek.* 2d ed. Cambridge: UP, 1983.

Bruce, F.F. *The Acts of the Apostles: The Greek Text with Introduction and Commentary.* London: Tyndale Press, 1951.

_____. *The Books and the Parchments: Some Chapters on the Transmission of the Bible.* Rev. ed. London: Pickering and Inglis, 1971.

_____. *Commentary on the Epistle to the Hebrews.* New London Commentary. London: Marshall, Morgan and Scott, 1964.

_____. "Did Jesus Speak Aramaic?" *Expository Times* 56 (1944-45) 328.

_____. *The Epistle of Paul to the Galatians: A Commentary on the Greek Text.* New International Greek Testament Commentary. Exeter: Paternoster, 1982.

_____. *The Epistle of Paul to the Romans: An Introduction and Commentary.* Tyndale NT Commentaries. London: Tyndale Press, 1963.

_____. *1 and 2 Corinthians.* New Century Bible. London: Oliphants, 1971.

_____. *1 and 2 Thessalonians.* Word Biblical Commentary 45. Waco, Texas: Word, 1982.

_____. "The OT in Greek." *Bible Translator* 4 (1953) 129-35; 156-62.

_____. *Paul: Apostle of the Heart Set Free.* Grand Rapids: Eerdmans, 1977.

Brugmann, K. *Griechische Grammatik. II.i: Lautlehre, Stammbildungs und Flexionslehre, Syntax.* (1st ed. 1885) 4th ed. Ed. A. Thumb. Munich: C.H. Beck, 1913.

_____. *Vergleichende Laut-, Stammbildungs- und Flexionslehre nebst Lehre vom Gebrauch der Wortformen der Indogermanischen Sprachen.* Vol. 2. Part 2.3.1 of *Grundriss der vergleichenden Grammatik der Indogermanischen Sprachen.* By K. Brugmann and B. Delbrück. Strassburg: Trübner, 1916.

_____. *Kurze Vergleichende Grammatik der Indogermanischen Sprachen.* 3 vols. Strassburg: Trübner, 1903.

Brunel, J. "L'aspect et 'L'ordre du procès' en grec." *Bulletin de la Societé Linguistique* 42 (1946) 43-75.

_____. *L'aspect verbal et l'emploi des préverbes en grec, particulièrement en attique.* Collection linguistique. Paris: Klincksieck, 1939.

Buck, C.D. *Comparative Grammar of Greek and Latin.* Chicago: U of Chicago P, 1933.

_____. *The Greek Dialects: Grammar, Selected Inscriptions, Glossary.* Chicago: U of Chicago P, 1955.

Büchsel, F. "Die griechische Sprache der Juden in der Zeit der Septuaginta und des NT." *Zeitschrift für die alttestamentliche Wissenschaft* 60 (1944) 132-49.

Bull, W.E. *Time, Tense, and the Verb: A Study in Theoretical and Applied Linguistics, with Particular Attention to Spanish.* Berkeley: U of California P, 1971.

Bultmann, R. *The Gospel of John: A Commentary.* Trans. G.R. Beasley-Murray. Oxford: Blackwell, 1971.

_____. *The History of the Synoptic Tradition.* Trans. J. Marsh. Rev. ed. Oxford: Blackwell, 1972.

_____. "Is Exegesis without Presuppositions Possible?" (1957). *Existence and Faith: Shorter Writings of R. Bultmann.* Ed. and trans. S.M. Ogden. London: Hodder and Stoughton, 1960: 289-96.

_____. *The Johannine Epistles.* Trans. R.P. O'Hare with L.C. McGaughy and R.W. Funk. Ed. R.W. Funk. Hermeneia. Philadelphia: Fortress, 1973.

_____. *The Second Letter to the Corinthians.* Trans. R.A. Harrisville. Ed. E. Dinkler. Minneapolis: Augsburg, 1985.

_____. *Theology of the NT.* 2 vols. Trans. F. Grobel. London: SCM, 1952, 1955.

Burdick, D.W. "Οἶδα and γινώσκω in the Pauline Epistles." *New Dimensions in NT Study.* Ed. R.N. Longenecker and M.C. Tenney. Grand Rapids: Zondervan, 1974: 344-56.

Burgess, J.A. *A History of the Exegesis of Matt 16:17-19 from 1781 to 1965.* Ann Arbor: Edwards Bros., 1976.

Burguière, P. *Histoire de l'infinitif en grec.* Etudes et commentaires 33. Paris: Klincksieck, 1960.

Burney, C.F. *The Aramaic Origin of the Fourth Gospel.* Oxford: Clarendon, 1922.

_____. "A Fresh Examination of the Current Theory of the Hebrew Tenses." *Journal of Theological Studies* 20 (1919) 200-14.

_____. "A Hebraic Construction in the Apocalypse." *Journal of Theological Studies* 22 (1920-21) 371-76.

_____. *The Poetry of Our Lord.* Oxford: Clarendon, 1925.

Burres, K.L. *Structural Semantics in the Study of the Pauline Understanding of Revelation.* Ph.D. thesis, Northwestern Univ., Evanston, Illinois, 1970.

Burrows, M. "Principles for Testing the Translation Hypothesis in the Gospels." *Journal of Biblical Literature* 33 (1934) 13-30.

_____. "The Original Language of the Gospel of John." *Journal of Biblical Literature* 49 (1930) 95-139.

_____. "The Semitic Background of the NT." *Bible Translator* 2 (1951) 67-73.

Burton, E.D.W. *A Critical and Exegetical Commentary on the Epistle to the Galatians.* International Critical Commentary. Edinburgh: T. and T. Clark, 1921.

_____. *Syntax of the Moods and Tenses in NT Greek.* 3d ed. Chicago: U of Chicago P; rpt. Grand Rapids: Kregel, 1976.

Buth, R. "Hebrew Poetic Tenses and the Magnificat." *Journal for the Study of the NT* 21 (1984) 67-83.

_____. "Mark's Use of the Historical Present." *Notes on Translation* 65 (1977) 7-13.

Butler, C.S. "Communicative function and semantics." *New Developments in Systemic Linguistics.* Vol. 1: Theory and Description. Ed. M.A.K. Halliday and R.P. Fawcett. London: Pinter, 1987: 212-29.

_____. *Systemic Linguistics: Theory and Applications.* London: Batsford, 1985.

Buttmann, A. *A Grammar of the NT Greek.* Trans. J.H. Thayer. Andover: Warren F. Draper, 1873.

Buttmann, P. *A Catalogue of Irregular Greek Verbs.* Trans. J.R. Fishlake. London: John Murray, 1837.

_____. *Griechische Grammatik.* 21st ed. Ed. A. Buttmann. Berlin: Ferdinand Dümmler, 1863.

Cadbury, H.J. "Luke--Translator or Author?" *American Journal of Theology* 24 (1920) 436-55.

_____. "The Meaning of John 20:23, Matt 16:19, and Matt 18:18." *Journal of Biblical Literature* 58 (1939) 251-54.

_____. "A Possible Perfect in Acts 9:34." *Journal of Theological Studies* 49 (1948) 57-58.

_____. *The Style and Literary Method of Luke.* Harvard Theological Studies 6. Cambridge: Harvard UP, 1920.

_____. "The Vocabulary and Grammar of NT Greek." *Bible Translator* 2 (1951) 153-59.

Cadoux, C.J. "The Imperatival Use of ἵνα in the NT." *Journal of Theological Studies* 42 (1941) 165-73.

Caird, G.B. *A Commentary on the Revelation of St. John the Divine.* Black's NT Commentaries. London: Adam and Charles Black, 1966.

_____. *The Language and Imagery of the Bible.* Philadelphia: Westminster, 1980.

Calboli, G. "I Modi del Verbo Greco e Latino 1903-1966." *Lustrum* 11 (1966) 173-349; 12 (1967) 405-511.

Caleb, R.H. "Subsequent Action Expressed by the Aorist Participle." *Transactions of the American Philological Association* 57 (1928) xxxix.

Callow, J. "The Function of the Historic Present in Mark 1:16-3:6; 4:1-41; 7:1-23; 12:13-34." *START* (Dallas SIL) 11 (1984) 9-17.

Campbell, A.Y. "The OY MH Constructions and Aristophanes, *Clouds*, 295-7." *Classical Review* 61 (1947) 58-61.

Campbell, J.Y. "The Origin and Meaning of the Christian Use of the Word ΕΚΚΛΗΣΙΑ." *Journal of Theological Studies* 49 (1948) 130-42.

Campbell, L. Untitled. *Classical Review* 4 (1890) 425.

von Campenhausen, H. "The Power of the Keys in the Primitive Church." *Ecclesiastical Authority and Spiritual Power in the Church of the First Three Centuries.* Trans. J.A. Baker. London: Adam and Charles Black, 1969: 124-48.

Cantineau, J. "Quelle langue parlait le peuple en Palestine an 1ᵉʳ siècle de noue èιc?" *Semitica* 5 (1956) 99-101.

Carmignac, J. *Recherches sur le 'Notre Pere.'* Paris: Letouzey, 1969.

_____. "Studies in the Hebrew Background of the Synoptic Gospels." *Annual of the Swedish Theological Institute* 7 (1968-69) 64-93.

Carpenter, J.W., Jr. *The Aktionsart of the Aorist in Acts.* Ph.D. thesis, Southern Baptist Theological Seminary, Louisville, Kentucky, 1942.

Carrière, J. *Stylistique grecque: l'usage de la prose attique.* Tradition de l'humanisme 6. 3d ed. Paris: Klincksieck, 1983.

Carson, D.A. *Exegetical Fallacies.* Grand Rapids: Baker, 1984.

_____. "Matthew." *Expositor's Bible Commentary.* Vol. 8. Ed. F.E. Gaebelein. Grand Rapids: Zondervan, 1984.

_____. "The ΟΜΟΙΟΣ Word-Group as Introduction to Some Matthean Parables." *NT Studies* 31 (1985) 277-82.

_____. "The Purpose of the Fourth Gospel: John 20:31 Reconsidered." *Journal of Biblical Literature* 106 (1987) 639-51.

Carter, F. "On Some Uses of the Aorist Participle." *Classical Review* 5 (1891) 3-6.

_____. Untitled. *Classical Review* 5 (1891) 249-53.

Casey, M. *Son of Man: The Interpretation and Influence of Daniel 7.* London: SPCK, 1979.

Cavallin, A. "Zum verhältnis zwischen regierendem Verb und Participium coniunctum." *Eranos* 44 (1946) 280-85.

502

Chadwick, J. "The Prehistory of the Greek Language." *The Cambridge Ancient History*. Vol. 2 part 2. Ed. I.E.S. Edwards *et al.* 3d ed. Cambridge: UP, 1975: 805-19.

Chamberlain, W.D. *An Exegetical Grammar of the Greek NT*. New York: Macmillan, 1941.

Chambers, C.D. "The Classification of Conditional Sentences." *Classical Review* 9 (1895) 293-94.

_____. "On a Use of the Aorist Participle in Some Hellenistic Writers." *Journal of Theological Studies* 24 (1922-23) 183-87.

_____. "On the Construction of οὐ μή." *Classical Review* 11 (1897) 109-11.

_____. "The Origin of the Construction οὐ μή." *Classical Review* 10 (1896) 150-52.

Chantraine, P. *Grammaire Hómerique*. 2 vols. Paris: Klincksieck, 1942, 1953.

_____. *Histoire du parfait grec*. Collection linguistique. Paris: Honoré Champion, 1927.

_____. "Questions de syntaxe grecque. II. Remarques sur l'emploi des thèmes de présent et de l'aoriste." *Revue de philologie* 40 (1966) 40-45.

_____. "Remarques sur les rapports entre les modes et les aspects en grec." *Bulletin de la Société de linguistique de Paris* 40 (1938) 69-79.

Charles, R.H. *A Critical and Exegetical Commentary on the Revelation of St. John*. 2 vols. International Critical Commentary. Edinburgh: T. and T. Clark, 1920.

_____. *Lectures on the Apocalypse*. Schweich Lectures of the British Academy 1919. London: Oxford UP, 1922.

_____. *Studies in the Apocalypse*. Edinburgh: T. and T. Clark, 1913.

Chilton, B. *A Galilean Rabbi and His Bible: Jesus' Own Interpretation of Isaiah*. London: SPCK, 1984.

_____. *God in Strength: Jesus' Announcement of the Kingdom*. Studien zum NT und seiner Umwelt Series B Band 1. Freistadt: Plöchl, 1978.

Chomsky, W. "What Was the Jewish Vernacular During the Second Commonwealth?" *Jewish Quarterly Review* 42 (1951-52) 193-212.

Clapp, E.B. "Conditional Sentences in Aischylos." *Transactions of the American Philological Association* 18 (1887) 43-58.

_____. "Mr. Bayfield on Conditions 'Contrary to Fact.'" *Classical Review* 5 (1891) 397-99.

Clavier, H. "Πέτρος καὶ πέτρα." *Neutestamentliche Studien für R. Bultmann*. Berlin: Töpelmann, 1954: 94-109.

Clines, D.J.A. *I, He, We, and They: A Literary Approach to Isaiah 53*. Journal for the Study of the OT Supplement Series 1. Sheffield: JSOT, 1976.

Cohen, S. "The Hebrew Language." *The Universal Jewish Encyclopedia*. Vol. 5. Ed. I. Landman. New York: Ktav, 1969: 276-81.

Collange, J.-F. *The Epistle of St. Paul to the Philippians*. Trans. A.W. Heathcote. London: Epworth, 1979.

Collinge, N.E. *Collectanea Linguistica: Essays in General and Genetic Linguistics*. Janua Linguarum Series Minor 21. The Hague: Mouton, 1970.

_____. "Greek (and Some Roman) Preferences in Language Categories." *Studies in the History of Western Linguistics*. Ed. T. Bynon and F.R. Palmer. Cambridge: UP, 1986: 11-22.

_____. "Some Reflexions on Comparative Historical Syntax." *Archivum Linguisticum* 12 (1960) 79-101.

_____. Review of Ruipérez, *Estructura*. *Archivum Linguisticum* 7 (1955) 60-62.

_____. Review of Wonneberger, *Syntax*. *Journal of Semitic Studies* 30 (1985) 292-94.

Collins, J.J. Review of Martin, *Syntactical Evidence*. *Catholic Biblical Quarterly* 37 (1975) 592-93.

Colwell, E.C. "The Greek Language." *Interpreter's Dictionary of the Bible*. Nashville: Abingdon, 1962: 2.479-87.

_____. *The Greek of the Fourth Gospel: A Study of its Aramaisms in the Light of Hellenistic Greek*. Chicago: U of Chicago P, 1931.

503

Comrie, B. *Aspect: An Introduction to the Study of Verbal Aspect and Related Problems.* Cambridge Textbooks in Linguistics. Cambridge: UP, 1976.

_____. *Tense.* Cambridge Textbooks in Linguistics. Cambridge: UP, 1985.

_____. Review of Anderson, *Essay. Lingua* 37 (1975) 89-92.

Contreras, H. Review of R. Valin, *La méthode comparative en linguistique historique et en psychomécanique du langage. Language* 42 (1966) 106-08.

Conybeare, F.C., and St.G. Stock. *A Grammar of Septuagint Greek.* Boston: Ginn, 1905; rpt. Grand Rapids: Zondervan, 1980.

Conybeare, W.J. "Use of the Aorist of the Greek NT." *Journal of Philology* 1 (1868) 222-26.

Conzelmann, H. *1 Corinthians.* Trans. J.W. Leitch. Ed. G.W. MacRae. Hermeneia. Philadelphia: Fortress, 1975.

_____. *An Outline of the Theology of the NT.* Trans. J. Bowden. NT Library. London: SCM, 1969.

Cope. "γίγνεσθαι, γιγνώσκειν." *Journal of Philology* 1 (1868) 79-88.

Coseriu, E. "Aspect verbal ou aspects verbaux? Quelques questions de théorie et de méthode." *La notion d'aspect.* Ed. J. David and R. Martin. Recherches linguistiques. Paris: Klincksieck, 1980: 13-25.

_____. "El aspecto verbal perifrástico en griego antiguo." *Actas del III Congreso Español de Studios Clásicos.* Sociedad Española de Estudios Clásicos. Madrid: [Publicaciones de la Sociedad Española de Estudios Clásicos], 1968: 93-116.

Coseriu, E., and H. Geckeler. "Linguistics and Semantics." *Current Trends in Linguistics* 12 (1974) 103-71.

Costas, P.W. *An Outline of the History of the Greek Language, with Particular Emphasis on the Koine and the Subsequent Periods.* Chicago, 1936; rpt. Chicago: Ares, 1979.

Cotterell, F.P. "The Nicodemus Conversation." *Expository Times* 96 (1985) 237-42.

Coughanowr, E.N. *The Verbal Categories in the Greek of the Synoptic Gospels.* Ph.D. thesis, Univ. of Illinois, Urbana Champaign, 1955.

Courtenay James, J. *The Language of Palestine and Adjacent Regions.* Edinburgh: T. and T. Clark, 1920.

Cousar, C.B. "Eschatology and Mark's *Theologia Crucis*: A Critical Analysis of Mark 13." *Interpretation* 24 (1970) 321-35.

Craigie, P.C. *Psalms 1 50.* Word Biblical Commentary 19. Waco, Texas: Word, 1983.

Cranfield, C.E.B. *A Critical and Exegetical Commentary on the Epistle to the Romans* 2 vols. International Critical Commentary. Edinburgh: T. and T. Clark, 1975, 1979.

_____. *The Gospel According to St. Mark.* Cambridge Greek Testament Commentary. Cambridge: UP, 1959.

_____. "Message of Hope: Mark 4:21-32." *Interpretation* 9 (1955) 150-64.

Crisafulli, V.S. *Aspect and Tense Distribution in Homeric Greek.* Ph.D. thesis, Univ. of North Carolina, Chapel Hill, 1967.

Cross, F.L. *1 Peter: A Paschal Liturgy.* London: Mowbray, 1954.

Cruse, D.A. *Lexical Semantics.* Cambridge Textbooks in Linguistics. Cambridge: UP, 1986.

Crystal, D. *A First Dictionary of Linguistics and Phonetics.* Language Library. London: Deutsch, 1980.

_____. *Linguistics.* Harmondsworth: Penguin, 1971.

Culler, J. *Saussure.* Glasgow: Fontana Collins, 1976.

Cullmann, O. *Peter: Disciple, Apostle, Martyr: A Historical and Theological Study.* 2d ed. Trans. F.V. Filson. London: SCM, 1962.

Curtius, G. *Elucidations of the Student's Greek Grammar.* 2d ed. Trans. E. Abbott. London: John Murray, 1875.

_____. *Erläuterungen zu meiner griechischen Schulgrammatik.* Prague: F. Tempsky, 1863.

_____. *The Greek Verb: Its Structure and Development.* Trans. A.S. Wilkins and E.B. England. London: John Murray, 1880.

Dahl, Ö. "Comrie's *Tense*: Review Article." *Folia Linguistica* 21 (1987) 489-502.

_____. *Tense and Aspect Systems*. Oxford: Blackwell, 1985.
Dahood, M. *Psalms III: 101-150*. Anchor Bible 17A. Garden City, New York: Doubleday, 1970.
Dalman, G. *Jesus-Jeshua: Studies in the Gospels*. Trans. P.P. Levertoff. London: SPCK, 1929.
_____. *The Words of Jesus: Considered in the Light of Post-Biblical Jewish Writings and the Aramaic Language*. Trans. D.M. Kay. Edinburgh: T. and T. Clark, 1902.
Dana, H.E., and J.R. Mantey. *A Manual Grammar of the Greek NT*. Toronto: Macmillan, 1955.
Danker, F.W. *A Century of Greco-Roman Philology*. Society of Biblical Literature Centennial Publications. Atlanta: Scholars, 1988.
Daube, D. "Concerning the Reconstruction of 'the Aramaic Gospels.'" *Bulletin of John Rylands Library* 29 (1945) 69-105.
_____. *The NT and Rabbinic Judaism*. London: Athlone, 1956.
_____. "Participle and Imperative in 1 Peter." *The First Epistle of St. Peter*, by E.G. Selwyn. 2d ed. London: Macmillan, 1947: 467-88.
David, J., and R. Martin, ed. *La notion d'aspect*. Recherches linguistiques 5. Paris: Klincksieck, 1980.
Davids, P.H. *The Epistle of James: A Commentary on the Greek Text*. New International Greek Testament Commentary. Grand Rapids: Eerdmans, 1982.
Davidson, M.E. "Computer Analysis of Verb Forms in the Greek NT." *ALLC Bulletin* (Association for Literacy and Linguistic Computing) 11 (1983) 68-72.
Davies, G.A. *The Trachiniae of Sophocles* (from R.C. Jebb). Cambridge: UP, 1908.
Davies, W.D. "Law in the NT." *Interpreter's Dictionary of the Bible*. New York: Abingdon, 1962: 3.95-102.
_____. *Paul and Rabbinic Judaism: Some Rabbinic Elements in Pauline Theology*. 4th ed. Philadelphia: Fortress, 1980.
_____. *The Setting of the Sermon on the Mount*. Cambridge: UP, 1964.
Debrunner, A. "Der Aorist ἔφατο." *Glotta* 25 (1936) 73-79.
_____. "Das hellenistische Nebensatziterativpräteritum mit ἄν." *Glotta* 11 (1921) 1-23.
_____. "Verschobener Partizipialgebrauch in Griechischen." *Museum Helveticum* 1 (1944) 31-46.
_____. Review of Björk, *HN ΔΙΔΑΣΚΩΝ*. *Indogermanische Forschungen* 58 (1942) 312-13.
_____. Review of Brunel, *L'aspect*. *Indogermanische Forschungen* 58 (1942) 284-87.
_____. Review of Koschmieder, *Zeitbezug*. *Indogermanische Forschungen* 48 (1930) Anzeiger 89-95.
Deer, D.S. "More about the Imperatival *HINA*." *Bible Translator* 24 (1973) 328-29.
_____. "Still more about the Imperatival ἵνα." *Bible Translator* 30 (1979) 148.
Deissmann, A. *Bible Studies*. Trans. A. Grieve. 2d ed. Edinburgh: T. and T. Clark, 1903.
_____. "Hellenistisches Griechisch." *Realencyklopädie für protestantische Theologie und Kirche*. Vol. 7. Ed. A. Hauck. 3d ed. Leipzig: Hinrichs, 1899: 627-39.
_____. *Light from the Ancient East*. Trans. L.R.M. Strachan. London: Hodder and Stoughton, 1910.
_____. *The Philology of the Greek Bible: Its Present and Future*. Trans. L.R.M. Strachan. London: Hodder and Stoughton, 1908.
Delancey, S. "Aspect, Transitivity and Viewpoint." *Tense-Aspect: Between Semantics and Pragmatics*. Ed. P.J. Hopper. Amsterdam: Benjamin, 1982: 167-83.
Delbrück, B. *Die Grundlagen der Griechischen Syntax*. Syntaktische Vorschungen 4. Halle: Waisenhauses, 1879.
_____. *Vergleichende Syntax der Indogermanischen Sprachen*. Parts 4.1-3 of *Grundriss der vergleichenden Grammatik der Indogermanischen Sprachen*. By K. Brugmann and B. Delbrück. Strassburg: Trübner, 1893, 1897, 1900.
Delebecque, E. "L'hellénisme de la 'relative complexe' dans le NT et principalement chez Saint Luc." *Biblica* 62 (1981) 229-38.

505

_____. "La vivante formule ΚΑΙ ΕΓΕΝΕΤΟ." *Etudes grecques sur l'Evangile de Luc.* Collection d'études anciennes. Paris: Société d'édition "Les Belles Lettres," 1976: 123-65.

Delling, G. "Partizipiale Gottesprädikationen in den Briefen des NT." *Studia Theologische* 17 (1963) 1-59.

[Denio, F.B.] "Translation of the Aorist Tense in the Indicative Mood." *Bibliotheca Sacra* 41 (1884) 386-89.

Denniston, J.D. *The Greek Particles.* Rev. K.J. Dover. Oxford: Clarendon, [1954].

_____. *Greek Prose Style.* Oxford: Clarendon, 1952.

Dibelius, M. *James.* Rev. H. Greeven. Trans. M.A. Wilkens. Ed. H. Koester. Hermeneia. Philadelphia: Fortress, 1976.

Dietrich, W. "Der periphrastische Verbalaspekt im Griechischen und Lateinischen." *Glotta* 51 (1973) 188-228.

Díez Macho, A. "The Recently Discovered Palestinian Targum: Its Antiquity and Relationship with the Other Targums." *Congress Volume.* Supplements to Vetus Testamentum 7. Leiden: Brill, 1960: 222-45.

Dik, S.C. *Functional Grammar.* North-Holland Linguistic Series. Amsterdam: North-Holland, 1978.

Dinneen, F.P. "Linguistics and Classic Philosophy." *Georgetown Univ. Round Table Selected Papers on Linguistics 1961-65.* Ed. R.J. O'Brien. Washington: Georgetown UP, 1968: 57-64.

Diver, W. "The System of Relevance of the Homeric Verb." *Acta Linguistica Hafniensia* 12 (1969) 45-68.

Dodd, C.H. *The Bible and the Greeks.* London: Hodder and Stoughton, 1954.

_____. *Historical Tradition in the Fourth Gospel.* Cambridge: UP, 1963.

_____. *The Interpretation of the Fourth Gospel.* Cambridge: UP, 1953.

_____. *NT Studies.* Manchester: UP, 1953.

_____. "NT Translation Problems II." *Bible Translator* 28 (1977) 101-16.

_____. "Notes from Papyri." *Journal of Theological Studies* 23 (1921-22) 60-63.

_____. *The Parables of the Kingdom.* 3d ed. London: Nisbet, 1936.

Dodds, E.R. *Plato Gorgias: A Revised Text with Introduction and Commentary.* Oxford: Clarendon, 1959.

Donovan, J. "German Opinion on Greek Jussives." *Classical Review* 9 (1895) 289-93; 342-46; 444-47.

_____. "Greek Jussives." *Classical Review* 9 (1895) 145-49.

_____. "The Prospective Subjunctive and Optative." *Classical Review* 8 (1894) 145.

_____. "Sonnenschein's Greek Grammar." *Classical Review* 9 (1895) 60-67.

Dorsch, T.S., trans. *Classical Literary Criticism.* Harmondsworth: Penguin, 1965.

Doudna, J.C. *The Greek of the Gospel of Mark.* Journal of Biblical Literature Monograph Series 12. Philadelphia: Society of Biblical Literature and Exegesis, 1961.

Dover, K.J. "The Colloquial Stratum in Classical Attic Prose." *Classical Contributions: Studies in honour of M.F. McGregor.* Ed. G.S. Shrimpton and D.J. McCargar. Locust Valley, New York: J.J. Augustin, 1981: 15-25.

_____. *Greek Word Order.* Cambridge: UP, 1960.

_____. "The Language of Classical Attic Documentary Inscriptions." *Transactions of the Philological Society* (1981) 1-14.

_____. Review of Aerts, *Periphrastica. Gnomon* 40 (1968) 87-88.

Downing, G. "Meanings." *What About the NT? Essays in Honour of C. Evans.* Ed. M. Hooker and C. Hickling. London: SCM, 1975: 127-42.

Draper, H.M. "Did Jesus Speak Greek?" *Expository Times* 67 (1955-56) 317.

Drewitt, J.A.J. "The Augment in Homer." *Classical Quarterly* 6 (1912) 44-59; 104-20.

Driver, S.R. *A Treatise on the Use of the Tenses in Hebrew: and Some other Syntactical Questions.* 3d ed. Oxford: Clarendon, 1892.

Druet, F.-X. "L'aspect en grec classique: une école des nuances." *Les études classiques* 51 (1983) 97-104.

506

Dunbar, R.G. "Submerged Aorists." *Expository Times* 45 (1933-34) 46.
Dunn, J.D.G. *Baptism in the Holy Spirit.* Studies in Biblical Theology Second Series 15. London: SCM, 1970.
_____. *Christology in the Making: A NT Inquiry into the Origins of the Doctrine of the Incarnation.* London: SCM, 1980.
_____. "Rom 7:14-25 in the Theology of Paul." *Theologische Zeitschrift* 31 (1975) 257-73.
Durie, D. *Greek Grammar: A Concise Grammar of NT Greek.* Canberra, Australia: privately printed, 1981.
Eakin, F. "Aorists and Perfects in First-Century Papyri." *American Journal of Theology* 20 (1916) 266-73.
Earle, M.L. "Notes on the Subjunctive of Purpose in Relative Clauses in Attic Greek." *Transactions of the American Philological Association* 23 (1892) xvii-xviii.
_____. "The Subjunctive of Purpose in Relative Clauses in Greek." *Classical Review* 6 (1892) 93-95.
_____. "Of the Subjunctive in Relative Clauses after οὐκ ἔστιν and its Kin." *Classical Review* 10 (1896) 421-24.
Elbert, P. "The Perfect Tense in Matt 16:19 and Three Charismata." *Journal of the Evangelical Theological Society* 17 (1974) 149-55.
van Elderen, B. "The Verb in the Epistolary Invocation." *Calvin Theological Journal* 2 (1967) 46-48.
Ellis, E.E. *The Gospel of Luke.* New Century Bible. London: Nelson, 1966.
Ellis, J.[O.] "On Contextual Meaning." *In Memory of J.R. Firth.* Ed. C.E. Bazell *et al.* London: Longman, 1966: 79-95.
_____. "Some Recent Work on German Grammar." *Archivum Linguisticum* 13 (1961) 33-49.
_____. Review of Bull, *Time. Archivum Linguisticum* 13 (1961) 210-12.
Elmer, H.C. "A Note on the Gnomic Aorist." *Transactions of the American Philological Association* 25 (1894) lix-lxiii.
Emden, C.S. "St. Mark's Use of the Imperfect Tense." *Expository Times* 65 (1953-54) 146-49; *Bible Translator* 5 (1954) 121-25.
Emerton, J.A. "Binding and Loosing--Forgiving and Retaining." *Journal of Theological Studies* NS 13 (1962) 325-31.
_____. "Did Jesus Speak Hebrew?" *Journal of Theological Studies* NS 12 (1961) 189-202.
_____. "The Problem of Vernacular Hebrew in the First Century A.D. and the Language of Jesus." *Journal of Theological Studies* NS 24 (1973) 1-23.
Engler, R. "European Structuralism: Saussure." *Current Trends in Linguistics* 13 (1975) 829-86.
Enslin, M.S. "The Perfect Tense in the Fourth Gospel." *Journal of Biblical Literature* 55 (1936) 121-31.
Entwistle, W.J. *Aspects of Language.* London: Faber and Faber, 1953.
Erhart, A. "Réflexions sur le participe du parfait actif." *Charisteria Francisco Novotny octogenario oblata.* Prague: Státní Pedagogické Nakladatelství, 1962: 71-77.
Erickson, R.J. *Biblical Semantics, Semantic Structure, and Biblical Lexicology: A Study of Methods, with Special Reference to the Pauline Lexical Field of "Cognition."* Ph.D. thesis, Fuller Theological Seminary, Pasadena, California, 1980.
_____. *James Barr and the Beginnings of Biblical Semantics.* Anthroscience Minigraph Series. Notre Dame: Foundations Press, 1984.
_____. "OIDA and GINOSKO and Verbal Aspect in Pauline Usage." *Westminster Theological Journal* 44 (1982) 110-22.
Eriksson, K. *Das Präsens Historicum in der nachklassischen griechischen Historiographie.* Lund: Håkan Ohlsson, 1943.

Ervin, H.E. *Conversion-Initiation and the Baptism in the Holy Spirit.* Peabody, Massachusetts: Hendrickson, 1984.

Ewald, H. *Syntax of the Hebrew Language of the OT.* Trans. J. Kennedy. Edinburgh: T. and T. Clark, 1881.

Exler, F.X.J. *The Form of the Ancient Greek Letter of the Epistolary Papyri (3rd c. B.C-3rd c. A.D.): A Study in Greek Epistolography.* 1823; rpt. Chicago: Ares, 1976.

Fajen, F. "Tempus im Griechischen: Bemerkungen zu einem Buch von H. Weinrich." *Glotta* 49 (1971) 34-41.

Farris, S.C. *The Hymns of Luke's Infancy Narrative: Their Origin, Meaning and Significance.* Journal for the Study of the NT Supplement Series 9. Sheffield: JSOT, 1985.

_____. "On Discerning Semitic Sources in Luke 1-2." *Gospel Perspectives II.* Ed. R.T. France and D. Wenham. Sheffield: JSOT, 1981: 201-37.

Fawcett, R.P. *Cognitive Linguistics and Social Interaction: Towards an Integrated Model of a Systemic Functional Grammar and the Other Components of a Communicating Mind.* Heidelberg: Julius Groos and Exeter Univ., 1980.

_____. "Generationg a sentence in systemic functional grammar." *Readings in Systemic Linguistics.* Ed. M.A.K. Halliday and J.R. Martin. London: Batsford, 1981: 146-83.

_____. "The semantics of clause and verb for relational processes in English." *New Developments in Systemic Linguistics.* Vol. 1: Theory and Description. Ed. M.A.K. Halliday and R.P. Fawcett. London: Pinter, 1987: 130-83.

_____. "What Makes a 'Good' System Network Good?--Four Pairs of Concepts for Such Evaluations." Unpublished paper, 1984.

Feldman, L.H. "How Much Hellenism in Jewish Palestine?" *Hebrew Union College Annual* 57 (1986) 83-111.

Ferguson, C.A. "Diglossia." *Word* 15 (1959) 325-40.

Fernando, A.P. "Translation of Questions and Prohibitions in Greek." *Bible Translator* 27 (1976) 138-42.

Filson, F.V. *A Commentary on the Gospel According to St. Matthew.* Black's NT Commentaries. London: Adam and Charles Black, 1960.

Finkel, A. "Jesus' Sermon at Nazareth (Luke 4:16-30)." *Abraham unser Vater: Juden und Christen in Gespräch über die Bibel.* Ed. O. Betz, M. Hengel, and P. Schmidt. Leiden: Brill, 1963: 106-15.

Firth, J.R. *Papers in Linguistics, 1934-51.* Oxford: UP, 1951.

_____. *Selected Papers of J.R. Firth 1952-59.* Ed. F.R. Palmer. London: Longmans, 1968.

Fitzmyer, J.A. "Another View of the 'Son of Man' Debate." *Journal for the Study of the NT* 4 (1979) 58-68.

_____. "Aramaic *Kepha'* and Peter's Name in the NT." *Text and Interpretation.* Ed. E. Best and R.McL. Wilson. Cambridge: UP, 1979: 121-32.

_____. "The Aramaic Language and the Study of the NT." *Journal of Biblical Literature* 99 (1980) 5-21.

_____. *The Gospel According to Luke.* 2 vols. Anchor Bible 28, 28A. Garden City, New York: Doubleday, 1981, 1985.

_____. "The Languages of Palestine in the First Century A.D." *Catholic Biblical Quarterly* 32 (1970) 501-31.

_____. "The Phases of the Aramaic Language." *A Wandering Aramean: Collected Aramaic Essays.* Society of Biblical Literature Monograph Series 25. Missoula, Montana: Scholars, 1979: 57-84.

_____. "The Study of the Aramaic Background of the NT." *A Wandering Aramean: Collected Aramaic Essays.* Society of Biblical Literature Monograph Series 25. Missoula, Montana: Scholars, 1979: 1-27.

Fitzmyer, J.A., and D.J. Harrington. *A Manual of Palestinian Aramaic Texts.* Biblica et Orientalia 34. Rome: Biblical Institute Press, 1978.

Flier, M.S., and A. Timberlake, ed. *The Scope of Slavic Aspect.* UCLA Slavic Studies 12. Columbus, Ohio: Slavica, 1984.

Forsyth, J. *A Grammar of Aspect: Usage and Meaning in the Russian Verb.* Cambridge: UP, 1970.

de Foucault, J.-A. *Recherches sur la langue et la style de Polybe.* Collection d'études ancienne. Paris: Société d'édition "Les Belles Lettres," 1972.

Fowler, D.C. "The Meaning of 'Touch Me Not' in John 20:17." *Evangelical Quarterly* 47 (1975) 16-25.

France, R.T. "The Exegesis of Greek Tenses in the NT." *Notes on Translation* 46 (1972) 3-12.

Frede, M. "Principles of Stoic Grammar." *The Stoics.* Ed. J.M. Rist. Berkeley: U of Calif. P, 1978: 27-75.

Friedrich, G. "Semasiologie und Lexicologie." *Theologische Literaturzeitung* 94 (1969) cols. 801-16.

Friedrich, P. "On Aspect Theory and Homeric Aspect." *International Journal of American Linguistics*, Memoir 28, 40 (1974) S1-S44.

Fries, C.C. *Linguistics: The Study of Language.* New York: Holt, Rinehart and Winston, 1964.

Frisk, H. "Participium und verbum finitum im Spätgriechischen." *Kleine Schriften zur Indogermanistik und zur griechischen Wortkunde.* Studia Graeca et Latina Gothoburgensia 21. Gothenburg: Acta Universitatis Gothoburgensis, 1966: 431-42; *Glotta* 17 (1928-29) 56-66.

von Fritz, K. "The So-Called Historical Present in Early Greek." *Word* 5 (1949) 186-201.

Frösén, J. *Prolegomena to a Study of the Greek Language in the First Centuries A.D.: The Problem of Koiné and Atticism.* Helsinki: Univ. of Helsinki (diss.), 1974.

Fuller, R.H. *The Foundations of NT Christology.* London: Lutterworth, 1965.

Funk, R.W. *A Beginning-Intermediate Grammar of Hellenistic Greek.* 2 vols. Vol. 1: Sight and Sound, Nominal System, Verbal System. Sources for Biblical Study 2. 2d ed. Missoula, Montana: Society of Biblical Literature, 1973.

_____. "Parsing Code for Hellenistic Greek: Preliminary Proposals." *Society of Biblical Literature 1972 Proceedings.* 2 vols. N.p. 2.315-330d.

Furnish, V.P. "The Ministry of Reconciliation." *Currents in Theology and Mission* 4 (1977) 204-18.

_____. *II Corinthians.* Anchor Bible 35A. Garden City, New York: Doubleday, 1984.

_____. *Theology and Ethics in Paul.* Nashville: Abingdon, 1968.

Gadamer, H.G. *Truth and Method.* New York: Crossroad, 1975.

Gärtner, B. *The Temple and the Community in Qumran and the NT: A Comparative Study in the Temple Symbolism of the Qumran Texts and the NT.* Society for NT Studies Monograph Series 1. Cambridge: UP, 1965.

Galton, H. *Aorist und Aspekt im Slavischen: Eine Studie zur funktionellen und historischen Syntax.* Wiesbaden: Harrassowitz, 1962.

_____. *The Main Functions of the Slavic Verbal Aspect.* Macedonian Academy of Sciences and Arts. Skopje: n.p., 1976.

_____. "A New Theory of the Slavic Verbal Aspect." *Archivum Linguisticum* 16 (1964) 133-43.

_____. "Verbalaspekt im Griechischen und Slavischen." *Folia Linguistica* 8 (1975) 147-56.

Gardner, P.D. "Damascus Road" (review of Kim, *Origin*). *Evangel* 2 (1984) 22.

Gaston, L. *No Stone on Another: Studies in the Significance of the Fall of Jerusalem in the Synoptic Gospels.* Supplements to Novum Testamentum 23. Leiden: Brill, 1970.

Gehman, H.S. "Ἅγιος in the Septuagint, and its Relation to the Hebrew Original." *Vetus Testamentum* 4 (1954) 337-48.

_____. "The Hebraic Character of Septuagint Greek." *Vetus Testamentum* 1 (1951) 81-90.

_____. "Hebraisms of the Old Greek Version of Genesis." *Vetus Testamentum* 3 (1953) 141-48.

509

George, A.R. "The Imperatival Use of ἵνα in the NT." *Journal of Theological Studies* 45 (1944) 56-60.

Gibson, A. *Biblical Semantic Logic: A Preliminary Analysis.* Oxford: Blackwell, 1981.

Gignac, F.T. *A Grammar of the Greek Papyri of the Roman and Byzantine Periods.* Vol. 1: Phonology. Vol. 2: Morphology. Milan: Istituto Editoriale Cisalpino--La Goliardica, n.d., 1981.

_____. "The Language of the Non-Literary Greek Papyri." *Proceedings of the Twelfth International Congress of Papyrology.* Ed. D.H. Samuel. American Studies in Papyrology 7. Toronto: Hackkert, 1970: 139-52.

_____. "The Papyri and the Greek Language." *Yale Classical Studies* 28 (1985) 155-65.

_____. "The Transformation of the Second Aorist in Koine Greek." *Bulletin of the American Society of Papyrologists* 22 (1985) 49-54.

[Gildersleeve, B.L.] "Aorist and Imperfect." *American Journal of Philology* 11 (1890) 107-08.

_____. "The Articular Infinitive Again." *American Journal of Philology* 8 (1887) 329-37.

_____. "The Articular Infinitive in Xenophon and Plato." *American Journal of Philology* 3 (1882) 193-202.

[_____.] "Brief Mention." *American Journal of Philology* 13 (1892) 123-25; 23 (1902) 106; 24 (1903) 481-82; 29 (1908) 242-45; 30 (1909) 234-35.

_____. "Consecutive Sentences." *American Journal of Philology* 7 (1886) 161-75; 9 (1888) 329-37.

_____. "Contributions to the History of the Articular Infinitive." *Transactions of the American Philological Association* 9 (1878) 6-19.

_____. "Encroachment of μή and οὐ in Later Greek." *American Journal of Philology* 1 (1879) 45-57.

_____. "The Final Sentence in Greek." *American Journal of Philology* 4 (1883) 416-44; 6 (1885) 53-73.

_____. "Note by the Editor." *American Journal of Philology* 18 (1897) 460-61.

_____. "Notes from the Greek Seminary. II. Οὐ μή." *American Journal of Philology* 3 (1882) 202-05.

_____. "Notes on the Evolution of oratio obliqua." *American Journal of Philology* 27 (1906) 200-08.

_____. "On εἰ with the Future Indicative and ἐάν with the Subjunctive in the Tragic Poets." *Transactions of the American Philological Association* 7 (1876) 5-23.

_____. "Problems of Greek Syntax." *American Journal of Philology* 23 (1902) 121-41; 241-60.

_____. "Stahl's Syntax of the Greek Verb. Second Article. Tenses." *American Journal of Philology* 29 (1908) 389-409.

_____. "Studies in Pindaric Syntax. I. The Conditional Sentence in Pindar." *American Journal of Philology* 3 (1882) 434-45.

_____. "Studies in Pindaric Syntax. III. Aorist and Imperfect." *American Journal of Philology* 4 (1883) 158-65.

_____, with C.W.E. Miller. *Syntax of Classical Greek from Homer to Demosthenes.* 2 vols. in one. New York: American Book, 1900, 1911.

_____. "Temporal Sentences of Limit in Greek." *American Journal of Philology* 24 (1903) 388-408.

_____. Untitled. *American Journal of Philology* 9 (1888) 491-92.

_____. Review of A. Joost, *Was ergiebt sich aus den Sprachgebrauch Xenophons. . . .* Berlin 1892. *American Journal of Philology* 14 (1893) 101-06.

Giles, P. *A Short Manual of Comparative Philology for Classical Students.* 2d ed. London: Macmillan, 1901.

Gingrich, F.W. "The Greek NT as a Landmark in the Course of Semantic Change." *Journal of Biblical Literature* 73 (1954) 189-96.

Gleason, H.A., Jr. *An Introduction to Descriptive Linguistics.* Rev. ed. New York: Holt, Rinehart and Winston, 1961.

_____. "Linguistics in the Service of the Church." *Hartford Quarterly* 1 (1961) 7-27.
_____. "Some Contributions of Linguistics to Biblical Studies." *Hartford Quarterly* 4 (1963) 47-56.
Gnilka, J. *Die Verstockung Israels: Isaias 6, 7-10 in der Theologie der Synoptiker.* Studien zum Alten und Neuen Testament. Munich: Kösel, 1961.
Godel, R. "F. de Saussure's Theory of Language." *Current Trends in Linguistics* 3 (1966) 479-93.
Godley, A.D. *Herodotus.* Vol. 4. Loeb Classical Library. London: Heinemann, 1925.
Goetchius, E. Van N. *The Language of the NT.* New York: Scribners, 1965.
Gomme, A.W. *A Historical Commentary on Thucydides.* Vol. 2. Oxford: Clarendon, 1956.
Gonda, J. *The Aspectual Function of the Rgvedic Present and Aorist.* Disputationes Rheno-Trajectinae VII. 'S-Gravenhage: Mouton, 1962.
_____. *The Character of the Indo-European Moods, with Special Regard to Greek and Sanskrit.* Wiesbaden: Harrassowitz, 1956.
_____. "A Remark on 'Periphrastic' Constructions in Greek." *Mnemosyne* Series 4, 12 (1959) 97-112.
Goodenough, E.R. *Jewish Symbols in the Greco-Roman Period.* 13 vols. Vol. 2: The Archeological Evidence from the Diaspora. New York: Pantheon, 1953.
Goodenough, W.H. "Componential Analysis and the Study of Meaning." *Language* 32 (1956) 195-216.
Goodspeed, E.J. "A New Glimpse of Greek Tense-Movements in NT Times." *American Journal of Theology* 10 (1906) 102-03.
_____. "The Original Language of the NT." *New Chapters in NT Study.* New York: Macmillan, 1937: 127-68.
_____. "The Possible Aramaic Gospel." *Journal of Near Eastern Studies* 1 (1942) 315-40.
Goodwin, W.W. *Demosthenes: On the Crown.* Cambridge: UP, 1901; rpt. New York: Arno, 1979.
_____. *A Greek Grammar.* Rev. ed. London: St. Martin's Press, 1894.
_____. *Greek Grammar.* Rev. C.B. Gulick. Boston: Ginn, 1958. [Goodwin/Gulick]
_____. "On the Classification of Conditional Sentences in Greek Syntax." *Transactions of the American Philological Association* 4 (1873) 60-80; *Journal of Philology* 5 (1874) 186-205.
_____. "On the Extent of the Deliberative Construction in Relative Clauses in Greek." *Harvard Studies in Classical Philology* 7 (1896) 1-12.
_____. "'Shall' and 'Should' in Protasis, and their Greek Equivalents." *Transactions of the American Philological Association* 7 (1876) 87-107; *Journal of Philology* 8 (1879) 18-38.
_____. *Syntax of the Moods and Tenses of the Greek Verb.* 5th ed. London: Macmillan, 1892.
Goppelt, L. *Der erste Petrusbrief.* Ed. F. Hahn. Meyer. Göttingen: Vandenhoeck und Ruprecht, 1978.
Gotteri, N.J.C. "The Concept of Aspect as a Privative Opposition." Unpublished paper, 1972.
_____. "A Note on Bulgarian Verb Systems." *Journal of the Midland Association for Linguistic Studies* NS 8 (1983) 49-60.
_____. "A Speaker's Right to Choose: Aspects of Tense and Aspect in Polish." *Sheffield Working Papers in Language and Linguistics* 1 (1984) 72-78.
_____. "Towards a Comparison of Systemic Linguistics and Tagmemics: An Interim Report and Bibliography." *Journal of the Midland Association for Linguistic Studies* NS 7 (1982) 31-42.
_____. "When is a System Network not a System Network? And is that a Fair Question? Fragments from a Continuing Discussion." *Occasional Papers in Systemic Linguistics* 1 (1987) 5-14.
Goulder, M.D. *Midrash and Lection in Matthew.* London: SPCK, 1974.
Gow, A.S.F., and D.L. Page, ed. *The Greek Anthology: The Garland of Philip and some Contemporary Epigrams.* 2 vols. Cambridge: UP, 1968.

Grant, W.L. "Hebrew, Aramaic, and the Greek of the Gospels." *Greece and Rome* 20 (1951) 115-22.

Grassi, C. "Imperativo presente e aoristo nelle preghiere agli dei." *Studi Italiani di Filologia Classica* 35 (1963) 186-98.

Grayston, K. "The Study of Mark XIII." *Bulletin of John Rylands Library* 56 (1973-74) 371-87.

Green, E.L. "Μή for οὐ before Lucian." *Studies in Honor of B.L. Gildersleeve*. Baltimore: Johns Hopkins Press, 1902: 471-79.

_____. "The Optative Mood in Diodorus Siculus." *Transactions of the American Philological Association* 34 (1903) lxii-iii.

Green, T.S. *A Treatise on the Grammar of the NT Dialect; Embracing Observations on the Literal Interpretation of Numerous Passages*. London: Samuel Bagster, 1842.

Greenberg, J.H. *Language Universals: With Special Reference to Feature Hierarchies*. The Hague: Mouton, 1966.

_____. "The Realis-Irrealis Continuum in the Classical Greek Conditional." *On Conditionals*. Ed. E.C. Trangott. Cambridge: UP, 1986: 247-64.

Greenlee, J.H. "'If' in the NT." *Bible Translator* 13 (1962) 39-43.

_____. "The Importance of Syntax for the Proper Understanding of the Sacred Text of the NT." *Evangelical Quarterly* 44 (1972) 131-46.

_____. "NT Participles." *Bible Translator* 5 (1954) 98-101.

_____. "Verbs in the NT." *Bible Translator* 3 (1952) 71-75.

Gregory, M. "Meta-functions: aspects of their development, status and use in systemic linguistics." *New Developments in Systemic Linguistics*. Vol. 1: Theory and Description. Ed. M.A.K. Halliday and R.P. Fawcett. London: Pinter, 1987: 94-106.

Gregory, M., and S. Carroll. *Language and Situation: Language Varieties and their Social Contexts*. Language and Society. London: Routledge and Kegan Paul, 1978.

Grelot, P. "L'arrière-plan araméen du 'Pater.'" *Revue Biblique* 91 (1984) 531-56.

Grice, H.P. "Further Notes on Logic and Conversation." *Syntax and Semantics 9: Pragmatics*. Ed. P. Cole. New York: Academic, 1978: 113-27.

_____. "Logic and Conversation." *Syntax and Semantics 3: Speech Acts*. Ed. P. Cole and J.L. Morgan. New York: Academic, 1975: 41-58.

_____. "Meaning." *Semantics: An Interdisciplinary Reader in Philosophy, Linguistics and Psychology*. Ed. D.D. Steinberg and L.A. Jakobovits. Cambridge: UP, 1971: 53-59.

Griffiths, J.G. "Did Jesus Speak Aramaic?" *Expository Times* 56 (1944-45) 327-28.

Grintz, J.M. "Hebrew as the Spoken and Written Language in the Last Days of the Second Temple." *Journal of Biblical Literature* 79 (1960) 32-47.

van Gronigen, B.A. "Quelques considérations sur l'aoriste gnomique." *Studia Varia Carolo Guilielmo Vollgraff: A Discipulis Oblata* (Studia Vollgraff). Amsterdam: North-Holland, 1948: 49-61.

Grudem, W. *1 Peter*. Tyndale NT Commentaries. Grand Rapids: Eerdmans (forthcoming).

Guelich, R.A. *The Sermon on the Mount: A Foundation for Understanding*. Waco, Texas: Word, 1982.

Guillaume, G. *Temps et verbe: Theorie des aspects, des modes et des temps*. Paris: Honoré Champion, 1965.

Gundry, R.H. "The Language Milieu of First-Century Palestine: Its Bearing on the Authenticity of the Gospel Tradition." *Journal of Biblical Literature* 83 (1964) 404-08.

_____. *Matthew: A Commentary on His Literary and Theological Art*. Grand Rapids: Eerdmans, 1982.

_____. "The Narrative Framework of Matt 16:17-19: A Critique of Professor Cullmann's Hypothesis." *Novum Testamentum* 7 (1964-65) 1-9.

_____. *The Use of the OT in St. Matthew's Gospel, with Special Reference to the Messianic Hope*. Supplements to Novum Testamentum 18. Leiden: Brill, 1967.

Haberland, H. "A Note on the 'Aorist.'" *Language and Discourse: Test and Protest*. Ed. J.L. Mey. Linguistic and Literary Studies in Eastern Europe 19. Amsterdam: Benjamins, 1986: 173-84.

Haenchen, E. *The Acts of the Apostles.* Trans. B. Noble *et al.* 14th ed. Oxford: Blackwell, 1971.

_____. *Das Johannesevangelium: Ein Kommentar.* Ed. U. Busse. Tübingen: J.C.B. Mohr (Paul Siebeck), 1980.

_____. *John.* 2 vols. Trans. R.W. Funk. Ed. R.W. Funk and U. Busse. Hermeneia. Philadelphia: Fortress, 1984.

Hahn, E.A. *Subjunctive and Optative: Their Origin as Futures.* Philological Monographs published by the American Philological Association 16. New York: American Philological Association, 1953.

Hahn, F. *The Titles of Jesus in Christology: Their History in Early Christianity.* Trans. H. Knight and G. Ogg. London: Lutterworth, 1969.

Hainsworth, J.B. "The Greek Language and the Historical Dialects." *The Cambridge Ancient History.* Vol. 3 part 1. Ed. J. Boardman *et al.* 2d ed. Cambridge: UP, 1982: 850-65.

Hale, W.G. "'Extended' and 'Remote' Deliberatives in Greek." *Transactions of the American Philological Association* 24 (1893) 156-205.

_____. "The Origin of Subjunctive and Optative Conditions in Greek and Latin." *Harvard Studies in Classical Philology* 12 (1901) 109-23.

_____. "The 'Prospective Subjunctive' in Greek and Latin." *Classical Review* 8 (1894) 166-69.

Halliday, M.A.K. *Halliday: System and Function in Language.* Ed. G.R. Kress. Oxford: UP, 1976.

_____. "Language Structure and Language Function." *New Horizons in Linguistics.* Ed. J. Lyon. Harmondsworth: Penguin, 1970: 140-65.

_____. "Lexis as a Linguistic Level." *In Memory of J.R. Firth.* Ed. C.E. Bazell *et al.* London: Longman, 1966: 148-62.

_____. "Structure." *Readings in Systemic Linguistics.* Ed. M.A.K. Halliday and J.R. Martin. London: Batsford, 1981: 122-31.

_____. "Text as Semantic Choice in Social Contexts." *Grammars and Descriptions.* Ed. T.A. Van Dijk and J.B. Petofi. Berlin: de Gruyter, 1977: 176-202.

Halliday, M.A.K., and R. Hasan. "Text and Context: Aspects of Language in a Social-Semiotic Perspective." *Sophia Linguistica* 6 (1980) 4-91.

Halliday, M.A.K., and R.P. Fawcett, ed. *New Developments in Systemic Linguistics.* Vol. 1: Theory and Description. London: Pinter, 1987.

Halliday, M.A.K., and J.R. Martin, ed. *Readings in Systemic Linguistics.* London: Batsford, 1981.

Harding, C.R. "Subsequent Action Expressed by the Aorist Participle." *Transactions of the American Philological Association* 57 (1928) xxxix.

Harman, H.M. "The Optative Mood in Hellenistic Greek." *Journal of Biblical Literature* 6 (1886) 3-12.

Harris, J. "Syntactic Variation and Dialect Divergence." *Journal of Linguistics* 20 (1984) 303-27.

Harris, J.R. "The So-Called Biblical Greek." *Expository Times* 25 (1913) 54-55.

Harris, M.J. "Appendix: Prepositions and Theology in the Greek NT." *New International Dictionary of NT Theology.* Vol. 3. Ed. C. Brown. Grand Rapids: Zondervan, 1978: 1171-1215.

_____. "2 Corinthians." *Expositor's Bible Commentary.* Ed. F.E. Gaebelein. Vol. 10. Grand Rapids: Zondervan, 1976.

_____. *Raised Immortal: Resurrection and Immortality in the NT.* Marshalls Theological Library. London: Marshall, Morgan and Scott, 1983.

Harrison, C. "Remarks on Bayfield's Paper." *Classical Review* 4 (1890) 297-98.

_____. Untitled. *Classical Review* 4 (1890) 130.

Harrison, J.E. *Aspects, Aorists and the Classical Tripos.* Cambridge: UP, 1919.

Harry, J.E. "The Perfect Forms in Later Greek from Aristotle to Justinian." *Transactions of the American Philological Association* 37 (1906) 53-72.

513

_____. "The Perfect Subjunctive, Optative and Imperative in Greek." *Classical Review* 19 (1905) 347-54.

_____. "The Perfect Subjunctive, Optative and Imperative in Greek Again." *Classical Review* 20 (1906) 100-03.

Hartman, L. *Participial Constructions in the Synoptic Gospels*. Testimonium Linguae. Coniectanea Neotestamentica 19. Lund: Gleerup, 1963.

Hartmann, F. "Aorist und Imperfektum." *Zeitschrift für vergleichende Sprachforschung* 48 (1919) 1-47.

_____. "Aorist und Imperfektum im Griechischen." *Neue Jahrbuch für das klassische Altertum* 43 (1919) 316-39; 49 (1920) 1-73.

_____. "Zur Frage der Aspektbedeutung beim griechischen Futurum." *Zeitschrift für vergleichende Sprachforschung* 62 (1935) 116-31.

Hartmann, H. "Zur Funktion des Perfekts: eine strukturelle Betrachtung." *Festschrift B. Snell: Zum 60. Geburtstag am 18. Juni 1956 von Freunden und Schülern Überreicht*. Munich: Beck, 1956: 243-50.

Hasan, R. "The grammarian's dream: lexis as most delicate grammar." *New Developments in Systemic Linguistics*. Vol. 1: Theory and Description. Ed. M.A.K. Halliday and R.P. Fawcett. London: Pinter, 1987: 184-211.

Hata, G. "Is the Greek Version of Josephus' *Jewish War* a Translation or a Rewriting of the First Version?" *Jewish Quarterly Review* 66 (1975-76) 89-108.

Hatch, E. *Essays in Biblical Greek*. 1889; rpt. Amsterdam: Philo, 1970.

Haugen, E. "Dialect, Language, Nation." *Sociolinguistics: Selected Readings*. Ed. J.B. Pride and J. Holmes. Harmondsworth: Penguin, 1972: 97-111.

_____. "Problems of Bilingualism." *Lingua* 2 (1950) 271-90.

_____. "Norm and Deviation in Bilingual Communities." *Bilingualism: Psychological, Social and Educational Implications*. Ed. P.A. Hornby. New York: Academic, 1977: 91-102.

Hauri, H.W. *Kontrahiertes und sigmatisches Futur: Einflüss von Lautstruktur und Aktionsart auf die Bildung des griechischen Futur*. Göttingen: Vandenhoeck und Ruprecht, 1975.

Hawkins, J.C. *Horae Synopticae: Contributions to the Study of the Synoptic Problem*. 2d ed. Oxford: Clarendon, [1909] 1968.

Hawthorne, G.F. *Philippians*. Word Biblical Commentary 43. Waco, Texas: Word, 1983.

Headlam, W. "Greek Prohibitions." *Classical Review* 19 (1905) 30-36.

_____. "Some Passages of Aeschylus and Others." *Classical Review* 17 (1903) 286-95.

Heidt, W. "Translating NT Imperatives." *Catholic Biblical Quarterly* 13 (1951) 253-57.

Heirs, R.H. "'Binding' and 'Loosing': The Matthean Authorizations." *Journal of Biblical Literature* 104 (1985) 233-50.

Helbing, R. *Grammatik der Septuaginta: Laut- und Wortlehre*. Göttingen: Vandenhoeck und Ruprecht, 1907.

Hemer, C.J. "Reflections on the Nature of NT Greek Vocabulary." *Tyndale Bulletin* 38 (1987) 65-92.

Hengel, M. "Hymn and Christology." *Studia Biblica 1978. III. Papers on Paul and Other NT Authors*. Ed. E.A. Livingstone. Journal for the Study of the NT Supplement Series 3. Sheffield: JSOT, 1980: 173-97.

_____. *Judaism and Hellenism: Studies in their Encounter in Palestine during the Early Hellenistic Period*. Trans. J. Bowden. London: SCM, 1974.

Henrici, A. "Some Notes on the Systemic Generation of a Paradigm of the English Clause." *Readings in Systemic Linguistics*. Ed. M.A.K. Halliday and J.R. Martin. London: Batsford, 1981: 74-93.

Henry, A.S. "Further Notes on the Language of the Prose Inscriptions of Hellenistic Athens." *Classical Quarterly* NS 19 (1969) 289-305.

_____. "Some Observations on Final Clauses in Hellenistic Attic Prose Inscriptions." *Classical Quarterly* NS 16 (1966) 291-97.

Herbig, G. "Aktionsart und Zeitstufe." *Indogermanische Forschungen* 6 (1896) 157-269.

Héring, J. *The Second Epistle of St. Paul to the Corinthians*. Trans. A.W. Heathcote and P.J. Allcock. London: Epworth, 1967.

Hermann, E. "Die altgriechischen Tempora: ein strukturanalytischer Versuch." *Nachrichten von der Akademie der Wissenschaften in Göttingen, Philologisch- Historische Klasse* (1943) 583-649.

_____. "Aspekt und Aktionsart." *Nachrichten der Gesellschaft der Wissenschaften zu Göttingen, Philologisch- Historische Klasse* 4 (1933) 470-80.

_____. "Aspekt und Zeitrichtung." *Indogermanische Forschungen* 54 (1936) 262-64.

_____. "Objektive und subjektive Aktionsart." *Indogermanische Forschungen* 45 (1927) 207-28.

Hessinger, J.J. "The Syntactic and Semantic Status of Prepositions in Greek." *Classical Philology* 73 (1978) 211-23.

Hettrich, H. *Kontext und Aspekt in der altgriechischen Prosa Herodots*. Göttingen: Vandenhoeck und Ruprecht, 1976.

Hewitt, B.G. Review of Nida *et al. Style and Discourse*. *Journal for the Study of the NT* 28 (1986) 121-23.

Hewlett, E.W.G. "On the Articular Infinitive in Polybius." *American Journal of Philology* 11 (1890) 267-90; 440-70.

Hicks, R.D. *Diogenes Laertius, Lives of Eminent Philosophers*. 2 vols. Loeb Classical Library. London: Heinemann, 1925.

Hiersche, R. "'Aspekt' in der stoischen Tempuslehre?" *Zeitschrift für vergleichende Sprachforschung* 91 (1977) 275-87.

Higgins, A.J.B. *Jesus and the Son of Man*. London: Lutterworth, 1964.

_____. *The Son of Man in the Teaching of Jesus*. Society for NT Studies Monograph Series 39. Cambridge: UP, 1980.

Higgins, M.J. "NT Result Clauses with Infinitive." *Catholic Biblical Quarterly* 23 (1961) 233-41.

_____. "The Renaissance of the First Century and the Origin of Standard Late Greek." *Traditio* 3 (1945) 49-100.

_____. "Why Another Optative Dissertation?" *Byzantion* 15 (1940-41) 443-48.

Hill, D. *The Gospel of Matthew*. New Century Bible. London: Oliphants, 1972.

_____. *Greek Words and Hebrew Meanings: Studies in the Semantics of Soteriological Terms*. Society for NT Studies Monograph Series 5. Cambridge: UP, 1967.

_____. *NT Prophecy*. Marshalls Theological Library. London: Marshall, Morgan and Scott, 1979.

_____. "On the Evidence for the Creative Role of Christian Prophets." *NT Studies* 20 (1970) 262-74.

Hirtle, W.H. *Time, Aspect and the Verb*. Cahiers de psychoméchanique du langage. Québec: Les presses de l'Université Laval, 1975.

Hjelmslev, L. *Essais linguistiques*. Travaux du cercle linguistique de Copenhague 12. Copenhagen: Nordisk Sprog-og Kulturforlag, 1959.

_____. *Essais linguistiques*. Paris: Les éditions de minuit, 1971.

Hockett, C.F. *A Course in Modern Linguistics*. New York: Macmillan, 1958.

Hoerber, R.G. "The Greek of the NT: Some Theological Implications." *Concordia Journal* 2 (1976) 251-56.

Hoffmann, E.G., and H. von Siebenthal. *Griechische Grammatik zum NT*. Riehen: Immanuel-Verlag, 1985.

Hoffmann, J.B. "Zum Wesen der sog. polaren Ausdrucksweise." *Glotta* 15 (1926) 45-53.

Hoffmann, O., and A. Debrunner. *Geschichte der griechischen Sprache*. Ed. A. Scherer. 4th ed. Berlin: de Gruyter, 1969.

Hoffmann, P. "Paratasis: de la description aspectuelle des verbes grecs à une définition du temps dans le néoplatonisme tardif." *Revue des études grecques* 96 (1983) 1-26.

Holt, J. *Etudes d'aspect*. Acta Jutlandica Aarskrift for Aarhus Universitet 15.2. Copenhagen: Universitetsforlaget I Aarhus, 1943.

515

Holzmeister, U. "Vom Angeblicken Verstockungszweck der Parabeln des Herrn." *Biblica* 15 (1934) 321-68.

Hooker, M.D. *Jesus and the Servant: The Influence of the Servant Concept of Deutero-Isaiah in the NT.* London: SPCK, 1959.

_____. *The Son of Man in Mark: A Study of the Background of the Term "Son of Man" and its Use in St. Mark's Gospel.* London: SPCK, 1967.

Hopper, P.J. "Aspect and Foregrounding in Discourse." *Syntax and Semantics 12: Discourse and Syntax.* Ed. T. Givón. New York: Academic, 1979: 213-41.

Hopper, P.J., ed. *Tense-Aspect: Between Semantics and Pragmatics.* Amsterdam: Benjamins, 1982.

Horrocks, G.C. Review of Lightfoot, *Natural Logic. Linguistics* 185 (1977) 68-83.

Horsley, G.H.R. "Divergent Views on the Nature of the Greek of the Bible." *Biblica* 65 (1984) 393-403.

_____. *The Linguistic and Historical Context of the Greek of the NT. The Evidence of Contemporary Documents.* Ph.D. thesis, Macquarrie Univ., Australia, 1985.

Horsley, G.H.R., ed. *New Documents Illustrating Christianity.* South Ryde: Macquarrie Univ., 1981-.

H[ort], F.J.A. Untitled. *Journal of Philology* 1 (1868) 226-30.

Horton, F.L. "Reflections on the Semitisms of Luke-Acts." *Perspectives on Luke-Acts.* Ed. C.H. Talbert. Edinburgh: T. and T. Clark, 1978: 1-23.

Horton-Smith, R. *The Theory of Conditional Sentences in Greek and Latin.* London: Macmillan, 1894.

Houben, J.L. *The Conditional Sentence in Ancient Greek.* Ph.D. thesis, Princeton Univ., New Jersey, 1976.

Householder, F.W. "Ancient Greek." *Lingua* 17 (1967) 103-28.

Householder, F.W., trans. *The Syntax of Apollonius Dyscolus.* Amsterdam Studies in the Theory and History of Linguistics III. Studies in the History of Linguistics vol. 23. Amsterdam: Benjamins, 1981.

Householder, F.W., and G. Nagy. *Greek: A Survey of Recent Work.* Janua Linguarum. The Hague: Mouton, 1972.

Hovdhaugen, E. *Foundations of Western Linguistics: From the Beginning to the End of the First Millenium A.D.* Oslo: Universitetsforlaget, 1982.

How, W.W., and J. Wells. *A Commentary on Herodotus.* 2 vols. Oxford: Clarendon, 1928.

Howard, G. *The Gospel of Matthew according to a Primitive Hebrew Text.* Macon, Georgia: Mercer UP, 1987.

_____. "Was the Gospel of Matthew Originally Written in Hebrew?" *Bible Review* 2 (1986) 15-25.

Howard, G., and J.C. Shelton. "The Bar-Kokhba Letters and Palestinian Greek." *Israel Exploration Society* 23 (1973) 101-02.

Howard, W.F. "The Language of the NT." *A Companion to the Bible.* Ed. T.W. Manson. Edinburgh: T. and T. Clark, 1939: 22-30.

_____. "On the Futuristic Use of the Participle in Hellenistic." *Journal of Theological Studies* 24 (1922-23) 403-06.

Howell, E.B. "St. Paul and the Greek World." *Greece and Rome* 2d series 11 (1964) 7-29; expanded from *Expository Times* 71 (1959-60) 328-32.

Huddleston, R.D. "Systemic features and their realization." *Readings in Systemic Linguistics.* Ed. M.A.K. Halliday and J.R. Martin. London: Batsford, 1981: 58-73.

Hudson, R.A. *Sociolinguistics.* Cambridge Textbooks in Linguistics. Cambridge: UP, 1980.

_____. "Systemic generative grammar." *Readings in Systemic Linguistics.* Ed. M.A.K. Halliday and J.R. Martin. London: Batsford, 1981: 190-217.

_____. "Systemic Grammar" (review article). *Linguistics* 24 (1986) 791-815.

Hughes, J.A. "Another Look at the Hebrew Tenses." *Journal of Near Eastern Studies* 29 (1970) 12-24.

Hughes, P.E. "The Language Spoken by Jesus." *New Dimensions in NT Study.* Ed. R.N. Longenecker and M.C. Tenney. Grand Rapids: Zondervan, 1974: 127-43.
_____. *Paul's Second Epistle to the Corinthians.* New London Commentary. London: Marshall, Morgan and Scott, 1961.
Hulton, A.O. "῏ΑΝ with the Future: A Note." *Classical Quarterly* NS 7 (1957) 139-42.
_____. "Some 'Past Optatives.'" *Classical Quarterly* NS 8 (1958) 139-41.
Hultsch, F. *Die erzählenden Zeitformen bei Polybius: Ein Beitrag zur Syntax der gemeingriechischen Sprache.* 3 vols. Des XIII. Bandes der Abhandlungen der philologisch-historischen Classe der Königl. Sächsischen Gesellschaft der Wissenschaften. Leipzig: Hirzel, 1891-93.
Hultszch, T. "Die erzählenden Zeitformen bei Diodor von Sicilien." *Zweiter Jahresbericht des städtischen Progymnasiums mit Realabteilungen zu Pasewalk.* Pasewalk: Gnädig, 1902.
_____. *De elocutione Diodori Siculi de usu aoristi et imperfecti pars 1.* Dissertatio inauguralis philologica. Halis Saxonum: Formis Kaemmererianis, 1893.
Humbert, J. "L'aoriste indicatif: rend-il nécessairement le passé?" *Revue des études anciennes* 42 (1940) 187-91.
_____. *Histoire de la langue grecque.* Que sais-je? 1483. Paris: Universitaires, 1972.
_____. *Syntaxe grecque.* Collection de philologie classique 2. 3d ed. Paris: Klincksieck, (1945) 1960.
_____. "Verbal Aspect: Has it Evolved from Ancient to Modern Greek?" *The Link* 1 (1938) 21-28.
Humphreys, M.W. "Notes on Greek Grammar." *Transactions of the American Philological Association* 23 (1892) lxi-lxii.
_____. "On Negative Commands in Greek." *Transactions of the American Philological Association* 7 (1876) 46-49.
_____. Untitled. *Classical Review* 5 (1891) 7.
Hunkin, J.W. "'Pleonastic' ἄρχομαι in the NT." *Journal of Theological Studies* 25 (1923-24) 390-402.
Hurst, L.D. "The Neglected Role of Semantics in the Search for the Aramaic Words of Jesus." *Journal for the Study of the NT* 28 (1986) 63-80.
ΤΑ ΙΕΡΑ ΓΡΑΜΜΑΤΑ. Athens: ΒΙΒΛΙΚΗ ΕΤΑΙΡΙΑ, 1979.
Ikegami, Y. "Structural Semantics: A Survey and Problems." *Linguistics* 33 (1967) 49-67.
Irigoin, J. "Aspects et temps du grec ancien au grec moderne." *Actants, voix et aspects verbaux: Actes des journées d'études linguistiques de l'Université d'Angers (22-23 mai 1979).* Angers: U of Angers P, 1981: 63-82.
Irmscher, J. "Der Streit um das Bibelgriechisch." *Acta Antigua Akademie Hungariae* 7 (1959) 127-34.
Ivanescu, G. "Le temps, l'aspect et la durée de l'action dans les langues indo-européennes." *Mélanges linguistiques publiés à l'occasion du VII Congrès International des Linguistes à Oslo.* Académie de la République Populaire Roumaine. Bucharest: Editions de l'académie de la République Populaire Roumaine, 1957: 23-61.
Ivic, M. *Trends in Linguistics.* Trans. M. Heppell. Janua Linguarum Series Minor 42. The Hague: Mouton, 1965.
Jackson, H. "Prohibitions in Greek." *Classical Review* 18 (1904) 262-63.
Jacobsohn, H. "Aspektfragen." *Indogermanische Forschungen* 51 (1933) 292-318.
_____. Review of Wackernagel, *Vorlesungen. Gnomon* 2 (1926) 369-95.
Jacoby, F. *Die Fragmente der griechischen Historiker.* III B. Leiden: Brill, 1950.
Jacquinod, B. "L'evolution de φημι et le système verbal du grec ancien." *Actes des sessions de linguistique de Bourg-Saint-Maurice, septembre 1976.* Paris: Conseil Scient. de la Sorbonne Nouvelle, 1977: 9.01-19.
Jakobson, R. "Implications of Language Universals for Linguistics." *Universals of Language.* Ed. J. Greenberg. 2d ed. Cambridge: M.I.T. Press, 1966: 263-78.
_____. "Shifters, Verbal Categories, and the Russian Verb." *Selected Writings II: Word and Language.* The Hague: Mouton, 1971: 130 47.

_____. "Signe Zéro." *Selected Writings II: Word and Language.* The Hague: Mouton, 1971: 212-19.

_____. "Zur Struktur des russischen Verbums." *Selected Writings II: Word and Language.* The Hague: Mouton, 1971: 3-16.

Jankowsky, K.R. *The Neogrammarians: A Re-evaluation of their Place in the Development of Linguistic Science.* Janua Linguarum Series Minor 16. The Hague: Mouton, 1972.

Jannaris, A.N. *A Historical Greek Grammar Chiefly of the Attic Dialect.* London: Macmillan, 1897.

J.D. "ὅστ ς ἄδει)(ὅστις ἂν ἄδῃ." *Classical Review* 6 (1892) 202-03.

_____. "The Remote Deliberative." *Classical Review* 6 (1892) 435-37.

Jelf, W.E. *A Grammar of the Greek Language Chiefly from the German of R. Kühner.* 2 vols. 2d ed. Oxford: James Henry Parker, 1851.

Jellicoe, S. *The Septuagint and Modern Study.* Oxford: Clarendon, 1968.

Jeremias, J. "Die aramäische Vorgeschichte unserer Evangelien." *Theologische Literaturzeitung* 9 (1949) 527-32.

_____. *Jesus' Promise to the Nations.* Trans. S.H. Hooke. Studies in Biblical Theology. London: SCM, 1958.

_____. *NT Theology. Part 1: The Proclamation of Jesus.* Trans. J. Bowden. NT Library. London: SCM, 1971.

_____. *The Parables of Jesus.* Trans. S.H. Hooke. Rev. ed. London: SCM, 1963.

_____. *The Prayers of Jesus.* Trans. J. Bowden and J. Reumann. Studies in Biblical Theology Second Series 6. London: SCM, 1967.

Jesperson, O. *The Philosophy of Grammar.* London: George Allen and Unwin, 1925.

Johannessohn, M. "Das biblische καὶ ἐγένετο und seine Geschichte." *Zeitschrift für vergleichende Sprachforschung* 53 (1925) 161-212.

Johnson, D. *A Study of the Use of the Historic Present Tense in the Gospel of St. Mark.* M.A. thesis, London Bible College, 1984.

Johnson, M.R. "A Unified Temporal Theory of Tense and Aspect." *Syntax and Semantics 14: Tense and Aspect.* Ed. P.J. Tedeschi and A. Zaenen. New York: Academic, 1981: 145-75.

Johnson, O.E. *Tense Significance as the Time of the Action.* Language Dissertations 21. Philadelphia: Linguistic Society of America, 1936.

Johnson, S.E. "The Septuagint and the NT." *Journal of Biblical Literature* 56 (1937) 331-46.

Joly, R. *Le vocabulaire chrétien de l'amour est-il original? Φιλεῖν et Ἀγαπᾶν dans le grec antique.* Brussels: Universitaires, 1968.

Jones, A.H.M. *The Greek City: From Alexander to Justinian.* Oxford: Clarendon, 1940.

Jones, D.M. Review of Ruipérez, *Estructura. Classical Review* NS 6 (1956) 126-28.

Jones, F.P. *The ab urbe condita Construction in Greek: A Study in the Classification of the Participle.* Supplement to Language 28. Linguistic Society of America, 1939; rpt. New York: Kraus, 1966.

Joseph, B.D. "Greek." *The World's Major Languages.* Ed. B. Comrie. London: Croom Helm, 1987: 410-39.

Joüon, P. "Quelques aramaïsmes: sous-jacent au grec des Evangiles." *Recherches de science religieuse* 17 (1927) 210-29.

Käsemann, E. "Sentences of Holy Law in the NT." *NT Questions of Today.* Trans. W.J. Montague. London: SCM, 1969: 66-81.

_____. "Some Thoughts on the Theme 'The Doctrine of Reconciliation in the NT.'" *The Future of Our Religious Past: Essays in Honour of R. Bultmann.* Ed. J.M. Robinson. Trans. C.E. Carlston and R.P. Scharlemann. London: SCM, 1971: 49-64.

Kahane, H.R. Review of Ruipérez, *Estructura. Language* 32 (1956) 324-29.

Kahle, P. *The Cairo Geniza.* 2d ed. Oxford: Blackwell, 1959.

_____. "Das palästinische Pentateuchtargum und das zur Zeit Jesu gesprochene Aramäisch." *Zeitschrift für die neutestamentliche Wissenschaft* 49 (1958) 100-15.

Kahn, C.H. "The Greek Verb 'To Be' and the Concept of Being." *Foundations of Language* 2 (1966) 254-65.
_____. *The Verb 'Be' in Ancient Greek.* Foundations of Language Supplement Series 16. Dordrecht: Reidel, 1973.
Kanjuparambil, P. "Imperatival Participles in Rom 12:9-21." *Journal of Biblical Literature* 102 (1983) 285-88.
Kapsomenos, S.G. "Das Griechische in Aegypten." *Museum Helveticum* 10 (1953) 248-63.
Karleen, P.S. *The Syntax of the Participle in the Greek NT.* Ph.D. thesis, Univ. of Pennsylvania, 1980.
Kaufman, S.A. "The Job Targum from Qumran." *Journal of the American Oriental Society* 43 (1973) 317-27.
_____. "On Methodology in the Study of the Targums and their Chronology." *Journal for the Study of the NT* 23 (1985) 117-24.
Kay, C., and M.L. Samuels. "Componential Analysis in Semantics: its Validity and Applications." *Transactions of the Philological Society* (1975) 49-81.
Kay, P. "Taxonomy and Semantic Contrast." *Language* 47 (1971) 866-87.
Keith, A.B. "Some Uses of the Future in Greek." *Classical Quarterly* 6 (1912) 121-26.
Kempson, R.M. *Semantic Theory.* Cambridge Textbooks in Linguistics. Cambridge: UP, 1977.
Kennedy, G. "Classical and Christian Source Criticism." *The Relationships Among the Gospels: An Interdisciplinary Dialogue.* Ed. W.O. Walker, Jr. San Antonio: Trinity UP, 1978: 125-55.
Kennedy, H.A.A. *Sources of NT Greek: or the Influence of the Septuagint on the Vocabulary of the NT.* Edinburgh: T. and T. Clark, 1895.
Kenny, A. *A Stylometric Study of the NT.* Oxford: Clarendon, 1986.
Kieckers, E. *Historische Griechische Grammatik. IV: Syntax.* Zweiter Teil. Berlin: de Gruyter, 1926.
_____. "Zum Gebrauch des imperativus aoristi und praesentis." *Indogermanische Forschungen* 24 (1909) 10-16.
Kieffer, R. "Die Bedeutung der modernen Linguistik für die Auslegung biblischer Texte." *Theologische Zeitschrift* 30 (1974) 223-33.
_____. *Essais de méthodologie néo-testamentaire.* Lund: Gleerup, 1972.
Kijne, J.J. "Greek Conditional Sentences." *Bible Translator* 13 (1962) 223-24.
Kilpatrick, G.D. "Atticism and the Text of the Greek NT." *Neutestamentliche Aufsätze.* Ed. J. Blinzer, O. Kuss, and F. Mussner. Regensburg: Friedrich Pustet, 1963: 125-37.
_____. "The Greek NT Text of Today and the *Textus Receptus.*" *The NT in Historical and Contemporary Perspective.* Ed. H. Anderson and W. Barclay. Oxford: Blackwell, 1965: 189-208.
_____. "The Historic Present in the Gospels and Acts." *Zeitschrift für die neutestamentliche Wissenschaft* 68 (1977) 258-62.
_____. *The Origins of the Gospel According to St. Matthew.* Oxford: Clarendon, 1946.
_____. Review of Gignac, *Grammar I. Novum Testamentum* 24 (1982) 190-92.
Kim, S. *The Origin of Paul's Gospel.* Wissenschaftliche Untersuchungen zum NT 2. Reihe 4. Tübingen: J.C.B. Mohr (Paul Siebeck), 1981.
_____. *"The 'Son of Man'" as the Son of God.* Wissenschaftliche Untersuchungen zum NT 30. Tübingen: J.C.B. Mohr (Paul Siebeck), 1983.
Kiparsky, P. "Tense and Mood in Indo-European Syntax." *Foundations of Language* 4 (1968) 30-57.
Kittel, G., and G. Friedrich. *Theological Dictionary of the NT* [*TDNT*]. 10 vols. Trans. G.W. Bromiley. Grand Rapids: Eerdmans, 1964-76.
Klein, H.G. *Tempus, Aspekt, Aktionsart.* Romantische Arbeitshefte 10. Tübingen: Max Niemeyer, 1974.
Knight, G.W., III. *The Faithful Sayings in the Pastoral Letters.* Kampen: Kok, 1968.

Knorr, D. "Aorist and Present Participles Modifying the Same Main Verb." M.A. seminar paper, Trinity Evangelical Divinity School, Illinois, 1982.

Köster, F. "Did Paul Model his Language after that of Demosthenes?" *Bibliotheca Sacra* 11 (1854) 514-27.

Koester, H. *History, Culture, and Religion of the Hellenistic Age.* Vol. 1 of *Introduction to the NT.* Hermeneia: Foundations and Facets. Philadelphia: Fortress, 1982.

Koller, H. "Praesens historicum und erzählendes Imperfekt: Beitrag zur Aktionsart der Präsensstammzeiten im Lateinischen und Griechischen." *Museum Helveticum* 8 (1951) 63-99.

Koppers, B.T. *Negative Conditional Sentences in Greek and Some Other Indo-European Languages.* [The Hague: Westerbaan, 1959].

Koschmieder, E. *Zeitbezug und Sprache: Ein Beitrag zur Aspekt- und Tempusfrage.* 1929; rpt. Darmstadt: Wissenschaftliche Buchgesellschaft, 1971.

_____. "Zu den Grundfragen der Aspekttheorie." *Indogermanische Forschungen* 53 (1935) 280-300.

Kraabel, A.T. "The Diaspora Synagogue: Archaeological and Epigraphic Evidence since Sukenik." *Aufstieg und Niedergang der römischen Welt.* Ed. W. Haase. II.19.1. Berlin: de Gruyter, 1979: 477-510.

Kravar, M. "Approche syntaxique en matière d'aspect verbal." *Actes du Xe Congrès International des Linguistes.* Vol. 2. Bucharest: L'Académie de la République Socialiste de Roumanie, 1970: 961-69.

_____. "Autour de l'aoriste intemporal en grec." *Ziva Antika* 17 (1967) 33-48.

Kress, G.R., ed. *Halliday: System and Function in Language.* Oxford: UP, 1976.

Kretschmer, P. *Einleitung in die Geschichte der griechischen Sprache.* Göttingen: Vandenhoeck und Ruprecht, 1896.

_____. "Der griechische Imperativus Aoristi Activi auf -σον." *Glotta* 10 (1919) 112-22.

_____. "Literaturbericht für das Jahr 1909: Griechisch." *Glotta* 3 (1912) 296-43.

Krischer, T. "Die Rolle der irrealen Bedingungssätze in der Geschichte des griechischer Denkens." *Glotta* 57 (1979) 39-61.

Krüger, K.W. *Griechische Sprachlehre für Schulen.* Berlin: K.W. Krüger, 1861.

Kruger, G. van W. *Conditionals in the NT: A Study of their Rationale.* Ph.D. thesis, Univ. of Cambridge, 1966.

Kühner, R., and B. Gerth. *Ausführliche Grammatik der griechischen Sprache: Satzlehre.* 2 vols. 4th ed. Leverkusen: Gottschalksche, 1955.

Kümmel, W.G. *Promise and Fulfillment: The Eschatological Message of Jesus.* Studies in Biblical Theology 23. 2d ed. London: SCM, 1961.

Kugel, J.L. *The Idea of Biblical Poetry: Parallelism and its History.* New Haven: Yale UP, 1981.

Kuhn, T.S. "Second Thoughts on Paradigms." *The Structure of Scientific Theories.* 2d. ed. Urbana: U of Illinois P, 1977: 459-82.

_____. *The Structure of Scientific Revolutions.* 2d. ed. Chicago: U of Chicago P, 1970.

Kurylowicz, J. *The Inflectional Categories of Indo-European.* Heidelberg: Carl Winter, 1964.

_____. "Verbal Aspect in Semitic." *Orientalia* 42 (1973) 114-20.

Kurzová, H. "Die Entstehung des deklarativen Infinitivs im Griechischen." *Eirene* 6 (1967) 101-14.

_____. "Das Griechische im Zeitalter des Hellenismus." *Soziale Probleme im Hellenismus und im römischen Reich.* Ed. P. Oliva and J. Burian. Prague: n.p., 1973: 213-33.

_____. *Zur syntaktischen Struktur des Griechischen: Infinitiv und Nebensatz.* Tschechoslowakische Akademie der Wissenschaften. Prague: Academie Verlag, 1968.

Kutscher, E.Y. "Aramaic." *Current Trends in Linguistics* 6 (1970) 347-412.

_____. "Hebrew Language: Mishnaic." *Encyclopaedia Judaica.* Vol. 16. Jerusalem: Encyclopaedia Judaica, 1972: cols. 1590-1607.

_____. *A History of the Hebrew Language.* Ed. R. Kutscher. Leiden: Brill, 1982.

520

_____. "The Language of the Genesis Apocryphon--A Preliminary Study." *Hebrew and Aramaic Studies*. Ed. Z. Ben-Hayyim *et al*. Jerusalem: Magnes, 1977: 3-36.

_____. "Das zur Zeit Jesu gesprochene Aramäisch." *Zeitschrift für die neutestamentliche Wissenschaft* 51 (1960) 46-54.

Lachs, S.T. "Hebrew Elements in the Gospels and Acts." *Jewish Quarterly Review* 71 (1980) 31-43.

Lagrange, M.-J. *Evangile selon Saint Luc*. Paris: Gabalda, 1921.

Lamb, W.R. *Plato 3*. Loeb Classical Library. London: Heinemann, 1925.

Lambert, G. "Lier-délier: L'expression de la totalité par l'opposition de deux contraires." *Vivre et penser (RB)* 3d Series (1943-44) 91-103.

Lambrecht, J. *Die Redaktion der Markus-Apokalypse: Literarische Analyse und Strukturuntersuchung*. Analecta Biblica 28. Rome: Päpstliches Bibelinstitut, 1967.

Lane, W.L. *The Gospel According to Mark*. New International Commentary. Grand Rapids: Eerdmans, 1974.

Langdon, S. "History of the Use of ἐάν for ἄν in Relative Clauses." *American Journal of Philology* 24 (1903) 447-51.

Lapide, P. "Insights from Qumran into the Languages of Jesus." *Revue de Qumran* 8 (1975) 483-501.

Law, R. "Note on the Imperfect of 'Obligation,' etc., in the NT." *Expository Times* 30 (1918-19) 330-32.

Lawton, R. Review of McFall, *Enigma*. *Biblica* 65 (1984) 418-20.

Lazzeroni, R. "L'aspetto verbale con gli avverbi di rapidità e con quelli significanti 'improvissamente' in greco classico." *Annali della Scuola Normale Superiore di Pisa* 26 (1957) 88-97.

_____. "Considerazioni sull'aspetto verbale in frase negativa del greco clasico." *Annali della Scuola Normale Superiore di Pisa* 25 (1956) 213-33.

Leclercq, H. "Note sur le grec néo-testamentaire et la position du grec en Palestine au premier siècle." *Les études classiques* 42 (1974) 243-55.

Lee, G.M. "NT Gleanings: The Aorist Participle of Subsequent Action (Acts 16:6)?" *Biblica* 51 (1970) 235-37.

_____. "The Past Participle of Subsequent Action." *Novum Testamentum* 17 (1975) 199.

_____. "Tense, Voice, and Case." *Biblica* 51 (1970) 238-39.

_____. "Three Notes on ἵνα." *Biblica* 51 (1970) 239-40.

_____. "Translation Greek in the NT." *Studia Evangelica*. Vol. VII. Ed. E.A. Livingstone. Berlin: Akademie Verlag, 1982: 317-26.

_____. "Two Linguistic Parallels from Babrius." *Novum Testamentum* 9 (1967) 41-42.

Lee, J.A.L. *A Lexical Study of the Septuagint Version of the Pentateuch*. Society of Biblical Literature Septuagint and Cognate Studies Series 14. Chico, California: Scholars Press, 1983.

_____. "Some Features of the Speech of Jesus in Mark's Gospel." *Novum Testamentum* 27 (1985) 1-26.

Leech, G. *Semantics*. 2d ed. Harmondsworth: Penguin, (1974) 1980.

Lehmann, W.P. *Descriptive Linguistics: An Introduction*. 2d ed. New York: Random House, 1976.

Lehrer, A. "Semantics: An Overview." *The Linguistic Reporter, Supplement* 27 (1971) 13-23.

Lejnieks, V. *Morphosyntax of the Homeric Greek Verb*. Janua Linguarum Series Practica 9. The Hague: Mouton, 1964, from *Mood, Tense, and Aspect in Homeric Greek*. Ph.D. thesis, Princeton Univ., New Jersey, 1962.

Lentzen-Deis, F. *Die Taufe Jesu nach der Synoptikern: Literaturkritische und gattungs-geschichtliche Untersuchungen*. Frankfurter Theologische Studien. Frankfurt am Main: Knecht, 1970.

Lepschy, G.C. "Problems of Semantics." *Linguistics* 15 (1965) 40-65.

Leroy, M. "L'aspect verbal en grec ancien." *Revue Belge de philologie et d'histoire* 36 (1958) 128-38.

_____. "L'évolution des couples aspectuels du grec." *Proceedings of the Ninth International Congress of Linguistics*. Ed. H.G. Lunt. Janua Linguarum Series Maior 12. The Hague: Mouton, 1964: 813-17.

Leumann, M. "'Aoristi mixti' und Imperative vom Futurstamm in Griechischen." *Glotta* 32 (1952) 204-13.

Levias, C.A. *A Grammar of the Aramaic Idiom contained in the Babylonian Talmud*. Cincinnati: Block Publishing, 1900.

Levin, S. "Remarks on the 'Historical' Present and Comparable Phenomena of Syntax." *Foundations of Language* 5 (1969) 386-90.

Levinsohn, S.H. "Preliminary Observations on the Use of the Historic Present in Mark." *Note on Translation* 65 (1977) 13-28.

_____. *Textual Connections in Acts*. Society of Biblical Literature Monograph Series 31. Atlanta: Scholars, 1987.

Levinson, S.C. *Pragmatics*. Cambridge Textbooks in Linguistics. Cambridge: UP, 1983.

Lias, J.J. *The Second Epistle of Paul the Apostle to the Corinthians*. Cambridge Greek Testament for Schools and Colleges. Cambridge: UP, 1892.

Liddell, H.G., and R. Scott. *A Greek-English Lexicon*. Rev. H.S. Jones with R. McKenzie, and supplement by E.A. Barber. 9th ed. Oxford: Clarendon, 1968.

Lieberman, S. *Greek in Jewish Palestine: Studies in the Life and Manners of Jewish Palestine in the II-IV Centuries C.E.* 2d ed. New York: Philipp Feldheim, 1965.

_____. "How much Greek in Jewish Palestine?" *Biblical and Other Studies*. Ed. A. Altmann. Studies and Texts 1. Cambridge: Harvard UP, 1963: 123-41.

Liefield, W.L. "Luke." *Expositor's Bible Commentary*. Vol. 8. Ed. F.E. Gaebelein. Grand Rapids: Zondervan, 1984.

Lieu, J.M. "'Grace to you and Peace': The Apostolic Greeting." *Bulletin of John Rylands Library* 68 (1985) 161-78.

_____. *The Second and Third Epistles of John*. Edinburgh: T and T Clark, 1986.

Lifshitz, B. "Papyrus grecs du désert de Juda." *Aegyptus* 42 (1962) 240-56.

Lightfoot, D. *Natural Logic and the Greek Moods: The Nature of the Subjunctive and Optative in Classical Greek*. Janua Linguarum Series Practica 230. The Hague: Mouton, 1975.

Lightfoot, J.B. *Notes on Epistles of St. Paul from Unpublished Commentaries*. London: Macmillan, 1904.

_____. *Saint Paul's Epistle to the Galatians*. London: Macmillan, 1896.

_____. *St. Paul's Epistles to the Colossians and to Philemon*. London: Macmillan, 1897.

Lilja, S. *On the Style of the Earliest Greek Prose*. Commentationes Humanarum Litterarum 41.3. Helsinki: Helsingfors, 1968.

Lindars, B. *The Gospel of John*. New Century Bible. London: Oliphants, 1972.

_____. *Jesus Son of Man: A Fresh Examination of the Son of Man Sayings in the Gospels in the Light of Recent Research*. London: SPCK, 1983.

_____. "The New Look on the Son of Man." *Bulletin of John Rylands Library* 63 (1980) 437-62.

Lohmann, J. Review of Schwyzer, *Grammatik*. *Gnomon* 25 (1953) 353-61.

Lohmeyer, E. *Das Evangelium des Paulus*. 17th ed. Göttingen: Vandenhoeck und Ruprecht, 1967.

_____. *The Lord's Prayer*. Trans. J. Bowden. London: Collins, 1965.

Lohse, E. *Colossians and Philemon*. Trans. W.R. Poehlmann and R.J. Karris. Ed. H. Koester. Hermeneia. Philadelphia: Fortress, 1971.

López Eire, A. "Del ático a la *koiné*." *Emerita* 49 (1981) 377-92.

Loriaux, R. "Notes sur la syntaxe grecque des modes et des temps." *Les études classiques* 50 (1982) 49-62; 133-39; 225-35; 347-52.

Louw, J.P. "Discourse Analysis and the Greek NT." *Bible Translator* 24 (1973) 101-18.

_____. "The Greek NT Wordbook." *Bible Translator* 30 (1979) 108-17.

_____. "On Greek Prohibitions." *Acta Classica* 2 (1959) 43-57.

_____. "On Johannine Style." *Neotestamentica* 20 (1986) 5-12.

_____. "Semantics--A Methodological Reply." *Acta Classica* 29 (1986) 127-36.

_____. *Semantics of NT Greek.* Philadelphia: Fortress, 1982.

_____. "Die Semantiese Waarde von die Perfektum in Hellenistiese Grieks." *Acta Classica* 10 (1967) 23-32.

_____. "Verbal Aspect in the First Letter of John." *Neotestamentica* 9 (1975) 98-104.

_____. "Verbale Aspek in Grieks." *Taalfasette* 15 (1971) 13-26.

Luz, U. *Das Evangelium nach Matthäus.* Evangelische-Katholik Kommentar. 3 Vols. Vol. 1. Zürich: Benziger, 1985.

Lyons, J. "Deixis and Subjectivity: *Loquor, ergo sum?*" *Speech, Place and Action.* Ed. R.J. Jarvella and W. Klein. New York: Wiley, 1982: 201-24.

_____. "Firth's Theory of 'Meaning.'" *In Memory of J.R. Firth.* Ed. C.E. Bazell *et al.* London: Longman, 1966: 288-302.

_____. *Introduction to Theoretical Linguistics.* Cambridge: UP, 1968.

_____. *Language and Linguistics: An Introduction.* Cambridge: UP, 1981.

_____. *Language, Meaning and Context.* N.p.: Fontana Paperbacks, 1981.

_____. "A Note on Possessive, Existential and Locative Sentences." *Foundations of Language* 3 (1967) 390-96.

_____. *Semantics.* 2 vols. Cambridge: UP, 1977.

_____. *Structural Semantics: An Analysis of Part of the Vocabulary of Plato.* Publications of the Philological Society 20. Oxford: Blackwell, 1963.

Lyons, J., ed. *New Horizons in Linguistics.* Harmondsworth: Penguin, 1970.

McFague, S. *Metaphorical Theology: Models of God in Religious Language.* London: SCM, 1982.

McFall, L. *The Enigma of the Hebrew Verbal System: Solutions from Ewald to the Present Day.* Sheffield: Almond, 1982.

McGaughy, L.C. *Toward a Descriptive Analysis of 'EINAI as a Linking Verb in NT Greek.* Society of Biblical Literature Dissertation Series 6. Missoula, Montana: Society of Biblical Literature, 1972.

McGehee, M. "A Less Theological Reading of John 20:17." *Journal of Biblical Literature* 105 (1986) 299-302.

MacIntyre, A. "Epistemological Crises, Dramatic Narrative and the Philosophy of Science." *The Monist* 60 (1977) 453-72.

McKay, K.L. "Aspect in Imperatival Constructions in NT Greek." *Novum Testamentum* 27 (1985) 201-26.

_____. "Aspects of the Imperative in Ancient Greek." *Antichthon* 20 (1986) 41-58.

_____. "Further Remarks on the 'Historical' Present and other Phenomena." *Foundations of Language* 11 (1974) 247-51.

_____. *Greek Grammar for Students: A Concise Grammar of Classical Attic with Special Reference to Aspect in the Verb.* Canberra: Australian National Univ., 1974.

_____. "On the Perfect and Other Aspects in NT Greek." *Novum Testamentum* 23 (1981) 289-329.

_____. "On the Perfect and Other Aspects in the Greek Non-Literary Papyri." *Bulletin of the Institute of Classical Studies* 27 (1980) 23-49.

_____. "Repeated Action, the Potential and Reality in Ancient Greek." *Antichthon* 15 (1981) 36-46.

_____. "Some Linguistic Points in Marxsen's Resurrection Theory." *Expository Times* 84 (1972-73) 330-32.

_____. "Style and Significance in the Language of John 21:15-17." *Novum Testamentum* 27 (1985) 319-33.

_____. "Syntax in Exegesis." *Tyndale Bulletin* 23 (1972) 39-57.

_____. "The Use of the Ancient Greek Perfect down to the End of the Second Century A.D." *Bulletin of the Institute of Classical Studies* 12 (1965) 1-21.

McKenzie, R. "The Greek Perfect" (review of Chantraine, *Histoire*). *Classical Review* 41 (1927) 184.

McKnight, E.V. "Is the NT Written in 'Holy Ghost' Greek?" *Bible Translator* 16 (1965) 87-93.
_____. "The NT and 'Biblical Greek.'" *Journal of Bible and Religion* 34 (1966) 36-42.
Maclennan, L.J. *El Problema del Aspecto Verbal: Estudio Critico de sus Presupuestos.* Madrid: Biblioteca Romanica Hispanica, Editorial Gredos, 1962.
McNeile, A.H. *The Gospel According to St. Matthew.* London: Macmillan, 1961.
_____. "A Note on Heb 9:12." *Journal of Theological Studies* 24 (1922-23) 402.
Maddox, R. "The Function of the Son of Man in the Gospel of John." *Reconciliation and Hope: NT Essays on Atonement and Eschatology.* Ed. R. Banks. Grand Rapids: Eerdmans, 1974: 186-204.
Madvig, J.N. *Syntax of the Greek Language, especially of the Attic Dialect.* Trans. H. Browne. Rev. T.K. Arnold. 2d ed. London: Rivingtons, 1873.
Magnien, V. *Le futur grec.* Vol. 2: Emplois et origines. Paris: Honoré Champion, 1912.
Mahlow, G. "Über den futurgebrauch griechischen praesentia." *Zeitschrift für vergleichende Sprachforschung* 26 (1883) 570-603.
Maier, G. *Matthäus-Evangelium.* 2 vols. Bibel-Kommentar. Neuhausen: Häussler, 1979.
Malden, H. "On Perfect Tenses in Greek, and especially the First Perfect Active." *Transactions of the Philological Society* (1865) 168-79.
Malherbe, A.J. *Social Aspects of Early Christianity.* London: Louisiana State UP, 1977.
Maloney, E.C. *Semitic Interference in Marcan Syntax.* Society of Biblical Literature Dissertation Series 51. Chico, California: Scholars, 1981.
Mandilaras, B.G. "Confusion of Aorist and Perfect in the Language of the Non-Literary Greek Papyri." *Studies in the Greek Language.* Athens: n.p., 1972: 9-21.
_____. "The NT and the Papyri." *Studies in the Greek Language.* Athens: n.p., 1972: 22-50.
_____. *The Verb in the Greek Non-Literary Papyri.* Athens: Hellenic Ministry of Culture and Sciences, 1973.
Manson, T.W. "The Lord's Prayer." *Bulletin of the John Rylands Library* 38 (1955-56) 99-113.
_____. *The Sayings of Jesus.* London: SCM, 1949.
_____. "Some Outstanding NT Problems." *Expository Times* 47 (1935-36) 7-11.
_____. *The Teaching of Jesus: Studies of its Form and Content.* 2d ed. Cambridge: UP, 1935.
Mantey, J.R. "Evidence that the Perfect Tense in John 20:23 and Matt 16:19 is Mistranslated." *Journal of the Evangelical Theological Society* 16 (1973) 129-38.
_____. "The Mistranslation of the Perfect Tense in John 20:23, Matt 16:19, and Matt 18:18." *Journal of Biblical Literature* 58 (1939) 243-49.
Marchant, E.C. Untitled. *Classical Review* 4 (1890) 320.
Marchant, E.C., and O.J. Todd. *Xenophon IV: Memorabilia and Oeconomicus, Symposium and Apology.* Loeb Classical Library. London: Heinemann, 1923.
Marcus, J. *The Mystery of the Kingdom of God.* Society of Biblical Literature Dissertation Series 90. Atlanta: Scholars, 1986.
Marcus, R. "Notes on Torrey's Translation of the Gospels." *Harvard Theological Review* 27 (1934) 211-39.
Margolis, M.L. *A Manual of the Aramaic Language of the Babylonian Talmud: Grammar, Chrestomathy and Glossaries.* Munich: Bech, 1910.
Markey, T.L. "Deixis and Diathesis: The Case of the Greek κ-perfect." *Indogermanische Forschungen* 85 (1980) 279-97.
Marshall, I.H. *1 and 2 Thessalonians.* New Century Bible. Grand Rapids: Eerdmans, 1983.
_____. *The Gospel of Luke: A Commentary on the Greek Text.* New International Greek Testament Commentary. Exeter: Paternoster, 1978.
_____. "The Meaning of 'Reconciliation.'" *Unity and Diversity in NT Theology.* Ed. R.A. Guelich. Grand Rapids: Eerdmans, 1978: 117-32.
_____. *The Origins of NT Christology.* Issues in Contemporary Theology. Downers Grove, Illinois: InterVarsity Press, 1976.

_____. "Son of God or Servant of Yahweh? A Reconsideration of Mark 1:11." *NT Studies* 15 (1968-69) 326-36.

Martin, J.R. "The meaning of features in sytemic linguistics." *New Developments in Systemic Linguistics.* Vol. 1: Theory and Description. Ed. M.A.K. Halliday and R.P. Fawcett. London: Pinter, 1987: 14-40.

Martin, R.A. "Some Syntactical Criteria of Translation Greek." *Vetus Testamentum* 10 (1960) 295-310.

_____. *Syntactical Evidence of Semitic Sources in Greek Documents.* Septuagint and Cognate Studies 3. Cambridge, Massachusetts: Society of Biblical Literature, 1974.

_____. *Syntax Criticism of the Synoptic Gospels.* Studies in the Bible and Early Christianity 10. Lewiston: Edwin Mellen, 1987.

Martin, R.P. *Philippians.* New Century Bible. London: Oliphants, 1976.

_____. *Reconciliation: A Study of Paul's Theology.* New Foundations Theological Library. Atlanta: John Knox, 1981.

_____. *2 Corinthians.* Word Biblical Commentary 40. Waco, Texas: Word, 1985.

Martin, W.J. "1 Cor 11:2-16: An Interpretation." *Apostolic History and the Gospel.* Ed. W.W. Gasque and R.P. Martin. Exeter: Paternoster, 1970: 231-41.

Masson, E. *Recherches sur les plus anciens emprunts sémitiques en grec.* Paris: Klincksieck, 1967.

Masterman, K.C. "On Grammatical Terminology and Aspect in Particular." *Greece and Rome* NS 9 (1962) 72-86.

Mateos, J. *El Aspecto Verbal en el NT.* Estudios de NT I. Madrid: Ediciones Cristiandad, 1977.

Mateos, J., and M. Alepuz. "El Perfecto Sucesivo en el NT." *Cuestiones de Grammatico y Lexico,* by A. Urban, J. Mateos and M. Alepuz. Estudios de NT 2. Madrid: Ediciones Cristiandad, 1977: 65-101.

Matthews, P.H. *Syntax.* Cambridge Textbooks in Linguistics. Cambridge: UP, 1981.

Mayser, E. *Grammatik der griechischen Papyri aus der Ptolemäerzeit.* 2 vols. Berlin: de Gruyter, 1906-34.

Meecham, H.G. "The Imperatival Use of ἵνα in the NT." *Journal of Theological Studies* 43 (1942) 179-80.

_____. *Light from Ancient Letters: Private Correspondence in the Non-Literary Papyri of Oxyrynchus of the First Four Centuries, and its Bearing on NT Language and Thought.* London: Allen and Unwin, 1923.

_____. "The Present Participle of Antecedent Action: Some NT Instances." *Expository Times* 64 (1952-53) 285-86.

_____. "The Use of the Participle for the Imperative in the NT." *Expository Times* 58 (1946-47) 207-08.

Meillet, A. *Aperçu d'une histoire de la langue grecque.* 3d ed. Paris: Hachette, 1930.

_____. *Etudes sur l'étymologie et le vocabulaire du vieux slave.* 2 vols. Bibliothèque de l'Ecole des Hautes Etudes. Paris: Emile Bouillon, 1902.

Meillet, A., and J. Vendryes. *Traité de grammaire comparée des langues classiques.* Paris: Edouard Champion, 1924; 4th ed. rev. J. Vendryes. Paris: Honoré Champion, 1966.

Meltzer, H. "Die Aktionsart als Grundlage der Lehre vom indogermanischen, besonders griechischen Zeitworten." *Verhandlung der 47. Philologen-Versammlung.* Nürnberg: Verein Deutsches Philologen und Schulmänner, 1903: 148-50.

_____. "Vermeintliche Perfektivierung durch präpositionale Zusammensetzung im Griechischen." *Indogermanische Forschungen* 12 (1902) 319-72.

_____. "Zur Lehre von den Aktionen besonders im Griechischen." *Indogermanische Forschungen* 17 (1905) 186-277.

_____. Review of Kühner/Gerth, *Grammatik. Neue Jahrbücher für das klassische Altertum, Geschichte und deutsche Literatur* 15 (1905) 609-13.

Meredith, G.P. "Semantics in Relation to Psychology." *Archivum Linguisticum* 8 (1956) 1-12.

Messing, G.M. Review of Ruipérez, *Estructura. Word* 11 (1955) 462-65.

Mettinger, T.N.D. "The Hebrew Verb System: A Survey of Recent Research." *Annual of the Swedish Theological Institute* 9 (1973) 64-84.

Metzger, B.M. "Bilingualism and Polylingualism in Antiquity: With a Check-List of NT MSS, written in more than one language." *The NT Age.* Vol. 2. Ed. W.C. Weinrich. Macon, Georgia: Mercer UP, 1984: 327-34.

_____. "Grammars of the Greek NT." *Interpretation* 1 (1947) 471-85.

_____. "The Language of the NT." *The Interpreter's Bible.* 12 vols. Nashville: Abingdon, 1951-57: 7.43-59.

_____. *A Textual Commentary on the Greek NT.* Corr. ed. London: United Bible Societies, 1975.

Meyer, B.F. *The Aims of Jesus.* London: SCM, 1979.

Meyer, H.A.W. *Critical and Exegetical Hand-book to the Epistles to the Corinthians.* Trans. D.D. Banneman. Ed. W.P. Dickson. New York: Funk and Wagnalls, 1884.

_____. *Critical and Exegetical Hand-Book to the Epistle to the Romans.* Trans. J.C. Moore and E. Johnson. Ed. W.P. Dickson. New York: Funk and Wagnalls, 1884.

Meyers, E.M., and J.F. Strange. *Archaeology, the Rabbis and Early Christianity.* London: SCM, 1981.

Michaelis, W. "Der Attizismus und das NT." *Zeitschrift für die neutestamentliche Wissenschaft* 22 (1923) 91-121.

Michel, O. *Der Brief an die Römer.* Meyer. 4th ed. Göttingen: Vandenhoeck und Ruprecht, 1966.

Mickey, K. "Dialect Consciousness and Literary Language: An Example from Ancient Greek." *Transactions of the Philological Society* (1981) 35-66.

Miller, C.W.E. "The Imperfect and the Aorist in Greek." *American Journal of Philology* 16 (1895) 139-85.

_____. "The Limitation of the Imperative in the Attic Orators." *American Journal of Philology* 13 (1892) 399-436.

Miller, J.E. *Tense and Aspect in Russian.* Ph.D. thesis, Univ. of Edinburgh, 1970.

Milligan, G. "The Grammar of the Greek NT." *Expository Times* 31 (1919-20) 420-24.

_____. *Here and There among the Papyri.* London: Hodder and Stoughton, 1922.

Milroy, J. "Linguistic Equality and Speakers." *Sheffield Working Papers in Language and Linguistics* 2 (1985) 66-71.

Milroy, J., and L. Milroy. *Authority in Language: Investigating Language Prescription and Standardisation.* London: Routledge and Kegan Paul, 1985.

Milroy, L. "Comprehension and Context: Successful Communication and Communicative Breakdown." *Applied Sociolinguistics.* Applied Language Studies. Ed. P. Trudgill. London: Academic, 1984.

_____. *Language and Social Networks.* 2d ed. Oxford: Blackwell, 1987.

Minn, H.R. "Classical Reminiscence in St. Paul." *Prudentia* 6 (1974) 93-98.

Mitton, C.L. *Ephesians.* New Century Bible. London: Oliphants, 1976.

_____. *The Epistle of James.* London: Marshall, Morgan and Scott, 1966.

Moeller, H.R., and A. Kramer. "An Overlooked Structural Pattern in NT Greek." *Novum Testamentum* 5 (1962) 25-35.

Moffatt, J. *A Critical and Exegetical Commentary on the Epistle to the Hebrews.* International Critical Commentary. Edinburgh: T. and T. Clark, 1924.

Mohrmann, C. "General Trends in the Study of NT Greek and of Early Christian Greek and Latin." *Classica et Iberica.* Ed. P.T. Braunan. Worcester, Massachusetts: n.p., 1975: 95-105.

Moller, K. "Contribution to the Discussion Concerning 'Langue' and 'Parole.'" *Recherches structurales 1949: Interventions dans le débat glossématique.* Copenhagen: Nordisk-Sprog- og Kulturforlag, 1970: 87-94.

Moloney, F.J. *The Johannine Son of Man.* Biblioteca di Scienze Religiose 14. Rome: Las, 1976.

Monro, D.B.A. *A Grammar of the Homeric Dialect.* 2d ed. Oxford: Clarendon, 1891.

_____. *Homer: Iliad.* 2 vols. Clarendon Press. Oxford: Clarendon, 1886, 1888.

Montgomery, J.A. *The Origin of the Gospel According to St. John.* Philadelphia: John C. Winston, 1923.

_____. "Torrey's Aramaic Gospels." *Journal of Biblical Literature* 53 (1934) 79-99.

Moo, D.J. *The OT in the Gospel Passion Narratives.* Sheffield: Almond, 1983.

Moore, A.L. *The Parousia in the NT.* Supplements to Novum Testamentum 13. Leiden: Brill, 1966.

Moorhouse, A.C. "AN with the Future." *Classical Quarterly* 40 (1946) 1-10.

_____. "The Construction with MH OY." *Classical Quarterly* 34 (1940) 70-77.

_____. "On Negating Greek Participles where the Leading Verbs are of a Type to Require μή." *Classical Quarterly* 42 (1948) 35-40.

_____. "The Origin of the Infinitive in Greek Indirect Statement." *American Journal of Philology* 76 (1955) 176-83.

_____. "The Past Optative." *Classical Review* 57 (1943) 61.

_____. "A Reply on ἄν with the Future." *Classical Quarterly* NS 9 (1959) 78-79.

_____. *Studies in the Greek Negatives.* Cardiff: U of Wales P, 1959.

_____. *The Syntax of Sophocles.* Mnemosyne. Leiden: Brill, 1982.

_____. "The Use of OYΔEIΣ and MHΔEIΣ." *Classical Quarterly* NS 15 (1965) 31-40.

Moravcsik, E.A. "Introduction: On Syntactic Approaches." *Syntax and Semantics 13: Syntactic Approaches.* Ed. E.A. Moravcsik and J.R. Wirth. New York: Academic, 1980: 1-18.

Morley, G.D. *An Introduction to Systemic Grammar.* London: Macmillan, 1985.

Morrice, W.G. "The Imperatival ἵνα." *Bible Translator* 23 (1972) 326-30.

_____. "Translating the Greek Imperative." *Bible Translator* 24 (1973) 129-34.

Morris, C.D. "On Some Forms of Greek Conditional Sentences." *Transactions of the American Philological Society* 6 (1875) 44-53.

Morris, L. *The Apostolic Preaching of the Cross.* 3d ed. Grand Rapids: Eerdmans, 1965.

_____. *The First and Second Epistles to the Thessalonians.* New London Commentary. London: Marshall, Morgan and Scott, 1959.

_____. *The Gospel According to John.* New International Commentary. Grand Rapids: Eerdmans, 1971.

_____. "ΚΑΙ ΑΠΑΞ ΚΑΙ ΔΙΣ." *Novum Testamentum* 1 (1956) 205-08.

Moscati, S., *et al. An Introducton to the Comparative Grammar of the Semitic Languages: Phonology and Morphology.* Porta Linguarum Orientalium. Wiesbaden: Harrassowitz, 1964.

Most, W.G. "Did Luke Imitate the Septuagint?" *Journal for the Study of the NT* 15 (1982) 30-41.

Moule, C.F.D. "'. . . As we forgive . . .'--A Note on the Distinction between Deserts and Capacity in the Understanding of Foregiveness." *Donum Gentilicium: NT Studies in Honour of D. Daube.* Ed. E. Bammel, C.K. Barrett, and W.D. Davies. Oxford: Clarendon, 1978: 68-77.

_____. *An Idiom Book of NT Greek.* 2d ed. Cambridge: UP, 1959.

_____. *The Language of the NT.* Cambridge: UP, 1952.

Moulton, J.H. "Characteristics of NT Greek." *The Expositor* Sixth Series 9 (1904) 67-75; 215-25; 310-20; 359-68; 461-72; 10 (1904) 124-34; 168-74; 276-83; 353-64; 440-50.

_____. "A Grammar of the Septuagint." *Journal of Theological Studies* 11 (1910) 293-300.

_____. "Grammatical Notes from the Papyri." *Classical Review* 15 (1901) 31-38; 434-42; 18 (1904) 106-12; 151-55.

_____. *An Introduction to the Study of NT Greek.* Books for Bible Students. 2d ed. London: Charles H. Kelly, 1903; 5th ed. rev. H.G. Meecham. London: Epworth, 1955.

_____. "Language of the NT." *Dictionary of the Bible.* Ed. J. Hastings. Edinburgh: T. and T. Clark, 1909: 528-30.

_____. "NT Greek in the Light of Modern Discovery." *Essays on Some Biblical Questions of the Day: By Members of the Univ. of Cambridge.* London: Macmillan, 1909: 461-505.

_____. "Notes from the Papyri." *Expositor* Sixth Series 3 (1901) 271-82; 7 (1903) 104-21; 8 (1903) 423-39.

_____. *Prolegomena.* Vol. 1 of *A Grammar of NT Greek.* 3d ed. Edinburgh: T. and T. Clark, 1906.

_____. *The Science of Language and the Study of the NT.* Inaugural Lecture. Manchester: UP, 1906.

Moulton, J.H., and W.F. Howard. *Accidence and Word-Formation.* Vol. 2 of *A Grammar of NT Greek.* Edinburgh: T. and T. Clark, 1929.

Mozley, F.W. "Notes on the Biblical Use of the Present and Aorist Imperative." *Journal of Theological Studies* 4 (1903) 279-82.

Müller, M. "The Expression 'the Son of Man' as Used by Jesus." *Studia Theologica* 38 (1984) 47-64.

Mullins, T.Y. "Disclosure: A Literary Form in the NT." *Novum Testamentum* 7 (1964-65) 44-50.

_____. "Greeting as a NT Form." *Journal of Biblical Literature* 87 (1968) 418-26.

Munck, J. "Deux notes sur la langue du NT." *Classica et mediaevalia* 5 (1942) 187-208; 6 (1944) 110-50.

Muraoka, T. "Purpose or Result? ὥστε in Biblical Greek." *Novum Testamentum* 15 (1973) 205-19.

_____. "The Use of ΌΣ in the Greek Bible." *Novum Testamentum* 7 (1964) 51-72.

Murphy, A.B. *Aspectual Usage in Russian.* Oxford: Pergamon, 1965.

Music, A. "Zum Gebrauche des negierten Konjunktivs für der negierten Imperativ im Griechischen." *Glotta* 6 (1915) 206-10.

Mussies, G. "Greek as the Vehicle of Early Christianity." *NT Studies* 29 (1983) 356-69.

_____. "Greek in Palestine and the Diaspora." *Compendia Rerum Judaicarum ad Novum Testamentum.* Section I: The Jewish People in the First Century. Vol. 2. Ed. S. Safrai and M. Stern. Assen: Van Gorcum, 1976: 1040-64.

_____. "The Greek of the Book of Revelation." *L'Apocalypse johannique et l'Apocalyptique dans le NT.* Bibliotheca Ephemeridum Theologicarum Lovaniensium 53. Louvain: Leuven UP, 1980: 167-77.

_____. *The Morphology of Koine Greek as Used in the Apocalypse of St. John: A Study in Bilingualism.* Supplements to Novum Testamentum 27. Leiden: Brill, 1971.

_____. "The Use of Hebrew and Aramaic in the Greek NT." *NT Studies* 30 (1984) 416-32.

_____. Review of Frösén, *Prolegomena. Mnemosyne* 31 (1978) 89-94.

Mussner, F. *Der Galaterbrief.* Herders. Freiburg: Herder, 1974.

_____. *Der Jakobusbrief.* 2d ed. Herders. Freiburg: Herder, 1967.

Mutzbauer, K. *Die Grundlagen der griechischen Tempuslehre und homerische Tempusgebrauch.* 2 vols. Strassburg: Trübner, 1893, 1909.

Naylor, H.D. "More Prohibitions in Greek." *Classical Review* 20 (1906) 348.

_____. "On the Optative and the Graphic Construction in Greek Subordinate Clauses." *Classical Review* 14 (1900) 247-49; 345-52.

_____. "Prohibitions in Greek." *Classical Review* 19 (1905) 26-30.

Neal, G.C. "In the Original Greek." *Tyndale House Bulletin* 12 (1963) 12-16.

Neusner, J. "'Judaism' after Moore: A Programmatic Statement." *Journal of Jewish Studies* 31 (1980) 141-56.

_____. "New Problems, New Solutions: Current Events in Rabbinic Studies." *Method and Meaning in Ancient Judaism,* Third Series. Chico, California: Scholars, 1981.

Newton, B. Review of Lightfoot, *Natural Logic. Lingua* 46 (1978) 278-81.

Nida, E.A. *Componential Analysis of Meaning: An Introduction to Semantic Structures.* The Hague: Mouton, 1975.

_____. "Implications of Contemporary Linguistics for Biblical Scholarship." *Journal of Biblical Literature* 91 (1972) 73-89.

_____. "Linguistic and Semantic Structure." *Language Structure and Translation: Essays by E.A. Nida.* Ed. A.S. Dil. Stanford, California: Stanford UP, 1975: 47-70.

_____. *Morphology: A Descriptive Analysis of Words.* 2d ed. Michigan: U of Michigan P, 1949.

_____, with C.R. Taber. "Semantic Structures." *Language Structure and Translation: Essays by E.A. Nida.* Ed. A.S. Dil. Stanford, California: Stanford UP, 1975: 102-30.

_____. "A System for the Description of Semantic Elements." *Word* 7 (1951) 1-14.

_____. *Toward a Science of Translating: with Special Reference to Principles and Procedures involved in Bible Translating.* Leiden: Brill, 1964.

Nida, E.A., and C.R. Taber. *The Theory and Practice of Translation.* United Bible Societies. Leiden: Brill, 1974.

Nida, E.A., *et al. Style and Discourse: with Special Reference to the Text of the Greek NT.* N.p.: Bible Society, 1983.

Nixon, G. *Aspects of English Structure.* 2d ed. Sheffield: Department of English Language, Univ. of Sheffield, 1979.

Nock, A.D. "The Vocabulary of the NT." *Journal of Biblical Literature* 52 (1933) 131-39.

Norden, E. *Die Antike Kunstprosa vom VI. Jahrhundert v. Chr. bis in die Zeit der Renaissance.* 2 vols. Leipzig: Teubner, 1898.

Nunn, H.P.V. *A Short Syntax of NT Greek.* 5th ed. Cambridge: UP, 1956.

Nutting, H.C. "The Modes of Conditional Thought." *American Journal of Philology* 24 (1903) 278-303.

_____. "The Order of Conditional Thought." *American Journal of Philology* 24 (1903) 25-39; 149-62.

Obata, A. "The Gnomic Aorist in Greek." *Journal of Classical Studies* (Kyoto, Japan) 27 (1979) 61-67.

O'Brien, P. *Colossians, Philemon.* Word Biblical Commentary 44. Waco, Texas: Word, 1982.

Ogden, C.K. *Opposition: A Linguistic and Psychological Analysis.* 1932; rpt. with introduction by I.A. Richards. Bloomington: Indiana UP, 1967.

Ogden, C.K., and I.A. Richards. *The Meaning of Meaning: A Study of the Influence of Language upon Thought and of the Science of Symbolism.* 10th ed. London: Routledge and Kegan Paul, 1952.

Oguse, A. *Recherches sur le participe circonstanciel en grec ancien.* Wetteren, Belgium: Cultura, 1962.

Ohman, S. "Theories of the 'Linguistic Field.'" *Word* 9 (1953) 123-34.

Oksaar, E. "Bilingualism." *Current Trends in Linguistics* 9 (1972) 476-511.

Olley, J.W. *"Righteousness" in the Septuagint of Isaiah: A Contextual Study.* Septuagint and Cognate Studies 8. Missoula, Montana: Scholars, 1979.

Olmstead, A.T. "Could an Aramaic Gospel be Written?" *Journal of Near Eastern Studies* 1 (1942) 41-75.

Orlinsky, H.M. "The Septuagint as Holy Writ and the Philosophy of the Translators." *Hebrew Union College Annual* 46 (1975) 89-114.

Ornan, U. "Hebrew Grammar." *Encyclopaedia Judaica.* Vol. 8. Jerusalem: Encyclopaedia Judaica, 1971: cols. 77-176.

O'Rourke, J. "The Historic Present in the Gospel of John." *Journal of Biblical Literature* 93 (1974) 585-90.

_____. "The Participle in Rom 15:25." *Catholic Biblical Quarterly* 29 (1967) 116-18.

Orr, W.F., and J.A. Walther. *I Corinthians.* Anchor Bible 32. Garden City, New York: Doubleday, 1976.

Osburn, C.D. "The Historical Present in Mark as a Text-Critical Criterion." *Biblica* 64 (1983) 486-500.

_____. "The Present Indicative in Matt 19:9." *Restoration Quarterly* 24 (1981) 193-203.

529

_____. "The Third Person Imperative in Acts 2:38." *Restoration Quarterly* 26 (1983) 81-84.

Ott, H. "Um die Muttersprache Jesu: Forschungen seit G. Dalman." *Novum Testamentum* 9 (1967) 1-25.

Ottley, R.R. *A Handbook to the Septuagint*. London: Methuen, 1920.

Ozanne, C.G. "The Language of the Apocalypse." *Tyndale House Bulletin* 16 (1965) 3-9.

Page, T.E. *The Acts of the Apostles*. London: Macmillan, 1930.

Paley, F.A. "On Some Peculiarities in the Use of the Future Participles of Greek Verbs." *Journal of Philology* 8 (1879) 79-83.

Palmer, F.R. *Modality and the English Modals*. Longman Linguistic Library. London: Longman, 1979.

_____. *Mood and Modality*. Cambridge Textbooks in Linguistics. Cambridge: UP, 1986.

_____. *Semantics: A New Outline*. 2d ed. Cambridge: UP, (1976) 1981.

Palmer, L.R. *A Grammar of the Post-Ptolemaic Papyri*. Vol. 1: Accidence and Word-Formation. Part 1: The Suffixes. Philological Society 13. London: Oxford UP, 1945.

_____. *The Greek Language*. The Great Languages. London: Faber and Faber, 1980.

_____. "The Language of Homer." *A Companion to Homer*. Ed. A.J. B. Wace and F.H. Stubbings. Cambridge: UP, 1962: 76-178.

_____. "Prolegomena to a Grammar of the Post-Ptolemaic Papyri." *Journal of Theological Studies* 35 (1934) 170-75.

Panhuis, D. "The Personal Endings of the Greek Verb: An Exploration in the Subjectivity and the Non-arbitrariness of a Paradigm." *Studies in Language* 4 (1980) 105-17.

Papanikolaou, A. "The Development of the Final Future Participle in NT Greek." Θεολογία ἐν Ἀθήναις (Theology in Athens) 34 (1963) 624-31.

_____. "The Narrative Perfect in NT." Θεολογία ἐν Ἀθήναις (Theology in Athens) 35 (1964) 147-53.

Paraskevas-Shepard, C. "Choosing between the Aorist and the Present Perfect: the Case of Modern Greek." *Journal of Modern Greek Studies* 4 (1986) 51-59.

Pariente, A. "Sobre los Futuros Sigmaticoos Griegos." *Emerita* 31 (1963) 53-130.

Pax, E. "Probleme des neutestamentlichen Griechisch." *Biblica* 53 (1972) 557-64.

Payne, D.F. "Semitisims in the Book of Acts." *Apostolic History and the Gospel*. Ed. W.W. Gasque and R.P. Martin. Exeter: Paternoster, 1970: 134-50.

Pedersen, H. *The Discovery of Language: Linguistic Science in the Nineteenth Century*. Trans. J.W. Spargo. Bloomington: Indiana UP, 1959.

Pedersen, H. "Erklärung." *Zeitschrift für vergleichende Sprachforschung* 38 (1905) 421-25.

_____. "Vorschlag." *Indogermanische Forschungen* 12 (1901) Anzeiger 152-53.

_____. "Zur Lehre von den Aktionsarten." *Zeitschrift für vergleichende Sprachforschung* 37 (1904) 219-50.

Peppler, C.W. "Durative and Aoristic." *American Journal of Philology* 54 (1933) 47-53.

Péristérakis, A.E. *Essai sur l'aoriste intemporel en grec*. Athens: n.p., 1962.

Pernée, L. "L'aspect en grec ancien: problèmes d'analyse." *Les études classiques* 51 (1983) 297-302.

Pernot, H. "Greek and the Gospels." *Expository Times* 38 (1926-27) 103-08.

Perrin, N. *Jesus and the Language of the Kingdom: Symbol and Metaphor in NT Interpretation*. NT Library. London: SCM, 1976.

_____. *Rediscovering the Teaching of Jesus*. NT Library. London: SCM, 1967.

Perrot, J. "Les faits d'aspect dans les langues classiques." *L'information litteraire* 13 (1961) 109-63.

Perry, B.E. *The Ancient Romances: A Literary-Historical Account of their Origins*. Berkeley: U of California P, 1967.

Pesch, R. *Naherwartungen: Tradition und Redaktion im Mark 13*. Düsseldorf: Patmos, 1968.

Petersen, N.R. *Rediscovering Paul: Philemon and the Sociology of Paul's Narrative World*. Philadelphia: Fortress, 1985.

Pfeiffer, R. *History of Classical Scholarship: From the Beginnings to the End of the Hellenistic Age.* Oxford: Clarendon, 1968.

Pinborg, J. "Classical Antiquity: Greece." *Current Trends in Linguistics* 13 (1975) 69-126.

Pistorius, P.V. "Some Remarks on the Aorist Aspect in the Greek NT." *Acta Classica* 10 (1967) 33-39.

Platt, A. "The Augment in Homer." *Journal of Philology* 19 (1891) 211-37.

_____. "ΜΕΛΛΩ." *Journal of Philology* 21 (1893) 39-45.

_____. "Some Homeric Aorist Participles." *Journal of Philology* 35 (1919-20) 128-32.

Plummer, A. *A Critical and Exegetical Commentary on the Gospel According to St. Luke.* International Critical Commentary. 4th ed. Edinburgh: T. and T. Clark, 1913.

_____. *A Critical and Exegetical Commentary on the Second Epistle of St. Paul to the Corinthians.* International Critical Commentary. Edinburgh: T. and T. Clark, 1915.

Pollak, W. *Studien zum "Verbalaspekt" im Französischen.* Österreichische Akademie der Wissenschaften. Philosophisch-Historische Klasse Sitzungberichte 233. Band 5. Abhandlung. Vienna: Rohrer, 1960.

Popper, K.R. *Conjectures and Refutations: The Growth of Scientific Knowledge.* 4th ed. London: Routledge and Kegan Paul, 1972.

Porter, S.E. "The Adjectival Attributive Genitive in the NT: A Grammatical Study." *Trinity Journal* NS 4 (1983) 3-17.

_____. "Tense Terminology and Greek Language Study: A Linguistic Re-Evaluation." *Sheffield Working Papers in Language and Linguistics* 3 (1986) 77-86.

_____. Review of Thompson, *Apocalypse. Journal for the Study of the NT* 29 (1987) 122-24.

Porter, S.E., and N.J.C. Gotteri. "Ambiguity, Vagueness and the Working Systemic Linguist." *Sheffield Working Papers in Language and Linguistics* 2 (1985) 105-18.

Porzig, W. "Zur Aktionsart indogermanischer Präsensbildungen." *Indogermanische Forschungen* 45 (1927) 152-67.

Post, L.A. "Dramatic Uses of the Greek Imperative." *American Journal of Philology* 59 (1938) 31-59.

de la Potterie, I. "Οἶδα et γίνωσκω: les deux modes de la connaissance dans le quatrième Evangile." *Biblica* 40 (1959) 709-25.

Poutsma, A. "Over de tempora van de imperativus en de conjunctivus hortativus-prohibitivus in het Grieks." *Verhandelingen der Koninklijke Akademie van Wetenschappen te Amsterdam.* Afdeeling Letterkunde Nieuwe Reeks, Deel 27 No. 2 (1928) 1-84.

Poythress, V.S. "Analyzing a Biblical Text: Some Important Linguistic Distinctions." *Scottish Journal of Theology* 32 (1979) 113-37.

Pride, J.B., and J. Holmes, ed. *Sociolinguistics: Selected Readings.* Harmondsworth: Penguin, 1972.

Pritchett, W.K. "The Conditional Sentence in Attic Greek." *American Journal of Philology* 76 (1955) 1-17.

_____. "ΜΗ with the Participle." *American Journal of Philology* 79 (1958) 392-404.

Pryke, E.J. *Redactional Style in the Marcan Gospel: A Study of Syntax and Vocabulary as Guides to Redaction in Mark.* Society for NT Studies Monograph Series 33. Cambridge: UP, 1978.

Psichari, J. "Essai sur le grec de la Septante." *Revue des Etudes Juives* 55 (1908) 161-208.

Pulgram, E. "The Functions of Past Tenses: Greek, Latin, Italian, French." *Language Sciences* 6 (1984) 239-69.

Purdie, E. "The Perfective 'Aktionsart' in Polybius." *Indogermanische Forschungen* 9 (1898) 63-153.

Rabin, C. "Hebrew." *Current Trends in Linguistics* 6 (1970) 304-46.

_____. "Hebrew and Aramaic in the First Century." *Compendia Rerum Judaicarum ad Novum Testamentum.* Section I: The Jewish People in the First Century. Vol. 2. Ed. S. Safrai and M. Stern. Assen: Van Gorcum, 1976: 1007-39.

_____. "The Translation Process and the Character of the Septuagint." *Textus* 6 (1968) 1-26.

Rabinowitz, I. "'Be Opened' = Ἐφφαθά (Mark 7:34): Did Jesus Speak Hebrew?" *Zeitschrift für die neutestamentliche Wissenschaft* 53 (1962) 229-38.

Radermacher, L. "Besonderheiten der Koine-Syntax." *Wiener Studien. Zeitschrift für klassische Philologie* 31 (1909) 1-12.

_____. *Koine.* Akademie der Wissenschaften in Wien. Vienna: Rohrer, 1947.

_____. *Neutestamentliche Grammatik: Das Griechisch des NT im Zusammenhang mit der Volkssprache.* Handbuch zum NT. 2d ed. Tübingen: J.C.B. Mohr (Paul Siebeck), (1911) 1925.

Rajak, T. *Josephus: The Historian and His Society.* London: Duckworth, 1983.

Ratzsch, D. *Philosophy of Science.* Contours of Christian Philosophy. Leicester: InterVarsity Press, 1986.

Regard, P.F. *La phrase nominale dans la langue du NT.* Paris: Ernest Leroux, 1919.

Reiling, J. "The Use and Translation of kai egeneto, 'and it happened,' in the NT." *Bible Translator* 16 (1965) 153-63.

Reiser, M. *Syntax und Stil des Markusevangeliums im Licht der hellenistischen Volksliteratur.* Wissenschaftliche Untersuchungen zum NT 2.11. Tübingen: J.C.B. Mohr (Paul Siebeck), 1984.

Reynolds, S.M. "The Zero Tense in Greek: A Critical Note." *Westminster Theological Journal* 32 (1965) 68-72.

Rhees, R. *Discussions of Wittgenstein.* London: Routledge and Kegan Paul, 1970.

Richards, G.C. "A Grammar of the NT" (review of Moulton, *Prolegomena*). *Journal of Theological Studies* 10 (1909) 283-90.

Richards, H. "Ἄν with the Future in Attic." *Classical Review* 6 (1892) 36-42.

Richardson, A. *An Introduction to the Theology of the NT.* London: SCM, 1958.

Riddle, D.W. "The Aramaic Gospels and the Synoptic Problem." *Journal of Biblical Literature* 54 (1935) 127-38.

_____. "The Logic of the Theory of Translation Greek." *Journal of Biblical Literature* 51 (1932) 13-30.

Riemann, O. "La question de l'aoriste grec." *Mélanges Graux; recueil de travaux d'érudition classique dédié à la mémoire de C. Graux.* Paris: Thorin, 1884: 585-99.

Riesenfeld, H. "Zu den johanneischen ἵνα-Sätzen." *Studia Theologica* 19 (1965) 213-20.

Rijksbaron, A. *The Syntax and Semantics of the Verb in Classical Greek: An Introduction.* Amsterdam: Gieben, 1984.

_____. "A Review of: H. Hettrich, *Kontext und Aspekt in der altgriechischen Prosa Herodots*." *Lingua* 48 (1979) 223-57.

Roberts, J.W. "Exegetical Helps: Contrary to Fact Conditions." *Restoration Quarterly* 4 (1960) 149-51.

_____. "The Independent Subjunctive." *Restoration Quarterly* 6 (1962) 98-101.

_____. "The Language Background of the NT." *Restoration Quarterly* 5 (1961) 193-204.

_____. "Notes on Some Selected Passages in Acts Involving Luke's Use of the Optative Mood." *Restoration Quarterly* 4 (1960) 244-48.

_____. "Some Aspects of Conditional Sentences in the Greek NT." *Bible Translator* 15 (1964) 70-76.

Robertson, A., and A. Plummer. *A Critical and Exegetical Commentary on the First Epistle of St. Paul to the Corinthians.* International Critical Commentary. Edinburgh: T. and T. Clark, 1911.

Robertson, A.T. "The Aorist Participle for Purpose in the Κοινή." *Journal of Theological Studies* 25 (1923-24) 286-89.

_____. "The Causal Use of ἽΝΑ." *Studies in Early Christianity.* Ed. S.J. Case. New York: Century, 1928: 51-57.

_____. *A Grammar of the Greek NT in the Light of Historical Research.* 4th ed. Nashville, Tennessee: Broadman, 1934.

_____. "Language of the NT." *International Standard Bible Encyclopedia.* 5 vols. Ed. J. Orr. Grand Rapids: Eerdmans, 1939: 3.1826-32.

_____. *The Minister and His Greek NT.* A.T. Robertson Library III. Grand Rapids: Baker, 1977.

Robins, R.H. *Ancient and Mediaeval Grammatical Theory in Europe: with Particular Reference to Modern Linguistic Doctrine.* London: Bell, 1951.

_____. "Dionysius Thrax and the Western Grammatical Tradition." *Transactions of the Philological Society* (1957) 67-106.

_____. *General Linguistics: An Introductory Survey.* 3d ed. London: Longman, 1980.

_____. *A Short History of Linguistics.* 2d ed. London: Longmans, 1979.

_____. "Some Continuities and Discontinuities in the History of Linguistics." *History of Linguistic Thought and Contemporary Linguistics.* Ed. H. Parret. Berlin: de Gruyter, 1976: 13-31.

Robinson, J.M. "The Formal Structure of Jesus' Message." *Current Issues in NT Interpretation.* Ed. W. Klassen and G.F. Snyder. London: SCM, 1962: 91-110.

Roby, H.J. "The Imperative in St. John 20:17." *Classical Review* 19 (1905) 229.

Rodenbusch, E. "Beiträge zur Geschichte der griechischen Aktionsarten." *Indogermanische Forschungen* 21 (1907) 116-45.

_____. "Präsensstemm und perfektive Aktionsart." *Indogermanische Forschungen* 22 (1911) 402-08.

_____. "Präsentia in perfektischer Bedeutung." *Indogermanische Forschungen* 28 (1916) 252-85.

_____. "Die temporale Geltung des Part. Aor. im Griechischen." *Indogermanische Forschungen* 24 (1909) 56-62.

Rogers, A.D. "'We' Inclusive and Exclusive in the NT." *Expository Times* 77 (1966-67) 339-40.

Rogerson, J.W. "Modern Logic and the Bible" (review of Gibson, *Biblical Semantic Logic*). *Expository Times* 93 (1981-82) 284.

Romano, B. "Il significato fondamentale dell'aoristo greco." *Rivista di filologia* 50 (1922) 197-227; 335-63.

Ronca, I. Review of Louw, *Semantics. Acta Classica* 28 (1985) 95-106.

Rose, J.L. *The Durative and Aoristic Tenses in Thucydides.* Language Dissertations 35, Supplement to Language. Baltimore: Linguistic Society of America, 1942.

Rosén, H.B. "᾽Ην διδάσκων et questions apparentées. Mises au point sur les contacts linguistiques néotestamentaires." *Bulletin de la Société Linguistique* 62 (1967) xxi-xxvi.

_____. "On the Use of the Tenses in the Aramaic of Daniel." *Journal of Semitic Studies* 6 (1961) 183-203.

_____. "Palestinian KOINH in Rabbinic Illustration." *Journal of Semitic Studies* 8 (1963) 56-72.

_____. "Die 'zweiten' Tempora des Griechischen: Zum Prädikatsausdruck beim griechischen Verbum." *Museum Helveticum* 14 (1957) 133-54.

Rosenthal, F. *A Grammar of Biblical Aramaic.* Porta Linguarum Orientalium. Wiesbaden: Harrassowitz, 1961.

Rost, B.C.F. *Griechische Grammatik.* 5th ed. Göttingen: Vandenhoeck und Ruprecht, 1836.

Rousseau, F. "La structure de Mark 13." *Biblica* 56 (1975) 157-72.

Roussel, L. *L'aspect en grec attique.* Publications de la Faculté des Lettres de l'Université de Montpellier 12. Paris: Universitaires, n.d.

Rubinstein, A. "The Anomalous Perfect with *Waw*-Conjunctive in Biblical Hebrew." *Biblica* 44 (1963) 62-69.

Rudberg, G. "Zu den Partizipien im NT." *Coniectanea Neotestamentica* 12 (1948) 1-38.

Rüger, H.P. "Zum Problem der Sprache Jesu." *Zeitschrift für die neutestamentliche Wissenschaft* 59 (1968) 113-22.

Ruijgh, C.J. *Autour de "Te épique": Etudes sur la syntaxe grecque.* Amsterdam: Hakkert, 1971.

_____. "L'emploi 'inceptif' du thème du présent du verbe grec." *Mnemosyne* Series 4, 28 (1985) 1-61.

_____. "A Review of Ch.H. Kahn, *The Verb 'Be' in Ancient Greek.*" *Lingua* 48 (1979) 43-83.

_____. "Sur la valeur fondamentale de εἶναι: une réplique." *Mnemosyne* Series 4, 37 (1984) 264-70.

_____. Review of Hettrich, *Kontext.* *Gnomon* 51 (1979) 217-27.

Ruipérez, M.S. *Estructura del Sistema de Aspectos y Tiempos del Verbo Griego Antiguo: Análysis Funcional Sincrónico.* Theses et Studia Philologica Salmanticensia 7. Salamanca: Colegio Trilingue de la Universidad, 1954.

_____. "The Neutralization of Morphological Oppositions as Illustrated by the Neutral Aspect of the Present Indicative in Classical Greek." *Word* 9 (1953) 241-52.

_____. "Quelques vues fonctionalistes sur l'aspect (résumé)." *La notion d'aspect.* Ed. J. David and R. Martin. Recherches linguistiques 5. Paris: Klincksieck, 1980: 27-30.

Rutherford, W.G. "Aristophanes *Knights*, 414: A Neglected Idiom." *Classical Review* 17 (1903) 249.

Rydbeck, L. "Bemerkungen zu Periphrasen mit εἶναι + Präsens Partizip bei Herodot und in der Koine." *Glotta* 47 (1969) 186-200.

_____. *Fachprosa, Vermeintliche Volkssprache und NT: Zur Beurteilung der sprachlichen Niveauunterscheide im nachklassischen Griechisch.* Acta Universitatis Upsaliensis Studia Graeca Upsaliensia 5. Uppsala: n.p., 1967.

_____. "What Happened to NT Greek Grammar after A. Debrunner?" *NT Studies* 21 (1975) 424-27.

Ryle, G. "Categories." *Collected papers.* Vol. 2: Collected Essays 1929-68. London: Hutchinson, 1971: 170-84.

_____. *The Concept of Mind.* London: Hutchinson, 1949.

Salom, A.P. "The Imperatival Use of the Participle in the NT." *Australian Biblical Review* 11 (1963) 41-49.

Sampley, J.P. *"And the Two Shall Become One Flesh": A Study of Traditions in Eph 5:21-33.* Society for NT Studies Monograph Series 16. Cambridge: UP, 1971.

Sanday, W., and A.C. Headlam. *A Critical and Exegetical Commentary on the Epistle to the Romans.* International Critical Commentary. 5th ed. Edinburgh: T. and T. Clark, 1902.

Sanders, E.P. *The Tendencies of the Synoptic Tradition.* Society for NT Studies Monograph Series 9. Cambridge: UP, 1969.

Sanders, J.T. *Ethics in the NT: Change and Development.* London: SCM, 1975.

Sandford, D.K., trans. *The Greek Grammar of Fredrick Thiersch.* Edinburgh: William Blackwood, 1830.

Sandys, J.E. *A History of Classical Scholarship: From the Sixth Century B.C. to the End of the Middle Ages.* Vol. 1. Cambridge: UP, 1903.

Sanspeur, C. "Le 'potentiel' en grec." *Les études classiques* 31 (1963) 43-51.

Sapir, E. *Language: An Introduction to the Study of Speech.* New York: Harcourt, Brace, 1921.

Sarauw, C. "Syntaktisches." *Zeitschrift für vergleichende Sprachforschung* 18 (1908) 145-93.

Saurer, W. *A Formal Semantics of Tense, Aspect and Aktionsarten.* Bloomington: Indiana Univ. Linguistics Club, 1984.

de Saussure, F. *Course in General Linguistics.* Ed. C. Bally, A. Sechehaye with A. Reidlinger. Trans W. Baskin. Intro. J. Culler (1974). New York: Philosophical Library, 1959.

Sawyer, J.F.A. *Semantics in Biblical Research: New Methods of Defining Hebrew Words for Salvation.* Studies in Biblical Theology Second Series 24. London: SCM, 1972.

Schlachter, L. "Statistische Untersuchungen über den Gebrauch der Tempora und Modi bei einzelen griechischen Schriftstellern." *Indogermanische Forschungen* 22 (1907-08) 202-42; 23 (1908) 165-204; 24 (1909) 189-221.

Schlachter, W. "Der Verbalaspekt als grammatische Kategorie." *Münchener Studien zur Sprachwissenschaft* 13 (1959) 22-78.

Schlier, H. *Der Brief an die Galater*. Meyer 12. Göttingen: Vandenhoeck und Ruprecht, 1962.

Schmid, W. *Der Atticismus in seiner Hauptvertreten: von Dionysius von Halikarnass bis auf den zweiten Philostratus*. 5 vols. Stuttgart: Kohlhammer, 1887-97.

Schmidt, D.L. *Hellenistic Greek Grammar and Noam Chomsky: Nominalizing Transformations*. Society of Biblical Literature Dissertation Series 62. Chico, California: Scholars, 1981.

_____. "The Study of Hellenistic Greek Grammar in the Light of Contemporary Linguistics." *Perspectives on Religious Studies* 11 (1984) 27-38.

Schnackenburg, R. *The Gospel According to St. John*. 3 vols. London: Burns and Oates, 1968, 1980, 1982.

Schoeps, H.J. *Paul: The Theology of the Apostle in the Light of Jewish Religious History*. Trans. H. Knight. Philadelphia: Westminster, 1961.

Schogt, H.G. "'Temps et verbe' de G. Guillaume trente-cinz ans après sa parution." *La linguistique* 1 (1965) 55-74.

Schopf, A., ed. *Der Englische Aspekt*. Darmstadt: Wissenschaftliche Buchgesellschaft, 1974.

Schürer, E. *The History of the Jewish People in the Age of Jesus Christ (170 B.C.-A.D. 135)*. Ed. G. Vermes *et al*. Vol. 2. Edinburgh: T. and T. Clark, 1979.

Schürmann, H. *Das Lukasevangelium*. 2 vols. Herders. Freiburg: Herder, 1969.

Schwarz, G. *"Und Jesu Sprach": Untersuchungen zur aramäischen Urgestalt der Worte Jesu*. 2d ed. Beiträge zur Wissenschaft vom Alten und Neuen Testament. Stuttgart: Kohlhammer, 1987.

Schweizer, E. *Church Order in the NT*. Trans. F. Clarke. Studies in Biblical Theology. London: SCM, 1959.

_____. *The Good News According to Luke*. Trans. D.E. Green. Atlanta: John Knox, 1984.

_____. *The Good News According to Matthew*. Trans. D.E. Green. London: SPCK, 1975.

_____. *The Letter to the Colossians*. Trans. A. Chester. London: SPCK, 1982.

Schwyzer, E. *Griechische Grammatik auf der Grundlage von Karl Brugmanns Griechische Grammatik. Vol. 1: Allgemeiner Teil, Lautlehre, Wortbildung, Flexion*. Munich: Beck, 1939. *Vol. 2: Syntax und Syntaktischer Stilistik*. Ed. A. Debrunner. Munich: Beck, 1950.

Scott, J.A. "The Aorist Participle in *Odyssey* ii.3." *Classical Journal* 16 (1920-21) 245-46.

_____. "Prohibitives with ΠΡΟΣ and the Genitive." *Classical Philology* 2 (1907) 324-30.

Searle, J.R. *Intentionality: An Essay in the Philosophy of Mind*. Cambridge: UP, 1983.

Sears, V.W. *The Use of the Future Tense in the NT*. Th.D. thesis, Southern Baptist Theological Seminary, Louisville, Kentucky, 1950.

Seaton, R.C. "The Iterative Use of ἄν with the Impf. and Aor. Ind." *Classical Review* 3 (1889) 343-45.

_____. "Prohibition in Greek." *Classical Review* 20 (1906) 438.

_____. Untitled. *Classical Review* 3 (1889) 314.

_____. Untitled. *Classical Review* 6 (1892) 201-02.

Sedgwick, W.B. "Some Uses of the Imperfect in Greek." *Classical Quarterly* 34 (1940) 118-22.

_____. "The Use of the Imperfect in Herodotus." *Classical Quarterly* NS 7 (1957) 113-17.

Segal, M.H. *A Grammar of Mishnaic Hebrew*. Oxford: Clarendon, 1927.

_____. "Misnaic Hebrew and its Relation to Biblical Hebrew and to Aramaic." *Jewish Quarterly Review* 20 (1908) 647-737.

Segert, S. "Hebrew Poetic Parallelism as Reflected in the Septuagint." *La Septuaginta en la Investigacion Contemporanea (V Congreso de la IOSCS)*. Ed. N. Fernández Marcos. Consejo Superior de Investigaciones Cientificas. Madrid: Textos y Estudios 'Cardenal Cisneros' de la Biblia Poliglota Matritense Instituto 'Arias Montano' C.S.I.C., 1985: 133-48.

_____. "Semitic Poetic Structure in the NT." *Aufstieg und Niedergang der römischen Welt*. II.25.2. Ed. W. Haase. Berlin: de Gruyter, 1984: 1433-62.

Seiler, H. *L'aspect et le temps dans le verbe néo-grec*. Paris: Les Belles Lettres, 1952.
_____. "Zur Problematik des Verbalaspekts." *Cahiers Ferdinand de Saussure* 26 (1969) 119-35.
Selby, R. "The Language in Which Jesus Taught." *Theology* 86 (1983) 185-93.
de Sélincourt, A., trans. *Herodotus: The Histories*. Rev. A.R. Burn. Harmondsworth: Penguin, 1972.
Selwyn, E.G. "Eschatology in 1 Peter." *The Background of the NT and its Eschatology*. Ed. W.D. Davies and D. Daube. Cambridge: UP, 1956: 394-401.
_____. *The First Epistle of St. Peter*. London: Macmillan, 1947.
Semenov, A.F. *The Greek Language in its Evolution: An Introduction to its Scientific Study*. London: George Allen and Unwin, 1936.
Sevenster, J.N. *Do You Know Greek? How Much Greek Could the First Jewish Christians Have Known?* Supplements to Novum Testamentum 19. Leiden: Brill, 1968.
Sewall, J.B. "On the Distinction between the Subjunctive and Optative Modes in Greek Conditional Sentences." *Transactions of the American Philological Association* 5 (1874) 77-82.
Seymour, T.D. "On the Use of the Aorist Participle in Greek." *Transactions of the American Philological Association* 12 (1881) 88-96.
Sharp, D.S. *Epictetus and the NT*. London: Charles H. Kelly, 1914.
_____. "Lexical Notes from Epictetus." *Journal of Theological Studies* 23 (1921-22) 290-91.
Shields, K. "Speculations Concerning the I.E. Root *es-." *Archivum Linguisticum* NS 9 (1978) 73-78.
Shipp, G.P. *Modern Greek Evidence for the Ancient Greek Vocabulary*. Sydney: UP, 1979.
Shuckburgh, E.S. "Hultsch on the Tenses of Polybius." *Classical Review* 9 (1895) 127-28.
Shutt, R.J.H. *Studies in Josephus*. London: SPCK, 1961.
Sidgwick, A. "Remote Deliberative." *Classical Review* 7 (1893) 97-99; 435-37.
Siertsema, B. "A-linguistic Views on Language in European Philosophy." *To Honor R. Jakobson: Essays on the Occasion of his Seventieth Birthday, 11 October 1966*. 3 vols. The Hague: Mouton, 1967: 3.1818-26.
Silva, M. *Biblical Words and their Meaning: An Introduction to Lexical Semantics*. Grand Rapids: Zondervan, 1983.
_____. "Bilingualism and the Character of Palestinian Greek." *Biblica* 61 (1980) 198-219.
_____. "New Lexical Semitisms." *Zeitschrift für die neutestamentliche Wissenschaft* 69 (1978) 253-57.
_____. "The Pauline Style as Lexical Choice: ΓΙΝΩΣΚΕΙΝ and Related Verbs." *Pauline Studies*. Ed. D.A. Hagner and M.J. Harris. Exeter: Paternoster, 1980: 184-207.
_____. "Semantic Borrowing in the NT." *NT Studies* 22 (1976) 104-10.
_____. *Semantic Change and Semitic Influence in the Greek Bible: with a Study of the Semantic Field of 'Mind.'* Ph.D. thesis, Univ. of Manchester, 1972.
Simcox, W.H. *The Writers of the NT: Their Style and Characteristics*. Rpt. Winona Lake, Indiana: Alpha Publications, 1980.
Simpson, E.K. *Words Worth Weighing in the Greek NT*. London: Tyndale Press, [1945].
Skalicka, V. "The Need for a Linguistics of 'la parole.'" *A Prague School Reader in Linguistics*. Ed. J. Vachek. Bloomington: Indiana UP, 1964: 375-90.
Smalley, S.S. "The Delay of the Parousia." *Journal of Biblical Literature* 83 (1964) 41-54.
_____. *1, 2, 3 John*. Word Biblical Commentary 51. Waco, Texas: Word, 1986.
Smith, C.R. "Errant Aorist Interpreters." *Grace Theological Journal* 2 (1981) 205-26.
Smith, C.S. "A Theory of Aspectual Choice." *Language* 59 (1983) 480-501.
Smith, M. "Aramaic Studies and the Study of the NT." *Journal of Bible and Religion* 26 (1958) 304-13.
Smith, N.V. Review of Hopper, *Tense-Aspect*. *Journal of Linguistics* 19 (1983) 505-06.
Smyth, H.W. *Greek Grammar*. Rev. G.M. Messing. Cambridge: Harvard UP, 1956.

Soisalon-Soininen, I. *Die Infinitive in der Septuaginta.* Annales Academiae Scientiarum Fennicae. Series B. Vol. 132.1. Helsinki: Suomalainen Tiedeakatemia, 1965.

Sollamo, R. "The LXX Renderings of the Infinitive Absolute Used with a Paronymous Finite Verb in Septuagintal Greek." *La Septuaginta en la Investigacion Contemporanea (V Congreso de la IOSCS).* Ed. N. Fernández Marcos. Consejo Superior de Investigaciones Cientificas. Madrid: Textos y Estudios 'Cardenal Cisneros' de la Biblia Poliglota Matritense Instituto 'Arias Montano' C.S.I.C., 1985: 101-13.

_____. "Some 'Improper' Prepositions, such as ENΩΠION, ENANTION, ENANTI, etc., in the Septuagint and Early Koine Greek." *Vetus Testamentum* 25 (1975) 73-82.

Sonnenschein, E.A. "Horton-Smith's *Conditional Sentences.*" *Classical Review* 9 (1895) 220-23.

_____. "Mr. Bayfield's Conditional Sentences." *Classical Review* 6 (1892) 199-201.

_____. "The Perfect Subjunctive, Optative, and Imperative in Greek." *Classical Review* 20 (1906) 155-56.

_____. "The Perfect Subjunctive, Optative, and Imperative in Greek.--A Reply." *Classical Review* 19 (1905) 439-40.

Sorensen, H.S. "On the Semantic Unity of the Perfect Tense." *English Studies Supplement to vol. 45* (1964) 74-83.

Sparks, H.F.D. "The Semitisms of St. Luke's Gospel." *Journal of Theological Studies* 44 (1943) 129-38.

_____. "The Semitisms of the Acts." *Journal of Theological Studies* NS 1 (1950) 16-28.

_____. "Some Observations on the Semitic Background of the NT." *Bulletin of Studiorum Novi Testamenti Societas* 2 (1951) 33-42.

Spence, N.C.W. "A Hardy Perennial: The Problem of *La Langue* and *La Parole.*" *Archivum Linguisticum* 9 (1957) 1-27.

_____. "Linguistic Fields, Conceptual Spheres, and the *Weltbild.*" *Transactions of the Philological Society* (1961) 87-106.

_____. "Review Article: The Basic Problems of Ethnolinguistics." *Archivum Linguisticum* 16 (1964) 144-56.

Spencer, A.B. *Paul's Literary Style: A Stylistic and Historical Comparison of II Cor 11:6-12:13, Rom 8:9-39, and Phil 3:2-4:13.* ETS Monograph. Jackson, Mississippi: Evangelical Theological Society, 1984.

Sperber, A. *A Historical Grammar of Biblical Hebrew: A Presentation of Problems with Suggestions to their Solutions.* Leiden: Brill, 1966.

Spicq, C. *Les épitres de Saint Pièrre.* Sources bibliques. Paris: Gabalda, 1966.

Spieckermann, H. *Juda unter Assur in der Sargonidenzeit.* Forschungen zur Religion und Literatur des AT 129. Göttingen: Vandenhoeck und Ruprecht, 1982.

Spieker, E.H. "On the So-Called Genitive Absolute and its Use Especially in the Attic Orators." *American Journal of Philology* 6 (1885) 310-43.

Stagg, F. "The Abused Aorist." *Journal of Biblical Literature* 91 (1972) 222-31.

Stahl, J.M. *Kritisch-historische Syntax des griechischen Verbums der klassischen Zeit.* Indogermanische Bibliothek 4. Heidelberg: Carl Winter, 1907.

Stambaugh, J.E., and D.L. Balch. *The NT in Its Social Environment.* Philadelphia: Westminster, 1986.

Stanford, W.B., ed. *The Odyssey of Homer.* 2 vols. 2d ed. London: Macmillan, 1959.

Stanton, G.N. "Presuppositions in NT Criticism." *NT Interpretation: Essays on Principles and Methods.* Ed. I.H. Marshall. 2d ed. Exeter: Paternoster, 1979: 60-71.

Steinthal, H. *Geschichte der Sprachwissenschaft bei den Griechen und Römern mit besonderer Rücksicht auf die Logik.* 2 vols. Berlin: 1890; rpt. Hildesheim: Georg Olms, 1961.

Stendahl, K. *The School of St. Matthew and its Use of the OT.* Acta Seminarii Neotestamentici Upsaliensis. 2d ed. Lund: Gleerup, [1967].

Stenius, E. *Wittgenstein's Tractatus: A Critical Exposition of its Main Lines of Thought.* Oxford: Blackwell, 1960.

Stephens, L. "The Origins of a Homeric Peculiarity: MH Plus Aorist Imperative." *Transactions of the American Philological Association* 113 (1983) 69-78.
Stevens, W.A. "On the Substantive Use of the Greek Participle." *Transactions of the American Philological Association* 4 (1873) 45-55.
Stevenson, W.B. *Grammar of Palestinian Jewish Aramaic*. Rev. J.A. Emerton. 2d ed. Oxford: Clarendon, 1962.
Stewart, R. "The Oracular εἰ." *Greek, Roman, and Byzantine Studies* 26 (1985) 67-73.
Stork, P. *The Aspectual Usage of the Dynamic Infinitive in Herodotus*. Gronigen: Bouma, 1982.
Strack, H.L., and P. Billerbeck. *Kommentar zum NT aus Talmud und Midrasch*. Vol. 1: *Das Evangelium nach Matthäus*. Munich: Beck, 1922.
Streeter, B.H. *The Four Gospels: A Study of Origins*. London: Macmillan, 1936.
Streitberg, W. "Die Benennung der Aktionsarten." *Indogermanische Forschungen* 22 (1907-08) 72-74.
_____. "Perfective und imperfective Aktionsart im Germanischen." *Beiträge zur Geschichte der Deutschen Sprache und Literatur* (Pauls und Braunes Beiträge) 15 (1891) 70-177.
_____. "Zum Perfektiv." *Indogermanische Forschungen* 24 (1909) 311-14.
_____. Review of Delbrück, *Vergleichende Syntax*. *Indogermanische Forschungen* 11 (1900) 56-67.
Strug, C. "Kuhn's Paradigm Thesis: A Two-Edged Sword for the Philosophy of Religion." *Religious Studies* 20 (1984) 269-79.
Strunk, K. "Überlegungen zu Defektivität und Suppletion in Griechischen und Indogermanischen." *Glotta* 55 (1977) 2-34.
_____. "Zeit und Tempus in Altindogermanischen Sprachen." *Indogermanische Forschungen* 73 (1968) 279-311.
_____. Review of Bakker, *Imperative*. *Gnomon* 42 (1970) 623-25.
Suppe, F. "The Search for Philosophical Understanding of Scientific Theories," 1-232; "Afterword-1977," 617-730, in F. Suppe, ed. *The Structure of Scientific Theories*. 2d ed. Urbana: U of Illinois P, 1977.
Svensson, A. *Zum Gebrauch der erzählenden Tempora im Griechischen*. Lund: Håkan Ohlssons, 1930.
Sweet, J. *Revelation*. SCM Pelican Commentaries. London: SCM, 1979.
Swete, H.B. *The Apocalypse of St. John*. London: Macmillan, 1906.
_____ *An Introduction to the OT in Greek*. 2d ed. Cambridge: UP, 1902.
Synge, F.C. "A Matter of Tenses--Fingerprints of an Annotator in Mark." *Expository Times* 88 (1976-77) 168-71.
Szemerényi, O. *Einführung in die vergleichende Sprachwissenschaft*. Darmstadt: Wissenschaftliche Buchgesellschaft, 1970.
_____. "Greek μέλλω: A Historical and Comparative Study." *American Journal of Philology* 72 (1951) 346-68.
_____. "The Origin of Aspect in the Indo-European Languages." *Glotta* 65 (1987) 1-18.
_____. "Unorthodox Views of Tense and Aspect." *Archivum Linguisticum* 17 (1969) 161-71.
Tabachovitz, D. *Die Septuaginta und das NT: Stilstudien*. Skrifter Utgivna av Svenska Institutet i Athen. 8. IV. Lund: Gleerup, 1956.
Talbert, C.H. "Tradition and Redaction in Rom 12:9-21." *NT Studies* 16 (1969-70) 83-93.
Tångberg, K.A. "Linguistics and Theology: An Attempt to Analyse and Evaluate J. Barr's Argumentation in *The Semantics of Biblical Language* and *Biblical Words for Time*." *Bible Translator* 24 (1973) 301-10.
Tannehill, R.C. *Dying and Rising with Christ*. Zeitschrift für die neutestamentliche Wissenschaft Beihefte 32. Berlin: Töpelmann, 1967.
_____. "The Magnificat as Poem." *Journal of Biblical Literature* 93 (1974) 263-75.

Tarbell, F.B. "The Deliberative Subjunctive in Relative Clauses in Greek." *Classical Review* 5 (1891) 302.

Tarelli, C.C. "Johannine Synonyms." *Journal of Theological Studies* 47 (1946) 175-77.

Tarrant, D. "Plato's Use of Extended *Oratio Obliqua*." *Classical Quarterly* NS 5 (1955) 222-24.

T.A.S. Review of Chantraine, *Histoire*. *Journal of Hellenic Studies* 47 (1927) 305-06.

Tate, J. *Grammarian's Progress*. Inaugural Lecture, 23 January 1946, Univ. of Sheffield.

Taylor, J. "Sequence of Action in Pauline Aorist Participle/Main Verb Combinations." M.A. seminar paper, Trinity Evangelical Divinity School, Illinois, 1984.

Taylor, R.O.P. *The Groundwork of the Gospels with Some Collected Papers*. Oxford: Blackwell, 1946.

_____. "Did Jesus Speak Aramaic?" *Expository Times* 56 (1944-45) 95-97.

Taylor, V. *The Gospel According to St. Mark*. London: Macmillan, 1952.

_____. "The Syntax of NT Greek." *Bible Translator* 6 (1955) 20-23.

Taylor, W.R. "Aramaic Gospel-Sources and Form-Criticism." *Expository Times* 49 (1937-38) 55-59.

Tedeschi, P.J., and A. Zaenen, ed. *Syntax and Semantics 14: Tense and Aspect*. New York: Academic, 1981.

Teodorsson, S.-T. "Phonological Variation in Classical Attic and the Development of Koine." *Glotta* 57 (1979) 61-75.

_____. *The Phonology of Ptolemaic Koine*. Studia Graeca et Latina Gothoburgensia 36. Gothenburg: Acta Universitatis Gothoburgensis, 1977.

Thackeray, H.St.J. *A Grammar of the OT in Greek According to the Septuagint*. Vol. 1: Introduction, Orthography and Accidence. Cambridge: UP, 1909.

_____. "The Greek Translators of the Four Books of Kings." *Journal of Theological Studies* 8 (1907) 262-78.

_____. "Renderings of the Infinitive Absolute in the LXX." *Journal of Theological Studies* 9 (1908) 597-601.

_____. *The Septuagint and Jewish Worship: A Study in Origins*. Schweich Lectures of the British Academy 1920. London: Oxford UP, 1921.

_____. *Some Aspects of the Greek OT*. London: George Allen and Unwin, 1927.

_____. "An Unrecorded 'Aramaism' in Josephus." *Journal of Theological Studies* 30 (1928-29) 361-70.

Thiselton, A.C. "Introducing Semantics" (review of Louw, *Semantics*). *Reformed Journal* 33 (1983) 29-30.

_____. "Semantics and NT Interpretation." *NT Interpretation: Essays on Principles and Methods*. Ed. I.H. Marshall. 2d ed. Exeter: Paternoster, 1979: 75-104.

_____. "The Semantics of Biblical Language as an Aspect of Hermeneutics." *Faith and Thought* 103 (1976) 108-20.

_____. "The Supposed Power of Words." *Journal of Theological Studies* NS 25 (1974) 283-99.

_____. *The Two Horizons: NT Hermeneutics and Philosophical Description with Special Reference to Heidegger, Bultmann, Gadamer, and Wittgenstein*. Grand Rapids: Eerdmans, 1980.

_____. "The Use of Philosophical Categories in NT Hermeneutics." *The Churchman* 87 (1973) 87-100.

_____. Review of Gibson, *Biblical Semantic Logic*. *Theology* 85 (1982) 301-03.

Thompson, F.E. *A Syntax of Attic Greek*. London: Longmans, Green, 1902.

Thompson, S. *The Apocalypse and Semitic Syntax*. Society of NT Studies Monograph Series 52. Cambridge: UP, 1985.

Thompson, W.G. *Matthew's Advice to a Divided Community: Matt 17:22-18:35*. Analecta Biblica 44. Rome: Biblical Institute Press, 1970.

Thomson, G. *The Greek Language*. 2d ed. Cambridge: Heffer, 1972.

Thomson, P. *The Greek Tenses in the NT: Their Bearing on its Accurate Interpretation, with a Rendering of the Gospels, and Notes*. Edinburgh: J. Gardner Hitt, 1895.

Thrall, M.E. *Greek Particles in the NT: Linguistic and Exegetical Studies.* NT Tools and Studies. Leiden: Brill, 1962.

Thumb, A. *Die griechische Sprache im Zeitalter des Hellenismus: Beiträge zur Geschichte und Beurteilung der KOINH.* Strassburg: Trübner, 1901.

_____. *Handbook of the Modern Greek Vernacular: Grammar, Texts, Glossary.* Trans. S. Angus. 2d ed. Edinburgh: T. and T. Clark, 1912.

_____. "Hellenistic and Biblical Greek." *Dictionary of the Apostolic Church.* Vol. 1. Ed. J. Hastings. Edinburgh: T. and T. Clark, 1915: 551-60.

_____. "On the Value of Modern Greek for the Study of Ancient Greek." *Classical Quarterly* 8 (1914) 181-205.

_____. "Zur Aktionsart der mit Präpositionen zusammengesetzten Verba im Griechischen." *Indogermanische Forschungen* 27 (1915) 195-99.

_____. Review of Blass, *Grammatik des NT Griechisch,* 2d ed. *Theologische Literaturzeitung* 15 (1903) 420-24.

Timberlake, A. "Invariance and the Syntax of Russian Aspect." *Tense-Aspect: Between Semantics and Pragmatics.* Ed. P.J. Hopper. Amsterdam: Benjamin, 1982: 305-31.

Tödt, H.E. *The Son of Man in the Synoptic Tradition.* Trans. D.M. Barton. NT Library. London: SCM, 1965.

Torrey, C.C. *The Apocalypse of John.* New Haven: Yale UP, 1958.

_____. "The Aramaic of the Gospels." *Journal of Biblical Literature* 61 (1942) 71-85.

_____. "The Aramaic Origin of the Gospel of John." *Harvard Theological Review* 16 (1923) 305-44.

_____. *The Composition and Date of Acts.* Harvard Theological Studies 1. Cambridge: Harvard UP, 1916.

_____. "Fact and Fancy in the Theories Concerning Acts." *American Journal of Theology* 23 (1919) 61-86; 189-212.

_____. *The Four Gospels: A New Translation.* London: Hodder and Stoughton, n.d.

_____. "Julius Wellhausen's Approach to the Aramaic Gospels." *Zeitschrift der Deutschen Morgenländischen Gesellschaft* 101 (NS 26) (1951) 125-37.

_____. *Our Translated Gospels: Some of the Evidence.* London: Hodder and Stoughton, n.d.

_____. "Studies in the Aramaic of the First Century A.D." *Zeitschrift für die alttestamentliche Wissenschaft* 65 (1953) 228-47.

Tov, E. "Did the Septuagint Translators always Understand their Hebrew Text?" *De Septuaginta: Studies in Honour of J.W. Wevers on his sixty-fifth birthday.* Ed. A. Pietersma and C. Cox. Ontario: Benben, 1984: 53-70.

_____. *The Text-Critical Use of the Septuagint in Biblical Research.* Jerusalem Biblical Studies. Jerusalem: Simor, 1981.

Treu, K. "Die Bedeutung des Griechischen für die Juden im römischen Reich." *Kairos* 15 (1973) 123-44.

Trotter, J.C., Jr. *The Use of the Perfect Tenses in the Pauline Epistles.* Th.D. thesis, Southern Baptist Theological Seminary, Louisville, Kentucky, 1951.

Trubetzkoy, N.S. *Principles of Phonology.* Trans. C.A.M. Baltaxe. Berkeley: U of California P, 1969.

Turner, C.H. "Marcan Usage: Notes, Critical and Exegetical, on the Second Gospel." *Journal of Theological Studies* 25 (1924) 377-86; 26 (1925) 12-20; 145-56; 225-40; 337-46; 27 (1926) 58-62; 28 (1927) 9-30; 349-62.

Turner, E.G. *Greek Papyri: An Introduction.* Oxford: Clarendon, 1968.

Turner, G. "Pre-Understanding and NT Interpretation." *Scottish Journal of Theology* 28 (1975) 227-42.

Turner, G.J. "Sociosemantic networks and discourse structure." *New Developments in Systemic Linguistics.* Vol. 1: Theory and Description. Ed. M.A.K. Halliday and R.P. Fawcett. London: Pinter, 1987: 64-93.

Turner, G.W. *Stylistics.* Pelican. Harmondsworth: Penguin, 1973.

Turner, N. "Biblical Greek--the Peculiar Language of a Peculiar People." *Studia Evangelica.* Vol. VII. Ed. E.A. Livingstone. Berlin: Akademie Verlag, 1982: 505-12.

_____. *Grammatical Insights into the NT.* Edinburgh: T. and T. Clark, 1965.

_____. "Jewish and Christian Influence in the NT Vocabulary." *Novum Testamentum* 16 (1974) 149-60.

_____. "The Language of the NT." *Peake's Commentary on the Bible.* Ed. M. Black and H.H. Rowley. London: Nelson, 1962: 659-62.

_____. "The Literary Character of NT Greek." *NT Studies* 20 (1974) 107-14.

_____. "Philology in NT Studies." *Expository Times* 71 (1959-60) 104-07.

_____. "The Quality of the Greek of Luke-Acts." *Studies in NT Language and Text.* Ed. J.K. Elliott. Supplements to Novum Testamentum 44. Leiden: Brill, 1976: 387-400.

_____. "The Relation of Luke I and II to Hebraic Sources and to the Rest of Luke-Acts." *NT Studies* 2 (1955-56) 100-09.

_____. "Second Thoughts--VII. Papyrus Finds." *Expository Times* 76 (1964-65) 44-48.

_____. *Style.* Vol. 4 of *A Grammar of NT Greek,* by J.H. Moulton. Edinburgh: T. and T. Clark, 1976.

_____. *Syntax.* Vol. 3 of *A Grammar of NT Greek,* by J.H. Moulton. Edinburgh: T. and T. Clark, 1963.

_____. "The 'Testament of Abraham': Problems in Biblical Greek." *NT Studies* 1 (1954-55) 219-23.

_____. "The Unique Character of Biblical Greek." *Vetus Testamentum* 5 (1955) 208-13.

_____. "Were the Gospels Written in Greek or Aramaic?" *Evangelical Quarterly* 21 (1949) 42-48.

Ullendorf, E. *Is Biblical Hebrew a Language: Studies in Semitic Languages and Civilizations.* Wiesbaden: Harrassowitz, 1977.

Ullmann, S. "Descriptive Semantics and Linguistic Theory." *Word* 9 (1953) 225-40.

_____. *The Principles of Semantics.* Glasgow: Jackson, Son and Company, 1951.

_____. "Semantic Universals." *Universals of Language.* Ed. J.H. Greenberg. Cambridge: M.I.T. Press, 1963: 172-207.

_____. *Semantics: An Introduction to the Science of Meaning.* Oxford: Blackwell, 1962.

Ultan, R. "The Nature of Future Tenses." *Universals of Human Language.* Vol. 3: Word Structure. Ed. J.H. Greenberg. Stanford, California: Stanford UP, 1978: 83-123.

van Unnik, W.C. "Aramaisms in Paul." *Sparsa Collecta: The Collected Essays of W.C. van Unnik.* Part I. Supplements to Novum Testamentum 29. Leiden: Brill, 1973: 129-43.

Vaid, J. "Visual, Phonetic, and Semantic Processing in Early and Late Bilinguals." *Early Bilingualism and Child Development.* Ed. M. Paradis and Y. Lebrun. Neurolinguistics 13. Lisse: Swets and Zeitlinger, 1984.

Veitch, W. *Greek Verbs: Irregular and Defective.* Oxford: Clarendon, 1897.

Velecky, L. Review of Gibson, *Biblical Semantic Logic. Journal of Theological Studies* NS 33 (1982) 642.

Vendler, Z. "Verbs and Time." *Der Englische Aspekt.* Ed. A. Schopf. Darmstadt: Wissenschaftliche Buchgesellschaft, 1974: 217-34.

Vendryes, J. "L'infinitif substantiv dans la langue de Lysias." *Revue de philologie* 70 (1944) 113-33.

Vergote, J. "Grec Biblique." *Dictionnaire de la Bible, Supplément 3.* Ed. L. Pirot. Paris: Librairie Letouzey et Ane, 1938: cols. 1320-69.

Verkuyl, H.J. *On the Compositional Nature of the Aspects.* Foundations of Language Supplement Series. Dordrecht: Reidel, 1972.

Vermes, G. "The 'Son of Man' Debate." *Journal for the Study of the NT* 1 (1978) 19-32.

_____. "The Targumic Versions of Gen 4:3-16." *Annual of the Leeds Univ. Oriental Society* 3 (1963) 81-114.

Vet, J.P. Review of Comrie, *Aspect. Lingua* 41 (1977) 382-85.

Viteau, J. *Etude sur le grec du NT. Le verbe: Syntaxe de propositions.* Paris: Emile Bouillon, 1893.

Vögtle, A. "Die griechische Sprache und ihre Bedeutung für die Geschichte des Urchristentums." *Der Lebenswert des Griechischen.* Ed. H. Gundert. Karlsruhe: Badenia, 1973: 77-93.

Voelz, J.W. "The Language of the NT." *Aufstieg und Niedergang der römischen Welt.* II.25.2. Ed. W. Haase. Berlin: de Gruyter, 1984: 893-977.

_____. *The Use of the Present and Aorist Imperatives and Prohibitions in the NT.* Ph.D. thesis, Univ. of Cambridge, 1977.

de Vries, S.J. "The Syntax of Tenses and Interpretation in the Hodayoth." *Revue de Qumran* 5 (1965) 375-414.

de Waard, J. "Σημιτισμοί στήν Ἑλληνική Κ. Διαθήκη." *Δελτίο Βιβλικῶν Μελετῶν* NS 1 (1979) 104-12.

_____. "Translation Techniques Used by the Greek Translators of Ruth." *Biblica* 54 (1973) 499-515.

Wackernagel, J. *Studien über die Griechischen Perfektum.* Göttingen: Officina Academica Dieferichiana, 1904.

_____. *Vorlesungen über Syntax mit besonderer Berücksichtigung von Griechisch, Lateinisch und Deutsch.* Vol. 1. 2d ed. Basel: Emil Birkhäuser, [1926].

Wakker, G.C. "Potential and Contrary-To-Fact Conditionals in Classical Greek." *Glotta* 64 (1986) 222-46.

Wallace, P.W. "MH with the Participle in Longus and Achilles Tatius." *American Journal of Philology* 89 (1968) 321-33.

Wallace, S. "Figure and Ground: The Interrelationships of Linguistic Categories." *Tense-Aspect: Between Semantics and Pragmatics.* Ed. P.J. Hopper. Amsterdam: Benjamins, 1982: 201-23.

Walbank, F.W. *A Historical Commentary on Polybius.* 3 vols. Vol. 1. Oxford: Clarendon, 1957.

Walters, P. *The Text of the Septuagint: Its Corruptions and their Emendation.* Ed. D.W. Gooding. Cambridge: UP, 1973.

Waterman, G.H. "What is Koiné Greek?" *Bible Translator* 3 (1952) 127-31.

Watson, M. "The Semitic Element in NT Greek." *Restoration Quarterly* 10 (1967) 225-30.

Weeden, T.J. "The Heresy that Necessitated Mark's Gospel." *Zeitschrift für die neutestamentliche Wissenschaft* 59 (1968) 145-58.

Weinreich, U. *Languages in Contact: Findings and Problems.* Publications of the Linguistic Circle of New York 1. New York: n.p., 1953.

_____. "On the Semantic Structure of Language." *Universals of Language.* Ed. J.H. Greenberg. Cambridge: M.I.T. Press, 1963: 114-71.

Weinrich, H. *Tempus: Besprochene und erzählte Welt.* 2d ed. Stuttgart: Kohlhammer, 1971.

_____. "Tense and Time." *Archivum Linguisticum* NS 1 (1970) 31-41.

Wellhausen, J. *Einleitung in die drei ersten Evangelien.* Berlin: Reimer, 1st ed. 1905, 2d ed. 1911.

_____. "Septuagint." *Encyclopedia Britannica.* 9th ed. Edinburgh: Adam and Charles Black, 1886: 21.667-70.

Wenham, D. *The Rediscovery of Jesus' Eschatological Discourse.* Gospel Perspectives 4. Sheffield: JSOT, 1984.

Wernberg-Moller, P. "Observations on the Hebrew Participle." *Zeitschrift für die alttestamentliche Wissenschaft* 71 (1959) 54-67.

Westcott, B.F. *The Gospel According to St. John.* London: John Murray, 1919.

Weymouth, R.F. "On the Rendering of the Aorist." *Expository Times* 8 (1896-97) 66-67.

_____. "The Rendering into English of the Greek Aorist and Perfect." *Theological Monthly* NS 4 (1890) 33-47; 162-80.

Wharton, E.R. "On the Origin of the Construction οὐ μή." *Classical Review* 109 (1896) 239.

Whiston, W., trans. *The Works of Flavius Josephus.* 4 vols. London: Lockington, Allen, et al., 1806.

White, H. *Appian's Roman History III.* Loeb Classical Library. London: Heinemann, 1913.

White, J.L. *Light from Ancient Letters.* Foundations and Facets. Philadelphia: Fortress, 1986.

Whitelaw, R. "On μή Prohibitive with Future Indicative." *Classical Review* 2 (1888) 322-23.
_____. "On Some Uses of the Aorist Participle." *Classical Review* 5 (1891) 248.
_____. "On the Construction of οὐ μή." *Classical Review* 10 (1896) 239-44.
Whitney, W.D. "On Delbrück's Vedic Syntax." *American Journal of Philology* 13 (1892) 271-306.
Whorf, B.L. *Language, Thought and Reality: Selected Writings of B.L. Whorf.* Ed. J.B. Carroll. Cambridge: M.I.T. Press, 1956.
Wifstrand, A. "Apostelgeschichte 25:13." *Eranos* 54 (1956) 123-37.
_____. "A Problem Concerning the Word Order in the NT." *Studia Theologica* 3 (1949) 172-84.
_____. "Stylistic Problems in the Epistles of James and Peter." *Studia Theologica* 1 (1947) 170-82.
van Wijk, N. "'Aspect' en 'Aktionsart.'" *De Nieuwe Taalgids* 22 (1928) 225-39.
Wilckens, U. *Der Brief an die Römer. 3. Röm 12-16.* Evangelisch-Katholischer Kommentar zum NT. Zürich: Benzinger, 1982.
Wilcox, M. "Jesus in the Light of his Jewish Environment." *Aufstieg und Niedergang der römischen Welt.* II.25.1. Ed. W. Haase. Berlin: de Gruyter, 1982: 131-95.
_____. "Peter and the Rock: A Fresh Look at Matt 16:17-19." *NT Studies* 22 (1976) 73-88.
_____. "Semitisms in the NT." *Aufstieg und Niedergang der römischen Welt.* II.25.2. Ed. W. Haase. Berlin: de Gruyter, 1984: 978-1029.
_____. *The Semitisms of Acts.* Oxford: Clarendon, 1965.
Wilkinson, N.K. *"Aspect" in the Syntax of the Verb in the Poems of Homer.* Ph.D. thesis, Australian National Univ., Canberra, 1980.
Wilmet, M. "Aspect grammatical, aspect sémantique, aspect lexical: un problème de limites." *La notion d'aspect.* Ed. J. David and R. Martin. Recherches linguistiques 5. Paris: Klincksieck, 1980: 51-68.
Wilson, R.McL. "Did Jesus Speak Greek?" *Expository Times* 68 (1956-57) 121-22.
Wilss, W. "E.A. Nida: Componential Analysis of Meaning--An Introduction to Semantic Structures." *Bible Translator* 27 (1976) 350-54.
Windisch, H. *Der Zweite Korintherbrief.* Ed. G. Strecker. Meyers. 9th ed. Göttingen: Vandenhoeck und Ruprecht, 1924.
Winer, G.B. *A Treatise on the Grammar of NT Greek Regarded as a Sure Basis for NT Exegesis.* Trans. W.F. Moulton. 3d ed. Edinburgh: T. and T. Clark, 1882.
Winger, M. "Unreal Conditions in the Letters of Paul." *Journal of Biblical Literature* 105 (1986) 110-12.
Winter, P. "Magnificat and Benedictus--Maccabean Psalms?" *Bulletin of John Rylands Library* 37 (1954-55) 328-47.
_____. "On Luke and Lucan Sources." *Zeitschrift für die neutestamentliche Wissenschaft* 47 (1956) 217-42.
_____. "The Proto-Source of Luke I." *Novum Testamentum* 1 (1956) 184-99.
_____. "Some Observations on the Language in the Birth and Infancy Stories of the Third Gospel." *NT Studies* 1 (1954-55) 111-21.
Wolfson, N. "The Conversational Historical Present Alteration." *Language* 55 (1979) 168-82.
Wonneberger, R. "Generative Stylistics: An Algorithmic Approach to Stylistic and Source Data Retrieval Problems based on Generative Syntax." *Bedeutung, Sprechakte und Texte: Akten des 13. Linguistischen Kolloquiums.* Vol. 2. Ed. W. Vandemeghe and M. Van de Velde. Tübingen: Niemeyer, 1979.
_____. *Syntax und Exegese: eine generative Theorie der griechischen Syntax und ihr Beitrag zur Auslegung des NT, dargestellt an 2. Korinther 5.2f und Römer 3.21-26.* Beiträge zur biblischen Exegese und Theologie 13. Frankfurt am Main: Peter Lang, 1979.
Wooten, C. "The Conditional Nature of πρίν Clauses in Attic Prose of the Fifth and Fourth Centuries." *Glotta* 48 (1970) 81-88.

Wright, B.G., III. "A Note on the Statistical Analysis of Septuagintal Syntax." *Journal of Biblical Literature* 104 (1985) 111-14.

Wright, J. *Comparative Grammar of the Greek Language*. London: Oxford UP, 1912.

Wuest, K.S. "The Eloquence of Greek Tenses and Moods." *Bibliotheca Sacra* 117 (1960) 134-43.

Young, C.M. "An Architectonic of Verbs." *Verbatim* 10 (1984) 13.

Young, D.J. "Continuative and inceptive adjuncts in English." *New Developments in Systemic Linguistics*. Vol. 1: Theory and Description. Ed. M.A.K. Halliday and R.P. Fawcett. London: Pinter, 1987: 230-45.

Zandvoort, R.W. "Is 'Aspect' an English Verbal Category?" *Contributions to English Syntax and Philology*. Ed. C.L. Barber *et al*. Goteborg: Almquist and Wicksell, 1962: 1-20.

Zerwick, M. *Biblical Greek Illustrated from Examples*. Trans. J. Smith. Rome: Scripta Pontificii Instituti Biblici, 1963.

Ziff, P. "On H.P. Grice's Account of Meaning." *Semantics: An Interdisciplinary Reader in Philosophy, Linguistics and Psychology*. Ed. D.D. Steinberg and L.A. Jakobovits. Cambridge: UP, 1971: 60-65.

Zilliacus, H. "Notes on the Periphrases of the Imperatives in Classical Greek." *Eranos* 44 (1946) 266-79.

Zimmermann, F. *The Aramaic Origin of the Four Gospels*. New York: Ktav, 1979.

Zsilka, J. "Probleme des Aorists bei Homer." *Acta Antiqua* 14 (1966) 33-59.

de Zwaan, J. "John Wrote in Aramaic." *Journal of Biblical Literature* 57 (1938) 155-71.

_____. "The Use of the Greek Language in Acts." *The Beginnings of Christianity*. Part 1: The Acts of the Apostles. Vol. 2: Prolegomena II, Criticism. Ed. F.J. Foakes Jackson and K. Lake. London: Macmillan, 1922: 30-65.

Zwicky, A.M. "On Markedness in Morphology." *Die Sprache* 24 (1978) 129-43.

INDEX

STUDIES IN BIBLICAL GREEK is an occasional series of monographs designed to promote and publish the latest research into biblical Greek (Old and New Testaments). The series does not assume that biblical Greek is a distinct dialect within the larger world of *koine,* but focuses on these corpora because it recognizes the particular interest they generate. Research into the broader evidence of the period, including epigraphical and inscriptional materials, is welcome in the Series, provided the results are cast in terms of their bearing on biblical Greek. Primarily, however, the Series is devoted to fresh philological, syntactical and linguistic study of the Greek of the biblical books, with the subsidiary aim of displaying the contribution of such study to accurate exegesis.

The series editor is:

D. A. Carson
Trinity Evangelical Divinity School
2065 Half Day Road
Deerfield, IL 60015